Instructor's Manual to Accompany

MICROELECTRONIC CIRCUITS

Second Edition

Adel S. Sedra
Kenneth C. Smith

HOLT, RINEHART AND WINSTON, INC.

New York Chicago San Francisco Philadelphia
Montreal Toronto London Sydney Tokyo

Printed in the United States of America
Published simultaneously in Canada

7 8 9 018 9 8 7 6 5 4 3 2 1

ISBN 0-03-007329-4

Holt, Rinehart and Winston, Inc.
The Dryden Press
Saunders College Publishing

CONTENTS

PREFACE

This manual contains complete solutions for all 400 exercises and 771 end-of-chapter problems included in the book MICROELECTRONIC CIRCUITS,Second Edition.It also includes additional design and examination problems, complete with solutions.Text materials on Data Converters and Digital Memory which were not included in the book (for size considerations) are printed in this manual.Finally,for the convenience of instructors we have included masters for overhead transparencies of the complex diagrams.

Communications concerning detected errors should be sent to :Adel S. Sedra,Department of Electrical Engineering,University of Toronto,Toronto,Ontario,Canada,M5S 1A4,and needless to say they will be greatly appreciated.

Exercise Solutions

1 $P = \frac{1}{T}\int_0^T \frac{v^2}{R}\,dt$

$$= \frac{1}{T} \times \frac{V^2}{R} \times T = \frac{V^2}{R}$$

Alternatively,

$$P = P_1 + P_3 + P_5 + \cdots$$

$$= \left(\frac{4V}{\sqrt{2}\pi}\right)^2 \frac{1}{R} + \left(\frac{4V}{3\sqrt{2}\pi}\right)^2 \frac{1}{R} + \left(\frac{4V}{5\sqrt{2}\pi}\right)^2 \frac{1}{R} + \cdots$$

$$= \frac{V^2}{R} \times \frac{8}{\pi^2} \times \left(1 + \frac{1}{9} + \frac{1}{25} + \frac{1}{49} + \cdots\right)$$

It can be shown by direct calculation that the infinite series in the parantheses has a sum that approaches $\frac{\pi^2}{8}$; thus P becomes $\frac{V^2}{R}$ as found from direct calculation.

Fraction of energy in fundamental $= \frac{8}{\pi^2} = \underline{\underline{0.81}}$

Fraction of energy in first five harmonics

$$= \frac{8}{\pi^2}\left(1 + \frac{1}{9} + \frac{1}{25}\right) = \underline{\underline{0.93}}$$

Fraction of energy in first seven harmonics

$$= \frac{8}{\pi^2}\left(1 + \frac{1}{9} + \frac{1}{25} + \frac{1}{49}\right) = \underline{\underline{0.95}}$$

Fraction of energy in the first nine harmonics $= \frac{8}{\pi^2}\left(1 + \frac{1}{9} + \frac{1}{25} + \frac{1}{49} + \frac{1}{81}\right) = \underline{\underline{0.96}}$

Note that 90% of the square wave's energy is in the first three harmonics, that is in the fundamental and the third.

2

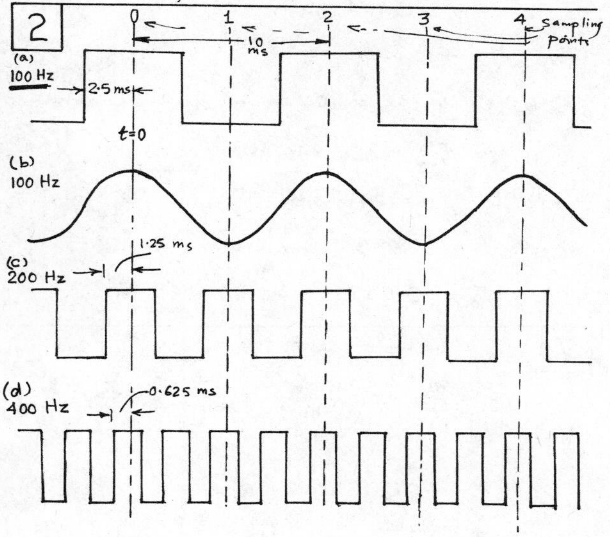

Samples of waveform (a) : +1, −1, +1, −1, +1

Samples of waveform (b) : +1, −1, +1, −1, +1

Samples of waveform (c) : +1, +1, +1, +1, +1

Samples of waveform (d) : +1, +1, +1, +1, +1

Sampling at a rate less than twice the frequency of the information of interest (f) is called <u>undersampling</u> and the ambiguity to which it leads is called <u>aliasing</u>. The minimum sampling frequency (2f) is called the <u>Nyquist rate</u> (or frequency).

3 The amplifier operates linearly with a gain of 1000 until a level of ±10 V is reached at the output. Thus we have

Peak-to-peak Input	1 μV	100 μV	1 mV	100 mV	1 V
Peak input	±0.5 μV	±50 μV	±0.5 mV	±50 mV	±0.5 V
Peak output (potential)	±0.5 mV	±50 mV	±0.5 V	±50 V	±500 V
Peak output (actual)	±0.5 mV	±50 mV	±0.5 V	±10 V	±10 V

4 From Eq. (1.6) with $\omega_c = 2\pi \times 10^6$, $\omega_s = 2\pi \times 10^3$ and $m = 0.1$, we see that the three components of the AM wave are:

a carrier of amplitude $\hat{V}_c$ and frequency of 1,000 kHz; an upper side-frequency of amplitude $\frac{1}{2} m \hat{V}_c = 0.05\,\hat{V}_c$ and frequency of 1,001 kHz; and a lower side-frequency of amplitude $0.05\,\hat{V}_c$ and frequency of 999 kHz.

---

5 The minimum sampling frequency necessary is $2 \times 3400 = 6800$ Hz. Thus the maximum adequate sampling interval is $\frac{1}{6800} = 147\ \mu s$. If each sample requires $10\ \mu s$, then the number of channels must not exceed $\frac{147}{10} = 14.7$. Thus the number of channel which can be implemented is $\underline{\underline{14}}$.

Chapter 2 — Exercises

1 For $v_I < 0$, the diode is cut off, no current flows and $v_O = 0$. For $v_I > 0$, the diode conducts with a zero voltage drop, resulting in $v_O = v_I$. The result is the transfer characteristic shown in Fig. E2.1.

---

2 The reasoning given in the solution to Exercise 2.1 above shows that when $v_I > 0$, $v_D = 0$, and when $v_I < 0$, $v_D = v_I$. The result is the waveform shown in Fig. E2.2.

---

3 Peak value of i_D = Peak value of v_I / R

$$= \frac{10\text{ V}}{1\text{ k}\Omega} = 10\text{ mA}$$

The dc component of v_D is obtained as the average value of the waveform shown in Fig. E2.2. The result is $-\frac{10}{\pi} = \underline{\underline{-3.18\text{ V}}}$

---

4 Voltage gain $= 20 \log 100 = \underline{\underline{40\text{ dB}}}$

Current gain $= 20 \log 1000 = \underline{\underline{60\text{ dB}}}$

Power gain $= 10 \log A_p = 10 \log (A_v A_i)$

$$= 10 \log 10^5 = \underline{\underline{50\text{ dB}}}$$

5

$$P_{dc} = 15 \times 9 = 135\text{ mW}$$

$$P_L = \frac{10^2}{1} = 100\text{ mW}$$

$$P_{dissipated} = 135 - 100 = \underline{\underline{35\text{ mW}}}$$

$$\eta \equiv \frac{P_L}{P_{dc}} \times 100 = \frac{100}{135} \times 100 = \underline{\underline{74.1\,\%}}$$

6 Refer to Example 2.2. For $V_O = 5$ V, Eq. (2.7) gives $V_I = 0.6734$ V (a slightly more accurate value than than given in the Example.). At this value, the small-signal gain is -200 V/V.

For an input signal of 2 mV superimposed on V_I:

(a) Using the small-signal gain gives

$$v_o = -200 \times 2\text{ mV} = \underline{\underline{-0.4\text{ V}}}$$

(b) Using Eq. (2.7) with $V_I = 0.6754$ V gives $V_O = 4.5937$ and thus $v_o = 4.5937 - 5 = \underline{\underline{-0.406\text{ V}}}$

For $v_i = +5$ mV:

(a) Using the small-signal gain we obtain

$$v_o = -200 \times 5\text{ mV} = \underline{\underline{-1\text{ V}}}$$

(b) Using Eq. (2.7) with $V_I = 0.6734 + 0.005 = 0.6784$ V results in $V_O = 3.904$, thus

$$v_o = 3.904 - 5 = -1.096\text{ V}.$$

For $v_i = +10$ mV:

(a) Using the small-signal gain we obtain

$$v_o = -200 \times 10\text{ mV} = \underline{\underline{-2\text{ V}}}$$

(b) Using Eq. (2.7) with $V_I = 0.6734 + 0.010 = 0.6834$ results in $V_O = 2.555$ V, thus

$$v_o = 2.555 - 5 = \underline{\underline{-2.445\text{ V}}}$$

7

$$v_o = 1 \times \frac{10}{10^6 + 10} \simeq 10^{-5}\text{ V} = \underline{\underline{10\ \mu\text{V}}}$$

$$P_L = \frac{v_o^2}{R_L} = \frac{(10 \times 10^{-6})^2}{10} = 10^{-11}\text{ W}$$

With the buffer amplifier:

$$v_o = 1 \times \frac{R_i}{R_i + R_s} \times A_{vo} \times \frac{R_L}{R_L + R_o}$$

$$= 1 \times \frac{1}{1+1} \times 1 \times \frac{10}{10+10} = \underline{\underline{0.25\text{ V}}}$$

2

$P_L = \frac{v_o^2}{R_L} = \frac{0.25^2}{10} = \underline{6.25 \text{ mW}}$

Voltage gain $\equiv \frac{v_o}{v_s} = \frac{0.25 \text{ V}}{1 \text{ V}} = 0.25$ V/V

$= \underline{\underline{-12 \text{ dB}}}$

Power gain $(A_p) \equiv \frac{P_L}{P_i}$,

where $P_L = 6.25$ mW and $P_i = v_i i_i$,

$v_i = 0.5$ V and $i_i = \frac{1 \text{ V}}{1\text{M}\Omega + 1\text{M}\Omega} = 0.5\ \mu\text{A}$

Thus, $P_i = 0.5 \times 0.5 = 0.25\ \mu\text{W}$

and, $A_p = \frac{6.25 \times 10^{-3}}{0.25 \times 10^{-6}} = 25 \times 10^3$

$10 \log A_p = \underline{\underline{44 \text{ dB}}}$

8 Open-circuit (no load) output voltage $= A_{vo} v_i$

Output voltage with load connected $= A_{vo} v_i \frac{R_L}{R_L + R_o}$

$0.8 = \frac{1}{R_o + 1} \Rightarrow R_o = 0.25 \text{ k}\Omega = \underline{\underline{250\ \Omega}}$

9 $A_{vo} = 40 \text{ dB} = \underline{\underline{100 \text{ V/V}}}$

$P_L = \frac{v_o^2}{R_L} = \left(A_{vo} v_i \frac{R_L}{R_L + R_o}\right)^2 / R_L$

$= v_i^2 \times \left(100 \times \frac{1}{1+1}\right)^2 / 1000 = 2.5 v_i^2$

$P_i = \frac{v_i^2}{R_i} = \frac{v_i^2}{10000}$

2

$A_p \equiv \frac{P_L}{P_i} = \frac{2.5 v_i^2}{10^{-4} v_i^2} = 2.5 \times 10^4$ W/W

$10 \log_{10} A_p = \underline{\underline{44 \text{ dB}}}$

10

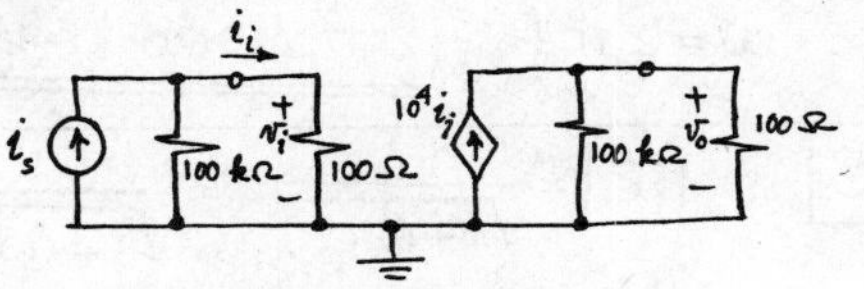

$v_o = 10^4 i_i \times (100 \text{ k}\Omega \,//\, 100\ \Omega)$

$= i_i \times 10^4 \times \frac{10^5 \times 10^2}{10^5 + 10^2} \simeq 10^6 i_i$

From the input circuit:

$i_i = v_i / 100$

Thus, $v_o = 10^6 v_i / 100 = 10^4 v_i$

Voltage gain $\equiv \frac{v_o}{v_i} = 10^4 \text{ V/V} = \underline{\underline{80 \text{ dB}}}$

$A_p \equiv \frac{P_L}{P_i} = \frac{v_o^2/100}{v_i^2/100} = \left(\frac{v_o}{v_i}\right)^2 = 10^8$ W/W

$10 \log A_p = \underline{\underline{80 \text{ dB}}}$

11

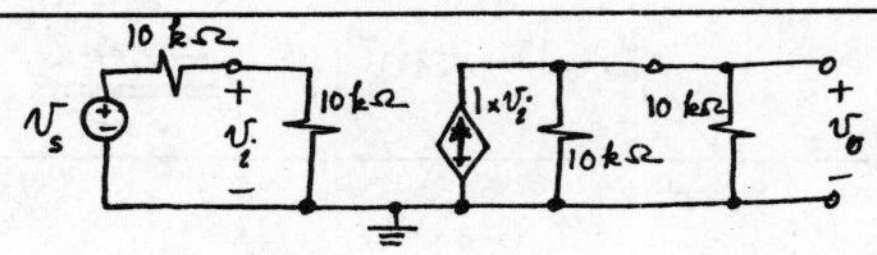

2

$v_i = v_s \times \frac{10 \text{ k}\Omega}{10 \text{ k}\Omega + 10 \text{ k}\Omega} = 0.5\, v_s$

$v_o = 1 \times v_i \times (10 \text{ k}\Omega \,//\, 10 \text{ k}\Omega)$

$= v_i \times 5 \text{ k}\Omega = 5000\, v_i$

Voltage gain $= \frac{v_o}{v_s} = \frac{5000\, v_i}{v_s} = \frac{5000 \times 0.5 v_s}{v_s}$

$= \underline{\underline{2500 \text{ V/V}}}$

$20 \log 2500 = \underline{\underline{68 \text{ dB}}}$

12

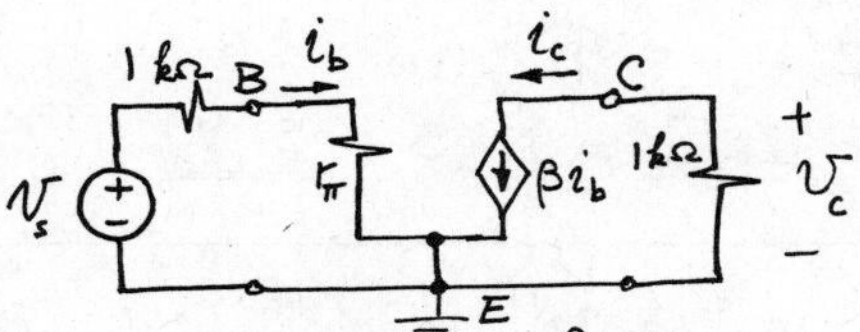

$r_\pi = 2 \text{ k}\Omega \qquad \beta = 90$

$v_c = -i_c \times 1 \text{ k}\Omega = -\beta i_b \times 1 \text{ k}\Omega$

$= -\beta \left(\frac{v_s}{1 \text{ k}\Omega + r_\pi}\right) \times 1 \text{ k}\Omega$

Thus, $\frac{v_c}{v_s} = -90 \times \frac{1}{1 \text{ k}\Omega + 2 \text{ k}\Omega} \times 1 \text{ k}\Omega = \underline{\underline{-30 \text{ V/V}}}$

2

$i_c = \beta i_b$

$\frac{i_c}{i_b} = \beta = \underline{\underline{90 \text{ A/A}}}$

$A_p \equiv \frac{P_L}{P_i} = \frac{-v_c \times i_c}{i_b^2 r_\pi}$

$= \frac{-v_c \times (i_c/i_b)}{i_b \times r_\pi} = \frac{-v_c \times (i_c/i_b)}{[v_s/(1 \text{ k}\Omega + r_\pi)] \times r_\pi}$

$= -\frac{v_c}{v_s} \times \frac{i_c}{i_b} \times \left(\frac{1 \text{ k}\Omega + r_\pi}{r_\pi}\right)$

$= 30 \times 90 \times \frac{3}{2} = 4050$ W/W

$10 \log_{10} A_p = \underline{\underline{36.1 \text{ dB}}}$

13

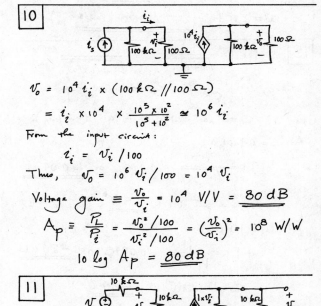

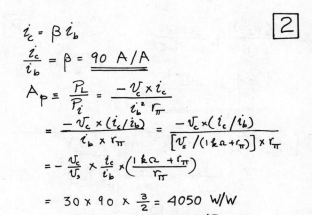

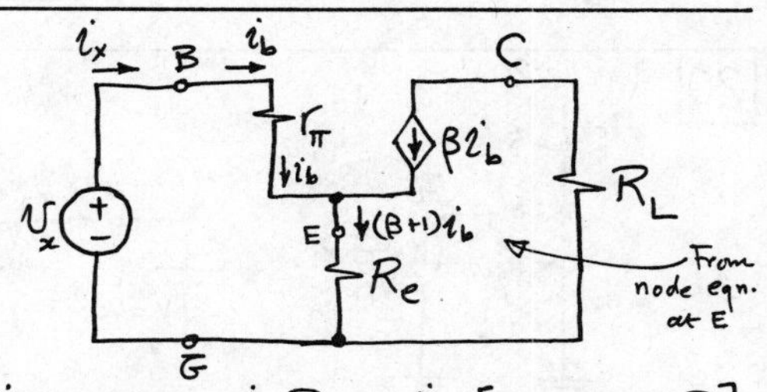

$v_b = i_b r_\pi + (\beta+1) i_b R_e = i_b [r_\pi + (\beta+1) R_e]$

But $v_b = v_x$ and $i_b = i_x$, thus

2

$$R_{in} \equiv \frac{v_x}{i_x} = \frac{v_b}{i_b} = r_\pi + (\beta+1) R_e$$

14 $f = 1/T = 1/10^{-3} = \underline{\underline{1000\ \text{Hz}}}$

$$\omega = 2\pi f = \underline{\underline{2\pi \times 1000\ \ \text{rad/s}}}$$

15 $$|T| = \frac{1}{\sqrt{1+(\omega CR)^2}} = \frac{1}{\sqrt{1+(\omega/\omega_0)^2}}$$

where $\omega_0 = \frac{1}{CR}$ is the corner frequency.

$$\phi = -\tan^{-1}(\omega CR) = -\tan^{-1}(\omega/\omega_0)$$

At $\omega = 0.1\,\omega_0$:

$$|T| = \frac{1}{\sqrt{1+0.01}} = 0.995 \quad \text{or} \quad \underline{\underline{-0.04\ \text{dB}}}$$

$$\phi = -\tan^{-1} 0.1 = \underline{\underline{-5.7^\circ}}$$

At $\omega = 10\,\omega_0$:

$$|T| = \frac{1}{\sqrt{1+100}} = 0.0995 \quad \text{or} \quad \underline{\underline{-20\ \text{dB}}}$$

$$\phi = -\tan^{-1} 10 = \underline{\underline{-84.3^\circ}}$$

2

16 $T = 1/f$

(a) $T = 1/60 = \underline{\underline{16.7\ \text{ms}}}$

(b) $T = 1/10^{-3} = \underline{\underline{1000\ \text{s}}}$

(c) $T = 1/10^{6} = \underline{\underline{1\ \mu\text{s}}}$

17 $$|T| = \frac{1}{\sqrt{1+(\omega CR)^2}}$$

$$= \frac{1}{\sqrt{1+(10^3 \times 10^{-6} \times 10^3)^2}} = 0.707\ \text{V/V}$$

Thus, $|v_o| = |T| \times |v_i| = 7.07\ \text{V}$

$$\phi = -\tan^{-1} \omega CR = -\tan^{-1}(10^3 \times 10^{-6} \times 10^3)$$

$$= -\tan^{-1} 1 = -45^\circ = -\frac{\pi}{4}$$

Thus,

$$\underline{\underline{v_o = 7.07 \sin\left(10^3 t - \frac{\pi}{4}\right)}}$$

18 $$\frac{V_o(s)}{V_i(s)} = \frac{R}{R + \frac{1}{sC}} = \frac{sCR}{1+sCR}$$

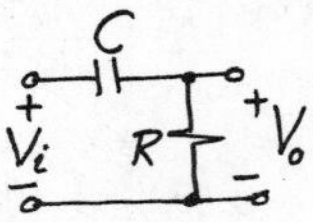

2

$$\frac{V_o(j\omega)}{V_i(j\omega)} = \frac{j\omega CR}{1+j\omega CR}$$

$$\underline{\underline{\left|\frac{V_o}{V_i}\right| = \frac{\omega CR}{\sqrt{1+(\omega CR)^2}}}}$$

19 V_t = open-circuit voltage = $\underline{\underline{10\ \text{V}}}$

$$Z_t = \frac{V_t}{I_{sc}} = \frac{10}{1\ \text{mA}} = \underline{\underline{10\ \text{k}\Omega}}$$

$$Z_n = Z_t = \underline{\underline{10\ \text{k}\Omega}}$$

I_n = short-circuit current = $\underline{\underline{1\ \text{mA}}}$

20

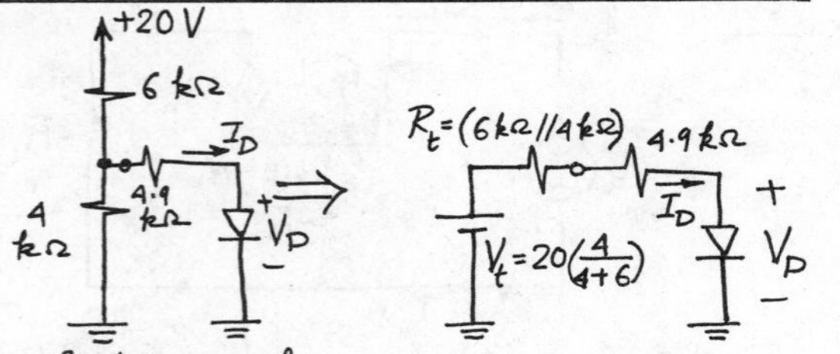

$$R_t = \frac{6\times 4}{6+4} = 2.4\ \text{k}\Omega$$

$$V_t = 8\ \text{V}$$

2

$$I_D = \frac{V_t - V_D}{2.4 + 4.9} = \frac{8 - 0.7}{7.3\ \text{k}\Omega} = \underline{\underline{1\ \text{mA}}}$$

21

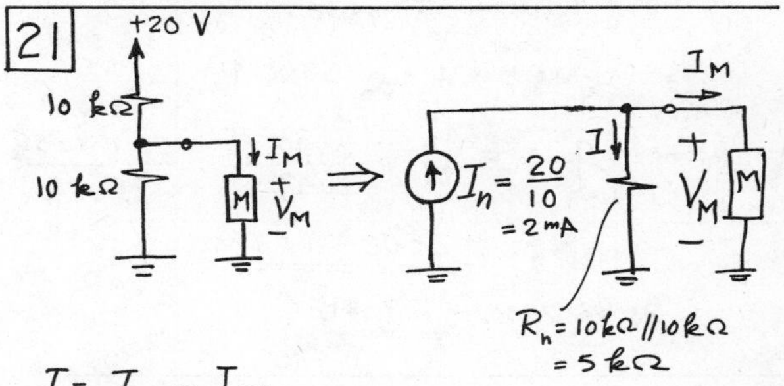

$$I = I_n - I_M$$

$$= 2 - 1 = 1\ \text{mA}$$

$$V_M = I R_n = 1 \times 5 = \underline{\underline{5\ \text{V}}}$$

22 $$C_{in} = C(1-\mu)$$

$$= 10\,(1-(-100)) = \underline{\underline{1010\ \text{pF}}}$$

23 $$Y_{in} = Y(1-\mu)$$

$$= \frac{1}{R}(1 - 0.95) = \frac{0.05}{100\ \text{k}\Omega}$$

$$R_{in} = \frac{1}{Y_{in}} = \frac{100\ \text{k}\Omega}{0.05} = \underline{\underline{2\ \text{M}\Omega}}$$

24 **2**

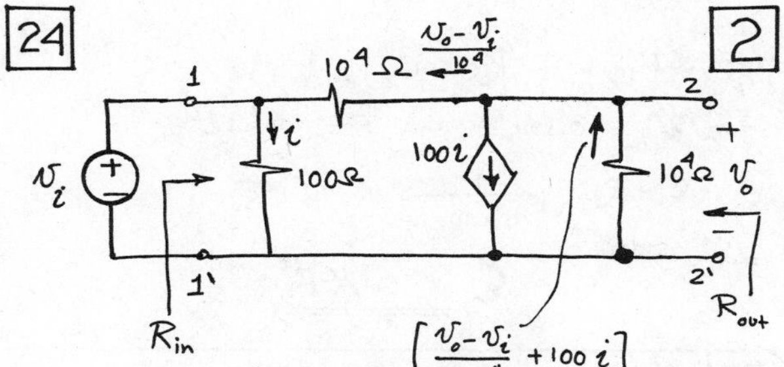

$$\left[\frac{v_o - v_i}{10^4} + 100\,i\right]$$

$$= \left[\frac{v_o - v_i}{10^4} + 100\left(\frac{v_i}{100}\right)\right]$$

$$v_o = -\left[\frac{v_o - v_i}{10^4} + 100\left(\frac{v_i}{100}\right)\right] \times 10^4$$

$$= \frac{-v_o}{10^4} \times 10^4 + \frac{v_i}{10^4} \times 10^4 - 10^4\, v_i$$

$$2v_o = -v_i\,(10^4 - 1)$$

$$v_o \simeq -5000\, v_i \Rightarrow \frac{v_o}{v_i} = \underline{\underline{-5000 \text{ V/V}}}$$

We can now determine the input Miller resistance as follows

$$Y_1 = \frac{1}{10^4\,\Omega}(1 - K) \simeq \frac{5000}{10{,}000}$$

$$R_1 = \frac{1}{Y_1} = 2\,\Omega$$

$$R_{in} = 100\,\Omega \,//\, 2\,\Omega \simeq \underline{\underline{2\,\Omega}}$$

To determine the output resistance we **2** return to the original circuit and reduce the input excitation (v_i) to zero. This will make $i = 0$ and the controlled source will also become zero. The result is the following circuit:

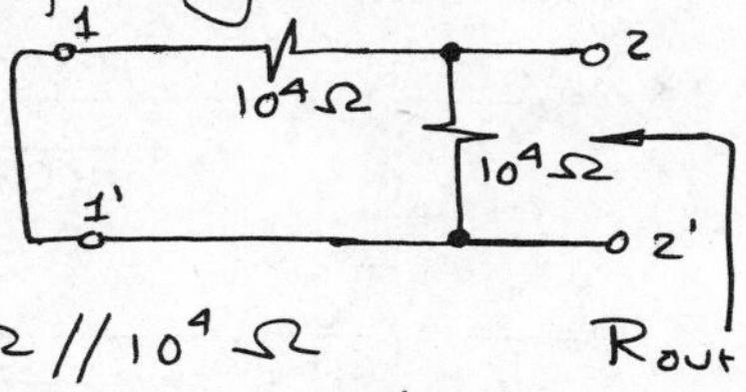

$$R_{out} = 10^4\,\Omega \,//\, 10^4\,\Omega$$

$$= 5000\,\Omega = \underline{\underline{5\,k\Omega}}$$

25 (a) Reducing v_I to zero the circuit reduces to a resistor R in parallel with L_2 which in turn is in parallel with L_1. Thus L_1 and L_2 can be combined into a single inductance $L = \frac{L_1 L_2}{L_1 + L_2}$ and the time constant is obtained as

$$\tau = \frac{L}{R} = \underline{\underline{\frac{1}{R}\,\frac{L_1 L_2}{L_1 + L_2}}}$$

(b) Reducing v_I to zero reduces the circuit to two parallel resistance R_1 and R_2 in parallel with two parallel inductances L_1 and L_2, thus **2**

$$\tau = \frac{L}{R} = \underline{\underline{\frac{(L_1 // L_2)}{(R_1 // R_2)}}}$$

26 (i) At dc : $i_o = 0$

At $\omega = \infty$: $i_o = \frac{v_I}{R}$

<u>HP</u>

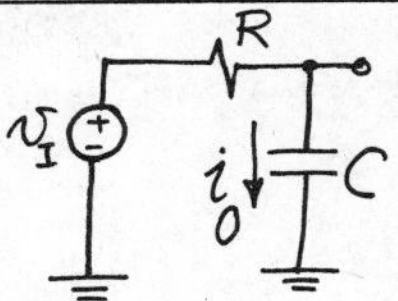

(ii) At dc : $i_o = \frac{v_I}{R}$

At $\omega = \infty$: $i_o = 0$

<u>LP</u>

(iii) At dc : $i_o = 0$

At $\omega = \infty$: $i_o = i_I$

<u>HP</u>

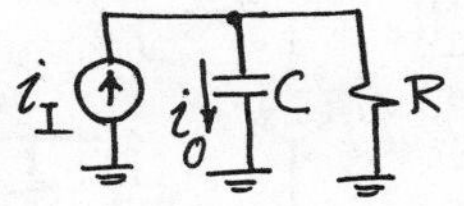

(iv) At dc: $i_o = 0$

At $\omega = \infty$: $i_o = i_I$

<u>HP</u>

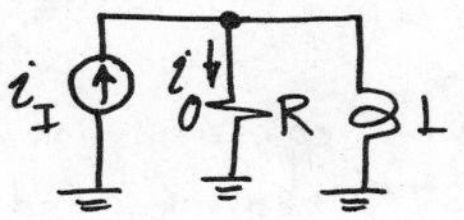

(v) At dc : $i_o = \frac{v_I}{R}$ **2**

At $\omega = \infty$: $i_o = 0$

<u>LP</u>

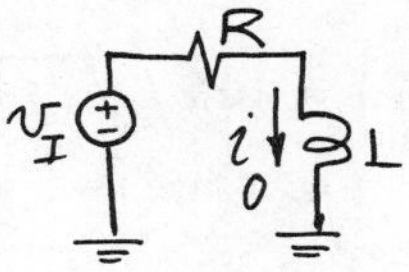

(vi) At dc : $v_o = i_I R$

At $\omega = \infty$ $v_o = 0$

<u>LP</u>

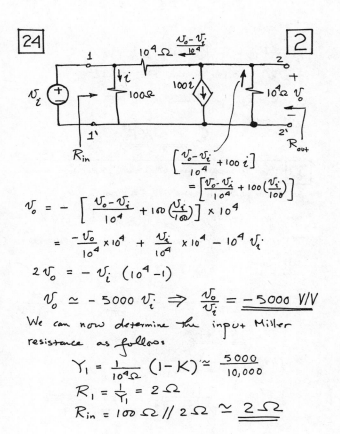

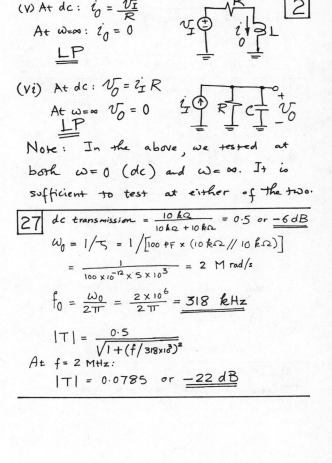

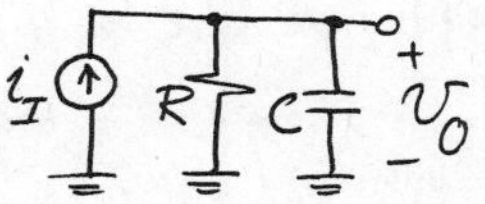

Note: In the above, we tested at both $\omega = 0$ (dc) and $\omega = \infty$. It is sufficient to test at either of the two.

27 dc transmission $= \frac{10\,k\Omega}{10\,k\Omega + 10\,k\Omega} = 0.5$ or $\underline{-6\,dB}$

$$\omega_0 = 1/\tau = 1/[100\,pF \times (10\,k\Omega \,//\, 10\,k\Omega)]$$

$$= \frac{1}{100 \times 10^{-12} \times 5 \times 10^3} = 2 \text{ M rad/s}$$

$$f_0 = \frac{\omega_0}{2\pi} = \frac{2 \times 10^6}{2\pi} = \underline{\underline{318 \text{ kHz}}}$$

$$|T| = \frac{0.5}{\sqrt{1 + (f/318 \times 10^3)^2}}$$

At $f = 2$ MHz:

$$|T| = 0.0785 \text{ or } \underline{\underline{-22\,dB}}$$

28

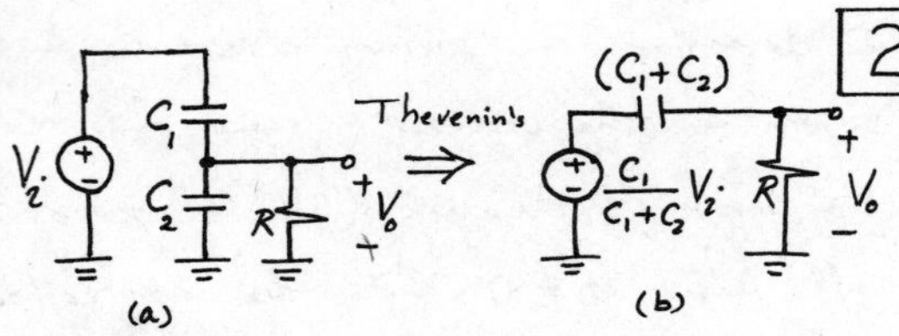

Using the voltage-divider rule on the circuit in Fig.(b) above yields

$$V_o = \left(\frac{C_1}{C_1+C_2}\right) V_i \frac{R}{R + \frac{1}{s(C_1+C_2)}}$$

Thus

$$T(s) \equiv \frac{V_o}{V_i} = \left(\frac{C_1}{C_1+C_2}\right)\frac{s}{s+\frac{1}{(C_1+C_2)R}}$$

which is a high-pass transfer function.

29 Refer to $T(s)$ derived in the solution to Exercise 2.28 above. As $s \to \infty$, $T(s) \to \frac{C_1}{C_1+C_2}$. Thus the high-frequency gain is $\frac{C_1}{C_1+C_2}$. For a high-frequency transmission of 0.5, we select $C_1 = C_2$.

$$\omega_0 = 1/[(C_1+C_2)R]$$

For $\omega_0 = 10$ rad/s and $R = 10\ k\Omega$,

$$C_1 + C_2 = \frac{1}{10 \times 10 \times 10^3} = 10\ \mu F$$

Thus, $C_1 = C_2 = 5\ \mu F$

30 As ω approaches ∞, the capacitor approaches a short circuit and V_s appears at the amplifier input, giving rise to $V_o = 100 V_s$. Thus the high-frequency gain is 100 or **40 dB**.

$$f_0 = \frac{\omega_0}{2\pi} = \frac{1}{2\pi\tau} = \frac{1}{2\pi \times 0.1 \times 10^{-6} \times 100 \times 10^3}$$

$$= 15.9\ Hz$$

$$T(s) = \frac{100\,s}{s+\omega_0}$$

$$|T(j\omega)| = \frac{100\,\omega}{\sqrt{\omega^2+\omega_0^2}} = \frac{100}{\sqrt{1+(\omega_0/\omega)^2}}$$

$$|T| = 100/\sqrt{1+(f_0/f)^2}$$

At $f = 1$ Hz:

$$|T| = 100/\sqrt{1+(15.9/1)^2} = 6.28 \text{ or } 16\ dB$$

31 LP with a time constant

$$\tau = CR = 100 \times 10^{-12} \times 10^3 = 10^{-7}\ s$$

The final value of v_O is $3\ mA \times R = 3\ V$.

Thus, $v_O(t) = 3 - (3-0)\,e^{-t/10^{-7}}$

$$= 3(1 - e^{10^7 t})$$

32 HP with a time constant

$$\tau = \frac{L}{R} = \frac{10 \times 10^{-6}}{2 \times 10^3} = 5 \times 10^{-9}\ s$$

The initial value of v_O is $2\ mA \times R = 4\ V$ and the final value of v_O is zero. Thus

$$v_O(t) = 0 - (0-4)\,e^{-t/5\times10^{-9}}$$

$$= 4\,e^{2\times10^8 t}$$

33 Refer to Fig. E2.30. The circuit is a high-pass STC network with a high-

frequency gain of 100 and when fed with a source having a resistance of 100 kΩ the high-frequency gain reduces to $100 \times \frac{100\,k\Omega}{100k + 100k\Omega}$ $= 50$ V/V. Thus the initial value of v_O is $50 \times 20\ mV = 1000\ mV = 1\ V$.

The final value of v_O is zero. The time constant $\tau = 0.1\ \mu F \times (100\ k\Omega + 100\ k\Omega)$

$$= 10^{-7} \times 200 \times 10^3 = 2 \times 10^{-2}\ s.$$

The output voltage $v_O(t)$ is

$$v_O(t) = 0 - (0-1)\,e^{-t/2\times10^{-2}}$$

$$= 1 \times e^{-50t}$$

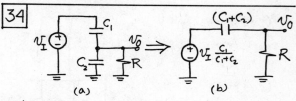

34

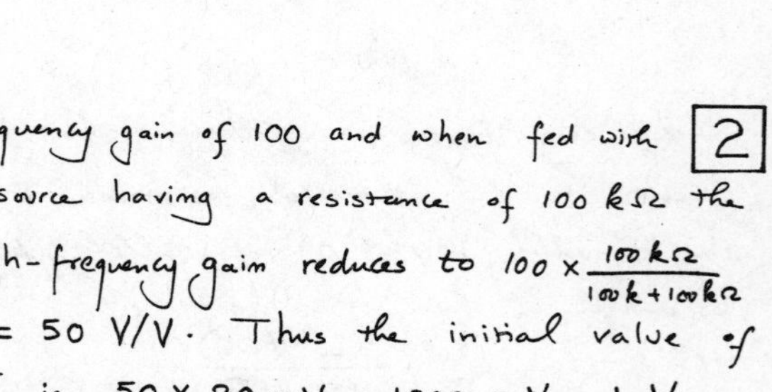

The equivalent circuit in Fig(b) is a HP STC network fed with a step of height

$$\frac{C_1}{C_1+C_2} v_I = \frac{0.5\mu F}{0.5\mu F + 0.5\mu F} \times 10 \text{ V}$$

$$= 5 \text{ V}.$$

The time constant $\tau = (C_1 + C_2) R$

$$= (0.5+0.5)\times 10^{-6} \times 1 \times 10^{6}$$

$$= 1 \text{ s}$$

Thus, $v_O(t) = 0 - (0-5)\, e^{-t/1}$

$$= \underline{\underline{5e^{-t}}}$$

35 $y(t) = S e^{-t/\tau}$

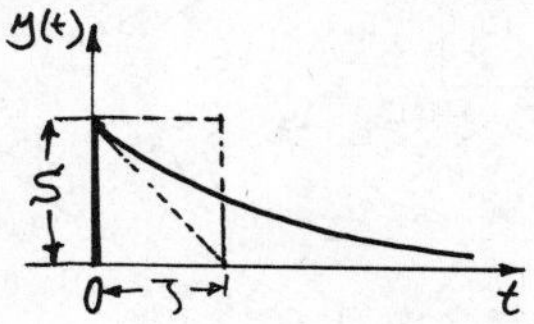

Area under exponential

$$= \int_0^\infty y(t)\, dt$$

$$= \int_0^\infty S e^{-t/\tau}\, dt$$

$$= S \times -\tau \left[e^{-t/\tau} \right]_{t=0}^{\infty}$$

$$= -S\tau\, [0-1]$$

$= S\tau$ = Area of rectangle. Q.E.D

36 $t_r = t_f \simeq 2.2\tau$

$$= 2.2/\omega_0 = \frac{2.2}{2\pi f_0} = \frac{2.2}{2\pi \times 10 \times 10^{6}}$$

$$= 0.35 \times 10^{-7} \text{ s} = \underline{\underline{35 \text{ ns}}}$$

37 Refer to the response shown in Fig. 2.42c. For $t \leq T$,

$$v(t) = P(1 - e^{-t/\tau})$$

For $t = T$ and substituting $\tau = 100T$,

$$v(T) = P(1 - e^{-0.01})$$

$$\simeq P(1 - (1 - 0.01))$$

$$= \underline{\underline{0.01 P}}$$

$$\frac{dv(t)}{dt} = \frac{P}{\tau} e^{-t/\tau}$$

$$\left.\frac{dv}{dt}\right|_{t=0} = \frac{P}{\tau}$$

$$\left.\frac{dv}{dt}\right|_{t=T} = \frac{P}{\tau} e^{-T/\tau} = \frac{P}{\tau} e^{-0.01}$$

$$\simeq \frac{P}{\tau}(1 - 0.01) = 0.99 \frac{P}{\tau}$$

Thus the difference in slope is only $\underline{1\%}$

which means that the response of $t \leq T$ is almost linear.

38 The equivalent circuit is as shown.

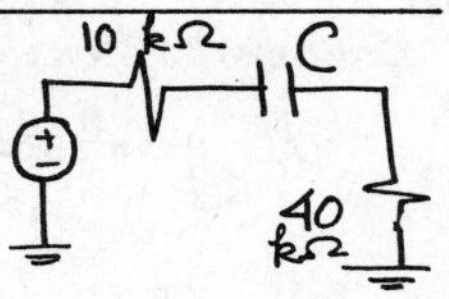

$$\tau = C(40+10)\times 10^{3}$$

$$\% \text{ sag} = \frac{T}{\tau} \times 100$$

$$1 = \frac{10 \times 10^{-6}}{\tau} \times 100 \Rightarrow \tau = 10^{-3} \text{ s}$$

$$C = \frac{10^{-3}}{50 \times 10^{3}} = \underline{\underline{0.02 \mu F}}$$

39 $v(t) = 1 \times e^{-t/\tau}$, $t \leq T$

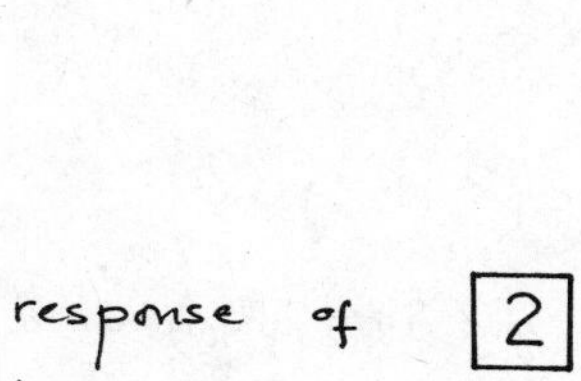

Thus,

$$v(T) = e^{-T/\tau}$$

$$= e^{-100\mu s/100\mu s}$$

$$= e^{-1} = 0.368$$

Undershoot, $\Delta V = 1 - v(T) = 1 - 0.368 = \underline{\underline{0.632 \text{ V}}}$

Chapter 3 — Exercises

1 (a) $v_2 - v_1 = \frac{v_3}{1000} = 0.001 \text{ V}$

Since $v_2 = 0$, $v_1 = \underline{\underline{-0.001 \text{ V}}}$

(b) $v_2 - v_1 = \frac{v_3}{1000} = \frac{-10}{1000} = -0.01 \text{ V}$

Since $v_2 = +5$ V, $v_1 = \underline{\underline{+5.01 \text{ V}}}$.

(c) $v_3 = 1000(v_2 - v_1) = 1000(0.999 - 1.001)$

$$= \underline{\underline{-2 \text{ V}}}$$

(d) $v_2 - v_1 = \frac{v_3}{1000} = \frac{-3.6}{1000} = -0.0036 \text{ V}$

Since $v_1 = -3.6$ V then

$$v_2 = \underline{\underline{-3.6036 \text{ V}}}$$

2 Refer to Fig. E3.2.

$$v_d = (g_m v_2 - g_m v_1) R$$

$$= g_m R (v_2 - v_1)$$

$$v_3 = \mu v_d$$

$$= \underline{\underline{\mu g_m R (v_2 - v_1)}}$$

Thus, $A = \mu g_m R = 100 \times 20 \times 10^{-3} \times 10 \times 10^{3}$

$A = 20{,}000\ \text{V/V}$

3 Input resistance $= R_1 \Rightarrow R_1 = 10\ \text{k}\Omega$

Voltage gain $= -\dfrac{R_2}{R_1} \Rightarrow R_2 = 10R_1 = 100\ \text{k}\Omega$

4 Apply a test current i_x at the input, as shown. For an ideal op amp, $v_1 = 0$. Thus the input resistance $\equiv \dfrac{v_1}{i_x} = 0$.

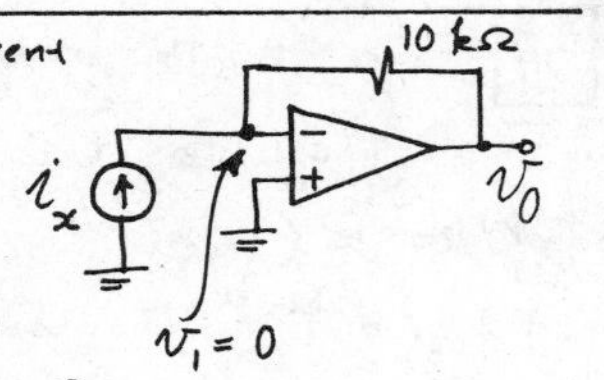

The current i_x will flow through the 10-kΩ feedback resister, resulting in $v_O = 0 - i_x \times 10\ \text{k}\Omega = -i_x \times 10\ \text{k}\Omega$

Thus, the transresistance R_m is

$R_m = -10\ \text{k}\Omega$.

Since the op amp is ideal, its output resistance will be zero and the transresistance amplifier will have $R_o = 0$.

Now, if the source shown in Fig. E3.4b is connected to the input as shown below

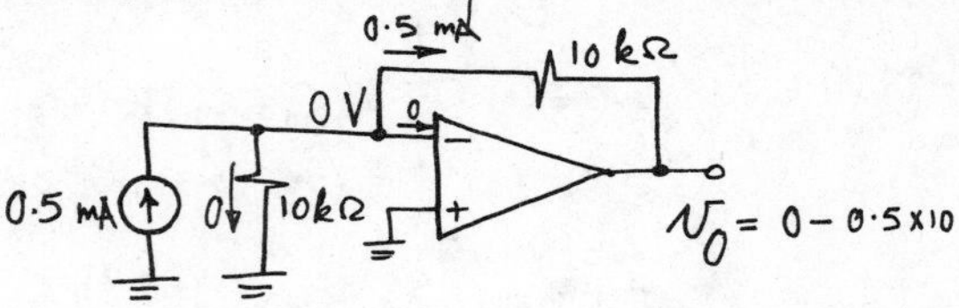

then the output voltage will be

$v_O = -5\ \text{V}$

5 The signal waveforms will be as shown.

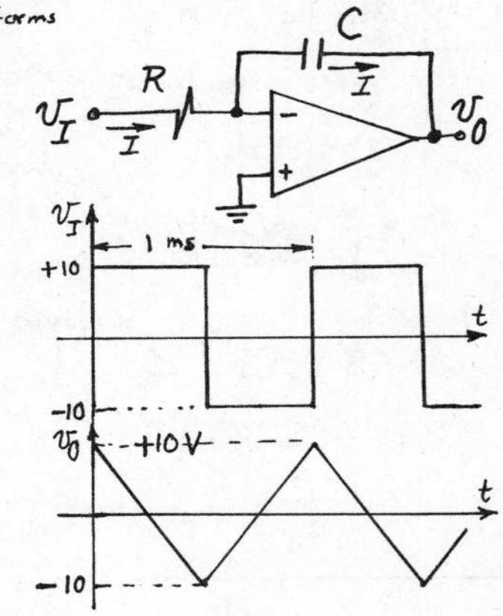

When $v_I = +10$ V, the current through the capacitor will be in the direction indicated,

$I = \dfrac{10}{R}$,

and the output

voltage will decrease linearly from +10 V to −10 V. Thus in $(\frac{T}{2})$ seconds the capacitor voltage changes by 20V. The charge equilibrium equation can be expressed as

$I\left(\frac{T}{2}\right) = C \times 20$

$\dfrac{10}{R}\,\dfrac{T}{2} = 20\,C$

$CR = \dfrac{10T}{40} = \dfrac{1}{4} \times 1.0 \times 10^{-3}$

$= 250\ \mu\text{s}$

6 Refer to Fig. E3.6.

$$\frac{V_o}{V_i} = -\frac{Z_2}{Z_1} = -\frac{Y_1}{Y_2}$$

$$= -\frac{1}{R_1}\,\frac{1}{\frac{1}{R_2} + sC_2}$$

$$= -\frac{(R_2/R_1)}{1 + sC_2R_2}$$

which is the transfer function of an STC LP network with a dc gain

of $(-R_2/R_1)$ and a corner frequency $\omega_0 = 1/C_2R_2$. For the component values given:

$$\text{dc gain} = -\frac{100\ \text{k}\Omega}{1\ \text{k}\Omega} = -100\ \text{V/V}$$

$$\text{3-dB frequency } (\omega_0) = \frac{1}{100 \times 10^{-12} \times 100 \times 10^{3}} = 10^5\ \text{rad/s}$$

7 $R =$ Input resistance $= 10\ \text{k}\Omega$

$$CR = 10^{-3}\ \text{s} \Rightarrow C = \frac{10^{-3}}{10 \times 10^{3}} = 0.1\ \mu\text{F}$$

$$\frac{V_o}{V_i} = -\frac{1}{sCR}$$

$$= -\frac{1}{j\omega CR} = -\frac{1}{j\omega \times 10^{-3}} = -\frac{10^3}{j\omega}$$

$$\left|\frac{V_o}{V_i}\right| = 10^3/\omega$$

$$\phi = 180^\circ - 90^\circ = +90^\circ$$

At $\omega = 10$ rad/s : $\left|\frac{V_o}{V_i}\right| = 100\ \text{V/V};\ \phi = +90^\circ$.

At $\omega = 1$ rad/s : $\left|\frac{V_o}{V_i}\right| = 1{,}000\ \text{V/V};\ \phi = +90^\circ$.

8 C = Input capacitance = $\underline{0.01\,\mu F}$ **3**

$$CR = 10^{-2}\,s \Rightarrow R = \frac{10^{-2}}{10^{-8}} = \underline{\underline{1\,M\Omega}}$$

$$\frac{V_o(s)}{V_i(s)} = -sCR$$

$$\frac{V_o(j\omega)}{V_i(j\omega)} = -j\omega CR$$

$$\left|\frac{V_o}{V_i}\right| = \omega CR = 10^{-2}\omega$$

$$\phi = 180^\circ + 90^\circ = 270^\circ \text{ or } -90^\circ$$

At $\omega = 10$ rad/s : $\left|\frac{V_o}{V_i}\right| = \underline{\underline{0.1\ V/V}}$; $\underline{\underline{\phi = -90^\circ}}$

At $\omega = 10^3$ rad/s : $\left|\frac{V_o}{V_i}\right| = \underline{\underline{10\ V/V}}$; $\underline{\underline{\phi = -90^\circ}}$

As $\omega \to \infty$, the capacitor approaches a short circuit and the

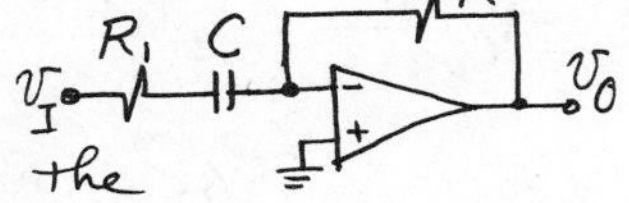

gain approaches $-R/R_1$. For $R = 1\,M\Omega$ and a gain of 100, $R_1 = \underline{\underline{10\ k\Omega}}$.

---

9 **3**

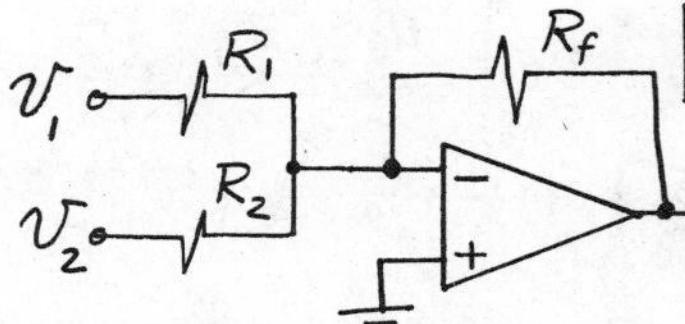

$$v_O = -\left(\frac{R_f}{R_1} v_1 + \frac{R_f}{R_2} v_2\right)$$

For a maximum value of v_O of 10 V we wish to limit the current in R_f to 1 mA. Thus $R_f \geq 10\ k\Omega$. Choosing $\underline{\underline{R_f = 10\ k\Omega}}$ and to obtain $v_O = -(v_1 + 5v_2)$,

$$R_1 = \underline{\underline{10\ k\Omega}} \text{ and } R_2 = \underline{\underline{2\ k\Omega}}$$

---

10 Set $v_2 = 0$. The voltage at the non-inverting input terminal of the op amp will be:

$$v_+ = v_1 \frac{3\ k\Omega}{2\ k\Omega + 3\ k\Omega} = 0.6\ v_1$$

and the output voltage will be

$$v_O = v_+ \times \left(1 + \frac{9\ k\Omega}{1\ k\Omega}\right) = 10 v_+ = 6 v_1$$

3

Now set $v_1 = 0$.

$$v_+ = v_2 \frac{2}{3+2} = 0.4\ v_2$$

$$v_O = v_+ \times 10 = 4\ v_2$$

Combining the contribution to v_O of v_1 and v_2 results in:

$$v_O = \underline{\underline{6 v_1 + 4 v_2}}$$

---

11 Refer to the solution of Exercise 3.10 above. To find the contribution to v_O of v_1, set

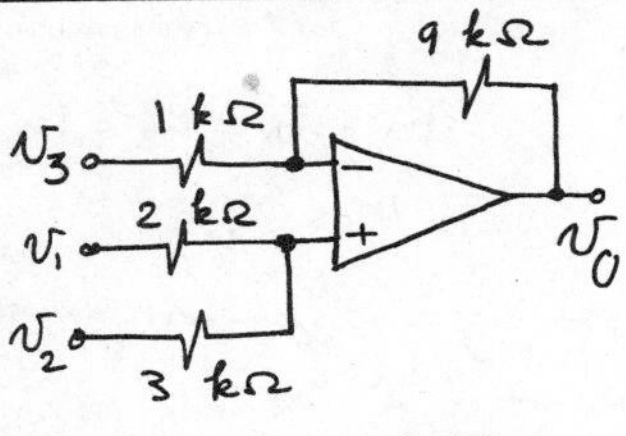

$v_2 = v_3 = 0$. The result is $v_O = 6\ v_1$.
To find the contribution of v_2, set $v_1 = v_3 = 0$.
The result is $v_O = 4 v_2$. Finally, to find the contribution of v_3, set $v_1 = v_2 = 0$.
In this case $v_+ = 0$ and a virtual ground appears at the inverting input terminal of

the op amp. Thus $v_O = -9\ v_3$. **3**

Combining the contributions of v_1, v_2 and v_3 results in

$$v_O = \underline{\underline{6 v_1 + 4 v_2 - 9 v_3}}$$

12

$$\frac{v_O}{v_I} = 1 + \frac{R_2}{R_1}$$

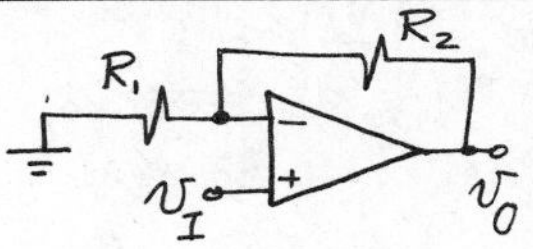

$$= 2$$

$$\Longrightarrow R_1 = R_2.$$

At $v_O = 10$ V, the current in the R_1, R_2 voltage divider is $10/(R_1 + R_2)$. To set this current to 10 μA we select $R_1 + R_2 = 1\ M\Omega$. Thus

$$R_1 = R_2 = \underline{\underline{0.5\ M\Omega}}$$

---

13 (a)

$$i = \frac{v_I - v_O/A}{R_1}$$

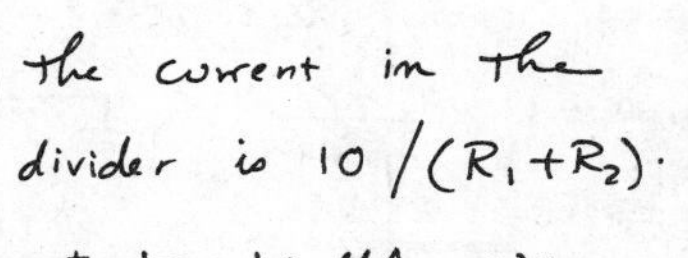

$$v_O = \left(v_I - \frac{v_O}{A}\right) + iR_2$$

$$v_O = v_I - \frac{v_O}{A} + \frac{R_2}{R_1}\left(v_I - \frac{v_O}{A}\right)$$

$$v_O\left[1 + \frac{1}{A} + \frac{R_2}{R_1}\frac{1}{A}\right] = v_I\left(1 + \frac{R_2}{R_1}\right)$$

$$G \equiv \frac{v_O}{v_I} = \frac{1 + R_2/R_1}{1 + \left(1 + \frac{R_2}{R_1}\right)/A} \qquad \text{Q.E.D}$$

(b) For $R_1 = 1\ k\Omega$ and $R_2 = 9\ k\Omega$, the ideal gain is 10 and the actual gain

$$G = \frac{10}{1 + (10/A)}$$

(i) $A = 10^3$: $G = 9.9$ $\quad \epsilon = \underline{-1\%}$

$v_I = 1\ V \quad v_O = 9.9\ V \quad v_2 - v_1 = \frac{9.9\ V}{10^3} = \underline{\underline{9.9\ mV}}$

(ii) $A = 10^4$: $G = 9.99$ $\quad \epsilon = \underline{-0.1\%}$

$v_I = 1\ V \quad v_O = 9.99\ V \quad v_2 - v_1 = \frac{9.99}{10^4} \simeq \underline{\underline{1\ mV}}$

(iii) $A = 10^5$: $G = 9.999$ $\quad \epsilon = \underline{-0.01\%}$

$v_I = 1\ V \quad v_O = 9.999\ V \quad v_2 - v_1 = \frac{9.999}{10^5} \simeq \underline{\underline{0.1\ mV}}$

14 Input resistance $= R_1 + R_3 = 4\ k\Omega$. Selecting $R_1 = R_3$ results in $\underline{\underline{R_1 = R_3 = 2\ k\Omega}}$.

To operate as a differential amplifier

$$\frac{R_2}{R_1} = \frac{R_4}{R_3}.$$

Thus $R_2 = R_4$. Since the gain of the differential amplifier is equal to (R_2/R_1), then for a gain of 100 we select

$$\underline{\underline{R_2 = R_4 = 200\ k\Omega}}$$

15 $I = \frac{V_i - V_-}{R_1}$

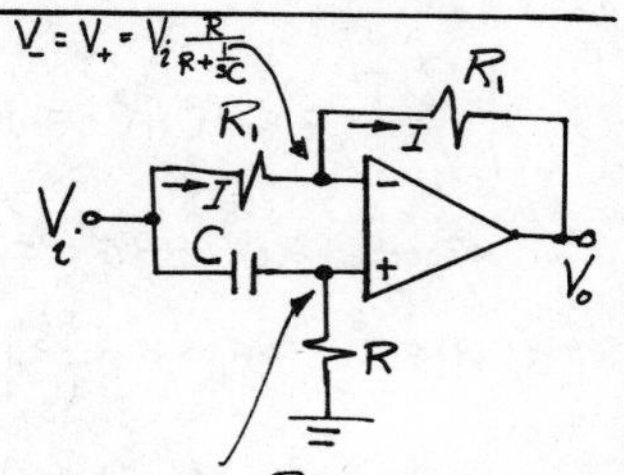

$$= \frac{1}{R_1}\left[V_i - V_i \frac{R}{R + \frac{1}{sC}}\right]$$

$$= \frac{V_i}{R_1}\,\frac{1/sC}{R + \frac{1}{sC}}$$

$$V_o = V_- - IR_1 \qquad V_+ = V_i \frac{R}{R + \frac{1}{sC}}$$

$$= V_i \frac{R}{R + \frac{1}{sC}} - V_i \frac{1/sC}{R + \frac{1}{sC}}$$

$$\frac{V_o(s)}{V_i(s)} = \frac{R - 1/sC}{R + 1/sC} = \underline{\underline{\frac{s - 1/RC}{s + 1/RC}}}$$

For the given component values

$$\frac{V_o(s)}{V_i(s)} = \frac{s - \frac{1}{10^{-8} \times 20 \times 10^3}}{s + \frac{1}{10^{-8} \times 20 \times 10^3}} = \frac{s - 5000}{s + 5000}$$

$$\frac{V_o(j\omega)}{V_i(j\omega)} = \frac{j\omega - 5000}{j\omega + 5000}$$

$$\left|\frac{V_o}{V_i}\right| = \underline{\underline{1}}$$

At $\omega = 5000$ rad/s : $\phi = 135° - 45° = \underline{\underline{+90°}}$

16 $v_+ = 10\ mV \times \frac{R_{in}}{R_{in} + 0.9\ M\Omega}$

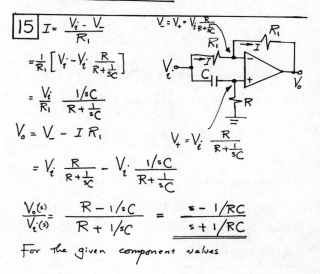

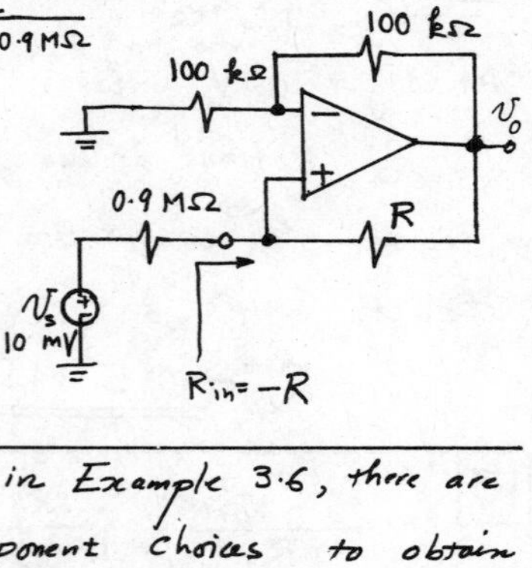

$$100 = 10 \times \frac{-R}{-R + 0.9}$$

$$\Rightarrow R = \underline{\underline{1.0\ M\Omega}}$$

$$v_o = v_+ \times 2$$

$$= \underline{\underline{200\ mV}}$$

17 As mentioned in Example 3.6, there are two possible component choices to obtain $Z_{in} = sL$. In the first, Z_2 is selected as

a capacitor. In the second, Z_4 is selected as a capacitor. Using this second choice, the input impedance is

$$Z_{in} = \frac{Z_1 Z_3 Z_5}{Z_2 Z_4}$$

$$= s\,C_4\,R_1 R_3 R_5 / R_2$$

Selecting all resistances to be equal,

$$R_1 = R_2 = R_3 = R_5 = R$$

$$Z_{in} = sC_4R^2 = s \times 0.1\ H \Rightarrow C_4R^2 = 0.1$$

Using the suggestion given in the Exercise statement, namely to select R equal to the reactance realized at the frequency of operation ($\omega = 10^4$ rad/s) yields

$$\omega C_4 R^2 = R$$

$$10^4 \times 0.1 = R \Rightarrow \underline{\underline{R = 1\ k\Omega}}$$

$$C_4 = \frac{0.1}{10^6} = \underline{\underline{0.1\ \mu F}}$$

18 3

106 dB $\Rightarrow A_0 = 200{,}000$

$|A| \simeq \frac{f_t}{f}$

$f = 1$ kHz $\quad |A| = \frac{2\text{ MHz}}{1\text{ kHz}} = \underline{\underline{2{,}000\ \text{V/V}}}$

$f = 10$ kHz $\quad |A| = \frac{2\text{ MHz}}{10\text{ kHz}} = \underline{\underline{200\ \text{V/V}}}$

$f = 100$ kHz $\quad |A| = \frac{2\text{ MHz}}{100\text{ kHz}} = \underline{\underline{20\ \text{V/V}}}$

19 Closed loop gain = 100 $\Rightarrow 1 + \frac{R_2}{R_1} = 100$

$f_{3\text{-dB}} = f_t \Big/ \left(1 + \frac{R_2}{R_1}\right)$

$= 2\text{ MHz}/100 = \underline{\underline{20\text{ kHz}}}$

$t_r \simeq 2.2\tau$

$= 2.2/\omega_{3dB} = \frac{2.2}{2\pi \times 20\times10^3} = \underline{\underline{17.5\ \mu s}}$

20 Feedback factor, $\beta \equiv \frac{R_1}{R_1+R_2} = \underline{\underline{0.01\ \text{V/V}}}$

Loop Gain $= -A\beta = -10^4 \times 0.01 = \underline{\underline{-100\ \text{V/V}}}$

21 β = Feedback signal / Output signal

$= \underline{\underline{1}}$

22 3

$v_O = v_I - \frac{v_O}{A_0}$

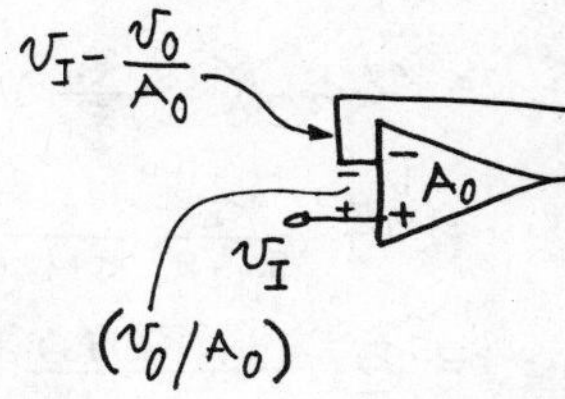

$\underline{\underline{\frac{v_O}{v_I} = \frac{1}{1+\frac{1}{A_0}}}}$

$A_0 = 10^3 \quad \frac{v_O}{v_I} = \underline{\underline{0.9990}}$

$A_0 = 10^5 \quad \frac{v_O}{v_I} = \underline{\underline{0.999990}}$

23 Largest peak-to-peak input $= \frac{20\text{ V}}{100}$

$= \underline{\underline{0.2\text{ V}}}$

24 See figure.

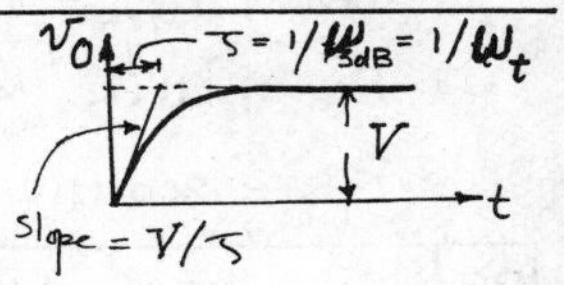

$\frac{V}{\tau} = SR$

$V \cdot \omega_t = SR$

$V = \frac{SR}{2\pi f_t} = \frac{10^6\text{ V/s}}{2\pi \times 10^6} = \underline{\underline{0.16\text{ V}}}$

$t_r \simeq 2.2\tau = \frac{2.2}{2\pi \times 10^6} = \underline{\underline{0.35\ \mu s}}$

3

With an input voltage step of height 1.6 V:

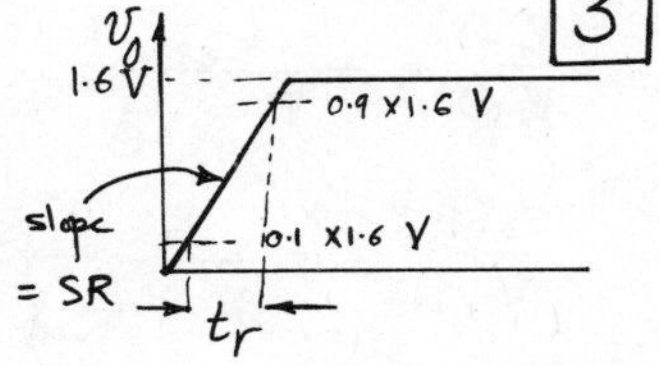

$t_r = 0.8 \times \frac{1.6}{10^6}$

$= \underline{\underline{1.28\ \mu s}}$

25 $SR = \frac{I_{max}}{C}$

$= \frac{19\times10^{-6}}{30\times10^{-12}} = \underline{\underline{0.63\ \text{V}/\mu s}}$

26 $\omega_M V_{omax} = SR$

$f_M = \frac{SR}{2\pi V_{omax}}$

$= \frac{10^6}{2\pi \times 10} = \underline{\underline{15.9\text{ kHz}}}$

With $f = 5f_M$, the maximum possible amplitude without slew distortion is

$V_{omax}/5 = \frac{10}{5} = \underline{\underline{2\text{ V}}}$

27 3

To find the common-mode gain of the difference amplifier, we connect the two input together and

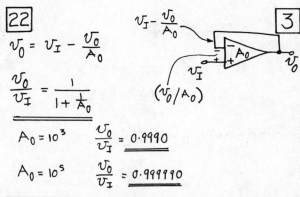

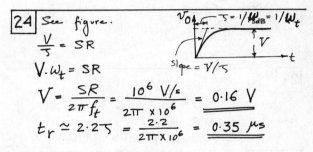

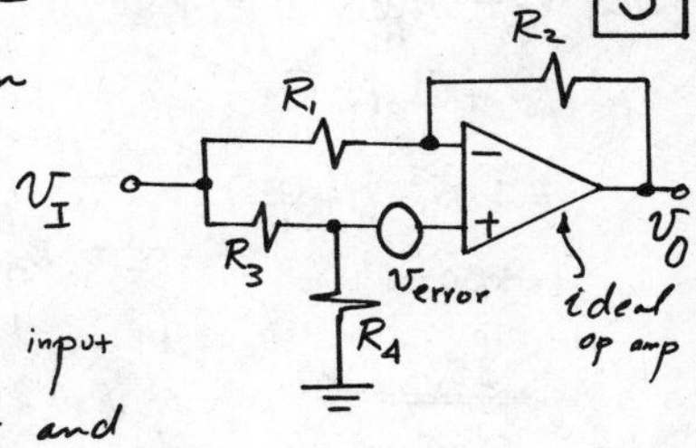

apply an input signal v_I. If the op amp were ideal and $\frac{R_2}{R_1} = \frac{R_4}{R_3}$ the output would be zero. The finite common-mode rejection ratio (CMRR) of the op amp can be taken into account by replacing the op amp with an ideal one (infinite CMRR) and including an error voltage source, V_{error}:

$V_{error} = v_+/\text{CMRR}$ (from Eq 3.34)

$= v_I \frac{R_4}{R_3+R_4} \frac{1}{\text{CMRR}}$

This error voltage will be amplified by the closed loop gain of the circuit (with the source v_I set to zero:) Thus

$$v_O = v_{error}\left(1+\frac{R_2}{R_1}\right)$$

$$= v_I \frac{R_4}{R_3+R_4}\frac{1}{CMRR}\left(1+\frac{R_2}{R_1}\right)$$

$$= v_I \frac{1+(R_2/R_1)}{1+(R_4/R_3)}\left(\frac{R_4}{R_3}\right)\frac{1}{CMRR}$$

Common-mode gain $\equiv \dfrac{v_O}{v_I}$

$$= \frac{R_4}{R_3}\;\frac{1}{CMRR}$$

$$= \frac{1000}{10^4} = \underline{\underline{0.1\ V/V}}$$

---

28 $R_{in} = (2R_{icm}) // [(1+A\beta)R_{id}]$

Substituting $R_{icm} = 100\ M\Omega$, $A = 10^4$, $\beta = 1$, and $R_{id} = 1\ M\Omega$ gives

$$R_{in} \simeq 200\ M\Omega // 10^4\ M\Omega \simeq \underline{\underline{200\ M\Omega}}$$

---

29 $R_{in} = (2R_{icm}) // [(1+A\beta)R_{id}]$

Substituting $R_{icm} = 100\ M\Omega$, $A = 10^4$, $\beta = 0.01$ and $R_{id} = 1\ M\Omega$ gives

$$R_{in} = 200\ M\Omega // [101 \times 1]\ M\Omega = \underline{\underline{67\ M\Omega}}$$

---

30 Refer to Fig. 3.40(a)

$R_o = \underline{\underline{100\ \Omega}}$

$$\frac{R_o}{A_0\beta} = \frac{100}{10^5 \times 0.01} = \underline{\underline{0.1\ \Omega}}$$

$$L = \frac{R_o}{\beta\omega_t} = \frac{100}{0.01 \times 2\pi \times 10^6} = \underline{\underline{1.59\ mH}}$$

---

31 DC offset voltage at output $= 4\ mV \times 1000$
$= 4\ V$

Maximum amplitude of output sinusoid
$= 12 - 4 = 8\ V$

Maximum amplitude of input sinusoid $= \dfrac{8}{1000} = \underline{8\ mV}$

If the amplifier is capacitively coupled as in Fig. 3.48, the output dc offset voltage reduces to 4 mV which is negligibly small. In this case we can apply a 12-mV amplitude sinusoid at the input without output clipping.

---

32 $V_O = V_{off}\left(1+\frac{R_2}{R_1}\right) + I_{off} R_2$

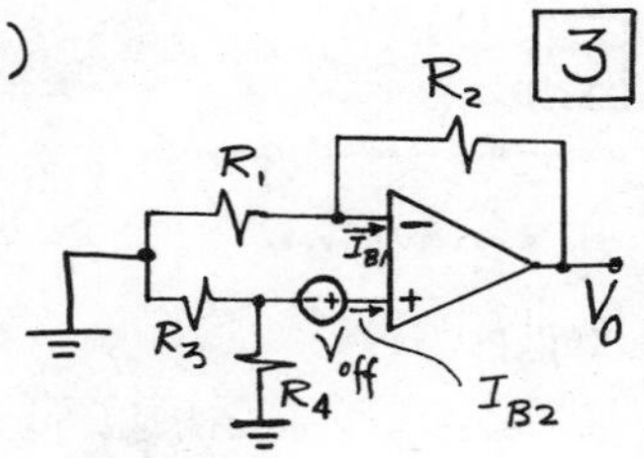

$$= 3\times10^{-3} \times \left(1+\frac{1000}{10}\right) + 50\times10^{-9} \times 10^6$$

$$= \underline{353\ mV}$$

Note that if the two components of V_O subtract then $V_O = \underline{253\ mV}$.

---

33 $f_0 = \dfrac{1}{2\pi CR_1}$

$$10 = \frac{1}{2\pi CR_1} \Rightarrow CR_1 = \frac{1}{20\pi}$$

For $f \gg f_0$, C acts as a short circuit and the gain approaches $-R_2/R_1$. For a gain of 100. $\Longrightarrow$ $R_2/R_1 = 100$.

At such high frequencies, the input resistance is almost equal to R_1. $\Rightarrow R_1 = \underline{1\ k\Omega}$

$R_2 = \underline{100\ k\Omega}$

$$C = \frac{1}{20\pi \times 10^3} = 15.9\ \mu F$$

$$\frac{V_o(s)}{V_i(s)} = -\frac{R_2}{R_1 + \frac{1}{sC}}$$

$$\frac{V_o(j\omega)}{V_i(j\omega)} = -\frac{R_2}{R_1 + \frac{1}{j\omega C}} = -\frac{R_2/R_1}{1 - j\frac{1}{\omega CR_1}}$$

$$\left|\frac{V_o}{V_i}\right| = \frac{R_2/R_1}{\sqrt{1+\left(\frac{\omega_0}{\omega}\right)^2}}$$

$$\phi = 180° + \tan^{-1}\left(\frac{\omega_0}{\omega}\right)$$

At $\omega = 2\pi \times 100$

$$\left|\frac{V_o}{V_i}\right| = \frac{100}{\sqrt{1+0.01}} = \underline{\underline{99.5\ V/V}}$$

$$\phi = 180° + \tan^{-1} 0.1$$

$$= \underline{\underline{180° + 5.7°}}$$

Chapter 4 — Exercises

1

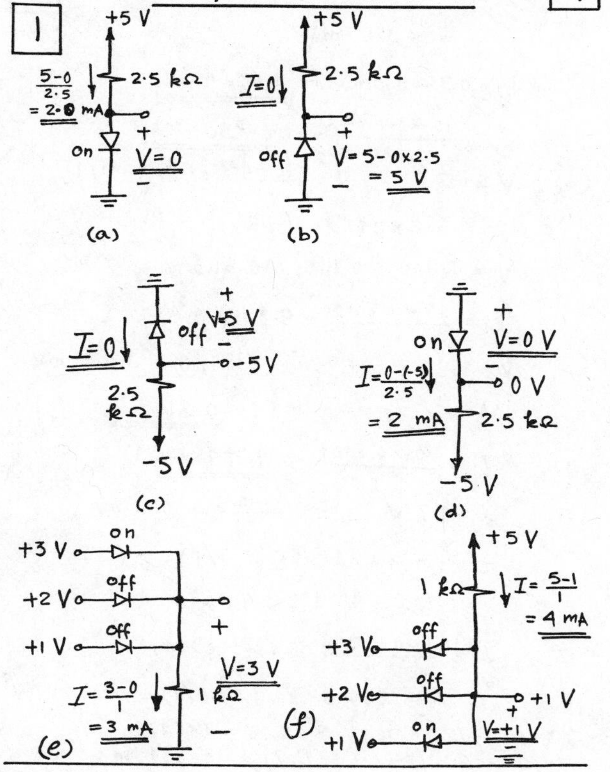

2 The current will consist of half sine waves having a peak value of

$$\hat{I} = \frac{10}{R+50}$$

Thus

$$I_{av} = \frac{1}{\pi}\,\frac{10}{R+50}$$

To obtain full-scale reading, $I_{av} = 1$ mA which results in

$$R + 50 = \frac{10}{\pi} \times 10^3 \Rightarrow R = 3133\ \Omega$$

3

$$i \simeq I_S\, e^{v/nV_T}$$

$$I_1 = I_S\, e^{V_1/nV_T}$$

$$I_2 = I_S\, e^{V_2/nV_T}$$

$$\frac{I_1}{I_2} = e^{(V_1 - V_2)/nV_T}$$

$$V_1 - V_2 = n V_T \ln (I_1/I_2)$$

$$= 1.5 \times 25 \ln (10/0.1)$$

$$= 172.7 \text{ mV}$$

4

$$v_2 - v_1 = n V_T \ln (i_2/i_1)$$

$v_1 = 0.7$ V, $i_1 = 1$ mA and $n = 1$, thus

$$v_2 = 0.7 + V_T \ln (i_2)$$

For $i_2 = 0.1$ mA,

$$v_2 = 0.7 + 0.025 \ln (0.1) = 0.64 \text{ V}$$

For $i_2 = 10$ mA,

$$v_2 = 0.7 + 0.025 \ln (10) = 0.76 \text{ V}$$

5

$$I_S = 10^{-14} \times (1.15)^{100}$$

$$= 1.17 \times 10^{-8} \text{ A}$$

6 At 20°C the reverse current is

$$I = \frac{1\text{ V}}{1\text{ M}\Omega} = 1\ \mu\text{A}$$

Since the reverse current doubles for every 10°C rise in temperature it becomes 4 μA at 40°C, resulting in V = 4 V. The reverse current reduces to 0.25 μA at 0°C with the result that V = 0.25 V.

7 Design #1 (R = 110 Ω)

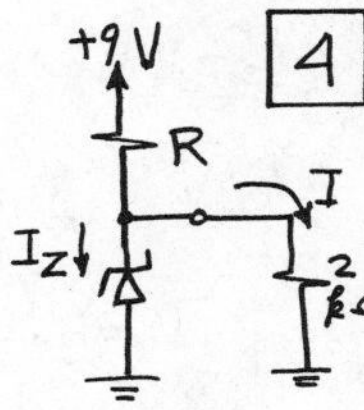

$$I = \frac{6.8}{2} = 3.4 \text{ mA}$$

$$I_Z \cong \frac{9-6.8}{0.110} - 3.4$$

$$= 20 - 3.4 = 16.6 \text{ mA}$$

Thus the zener will still have plenty of current. Its' current has simply decreased by 3.4 mA. Thus its voltage will decrease by 3.4 mA × r_Z = 3.4 × 5 = 17 mV

Design #2 (R = 8.8 kΩ)

$$I_Z = \frac{9-6.8}{8.8} - 3.4 = \text{negative value.}$$

Thus the zener will no longer be operating in the zener mode; it will operate as a reverse-biased diode conducting a negligible current. The output voltage will be determined by the voltage divider formed by R (8.8 kΩ) and the 2-kΩ load resistance. Thus

$$V_O = 9\,\frac{2}{2+8.8} = 1.67\text{ V}$$ 4

and the change in output voltage is

$$\Delta V_O = 1.67 - 6.8 = \underline{\underline{-5.13\text{ V}}}$$

8 Please note that the value of V^+ was missing in the first printing : $V^+ = 20$ V.

(a) $\Delta V_O = \pm 2 \times \frac{r_Z}{r_Z + R} = \pm 2 \times \frac{0.1}{0.1+1}$

$= \pm 0.18$ V

Thus, the voltage regulation is $\frac{\pm 0.18}{10} \times 100$

$= \underline{\underline{\pm 1.8\ \%}}$

(b) For a 2-mA load current, the output voltage changes by

$\Delta V_O = -2 \times 100 = -200$ mV

Thus the load regulation is -100 mV/mA

or $\underline{\underline{-1\ \%/\text{mA}}}$

9 (a) $V_2 - V_1 = n V_T \ln(I_2/I_1)$

$V = 0.7$ V $\quad I = \frac{10-0.7}{10} = 0.93$ mA

4

$V_2 - V_1 = 2 \times 25 \ln(0.93/1)$

$= -3.6$ mV

$V = 0.7 - 0.0036 = \underline{\underline{0.6964\text{ V}}}$

$I = \frac{10-0.6946}{10} = \underline{\underline{0.930\text{ mA}}}$

(b) $V = 0.7$ V $\quad I = \frac{10-0.7}{1} = 9.3$ mA

$V_2 - V_1 = 2 \times 25 \ln(9.3/1) = 111.5$ mV

$V = 0.700 + 0.1115 = 0.8115$ V

$I = \frac{10-0.8115}{1} = 9.189$ mA

$V_2 - V_1 = 2 \times 25 \ln(9.189/1) = 110.9$ mV

$V = 0.700 + 0.1109 = \underline{\underline{0.8109\text{ V}}}$

$I = \frac{10-0.8109}{1} = \underline{\underline{9.189\text{ mA}}}$

(c) $V = 0.7$ V $\quad I = \frac{1-0.7}{1} = 0.3$ mA

$V_2 - V_1 = 2 \times 25 \ln(0.3/1) = -60.2$ mV

$V = 0.700 - 0.0602 = 0.6398$

$I = \frac{1-0.6398}{1} = 0.360$ mA

$V_2 - V_1 = 2 \times 25 \ln(0.36/1) = -51.08$ mV

$V = 0.700 - 0.05108 = 0.6489$ V

$I = (1 - 0.6489)/1 = 0.351$ mA

$V_2 - V_1 = 2 \times 25 \times \ln\left(\frac{0.351}{1}\right) = -52.3$ mV 4

$V = 0.7 - 0.0523 = \underline{\underline{0.6477\text{ V}}}$

$I = \frac{1-0.6477}{1} = \underline{\underline{0.352\text{ mA}}}$

10 Iterate to find V_1:

$V_D = 0.7$ V $\quad V_1 = 3 \times 0.7 = 2.1$ V $\quad I = \frac{10-2.1}{1} = 7.9$ mA

$V_D = 0.7 + 0.025 \ln\left(\frac{7.9}{1}\right) = 0.7517$

$V_1 = 2.255$ V $\quad I = 7.745$ mA

$V_D = 0.7 + 0.025 \ln\left(\frac{7.745}{1}\right) = 0.7512$V

$V_1 = \underline{\underline{2.254\text{ V}}}$

<u>With the supply voltage at +15 V:</u>

$V_D = 0.7$ V $\quad V_1 = 3 \times 0.7 = 2.1$ V $\quad I = \frac{15-2.1}{1} = 12.9$ mA

$V_D = 0.7 + 0.025 \ln\left(\frac{12.9}{1}\right) = 0.7639$ V

$V_1 = 2.292$ V $\quad I = 12.71$ mA

$V_D = 0.76356$ V $\quad V_1 = 2.2907$ V

$\Delta V_1 = \underline{\underline{36.7\text{ mV}}}$

<u>With the supply voltage at +5 V:</u>

4

$V_D = 0.7$ V $\quad V_1 = 2.1$ V $\quad I = \frac{5-2.1}{1} = 2.9$ mA

$V_D = 0.7 + 0.025 \ln(2.9) = 0.7266$ V

$V_1 = 2.18$ V $\quad I = 2.82$ mA

$V_D = 0.7 + 0.025 \ln(2.82) = 0.726$ V

$V_1 = 2.178$ V

$\Delta V_1 = \underline{\underline{-76\text{ mV}}}$

11 Modeling the diode as a series combination of a 0.5-V battery and a 200-Ω resistance we obtain the equivalent circuit shown.

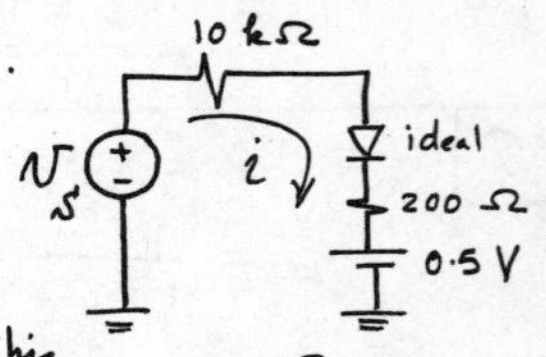

$v_S = t$

Obviously, for the diode to conduct, v_S must exceed 0.5 V. This occurs at $t = 0.5$ s. Thus,

$\underline{\underline{i = 0, \quad t \le 0.5\text{ s}}}$

For $t \ge 0.5$ s, the current can be found from the equivalent circuit as

$$i = \frac{t - 0.5}{10.2}\ \text{mA}, \quad t \geq 0.5\ \text{s}$$

12 Equation (4.12) provides the exact value of total current as (for n=1)

$$i_D = I_D\, e^{v_d/V_T}$$

Equation (4.14) provides an approximate value of i_D based on the assumption that $v_d \ll V_T$ as

$$i_D \cong I_D\left(1 + \frac{v_d}{V_T}\right)$$

For $v_d = 2$ mV:

Exact $i_D = 1.083\, I_D$ Approximate $i_D = 1.08\, I_D$

Error $= 0.003\, I_D$ or 0.3%

For $v_d = 5$ mV:

Exact $i_D = 1.2214\, I_D$ Approximate $i_D = 1.2\, I_D$

Error $= 0.0214\, I_D$ or 1.75%

For $v_d = 10$ mV

Exact $i_D = 1.49182\, I_D$ Approximate $i_D = 1.4\, I_D$

Error $= 0.09182\, I_D$ or 6.2%

For $v_d = 25$ mV:

Exact $i_D = 2.71828\, I_D$ Approximate $= 2\, I_D$

Error $= 0.71828\, I_D$ or 26.4%

13

$$i_D = I_S\, e^{v_D/nV_T}$$

$$r_d \equiv \left[\left.\frac{\partial i_D}{\partial v_D}\right|_{i_D = I_D}\right]^{-1}$$

$$\frac{\partial i_D}{\partial v_D} = \frac{I_S}{nV_T}\, e^{v_D/nV_T}$$

$$= \frac{i_D}{nV_T}$$

$$\left.\frac{\partial i_D}{\partial v_D}\right|_{i_D = I_D} = \frac{I_D}{nV_T}$$

Thus,

$$r_d = \frac{nV_T}{I_D}$$

Chapter 5— Exercises

1

$$i = \frac{v_O}{R}$$

$$i = I_S\, e^{v_D/nV_T} \quad (1)$$

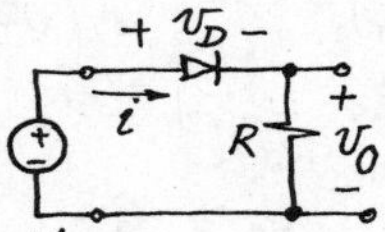

For $i = 1$ mA, denote v_D by V_{D1}:

$$1 = I_S\, e^{V_{D1}/nV_T} \quad (2)$$

Combining Eqs.(1) and (2) gives

$$i = e^{(v_D - V_{D1})/nV_T}$$

Thus,

$$v_D = V_{D1} + nV_T \ln(i)$$

where i is in milliamps. Substituting $i = \frac{v_O}{R}$ gives (with v_O in volts and R in kΩs)

$$v_D = V_{D1} + nV_T \ln\left(\frac{v_O}{R}\right)$$

Now from the circuit we have

$$v_I = v_O + v_D$$

$$= v_O + V_{D1} + nV_T \ln\left(\frac{v_O}{R}\right)$$

2 Since the op amp is ideal, $v_O = v_I$ for $v_I > 0$.

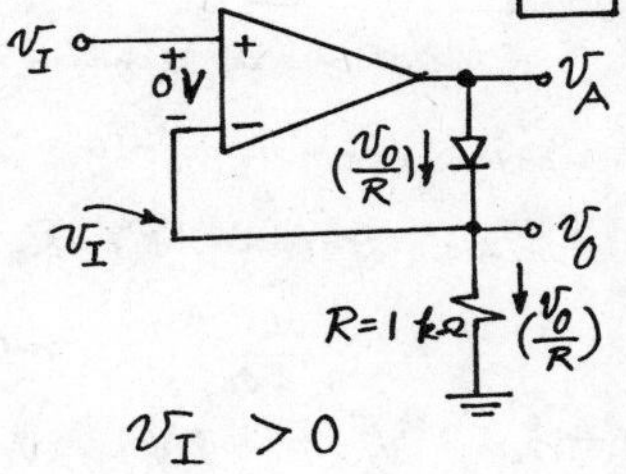

$v_I = 10$ mV:

$v_O = 10$ mV

$$i_D = \frac{10\ \text{mV}}{1\ \text{k}\Omega} = 10\ \mu\text{A} \qquad v_I > 0$$

i_D	1 mA	0.1 mA	10 μA
v_D	0.7 V	0.6 V	0.5 V

Thus $v_D = 0.5$ V and $v_A = v_O + v_D = 0.51$ V

$v_I = 1$ V:

$v_O = 1$ V

$i_D = 1$ mA $v_D = 0.7$ V $v_A = 1.7$ V

$v_I = -1$ V

The negative-feedback loop is not operative. See figure →

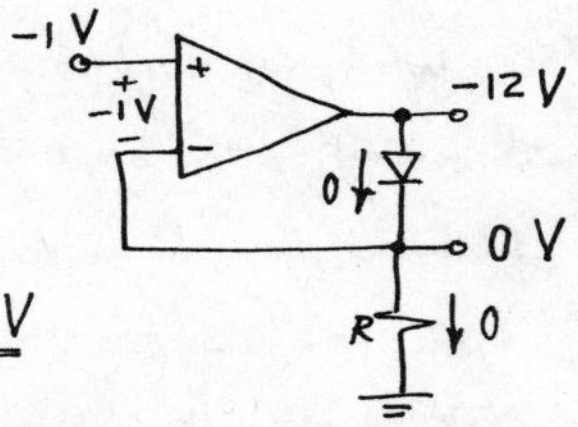

$v_O = 0$ V $v_A = -12$ V

3 **5**

For the diode to conduct and close the negative-feedback loop, v_O must be negative. This will happen when v_I is negative, in which case the negative feedback causes a virtual short circuit to appear between the input terminals of the op amp and thus $v_O = v_I$.

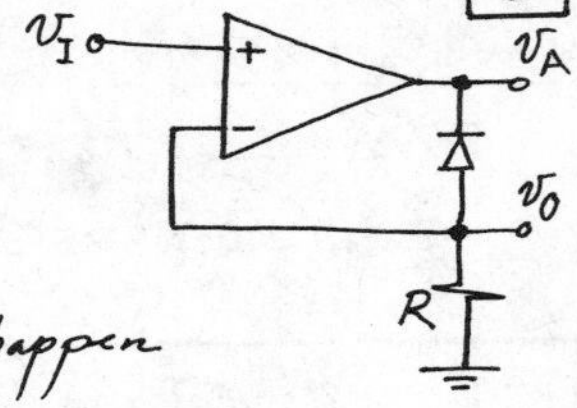

For positive v_I, the op amp saturates in the positive direction with v_A equal to the positive saturation level. The diode will be cut off and $v_O = 0$.

In summary: $v_O = 0$ for $v_I \geq 0$
$v_O = v_I$ for $v_I \leq 0$

---

4 Refer to Fig. 5.4a. **5**

For $v_I = +1\,V$:

D_2 will conduct and close the negative-feedback loop around the op amp. $v_- = 0$, the current through R_1 and D_2 will be 1 mA. Thus the voltage at the op amp output, $v_A = \underline{-0.7\,V}$. D_1 will be off and no current will flow through R_2. Thus $v_O = \underline{0\,V}$.

For $v_I = -10\,mV$:

D_1 will conduct through R_2 and R_1 to v_I. The negative-feedback loop of the op amp will thus be closed and a virtual ground will appear at the inverting input terminal. D_2 will be cut off. The current through R_1, R_2 and D_2 will be $10\,mV/1\,k\Omega = 10\,\mu A$. Thus the diode ($D_1$) voltage will be 0.5 V. $v_O = 0 + 10\,\mu A \times 10\,k\Omega = \underline{+0.1\,V}$

$v_A = v_{D1} + v_O = 0.5 + 0.1 = \underline{0.6\,V}$

5

For $v_I = -1\,V$:

Operation is similar to that described above for $v_I = -10\,mV$. Here, however, the current through R_1, R_2 and D_1 will be

$$I = \frac{1\,V}{1\,k\Omega} = 1\,mA$$

Thus $V_{D1} = 0.7\,V$. $v_O = 0 + 1\,mA \times 10\,k\Omega = \underline{10\,V}$

$$v_A = v_{D1} + v_O = \underline{10.7\,V}$$

---

5 When v_I goes positive, current flows from v_I through R_1, R_2 and D_1 into the output terminal of the op amp. Thus a negative-feedback loop is closed around the op amp with the result that a virtual ground appears at the inverting input terminal. Thus

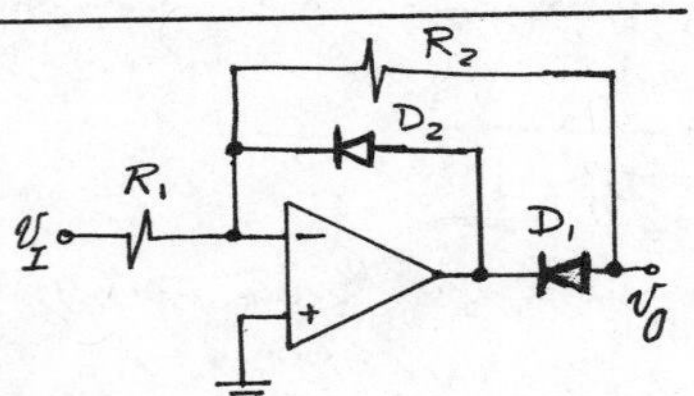

5

the current that flows from v_I through R_1 is (v_I/R_1). This current flows through R_2, causing v_O to be

$$v_O = 0 - \left(\frac{v_I}{R_1}\right) \times R_2$$

Thus, $v_O = -\left(\frac{R_2}{R_1}\right) v_I$

The negative v_O causes the op amp output voltage to be even more negative. Thus diode D_2 will be off.

When v_I goes negative current flows from the op amp output terminal through D_2 and R_1 to v_I. Again a negative-feedback loop is closed around the op amp and a virtual ground appears at the op amp inverting input. The op amp output voltage will be positive (at one diode drop higher than ground) and thus D_1 will be off. No current will flow through

R_2 and thus $v_O = 0$.

In summary:

$v_O = -\frac{R_2}{R_1} v_I$ for $v_I \geq 0$

$v_O = 0$ for $v_I \leq 0$

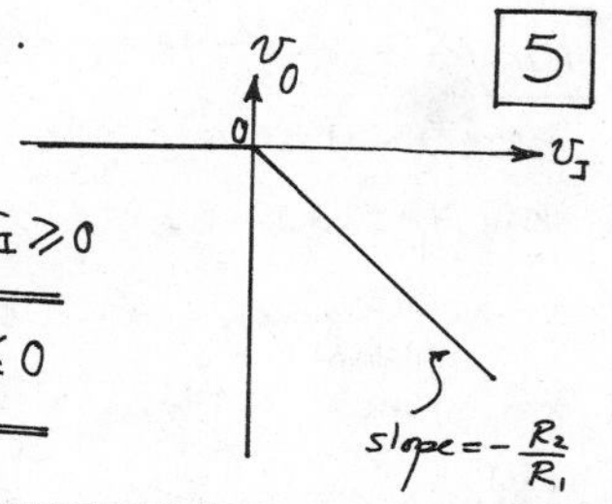

5

6

When v_I is positive D_2 will be on and D_1 will be off. D_2 will close the feedback loop and will conduct a current of $\left(\frac{15}{3R} + \frac{v_I}{R}\right)$. In this case $v_O = 0$. This situation remains even if v_I goes negative. In fact this situation obtains as long as a net positive current is forced thru D_2. Thus the situation changes when the current $\left(\frac{15}{3R} + \frac{v_I}{R}\right)$ is reduced to zero, which occurs when $v_I = -5$ V.

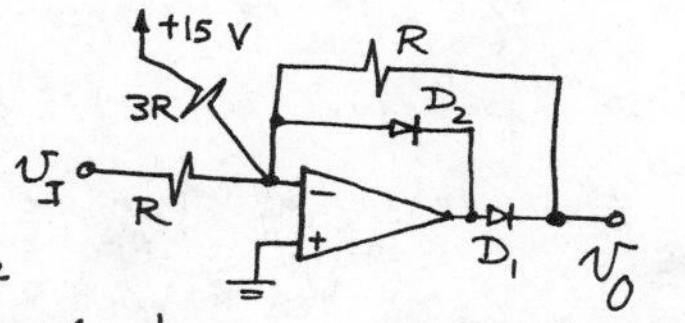

5

For $v_I \leq -5$ V, diode D_2 will be off and D_1 will turn on and close the feedback loop through the resistor R. In this case: $v_O = -\left(\frac{15}{3R} + \frac{v_I}{R}\right) R$

In summary:

For $v_I \geq -5$ V, $v_O = 0$

and for $v_I \leq -5$ V, $v_O = -v_I - 5$

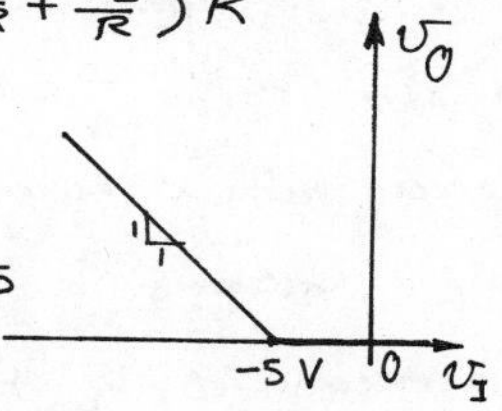

7

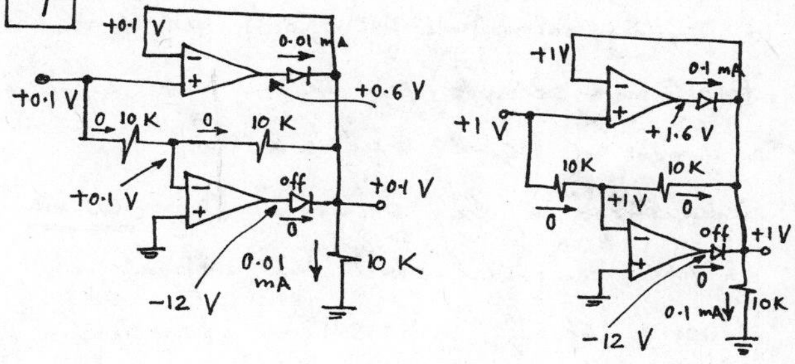

5

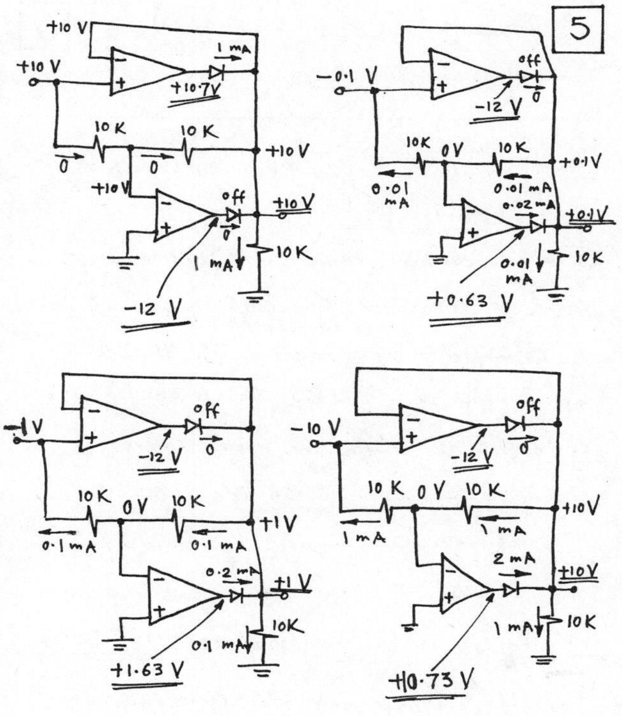

8

5

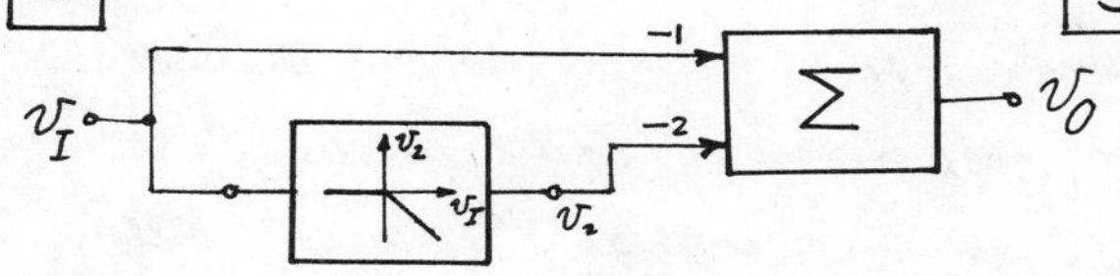

For $v_I \geq 0$, i.e. $v_I = |v_I|$, $v_2 = -|v_I|$, and

$$v_O = -1 \times |v_I| - 2 \times -|v_I| = +|v_I|.$$

For $v_I \leq 0$, i.e. $v_I = -|v_I|$, $v_2 = 0$, and

$$v_O = -1 \times -|v_I| - 2 \times 0 = +|v_I|.$$

Thus, the block diagram implements the absolute value operation.

Using the circuit of Fig. 5.4a, with the diodes reversed, to implement the half-wave rectifier, and a weighted summer results in the circuit shown below.

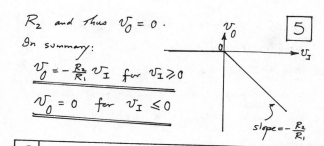

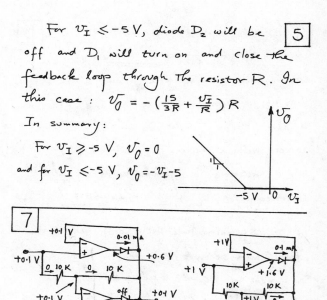

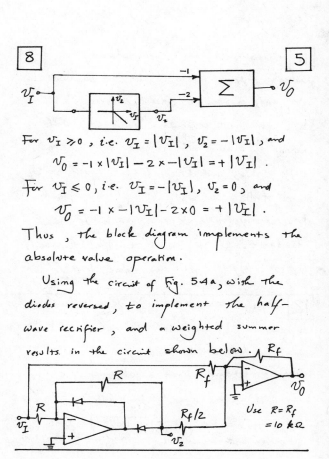

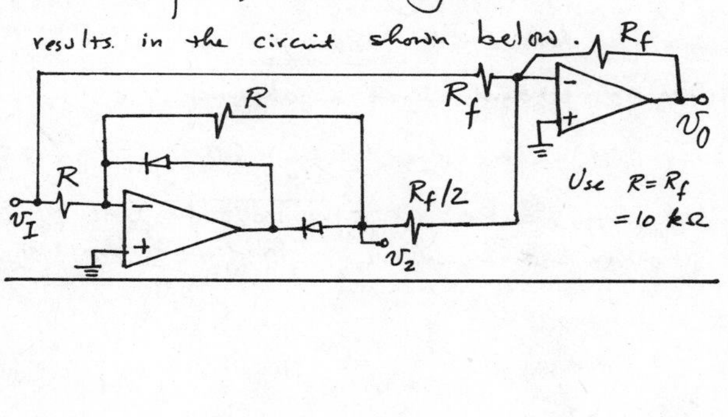

9 (a) Peak current in each diode

$$= \frac{100\text{ V}}{1\text{ k}\Omega} = 100\text{ mA}.$$

(b) Consider the half cycle during which v_B and v_C are positive. D_1 is on and acts as a short circuit while D_2 is off. The reverse voltage across D_2 will be $(v_L + v_C)$ which attains a peak value of 200 V.

(c) Average of $v_L = \frac{2}{\pi} \times 100 = 63.7$ V.

(d) During each half cycle, only half of the transformer secondary is active and supplying a current of 100-mA peak. Thus, the peak current in the primary will be 100 mA.

(e) The sinusoidal source has a peak value of 100 V (i.e. $\frac{100}{\sqrt{2}}$-V RMS) and supplies a peak current of 100 mA (i.e. $\frac{0.1}{\sqrt{2}}$-A RMS). Thus the power supplied by the source

$$= \frac{100}{\sqrt{2}} \times \frac{0.1}{\sqrt{2}} = 5\text{ W}$$

5

---

10 v_A is a sinusoid of 5-V rms ($5\sqrt{2}$-V peak). The average current through the meter will be $\frac{2}{\pi} \times \frac{5\sqrt{2}}{R}$. To obtain full-scale reading, this current must be equal to 1 mA. Thus: $\frac{2}{\pi} \times \frac{5\sqrt{2}}{R} = 1$ mA, which leads to $R = 4.5$ kΩ.

v_C will be maximum when v_A is at its positive peak, i.e. $v_A = 5\sqrt{2}$ V. At this value of v_A we obtain

$$v_C = V_{D1} + V_M + V_{D3} + V_R$$

where $V_{D1} = V_{D3} \simeq 0.7$ V and

$$V_M = \frac{5\sqrt{2}}{4.5} \times 0.05 = 0.08\text{ V}.$$

Thus, $v_C|_{max} = 0.7 + 0.08 + 0.7 + 5\sqrt{2} = +8.55$ V

Similarly we can calculate the minimum value of v_C as -8.55 V

5

---

11 Consider the half cycle during which v_A is positive. D_1 and D_3 will be on and, assuming ideal diodes, will act as short circuit. Thus v_L will equal v_A, and the reverse bias across each of D_2 and D_4 will be equal to v_L and thus to v_A. Thus, the peak reverse voltage across each of the diodes will be equal to the peak of the input, in this case 100 V.

5

---

12 Refer to Example 5.1. If R is halved then to maintain V_r unchanged the value of C must be doubled to 186.6 μF.

The average diode current is obtained from Eq. (5.9) where $I_L = \frac{100\text{ V}}{5\text{ k}\Omega} = 20$ mA,

$$i_{Dav} = 20\left(1 + \pi\sqrt{2 \times 100/2}\right) = 648\text{ mA}$$

The peak diode current is found using Eq. (5.10),

$$i_{Dmax} = 20\left(1 + 2\pi\sqrt{2 \times 100/2}\right)$$

$$= 1.276\text{ A}$$

5

---

13 $$C = \frac{V_p(T/2)}{V_r R} = \frac{V_p}{2V_r f R} = \frac{100}{2 \times 2 \times 60 \times 10^3}$$

$$= 41.7\ \mu\text{F}$$

The conduction angle ($\omega\Delta t$) remains equal to that for the half-wave circuit (at 0.2 rad) of Example (5.1). However, it occurs every half cycle. Thus the fraction of a cycle during which the diodes conduct is

$$\frac{0.2}{\pi} \times 100 = 6.36\ \%.$$

The average diode current is found from Eq. (5.12),

$$i_{Dav} = 10\left(1 + \pi\sqrt{100/2 \times 2}\right) = 167.1\text{ mA}$$

Finally, we compute the peak current through the diodes using Eq. (5.13),

$$i_{Dmax} = 10\left(1 + 2\pi\sqrt{100/2 \times 2}\right) = 324.2\text{ mA}$$

14 The maximum rate of change of the output voltage is the lesser of the op-amp slew rate ($SR = 0.1\ V/\mu s$), and the rate determined by the charging of C with the maximum possible output current, I_{max},

$$\frac{I_{max}}{C} = \frac{10 \times 10^{-3}}{10^{-6}}\ V/s = 10\ mV/\mu s.$$

It follows that the maximum rate of change of v_O is $10\ mV/\mu s$ which can be expressed more conveniently as $\underline{10\ V/ms}$

5

15

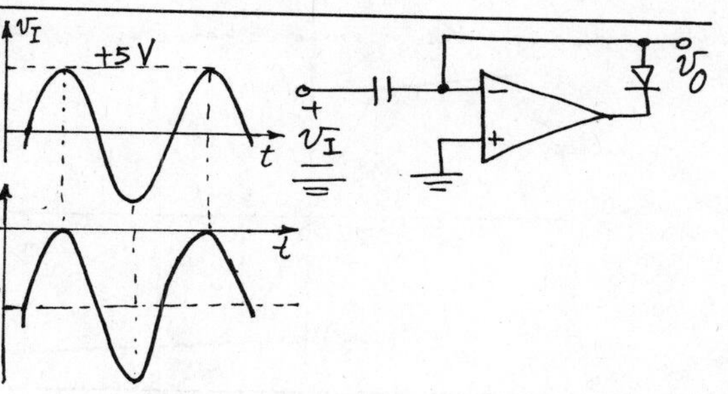

5

Assuming ideal operation, v_O will be as shown in the figure. It consists of a dc component of $-5\ V$ on which a 1 kHz sinusoid with 5-V peak amplitude is sumperimposed. The RC low-pass filter will attenuate this latter component to an amplitude of $\frac{5}{\sqrt{1+\left(\frac{1000}{10}\right)^2}} \simeq 0.05\ V$.

Thus, at the output of the filter we will have $\underline{\underline{-5\ V}}$ dc and a $\underline{\underline{0.05\text{-}V}}$ peak, 1 kHz sinusoid.

16 Refer to Fig. E5.16.

L_+ = positive saturation voltage of op amp $= \underline{\underline{+12\ V}}$

L_- = negative saturation voltage of op amp $= \underline{\underline{-12\ V}}$

K = Gain of op-amp circuit

$= 1 + \frac{40}{10} = 5$

Assuming that the op amp saturate abruptly $\Rightarrow$ hard limiting.

17 The output resembles a square wave of 2-V peak-to-peak amplitude.

5

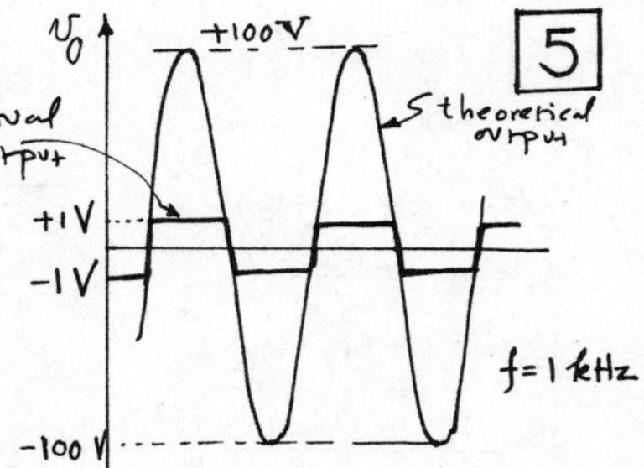

The slope of the square wave edges is equal to the slope of the 100-V peak, 1-kHz sine wave at its zero crossings. Thus

$$\text{edge slope} = \omega \hat{V} = 2\pi \times 10^3 \times 100$$

$$= 2\pi \times 10^5\ V/s$$

$$= 0.2\pi\ V/\mu s$$

$t_r = \frac{2}{0.2\pi}\ \mu s$

Thus, $t_r = t_f = \frac{2\ V}{0.2\pi\ V/\mu s}$

$= \underline{\underline{3.18\ \mu s}}$

18 L_+ = positive saturation voltage of op amp $= +12\ V$

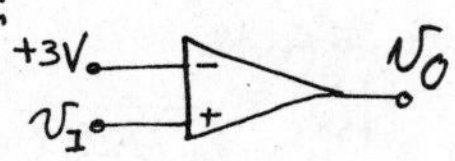

5

L_- = negative saturation voltage of op amp $= \underline{\underline{-12\ V}}$

$V_R = \underline{\underline{+3\ V}}$

19 Assuming ideal diodes:

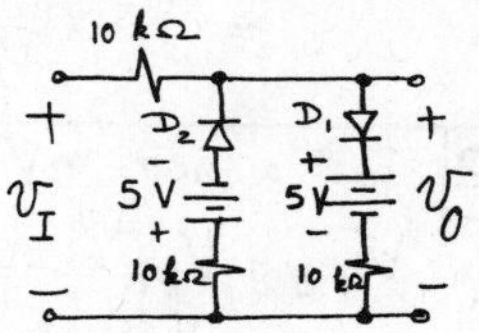

For D_1 to conduct, v_I has to exceed +5 V.

For D_2 to conduct, v_I has to be lower than $-5\ V$. It follows that in the range $\underline{-5 \le v_I \le +5\ V}$, both D_1 and D_2 will be off and $\underline{\underline{v_O = v_I}}$

For $\underline{v_I \geq +5\ V}$, D_1 will be on and acting as a perfect short circuit, then the current flowing becomes

$$I = \frac{v_I - 5}{20\ k\Omega}$$

Thus, $v_O = I \times 10\ k\Omega + 5 = \underline{\underline{\tfrac{1}{2}v_I + 2.5}}$

From symmetry we see that for $\underline{v_I \le -5\ V}$, $\underline{\underline{v_O = \tfrac{1}{2}v_I - 2.5}}$

20 As v_I goes positive, v_O goes negative,

5

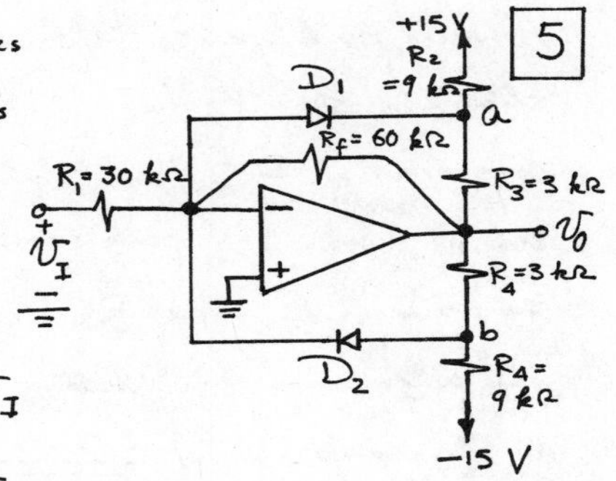

$$v_O = -\frac{R_f}{R_1} v_I$$

$$= -2\,v_I$$

Node "b" will be at a negative voltage and D_2 will be off. Assume for the moment that D_1 also is off. We see that the voltage at node "a" will be

$$v_A = v_O + \frac{15 - v_O}{R_2 + R_3} \cdot R_3$$
$$= v_O + \tfrac{1}{4}(15 - v_O)$$

As long as v_A is positive, D_1 will be off and $v_O = -2v_I$. As v_O increases in the negative direction, a value will be reached at which v_A is reduced to zero and begins to go negative. This value is obtained from

5

$$v_A = 0 = v_O + \tfrac{1}{4}(15 - v_O) \Rightarrow v_O = -5\text{ V}$$

which corresponds to $v_I = +2.5$ V.

For $v_I \geq 2.5$ V, diode D_1 conducts and thus clamps node "a" to 0 V. From that point on, v_O decreases only slightly below the limiting level of −5 V. Specifically,

$$v_O = -5 - \frac{(R_f \,//\, R_3)}{R_1} v_I$$
$$= -5 - 0.095\, v_I$$

For negative v_I, similar arguments apply to derive the transfer characteristic shown:

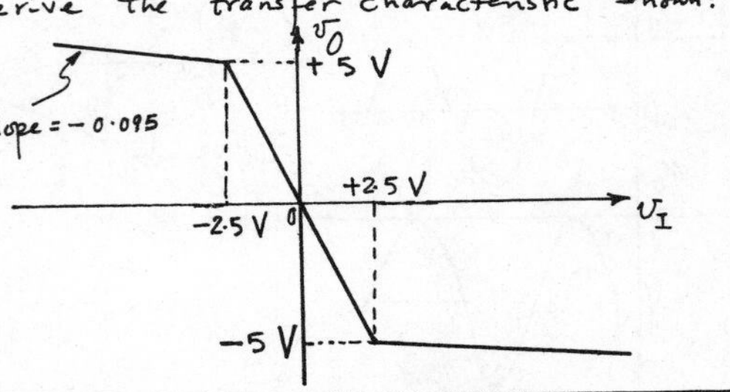

---

21 $V_{T1} = -L_+ \dfrac{R_1}{R_2}$

5

$$= -10 \times \frac{10}{20} = \underline{\underline{-5\text{ V}}}$$

$$V_{T2} = -L_- \frac{R_1}{R_2}$$

$$= 10 \times \frac{10}{20} = \underline{\underline{+5\text{ V}}}$$

---

22 For a 100-mV hystresis,

$$V_{T2} = -V_{T1} = 50\text{ V}$$

$$V_{T2} = -L_- \frac{R_1}{R_2} \Rightarrow 0.05 = +10 \times \frac{1}{R_2}$$

$$R_2 = \underline{\underline{200\text{ k}\Omega}}$$

---

23 From Eq. (5.19), the period is given by

$$T = 2\tau \ln \frac{1+\beta}{1-\beta}$$

where $\tau = C_1 R_3 = 0.01 \times 10^{-6} \times 10^6 = 0.01$ s

$$\beta = \frac{R_1}{R_1 + R_1} = \frac{0.1}{0.1 + 1} = \frac{1}{11}$$

Thus, $T = 2 \times 0.01 \ln\left(\frac{1 + \frac{1}{11}}{1 - \frac{1}{11}}\right) = 0.00365$ s

$f = 1/T = 274.2$ Hz

---

24 $T_1 = T_2 = \frac{T}{2}$

5

During T_1:

$$v_B(t) = 12 - (12 + V_D)\,e^{-t/\tau}$$

$$v_B = V_D \text{ at } t = \frac{T}{2}$$

$$V_D = 12 - (12 + V_D)\,e^{-T/2\tau}$$

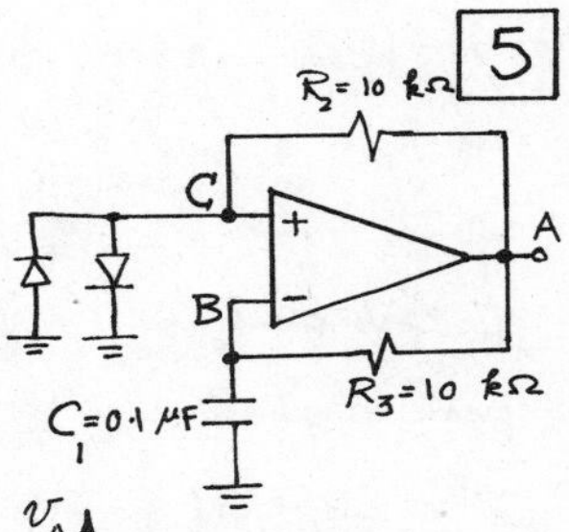

$$T = 2\tau \ln\left(\frac{12 + V_D}{12 - V_D}\right)$$

$$= 2 \times 0.1 \times 10^{-6} \times 10 \times 10^3$$
$$\times \ln \frac{(12 + V_D)}{(12 - V_D)}$$

$$f = \frac{1}{T} = \frac{500}{\ln\left(\frac{12 + V_D}{12 - V_D}\right)}\ \text{Hz}$$

$$f\Big|_{25^\circ C} = \frac{500}{\ln\left(\frac{12.7}{11.3}\right)} = \underline{\underline{4{,}281\text{ Hz}}}$$

At 0 °C, $V_D = 0.7 + 0.05$
$= 0.75$ V

$$f\Big|_{0^\circ C} = \frac{500}{\ln\left(\frac{12.75}{11.25}\right)} = \underline{\underline{3{,}995\text{ Hz}}}$$

At 50 °C, $V_D = 0.7 - 0.05 = 0.65$ V

$$f\Big|_{50^\circ C} = \frac{500}{\ln\left(\frac{12.65}{11.35}\right)} = \underline{\underline{4{,}611\text{ Hz}}}$$

At 100 °C, $V_D = 0.7 - 0.15 = 0.55$ V

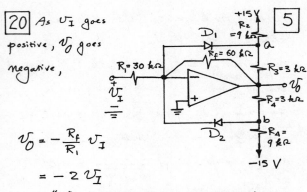

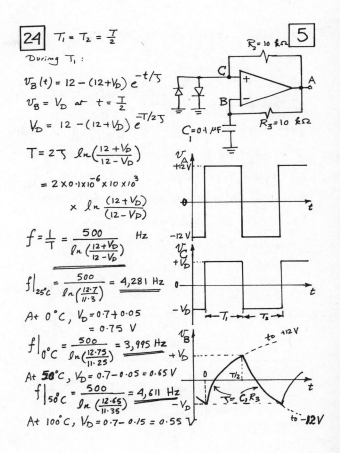

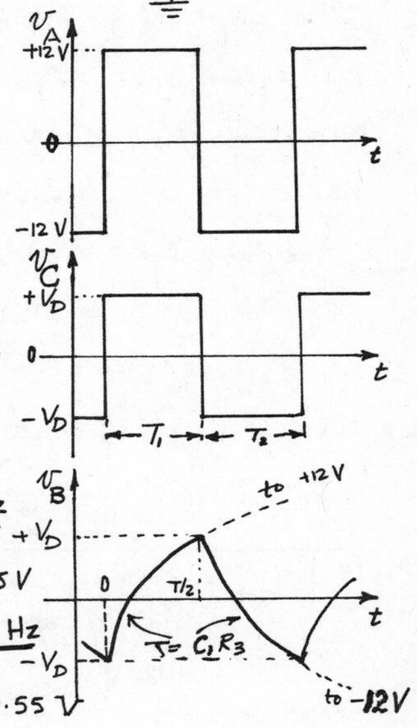

5

$$f\Big|_{100^\circ C} = \frac{500}{\ln\left(\frac{12.55}{11.45}\right)} = \underline{\underline{5,451\ \text{Hz}}}$$

25 To obtain a triangular waveform with 10-V peak-to-peak amplitude we should have

$$V_{TH} = -V_{TL} = 5\ \text{V}$$

But

$$V_{TL} = -L_+ \frac{R_1}{R_2}$$

Thus

$$-5 = -10 \times \frac{10}{R_2}$$

$$R_2 = \underline{\underline{20\ \text{k}\Omega}}$$

For 1 kHz frequency, $T = 1$ ms.

Thus

$$\frac{T}{2} = 0.5 \times 10^{-3} = CR\,\frac{V_{TH} - V_{TL}}{L_+}$$

$$= 0.01 \times 10^{-6} \times R \times \frac{10}{10}$$

$$R = \underline{\underline{50\ \text{k}\Omega}}$$

26 Using Eq. (5.20)

$$100 \times 10^{-6} = 0.1 \times 10^{-6} \times R_3\ \ln\left(\frac{12.7}{10.8}\right)$$

$$R_3 = \underline{\underline{6171\ \Omega}}$$

5

27 $i = 0.1 v^2$

At $v = 2$ V, $i = 0.4$ mA

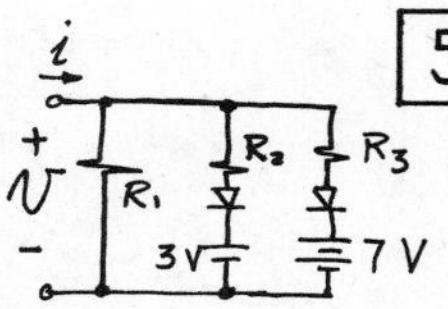

Thus, $R_1 = \frac{2}{0.4} = \underline{\underline{5\ \text{k}\Omega}}$

For $3\ \text{V} \le v \le 7\ \text{V}$

$$i = \frac{v}{R_1} + \frac{v-3}{R_2}$$

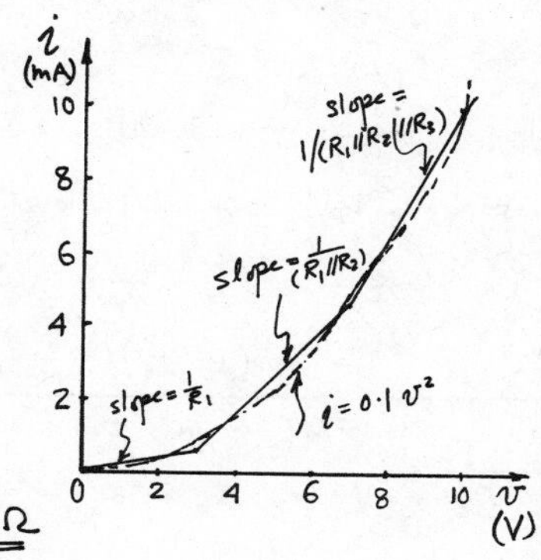

To obtain a perfect match at $v = 4$ V (i.e. to obtain $i = 1.6$ mA)

$$1.6 = \frac{4}{5} + \frac{4-3}{R_2}$$

$$\Rightarrow R_2 = \underline{\underline{1.25\ \text{k}\Omega}}$$

For $v \geq 7$ V:

$$i = \frac{v}{R_1} + \frac{v-3}{R_2} + \frac{v-7}{R_3}$$

To obtain a perfect match at $v = 8$ V we must have to select R_3 so that $i = 6.4$ mA,

5

$$6.4 = \frac{8}{5} + \frac{8-3}{1.25} + \frac{8.7}{R_3}$$

$$\Rightarrow R_3 = \underline{1.25\ \text{k}\Omega}$$

* At $v = 3$ V, the circuit provides $i = \frac{3}{5} = 0.6$ mA while ideally $i = 0.1 \times 9 = 0.9$ mA. Thus the error is $\underline{\underline{-0.3\ \text{mA}}}$.

* At $v = 5$ V, the circuit provides $i = \frac{5}{5} + \frac{5-3}{1.25} = 2.6$ mA, while ideally $i = 0.1 \times 25 = 2.5$ mA. Thus the error is $\underline{\underline{+0.1\ \text{mA}}}$.

* At $v = 7$ V, the circuit provides $i = \frac{7}{5} + \frac{7-3}{1.25} = 4.6$ mA, while ideally $i = 0.1 \times 49 = 4.9$ mA. Thus the error is $\underline{\underline{-0.3\ \text{mA}}}$.

* At $v = 10$ V, the circuit provides $i = \frac{10}{5} + \frac{10-3}{1.25} + \frac{10-7}{1.25} = 10$ mA, while ideally $i = 10$ mA. Thus the error is $\underline{\underline{0}}$.

5

28 $v_I = 10$ mV results in $v_O = -0.4$ V.

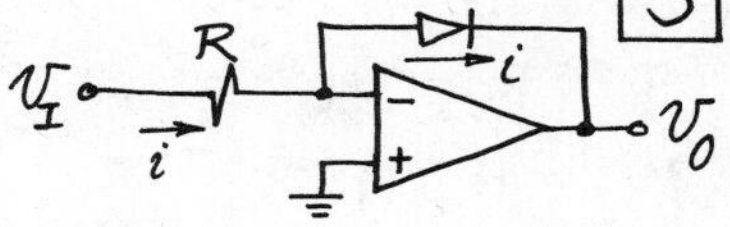

From the diode characteristics given, we see that the current i must be 0.01 mA. Thus

$$\frac{v_I}{R} = 0.01\ \text{mA}$$

$$\frac{10\ \text{mV}}{R} = 0.01\ \text{mA}$$

$$\Rightarrow R = \underline{1\ \text{k}\Omega}$$

Observe that for $v_I = 100$ mV, a current of 0.1 mA flows with the result that $v_D = 0.5$ V and $v_O = -0.5$ V. Similarly, for $v_I = 1$ V, the current is 1 mA, $v_D = 0.6$ V, and $v_O = -0.6$ V and so on.

Chapter 6 — Exercises

1 To operate in pinch off:

$$v_{DS} \geq v_{GS} + |V_P|$$

Thus, $v_{DS} \geq -2 + 4 = 2\text{ V}$

$$v_{DS_{min}} = \underline{\underline{2\text{ V}}}$$

For $v_{GS} = -2$ V and $v_{DS} = 3$ V the FET is operating in pinch-off and

$$i_D = I_{DSS}\left(1 - \frac{v_{GS}}{V_P}\right)^2$$

$$= 10\left(1 - \frac{-2}{-4}\right)^2 = \underline{\underline{2.5\text{ mA}}}$$

2 The FET is in pinch off.

$v_{GS} = -2\text{ V}$: $i_D = 10\left(1 - \frac{-2}{-4}\right)^2 = 2.5\text{ mA}$

$v_{GS} = -1.6\text{ V}$: $i_D = 10\left(1 - \frac{-1.6}{-4}\right)^2 = 3.6\text{ mA}$

Thus i_D increases by $\underline{\underline{1.1\text{ mA}}}$.

3 Operation in the triode region.

$$i_D = I_{DSS}\left[2\left(1 - \frac{v_{GS}}{V_P}\right)\left(\frac{v_{DS}}{-V_P}\right) - \left(\frac{v_{DS}}{V_P}\right)^2\right]$$

For small v_{DS}:

$$i_D \simeq 2 I_{DSS}\left(1 - \frac{v_{GS}}{V_P}\right)\left(\frac{v_{DS}}{-V_P}\right)$$

$$r_{DS} = \frac{v_{DS}}{i_D} = -V_P \Big/ \left[2 I_{DSS}\left(1 - \frac{v_{GS}}{V_P}\right)\right]$$

At $v_{GS} = 0$: $r_{DS} = \dfrac{4}{2 \times 10 \times 10^{-3} \times 1} = \underline{\underline{200\ \Omega}}$

At $v_{GS} = -3$ V: $r_{DS} = \dfrac{4}{2 \times 10 \times 10^{-3}\left(1 - \frac{-3}{-4}\right)} = \underline{\underline{800\ \Omega}}$

4

$$r_o = \frac{V_A}{I_D}$$

$I_D = 1$ mA $\quad r_o = \frac{1000}{1} = \underline{\underline{1\text{ M}\Omega}}$

$I_D = 2.5$ mA $\quad r_o = \frac{1000}{2.5} = \underline{\underline{400\text{ k}\Omega}}$

$I_D = 10$ mA $\quad r_o = \frac{1000}{10} = \underline{\underline{100\text{ k}\Omega}}$

5 $v_{SD} = 1\text{ V} \Rightarrow v_{GD} = 4\text{ V}$, and the FET is operating in the triode region,

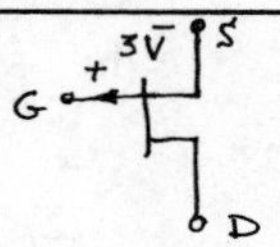

$$i_D = I_{DSS}\left[2\left(1 - \frac{v_{GS}}{V_P}\right)\left(\frac{v_{DS}}{-V_P}\right) - \left(\frac{v_{DS}}{-V_P}\right)^2\right]$$

$$= 10\left[2\left(1 - \frac{+3}{+5}\right)\left(\frac{-1}{-5}\right) - \left(\frac{-1}{-5}\right)^2\right]$$

$$= \underline{\underline{1.2\text{ mA}}}$$

$v_{SD} = 2\text{ V} \Rightarrow v_{GD} = 5\text{ V}$ and the JFET is operating at the edge of the pinch-off region. Thus

$$i_D = I_{DSS}\left(1 - \frac{v_{GS}}{V_P}\right)^2$$

$$= 10 \times \left(1 - \frac{3}{5}\right)^2 = \underline{\underline{1.6\text{ mA}}}$$

6 When the device is operating in the triode region with small v_{SD}:

$$i_D \cong I_{DSS}\left[2\left(1 - \frac{v_{GS}}{V_P}\right)\left(\frac{v_{DS}}{-V_P}\right)\right]$$

For $v_{GS} = 0$

$$i_D = 2 I_{DSS}\left(\frac{v_{DS}}{-V_P}\right) = 2 I_{DSS}\left(\frac{v_{SD}}{V_P}\right)$$

$$r_{DS} \equiv \frac{v_{SD}}{i_D} = \frac{V_P}{2 I_{DSS}} = \frac{1}{2 \times 1} = 0.5\text{ k}\Omega$$

$$= \underline{\underline{500\ \Omega}}$$

In pinch-off, $r_o = \dfrac{|V_A|}{I_D}$ which for $v_{SG} = 0$ becomes $|V_A| / I_{DSS} = \dfrac{100}{1} = \underline{\underline{100\text{ k}\Omega}}$

7 To operate in pinch-off, the drain must be lower than the gate by at least V_P volts, thus

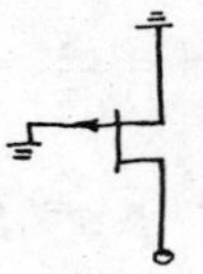

$$v_{D_{max}} = \underline{\underline{-1\text{ V}}}$$

At this voltage

$$i_D = I_{DSS} = \underline{\underline{1\text{ mA}}}$$

If the drain voltage is decreased by 4 volts the drain current changes because of the finite value of r_o. Specifically,

$$\Delta i_D = \frac{\Delta v_{SD}}{r_o} = \frac{4}{100\text{ k}\Omega} = \underline{\underline{+0.04\text{ mA}}}$$

8 $V_G = 15 \times \dfrac{100}{100 + 50}$

$$= \underline{\underline{+10\text{ V}}}$$

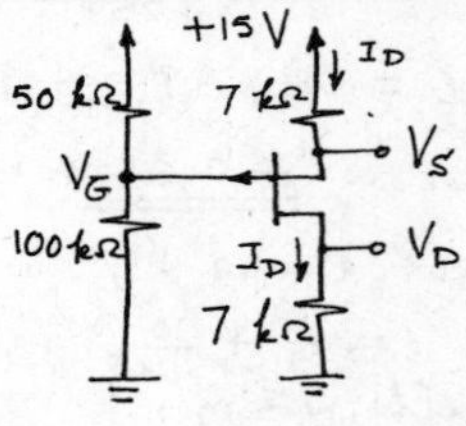

$V_{GS} = V_G - V_S = 10 - V_S$

Assume operation in pinch off,

$$I_D = I_{DSS}\left(1 - \frac{V_{GS}}{V_P}\right)^2$$

6

$I_D = 9 \times \left(1 - \frac{10 - V_S}{3}\right)^2$

But from the circuit,

$V_S = 15 - 7 I_D$

Thus

$$I_D = 9 \times \left(1 - \frac{10 - 15 + 7 I_D}{3}\right)^2$$
$$= 9 \left(1 - \frac{7 I_D - 5}{3}\right)^2$$
$$= 9 + (7 I_D - 5)^2 - 6(7 I_D - 5)$$

$\Rightarrow$ $I_D = 1\,\text{mA}$ or 1.306 mA

$I_D = 1\,\text{mA}$ leads to $V_S = 15 - 7 \times 1 = +8$ V and $V_{SG} = -2$ V. $I_D = 1.306$ mA leads to $V_S = 5.86$ and $V_{SG} = -4.14$ which is physically meaningless as the device would be cut-off. Thus, $I_D = 1$ mA and $V_S = \underline{+8V}$.

$V_D = 7 \times I_D = \underline{\underline{+7\text{ V}}}$. Thus $V_{GD} = 3$ V which is equal to V_P, thus the device is at the edge of pinch-off, and our original assumption of pinch-off operation is justified.

---

9 $V_{DG} = 5$ V, thus operation is in pinch-off,

6

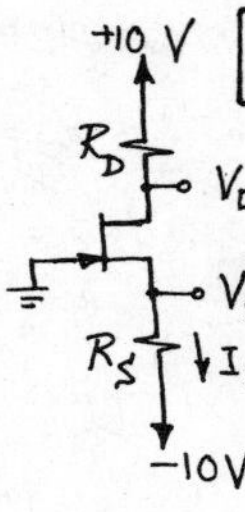

$$I_D = I_{DSS}\left(1 - \frac{V_{GS}}{V_P}\right)^2$$

$$0.5 = 2\left(1 - \frac{V_{GS}}{-2}\right)^2$$

$\Rightarrow V_{GS} = -1$ V

Thus, $V_S = +1$ V

$$R_S = \frac{V_S - (-10)}{I_D} = \frac{1 + 10}{0.5} = \underline{\underline{22\text{ k}\Omega}}$$

$$R_D = \frac{+10 - V_D}{I_D}$$

but $V_D = V_G + V_{DG} = 0 + 5 = 5$ V,

thus, $R_D = \frac{10 - 5}{0.5} = \underline{\underline{10\text{ k}\Omega}}$

---

10 Assume operation in pinch-off, thus

$$I_D = I_{DSS}\left(1 - \frac{V_{GS}}{V_P}\right)^2$$
$$= 12 \times \left(1 - \frac{-2}{-4}\right)^2 = \underline{\underline{3\text{ mA}}}$$

$V_D = V_{DD} - R_D I_D = 15 - 3 \times 3 = \underline{\underline{+6\text{ V}}}$

Since $V_{DG} = 9\text{ V} > |V_P|$, operation is in pinch-off, as assumed.

---

11 $v_{GS} = 0$ and $v_{DS} = 0.1$ V implies operation in the triode region. Thus

6

$$i_D = I_{DSS}\left[2\left(1 - \frac{v_{GS}}{V_P}\right)\left(\frac{v_{DS}}{-V_P}\right) - \left(\frac{v_{DS}}{V_P}\right)^2\right]$$
$$= 12\left[2\left(1 - \frac{0}{-4}\right)\left(\frac{0.1}{4}\right) - \left(\frac{0.1}{4}\right)^2\right]$$
$$\simeq 12 \times 2 \times \frac{0.1}{4} = 0.6\text{ mA}$$

$$R_D = \frac{15 - 0.1}{0.6} = 24.83\text{ k}\Omega \simeq \underline{\underline{25\text{ k}\Omega}}$$

$$r_{DS} = \frac{v_{DS}}{i_D} = \frac{0.1}{0.6} \simeq \underline{\underline{167\,\Omega}}$$

---

12 Refer to Example 6.4. The maximum value of R_D that will ensure operation in pinch-off is found from the case of the "high" device.

$V_{D\min} = V_G + |V_P| = 8 + 8 = 16$ V

$I_D = 5.63$ mA

Thus, $R_D = \frac{20 - 16}{5.63} = \underline{\underline{710\,\Omega}}$

For the "low" device

$V_D = 20 - 0.710 \times 4 = \underline{\underline{17.2\text{ V}}}$

For the "high" device, $V_D = \underline{\underline{16\text{ V}}}$

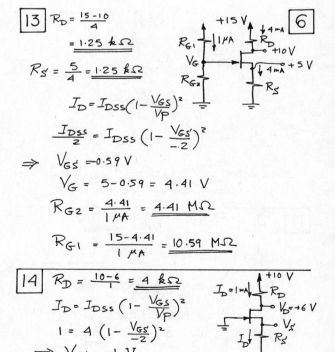

13 $R_D = \frac{15 - 10}{4}$

6

$= \underline{\underline{1.25\text{ k}\Omega}}$

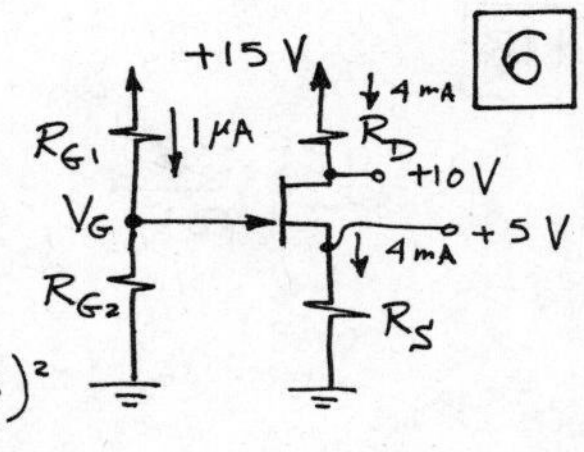

$R_S = \frac{5}{4} = \underline{\underline{1.25\text{ k}\Omega}}$

$$I_D = I_{DSS}\left(1 - \frac{V_{GS}}{V_P}\right)^2$$

$$\frac{I_{DSS}}{2} = I_{DSS}\left(1 - \frac{V_{GS}}{-2}\right)^2$$

$\Rightarrow V_{GS} = -0.59$ V

$V_G = 5 - 0.59 = 4.41$ V

$$R_{G2} = \frac{4.41}{1\,\mu\text{A}} = \underline{\underline{4.41\text{ M}\Omega}}$$

$$R_{G1} = \frac{15 - 4.41}{1\,\mu\text{A}} = \underline{\underline{10.59\text{ M}\Omega}}$$

---

14 $R_D = \frac{10 - 6}{1} = \underline{\underline{4\text{ k}\Omega}}$

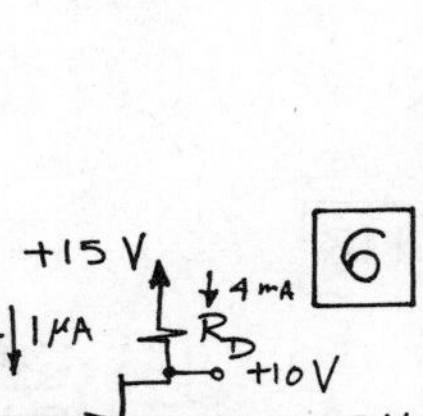

$$I_D = I_{DSS}\left(1 - \frac{V_{GS}}{V_P}\right)^2$$

$$1 = 4\left(1 - \frac{V_{GS}}{-2}\right)^2$$

$\Rightarrow V_{GS} = -1$ V

$V_S = +1$ V

$$R_S = \frac{1 - (-10)}{1\text{ mA}} = \underline{\underline{11\text{ k}\Omega}}$$

(a) The FET is replaced with another having $V_P = -2\,V$ and $I_{DSS} = 8$ mA. **6**

$$V_{GS} = 0 - V_S = 0 - (-10 + I_D R_S)$$

$$= 10 - 11 I_D$$

$$I_D = I_{DSS}\left(1 - \frac{V_{GS}}{V_P}\right)^2$$

$$= 8\left(1 - \frac{10 - 11 I_D}{-2}\right)^2$$

$\Rightarrow I_D = 1.025$ mA (the other solution is physically meaningless).

Thus, I_D changes by $\underline{2.5\,\%}$

(b) The FET is replaced with another having $V_P = -4$ V and $I_{DSS} = 8$ mA.

$$I_D = 8\left(1 - \frac{10 - 11 I_D}{-4}\right)^2$$

$\Rightarrow I_D = 1.136$ mA (the other solution is physically meaningless).

Thus, I_D changes by $\underline{13.6\,\%}$

---

15 $I_{DSS} = 16$ mA, $V_P = -4$ V **6**

$V_{GS} = -1\,V \quad I_D = 16\left(1 - \frac{1}{4}\right)^2 = 9$ mA

$$g_m = \left(\frac{2 I_{DSS}}{-V_P}\right)\sqrt{\frac{I_D}{I_{DSS}}} = \frac{2\times 16}{4}\sqrt{\frac{9}{16}} = \underline{6\text{ mA/V}}$$

Voltage gain $= -g_m R_D = -6 \times 1.33 = \underline{-8\text{ V/V}}$

16

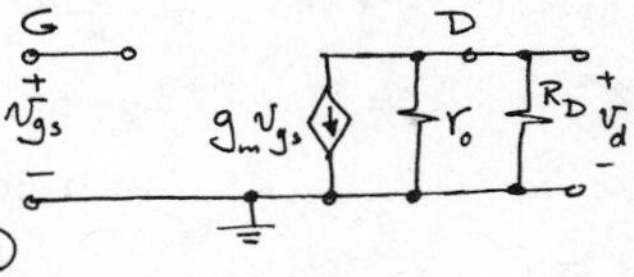

$$A_v \equiv \frac{v_d}{v_{gs}}$$

$$= \frac{-g_m v_{gs}\,(r_o \,//\, R_D)}{v_{gs}}$$

$$= \underline{-g_m\,(R_D \,//\, r_o)}$$

---

17 $g_{m0} = \frac{2 I_{DSS}}{V_P} = \frac{2\times 0.5}{1} = \underline{1\text{ mA/V}}$

$$g_m = g_{m0}\sqrt{\frac{I_D}{I_{DSS}}} = 1 \times \sqrt{\frac{0.25}{0.5}} = \underline{0.707\text{ mA/V}}$$

$$r_o = \frac{|V_A|}{I_D} = \frac{100}{0.25} = \underline{400\text{ k}\Omega}$$

$$\left.\frac{v_d}{v_s}\right|_{\text{without } r_o} = -g_m R_D = -0.707 \times 10 = \underline{-7.07\text{ V/V}}$$

$$\left.\frac{v_d}{v_s}\right|_{\text{with } r_o} = -g_m\,(R_D // r_o) = -0.707 \times (10 // 400) = \underline{-6.9\text{ V/V}}$$

---

18 $i_D = I_{DSS}\left(1 - \frac{v_{GS}}{V_P}\right)^2$ **6**

$$g_m \equiv \left.\frac{\partial i_D}{\partial v_{GS}}\right|_{i_D = I_D}$$

$$= 2 I_{DSS} \times \frac{1}{-V_P}\left.\left(1 - \frac{v_{GS}}{V_P}\right)\right|_{i_D = I_D}$$

But $i_D = I_D$ at $v_{GS} = V_{GS}$, thus

$$g_m = \underline{\frac{2 I_{DSS}}{-V_P}\left(1 - \frac{V_{GS}}{V_P}\right)}$$

---

19 $g_m = \frac{2\times 9}{3}\left(1 - \frac{-2}{-3}\right) = \underline{2\text{ mA/V}}$

$$A_v = -g_m R_D = -2\times 10 = \underline{-20\text{ V/V}}$$

Peak-to-peak $v_d = 0.2 \times 20 = 4$ V

$$V_D = V_{DD} - I_D R_D = 15 - 9\left(1 - \tfrac{2}{3}\right)^2 \times 10 = 5\text{ V}$$

Max. $v_D = V_D + 2 = 5 + 2 = \underline{7\text{ V}}$

Min. $v_D = V_D - 2 = 5 - 2 = \underline{4\text{ V}}$

---

20 From the text on page 293, **6**

Percent second-harmonic distortion

$$= \frac{1}{4}\left(\frac{\hat{V}}{-V_P}\right)\sqrt{\frac{I_{DSS}}{I_D}} \times 100$$

$$1 = \frac{1}{4}\,\frac{\hat{V}}{3}\sqrt{\frac{9}{1}} \times 100$$

$$\Rightarrow \hat{V} = \underline{0.04\text{ V}}$$

---

21 Refer to Example 6.5. If R_L is removed, the voltage gain becomes

$$\frac{v_o}{v_i} = \frac{R_{in}}{R_{in} + R}\,(-g_m)(R_D // r_o)$$

$$= \frac{-420}{420 + 100} \times 2.98 \times (2.7 // 100)$$

$$= \underline{-6.33\text{ V/V}}$$

$$-1 = \frac{-420}{420 + 100} \times 2.98\,(2.7 // 100 // R_L)$$

$$\Rightarrow R_L = \underline{493\ \Omega}$$

22 **6**

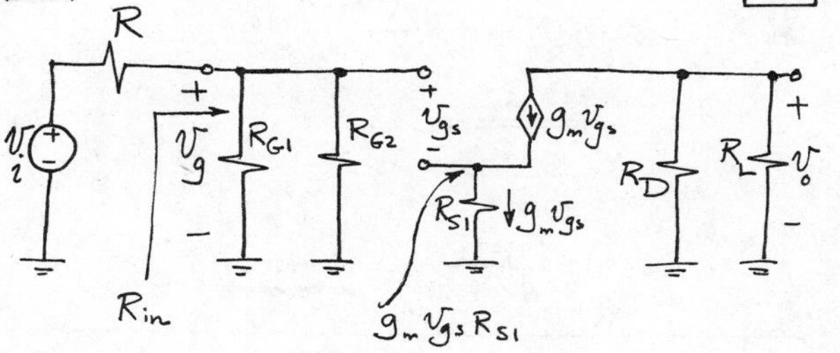

$R_{in} = R_{G1} // R_{G2}$

$$v_g = v_i \frac{R_{in}}{R_{in}+R} \qquad (1)$$

$$v_g = v_{gs} + g_m v_{gs} R_{S1} = v_{gs}(1+g_m R_{S1})$$

$$v_{gs} = \frac{v_g}{1+g_m R_{S1}} \qquad (2)$$

$$v_o = -g_m v_{gs}(R_D // R_L) \qquad (3)$$

Combining Eqs. (1), (2) and (3) gives

$$\frac{v_o}{v_i} = -\frac{R_{in}}{R_{in}+R}\,\frac{g_m(R_D//R_L)}{1+g_m R_{S1}}$$

$$= -\frac{R_{in}}{R_{in}+R}\,\frac{(R_D//R_L)}{(1/g_m)+R_{S1}}$$

---

23 **6**

$$\frac{v_o}{v_i} = -\frac{R_{in}}{R_{in}+R}\,\frac{(R_D//R_L//r_o)}{\left(\frac{1}{g_m}+R_{S1}\right)}$$

where $R = 100\ k\Omega$, $R_{in} = 420\ k\Omega$, $R_L = R_D = 2.7\ k\Omega$, $r_o = 100\ k\Omega$, $g_m = 2.98\ mA/V$ and $R_{S1} = 300\,\Omega$.

Thus,

$$\frac{v_o}{v_i} = -\frac{420}{420+100}\,\frac{(2.7//2.7//100)}{\left(\frac{1}{2.98}\right)+0.3}$$

$$= -1.7\ V/V$$

$$v_{gs} = v_i \frac{R_{in}}{R_{in}+R}\,\frac{1/g_m}{(1/g_m)+R_{S1}}$$

$$0.4 = v_i \frac{420}{420+100}\,\frac{(1/2.98)}{\left(\frac{1}{2.98}\right)+0.3}$$

$$\Rightarrow v_i = 0.94\ V$$

23A Please note that this is the first Exercise on page 307. In the first printing it was incorrectly numbered 6.23.

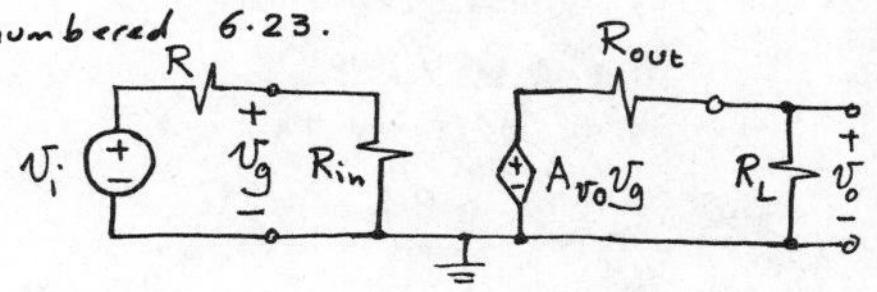

6

Refer to Fig. 6.32.

$R_{in} = R_G$

$$A_{vo} \equiv \left.\frac{v_o}{v_g}\right|_{R_L=\infty} = \frac{(R_S//r_o)}{(R_S//r_o)+\frac{1}{g_m}}$$

$$R_{out} = R_S // r_o // \left(\frac{1}{g_m}\right)$$

From the equivalent circuit shown:

$$\frac{v_o}{v_i} = \frac{R_{in}}{R_{in}+R}\,A_{vo}\,\frac{R_L}{R_L+R_{out}}$$

$$= \frac{R_{in}}{R_{in}+R}\,\frac{(R_S//r_o)}{(R_S//r_o)+\frac{1}{g_m}}\,\frac{R_L}{R_L+(R_S//r_o//\frac{1}{g_m})}$$

It can be shown that this expression reduces to that in Eq. (6.60) as follows:

Denote $R_S//r_o$ by R_S'

$$\frac{v_o}{v_i} = \frac{R_{in}}{R_{in}+R}\,\frac{R_S'}{R_S'+\frac{1}{g_m}}\,\frac{R_L}{R_L+\dfrac{R_S'\frac{1}{g_m}}{R_S'+\frac{1}{g_m}}}$$

$$= \frac{R_{in}}{R_{in}+R}\,\frac{R_S' R_L}{R_S' R_L + \frac{R_L}{g_m} + \frac{R_S'}{g_m}}$$

$$= \frac{R_{in}}{R_{in}+R}\,\frac{R_S' R_L/(R_L+R_S')}{R_S' R_L/(R_L+R_S') + 1/g_m}$$

6

$$\frac{v_o}{v_i} = \frac{R_{in}}{R_{in}+R}\,\frac{R_S'//R_L}{(R_S'//R_L)+(1/g_m)}$$

$$= \frac{R_{in}}{R_{in}+R}\,\frac{(R_S//r_o//R_L)}{(R_S//r_o//R_L)+(1/g_m)}$$

Q.E.D

24

$R_{in} = R_G = 1\ M\Omega$

To find I_D refer to the dc circuit shown →

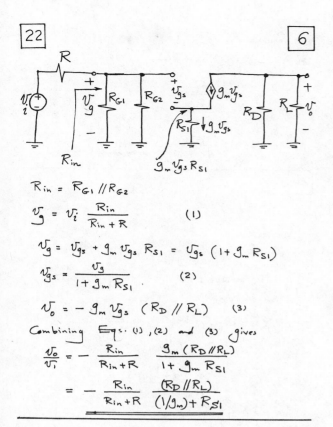

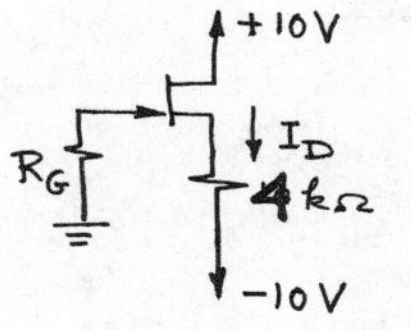

$$V_{GS} = 0-(-10+4I_D) = 10-4I_D$$

$$I_D = I_{DSS}\left(1-\frac{10-4I_D}{-4}\right)^2$$

$$= 12\left(1+\frac{10-4I_D}{4}\right)^2 = 12(1+2.5-I_D)^2$$

$$= 12(3.5-I_D)^2$$

$\Rightarrow I_D = 3\ mA$ (The other solution is physically meaningless.)

$$g_m = \frac{2\times 12}{4}\sqrt{\frac{3}{12}} = 3 \text{ mA/V}$$

6

$$\frac{v_o}{v_i} = \frac{R_{in}}{R_{in}+R}\,\frac{R_S//R_L}{(R_S//R_L)+\frac{1}{g_m}}$$

$$= \frac{1000}{1000+100}\,\frac{(4//4)}{(4//4)+\frac{1}{3}}$$

$$= \underline{\underline{0.78 \text{ V/V}}}$$

$$R_{out} = R_S//(\tfrac{1}{g_m})$$

$$= 4//(\tfrac{1}{3}) = \underline{\underline{307\ \Omega}}$$

25

$$A_{vo} = \frac{(R_S//r_o)}{(R_S//r_o)+(1/g_m)}$$

$$0.9 = \frac{(10//100)}{(10//100)+(1/g_m)}$$

$$\Rightarrow g_m = \underline{\underline{0.99 \text{ mA/V}}}$$

6

$$R_{out} = R_S//r_o//(\tfrac{1}{g_m})$$

$$= 10//100//(\tfrac{1}{0.99})$$

$$= \underline{\underline{909\ \Omega}}$$

$$A_v = A_{vo}\,\frac{R_L}{R_L+R_{out}}$$

$$= 0.9\,\frac{910}{910+909} = \underline{\underline{0.45 \text{ V/V}}}$$

26

In the triode region

$$i_D = I_{DSS}\left[2\left(1-\frac{v_{GS}}{V_P}\right)\left(\frac{v_{DS}}{-V_P}\right)-\left(\frac{v_{DS}}{V_P}\right)^2\right]$$

For small v_{DS}

$$i_D \simeq 2I_{DSS}\left(1-\frac{v_{GS}}{V_P}\right)\left(\frac{v_{DS}}{-V_P}\right)$$

Thus,

$$r_{DS} \equiv \frac{v_{DS}}{i_D} = \left(\frac{+V_P}{2I_{DSS}}\right)\Big/\left(1-\frac{v_{GS}}{V_P}\right)$$

From Fig. 6.35 we see that

$$r_{DS}|_{v_{GS}=0} = 80\ \Omega$$

6

Thus $\frac{+V_P}{2I_{DSS}} = 80\ \Omega$ (1)

We also see that for $v_{GS} = +6$ V, $r_{DS} =$ 400 Ω. Thus

$$\frac{80}{1-\frac{6}{V_P}} = 400 \Rightarrow V_P = \underline{\underline{7.5 \text{ V}}}$$

Substituting in Eq. (1) gives

$$I_{DSS} = \underline{\underline{46.9 \text{ mA}}}$$

27

With v_C low, the FET switch is on and

$$v_O = v_I\,\frac{R}{R+r_{DS}}$$

For R = 100 kΩ:

$$v_O = 1\sin\omega t \times \frac{100}{100+0.1} = \underline{\underline{0.9990\ \sin\omega t}}$$

For R = 1 kΩ:

$$v_O = 1\sin\omega t \times \frac{1}{1+0.1} = \underline{\underline{0.9091\ \sin\omega t}}$$

6

The low level of v_C must be selected so as to ensure that the diode is off even when the FET gate is at its most negative value. The most negative value of the gate voltage is equal to the most negative value of v_I, which is −1V. Thus $v_C|_{low} = \underline{\underline{-1\text{V}}}$.

The high level of v_C must be selected so as to cause the FET to be off even when v_I is at its most positive value of +1V. To turn the FET off the diode must turn on and a voltage of at least V_P must appear between gate and source. Thus

$$v_C|_{high} = 1+5+0.7 = \underline{\underline{+6.7 \text{ V}}}$$

28

Refer to Figures 6.37 and 6.38. The value of V_2 is equal to v_{DS} at operating point C. In the triode region

$$i_D = I_{DSS}\left[2\left(1-\frac{v_{GS}}{V_P}\right)\left(\frac{v_{DS}}{-V_P}\right)-\left(\frac{v_{DS}}{V_P}\right)^2\right]$$

$I_{DSS} = 10$ mA, $v_{GS} = 0$, $V_P = -2$ V, and

$$i_D\Big|_C = \frac{V_{DD}-V_2}{R_D} \simeq \frac{V_{DD}}{R_D} = \frac{10}{10} = 1\text{mA}$$

Assuming that $(v_{DS}/V_P)^2$ is small,

$$1 \simeq 10 \times 2 \times \frac{V_2}{2}$$

$$\Rightarrow \underline{\underline{V_2 = 0.1\text{ V}}}$$

For a sawtooth waveform of 1 V peak-to-peak

$$V_1 - V_2 = 1\text{ V}$$

$V_1 = 1.1$ V

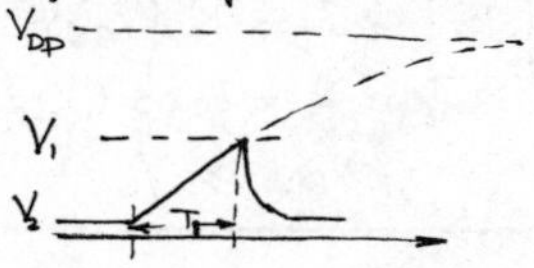

From the exponential rise

$$V_1 = V_{DD} - (V_{DD}-V_2)\,e^{-T_1/\tau}$$

$$\Rightarrow \tau = T_1 \Big/ \ln\left(\frac{V_{DD}-V_2}{V_{DD}-V_1}\right)$$

$$= 10^{-3} \Big/ \ln\left(\frac{10-0.1}{10-1.1}\right)$$

$$= 9.4\text{ ms}$$

$$C = \frac{9.4 \times 10^{-3}}{10 \times 10^3} = \underline{\underline{0.94\ \mu F}}$$

29

$$1\text{ mV/s} = \frac{I_{leakage}\text{ in mA}}{C}$$

Thus, $I_{leakage} = 10^{-7}$ mA

$$= 10^{-10}\text{ A}$$

$$= \underline{\underline{100\text{ pA}}}$$

Chapter 7 — Exercises

1 For pinch-off operation

$$v_{DS} \geq v_{GS} - V_P$$

Thus, for $v_{GS} = +1$ V

$$v_{DS}\Big|_{min} = 1-(-2) = \underline{\underline{3\text{ V}}}$$

Correspondingly

$$i_D = I_{DSS}\left(1-\frac{v_{GS}}{V_P}\right)^2$$

$$= 8\left(1-\frac{1}{-2}\right)^2 = \underline{\underline{18\text{ mA}}}$$

2 For $\underline{v \geq V_P}$, the depletion MOSFET will be operating in the triode region.

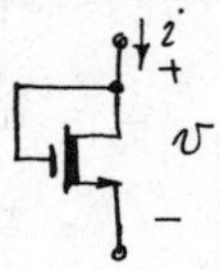

Thus

$$i = I_{DSS}\left[2\left(1-\frac{v_{GS}}{V_P}\right)\left(\frac{v_{DS}}{-V_P}\right)-\left(\frac{v_{DS}}{-V_P}\right)^2\right]$$

$$= I_{DSS}\left[2\left(1-\frac{v}{V_P}\right)\left(\frac{v}{-V_P}\right)-\left(\frac{v}{-V_P}\right)^2\right]$$

$$= \underline{\underline{I_{DSS}\left[2\left(\frac{v}{-V_P}\right)+\left(\frac{v}{-V_P}\right)^2\right]}}$$

Note that for negative v, i will be negative, as indicated →

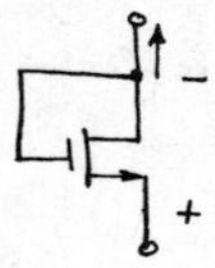

In this case, the same result can be obtained if the roles of the source and drain are interchanged. That is, we can think of the MOSFET as if its source is connected to the gate and a positive voltage (lower than that required for pinch-off operation) is applied to the drain.

For $v \leq V_P$, it is most convenient to think of the device in the manner shown

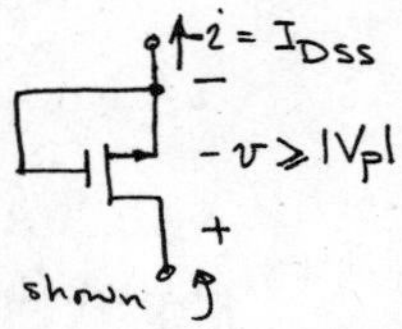

It follows that the depletion MOSFET will be operating in pinch-off with $v_{GS} = 0$, thus

$$i = \underline{\underline{-I_{DSS}}}$$

3 $V_t = 2\text{ V}$ $\quad v_{GS} = v_{DS} = 3\text{ V}$ implies operation in the pinch-off region. **7**

Thus, $i_D = K(v_{GS} - V_t)^2$

$$1 = K(3-2)^2$$

$$K = 1\text{ mA/V}^2$$

For $v_{GS} = 4\text{ V}$ and $v_{DS} = 5\text{ V}$:

$$i_D = 1 \times (4-2)^2 = \underline{\underline{4\text{ mA}}}$$

For operation in the triode region with small v_{DS}:

$$i_D \simeq K\left[2(v_{GS} - V_t)\,v_{DS}\right]$$

Thus,

$$r_{DS} \equiv \frac{v_{DS}}{i_D} = \frac{1}{2K(v_{GS}-V_t)}$$

$$= \frac{1}{2 \times 1(4-2)}$$

$$= \underline{250\,\Omega}$$

4 $K = \frac{1}{2}(\mu_n C_{ox})(W/L) = \frac{1}{2} \times 20 \times \frac{100}{10} = 100\ \mu\text{A/V}^2$

$$= \underline{\underline{0.1\text{ mA/V}^2}}$$

7

$$V_t = 1 + \gamma\sqrt{V_{SB}}$$

$$= 1 + 0.5\sqrt{4}$$

$$= \underline{\underline{2\text{ V}}}$$

For $V_{GS} = 3\text{ V}$ and $V_{DS} = 5\text{ V}$

$$I_D = K(V_{GS} - V_t)^2\left(1 + \frac{V_{DS}}{V_A}\right)$$

$$= 0.1\,(3 - V_t)^2\left(1 + \frac{5}{100}\right)$$

$V_{SB} = 0\text{ V} \Rightarrow V_t = 1\text{ V}$ $\quad I_D = 0.1 \times 4 \times 1.05$ $= \underline{\underline{0.420\text{ mA}}}$

$V_{SB} = 4\text{ V} \Rightarrow V_t = 2\text{ V}$ $\quad I_D = 0.1 \times 1 \times 1.05$ $= \underline{\underline{0.105\text{ mA}}}$

$$r_o\Big|_{V_{SB}=0\text{ V}} = \frac{V_A}{I_D} = \frac{100}{0.42} = \underline{\underline{238\text{ k}\Omega}}$$

$$r_o\Big|_{V_{SB}=4\text{ V}} = \frac{V_A}{I_D} = \frac{100}{0.105} = \underline{\underline{952\text{ k}\Omega}}$$

5 $I_D = K(V_{GS} - V_t)^2$

$4 = 0.25(V_{GS} - 2)^2 \Rightarrow V_{GS} = 6\text{ V}$

$V_{DS} \geq V_{GS} - V_t \Rightarrow V_{DS}\big|_{min} = \underline{\underline{4\text{ V}}}$

6 Originally, $I_D = 1\text{ mA}$. **7**

After replacing the MOSFET:

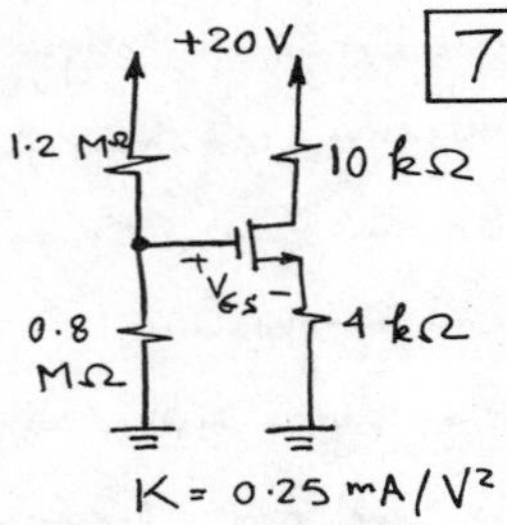

$K = 0.25\text{ mA/V}^2$

$V_t = 3\text{ V}$

$$I_D = K(V_{GS} - V_t)^2$$

$$V_{GS} = 20 \times \frac{0.8}{1.2 + 0.8} - 4 I_D$$

$$= 8 - 4 I_D$$

Thus,

$$I_D = 0.25\,(8 - 4I_D - 3)^2$$

$$= 0.25\,(5 - 4I_D)^2$$

$$= 0.25\,(25 - 40 I_D + 16 I_D^2)$$

$$4 I_D^2 - 11 I_D + 6.25 = 0$$

$I_D = 0.8\text{ mA}$ (The other solution is physically meaningless.) Thus I_D decreases by $\underline{\underline{20\%}}$.

7 $V_t = 2\text{ V}$ $\quad K = 0.25\text{ mA/V}^2$ **7**

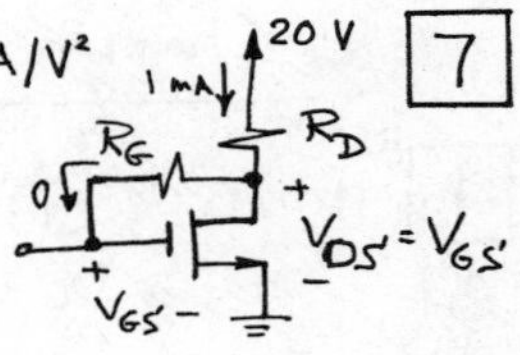

$$I_D = K(V_{GS} - V_t)^2$$

$$1 = 0.25(V_{GS} - 2)^2$$

$$\Rightarrow V_{GS} = 4\text{ V}$$

$$V_D = 4\text{ V}$$

$$1\text{ mA} = \frac{20-4}{R_D} \Rightarrow R_D = \underline{\underline{16\text{ k}\Omega}}$$

Now, if the device is replaced with another having the same K but $V_t = 3\text{ V}$:

$$V_{GS} = V_{DS} = 20 - 16 I_D$$

$$I_D = K(V_{GS} - V_t)^2$$

$$= 0.25\,(20 - 16 I_D - 3)^2$$

$$= 0.25\,(17 - 16 I_D)^2$$

$$\Rightarrow I_D = 0.94\text{ mA}$$

Thus, $\Delta I_D = \underline{\underline{-6\%}}$

8 (a) $g_m = 2K(V_{GS} - V_t)$ **7**

$= 2 \times \frac{1}{2}(\mu_n C_{ox})(W/L)(V_{GS} - V_t)$

$= 2 \times \frac{1}{2} \times 20 \times 64 \times (2-1)$

$= \underline{\underline{1.28 \ \text{mA/V}}}$

$r_o = \frac{V_A}{I_D} = \frac{100}{K(V_{GS}-V_t)^2}$

$= \frac{100}{\frac{1}{2} \times 20 \times 64 (2-1)^2} = \underline{\underline{156 \ k\Omega}}$

(b) $g_m = \left.\frac{\partial i_D}{\partial v_{GS}}\right|_{v_{GS}=V_{GS}}$

$= \frac{\partial}{\partial v_{GS}}\left[K(v_{GS}-V_t)^2\right]\Big|_{v_{GS}=V_{GS}}$

$= 2K(V_{GS} - V_t)$

$= 2K\sqrt{\frac{I_D}{K}}$

$= 2\sqrt{K I_D}$

$= 2\sqrt{\frac{1}{2}(\mu_n C_{ox})(W/L)\, I_D}$

$= \sqrt{2 \times 20 \times 64 \times 1000} = 1600 \ \mu\text{A/V}^2$

$= \underline{\underline{1.6 \ \text{mA/V}^2}}$

$r_o = \frac{V_A}{I_D} = \frac{100}{1} = \underline{\underline{100 \ k\Omega}}$ **7**

---

9 $V_t = \text{constant} + \gamma\sqrt{V_{SB}}$

$\chi \equiv \frac{\partial V_t}{\partial V_{SB}} = \frac{\gamma}{2\sqrt{V_{SB}}}$

$= \frac{0.5}{2\sqrt{4}} = \underline{\underline{0.125}}$

10

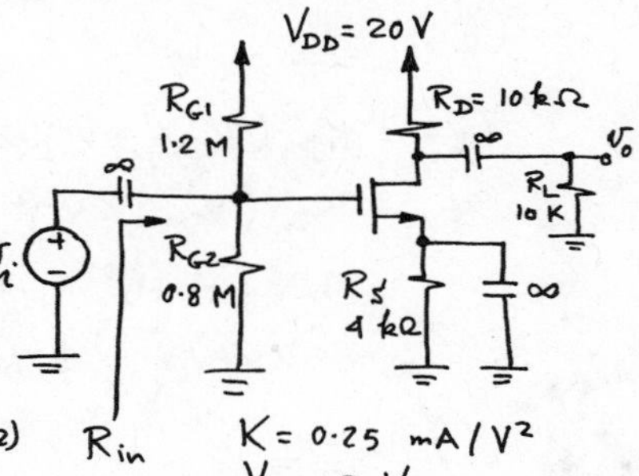

$R_{in} = R_{G1} // R_{G2}$

$= \frac{0.8 \times 1.2}{0.8 + 1.2}$

$= \underline{\underline{480 \ k\Omega}}$

$g_m = 2K(V_{GS} - V_t)$

$= 2 \times 0.25 \times (4-2)$

$= 1 \ \text{mA/V}$

$K = 0.25 \ \text{mA/V}^2$

$V_t = 2$ V

$I_D = 1$ mA

$V_{GS} = 4$ V

$r_o = \frac{V_A}{I_D} = \frac{50}{1} = 50 \ k\Omega$

$A_v \equiv \frac{v_o}{v_i} = -g_m (R_D // r_o // R_L)$

$= -1\,(10 // 50 // 10) = \underline{\underline{-4.54 \ \text{V/V}}}$

---

11 (a) $V_G = \underline{0 \ \text{V}}$ **7**

$I_D = K(V_{GS} - V_t)^2$

$10^{-3} = \frac{1}{2} \times 20 \times 10^{-6} \times 100\,(V_{GS} - 1)^2$

$\Rightarrow V_{GS} = 2$ V

$V_S = \underline{-2 \text{V}}$

$V_D = V_{DD} - I R_D$

$= 5 - 1 \times 3 = \underline{+2 \ \text{V}}$

(b) $g_m = 2K(V_{GS} - V_t)$

$= 2 \times \frac{1}{2} \times 20 \times 100\,(2-1) = \underline{\underline{2 \ \text{mA/V}}}$

(c) $R_{in} = R_G = \underline{1 \ M\Omega}$

$R_{out} = R_D // r_o$

$r_o = \frac{V_A}{I_D}$

$= \frac{50}{1} = 50 \ k\Omega$

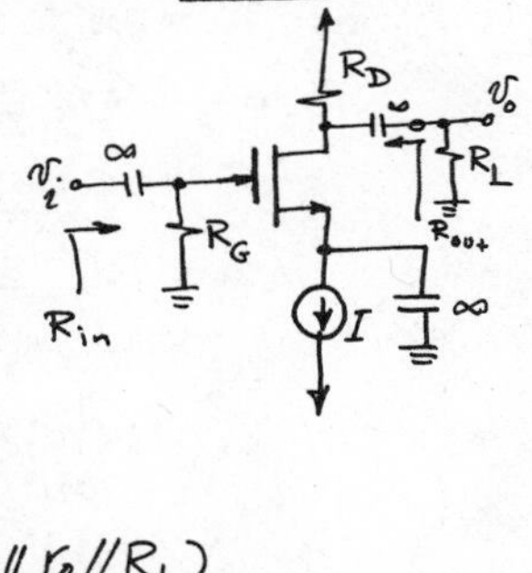

$R_{out} = 3 // 50$

$= \underline{\underline{2.83 \ k\Omega}}$

$A_v \equiv \frac{v_o}{v_i} = -g_m (R_D // r_o // R_L)$

$= -2 \times (3 // 50 // 3) = \underline{\underline{-2.91 \ \text{V/V}}}$

(d) $R_{in} \simeq 1/g_m$ (neglecting the effect of r_o). **7**

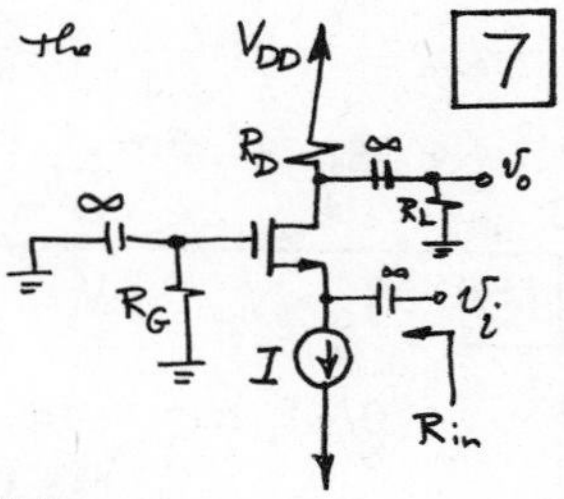

$R_{in} = \underline{0.5 \ k\Omega}$

$R_{out} = R_D // r_o$

$= \underline{2.83 \ k\Omega}$

$A_v \equiv \frac{v_o}{v_i} \simeq g_m (R_D // r_o // R_L)$

$= \underline{\underline{+2.91 \ \text{V/V}}}$

(e) $R_{in} = R_G$

$= \underline{\underline{1 \ M\Omega}}$

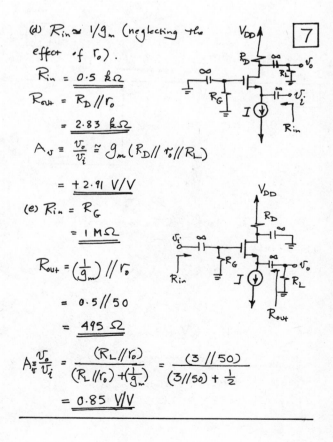

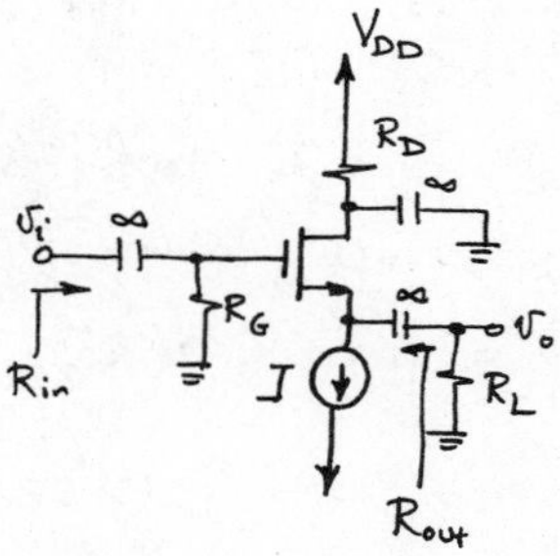

$R_{out} = \left(\frac{1}{g_m}\right) // r_o$

$= 0.5 // 50$

$= \underline{\underline{495 \ \Omega}}$

$A_v \equiv \frac{v_o}{v_i} = \frac{(R_L // r_o)}{(R_L // r_o) + (\frac{1}{g_m})} = \frac{(3 // 50)}{(3//50) + \frac{1}{2}}$

$= \underline{\underline{0.85 \ \text{V/V}}}$

12 $V_t = +1\text{ V} \qquad V_{DS}\big|_{Q_1} = 4\text{ V}$

$$I_{D1} = K_1 (V_{GS1} - V_t)^2$$

$$90 = K_1 (V_{DS1} - V_t)^2$$

$$= K_1 (4-1)^2$$

$$K_1 = 10\ \mu A/V^2 = \tfrac{1}{2} \times 20 \times \left(\tfrac{W}{L}\right)_1$$

$$\left(\tfrac{W}{L}\right)_1 = \underline{\underline{1}}$$

$$I_{D3} = K_3 (V_{GS3} - V_t)^2$$

$$90 = K_3 (V_{DS3} - V_t)^2$$

$$= K_3 (4-1)^2$$

$$K_3 = 10\ \mu A/V^2 = \tfrac{1}{2} \times 20 \left(\tfrac{W}{L}\right)_3$$

$$\left(\tfrac{W}{L}\right)_3 = \underline{\underline{1}}$$

$$I_{D2} = K_2 (V_{GS2} - V_t)^2$$

$$90 = K_2 (V_{DS2} - V_t)^2$$

$$= K_2 (2-1)^2 \Rightarrow K_2 = 90\ \mu A/V^2$$

$$90 = \tfrac{1}{2} \times 20 \times \left(\tfrac{W}{L}\right)_2$$

$$\Rightarrow (W/L)_2 = \underline{\underline{9}}$$

13 $i = K(v - V_t)^2$

$$\frac{\partial i}{\partial v} = 2K(v - V_t)$$

$$r \equiv \frac{1}{\left.\frac{\partial i}{\partial v}\right|_{v = 2V_t}} = \frac{1}{2KV_t}$$

$$= \frac{1}{2 \times \frac{1}{2} \times (\mu_n C_{ox}) \times \left(\frac{W}{L}\right) V_t} = \underline{\underline{\frac{1}{\mu_n C_{ox} \left(\frac{W}{L}\right) V_t}}}$$

$$= \frac{1}{20 \times 10^{-6} \times \frac{6}{30} \times 1} = \underline{\underline{250\ k\Omega}}$$

14 Without taking the body effect into account:

$$A_v = -\frac{g_{m1}}{g_{m2}}$$

But, $g_m = 2K(V_{GS} - V_t) = 2\sqrt{KI_D}$

Thus

$$A_v = -\sqrt{\frac{K_1}{K_2}} = -\sqrt{\frac{(W/L)_1}{(W/L)_2}}$$

$$= -\sqrt{\frac{100/6}{6/30}} = \underline{\underline{-9.13\text{ V/V}}}$$

Taking the body effect into account reduces the gain by a factor of $(1+\chi)$ (Eq. 7.66),

Thus,

$$A_v = -9.13 \frac{1}{1.1} = \underline{\underline{-8.3\text{ V/V}}}$$

15 $v_{IA} = V_{t1} = \underline{\underline{1\text{ V}}}$

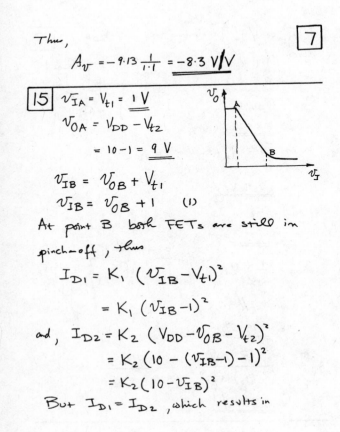

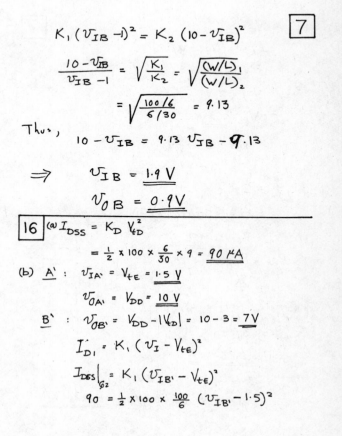

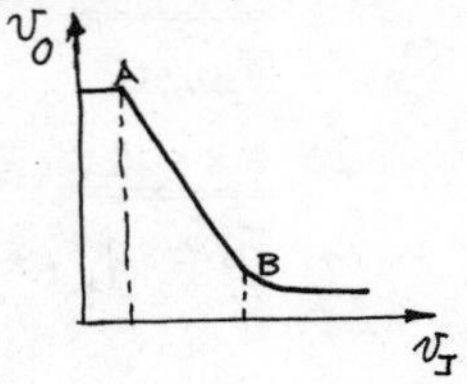

$$v_{OA} = V_{DD} - V_{t2}$$

$$= 10 - 1 = \underline{\underline{9\text{ V}}}$$

$$v_{IB} = v_{OB} + V_{t1}$$

$$v_{IB} = v_{OB} + 1 \qquad (1)$$

At point B both FETs are still in pinch-off, thus

$$I_{D1} = K_1 (v_{IB} - V_{t1})^2$$

$$= K_1 (v_{IB} - 1)^2$$

and, $I_{D2} = K_2 (V_{DD} - v_{OB} - V_{t2})^2$

$$= K_2 (10 - (v_{IB} - 1) - 1)^2$$

$$= K_2 (10 - v_{IB})^2$$

But $I_{D1} = I_{D2}$, which results in

$$K_1 (v_{IB} - 1)^2 = K_2 (10 - v_{IB})^2$$

$$\frac{10 - v_{IB}}{v_{IB} - 1} = \sqrt{\frac{K_1}{K_2}} = \sqrt{\frac{(W/L)_1}{(W/L)_2}}$$

$$= \sqrt{\frac{100/6}{6/30}} = 9.13$$

Thus,

$$10 - v_{IB} = 9.13\, v_{IB} - 9.13$$

$$\Rightarrow \quad v_{IB} = \underline{\underline{1.9\text{ V}}}$$

$$v_{OB} = \underline{\underline{0.9\text{V}}}$$

16 (a) $I_{DSS} = K_D V_{tD}^2$

$$= \tfrac{1}{2} \times 100 \times \tfrac{6}{30} \times 9 = \underline{\underline{90\ \mu A}}$$

(b) $\underline{A'}$: $v_{IA'} = V_{tE} = \underline{\underline{1.5\text{ V}}}$

$v_{OA'} = V_{DD} = \underline{\underline{10\text{ V}}}$

$\underline{B'}$: $v_{OB'} = V_{DD} - |V_{tD}| = 10 - 3 = \underline{\underline{7\text{V}}}$

$$I_{D1} = K_1 (v_I - V_{tE})^2$$

$$I_{DSS}\big|_{Q2} = K_1 (v_{IB'} - V_{tE})^2$$

$$90 = \tfrac{1}{2} \times 100 \times \tfrac{100}{6} (v_{IB'} - 1.5)^2$$

$0.33 = v_{IB'} - 1.5$

$\Rightarrow v_{IB'} = 1.83\text{ V}$

C' B'C' is a vertical line, thus

$v_{IC'} = 1.83\text{ V}$

$v_{OC'} = v_{IC'} - V_{tE} = 0.33\text{V}$

(c) $g_{m1} = 2K_1 (V_{GS1} - V_{tE})$

$= 2 \times \frac{1}{2} \times 100 \times \frac{100}{6} (1.83 - 1.5)$

$= 0.55 \text{ mA/V}$

$g_{m2} = \frac{2 I_{DSS2}}{|V_{tD}|}$

$= \frac{2 \times 90}{3} = 60\ \mu\text{A/V}$

$g_{mb2} = \chi g_{m2} = 0.1 \times 60 = 6\ \mu\text{A/V}$

$r_{o1} = \frac{|V_A|}{I_{D1}} = \frac{|V_A|}{I_{DSS}|_{Q_2}} = \frac{90}{90} = 1\text{ M}\Omega$

$r_{o2} = \frac{|V_A|}{I_{D2}} = \frac{|V_A|}{I_{DSS}|_{Q_2}} = \frac{90}{90} = 1\text{M}\Omega$

(d) $A_v = -g_{m1} \left[r_{o1} // r_{o2} // \frac{1}{g_{mb2}} \right]$

(Refer to Fig. 7.44)

$A_v = -0.55 \left[1000 // 1000 // \left(\frac{1}{6 \times 10^{-3}} \right) \right]$

$= -68.8 \text{ V/V}$

17 (a) $10 = K_1 (V_{GS} - V_t)^2$

$= \frac{1}{2} \times 20 \times \frac{6}{6} (V_{GS} - V_t)^2$

$V_{GS} - V_t = 1$

$\Rightarrow V_{GS} = 2\text{ V}$

(b) $100 = K_2 (V_{GS} - V_t)^2$

$= \frac{1}{2} \times 20 \times \frac{W_2}{6} (2-1)^2$

$\Rightarrow W_2 = 60\ \mu\text{m}$

(c) $r_{o2} = \frac{|V_A|}{I_{D2}} = \frac{50}{100} = 0.5\text{ M}\Omega$

When v_O increases by 5 V, the finite output

resistance (0.5 MΩ) causes the output current to increase by $\frac{5}{0.5} = 10\ \mu\text{A}$. Thus i_O becomes $110\ \mu\text{A}$.

18 $I_{REF} = 25\ \mu\text{A}$:

Using Eq.(7.81),

$A_v = -\frac{\sqrt{100 \times 10^{-6}} \times 100}{\sqrt{25 \times 10^{-6}}}$

$= -200 \text{ V/V}$

For $I_{REF} = 400\ \mu\text{A}$:

Using Eq.(7.81),

$A_v = -\frac{\sqrt{100 \times 10^{-6}} \times 100}{\sqrt{400 \times 10^{-6}}}$

$= -50 \text{ V/V}$

19 Refer to Fig. 7.46 a. Replacing Q_1 with its small-signal equivalent circuit, and Q_2 with its output resistance r_{o2} gives rise to the equivalent circuit shown in Fig. E7.19.

20 Refer to Fig. 7.47(b)

$A_{vo} = \frac{v_o}{v_i} = \frac{(1/g_{mb}) // r_o}{\left(\frac{1}{g_{mb}} // r_o\right) + \frac{1}{g_m}}$

$g_m = 2K(V_{GS} - V_t)$

$= 2K \times \sqrt{\frac{I}{K}} = 2\sqrt{KI}$

$= 2\sqrt{\frac{1}{2} \times 100 \times \frac{100}{8} \times 500} = 1.12 \text{ mA/V}$

$g_{mb} = \chi g_m = 0.1 \times 1.12 = 0.112 \text{ mA/V}$

$r_o = \frac{|V_A|}{I} = \frac{100}{0.5} = 200\text{ k}\Omega$

$A_{vo} = \frac{\left(\frac{1}{0.112} // 200\right)}{\left(\frac{1}{0.112} // 200\right) + \frac{1}{1.12}} = 0.91 \text{ V/V}$

$R_o = \frac{1}{g_m} // \frac{1}{g_{mb}} // r_o$

$= \left(\frac{1}{1.12}\right) // \left(\frac{1}{0.112}\right) // 200 = 810\ \Omega$

21 $v_{DS1} = v_{SD2} = v$

(a) $v_A = -5$ V:

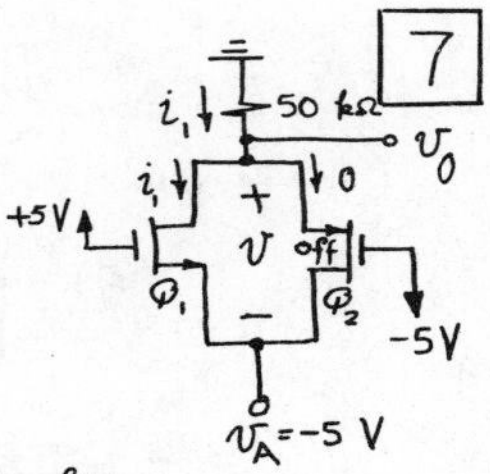

$$i_1 \cong 2K_1(v_{GS1} - V_t)\,v$$
$$= 2 \times 0.05 \times (10-2)\,v$$
$$= 0.8\,v$$

$$r_{DS1} = \frac{v_{DS1}}{i_1} = \frac{v}{i_1} = \frac{1}{0.8} = 1.25 \text{ k}\Omega$$

$$R_{switch} = 1.25 \text{ k}\Omega$$

Also, $i_1 \times 50 \text{ k}\Omega + i_1 \times 1.25 = 5 \text{ V} \Rightarrow i_1 = \frac{5}{51.25}$ mA

$$v = i_1 \times 1.25 = \frac{5}{51.25} \times 1.25 = 0.122 \text{ V}$$

$$v_O = -50 \times i_1 = -50 \times \frac{5}{51.25} = -4.878 \text{ V}$$

(b) $v_A = -2$ V:

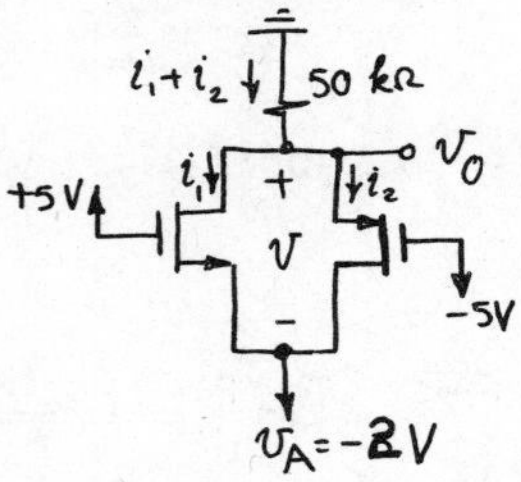

$$i_1 \simeq 2K_1(v_{GS1} - V_t)\,v$$
$$= 2 \times 0.05 \times (7-2)\,v$$
$$= 0.5\,v$$

$$i_2 \simeq 2K_2(v_{SG2} - V_t)\,v$$
$$= 2 \times 0.05\,(v_O + 5 - 2)\,v$$
$$= 0.1\,(v_O + 3)\,v$$

Substituting $v = v_O - (-2) = v_O + 2$,

$$i_1 = 0.5\,(v_O + 2)$$
$$i_2 = 0.1\,(v_O+3)(v_O+2)$$
$$i_1 + i_2 = 0.5(v_O+2) + 0.1\,(v_O+3)(v_O+2)$$
$$= (v_O+2)\,[0.5 + 0.1 v_O + 0.3]$$
$$= (v_O+2)\,(0.1 v_O + 0.8)$$
$$= 0.1\,v_O^2 + v_O + 1.6$$

But, $v_O = -(i_1+i_2) \times 50$
$$= -[5 v_O^2 + 50 v_O + 80]$$

$$\Rightarrow \quad 5v_O^2 + 51 v_O + 80 = 0$$

$v_O = -1.936$ V (The other solution is physically meaningless.)

$$R_{switch} \equiv \frac{v}{i_1 + i_2} = \frac{v_O + 2}{(-v_O/50)}$$
$$= 1.649 \text{ k}\Omega$$

(c) $v_A = 0$:

It should be obvious that $i_1 = i_2 = 0$.

Thus, $v_O = 0$ V

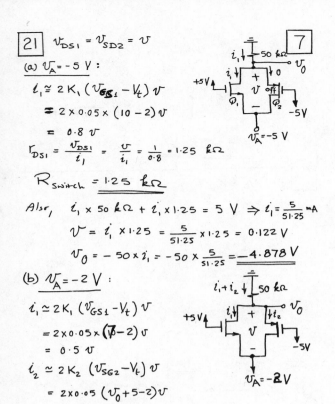

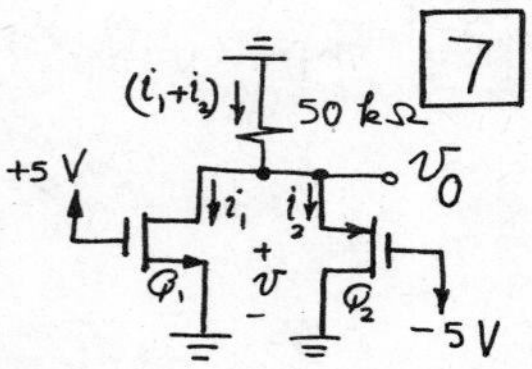

$$i_1 \cong 2K_1(v_{GS1} - V_t)\,v = 0.1 \times 3\,v = 0.3\,v$$

$$r_{DS1} \equiv \frac{v}{i_1} = \frac{1}{0.3} = 3.333 \text{ k}\Omega$$

$$i_2 \cong 2K_2(v_{SG2} - V_t)\,v = 0.1 \times 3\,v = 0.3\,v$$

$$r_{DS2} \equiv \frac{v}{i_2} = \frac{1}{0.3} = 3.333 \text{ k}\Omega$$

$$R_{switch} = r_{DS1} \,//\, r_{DS2} = 1.667 \text{ k}\Omega$$

Chapter 8 — Exercises

1

$$i_C = I_S\, e^{v_{BE}/V_T}$$
$$1 = I_S\, e^{0.7/V_T}$$
$$\frac{i_C}{1} = e^{(v_{BE} - 0.7)/V_T}$$

$$v_{BE} = 0.7 + V_T \ln(i_C)$$

$i_C = 0.1$ mA: $v_{BE} = 0.7 + 0.025 \ln(0.1) = 0.64$ V

$i_C = 10$ mA: $v_{BE} = 0.7 + 0.025 \ln(10) = 0.76$ V

2 $\alpha = \dfrac{\beta}{\beta+1}$

$\beta = 50 \qquad \alpha = \frac{50}{51} = 0.980$

$\beta = 150 \qquad \alpha = \frac{150}{151} = 0.993$

Thus, $\alpha = 0.980 \rightarrow 0.993$

3 **8**

$i_B = 14.46\ \mu A$

$i_E = 1.460\ mA$

$\beta + 1 = \frac{i_E}{i_B} = 101$

$\beta = \underline{\underline{100}}$

$\alpha = \frac{\beta}{\beta+1} = \underline{\underline{0.99}}$

$i_C = i_E - i_B = 1.446\ mA$

$1.446 = I_S\, e^{0.7/0.025}$

$I_S = \underline{\underline{10^{-15}\ A}}$

4

$\alpha = 0.99 \qquad \beta = \frac{\alpha}{1-\alpha} = \frac{0.99}{0.01} = \underline{\underline{99}}$

$\alpha = 0.98 \qquad \beta = \frac{\alpha}{1-\alpha} = \frac{0.98}{0.02} = \underline{\underline{49}}$

$\alpha = 0.99 \qquad I_C = 10\ mA \qquad I_B = \frac{10}{99} \simeq \underline{\underline{0.1\ mA}}$

$\alpha = 0.98 \qquad I_C = 10\ mA \qquad I_B = \frac{10}{49} \simeq \underline{\underline{0.2\ mA}}$

---

5 **8**

Scale current of $D_B = I_S/\beta$

$= 10^{-14}/100 = \underline{\underline{10^{-16}\ A}}$

$V_{BE} = V_{DB}$

$= V_T \ln(i_B/10^{-16})$

$= 0.025 \ln\left(\frac{10 \times 10^{-6}}{10^{-16}}\right) = \underline{\underline{0.633\ V}}$

$I_C = \beta I_B = 100 \times 10 = 1000\ \mu A$

$= \underline{\underline{1\ mA}}$

---

6 $I_S = 10^{-14}\ A$

$\beta = 50 \quad \alpha = \frac{50}{51} = 0.98$

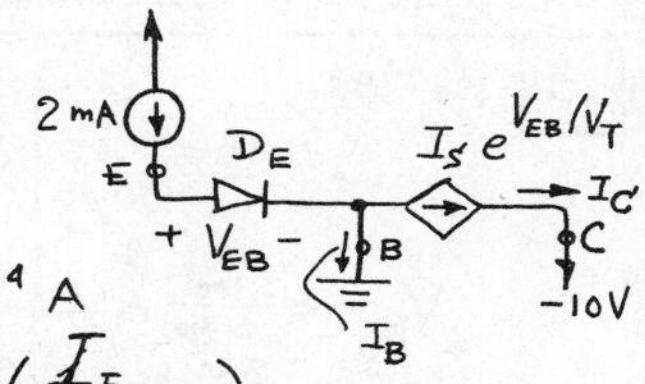

Scale current of D_E

$= \frac{I_S}{\alpha} = 1.02 \times 10^{-14}\ A$

$V_E = V_{D_E} = V_T \ln\left(\frac{I_E}{1.02 \times 10^{-14}}\right)$

$= 0.025 \ln\left(\frac{2 \times 10^{-3}}{1.02 \times 10^{-14}}\right)$

$= \underline{\underline{0.650\ V}}$

8

$I_B = \frac{I_E}{\beta+1} = \frac{2\ mA}{51} = \underline{\underline{39.2\ \mu A}}$

$I_C = I_E - I_B$

$= 2 - 0.0392 = \underline{\underline{1.96\ mA}}$

7

$i_C = I_S e^{v_{EB}/V_T}$

$v_{EB} = V_T \ln(i_C/I_S)$

$= 0.025 \times \ln(1.5/10^{-11})$

$= \underline{\underline{0.643\ V}}$

8

③ $I_C = I_E - I_B$
$= 0.93 - 0.018$
$= \underline{\underline{0.91\ mA}}$

② $I_B = \frac{I_E}{\beta+1} = \frac{0.93}{51} = \underline{\underline{18.2\ \mu A}}$

① $I_E = \frac{-0.7-(-10)}{10} = \underline{\underline{0.93\ mA}}$

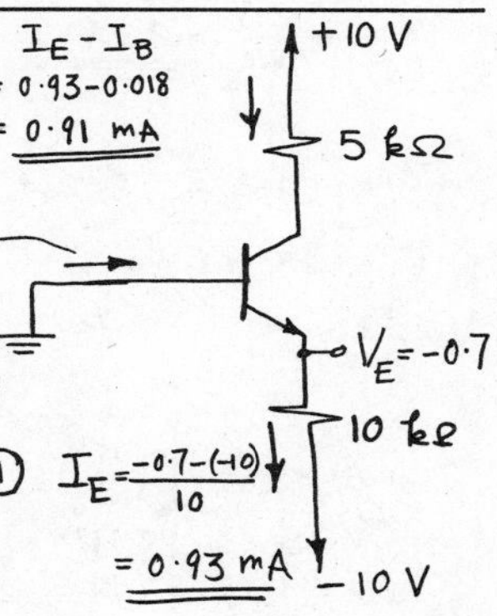

Note the numbering of the solution steps

---

9 **8**

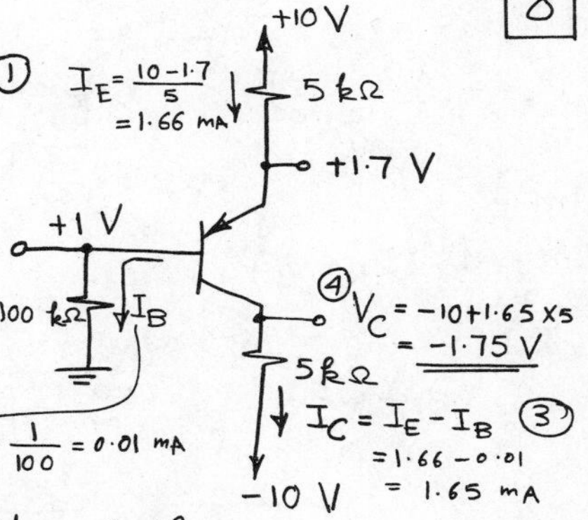

① $I_E = \frac{10-1.7}{5} = 1.66\ mA$

② $I_B = \frac{1}{100} = 0.01\ mA$

③ $I_C = I_E - I_B = 1.66 - 0.01 = 1.65\ mA$

④ $V_C = -10 + 1.65 \times 5 = \underline{\underline{-1.75\ V}}$

Note the order of the solution steps.

$\alpha = \frac{I_C}{I_E} = \frac{1.65}{1.66} = \underline{\underline{0.994}}$

$\beta = \frac{I_C}{I_B} = \frac{1.65}{0.01} = \underline{\underline{165}}$

10

$\Delta V_{EB} = 30 \times -2$

$= -60\ mV$

Thus, $\Delta V_E = \underline{\underline{-60\ mV}}$

i_C remains constant at $\alpha \times 1\ mA$ and thus v_C remains constant. $\underline{\underline{\Delta v_C = 0}}$.

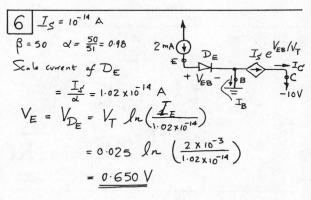

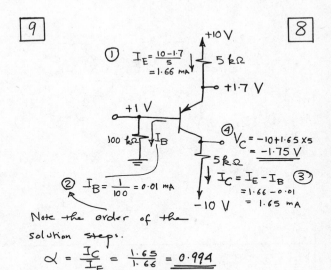

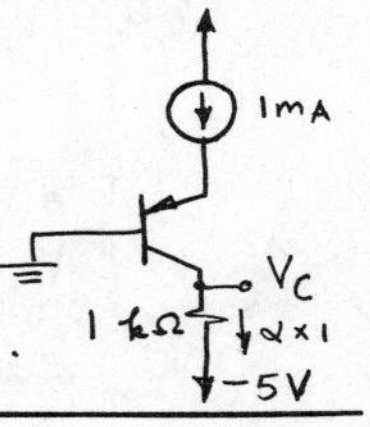

8

11 $r_o = \dfrac{V_A}{I_C} = \dfrac{100}{I_C}$

I_C :	0.1 mA	1 mA	10 mA
r_o :	1 MΩ	100 kΩ	10 kΩ

12 Since V_{BE} is kept constant, the change in I_C is due entirely to the finite r_o.

$$r_o = \frac{V_A}{I_C} = \frac{100}{1} = 100\ k\Omega$$

$$\Delta I_C = \frac{\Delta V_{CE}}{r_o} = \frac{10}{100} = 0.1\ mA$$

$$I_C \rightarrow \underline{1.1\ mA}$$

13 $\beta \simeq \infty$,

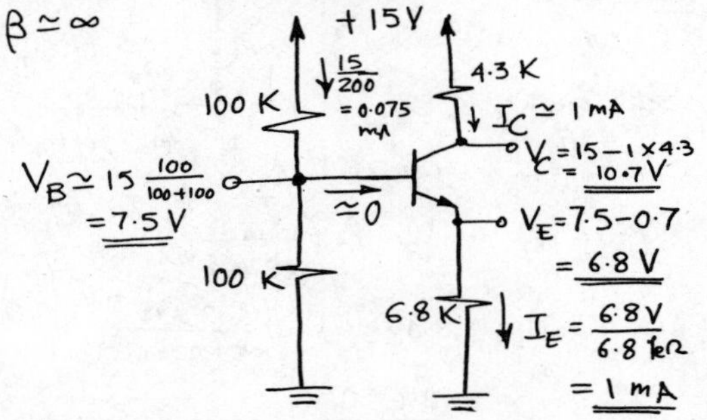

14 $i_C = I_S e^{v_{BE}/V_T}$

$$I_C = I_S e^{V_{BE}/V_T}$$

$$g_m \equiv \left.\frac{\partial i_C}{\partial v_{BE}}\right|_{i_C = I_C}$$

$$= \left.\frac{I_S}{V_T} e^{v_{BE}/V_T}\right|_{i_C = I_C}$$

$$= \left.\frac{i_C}{V_T}\right|_{i_C = I_C}$$

Thus,

$$g_m = \frac{I_C}{V_T}$$

Q.E.D.

15 $g_m = I_C / V_T$

$$= 0.5/0.025 = \underline{20\ mA/V}$$

$$r_e = \frac{V_T}{I_E} \simeq \frac{V_T}{I_C} = \frac{25\ mV}{0.5\ mA} = \underline{50\ \Omega}$$

$$r_\pi = (\beta+1)\, r_e = \frac{\beta}{g_m} = \frac{100}{20} = \underline{5\ k\Omega}$$

8

16

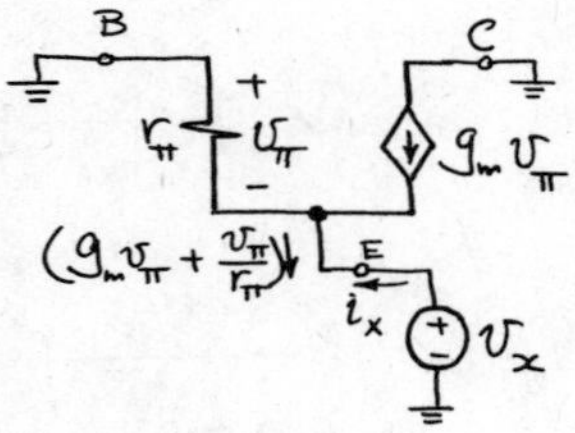

$$i_x = -\left(g_m v_\pi + \frac{v_\pi}{r_\pi}\right)$$

But $v_\pi = -v_x$, thus

$$i_x = v_x \left(g_m + \frac{1}{r_\pi}\right)$$

$$R_{in}\Big|_{\text{into emitter}} = \frac{v_x}{i_x} = \frac{1}{g_m + \frac{1}{r_\pi}}$$

$$= \frac{r_\pi}{g_m r_\pi + 1} = \frac{r_\pi}{\beta + 1} = r_e$$

Q.E.D.

17 $I_C = 1$ mA $I_B = \dfrac{1\ mA}{100} = 0.01$ mA

$$V_C = V_{CC} - I_C R_C = 15 - 1 \times 10 = +5\ V$$

$$g_m = I_C / V_T = \frac{1\ mA}{0.025\ V} = 40\ mA/V$$

$$i_c = g_m v_{be} = 40 \times 0.005 \sin \omega t$$

$$= 0.2 \sin \omega t$$

$$v_c = -i_c R_C = -2 \sin \omega t \quad V$$

$$v_C(t) = V_C + v_c$$

$$= \underline{5 - 2 \sin \omega t}, \ V$$

$$i_b = \frac{i_c}{\beta} = \frac{0.2 \sin \omega t}{100} = 2 \sin \omega t \quad \mu A$$

$$i_B(t) = I_B + i_b$$

$$= \underline{10 + 2 \sin \omega t \quad \mu A}$$

18 For bias calculation assume β very high.

$$I_C \simeq 1\ mA$$

$$r_e = \frac{V_T}{I_E}$$

$$= \frac{25\ mV}{1\ mA} = \underline{25\ \Omega}$$

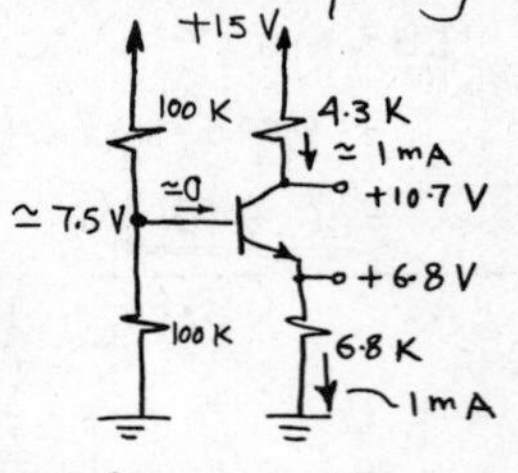

Replacing the BJT with the equivalent circuit of Fig. 8.25 results in:

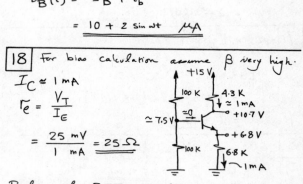

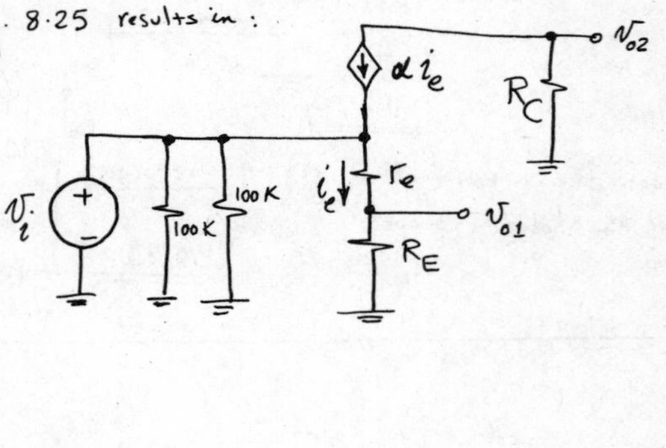

8

$$v_{o1} = v_i \frac{R_E}{R_E + r_e}$$

Thus,

$$\frac{v_{o1}}{v_i} = \frac{R_E}{R_E + r_e}$$

$$i_e = \frac{v_i}{r_e + R_E}$$

$$v_{o2} = -\alpha i_e R_C$$

$$= -\alpha \frac{v_i}{r_e + R_E} \cdot R_C$$

$$\frac{v_{o2}}{v_i} = \frac{-\alpha R_C}{r_e + R_E}$$

For $r_e = 25\,\Omega$, $R_E = 6.8\ k\Omega$, $\alpha = \frac{100}{101} = 0.99$ and $R_C = 4.3\ k\Omega$:

$$\frac{v_{o1}}{v_i} = \frac{6.8}{6.8 + 0.025} = \underline{\underline{0.996\ V/V}}$$

$$\frac{v_{o2}}{v_i} = \frac{-0.99 \times 4.3}{0.025 + 6.8} = \underline{\underline{0.62\ V/V}}$$

8

Alternative derivation of gain expressions using the equivalent circuit of Fig. 8.24a:

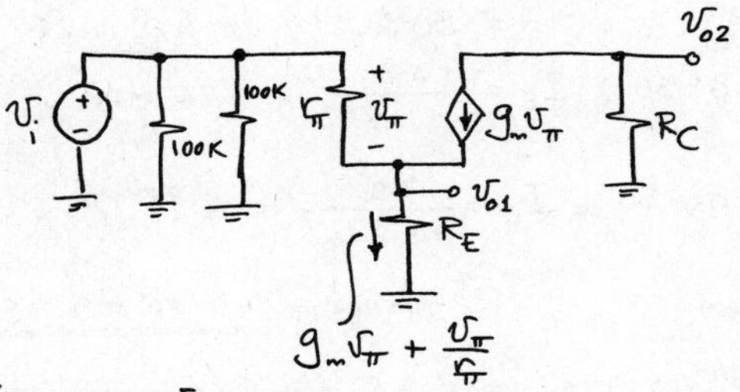

$$v_{o1} = \left(g_m v_\pi + \frac{v_\pi}{r_\pi}\right) R_E = \left(g_m + \frac{1}{r_\pi}\right) R_E\, v_\pi$$

$$v_i = v_{o1} + v_\pi$$

$$= \left(g_m + \frac{1}{r_\pi}\right) R_E\, v_\pi + v_\pi = v_\pi \left[1 + R_E\left(g_m + \frac{1}{r_\pi}\right)\right] \quad (1)$$

$$\frac{v_{o1}}{v_i} = \frac{\left(g_m + \frac{1}{r_\pi}\right) R_E}{\left(g_m + \frac{1}{r_\pi}\right) R_E + 1}$$

$$= \frac{R_E}{R_E + \frac{1}{g_m + \frac{1}{r_\pi}}}$$

8

Now,

$$\frac{1}{g_m + \frac{1}{r_\pi}} = \frac{r_\pi}{g_m r_\pi + 1} = \frac{r_\pi}{\beta + 1}$$

$$= r_e$$

Thus,

$$\frac{v_{o1}}{v_i} = \frac{R_E}{R_E + r_e} \qquad Q.E.D$$

$$v_{o2} = -g_m v_\pi R_C$$

Substituting for v_π from Eq. (1),

$$v_\pi = \frac{v_i}{1 + R_E\left(g_m + \frac{1}{r_\pi}\right)}$$

results in

$$v_{o2} = \frac{-g_m R_C v_i}{1 + R_E\left(g_m + \frac{1}{r_\pi}\right)}$$

$$= -\frac{\left(\frac{g_m}{g_m + \frac{1}{r_\pi}}\right) R_C v_i}{\left(\frac{1}{g_m + \frac{1}{r_\pi}}\right) + R_E}$$

$$= \frac{-\left(\frac{\beta}{\beta+1}\right) R_C v_i}{\left(\frac{r_\pi}{\beta+1}\right) + R_E}$$

8

Thus

$$\frac{v_{o2}}{v_i} = \frac{-\alpha R_C}{r_e + R_E} \qquad Q.E.D.$$

---

19 (a) DC Analysis:

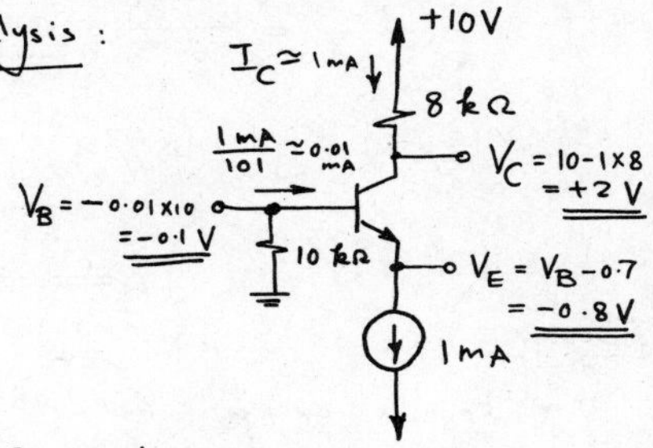

(b) $g_m = \frac{I_C}{V_T} = \frac{1}{0.025} = \underline{40\ mA/V}$

$$r_\pi = \frac{\beta}{g_m} = \frac{100}{40} = \underline{2.5\ k\Omega}$$

(c) $\frac{v_y}{v_i} = -g_m (R_C // R_L)$

$$= -40\ (8 // 8) = \underline{\underline{-160\ V/V}}$$

---

20 From Eq. (8.47)

$$I_E = \frac{V_{BB} - V_{BE}}{R_E + \frac{R_B}{\beta+1}} = \frac{4-0.7}{3.3 + \frac{R_B}{\beta+1}}$$

Design 1 $R_B = 80\,k\Omega \,//\, 40\,k\Omega = 26.7\,k\Omega$

For $\beta = 50$, $I_E = \frac{3.3}{3.3 + \frac{26.7}{51}} = 0.86\text{ mA}$

For $\beta = 150$, $I_E = \frac{3.3}{3.3 + \frac{26.7}{151}} = 0.95\text{ mA}$

Thus, I_E is in the range 0.86 mA to 0.95 mA

Design 2 $R_B = 8\,k\Omega \,//\, 4\,k\Omega = 2.67\,k\Omega$

For $\beta = 50$, $I_E = \frac{3.3}{3.3 + \frac{2.67}{51}} = 0.984\text{mA}$

For $\beta = 150$, $I_E = \frac{3.3}{3.3 + \frac{2.67}{151}} = 0.995\text{ mA}$

Thus, I_E is in the range 0.984 to 0.995 mA.

20A Please note that this Exercise, on page 445, was numbered 8.21 in the first printing.

Since the amplifier is to be used in the common base configuration, the based can be directly connected to ground and R_B set to zero,

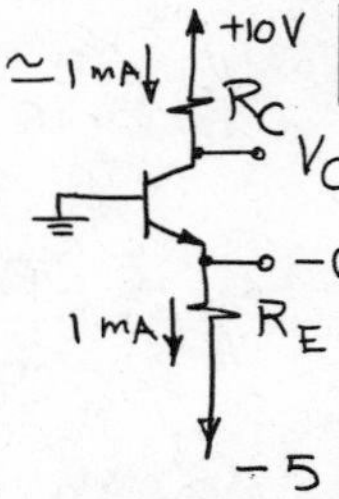

$$R_B = 0$$

$$R_E = \frac{-0.7 - (-5)}{1\text{ mA}}$$

$$= 4.3\,k\Omega$$

To allow for ±2-V signal swing at the collector while choosing as large a value for R_C as possible we set $V_C = +2\text{ V}$ (thus a −2-V signal would not saturate the BJT.) Thus

$$R_C = \frac{10-2}{I_C} = \frac{8}{1\text{ mA}} = 8\,k\Omega$$

8.21 This is the first Exercise on page 447.

Design 1

$I_E = 0.93$ mA

$r_e = 27\,\Omega$

$g_m = 37$ mA/V

$r_\pi = 2.7\,k\Omega$

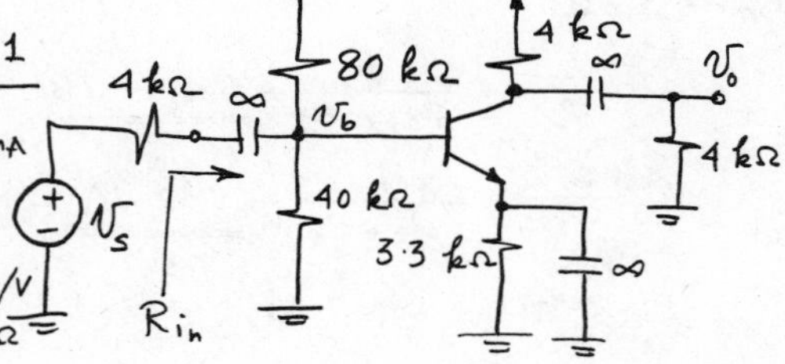

$$R_{in} = 80 \,//\, 40 \,//\, r_\pi$$

$$= 80 \,//\, 40 \,//\, 2.7 = 2.5\,k\Omega$$

$$\frac{v_b}{v_s} = \frac{R_{in}}{R_{in} + 4} = \frac{2.5}{6.5} = 0.38$$

$$\frac{v_o}{v_s} = \frac{v_b}{v_s} \times -g_m\,(4\,//\,4)$$

$$= -0.38 \times 37 \times 2 = -28\text{ V/V}.$$

Design 2

Same circuit except that the 80-kΩ resistor is replaced with an 8-kΩ resistor and the 40-kΩ resistor is replaced with a 4-kΩ resistor.

$I_E = 0.99\text{ mA} \simeq 1\text{ mA}$

$r_e = 25\,\Omega$ $g_m = 40\text{ mA/V}$

$r_\pi \simeq 2.5\,k\Omega$

$R_{in} = 8 \,//\, 4 \,//\, 2.5 = 1.3\,k\Omega$

$$\frac{v_b}{v_s} = \frac{1.3}{1.3 + 4} = 0.25$$

$$\frac{v_o}{v_s} = \frac{v_b}{v_s} \times -g_m\,(4\,//\,4)$$

$$= -0.25 \times 40 \times 2$$

$$= -20\text{ V/V}$$

22 Design 1

$$\hat{v}_s = \frac{\hat{v}_{be}}{(v_b/v_s)} = \frac{10\text{ mV}}{0.38} = 26.3\text{ mV}$$

$$\hat{v}_o = \hat{v}_s \times \left|\frac{v_o}{v_s}\right| = 26.3 \times 28 = 0.74\text{ V}$$

Design 2

$$\hat{v}_s = \frac{10\text{ mV}}{0.25} = 40\text{ mV}$$

$$\hat{v}_o = 40 \times 20 = 0.8\text{ V}$$

23 Design 1

$I_E = 0.93$ mA

$r_e = 27\,\Omega$

$g_m = 37$ mA/V

$r_\pi = 2.7\,k\Omega$

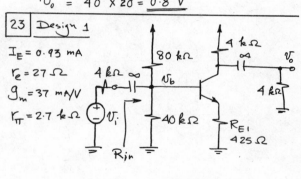

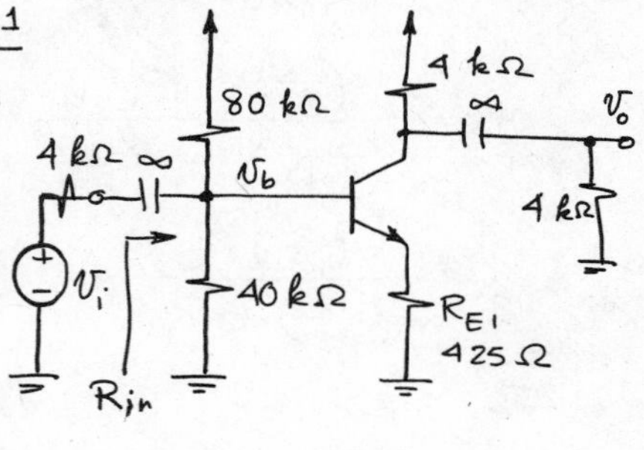

$$R_{in} = 80 // 40 // [(\beta+1)(R_{E1} + r_e)]$$ **8**

$$= 80//40//[101 \times (425 + 27) \times 10^{-3}]$$

$$= \underline{16.8\ k\Omega}$$

$$\frac{v_b}{v_s} = \frac{16.8}{16.8+4} = \underline{0.81}$$

$$\frac{v_o}{v_s} = \frac{v_b}{v_s} \times -\frac{(4//4)}{(R_{E1}+r_e)} = -0.81 \times \frac{2}{0.452}$$

$$= \underline{-3.6\ V/V}$$

Design 2

Replace 80 kΩ with 8 kΩ and 40 kΩ with 4 kΩ. $I_E \simeq 1\,mA$, $r_e = 25\,\Omega$, $g_m = 40\,mA/V$.

$$R_{in} = 8//4//(101 \times 0.450) = \underline{2.5\ k\Omega}$$

$$\frac{v_b}{v_s} = \frac{2.5}{2.5+4} = \underline{0.38}$$

$$\frac{v_o}{v_s} = \frac{v_b}{v_s} \times -\frac{4//4}{R_{E1}+r_e}$$

$$= -0.38 \times \frac{2}{0.45} = \underline{-1.7\ V/V}$$

---

24 Refer to the results of Exercise 8.23 above. **8**

Design 1

$$\hat{v}_s = \frac{\hat{v}_b}{(v_b/v_s)} = \frac{\hat{v}_{be}}{(v_{be}/v_b)} \frac{1}{(v_b/v_s)}$$

$$= \frac{10\ mV}{[r_e/(r_e+R_{E1})]} \times \frac{1}{0.81}$$

$$= \frac{10}{(27/452)} \times \frac{1}{0.81} = \underline{208\ mV}$$

$$\hat{v}_o = \hat{v}_s \times \left|\frac{v_o}{v_s}\right| = 208 \times 3.6$$

$$= \underline{0.75\ V}$$ (Approx. the same as the corresponding value without R_{E1})

Design 2

$$\hat{v}_s = \frac{\hat{v}_b}{(v_b/v_s)} = \frac{\hat{v}_{be}}{(v_{be}/v_b)} \frac{1}{(v_b/v_s)}$$

$$= \frac{10\ mV}{(25/450)} \times \frac{1}{0.38} = \underline{474\ mV}$$

$$\hat{v}_o = \hat{v}_s \times \left|\frac{v_o}{v_s}\right| = 474 \times 1.7$$

$$= \underline{0.81\ V}$$ (Approx. the same as the corresponding value without R_{E1})

---

25 Refer to the small-signal model shown (without explicitly replacing the BJT with its equivalent circuit), **8**

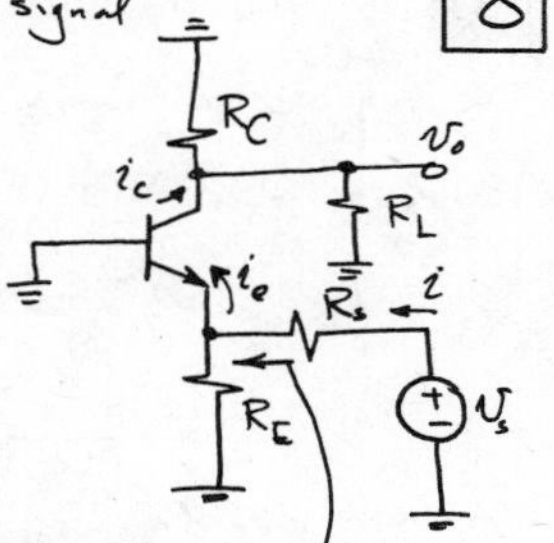

For $R_s >> r_e$ we see that $R_s >> R_{in}$, thus

$$i \cong \frac{v_s}{R_s}$$

Since usually $r_e << R_E$,

$$i_e \simeq i = \frac{v_s}{R_s}$$

For $\alpha \simeq 1$,

$$i_c \simeq i_e = \frac{v_s}{R_s}$$

$$v_o = i_c (R_C // R_L)$$

$$= \frac{v_s}{R_s}(R_C//R_L)$$

$$\frac{v_o}{v_s} = \underline{(R_C//R_L)/R_s}$$

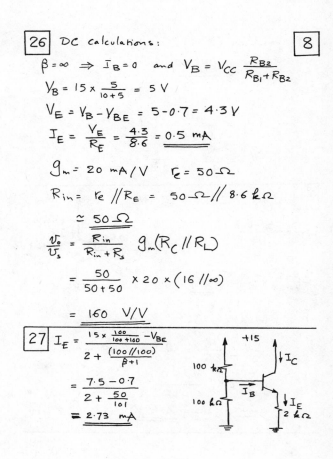

26 DC calculations: **8**

$$\beta = \infty \Rightarrow I_B = 0 \quad \text{and} \quad V_B = V_{CC}\frac{R_{B2}}{R_{B1}+R_{B2}}$$

$$V_B = 15 \times \frac{5}{10+5} = 5\ V$$

$$V_E = V_B - V_{BE} = 5 - 0.7 = 4.3\ V$$

$$I_E = \frac{V_E}{R_E} = \frac{4.3}{8.6} = \underline{0.5\ mA}$$

$$g_m = 20\ mA/V \qquad r_e = 50\,\Omega$$

$$R_{in} = r_e // R_E = 50\,\Omega // 8.6\,k\Omega$$

$$\simeq \underline{50\,\Omega}$$

$$\frac{v_o}{v_s} = \frac{R_{in}}{R_{in}+R_s} g_m (R_C//R_L)$$

$$= \frac{50}{50+50} \times 20 \times (16//\infty)$$

$$= \underline{160\ V/V}$$

27

$$I_E = \frac{15 \times \frac{100}{100+100} - V_{BE}}{2 + \frac{(100//100)}{\beta+1}}$$

$$= \frac{7.5 - 0.7}{2 + \frac{50}{101}}$$

$$= \underline{2.73\ mA}$$

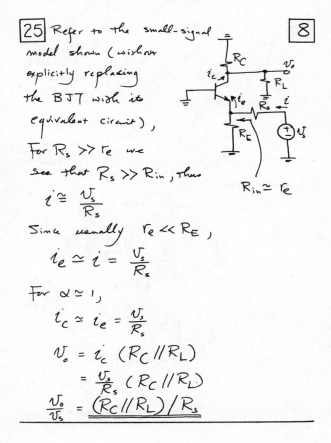

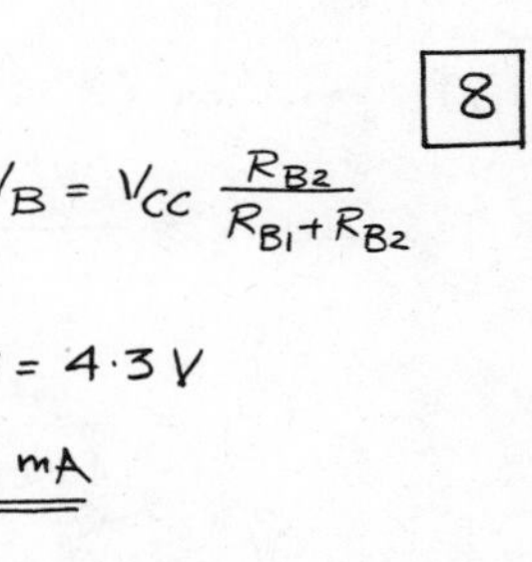

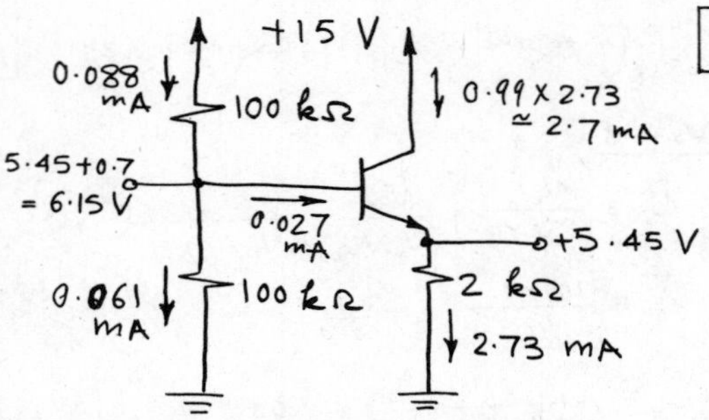

28

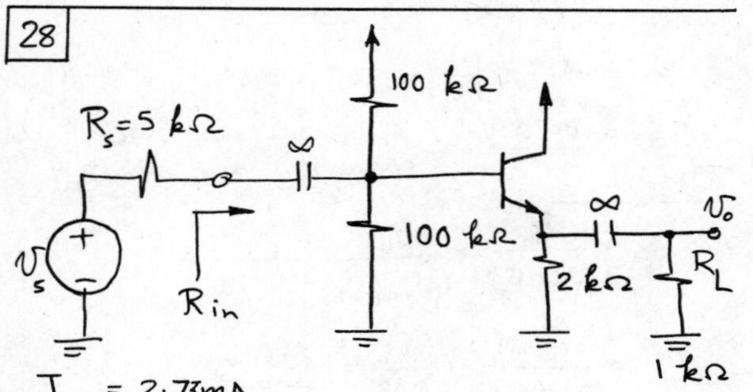

$I_E = 2.73\text{mA}$

$$r_e = \frac{25}{2.73} = 9.2\,\Omega$$

$$R_{in} = 100 \,//\, 100 \,//\, \{(\beta+1)\,[r_e + (2\,//\,1)]\}$$
$$= 50 \,//\, [101 \times \{0.009 + 0.667\}]$$

$R_{in} = \underline{28.9\ \text{k}\Omega}$

$$\frac{v_o}{v_s} = \left(\frac{28.9}{28.9+5}\right) \frac{(2//1)}{(2//1) + 0.009}$$
$$= \underline{0.84\ \text{V/V}}$$

29 Refer to the figure in the solution to Exercise 28 above.

$$R_{in}\Big|_{R_L=\infty} = 100 \,//\, 100 \,//\, [(\beta+1)\,(r_e + 2)]$$
$$= 100//100//[101\,(2.009)]$$
$$= 40.1\ \text{k}\Omega$$

$$A_{v_o} \equiv \frac{v_o}{v_s}\Big|_{R_L=\infty}$$
$$= \left(\frac{40.1}{40.1+5}\right)\left(\frac{2}{2+0.009}\right)$$
$$= \underline{0.885\ \text{V/V}}$$

$$R_{out} = 2 \,//\, \left[r_e + \frac{(100//100//5)}{\beta+1}\right]$$
$$= \underline{52.7\ \Omega}$$

30 From Eq. (8.76)

$$\hat{V}_e = \frac{V_E}{1 + \frac{R_E}{R_L}}$$
$$= \frac{5.45}{1 + \frac{2}{1}} = 1.82\ \text{V}$$
$$\hat{V}_s = \frac{\hat{V}_e}{\text{gain}} = \frac{1.82}{0.84} = \underline{2.1\ \text{V}}$$

31 $I_C = \frac{5-0.3}{1} = 4.7\ \text{mA}$

$$I_B = \frac{5-0.7}{10}$$
$$= 0.43\ \text{mA}$$

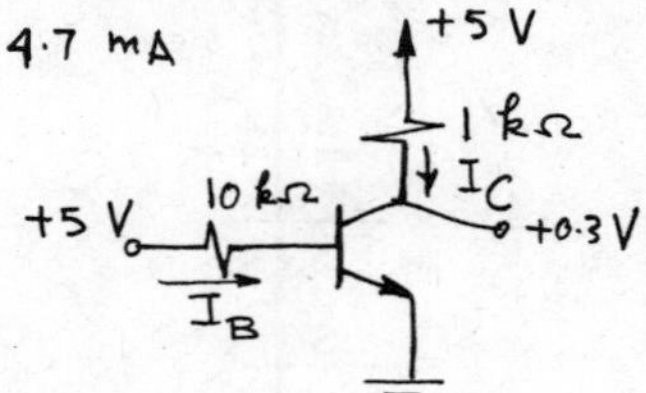

$$\beta_{Forced} = \frac{4.7}{0.43} = \underline{10.9}$$

For $\beta_{forced} = \frac{\beta}{2} = 25$,

$$I_B = \frac{I_C}{25} = \frac{4.7}{25} = 0.188\ \text{mA}$$

$$0.188 = \frac{V_I - 0.7}{10}$$

$$\Rightarrow\ V_I = \underline{2.6\ \text{V}}$$

32 At the lowest β we require a base current of

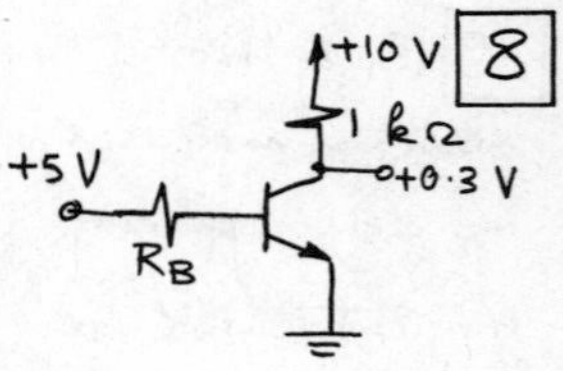

$$I_{B_{sat}} = \frac{I_{C_{sat}}}{\beta_{min}}$$
$$= \frac{10-0.3}{50} = 0.194\ \text{mA}$$

For an overdrive factor of 5, the base current must be

$$I_B = 5 \times 0.194 = 0.97\ \text{mA}$$

Thus, $R_B = \frac{5-0.7}{0.97} = \underline{4.4\ \text{k}\Omega}$

33

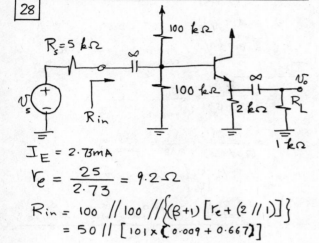

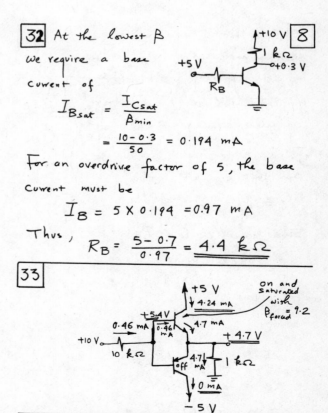

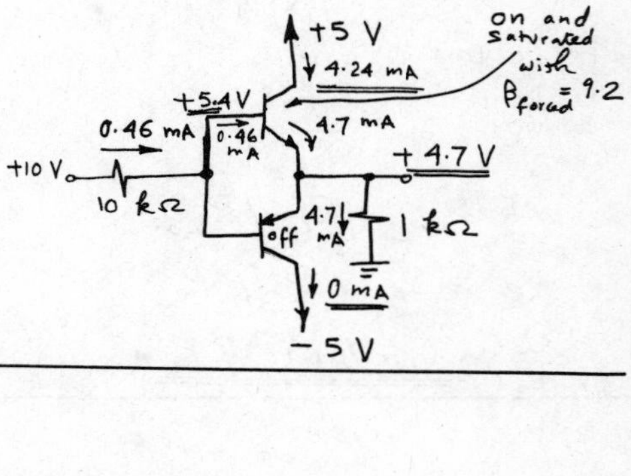

34 The CB junction will breakdown and exhibit a reverse voltage of 70 V, as shown.

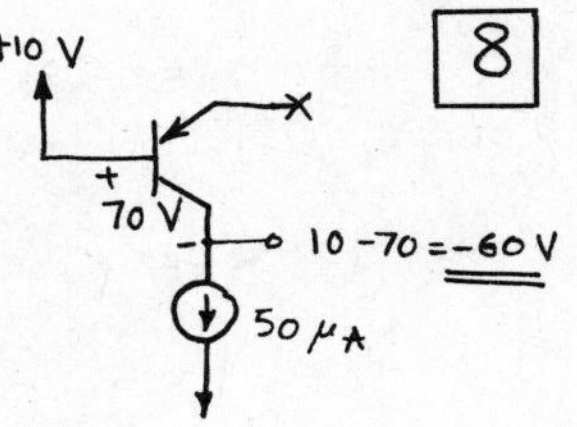

---

35 From sketch,

$V_{off} = 70\ mV$

$R_{CEsat} = \frac{60\ mV}{3\ mA}$

$= 20\ \Omega$

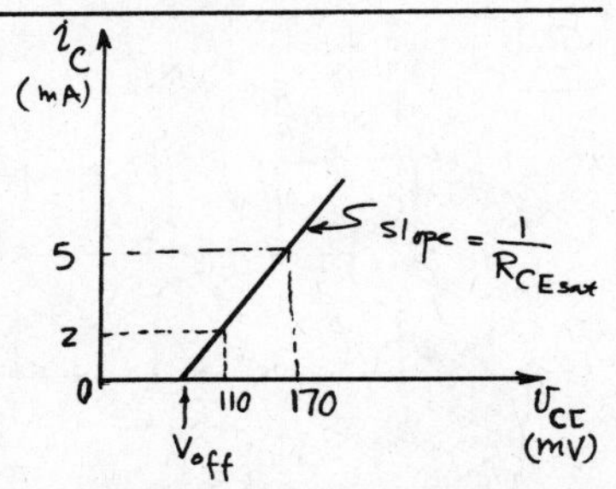

Chapter 9—Exercises

1

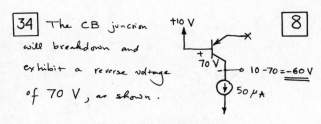

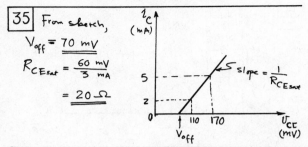

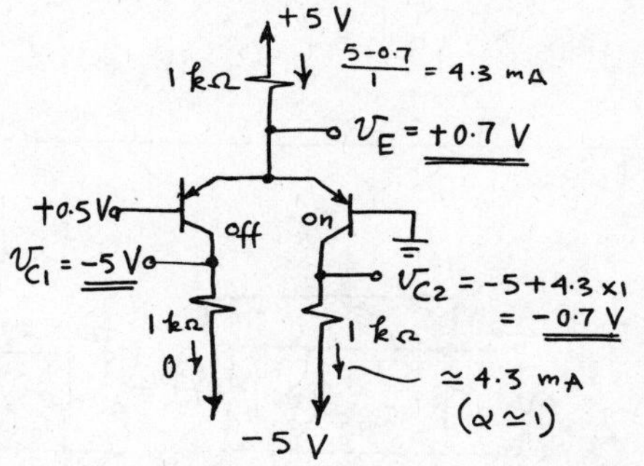

---

2 Substituting $i_{E1} + i_{E2} = I$ in Eq. (9.4) yields

$$i_{E1} = \frac{I}{1 + e^{(v_{B2} - v_{B1})/V_T}}$$

$$0.99\,I = \frac{I}{1 + e^{(v_{B2} - v_{B1})/V_T}}$$

$$v_{B1} - v_{B2} = -V_T \ln\left(\frac{1}{0.99} - 1\right)$$

$$= -25 \ln\left(\frac{1}{99}\right)$$

$$= 25 \ln 99 = 115\ mV$$

---

3 (a) $r_{e1} = r_{e2} = 50\ \Omega$

$$R_{id} = 2(\beta+1)(R_E + r_e)$$

$$= 2 \times 101 \times (150 + 50)$$

$$\cong 40\ k\Omega$$

(b) $$\frac{v_{b1}}{v_s} = \frac{R_{id}}{R_{id} + R_s}$$

$$= \frac{40}{40 + 10} = 0.8\ V/V$$

$$\frac{v_o}{v_{b1}} = \frac{+\alpha\, 2R_C}{2(R_E + r_e)}$$

$$\simeq \frac{+2 \times 10}{2 \times 0.2} = +50\ V/V$$

Thus, $\frac{v_o}{v_s} = 0.8 \times 50 = 40\ V/V$

(c) Using Eq. (9.40),

$$A_{cm} = \frac{R_C}{2R} \frac{\Delta R_C}{R_C}$$

where $\Delta R_C = 0.02\, R_C$ in the worst case.

Thus $A_{cm} = \frac{10}{400} \times 0.02 = 5 \times 10^{-4}\ V/V$

3 (d) $$CMRR = 20 \log \frac{A_d}{A_{cm}}$$

$$= 20 \log\left(\frac{40}{5 \times 10^{-4}}\right)$$

$$= 98\ dB$$

(e) $r_o = \frac{V_A}{(I/2)} = \frac{100}{0.5} = 200\ k\Omega$

$r_\mu = 10\,\beta\, r_o = 10 \times 100 \times 200 = 200\ M\Omega$

Using Eq. (9.44),

$$R_{icm} = \left(\frac{r_\mu}{2}\right) // [(\beta+1)R] // \left[(\beta+1)\frac{r_o}{2}\right]$$

$$= 100 // (101 \times 0.2) // (101 \times 0.1)\quad M\Omega$$

$$= 6.3\ M\Omega$$

---

4 From Eq. (9.55)

$$V_{off} = V_T \sqrt{\left(\frac{\Delta R_C}{R_C}\right)^2 + \left(\frac{\Delta I_S}{I_S}\right)^2}$$

$$= 25 \sqrt{(0.02)^2 + (0.1)^2}$$

$$= 2.5\ mV$$

$$I_B = \frac{100}{2 \times (\beta+1)} = \frac{100}{2 \times 101} \simeq 0.5\ \mu A$$

$$I_{off} = I_B\left(\frac{\Delta\beta}{\beta}\right)$$
$$= 0.5 \times 0.1\ \mu A$$
$$= \underline{50\ nA}$$

5

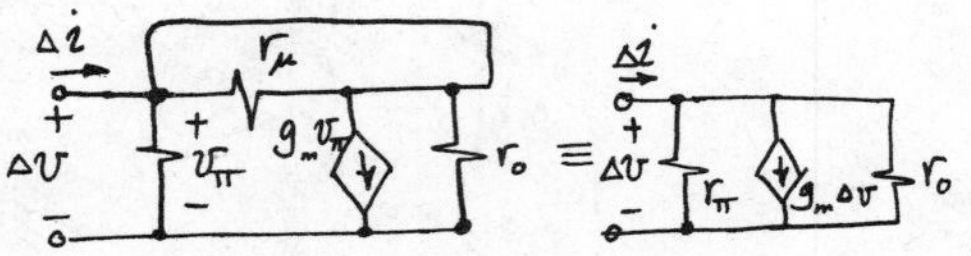

$$v_\pi = \Delta v$$

⇓

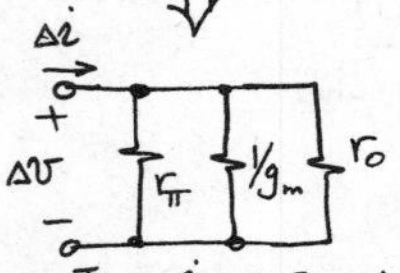

$$R_{incremental} = r_\pi // \frac{1}{g_m} // r_o$$
$$= r_e // r_o$$
$$\simeq \underline{r_e} = \underline{50\,\Omega} \quad \text{for } I_E = i = 0.5\ mA$$

6 $R_{out} = r_o = \dfrac{V_A}{I_{REF}} = \dfrac{100}{1} = \underline{\underline{100\ k\Omega}}$

At $V_O = V_B = -V_{EE} + V_{BE} = -4.3\ V$, $I_O = I_{REF}$.

At $V_O = +5\ V$, $I_O = I_{REF} + \dfrac{5-(-4.3)}{R_{out}}$

$$= 1 + \frac{9.3}{100} = \underline{\underline{1.093\ mA}}$$

7 $I_O = I_{REF}$

Thus, $I_{REF} = 1\ mA$

But, $I_{REF} = \dfrac{V_{CC} - V_{BE}}{R}$

$$1 = \frac{5-0.7}{R} \Rightarrow R = \underline{4.3\ k\Omega}$$

8

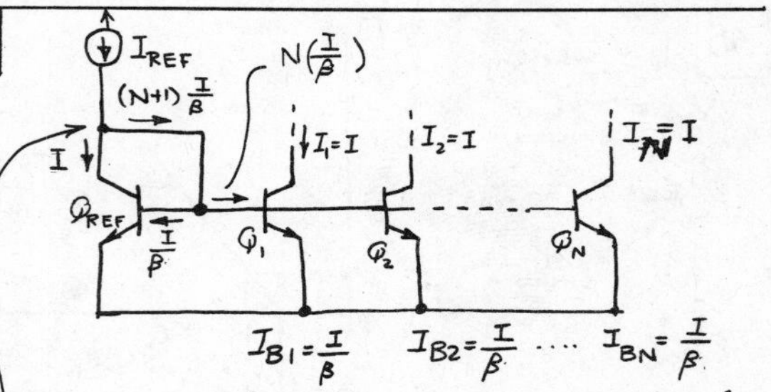

All collector currents are equal because transistors are matched and have the same V_{BE}

Node equation:

$$I_{REF} = I + (N+1)\frac{I}{\beta}$$

Thus,

$$I = \frac{I_{REF}}{1 + \dfrac{N+1}{\beta}} \qquad \text{Q.E.D}$$

For the error not to exceed 10%

$$\frac{N+1}{\beta} \leq 0.1$$

For $\beta = 100$

$$N+1 \leq 0.1 \times 100$$
$$N \leq \underline{\underline{9}}$$

9

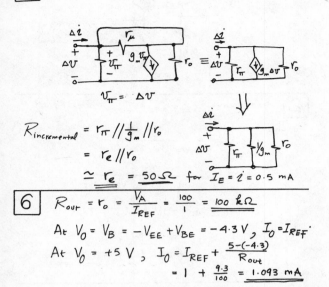

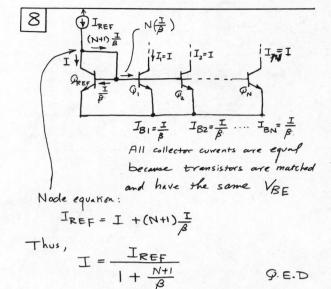

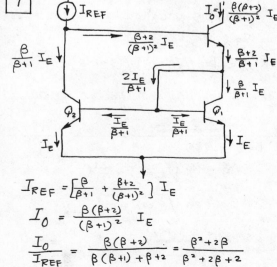

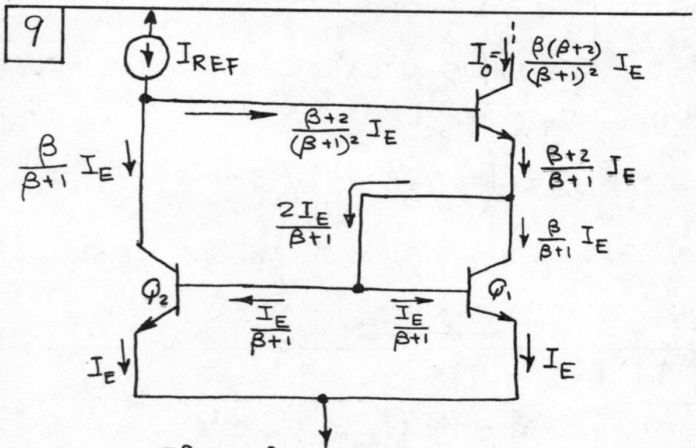

$$I_{REF} = \left[\frac{\beta}{\beta+1} + \frac{\beta+2}{(\beta+1)^2}\right] I_E$$

$$I_O = \frac{\beta(\beta+2)}{(\beta+1)^2} I_E$$

$$\frac{I_O}{I_{REF}} = \frac{\beta(\beta+2)}{\beta(\beta+1) + \beta + 2} = \frac{\beta^2 + 2\beta}{\beta^2 + 2\beta + 2}$$

$$\frac{I_O}{I_{REF}} = \frac{1}{1 + \dfrac{2}{\beta^2 + 2\beta}}$$

$$\simeq \frac{1}{1 + \dfrac{2}{\beta^2}} \qquad \text{Q.E.D}$$

10 For the current source of Fig. 9.21a,

$$R_{out} = r_{o2}$$
$$= \frac{V_A}{I_O} = \frac{100\ V}{10\ \mu A} = \underline{\underline{10\ M\Omega}}$$

For the current source of Fig. 9.21b we use Eq. (9.78) to determine the output resistance,

$$R_{out} = r_o(1 + g_m R_E')$$

where $r_o = \dfrac{V_A}{I_O} = \dfrac{100}{10} = 10\ M\Omega$

$$g_m = \frac{10\ \mu A}{25\ mV} = 0.4\ mA/V$$

$$R_E' = R_E // r_\pi = 11.5\ k\Omega // \frac{100}{0.4}\ k\Omega$$
$$= 11.5 // 250 = 11\ k\Omega$$

Thus, $R_{out} = 10(1 + 0.4 \times 11) = \underline{\underline{54\ M\Omega}}$

11 (a) **9**

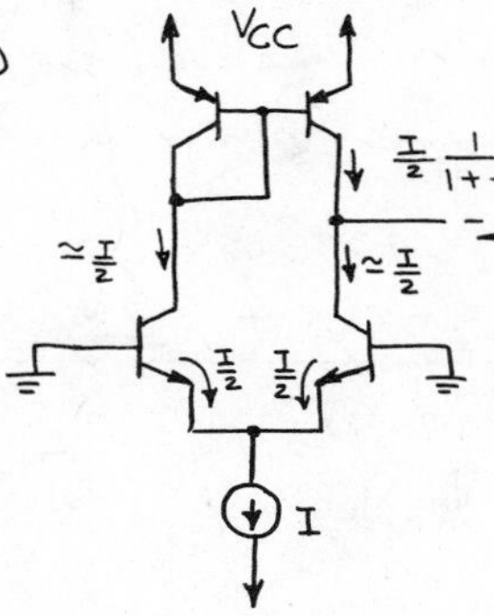

$\frac{I}{2}\frac{1}{1+\frac{2}{\beta_P}}$ ← From Eq. (9.65)

$$I_o = \frac{I}{2} - \frac{I}{2}\frac{1}{1+\frac{2}{\beta_P}}$$

$$= \frac{I}{2}\frac{2/\beta_P}{1+\frac{2}{\beta_P}}$$

$$\simeq \frac{I}{\beta_P}$$

(b) $\frac{i_o}{v_{id}} = g_m = \frac{I/2}{V_T}$

Thus, the input offset voltage that reduce the dc output current $\frac{I}{\beta_P}$ to zero is

$$V_{off} = \frac{I/\beta_P}{g_m} = \frac{I/\beta_P}{(I/2)/V_T}$$

$$= \frac{2V_T}{\beta_P}$$

(c) $V_{off} = \frac{2 \times 25}{25} = 2 \text{ mV}$

---

12 From equation (9.91) **9**

$$v_{id} = |V_P|\sqrt{\frac{I}{I_{DSS}}}$$

$$= 2 \times \sqrt{\frac{1}{2}} = \sqrt{2} = 1.4 \text{ V}$$

$$g_m = \frac{2I_{DSS}}{|V_P|}\sqrt{\frac{I/2}{I_{DSS}}}$$

$$= \frac{2 \times 2}{2}\sqrt{\frac{1/2}{2}}$$

$$= 1 \text{ mA}$$

$$\frac{v_o}{v_{id}} = -g_m(R_D // r_o)$$

Since r_o is not specified we shall assume it to be very large. Thus

$$\frac{v_o}{v_{id}} \simeq -g_m R_D = -1 \times 10$$

$$= -10 \text{ V/V}$$

---

13 **9**

$$\frac{I}{2} = \frac{1}{2}(\mu_n C_{ox})\left(\frac{W}{L}\right)(V_{GS} - V_t)^2$$

$$\frac{25}{2} = \frac{1}{2} \times 20 \times \frac{120}{6}(V_{GS} - 1)^2$$

$$\Rightarrow V_{GS} = 1.25 \text{ V}$$

$$g_m = 2K(V_{GS} - V_t)$$

$$= 2 \times \frac{1}{2} \times \mu_n C_{ox} \times \left(\frac{W}{L}\right)(V_{GS} - V_t)$$

$$= 20 \times \frac{120}{6} \times (1.25 - 1)$$

$$= 100 \ \mu\text{A/V}$$

$$= 0.1 \text{ mA/V}$$

$$v_{id}|_{max} = \sqrt{2}(V_{GS} - V_t)$$

$$= \sqrt{2} \times (1.25 - 1)$$

$$= 0.35 \text{ V}$$

---

14 Refer to Exercise 9.13 above.

Using Eq. (9.122) we obtain V_{off} due to $\frac{\Delta R_D}{R_D}$ as:

$$V_{off} = \left(\frac{V_{GS} - V_t}{2}\right)\left(\frac{\Delta R_D}{R_D}\right)$$

9

$$V_{off} = \frac{1.25 - 1}{2} \times 0.02$$

$$= 2.5 \text{ mV}$$

To obtain V_{off} due to $\Delta K/K$ we use Eq. (9.129),

$$V_{off} = \left(\frac{V_{GS} - V_t}{2}\right)\left(\frac{\Delta K}{K}\right)$$

$$= \frac{1.25 - 1}{2} \times 0.02$$

$$= 2.5 \text{ mV}$$

Finally, the offset voltage arising from ΔV_t is obtained from Eq. (9.132),

$$V_{off} = \Delta V_t = 2 \text{ mV}$$

---

15 $R_{out} = r_{o2} = \frac{V_A}{I_O} = \frac{V_A}{I_{REF}}$

$$= \frac{20 \text{ V}}{10 \ \mu\text{A}} = 2 \text{ M}\Omega$$

$$I_{REF} = K(V_{GS} - V_t)^2$$

$$10 = \frac{1}{2} \times 20 \times \frac{40}{10} \times (V_{GS} - 1)^2$$

$$\Rightarrow V_{GS} = 1.5 \text{ V}$$

$V_{G2} = -5 + 1.5 = -3.5\text{ V}$

The output voltage is allowed to go down to $V_{G2} - V_t$ before Q_2 saturates. Thus the lowest allowable output voltage is $\underline{\underline{-4.5\text{ V}}}$.

---

16 To obtain R_o we use Eq. (9.134),

$$R_o = r_o(2 + g_m r_o)$$

where

$$r_o = 2\text{ M}\Omega$$

$$g_m = 2K(V_{GS} - V_t)$$

$$= 2 \times \tfrac{1}{2} \times 20 \times \tfrac{40}{10}(1.5 - 1)$$

$$= 40\ \mu\text{A/V}$$

Thus, $R_o = 2(2 + 40 \times 2) = \underline{164\text{ M}\Omega}$

V_{GS} is the same as in the basic mirror considered in Exercise 9.15 above,

$$\underline{\underline{V_{GS} = 1.5\text{ V}}}$$

Refer to Fig. 9.31b. $V_{G2} = -5 + 1.5 = -3.5\text{ V}$

$V_{G3} = -3.5 + 1.5 = -2\text{ V}$

Minimum allowable voltage at the output $= V_{G3} - V_t$

$$= -2 - 1 = \underline{\underline{-3\text{ V}}}$$

---

17 $\frac{I}{2} = K(V_{GS} - V_t)^2$

$$\frac{25}{2} = \frac{1}{2} \times 20 \times \frac{120}{6}(V_{GS} - 1)^2$$

$$\Rightarrow \quad V_{GS} = 1.25\text{ V}$$

From Eq. (9.137),

$$A_v = \frac{V_A}{V_{GS} - V_t}$$

$$= \frac{20}{1.25 - 1} = \underline{\underline{80\text{ V/V}}}$$

---

18 $R_{id} = 20.2\text{ k}\Omega$

$$A_{vo} = 8513\text{ V/V}$$

$$R_o = 152\ \Omega$$

With $R_s = 10\text{ k}\Omega$ and $R_L = 1\text{ k}\Omega$,

$$A_v = \left(\frac{20.2}{20.2 + 10}\right) \times 8513 \times \left(\frac{1}{1 + 0.152}\right)$$

$$= \underline{\underline{4{,}943\text{ V/V}}}$$

Chapter 10—Exercises

1 $I = \dfrac{|-V_{CC} + V_{CEsat}|}{R_L}$

$$= \frac{|-15 + 0.2|}{1} = 14.8\text{ mA}$$

$$R = \frac{V_{CC} - V_D}{I}$$

$$= \frac{15 - 0.7}{14.8} = \underline{\underline{0.97\text{ k}\Omega}}$$

Output voltage swing $= \underline{\underline{-14.8\text{ V to } +14.8\text{ V}}}$

Min. emitter current $= \underline{\underline{0\text{ mA}}}$

Max. emitter current $= 2I$

$$= 2 \times 14.8 = \underline{\underline{29.6\text{ mA}}}$$

---

2 At $v_O = -10\text{ V}$, the load current is -10 mA and the emitter current of Q_1 is $14.8 - 10 = 4.8\text{ mA}$. Thus

$$v_{BE1} = 0.6 + 0.025\ \ln\left(\frac{4.8}{1}\right)$$

$$= 0.64\text{ V}$$

Thus, $v_I = -10 + 0.64 = \underline{\underline{-9.36\text{ V}}}$

10

At $v_O = 0$ V, $i_L = 0$ and $i_{E1} = 14.8$ mA

Thus, $v_{BE1} = 0.6 + 0.025 \ln \frac{14.8}{1}$

$= 0.67$ V

$v_I = +0.67$ V

At $v_O = +10$ V, $i_L = 10$ mA and $i_{E1} = 24.8$ mA

Thus, $v_{BE1} = 0.6 + 0.025 \ln(24.8)$

$= 0.68$ V

$v_I = 10.68$ V

To calculate the incremental voltage gain we use

$$\frac{v_o}{v_i} = \frac{R_L}{R_L + r_{e1}}$$

At $v_O = -10$ V, $i_{E1} = 4.8$ mA and $r_{e1} = \frac{25}{4.8} = 5.2\,\Omega$

Thus, $\frac{v_o}{v_i} = \frac{1}{1+0.0052} = 0.995$ V/V

Similarly, at $v_O = 0$ V, $r_{e1} = \frac{25}{14.8} = 1.7\,\Omega$

and, $\frac{v_o}{v_i} = \frac{1}{1+0.0017} = 0.998$ V/V

At $v_O = +10$ V; $i_{E1} = 24.8$ mA and $r_{e1} = 1\,\Omega$.

Thus, $\frac{v_o}{v_i} = \frac{1}{1+0.001} = 0.999$ V/V

10

3 For $v_O = 0$ V,

$P_{D1} = V_{CC} I = 10 \times 0.1 = 1$ W

$P_{D2} = V_{CC} I = 10 \times 0.1 = 1$ W

For a 10-V amplitude output sinusoid, the waveform shown in Fig. 10.4 apply and the average power dissipation in Q_1 is seen to be $\frac{1}{2} V_{CC} I = \frac{1}{2} \times 10 \times 0.1 = 0.5$ W. Transistor Q_2 carries a constant current I and has an average v_{CE} of 15 V, thus the average power dissipated in Q_2 remains unchanged at 1 W. The load power is

$$P_L = \frac{(\hat{V}_o/\sqrt{2})^2}{R_L} = \frac{1}{2}\frac{100}{100} = 0.5 \text{ W}$$

---

4 $P_L = \frac{(8/\sqrt{2})^2}{100} = 0.32$ W

$P_+ = 10 \times 0.1 = 1$ W

$P_- = 10 \times 0.1 = 1$ W

$P_{supplies} = 2$ W

10

$$\eta = \frac{P_L}{P_S} \times 100$$

$$= \frac{0.32}{2} \times 100 = 16\ \%$$

---

5 (a) $P_L = \frac{1}{2}\frac{\hat{V}_o^2}{R_L}$

$= \frac{1}{2}\frac{(4.5)^2}{4} = 2.53$ W

(b) $P_+ = P_- = V_{CC} \times \frac{1}{\pi}\frac{\hat{V}_o}{R_L}$

$= 6 \times \frac{1}{\pi} \times \frac{4.5}{4} = 2.15$ W

(c) $\eta = \frac{P_L}{P_S} \times 100 = \frac{2.53}{2 \times 2.15} \times 100$

$= 59\ \%$

(d) Peak input currents $= \frac{1}{\beta+1}\frac{\hat{V}_o}{R_L}$

$= \frac{1}{51} \times \frac{4.5}{4}$

$= 22.1$ mA

10

(e) Using Eq. (10.22)

$$P_{DNmax} = P_{DPmax} = \frac{V_{CC}^2}{\pi^2 R_L}$$

$$= \frac{6^2}{\pi^2 \times 4} = 0.91 \text{ W}$$

---

6 Under quiescent conditions

$i_N = i_P = I_Q$

and $v_O = v_I = 0$

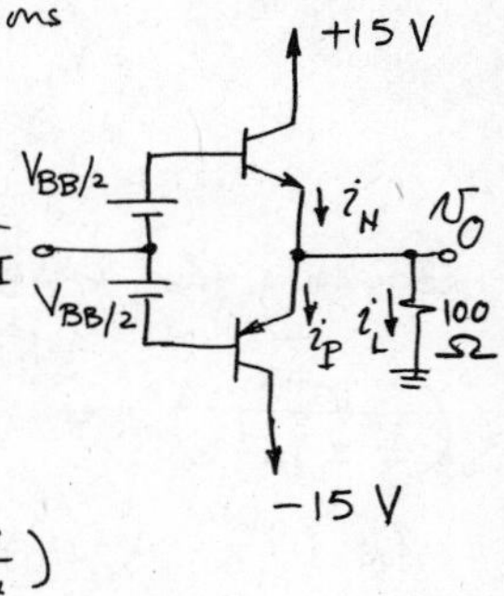

$I_Q = I_S e^{|v_{BE}|/V_T}$

$= I_S e^{V_{BB}/2V_T}$

$V_{BB} = 2 V_T \ln\left(\frac{I_Q}{I_S}\right)$

$= 2 \times 0.025 \ln\left(\frac{2 \times 10^{-3}}{10^{-13}}\right)$

$= 1.186$ V

We shall illustrate the construction of the table by calculating in detail one of its rows. For $v_O = +1\,V$:

10

$i_L = \frac{1}{0.1} = 10\ mA$

Substituting in Eq.(10.27) gives

$i_N^2 - 10\,i_N + 4 = 0$

$\Rightarrow i_N = \underline{10.39\ mA}$

$i_P = i_N - i_L = 10.39 - 10 = \underline{0.39\ mA}$

$v_{BEN} = V_T \ln\left(\frac{i_N}{I_S}\right)$

$= 0.025 \times \ln\left(\frac{10.39 \times 10^{-3}}{10^{-13}}\right)$

$= \underline{0.634\ V}$

$v_{EBP} = V_T \ln\left(\frac{i_P}{I_S}\right)$

$= 0.025 \ln\left(\frac{0.39 \times 10^{-3}}{10^{-13}}\right) = \underline{0.552\,V}$

Note that, $v_{BEN} + v_{BEP} = V_{BB}$ (as should be expected)

10

$v_I = v_O + v_{BEN} - V_{BB}/2$

$= 1 + 0.634 - \frac{1.186}{2}$

$= \underline{1.041\ V}$

$\frac{v_O}{v_I} = \frac{1}{1.041} = \underline{0.96}$

From Eq. (10.31),

$R_{out} = \frac{V_T}{i_P + i_N}$

$= \frac{25\ mV}{(0.39 + 10.39)\ mA} = \underline{2.32\,\Omega}$

$\frac{v_o}{v_i} = \frac{R_L}{R_L + R_{out}} = \frac{100}{100 + 2.32}$

$= \underline{0.98\ V/V}$

7 Refer to Fig.(10.14). For $v_O = +10\,V$, $i_L = \frac{10}{100} = 0.1\,A$. As a first approximation $i_N \cong 0.1\,A$ and $i_P = 0$. Thus $i_{BN} \simeq \frac{100}{51} \simeq 2\,mA$

10

Since $I_{bias} = 3\ mA$ it follows that the current through the diodes will decrease to $1\,mA$. Thus

$V_{BB} = 2\,V_T \ln\left(\frac{10^{-3}}{\frac{1}{3} \times 10^{-13}}\right)$ (1)

But, $V_{BB} = v_{BEN} + v_{EBP}$

$= V_T \ln\left(\frac{i_N}{I_S}\right) + V_T \ln\frac{(i_N - i_L)}{I_S}$

$= V_T \ln\left[\frac{i_N(i_N - 0.1)}{10^{-26}}\right]$ (2)

Equating the RHS of (1) and (2) gives

$\left(\frac{10^{-3}}{\frac{1}{3} \times 10^{-13}}\right)^2 = \frac{i_N(i_N - 0.1)}{10^{-26}}$

$i_N(i_N - 0.1) = 9 \times 10^{-6}$

If i_N is in mA then

$i_N(i_N - 100) = 9$

$i_N^2 - 100\,i_N - 9 = 0$

$\Rightarrow i_N = \underline{100.1\ mA}$ $\quad i_P = \underline{0.1\ mA}$

10

For $v_O = -10\,V$, $i_L = -100\ mA$

As a first approximation, $i_P \cong 100\,mA$ and $i_N \simeq 0$. Thus $i_{BN} \simeq 0$ and the current through the diodes will be equal to I_{bias},

$V_{BB} = 2V_T \ln\left(\frac{3 \times 10^{-3}}{\frac{1}{3} \times 10^{-13}}\right)$ (3)

But, $V_{BB} = V_T \ln\left(\frac{i_N}{10^{-13}}\right) + V_T \ln\left(\frac{i_P}{10^{-13}}\right)$

$= V_T \ln\left(\frac{i_P - 0.1}{10^{-13}}\right) + V_T \ln\left(\frac{i_P}{10^{-13}}\right)$

$= V_T \ln\left[\frac{i_P(i_P - 0.1)}{10^{-26}}\right]$ (4)

Equating the RHS of (3) and (4) gives

$\left(\frac{3 \times 10^{-3}}{\frac{1}{3} \times 10^{-13}}\right)^2 = \frac{i_P(i_P - 0.1)}{10^{-26}}$

$i_P(i_P - 0.1) = 81 \times 10^{-6}$

If i_P is in mA,

10

$$i_P(i_P - 100) = 81$$

$$i_P^2 - 100\, i_P - 81 = 0$$

$$\Rightarrow i_P = \underline{\underline{100.8 \text{ mA}}}$$

$$i_N = \underline{\underline{0.8 \text{ mA}}}$$

---

8 $\Delta I_C = g_m \times 2\text{ mV/°C} \times 5\text{°C}$, mA

where g_m is in mA/mV,

$$g_m = \frac{10 \text{ mA}}{25 \text{ mV}} = 0.4 \text{ mA/mV}$$

Thus, $\Delta I_C = 0.4 \times 2 \times 5 = \underline{\underline{4 \text{ mA}}}$

---

9 Refer to Fig. 10.15

(a) To obtain a terminal voltage of 1.2V, and since β_1 is very large, it follows that $V_{R_1} = V_{R_2} = 0.6$ V. Thus $I_{C1} = 1$ mA

$$I_R = \frac{1.2 \text{ V}}{R_1 + R_2} = \frac{1.2}{2.4} = 0.5 \text{ mA}$$

10

Thus,

$$I = I_{C1} + I_R = \underline{\underline{1.5 \text{ mA}}}$$

(b) For $\Delta V_{BB} = +50$ mV:

$V_{BB} = 1.25$ V $\quad I_R = \frac{1.25}{2.4} = 0.52$ mA

$$V_{BE} = \frac{1.25}{2} = 0.625 \text{ V}$$

$$I_{C1} = 1 \times e^{\Delta V_{BE}/V_T} = e^{0.025/0.025}$$

$$= 2.72 \text{ mA}$$

$$I = 2.72 + 0.52 = \underline{\underline{3.24 \text{ mA}}}$$

For $\Delta V_{BB} = +100$ mV:

$V_{BB} = 1.3$ V $\quad I_R = \frac{1.3}{2.4} = 0.54$ mA

$$V_{BE} = \frac{1.3}{2} = 0.65 \text{ V}$$

$$I_{C1} = 1 \times e^{\Delta V_{BE}/V_T} = 1 \times e^{0.05/0.025}$$

$$= 7.39 \text{ mA}$$

$$I = 7.39 + 0.54 = \underline{\underline{7.93 \text{ mA}}}$$

For $\Delta V_{BB} = +200$ mV:

$V_{BB} = 1.4$ V $\quad I_R = \frac{1.4}{2.4} = 0.58$ mA

10

$$V_{BE} = 0.7 \text{ V}$$

$$I_{C1} = 1 \times e^{0.1/0.025} = 54.60 \text{ mA}$$

$$I = 54.60 + 0.58 = \underline{\underline{55.18 \text{ mA}}}$$

For $\Delta V_{BB} = -50$ mV:

$V_{BB} = 1.15$ V $\quad I_R = \frac{1.15}{2.4} = 0.48$ mA

$$V_{BE} = \frac{1.15}{2} = 0.575 \text{ V}$$

$$I_{C1} = 1 \times e^{-0.025/0.025} = 0.37 \text{ mA}$$

$$I = 0.48 + 0.37 = \underline{\underline{0.85 \text{ mA}}}$$

For $\Delta V_{BB} = -100$ mV:

$V_{BB} = 1.1$ V $\quad I_R = \frac{1.1}{2.4} = 0.46$ mA

$$V_{BE} = 0.55 \text{ V}$$

$$I_{C1} = 1 \times e^{-0.05/0.025} = 0.13 \text{ mA}$$

$$I = 0.46 + 0.13 = \underline{\underline{0.59 \text{ mA}}}$$

For $\Delta V_{BB} = -200$ mV:

$V_{BB} = 1.0$ V $\quad I_R = \frac{1}{2.4} = 0.417$ mA

10

$$V_{BE} = 0.5 \text{ V}$$

$$I_{C1} = 1 \times e^{-0.1/0.025} = 0.018 \text{ mA}$$

$$I = \underline{\underline{0.43 \text{ mA}}}$$

10

$$T_J - T_A = \theta_{JA} P_D$$

$$200 - 25 = \theta_{JA} \times 50$$

$$\theta_{JA} = \frac{175}{50} = 3.5 \text{ °C/W}$$

But, $\theta_{JA} = \theta_{JC} + \theta_{CS} + \theta_{SA}$

$$3.5 = 1.4 + 0.6 + \theta_{SA}$$

$$\Rightarrow \theta_{SA} = \underline{1.5\text{°C/W}}$$

$$T_J - T_C = \theta_{JC} \times P_D$$

$$T_C = T_J - \theta_{JC} P_D$$

$$= 200 - 1.4 \times 50$$

$$= \underline{\underline{130\text{°C}}}$$

11

10

(a) From symmetry we see that all transistors will conduct equal currents and have equal V_{BE}'s. Thus $v_O = 0\ V$.

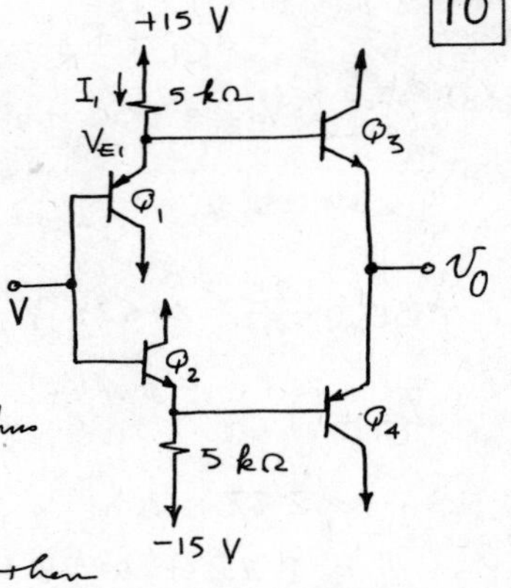

If $V_{BE} \simeq 0.7\ V$ then

$V_{E1} = 0.7\ V$ and $I_1 = \frac{15-0.7}{5} = 2.86\ mA$

If we neglect I_{B3} then

$I_{C1} \simeq 2.86\ mA$.

At this current, V_{BE} is given by

$$V_{BE} = 0.025\ ln\left(\frac{2.86\times10^{-3}}{3.3\times10^{-14}}\right) \simeq 0.63\ V$$

Thus $V_{E1} = 0.63V$ and $I_1 = 2.87\ mA$

No more iterations are required and

$$i_{C1} = i_{C2} = i_{C3} = i_{C4} \simeq 2.87\ mA$$

10

(b) For $v_I = +10\ V$:

To start the iterations let $V_{BE1} \simeq 0.7\ V$

Thus,

$V_{E1} = 10.7\ V$

and,

$I_1 = \frac{15-10.7}{5} = 0.86\ mA$

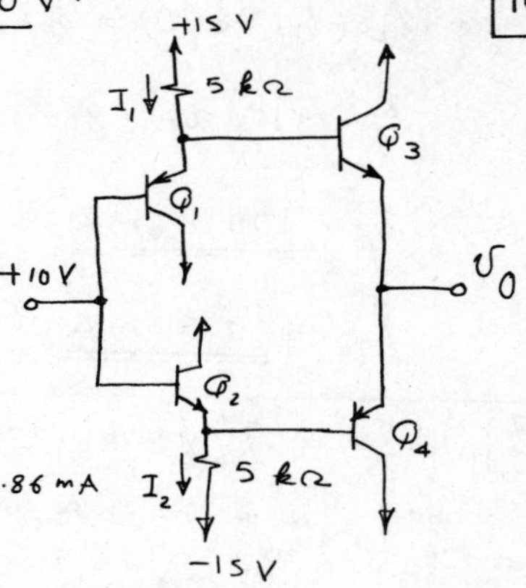

Neglecting I_{B3},

$I_{C1} \simeq I_{E1} \simeq I_1 = 0.86\ mA$

But at this current

$$V_{BE1} = V_T\ ln\left(\frac{I_{C1}}{I_S}\right)$$

$$= 0.025 \cdot ln\left(\frac{0.86\times10^{-3}}{3.3\times10^{-14}}\right)$$

$$= 0.6\ V$$

Thus, $V_{E1} = +10.6\ V$ and $I_1 = 0.88\ mA$

No further iterations are required and

$I_{C1} \simeq 0.88\ mA$.

To find I_{C2} we use an identical procedure:

10

$V_{BE2} \simeq 0.7\ V$

$V_{E2} = 10 - 0.7 = +9.3\ V$

$I_2 = \frac{9.3-(-15)}{5} = 4.86\ mA$

$V_{BE2} = 0.025\ ln\left(\frac{4.86\times10^{-3}}{3.3\times10^{-14}}\right)$

$= 0.643\ V$

$V_{E2} = 10 - .643 = +9.357$

$I_2 = 4.87\ mA$

$I_{C2} \simeq 4.87\ mA$

Finally,

$$I_{C3} = I_{C4} = 3.3\times10^{-14}\ e^{V_{BE}/V_T}$$

where

$$V_{BE} = \frac{V_{E1}-V_{E2}}{2} = 0.62\ V$$

Thus, $I_{C3} = I_{C4} = 1.95\ mA$

The symmetry of the circuit enables us to find the values for $v_I = -10\ V$ as follows:

10

$I_{C1} = 4.87\ mA$ $\quad I_{C2} = 0.88\ mA$

$I_{C3} = I_{C4} = 1.95\ mA$

For $v_I = +10\ V$, $v_O = V_{E1} - V_{BE3}$

$= 10.6 - 0.62 = +9.98\ V$

For $v_I = -10\ V$, $v_O = V_{E1} - V_{BE3}$

$= -9.357 - 0.62 = -9.98\ V$

(c) For $v_I = +10\ V$,

$v_O \simeq 10\ V$

$I_L \simeq 100\ mA$

$I_{C3} \simeq 100\ mA$

$I_{B3} = \frac{100}{201}$

$\simeq 0.5\ mA$

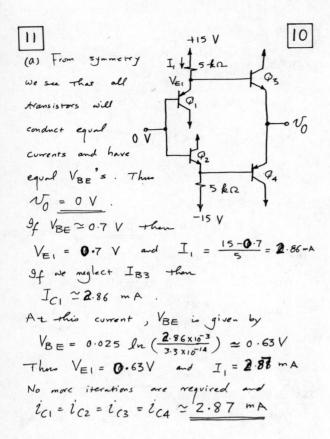

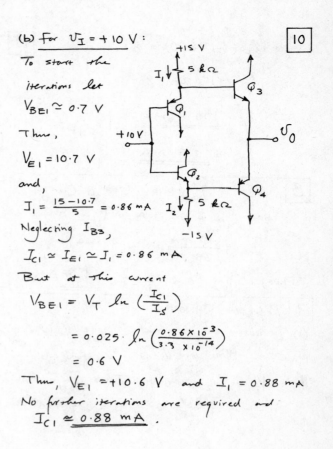

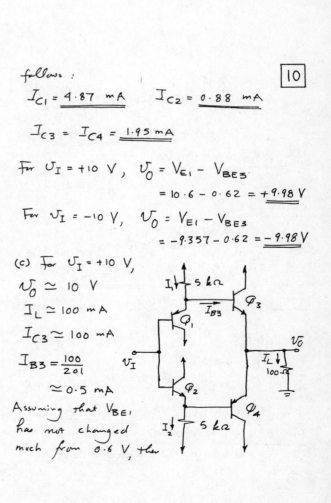

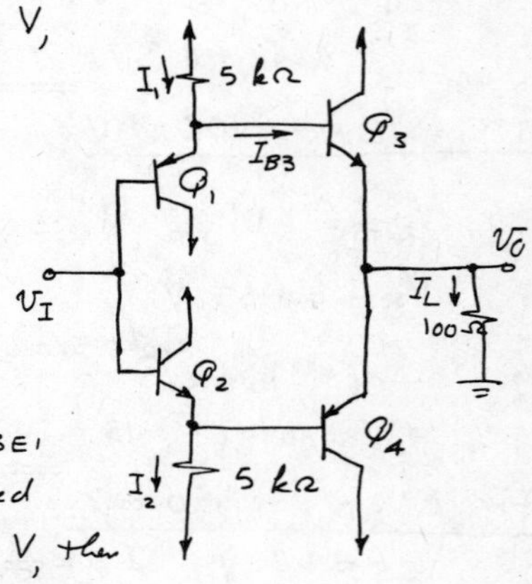

Assuming that V_{BE1} has not changed much from 0.6 V, then

$V_{E1} \simeq 10.6\ V$

$I_1 = \frac{15-10.6}{5} = 0.88\ mA$

$I_{E1} = I_1 - I_{B3} = 0.88 - 0.5 = 0.38\ mA$

$I_{C1} \simeq 0.38\ mA$

$V_{BE1} = 0.025\ \ln\left(\frac{0.38 \times 10^{-3}}{3.3 \times 10^{-14}}\right)$

$= 0.58\ V$

$V_{E1} = 10.58\ V$

$I_1 = \frac{15-10.58}{5} = 0.88\ mA$

Thus, $I_{C1} \simeq \underline{\underline{0.38\ mA}}$

Now for Q_2 we have:

$V_{BE2} \simeq 0.643V$

$V_{E2} = 10 - 0.643 = 9.357$

$I_2 = 4.87\ mA$

$I_{B4} \simeq 0$

$I_{C2} \simeq \underline{\underline{4.87\ mA}}$ (as in (b))

Assuming that $I_{C3} \simeq \underline{\underline{100\ mA}}$,

$V_{BE3} = 0.025\ \ln\left(\frac{100 \times 10^{-3}}{3.3 \times 10^{-14}}\right)$

$= 0.72\ V$

Thus, $v_O = V_{E1} - V_{BE3}$

$= 10.58 - 0.72 = \underline{\underline{+9.86\ V}}$

$V_{BE4} = v_O - V_{E2}$

$= 9.86 - 9.36 = 0.5\ V$

Thus, $I_{C4} = 3.3 \times 10^{-14}\ e^{0.5/0.025}$

$\simeq \underline{\underline{0.02\ mA}}$

From symmetry we find the values for the case $v_I = -10\ V$ as,

$I_{C1} = \underline{\underline{4.87\ mA}}$ $\quad I_{C2} = \underline{\underline{0.38\ mA}}$

$I_{C3} = \underline{\underline{0.02\ mA}}$ $\quad I_{C4} = \underline{\underline{100\ mA}}$

$v_O = \underline{\underline{-9.86\ V}}$.

---

12 (a)

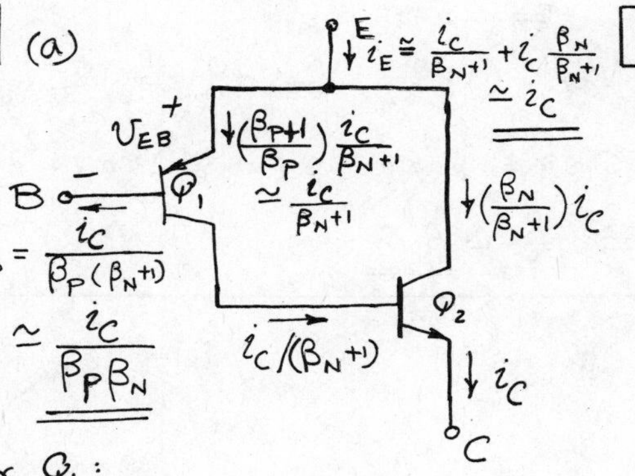

$i_B = \frac{i_C}{\beta_P(\beta_N+1)} \simeq \underline{\underline{\frac{i_C}{\beta_P\beta_N}}}$

For Q_1:

$i_{C1} = I_{SP}\ e^{v_{EB}/V_T}$

$\frac{i_C}{\beta_N+1} = I_{SP}\ e^{v_{EB}/V_T}$

Thus, $i_C \simeq \underline{\underline{\beta_N I_{SP}\ e^{v_{EB}/V_T}}}$

Thus,

Effective scale current $= \beta_N I_{SP}$

(b) Effective current gain $\equiv \frac{i_C}{i_B} = \beta_P \beta_N$

$= 20 \times 50 = \underline{\underline{1000}}$

$100 \times 10^{-3} = 50 \times 10^{-14}\ e^{v_{EB}/0.025}$

$v_{EB} = 0.025\ \ln(2 \times 10^{11})$

$= \underline{\underline{0.651\ V}}$

---

13 Refer to Fig. 10.28.

We require Q_5 to conduct a collecter current of 2 mA when its $V_{BE} = 150\ mA \times R_{E1}$

$V_{BE5} = V_T\ \ln\left(\frac{2 \times 10^{-3}}{10^{-14}}\right)$

$= 0.651\ V$

Thus, $R_{E1} = \frac{0.651}{0.150} = \underline{\underline{4.3\ \Omega}}$

For a peak output current of 100 mA, a $\underline{430\ mV}$ voltage drop develops across R_{E1}. Thus Q_5 will conduct a collector current of

$i_{C5} = 10^{-14}\ e^{0.43/0.025} = 2.95 \times 10^{-7} A$

$\cong \underline{\underline{0.3\ \mu A}}$

---

14 Total current out of node B $= \frac{2v_i}{R_3} + \frac{v_o}{R_2}$ **10**

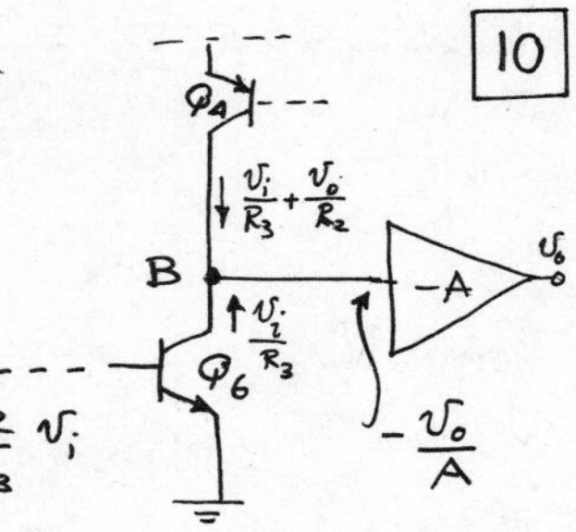

Thus

$$\left(\frac{2v_i}{R_3} + \frac{v_o}{R_2}\right)R = -\frac{v_o}{A}$$

$$\Rightarrow \quad v_o\left(\frac{1}{A} + \frac{R}{R_2}\right) = \frac{-2R}{R_3}\, v_i$$

$$\frac{v_o}{v_i} = \frac{-\frac{2R}{R_3}}{\frac{1}{A} + \frac{R}{R_2}}$$

$$= \frac{-2R_2/R_3}{1 + (R_2/AR)} \qquad \text{Q.E.D}$$

For $AR \gg R_2$

$$\frac{v_o}{v_i} \simeq -\frac{2R_2}{R_3}$$

15

$$P_{Dmax} = \frac{T_{Jmax} - T_A}{\theta_{JA}}$$

$$= \frac{150 - 50}{35} = \underline{2.9\,W}$$

---

16 From Fig. 10.32 we see that for $P_{dissipation}$ to be less than 2.9 W, a maximum supply voltage of 20 V is called for. The 20-V-supply curve intersects the 3% distortion line at a point for which the output power is 4.2 W. Since **10**

$$P_L = \frac{(\hat{V}_o/\sqrt{2})^2}{R_L}$$

thus

$$\hat{V}_o = \sqrt{4.2 \times 2 \times 8} = 8.2\,V$$

or 16.4 V peak-to-peak

---

17 Voltage gain $= 2K$

where $K = \frac{R_4}{R_3} = 1 + \frac{R_2}{R_1} = 1.5$

Thus, $A_v = \underline{3\ V/V}$

Input resistance $= R_3 = \underline{10\,k\Omega}$

Peak-to-peak $v_O = 3 \times 20 = \underline{60\,V}$

Peak load current $= \frac{30\,V}{8\,\Omega} = \underline{3.75\,A}$ **10**

$$P_L = \frac{(30/\sqrt{2})^2}{8} = \underline{56.25\,W}$$

---

18 We wish to make

$$\frac{\partial V_{GG}}{\partial T} = -3 - 3 = -6\ mV/^\circ C$$

but from Eq. (10.49)

$$\frac{\partial V_{GG}}{\partial T} = \left(1 + \frac{R_3}{R_4}\right)\frac{\partial V_{BE6}}{\partial T}$$

Thus

$$-6 = \left(1 + \frac{R_3}{R_4}\right) \times -2$$

$$\Longrightarrow \quad \frac{R_3}{R_4} = \underline{2}$$

---

19 $I_{DN} = I_{DP} = K(|V_{GS}| - V_t)^2$

$$0.1 = 1 \times (|V_{GS}| - 3)^2$$

$$\Longrightarrow \quad V_{GS} = \underline{3.32\,V}$$

$$V_{GG} = 2 \times 3.32 = \underline{6.64\,V}$$

$$R = \frac{V_{GG}}{20\,mA} = \frac{6.64}{20} = \underline{332\,\Omega}$$

From Eq. (10.48) **10**

$$V_{GG} = \left(1 + \frac{R_3}{R_4}\right)V_{BE6} + \left(1 + \frac{R_1}{R_2}\right)V_{BE5} - 4V_{BE}$$

$$6.64 = 3 \times 0.7 + \left(1 + \frac{R_1}{R_2}\right) \times 0.7 - 4 \times 0.7$$

$$\Rightarrow \quad \frac{R_1}{R_2} = \underline{9.5}\,.$$

Chapter 11 — Exercises

1 Using the voltage divider rule,

$$\frac{V_o(s)}{V_i(s)} = \frac{Z_2}{Z_1 + Z_2}$$

$$= \frac{Y_1}{Y_1 + Y_2}$$

$$= \frac{1/R_1}{\left(\frac{1}{R_1}\right) + \left(\frac{1}{R_2} + sC\right)}$$

$$= \frac{1/CR_1}{s + \frac{1}{C}\left(\frac{1}{R_1} + \frac{1}{R_2}\right)}$$

$$= \frac{1/CR_1}{s + \frac{1}{C(R_1 /\!/ R_2)}}$$

2

$$T(s) = \frac{a_1 s + a_0}{s + \omega_P}$$

$$= \frac{a_1 s + a_0}{s + 2\pi \times 10^4}$$

DC gain $= \frac{a_0}{2\pi \times 10^4} = 10 \implies a_0 = 2\pi \times 10^5$

Infinite-frequency gain $= a_1 = 1 \implies a_1 = 1$

Thus

$$T(s) = \frac{s + 2\pi \times 10^5}{s + 2\pi \times 10^4}$$

3 Gain-bandwidth product $= 1000 \times 100 \times 10^3$

$$= 10^8 \text{ Hz}$$

4

$$F_H(s) = \frac{1}{\left(1 + \frac{s}{\omega_{P1}}\right)\left(1 + \frac{s}{\omega_{P2}}\right)}$$

$$= \frac{1}{\left(1 + \frac{s}{\omega_{P1}}\right)\left(1 + \frac{s}{k\omega_{P1}}\right)}$$

$$|F_H(j\omega)| = \frac{1}{\sqrt{\left[1 + \left(\frac{\omega}{\omega_{P1}}\right)^2\right]\left[1 + \left(\frac{\omega}{k\omega_{P1}}\right)^2\right]}}$$

$$\frac{1}{\sqrt{2}} = \frac{1}{\sqrt{\left[1 + \left(\frac{\omega_{3dB}}{\omega_{P1}}\right)^2\right]\left[1 + \left(\frac{\omega_{3dB}}{k\omega_{P1}}\right)^2\right]}}$$

Denote $\frac{\omega_{3dB}}{\omega_{P1}} = \alpha$

$$2 = (1 + \alpha^2)\left(1 + \frac{\alpha^2}{k^2}\right)$$

$$= 1 + \alpha^2\left(1 + \frac{1}{k^2}\right) + \frac{\alpha^4}{k^2} \quad (1)$$

$$k = \sqrt{\frac{\alpha^2 + \alpha^4}{1 - \alpha^2}}$$

For $\alpha = 0.9$ $\quad k = 2.78$

For $\alpha = 0.99$ $\quad k = 9.88$

5 For the exact values refer to the solution of Exercise 11.4 above. From Eq.(1) there we have

$$\frac{\alpha^4}{k^2} + \alpha^2\left(1 + \frac{1}{k^2}\right) - 1 = 0 \quad (2)$$

where $\alpha \equiv \frac{\omega_{3dB}}{\omega_{P1}}$

For $k = 1$

$$\alpha^4 + 2\alpha^2 - 1 = 0$$

$$\alpha^2 = \frac{-2 + \sqrt{4 + 4}}{2} = 0.414$$

$$\omega_{3dB} = 0.64\ \omega_{P1}$$

For $k = 2$

$$\frac{1}{4}\alpha^4 + 1.25\alpha^2 - 1 = 0$$

$$\alpha^2 = \frac{-1.25 + \sqrt{1.25^2 + 1}}{0.5} = 0.70156$$

$$\omega_{3\text{-dB}} = 0.84\ \omega_{P1}$$

For $k = 4$

$$\frac{1}{16}\alpha^4 + \frac{17}{16}\alpha^2 - 1 = 0$$

$$\alpha^4 + 17\alpha^2 - 16 = 0$$

$$\alpha^2 = \frac{-17 + \sqrt{289 + 64}}{2} = 0.894$$

$$\omega_{3\text{-dB}} = 0.95\ \omega_{P1}$$

For the approximate values we use Eq.(11.22),

$$\omega_{3\text{-dB}} = \frac{1}{\sqrt{\frac{1}{\omega_{P1}^2} + \frac{1}{\omega_{P2}^2}}}$$

$$= \frac{1}{\sqrt{\frac{1}{\omega_{P1}^2} + \frac{1}{k^2\omega_{P1}^2}}}$$

$$= \frac{\omega_{P1}}{\sqrt{1 + \frac{1}{k^2}}}$$

$k = 1$ $\quad \omega_{3\text{-dB}} = 0.71\ \omega_{P1}$

$k = 2$ $\quad \omega_{3\text{-dB}} = 0.89\ \omega_{P1}$

$k = 4$ $\quad \omega_{3\text{-dB}} = 0.97\ \omega_{P1}$

6 Gain-bandwidth product $= 10.8 \times 0.1283 = \underline{\underline{1.39\ MHz}}$ **11**

Refer to Example 11.5. We want

$$\omega_H = 2\pi f_H = 2\pi \times 180\ kHz$$

but

$$\omega_H \simeq \frac{1}{\tau_{gs} + \tau_{gd}}$$

Thus $\tau_{gs} + \tau_{gd} = \frac{1}{2\pi \times 180 \times 10^3} = 884.2\ ns$

Now τ_{gs} is independent of R_L,

$$\tau_{gs} = 80.8\ ns$$

Thus, $\tau_{gd} = 884.2 - 80.8 = 803.4\ ns$

$$= C_{gd} R_{gd}$$

$$\Rightarrow R_{gd} = \frac{803.4 \times 10^{-9}}{1 \times 10^{-12}} = 803.4\ k\Omega$$

$$= R' + R_L'(1 + g_m R')$$

where $R' = 80.8\ k\Omega$ and $g_m = 4\ mA/V$.

Thus $R_L' = \frac{803.4 - 80.8}{1 + 4 \times 80.8} = \underline{2.23\ k\Omega}$

New midband gain $= -\frac{420}{420+100} \times 4 \times 2.23 = \underline{-7.2\ V/V}$

New gain-bandwidth product $= 7.2 \times 0.18 = \underline{\underline{1.3\ MHz}}$

---

7 The frequency of the zero is given by Eq. (11.37), **11**

$$\omega_Z = \frac{1}{C_S R_S}$$

$$10 = \frac{1}{C_S \times 10^3}$$

$$C_S = \frac{1}{10^4} = \underline{100\ \mu F}$$

The frequency of the pole is given by Eq. (11.38),

$$\omega_P = \frac{g_m + \frac{1}{R_S}}{C_S}$$

$$100 = \frac{g_m + 10^{-3}}{10^{-4}}$$

$$g_m = \underline{9\ mA/V}$$

---

8 The effective value of $R_S = \infty$.

Thus $\omega_Z = \frac{1}{R_S C_S} = \underline{\underline{0}}$

$$\omega_P = \frac{1}{C_S (R_S // \frac{1}{g_m})} = \underline{\underline{\frac{g_m}{C_S}}}$$

---

9 We substitute in Eq. (11.51) the following values **11**

$g_m = 4\ mA/V$ $C_{gd} = 1\ pF$ $C_{gs} = 1\ pF$

$R_L' = 3.33\ k\Omega$ $R' = 80.8\ k\Omega$

$$\frac{V_o}{V_i} = -A_M \frac{1 - \frac{s}{4 \times 10^9}}{1 + s\ 1.24 \times 10^{-6} + s^2\ 2.69 \times 10^{-16}}$$

Thus $\omega_Z = 4 \times 10^9\ rad/s$

$$f_Z = \frac{4 \times 10^9}{2\pi} = \underline{\underline{637\ MHz}}$$

The poles are determined from

$$2.69 \times 10^{-16} s^2 + 1.24 \times 10^{-6} s + 1 = 0$$

which has the solutions

$$\omega_{P1} = 808.6\ k\ rad/s$$

& $\omega_{P2} = 4608.9\ M\ rad/s$

Thus, $f_{P1} = \underline{\underline{128.4\ kHz}}$

$$f_{P2} = \underline{\underline{734.5\ MHz}}$$

Capacitor C_{C2} sees a resistance R_{C2}, **11**

$$R_{C2} = R_C + R_L = 8\ k\Omega$$

To find f_L we use Eq. (11.32),

$$f_L \simeq \frac{1}{2\pi} \sum_i \frac{1}{C_i R_{is}}$$

$$= \frac{1}{2\pi} \left[\frac{1}{C_{C1} R_{C1}} + \frac{1}{C_E R_E'} + \frac{1}{C_{C2} R_{C2}} \right]$$

$$= \frac{1}{2\pi} \left[\frac{1}{1 \times 10^{-6} \times 42 \times 10^3} + \frac{1}{47 \times 10^{-6} \times 25.4} + \frac{1}{10^{-6} \times 8 \times 10^3} \right]$$

$$= \underline{\underline{157\ Hz}}$$

The frequency of the zero caused by C_E is given by

$$f_Z = \frac{1}{2\pi C_E R_{E2}}$$

$$= \frac{1}{2\pi \times 47 \times 10^{-6} \times 3.6 \times 10^3} = \underline{\underline{0.94\ Hz}}$$

---

10 Refer to Fig. E11.10. Using the voltage divider rule,

$$v_\pi = v_{ce}\,\frac{r_\pi}{r_\pi + r_\mu}$$

Writing a node equation at the collector yields

$$i_c = \frac{v_{ce}}{r_o} + g_m v_\pi + \frac{v_{ce}}{r_\mu + r_\pi}$$

$$= \frac{v_{ce}}{r_o} + \frac{g_m r_\pi}{r_\mu + r_\pi} v_{ce} + \frac{v_{ce}}{r_\mu + r_\pi}$$

Thus, $\dfrac{i_c}{v_{ce}} = \dfrac{1}{r_o} + \dfrac{g_m r_\pi + 1}{r_\mu + r_\pi}$

Substituting $g_m r_\pi = \beta_0$ and assuming $\beta_0 \gg 1$ and $r_\mu \gg r_\pi$ results in

$$\frac{i_c}{v_{ce}} \simeq \frac{1}{r_o} + \frac{\beta_0}{r_\mu}$$

---

11 $g_m = I_C/V_T = \dfrac{1\text{ mA}}{0.025\text{ V}} = 40\text{ mA/V}$

$\beta_0 = h_{fe} = 100$

$r_\pi = \beta_0/g_m = \dfrac{100}{40} = 2.5\text{ k}\Omega$

$r_x = h_{ie} - r_\pi$

$= 2.6 - 2.5 = 0.1\text{ k}\Omega = 100\ \Omega$

$r_\mu = \dfrac{r_\pi}{h_{re}}$

$= \dfrac{2.5}{0.5\times10^{-4}} = 5\times10^4\text{ k}\Omega = 50\text{ M}\Omega$

$r_o = \left(h_{oe} - \dfrac{h_{fe}}{r_\mu}\right)^{-1}$

$= \left(1.2\times10^{-5} - \dfrac{100}{50\times10^6}\right)^{-1} = (1\times10^{-5})^{-1}$

$= 10^5\ \Omega = 100\text{ k}\Omega$

$r_o = \dfrac{V_A}{I_C}$

$\Rightarrow V_A = r_o I_C = 100\times1 = 100\text{ V}$

---

12 $|h_{fe}| = 10$ at $f = 50$ MHz. Thus $|h_{fe}| = 1$ at $f = 500$ MHz which means that

$$f_T = 500\text{ MHz}$$

$$\omega_T = \frac{g_m}{C_\pi + C_\mu}$$

$\Rightarrow C_\pi + C_\mu = \dfrac{g_m}{\omega_T}$

$= \dfrac{40\times10^{-3}}{2\pi\times500\times10^6}$

$= 12.7\text{ pF}$

$C_\pi = 12.7 - 2 = 10.7\text{ pF}$

---

13 At $I_C = 1$ mA the diffusion part of C_π is $10.7 - 2 = 8.7$ pF. Thus at $I_C = 0.1$ mA the diffusion part becomes 0.87 pF with the result that C_π becomes 2.87 pF. Thus

$$\omega_T = \frac{g_m}{C_\pi + C_\mu}$$

$= \dfrac{4\times10^{-3}}{(2.87+2)\times10^{-12}}$

$f_T = \dfrac{\omega_T}{2\pi} = 130.7\text{ MHz}$

---

14 $R_{in} = R_1 /\!/ R_2 /\!/ (r_x + r_\pi)$

$= 8 /\!/ 4 /\!/ \left(0.05 + \dfrac{100}{40}\right)$

$= 1.3\text{ k}\Omega$

$A_M = \dfrac{R_{in}}{R_s + R_{in}} \times \dfrac{r_\pi}{r_\pi + r_x} \times -g_m (R_C /\!/ R_L /\!/ r_o)$

$= \dfrac{1.3}{4 + 1.3} \times \dfrac{2.5}{2.5 + 0.05} \times -40 \times (6 /\!/ 4 /\!/ 100)$

$= -22.5\text{ V/V}$

---

15 $R_{C1} = R_s + [R_B /\!/ (r_x + r_\pi)]$

$= 4 + [8 /\!/ 4 /\!/ 2.55]$

$= 4 + 1.3 = 5.3\text{ k}\Omega$

$R_E' = R_E /\!/ \left[\dfrac{1}{g_m} + \dfrac{r_x + (R_B /\!/ R_s)}{\beta + 1}\right]$

$= 3.3 /\!/ \left[0.025 + \dfrac{0.05 + (8/\!/4/\!/4)}{101}\right]$

$= 40.5\ \Omega$

$R_{C2} = R_L + (R_C /\!/ r_o)$

$= 4 + (6/100) = 9.66\text{ k}\Omega$

$$\omega_L \simeq \frac{1}{C_{C1}R_{C1}} + \frac{1}{C_E R_E'} + \frac{1}{C_{C2}R_{C2}}$$

$$= \frac{1}{1\times10^{-6}\times5.3\times10^{3}} + \frac{1}{10\times10^{-6}\times40.5} + \frac{1}{1\times10^{-6}\times9.66\times10^{3}}$$

$$= 188.7 + 2469.1 + 103.5$$

$$= 2761.3$$

$$f_L = \frac{\omega_L}{2\pi} = \underline{\underline{439.5\ \text{Hz}}}$$

$$f_Z = \frac{1}{2\pi C_E R_E} = \frac{1}{2\pi\times10\times10^{-6}\times3.3\times10^{3}}$$

$$= \underline{\underline{4.8\ \text{Hz}}}$$

16 Using the design procedure described on page 635:

$$\frac{1}{C_E R_E'} = 0.8\,\omega_L = 0.8\times100\times2\pi$$

$$\Rightarrow C_E = \frac{1}{160\pi\times40.5} = \underline{\underline{49.1\ \mu F}}$$

$$\frac{1}{C_{C1}R_{C1}} = 0.1\,\omega_L = 0.1\times2\pi\times100$$

$$C_{C1} = \frac{1}{20\pi\times5.3\times10^{3}} = \underline{\underline{3\ \mu F}}$$

$$\frac{1}{C_{C2}R_{C2}} = 0.1\,\omega_L = 0.1\times2\pi\times100$$

$$C_{C2} = \frac{1}{20\pi\times9.66\times10^{3}} = \underline{\underline{1.65\ \mu F}}$$

17

$$C_{in} = C_\pi + C_\mu\left[1 + g_m(R_C // R_L // r_o)\right]$$

$$= 13.9 + 2\left[1 + 40\times(6//4//100)\right]$$

$$= 13.9 + 2\times94.75$$

$$= \underline{203.4\ \text{pF}}$$

The resistance seen by this capacitor is

$$R' = r_\pi // \left(r_x + (R_B // R_s)\right)$$

$$= 2.5 // \left(0.05 + (4//8//4)\right)$$

$$= 0.99\ \text{k}\Omega$$

Thus,
$$f_H = \frac{1}{2\pi\times203.4\times10^{-12}\times0.99\times10^{3}} = \underline{\underline{787\ \text{kHz}}}$$

18 Using Eq. (11.53) we obtain

$$\omega_{P1} = \frac{1}{\left[C_\pi + C_\mu(1+g_m R_L') + C_\mu\left(\frac{R_L'}{R'}\right)\right]R'}$$

where $C_\pi = 13.9$ pF, $C_\mu = 2$ pF, $g_m = 40$ mA/V,

$$R_L' = R_C // R_L // r_o = 6//4//100 = 2.34\ \text{k}\Omega$$

$$R' = r_\pi // \left[r_x + (R_1 // R_2 // R_s)\right]$$

$$= 2.5 // \left[0.05 + (8//4//4)\right]$$

$$= 2.5 // 1.65 = 0.99\ \text{k}\Omega$$

$$\omega_{P1} = \frac{1}{\left[13.9 + 2(1+40\times2.34) + 2\times\frac{2.34}{0.99}\right]\times0.99\times10^{-9}}$$

$$= 4.86\times10^{6}\ \text{rad/s}$$

Thus,
$$f_H \simeq f_{P1} = \frac{\omega_{P1}}{2\pi} = \underline{\underline{773.5\ \text{kHz}}}$$

To obtain the frequency of the second pole we employ Eq. (11.54) to write

$$\omega_{P2} = \frac{C_\pi + C_\mu(1+g_m R_L') + C_\mu(R_L'/R')}{C_\pi C_\mu R_L'}$$

$$= \frac{\left[13.9 + 2(1+40\times2.34) + 2\times\frac{2.34}{0.99}\right]\times10^{-12}}{13.9\times2\times2.34\times10^{-21}}$$

$$\omega_{P2} = 3.195\times10^{9}\ \text{rad/s}$$

$$f_{P2} = \underline{\underline{508.5\ \text{MHz}}}$$

19

$$t_r \simeq 2.2\,\tau_H$$

$$= \frac{2.2}{\omega_H} = \frac{2.2}{2\pi f_H}$$

$$= \frac{1.1}{\pi\times770\times10^{3}} = \underline{\underline{0.45\ \mu s}}$$

$$\text{height} = 10\ \text{mV}\times22.5 = \underline{\underline{225\ \text{mV}}}$$

$$\text{Sag},\ \Delta V \simeq 225\times\frac{T}{\tau_L} \quad (T \text{ is pulse width})$$

$$= 225\times\omega_L T$$

$$= 225\times2\pi\times439.5\times10\times10^{-6}$$

$$= \underline{\underline{6.2\ \text{mV}}}$$

20 Refer to Fig. 11.27 and neglect base currents. Thus,

$$V_{B1} = V_{CC}\frac{R_3}{R_1+R_2+R_3} = 15\times\frac{8}{18+4+8} = 4\ \text{V}$$

$$I_{E1} = \frac{V_{B1}-V_{BE1}}{R_E} = \frac{4-0.7}{3.3} = \underline{\underline{1\ \text{mA}}}$$

$$I_{E2} = \alpha I_{E1} \simeq \underline{1\ mA}$$

$$V_{B2} = 15 \times \frac{4+8}{8+4+8} = 6\ V$$

$$V_{C1} = 6 - V_{BE2} = 5.3\ V$$

$$V_{C2} \cong 15 - 1 \times 6 = 9\ V$$

Thus both transistors are operating in the active region at $I_E \simeq 1\,mA$.

Using Eq. (11.91),

$$A_M = -40\,(4/\!/6)\,\frac{4/\!/8}{(4/\!/8)+4}\;\frac{2.5}{2.5+0.05+(4/\!/8/\!/4)}$$

$$= \underline{\underline{-23.1\ V/V}}$$

From Eq. (11.88)

$$f_1 = \frac{\omega_1}{2\pi} = \frac{1}{2\pi R_s'\,(C_{\pi 1} + 2C_{\mu 1})}$$

$$= \frac{1}{2\pi\{r_{\pi 1} /\!/ [r_{x1} + (R_3 /\!/ R_2 /\!/ R_s)]\}(C_{\pi 1}+2C_{\mu 1})}$$

$$= \frac{10^9}{2\pi\{2.5 /\!/ [0.05 + (8/\!/4/\!/4)]\}(13.9+4)}$$

$$= \underline{\underline{8.95\ MHz}}$$

f_2 can be obtained from Eq. (11.87),

$$f_2 = \frac{\omega_2}{2\pi} = \frac{1}{2\pi C_{\pi 2}\, r_{e2}}$$

$$= \frac{1}{2\pi \times 13.9 \times 25 \times 10^{-12}}$$

$$= \underline{\underline{458\ MHz}}$$

To obtain f_3 we use Eq. (11.89),

$$f_3 = \frac{1}{2\pi\, C_{\mu 2}\, R_L'}$$

$$= \frac{1}{2\pi\, C_{\mu 2}\,(R_L /\!/ R_C)}$$

$$= \frac{1}{2\pi \times 2 \times 10^{-12} \times (4/\!/6) \times 10^3}$$

$$= \underline{\underline{33\ MHz}}$$

Now using Eq. (11.22) to combine f_1, f_2 & f_3 above, we calculate f_H as

$$f_H = \frac{1}{\sqrt{\frac{1}{f_1^2} + \frac{1}{f_2^2} + \frac{1}{f_3^2}}} = \underline{\underline{8.64\ MHz}}$$

21

$$A_M = \frac{r_\pi + (\beta+1)R_E}{R_s + r_x + r_\pi + (\beta+1)R_E}\;\frac{R_E}{R_E + r_e}$$

where $r_\pi = \frac{100}{40} = 2.5\ k\Omega$, $\beta = 100$, $R_E = 1\ k\Omega$, $R_s = 1\ k\Omega$, $r_x = 0.1\ k\Omega$ and $r_e = 25\ \Omega$.

Thus

$$A_M = \frac{2.5 + 101 \times 1}{1 + 0.1 + 2.5 + 101 \times 1}\;\frac{1}{1 + 0.025}$$

$$= \underline{0.97\ V/V}$$

$$\omega_T = \frac{g_m}{C_\pi + C_\mu}$$

$$\Rightarrow C_\pi + C_\mu = \frac{g_m}{\omega_T} = \frac{40 \times 10^{-3}}{2\pi \times 400 \times 10^6}$$

$$= 15.9\ pF$$

$$C_\pi = 13.9\ pF$$

Using Eq. (11.96)

$$\omega_P = \left[\left(2 + \frac{13.9}{1+40\times 1}\right)[(1+0.1) /\!/ (1+40\times 1)\times 2.5] \times 10^{-9}\right]^{-1}$$

$$f_P = \frac{\omega_P}{2\pi} = \underline{\underline{62.5\ MHz}}$$

---

22 Refer to Fig. 11.29. The resistance seen by $\left(\frac{C_\pi}{1+g_m R_E}\right)$ (with C_μ set to zero) is

$$r_\pi\,(1 + g_m R_E) \;/\!/\; R_s' + R_E$$

$$= (2.5 \times (1 + 40 \times 1)) /\!/ (1 + 0.1 + 1)$$

$$= 2.06\ k\Omega$$

Thus the time constant is

$$\tau_1 = \frac{13.9}{1 + 40 \times 1} \times 10^{-12} \times 2.06 \times 10^3$$

$$= 0.7\ ns.$$

The resistance seen by C_μ (with $\frac{C_\pi}{1+g_m R_E}$ set to zero) is

$$R_s' \;/\!/\; [r_\pi\,(1 + g_m R_E) + R_E]$$

$$= (1 + 0.1) /\!/ [2.5 \times (1 + 40) + 1]$$

$$= 1.09\ k\Omega$$

The corresponding time constant is

$$\tau_2 = 2 \times 10^{-12} \times 1.09 \times 10^3 = 2.18\ ns$$

Eq. (11.27) can now be used to find an estimate of f_H as

11

$$f_H = \frac{\omega_H}{2\pi} \simeq \frac{1}{2\pi(\tau_1+\tau_2)}$$

$$= \frac{1}{2\pi(0.7+2.18)\times 10^{-9}} = \underline{\underline{55.3\ MHz}}$$

23 Refer to Fig. 11.32. Capacitor C_{C1} sees a resistance R_{C1} given by (recall that C_E and C_{C2} are set to ∞):

$$R_{C1} = R_s + R_{in}$$

$$= 4 + 38 = 42\ k\Omega$$

(Note that the value of R_{in} was calculated in Example 11.9).

Capacitor C_E sees a resistance R_E':

$$R_E' = R_{E2} \,//\, \left\{ r_{e2} + \frac{\left[R_{E1} \,//\, \left(r_{e1} + \frac{R_1//R_2//R_s}{\beta_0+1}\right)\right]}{\beta_0+1} \right\}$$

$$= 3.6 \,//\, \left\{ 0.025 + \frac{\left[4.3 \,//\, \left(0.025 + \frac{100//100//4}{101}\right)\right]}{101} \right\}$$

$$= 25.4\ \Omega$$

24 Refer to Fig. E11.24(b). Note that R_{in} is the input resistance looking into the base of Q_1.

11

$$R_{in} = (\beta_1+1)\left[r_{e1} + (\beta_2+1)(r_{e2}+R_E)\right]$$

$I_{E2} = 5\ mA \qquad r_{e2} = 5\ \Omega$

$I_{E1} = \frac{5}{\beta_1+1} \simeq 0.05\ mA \qquad r_{e1} = 500\ \Omega$

$$R_{in} = 101 \times [500 + 101 \times (5 + 1000)]$$

$$= \underline{\underline{10.3\ M\Omega}}$$

$$\frac{v_{b1}}{v_s} = \frac{R_{in}}{R_{in}+R_s} = \frac{10.3}{10.3+0.1} = 0.990$$

$$\frac{v_o}{v_{b1}} = \frac{R_E}{R_E + r_{e2} + \frac{r_{e1}}{\beta_2+1}} = \frac{1000}{1000+5+\frac{500}{101}}$$

$$= 0.990$$

$$\frac{v_o}{v_s} = 0.99 \times 0.99 = \underline{\underline{0.98\ V/V}}$$

$$R_{out} = R_E \,//\, \left[r_{e2} + \frac{r_{e1} + \frac{R_s}{\beta_1+1}}{\beta_2+1}\right]$$

$$\simeq \underline{\underline{20\ \Omega}}$$

25 From Eq. (11.105),

11

$$A_0 = -g_m R_C \frac{2r_\pi}{2r_\pi + R_s + r_x}$$

$$= -20 \times 10 \times \frac{2\times 5}{2\times 5 + 10 + 0.1}$$

$$\simeq \underline{\underline{-100\ V/V}} \quad \text{or} \quad \underline{\underline{40\ dB}}$$

From Eq. (11.104)

$$f_H \simeq \frac{\omega_P}{2\pi} = \frac{1}{2\pi} \frac{1}{\left[2r_\pi//(R_s+2r_x)\right]\left[\frac{C_\pi}{2} + \frac{C_\mu}{2} g_m R_C\right]}$$

$$= \frac{1}{2\pi} \frac{1}{(10//10.1)\left[3 + 1\times 20\times 10\right]\times 10^{-9}}$$

$$= \underline{\underline{156\ kHz}}$$

Gain-bandwidth product $= 100 \times 156 = \underline{\underline{15.6\ MHz}}$

From Eq. (11.107)

11

$$R_\pi = r_\pi \,//\, \frac{R_s' + R_E}{1 + g_m R_E}$$

$$= 5 \,//\, \frac{5.05 + 0.15}{1 + 20 \times 0.15}$$

$$= 1.03\ k\Omega$$

Eq. (11.108):

$$R_\mu = R_C + \frac{1 + \frac{R_E}{r_e} + g_m R_C}{\frac{1}{r_\pi} + \left(\frac{1}{R_s'}\right)\left(1 + \frac{R_E}{r_e}\right)}$$

$$= 10 + \frac{1 + \frac{0.15}{0.05} + 20\times 10}{\frac{1}{5} + \frac{1}{5.05}\times\left(1 + \frac{0.15}{0.05}\right)}$$

$$= 215.6\ k\Omega$$

Eq. (11.109):

$$\tau = C_\pi R_\pi + C_\mu R_\mu$$

$$= 6 \times 1.03 + 2 \times 215.6 = 437.4\ ns$$

$$f_H = \frac{\omega_H}{2\pi} \simeq \frac{1}{2\pi\tau}$$

$$= \frac{1}{2\pi \times 437.4 \times 10^{-9}} = \underline{\underline{364\ kHz}}$$

Gain-bandwidth product $= 40 \times 364 = \underline{\underline{14.56\ MHz}}$

26 Using Eq. (11.106),

$$A_0 = \frac{-(\beta+1)(r_e+R_E)}{R_s/2 + r_x + (\beta+1)(r_e+R_E)} \cdot \frac{\alpha R_C}{R_E + r_e}$$

$$= \frac{-101\,(0.05+0.15)}{5 + 0.05 + 101\times(0.05+0.15)} \times \frac{0.99\times 10}{0.15+0.05}$$

$$= \underline{\underline{-40\ V/V}} \quad \text{or} \quad \underline{\underline{32\ dB}}$$

27 The CMRR decreases by 3 dB at the frequency of the zero caused by the biasing current source,

$$f_Z = \frac{1}{2\pi \times 2\times 10^{-12} \times 30\times 10^{6}}$$

$$= \underline{\underline{2.65\ \text{kHz}}}$$

Chapter 12—Exercises

1 (a) $\beta = \dfrac{R_1}{R_1+R_2}$

(b) $A_f = \dfrac{A}{1+A\beta}$

$$10 = \frac{10^4}{1+10^4\beta} \Rightarrow \beta = 0.0999$$

$$\frac{R_1}{R_1+R_2} = 0.0999 \Rightarrow \frac{R_2}{R_1} = \underline{\underline{9.01}}$$

(c) Amount of feedback $= 20\log(1+A\beta) = \underline{60\text{dB}}$

(d) $V_s = 1\text{V}$ $\quad V_o = A_f \times V_s = \underline{10\text{ V}}$

$$V_f = \beta V_o = 0.0999\times 10 = \underline{0.999\text{ V}}$$

$$V_i = V_s - V_f = 1.0 - 0.999 = \underline{0.001\text{ V}}$$

(e) $A = 0.8\times 10^4$ $\quad A_f = \dfrac{0.8\times 10^4}{1+0.8\times 10^4 \times 0.0999} = 9.9975$

Thus A_f decreases by about $\underline{\underline{0.02\%}}$

---

2 $A_{f0} = \dfrac{A_0}{1+A_0\beta} = \dfrac{10^4}{1+10^4\times\frac{R_1}{R_1+R_2}} = \dfrac{10^4}{1+10^4\times 0.1} = \underline{\underline{9.99\text{ V/V}}}$

$$f_{Hf} = f_H(1+A_0\beta) = 100(1+10^4\times 0.1) = \underline{\underline{100.1\text{ kHz}}}$$

---

3 Signal voltage at output

$$= V_s \times \frac{A_1A_2}{1+A_1A_2\beta}$$

$$= 1 \times \frac{1\times 100}{1+1\times100\times1} \simeq \underline{\underline{1\text{V}}}$$

Note that the value of A_1 was missing from the first printing; it is 1V/V.

Noise voltage at output

$$= V_n \times \frac{A_1}{1+A_1A_2\beta}$$

$$= 1 \times \frac{1}{1+1\times100\times1} \cong \underline{\underline{0.01\text{ V}}}$$

Thus the signal-to-noise ratio (S/N) becomes 100 or 40 dB, which is an improvement of 40 dB.

---

4 From Example 12.1,

$$1+A\beta = 7$$

Thus

$$f_{Hf} = 7\times 1 = 7\text{ kHz}$$

---

5 dc analysis:

$$I_{E1} = I_{E2} = 0.5\text{mA}$$

$$V_{C2} \simeq 10.7 - 0.5\times 20 = +0.7\text{V}$$

$$V_O = 0.7 - V_{BE3} = 0\text{ V}$$

$$I_{E3} = 5\text{ mA}$$

$$r_{e1} = r_{e2} = 50\,\Omega \qquad r_{e3} = 5\,\Omega$$

The A circuit is:

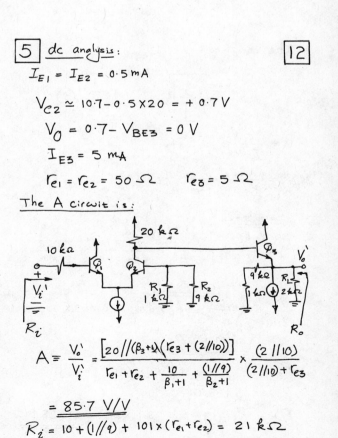

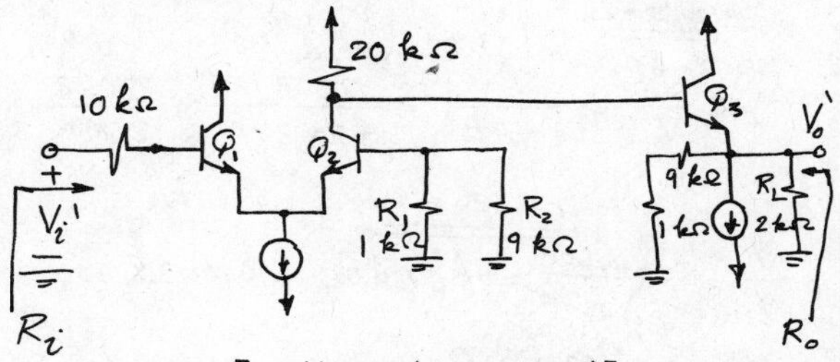

$$A \equiv \frac{V_o'}{V_i'} = \frac{[20/\!/(\beta_3+1)(r_{e3}+(2/\!/10))]}{r_{e1}+r_{e2}+\frac{10}{\beta_1+1}+\frac{(1/\!/9)}{\beta_2+1}} \times \frac{(2/\!/10)}{(2/\!/10)+r_{e3}}$$

$$= \underline{85.7\text{ V/V}}$$

$$R_i = 10 + (1/\!/9) + 101\times(r_{e1}+r_{e2}) = 21\text{ k}\Omega$$

12

$$R_o = 2 // 10 // \left[r_{e3} + \frac{20}{\beta_3 + 1} \right]$$

$$= 181\ \Omega$$

The β circuit is:

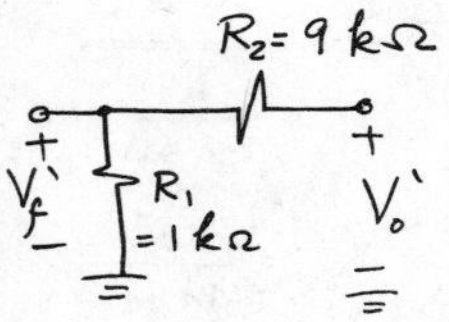

$$\beta \equiv \frac{V_f'}{V_o'} = \frac{1}{9+1} = 0.1\ V/V$$

$$A_f \equiv \frac{V_o}{V_s} = \frac{A}{1 + A\beta}$$

$$= \frac{85.7}{1 + 85.7 \times 0.1} = 8.96\ V/V$$

$$R_{if} = R_i (1 + A\beta)$$

$$= 21 \times 9.57 = 201\ k\Omega$$

$$R_{if}' = R_{if} - R_s = 201 - 10 = 191\ k\Omega$$

$$R_{of} = \frac{R_o}{1 + A\beta} = \frac{181}{9.57} = 18.9\ \Omega$$

$$\frac{1}{R_{of}} = \frac{1}{R_L} + \frac{1}{R_{of}'} \Rightarrow R_{of}' = 19.1\ \Omega$$

---

6 The A circuit is: 12

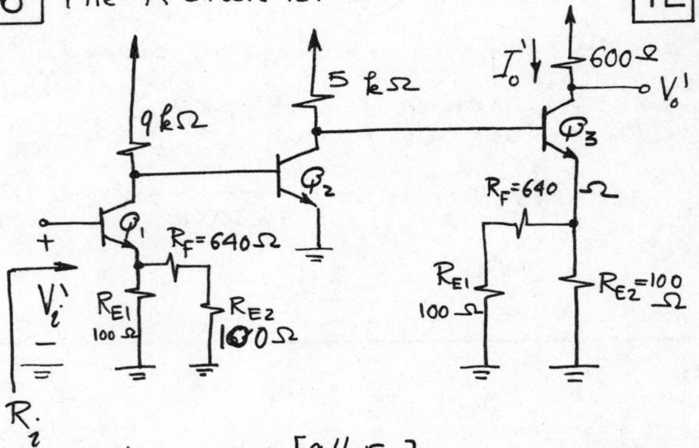

$$A = \frac{I_o'}{V_i'} = \frac{-\alpha_1 [9 // r_{\pi 2}]}{r_{e1} + (R_{E1} // (R_F + R_{E2}))} \times$$

$$- g_{m2} \left[5 // (\beta_3 + 1)(r_{e3} + (R_{E2} // (R_F + R_{E1}))) \right]$$

$$\times \frac{1}{r_{e3} + (R_{E2} // (R_F + R_{E1}))}$$

where $r_{e1} = 41.7\ \Omega$, $r_{e2} = 25\ \Omega$, $g_{m2} = 40$ mA/V, $r_{\pi 2} = 2.5\ k\Omega$ and $r_{e3} = 6.25\ \Omega$.

Thus, $A = 20.8\ A/V$

The β circuit is: 12

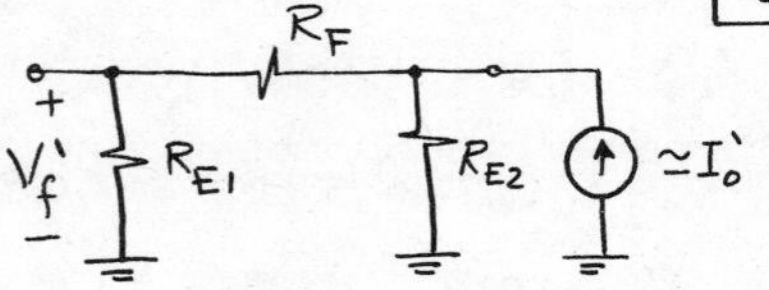

$$\beta \equiv \frac{V_f'}{I_o'}$$

$$= \frac{R_{E2}}{R_{E2} + R_F + R_{E1}} \times R_{E1}$$

$$= 12\ \Omega$$

$$A_f \equiv \frac{I_o}{V_s} = \frac{A}{1 + A\beta} = \frac{20.8}{1 + 20.8 \times 12} = \frac{20.8}{250.6}$$

$$= 0.083\ A/V$$

$$\frac{V_o}{V_s} = \frac{-I_o \times 600}{V_s} = -A_f \times 600 = -0.083 \times 600$$

$$= -49.8\ V/V$$

$$R_i = (\beta_1 + 1) \left[r_{e1} + (R_{E1} // (R_F + R_{E2})) \right]$$

$$= 13.1\ k\Omega$$

$$R_{if} = R_i (1 + A\beta) = 13.1 \times 250.6 = 3.28\ M\Omega$$

---

7 12

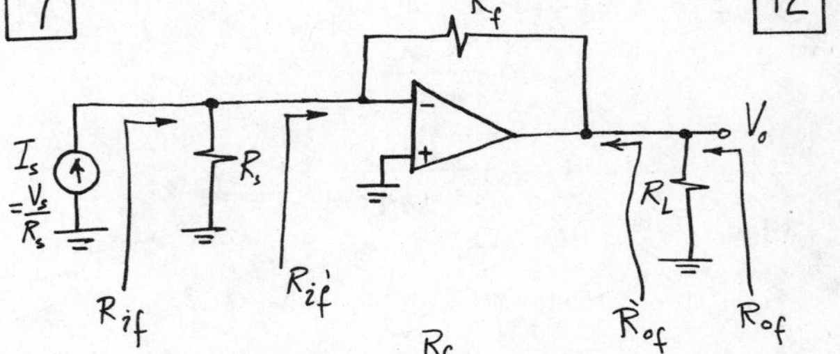

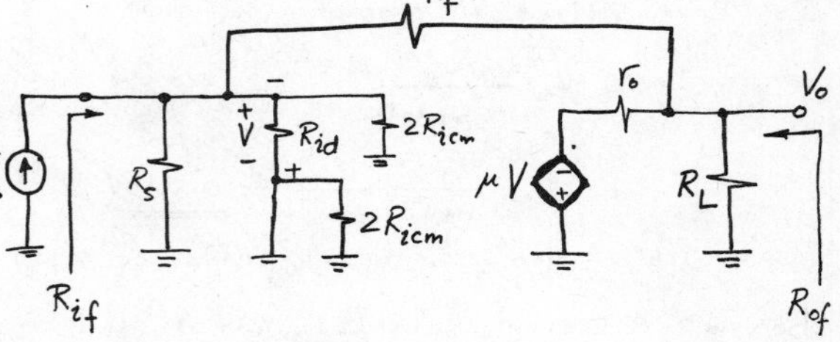

The A circuit is:

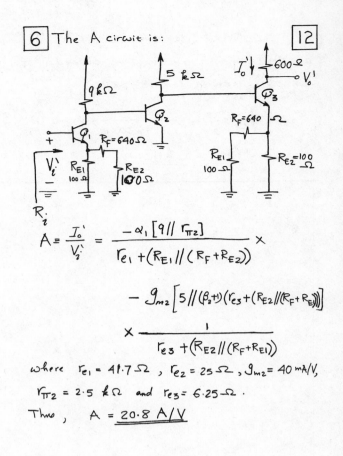

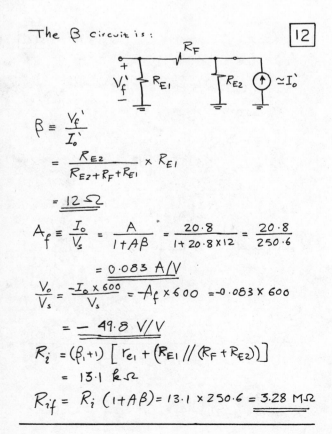

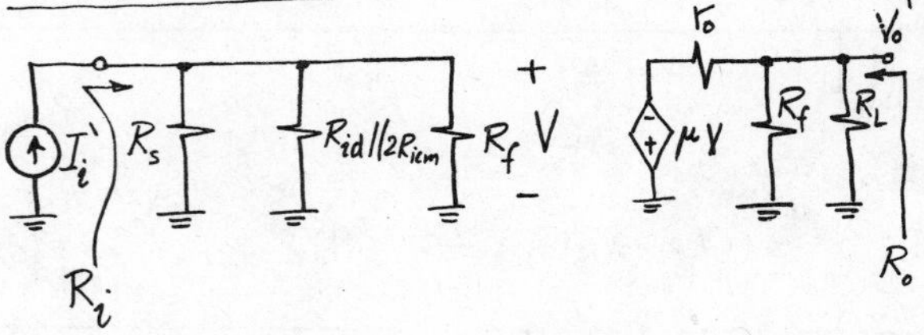

12

$$A \equiv \frac{V_o'}{I_i'} = -\mu V \frac{(R_L // R_f)}{(R_L // R_f) + r_o} \times \frac{1}{I_i'}$$

$$= -\mu (R_s // R_{id} // 2R_{icm} // R_f) \frac{(R_L // R_f)}{(R_L // R_f) + r_o}$$

$$= -10^4 (1 // 100 // 20{,}000 // 1000) \times \frac{(2 // 1000)}{(2 // 1000) + 1}$$

$$= \underline{\underline{-6589 \text{ k}\Omega}}$$

$$R_i = R_s // R_{id} // 2R_{icm} // R_f = 989.1\ \Omega$$

$$R_o = R_L // R_f // r_o = 2 // 1000 // 1 = 666.2\ \Omega$$

$$\beta \equiv \frac{I_f'}{V_o'} = -\frac{1}{R_f} = -10^{-6}\ \mho$$

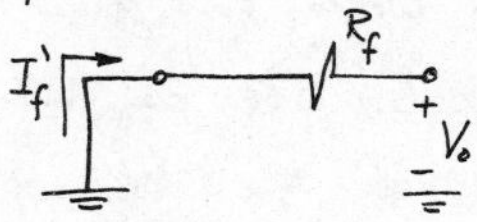

$$1 + A\beta = 1 + 6589 \times 10^3 \times 10^{-6} = 7.589$$

$$A_f \equiv \frac{V_o}{I_s} = \frac{A}{1 + A\beta} = \frac{-6589}{7.589} \cong -870 \text{ k}\Omega$$

$$\frac{V_o}{V_s} = \frac{V_o}{I_s R_s} = -\frac{870}{1} = \underline{\underline{-870 \text{ V/V}}}$$

$$R_{if} = R_i / (1 + A\beta) = 989.1 / 7.589 = 130.3\ \Omega$$

12

$$\frac{1}{R_{if}} = \frac{1}{R_{if}'} + \frac{1}{R_s}$$

$$\Rightarrow R_{if}' \cong \underline{150\ \Omega}$$

$$R_{of} = R_o / (1 + A\beta) = \frac{666.2}{7.589} = 87.8\ \Omega$$

$$\frac{1}{R_{of}} = \frac{1}{R_{of}'} + \frac{1}{R_L}$$

$$\Rightarrow R_{of}' = \underline{92\ \Omega}$$

---

8 Refer to Fig. 12.17b. We break the loop to the left of R_E and apply a voltage V_t (while reducing V_s to zero). The right-hand part of the circuit is terminated in $(r_\pi + R_s)$.

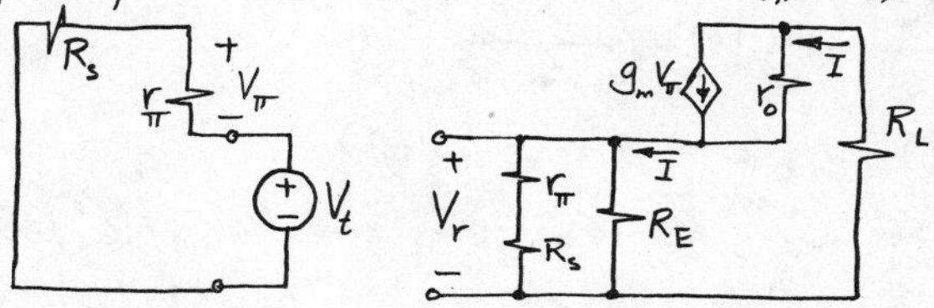

$$V_\pi = -V_t \frac{r_\pi}{r_\pi + R_s} \quad (1)$$

12

$$I = g_m V_\pi \frac{r_o}{r_o + R_L + \dfrac{R_E (R_s + r_\pi)}{R_E + R_s + r_\pi}}$$

$$V_r = I \frac{R_E (R_s + r_\pi)}{R_E + R_s + r_\pi}$$

$$= g_m V_\pi \frac{r_o}{r_o + R_L + \dfrac{R_E (R_s + r_\pi)}{R_E + R_s + r_\pi}} \cdot \frac{R_E (R_s + r_\pi)}{R_E + R_s + r_\pi}$$

Substituting for V_π from Eq. (1):

$$A\beta \equiv -\frac{V_r}{V_t} = \frac{g_m r_o \dfrac{r_\pi}{R_s + r_\pi}}{r_o + R_L + \dfrac{R_E (R_s + r_\pi)}{R_E + R_s + r_\pi}} \cdot \frac{R_E (R_s + r_\pi)}{R_E + R_s + r_\pi}$$

$$= \frac{g_m r_\pi R_E}{1 + \dfrac{R_L}{r_o} + \dfrac{R_E (R_s + r_\pi)}{r_o (R_E + R_s + r_\pi)}} \cdot \frac{1}{R_E + R_s + r_\pi}$$

$$A\beta = \underline{\underline{\frac{g_m r_\pi}{\left(1 + \dfrac{R_L}{r_o}\right)\left(1 + \dfrac{R_s + r_\pi}{R_E}\right) + \dfrac{R_s + r_\pi}{r_o}}}}$$

---

9 Refer to the circuit diagram in the solution of Exercise 12.7 above. To find the loop gain $A\beta$ we reduce I_s to zero, apply a voltage V_t and find the returned voltage V_r as shown: 12

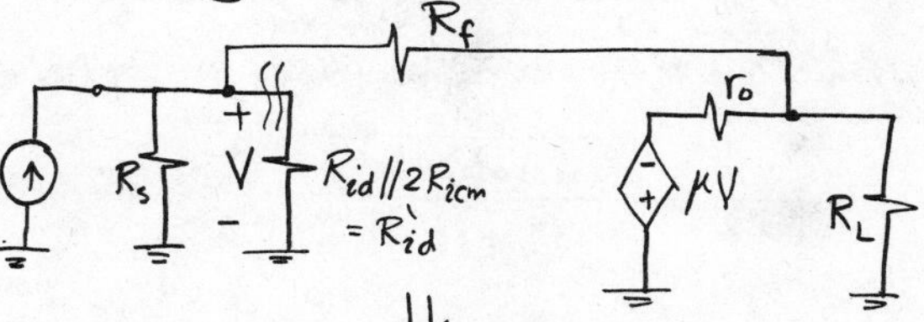

⇓

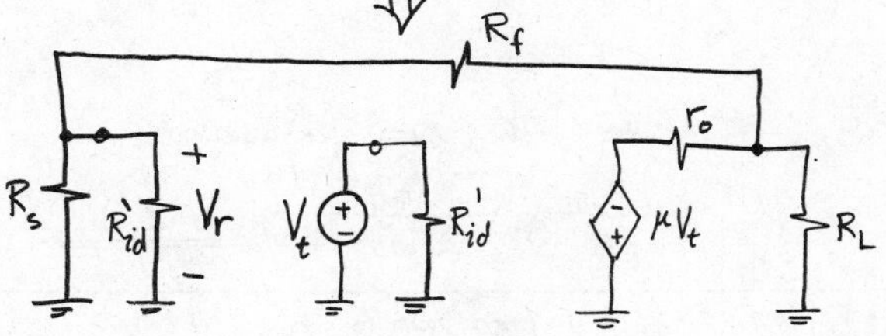

$$V_r = -\mu V_t \frac{R_L // [R_f + (R_s // R_{id} // 2R_{icm})]}{R_L // [R_f + (R_s // R_{id} // 2R_{icm})] + r_o} \times \frac{(R_s // R_{id} // 2R_{icm})}{(R_s // R_{id} // 2R_{icm}) + R_f}$$

Substituting $\mu = 10^4$, $R_L = 2\ k\Omega$, $R_f = 1000\ k\Omega$, $R_s = 1\ k\Omega$, $R_{id} = 100\ k\Omega$, $R_{icm} = 10{,}000\ k\Omega$ and $r_o = 1\ k\Omega$ yields:

$$A\beta \equiv -\frac{V_r}{V_t} = 10^4\,\frac{(2 // 1000 \cdot 99)}{(2 // 1000 \cdot 99) + 1} \times \frac{0.99}{0.99 + 1000}$$

$$= \underline{\underline{6.589\ V/V}}$$

which is the same value found in Exercise 12.7. (Please note that the answer given in the first printing was in error.)

10 $A(j\omega) = \left(\frac{10}{1 + j\omega/10^4}\right)^3$

Thus, $\phi = -3 \tan^{-1}(\omega/10^4)$

At $\omega_{180°}$, $\phi = 180°$; thus $\tan^{-1}(\omega_{180}/10^4) = 60°$

$$\frac{\omega_{180}}{10^4} = \sqrt{3} \Rightarrow \omega_{180} = \underline{\underline{\sqrt{3} \times 10^4\ \text{rad/s}}}$$

The feedback amplifier will be stable if at

ω_{180}, $|A\beta| < 1$. At the boundary, $\beta = \beta_{cr}$, thus

$$\beta_{cr} = \frac{1}{|A(j\omega_{180})|}$$

$$= \frac{1}{1000 / (1 + (\sqrt{3})^2)^{3/2}} = \underline{\underline{0.008}}$$

11 The pole is shifted by the factor $(1 + A_0\beta) = 1 + 10^5 \times 0.01 = \underline{1001}$.

The pole frequency will be $100 \times 1001 = \underline{100.1\ \text{kHz}}$

For a closed-loop gain of 1, $\beta = 1$. Thus the pole will be shifted by the factor

$$1 + 10^5 \times 1 \simeq 10^5 \text{ to } 100 \times 10^5 = 10^7\ \text{Hz}$$

or $\underline{10\ \text{MHz}}$

12 Refer to Eq.(12.44). The poles will coincide at the value of β which makes

$$(\omega_{P1} + \omega_{P2})^2 - 4(1 + A_0\beta)\,\omega_{P1}\,\omega_{P2} = 0$$

Substituting $A_0 = 100$, $\omega_{P1} = 10^4$ and $\omega_{P2} = 10^6$ rad/s,

$$(10^4 + 10^6)^2 = 4(1 + 100\beta) \times 10^{10}$$

$$1 + 100\beta = \frac{(1.01)^2 \times 100}{4}$$

$$\Rightarrow \beta = \underline{\underline{0.245}}$$

The corresponding $\underline{Q = 0.5}$

A maximally-flat response is obtained when $Q = 0.707$. Substituting in Eq.(12.46),

$$\frac{1}{\sqrt{2}} = \frac{\sqrt{(1 + 100\beta) \times 10^4 \times 10^6}}{10^4 + 10^6}$$

$$\Rightarrow \beta = \underline{0.5}$$

In this case, the low-frequency gain is

$$\frac{A_0}{1 + A_0\beta} = \frac{100}{1 + 100 \times 0.5} = \underline{\underline{1.96\ V/V}}$$

13 The closed-loop poles are obtained from $1 + A(s)\beta = 0$

$$1 + \frac{10^3}{(1 + s/10^4)^3}\beta = 0$$

$$(1 + \tfrac{s}{10^4})^3 + 10^3\beta = 0$$

$$\frac{s^3}{10^{12}} + s^2\frac{3}{10^8} + s\frac{3}{10^4} + (1 + 1000\beta) = 0$$

To simplify matters we shall normalize the complex frequency variabe s by replacing $\frac{s}{10^4}$ by s_n; thus

$$s_n^3 + 3s_n^2 + 3s_n + (1 + 1000\beta) = 0$$

The roots of this cubic equation are

$$\underline{\underline{-(1 + 10\beta^{1/3}),\ -1 + 5\beta^{1/3} \pm j\,5\sqrt{3}\,\beta^{1/3}}}$$

It is easy to verify that these roots follow the locus shown in Fig. E12.13.

The amplifier becomes unstable when the value of β is increased so that the complex conjugate pair of roots crosses the $j\omega$ axis into the righ-half of the s-plane. This happens at $\beta = \beta_{cr}$ where

$$10\,\beta_{cr}^{1/3} = \frac{1}{\cos 60°} = 2$$

Thus, $\underline{\underline{\beta_{cr} = 0.008}}$

14 $\beta = 0.01$

$$A = \frac{A_0}{1 + j\frac{\omega}{\omega_p}} = \frac{A_0}{1 + j f/f_p}$$

$$= \frac{10^5}{1 + jf/10}$$

$$|A\beta| = \frac{10^5 \times 0.01}{\sqrt{1 + f^2/100}} = 1 \quad \text{at}$$

$$1 + \frac{f^2}{100} = 10^6 \Rightarrow f \simeq \underline{10^4 \text{ Hz}}$$

At this frequency

$$\phi = -\tan^{-1}(10^4/10) \simeq -90°.$$

Thus the phase margin is $\underline{90°}$.

15 From Eq. (12.56),

$$|A_f(j\omega_1)| = \frac{1/\beta}{|1 + e^{-j\theta}|}$$

where $\frac{1}{\beta} \simeq$ low-frequency gain, and

$$\theta = 180° - \text{phase margin}$$

For a phase margin of 30°,

$\theta = 150°$, and $|A_f(j\omega_1)|/(1/\beta) = \underline{1.93}$

For a phase margin of 60°,

$\theta = 120°$, and $|A_f(j\omega_1)|/(1/\beta) = \underline{1}$

For a phase margin of 90°,

$\theta = 90°$, and $|A_f(j\omega_1)|/(1/\beta) = \underline{0.707}$

16 $\beta = \dfrac{1/sC}{R + \frac{1}{sC}}$

$$= \frac{1}{1 + sCR}$$

$$|1/\beta| = \sqrt{1 + (\omega CR)^2}$$

$$\frac{1}{2\pi CR} \leq 1 \text{ Hz}$$

$$CR \geq \frac{1}{2\pi}$$

Thus

$$\underline{CR \geq 0.159 \text{ s}}$$

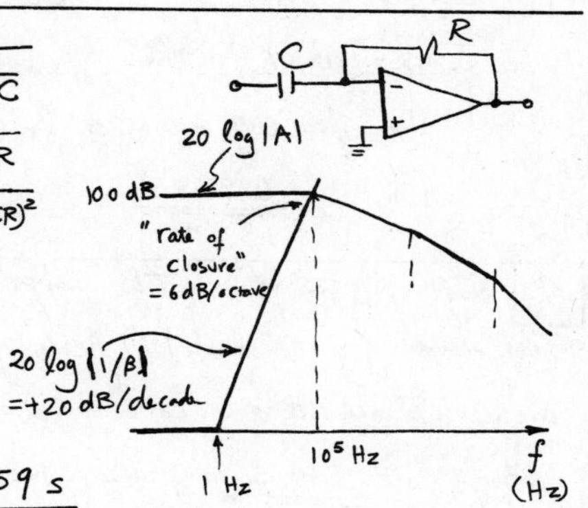

17 The new pole must be placed at $f_D = \dfrac{10^6}{10^4}$ ← 1 MHz (100dB − 20dB)

$$f_D = \underline{100 \text{ Hz}}$$

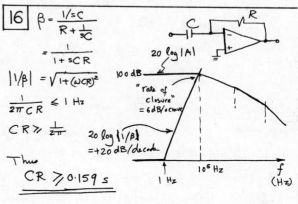

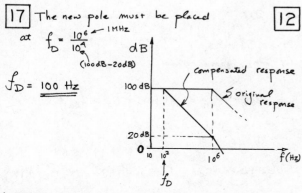

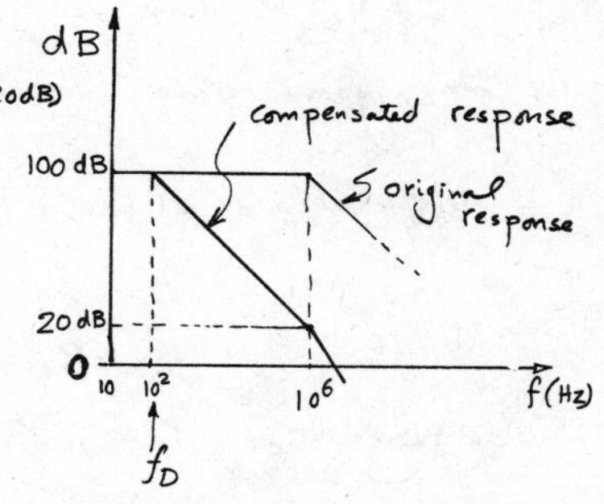

18 The frequency of the first pole must be lowered to

$$f_D = \frac{\text{frequency of second pole}}{10^4} \leftarrow (100 \text{ dB} - 20 \text{ dB})$$

$$= \frac{10 \times 10^6}{10^4} = \underline{1000 \text{ Hz}}$$

The capacitance at the controlling node must be increased by the same factor as the decrease in the frequency of the pole (10^6 Hz to 10^3 Hz). Thus the factor is $\underline{1000}$.

Chapter 13 — Exercises

1 $V_{BE} = V_T \ln(I_C/I_S)$

$$= 0.025 \ln(10^{-3}/10^{-14}) = \underline{0.633 \text{ V}}$$

$$g_m = I_C/V_T = \underline{40 \text{ mA/V}}$$

$$r_e = V_T/I_E \simeq \underline{25\ \Omega}$$

$$r_\pi = \beta/g_m = \underline{5 \text{ k}\Omega}$$

$$r_o = V_A/I_C = \frac{125 \text{ V}}{1 \text{ mA}} = \underline{125 \text{ k}\Omega}$$

$$r_\mu = 10\beta r_o = 10 \times 200 \times 125 = \underline{250 \text{ M}\Omega}$$

2 $V_{BE1} = V_T \ln(I_1/I_{S1})$

$$V_{BE2} = V_T \ln(I_1/I_{S2})$$

$$V_{BE1} + V_{BE2} = V_T \ln(I_1^2/I_{S1}I_{S2})$$

Similarly,

$$V_{BE3} + V_{BE4} = V_T \ln(I_3^2/I_{S3}I_{S4})$$

But,

$$V_{BE1} + V_{BE2} = V_{BE3} + V_{BE4}$$

thus,

$$V_T \ln(I_1^2/I_{S1}I_{S2}) = V_T \ln(I_3^2/I_{S3}I_{S4})$$

$$\Rightarrow I_3 = I_1\sqrt{\frac{I_{S3}I_{S4}}{I_{S1}I_{S2}}}$$

QED

3 From Eq. (13.1)

$$0.025 \ln\left(\frac{1000\ \mu A}{10\ \mu A}\right) = 10\times10^{-6}\times R_4$$

$$\Rightarrow R_4 = \underline{11.5\ k\Omega}$$

$I_{C11} = 1\ mA$, thus $V_{BE11} = \underline{0.7\,V}$

$I_{C10} = 10\ \mu A$, thus

$$V_{BE10} = 0.7 + 0.025 \ln\left(\frac{10}{1000}\right)$$

$$= \underline{0.585\ V}$$

4 Refer to Fig. 13.1. The upper limit is determined by Q_1 and Q_2 leaving the active mode. Since their collectors are at $15 - 0.6 = \underline{+14.4\ V}$; this value can be taken as the upper limit of the common-mode range. The lower limit is determined by Q_5 and Q_6 leaving the active mode; thus the lower limit is

$$-15 + V_{BE5} + V_{BE7} + V_{BE3} + V_{BE1}$$

$$= -15 + 2.4 = \underline{\underline{-12.6\ V}}$$

5 Using the result of Exercise 13.2,

$$I_{14} = 0.25\, I_{REF}\sqrt{\frac{I_{S14}I_{S20}}{I_{SX}I_{SY}}}$$

where X and Y are the two diode-connected transistors. Substituting $I_{REF} = 0.73\ mA$, $I_{S14} = I_{S20} = 3I_{SX} = 3I_{SY}$ (because the area of each of the output transistors is 3 times the area of a standard transistor) we obtain

$$I_{14} = 0.25\times0.73\times3 = \underline{\underline{0.548\ mA}}$$

6 Refer to Fig. 13.7.

(a) $v_{b6} = i_e(R_2 + r_{e6}) = i_e(1 + 2.63)$

$$= \underline{\underline{3.63\ k\Omega \times i_e}}$$

(b) $i_{e7} = \dfrac{v_{b6}}{R_3} + \dfrac{2\,i_e}{\beta+1} = \dfrac{3.63\times i_e}{50} + \dfrac{2\,i_e}{201} = \underline{\underline{0.08\,i_e}}$

(c) $i_{b7} = \dfrac{i_{e7}}{\beta+1} \simeq \underline{0.0004\ i_e}$

(d) $v_{b7} = v_{b6} + i_{e7}r_{e7}$

$$= 3.63\,i_e + 0.08\,i_e \times \frac{25\ mV}{9.5\ \mu A}$$

$$= \underline{3.84\ k\Omega \times i_e}$$

(where we have followed the instruction that $I_7 \simeq I_{C5} = I_{C6} = 9.5\ \mu A$)

(e) $R_{in} = \dfrac{v_{b7}}{\alpha i_e} \simeq \underline{3.84\ k\Omega}$

7 From Fig. E13.7 we see that the equivalent common-mode half circuit is

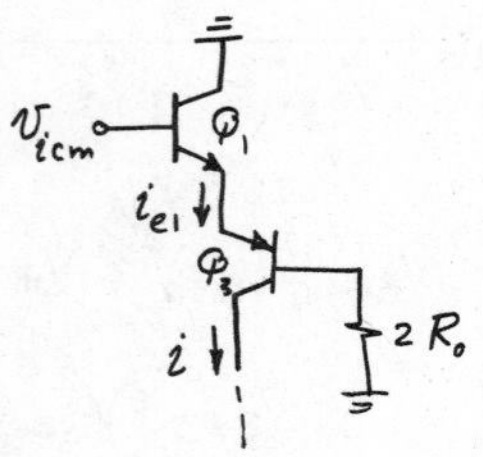

Thus,

$$i = \alpha_3\, i_{e1}$$

$$\simeq i_{e1}$$

$$= \frac{v_{icm}}{r_{e1} + r_{e3} + \dfrac{2R_o}{\beta_P + 1}}$$

Q.E.D

8 Refer to Fig. E13.7 and assume β_5 and β_6 to very very large (that is, we may ignore base currents).

$$v_{b5} = v_{b6} = i(r_{e5} + R_1) = i_{c6}(r_{e6} + R_2)$$

Thus

$$i_{c6} = i\,\frac{r_{e5} + R_1}{r_{e6} + R_2}$$

Substituting $r_{e6} = r_{e5}$, $R_1 = R$ and $R_2 = R + \Delta R$,

$$i_{c6} = i\,\frac{r_{e5} + R}{r_{e5} + R + \Delta R}$$

A node equation at the output yields

$$i_o = i_{c6} - i$$

$$= i\,\frac{r_{e5} + R}{r_{e5} + R + \Delta R} - i$$

$$= \underline{\underline{-i\,\frac{\Delta R}{r_{e5} + R + \Delta R}}}$$

9 Combining the results of Exercises 13.7 and 13.8 above and using the definition of the common-mode transconductance, **13**

$$G_{mcm} \equiv \frac{i_o}{v_{icm}}$$

results in

$$G_{mcm} = \frac{-\Delta R}{R + r_{es} + \Delta R} \; \frac{1}{r_{e1} + r_{e3} + \frac{2R_o}{\beta_P + 1}}$$

Assuming that $\Delta R << (R + r_{es})$ and that $\frac{R_o}{\beta_P + 1} >> r_{e1} + r_{e3}$,

$$G_{mcm} \simeq \left(\frac{-\Delta R}{R + r_{es}}\right)\left(\frac{\beta_{P+1}}{2R_o}\right)$$

$$\simeq \frac{\beta_P}{2R_o} \; \frac{\Delta R}{R + r_{es}}$$

where we have assumed that $\beta_P >> 1$. We have also ignored the negative sign as it is irrelevant for our purpose here.

---

10 The output resistance of a common-base transistor is given by Eq.(13.7), **13**

$$R_o = r_o \left[1 + g_m (R_E // r_\pi)\right] \qquad (1)$$

where r_μ is neglected. Applying this formula to Q_9, we have

$$r_{o9} = \frac{V_A}{I_{C9}} = \frac{50 \text{ V}}{19 \text{ } \mu A} = 2.63 \text{ M}\Omega$$

Since in this case $R_E = 0$ then

$$R_{o9} = r_{o9} = \underline{\underline{2.63 \text{ M}\Omega}}$$

Next we apply the formula in (1) to Q_{10},

$$r_{o10} = \frac{V_A}{I_{C10}} = \frac{125}{19} = 6.58 \text{ M}\Omega$$

$$g_m = \frac{19 \text{ } \mu A}{25 \text{ mV}} = 0.76 \text{ mA/V}$$

$$r_\pi = \frac{200}{0.76} = 263.2 \text{ k}\Omega$$

$$R_E = R_4 = 5 \text{ k}\Omega$$

Thus,

$$R_{o10} = 6.58 \times \left[1 + 0.76 (5 // 263)\right]$$ **13**

$$= \underline{\underline{31.1 \text{ M}\Omega}}$$

Finally

$$R_o \equiv R_{o9} // R_{o10}$$

$$= 2.63 // 31.1 = \underline{\underline{2.43 \text{ M}\Omega}}$$

---

11 Refer to the result of Exercise 13.9,

$$G_{mcm} = \frac{\beta_P}{2R_o} \; \frac{\Delta R}{R + r_{es}}$$

We have: $\beta_P = 50$, $\frac{\Delta R}{R} = 0.02$, $R = 1 \text{ k}\Omega$, $r_{es} = 2.63 \text{ k}\Omega$, and (from Exercise 13.10 above) $R_o = 2.43 \text{ M}\Omega$. Thus

$$G_{mcm} = \frac{50}{2 \times 2.43} \times \frac{0.02}{1 + 2.63}$$

$$= \underline{\underline{0.057 \text{ } \mu A/V}}$$

---

12 $G_{mcm} = 0.057 \text{ } \mu A/V$ and $G_{m1} = \frac{1}{5.26}$ mA/V

Thus, $CMRR \equiv 20 \log \left[\frac{(1/5.26) \times 10^{-3}}{0.057 \times 10^{-6}}\right] = \underline{\underline{70.5 \text{ dB}}}$

---

13 The common-mode feedback will increase the common-mode rejection by the amount-of-feedback which is approximately equal to β_P. Thus **13**

$$CMRR = 20 \log_{10} \left[\beta_P \frac{G_{m1}}{G_{mcm}}\right]$$

$$= 20 \log_{10} \beta_P + 20 \log_{10} \frac{G_{m1}}{G_{mcm}}$$

$$= 20 \log 50 + 70.5$$

$$= \underline{\underline{104.6 \text{ dB}}}$$

---

14 We substitute in Eq.(13.12)

$$\beta_{16} = \beta_{17} = 200$$

$$r_{e16} = \frac{25 \text{ mV}}{16.2 \text{ } \mu A} = 1.54 \text{ k}\Omega$$

$$r_{e17} = \frac{25 \text{ mV}}{0.55 \text{ mA}} = 45.5 \Omega$$

$$R_8 = 100 \Omega \qquad R_9 = 50 \text{ k}\Omega$$

Thus, $R_{i2} = 201 \left[1.54 + 50 // (201 \times 0.0455)\right] \cong \underline{\underline{4 \text{ M}\Omega}}$

15 From Eq. (13.13) **13**

$$i_{c17} = \frac{\alpha\, v_{b17}}{r_{e17} + R_8}$$

$$\simeq \frac{1 \times v_{b17}}{45.5 + 100} = \frac{v_{b17}}{145.5} \quad (1)$$

From Eq. (13.14)

$$v_{b17} = v_{i2}\, \frac{(50\ \text{k}\Omega \,//\, R_{i17})}{(50\ \text{k}\Omega // R_{i17}) + 1.54\ \text{k}\Omega}$$

where R_{i17} is obtained from Eq. (13.15),

$$R_{i17} = 201 \times (45.5 + 100)\ \Omega$$

$$= 29.2\ \text{k}\Omega$$

Thus

$$v_{b17} = v_{i2} \times 0.92 \quad (2)$$

From Eq. (13.16),

$$G_{m2} \equiv \frac{i_{c17}}{v_{i2}}$$

$$= \frac{v_{b17}}{145.5}\, \frac{1}{v_{i2}} = \frac{0.92}{145.5}\ \text{A/V}$$

$$= 6.3\ \text{mA/V}$$

(slightly less than the value used in the text)

---

16 From Eq. (13.17) **13**

$$R_{o2} = R_{o13B} \,//\, R_{o17}$$

where

$$R_{o13B} = r_{o13B} = \frac{50\ \text{V}}{0.55\ \text{mA}} = 90.9\ \text{k}\Omega$$

$$R_{o17} = r_{o17}\left[1 + g_{m17}\,(r_{\pi17} // R_8)\right]$$

and, $$r_{o17} = \frac{125}{0.55} = 227.3\ \text{k}\Omega$$

$$g_{m17} = \frac{0.55}{0.025} = 22\ \text{mA/V}$$

$$r_{\pi17} = \frac{200}{22} = 9.09\ \text{k}\Omega$$

$$R_8 = 100\ \Omega$$

Thus, $$R_{o17} = 227.3\left[1 + 22 \times (9.09 // 0.1)\right]$$

$$= 722\ \text{k}\Omega$$

$$R_{o2} = 80.7\ \text{k}\Omega$$

$$\simeq 81\ \text{k}\Omega$$

---

17 From Fig. 13.14, the open circuit voltage gain of the second stage is **13**

$$-G_{m2} R_{o2} = -6.5 \times 81$$

$$= -526.5\ \text{V/V}$$

---

18 The diode-connected transistor Q_{19} is replaced with r_{e19},

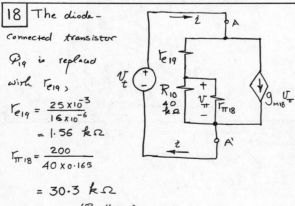

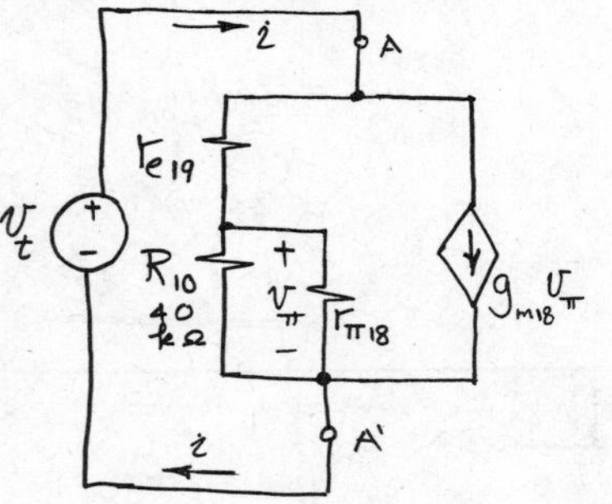

$$r_{e19} = \frac{25 \times 10^{-3}}{16 \times 10^{-6}}$$

$$= 1.56\ \text{k}\Omega$$

$$r_{\pi18} = \frac{200}{40 \times 0.165}$$

$$= 30.3\ \text{k}\Omega$$

$$V_\pi = V_t\, \frac{(R_{10} // r_{\pi18})}{r_{e19} + (R_{10} // r_{\pi18})} = 0.917\ V_t$$

$$i = \frac{V_t}{r_{e19} + (R_{10} // r_{\pi18})} + g_{m18} V_\pi = \frac{V_t}{1.56 + (40 // 30.3)} + g_{m18} \times 0.917\ V_t$$

13

$$i = 6.11\ V_t \times 10^{-3}$$

Thus, $$R \equiv \frac{V_t}{i} \simeq 163\ \Omega$$

19

$$R_o = \left[\left(\frac{R_{o2}}{\beta_{23}+1} + r_{e23} + R\right) \Big/ (\beta_{14}+1)\right] + r_{e14}$$

$$= \left[\left(\frac{81000}{51} + \frac{0.025}{0.18 \times 10^{-3}} + 163\right) \Big/ 201\right] + r_{e14}$$

$$= 9.4 + r_{e14}$$

For an output current of 5 mA, $r_{e14} = 5\ \Omega$

and

$$R_o = 14.4\ \Omega$$

---

20 For $v_O = 10 \sin \omega t$

$$\frac{dv_O}{dt} = \omega \times 10 \cos \omega t$$

$$SR = \left.\frac{dv_O}{dt}\right|_{max} = \omega_M \times 10 = 2\pi f_M \times 10$$

$$f_M = \frac{SR}{20\pi} = \frac{0.63 \times 10^6}{20\pi} = 10\ \text{kHz}$$

---

21 Denoting the resistance R, the dc gain is

$$A_0 = G_{m1} R$$

For $A_0 = 243,147$ and $G_{m1} = \frac{1}{5.26} \times 10^{-3}$

$$R = \underline{1279\ M\Omega}$$

22 $SR = 2I/C_C$

& $\omega_t = \dfrac{G_{m1}}{C_C}$

Thus $SR = \left(\dfrac{2I}{G_{m1}}\right)\omega_t$ (1)

With a resistance R_E in each of the emitter leads of Q_3 and Q_4,

$$G_{m1} = 2 \times \frac{1}{4r_e + 2R_E} = \frac{1}{2r_e + R_E}$$

$$= \frac{1}{2\frac{V_T}{I} + R_E} = \frac{I/2}{V_T + (IR_E/2)}$$

Substituting in Eq. (1) yields

$$SR = 4\omega_t (V_T + IR_E/2)$$

Q.E.D.

For a given ω_t, we can double the slew rate by including R_E whose value provide

$$IR_E/2 = V_T$$

Thus, $R_E = \dfrac{2V_T}{I} = \dfrac{2 \times 0.025}{9.5 \times 10^{-6}} = \underline{\underline{5.26\ k\Omega}}$

The new value of C_C is found from

$$\omega_t = \frac{G_{m1}}{C_C}$$

Since ω_t remains constant and G_{m1} is reduced by a factor of 2, C_C must be reduced by the same factor, thus

$$C_C = \underline{\underline{15\ pF}}$$

The dc gain is decreased by the same factor as G_{m1}, that is a factor of 2 or 6 dB, resulting in $\underline{101.7\ dB}$.

Since $\omega_t = A_0\,\omega_{3dB}$

and A_0 is reduced by a factor of 2 while ω_t remains constant then ω_{3dB} is increased by a factor of 2 to $\underline{8.2\ Hz}$.

23 Refer to Fig. 13.23. Since Q_8 and Q_5 are matched, $2I = I_{REF}$. Q_1, Q_2, Q_3 and Q_4 each conducts a current of $I = 12.5\ \mu A$. Q_7 is matched to Q_5 and Q_8, thus the current in Q_7 is equal to $I_{REF} = 25\ \mu A$. Q_6 conducts an equal current.

With I_D of each device known, we use

$$I_D = \tfrac{1}{2}(\mu C_{ox})\left(\tfrac{W}{L}\right)(|V_{GS}| - |V_t|)^2$$

to determine $|V_{GS}|$. The results are given in the answer table.

g_m of each device is determined from

$$g_m = 2K\,(|V_{GS}| - |V_t|)$$
$$= (\mu C_{ox})(W/L)(|V_{GS}| - |V_t|)$$
$$= \sqrt{2(\mu C_{ox})(W/L)\,I_D}$$

or alternatively

$$g_m = \frac{2I_D}{|V_{GS}| - |V_t|}$$

The value of r_o is determined from

$$r_o = |V_A| / I_D$$

The resulting values of g_m and r_o are given in the answer table.

A_1 is determined using Eq. (13.44),

$$A_1 = -g_{m1}(r_{o2} \,//\, r_{o4})$$
$$= -62.5 \times (2//2) = \underline{\underline{-62.5\ V/V}}$$

A_2 is determined using Eq. (13.45),

$$A_2 = -g_{m6}(r_{o6} \,//\, r_{o7})$$
$$= -100 \times (1//1) = \underline{\underline{-50\ V/V}}$$

Thus, the dc open-loop gain is

$$A_0 = A_1 A_2 = 62.5 \times 50 = \underline{\underline{3,125\ V/V}}$$

The lower limit of the input common-mode range is the value at which Q_1 and Q_2

leave the active (pinch-off) region. This occurs when the drain of Q_1 exceeds the input voltage by $|V_t|$ volts. Since the drain of Q_1 is at $-5+1.5=-3.5V$ then the input should not be allowed to go below $\underline{-4.5\text{ V}}$.

13

The upper limit of the input common-mode range is the value of input at which Q_5 leaves the active mode. Thus

$$v_{ICM}|_{max} = V_{DD} - |V_{GS5}| + |V_t| - |V_{GS1}|$$
$$= 5 - 1.6 + 1 - 1.4 = \underline{\underline{3\text{ V}}}$$

Finally, the output voltage range is determined from Q_7 leaving the active mode,

$$v_{O\,max} = V_{DD} - |V_{GS7}| + |V_t|$$
$$= 5 - 1.6 + 1 = \underline{4.4\text{ V}}$$

and from Q_6 leaving the active mode,

$$v_{O\,min} = -V_{SS} + |V_{GS6}| - |V_t| = \underline{-4.5\text{V}}$$

---

24 Refer to Fig. 13.23 and let the two input terminals be grounded.

13

$$I_{D5} = 2I = K_5\,(|V_{GS5}| - |V_t|)^2 \quad (1)$$

$$I_{D7} = K_7\,(|V_{GS7}| - |V_t|)^2 \quad (2)$$

But $|V_{GS5}| = |V_{GS7}|$, thus

$$\frac{K_5}{K_7} = \frac{2I}{I_{D7}} \quad (3)$$

Now, $I_{D1} = I_{D2} = I$ and thus

$$I_{D3} = I_{D4} = I$$

If Q_3 and Q_4 are matched then

$$V_{D4} = V_{D3}$$

and thus

$$V_{GS6} = V_{GS4}$$

For Q_4 we have

$$I = K_4\,(|V_{GS4}| - |V_t|)^2 \quad (4)$$

and for Q_6

$$I_{D6} = K_6\,(|V_{GS6}| - |V_t|)^2 \quad (5)$$

Equating $|V_{GS4}|$ and $|V_{GS6}|$ in (4) and (5) yields

13

$$\frac{I}{I_{D6}} = \frac{K_4}{K_6} \quad (6)$$

To obtain zero output offset we must have

$$I_{D6} = I_{D7}$$

Thus

$$\frac{I}{I_{D7}} = \frac{K_4}{K_6} \quad (7)$$

Finally, from (3) and (7) we find the condition of zero output offset as

$$\frac{K_4}{K_6} = \frac{1}{2}\,\frac{K_5}{K_7} \qquad Q.E.D.$$

---

25 From Eq. (13.50)

$$\omega_t = \frac{G_{m1}}{C_C}$$

where $G_{m1} = g_{m1} = g_{m2} = 62.5\ \mu A/V$

(from the results of Exercise 13.23)

Thus for $f_t = 1\text{MHz}$,

$$C_C = \frac{62.5\times10^{-6}}{2\pi\times1\times10^{6}} = \underline{\underline{10\text{ PF}}}$$

13

---

26 From Eq. (13.52) we see that to place the zero at $s=\infty$ we select

$$R = \frac{1}{G_{m2}}$$

Now $G_{m2} = g_{m6} = 100\ \mu A/V$

(from the answer table to Exercise 13.23)

Thus

$$R = \frac{1}{0.1} = \underline{\underline{10\ k\Omega}}$$

---

27 From Eq. (13.53)

$$\omega_{P2} \cong \frac{G_{m2}}{C_2}$$

$$= \frac{0.1\times10^{-3}}{10\times10^{-12}} = 10^7\ \text{rad/s}$$

$$f_{P2} = \frac{10^7}{2\pi} = 1.59\ \text{MHz}$$

At $f = f_t = 1\text{ MHz}$ the second pole introduces an excess phase of

$$\phi = -\tan^{-1}\frac{1}{1.59} = \underline{\underline{-32.2^\circ}}$$

Thus the phase margin becomes

$$180^\circ - 90^\circ - 32.2^\circ = \underline{57.8^\circ}$$

28 Using Eq. (13.55)

$$SR = (V_{GS} - V_t)\,\omega_t$$

where V_{GS} is that for Q_1 and Q_2 in Fig. 13.23, thus $V_{GS} = 1.4$ V.

$$SR = (1.4 - 1) \times 2\pi \times 10^6$$

$$= \underline{\underline{2.5\ \text{V}/\mu\text{s}}}$$

Chapter 14 — Exercises

1 Refer to Fig. 14.3 b.

$$T(s) = \frac{1}{[s-(-1)]\left[s-\left(-\frac{1}{2}-j\frac{\sqrt{3}}{2}\right)\right]\left[s-\left(-\frac{1}{2}+j\frac{\sqrt{3}}{2}\right)\right]}$$

$$= \frac{1}{(s+1)\left(s+\frac{1}{2}+j\frac{\sqrt{3}}{2}\right)\left(s+\frac{1}{2}-j\frac{\sqrt{3}}{2}\right)}$$

$$= \frac{1}{(s+1)\left[\left(s+\frac{1}{2}\right)^2-\left(j\frac{\sqrt{3}}{2}\right)^2\right]}$$

$$= \underline{\underline{\frac{1}{(s+1)(s^2+s+1)}}}$$

2

$$T(j\omega) = \frac{1}{(j\omega+1)(-\omega^2+j\omega+1)}$$

$$= \frac{1}{(1+j\omega)[(1-\omega^2)+j\omega]}$$

$$|T(j\omega)| = \frac{1}{\sqrt{1+\omega^2}}\ \frac{1}{\sqrt{(1-\omega^2)^2+\omega^2}}$$

$$|T(j\omega)| = \frac{1}{\sqrt{1+\omega^2}\sqrt{1-2\omega^2+\omega^4+\omega^2}}$$

$$= \frac{1}{\sqrt{(1+\omega^2)(1-\omega^2+\omega^4)}}$$

$$= \frac{1}{\sqrt{1+\omega^6}} \qquad \text{Q.E.D.}$$

$|T(j\omega)| = \frac{1}{\sqrt{2}}$ at $\omega = \omega_{3dB}$, thus

$$\omega_{3dB} = \underline{\underline{1\ \text{rad/s}}}$$

At $\omega = 3$ rad/s,

$$|T| = \frac{1}{\sqrt{1+3^6}}$$

$$\text{Attenuation} = 20\log_{10}\sqrt{1+3^6} = \underline{\underline{28.6\ \text{dB}}}$$

3

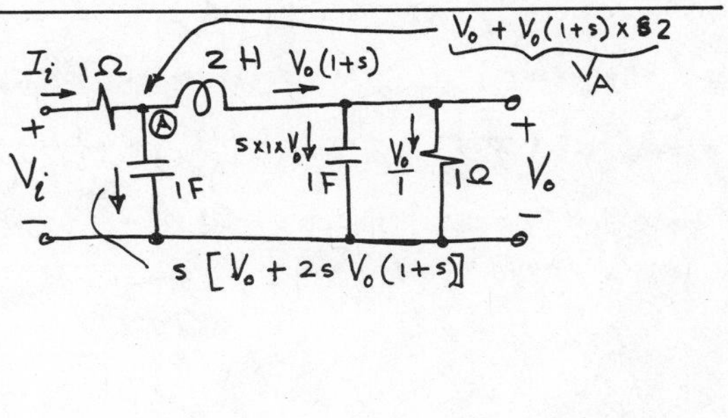

See analysis on circuit diagram above. Writing a node equation at Ⓐ yields

$$I_i = V_o(1+s) + s\,V_o\,[1+2s(1+s)]$$

Now we can write for V_i

$$V_i = V_A + I_i \times 1$$

$$= V_o[1+2s(1+s)] + V_o(1+s) + sV_o[1+2s(1+s)]$$

$$\frac{V_i}{V_o} = 1 + 2s + 2s^2 + 1 + s + s + 2s^2 + 2s^3$$

$$= 2s^3 + 4s^2 + 4s + 2$$

$$= 2\,[s^3 + 2s^2 + 2s + 1]$$

$$= 2\,(s+1)(s^2+s+1)$$

$$\frac{V_o(s)}{V_i(s)} = \frac{0.5}{(s+1)(s^2+s+1)} \qquad \text{Q.E.D.}$$

4 From the result of Exercise 14.1, **14**

$$T(s) = \frac{1}{(s+1)(s^2+s+1)}$$

$$= \frac{1}{s+1} \times \frac{1}{s^2+s+1}$$

Thus this filter can be realized as the cascade connection of a first-order RC section having the transfer function $\frac{1}{s+1}$ and a second-order section with a transfer function of

$$\frac{1}{s^2+s+1}$$

This is a <u>low-pass</u> function with

$\omega_0 = \underline{\underline{1 \text{ rad/s}}}$, and

$Q = \underline{\underline{1}}$

---

5 BP with $\omega_0 = 10^4$ rad/s and **14**

3-dB BW $\equiv \frac{\omega_0}{Q} = 10^3$ rad/s. Thus

$$Q = \frac{10^4}{10^3} = 10 \quad \text{and}$$

$$T(s) = \frac{n_1 s}{s^2 + s \times 10^3 + 10^8}$$

Center-frequency gain $= \frac{n_1}{10^3} = 10 \Rightarrow n_1 = 10^4$

Thus

$$\underline{\underline{T(s) = \frac{10^4 s}{s^2 + 10^3 s + 10^8}}}$$

---

6 At $\omega = \omega_0 = \frac{1}{\sqrt{LC}}$, the parallel tuned circuit exhibits an infinite impedance. Thus no current flows through R and $V_o = V_i$. That is, the center-frequency gain is <u>1 (0 dB)</u>.

$$T(s) = \frac{Z_{LC}}{Z_{LC} + R}$$

where Z_{LC} denotes the impedance of the parallel tuned circuit. **14**

$$T(s) = \frac{1}{1 + R\,Y_{LC}}$$

where Y_{LC} is the admittance of the parallel tuned circuit, $Y_{LC} = sC + \frac{1}{sL}$

$$T(s) = \frac{1}{1 + R\left(sC + \frac{1}{sL}\right)}$$

$$= \frac{s\frac{1}{CR}}{s^2 + s\frac{1}{CR} + \frac{1}{LC}}$$

$$\omega_0 = \frac{1}{\sqrt{LC}} = 10^4$$

$$\frac{\omega_0}{Q} = \frac{1}{CR} = 10^3$$

For $R = 10\ k\Omega$, $C = (10 \times 10^3 \times 10^3)^{-1} = \underline{\underline{0.1\ \mu F}}$

$$\frac{1}{LC} = 10^8$$

$$L = \frac{1}{10^8 \times 0.1 \times 10^{-6}} = \underline{\underline{0.1\ H}}$$

---

7 From Eq. (14.14), **14**

$$CR = \frac{2Q}{\omega_0} = \frac{2 \times 1}{10^4} = 2 \times 10^{-4}\ s$$

For $C = C_1 = C_2 = 1\ nF$,

$$R = \frac{2 \times 10^{-4}}{10^{-9}} = 2 \times 10^5\ \Omega = 200\ k\Omega$$

Thus, $R_3 = \underline{\underline{200\ k\Omega}}$

From Eq. (14.13),

$$m = 4Q^2 = 4$$

Thus, $R_4 = R/m = 200/4 = \underline{\underline{50\ k\Omega}}$

---

8 The transfer function of the feedback network is given in Fig. 14.8 a. The poles are the roots of the denominator polynomial,

$$s^2 + s\left(\frac{1}{C_1R_3} + \frac{1}{C_2R_3} + \frac{1}{C_1R_4}\right) + \frac{1}{C_1C_2R_3R_4} = 0$$

For $C_1 = C_2 = 10^{-9}$ F, $R_3 = 2 \times 10^5\ \Omega$ and $R_4 = 5 \times 10^4$ we have

14

$$s^2 + s\left(\frac{2}{10^{-9}\times 2\times 10^5} + \frac{1}{10^{-9}\times 5\times 10^4}\right) + \frac{1}{10^{-18}\times 10^{10}} = 0$$

$$s^2 + s\times 3\times 10^4 + 10^8 = 0$$

$$s = \frac{-3\times 10^4 \pm \sqrt{9\times 10^8 - 4\times 10^8}}{2}$$

$$= \underline{\underline{-0.382\times 10^4}} \text{ and } \underline{\underline{-2.618\times 10^4 \text{ rad/s}}}$$

9

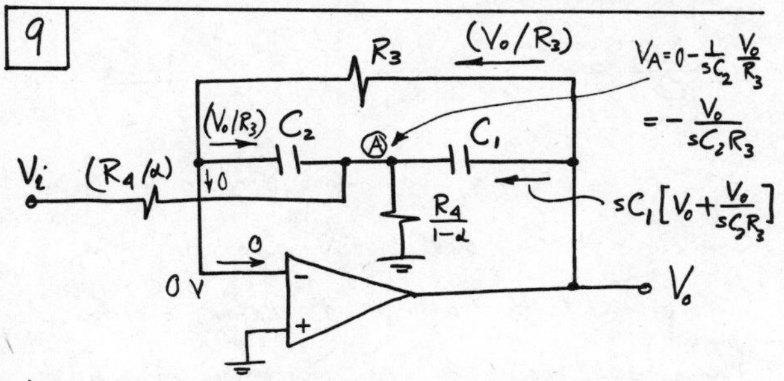

Writing a node equation at Ⓐ yields

$$\frac{V_o}{R_3} + sC_1\left[V_o + \frac{V_o}{sC_2R_3}\right] + \frac{V_A}{R_4/(1-\alpha)} + \frac{V_i - V_A}{R_4/\alpha} = 0$$

where $V_A = -\frac{V_o}{sC_2R_3}$, thus

$$\frac{V_o}{R_3} + sC_1V_o + V_o\frac{C_1}{C_2R_3} + \frac{(1-\alpha)V_o}{sC_2R_3R_4} + \frac{\alpha V_o}{sC_2R_3R_4} = \frac{-V_i}{R_4/\alpha}$$

14

$$\frac{V_o}{V_i} = \frac{-\frac{\alpha}{R_4}}{sC_1 + \frac{1}{R_3} + \frac{C_1}{C_2R_3} + \frac{1}{sC_2R_3R_4}}$$

$$= \frac{-s\frac{\alpha}{C_1R_4}}{s^2 + s\left(\frac{1}{C_1R_3} + \frac{1}{C_2R_3}\right) + \frac{1}{C_1C_2R_3R_4}}$$

This is a bandpass function whose poles are identical to the zeros of $t(s)$ in Fig. 14.8(a). Q.E.D.

For $C_1 = C_2 = 10^{-9}$ F, $R_3 = 2\times 10^5\ \Omega$ and $R_4 = 5\times 10^4\ \Omega$

$$\frac{V_o}{V_i} = \frac{-s\times 2\times 10^4\times\alpha}{s^2 + s\times 10^4 + 10^8}$$

To obtain a unity center-frequency gain,

$$2\times 10^4\times\alpha = 10^4 \Rightarrow \alpha = 0.5$$

Thus $\frac{R_4}{\alpha} = \underline{\underline{100\ k\Omega}}$ and $\frac{R_4}{1-\alpha} = \underline{\underline{100\ k\Omega}}$

---

10 14

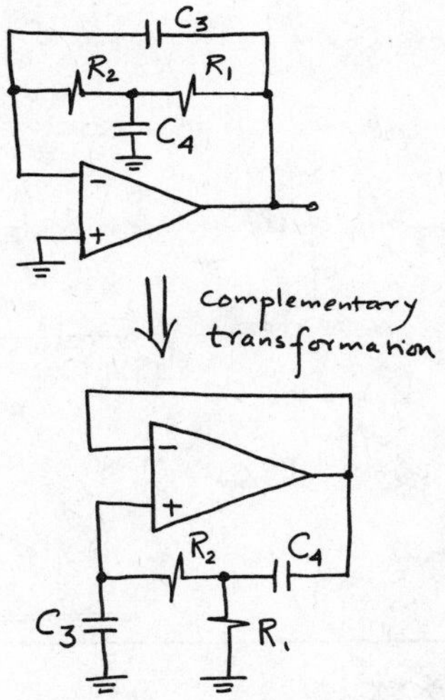

To realize a second-order LP function:

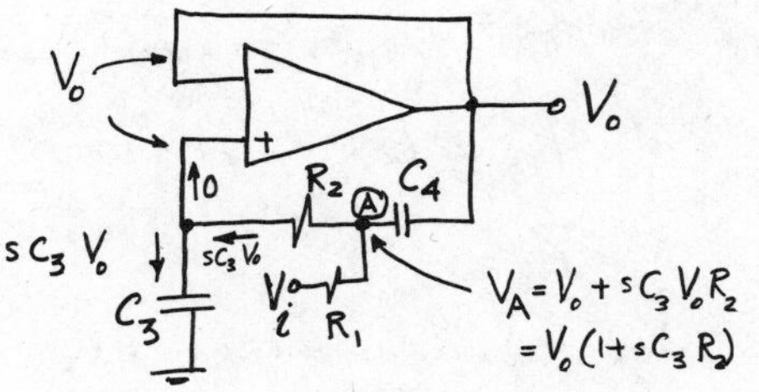

Writing a node equation at Ⓐ yields 14

$$sC_3V_o + sC_4(V_A - V_o) + \frac{V_A - V_i}{R_1} = 0$$

$$sC_3V_o + sC_4(sC_3R_2V_o) + \frac{V_o}{R_1}(1 + sC_3R_2) = \frac{V_i}{R_1}$$

$$\frac{V_o}{V_i} = \frac{1/R_1}{s^2C_3C_4R_2 + sC_3 + sC_3\frac{R_2}{R_1} + \frac{1}{R_1}}$$

$$= \frac{1/C_3C_4R_1R_2}{s^2 + s\left(\frac{1}{C_4R_2} + \frac{1}{C_4R_1}\right) + \frac{1}{C_3C_4R_1R_2}}$$

which is a second-order low-pass function having poles identical to the zeros of the bridged-T network of Fig. 14.8(b).

---

11 Refer to the results derived in Example 14.1.

(a) $S^{\omega_0}_{R_3} = -\frac{1}{2}$. Thus for $\frac{\Delta R_3}{R_3} = +2\%$,

$\Delta\omega_0/\omega_0 = -\frac{1}{2}\times 2 = \underline{\underline{-1\%}}$.

14

$S^{Q}_{R_3} = +\frac{1}{2}$. Thus, for $\frac{\Delta R_3}{R_3} = +2\%$,

$$\frac{\Delta Q}{Q} = +\frac{1}{2} \times 2 = +1\%.$$

(b) $S^{\omega_0}_{R_4} = -\frac{1}{2}$. Thus, for $\frac{\Delta R_4}{R_4} = +2\%$,

$$\frac{\Delta \omega_0}{\omega_0} = -\frac{1}{2} \times 2 = -1\%$$

$S^{Q}_{R_4} = -\frac{1}{2}$. Thus, for $\frac{\Delta R_4}{R_4} = +2\%$,

$$\frac{\Delta Q}{Q} = -\frac{1}{2} \times 2 = -1\%$$

(c) Combining the results in (a) and (b) above:

$$\frac{\Delta \omega_0}{\omega_0} = -1 - 1 = -2\%$$

$$\frac{\Delta Q}{Q} = +1 - 1 = 0\%$$

(d) Due to the two resistors being both 2% low we have

$$\frac{\Delta \omega_0}{\omega_0} = +2\% \quad \text{and} \quad \frac{\Delta Q}{Q} = 0\%$$

14

Due to the +2% deviation in each of the capacitors we have

$$\frac{\Delta \omega_0}{\omega_0} = S^{\omega_0}_{C_1} \frac{\Delta C_1}{C_1} + S^{\omega_0}_{C_2} \frac{\Delta C_2}{C_2}$$

$$= \left(-\frac{1}{2} \times +2\right) + \left(-\frac{1}{2} \times +2\right)$$

$$= -2\%$$

and,

$$\frac{\Delta Q}{Q} = S^{Q}_{C_1} \frac{\Delta C_1}{C_1} + S^{Q}_{C_2} \frac{\Delta C_2}{C_2}$$

$$= 0 \times +2 + 0 \times +2 = 0$$

Combining the deviations due to the resistance deviations together with those due to the capacitance deviations we obtain

$$\frac{\Delta \omega_0}{\omega_0} = +2 - 2 = 0\%$$

$$\frac{\Delta Q}{Q} = 0 + 0 = 0\%$$

12 From Eq. (14.26) 14

$$\omega_0 = \frac{1}{\sqrt{C_2 C_6 R_1 R_3 R_5 / R_4}}$$

For $C_2 = C_6 = C$ and $R_1 = R_3 = R_4 = R_5 = 10\ k\Omega$

$$\omega_0 = \frac{1}{C \times 10 \times 10^3}$$

For $\omega_0 \equiv 2\pi f_0 = 2\pi \times 10 \times 10^3$

$$C = \frac{1}{2\pi \times 10^4 \times 10^4} = 1.59\ nF$$

From Eq. (14.27) with the component values given above

$$Q = \frac{R_7}{10\ k\Omega}$$

To obtain $Q = 20 \Longrightarrow R_7 = 200\ k\Omega$

Center-frequency gain $= \frac{V_1}{V_i}(j\omega_0) \times \frac{V_{o1}}{V_1}$

$= 1 \times 2 = 2\ V/V$

13 Interchanging R_7 and C_6 in the circuit of Fig. 14.15 results in a filter having the following equivalent circuit. 14

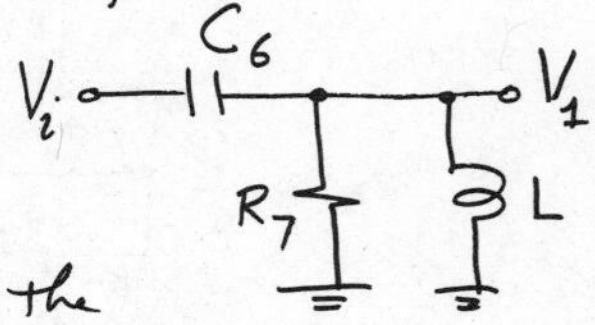

This is a second-order high-pass network. Thus the resulting filter is high pass.

14

$$CR = \frac{1}{\omega_0}$$

Thus, $C = \frac{1}{10 \times 10^3 \times 2\pi \times 10 \times 10^3} = 1.59\ nF$

$$R_d = QR = 20 \times 10 = 200\ k\Omega$$

$$R_g = \frac{R}{n_2}$$

where, Center-frequency gain $= n_2 Q$

For a unity center-frequency gain **14**

$$m_2 \times 20 = 1 \Rightarrow m_2 = \frac{1}{20}$$

Thus, $R_g = 20R = \underline{\underline{200\ k\Omega}}$

---

15 From Eqs. (14.36) and (14.37),

$$C_3 = C_4 = \omega_0 T_c C$$

$$= 2\pi \times 10 \times 10^3 \times \frac{1}{200 \times 10^3} \times 20 \quad pF$$

$$= \underline{\underline{6.283\ pF}}$$

From Eq. (14.39),

$$C_5 = \frac{C_4}{Q} = \frac{6.283}{20} = \underline{\underline{0.314\ pF}}$$

From Eq. (14.40)

$$\text{Center-frequency gain} = \frac{C_6}{C_5}$$

$$\Rightarrow C_6 = C_5 = \underline{\underline{0.314\ pF}}$$

---

16 $R_p = \omega_0 L Q_0$

$$= 2\pi \times 1 \times 10^6 \times 3.2 \times 10^{-6} \times 150$$

$$= \underline{\underline{3\ k\Omega}}$$

From Example 14.2, **14**

$$R = R_L // r_o // R_p = 2\ k\Omega$$

Thus

$$R_L // 10 // 3 = 2$$

$$\Rightarrow R_L = \underline{\underline{15\ k\Omega}}$$

17

$$Q = \frac{(R_1 // R_{in})}{\omega_0 L}$$

$$= \frac{(10^3 // 10^3)}{2\pi \times 455 \times 10^3 \times 5 \times 10^{-6}} = 35$$

$$BW = \frac{f_0}{Q} = \frac{455}{35} = \underline{\underline{13\ kHz}}$$

$$C_1 + C_{in} = \frac{1}{\omega_0^2 L}$$

$$= \frac{1}{(2\pi \times 455 \times 10^3)^2 \times 5 \times 10^{-6}}$$

$$= 24.47\ nF$$

$$C_1 = 24.47 - 0.2 = \underline{\underline{24.27\ nF}}$$

---

18 To just meet specifications **14**

$$Q = \frac{f_0}{BW}$$

$$= \frac{455}{10} = 45.5$$

Thus

$$\frac{(R_1 // n^2 R_{in})}{\omega_0 L} = 45.5$$

$$(R_1 // n^2 R_{in}) = 45.5 \times 2\pi \times 455 \times 10^3 \times 5 \times 10^{-6}$$

$$= 650\ \Omega$$

$$n^2 R_{in} = 1.86\ k\Omega$$

$$n = \sqrt{1.86/1} = \underline{1.36}$$

$$C_1 + \frac{C_{in}}{n^2} = \frac{1}{\omega_0^2 L} = 24.47$$

$$\Rightarrow C_1 = \underline{\underline{24.36\ nF}}$$

At resonance, the voltage developed across R_1 is $I(R_1 // n^2 R_{in})$. Thus, $V_{be} = IR/n$ and $I_c = g_m V_{be} = g_m IR/n$, hence

$$\frac{I_c}{I} = g_m R/n = \frac{40 \times 0.65}{1.36} = \underline{\underline{19.1\ A/A}}$$

---

19 From Eq. (14.50) **14**

$$200 = \left(\frac{f_0}{Q}\right)\sqrt{2^{1/2} - 1}$$

$$\Rightarrow \frac{f_0}{Q} = \underline{\underline{310.8\ kHz}}$$

$$C = \frac{1}{\omega_0^2 L}$$

$$= \frac{1}{(2\pi \times 10.7 \times 10^6)^2 \times 3 \times 10^{-6}} = \underline{\underline{73.7\ pF}}$$

$$\left(\frac{\omega_0}{Q}\right) = \frac{1}{CR}$$

$$\Rightarrow R = \frac{1}{73.7 \times 10^{-12} \times 2\pi \times 310.8 \times 10^3} = \underline{\underline{6.95\ k\Omega}}$$

---

20 From Eq. (14.55)

$$f_{01} = f_0 + \frac{2\pi B}{2\sqrt{2}}$$

$$= 10.7\ MHz + \frac{200\ kHz}{2\sqrt{2}}$$

$$= \underline{\underline{10.77\ MHz}}$$

$B_1 = \frac{B}{\sqrt{2}}$

$B_1 \text{ (in kHz)} = \frac{200}{\sqrt{2}} = \underline{\underline{141.4 \text{ kHz}}}$

From Eq. (14.56)

$f_{02} = f_0 - \frac{2\pi B}{2\sqrt{2}}$

$= 10.7 \text{ MHz} - \frac{200 \text{ kHz}}{2\sqrt{2}}$

$= \underline{\underline{10.63 \text{ MHz}}}$

$B_2 \text{ (in kHz)} = \frac{200}{\sqrt{2}} = \underline{\underline{141.4 \text{ kHz}}}$

For stage 1:

$C = \frac{1}{\omega_{01}^2 L} = \frac{1}{(2\pi \times 10.77 \times 10^6)^2 \times 3 \times 10^{-6}}$

$= \underline{72.8 \text{ PF}}$

$R = \frac{1}{C B_1} = \frac{1}{72.8 \times 10^{-12} \times 141.4 \times 2\pi \times 10^3}$

$= \underline{\underline{15.5 \text{ k}\Omega}}$

For Stage 2:

$C = \frac{1}{\omega_{02}^2 L} = \frac{1}{(2\pi \times 10.63 \times 10^6)^2 \times 3 \times 10^{-6}}$

$= \underline{\underline{74.7 \text{ PF}}}$

$R = \frac{1}{C B_2} = \frac{1}{74.7 \times 10^{-12} \times 2\pi \times 141.4 \times 10^3}$

$= \underline{\underline{15.1 \text{ k}\Omega}}$

---

21 Gain of stagger-tuned amplifier at f_0 is proportional to

$\frac{1}{\sqrt{2}} \times R_{stage\,1} \times \frac{1}{\sqrt{2}} \times R_{stage\,2}$

$= \frac{1}{2} \times 15.5 \times 15.1 = 117$

Gain of synchronous-tuned amplifier at f_0 is proportional to

$R_{stage\,1} \times R_{stage\,2}$

$= 6.95 \times 6.95 = 48.3$

Thus the ratio is $\frac{117}{48.3} = \underline{\underline{2.42}}$

22

(a) $L(s) = \left(1 + \frac{R_2}{R_1}\right) \frac{Z_p}{Z_p + Z_s}$

$= \left(1 + \frac{R_2}{R_1}\right) \frac{1}{1 + Z_s Y_p}$

$= \left(1 + \frac{20.3}{10}\right) \frac{1}{1 + (R + \frac{1}{sC})(\frac{1}{R} + sC)}$

$= \frac{3.03}{3 + sCR + \frac{1}{sCR}}$

where $R = 10 \text{ k}\Omega$ and $C = 16 \text{ nF}$

Thus $L(s) = \frac{3.03}{3 + s \times 16 \times 10^{-5} + \frac{1}{s \times 16 \times 10^{-5}}}$

The closed-loop poles are found by setting $L(s) = 1$, that is, they are the values of s satisfying

$3 + s \times 16 \times 10^{-5} + \frac{1}{s \times 16 \times 10^{-5}} = 3.03$

$\Rightarrow s = \frac{10^5}{16} (0.015 \pm j)$

(b) The frequency of oscillation is $(10^5/16)$ rad/s or $\underline{1 \text{ kHz}}$.

(c) Refer to Fig. 14.35. At the positive peak $\hat{V}_o$, the voltage at node b will be one diode drop (0.7 V) above the voltage v_1 which is about $\frac{1}{3}$ of v_O; thus $V_b = 0.7 + \frac{\hat{V}_o}{3}$. Now if we neglect the current through D_2 in comparison with the currents through R_5 and R_6 we find that

$\frac{\hat{V}_o - V_b}{R_5} \simeq \frac{V_b - (-15)}{R_6}$

Thus

$\frac{\hat{V}_o - V_b}{1} = \frac{V_b + 15}{3} \Rightarrow \hat{V}_o = \frac{4}{3} V_b + 5$

$\hat{V}_o = \frac{4}{3}\left(0.7 + \frac{\hat{V}_o}{3}\right) + 5$

which leads to $\hat{V}_o = 10.68$ V.

From symmetry we see that the negative peak is equal to the positive peak. Thus the output peak-to-peak voltage is $\underline{21.36 \text{ V}}$.

14

23 (a) For oscillations to start, $\frac{R_2}{R_1} = 2$. Thus the potentiometer should be set so that its resistance to ground is $\underline{20\ k\Omega}$.

(b) $f_0 = \frac{1}{2\pi CR}$

$$= \frac{1}{2\pi \times 16 \times 10^{-9} \times 10 \times 10^{3}} = \underline{1\ kHz}$$

24

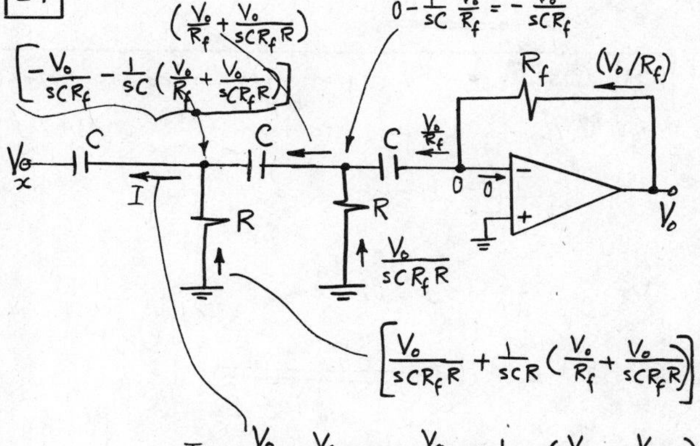

$$I = \frac{V_o}{R_f} + \frac{V_o}{sCR_fR} + \frac{V_o}{sCR_fR} + \frac{1}{sCR}\left(\frac{V_o}{R_f} + \frac{V_o}{sCR_fR}\right)$$

$$V_x = -\frac{V_o}{sCR_f} - \frac{1}{sC}\left(\frac{V_o}{R_f} + \frac{V_o}{sCR_fR}\right) - \frac{1}{sC} I$$

14

$$V_x = -\frac{V_o}{sCR_f}\left(2 + \frac{1}{sCR}\right)$$

$$- \frac{V_o}{sCR_f}\left[1 + \frac{1}{sCR} + \frac{1}{sCR} + \frac{1}{sCR}\left(1 + \frac{1}{sCR}\right)\right]$$

$$= -\frac{V_o}{sCR_f}\left(3 + \frac{4}{sCR} + \frac{1}{s^2C^2R^2}\right)$$

Thus,

$$\frac{V_o}{V_x} = \frac{-sCR_f}{3 + \frac{4}{sCR} + \frac{1}{s^2C^2R^2}}$$

$$\frac{V_o}{V_x}(j\omega) = \frac{-j\omega CR_f}{3 - j\frac{4}{\omega CR} - \frac{1}{\omega^2C^2R^2}}$$

$$= \underline{\underline{\frac{\omega^2C^2RR_f}{4 + j\left(3\omega CR - \frac{1}{\omega CR}\right)}}}$$

---

25 The circuit will oscillate at the value of ω that makes $\frac{V_o}{V_x}(j\omega)$ a real number. It follows that ω_0 is obtained from

$$3\omega_0 CR = \frac{1}{\omega_0 CR} \Rightarrow \omega_0 = \frac{1}{\sqrt{3}\,CR}$$

14

Thus,

$$f_0 = \frac{1}{2\pi \times \sqrt{3} \times 16 \times 10^{-9} \times 10 \times 10^{3}}$$

$$= \underline{\underline{574.3\ Hz}}$$

For oscillations to begin, the magnitude of $\frac{V_o}{V_x}(j\omega)$ should equal to (or greater than) unity, that is

$$\frac{\omega_0^2 C^2 R R_f}{4} \geq 1$$

Thus the minimum value of R_f is

$$R_f = \frac{4}{\omega_0^2 C^2 R}$$

$$= \frac{4R}{\omega_0^2 C^2 R^2} = \frac{4R}{\frac{1}{3}} = 12R$$

or $\underline{\underline{120\ k\Omega}}$.

---

26 $\omega_0 = 1/CR \Longrightarrow CR = \frac{1}{2\pi \times 10^3}$

For $C = 16$ nF, $R = \frac{1}{2\pi \times 10^3 \times 16 \times 10^{-9}} = \underline{\underline{10\ k\Omega}}$

14

To find the amplitude of the output sinusoid we note that the square wave v_2 will have a 1.4-V peak-to-peak amplitude. The filter which has a gain of 2 at ω_0 will provide a sinusoid v_1 of $2 \times \frac{4}{\pi} \times 1.4$

$= \underline{\underline{3.6\ V}}$ peak-to-peak amplitude.

27

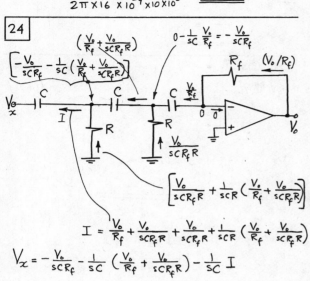

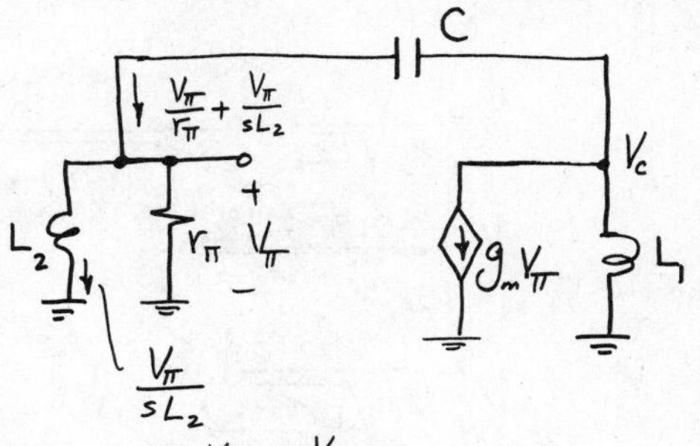

$$V_c = V_\pi + \frac{1}{sC}\left(\frac{V_\pi}{r_\pi} + \frac{V_\pi}{sL_2}\right)$$

Writing a node equation at the collector yields

$$\frac{V_\pi}{r_\pi} + \frac{V_\pi}{sL_2} + g_m V_\pi + \frac{V_\pi}{sL_1} + \frac{1}{s^2 L_1 C}\left(\frac{V_\pi}{r_\pi} + \frac{V_\pi}{sL_2}\right) = 0$$

$$\left(\frac{1}{r_\pi} + g_m\right) + \left(\frac{1}{sL_2} + \frac{1}{sL_1}\right) + \frac{1}{s^2 L_1 C r_\pi} + \frac{1}{s^3 L_1 L_2 C} = 0$$

Substituting $s = j\omega$,

$$\left(g_m + \frac{1}{r_\pi} - \frac{1}{\omega^2 L_1 C r_\pi}\right) - j\left(\frac{1}{\omega L_1} + \frac{1}{\omega L_2} - \frac{1}{\omega^3 L_1 L_2 C}\right) = 0$$

For oscillations to start, both the real and the imaginary parts must be zero, thus

$$\frac{1}{\omega_0 L_1} + \frac{1}{\omega_0 L_2} - \frac{1}{\omega_0^3 L_1 L_2 C} = 0$$

$$\Rightarrow \omega_0 = \frac{1}{\sqrt{(L_1 + L_2)C}}$$

and

$$g_m + \frac{1}{r_\pi} = \frac{1}{\omega_0^2 L_1 C r_\pi}$$

$$g_m r_\pi + 1 = \frac{1}{\omega_0^2 L_1 C}$$

Substituting $g_m r_\pi = \beta_0$ and $\omega_0^2 = \frac{1}{(L_1+L_2)C}$ gives,

$$\beta_0 + 1 = 1 + \frac{L_2}{L_1}$$

Thus,

$$\underline{\underline{\frac{L_2}{L_1} = \beta_0}}$$

---

28 Oscillation are just guaranteed to start if C_1/C_2 is chosen according to Eq.(14.72),

$$\frac{C_1}{C_2} = \beta_0$$
$$= 50$$

Using Eq.(14.71) we have

$$10^6 = \frac{1}{\sqrt{100 \times 10^{-6} \frac{C_1 C_2}{C_1 + C_2}}}$$

$$= \frac{100}{\sqrt{\frac{C_1 C_2}{C_1 + C_2}}}$$

Thus

$$\frac{C_1 C_2}{C_1 + C_2} = 10^{-8}\ \text{F}$$

Substituting $C_1 = 50 C_2$

$$\frac{50 C_2^2}{51 C_2} = 10^{-8}$$

$$\Rightarrow C_2 \simeq 10^{-8}\ \text{F} = \underline{\underline{0.01\ \mu\text{F}}}$$

$$C_1 = 50 \times 10^{-8}\ \text{F} = \underline{\underline{0.5\ \mu\text{F}}}$$

---

29 From Eq. (14.74),

$$f_s = \frac{1}{2\pi\sqrt{LC_s}} = \frac{1}{2\pi\sqrt{0.52 \times 0.012 \times 10^{-12}}}$$

$$= \underline{2.015\ \text{MHz}}$$

From Eq.(14.75)

$$f_p = \frac{1}{2\pi\sqrt{L\frac{C_s C_p}{C_s + C_p}}}$$

$$= \frac{1}{2\pi\sqrt{0.52 \times \frac{0.012 \times 4}{0.012 + 4} \times 10^{-12}}} = \underline{\underline{2.018\ \text{MHz}}}$$

$$Q = \frac{\omega_0 L}{r}$$

$$\simeq \frac{\omega_s L}{r}$$

$$= \frac{2\pi \times 2.015 \times 10^6 \times 0.52}{120}$$

$$\simeq \underline{\underline{55{,}000}}$$

Chapter 15 — Exercises

1 (a) $V_{IH} = 2\ V \quad V_{IL} = 0.8\ V$

$V_{OH} = 2.4\ V \quad V_{OL} = 0.4\ V$

$$NM_H = V_{OH} - V_{IH} = \underline{\underline{0.4\ V}}$$

$$NM_L = V_{IL} - V_{OL} = \underline{\underline{0.4\ V}}$$

(b) Average static power dissipation/gate

$= \text{Average supply current} \times V^+ / 4$ (↑ number of gates/package)

$= \left(\frac{12+4}{2}\right) \times 5 \ /4$

$= \underline{\underline{10\ mW}}$

(c) When the gate output changes from V_{OL} to V_{OH}, the energy stored in the load capacitor changes by $\left(\frac{1}{2}C_L V_{OH}^2 - \frac{1}{2}C_L V_{OL}^2\right)$. The charge supplied to C_L is

$$Q = C_L(V_{OH} - V_{OL})$$

This charge is drawn from the supply voltage, thus the energy drawn from the supply is

$$Q V^+ = C_L(V_{OH} - V_{OL})V^+$$

It follows that the energy lost in the gate circuit is

$$C_L(V_{OH} - V_{OL})V^+ - \left(\tfrac{1}{2}C_L V_{OH}^2 - \tfrac{1}{2}C_L V_{OL}^2\right)$$

Next consider the situation as the gate output voltage changes from V_{OH} to V_{OL}. The energy stored on C_L changes from $\frac{1}{2}C_L V_{OH}^2$ to $\frac{1}{2}C_L V_{OL}^2$. Thus the energy lost in the gate circuit is $\left(\frac{1}{2}C_L V_{OH}^2 - \frac{1}{2}C_L V_{OL}^2\right)$. The total energy lost in the gate circuit per cycle is the sum of the

two quantities found above, namely

$$C_L(V_{OH} - V_{OL})V^+$$

If the gate is switched f times/second, the dynamic power dissipation will be

$$P = f C_L (V_{OH} - V_{OL}) V^+$$

$= 10^6 \times 45 \times 10^{-12} \times (3.3 - 0.22) \times 5$

$= \underline{\underline{0.7\ mW}}$

(d) $DP = \left(\frac{11+7}{2}\right) \times 10^{-9} \times 10 \times 10^{-3}$

$= 90 \times 10^{-12}\ J$

$= \underline{\underline{90\ \text{picojoules}}}$

---

2 $P = f C_L V^{+2}$

$= 10^6 \times 50 \times 10^{-12} \times 10^2 = \underline{\underline{5\ mW}}$

Average supply current $= \frac{P}{V^+} = \frac{5\ mW}{10\ V} = \underline{\underline{0.5\ mA}}$

---

3 $V_{OH} = V^+ = \underline{\underline{5.5\ V}}$

$$V_{OL} = V^+ \frac{R_{on}}{R_{on} + R_L}$$

$= 5.5 \times \frac{1}{1+10} = \underline{\underline{0.5\ V}}$

---

4 To find t_{PLH}:

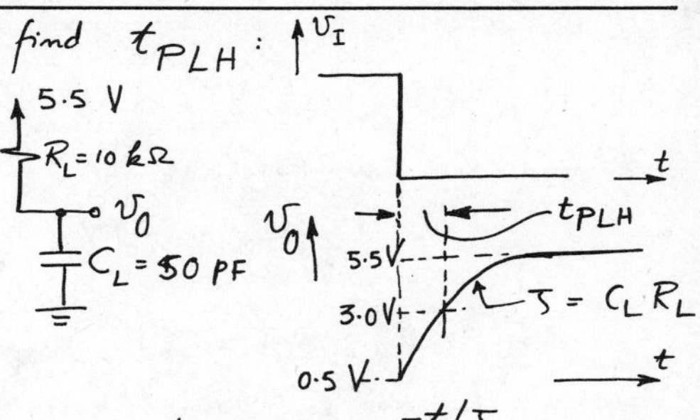

$v_O(t) = 5.5 - (5.5 - 0.5)e^{-t/\tau}$

$3 = 5.5 - 5e^{-t_{PLH}/\tau}$

$\Rightarrow t_{PLH} = \tau \ln 2$

$= 50 \times 10^{-12} \times 10 \times 10^{-3} \times \ln 2$

$= \underline{\underline{347\ ns}}$

To find t_{PHL}:

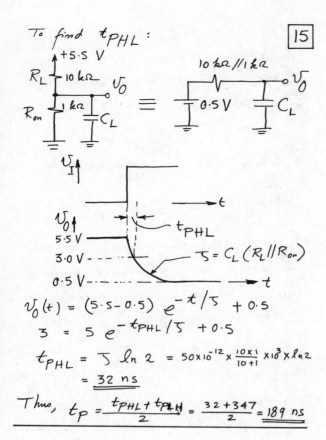

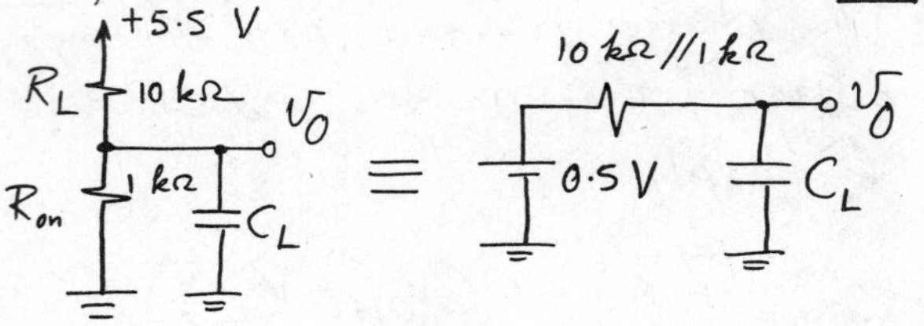

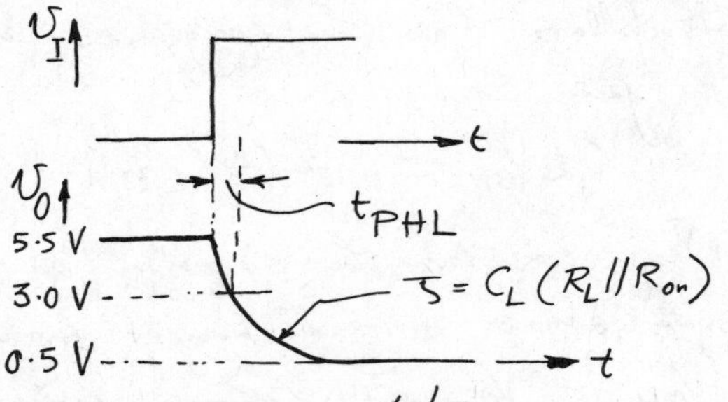

$$v_O(t) = (5.5 - 0.5)\, e^{-t/\tau} + 0.5$$

$$3 = 5\, e^{-t_{PHL}/\tau} + 0.5$$

$$t_{PHL} = \tau \ln 2 = 50 \times 10^{-12} \times \frac{10 \times 1}{10+1} \times 10^3 \times \ln 2$$

$$= \underline{32 \text{ ns}}$$

Thus, $t_P = \dfrac{t_{PHL} + t_{PLH}}{2} = \dfrac{32 + 347}{2} = \underline{\underline{189 \text{ ns}}}$

---

5 $L_1 = 5\ \mu m \quad W_1 = 15\ \mu m$

$W_2 = 5\ \mu m \quad L_2 = 15\ \mu m$

$$\text{Area} = W_1 L_1 + W_2 L_2 = \underline{\underline{150\ \mu m^2}}$$

$$K_R \equiv \frac{K_1}{K_2} = \frac{(W/L)_1}{(W/L)_2} = \frac{3}{1/3} = \underline{\underline{9}}$$

For K_R to become $4 \times 9 = 36$, we use $(W/L)_1 = 6$ and $(W/L)_2 = \frac{1}{6}$.

---

6 Substitute in Eq. (15.11):

$v_I = 4\ V$, $V_{t1} = V_{t2} = 1\ V$, $v_O = 0.1\ V$, and $V_{DD} = 5\ V$. Thus

$$K_1 [2 \times 3 \times 0.1 - 0.01] = K_2 (5 - 0.1 - 1)^2$$

Thus,

$$K_R \equiv \frac{K_1}{K_2} = \underline{\underline{26}}$$

7

$$t_P = \frac{0.4 \times 0.1 \times 10^{-12}}{\frac{1}{2} \times 20 \times \frac{1}{3} \times 10^{-6} \times 4} = \underline{\underline{3 \text{ ns}}}$$

$$DP = 0.2 \times 0.1 \times 10^{-12} \times 5 \times 4 = \underline{\underline{0.4 \text{ pJ}}}$$

---

8 $DP = 0.2 \times 10 \times 10^{-12} \times 5 \times 4$

$$= \underline{\underline{40 \text{ pJ}}}$$

---

9 Before solving this Exercise the reader is urged to thoroughly review part (a) of Example 15.2.

$$V_{OH} = V_{DD} = \underline{\underline{5\ V}}$$

To find V_{OL} we have:

$$i_{D1} = K_1 [2(5-1) V_{OL} - V_{OL}^2]$$

$$i_{D2} = K_2 |V_{tD}|^2 = 9 K_2$$

Equating i_{D1} and i_{D2}, substituting $K_1/K_2 = 4$, and solving the resulting quadratic equation, we get

$$V_{OL} \simeq \underline{\underline{0.3\ V}}$$

To determine V_{IH} we assume that Q_1 is in the triode region while Q_2 is in pinch-off and equate their drain currents

to obtain

$$K_1 [2(v_I - 1) v_O - v_O^2] = 9 K_2$$

Substituting $K_2 = K_1/4$ gives

$$2(v_I - 1) v_O - v_O^2 = \frac{9}{4} \qquad (1)$$

Differentiating with respect to v_I yields

$$2(v_I - 1) \frac{dv_O}{dv_I} + 2v_O - 2v_O \frac{dv_O}{dv_I} = 0$$

Substituting $v_I = V_{IH}$ and $dv_O/dv_I = -1$ results in

$$v_O = \frac{1}{2}(V_{IH} - 1) \qquad (2)$$

Substituting $v_I = V_{IH}$ in Eq. (1) and replacing v_O with the value given in Eq. (2) results in a quadratic equation in V_{IH} whose solution is

$$V_{IH} = \underline{\underline{2.7\ V}}$$

The corresponding value of $v_O = 0.9\ V$. Thus Q_1 and Q_2 are in their assumed states.

15

To determine V_{IL} we assume that Q_1 is in pinch-off and Q_2 is in the triode region, and equate their currents. Since we expect v_O to be close to 5 V, we use $V_{tD} \simeq -2.2$ V (see Fig 15.12c). The resulting equation is

$$(v_I - 1)^2 = 1.1\,(5 - v_O) - \tfrac{1}{4}\,(5 - v_O)^2 \quad (3)$$

Differentiating relative to v_I, we obtain

$$2(v_I - 1) = -1.1\,\frac{dv_O}{dv_I} + \frac{1}{2}\,(5 - v_O)\,\frac{dv_O}{dv_I}$$

Substituting $v_I = V_{IL}$ and $dv_O/dv_I = -1$ gives

$$v_O = 4\,V_{IL} - 1.2 \quad (4)$$

Substituting $v_I = V_{IL}$ in Eq. (3) and for v_O from Eq. (4) results in a quadratic equation in V_{IL} whose solution is

$$V_{IL} = \underline{\underline{1.5\ \text{V}}}$$

The corresponding value of $v_O = 4.8$ V.

15

The noise margins can now be calculated as follows:

$$NM_H = V_{OH} - V_{IH} = 5 - 2.7 = \underline{\underline{2.3\ \text{V}}}$$

$$NM_L = V_{IL} - V_{OL} = 1.5 - 0.3 = \underline{\underline{1.2\ \text{V}}}$$

---

10 Refer to Fig. 15.13. To find the average discharge current, I_{HL}:

$$i_{D1}(D) = K_1\,(5-1)^2$$

$$= \tfrac{1}{2} \times 20 \times 2 \times 16 = 320\ \mu\text{A}$$

At point N, $v_O = \frac{1}{2}\,(V_{OH} + V_{OL})$

$$= \tfrac{1}{2}\,(5 + 0.3) = 2.65\ \text{V}$$

Thus Q_1 will be in the triode region and

$$i_{D1}(N) = K_1\left[2\,(5-1) \times 2.65 - 2.65^2\right]$$

$$= \tfrac{1}{2} \times 20 \times 2\,\left[8 \times 2.65 - 2.65^2\right]$$

$$= 284\ \mu\text{A}$$

If we neglect $i_{D2}(M)$ then

15

$$I_{HL} \cong \frac{i_{D1}(D) + i_{D1}(N)}{2}$$

$$= \frac{320 + 284}{2} \simeq \underline{\underline{300\ \mu\text{A}}}$$

To find the average charging current, I_{LH}, we determine $i_{D2}(A)$ and $i_{D2}(M)$ as follows:

$$i_{D2}(A) = K_2\,|V_{tD}|^2$$

$$= \tfrac{1}{2} \times 20 \times \tfrac{1}{2} \times 3^2 = 45\ \mu\text{A}$$

At point M, $v_O = 2.65$ V, thus Q_2 will have (Eq. (15.24))

$$V_{tD} = -3 + 0.5\left[\sqrt{2.65 + 0.6} - \sqrt{0.6}\right]$$

$$= -2.5\ \text{V}$$

Thus Q_2 will be in the triode region and its current is determined from Eq. (15.23),

15

$$i_{D2}(M) = \tfrac{1}{2} \times 20 \times \tfrac{1}{2}\left[2 \times 2.5 \times (5 - 2.65) - (5 - 2.65)^2\right]$$

$$= 31\ \mu\text{A}$$

Thus,

$$I_{LH} = \frac{i_{D2}(A) + i_{D2}(M)}{2}$$

$$= \frac{45 + 31}{2} = \underline{\underline{38\ \mu\text{A}}}$$

Now we can find t_{PHL},

$$t_{PHL} = \frac{C\left[V_{OH} - \frac{1}{2}(V_{OH} + V_{OL})\right]}{I_{HL}}$$

$$= \frac{0.1 \times 10^{-12}\,[5 - 2.65]}{300 \times 10^{-6}} = \underline{\underline{0.8\ \text{ns}}}$$

and t_{PLH},

$$t_{PLH} = \frac{C\left[\frac{1}{2}(V_{OH} + V_{OL}) - V_{OL}\right]}{I_{LH}}$$

$$= \frac{0.1 \times 10^{-12} \times [2.65 - 0.3]}{38 \times 10^{-6}} = \underline{\underline{6.2\ \text{ns}}}$$

15

Finally, the propagation delay is found,

$$t_P \equiv \frac{1}{2}\left(t_{PHL} + t_{PLH}\right)$$

$$= \frac{1}{2}\left(0.8 + 6.2\right) = \underline{\underline{3.5\ ns}}$$

---

11 When the output is high, the inverter current is zero and thus the static power dissipation is zero. When the output is low at $V_{OL} = 0.3\ V$, the inverter current is $K_2 |V_{tD}|^2 = \frac{1}{2} \times 20 \times \frac{1}{2} \times 3^2 = 45\ \mu A$. Thus the power dissipation is $5 \times 45 = 225\ \mu W$.

The average static power dissipation is

$$P_D = \frac{0 + 225}{2} = 112.5\ \mu W$$

It follows that

$$DP = 3.5\ ns \times 112.5\ \mu W \simeq \underline{\underline{0.4\ pJ}}$$

Alternatively, using Eq. (15.29)

$$DP \simeq \frac{1}{8 \times 0.9} \times 0.1 \times 10^{-12} \times 5^2 = \underline{\underline{0.35\ pJ}}$$

---

12 Since v_O will be small we shall assume that $V_{tD} \simeq V_{tD0} = -3\ V$.

15

(a) With one input high:

$$\frac{1}{2} \times \mu_n C_{ox} \times \frac{12}{6}\left[2 \times (5-1) \times V_O - V_O^2\right]$$

$$= \frac{1}{2} \times \mu_n C_{ox} \times \frac{6}{12} \times 3^2$$

$$\Rightarrow V_O^2 - 8 V_O + \frac{9}{4} = 0$$

Thus, $V_O = \underline{\underline{0.29\ V}}$

(b) With both inputs high:

$$2 \times \frac{1}{2} \times \mu_n C_{ox} \times \frac{12}{6}\left[2 \times (5-1) \times V_O - V_O^2\right]$$

$$= \frac{1}{2} \times \mu_n C_{ox} \times \frac{6}{12} \times 3^2$$

$$\Rightarrow 2 V_O^2 - 16 V_O + \frac{9}{4} = 0$$

Thus, $V_O = \underline{\underline{0.14\ V}}$

---

13 Each of the input transistors will have

$$W = 3 \times 12 = \underline{\underline{36\ \mu m}}$$

and, $L = \underline{\underline{6\ \mu m}}$

---

14 Using Eqn. (15.37),

15

$$V_{IL} = \frac{1}{8}\left(3 V_{DD} + 2 V_t\right)$$

$$= \frac{1}{8}\left(3 \times 5 + 2 \times 1\right) = \underline{\underline{2.1\ V}}$$

Using Eq. (15.36),

$$V_{IH} = \frac{1}{8}\left(5 V_{DD} - 2 V_t\right)$$

$$= \frac{1}{8}\left(5 \times 5 - 2 \times 1\right) = \underline{\underline{2.9\ V}}$$

Using Eqs. (15.38) and (15.39),

$$NM_H = NM_L = \frac{1}{8}\left(3 V_{DD} + 2 V_t\right)$$

$$= \frac{1}{8}\left(3 \times 5 + 2 \times 1\right)$$

$$= \underline{\underline{2.1\ V}}$$

---

15 Q_N will be operating in the triode region and Q_P will be off, thus

$$i = \frac{1}{2} \times 20 \times 20\left[2(10-2) \times 0.5 - 0.5^2\right]$$

$$= \underline{\underline{1.55\ mA}}$$

---

16 The peak current occurs when $v_I = \frac{V_{DD}}{2} = 5\ V$. Both Q_N and Q_P will be in pinch-off and conducting equal currents of

15

$$I_{peak} = \frac{1}{2} \times 20 \times 20\ (5-2)^2 = \underline{\underline{1.8\ mA}}$$

---

17 $P_D = f C V_{DD}^2$

$$= 2 \times 10^6 \times 15 \times 10^{-12} \times 10^2$$

$$= 3\ mW$$

$$\text{Average supply current} = \frac{P_D}{V_{DD}}$$

$$= \frac{3}{10} = \underline{\underline{0.3\ mA}}$$

---

18 $K_p = K_n = \frac{1}{2} \times 20 \times \frac{10}{5} = 20\ \mu A/V^2$

Thus using Eq. (15.44)

$$t_{PHL} = t_{PLH} = \frac{0.1 \times 10^{-12}}{20 \times 10^{-6}(5-1)}\left[\frac{1}{5-1} + \frac{1}{2}\ln\left(\frac{15-4}{5}\right)\right]$$

$$= \underline{\underline{0.8\ ns}}$$

Thus, $t_P = \underline{\underline{0.8\ ns}}$

19 $t_P = t_{PHL} = t_{PLH}$

$$= \frac{15 \times 10^{-12}}{\frac{1}{2} \times 20 \times 20 \times 10^{-6} (10-2)} \left[\frac{2}{10-2} + \frac{1}{2} \ln\left(\frac{30-8}{10}\right) \right]$$

$$= \underline{\underline{6 \text{ ns}}}$$

---

20 $P_D = f C V_{DD}^2$

$$= 50 \times 10^6 \times 0.1 \times 10^{-12} \times 5^2 = 125 \ \mu W$$

$$DP = P_D t_P$$

$$= 125 \times 10^{-6} \times 0.8 \times 10^{-9}$$

$$= 0.1 \text{ pJ}$$

---

21 (a) NOR:

$\left(\frac{W}{L}\right)_n = 2$

$L_n = 5 \ \mu m \qquad \underline{\underline{W_n = 10 \ \mu m}}$

Using (15.47) with $N = 2$ yields

$(W/L)_p = 4 \times 2 = 8$

$L_p = 5 \ \mu m \qquad W_p = 40 \ \mu m$

Total area $= 2 W_n L_n + 2 W_p L_p$

$$= 2 \times 10 \times 5 + 2 \times 40 \times 5$$

$$= \underline{\underline{500 \ \mu m^2}}$$

(b) NAND:

$W_n / L_n = 4$ (because with both inputs high Q_1 and Q_3 are in series resulting in an effective channel length of $2L_n$)

$L_n = 5 \ \mu m$

$\underline{W_n = 20 \ \mu m}$

Using Eq. (15.48) with $N = 2$ yields

$\left(\frac{W}{L}\right)_p = 4$

$L_p = 5 \ \mu m$

$\underline{W_p = 20 \ \mu m}$

Total area $= 2 W_n L_n + 2 W_p L_p$

$$= 2 \times 20 \times 5 + 2 \times 20 \times 5$$

$$= \underline{\underline{400 \ \mu m^2}}$$

---

22 (a) $\Delta V = 0.5$ V

Thus, $V_{OL} = 0.5$ V,

and, $NM_L = V_{IL} - V_{OL} = 1.5 - 0.5 = \underline{\underline{1 \text{ V}}}$

$V_{OH} = V_{DD} - \Delta V = 5 - 0.5 = 4.5$ V

$NM_H = V_{OH} - V_{IH} = 4.5 - 3.5 = \underline{\underline{1 \text{ V}}}$

(b) $\Delta V = 1$ V

$V_{OL} = 1$ V

$NM_L = V_{IL} - V_{OL} = 3 - 1 = \underline{\underline{2 \text{ V}}}$

$V_{OH} = 10 - 1 = 9$ V

$NM_H = V_{OH} - V_{IH} = 9 - 7 = \underline{\underline{2 \text{ V}}}$

(c) $\Delta V = 1.5$ V

$V_{OL} = 1.5$ V

$NM_L = V_{IL} - V_{OL} = 4 - 1.5 = \underline{\underline{2.5 \text{ V}}}$

$V_{OH} = 15 - 1.5 = 13.5$ V

$NM_H = V_{OH} - V_{IH} = 13.5 - 11 = \underline{\underline{2.5 \text{ V}}}$

---

23 The width of the triggering pulse must be at least equal to $(t_{PHL} + t_{PLH})$. From the results of Exercise 15.10, $t_{PHL} = 0.8$ ns and $t_{PLH} = 6.2$ ns. Thus, the width of the triggering pulse is $\geq \underline{\underline{7 \text{ ns}}}$.

---

24 Refer to Fig. 15.34c. The exponential rise of v_{I2} can be expressed as

$$v_{I2} = V_{DD} - \Delta V_1 e^{-t/C(R+R_{on})}$$

where $t=0$ at the beginning of the pulse interval T. The end of the pulse interval (i.e. $t = T$) is determined by $v_{I2} = V_{th}$, thus

$$V_{th} = V_{DD} - \Delta V_1 e^{-T/C(R+R_{on})}$$

Substituting for ΔV_1 from Eq. (15.51) and arranging terms yields

$$e^{T/C(R+R_{on})} = \frac{R}{R+R_{on}} \frac{V_{DD}}{V_{DD} - V_{th}}$$

Thus

$$\underline{\underline{T = C(R+R_{on}) \ln\left(\frac{R}{R+R_{on}} \frac{V_{DD}}{V_{DD} - V_{th}}\right)}}$$

25 Refer to Fig. (15.37). The exponential rise of v_{I1} is described by

$$v_{I1} = V_{DD}\left(1 - e^{-t/CR}\right)$$

$v_{I1} = V_{th}$ at $t = T_1$, thus

$$V_{th} = V_{DD}\left(1 - e^{-T_1/CR}\right)$$

$$\Rightarrow \quad T_1 = CR \ln \frac{V_{DD}}{V_{DD} - V_{th}}$$

The exponential decay of v_{I1} is described by

$$v_{I1} = V_{DD}\, e^{-t/CR}$$

$v_{I1} = V_{th}$ at $t = T_2$, thus

$$V_{th} = V_{DD}\, e^{-T_2/CR}$$

$$\Rightarrow \quad T_2 = CR \ln\left(\frac{V_{DD}}{V_{th}}\right)$$

$$T = T_1 + T_2 = CR\left(\ln \frac{V_{DD}}{V_{DD} - V_{th}} + \ln \frac{V_{DD}}{V_{th}}\right)$$

Chapter 16 — Exercises

1 From Eq. (16.3)

$$I_{SC} = \frac{\alpha_F I_{SE}}{\alpha_R} = \frac{1 \times 10^{-14}}{0.02} = \underline{\underline{50 \times 10^{-14}\ \text{A}}}$$

Since the scale current is proportional to the junction area, the CBJ must be $\underline{\underline{50}}$ times as large as the EBJ.

Using Eq. (16.12),

$$\beta_R = \frac{\alpha_R}{1 - \alpha_R} = \frac{0.02}{1 - 0.02} \simeq \underline{\underline{0.02}}$$

---

2 Substituting $v_{BC} = 0$ in Eq. (16.8) yields

$$i_E = \frac{I_S}{\alpha_F}\left(e^{v_{BE}/V_T} - 1\right) = \frac{I_S}{\alpha_F}\left(e^{v/V_T} - 1\right) \simeq \frac{I_S}{\alpha_F}\, e^{v/V_T}$$

Q.E.D.

---

3 $I_B = 1$ mA

For $\beta_{forced} = 1$, $I_C = 1$ mA and $V_{CEsat} = 76$ mV

For $\beta_{forced} = 10$, $I_C = 10$ mA and $V_{CEsat} = 123$ mV

Thus $$R_{CEsat} = \frac{123 - 76}{10 - 1} = \underline{\underline{5.2\ \Omega}}$$

---

4 $V_{BC} = 0.6$ V, thus $V_B = +0.6$ V and

$$I_B = \frac{V_I - V_B}{R_B} = \frac{5 - 0.6}{1} = 4.4\ \text{mA}$$

For $R_C = 1$ kΩ assume that the transistor is in the reverse active mode. Thus

$$I_1 = \beta_R I_B = 0.1 \times 4.4 = 0.44\ \text{mA}$$

$$V_E = V_{CC} - I_1 R_C = 5 - 0.44 \times 1 = \underline{+4.56\ \text{V}}$$

Since $V_E > V_B$, the transistor is indeed in the reverse active mode, as assumed.

For $R_C = 10$ kΩ, assume reverse active mode, thus

$$I_1 = \beta_R I_B = 0.1 \times 4.4 = 0.44\ \text{mA}$$

$$V_E = V_{CC} - I_1 R_C = 5 - 4.4 = \underline{+0.6\ \text{V}}$$

Since $V_E = V_B$, the BJT is still in the reverse active mode, as assumed.

For $R_C = 100$ kΩ, assume that the BJT is in the reverse saturation mode. Since V_{ECsat} is likely to be very small we shall assume $V_E \simeq 0$ and thus

$$I_1 \simeq \frac{V_{CC} - 0}{R_C} = \frac{5}{100} = 0.05\ \text{mA}.$$

A better estimate of V_E can now be found by computing V_{ECsat} using Eq. (16.17),

$$V_E = V_{ECsat} = 25 \ln \frac{1 + \frac{1}{50} + \left(\frac{0.05}{4.4}\right)\left(\frac{1}{50}\right)}{1 - \left(\frac{0.05}{4.4}\right)\left(\frac{1}{0.1}\right)}$$

$$= \underline{\underline{3.5\ \text{mV}}}$$

Note that since $I_1 < \beta_R I_B$ the BJT is indeed saturated.

5

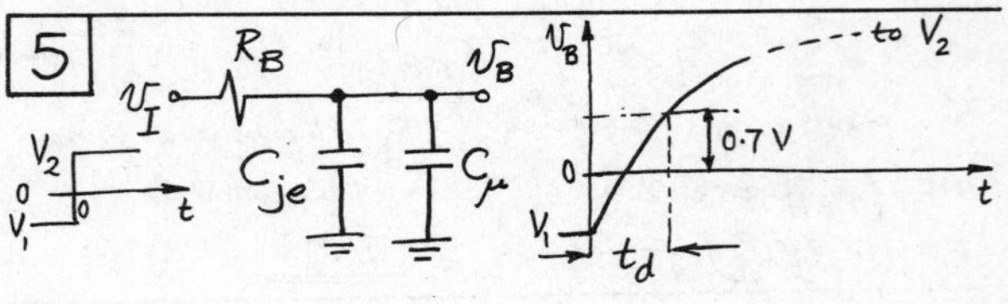

$$v_B = V_2 - (V_2 - V_1)\, e^{-t/\tau}$$

where $\tau = (C_{je} + C_\mu) R_B$

$$0.7 = V_2 - (V_2 - V_1)\, e^{-t_d/\tau}$$

$$(V_2 - V_1)\, e^{-t_d/\tau} = V_2 - 0.7$$

$$t_d = \tau \ln\left(\frac{V_2 - V_1}{V_2 - 0.7}\right)$$

$$t_d = (C_{je} + C_\mu) R_B \ln[(V_2 - V_1)/(V_2 - 0.7)]$$

6 Refer to Fig. E16.6.

$$V_{OH} = V_{CC} - I R_C$$

where $I = \dfrac{V_{CC} - V_{BE}}{R_C + \frac{R_B}{N}}$

Thus

$$V_{OH} = V_{CC} - R_C \frac{V_{CC} - V_{BE}}{R_C + R_B/N} \quad \text{Q.E.D.}$$

For $V_{CC} = +3$ V, $R_C = 640\ \Omega$, $R_B = 450\ \Omega$,

16

$V_{BE} = 0.7$ V, and $N = 5$,

$$V_{OH} = 3 - 640 \frac{3 - 0.7}{640 + \frac{450}{5}} = 0.98\ \text{V} \simeq 1\ \text{V}$$

7 (a)

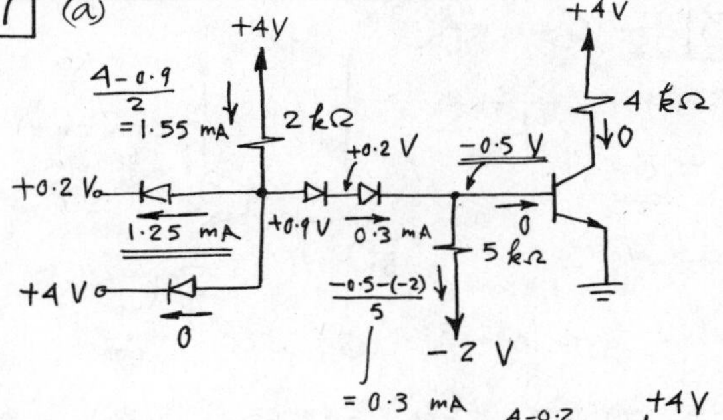

(b)

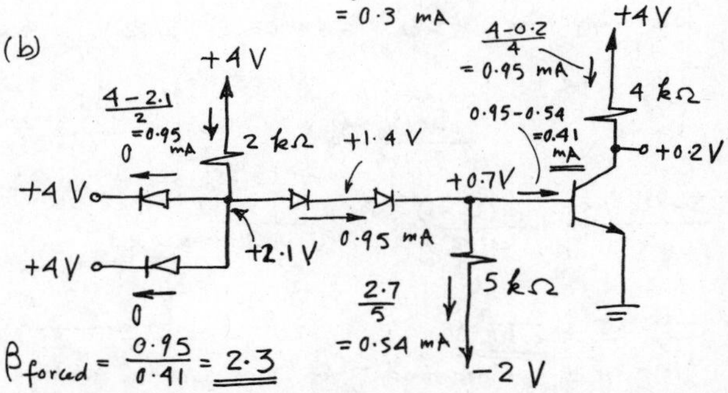

$$\beta_{forced} = \frac{0.95}{0.41} = 2.3$$

8 (a)

16

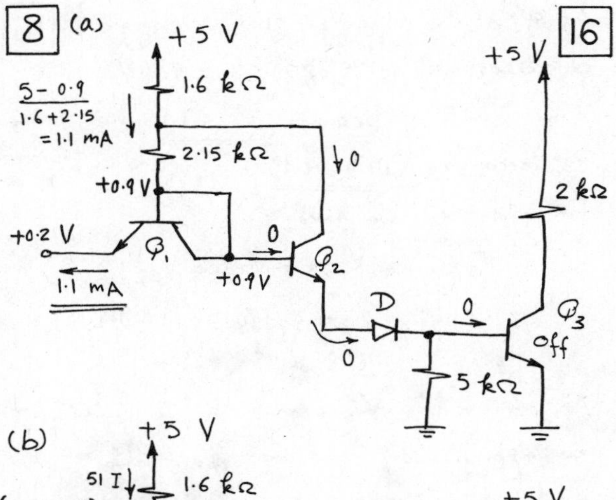

(b)

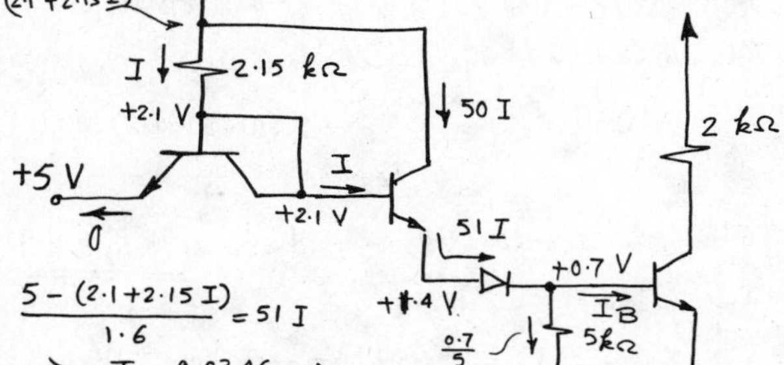

$$\frac{5 - (2.1 + 2.15 I)}{1.6} = 51 I$$

$\Rightarrow I = 0.0346$ mA

$I_B = 51 I - 0.14 = 1.6$ mA

16

9 $i_{L max} = \dfrac{0.3 - 0.1}{8} = 25$ mA

10 Maximum fan-out $= \dfrac{i_{L max}}{I_{IL}}$

$$= \frac{25\ \text{mA}}{1\ \text{mA}} = 25$$

11 From Eq. (16.16)

$$V_{CEsat} = V_T \ln \frac{1 + (\beta_{forced} + 1)/\beta_R}{1 - (\beta_{forced}/\beta_F)}$$

From Fig. 16.26 we see that for Q_1

$\beta_{forced} = 0$, thus

$$V_{CEsat} = 25 \ln\left(\frac{1 + \frac{1}{0.02}}{1 - 0}\right)$$

$$= 98\ \text{mV}$$

12 At the verge of saturation we have →

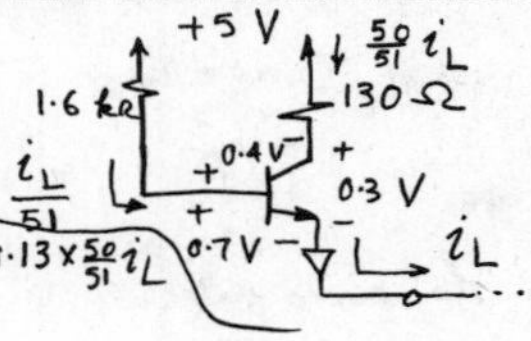

Thus

$$5 - 1.6 \times \frac{i_L}{51} - 0.4 = 5 - 0.13 \times \frac{50}{51} i_L$$

which leads to

$$\frac{1.6\, i_L}{51} + 0.4 = \frac{0.13 \times 50\, i_L}{51}$$

$$\Rightarrow i_L = \underline{\underline{4.16 \text{ mA}}}$$

13 For $i_L = 1$ mA:

$$v_O = 5 - 1.6 \times \tfrac{1}{51} - 1.4$$
$$\simeq \underline{\underline{3.6 V}}$$

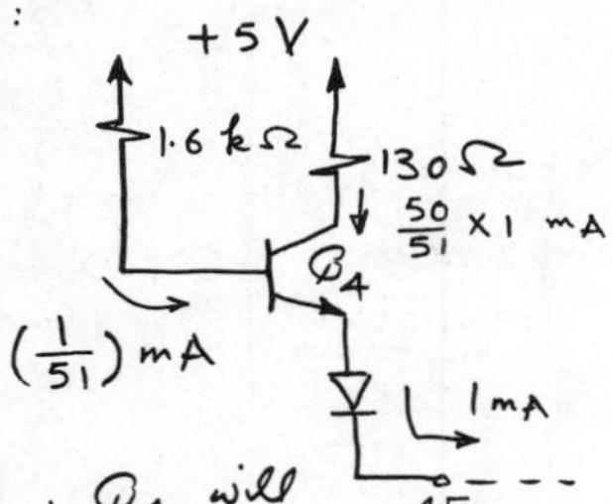

When $i_L = 10$ mA, Q_4 will be saturated (see Exercise 16.12).

Thus we have →

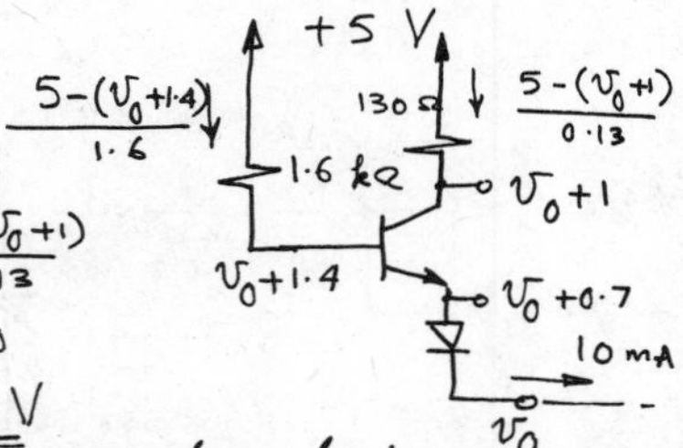

$$\frac{5-(v_O+1.4)}{1.6} + \frac{5-(v_O+1)}{0.13} = 10$$

$$\Rightarrow v_O = \underline{\underline{2.77 V}}$$

Note that we assumed that the junction voltages remain at 0.7 V. If we assume that at 10 mA the junction voltages increase to 0.76 V each then $v_O \simeq 2.7$ V.

14 Transistor Q_4 will be saturated. Thus we can use the approximate relationship in Eq. (16.22) with $v_O = 2.4$ V to determine i_L,

$$i_L = \frac{V_{CC} - v_O - V_{CE\,sat} - V_D}{0.13}$$

$$= \frac{5 - 2.4 - 0.3 - 0.7}{0.13} = \underline{\underline{12.3 \text{ mA}}}$$

A more accurate value can be obtained from the following circuit

$$i_L \simeq 12.3 + 0.75$$
$$= 13.05 \text{ mA}$$

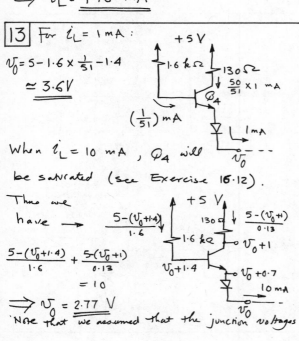

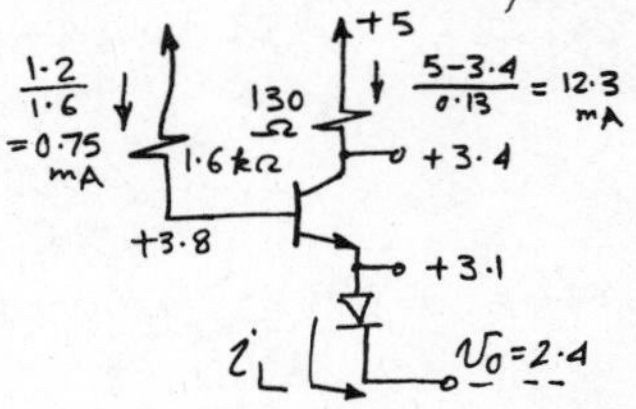

15 At −55°C, the junction voltage increases by $[25-(-55)] \times 2 = 0.16$ V.

Thus point A changes to $3.7 - 2 \times 0.16 = 3.38$ V i.e. it will have the coordinates (0, 3.38).

Point B will become $\underline{\underline{(0.66, 3.38)}}$

Now to point C:

$$v_I(C) = V_{BE3} + V_{BE2} - V_{CE\,sat}(Q_1)$$
$$= (0.6 + 0.16) + (0.7 + 0.16) - 0.1$$
$$= \underline{\underline{1.52 V}}$$

At this point the emitter current of Q_2 is approximately 0.76 mA; neglecting the base current of Q_4, the voltage at the collector of Q_2 is

$$v_{C2}(C) = 5 - 0.76 \times 1.6 = 3.78 \text{ V}$$

The corresponding output voltage is

$$v_O(C) = 3.78 - 2 \times (0.65 + 0.16)$$
$$= \underline{\underline{2.16 V}}$$

Thus point C becomes $\underline{\underline{(1.52, 2.16)}}$.

For point D we have

$$v_I(D) = V_{BE3} + V_{BE2} + V_{BC1} - V_{BE1}$$
$$= 0.86 + 0.86 + 0.86 - 0.86 = 1.72 \text{ V}$$

Thus the coordinates of D change to $\underline{\underline{(1.72, 0.1)}}$.

At +125°C the junction voltage decreases by $(125-25) \times 2 = 0.2$ V.

Thus point A becomes $\underline{\underline{(0, 4.1)}}$ and point B becomes $\underline{\underline{(0.3, 4.1)}}$.

For point C we have

$$v_I(C) = V_{BE3} + V_{BE2} - V_{CE\,sat}(Q_1)$$
$$= (0.6 - 0.2) + (0.7 - 0.2) - 0.1$$
$$= 0.8 \text{ V}$$

At this point the current in Q_2 will be approximately 0.4 mA and thus

$$v_{C2}(C) = 5 - 0.4 \times 1.6 = 4.36 \text{ V}$$

The output voltage will be

$$v_O(C) = 4.36 - 2(0.65 - 0.2)$$
$$= 3.46 \text{ V}$$

Thus the coordinates of C become $\underline{\underline{(0.8, 3.46)}}$.

For point D we have

$$v_I(D) = V_{BE3} + V_{BE2} + V_{BC1} - V_{BE1}$$

$v_I(D) = (0.7-0.2) + (0.7-0.2) + (0.7-0.2) - (0.7-0.2)$

$= 1$ V

Thus point D becomes $\underline{\underline{(1, 0.1)}}$

16 The analysis shown on Fig. 16.24 applies at +25°C. At −55°C each junction voltage increases by 0.16 V. Thus we have

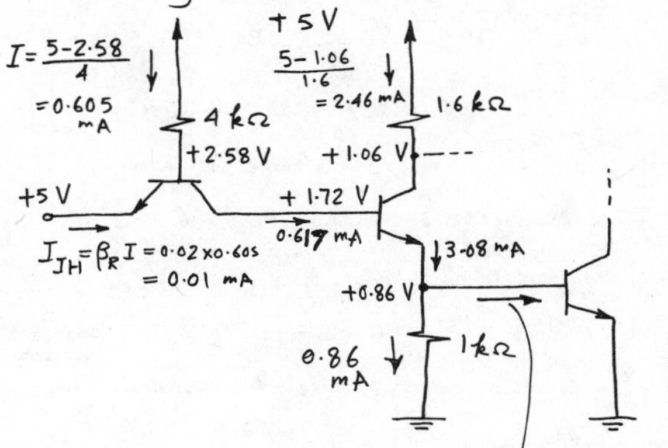

$\underline{\underline{2.2 \text{ mA}}}$

At +125°C each junction voltage decreases by 0.2 V, thus we have

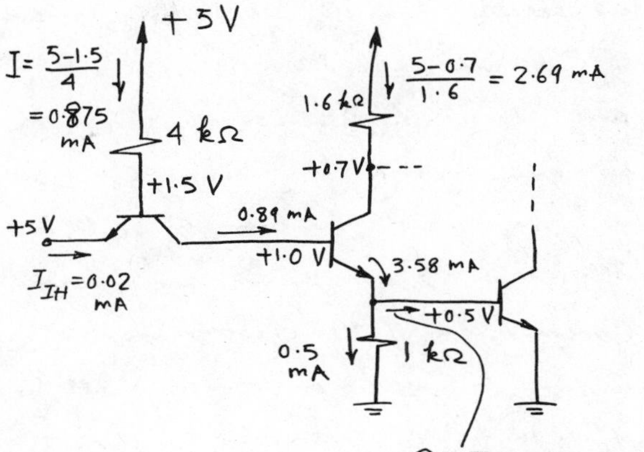

$\underline{\underline{\simeq 3 \text{ mA}}}$

17 The value of β_3 is determined by dividing the value of i_L (which is i_{C3}) at which the transistor leaves saturation and enters the active mode by the base current supplied to Q_3.

Thus at −55°C we have

$$\beta = \frac{35 \text{ mA}}{2.2 \text{ mA}} = \underline{\underline{16}}$$

At +25°C:

$$\beta = \frac{64}{2.6} = \underline{\underline{25}}$$

At +125°C:

$$\beta = \frac{85}{3} = \underline{\underline{28}}$$

18 (a) Refer to Fig. 16.26

$I_{CC} = I = \underline{\underline{1 \text{ mA}}}$

$P_D = 1 \times 5 = \underline{\underline{5 \text{ mW}}}$

(b) Refer to Fig. 16.24

$I_{CC} = 0.73 + 2.6 = \underline{\underline{3.33 \text{ mA}}}$

$P_D = 3.33 \times 5 = \underline{\underline{16.65 \text{ mW}}}$

19 Each cycle a charge of

$30 \times 10^{-3} \times 2 \times 10^{-9} = 60$ p Coulomb

is drawn from the supply. Since the

gate is switched at the rate of 1 MHz, i.e. 10^6 cycles / second it follows that a charge of $60 \times 10^{-12} \times 10^6$

$= 60$ μ Coulomb is drawn from the supply every second. Thus the average supply current is 60 μA. We can now compute the dynamic power dissipation as

$$P_D = 60 \times 10^{-6} \times 5 = \underline{\underline{0.3 \text{ mW}}}$$

20 When $\overline{\text{Third state}}$ is high, the EBJ of Q_5 will be off while current flows from the +5 V supply through the 4 kΩ resistor, the CBJ of Q_5 and into the base of Q_6 which turns on and saturates. Its V_{CEsat} appears between the base and emitter of Q_7. Thus Q_7 will be off and will have no effect on the operation of the TTL NAND gate in the lower part of the figure. **16**

When $\overline{\text{Third state}}$ is low, Q_5 turns on and saturates. Thus Q_6 will be off. Transistor Q_7 will turn on and its collector will pull current from the supply through the 1.6-kΩ resistor, thus robbing Q_4 from its base current. Transistor Q_4 will be off. Since Q_1 will be on and saturated (because one of its emitters is low), Q_2 will be off and thus Q_3 will be off. It follows that both output parts of the NAND gate will be off and thus the output terminal will function as an open circuit. This is the third state, or the high-output-impedance state.

---

21 $V_{OH} \simeq V_{CC} - V_{BE5} - V_{BE4}$ **16**

where we have neglected the small voltage drop across R_1. If the output current is small then $V_{BE5} \simeq V_{BE4} \simeq 0.7$ V and

$$V_{OH} = 5 - 0.7 - 0.7 = \underline{\underline{3.6\ V}}$$

V_{IL} is the input voltage at which Q_2 and Q_3 begin to turn on,

$$V_{IL} = V_{BE3} + V_{BE2} + V_{BC1} - V_{BE1}$$

$$= 0.7 + 0.7 + 0.5 - 0.8 = \underline{\underline{1.1\ V}}$$

V_{IH} is the input voltage at which Q_2 and Q_3 are fully turned on,

$$V_{IH} = V_{BE3} + V_{BE2} + V_{BC1} - V_{BE1}$$

$$= 0.8 + 0.8 + 0.5 - 0.8 = \underline{\underline{1.3\ V}}$$

V_{OL} is the output voltage when Q_3 is fully conducting,

$$V_{OL} = V_{CE3} = \underline{\underline{0.3\ V}}$$

---

22 **16**

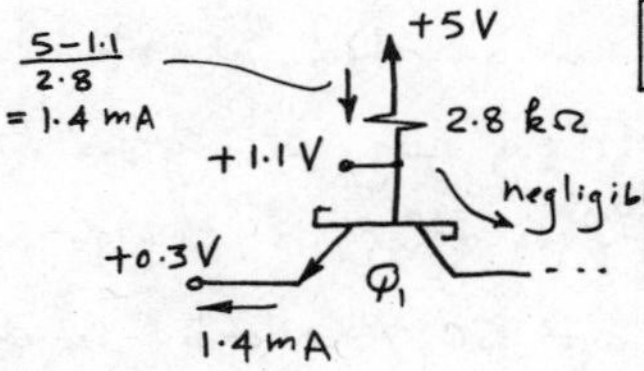

---

23 Input low:

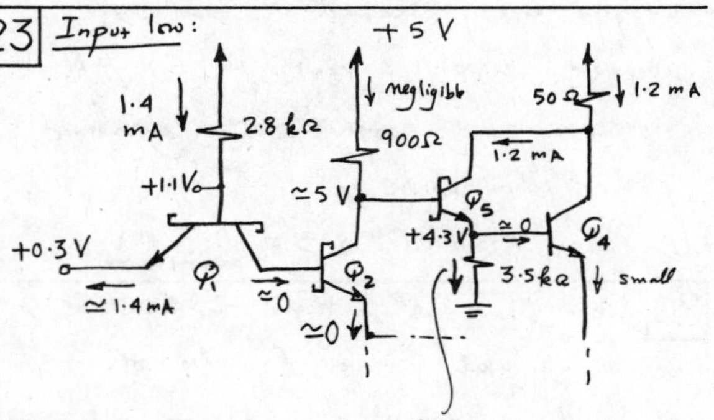

$\frac{4.3}{3.5} = 1.2$ mA

$I_{CC} = 1.4 + 1.2$

$= \underline{\underline{2.6\ mA}}$

$P_D = 2.6 \times 5 = \underline{\underline{13\ mW}}$

Input high: **16**

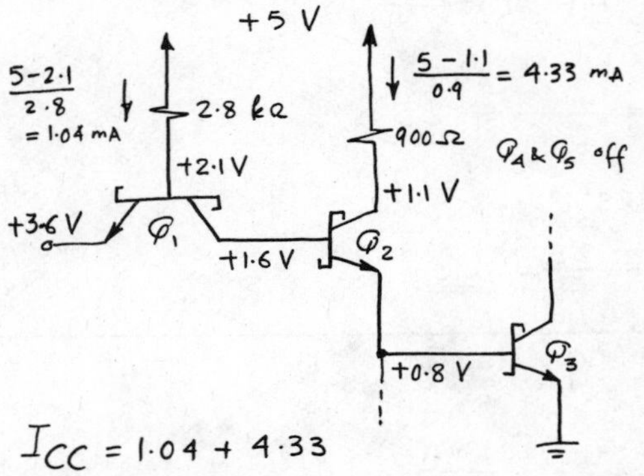

$I_{CC} = 1.04 + 4.33$

$= \underline{5.37\ mA}$

$P_D = 5.37 \times 5 = \underline{26.9}$ mW

$\text{Average } P_D = \frac{13 + 26.9}{2} \simeq \underline{\underline{20\ mW}}$

---

24 $NM_H = V_{OH} - V_{IH} = 2.7 - 2 = \underline{\underline{0.7\ V}}$

$NM_L = V_{IL} - V_{OL} = 0.8 - 0.5 = \underline{\underline{0.3\ V}}$

25 When the output is high and the gate output current is small, Q_4 will be off and Q_5 will be conducting with V_{BE} of 0.7 V. Neglecting the small voltage drop across R_1 we obtain **16**

$$V_{OH} \simeq V_{CC} - V_{BE5}$$
$$= 5 - 0.7 = \underline{\underline{4.3\ V}}$$

V_{IL} is the input voltage at which Q_2 and Q_3 begin to conduct, thus

$$V_{IL} = V_{BE3} + V_{BE2} - V_{D1}$$
$$= 0.7 + 0.7 - 0.5 = \underline{\underline{0.9\ V}}$$

V_{IH} is the input voltage at which Q_2 and Q_3 will be fully conducting, thus

$$V_{IH} = V_{BE3} + V_{BE2} - V_{D1}$$
$$= 0.8 + 0.8 - 0.5 = \underline{\underline{1.1\ V}}$$

Finally, $V_{OL} = V_{CE3} = \underline{\underline{0.3\ V}}$

---

26 *Input low:* **16**

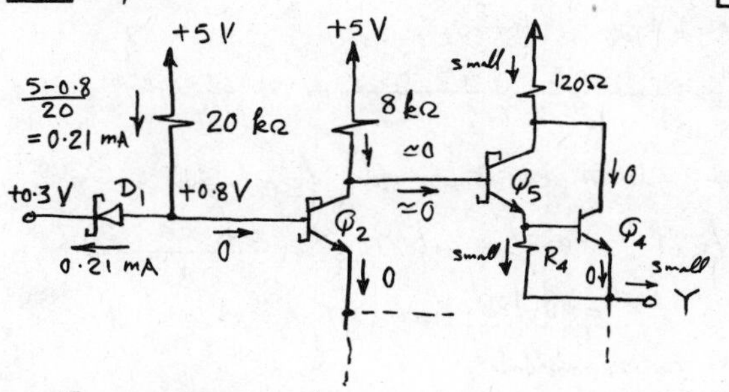

$$I_{CC} = 0.21\ mA$$

Input high:

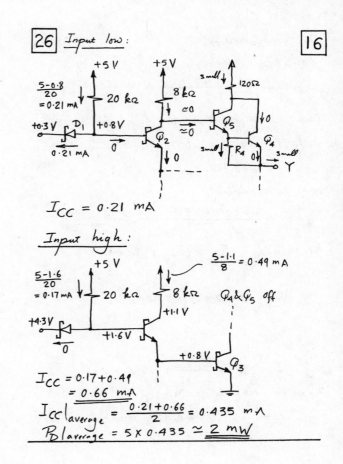

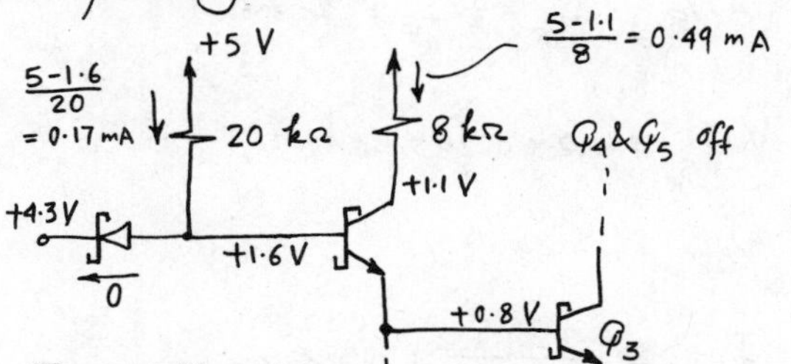

$$I_{CC} = 0.17 + 0.49$$
$$= \underline{\underline{0.66\ mA}}$$

$$I_{CC}\big|_{average} = \frac{0.21 + 0.66}{2} = 0.435\ mA$$

$$P_D\big|_{average} = 5 \times 0.435 \simeq \underline{\underline{2\ mW}}$$

---

27 Refer to Fig. E16.27. Neglecting the base current of Q_1, the current through R_1, D_1, D_2 and R_2 is **16**

$$I = \frac{5.2 - V_{D1} - V_{D2}}{R_1 + R_2}$$
$$= \frac{5.2 - 0.75 - 0.75}{0.907 + 4.98} = 0.6285\ mA$$

Thus,

$$V_B = -IR_1 = -0.57\ V$$
$$V_R = V_B - V_{BE1} = -0.57 - 0.75 = \underline{\underline{-1.32\ V}}$$

---

28 Refer to Fig. 16.36.

$$I_E = \frac{V_R - V_{BE}|_{Q_R} - (-V_{EE})}{R_E}$$
$$= \frac{-1.32 - 0.75 + 5.2}{0.779} \simeq \underline{\underline{4\ mA}}$$

$$V_C|_{Q_R} = -\alpha \times 4 \times R_{C2} \simeq -4 \times 0.245 \simeq \underline{\underline{-1\ V}}$$

$V_C|_{Q_A, Q_B} = \underline{\underline{0\ V}}$ (because the current through R_{C1} is zero)

---

29 Refer to Fig. 16.38. **16**

For $v_I = V_{IL}$, $I_{Q_R} = 99\ I_{Q_A}$,

$$I_E = \frac{-1.32 - V_{BE}|_{Q_R} + 5.2}{0.779}$$

Assume $V_{BE}|_{Q_R} = 0.75\ V$, $I_E = 4.018\ mA$

$$I_{Q_R} \simeq 0.99 \times 4.018 = 3.98\ mA$$

Thus a better estimate of $V_{BE}|_{Q_R}$ is

$$V_{BE}|_{Q_R} = 0.75 + 0.025\ \ln\left(\frac{3.98}{1}\right)$$
$$= 0.785\ V$$

and correspondingly,

$$I_E = \frac{-1.32 - 0.785 + 5.2}{0.779} = \underline{\underline{3.97\ mA}}$$

For $v_I = -1.32\ V$, $I_{Q_R} = I_{Q_A} = I_E/2$,

$$I_E = \frac{-1.32 - 0.75 + 5.2}{0.779} = 4.018\ mA$$

Thus a better estimate for $V_{BE}|_{Q_R}$ is

$$V_{BE}|_{Q_R} = 0.75 + 0.025\ \ln\left(\frac{2.009}{1}\right)$$
$$= 0.767\ V$$

and correspondingly,

$$I_E = \underline{\underline{4.00\ mA}}$$

16

For $v_I = V_{IH} = -1.205$ V,

$$I_{Q_A} = 99\, I_{Q_R},$$

$$I_E = \frac{-1.205 - 0.75 + 5.2}{0.779} = 4.166 \text{ mA}$$

Thus a better estimate for $V_{BE}|_{Q_A}$ is

$$V_{BE}|_{Q_A} = 0.75 + 0.025 \ln\left(\frac{0.99 \times 4.166}{1}\right)$$
$$= 0.788 \text{ V},$$

and correspondingly

$$I_E = \frac{-1.205 - 0.788 + 5.2}{0.779} = \underline{\underline{4.12 \text{ mA}}}$$

At $v_I = V_R$, $I_{Q_R} = \frac{1}{2} I_E = 2$ mA.

Thus,

$$V_C|_{Q_R} \cong -2 \times 0.245 = -0.49 \text{ V}$$

$$v_{OR} = -0.49 - 0.75 = -1.24 \text{ V}$$

$$I_E|_{Q_2} = \frac{-1.24 + 2}{0.05} = 15.2 \text{ mA}$$

A better estimate for $V_{BE}|_{Q_2}$ is

$$V_{BE}|_{Q_2} = 0.75 + 0.025 \ln\left(\frac{15.2}{1}\right) = 0.818 \text{ V}$$

16

Thus a better estimate for V_{OR} is

$$V_{OR} = -0.49 - 0.818 = \underline{-1.31 \text{ V}}$$

---

30 (a) Refer to Fig. 16.42. For $v_I = V_{IH} = -1.205$ the value of I_E was found in Exercise 16.29 to be 4.12 mA. Thus $V_C|_{Q_A} \simeq -0.22 \times 4.12$

$$= -0.906 \text{ V}$$

$$v_{NOR} \simeq -0.906 - 0.75 = -1.656 \text{ V}$$

$$I|_{Q_3} = \frac{-1.656 + 2}{0.05} = 6.88 \text{ mA}$$

A better estimate for $V_{BE}|_{Q_3}$ is

$$V_{BE}|_{Q_3} = 0.75 + 0.025 \ln\left(\frac{6.88}{1}\right)$$
$$= 0.798 \text{ V}$$

and correspondingly

$$v_{NOR} = -0.906 - 0.798 = \underline{\underline{-1.704 \text{ V}}}$$

(b) For $v_I = V_{OH} = -0.88$ V,

$$I_E \simeq \frac{-0.88 - 0.75 + 5.2}{0.779} = 4.58 \text{ mA}$$

16

A better estimate for $V_{BE}|_{Q_A}$ is

$$V_{BE}|_{Q_A} = 0.75 + 0.025 \ln\left(\frac{4.58}{1}\right) = 0.788 \text{ V}$$

Thus,

$$I_E = \frac{-0.88 - 0.788 + 5.2}{0.779} = 4.53 \text{ mA}$$

$$V_C|_{Q_A} = -0.22 \times 4.53 = -1 \text{ V}$$

$$v_{NOR} = -1 - 0.75 = -1.75 \text{ V}$$

$$I|_{Q_R} = \frac{-1.75 + 2}{0.05} = 5 \text{ mA}$$

$$V_{BE}|_{Q_3} = 0.75 + 0.025 \ln\left(\frac{5}{1}\right)$$
$$= 0.79 \text{ V}$$

$$v_{NOR} = -1 - 0.79 = \underline{-1.79 \text{ V}}$$

(c) The input resistance into the base of Q_3 is $(\beta + 1)\,[r_{e3} + R_T]$

$$= 101\left[\frac{25}{5} + 50\right] = 5.55 \text{ k}\Omega$$

$$\frac{v_c|_{Q_A}}{v_i} = -\frac{(5.55 \text{ k}\Omega \,//\, 0.22 \text{ k}\Omega)}{r_e|_{Q_A} + R_E}$$

16

$$= \frac{-5.55 \,//\, 0.22}{\left(\frac{25}{4.53} + 779\right) \times 10^{-3}} = -0.269$$

$$\frac{v_{NOR}}{v_c|_{Q_A}} = \frac{50\,\Omega}{50\,\Omega + 5\,\Omega} = 0.909$$

Thus,

$$\frac{v_{NOR}}{v_c|_{Q_A}} = -0.269 \times 0.909 = \underline{\underline{-0.24 \text{ V/V}}}$$

(d) See figure →

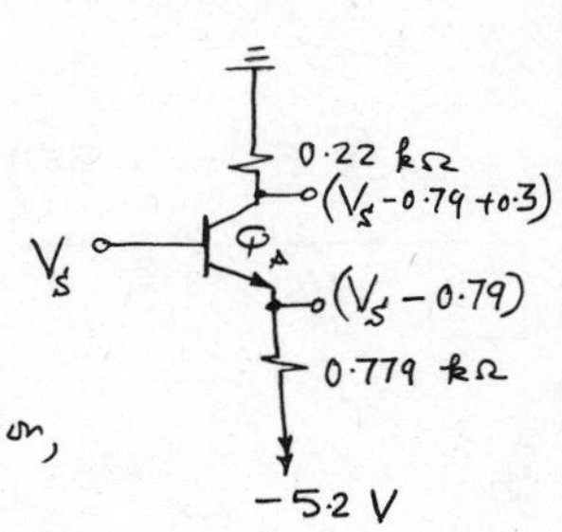

Assume $V_{BE} \simeq 0.79$ V (because the current will be 4 to 5 mA).

At the verge of saturation,

$$I_C = \alpha I_E = 0.99\, I_E$$

Thus,

$$\frac{0 - V_S + 0.79 - 0.3}{0.22} = 0.99\, \frac{V_S - 0.79 + 5.2}{0.779}$$

$$\Rightarrow V_S = \underline{-0.58 \text{ V}}$$

---

31 Refer to Fig. 16.36. For the reference circuit, the current through R_1, D_1, D_2 and R_2 is

$$\frac{5.2 - 2\times0.75}{4.98 + 0.907} = 0.629 \text{ mA}$$

$V_B|_{Q_1} = -0.57$ V $V_R = -0.57 - 0.75 = -1.32$ V

$$I_E|_{Q_1} = \frac{-1.32 + 5.2}{6.1} = 0.636 \text{ mA}$$

Thus the reference circuit draws a current of $(0.629 + 0.636) = 1.265$ mA from the 5.2-V supply. It follows that the power dissipated in the reference circuit is $1.265 \times 5.2 = 6.6$ mW. Since the reference circuit supplies four gates, the dissipation attributed to a gate is

$$\frac{6.6}{4} = 1.65 \text{ mW}$$

In addition, the gate draws a current $I_E \simeq 4$ mA from the 5.2-V supply. Thus the total power dissipation / gate is

$P_D = 4\times5.2 + 1.65 = \underline{22.4 \text{ mW}}$

Problem Solutions

---

1 Eq. (1.1): To 4 terms -

$$v(t) = \frac{4V}{\pi}\left(\sin\omega_0 t + \tfrac{1}{3}\sin 3\omega_0 t + \tfrac{1}{5}\sin 5\omega_0 t + \tfrac{1}{7}\sin 7\omega_0 t\right)$$

See sketch following 7

2 For a square wave of V volts peak across resistor R, Power $= 2(\tfrac{1}{2}V^2/R) = V^2/R$

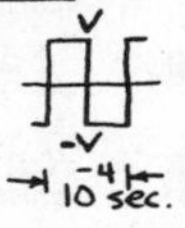

For a cutoff of 16 kHz, only the fundamental is perceived. Thus

Perceived Power is $\dfrac{\left(\frac{4V}{\pi}/\sqrt{2}\right)^2}{R} = V^2/R\left(8/\pi^2\right)$

Thus a 40 year old receives $8/\pi^2(1/100)$ or $\underline{\underline{81\%}}$ of the available energy.

3 For the 4 terms in 1 above, $T = 2\pi$ rad and T/8, T/4, 5T/8, 3T/4 correspond (at ω_0) to 45°, 90°, 135°, 270° resp.

At:	T/8	T/4	5T/8	3T/4
1× 1st H.:	(45°) .707	(90°) 1.000	(225°) −.707	(270°) −1.00
1/3 × 3rd H.:	(135°) .236	(270°) −.333	(675°) .236	(810°) .333
1/5 × 5th H.:	(225°) −.141	(450°) .200	(1125°) .141	(1350°) −.200
1/7 × 7th H.:	(315°) −.101	(630°) −.143	(1575°) −.101	(1890°) .143
Sum	.701	.724	−.701	−.724
$4/\pi$(Sum)	.893	.923	−.893	−.923

4 Harmonic at 9f of a 2Vpp Sq. Wave has amp. $= \frac{1}{9}\frac{4}{\pi}V$

Total energy of square wave $\propto (1V)^2/R = 1$ unit

and of the 9th harmonic $\propto \left(\frac{4V}{9\pi}\right)^2/R = .020$ unit

Thus 9th harmonic has $.020/1$ or $\underline{\underline{2\%}}$ of energy of Sq. W.

5

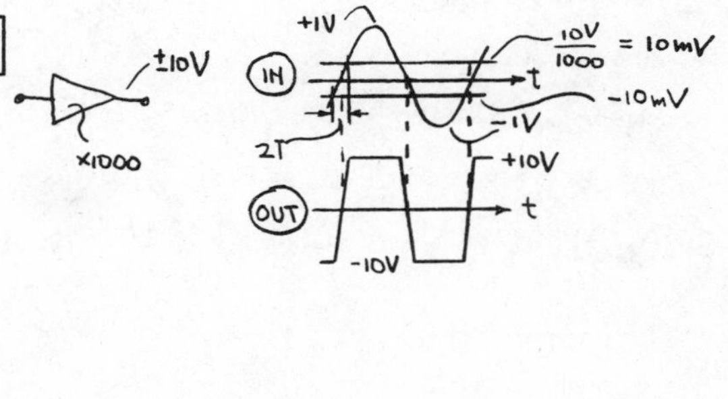

The output limits at 10V when the input **1** reaches $10/1000 = 10mV$ ie. when $1 \sin 2\pi 10^3 T = 10^{-2}$

or $T = \frac{1}{2\pi \times 10^{-3}} \sin^{-1} 10^{-2}$ sec $= \frac{.573^\circ \times 2\pi/360}{2\pi \times 10^3} = 1.6\mu s$

Thus, ignoring amplifier dynamics, the rise/fall times of the output are about 3.2µs, and the square wave approximation is quite good!

A square wave of amplitude 10V has a fundamental of $\frac{40}{\pi}$ V or 12.7(3)V.

Thus for a 1Vpeak sine wave, the "gain" is 12.7 V/V

6 Component at 1kHz has an rms value $\frac{40}{\pi} \cdot \frac{1}{\sqrt{2}} = 9.003V$

3	$(\times 1/3)$	3.001
5	$(\times 1/5)$	1.801
7	$(\times 1/7)$	1.286
9	$(\times 1/9)$	1.000

RMS Value of all (4) harmonics $= (3^2 + 1.8^2 + 1.29^2 + 1^2)^{1/2}$
$= 3.86V$

Total Harmonic Distortion (THD) $= \frac{3.86}{9.003} \times 100 = 42.9\%$

7 $v_o = 100 v_i + 50 v_i^2$ and $v_i = V_i \sin \omega t$ **1**

$\therefore v_o = 100 V_i \sin \omega t + 50 V_i^2 \sin^2 \omega t$, but $\sin^2 x = \frac{1 + \cos 2x}{2}$

$v_o = 100 V_i \sin \omega t + 25 V_i^2 + 25 V_i^2 \cos 2\omega t$

$\therefore$ second-harmonic distortion $= \frac{25 V_i^2}{100 V_i} \times 100 = 25 V_i$

a) For 1%, $25 V_i = 1$, $V_i = 1/25 \equiv 40mV$

b) For 10% SHD, $25 V_i = 10 \rightarrow V_i = 0.4V$

c) When $100 V_i = 10V$, $V_i = 0.1V$
and SHD $= 25 V_i = 25(0.1) = 2.5\%$

d) For a postamplifier of gain 2, $100 V_i = 5V$
and $V_i = .05V$, for which SHD $= 25(.05) = 1.25\%$

1 Cont'd.

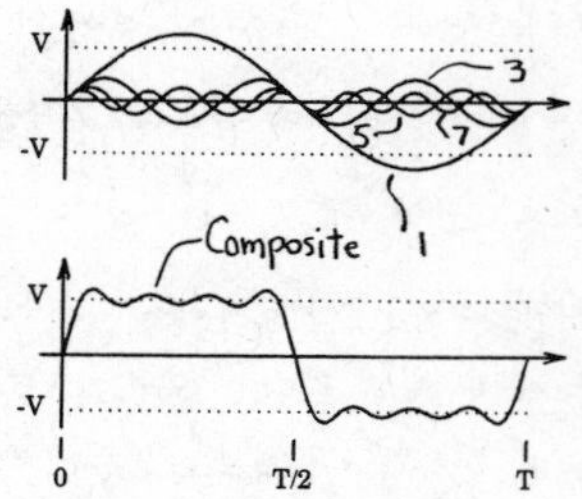

1

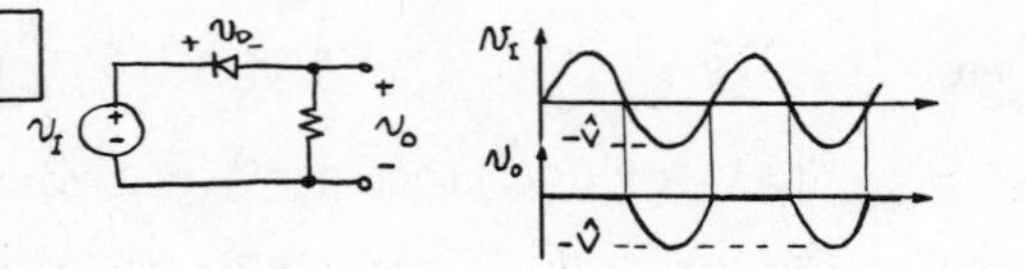

2

2

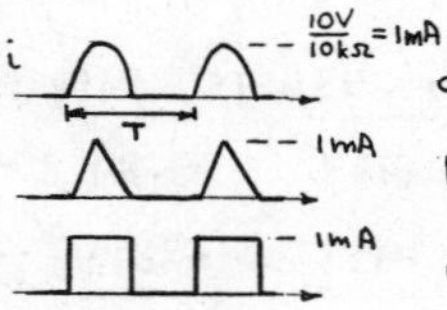

a) $I_{av} = \frac{1mA}{\pi} = 0.318mA \equiv 31.8\%$

b) $I_{av} = \frac{1/2 \times T/2 \times 1}{T} = 1/4 mA \equiv 25\%$

c) $I_{av} = \frac{1 \times T/2}{T} = 1/2 mA \equiv 50\%$

3 $i = I_o e^{v/V_o} \rightarrow v = V_o \ln i/I_o$

$v_3 = v_1 + v_2 = V_o(\ln i_1/I_o + \ln i_2/I_o) = V_o \ln \frac{i_1 i_2}{I_o^2}$

$i_3 = I_o e^{v_3/V_o} = I_o e^{\ln \frac{i_1 i_2}{I_o^2}} = I_o \frac{i_1 i_2}{I_o^2} = \frac{i_1 i_2}{I_o}$

4 $i = 10 \sin(\frac{\pi}{20} v)$ mA with v:

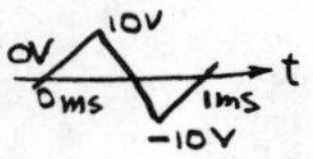

For $v = 0$, $i = 10 \sin 0 = 0$

$v = 10$, $i = 10 \sin \frac{\pi}{20} \cdot 10 = 10 \sin \pi/2 = 10$

$v = 5$, $i = 10 \sin \frac{\pi}{20} \cdot 5 = 10 \sin \pi/4 = 7.07$

See (next) $i_o(t) = 10 \sin(2\pi \times 10^3 t)$ results

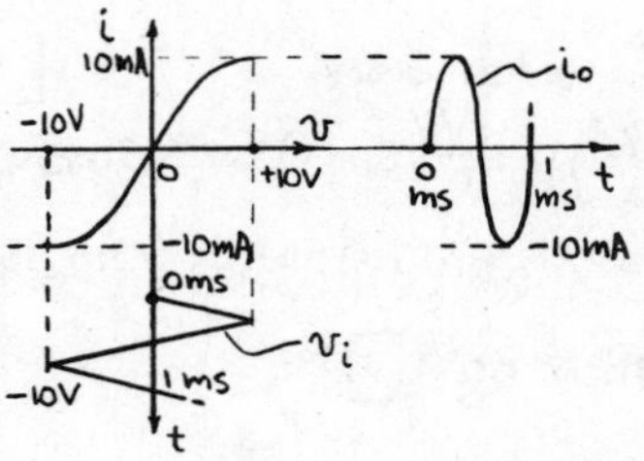

$\omega = 2\pi/10^{-3} = 2\pi \times 10^3$ **2**

$i_o = 10 \sin(2\pi \times 10^3 t)$ mA

5 $i_{out} = 1V/1K = 1mA$ (peak)

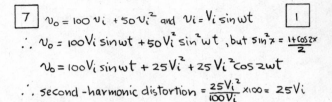

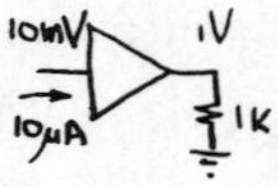

Voltage gain $= A_v = v_o/v_i = \frac{1V}{10mV} = 100 V/V$
or $20 \log_{10} 10^2 = 40dB$

Current gain $= A_i = i_o/i_i = \frac{1mA}{10\mu A} = \frac{10^{-3}}{10^{-5}} = 100 A/A$ or 40dB

Power gain $= \frac{v_{o\,rms}^2}{R} / i_{i\,rms} \cdot v_{i\,rms} = \frac{(1/\sqrt{2})^2}{10^3} / \frac{10^{-2}}{\sqrt{2}} \times \frac{10^{-5}}{\sqrt{2}}$
$= \frac{1}{10^3} \times 10^7 = 10^4 W/W$ or $10 \log_{10} 10^4 = 40dB$

or $A_p = A_v A_i = 100 \times 100 = 10^4$ or 40dB

6 Voltage gain $= 60dB$ or $1000 V/V = A_v$

Power gain $= 40dB$ or $10^4 W/W = A_P$

Current gain $A_i = A_P/A_v = 10^4/10^3 = 10$ or 20dB

Check: $|A_P| = \frac{|A_v| + |A_i|}{2} = \frac{60 + 20}{2} = 40dB$ ✓

7 $P_L = \dfrac{(10/\sqrt{2})^2}{2} = \dfrac{100}{4} = 25\ mW$ **2**

$P_{dc} = 15 \times 1.2 + 15 \times 1.2 = 36\ mW$

$P_{dissipated} = 36 - 25 = 11\ mW$

Power efficiency $\eta = \dfrac{25}{36} \times 100 = 69.4\%$

8 $v_O = 10 - 5(v_I - 2)^2$ for $2 \le v_I \le v_O + 2$

For $v_I = 2$, $v_O = 10 - 0 = 10V$

For $v_I = v_O + 2$, $v_O = 10 - 5(v_O + 2 - 2)^2 = 10 - 5v_O^2$

or $5v_O^2 + v_O - 10 = 0 \rightarrow v_O = \dfrac{-1 \pm \sqrt{1+200}}{10} = 1.32V$ (or neg)

$\therefore\ v_O = 1.32$ for $v_I = 3.32$

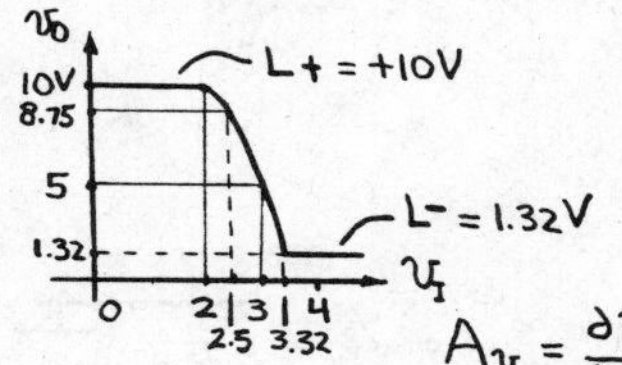

$L_+ = 10V$; $L_- = 1.32V$

For $v_I = 2.5V$

$v_O = 10 - 5(2.5-2)^2 = 8.75$

$A_v = \dfrac{\partial v_O}{\partial v_I} = -10(v_I - 2)$

At $v_I = 2.5V$, $A_v = -5\ V/V$

or more fundamentally, if $v_O = V_O + \Delta v_O$ for $v_I = V_I + \Delta v_i$

$V_O + \Delta v_O = 10 - 5(V_I + \Delta v_i - 2)^2$ and for $V_I = +2.5V$,

$V_O + \Delta v_O = 10 - 5(0.5 + \Delta v_i)^2 = 8.75 - 5\Delta v_i - 5\Delta v_i^2$

See: a) dc output bias of +8.75V, b) a small-signal voltage gain of −5 V/V and c) a nonlinear term (a distortion). Now for input increments of 0.1V, 0.2V, 0.5V, the small-signal output approximation is −0.5V, −1.0V and −2.5V resp. with a nonlinear component of −0.5(0.1) or −.05 V, −0.2 V and −1.25 V respectively, for a total output change of −0.55V, −1.20V, −3.75 V respectively. **2**

9 $i_D = 10^{-15} e^{40 v_D} \rightarrow I_D = 10^{-15} e^{40 V_D}$ and for $I_D = 1mA$

$V_D = 1/40 \ln 10^{15} I_D = 1/40 \ln 10^{15}(10^{-3}) = 1/40 \ln 10^{12} = 0.691V$

Now for $v_D = V_D + v_d$, $I_D + i_d = 10^{-15} e^{40(V_D + v_d)} = 10^{-3} e^{40 v_d}$

$\simeq 10^{-3}(1 + 40 v_d)$. That is $I_D = 1mA$ and $i_d = .04 v_d$

whence $r_d = v_d / i_d = \dfrac{1}{.04} = 25\Omega$

Correspondingly, at $I_D = 10mA$, $i_D = 10^{-2} e^{40 v_d} \simeq 10^{-2}(1 + 40 v_d)$.

That is $i_d = 10^{-2}(40 v_d)$, and $r_d = v_d / i_d = 2.5\Omega$

10 **2**

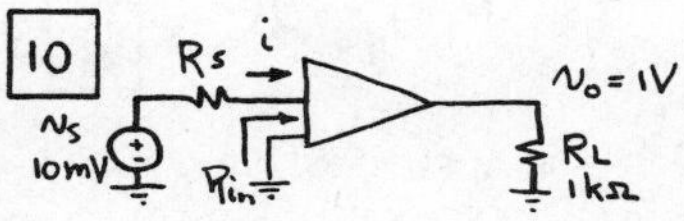

$v_o = 1V$ $R_s = \dfrac{10mV}{1\mu A} = 10^4\Omega$

$i = \dfrac{v_s}{R_s + R_{in}} = 0.5\mu A$

Thus amplifier input resistance $R_{in} = \dfrac{10mV}{0.5\mu A} - 10^4 = 10^4\Omega$

Current gain $= \dfrac{1V/1k}{0.5\mu A} = 2000$ or 66 dB

Voltage gain $= 1V / \left(\dfrac{10k}{10k + 10k} \times 10mV\right) = 200$ or 46dB

Power gain $= \dfrac{1V \times 1mA}{(.5\mu A)^2 \times 10k} = \dfrac{10^{-3}}{0.25 \times 10^{-12} \times 10^4} = 4 \times 10^5$ or 56 dB

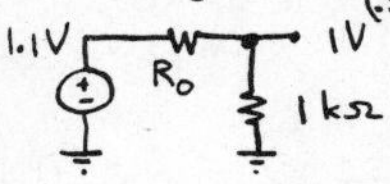

For R_o : $\dfrac{1}{1 + R_o} \times 1.1 = 1 \rightarrow R_o = 0.1k\Omega$

$A_{v_o} = \dfrac{1.1V}{5mV} = 220\ V/V$

11 $P_{dc} = 2 \times 10 \times 0.1 = 2W$

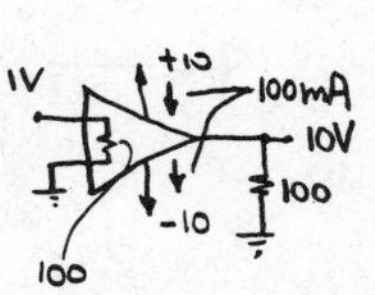

$P_{in} = \dfrac{1^2}{100} = 0.01\ W$

$P_L = \dfrac{10^2}{100} = 1W$

$P_{diss} = 2 + .01 - 1 = 1.01W$

$A_P = \dfrac{1}{0.01} = 100\ W/W$ or $10\log_{10} 100 = 20dB$

$\eta = \dfrac{1}{2 + .01} \times 100 = 49.75\% \simeq 50\%$

12 **2**

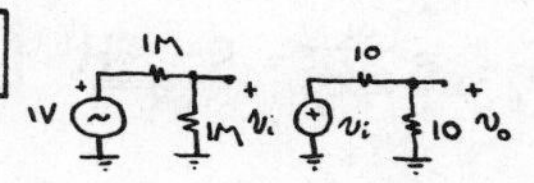

$v_i = \dfrac{1}{1+1} v_s = 0.5V_{rms}$

$v_o = \dfrac{10}{10 + 10} \cdot v_i = 0.25\ V_{rms}$

$P_L = \dfrac{v_o^2}{10} = \dfrac{0.25^2}{10} = 6.25\ mW$

$v_o / v_s = 0.25 = 1/4\ V/V$ or -12 dB

$i_o / i_i = \dfrac{0.25/10}{0.5/10^6} = \frac{1}{2} \times 10^5 = 50{,}000\ A/A$ or 94 dB

$P_o / P_i = \dfrac{6.25 \times 10^{-3}}{0.5^2 / 10^6} = 25{,}000\ W/W$ or 44 dB

Note that $v_o / v_i = 0.5\ V/V$ or $-6dB$ and $P_o / P_i = v_o / v_i \cdot i_o / i_i$

that is $|P_o / P_i| = \dfrac{94 - 6}{2} = 44$ dB

13

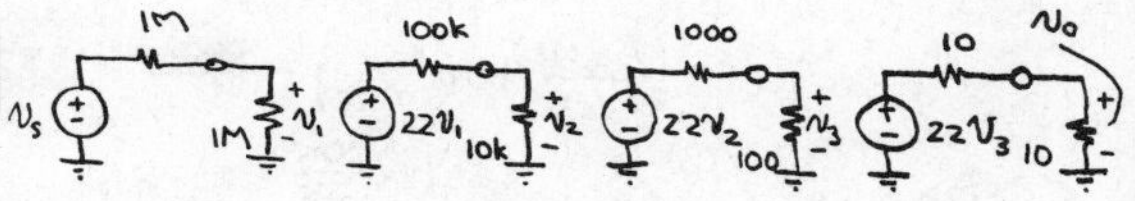

$v_o / v_s = \dfrac{1}{1+1} \times 22 \times \dfrac{10}{100 + 10} \times 22 \times \dfrac{100}{1000 + 100} \times 22 \times \dfrac{10}{10 + 10}$

$= 22\ V/V$ or 27 dB

$P_o / P_i = \dfrac{v_o^2 / R_L}{v_i^2 / R_i} = \dfrac{(22 v_s)^2 / 10}{(v_s/2)^2 / 10^6} = 44^2 \times 10^5$

$= 193.6 \times 10^6\ W/W$ or 82.9 dB

2

14

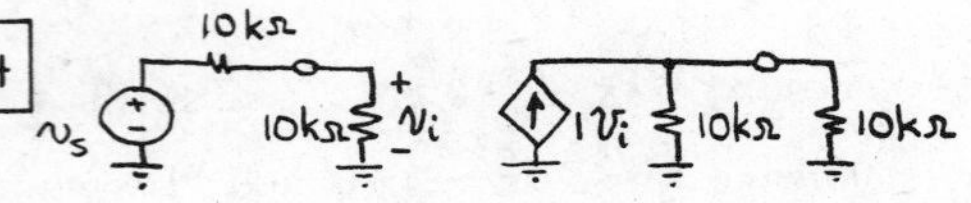

$$v_o/v_s = \frac{10}{10+10} \times 1 \times 10k \| 10k = \underline{\underline{2500\ V/V}} \text{ or } \underline{\underline{68\,dB}}$$

15

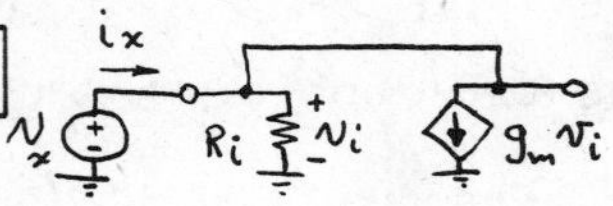

$$v_i = v_x$$

$$i_x = v_x/R_i + g_m v_x = (g_m + 1/R_i)\,v_x$$

$$R_{in} = \frac{v_x}{i_x} = \underline{\underline{\frac{1}{g_m + 1/R_i}}}$$

16

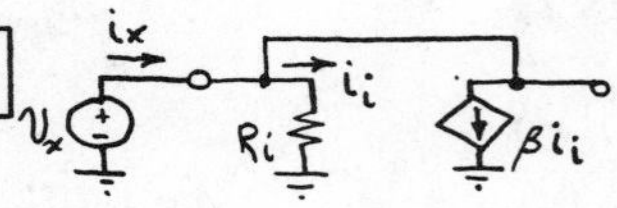

$$i_x = i_i + \beta i_i = (\beta+1)\frac{v_x}{R_i}$$

$$R_{in} = \frac{v_x}{i_x} = \underline{\underline{\frac{R_i}{\beta+1}}}$$

17

$$\frac{v_o}{v_i} = 40\times10^{-3}\times10^{4} = \underline{\underline{400\ V/V}} \text{ or } \underline{\underline{52\,dB}}$$

$$\frac{i_o}{i_i} = \frac{40\times10^{-3} v_i}{v_i/2.5\times10^{3}} = \underline{\underline{100}}\ A/A \equiv 20\log_{10} 100 = \underline{\underline{40\,dB}}$$

$$A_p = P_o/P_i = \frac{i_o^2 R_L}{v_i^2/R_i} = \frac{(40\times10^{-3})^2 v_i^2 \times 10^4}{v_i^2/2.5\times10^3}$$

$$= 1600\times10^{-6}\times2.5\times10^{7} = \underline{\underline{40{,}000\ W/W}} \equiv \underline{\underline{46\,dB}}$$

18 **2**

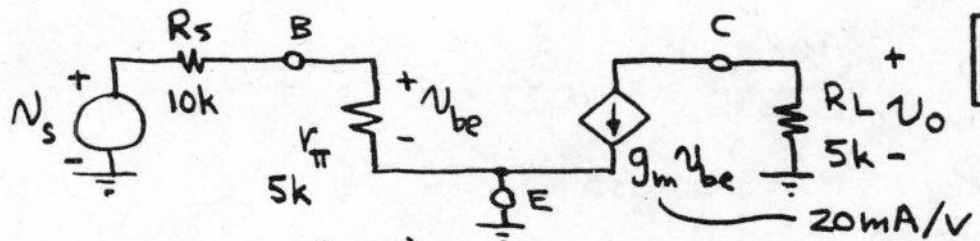

$$v_o/v_s = \frac{5}{10+5}\times(-20)\times5 = \underline{\underline{-33.3\ V/V}} \text{ or } \underline{\underline{30.4\,dB}}$$

19

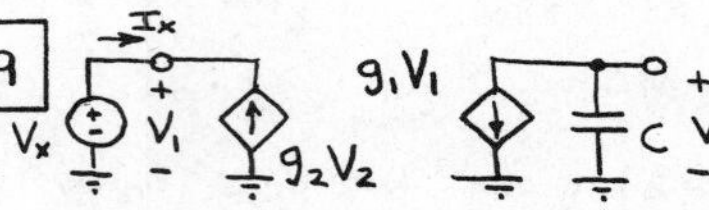

$$V_2 = -\frac{g_1 V_1}{sC}$$

$$I_x = -g_2 V_2 = \frac{g_1 g_2 V_1}{sC} = \frac{g_1 g_2 V_x}{sC}$$

$$\therefore\ Z_{in}(s) = \underline{\underline{\frac{sC}{g_1 g_2}}}$$

20

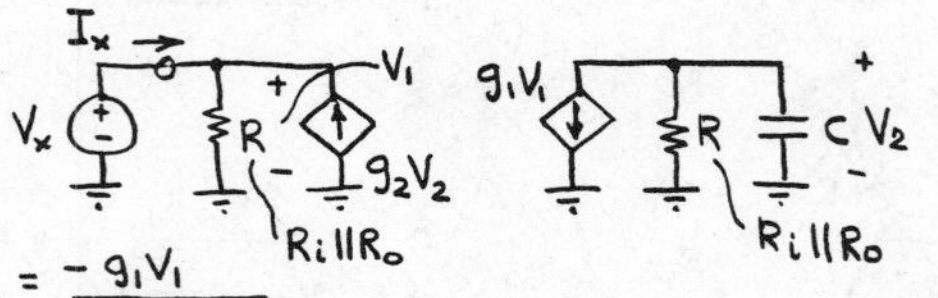

$$V_2 = \frac{-g_1 V_1}{sC + 1/R}$$

$$I_x = V_x/R + \frac{g_1 g_2 V_1}{sC + 1/R}$$

$$Y_{in} = I_x/V_x = 1/R + \frac{g_1 g_2 R}{sCR+1} = 1/R + \frac{1}{s\dfrac{C}{g_1 g_2} + \dfrac{1}{g_1 g_2 R}}$$

$$\equiv 1/R_2 + \frac{1}{sL + R_1}$$

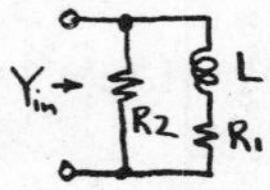

for which $L = \dfrac{C}{g_1 g_2}$

and $R_1 = \dfrac{1}{g_1 g_2 R}$; $R_2 = R = R_o \| R_i$

21

$$L = \frac{C}{g_1 g_2} = \frac{.01\times10^{-6}}{5\times10^{-3}\times5\times10^{-3}} = \frac{1}{2500} = \underline{0.4\ mH}$$

2

22

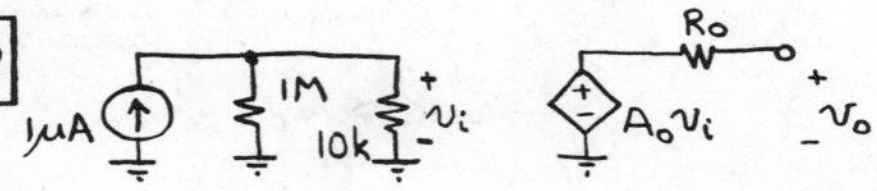

Now, for output open:

$v_o = A_o v_i = 10V$ while $v_i = 10^{-6}\times10^{6}\|10^{4} \approx 10^{-2}V$

$\therefore\ A_o = \dfrac{10}{10^{-2}} = \underline{\underline{10^3}}$. But for output shorted:

$i_o = \dfrac{A_o v_o}{R_o} = 10mA \longrightarrow R_o = \dfrac{10V}{10mA} = \underline{\underline{1k\Omega}}$

Now for $R_L = 2k\Omega$

$$A_v = v_o/v_i = A_o\frac{R_L}{R_o+R_L} = 1000\frac{2}{1+2} = \underline{\underline{667}} \text{ or } \underline{\underline{56.5dB}}$$

$$A_i = i_o/i_i = \left(\frac{A_o v_i}{R_o+R_L}\right)\Big/\left(v_i/R_i\right) = \frac{1000\times10}{1+2} = \underline{\underline{3333\ A/A}} \text{ or } \underline{\underline{70.5dB}}$$

$$A_p = \frac{v_o^2}{R_L}\Big/\left(v_i^2/R_i\right) = 667^2\times\frac{10k}{2k} = \underline{\underline{2.24\times10^6}} \text{ or } \underline{\underline{63.5dB}}$$

Note $A_p = A_i A_p = 667(3333) = 2.24\times10^6$ or $\dfrac{56.5+70.5}{2} = 63.5dB$

23

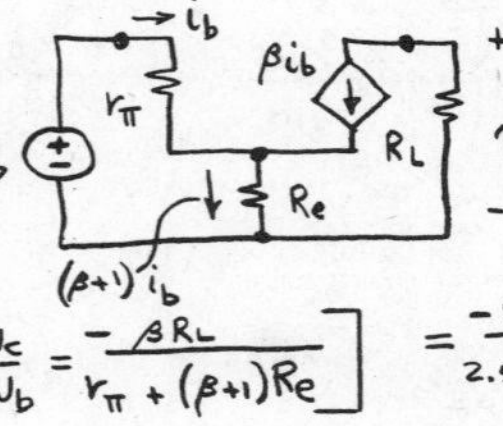

$$v_b = i_b r_\pi + (\beta+1) i_b R_e$$

$$v_c = -\beta i_b R_L$$

$$\boxed{A_v = \frac{v_c}{v_b} = \frac{-\beta R_L}{r_\pi + (\beta+1)R_e}} = \frac{-100(10^4)}{2.5\times10^3 + (101)10^3} = \underline{\underline{-9.66\ V/V}}$$

24 **2**

$f = 1/T$; $\omega = 2\pi f$

(a) $f = 1/1 = 1\,Hz$; $\omega = 2\pi$ r/s

(b) $f = 1/10^{-6} = 1\,MHz$; $\omega = 2\pi\times10^{6}$ r/s

(c) $f = 1/10^{-9} = 1\,GHz = 1000\,MHz$; $\omega = 2\pi\times10^{9}$ r/s

(d) $f = 60\,Hz$; $\omega = 120\pi$ r/s $= 377$ r/s

(e) $f = 10^3/16.6ms = 60.2\,Hz$; $\omega = 2\pi(60.2) = 384$ r/s

25

$T = 1/f = 2\pi/\omega$

(a) $T = \dfrac{2\pi}{2\pi\times10^{3}} = 1ms$

(b) $T = \dfrac{1}{10^{-3}} = 1000s$

(c) $T = \dfrac{1}{60} = 16.\dot{6}\ ms$

(d) $T = 2\pi/2\pi = 1\,sec.$

(e) $T = 1/10^{10} = 0.1\,ns = 100ps$

(f) $T = \dfrac{1}{0.1\times10^{6}} = 10\mu s$

26

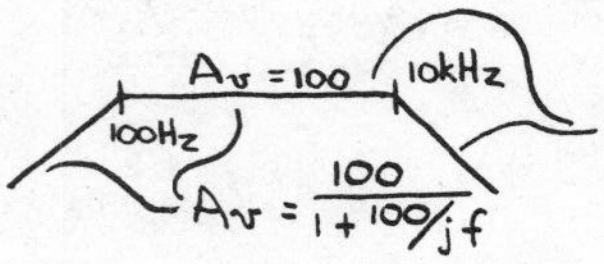

$$A_v = \frac{100}{1 + jf/10^4}$$

$$A_v = \frac{100}{1 + 100/jf}$$

Input is a square wave of amplitude 5mV and frequency $f = \omega/2\pi$.

ie $V_i(t) = \frac{4}{\pi}(5mV)\big(\sin\omega t + \frac{1}{3}\sin 3\omega t + \frac{1}{5}\sin 5\omega t + \frac{1}{7}\sin 7\omega t + \frac{1}{9}\sin 9\omega t + \frac{1}{11}\sin 11\omega t + \cdots\big)$

and the output is a wave with attenuated and shifted harmonic components

ie $V_o(t) = \frac{4}{\pi}(500mV)\big(C_1\sin(\omega t+\phi_1) + C_3\sin(3\omega t+\phi_3) + C_5\sin(5\omega t+\phi_5) + C_7\sin(7\omega t+\phi_7) + C_9\sin(9\omega t+\phi_9) + C_{11}\sin(11\omega t+\phi_{11}) + \cdots\big)$

where $T(jf) = \dfrac{100jf}{(1+10^2/jf)(1+jf/10^4)}$ for which

$|T| = 100\times\big((1+10^4/f^2)(1+f^2/10^8)\big)^{-1/2}$ and $\phi = 90^\circ - \tan^{-1}\frac{f}{10^2} - \tan^{-1}\frac{f}{10^4}$

Here:

Magnitude						
Frequency (Hz)	C_1	C_3	C_5	C_7	C_9	C_{11}
10	9.95	9.58	8.94	8.19	7.43	6.73
50	44.72	27.73	18.56	13.73	10.84	8.93
200	89.42	32.82	19.80	14.11	10.92	8.87
1000	99.01	31.91	17.88	11.70	8.26	6.11
5000	89.42	18.49	7.43	3.92	2.41	1.63
20000	44.72	5.48	1.99	1.02	0.62	0.41

Phase (in degrees)						
Frequency (Hz)	φ_1	φ_3	φ_5	φ_7	φ_9	φ_{11}
10	84.23	73.13	63.15	54.61	47.50	41.64
50	63.15	32.83	20.37	13.94	9.95	7.16
200	25.42	6.03	0.00	-3.88	-7.02	-9.80
1000	0.00	-14.79	-25.42	-34.17	-41.35	-47.21
5000	-25.42	-55.93	-67.97	-73.89	-77.34	-79.59
20000	-63.15	-80.44	-84.23	-85.87	-86.79	-87.37

V_o:

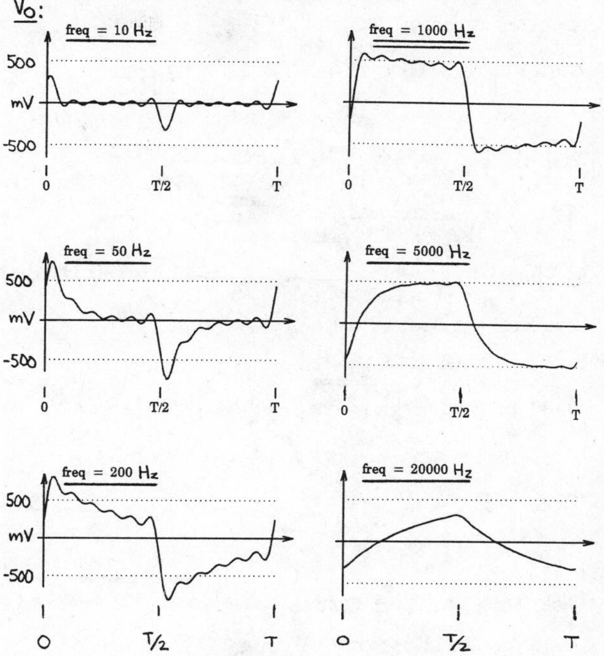

27 (a) $V_o(s)/V_i(s) = \dfrac{1/Cs}{R + 1/Cs} = \dfrac{1}{1+RCs}$

For $R = 10k$, $C = 0.1\mu F$, $RC = 10^4 \cdot 10^{-7} = 10^{-3}$ sec

At $\omega = 10^3$ r/s, $T(j\omega) = \dfrac{1}{1+j10^{-3}\omega} = \dfrac{1}{1+j1}$

whose magnitude is $\frac{1}{\sqrt{2}}$ and phase is $-\tan^{-1}1$ or -45°

(b) $T(s) = V_o(s)/V_i(s) = \dfrac{R}{R+1/Cs} = \dfrac{sCR}{1+sCR}$

At $\omega = 10^3$ r/s, $T(j\omega) = \dfrac{j\omega 10^{-3}}{1+j\omega 10^{-3}} = \dfrac{j1}{1+j1}$

with magnitude: $\frac{1}{\sqrt{2}}$ and phase: $\tan^{-1}1/0 - \tan^{-1}1/1$ or $90^\circ - 45^\circ = 45^\circ$

(c) $T(s) = V_o(s)/V_i(s) = \dfrac{R}{R + 1/Cs \| kR} = \dfrac{R}{R + \frac{kR/Cs}{1/Cs + kR}}$

$= \dfrac{1/Cs + kR}{1/Cs + kR + k/Cs} = \dfrac{sCR + 1/k}{sCR + (1+1/k)}$

For $RC = 10^{-3}$s, $k = 10$, $T(j\omega) = \dfrac{j\omega 10^{-3} + 0.1}{j\omega 10^{-3} + 1.1}$

and for $\omega = 10^{-3}$, $T(j\omega) = (0.1+j1)/(1.1+j1)$

with magnitude: $\left(\dfrac{0.1^2+1^2}{1.1^2+1^2}\right)^{1/2} = .676$

and phase: $\tan^{-1}1/0.1 - \tan^{-1}1/1.1 = 84.3 - 42.3$ or 42.0°

28 $T(s) = \dfrac{sCR + 1/k}{sCR + (1+1/k)}$

$|T(j\omega)| = \dfrac{|1/k + j\omega CR|}{|(1+1/k) + j\omega CR|} = \dfrac{1}{k+1}\cdot\dfrac{|1+j\omega CRk|}{|1+j\omega CR\frac{k}{k+1}|}$

Now for $k=10$:

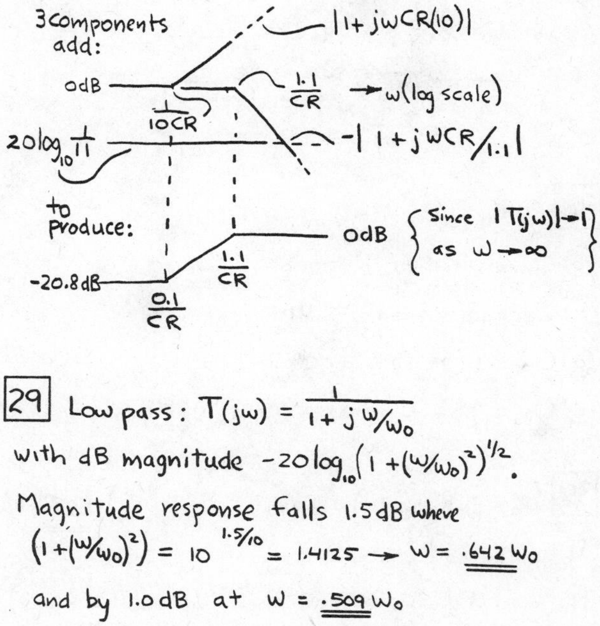

29 Low pass: $T(j\omega) = \dfrac{1}{1+j\omega/\omega_o}$

with dB magnitude $-20\log_{10}(1+(\omega/\omega_o)^2)^{1/2}$.

Magnitude response falls 1.5dB where

$(1+(\omega/\omega_o)^2) = 10^{1.5/10} = 1.4125 \rightarrow \omega = .642\,\omega_o$

and by 1.0dB at $\omega = .509\,\omega_o$

and by 0.75dB at $\omega = .434\,\omega_o$

30 4 stages each with an STC low-pass response each contribute $3/4 = 0.75\,dB$ to an overall 3dB loss. As in **29**, this occurs where $20\log_{10}(1+(\omega/\omega_o)^2)^{1/2} = 0.75$, namely at $\omega = 0.43\,\omega_o = \underline{\underline{0.43/RC}}$ **2**

31 $T(s) = V_o(s)/V_i(s) = \dfrac{g_m}{1/R + sC + 1/sL}$

$T(j\omega) = \dfrac{g_m}{1/R + j\omega C + 1/j\omega L} = \dfrac{g_m}{1/R + j(\omega C - 1/\omega L)}$

$|T(j\omega)| = \dfrac{g_m R}{(1+(\omega C - 1/\omega L)^2R^2)^{1/2}}$ and $|T(0)| = 0$, $|T(\infty)| = 0$

Gain is maximum when $\omega_o C = \dfrac{1}{\omega_o L}$ or $\omega_o = \underline{\underline{1/\sqrt{LC}}}$

Max. gain is $\underline{\underline{g_m R}}$

Gain is 3dB below max. when $(\omega C - 1/\omega L)^2 R^2 = 1$

or $\omega C - 1/\omega L = \pm 1/R$ or $\omega^2 LC - 1 = \pm \omega L/R$

or $\omega^2 LC \mp \dfrac{\omega L}{R} - 1 = 0$ or $\omega = \dfrac{\pm L/R \pm \sqrt{L^2/R^2 + 4LC}}{2LC}$

or $\omega = \pm\dfrac{1}{2CR} + \sqrt{\dfrac{1}{LC} + \dfrac{1}{4C^2R^2}} = \pm\dfrac{1}{2CR} + \sqrt{\omega_o^2 + \left(\dfrac{1}{2CR}\right)^2}$

Note above that the second (larger) term is taken to be +ve

3dB bandwidth: BW is $2\dfrac{1}{2CR} = \underline{\underline{\dfrac{1}{CR}}}$

32 $T(j\omega) = \dfrac{j\omega CR}{1 + j\omega CR}$ where $CR = 10^3 \times 10^{-6} = 10^{-3}\,s$ **2**

Now for $\omega = 10^3\,r/s$ and $V_i = 10\sin\omega t$, then

$V_o(t) = \dfrac{j\,10}{1+j1}\sin 10^3 t = \dfrac{10}{\sqrt{2}}\sin(10^3 t - \pi/4)$

33 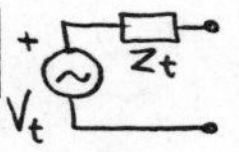 $V_{oc} = V_t$; $I_{sc} = V_t/Z_t$; $\boxed{Z_t = \dfrac{V_{oc}}{I_{sc}}}$

34 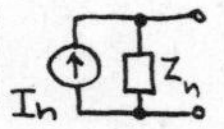 $V_{oc} = I_n Z_n$; $I_{sc} = I_n$; $\boxed{Z_n = \dfrac{V_{oc}}{I_{sc}}}$

35 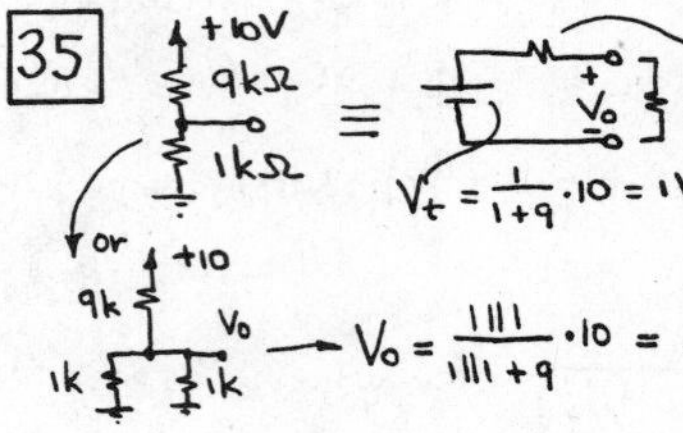

$R_t = 1k \| 9k = 0.9k$, $R_L = 1k$

$V_t = \dfrac{1}{1+9}\cdot 10 = 1V \rightarrow V_o = \dfrac{1}{1+0.9}\cdot 1 = \underline{0.526V}$

or $V_o = \dfrac{1\|1}{1\|1 + 9}\cdot 10 = \dfrac{0.5}{9.5} = \underline{0.526\,V}$

36 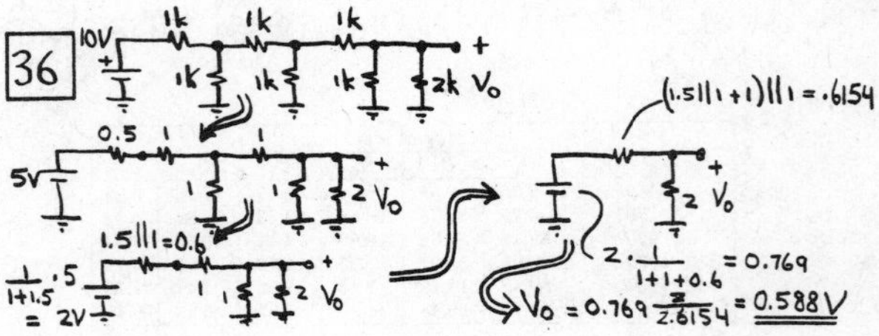

$(1.5\|1 + 1)\|1 = .6154$

$1.5\|1 = 0.6$; $\dfrac{1}{1+1.5}\cdot 5 = 2V$

$2\cdot\dfrac{1}{1+1+0.6} = 0.769$

$V_o = 0.769\,\dfrac{2}{2.6154} = \underline{\underline{0.588\,V}}$

37 **2**

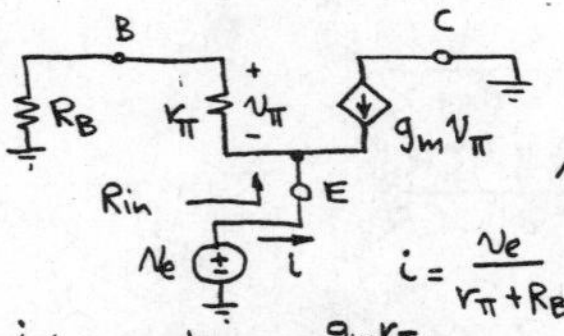

$v_\pi = -v_e\dfrac{r_\pi}{r_\pi + R_B}$

$i = \dfrac{v_e}{r_\pi + R_B} + \dfrac{g_m r_\pi}{r_\pi + R_B}\cdot v_e$

$1/R_{in} = i/v_e = \dfrac{1}{r_\pi + R_B} + \dfrac{g_m r_\pi}{r_\pi + R_B} = \dfrac{g_m r_\pi + 1}{r_\pi + R_B} = \dfrac{\beta + 1}{r_\pi + R_B}$

∴ 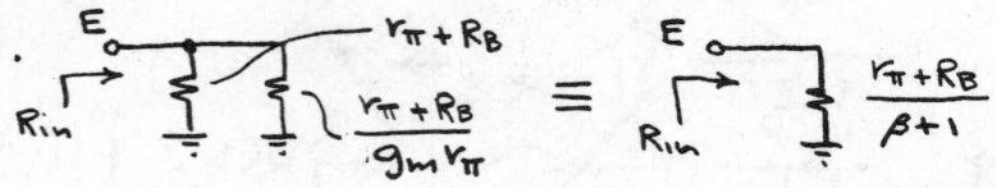

38 ⓐ $C_{in} = 10(1-(-1)) = \underline{20pF}$

ⓑ $C_{in} = 1(1-(-10^6)) \approx 10^6 pF = \underline{1\mu F}$

ⓒ $C_{in} = 10(1-(-0.1)) = \underline{11pF}$

ⓓ $C_{in} = 1(1-1) = \underline{0pF}$

ⓔ $C_{in} = 10 + 1(1-10) = 10 - 9 = \underline{1pF}$

39 $v_o = g_m R(v_1 - v_2) = 100\times10^{-3}\times5\times10^3(v_1 - v_2) = \underline{\underline{500(v_1 - v_2)}}$

If $v_1 = v_2 = 1V$, then $v_o = \underline{0V}$.

If $v_1 = 1.01\,V$, $v_2 = 0.99V$, then $v_o = 500(1.01 - 0.99)$

or $v_o = 500(.02) = \underline{10V}$

40 **2**

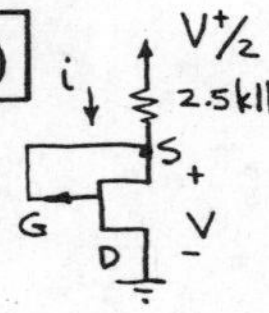

$2.5k\|2.5k = 1.25K$. Now for $V^+ = 10V$

assume $V \gg 2V$ and $i = 2mA$

for which $V = 10/2 - 2(1.25) = \underline{\underline{2.5V}}$

Thus operation is at I_{DSS}. Such operation persists for $V \gg 2$ or $V^+/2 \gg 2 + 2(1.25) = 4.5\,V$ or while $V^+ \gg \underline{\underline{9\text{ volts}}}$. Now for $V^+ = 2V$, let the JFET conduct I at V volts where

$I = \dfrac{2/2 - V}{1.25} = 2(2\,V/2 - (V/2)^2)$

Thus $1 - V = 2.5\,V - \dfrac{2.5}{4}V^2 \rightarrow \dfrac{2.5}{4}V^2 - 3.5V + 1 = 0$

and $V^2 - \dfrac{14}{2.5}V + \dfrac{4}{2.5} = 0 \rightarrow V^2 - 5.6V + 1.6 = 0$

or $V = \dfrac{5.6 - \sqrt{5.6^2 - 6.4}}{2}$ or $\underline{0.3V}$

for which $I = \dfrac{1 - 0.3}{1.25} = \underline{0.56\,mA}$

41 Condition is $\dfrac{R_2}{R_1 + R_2} = \dfrac{1/sC_2}{1/sC_2 + 1/sC_1} = \dfrac{C_1}{C_1 + C_2}$

whence $C_1R_1 + C_1R_2 = C_1R_2 + C_2R_2 \rightarrow \boxed{C_1R_1 = C_2R_2}$

$\dfrac{V_o}{V_i} = \dfrac{Y_1}{Y_1 + Y_2} = \dfrac{sC_1 + 1/R_1}{s(C_1 + C_2) + 1/R_1 + 1/R_2}$ which for $R_1 = R_2 = R$, $C_1 = C_2 = C$

is $\dfrac{V_o}{V_i} = \dfrac{sC + 1/R}{2sC + 2/R} = 1/2$ ie 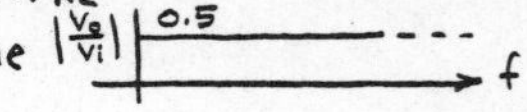

42 $\dfrac{V_o}{V_i} = \dfrac{sC_1 + 1/R_1}{s(C_1+C_2) + 1/R_1 + 1/R_2} = \dfrac{1 + sC_1R_1}{1 + \dfrac{s(C_1+C_2)}{1/R_1 + 1/R_2}} \cdot \dfrac{1/R_1}{1/R_1 + 1/R_2}$ [2]

For this to be independant of frequency:

$C_1R_1 = \dfrac{C_1 + C_2}{1/R_1 + 1/R_2} \rightarrow C_1 + \dfrac{C_1R_1}{R_2} = C_1 + C_2$

or $\boxed{C_1R_1 = C_2R_2}$, whence $\boxed{\dfrac{V_o}{V_i} = \dfrac{R_2}{R_1 + R_2}}$

43 $R_2 = 1\,M\Omega$, $C_2 = 30\,pF$; $\dfrac{R_2}{R_1+R_2} = 0.1 = \dfrac{1}{R_1+1}$

$\therefore R_1 = 10 - 1 = 9\,M\Omega$; $C_1 = \dfrac{30\times 1}{9} = \dfrac{10}{3}\,pF$

$Z_{in} = Z_1 + Z_2 = \dfrac{1}{1/R_1 + sC_1} + \dfrac{1}{1/R_2 + sC_2}$

$= \dfrac{R_1}{1 + sC_1R_1} + \dfrac{R_2}{1 + sC_2R_2} = \dfrac{R_1 + R_2}{1 + sC_1R_1}$ {See $= 10Z_2$}

$Y_{in} = 1/Z_{in} = \dfrac{1}{R_1+R_2} + s\,\dfrac{C_1R_1}{R_1+R_2}$

$= \dfrac{1}{10\,M\Omega} + s\cdot\dfrac{30\times 1}{10}$

$= \dfrac{1}{10\,M\Omega} + s \times 3\,pF \longrightarrow$

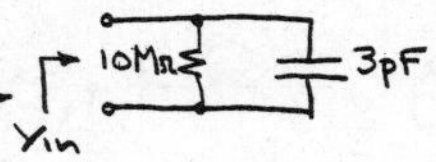

44 $\tau = L/R = \dfrac{10\times 10^{-3}}{10^3} = 10\,\mu s$

$\tau = CR = 10^{-8} \times 10^{3} = 10\,\mu s$

$\omega_o = 1/\tau = 1/10^{-5} = 10^5$ rad/s

45 [2]

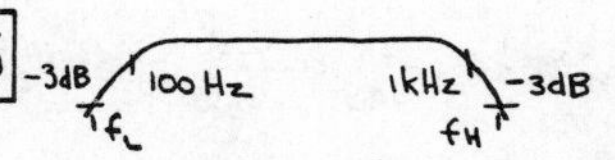

At the edges of the passband defined

$\tan^{-1} f_L/f = 11.4°$ and $\tan^{-1} f/f_H = 11.4°$

Now $\tan 11.4° = 0.20 \rightarrow f_L = 0.2(100) = \underline{\underline{20\,Hz}}$

and $f_H = 1\,kHz/0.2 = \underline{\underline{5\,kHz}}$

Drop in gain at passband ends is $20\log_{10}\sqrt{1+(0.2)^2}$

or $\underline{\underline{0.17\,dB}}$, and 3dB at 20Hz and 5kHz

Thus the 3dB bandwidth extends from $\underline{\underline{20\,Hz \text{ to } 5\,kHz}}$

46

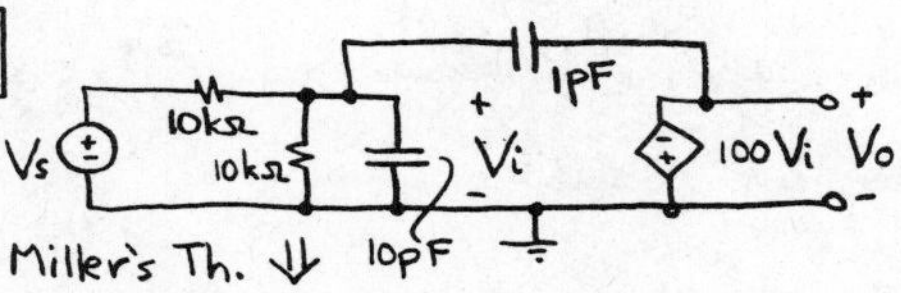

By Miller's Th. ⇓

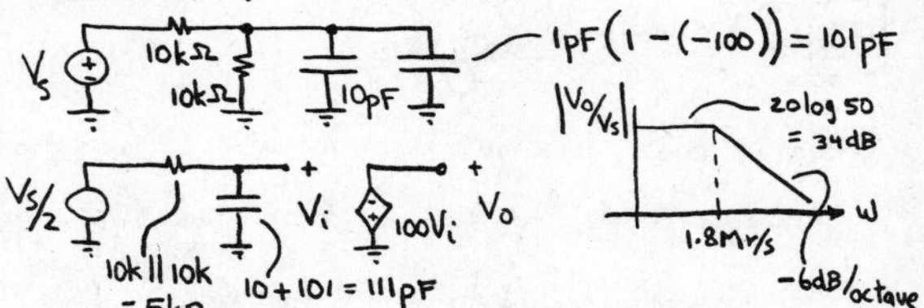

$V_o/V_s = \dfrac{-100 \times 0.5}{1 + s(5\times10^3 \times 111 \times 10^{-12})} = \dfrac{-50}{1 + s/1.8\times10^6}$

47 Using Miller's theorem: [2]

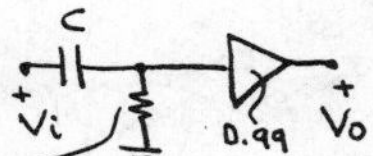

$R_{eq} = 100R$

$1/R_{eq} = 1/R\,(1-\mu) = \dfrac{0.01}{R}$

$V_o/V_i = \dfrac{0.99(100R)}{100R + 1/sC}$

$= \dfrac{99sCR}{1 + sCR\times 100} \longrightarrow \underline{HP}$

A high-pass response for which $\omega_o = \dfrac{1}{100CR}$

or $\omega_o = \dfrac{1}{100\times 0.01\times 10^{-6}\times 10^5} = \underline{10\,rad/s}$

48 High-pass response:

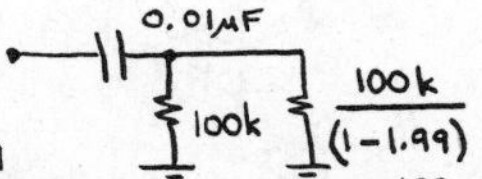

$100k \,\|\, \dfrac{-100k}{0.99} = \dfrac{100 \times -100/.99}{100 - 100/.99}$

$= \dfrac{100\times 100}{1} = 10^4\,k\Omega = 10^7\,\Omega$

$\omega_o = \dfrac{1}{10^{-8}\times 10^7} = \underline{10\,rad/s}$; $\underline{HP}$

49

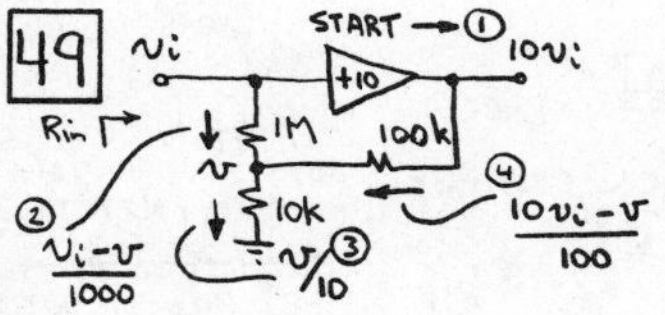

⑤ $\dfrac{v_i - v}{1000} + \dfrac{10v_i - v}{100} = v/10$

⑥ $v_i - v + 100v_i - 10v = 100v$

or $101v_i = 111v$

Thus $v = \dfrac{101}{111}v_i = .991v_i$

and $R_{in} = v_i/i_i = \dfrac{v_i}{\dfrac{v_i - (101/111)v_i}{1000}} = \dfrac{1000}{10/111} = \underline{\underline{11.1\,M\Omega}}$

[2]

Note an approximate calculation is appropriate since $1M >> 10k$. Directly from Miller's Theorem $R_{in} \approx \dfrac{1M}{10\times\dfrac{10}{10+100}} = \underline{11\,M\Omega}$ (Approx.)

50

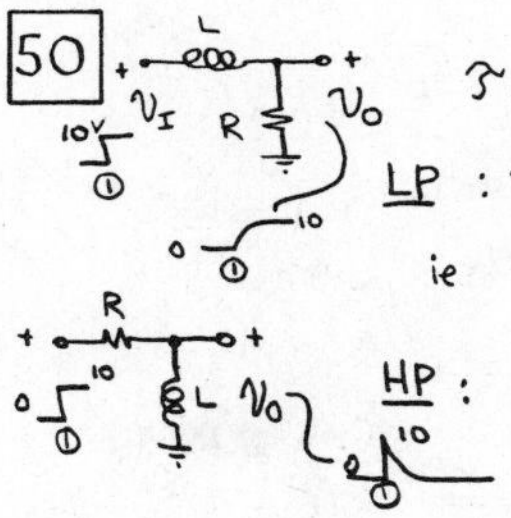

$\tau = L/R = 10^{-3}/10^3 = 10^{-6}\,s$

$\underline{LP}$: $v_o(t) = 10(1 - e^{-t/10^{-6}})$

ie $v_o(t) = 10(1 - e^{-10^6 t})$

$\underline{HP}$: $v_o(t) = 10e^{-10^6 t}$

51

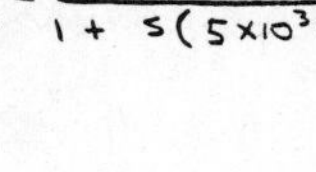

$v_o(t) = 10(1 - e^{-t/\tau})$

ⓐ $5 = 10(1 - e^{-t/\tau}) \rightarrow 0.5 = e^{-t/\tau} \rightarrow 2 = e^{t/\tau} \rightarrow t = \underline{0.69\tau}$

ⓑ $9 = 10(1 - e^{-t/\tau}) \rightarrow 10 = e^{t/\tau} \rightarrow t = \underline{2.3\tau}$

ⓒ $9.9 = 10(1 - e^{-t/\tau}) \rightarrow 100 = e^{t/\tau} \rightarrow t = \underline{4.6\tau}$

ⓓ $9.99 = 10(1 - e^{-t/\tau}) \rightarrow 1000 = e^{t/\tau} \rightarrow t = \underline{6.9\tau}$

52 $t_r = 2.2\tau = \dfrac{2.2}{\omega_o} = \dfrac{2.2}{2\pi f_o} = \dfrac{0.35}{f_o} = \dfrac{0.35}{10^8} = \underline{\underline{3.5\,ns}}$

53 $t_s = t_r = \frac{0.35}{f_0} \rightarrow$ Scope $f_{3dB} = \frac{0.35}{35\times10^{-9}} = 10MHz$ **2**

$t_d = \sqrt{t_s^2 + t_w^2}$:

For t_w = 100ns, $t_d = \sqrt{35^2+100^2}$ = 106 ns

35 ns, $t_d = \sqrt{35^2+35^2}$ = 49.5 ns

10 ns, $t_d = \sqrt{35^2+10^2}$ = 36.4 ns

For t_d = 49.5, the actual rise $t_w = \sqrt{49.5^2 - 35^2} = 35ns$

54 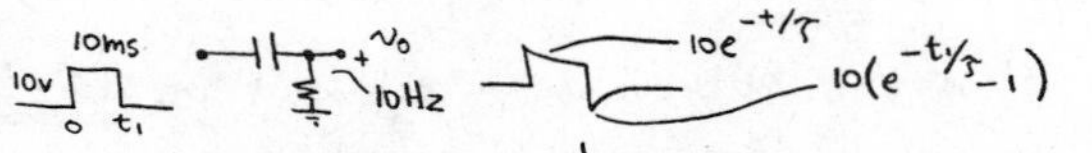

$\omega = 2\pi f = 1/\tau \rightarrow \tau = \frac{1}{2\pi f} = \frac{1}{2\pi\times10} = 15.9$ ms

At 10 ms, $v_o = 10e^{-t/\tau}$ becomes $10e^{-10/15.9} = 5.33V$

∴ undershoot is 5.33 − 10 or −4.67 V

55 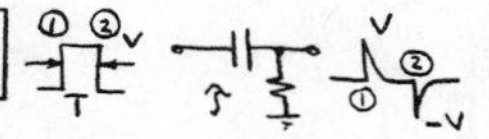

Negative peak is short by 10% when T is small enough that the output from the first edge has decayed (only) to 10% V in time T.

ie $e^{-T/\tau} = 0.1 \rightarrow T = 2.3\tau$ 

56 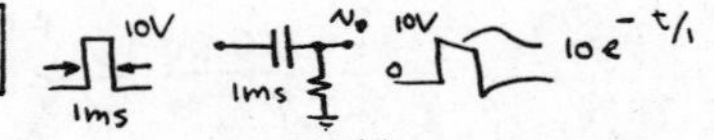

2

At 1ms, $v_o = 10e^{-1/1} = 3.68V$ and undershoot is 10 − 3.68 = 6.32V

For undershoot ≤ 1V, $10(1-e^{-1/\tau}) = 1 \rightarrow 10e^{-1/\tau} = 9$

or $e^{-1/\tau} = 0.9$, $1/\tau = 0.105$, $\tau = \frac{1}{.105} = 9.49$

That is the required time constant is 9.49 ms or more

57 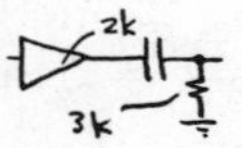

$e^{-10^{-3}/\tau} = 0.99 \rightarrow 1/\tau = 0.010$

or $\tau = 99.5 \approx 100$ ms

for which $f_{3dB} = \frac{1}{2\pi\tau} = \frac{1}{2\pi\times0.1} = 1.59Hz$

Capacitor $C = \tau/R = \frac{100\times10^{-3}}{(2+3)\times10^3} = 20\mu F$

58 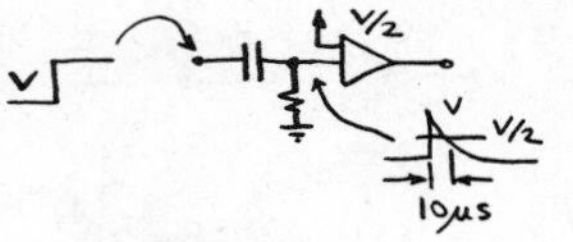

$e^{-10/\tau} = 1/2 \rightarrow 10/\tau = 0.693$

$\tau = 14.4\mu s$

59 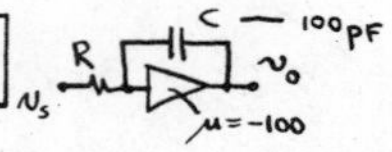

At Amp input, $C_{eq} = 100(1-(-100))$

$= 10100$ pF

For $f_{3dB} = 1kHz$, $R = \frac{1}{2\pi f_{3dB} C}$

or $R = \frac{1}{2\pi\times10^3\times10100\times10^{-12}} = 15.8k\Omega$

1 For all circuits : $v_o/v_i = -R_2/R_1$; $R_i = R_1$ **3**

(a) $v_o/v_i = -10$, $R_i = 1k\Omega$

(b) $v_o/v_i = -1$, $R_i = 1k\Omega$

(c) $v_o/v_i = -1/10$, $R_i = 10k\Omega$

(d) $v_o/v_i = -0/1k = 0$, $R_i = 1k\Omega$

(e) $v_o/v_i = -1k/100 = -10$, $R_i = 100\Omega$

(f) $v_o/v_i = -1k/0 = -\infty$, $R_i = 0$

2 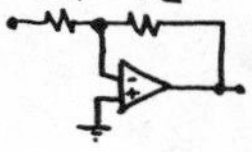

$R_1 = R_i = 10k\Omega$; $\frac{v_o}{v_i} = -\frac{R_2}{R_1} = -100$

$R_2 = 100R_1 = 1M\Omega$

3 R_2 is largest = 10MΩ

Gain $\frac{v_o}{v_i} = \frac{-R_2}{R_1} = -100 \rightarrow R_1 = \frac{R_2}{100} = \frac{10M}{100} = 100k\Omega$

For which $R_{in} = R_1 = 100k\Omega$

4 For 2x gain, shunt R_1 by 100kΩ, its original value

Then R_{in} = 100k‖100k = 50kΩ

5 **3**

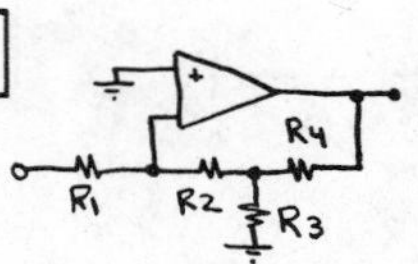

$R_{in} = 1M\Omega = R_1$

$-v_o/v_i = \frac{R_2}{R_1} + \frac{R_4}{R_1}\left(1 + \frac{R_2}{R_3}\right) = 102$

Say $R_2 = R_4 = R_1 = 1M$

∴ $102 = 1 + 1(1 + 1/R_3) \rightarrow R_2/R_3 = 100$

and $R_3 = \frac{1}{100}M = 10k\Omega$

6 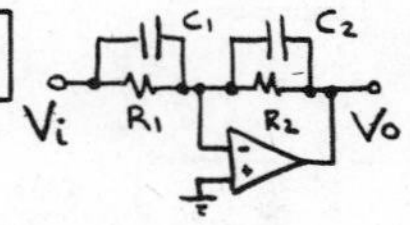

$\frac{V_o(s)}{V_i(s)} = -\frac{Z_2}{Z_1} = -\frac{Y_1}{Y_2} = -\frac{1/R_1 + C_1 s}{1/R_2 + C_2 s}$

$= -\frac{R_2}{R_1} \cdot \frac{1 + R_1C_1s}{1 + R_2C_2s}$

which is frequency independant when $R_1C_1 = R_2C_2$

For $V_o/V_i = -10$, $R_1 = 1M$, $C_1 = 30pF$, then

$R_2 = 10M$, $C_2 = \frac{R_1}{R_2}C_1 = \frac{30}{10} = 3pF$

7 Circuit as in **6**

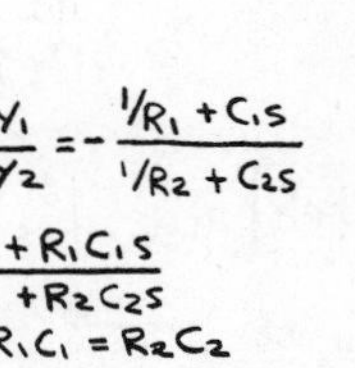

(a) $R_1 = R_2 = 10k$, $C_1 = 10C_2 = 0.1\mu F$

Low freq. gain $= -R_2/R_1 = -1$

High freq. gain $= -C_1/C_2 = -10$

$\frac{1}{R_1C_1} = \frac{1}{10^4\times10^{-7}} = 10^3$ r/s ; $\frac{1}{R_2C_2} = \frac{1}{10^4\times10^{-8}} = 10^4$ r/s

3

(b) $R_1 = R_2 = 10k\Omega$, $C_2 = 10C_1 = 0.1\mu F$

Low freq. gain $= -R_2/R_1 = -1$

High freq. gain $= -C_1/C_2 = -\frac{1}{10}$

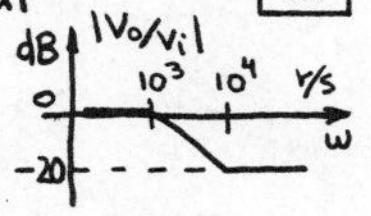

$\frac{1}{R_2C_2} = \frac{1}{10^4 \times 10^{-7}} = 10^3$ r/s ; $\frac{1}{R_1C_1} = \frac{1}{10^4 \times 10^{-8}} = 10^4$ r/s

8

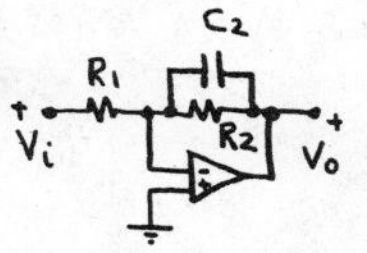

Gain of 20dB $\rightarrow R_2 = 10R_1$

Rin of $10k\Omega \rightarrow \underline{R_1 = 10k\Omega}$

whence $R_2 = \underline{100k\Omega}$.

Also $\omega_{3dB} = 10^3$ r/s $\rightarrow R_2C_2 = 10^{-3} \rightarrow C_2 = \frac{10^{-3}}{10^5} = 10^{-8} = \underline{.01\mu F}$

Now at $\omega = 10^4$ r/s $= 10\,\omega_{3dB}$, gain 20-20 $= \underline{0dB}$

For a +1V step, $v_o(t) = -10(1 - e^{-10^3 t})$

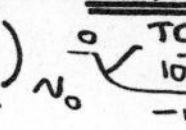

9

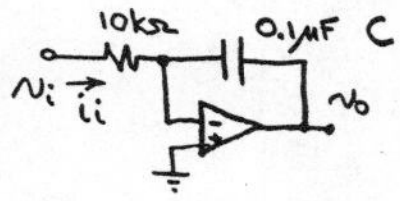

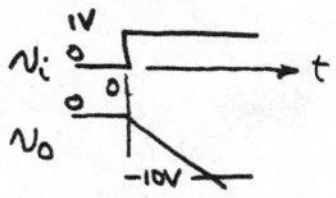

$v_o|_{t=0} = 0$

$i_i|_{t=0+} = \frac{1V}{10k\Omega} = 100\mu A$ flowing into C

Thus v_o is a negative ramp falling at rate $V/T = I/C = \frac{100 \times 10^{-6}}{0.1 \times 10^{-6}} = 1000$ $\underline{V/s}$

It reaches $-10V$ in $\frac{10V}{1000V/s} = \underline{10ms}$.

10

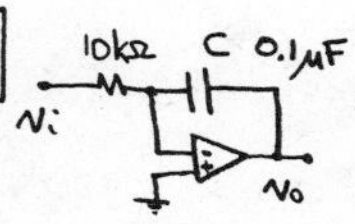

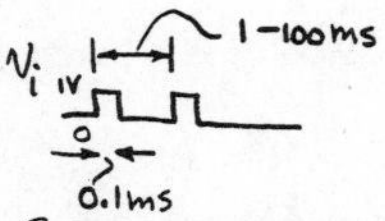

3

$v_o|_{t=0} = +10V$

Voltage change across C for each pulse is $V = \frac{IT}{C} = \frac{\frac{1}{10^4}(0.1 \times 10^{-3})}{0.1 \times 10^{-6}}$ or $\frac{10^{-8}}{10^{-7}} = 10^{-1}V$. Thus the output reaches 0V after $\frac{10-0}{0.1}$ or $\underline{100 \text{ pulses}}$. For the output initially at zero, after 10 pulses it is $-10(0.1) = \underline{-1V}$.

11

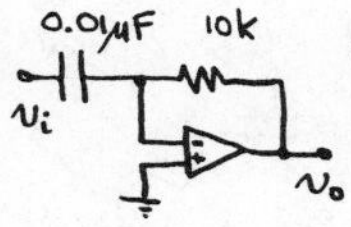

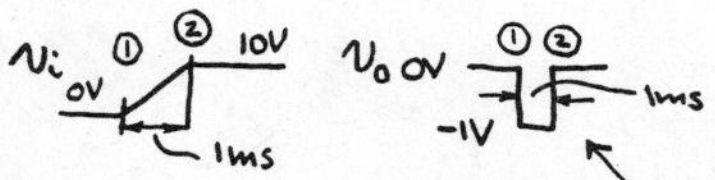

During the ramp, capacitor current $i = \frac{C\,dv_i}{dt}$ is $.01 \times 10^{-6} \times \frac{10}{10^{-3}} = 0.1mA$ and $v_o = -0.1(10k) = -1.0V$

If "step" rises in 0.1 msec, v_o becomes $-10V$ for 0.1ms

If the step is ideal (with $t_r = 0$), v_o is an infinite negative impulse (of zero duration)

12

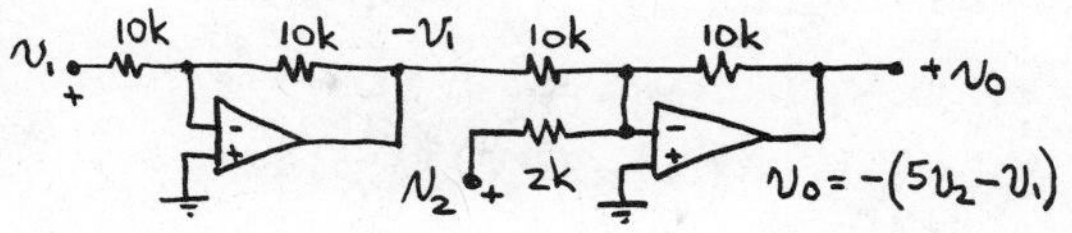

13

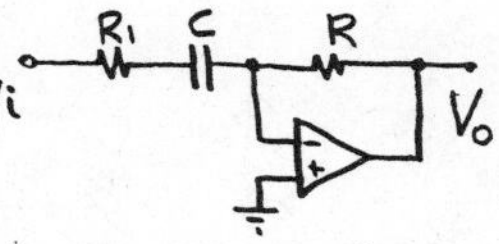

3

$\frac{V_o(s)}{V_i(s)} = \frac{R}{R_1 + \frac{1}{Cs}} = \frac{RCs}{1 + R_1Cs}$

$V_o/V_i \rightarrow 0$ at low freq.

$\rightarrow R/R_1$ at high freq.

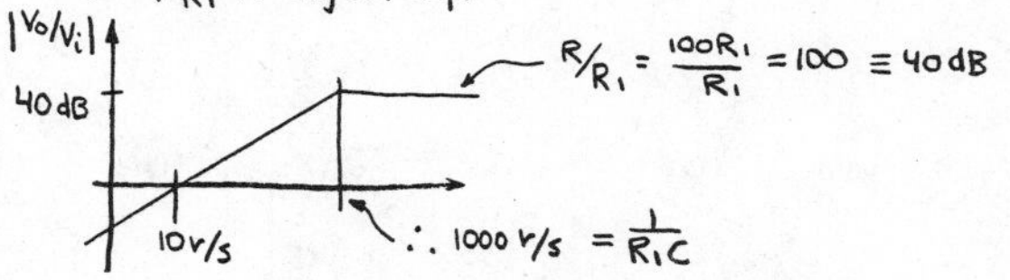

$|V_o/V_i|$ at 100 r/s is 20dB and at 10^4 r/s is 40dB

14

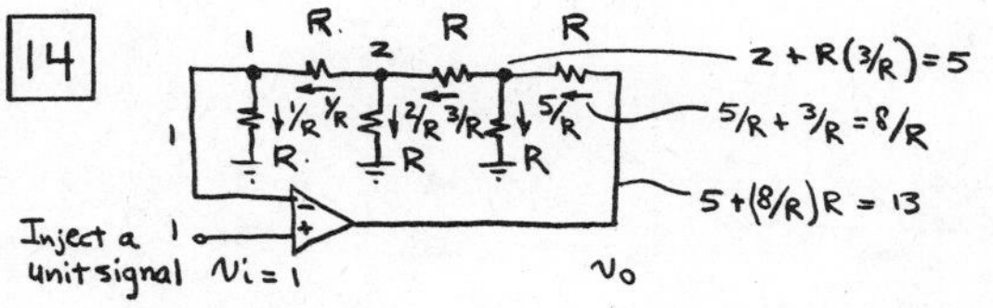

See for all resistors equal and ideal op amp, that Gain $= v_o/v_i = 13$

15

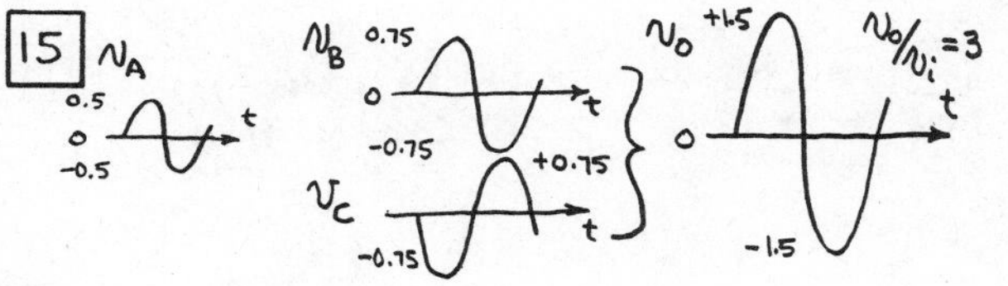

16 At B, signal range is ±14V, that is $v_B = 28V_{pp}$ and $v_C = 28V_{pp}$. Thus $v_o = v_B - v_C$ can be $28 + 28 = \underline{56V_{pp}} = 28V_{peak} = \frac{28}{\sqrt{2}}$ or $\underline{19.8}V_{rms}$ before clipping results

3

17 Gain $= \frac{100k}{100k + 100k}\left(1 + \frac{100k}{100k}\right) = \frac{1}{2} \times (1+1) = \underline{1}$ V/V

18 Voltage at op amp + node $= \frac{v_1 + v_2}{2}$

$\therefore v_o = \frac{v_1 + v_2}{2}(2) = v_1 + v_2$

19 $v_o = \frac{v_1 + v_2}{2} + \left(\frac{v_1 + v_2}{2} - v_3\right) \times 1 = v_1 + v_2 - v_3$

Notice that if $v_2 = 0$, $v_o = v_1 - v_3$, ie difference amp.

20

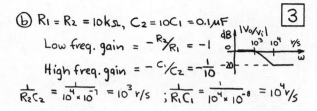

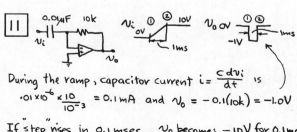

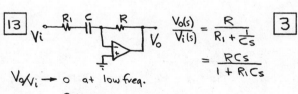

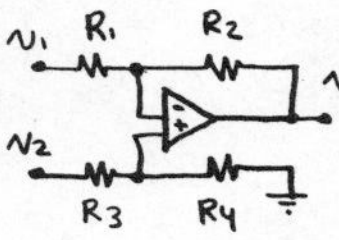

$v_o = v_2 \times \frac{R_4}{R_3 + R_4} + \left(v_2 \times \frac{R_4}{R_3 + R_4} - v_1\right)\frac{R_2}{R_1}$

which for $R_4/R_3 = R_2/R_1$

becomes $v_o = \frac{v_2 R_4}{R_3 + R_4}\left(1 + \frac{R_4}{R_3}\right) - \frac{v_1 R_4}{R_3} = \frac{R_4}{R_3}(v_2 - v_1)$

For gain of 10, $R_4 = 10R_3$

Differential input resistance $= R_1 + R_3 = 20k\Omega$ **3**

Choose $R_1 = R_3 = 10k \rightarrow R_2 = R_4 = 100k$

Now at v_1, $R_{in1} = R_1$; at v_2, $R_{in2} = R_3 + R_4$ } These are equal if $R_1 = R_3 + R_4 = R_3 + 10R_3 = 11R_3$

If $R_1 + R_3 = 20K$, $11R_3 + R_3 = 20K$ and

$R_3 = \frac{20}{12}k = 1.\dot{6}k$; $R_1 = 18.\dot{3}k$

$R_4 = 16.\dot{6}k$; $R_2 = 183.\dot{3}k$

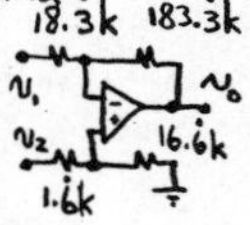

21 (a) Gain $= \frac{-xR}{(1-x)R} = \frac{x}{x-1} = \frac{1}{1-1/x}$

Note that gain varies from 0 to ∞ as $x \rightarrow 0$ to 1

(b) Gain $= 1 + \frac{xR}{(1-x)R} = \frac{1-x+x}{1-x} = \frac{1}{1-x}$

Varying from 1 to ∞ as x varies from 0 to 1

(c)

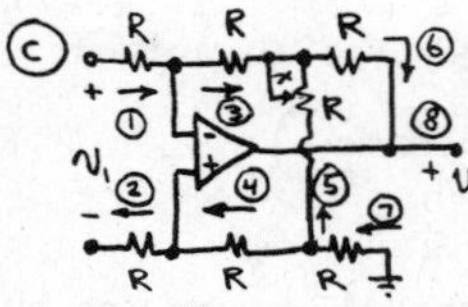

① $i = v_1/2R$; ② $i = v_1/2R$

③ $i = v_1/2R$; ④ $i = v_1/2R$

⑤ Now operation as a difference amplifier implies v_1 appears across $(1-x)R$ and $i = v_1/(1-x)R$

⑥ $i = \frac{v_1}{R}\left(\frac{1}{2} + \frac{1}{1-x}\right)$ and ⑦ $i = \frac{v_1}{R}\left(\frac{1}{2} + \frac{1}{1-x}\right) = \frac{v_1}{R}\left(\frac{3-x}{2(1-x)}\right)$

⑧ Sum voltage across resistors, from ground: **3**

$v_o = 0 - \frac{v_1}{R}\left(\frac{3-x}{2(1-x)}\right) \times R - \frac{v_1}{(1-x)R} \times (1-x)R - \frac{v_1}{R}\left(\frac{3-x}{2(1-x)}\right) \times R$

$= v_1\left(-1 - \frac{3-x}{1-x}\right) = v_1\left(\frac{-4+2x}{1-x}\right)$

Gain $= \frac{-2(x-2)}{(x-1)} = \frac{4-2x}{x-1} = -2 - \frac{2}{1-x}$

See gain varies from -4 to $-\infty$ as x varies from 0 to 1

22 (a) v is imposed across R: $i_o = v/R$

(b) The difference amp connection forces $-v$ across R. Thus $i_o = -v/R$

23 Voltage across R_4 is $v_2 - v_1$

Voltage between the op amp outputs is $(v_2 - v_1)\left(1 + \frac{2R_3}{R_4}\right)$

Gain of second stage $= -\frac{R_2}{R_1}$

$\therefore v_o = -R_2/R_1 \left(1 + 2R_3/R_4\right)(v_2 - v_1)$

24 $G = \frac{1 + R_2/R_1}{1 + (1 + R_2/R_1)/A}$ **3**

For follower: $R_2 = 0$, $R_1 = \infty$

$G_1 = \frac{1+0}{1 + (1+0)/1000} = \frac{1}{1 + 1/1000} = \frac{1000}{1001} = .999$

$G_2 = \frac{2000}{2001} = .9995$

% change in gain is $\frac{G_2 - G_1}{G_1} \times 100 = \frac{.05}{.999} = \underline{\underline{.05\%}}$

25 $Z_{in} = \frac{Z_1 Z_3}{Z_2 Z_4} \times Z_5 = \frac{1/Cs \times R}{R\,R} \times \frac{1}{Cs} = \frac{1}{RC^2 s^2}$

$Z(j\omega) = -\frac{1}{RC^2\omega^2}$, a negative resistor inversely proportional to the square of freq.

26

$v = \frac{1/Cs}{R + 1/Cs} v_1 = \frac{1}{1 + RCs} v_1$

$v_o = v - \frac{v_1 - v}{R_1} \cdot R = 2v - v_1$

or $v_o = \left(\frac{2}{1+RCs} - 1\right) v_1 = \frac{1 - RCs}{1 + RCs} \times v_1$

Now with $C = .01\mu F$, $R = 20k\Omega$, $R_1 = 10k\Omega$

$v_o/v_1 = \frac{1 - 2 \times 10^4 \times 10^{-8}(j\omega)}{1 + 2 \times 10^4 \times 10^{-8}(j\omega)} = \frac{1 - 2 \times 10^{-4}(j\omega)}{1 + 2 \times 10^{-4}(j\omega)}$

At $\omega = 5000$ r/s, $v_o/v_1 = \frac{1-j}{1+j}$

For which $|v_o/v_1| = \left(\frac{1^2 + 1^2}{1^2 + 1^2}\right)^{1/2} = 1$ and $\phi = \tan^{-1}(-1) - \tan^{-1} 1 = -90°$

27 **3**

A_o		f_b		f_t	
V/V	dB	Hz	r/s	Hz	10^6 r/s
10^5	100	10	62.8	10^6	6.
10^5	100	10	62.8	10^6	
10^5	100	10	62.8	10^6	
10^5	100	10	62.8	10^6	
10^6	120	1	6.28	10^6	
10^4	80	100	62.8	10^6	
10^5	100	100	62.8	10^7	

28

Gain $\times$ Bandwidth $GB = 10 \times 10^5 = 10^6$

$A_o = \underline{10^3}$

$f_b = 10^6/10^3 = \underline{\underline{10^3\,Hz}}$; $f_t = 10^6/1 = \underline{\underline{10^6\,Hz}}$

29 (a)

$f_t = 2MHz$; $f_{3dB} = \frac{2}{1+0} = \underline{\underline{2MHz}}$

(b)

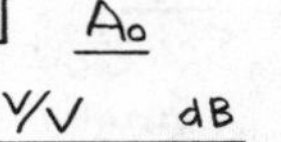

$f_{3dB} = \frac{2}{1 + R/R} = \underline{\underline{1MHz}}$

(c)

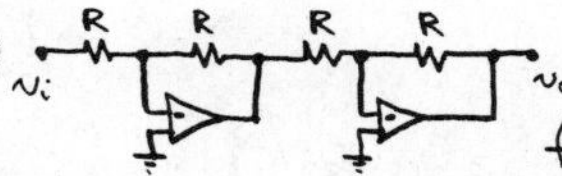

3

f_{3dB} for each $= \frac{2}{1+1} = 1\,MHz$

For both: $v_o/v_i = \frac{-1}{1+jf/1} \times \frac{-1}{1+jf/1}$

At 3dB cutoff: $\left|\left(\frac{1}{1+jf}\right)^2\right| = \frac{1}{\sqrt{2}}$, ie $\left(\left(\frac{1}{1+f^2}\right)^2\right)^{1/2} = \frac{1}{\sqrt{2}}$

or $1+f^2 = \sqrt{2} \rightarrow f = \sqrt{.414} = \underline{\underline{.643\,MHz}}$

30

	Low Freq. Gain	3dB Freq.	Product
Inverting:	$-(R_2/R_1)$	$f_t/(1+R_2/R_1)$	$\frac{f_t(R_2/R_1)}{1+R_2/R_1} = \frac{f_t}{1+R_1/R_2}$
NonInvert:	$(1+R_2/R_1)$	$f_t/(1+R_2/R_1)$	f_t

GB product is highest for noninverting amp.

GB product is constant for noninverting amp.

Difference is greatest for R_1/R_2 largest, or R_2 smallest, that is for small gain (such as -1, for $R_2/R_1 = 1$)

31 Eq 3.13 : $G = \frac{1+R_2/R_1}{1+(1+R_2/R_1)/A}$; for a follower ($R_2 = 0$)

$G = \frac{1}{1+1/A}$ is 0.99 when $1 = 0.99 + 0.99/A$ or $A = \frac{.99}{.01} = \underline{\underline{99}}$

For inverter: $G = \frac{-R_2/R_1}{1+(1+R_2/R_1)/A}$

For $R_1 = R_2$ and $A = 99$, $G = \frac{-1}{1+(1+1)/99} = \underline{\underline{-0.98}}$

3

32

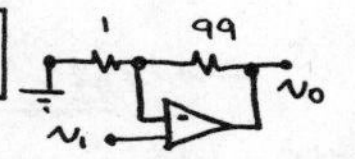

$f_t = 1\,MHz$

$f_{3dB} = \frac{1\,MHz}{1+99/1} = 10\,kHz$

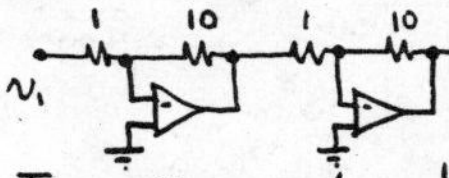

For each: $f_{3dB} = \frac{1\,MHz}{1+10} = \underline{\underline{90.9\,kHz}}$

Together: $\left(\frac{10}{\left(1+\left(\frac{f_{3dB}}{90.9}\right)^2\right)^{1/2}}\right)^2 = \frac{100}{\sqrt{2}}$ or $\left(\frac{f_{3dB}}{90.9}\right)^2 = \sqrt{2}-1$

whence $f_{3dB} = 90.9\sqrt{\sqrt{2}-1} = \underline{\underline{58.5\,kHz}}$

33 $112\,dB \rightarrow 20\log_{10} x = 112 \rightarrow x = \log^{-1}\frac{112}{20} = 10^{112/20} = 4\times10^5$

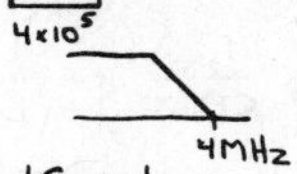

$f_{3dB} = \frac{4\times10^6}{4\times10^5} = 10\,Hz$

|Gain| at $1\,MHz = 0 + 20\log_{10}\frac{4\times10^6}{1\times10^6} = \underline{\underline{12\,dB}}$

at $100\,kHz = 0 + 20\log_{10} 40 = \underline{\underline{32\,dB}}$

at $1\,kHz = 0 + 20\log_{10} 4000 = \underline{\underline{72\,dB}}$

But at $10\,Hz = 112\,dB - 3\,dB = \underline{\underline{109\,dB}}$

34 $f_t = 4\,MHz$, $A = 400\times10^3$

3

Gain $= 400 \rightarrow 1 + R_2/R_1 = 400$

$f_{3dB} = f_t/(1+R_2/R_1) = 4\times10^6/400 = \underline{\underline{10\,kHz}}$

For a 2.5mV step input, output rises to 1 volt with a rise time $t_r = \frac{0.35}{f_{3dB}} = \frac{0.35}{10^4} = \underline{\underline{35\,\mu s}}$

35

$\beta = v_1/v_o$: For gain ∞, v_o finite then input is zero.

Thus $v_s = v_1 = v_o\beta \rightarrow$ $\boxed{v_o/v_s = 1/\beta}$

(a)

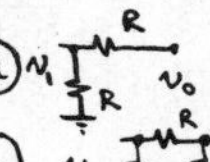

$\beta = \underline{\underline{1/2}}$, $v_o/v_s = \frac{1}{1/2} = \underline{\underline{2}}$

(b)

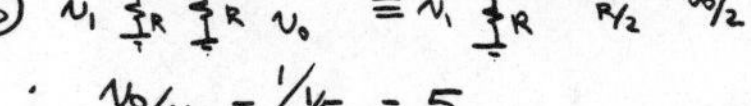

$\beta = \frac{R}{5/2\,R}\cdot 1/2 = \underline{\underline{1/5}}$

$\therefore v_o/v_s = 1/(1/5) = \underline{\underline{5}}$

(c)

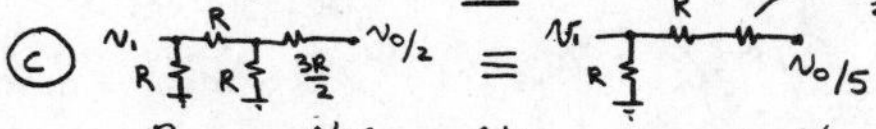

$\frac{3R}{2}\|R = \frac{3R}{5}$

$v_1 = \frac{R}{2R+3/5R}\cdot v_o/5 = \frac{v_o}{13} \rightarrow \beta = \underline{\underline{1/13}}$, $v_o/v_s = \underline{\underline{13}}$

36

$v_o = A(v_s - v_1)$ and $v_1 = \beta v_o \rightarrow v_o = A(v_s - \beta v_o)$

or $v_o(1+\beta A) = Av_s \rightarrow \frac{v_o}{v_s} = \frac{A}{1+\beta A}$. For $\underline{\underline{A\beta \gg 1}}$, $\frac{v_o}{v_s} = \frac{A}{\beta A} = 1/\beta$

37

3

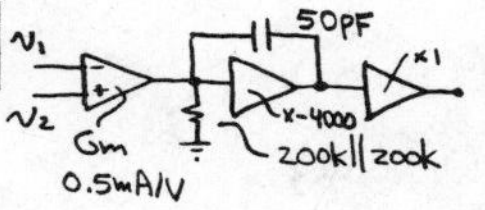

$A_o = 0.5\times10^{-3}\times(200\|200)\times10^3\times4000$

or $A_o = \underline{200{,}000}$

$C_{eq} = 50\,pF(1-(-4000)) = 50(4001) = 0.2\,\mu F$

$f_b = \frac{1}{2\pi(100\times10^3)(.2\times10^{-6})} = \underline{7.96\,Hz}$

$f_t = 7.96\times2\times10^5 = \underline{\underline{1.6\,MHz}}$

38 $CV = IT \rightarrow V/T = I/C = \frac{0.1\times10^{-3}}{50\times10^{-12}} = \underline{\underline{2V/\mu sec}}$

$f_M = \frac{2V/\mu s}{2\pi V_{omax}} = \frac{2\times10^6}{2\pi\times10} = \underline{\underline{31.8\,kHz}}$

39

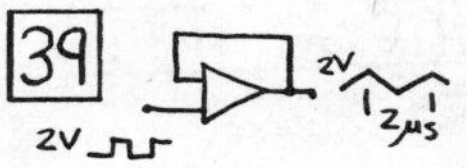

$2V$ in $\frac{1}{2}\times\frac{1}{500\times10^6}$ s $\rightarrow SR = \underline{\underline{2V/\mu s}}$

and $V_{omax} = 15 - 2 = \underline{13\,V}$

whence $f_M = \frac{2V/\mu s}{2\pi/13} = \underline{\underline{24.5\,kHz}}$

40 $f_M = \frac{SR}{2\pi V_{omax}}$

For 1 volt sine wave, $f_{Max} = \frac{10\times10^6}{2\pi\times1} = \underline{\underline{1.59\,MHz}}$

For 10 volt sine wave, $f_{Max} = \frac{10\times10^6}{2\pi\times10} = \underline{\underline{15.9\,MHz}}$

41 $V_f = V_{o\,max}\dfrac{f_m}{f} = 12\,\dfrac{50}{100} = \underline{\underline{6\text{ volts peak}}}$ **3**

42 ⓐ $CMRR = \dfrac{A_d}{A_{cm}} = \dfrac{10^3}{10^{-3}} = 10^6 \longrightarrow$ or $\underline{\underline{120\text{ dB}}}$

ⓑ With ×100 postamp, $CMRR = \dfrac{10^3\times 100}{10^{-3}\times 100} = 10^6$ or $\underline{120\text{ dB}}$ as before

ⓒ With preamp, $CMRR = \dfrac{A_{d_1}\times 10^3}{A_{cm_1}\times 10^{-3}}$

but $A_{d_1}/A_{cm_1} = 10^{40/20} = 100$

$\therefore CMRR = \dfrac{100\times 10^3}{10^{-3}} = 10^8$ or $\underline{160\text{ dB}}$

Alternatively $CMRR = 40 + 120 = 160\text{ dB}$

43

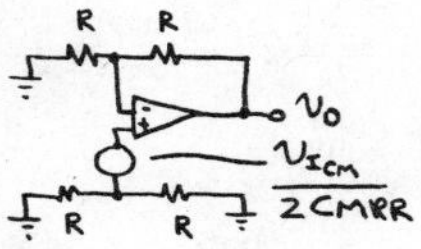

$v_O = \dfrac{v_{Icm}}{2\,CMRR}\left(1+R/R\right) = \dfrac{v_{Icm}}{CMRR}$

That is $A_{cm} = \dfrac{1}{CMRR}$

and $A_d = 1$

Thus CMRR of the difference amplifier $= \dfrac{A_d}{A_{cm}} = \dfrac{1}{1/CMRR}$

that is CMRR of the op amp.

44 **3**

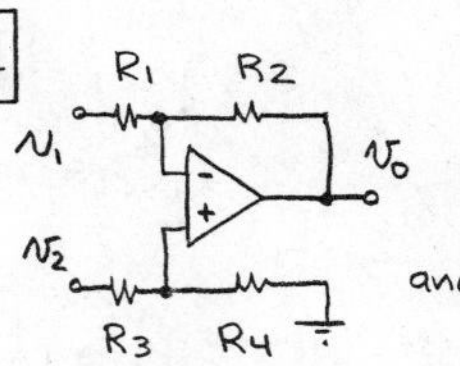

$v_O = G_d(v_2 - v_1) + G_{cm}\left(\dfrac{v_1+v_2}{2}\right)$

and $v_O = -\dfrac{R_2}{R_1}v_1 + \dfrac{1+R_2/R_1}{1+R_3/R_4}v_2$

See $R_2/R_1 = G_d - G_{cm}/2$ and $\dfrac{1+R_2/R_1}{1+R_3/R_4} = G_d + G_{cm}/2$

Adding: $G_d = \tfrac{1}{2}\left(R_2/R_1 + \dfrac{1+R_2/R_1}{1+R_3/R_4}\right)$

or $\boxed{G_d = \dfrac{R_2}{R_1}\left(\dfrac{1+\frac{1}{2}\left(\frac{R_1}{R_2}+\frac{R_3}{R_4}\right)}{1+R_3/R_4}\right)}$

Subtracting: $G_{cm} = -R_2/R_1 + \dfrac{1+R_2/R_1}{1+R_3/R_4}$

or $\boxed{G_{cm} = \dfrac{R_2}{R_1}\left(\dfrac{\frac{R_1}{R_2}-\frac{R_3}{R_4}}{1+R_3/R_4}\right)}$

$CMRR = G_d/G_{cm}$

Thus $CMRR = \boxed{\dfrac{1+\frac{1}{2}\left(\frac{R_1}{R_2}+\frac{R_3}{R_4}\right)}{\left(\frac{R_1}{R_2}-\frac{R_3}{R_4}\right)}}$

Now for $R_2/R_1 = 1000\,(1\pm 0.01)$ **3**

and $R_4/R_3 = 1000\,(1\pm 0.01)$

Nominal $G_d = 1000\left(\dfrac{1+\frac{1}{2}(.001+.001)}{1+.001}\right)$

$= \underline{\underline{1000\text{ V/V}}} \equiv 60\text{ dB}$

Generally:

$G_{cm} = 1000(1\pm.01)\left[\dfrac{\frac{1}{1000(1\pm.01)} - \frac{1}{1000(1\pm.01)}}{1+\frac{1}{1000(1\pm.01)}}\right]$

whose largest value is $\approx \dfrac{1-(-.01)-(1-(+.01))}{1.001}$

or $G_{cm} = \dfrac{\pm .02}{1.001}$ is $\underline{.02}$ V/V or −34 dB

Generally:

$CMRR = \dfrac{1+\frac{1}{2}\left(\frac{1}{1000(1\pm.01)}+\frac{1}{1000(1\pm.01)}\right)}{\frac{1}{1000(1\pm.01)}-\frac{1}{1000(1\pm.01)}}$

whose least value is $\approx 1000\,(1+.001)/.02$

or $50050 \equiv \underline{94.0\text{ dB}}$

45

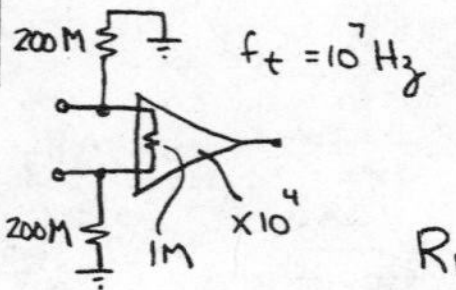

$f_t = 10^7\text{ Hz}$

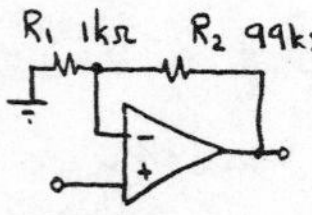

$\beta = \dfrac{R_1}{R_1+R_2} = \dfrac{1}{100}$

$R_{in} = 2R_{icm}\,\|\,(1+A\beta)R_{id}$

Op amp 3 dB frequency is $\dfrac{f_t}{A_0} = \dfrac{10^7}{10^4} = 10^3\text{ Hz}$ **3**

Thus at 60 Hz, $A = 10^4$ and $R_{in} = 2(10^8)\,\|\,(1+10^4\times 10^{-2})10^6$

or $R_{in} = 2\times 10^8\,\|\,1.01\times 10^8 = 67.1\text{ M}\Omega$

But at 60 kHz, $A = \dfrac{2\pi f_t}{s}$, whence

$Z_{in} = 2\times 10^8\,\|\left(10^6\left(1+\dfrac{2\pi\times 10^7}{100\,s}\right)\right) \longrightarrow$

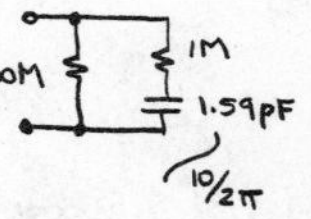

and at 60 kHz, $Z_{in} \approx 10^6(1-1.6j)$

46

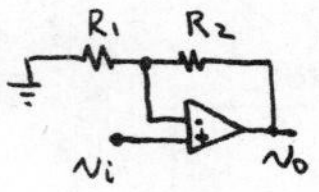

ⓐ $v_O\dfrac{R_1}{R_1+R_2} + \dfrac{v_O}{A} = v_i$

or $v_O/v_i = \dfrac{1}{\frac{R_1}{R_1+R_2}+1/A} = \dfrac{A}{1+A\frac{R_1}{R_1+R_2}}$

and as $\beta = \dfrac{R_1}{R_1+R_2}$, $v_O/v_i = \dfrac{A}{1+A\beta}$ and thus $(\div A\beta)$

$v_O/v_i = \dfrac{1/\beta}{1+(1/\beta)/A}$

ⓑ

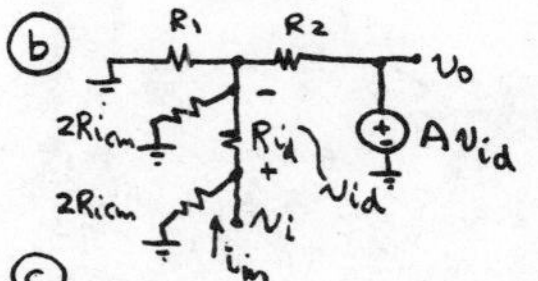

$v_O = v_i\dfrac{A}{1+A\beta} = Av_{id}$

or $v_{id} = v_i/(1+A\beta)$

$i_{in} = \dfrac{v_i}{2R_{icm}} + \dfrac{v_{id}}{R_{id}}$

ⓒ $\therefore 1/R_{in} = i_{in}/v_i = \dfrac{1}{2R_{icm}} + \dfrac{1}{R_{id}}\cdot\dfrac{1}{1+A\beta}$

ie $R_{in} = (2R_{icm})\,\|\,R_{id}(1+A\beta)$ as in Eq. 3.35

47 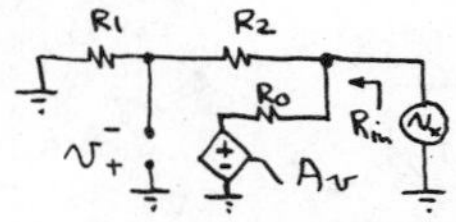

Gain of the equivalent amplifier is $-\frac{R_1}{R_1+R_2} \times A = -\beta A$ **3**

$R_{in} = (R_1+R_2) \| \frac{R_o}{(1-\text{Gain})} = (R_1+R_2) \| \frac{R_o}{1+A\beta} = R_{out}$

with feedback as in Eq. 3.37

48 ⓐ 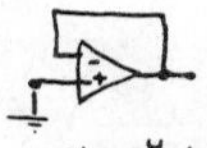 $R_{out} = (R_1+R_2) \| R_o/(1+A\beta)$

$R_{out} = \infty \| 10^4/(1+10^4 \times 1) = 0.9999\,\Omega \simeq \underline{\underline{1\,\Omega}}$

ⓑ 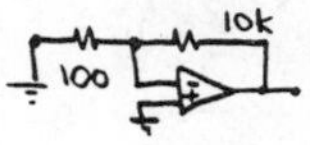

$R_{out} = (100+10^4) \| 10^4/(1+10^4 \times \frac{0.1}{10.1})$

$= 10.1k \| 100 = \underline{\underline{99\,\Omega}}$

ⓒ 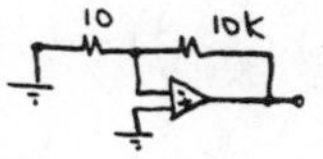

$R_{out} = (10+10^4) \| 10^4/(1+10^4 \times \frac{0.01}{10.01})$

$= 10.01k \| 909.9 = \underline{\underline{834\,\Omega}}$

The approximation, $R_{out} = \frac{R_o}{A\beta}$, yields ⓐ 1.00 ⓑ 101 ⓒ 1001

49 $R_o = 1k$, $A_o = 10^5$, $f_t = 10^6$ Hz, $f_{3dB} = \frac{10^6}{10^5} = 10$

$R_{out} = (R_1+R_2) \| R_o/(1+A\beta) \approx R_o/(1+A\beta)$. Here $\beta = \frac{1}{101}$.

Thus at dc: $R_{out} = \frac{10^3}{1+10^5 \times \frac{1}{101}} = \underline{\underline{1.01\,\Omega}}$

For higher frequencies $A = A_o/(1+jf/f_{3dB}) = \frac{10^5}{1+jf/10}$

Thus $Y_{out} = 1/Z_{out} = 1/R_o(1+A\beta)$ **3**

or $Y_{out} = 10^{-3}\left(1+\frac{10^5}{1+jf/10} \cdot \frac{1}{101}\right) = 10^{-3} + \frac{1}{1.01+0.101jf}$

representing the network: 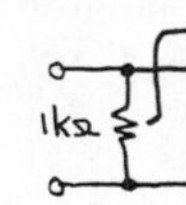

$L = \frac{.101}{2\pi}$ H = 16.1 mH

At f = 10kHz, $Z_{out} = \left(10^{-3} + (1.01 + .101 \times 10^4 j)^{-1}\right)^{-1}$

$= (497+503j)$ ohms

50 $R_o = 10k$, A_o large, $f_t = 1$MHz, $R_1 = 1k$, $R_2 = 100k$

$A \approx \frac{2\pi \times 10^6}{s}$; $Z_{out} = \frac{R_o}{A\beta} = \frac{10^4}{\frac{2\pi \times 10^6}{s} \cdot \frac{1}{101}} = .159\,s$,

corresponding to an inductor of .159 H

Resonance with a 0.1μF load at $f = \frac{1}{2\pi} \frac{1}{\sqrt{LC}}$

or $\frac{1}{2\pi\sqrt{.159 \times 10^{-7}}} = 1.26$ kHz

51 Output offset $= 1mV(1+\frac{100R_1}{R_1}) = 101$ mV, polarity unknown.

52 10μV/°C, zeroed at +25°C, yields output offsets at 0°C of 10×25×1000 = 0.25 V, and at 75°C of 0.5 V {of opposite polarities}

53 Offset $\le \pm 1$mV at 25°C with. TC ≤ 20μV/°C **3**

At 0°C, $V_o = (1+25(20 \times 10^{-3}))$mV × 1000 $= \underline{\underline{1.5V}}$

At 75°C, $V_o = (1+50(20 \times 10^{-3}))$mV × 1000 $= \underline{\underline{2.0V}}$ of opposite polarity. For limiting at ±12V, the maximum sine-wave peak is 12−2 or $\underline{\underline{10V}}$

54 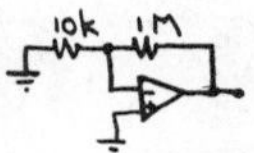

ⓐ $v_o = 100 \times 10^{-9} \times 10^6 = \underline{\underline{0.1V}}$

ⓑ Total output offset $v_o = 1mV(101) + 0.1 = \underline{\underline{0.2V}}$

ⓒ An alternative view to ⓐ is that:

$v_o = 100 \times 10^{-9}(10k \| 1M)(1+\frac{1M}{10k}) = 100 \times 10^{-9}(9.9k)101 = \underline{\underline{0.1V}}$

from which one sees that the compensating resistor is $(10k \| 1M) = 9.9k$. With bias current compensated and offset current 1/10 as large, corresponding output offset $= 1/10(0.1) = \underline{\underline{.01\text{ volts}}}$

ⓓ With bias compensation, the maximum output offset due to input offset current and input offset voltage is $1mV(101) + .01V = \underline{\underline{0.111V}}$

55 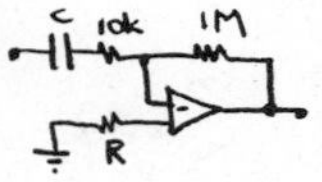

3

$V_{o_{off}} = 100 \times 10^{-9} \times 10^6 = \underline{\underline{0.1\text{ volts}}}$

$R_{comp} = \underline{\underline{1M\Omega}}$

With Compensation $V_{o_{off}} = 10 \times 10^{-9} \times 10^6 = \underline{\underline{0.01V}}$

56 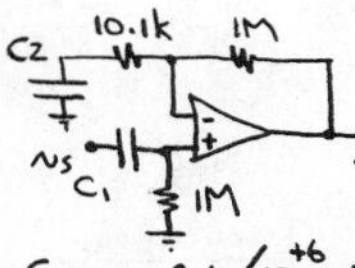

$\frac{v_o}{v_s} = \left(1+\frac{10^6}{10.1 \times 10^3}\right) = 1+99 = \underline{\underline{100}}$

T.C. = RC = 0.1 s

Thus $C_1 = 0.1/10^{+6} = \underline{\underline{0.1\mu F}}$ and $C_2 \approx 0.1/10^4 = \underline{\underline{10\mu F}}$

57 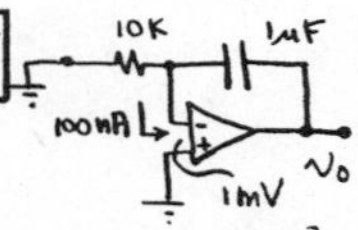

$v_o = V_{off} + \frac{V_{off}}{CR} \times t + \frac{I_{B1}}{C} \times t$

Initial offset = 1mV at output

Now $\frac{V_{off}}{CR} = \frac{1 \times 10^{-3}}{10^{-6} \times 10^4} = \underline{\underline{10^{-1}}}$ } See of equal magnitude

$\frac{I_{B1}}{C} = \frac{100 \times 10^{-9}}{10^{-6}} = \underline{\underline{10^{-1}}}$

Combined: $10^{-1}t + 10^{-1}t = 12$ when $t = \underline{\underline{60}}$ sec.

58 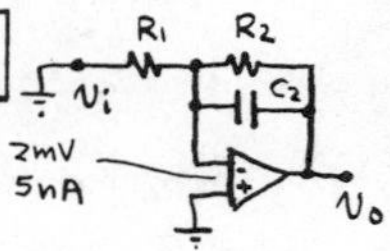

$R_1 = R_{in} = 100k\Omega$

$R_1C_2 = 10^{-2} \rightarrow C_2 = \frac{10^{-2}}{10^5} = \underline{0.1\mu F}$

$$v_{o_{off}} = 2\times10^{-3}\left(1+\frac{R_2}{100k}\right) + 5\times10^{-9}R_2 \le 100\times10^{-3}$$ **3**

or $2 + \frac{2R_2}{10^5} + 5\times10^{-6}R_2 = 100 \rightarrow R_2 = \underline{3.9M\Omega}$

For a 10V pulse (10V, 0V) input, $i_{in} = \frac{10V}{10^5} = 10^{-4} = 0.1mA$, for which

the output heads toward $-0.1\times10^{-3}\times3.9\times10^6 = -390V$,

reaching $-10V$ in $t = \frac{CV}{I} = \frac{0.1\times10^{-6}\times10}{0.1\times10^{-3}} = \underline{\underline{10^{-2}s}}$

When pulse is removed (and $v_i = 0$), $v_o = -10e^{-\frac{t}{R_2C_2}}$

reaching $-1V$ at $t = 3.9\times10^6\times10^{-7}\ln 1/10 = \underline{\underline{0.90s}}$

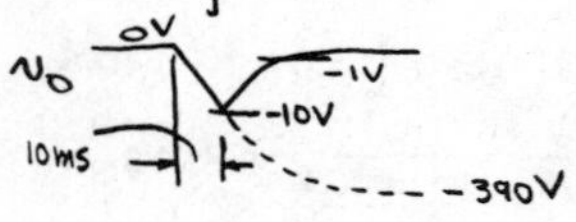

59

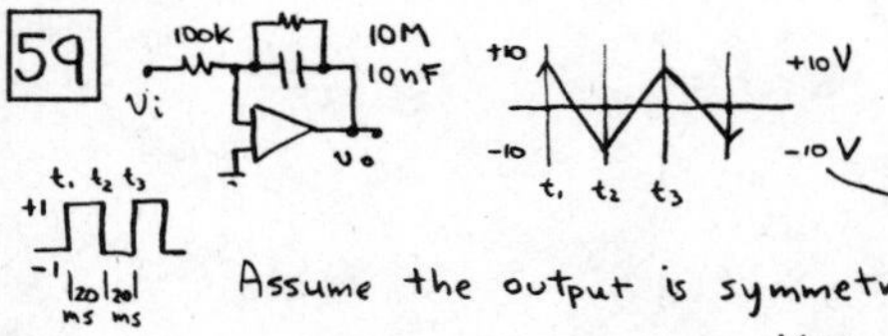

Assume the output is symmetrical:

In the ideal case: $CV = IT \rightarrow V = \frac{1/10^5 \times 20\times10^{-3}}{10\times10^{-9}} = 20V, ie \pm 10$

For non-ideal:

$v_o = -V + 100(1-e^{-t/RC}) = +V$

$2V = 100(1-e^{\frac{-20\times10^{-3}}{10^{-1}}}) = 100(1-e^{-0.2}) \rightarrow V = 9.06$, (not 10)

60 **3**

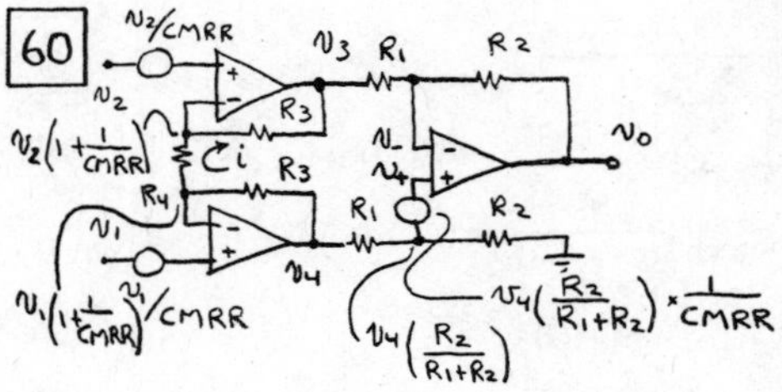

$$i = \frac{v_2 - v_1}{R_4}\left(1+\frac{1}{CMRR}\right)$$

$$v_3 = v_2\left(1+\frac{1}{CMRR}\right) + (v_2-v_1)\left(1+\frac{1}{CMRR}\right)\left(\frac{R_3}{R_4}\right)$$

$$= \left(1+\frac{1}{CMRR}\right)\left(v_2 + (v_2-v_1)\left(\frac{R_3}{R_4}\right)\right) \quad \text{-- (1)}$$

$$v_4 = v_1\left(1+\frac{1}{CMRR}\right) - \frac{(v_2-v_1)}{R_4}\left(1+\frac{1}{CMRR}\right)R_3$$

$$= \left(1+\frac{1}{CMRR}\right)\left(v_1 - (v_2-v_1)\left(\frac{R_3}{R_4}\right)\right) \quad \text{-- (2)}$$

$$v_- = v_+ = v_4\frac{R_2}{R_1+R_2}\left(1+\frac{1}{CMRR}\right)$$

$$v_o = v_- - \frac{v_2-v_1}{R_1}\cdot R_2$$

$$= v_4\frac{R_2}{R_1+R_2}\left(1+\frac{1}{CMRR}\right)\left(1+\frac{R_2}{R_1}\right) - v_3\frac{R_2}{R_1}$$

$$= v_4\left(\frac{R_2}{R_1}\right)\left(1+\frac{1}{CMRR}\right) - v_3\frac{R_2}{R_1}$$

Substituting for v_3 from (1) and v_4 from (2)

$$v_o = \frac{R_2}{R_1}\left(1+\frac{1}{CMRR}\right)\left[\frac{v_1}{CMRR} - (v_2-v_1)\left(1+\frac{2R_3}{R_4}\left(1+\frac{1}{2CMRR}\right)\right)\right]$$

3

Now, for $v_1 = v_{icm}$ and $v_2 = v_{icm} + v_d$

$$\rightarrow v_o = \frac{R_2}{R_1}\left(1+1/CMRR\right)\left(\frac{v_{icm}}{CMRR} - v_{id}\left(1+\frac{2R_3}{R_4}\left(1+\frac{2}{CMRR}\right)\right)\right)$$

Thus, common-mode gain $= \frac{R_2}{R_1}\left(1+\frac{1}{CMRR}\right)\frac{1}{CMRR} \approx \frac{R_2}{R_1}\left(\frac{1}{CMRR}\right)$

and differential gain $= -\frac{R_2}{R_1}\left(1+\frac{1}{CMRR}\right)\left(1+\frac{2R_3}{R_4}\left(1+\frac{1}{2CMRR}\right)\right)$

$$\approx -R_2/R_1\left(1+2R_3/R_4\right)$$

Now the common-mode rejection ratio of the instrumentation amplifier is $\frac{|\text{differential gain}|}{|\text{common-mode gain}|}$

ie $$\frac{R_2/R_1\left(1/CMRR\right)}{R_2/R_1\left(1+2R_3/R_4\right)} = \underline{\underline{CMRR\left(1+\frac{2R_3}{R_4}\right)}}$$

as required

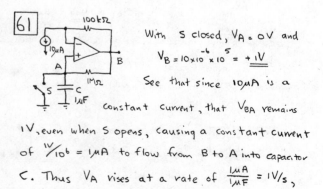

61

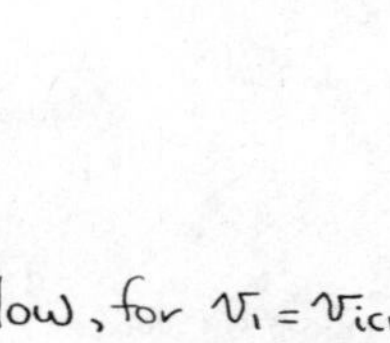

With S closed, $V_A = 0V$ and $V_B = 10\times10^{-6}\times10^5 = \underline{+1V}$

See that since 10µA is a constant current, that V_{BA} remains 1V, even when S opens, causing a constant current of $1V/10^6 = 1\mu A$ to flow from B to A into capacitor C. Thus V_A rises at a rate of $\frac{1\mu A}{1\mu F} = 1V/s$,

3

with V_B preceeding it by 1V. V_B reaches 11 volts in $T = CV/I = \frac{1\times10^{-6}(11-1)}{1\times10^{-6}} = \underline{\underline{10s}}$,

proceeding to 13V where limiting occurs.

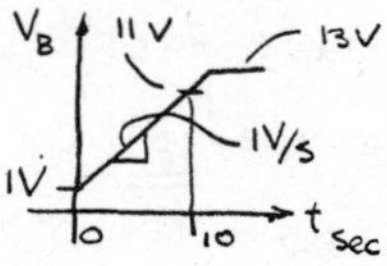

Note (for future reference in Ch.9) that this op amp circuit implements a <u>current mirror</u>

62

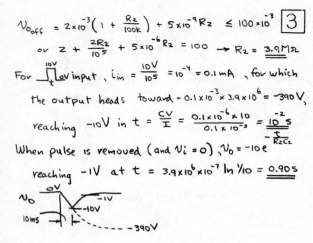

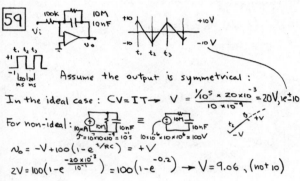

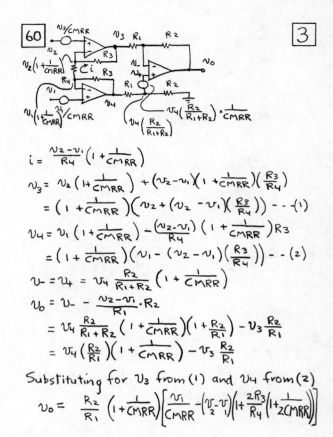

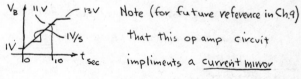

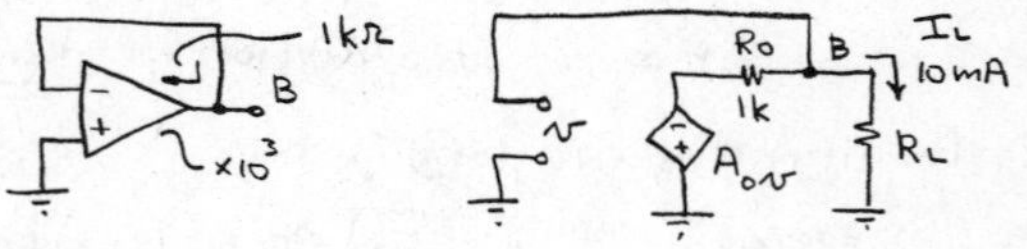

With no load, $V_B = 0$.

With 10mA load, $V_B = v = -A_o v - I_L R_o$

or $v(1+A_o) = -I_L R_o$

whence $v = \frac{-I_L R_o}{1+A_o} = \frac{-10\times10^{-3}\times10^3}{1+10^3} \approx \underline{\underline{-10mV}}$

Thus the output V_B is $-10mV$

Closed loop output resistance $= \frac{|v|}{I_L} = \frac{10\times10^{-3}}{10\times10^{-3}} = \underline{\underline{1\Omega}}$

63 Since the voltage at B falls, the op amp bias current flows <u>out</u> of the negative input terminal. $CV = IT \rightarrow$ $V/T = I/C$. Thus the bias current is $10\,mV/s \times 1000\,pF$

ie $I_B = 10 \times 10^{-3} \times 1000 \times 10^{-12} = \underline{10\ pA}$

3

64

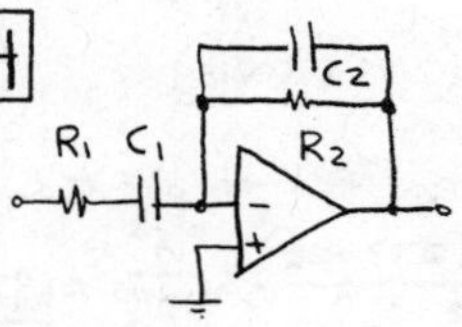

$R_{in} = 10k$ at high frequencies

$\rightarrow R_1 = \underline{10 k\Omega}$

Midband gain of -10^2

$\rightarrow R_2 = 100 R_1 = \underline{1 M\Omega}$

Low cutoff of 100 Hz $\rightarrow C_1 = \frac{1}{2\pi \times 100 \times 10^4} = \underline{0.159\,\mu F}$

Upper cutoff of 10kHz $\rightarrow C_2 = \frac{1}{2\pi \times 10^4 \times 10^6} = \underline{15.9\ pF}$

For op amp unity gain at f_t, closed loop rolls off at $f_t/(1 + R_2/R_1) = f_t/100$. For this at least a factor of 10 above the filter rolloff

$f_t/100 \geq 10(10\,kHz) \rightarrow f_t \geq \underline{10\,MHz}$

1 Ideal Diodes:

4

ⓐ $V = 0\,V$, $I = 2\,mA$

ⓑ $V = +10\,V$, $I = 0\,mA$

ⓒ $V = +10\,V$, $I = 2\,mA$

ⓓ $V = 0\,V$, $I = 0\,mA$

2

	ⓐ	ⓑ	ⓒ	ⓓ	ⓔ	ⓕ	ⓖ	ⓗ
V_{volts}	0	0	10	0	5	0	0	0
I_{mA}	1	0	0	0	0	½	0	1

3

	ⓐ	ⓑ	ⓒ	ⓓ	ⓔ	ⓕ
V_{volts}	15	10	2	-2	0	0
I_{mA}	0.75	0	0	1.2	$\frac{1-0.1}{2} = 0.45$	$\frac{10}{40} - \frac{10}{80} = .125$

4

4

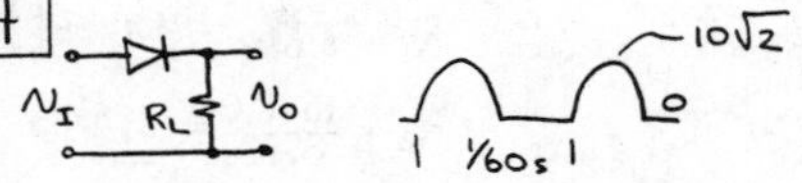

Peak $= 10\sqrt{2} = \underline{14.14\ V}$

On for 1/120 sec $= \underline{8.\dot{3}\ ms}$

Off for 1/120 sec $= \underline{8.\dot{3}\ ms}$

Av. output voltage : $\frac{1}{T}\int_0^T V \sin\omega t\, dt$

$= -\frac{1}{1/60} \cdot V/\omega \cos\omega t \Big|_{\omega t = 0}^{\pi} = \frac{10\sqrt{2} \times 60(2)}{2\pi \times 60} = 4.50\,V$

Av. current (in diode) $= \frac{4.5}{100} = \underline{45\ mA}$

5

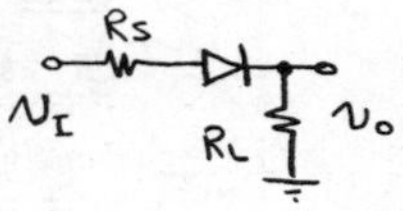

$R_S = R_L$

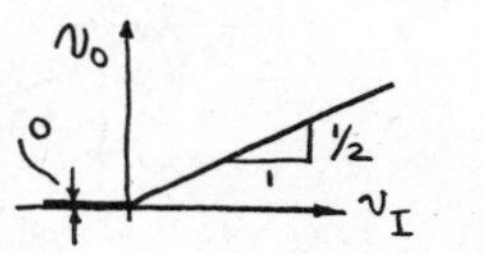

6

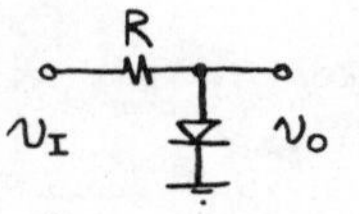

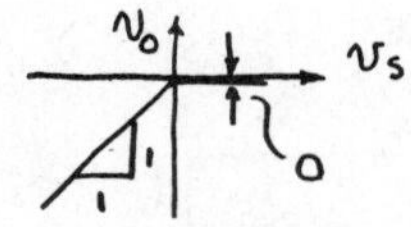

ⓐ No effect

ⓑ Zero output

7

4

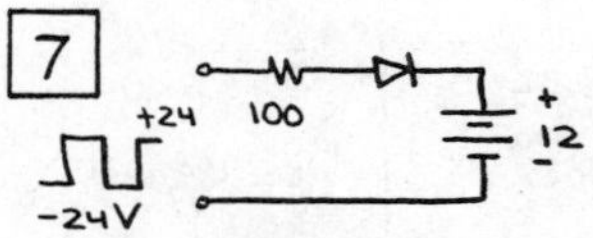

Conducts for ½ cycle

Peak diode current $= \frac{24-12}{100} = \underline{120\,mA}$

Av. diode current $= \frac{120}{2} = \underline{60\ mA}$

8

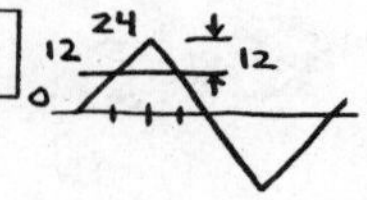

Conducts for ¼ cycle

Peak current $= \frac{24-12}{100} = \underline{120\,mA}$

Average current $= \frac{120}{2} \times \frac{1}{4} = \underline{15\ mA}$

9

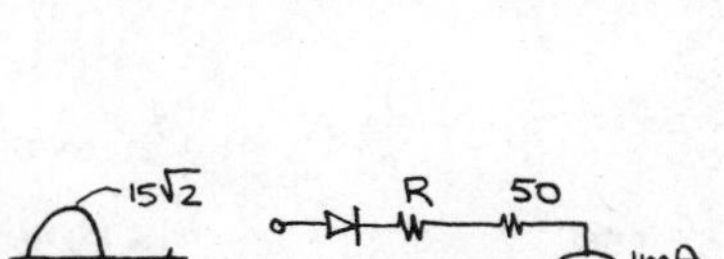

See $\frac{15\sqrt{2}/\pi}{R_{total}} = 1mA \rightarrow R_{total} = \frac{15\sqrt{2}}{\pi} = 6.75\,k$

Thus $R = 6.75 - .05 = \underline{6.7\,k\Omega}$

10

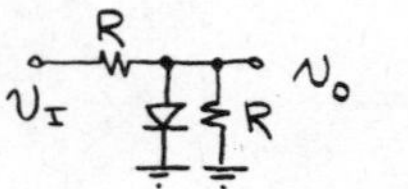

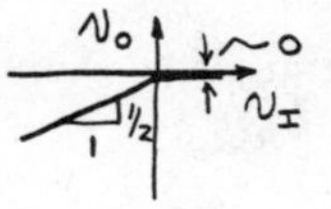

11 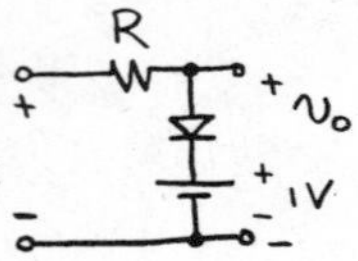 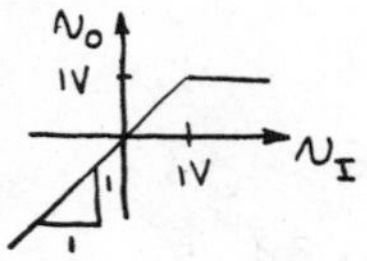 **4**

$v_o = v_I$ for positive peak voltages $\leq 1V$

Largest Δ wave input unaffected is $2V_{pp}$

12 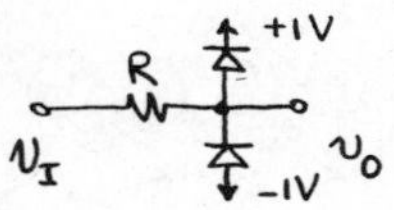 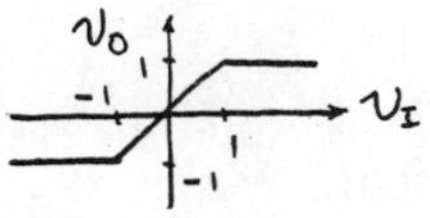

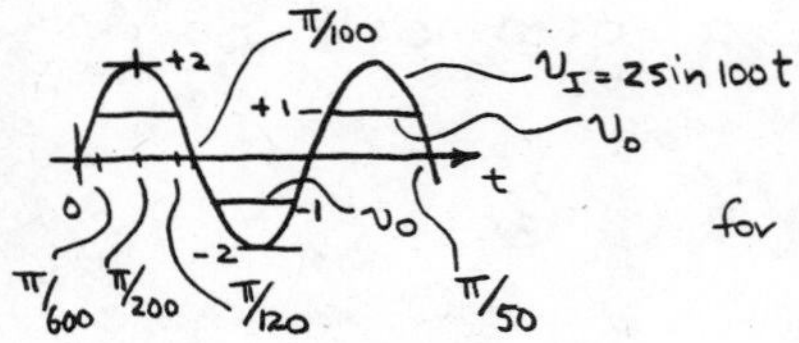

$2 \sin\theta = 1$

for $\theta = \sin^{-1}\frac{1}{2} = 30° = \pi/6^r$

13 $i = I_s(e^{v/nV_T} - 1)$

$I_{S_A} = 1000\, I_{S_B}$ for $A_{J_A} = 1000\, A_{J_B}$

$i_A = 1000\, i_B$

14 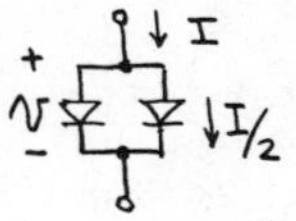 **4**

$I = I_s e^{v_1/V_T}$

$I/2 = I_s e^{v_2/V_T}$

Ratio: $2 = e^{(v_1 - v_2)/V_T} \rightarrow (v_1 - v_2) = V_T \ln 2 = 17.32\text{mV}$

Thus voltage reduces by 17.3 mV

15 $n = 1$, $I_s = 10^{-15}$A at 20°C increasing by 15%/°C

$V_T = \frac{kT}{q} = \frac{1.38 \times 10^{-23}(273 + \text{temp})}{1.602 \times 10^{-19}}$

For $i = 1$ mA, $i = I_s e^{v/V_T} \rightarrow v = V_T \ln \frac{i}{I_s}$

Thus $v(20°C) = \frac{1.38 \times 10^{-23}(273 + 20)}{1.602 \times 10^{-19}} \ln \frac{10^{-3}}{10^{-15}} = 697.4\text{mV}$

and $v(30°C) = \frac{1.38 \times 10^{-4}(303)}{1.602} \ln\left(\frac{10^{-3}}{10^{-15}(1.15)^{10}}\right) = 684.4\text{mV}$

Thus voltage temperature coefficient is $\frac{697.4 - 684.4}{20 - 30} = -1.3\text{ mV/°C}$

16 $i = I_s e^{v/nV_T}$

Two diodes: 0.7V @ 1mA and 0.7V @ 10A

(a) $n=1$: $I_s = 10^{-3} e^{-\frac{700}{25}} = 6.91 \times 10^{-16}$ A	$I_s = 6.9 \times 10^{-12}$ A
At 0.5V: $i = I_s e^{\frac{500}{25}} = 0.335\mu$A	$i = 3.35$ mA

4

(b) $n=2$: $I_s = 10^{-3} e^{-\frac{700}{50}} = 8.32 \times 10^{-10}$ A	$I_s = 8.32 \times 10^{-6}$
At 0.5V: $i = I_s e^{\frac{500}{50}} = 18.3\mu$A	$i = 183$ mA
(c) 0.1V/decade: $i = \frac{10^{-3}}{100} = 10\mu$A	$i = 100$ mA

17 $i = I_s e^{v/nV_T}$

$5 = I_s e^{\frac{710}{25n}}$

$15 = I_s e^{\frac{764}{25n}}$

Ratio: $3 = e^{54/25n} \rightarrow n = \frac{54}{25 \ln 3} = 1.97$

and $I_s = 5 e^{-\frac{710}{25(1.97)}}$ mA $= 2.74 \times 10^{-9}$ A

18 At 0°C → 20°C drop → 40mV rise, $V_j = 700 + 40 = 740$mV

At 100°C → 80°C rise → 160mV drop, $V_j = 700 - 160 = 540$mV

19 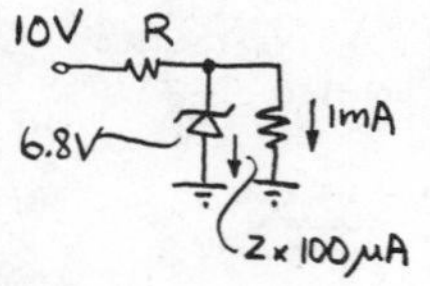

$R < \frac{10 - 6.8}{1 + 2(0.1)} = \frac{3.2}{1.2} = 2.67\text{k}\Omega$

$I_Z\big|_{\text{no load},\ 20V} = \frac{20 - 6.8}{2.67k} = 4.94$mA

$P_{D_Z} = 4.94\text{ mA}(6.8V) = 33.6$ mW

20 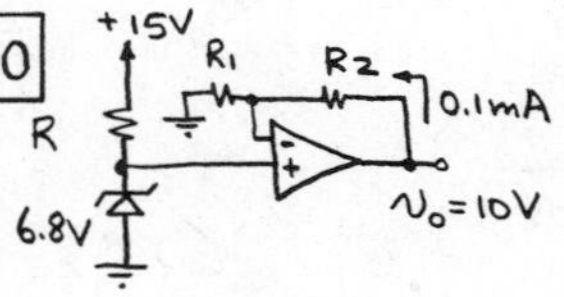 **4**

$R_1 = \frac{6.8}{0.1\text{mA}} = 68\text{k}\Omega$

$R_2 = \frac{10 - 6.8}{0.1} = 32\text{k}\Omega$

$R = \frac{15 - 6.8}{1.0} = 8.2\text{k}\Omega$

21 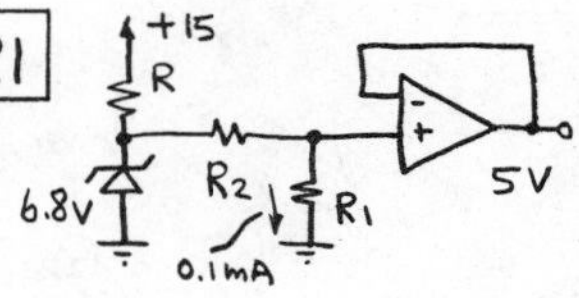

$R_1 = \frac{5.0}{0.1\text{mA}} = 50\text{k}\Omega$

$R_2 = \frac{6.8 - 5.0}{0.1} = 18\text{k}\Omega$

$R = \frac{15 - 6.8}{1 + 0.1} = 7.45\text{k}\Omega$

22 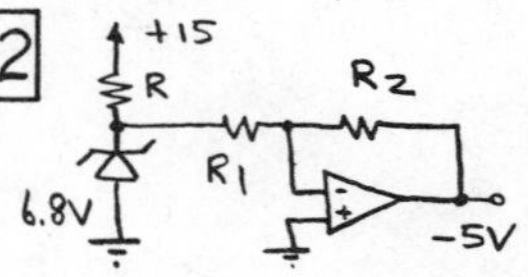

$R_1 = \frac{6.8}{0.1} = 68\text{k}\Omega$

$R_2 = \frac{5.0}{0.1} = 50\text{k}\Omega$

$R = \frac{15 - 6.8}{1 + 0.1} = 7.45\text{k}\Omega$

23 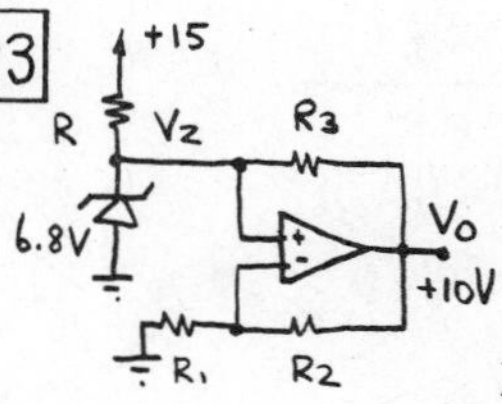

As in **20**, $R_1 = 68k$, $R_2 = 32k$

$R_3 = \frac{10 - 6.8}{1.0\text{mA}} = 3.2\text{k}\Omega$

$R = \frac{15 - 6.8}{10\mu A} = 820\text{k}\Omega$

$\Delta V_Z \approx \frac{100}{820k + 100} \times (20 - 15) = 0.61$mV

and $\Delta V_o \approx 0.61(1 + 32/68) = 0.897$ mV

4

For the unmodified circuit (20),

$$\Delta V_o = \frac{32+68}{68} \times \frac{100}{8.2k+100} \times 5 = \underline{\underline{88.6\,mV}}$$

For the modified circuit, including the effect of the 3.2k (positive-) feedback resistor: Using Miller's Theorem, $R_{eq} = 3.2k(1-\text{gain}) = 3.2\left(1-\frac{68+32}{68}\right)$ or $-1.73k\Omega$. This, shunting the zener results in an equivalent resistance at the zener of $100 \| (-1.73k) = \frac{-0.1(1.73)}{-1.73+0.1}$ or $.106k\Omega$.

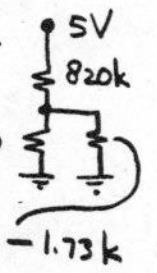

Thus $\Delta V_o = \frac{32+68}{68} \times \frac{.106}{820+.106} \times 5 = \underline{\underline{0.95\,mV}}$

24 0.1mV/°C in 5.1V is $\frac{0.1\times10^{-3}}{5.1} = 19.6$ ppm/°C

25

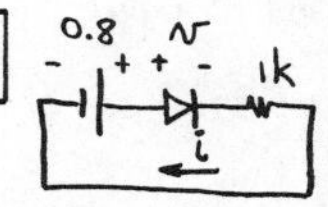

$n=2$

$I_S = 8.3\times10^{-10}A$

$i = I_S e^{v/nV_T} \rightarrow v = nV_T \ln i/I_S$

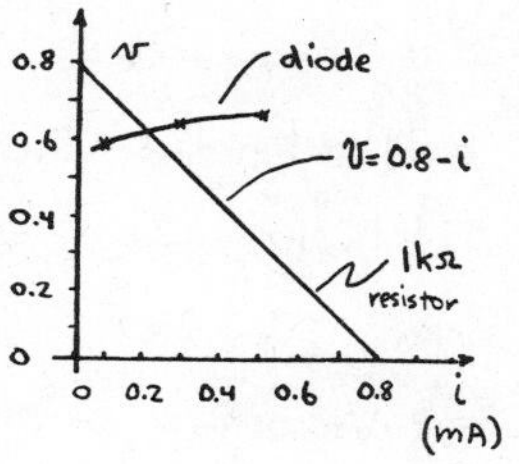

4

$i = 0.1mA \rightarrow v = 50\ln\frac{0.1\times10^{-3}}{8.3\times10^{-10}} = 585\,mV$

$i = 0.3mA \rightarrow v = 640\,mV$

$i = 0.5mA \rightarrow v = 665\,mV$

See from graph $i \approx 0.2\,mA$, for which $v = 0.8-0.2 = 0.6V$

Check: At $i = 0.2mA$, $v = 50\ln\frac{0.2\times10^{-3}}{8.3\times10^{-10}} = 620mV$

Conclude i is lower, say 0.19 mA whence $v = 0.80-0.19 = 0.61V$

or $v = 50\ln\frac{0.19\times10^{-3}}{8.3\times10^{-10}} = 617\,mV$

26 $0.8 = v + i(1k)$

$i = 0.1mA \rightarrow v = 0.7$

$i = 0.2mA \rightarrow v = 0.6$

$i = 0.3mA \rightarrow v = 0.5$

See $i \approx 0.1\times\log_{10}^{-1} 0.27 = 0.186mA$

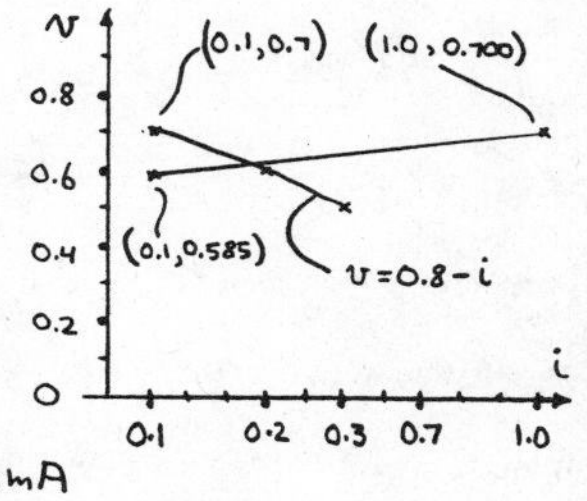

27 $v = 0.8 - i$, i in mA

4

$i = I_S e^{v/nV_T}$, $v = 50\,mV \times \ln\frac{i\,mA}{8.3\times10^{-7}\,mA}$

$i = \frac{800mV}{1k} = 0.8mA \rightarrow v = 50\ln\frac{0.8}{8.3}\times10^7 = 689\,mV$

$i = \frac{800-689}{1k} = 0.111mA \rightarrow v = 50\ln\frac{0.111}{8.3}\times10^7 = 590\,mV$

$i = \frac{800-590}{1k} = 0.21mA \rightarrow v = 622\,mV$

$i = \frac{800-622}{1k} = 0.178mA \rightarrow v = 614\,mV$

$i = \frac{800-614}{1k} = 0.186mA \rightarrow v = 616\,mV$

$i = \frac{800-616}{1k} = \underline{0.184\,mA} \rightarrow v = \underline{\underline{615.5mV}}$

28

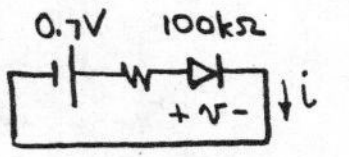

$v = 700 + 100\log_{10} \frac{i}{1000}\,mV$, i in μA

$i = 0.7/100k = 7\mu A$, $v = 700 + 100\log 7/1000 = 485\,mV$

$i = \frac{700-485}{100k} = 2.15\mu A$, $v = 700 + 100\log\frac{2.15}{1000} = 700-267$

$i = \frac{267}{100k} = 2.67\mu A$, $v = 700-257$

$i = \frac{257}{100k} = 2.57\mu A$, $v = 700-259$

ie $i = \underline{\underline{2.57\mu A}}$ for which $v = \underline{\underline{441\,mV}}$

29

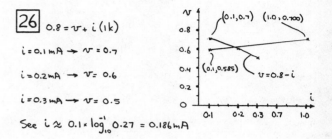

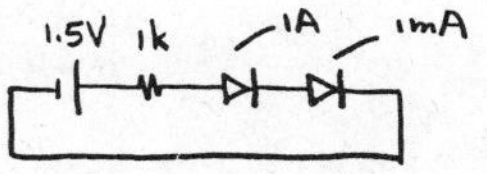

4

$n = 2$

$i = I_S e^{v/nV_T}$, $I_S = i e^{-v/nV_T}$

For 1mA diode: $I_{S_1} = 1e^{-\frac{700}{50}}\,mA = 8.32\times10^{-10}A$ and

for 1A diode, $I_{S_{1000}} = 8.32\times10^{-7}A$

For each diode $v = 50\ln i/I_S = 50\ln i - 50\ln I_S$

For 2 diodes $V_t = 50\ln i - 50\ln I_{S_1} + 50\ln i - 50\ln I_{S_{1000}}$

$= 100\ln i - 100\ln I_{S_1} - 50\ln(1000)$

$= (100\ln i + 1746)\,mV$

(a) Say $i \approx 0.5mA \rightarrow v_t = 100\ln 0.5\times10^{-3} + 1746 = 986mV$

Then $i = \frac{1.5-.986}{1k} = 0.514mA \rightarrow V_t = 1746 + 100\ln 0.514\times10^{-3}$

$= \underline{\underline{989\,mV}}$

Now at $i = \underline{\underline{0.514mA}}$, diode drops are $50\ln\frac{0.514\times10^{-3}}{8.32\times10^{-10}}$ or $\underline{\underline{667\,mV}}$ and $50\ln\frac{0.514\times10^{-3}}{8.32\times10^{-7}} = \underline{\underline{321\,mV}}$

(b) For each ideal, $i = \frac{1.5}{1} = \underline{\underline{1.5mA}}$

(c) For each 0.7V, $i = \frac{1.5-0.7-0.7}{1} = \underline{\underline{0.1mA}}$

(d) For battery v, $0.9\left(\frac{v-0}{1k}\right) = i = \frac{v-0.7-0.7}{1k}$

for which $0.9v = v - 1.4$ and $v = \underline{\underline{14\text{ volts}}}$

30 For convenience in the following **4**

use $v = V$ and $i = I$ for each diode:

Thus $i = I_s e^{v/nV_T}$ and $v = nV_T(\ln i + \ln I_s)$

But $v = 700$ mV for $i = 1$ mA and $n = 1$

ie. $700 = 25(\ln 1 + \ln I_s) \rightarrow \ln I_s = 700/25$

Thus $v = (700 + 25\ln i)$ mV or $(0.7 + .025\ln i)$ V

(1) From Fig. P4.1

(a) $10 - 5i - v = 0$. Thus for $v = 0.7$V constant,

$i = \frac{10 - 0.7}{5} = 1.86$mA for which $v = 0.7 + .025\ln i$

and $i = \frac{9.3 - 0.025\ln i}{5} = 1.86 - .005\ln i$

Now for $i \approx 1.86$mA, $i = 1.86 - .005\ln(1.86) = 1.857$mA

for which $v = 700 + 25\ln 1.857 = 715.5$mV

Thus $I = \underline{\underline{1.857\text{ mA}}}$, $V = \underline{\underline{715\text{ mV}}}$

(b) Diode is cut off. Ignoring leakage,

$I = \underline{\underline{0\text{ mA}}}$, $V = \underline{\underline{+10\text{ V}}}$

(c) Using data from (a), $i = 1.857$mA, $v = (10 - 0.715)$V

Thus $I = \underline{\underline{1.857\text{ mA}}}$, $V = \underline{\underline{9.285\text{ V}}}$

(d) Diode is cut off. Ignoring leakage **4**

$I = \underline{\underline{0\text{ mA}}}$, $V = \underline{\underline{0\text{ V}}}$

(2) From Fig. P4.2:

(a) $10 - 10i - v = 0$

For $v = 2(0.7\text{V})$ constant, $i = \frac{10 - 1.4}{10} = 0.86$mA

For $v = 2(0.7 + .025\ln i)$, $i = \frac{10 - 1.4 - .05\ln i}{10}$

or $i = 0.86 - .005\ln i$

Now, for $i = 0.86$mA, $i(\text{new}) = 0.86 - .005\ln 0.86 = 0.8638$mA

for which $v = 2(0.7 + .025\ln(.8638)) = 1.393$ V

Thus $I = \underline{\underline{0.864\text{ mA}}}$, $V = \underline{\underline{1.393\text{ V}}}$

(b) Top diode is cut off. Ignoring leakage

$I = 0$ mA, $V = 0$ V

But more precisely: $i = I_s(e^{v/V_T} - 1)$. Now

for the top diode, $I = -i = -I_s(e^{-10/V_T} - 1) = +I_s$

For the lower diode, $I = I_s(e^{V/V_T} - 1)$

whence $I_s = I_s(e^{V/V_T} - 1) \rightarrow e^{V/V_T} = 2$

and $V = 25\ln 2$ or 17.3 mV

for which $I = I_s = 1 \times e^{-700/25} = 6.9 \times 10^{-13}$ mA **4**

Thus $I = \underline{\underline{0.69\text{ fA}}}$ (femptoamperes), $V = \underline{\underline{17.3\text{ mV}}}$

(c) Lower diode is cut off.

Ignoring leakage, $I = 0$, $V = +10$V

More precisely: $I \approx I_s = 0.69$ fA (from (b))

and $V = 10 - 0.017 - 10 \times 6.9 \times 10^{-13} = 9.983$V

Thus $I = \underline{\underline{0.69\text{ fA}}}$, $V = \underline{\underline{9.983\text{ V}}}$

(d) Leftmost diode conducts: $10 - 10i - v = 0$

For $v = 0.7$V constant, $i = \frac{10 - 0.7}{10} = 0.93$mA

For $v = 0.7 + 0.025\ln i$, $i = \frac{10 - 0.7 - .025\ln i}{10}$

$= 0.93 - .0025\ln i$

Now for $i = 0.93$mA, $i_{new} = 0.93 - .0025\ln(.93) = 0.9302$

for which $v = 0.7 + .025\ln .9302 = 0.6982$V

Thus $I = \underline{\underline{0\text{ mA}}}$, $V = \underline{\underline{0.698\text{ V}}}$

(e) Both diodes cut off.

$I = \underline{\underline{0\text{ mA}}}$, $V = 10/2 = \underline{\underline{5.0\text{V}}}$

(next)

(f) Both diodes conduct; $I = i$ flows **4**

in the rightmost.

For $v = 0.7$V constant, $i = \frac{1}{2}\left(\frac{10 - 0.7}{10}\right) = 0.465$mA

For $v = (0.7 + .025\ln i)$, $i = .465 - .00125\ln i$

Now for $i = 0.465$mA, $i_{new} = .465 - .00125\ln(.465) = 0.466$

for which $v = 0.7 + .025\ln 0.466 = 0.6809$V

Thus $I = \underline{\underline{0.466\text{ mA}}}$, $V = \underline{\underline{0.681\text{ V}}}$

(g) Both diodes conduct but with $i_{DR} \ll i_{DL}$

ie $i \ll i_L$

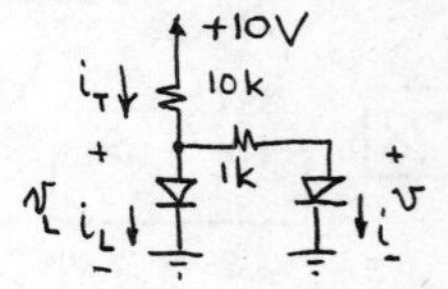

For $v_L = 0.7$V constant

Total current $i_T = i_L + i$

$= \frac{10 - v_L}{10} = \frac{10 - 0.7}{10} = 0.93$mA

Now for $i \ll i_L$, $i_L \approx i_T = 0.93$mA

and $v_L = 0.7 + .025\ln(0.93) = 0.698$V

Now $v = 0.698 - 1k(i) = 0.698 - i$

Also, $v = 0.700 + .025\ln i \rightarrow 0.698 - i = 0.700 + .025\ln i$

Thus $i = -.002 - .025\ln i$

4

For $i = 0.1\,mA$, $i_{new} = -.002 - .025\ln 0.1 = 0.056$

For $i = 0.056\,mA$, $i_{new} = -.002 - .025\ln .056 = 0.070\,mA$

.070	.0644
.0644	.0666
.0666	.0657

That is $i \approx .066\,mA$ and $i_L \approx .930 - .066 = 0.864\,mA$

for which $v_L = 0.7 + .025\ln(0.864) = 0.696\,V$

and $i = -0.700 + .696 - .025\ln i = -.004 - .025\ln i$

Thus for $i = .066\,mA$, $i_{new} = -.004 - .025\ln(.066) = .0647$

for $i = .0647\,mA$, $i_{new} = .0644$

That is $i \approx .0644$ for which $V = 0.7 + .025\ln(.0644) = 0.631$

Thus $I = \underline{0.064\,mA}$, $V = \underline{0.631\,V}$

(h) See diode drops roughly cancel and $V \approx 0$.

Thus $I = i \approx \frac{10-0}{10k} = 1mA$ and $v_L = 0 + 0.7 = 0.7V$

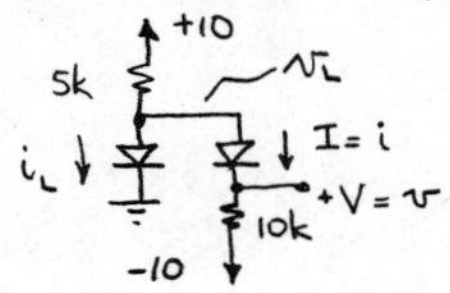

$\therefore\ i_L = \frac{10-0.7}{5} - 1 = 0.86mA$

whence $v_L = 0.7 + .025\ln .86 = .6962V$

and $v = .6962 - .700 = -.0038V = V$

4

and $i = \frac{10 - .0038}{10k} = 0.9996\,mA \approx 1mA = I$

Thus $I = \underline{1.00\,mA}$, $V = \underline{-0.0038V}$

(3) From Fig. P4.3:

(a) Assuming a 0.7V diode, ie $v_d = 0.7V$,

$$I = i = \frac{\left(\frac{20k}{20k + 10k} \times 30\right) - 0.7}{20k \,\|\, 10k + 20k} = \frac{20 - 0.7}{20/3 + 20} = 0.724mA$$

Now $v_d = 0.7 + .025\ln 0.724 = 0.692\,V$

whence $i = \frac{20 - .692}{26.67} = 0.724\,mA = I$

and $V = 0.724 \times 20k = 14.48V$

Thus $I = \underline{0.724\,mA}$, $V = \underline{14.48V}$

(b) See diode is cut off and $V = \frac{10}{10+10} \times 30 - \frac{10}{10+10} \times 10$

or $V = \frac{1}{2}(20) = 10V$

Thus $I = \underline{0\,mA}$, $V = \underline{10V}$

(c) See V follows the highest input and I=0

ie. $V \approx 2 - 0.7 = 1.3V$ and $i_{10} \approx \frac{1.3-(-10)}{10k} = 1.13mA$

whence $v_d = 0.7 + .025\ln 1.13 = 0.703\,mA$

and $V = +2 - .703 = 1.297V$. Thus $I = \underline{0mA}$, $V = \underline{1.297V}$

4

(d) See V follows lowest input, and

$I = \frac{10 - (-2) - 0.7}{10k} = 1.13mA$

$V = -2 + 0.7 + 0.025\ln 1.13 = -1.297V$

Thus $I = \underline{1.13\,mA}$, $V = \underline{-1.297V}$

(e) See that the resistors connected to -10V provide currents much in excess of that from +10V.

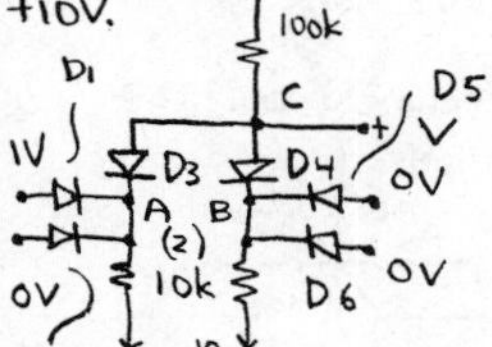

Thus $V_A \approx 1 - 0.7 = +0.3V$

and $V_B \approx 0 - 0.7 = -0.7V$

Thus D4 conducts, D3 is off

and $V_C \approx -0.7 + 0.7 = 0V$

Thus $i_{D4} \approx \frac{10-0}{100k} = 0.1V$

$\therefore\ v_{D4} = 0.7 + .025\ln 0.1 = 0.642V$

and $I = i_{D5} = i_{D4} = \frac{1}{2}\left(\frac{-0.7-(-10)}{10k}\right) = 0.465mA = I$

and $v_{D5} = 0.7 + .025\ln 0.465 = 0.681\,V$

Thus $v_B = -0.681V$, $v_C = -0.681 + .642 = -0.039V$

Thus $I = \underline{0.465\,mA}$ and $V = \underline{-0.039V}$

(next)

4

(f) Resistor ratios imply that all diodes conduct, that diode drops roughly compensate, and that $V \approx 0$. Thus:

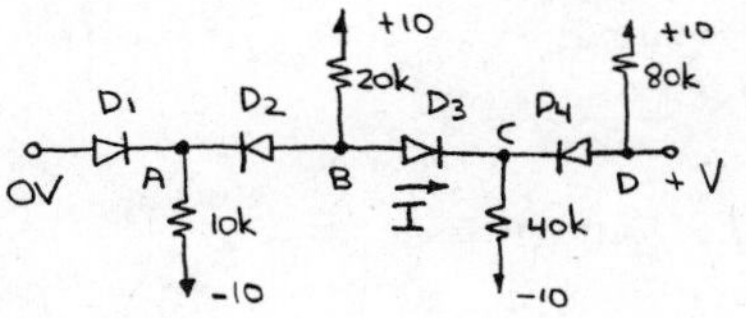

$i_{D4} = \frac{10V}{80k} = 0.125mA$, $v_{D4} = 0.7 + 0.025\ln .125 = .648V$, $V_C = -.648$

$\therefore\ i_{40} = \frac{10 - 0 - .648}{40k} = .234\,mA$, $i_{D3} = 0.234 - .125 = 0.109\,mA$

$\therefore\ v_{D4} = 0.7 + .025\ln 0.109 = 0.645\,V$, $V_B \approx -0.648 + 0.645 = -.003V$

$\therefore\ i_{20} = \frac{10 + .003}{20k} = 0.5001mA$, $i_{D2} = 0.500 - .109 = 0.391mA$

$\therefore\ v_{D2} = 0.7 + .025\ln 0.391 = 0.677V$, $V_A \approx -.003 - .677 = -0.680V$

$\therefore\ i_{10} = \frac{10 - .68}{10k} = 0.932\,mA$, $i_{D1} = 0.932 - 0.391 = 0.541\,mA$

$\therefore\ v_{D1} = 0.7 + .025\ln 0.541 = 0.685V$,

See that $V_A = -0.685\,V$, not $-0.680V$ as estimated.

Thus correct all previous estimates by -5mV:

Thus $I = i_{D3} = \underline{0.109mA}$, $V = \underline{-0.005V}$

31 — 4

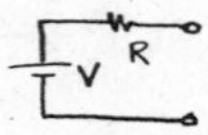

0.58V @ 1mA; 0.64V @ 10mA

Thus $580 = V + R(1)$, $640 = V + R(10)$ } Subtract → $60 = 9R$ or $R = 6.\dot{6}\,\Omega$

and $V = 580 - 6.7 = 573$ mV : Check $573 + 10(6.\dot{6}) = 639.\dot{6}$

At 5.5 mA, $v_d = 573 + 5.5(6.\dot{6}) = 610$ mV

At 19 mA, $v_d = 573 + 19(6.\dot{6}) = 700$ mV, that is, this could be called a "19 mA diode"

32

$i_{D1} = I_D e^{v_d/nV_T}$ and $i_{D2} = I_D\left(1 + \frac{v_d}{nV_T}\right)$ for $n = 2$

v_d mV	i_D/I_D	i_{D2}/I_D	% error	% error {For n=1 from Ex 4.12}
2	1.041	1.04	0.096	0.30
5	1.105	1.10	0.45	1.75
10	1.221	1.20	1.72	6.20
25	1.649	1.50	9.03	26.4

33 — 4

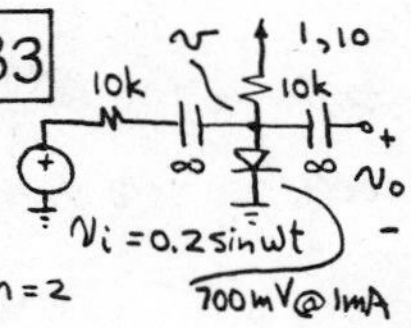

n = 2

$i = I_S e^{v/nV_T} = I_S e^{700/50}$

$I_S = 8.31 \times 10^{-10}$ A

and $v = 50 \ln \frac{i\,mA}{8.31 \times 10^{-7}}$

At 10V: $I = \frac{10 - 0.7}{10k} = 0.93$ mA → $v = 696$ mV

or $I = \frac{10 - .696}{10k} = 0.930$ mA → $v = 696.4$ mV

$r_d = \frac{nV_T}{I} = \frac{50\,mV}{0.93\,mA} = 53.8\,\Omega$

$v_o = \frac{53.8 \| 10k}{10k + 53.8 \| 10k} \cdot v_i = (5.35 \times 10^{-4})\, v_i$

that is a 1.07 mV peak sine wave.

At 1V: $I = \frac{1 - 0.5}{10k} = .05$ mA → $v = 50 \ln \frac{.05 \times 10^7}{8.31} = 550$ mV

or $I = \frac{1 - .55}{10k} = .045$ mA → $v = 555$ mV

$r_d = \frac{50\,mV}{.045\,mA} = 1111\,\Omega$ and $1111 \| 10k = 999\,\Omega$

$v_o = \frac{.999}{.999 + 10} v_i = .091\, v_i$

that is a $0.2 \times .091$ or 18.2 mV peak sine wave.

34 — 4

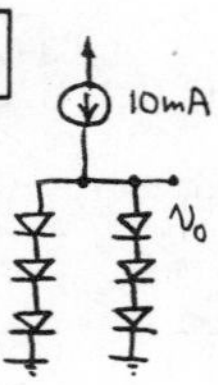

See 5mA in each diode.

700mV @ 1mA with $n = 2 \rightarrow I_S = 8.31 \times 10^{-7}$ mA

and at 5mA, $v = 50 \ln \frac{5}{8.31 \times 10^{-7}} = 780.5$ mV

Thus, output $v_o = 3(780.5) = 2341$ mV.

For each diode $r_d = \frac{50\,mV}{5\,mA} = 10\,\Omega$

For the supply, the output resistance is $\frac{3(10)}{2} = 15\,\Omega$

For a 2.34 k load added, the change in output voltage is $\frac{15}{2.34k + 15} \times 2.34 = \underline{15\,mV}$

(or) Using the exponential formula, see that the load current is 1mA. Thus each diode current decreases by 0.5 mA, for which

$v = 50 \ln \frac{4.5}{8.31 \times 10^{-7}} = 775.2$, a decrease of

$780.5 - 775.2 = \underline{5.26}$ mV

Thus for 3 diodes, the output voltage drops by $3(5.26) = \underline{15.8\,mV}$

35 — 4

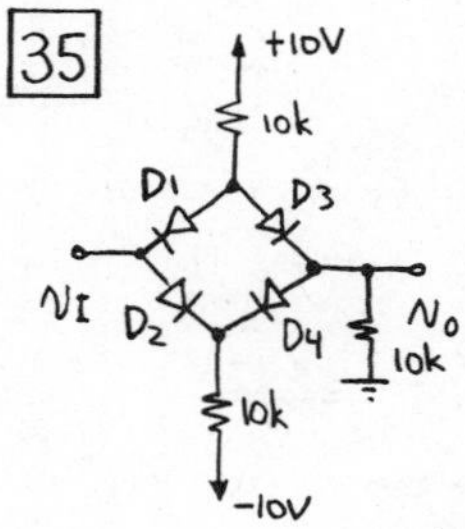

For $v_I \geq 4.65$ V

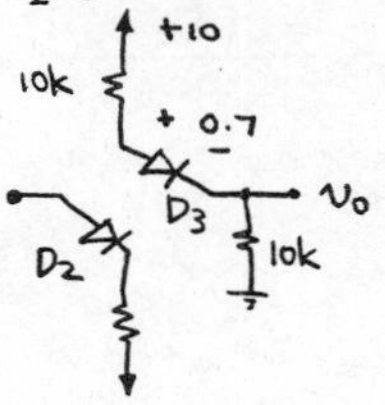

$\frac{v_o}{10} = \frac{10 - v_o - 0.7}{10} \rightarrow 2v_o = 9.3$

and $v_o = 4.65$ volts

Likewise for $v_I \leq -4.65$V, D1 and D4 conduct, and $v_o = -4.65$:

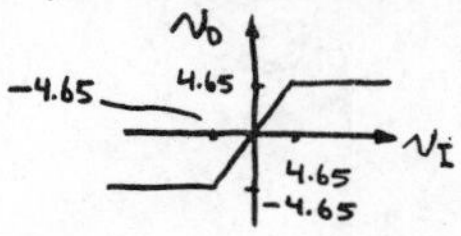

That is:

for $-4.65 \leq v_I \leq +4.65$V, $v_o = v_i$

for $v_I \geq +4.65$V, $v_o = +4.65$V

for $v_I \leq -4.65$V, $v_o = -4.65$V

5

1

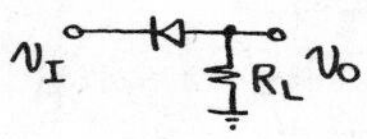

For $v_I \geq 0$, $v_O = 0$

For $v_I \leq 0$, $v_O = v_I$

2

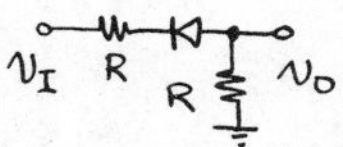

For $v_I \geq 0$, $v_O = 0$

For $v_I \leq 0$, $v_O = v_I/2$

3

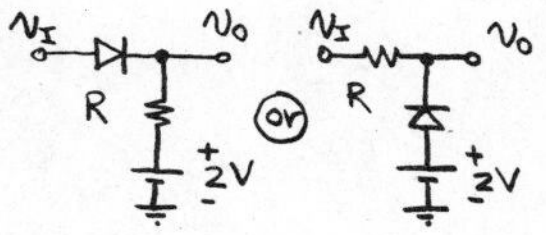

For $v_I \leq 2V$, $v_O = +2V$

For $v_I \geq 2V$, $v_O = v_I$

4

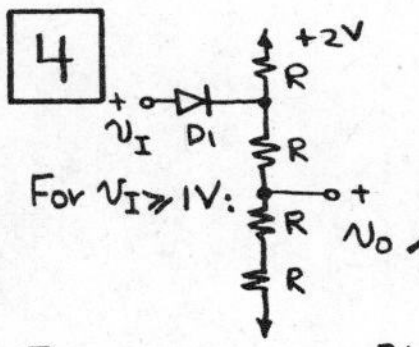

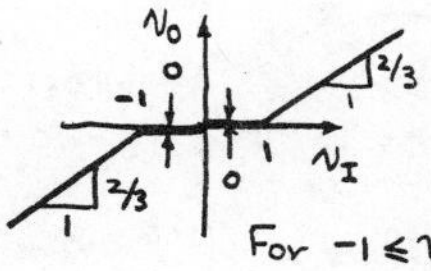

For $-1 \leq v_I \leq +1$, $v_O = 0$

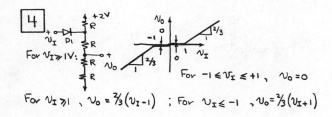

For $v_I \geq 1$, $v_O = \frac{2}{3}(v_I - 1)$; For $v_I \leq -1$, $v_O = \frac{2}{3}(v_I + 1)$

5

5

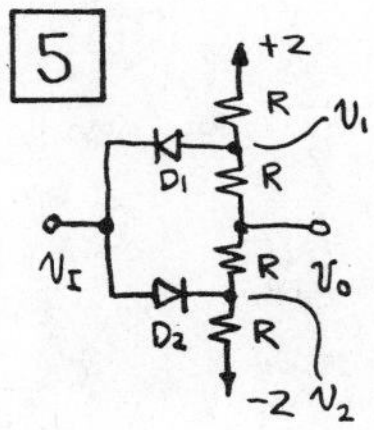

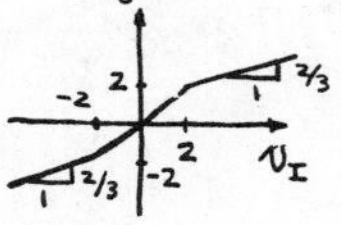

For $-2 \leq v_I \leq +2$, $v_O = v_I$

For $v_I \geq 2$, $v_O = \frac{2}{3}(1 + v_I)$

For $v_I \leq 2$, $v_O = \frac{2}{3}(v_I - 1)$

6

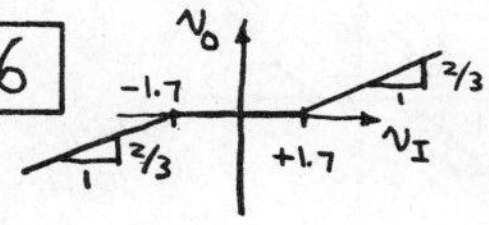

For $-1.7 \leq v_I \leq 1.7$, $v_O = 0$

For $v_I \geq 1.7$, $v_O = \frac{2}{3}(v_I - 1.7)$

For $v_I \leq -1.7$, $v_O = \frac{2}{3}(v_I + 1.7)$

7 See **5** above: $V_d = 0.7\,V$. See that for $v_I = 0$, $v_O = 0$, and as v_I rises, D1 and D2 continue to conduct until $\frac{2}{3}(2 - v_2) = 1.4$ or $2 - v_2 = 2.1$

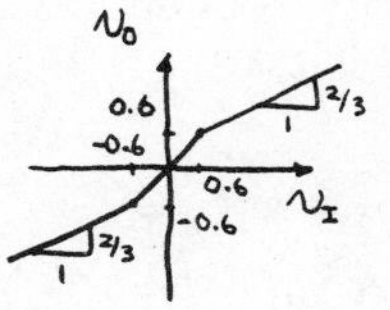

or $v_2 = -0.1$, for which $v_I = 0.6$ and $v_O = 2 - \frac{2}{3}(2 - (-0.1)) = 0.6$. Above this only D2 conducts and $v_O = 0.6 + \frac{2}{3}(v_I - 0.6) = 0.2 + \frac{2}{3}v_I$

5

That is: For $-0.6 \leq v_I \leq 0.6$, $v_O = v_I$

For $v_I \geq 0.6$, $v_O = \frac{2}{3}(v_I + 0.3)$

For $v_I \leq -0.6$, $v_O = \frac{2}{3}(v_I - 0.3)$

Compare with **5**

8

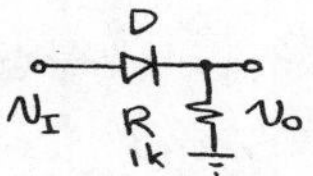

$$v_I = v_O + v_D(\text{at } i_D) + nV_T \ln \frac{v_O/R}{i_D}$$

$v_D = 0.7V$ @ 1.0mA, $n = 2$

ⓐ At $v_I = 10V$, $v_O \approx 10 - 0.7 = 9.3 = 10 - 0.7 - 50 \ln \frac{9.3/1}{1}$

or $v_O = 10 - .812 = 9.19V$

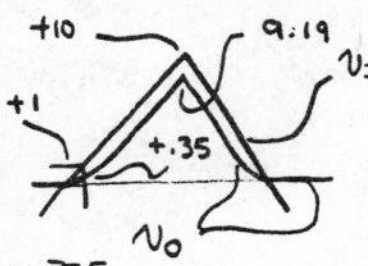

ⓑ At $v_I = 1V$, $v_O = 1 - 0.7 - 50 \ln v_O$

Try $v_O = 0.5 \rightarrow v_O = 1 - 0.7 - (-0.35) = .335$

$\rightarrow v_O = 0.3 - 50 \ln(.335) = 0.3 + .055 = .355$

$\rightarrow v_O = 0.3 + .052 = .352V$

Similarly for $v_I = 0.5$, find $v_O \approx .014V$

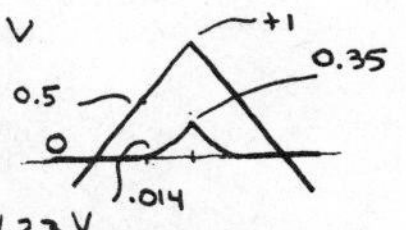

ⓒ At $v_I = 5V$, $v_O = 5 - 0.7 - 50 \ln v_O$

Try $v_O = 4.3 \rightarrow v_O = 4.3 - 50 \ln 4.3 = 4.23V$

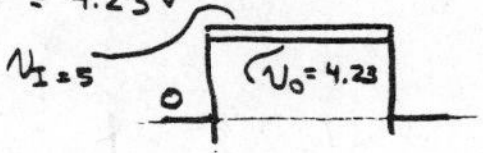

5

9

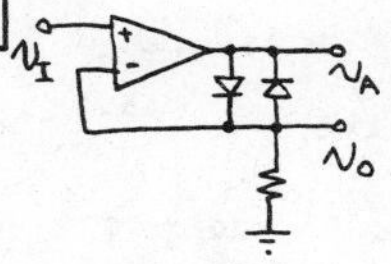

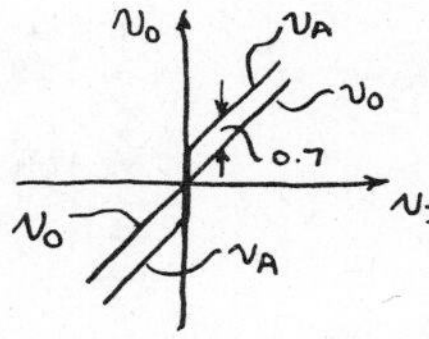

10

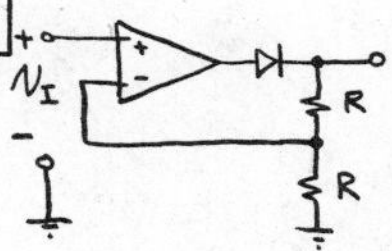

$v_O = 2v_I$

11

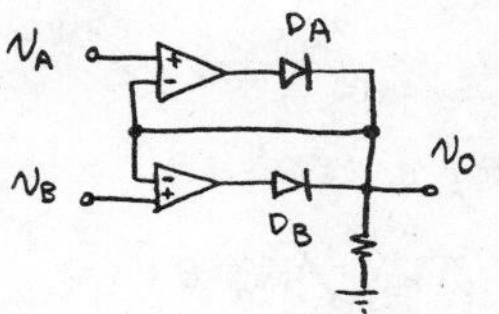

For $v_A = +1$, $v_B = +2$, D_B conducts, D_A cutoff, $v_O = +2V$

With diodes reversed and inputs -2 and -1, $v_O = -2V$

12

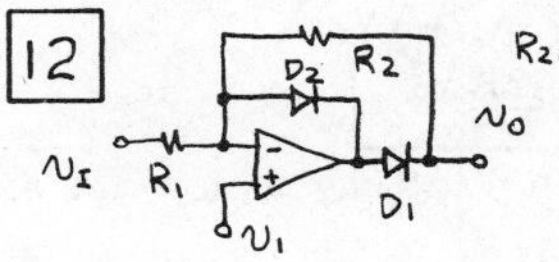

$R_2 = R_1$

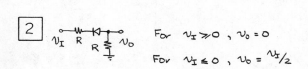

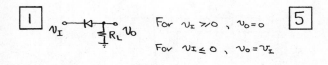

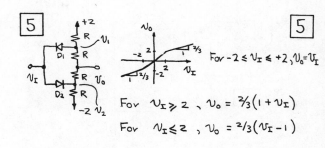

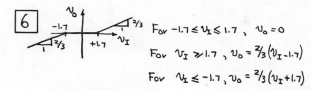

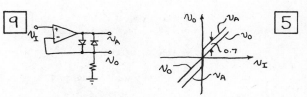

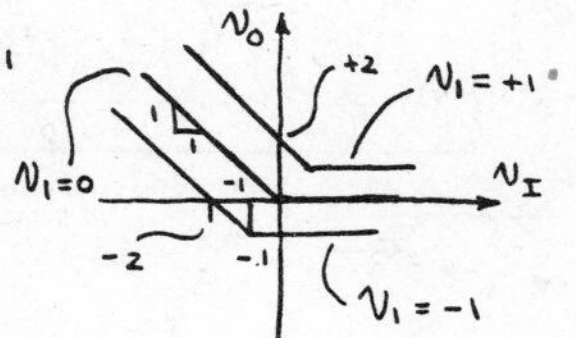

13 **5**

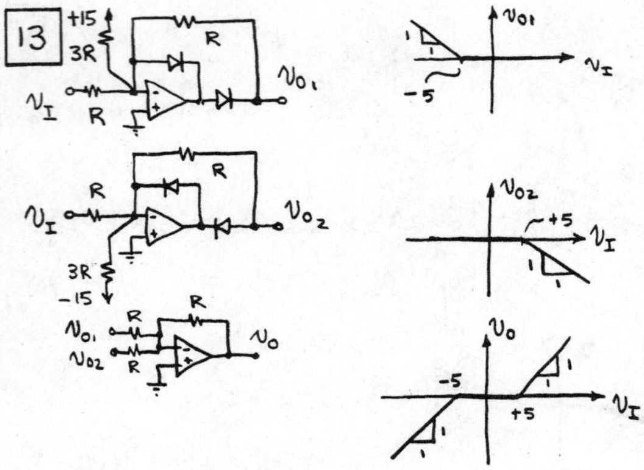

14

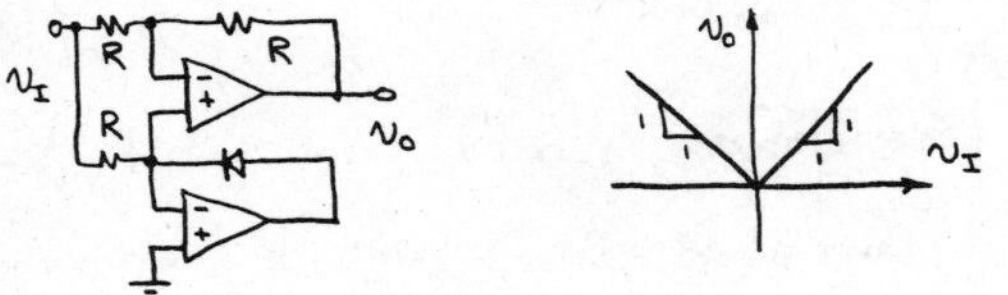

15

ⓐ 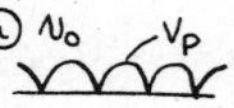 $R_1 = R_2$ $\quad A_V = \frac{2V_P}{\pi} = 0.636 V_P$

ⓑ $R_2 = \pi R_1$ 

$$A_V = \frac{1}{\pi}V_P + \frac{\pi V_P}{\pi} = V_P\left(\frac{\pi+1}{\pi}\right) = 1.32 V_P$$

16 **5**

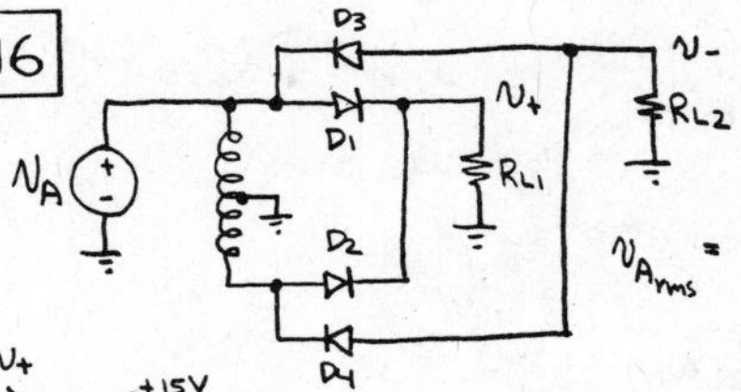

$$v_{A_{rms}} = \frac{(15+0.7)}{\sqrt{2}} = \underline{\underline{11.1V}}$$

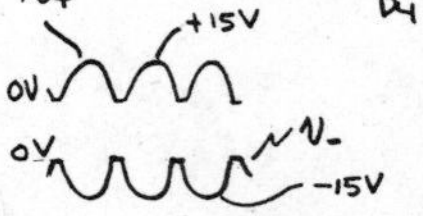

$v_O = v_+ - v_-$; $v_{O\,max} = 2V_P - 2V_D$

or $v_{O\,max} = 2(15+0.7-0.7) = \underline{\underline{30V}}$

$v_{O\,min} = \underline{\underline{0V}}$; $v_{O\,av.} \approx 2\times 2\times\frac{V_P}{\pi} - 2V_D = \frac{4}{\pi}(15+0.7) - 1.4$

or $v_{O\,av} = \underline{\underline{18.59V}}$

17

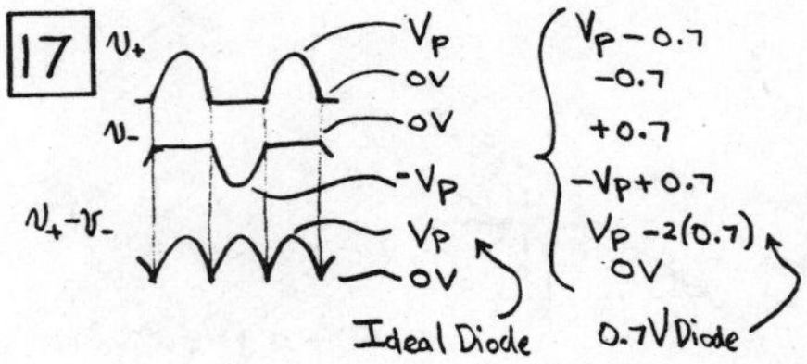

18

Current in M →  $5\sqrt{2}/1k = 7.07mA$ $\quad I_{av} = \frac{2(5)\sqrt{2}}{\pi(1k)} = 4.5mA$

Waveform across R is a sinewave of peak value $5\sqrt{2} = 7.07V$

5

At saturation:

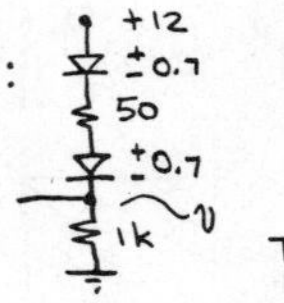

Peak across 1kΩ is $(12-0.7-0.7)\frac{1k}{1k+50} = 10.095V$

Thus the largest sine wave for expected operation is $\frac{10.095}{\sqrt{2}} = \underline{\underline{7.14 V_{rms}}}$

19

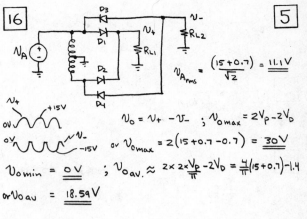

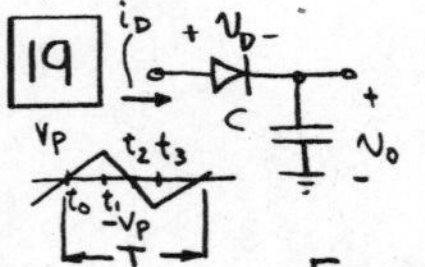

Diode Current $i_D = I_S e^{v_D/nV_T} = i$

Capacitor Curr. $i_C = C\frac{dv_O}{dt} = i$

From t_0 to t_1: $v_I = \frac{V_P}{T/4}\times t = v_D + v_O$

Thus $C\frac{dv_O}{dt} = I_S e^{v_D/nV_T} = I_S e^{\frac{4V_P t}{nV_T T}} \times e^{-v_O/nV_T}$

or $C\int e^{v_O/nV_T} dv_O = I_S \int e^{\frac{4V_P}{nTV_T}t} dt$

ie $CnV_T e^{v_O/nV_T}\Big]_0^{v_O} = I_S T nV_T/4V_P\, e^{\frac{4V_P}{nTV_T}t}\Big]_0^{t}$

or $e^{v_O/nV_T} - 1 = \frac{I_S T}{4V_P C}\left[e^{\frac{4V_P t}{nTV_T}} - 1\right]$

Taking ln: $\frac{v_O}{nV_T} = \ln\frac{I_S T}{4CV_P} + \frac{4V_P}{nTV_T}\cdot t$

ie $\boxed{v_O = nV_T \ln\frac{I_S T}{4CV_P} + \frac{V_P}{T/4}\cdot t}$

For 1mA diode: 0.7V@1mA and 0.1V/decade with $i = I_S e^{v/nV_T}$

$\rightarrow \frac{10}{1} = e^{\frac{0.1}{nV_T}} \rightarrow \frac{0.1}{nV_T} = \ln 10 = 2.303$, ie $n = \frac{0.1}{2.3\times 25\times 10^{-3}} = \underline{\underline{1.737}}$

and $1\times 10^{-3} = I_S e^{\frac{700}{1.737(25)}} \rightarrow I_S = 9.98\times 10^{-11}$ A

5

Now for $T = 40ms$, $C = 10\mu F$, $V_P = 10V$, at t_1,

$$v_{O_1} = 1.737(25\times 10^{-3})\ln\frac{9.98\times 10^{-11}\times 40\times 10^{-3}}{4(10)10^{-6}\times 10} + \frac{10}{40/4}\times 10$$

ie $v_{O_1} = -0.8 + 10.0 = \underline{9.2V}$

Beyond $t = t_1$:

$C\frac{dv_O}{dt} = I_S e^{(v_I - v_O)/nV_T}$, but $v_I = 10 - \frac{V_P}{T/4}\times t$,

where for simplicity we have taken $t=0$ at t_1

Thus $C\frac{dv_O}{dt} e^{v_O/nV_T} = I_S e^{((10-\frac{V_P}{T/4}t)/nV_T)}$

and $\int_{9.2}^{v_O(t)} C/I_S\, e^{v_O/nV_T} dv_O = \int_0^t e^{((10-\frac{V_P}{T/4}t)/nV_T)} dt$

which results in $e^{(v_O-9.2)/nV_T} = 1 + \frac{I_S T}{4CV_P} e^{0.8/nV_T}\left(1 - e^{-\frac{4V_P}{nV_T}\cdot\frac{t}{T}}\right)$

But $I_S = 10^{-3} e^{-0.7/nV_T} = 10^{-2} e^{-0.8/nV_T}$

Thus $e^{(v_O-9.2)/nV_T} = 1 + \frac{10^{-2}T}{4CV_P}\left[1 - e^{-\frac{4V_P}{nV_T}\cdot\frac{t}{T}}\right]$

Now as t increases, $e^{-\frac{4V_P}{nV_T}\cdot\frac{t}{T}}$ becomes negligibly small and we can approximate:

$$e^{(v_O-9.2)/nV_T} \approx 1 + \frac{10^{-2}T}{4CV_P}$$

from which the maximum value reached by v_O is

$$v_O = 9.2 + nV_T \ln\left(1 + \frac{10^{-2}T}{4CV_P}\right)$$

$$= 9.2 + 1.737(25\times 10^{-3})\ln\left(1 + \frac{10^{-2}\times 40\times 10^{-3}}{4\times 10\times 10^{-6}\times 10}\right) = \underline{\underline{9.23V}}$$

20 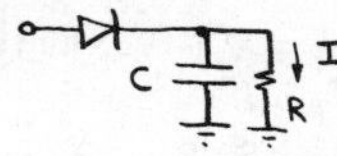

$V_o = V_P - V_r/2$ **5**

$V_r \approx \frac{V_P}{fCR}$

ie $V_o \approx V_P - \frac{V_P}{R}\cdot\frac{1}{2fC} = V_P - \frac{I_L}{2fC}$ of the form $V_{Th} - R_{Th}I_L$ where $\underline{V_{Th} = V_P}$ and $\underline{R_{Th} = \frac{1}{2fC}}$

For $C = 100\,\mu F$ and $f = 60\,Hz$, $R_{Th} = \frac{1}{2(60)100\times10^{-6}} = \underline{\underline{83.3\,\Omega}}$

21 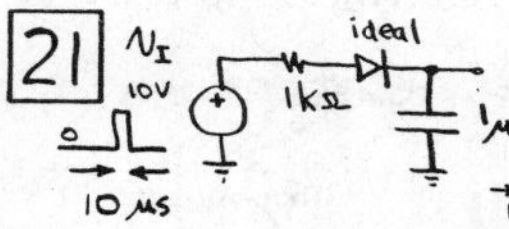

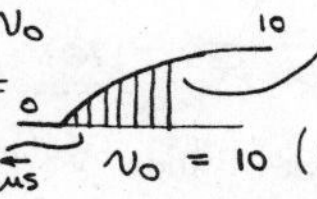

Pulses shown as contiguous: $v_o = 10(1-e^{-t/\tau})$

where $\tau = RC = 10^3\times1\times10^{-6} = 10^{-3}\,s$

After one pulse: $v_o = 10(1-e^{-10^{-5}/10^{-3}}) = .0995\,V$

After 2 pulses: $v_o = 10(1-e^{-2(10^{-2})}) = 0.198$

After 10 pulses: $v_o = 10(1-e^{-10(10^{-2})}) = 0.952\,V$

For $v_o = 6.32\,V$, $10(1-e^{-n(10^{-2})}) = 6.32 \rightarrow -e^{-n/100} = .632-1 \rightarrow n = 100$

For $v_o = 9.0\,V$, $n = 230$

For $v_o = 9.9\,V$, $n = 460.5$ or 461

22 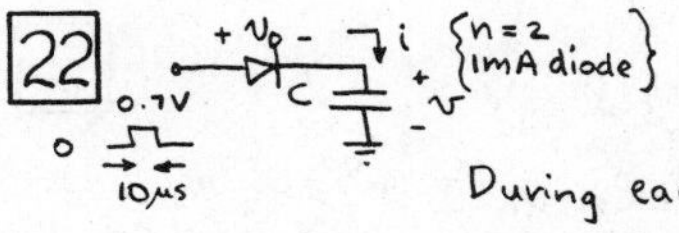

5

During each pulse: $i = C\frac{dv}{dt} = I_S e^{v_D/nV_T}$

But $v_D = 0.7 - v \rightarrow C\frac{dv}{dt} = \underbrace{I_S e^{\frac{700}{nV_T}}}_{1mA} \times e^{-v/nV_T}$

$\therefore \int_{t_1}^{t_2} 10^{-3}dt = C\int_{V_1}^{V_2} e^{v/nV_T}dv$, whence

$10^{-3}(t_2-t_1) = CnV_T\left[e^{v/nV_T}\right]_{V_1}^{V_2} = CnV_T\left(e^{\frac{V_2}{nV_T}} - e^{\frac{V_1}{nV_T}}\right)$

Thus $e^{V_2/nV_T} = e^{V_1/nV_T} + \frac{10^{-3}(t_2-t_1)}{CnV_T}$; $\frac{10^{-3}(10\times10^{-6})}{1\times10^{-6}(50\times10^{-3})} = 0.2$

For output initially 0V, ie $V_1 = 0$, after

1 pulse $e^{V_2/nV_T} = 1 + 0.2 = 1.2$

2 pulses $e^{V_3/nV_T} = e^{V_2/nV_T} + 0.2 = 1.4$

3 pulses $e^{V_4/nV_T} = e^{V_3/nV_T} + 0.2 = 1.6$, etc.

For which, after

1 pulse, $V_2 = 50\ln 1.2 = \underline{9.11\,mV}$

2 pulses, $V_3 = 50\ln 1.4 = \underline{16.8\,mV}$

n pulses, $V_{n+1} = 50\ln[1 + n(0.2)]$

10 pulses, $V_{11} = 50\ln[3] = \underline{\underline{54.9\,mV}}$

Now to reach 0.63 V, ie 90% of 0.7, $50\ln(1+0.2n) = 630$

or $\ln(1+0.2n) = 12.6$, whence $n = \underline{\underline{1{,}482{,}788}}$ pulses

23 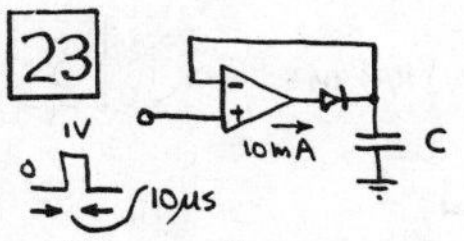

$CV = IT \rightarrow V = \frac{10\times10^{-3}\times10\times10^{-6}}{10\times10^{-6}}$ **5**

$= 0.01\,V$

Thus, following 1 pulse, $v_o = 0.01\,V$

2 pulses, $v_o = .02\,V$

10 pulses, $v_o = 0.10\,V$

To reach 0.5V, requires $500/10 = 50$ pulses

To reach 1.0 V, requires $1000/10 = 100$ pulses

To reach 2.0V is impossible since beyond $v_o = 1V$, the amplifier output is always low.

24 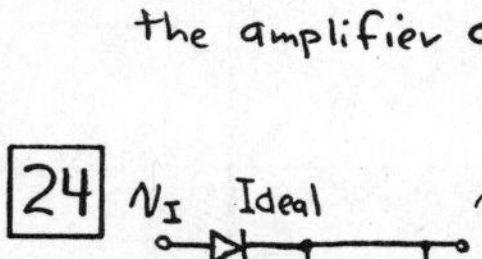

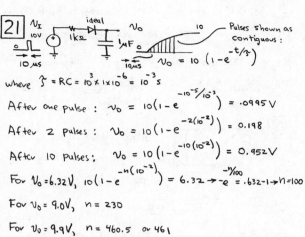

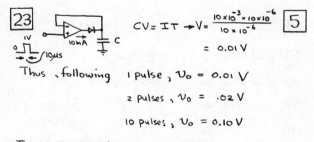

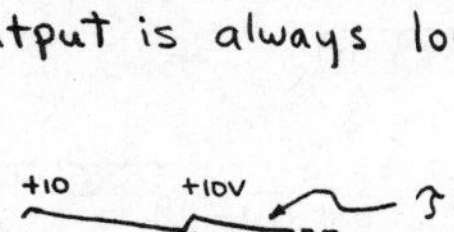

$\tau = 10^4\times100\times10^{-6} = 1$ sec.

Peak v_o is 10 volts, at which point the load current is $\frac{10V}{10k} = 1mA$. Assuming the diode conducts for only a short time and that v_o stays very nearly at +10V, the peak-to-peak ripple

$V_r = \frac{IT}{C} \approx \frac{10^{-3}\times10^{-2}}{100\times10^{-6}} = \underline{\underline{0.1\text{ Volts}}}$

Thus the dc output voltage is $\frac{10+10-0.1}{2}$ **5**

or $\underline{9.95\,V}$, and the average load current nearly 1mA as expected. The capacitor charge lost is replaced by a current pulse through the diode of amplitude $i = C\frac{dv}{dt} = 100\times10^{-6}\times\frac{20}{10^{-2}/2} = \underline{0.4\,A}$, and duration $t = \frac{0.1\,V}{20V/5\,ms} = \underline{25\,\mu s}$.

Check: Charge provided thru diode: $0.4\times25\times10^{-6} = 10^{-5}\,C$

Charge lost in the load/cycle: $1mA\times10^{-2} = 10^{-5}\,C$ ✓

25 $V_{out} \approx \underline{100V}$; $I_L \approx \frac{100V}{1k\Omega} = \underline{100mA}$

For 2V ripple: $C = \frac{IT}{V} = \frac{10^{-1}\times1/60}{2} = \underline{\underline{833\,\mu F}}$

The diode conducts while the 100 V peak sine wave rises from 98V to 100V. Conduction angle is $90° - \sin^{-1}\frac{98}{100} = 11.5°$ or $\frac{11.5}{360}\times100$ or $\underline{3.2\%}$ of the cycle

Average diode current during conduction $= \frac{360}{11.5}\times100mA = \underline{3.13A}$

26 **5**

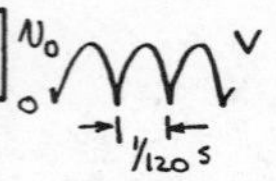

Peak $V_{out} \approx V$

Load current $I \approx V/R$

Ripple voltage $V_r = \frac{IT}{C} = \frac{V/R \times 1/f}{C} \rightarrow \frac{V_r}{V} = \frac{1}{fCR} \rightarrow C = \frac{1}{fR\frac{V_r}{V}}$

For 10% ripple, $C_{10} = \frac{1}{120 \times 10^4 \times 0.1} = 8.\dot{3}\,\mu F$

For 1% ripple, $C_1 = 10\,C_{10} = 83.\dot{3}\,\mu F$

27

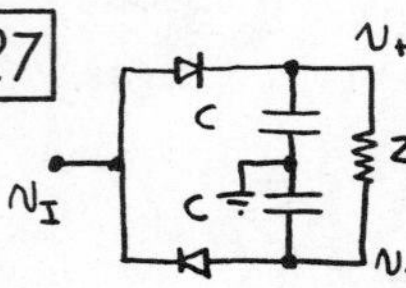

Ideal diodes:

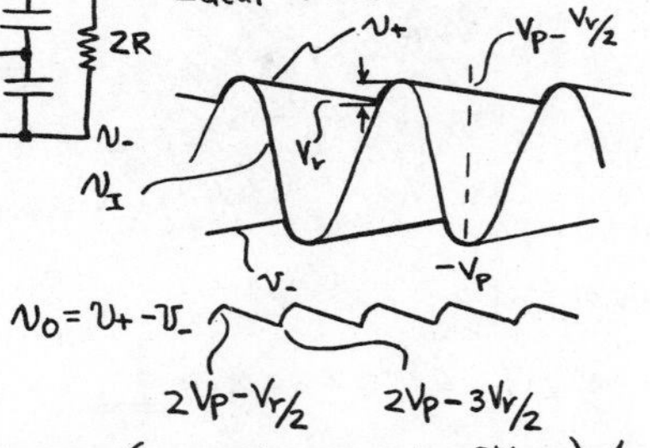

$V_r = \frac{V_p}{fCR}$

Average output is $(2V_p - V_r/2 + 2V_p - 3V_r/2)/2$ or $2V_p - V_r$. The ripple voltage is $2V_p - V_r/2 - (2V_p - 3V_r/2) = V_r$. Thus for the same load current, the percent ripple is half of a half-wave supply.

28 **5**

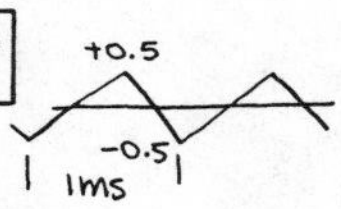

(Leakage) load on $C = 1 + 10 = 11\,nA$

Peak output $= 0.5\,V$

For 1% ripple, $V_r = \frac{0.5}{100} = 5\,mV$

Capacitor $C = \frac{IT}{V} = \frac{11 \times 10^{-9} \times 10^{-3}}{5 \times 10^{-3}} = 2.2 \times 10^{-9} = \underline{\underline{2200\,pF}}$

29 V_C will rise, and is out of control! For Fig P5.29a,

$R_{3_a} = \frac{0.7\,V}{10\,nA} = \frac{0.7}{10 \times 10^{-9}} = \underline{\underline{70\,M\Omega}}$. For Fig P5.29b,

$R_{3_b} = \underline{\underline{10\,M\Omega}}$ and divider voltage is $V = 10 \times 10^{-9} \times 10 \times 10^{6} = 10^{-1}\,V$

$R_4 = \frac{0.1}{0.1\,mA} = \underline{\underline{1k}}$, $R_5 = \frac{0.7 - 0.1}{0.1} = \underline{\underline{6k}}$ for a 0.1 mA divider.

30

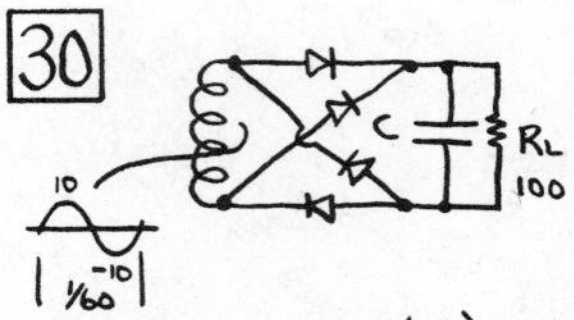

Peak voltage across C is $(10 - 0.7 - 0.7) = 8.6\,V$

For 10% ripple

$C = \frac{IT}{V} = \frac{\frac{0.95(8.6)}{100} \times \frac{1}{120}}{8.6 \times 0.1} = \underline{\underline{791\,\mu F}}$

since average output voltage (for ripple 10% V_P) is $V_P(1 - \frac{0.1}{2}) = .95(8.6) = \underline{\underline{8.17\,V}}$

31 **5**

For input $v_I = 2 + 5\sin\omega t$, the highest voltage on C, $\bar{V}_C = 2 + 5\sqrt{2} = 9.07\,V$.

The most negative input, $v_I = 2 - 5\sqrt{2} = -5.07\,V$.

The most negative voltage on the anode of D_1 is 0.7 volts lower since D_2 conducts.

∴ Peak voltage across D_1 is $9.07 + 5.07 + 0.70 = 14.84\,V$. The peak reverse voltage occurs across D_2 when D_1 conducts allowing the anode of D_2 to follow 0.7 volts below the anode of D_1 as it conducts.

∴ Peak voltage across D_2 is 0.7 volts.

32

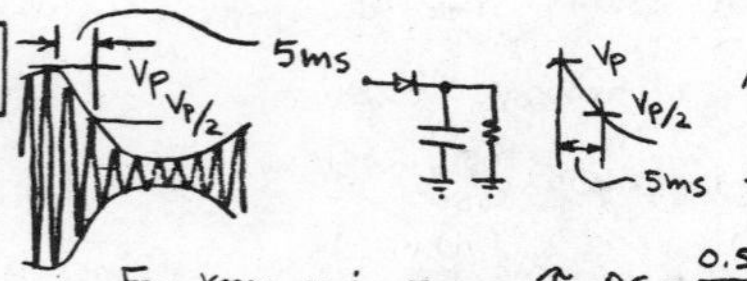

$v = V_p(e^{-t/\tau}) = 0.5\,V_p$ for $t = .693\,\tau$

For response in 5ms, $\tau = RC = \frac{0.5 \times 10^{-3}}{0.693} \rightarrow C = \frac{5 \times 10^{-3}}{.693 \times 10^{4}} = \underline{\underline{.721\,\mu F}}$

Ripple: $V_r = \frac{IT}{C} = \frac{V_p}{10^4} \times \frac{1/2 \times 10^6}{0.721 \times 10^{-6}} \rightarrow \frac{V_r}{V_p} \times 100 = \underline{\underline{.0069\%}}$

33 **5**

$CR \gg T = 1\,ms$: net charge flow in $C = 0$

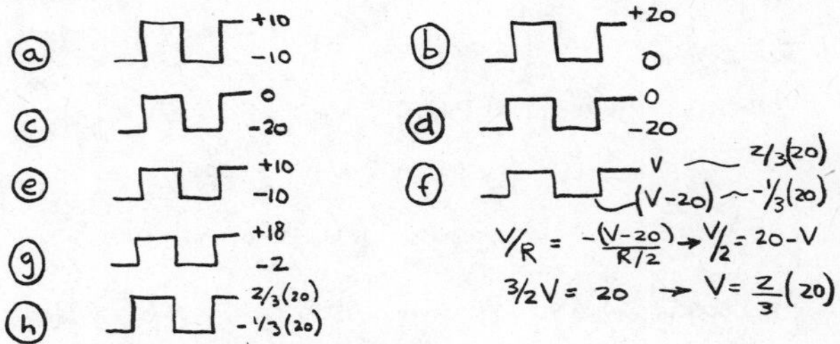

(f) $V \sim 2/3(20)$, $(V-20) \sim -1/3(20)$

$\frac{V}{R} = -\frac{(V-20)}{R/2} \rightarrow V/2 = 20 - V$

$3/2\,V = 20 \rightarrow V = \frac{2}{3}(20)$

(h) $\frac{2/3(20)}{2R} = \frac{1/3(20)}{R}$

34

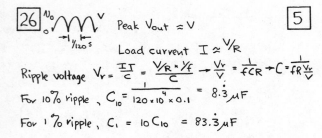

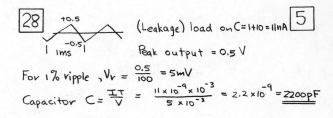

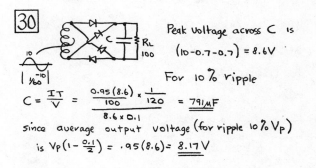

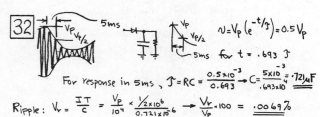

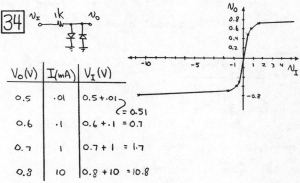

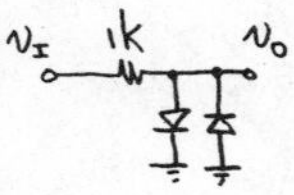

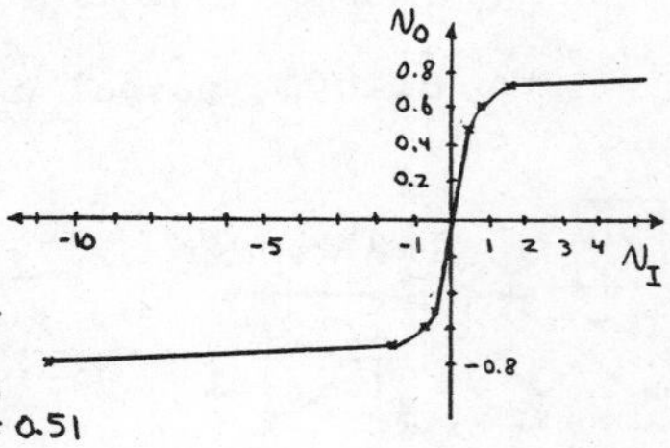

V_O(V)	I(mA)	V_I(V)
0.5	.01	0.5 + .01 = 0.51
0.6	.1	0.6 + .1 = 0.7
0.7	1	0.7 + 1 = 1.7
0.8	10	0.8 + 10 = 10.8

Conclude: Soft limiter; $K \approx \frac{0.50}{0.51} = 0.98$

$L+ = 0.8$; $L- = -0.8$

35

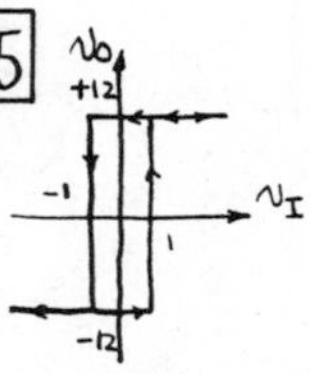

5

Amount of hysteresis is 2V

For a 0.5V peak input wave, output is either +12 or −12V.

For a sinewave input of 1.1 Vpeak the output is a ±12 volt square wave of the same frequency, but lagging by $\sin^{-1}\frac{10}{11} = 65.4°$. The average of the input 1.1 volt peak sine wave can vary by ±0.1 volts until operation ceases when the input fails to exceed the ±1V threshold.

36

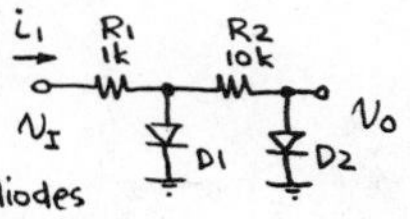

1mA diodes
0.1V/decade

$v_O = 0.4$

$i_{D2} = 10^{(0.4-0.7)/0.1}$ mA = 1μA

$v_{D1} = 0.4 + .01 = 0.41$

$i_{D1} = 10^{4.1-7}$ mA = 1.26μA

$i_1 = 1.0 + 1.26 = 2.26$μA

$v_I = 0.41 + 2.26\times10^{-6}\times10^{3} = 0.412$V

5

v_O:	0.5	0.52	0.54
i_{D2}	10^{5-7} mA = 10μA	$10^{5.2-7}$ = 15.8μA	$10^{5.4-7}$ mA = 25.1μA
v_{D1}	0.5+0.1 = 0.6	.52+.158 = .678	.54+.251 = .791
i_{D1}	10^{6-7} mA = 100μA	$10^{6.78-7}$ mA = 602μA	$10^{7.91-7}$ mA = 8.13mA
i_1	110μA	618μA	8.16mA
v_I	0.6+.11 = .71V	.678+.618 = 1.296	.791+8.16 = 8.95V

v_O	0.56
i_{D2}	$10^{5.6-7}$ mA = 39.8μA
v_{D1}	.56+.398 = .958
i_{D1}	$10^{9.58-7}$ mA = 380mA
i_1	380mA
v_I	380 V

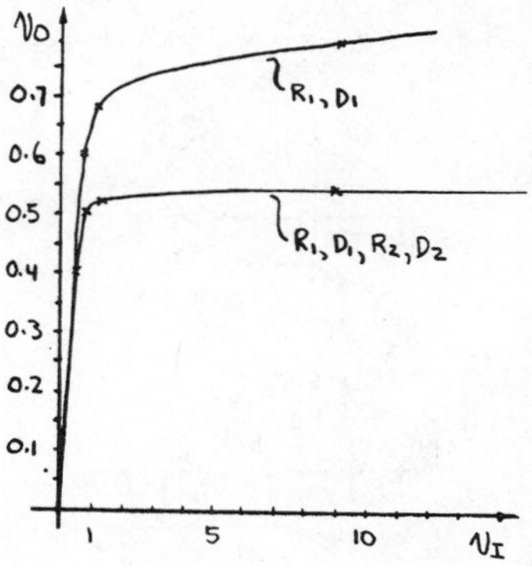

37

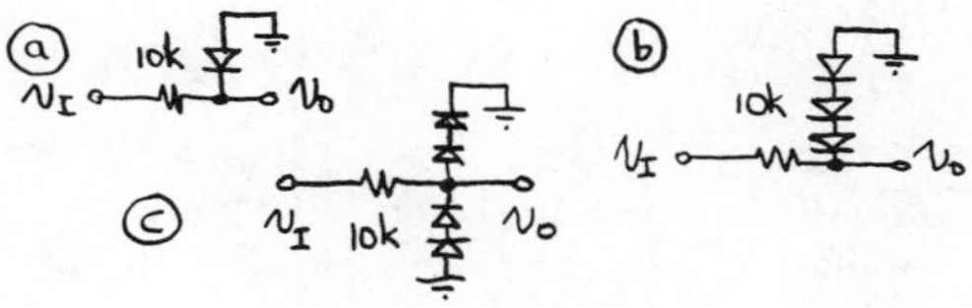

38

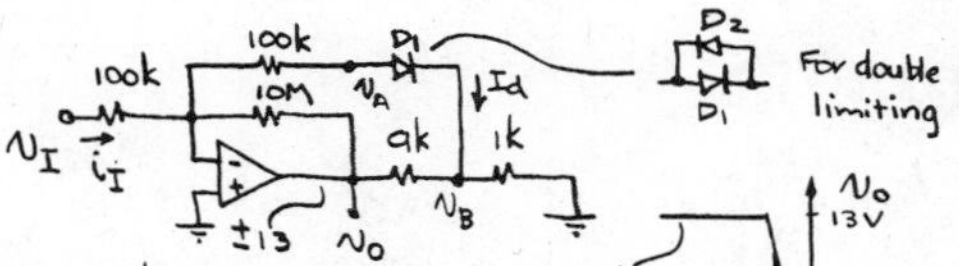

For double limiting

5

1mA diode: $V_d = 0.7 - 0.1\log 1/I_d$

I_d μA	V_d	v_A	v_B	v_O	I_I μA	v_I
0.1	0.3	−.01	−.31	−3.1	.4	.04
1	.4	−.1	−.5	−5.0	1.5	.15
2	.43	−.2	−.63	−6.3	2.6	.26
5	.47	−.5	−.97	−9.7	6.0	.60
8	.49	−.8	−1.29	−12.9	9.3	.93

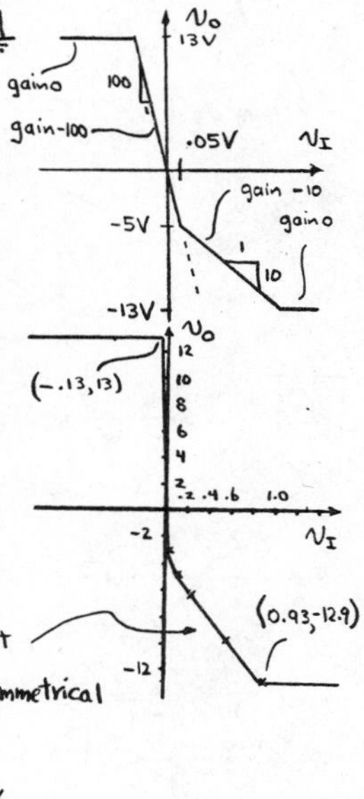

See with 2 diodes as above, that the 2nd and 4th quadrants are symmetrical

39

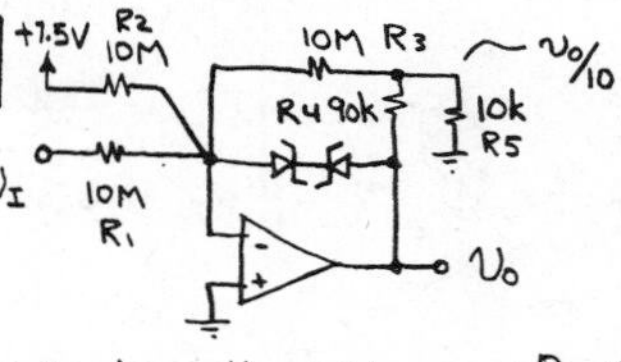

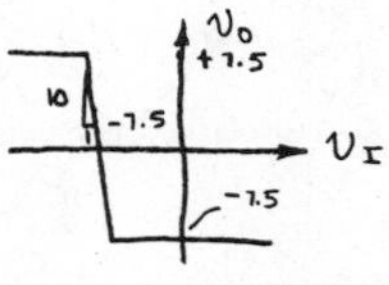

R2 sets the threshold, and R4, R5 set the gain.

40

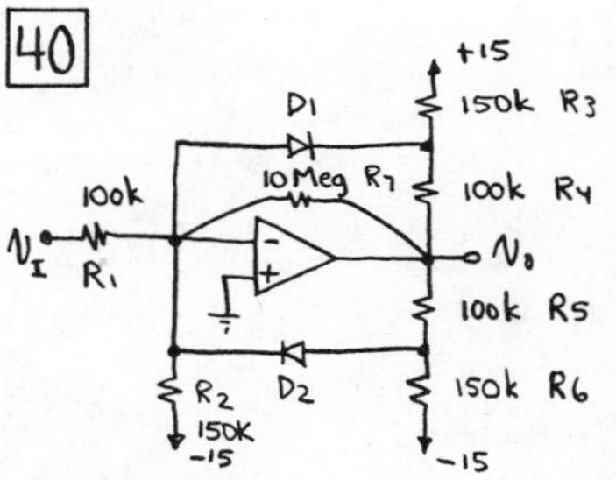

5

Assume diodes are ideal:

D1 conducts with $v_O = -10$ and gain $= -\frac{R_4}{R_1} = -1$

R2 raises threshold to $R_1/R_2 \times 15 = +10$V

41

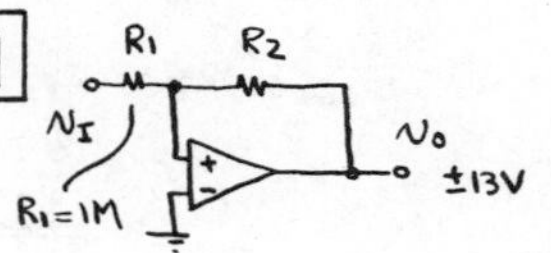

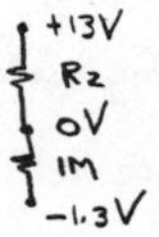

$R_2 = \frac{13}{1.3}\cdot 1M = \underline{\underline{10M}}$

42

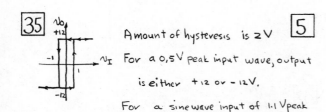

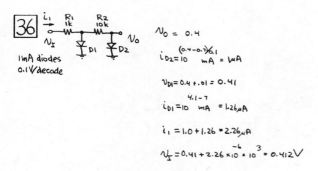

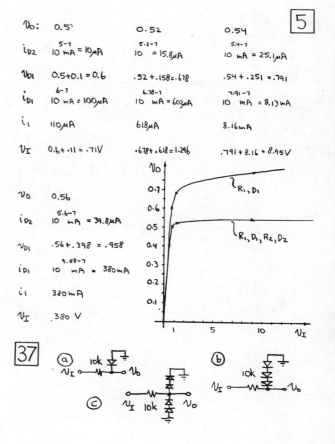

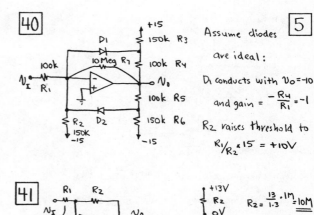

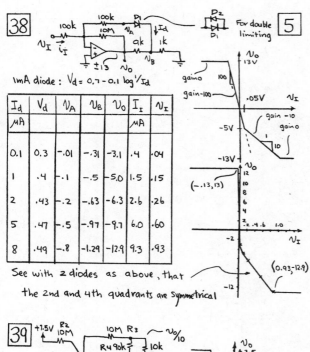

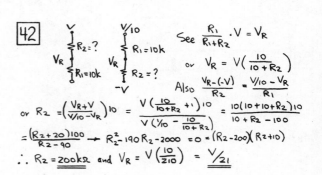

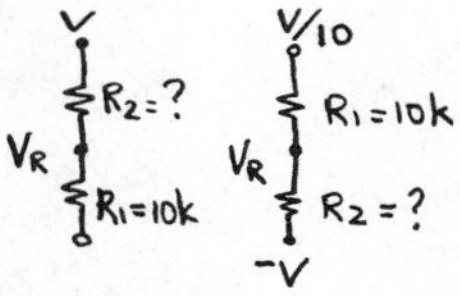

See $\frac{R_1}{R_1+R_2}\cdot V = V_R$

or $V_R = V\left(\frac{10}{10+R_2}\right)$

Also $\frac{V_R-(-V)}{R_2} = \frac{V/10 - V_R}{R_1}$

or $R_2 = \left(\frac{V_R+V}{V/10 - V_R}\right)10 = \frac{V\left(\frac{10}{10+R_2}+1\right)10}{V\left(1/10 - \frac{10}{10+R_2}\right)} = \frac{10(10+10+R_2)10}{10+R_2-100}$

$= \frac{(R_2+20)100}{R_2-90} \rightarrow R_2^2 - 190R_2 - 2000 = 0 = (R_2-200)(R_2+10)$

$\therefore R_2 = \underline{\underline{200k\Omega}}$ and $V_R = V\left(\frac{10}{210}\right) = \underline{\underline{V/21}}$

43

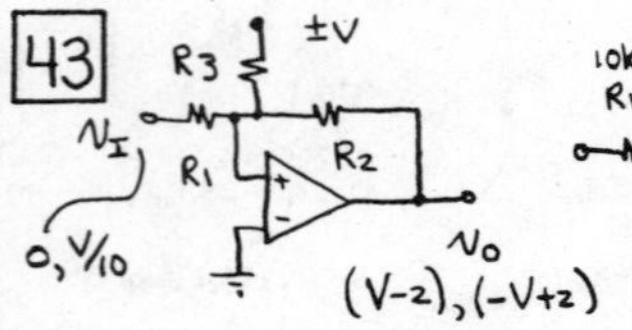

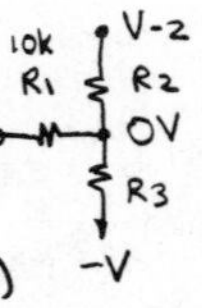

$R_1 = \underline{10k\Omega}$ **5**

$R_2 = \frac{V-2}{V} \times R_3$

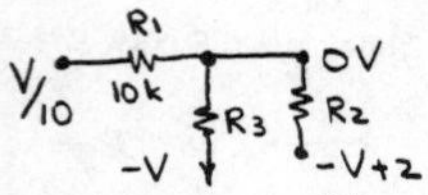

$\frac{V/10}{R_1} = \frac{V}{R_3} + \frac{V-2}{R_2}$

Combining: $\frac{V}{10(10)} = V/R_3 + \frac{V-2}{V-2} \times V/R_3 \rightarrow \frac{1}{100} = \frac{2}{R_3}$

or $R_3 = \underline{\underline{200k\Omega}}$; $R_2 = \left(\frac{V-2}{V}\right) R_3 = \frac{13}{15}(200k) = \underline{\underline{173.3k}}$

44

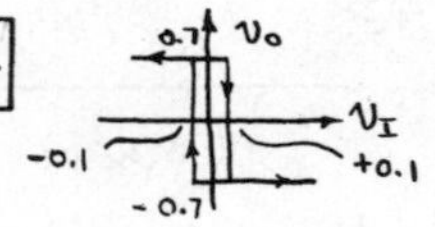

Note that the amplifier saturation voltage is not critical.

45

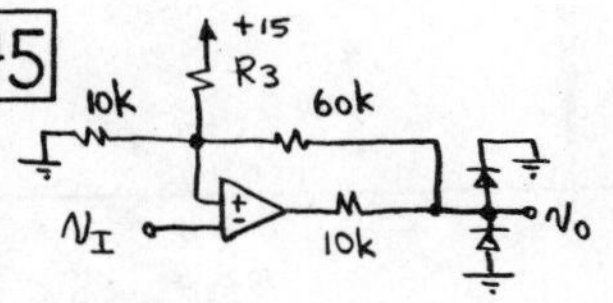

Centered at +2V →

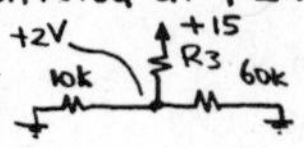

See $\frac{15-2}{R_3} = \frac{2}{10k} + \frac{2}{60k} \rightarrow R_3 = \frac{13}{14} \times 60k = 55.7k$

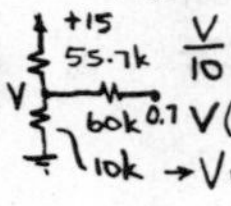

$\frac{V}{10} = \frac{15-V}{55.7} - \frac{V-0.7}{60}$

$V(0.1 + .01795 + .01667) = .269 + .012$

$\rightarrow V = \frac{.269 + .012}{.1346} = \underline{\underline{2.088}}\ V$

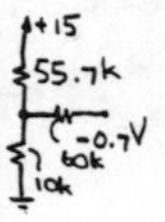

$V = \frac{.269 - .012}{.1346} = \underline{\underline{1.914}}\ V$

46

5

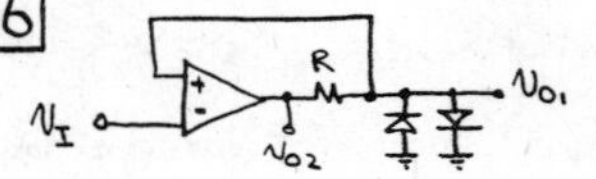

$v_{I_t} = \pm 0.7V$

$v_{O1} = \pm 0.7$; $v_{O2} = \pm 12V$

47

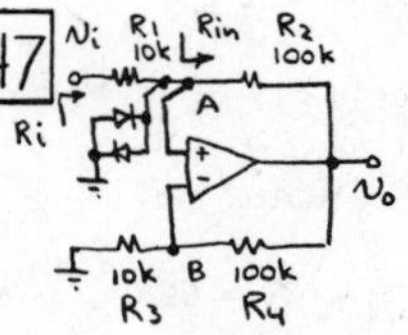

$v_A = \pm 0.7V$ due diodes

$v_B = \pm 0.7V$ due negative feedback

$v_O = \pm(0.7)\left(\frac{100k + 10k}{10k}\right) = \pm 7.7V$

Since $R_1 = 20k$, V_{It} lie ∓ 1.4 volts from critical levels of V_A, that is $V_{I_t} = \mp 0.7V$

$R_{in} = \frac{v_{in}}{i_{in}} = \frac{v_{in}}{-\left(\left(1 + R_4/R_3\right)v_{in} - v_{in}\right)/R_2} = \frac{-R_2 \times R_3}{R_4} = -R_3 = -10k\Omega$

$R_i = R_1 + R_{in} = R_1 - 10k$ which is positive for $R_1 > 10k$

zero for $R_1 = 10k$

negative for $R_1 < 10k$

48

For v_2 high (at +9V), D_1 and D_4 are cut off and $v_3 = \left(\frac{1}{1+9}\right)(10 - 0.7) = 0.93V$. For v_2 low, $v_3 = -0.93V$

Thus thresholds are $V_{I_t} = \pm 0.93V$

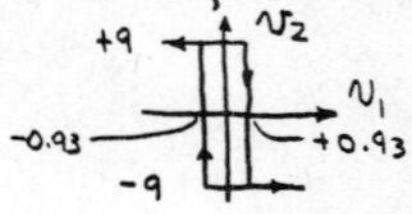

49

5

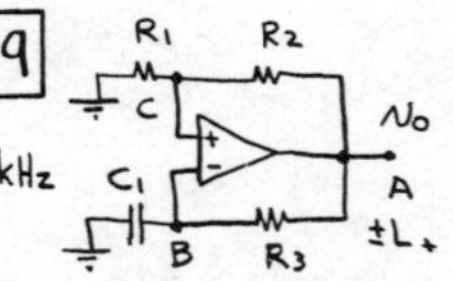

$\beta = \frac{R_1}{R_1 + R_2} = 0.1$

For resistors ≫ 10k and small

$R_1 = \underline{10k}$, $R_2 = \underline{90k}$, $R_3 = \underline{10k}$

$T = 2\tau \ln \frac{1+\beta}{1-\beta} = 1/1kHz \rightarrow \tau = \frac{1ms}{2 \ln 1.1/0.9} = 2.49$ ms

$C_1 = \tau/R = \frac{2.49 \times 10^{-3}}{10^4} = \underline{\underline{0.249\mu F}}$

v_C ranges over $\pm \frac{R_1}{R_1 + R_2} \times L_+$

Initial charging current $= \left(1 + \frac{R_1}{R_1 + R_2}\right) L_+/R_3 = I_i$

Final charging current $= \left(1 - \frac{R_1}{R_1 + R_2}\right) L_+/R_3 = I_f$

Slope difference at B $= \frac{1}{C_1}(I_i - I_f) = \frac{L_+}{R_3 C_1} \times 2\beta = \underline{\underline{\frac{0.2 L_+}{R_3 C_1}}}$

as a % of maximum: $\frac{\frac{2 L_+ \beta}{C_1 R_3}}{\frac{L_+(\beta + 1)}{C_1 R_3}} \times 100 = \frac{2\beta}{\beta + 1} \times 100 = \underline{\underline{18.2\%}}$

50

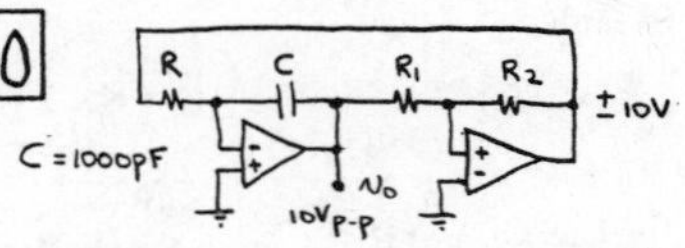

$R_1 = \underline{100k\Omega}$

$R_2 = \frac{10}{10/2} \cdot R_1 = \underline{\underline{200k\Omega}}$

For f = 10kHz, v_o rises by 10V in $\frac{1}{2} \times \frac{1}{10^4} = 50\mu sec.$

$I_R = \frac{CV}{T} = \frac{1000 \times 10^{-12} \times 10}{50 \times 10^{-6}} = 200\mu A \rightarrow R = V/I_R = \frac{10}{200 \times 10^{-6}} = \underline{\underline{50k\Omega}}$

51

5

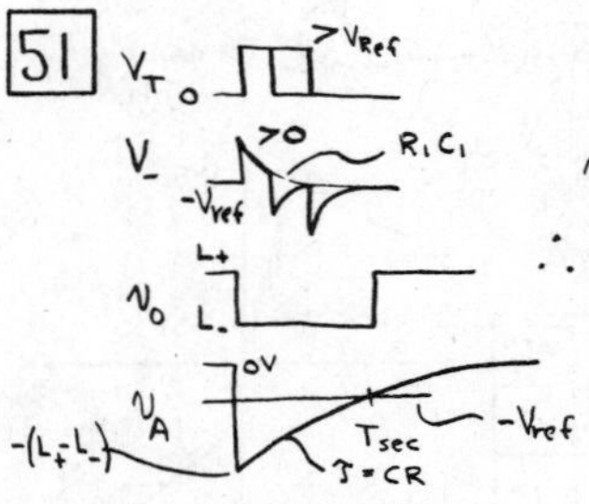

$v_A = -(L_+ - L_-)e^{-t/RC}$

$\therefore -V_{ref} = -(L_+ - L_-)e^{-T/RC}$

$T = RC \ln\left(\frac{L_+ - L_-}{V_{ref}}\right)$

Note that for normal operation $R_1 C_1 \ll RC$

52

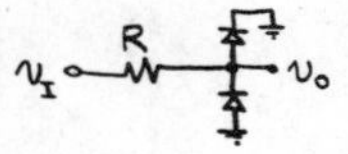

Diodes 0.7V @ 1mA, 0.1 V/decade

$v_O = 0.7 \sin \omega t \rightarrow \frac{dv_O}{dt} = 0.7\omega \cos \omega t$

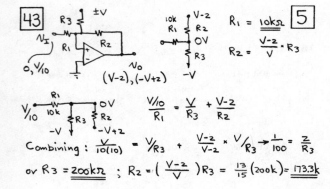

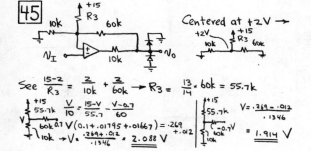

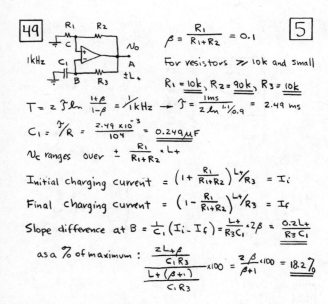

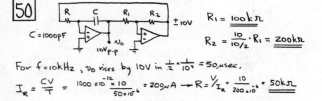

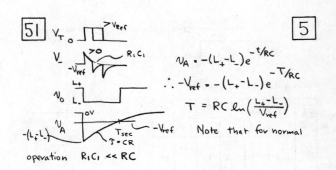

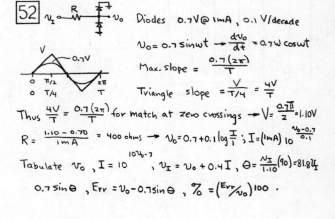

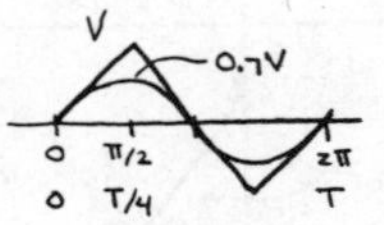

Max. slope $= \frac{0.7(2\pi)}{T}$

Triangle slope $= \frac{V}{T/4} = \frac{4V}{T}$

Thus $\frac{4V}{T} = \frac{0.7(2\pi)}{T}$ for match at zero crossings $\rightarrow V = \frac{0.7\pi}{2} = 1.10V$

$R = \frac{1.10 - 0.70}{1mA} = 400$ ohms $\rightarrow v_O = 0.7 + 0.1 \log \frac{I}{1}$; $I = (1mA)\, 10^{\frac{v_O - 0.7}{0.1}}$

Tabulate v_O, $I = 10^{10 v_O - 7}$, $v_I = v_O + 0.4I$, $\theta = \frac{v_I}{1.10}(90) = 81.8 v_I$

$0.7 \sin\theta$, $Err = v_O - 0.7\sin\theta$, $\% = (Err/v_O)100$.

(next)

5

v_O	0.70	0.65	0.60	0.55	0.50	0.40	0.30	0.20	0.10	0.0
I	1mA	0.316	0.1	.0316	0.01	1μA	0.1	0.01	1nA	0
v_I	1.10	.776	.64	.563	.504	.4004	.3	.2	.1	0
θ	90	63.5	52.4	46.1	41.2	32.8	24.6	16.4	8.2	0
$0.7\sin\theta$	0.7	.626	.555	.504	.461	.379	.291	.197	0.100	0
Err	0	.024	.045	.051	.039	.021	.009	.003	.000	0
%Err	0	3.7	7.5	9.3	7.8	5.3	3	1.5	0	0

53

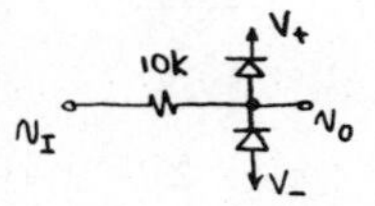

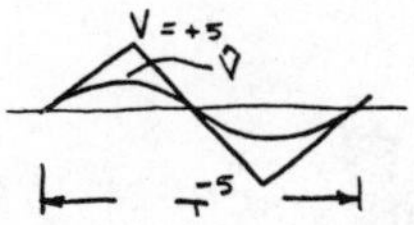

Slopes equal: $\frac{V}{T/4} = \frac{\hat{V}2\pi}{T} \rightarrow \hat{V} = \frac{4V}{2\pi} = \frac{2(5)}{\pi} = 3.18V$

Clamping Voltage $= 3.18 - 0.70 = 2.48V$

Use $\underline{\pm 2.5V}$ clamps

6

1

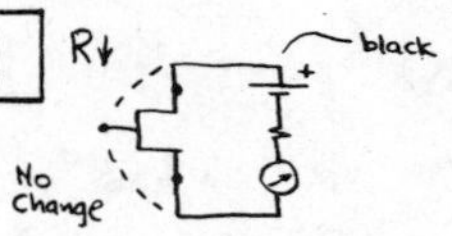

Conclude JFET is

<u>n-channel</u>

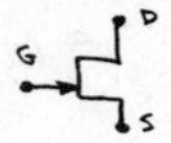

2 (a)

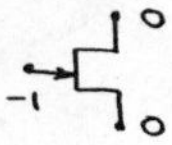

$V_P = -4V \rightarrow$ Operating in <u>triode region</u>

Pinchoff region: $v_{DG} \geq |V_P| = \underline{4V}$

where $v_{DS} = v_{DG} + v_{GS} = 4 + (-1) = \underline{3V}$

(b) $V_P = -5V$, $V_{GS} = -1$ volt.

For pinchoff operation $v_{DS} \geq v_{GS} + |V_P| = -1 + 5 = \underline{4V}$

3 Triode region: $i_D = I_{DSS}\left[2\left(1 - \frac{v_{GS}}{V_P}\right)\frac{v_{DS}}{-V_P} - \left(\frac{v_{DS}}{V_P}\right)^2\right]$

For square term a fraction k of the linear:

$$\left(\frac{v_{DS}}{V_P}\right)^2 = k \times 2\left(1 - \frac{v_{GS}}{V_P}\right)\frac{v_{DS}}{-V_P}$$

for which $v_{DS} = 2kV_P\left(\frac{v_{GS}}{V_P} - 1\right) = 2(v_{GS} - V_P)k$

For $k = 0.1$, $v_{DS} = 0.2(v_{GS} - V_P)$ $\Big|\, -V_P/5$ } at $v_{GS} = 0$ $\Big|\, -V_P/10$ } at $v_{GS} = \frac{V_P}{2}$

For $k = 0.01$, $v_{DS} = 0.02(v_{GS} - V_P)$ $\Big|\, -V_P/50$ } at $v_{GS} = 0$ $\Big|\, -V_P/100$ } at $v_{GS} = \frac{V_P}{2}$

6

4 $r_{DS} = \left[\frac{2I_{DSS}}{-V_P}\left(1 - \frac{v_{GS}}{V_P}\right)\right]^{-1}$

For $v_{GS} = 0$, $r_{DS} = \frac{-V_P}{2I_{DSS}} = -\frac{0.5V_P}{I_{DSS}}$

For $v_{GS} = V_P/2$, $r_{DS} = \left(\frac{2I_{DSS}}{-V_P}(1/2)\right)^{-1} = \frac{-V_P}{I_{DSS}}$

For $v_{GS} = 0.9V_P$, $r_{DS} = -\frac{5V_P}{I_{DSS}}$

5 $i_D = I_{DSS}\left(1 - \frac{v_{GS}}{V_P}\right)^2 = \frac{I_{DSS}}{2}$ when $\left(1 - \frac{v_{GS}}{V_P}\right)^2 = 1/2$

or $1 - \frac{v_{GS}}{V_P} = \frac{1}{1.414} = .707$ or $v_{GS} = \underline{0.293V_P}$

For $v_{GS} = V_P/2$, $i_D = I_{DSS}\left(1 - \frac{V_P/2}{V_P}\right)^2 = \underline{0.25\ I_{DSS}}$

6

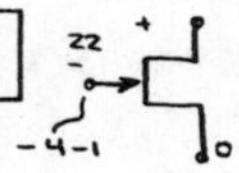

Max $v_{DS} = 22 - 4 - 1 = \underline{17V}$

7 v_{GS} goes to $20 - 22 = \underline{-2V}$ and <u>i_{DS} increases</u>

8 For $v_{GS} = 0$, $i_D = I_{DSS}$ and $r_o = \frac{V_A}{I_{DSS}}$

Thus $V_A = r_o I_{DSS} = 100k\,(1mA) = 100V$. Now at $v_{GS} = -0.5$

$i_D = I_{DSS}\left(1 - \frac{0.5}{1}\right)^2 = \frac{I_{DSS}}{4}$ and $r_o = \frac{V_A}{i_D} = \frac{100}{1/4} = \underline{400k\Omega}$

6

9 $v_{DS} = v_{GS} - V_P = -1 - (-2) = \underline{1V}$

$i_D = I_{DSS}\left(1 - \frac{v_{GS}}{V_P}\right)^2 = 8\left(1 - \frac{-1}{-2}\right)^2 = \underline{2mA}$

10 $i_D = I_{DSS}\left(1 - \frac{v_{GS}}{V_P}\right)^2 = 8\left(1 - \frac{-1}{-2}\right)^2 = 2mA$

For $i_D = 2 + 1 = 3mA \rightarrow \left(1 - \frac{v_{GS}}{V_P}\right)^2 = 3/8$

$1 - \frac{v_{GS}}{V_P} = .612$ or $v_{GS} = -2(1 - .612) = -.775V$,

that is $\Delta v_{GS} = -.775 - (-1.0) = \underline{0.225V}$

For $i_D = 2 - 1 = 1mA \rightarrow \left(1 - \frac{v_{GS}}{V_P}\right)^2 = 1/8$

or $v_{GS} = -2\left((1/8)^{1/2} - 1\right) = -1.293V$,

that is $\Delta v_{GS} = -1.293 - (-1.0) = \underline{-0.293}V$

11 $i_D = I_{DSS}\left[2\left(1 - \frac{v_{GS}}{V_P}\right)\frac{v_{DS}}{-V_P} - \left(\frac{v_{DS}}{V_P}\right)^2\right]$

For linear operation $1/r_{DS} = \frac{2I_{DSS}}{-V_P}\left(1 - \frac{v_{GS}}{V_P}\right)$

or $r_{DS} = \left(\frac{2(8)}{2}\left(1 - \frac{-1}{-2}\right)\right)^{-1} = 1/4\text{mA/V} = \underline{250\Omega}$

Now r_{DS} becomes 125Ω for $\frac{1}{.125} = \frac{2(8)}{2}\left(1 - \frac{v_{GS}}{-2}\right)$

or $1 - \frac{v_{GS}}{-2} = 1$ or $v_{GS} = \underline{0V}$

12 $\frac{1}{r_{DS}} = \frac{2I_{DSS}}{V_P}\left(1-\frac{v_{GS}}{V_P}\right)$ **6**

Now $\frac{1}{0.1} = \frac{2I_{DSS}}{V_P}(1-0) \rightarrow V_P = 0.2\,I_{DSS}$

And $\frac{1}{0.4} = \frac{2I_{DSS}}{V_P}(1-1/V_P) = \frac{2\,I_{DSS}}{0.2\,I_{DSS}}\left(1-\frac{1}{V_P}\right)$

or $2.5 = 10(1-1/V_P) \rightarrow 1/V_P = 0.75$, $V_P = 4/3\,V$

Whence $I_{DSS} = \frac{4/3}{0.2} = 20/3\,mA$

13 For $v_{SG}=0$, $v_{SD}=V_P$, $i_D = I_{DSS} = 1mA$

For v_{SD} raised from 1V to 11V, and i_D increasing from 1.0 to 1.1 mA, $r_o = \frac{11-1}{1.1-1} = \frac{10}{0.1} = 100k\Omega$

For a 20V breakdown and $V_S = +10$, the lowest acceptable V_D is $+10-0-20 = -10V$

14

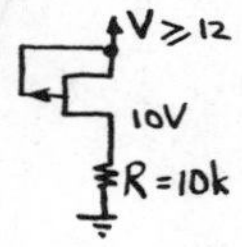

$I_{DSS} = \frac{10V}{10k} = 1mA$

$V_P = 12-10 = 2V$

15 For previous circuit $V=5V$, $i_D = i$, $v_{DS} = v$ **6**

$i_D = I_{DSS}\left(2\left(1-\frac{v_{GS}}{V_P}\right)\frac{v_{DS}}{V_P} - \left(\frac{v_{DS}}{V_P}\right)^2\right)$

or $i = 1\left(2(1-0)\,v/2 - \left(\frac{v}{2}\right)^2\right) = v - \frac{v^2}{4}$ and $v + 10i = 5$

or $i = \frac{5-v}{10}$. Thus $\frac{5-v}{10} = v - \frac{v^2}{4} \rightarrow 10-2v = 20v-5v^2$

$5v^2 - 22v + 10 = 0 \rightarrow v = \frac{22 \pm \sqrt{22^2-4(10)(5)}}{10}$

Whence $v = 0.515V$

Now for $R = 100k$, $i = v - \frac{v^2}{4}$ as before and also $\frac{5-v}{100}$

Thus $5 - v = 100v - 25v^2$ or $25v^2 - 101v + 5 = 0$

$\rightarrow v = \frac{101 \pm \sqrt{101^2 - 4(5)(25)}}{50} = 0.0501V$

16

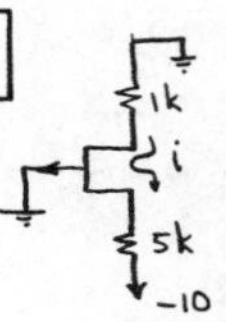

$I_{DSS} = 8mA$, $V_P = 2V$

Assume pinchoff: $i_D = I_{DSS}\left(1-\frac{v_{SG}}{V_P}\right)^2$

or $i = 8\left(1-\frac{i(1)}{2}\right)^2 = 8\left(1-i+\frac{i^2}{4}\right)$

ie. $2i^2 - 9i + 8 = 0 \rightarrow i = \frac{+9 \pm \sqrt{9^2-4(8)(2)}}{2(2)} = 1.22mA$

Thus $i_{DS} = 1.22mA$

$v_S = -1.22V$

$v_D = -10 + 5(1.22) = -3.9V$

17 For $R = 20k$ in previous $\rightarrow$ triode operation **6**

$i_D = I_{DSS}\left(2\left(1-\frac{v_{SG}}{V_P}\right)\frac{v_{SD}}{V_P} - \left(\frac{v_{SD}}{V_P}\right)^2\right)$ and $v_{SG} = i_D(1k)$

ie $i = 8\left(2\left(1-\frac{i}{2}\right)\frac{v}{2} - \left(\frac{v}{2}\right)^2\right)$ but also $10 = i(1) + v + i(20)$

ie $i = \frac{10-v}{21} \rightarrow \therefore \frac{10-v}{21} = 8\left(v\left(1-\frac{10-v}{42}\right) - v^2/4\right)$

or $20 - 2v = 8v(42-10-v) - 84v^2$

or $20 - 2v = 256v - 8v^2 - 84v^2$

$92v^2 - 258v + 20 = 0$

Whence $v = \frac{258 \pm \sqrt{258^2 - 4(20)(92)}}{2(92)} = 0.08V$

and $i = \frac{10-.08}{21} = 0.472mA$

$v_S = -0.472V$ and $v_D = -.472 - .080 = -0.552V$

18 $I_{DSS} = 2mA$, $|V_P| = 2V$, $r_o = 50k$

(a) $I_1 = 2mA + \frac{10}{50k} = 2.2mA$

(b) $I_2 = 2(2.2) = 4.4\,mA$

(c) $I_3 = 2 + 0.2 + 2 + 0.2 = 4.4mA$

(d) V_4 is low with Q_6 and Q_7 in triode mode and each conducting $\frac{1}{2}(I_{Q8}) \approx \frac{2.2}{2} = 1.1mA$, $V_4 = v$

6

ie $1.1 = 2\left(2(1-0)\frac{v}{2} - \left(\frac{v}{2}\right)^2\right) \rightarrow 1.1 = 2v - \frac{v^2}{2}$

or $v^2 - 4v + 2.2 = 0 \rightarrow v = \frac{4 \pm \sqrt{16-4(2.2)}}{2} = 0.658V$

ie $V_4 = 0.658V$

(e) $V_5 = 5V$; $I_5 = 2.0 + \frac{5}{50k} = 2.1mA$

(f) $V_6 = 5V$

19 $I_{DSS} = 2mA$, $|V_P| = 2V$, $r_o = \infty$

(a) $V_1 = 10 - 2(2) = 6V$

(b) Pinchoff? $i_D = I_{DSS}\left(1-\frac{v_{GS}}{V_P}\right)^2$ and $i_D = \frac{v_{SG}}{2k}$

Let $v_{SG} = v \rightarrow +v/2 = 2\left(1-\frac{-v}{-2}\right)^2 \rightarrow v = 4 - 4v + v^2$

or $v^2 - 5v + 4 = 0$, whence $v = \frac{+5 \pm \sqrt{5^2-4(4)}}{2} = 1\,volt$

$\therefore i_{DS} = 0.5mA$, $V_2 = 1V$, $V_3 = 10 - 0.5(10) = 5V$

Yes, it is in pinchoff!

(c) Triode? Let $v_{DS} = v$

$i = 2\left(2\left(1-\frac{2i}{2}\right)\frac{v}{2} - \left(\frac{v}{2}\right)^2\right)$ and $i = \frac{10-v}{20+2}$

$\therefore \frac{10-v}{22} = 2v\left(1 - \frac{10}{22} + \frac{v}{22}\right) - \frac{v^2}{2}$

or $10 - v = 44v - 2v + 2v^2 - 11v^2$

or $9v^2 - 43v + 10 = 0 \to v = \frac{43 \pm \sqrt{43^2 - 4(9)(10)}}{18} = .245$ **6**

Thus $i = \frac{10 - .245}{22} = 0.443\,mA$, and

$V_4 = 2(.443) = \underline{\underline{0.886V}}$, $V_5 = .886 + .245 = \underline{\underline{1.131V}}$

Yes, triode!

(d) Pinchoff: Estimate $V_6 \approx 1.0$ volts

$\therefore i_{DS} = \frac{10+1}{22k} = 0.5\,mA$ and $i_{DS} = 2(1 - \frac{1}{2})^2 = 0.5\,mA$ ✓

both check. Thus $V_6 = \underline{\underline{+1 \text{ volt}}}$, $V_7 = 10 - 0.5(10) = \underline{\underline{5V}}$

(e) $i_{DS6} = 2mA \to V_8 = \underline{0V}$, $V_9 = 10 - 2(2) = \underline{6V}$

(f) $i_{DS9} = 2mA \to V_{11} = 10 - 2(2) = 6V$

$i_{DS7} = i_{DS8} = 1mA \to v_{GS} = V_P\left(\sqrt{\frac{i_D}{I_{DSS}}} - 1\right) = 2(\sqrt{\tfrac{1}{2}} - 1) = -.586$

Thus $V_{10} = -0.586V$

(g) Q_{11} in triode operation, Q_{10} in pinchoff op.

$V_{12} = v$.

For Q_{11}, $i = i_{DS} = I_{DSS}\left(2\left(1 - \frac{v_{GS}}{V_P}\right)\frac{v_{DS}}{V_P} - \left(\frac{v_{DS}}{2}\right)^2\right)$

ie $i = 2\left(\frac{2v}{2} - \frac{v^2}{4}\right) = 2v - v^2/2$

For Q_{10}, $i = i_{DS} = I_{DSS}\left(1 - \frac{v_{GS}}{V_P}\right)^2 = 2\left(1 - \frac{v}{2}\right)^2 = 2 - 2v + \frac{v^2}{2}$

$\therefore v^2 - 4v + 2 = 0 \to v = \frac{4 \pm \sqrt{16 - 8}}{2} = 0.585V$

and $i = 2(.585) - \frac{(.585)^2}{2} = 1.17 - .17 = 1.0\,mA$ **6**

Thus $V_{12} = \underline{0.585V}$ and $V_{13} = 10 - 4(1) = \underline{6.0V}$

(h) Q_{12} in triode and Q_{13} in pinchoff operation:

(See (b)), $i_{DS13} = 0.5\,mA$; $v_{GS12} = -(1k)(0.5mA) = 0.5V$

For Q_{12}, $i_{DS} = I_{DSS}\left(2\left(1 - \frac{v_{GS}}{V_P}\right)\frac{v_{DS}}{-V_P} - \left(\frac{v_{DS}}{V_P}\right)^2\right)$ or

$0.5 = 2\left(2\left(1 - \frac{0.5}{2}\right)v/2 - v^2/2\right)$

or $1 = 4(1 - 1/4)v - v^2 \to v^2 - 3v + 1 = 0$

whence $v = \frac{3 \pm \sqrt{9 - 4}}{2} = 0.382V$

Thus $V_{14} = 10 - .382 - 0.5 = \underline{\underline{9.12V}}$

(i) Q_{14} in pinchoff and Q_{15} in triode operation:

(See (b)), $i_{DS14} = 0.5\,mA$, $v_{GS15} = 0.5V$

Calculation is same as in (h)

Thus $V_{15} = 0.5 + 0.382 = \underline{\underline{0.882V}}$

20 In the triode region, **6**

$i_D = I_{DSS}\left[2\left(1 - \frac{v_{GS}}{V_P}\right)\frac{v_{DS}}{-V_P} - \left(\frac{v_{DS}}{V_P}\right)^2\right]$

$\frac{\partial i_D}{\partial v_{DS}} = \frac{2I_{DSS}\left(1 - \frac{v_{GS}}{V_P}\right)}{-V_P} - \frac{2I_{DSS}}{V_P^2} \cdot v_{DS}$ which for $v_{DS} = 0$

becomes $\left.\frac{\partial i_D}{\partial v_{DS}}\right|_{v_{DS}=0} = \frac{1}{r_{DS}} = \frac{2I_{DSS}}{-V_P}\left(1 - \frac{v_{GS}}{V_P}\right)$ which for $v_{GS} = 0$

becomes: $\frac{1}{r_{DS}} = \frac{2I_{DSS}}{-V_P}$

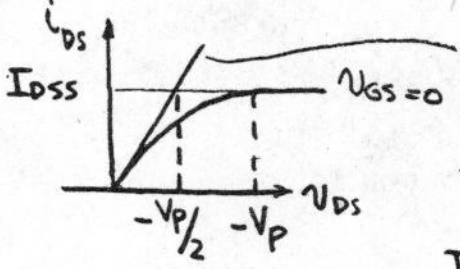

$i_{DS} = \frac{v_{DS}}{r_{DS}}$ Line $i_{DS} = \frac{v_{DS}}{r_{DS}}$ intersects the line $i_{DS} = I_{DSS}$ at

$I_{DSS} = v_{DS}(1/r_{DS}) = v_{DS}\left(\frac{2I_{DSS}}{-V_P}\right)$

ie where $v_{DS} = -V_P/2$, half way to the edge of pinchoff for $v_{GS} = 0$ at $v_{DS} = -V_P$

Now for $v_{GS} = 0$ and $v_{DS} = -V_P$

$i_D = I_{DSS}\left[2(1 - 0)\frac{-V_P}{-V_P} - \left(\frac{-V_P}{+V_P}\right)^2\right] = I_{DSS}$

For Fig 6.7, $I_{DSS} = 16mA$, $V_P = -4$ and $v_{GS} = 0$

$i_D = I_{DSS}\left[2\left(\frac{v_{DS}}{-V_P}\right) - \left(\frac{v_{DS}}{V_P}\right)^2\right] = \frac{I_{DSS}}{2}$ when, with $v_{DS} = v$,

$8 = 16\left[\frac{2}{4}v - \frac{v^2}{16}\right] \to 8 = 8v - v^2 \to v^2 - 8v + 8 = 0$

whence $v = \frac{8 \pm \sqrt{64 - 32}}{2} = \underline{1.17V}$. Compare this with the tangent at $i_D = \frac{I_{DSS}}{2}$ where $v_{DS} = V_P/4 = 4/4 = \underline{\underline{1 \text{ Volt}}}$

For $i_D = 0.75 I_{DSS} \to 12 = 8v - v^2$ **6**

or $v^2 - 8v + 12 = 0 \to v = \frac{8 \pm \sqrt{64 - 48}}{2} = \underline{\underline{2V}}$

On the tangent $v_{DS} = \frac{3}{4} V_P/2 = \frac{3}{4} \times 4/2 = \underline{\underline{1.5V}}$

21 $V_{DD} = 12V$, $V_P = -4$:

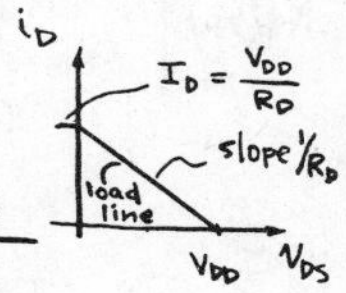

	R_D Ω	250	500	1000	2k	4k
	I_D mA	48	24	12	6	3
$v_{GS} = 0$	i_D mA	16	16	10.1	5.8	2.9
	v_{DS}	8	4	1.6	0.9	0.5
$v_{GS} = -2$	i_D mA	4	4	4	4	2.9
	v_{DS}	11	10	8	4	1.0
$v_{GS} = -4$	i_D mA	0	0	0	0	0
	v_{DS}	12	12	12	12	12

6

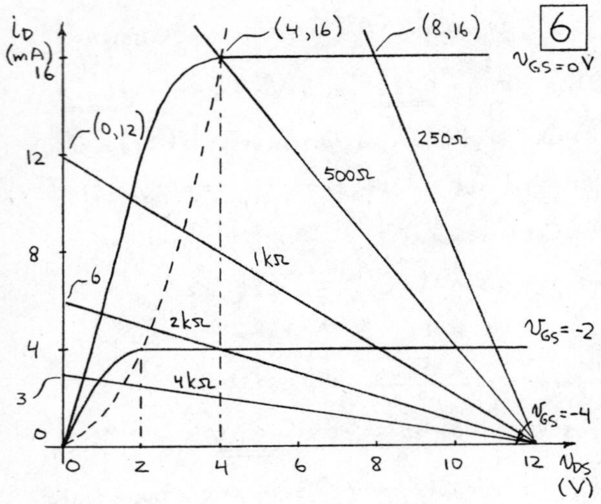

6

22

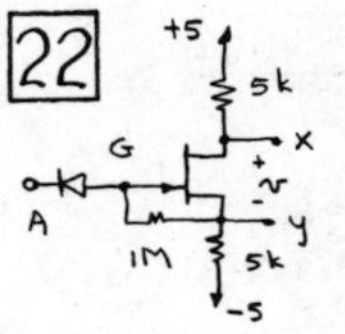

$I_{DSS} = 10mA$, $V_P = -2V$, $V_d = 0.7$

For A high: $i_D = I_{DSS}\left[2\left(1-\frac{v_{GS}}{V_P}\right)\frac{v_{DS}}{-V_P} - \left(\frac{v_{DS}}{V_P}\right)^2\right]$

$i = 10\left[2\frac{v}{2} - \left(\frac{v}{2}\right)^2\right]$

and $5 - v - (-5) = i(5+5) \rightarrow 1 - \frac{v}{10} = 10v - \frac{10}{4}v^2$

or $20 - 2v = 200v - 50v^2 \rightarrow 50v^2 - 202v + 20 = 0$

whence $v = \frac{202 \pm \sqrt{202^2 - 4(20)50}}{100} = 0.102$

Thus with A high, $V_x = \underline{\underline{+0.051}}V$, $V_y = \underline{\underline{-0.051}}V$

For the diode barely cut off, $V_d = 0.0V$ and

$V_A \geqslant 0 + V_y = \underline{\underline{-51mV}}$

JFet cuts off for $V_A = -5 - 2 - 0.7 = -7.7V$ for

which $V_x = \underline{\underline{+5V}}$, $V_y = \underline{\underline{-5V}}$

23 From Fig. 6.20, largest current for which the gate of the "low" device remains cut off is <u>4mA</u>

24 $i_D = I_{DSS}\left(1 - \frac{v_{GS}}{V_P}\right)^2$

For $I_D = \frac{I_{DSS}}{4}$, $v_{GS} = \frac{V_P}{2}$, $R_S = \frac{V_P/2}{I_{DSS}/4} = \underline{\underline{\frac{2V_P}{I_{DSS}}}}$

6

I_{DSS}	16	8	4	16	8	16	4
$-V_P$	8	4	2	4	2	2	1
$R_S(k\Omega)$	1	1	1	0.5	0.5	0.25	0.25

25 The four extreme devices are:

Device	①	②	③	④
I_{DSS} (mA)	2	2	16	16
V_P (V)	-1	-4	-1	-4

<u>Nominally</u>: $I_{DSS} = 4mA$, $V_P = -2V$, $V_{GS} = -1V$

$I_D = 1mA$, $V_D = 6V$, $g_m = \frac{2\times 4}{2}\left(1 - \frac{-1}{-2}\right) = \underline{\underline{2mA/V}}$

<u>Circuit ⓐ</u>: (Fixed bias)

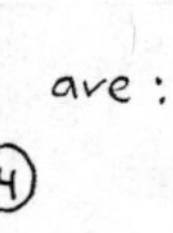

For pinchoff: $I_D = I_{DSS}\left(1 - \frac{-1}{V_P}\right)^2$

For triode op.: $I_D \approx 2I_{DSS}\left(1 - \frac{-1}{V_P}\right)\left(\frac{V_D}{-V_P}\right)$

(next)

6

① $I_D = 2\left(1 - \frac{-1}{-1}\right)^2 = 0$, ie <u>cutoff</u>

$V_{GS} = -1V$, $V_D = 10V$, $g_m = 0$

② $I_D = 2\left(1 - \frac{-1}{-4}\right)^2 = \frac{9}{8}$ mA

$V_{GS} = -1V$, $V_D = 10 - 4\times\frac{9}{8} = 5.5V$

Thus the FET is in pinchoff and

$g_m = \frac{2\times 2}{4}\left(1 - \frac{-1}{-4}\right) = \underline{\underline{0.75}}$ mA/V or 0.37 of nominal

The maximum allowable output swing is $5.5 - (-1) - 4 = \underline{\underline{2.5V}}$

③ $I_D = 16(1-1)^2 = 0 \rightarrow$ <u>cutoff</u>

$V_{GS} = -1V$, $V_D = +10V$, $g_m = \underline{\underline{0}}$

④ $I_D = 16(1 - 1/4)^2 = 9mA \rightarrow V_D = 10 - 9(4) =$ neg X

Thus the FET operates in <u>triode mode</u> with

$I_D = 2(16)\left(1 - \frac{-1}{-4}\right)\frac{V_D}{4}$ -- Ⓐ, but $I_D = \frac{10 - V_D}{4}$ -- Ⓑ

Solving yields $V_D \simeq 0.4V$, $I_D = 2.4mA$

<u>Circuit ⓑ</u>: (Self bias)

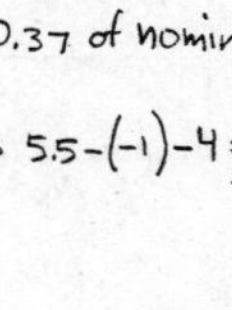

$V_{GS} = -I_D \times 1 = -I_D$

For pinchoff operation: $I_D = I_{DSS}\left(1 - \frac{I_D}{|V_P|}\right)^2$

For triode operation: $I_D \approx 2I_{DSS}\left(1 - \frac{I_D}{|V_P|}\right)\left(\frac{10 - 5I_D}{|V_P|}\right)$

6

① $I_D = 2(1-\frac{I_D}{1})^2 = 2(1-2I_D+I_D^2)$

Thus $I_D^2 - 2.5I_D + 1 = 0 \rightarrow I_D = 0.5\,mA$

$V_{GS} = -0.5V$, $V_D = 10-0.5(4) = 8V$

Maximum signal swing = 2V (for cut off)

$g_m = \frac{2\times2}{1}(1-\frac{0.5}{1}) = 2\,mA/V$, the nominal value

② $I_D = 2(1-\frac{I_D}{4})^2 = 2(1+\frac{I_D^2}{16}-\frac{I_D}{2})$

Thus $I_D^2/8 - 2I_D + 2 = 0 \rightarrow I_D = 1.07\,mA$

$V_{GS} = -1.07V$, $V_D = +5.7V$

Maximum signal swing = 5.7−(−1.07)−4 ≃ 1.7V

$g_m = \frac{2\times2}{4}(1-\frac{1.07}{4}) = 0.73\,mA/V$, or 0.37 of nominal

③ $I_D = 16(1-\frac{I_D}{1})^2 = 16(1+I_D^2-2I_D)$

Thus $16I_D^2 - 33I_2 + 16 = 0 \rightarrow I_D = 0.78\,mA$

$V_{GS} = -0.78V$, $V_D = 6.9V$

Maximum signal swing = 10−6.9 = 3.1V (cutoff)

$g_m = \frac{2\times16}{1}(1-\frac{0.78}{1}) = 7mA/V$ or 3.5 times nominal

④ $I_D = 16(1-\frac{I_D}{4})^2 = 16(1+\frac{I_D^2}{16}-\frac{I_D}{2})$

Thus $I_D^2 - 9I_D + 16 = 0 \rightarrow I_D = 2.43\,mA$

$V_D = 10-4(2.43) = 0.28V$, clearly too low ×

6

Conclude operation is in triode region:

$I_D = 2\times16(1-\frac{I_D}{4})(\frac{10-5I_D}{4}) = 40(1-\frac{I_D}{4})(2-I_D)$

whence $I_D^2 - 6.1I_D + 8 = 0 \rightarrow I_D = 1.91\,mA$

$V_{GS} = -1.91V$, $V_D = 2.36V$

Circuit (c) (Mixed bias)

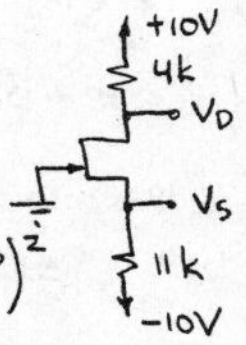

$V_{GS} = 10 - 11I_D$

For pinchoff op.: $I_D = I_{DSS}(1+\frac{10-11I_D}{|V_P|})^2$

① $I_D = 2(1+\frac{10-11I_D}{1})^2 = 2(11-11I_D)^2 = 242(1-I_D)^2$

Thus $I_D^2 - 2I_D + 1 = \frac{I_D}{242} \rightarrow I_D^2 - (2+\frac{1}{242})I_D + 1 = 0 \rightarrow$

$I_D = 0.94\,mA$, $V_{GS} = -0.3V$, $V_D = 6.2V$

Maximum signal = 10−6.2 = 3.8V

$g_m = \frac{2\times2}{1}(1-\frac{0.3}{1}) = 2.8\,mA/V$ or 1.4× nominal

② $I_D = 2(1+\frac{10-11I_D}{4})^2 = \frac{1}{8}(14-11I_D^2)$

whence $I_D \approx 1mA$, $V_{GS} = -1V$, $V_D = 6V$

Maximum signal swing = 6−4 = 2V

$g_m = \frac{2\times2}{4}(1-\frac{1}{4}) = 0.75\,mA/V$ or 0.38× nominal

③ $I_D = 16(1+10-11I_D)^2 = 16\times121(1-I_D)^2$

6

Thus $I_D^2 - (2+\frac{1}{16\times121})I_D + 1 = 0 \rightarrow I_D = 0.98mA$

$V_{GS} = -0.78V$, $V_D = +6.1V$

Maximum signal swing = 10−6.1 = 3.9V

$g_m = \frac{2\times16}{1}(1-0.78) = 7mA/V$ or 3.5× nominal

④ $I_D = 16(1+\frac{10-11I_D}{4})^2 = (14-11I_D)^2$

Thus $121I_D^2 - 309I_D + 196 = 0 \rightarrow I_D = 1.17mA$

$V_{GS} = -2.87V$, $V_D = 5.3V$

Maximum signal swing = 5.3−4 = 1.3V

$g_m = \frac{2\times16}{4}(1-\frac{2.87}{4}) = 2.3\,mA/V$ or 1.15× nominal

Circuit (d): (Feedback bias)

$V_{GS} = \frac{V_D+10}{1600}\times900 - 10 = \frac{9}{16}V_D - \frac{70}{16}$

$= \frac{9V_D-70}{16} = \frac{9(10-4I_D)-70}{16} = \frac{20-36I_D}{16}$

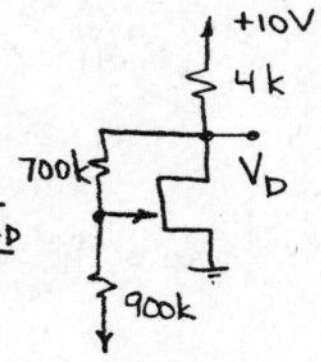

ie $V_{GS} = \frac{5-9I_D}{4}$

For pinchoff operation: $I_D = I_{DSS}(1+\frac{5-9I_D}{4|V_P|})^2$

For triode region op.: $I_D \approx 2I_{DSS}(1+\frac{5-9I_D}{4|V_P|})(\frac{10-4I_D}{|V_P|})$

① $I_D = 2(1+\frac{5-9I_D}{4})^2 = \frac{2}{16}\times81(1-2I_D+I_D^2)$

Thus $I_D^2 - (2+\frac{16}{162})I_D + 1 = 0 \rightarrow$

6

$I_D = 0.73mA$, $V_{GS} = -0.4V$, $V_D = +7.1V$

Maximum signal swing = 10−7.1 = 2.9V

$g_m = \frac{2\times2}{1}(1-0.4) = 2.4\,mA/V$ or 1.2× nominal

② $I_D = 2(1+\frac{5-9I_D}{16})^2 = \frac{2}{256}(21-9I_D)^2$

Thus $81I_D^2 - I_D(2\times9\times21+128) + 441 = 0 \rightarrow$

$I_D = 1.05mA$, $V_{GS} = -1.1V$, $V_D = 5.8V$

Maximum signal swing = 5.8−(−1.1)−4 = 2.9V

$g_m = \frac{2\times2}{4}(1-\frac{1.1}{4}) = 0.73\,mA/V$ or 0.36 of nominal

③ $I_D = 16(1+\frac{5-9I_D}{4})^2 = 81(1-I_D)^2$

Thus $I_D^2 - (2+\frac{1}{81})I_D + 81 = 0 \rightarrow$

$I_D = 0.89\,mA$, $V_{GS} = -0.75V$, $V_D = +6.4V$

Maximum signal swing = 10−6.4 = 3.6V

$g_m = \frac{2\times16}{1}(1-0.75) = 8\,mA/V$ or 4× nominal

④ $I_D = 16(1+\frac{5-9I_D}{16})^2 = \frac{1}{16}(21-9I_D)^2$

Thus $I_D^2 - (2\times9\times21+16)I_D + 441 = 0 \rightarrow$

$I_D = 1.74mA$, $V_D = 3V$, $V_{GS} = -2.67V$

6

Maximum signal swing $= 3 - (-2.7) - 4 = 1.7V$

$g_m = \frac{2\times16}{4}\left(1 - \frac{2.67}{4}\right) = 2.7\ mA/V$ or $1.35 \times$ nominal

Circuit ⓔ (Constant-current bias)

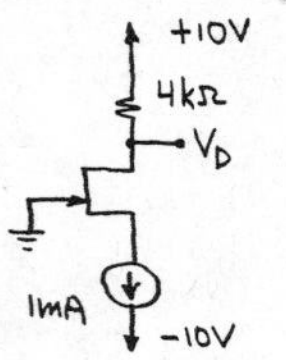

$I_D = 1mA$

① $1 = 2\left(1 + \frac{V_{GS}}{1}\right)^2 \rightarrow$

$V_{GS} = -0.3\ V$, $V_D = 6V$

Maximum signal swing $= 10 - 6 = 4V$

$g_m = \frac{2\times2}{1}(1 - 0.3) = 2.8\ mA/V$ or $1.4\times$ nominal

② $1 = 2\left(1 + \frac{V_{GS}}{4}\right)^2 \rightarrow$

$V_{GS} = -1.17V$, $V_D = 6V$

Maximum signal swing $= 6 - 4 = 2V$

$g_m = \frac{2\times2}{4}\left(1 - \frac{1.17}{4}\right) = 0.71\ mA/V$ or 0.35 of nominal

③ $1 = 16(1 + V_{GS})^2 \rightarrow$

$V_{GS} = -0.75V$, $V_D = 6V$

Maximum signal swing $= 10 - 6 = 4V$

$g_m = \frac{2\times16}{1}(1 - 0.75) = 8\ mA/V$ or $4\times$ nominal

④ $1 = 16\left(1 + \frac{V_{GS}}{4}\right)^2 \rightarrow$

6

$V_{GS} = -3V$, $V_D = 6V$

Maximum signal swing $= 6 - 4 = 2V$

$g_m = \frac{2\times16}{4}\left(1 - \frac{3}{4}\right) = 2\ mA/V$ or the nominal

Summary:

Circuit	Mode of Operation	Range of Output Swing	Range of g_m/nom. g_m
ⓐ	Cut-off for devices ① and ③, and triode for device ④	2.5V	0.37
ⓑ	Triode for device ④	1.7V to 3.1V	0.37 to 3.5
ⓒ	Always in pinchoff	1.3V to 3.9V	0.38 to 3.5
ⓓ	Always in pinchoff	1.7V to 3.6V	0.36 to 4.0
ⓔ	Always in pinchoff	2V to 4 V	0.35 to 4.0

Commentary: ⓐ is the worst design. ⓑ and ⓓ are about equal, although ⓓ is the better. ⓒ and ⓔ are the best, with ensured pinchoff operation. ⓔ is superior to ⓒ since it guarantees larger outputs, and has a constant drain voltage

26   6

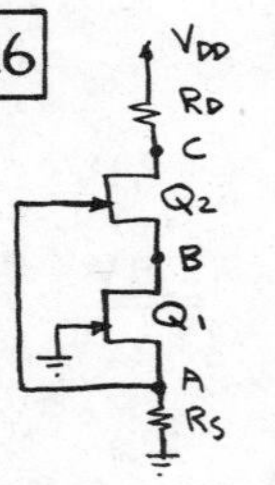

For Q_1, Q_2 matched and in pinchoff: $v_{DG1} \geq |V_P|$; $v_{DG2} \geq |V_P|$

ie $V_{DD} - i_D R_D \geq |V_P| + v_{SG1}$

and $v_{DG1} = v_{SG2} + v_{SG1} = 2 v_{SG1} \geq |V_P|$

$\therefore\ v_{SG1} = \boxed{I_D R_S \geq 0.5|V_P|}$

and $\boxed{V_{DD} - I_D R_D \geq |V_P| + \frac{|V_P|}{2} \geq 1.5|V_P|}$

Now for $V_{DD} = 10V$, $|V_P| = 2V$, $I_{DSS} = 4mA$

For $V_{DG1} = |V_P|$, $V_{DG2} = 2|V_P|$:

$V_{SG1} = V_P/2 = 1V \rightarrow i_D = 4(1 - 1/2)^2 = 1mA$

$\therefore\ R_S = 1k\Omega$ and $R_D = (10 - 2(2) - 2/2)/1mA = 5k\Omega$

For $V_{DG1} = 1.5|V_P|$, $V_{DG2} = 1.5|V_P|$

$V_{SG1} = \frac{1.5}{2}|V_P| = 1.5V \rightarrow i_D = 4\left(1 - \frac{1.5}{2}\right)^2 = 0.25mA$

$\therefore\ R_S = \frac{1.5}{0.25} = 6k\Omega$

and $R_D = \frac{10 - 1.5(2) - \frac{1.5}{2}(2)}{0.25} = 22k\Omega$

27   6

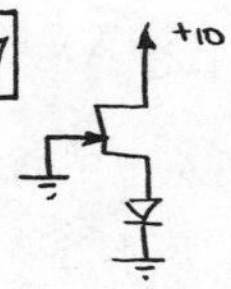

$I_{DSS} = 4mA$, $V_P = -2$ or -1

Diode: 0.7V@1mA, $n = 2$

$i = I_S e^{\frac{v}{nV_T}} \rightarrow v = 700 + 50 \ln i/1$

$i = I_{DSS}\left(1 - \frac{v_{GS}}{V_P}\right)^2$

For $V_P = -2$: Say $i = 1mA \rightarrow v_{GS} = 0.7V$

$i = 4\left(1 - \frac{0.7}{2}\right)^2 = 1.69mA \rightarrow v = 700 + 50\ln 1.69 = 726mV$

$i = 4\left(1 - \frac{0.726}{2}\right)^2 = 1.62mA \rightarrow v = 700 + 50\ln 1.62 = 724mV$

For $V_P = -1$: Say $i = 1mA \rightarrow v_{GS} = 0.7V$

$i = 4\left(1 - \frac{0.7}{1}\right)^2 = 0.36mA \rightarrow v = 700 + 50\ln 0.36 = 650mV$

$i = 4\left(1 - \frac{0.65}{1}\right)^2 = 0.49mA \rightarrow v = 700 + 50\ln 0.49 = 664mV$

$i = 4\left(1 - \frac{0.664}{1}\right)^2 = 0.450mA \rightarrow v = 700 + 50\ln 0.45 = 660mV$

28 V_P is the same; I_{DSS} doubles; g_{mo} doubles

29 $i_D = I_{DSS}\left(1 - \frac{v_{GS}}{V_P}\right)^2$; $g_m = \frac{\partial i_D}{\partial v_{GS}} = \frac{I_{DSS}}{V_P}(2)\left(1 - \frac{v_{GS}}{V_P}\right)$

$\frac{\partial g_m}{\partial v_{GS}} = \frac{2 I_{DSS}}{V_P^2} \rightarrow \frac{\Delta g_m}{g_m} = \frac{2 I_{DSS}}{V_P^2} \cdot \frac{\Delta v_{GS}}{g_m} = 0.1$

When $\Delta v_{GS} = 0.1(2)\frac{I_{DSS}}{V_P}\left(1 - \frac{v_{GS}}{V_P}\right)\left(V_P^2/2I_{DSS}\right) = 0.1(V_P - v_{GS})$

Thus g_m changes by 10% for each change by 10% of the difference between V_P and v_{GS} **6**

30 $i_D = I_{DSS}\left(1-\frac{v_{GS}}{V_P}\right)^2 = I \rightarrow \left(1-\frac{v_{GS}}{V_P}\right) = \left(\frac{I}{I_{DSS}}\right)^{1/2}$

$g_m = \frac{\partial i_D}{\partial v_{GS}} = \frac{2I_{DSS}}{V_P}\left(1-\frac{v_{GS}}{V_P}\right) = \frac{2\sqrt{I_{DSS}}}{V_P}\sqrt{I}$

Now if I_{DSS} ↑ by 4x, g_m ↑ by 2x and gain ↑ x 2x

31 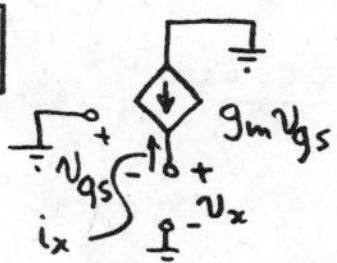

$i_x = -g_m v_{gs} = -g_m(-v_x) = g_m v_x$

$R_{in} = \frac{v_x}{i_x} = \frac{v_x}{g_m v_x} = 1/g_m$

$g_m = \frac{2I_{DSS}}{-V_P}\left(1-\frac{v_{GS}}{V_P}\right) = \frac{2I_{DSS}}{-V_P}\sqrt{\frac{I_D}{I_{DSS}}}$

For $I_{DSS} = 4\,mA$, $I = 1\,mA$, $V_P = -2$, $g_m = \frac{2(4)}{2}\sqrt{\frac{1}{4}} = 2\,mA/V$

$\therefore R_{in} = 1/2 = \underline{\underline{0.5\,k\Omega}}$

32 Consider $R_1 = 10M$, $R_2 = 5M \rightarrow I_{bias} = \frac{15V}{(10+5)10^6} = 1\mu A < 10\mu A$

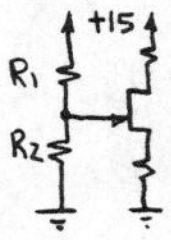

$R_{input} = R_1 \| R_2 = 2R_2 \| R_2 = \frac{2}{3}R_2 = 3.\dot{3}M > 1M$

At high temp. $R_{input} \le \frac{0.1(5V)}{100\times10^{-9}} = 5M > 3.\dot{3}M$

$\therefore R_1 = 10M$, $R_2 = 5M$ is OK

33 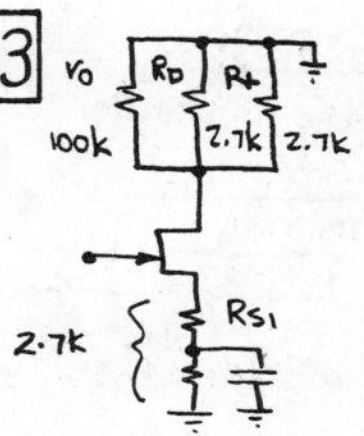

6

$\text{gain} = \frac{-R_D \| R_L \| r_o}{R_{S1} + 1/g_m}$

$g_m = 2.98\,mA/V \rightarrow 1/g_m = 336\,\Omega$

$R_D \| R_L \| r_o = 2.7 \| 2.7 \| 100 = 1.33k$

For gain $= -1 \rightarrow R_{S1} = 1.330 - .336$

or $R_{S1} = .994\,k \simeq \underline{\underline{1\,k\Omega}}$

34 $i_D = I_{DSS}\left(1-\frac{v_{GS}}{V_P}\right)^2$ and $v_{GS} = -1 - V\sin\omega t$

For $I_{DSS} = 8mA$, $V_P = -2V$, $i_D = 8\left(1-\frac{1}{2}-\frac{V}{2}\sin\omega t\right)^2$

or $i_D = 2(1-V\sin\omega t)^2 = 2(1-2V\sin\omega t + V^2\sin^2\omega t)$

$= 2\left(1+\frac{V^2}{2} - 2V\sin\omega t + \frac{V^2}{2}\cos 2\omega t\right)$

$\%\,H.D = \frac{\frac{V^2}{2}\times100}{2V} = \frac{V}{4}\times100 = 25V\%$

For $V = 0.5\,V$, %HD = $\underline{12.5\%}$

For HD = 1%, $V = \frac{1\%\times4}{100} = \underline{\underline{40mV}}$ peak

35 In Ex 6.5, PHD = $12.5\hat{V}\%$. This becomes 1% for $12.5\hat{V} = 1$ or $\hat{V} = 80mV$ peak $\equiv \frac{80}{\sqrt{2}} = \underline{\underline{56.6\,mV_{rms}}}$

36 Gain $= \frac{R_D}{R_S + 1/g_m} \rightarrow \text{Gain}_1 = \frac{R_D}{R_S + 1/g_{m1}}$ **6**

For $g_{m2} = 0.5g_{m1}$, $\text{Gain}_2 = \frac{R_D}{R_S + \frac{1}{0.5g_{m1}}} = 0.95\frac{R_D}{R_S + 1/g_{m1}}$

or $R_S + \frac{2}{g_{m1}} = \frac{R_S}{0.95} + \frac{1}{0.95g_{m1}} \rightarrow R_S = \frac{1}{g_{m1}}\left(\frac{2(.95)-1}{1-0.95}\right)$

or $R_S = \frac{18}{g_{m1}}$

ie R_S must be 18 times the equivalent source resistance

37 (a) Voltage gain $= \frac{-R_L \| R_D}{1/g_m + R_{S1}} = \frac{-4\|8}{1/10 + 0.1} = \frac{-8/3}{0.2} = -13.\dot{3}$

Input power $= \frac{v^2}{1M}$; Output power $= \frac{(13.\dot{3}v)^2}{8k}$

Power gain $= \frac{13.\dot{3}^2}{8\times10^3}\Big/\frac{1}{10^6} = 22.22\times10^3 \equiv 43.5\,dB$

(b) For $R_L = 4k$, Voltage gain $= \frac{-4\|4}{0.2} = -10\,V/V$

Power gain $= \frac{10^2}{4\times10^3}\Big/\frac{1}{10^6} = 25000 \equiv 44\,dB$

38 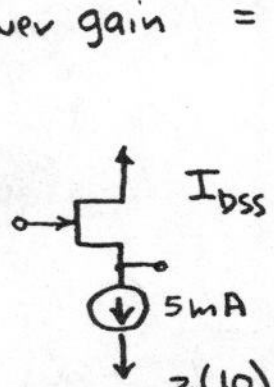

$I_{DSS} = 10mA$, $V_P = -5V$

$g_m = \frac{2I_{DSS}}{V_P}\left(1-\frac{V_{gs}}{V_P}\right) = \frac{2I_{DSS}}{V_P}\sqrt{\frac{I_D}{I_{DSS}}}$

Here $g_m = \frac{2(10)}{5}\sqrt{\frac{5}{10}} = 2.83\,mA/V$

and $R_{out} = 1/g_m = \frac{1}{2.83\times10^{-3}} = 353\,\Omega$

Gain reduces to 1/2 for a capacitor-coupled load of 353Ω

39 Gain $= \frac{r_o/2}{1/g_m + r_o/2} = \frac{g_m r_o}{2 + g_m r_o} = \frac{g_m r_o/2}{1 + g_m r_o/2}$ **6**

$R_{out} = r_o \| r_o \| 1/g_m = \frac{\frac{r_o}{2}\frac{1}{g_m}}{r_o/2 + 1/g_m} = \frac{r_o/2}{1 + g_m r_o/2} \equiv r_o/2 \| 1/g_m$

For $I_{DSS} = 1mA$, $V_P = -2V$, $|V_A| = 100V$:

$g_m = g_{mo} = \frac{2I_{DSS}}{-V_P} = \frac{2(1)}{2} = 1\,mA/V$

$r_o = \frac{100V}{1mA} = 100k\Omega$

Gain $= \frac{1(100)}{2+1(100)} = \underline{0.98\,V/V}$

$R_{out} = \frac{100}{2} \| 1/1 = \underline{0.98\,k\Omega}$

40 $V_{gate} = V_o = 10\times10^6 \times 1\times10^{-9} = 10^{-2}V$ or 10mV at low temp.

For high temperatures: $V_o = 10\times10^6 \times 100\times10^{-9} = +1V$

41 Change at output is to v_{omin}

Change at source is $+v_{omin}$

Thus $\frac{I_D R_S + v_{omin}}{R_S} = -\frac{v_{omin}}{R_L} \rightarrow I_D = -v_{omin}\left(\frac{1}{R_S} + \frac{1}{R_L}\right)$

or $v_{omin} = \frac{-I_D R_S}{1 + R_S/R_L}$. Voltage at the source is $I_D R_S + v_{omin}$, and at the gate is $v_G = I_D R_S + v_{omin} - |V_P|$

$= I_D R_S\left(1 - \frac{1}{1+R_S/R_L}\right) - |V_P| = I_D R_S \frac{R_S/R_L}{1+R_S/R_L} - |V_P|$

42 **6**

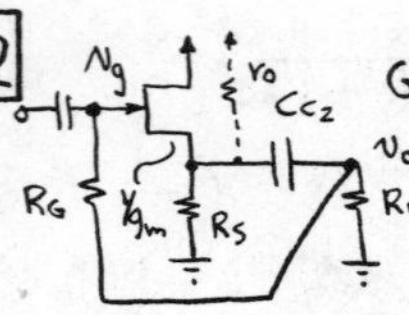

$$\text{Gain } G = \frac{v_o}{v_g} = \frac{R_L \| r_o \| R_S}{\frac{1}{g_m} \| R_G + R_L \| r_o \| R_S} = \frac{\dfrac{1}{1/R_L + 1/r_o + 1/R_S}}{\dfrac{1}{1/R_G + g_m} + \dfrac{1}{1/R_L + 1/r_o + 1/R_S}}$$

$$\text{or } G = \frac{v_o}{v_g} = \frac{g_m + 1/R_G}{1/R_L + 1/r_o + 1/R_S + 1/R_G + g_m}$$

(a) From Miller's Theorem $R_{in} = R_G/(1-G)$

$$\text{or } R_{in} = R_G \Big/ \left(\frac{1/R_L + 1/r_o + 1/R_S}{1/R_L + 1/r_o + 1/R_S + 1/R_G + g_m} \right)$$

$$= R_G \left(1 + \frac{g_m}{1/R_L + 1/r_o + 1/R_S} \right)$$

(b) For input from a source v_s with resistance $R = 100k$, $r_o = \infty$, $R_G = 1M$, $R_S = 4k$ to $-10V$ with $V_p = -4$ and $I_{DSS} = 12mA$, and $R_L = 4k$,

$$i_D = I_{DSS}\left(1 - \frac{v_{GS}}{V_p}\right)^2 \text{ and } i_D = \frac{v_{GS} + 10}{4k} \text{ and } v_{GS} = v$$

$$\text{whence } v + 10 = 4(12)\left(1 - \frac{v}{4}\right)^2 = 48 - 24v + 3v^2$$

$$\text{or } 3v^2 - 25v + 38 = 0 \rightarrow v = \frac{+25 \pm \sqrt{25^2 - 12(38}}{6} = 2V$$

$$\text{Thus } g_m = \frac{2 I_{DSS}}{-V_p}\left(1 - \frac{v_{GS}}{V_p}\right) = \frac{2(12)}{4}\left(1 - 2/4\right) = 3mA/V$$

$$\therefore \frac{v_o}{v_g} = \frac{10^{-3} + 3}{1/4 + 1/4 + 10^{-3} + 3} = \underline{\underline{.857}} \rightarrow R_{in} = 10^6\left(1 + \frac{3}{1/4 + 1/4}\right) = \underline{\underline{7M}}$$

$$\therefore \frac{v_o}{v_s} = 0.857\left(\frac{7}{7 + 0.1}\right) = \underline{\underline{0.845}}\ V/V$$

43 **6**

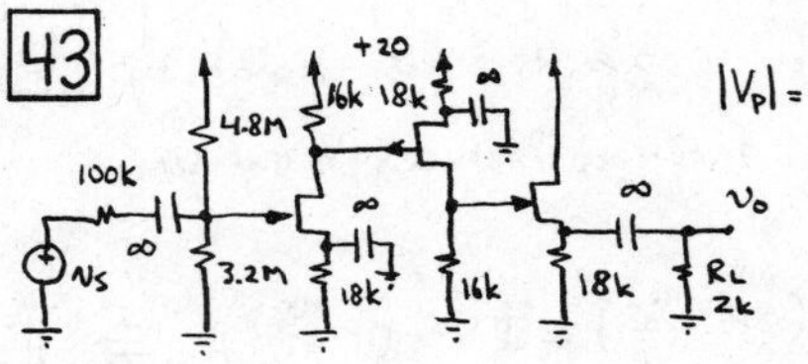

$|V_p| = 2V$, $I_{DSS} = 8mA$

$$v_{G1} = \frac{3.2}{3.2 + 4.8} \times 20 = 8V$$

$$v_{SG1} = v$$

$$i_{D1} = 8\left(1 - \frac{v}{2}\right)^2 = \frac{v + 8}{18} \rightarrow v + 8 = 8(18)\left(1 - v + \frac{v^2}{4}\right)$$

$$36v^2 - 145v + 136 = 0 \rightarrow v = \frac{145 \pm \sqrt{145^2 - 4(36)(136)}}{72} = 1.49V$$

$$i_{D1} = \frac{1.49 + 8}{18} = 0.527mA \;;\; v_{G2} = 20 - 16(.527) = 11.57 \;;\; v_{GS_2} = v$$

$$i_{D2} = 8\left(1 - \frac{v}{2}\right)^2 = \frac{16(.527) + v}{18} = \frac{8.43 + v}{18}$$

$$\text{or } v + 8.43 = 8(18)\left(1 - v + \frac{v^2}{4}\right) \rightarrow 36v^2 - 145v + 135.6 = 0$$

$$\text{and } v = \frac{+145 \pm \sqrt{145^2 - 4(36)(135.6)}}{72} \approx 1.49V$$

$$i_{D2} = \frac{1.49 + 8.43}{18} = .551 mA \;;\; v_{G3} = 0.551(16k) = 8.82V \;;\; v_{GS_3} = v$$

$$i_{D3} = 8\left(1 - \frac{v}{2}\right)^2 = \frac{8.82 + v}{18} \rightarrow v + 8.82 = 8(18)\left(1 - v + \frac{v^2}{4}\right)$$

$$36v^2 - 145v + 135.2 = 0 \rightarrow v = \frac{145 \pm \sqrt{145^2 - 4(36)(135.2)}}{72} = 1.47V$$

$$i_{D3} = \frac{8.82 + 1.47}{18} = 0.57mA$$

$$\text{Thus total current} = \frac{20}{8 \times 10^3} + .527 + .551 + .570 = 1.65mA$$

$$\text{and as } g_m = \frac{2 I_{DSS}}{V_p}\sqrt{\frac{I_D}{I_{DSS}}} = \frac{2(8)}{2}\sqrt{\frac{I_D}{8}} \rightarrow g_{m1} = 2.05mA/V$$

$g_{m2} = 2.10mA/V$, $g_{m3} = 2.14mA/V$.

6

$R_{in} = 3.2 \| 4.8 = 1.92M$

$$\text{Gain with a } 2k\Omega \text{ load} = \frac{1.92}{1.92 + 0.1} \times (-2.05)(16)(-2.10)(18) \times \frac{2k\|18k}{2k\|18k + \frac{1}{2.14}}$$

or 935.7

44

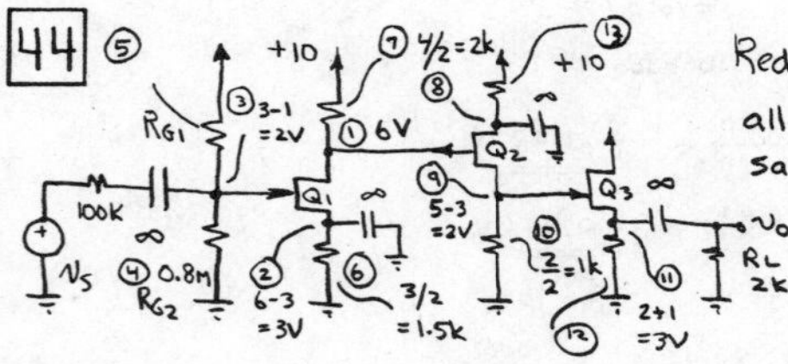

Redesign with all I_D, V_{DS} the same and $V_{D1} = 6V$

That is, $I_{D1} = I_{D2} = I_{D3} = 2mA$, $V_{GS1} = V_{GS2} = V_{GS3} = 1V$, $V_{DS1} = V_{DS2} = 3V$, and proceed ①, ② etc:

① $V_{D1} = 6V$, ② $V_{S1} = 6V - 3V = 3V$, ③ $V_{G1} = 3V - 1V = 2V$

④ $R_{G2} = 0.8M$ (as in original design) ⑤ $R_{G1} = \frac{0.8M}{2}(10 - 2) = 3.2M$

⑥ $R_{S1} = \frac{3V}{2mA} = 1.5k$, ⑦ $R_{D1} = \frac{10-6}{2} = 2k$, ⑧ $V_{S2} = 6 - 1 = 5V$

⑨ $V_{D2} = 5 - 3 = 2V$, ⑩ $R_{D2} = \frac{2V}{2mA} = 1k$, ⑪ $V_{S3} = 2 + 1 = 3V$

⑫ $R_{S3} = \frac{3V}{2mA} = 1.5k$, ⑬ $R_{S2} = \frac{10-5}{2} = 2.5k$

$$R_{in} = 0.8 \| 3.2 = 0.64M \;;\; \text{Gain} = \frac{0.64}{0.64 + 0.1} \times (-4)(2)(-4)(1)\frac{2k\|5k}{2k\|5k + 1/4}$$

ie gain $= \underline{\underline{21.4 V/V}}$

45 **6**

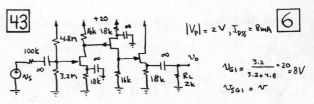

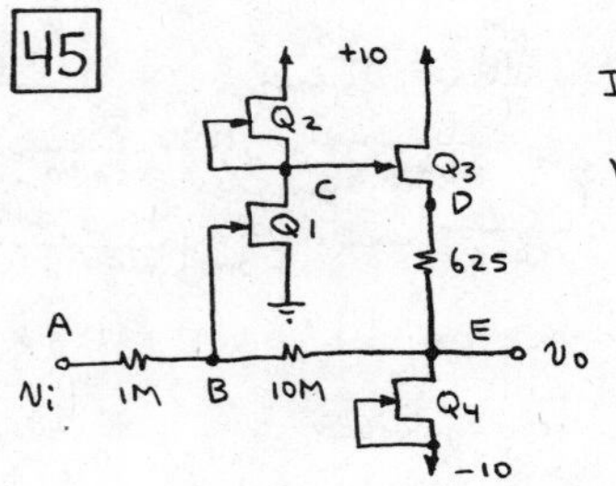

$I_{DSS} = 8mA$, $V_p = -2V$

r_o @ $8mA = 125k$

Now, ignoring r_o, current in Q_1 balances that in Q_2 if $V_B = 0$, allowing V_C to be any appropriate Voltage.

(a) If $V_A = 0$, $V_B = \underline{\underline{0}} \rightarrow V_E = \underline{\underline{0}}$ and $V_D = 8mA(625) = \underline{\underline{5V}}$

Thus Q_3 operates with $v_{GS} = 0 \rightarrow V_C = \underline{\underline{5V}}$. Now see that currents in r_{o1} and r_{o2} cancel but that in r_{o3} is $\frac{10-5}{125k} = 40\mu A$ and in r_{o4} is $\frac{10-0}{125k} = 80\mu A$. Thus Q_3 must provide an extra $40\mu A$ for balance. For all devices, $I_D = 8mA$, and $g_m = g_{mo} = \frac{2 I_{DSS}}{-V_p} = \frac{2(8)}{2} = 8mA/V$

(b) Gains: $G_{BC} = -8(125k \| 125k) = \underline{\underline{-500}}\ V/V$

$$G_{CE} \doteq \frac{125k \| 10M}{125k \| 10M + (625 + 125)} = .993 \;;\; G_{BE} = -500(.993) = \underline{\underline{-497}}\ V/V$$

$$\text{Closed Loop Gain} = \frac{-R_2/R_1}{1 + (1 + R_2/R_1)/A} = \frac{-10/1}{1 + (1 + 10/1)/497}$$

$$= \underline{\underline{-9.78\ V/V}}$$

46

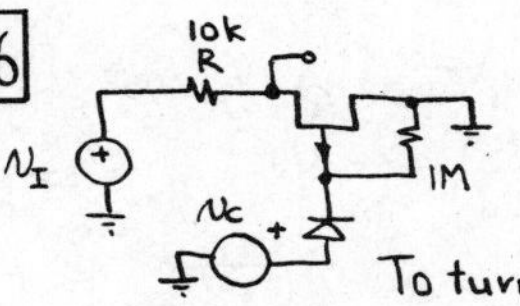

$V_P = 2V$

$v_o \approx \frac{0.10k}{10k+0.10k} \times 5\sin\omega t = .0495\sin\omega t$

To turn off, need $v_C = +5+2+0.7 = 7.7V$

47

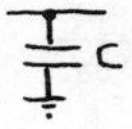

$CV = IT \rightarrow C = \frac{10\times10^{-9}}{0.1\times10^{-3}} = 100\mu F$

48

To cut off: $15-0.7+\bar{V}_P = 12 \rightarrow \bar{V}_P = -2.3V$

49

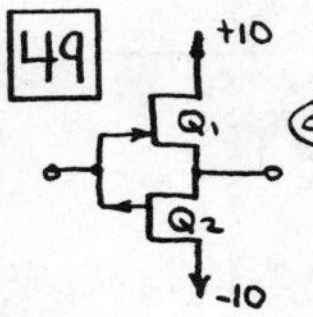

$I_{DSS} = 16mA$, $|V_P| = 2V$

(a) For $v_I = 0$, $v_O = 0$, Q_1 and Q_2 in pinchoff

For $v_I = \pm 8$, $v_O = \pm 8$, at edge of pinchoff

For $v_I = \pm 9V$, one device is in triode operation:

For $v_I = +9$, let $v_O = 9 - v$. Thus $v_{GS2} = v$

For Q_2, $i_{D2} = 16(1 - v/2)^2$

For Q_1, $i_{D1} = I_{DSS}\left(2\left(1 - \frac{v_{GS}}{V_P}\right)\left(\frac{v_{DS}}{-V_P}\right) - \left(\frac{v_{DS}}{V_P}\right)^2\right)$

$= 16\left(2\left(1 - \frac{v}{-2}\right)\left(\frac{1+v}{2}\right) - \left(\frac{1+v}{2}\right)^2\right)$

Now $i_{D1} = i_{D2}$

$\therefore 1 - v + v^2/4 = 2(1 + v/2)\left(\frac{1+v}{2}\right) - \frac{1+2v+v^2}{4}$

$\times 4$: $4 - 4v + v^2 = 4 + 2v + 4v + 2v^2 - 1 - 2v - v^2$

or $8v - 1 = 0$ and $v = 0.125V$

Thus for $v_i = \pm 9$, $v_o = \pm 8.875V$

(b) For $v_I = 0$, $g_m = g_{mo} = \frac{2I_{DSS}}{V_P} = \frac{2(16)}{2} = 16 mA/V$

and $r_s = 1/g_m = 1/16 = 62.5\Omega$

Thus $R_o = \frac{62.5}{2} = 31.25\Omega$

(c) For 2mA load, hypothesize that I_{D1} increases by 1mA to 17mA and I_{D2} decreases by 1mA to 15mA. Thus $\Delta v_O = \frac{1mA}{16mA/V} = 1/16V = 62.5mV$

and v_O becomes $-.0625V$

50

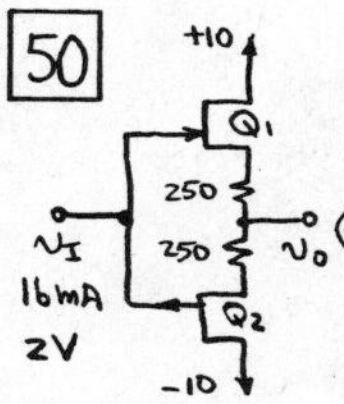

16mA
2V

See $i_D = 4mA$, $v_{GS} = 1V$

Check: $i_D = I_{DSS}\left(1 - \frac{v_{GS}}{V_P}\right)^2 = 16(1 - 1/2)^2 = 4mA$

(a) For $v_I = 0V$, $v_O = 0V$

For $v_I = \pm 8V$, $v_O = \pm 8V$

For $v_I = \pm 9V$, one of devices is in triode mode

Approximation: Assume Q_2 continues with $v_{GS2} = 1V$ and Q_1 is in triode region with $v_{DS1} = v$ small:

ie $i_D = I_{DSS}\left[2\left(1 - \frac{v_{GS}}{V_P}\right)\frac{v_{DS}}{-V_P} - \left(\frac{v_{DS}}{V_P}\right)^2\right]$ and $\left(\frac{v_{DS}}{V_P}\right)^2 \approx 0$

and $v_{DG} = v_{DS} + v_{SG} \rightarrow 1 = v + v_{SG} \rightarrow v_{SG} = 1 - v$

$\therefore i_{D1} \approx 16\left(2\left(1 - \frac{1-v}{2}\right)\frac{v}{2}\right)$. As well this current

$i_{D1} \approx \frac{10 - 9 - (-1) - v}{0.25 + 0.25} = \frac{2 - v}{0.5} = 4 - 2v$

ie $4 - 2v = 16(v(1/2 + v/2)) = 8(v + v^2)$

or $4v^2 + 5v - 2 = 0 \rightarrow v = \frac{-5 \pm \sqrt{25+32}}{8} = 0.32V$

$\therefore$ for $v_I = \pm 9V$, $v_O = \pm\left(9 - \frac{0.32}{2}\right) = \pm 8.84V$

(b) At $v_O = 0$, $g_m = \frac{2I_{DSS}}{V_P}\left(1 - \frac{v_{GS}}{V_P}\right) = \frac{2(16)}{2}(1 - 1/2)$

or 8mA/V. Thus $R_o = \frac{1}{2}(250 + 1/g_m) = 162.5\Omega$

(c) Now for a 2mA load, v_O drops approx. to

$v_O = 0 - 2(.1625) = -.325V$

51

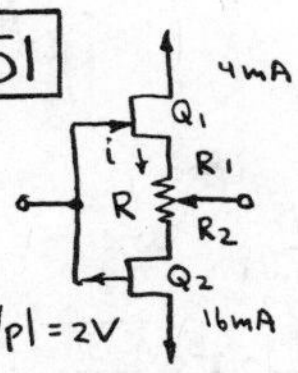

(a) Minimum R is reached with $v_{GS1} = 0$, ie $i = I_{DSS1} = 4mA$

for which $v_{GS2} = 1V$ (Since $16(1 - 1/2)^2 = 4mA$)

and $R_{min} = \frac{1V}{4mA} = 0.25k\Omega$

(b) For $R = 0.5k\Omega$, $v_I = 0$, $i = 4\left(1 - \frac{v_1}{2}\right)^2 = 16\left(1 - \frac{v_2}{2}\right)^2$

and $i = \frac{v_1 + v_2}{R} = 2(v_1 + v_2)$. See $\sqrt{\ } \rightarrow 1 - \frac{v_1}{2} = 2\left(1 - \frac{v_2}{2}\right)$

or $v_1 = 2v_2 - 2$. Thus $i = 2((2v_2 - 2) + v_2) = 6v_2 - 4$

but also $i = 16\left(1 - \frac{v_2}{2}\right)^2$. Thus $16 - 16v_2 + 4v_2^2 = 6v_2 - 4$

or $4v_2^2 - 22v_2 + 20 = 0 \rightarrow v_2 = \frac{22 \pm \sqrt{22^2 - 320}}{8} = 1.15V$

$v_1 = 2(1.15) - 2 = 0.30V$; $i = 2(1.15 + 0.30) = 2.9mA$

$R_1 = \frac{0.30}{2.9} = 103\Omega$ and $R_2 = \frac{1.15}{2.9} = 397\Omega$. See $R_1 + R_2 = 500$

52

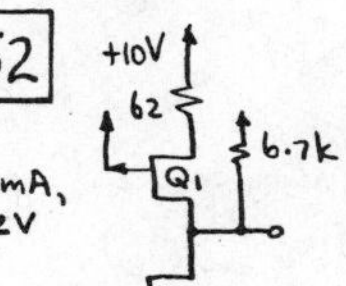

4mA,
2V

$I_{D2} = 4mA$, $I_{D1} = I_{DSS}\left(1 - \frac{v_{GS}}{V_P}\right)^2$

or $i = 4\left(1 - \frac{v}{2}\right)^2$ and $i = \frac{v}{.062}$

$\therefore v = 4(.062)\left(1 - \frac{v}{2}\right)^2 = 0.248(1 - v + v^2/4)$

$4.032v = 1 - v + v^2/4$

$v^2 - 2.013v + 4 = 0 \rightarrow v = \frac{20.13 \pm \sqrt{20.13^2 - 16}}{2} = .2007V$

$i = \frac{.2007}{.062} = 3.24\,mA$ **6**

$\therefore v_o = 10 - 6.7(4 - 3.24) = \underline{4.89V}$

Now $g_m = \frac{2I_{DSS}}{-V_P} = \frac{2(4)}{2} = 4mA/V$

Gain $= -4(6.7k) = \underline{\underline{-26.8\,V/V}}$

53

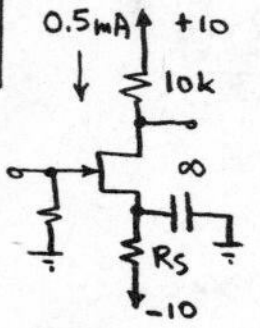

ⓐ Use $V_P = \underline{2V}$ to minimize I_{DSS}

$\therefore V_{GS} = 1V \rightarrow 0.5 = I_{DSS}(1 - \frac{1}{2})^2$

so $I_{DSS} = \underline{\underline{2mA}}$

$R_S = \frac{10+1}{0.5} = 22k\Omega$; $g_m = \frac{2I_{DSS}}{-V_P}\left(1 - \frac{v_{GS}}{V_P}\right) = \frac{2(2)}{2}\left(1-\frac{1}{2}\right)$

or $g_m = 1mA/V$. Thus Gain $= \underline{\underline{-10}}\ V/V$

ⓑ For $I_{DSS} = 4mA$, $i = 4(1 - v/2)^2$ and $i = \frac{10+v}{22}$

ie $10 + v = 88 - 88v + 22v^2$ or $22v^2 - 89v + 78 = 0$

Thus $v = \frac{89 \pm \sqrt{89^2 - 4(22)(78)}}{44} = 1.28V$

and $i = \frac{10 + 1.28}{22} = 0.513\,mA$,

for which $g_m = \frac{2(4)}{2}\left(1 - \frac{1.28}{2}\right) = 1.44\,mA/V$

and $1/g_m = 694\,\Omega$

Thus $r_{series} = 100 - 694 = \underline{\underline{306\,\Omega}}$

54 $I_{DSS} = 4mA$, $V_P = -2V$, $I_D = 1mA$, $V_{GS} = 1V$; **6**

$g_m = \frac{2I_{DSS}}{V_P}\left(1 - \frac{v_{GS}}{V_P}\right) = \frac{2(4)}{2(2)} = 2mA/V$; $1/g_m = 500\Omega$

ⓐ $\frac{I(s)}{V(s)} = \frac{1}{500 + \frac{1}{10^{-5}s}} = \frac{1}{10^5} \times \frac{s}{1 + s/200}$

ⓑ $\frac{I(s)}{V(s)} = \frac{1}{1500 + \frac{1}{10^{-5}s}} = \frac{1}{10^5} \times \frac{s}{1 + s/66.\dot{6}}$

ⓒ $\frac{I(s)}{V(s)} = \frac{1}{1500 + \frac{1}{10^{-5}s}} = \frac{1}{10^5} \times \frac{s}{1 + s/66.\dot{6}}$

ⓓ Note: negative supply is $-10V$, $I_D = 1mA$, $V_{GS} = 1V$

$\frac{I(s)}{V(s)} = \frac{1}{500 + 1000 + 10k \,\|\, \frac{1}{10^{-5}s}}$

$= \frac{1}{1500 + \frac{10^4/10^{-5}s}{10^4 + 1/10^{-5}s}} = \frac{1}{1500 + \frac{10^4}{10^{-1}s + 1}}$

$= \frac{10^{-1}s + 1}{150s + 11.5 \times 10^3} = \frac{1}{11.5k} \times \frac{s/10 + 1}{s/76.\dot{6} + 1}$

55

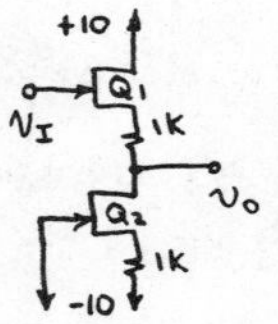

$I_{DSS} = 4mA$, $V_P = -2V$, $I_D = 1mA$, $V_{GS} = 1V$

$\underline{\underline{V_O = v_I}} \rightarrow$ ie $v_o = 0, \pm 1V$ for $v_I = 0, \pm 1V$

$g_m = \frac{2(4)}{2}(1 - \frac{1}{2}) = 2mA/V$

$1/g_m = 500\,\Omega$ and $R_{out} = 1k + 500 = \underline{\underline{1.5k\Omega}}$

56 $I_{DSS} = 4mA$, $V_P = -2V$ **6**

$V_A = \underline{1V}$, $I_A = 1mA$

For V_B: Let $v_{GS} = v \rightarrow i = 4(1 - \frac{v}{2})^2$ and $i = \frac{v+1}{1}$

$\therefore v + 1 = 4 - 4v + v^2 \rightarrow v^2 - 5v + 3 = 0 \rightarrow v = \frac{5 \pm \sqrt{5^2 - 12}}{2} = .697$

$\therefore V_B = 0.697V + 1V = \underline{\underline{1.697V}}$

For V_C: $i = 4(1 - v/2)^2 = \frac{v + 1.697}{1} \rightarrow v + 1.697 = 4 - 4v + v^2$

$v^2 - 5v + 2.03 = 0 \rightarrow v = \frac{5 \pm \sqrt{25 - 9.212}}{2} = 0.513$

$\therefore V_C = 1.697 + .513 = \underline{\underline{2.21}}\,V$

For V_D: $i = 4(1 - \frac{v}{2})^2 = \frac{v + 2.21}{1} \rightarrow v + 2.21 = 4 - 4v + v^2$

$v^2 - 5v + 1.79 = 0 \rightarrow v = \frac{5 \pm \sqrt{25 - 7.159}}{2} = .388$

$\therefore V_D = 2.21 + .388 = \underline{\underline{2.598}}\,V$

57

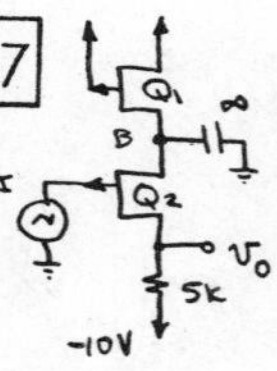

$I_{DSS} = 1mA$, $V_P = 1V$

$I_{D_1} = 1mA$, $V_B = \underline{0V}$, $V_O = -10 + 5(1) = \underline{-5V}$

$g_m = \frac{2I_{DSS}}{V_P} = \frac{2(1)}{1} = 2mA/V$

Gain $= -g_m R_L = -2(5) = \underline{\underline{-10\,V/V}}$

1 $I_{DSS} = 2mA$, $V_P = -1V$ **7**

Pinchoff : $v_{DS} \geq v_{GS} - V_P$, $i_D = I_{DSS}\left(1 - \frac{v_{GS}}{V_P}\right)^2$

For $v_{GS} = 1V$, $v_{DS} \geq 1 + 1 = \underline{\underline{2V}}$

For $v_{GS} = 5V$, $v_{DS} \geq 5 + 1 = \underline{\underline{6V}}$

For $v_{GS} = 1V$, $i_D = 2(1 - \frac{1}{-1})^2 = \underline{\underline{8mA}}$

For $v_{GS} = 5V$, $i_D = 2(1 - \frac{5}{-1})^2 = \underline{\underline{72mA}}$

2 From Fig 7.6, $I_{DSS} = 16mA$, $V_P = -4V$

$i_D = I_{DSS}\left(1 - \frac{v_{GS}}{V_P}\right)^2 \rightarrow g_m = \frac{\partial i_D}{\partial v_{GS}} = \frac{2I_{DSS}}{-V_P}\left(1 - \frac{v_{GS}}{V_P}\right)$

For $v_{GS} = -1$, $g_m = \frac{2(16)}{4}(1 - \frac{-1}{-4}) = \underline{\underline{6mA/V}}$

For $v_{GS} = 0$, $g_m = \frac{2(16)}{4}(1 - 0) = \underline{\underline{8mA/V}}$

For $v_{GS} = +1$, $g_m = \frac{2(16)}{4}(1 - \frac{1}{-4}) = \underline{\underline{10mA/V}}$

3 $I_{DSS} = 16mA$, $V_P = -4V$

$i_D = I_{DSS}\left(1 - \frac{V_{GS}}{V_P}\right)^2 \rightarrow 32 = 16\left(1 - \frac{v_{GS}}{-4}\right)^2$

$2 = 1 + \frac{v}{2} + \frac{v^2}{16}$ or $v^2 + 8v - 16 = 0 \rightarrow v = \frac{-8 \pm \sqrt{64 + 64}}{2} = 1.6V$

ie $v_{GS} = \underline{\underline{1.6\dot{6}\,V}}$

$\boxed{4}$ $I_{DSS} = 8\,mA$ $V_P = 4\,V$ $\uparrow(8,64)$ $\boxed{7}$

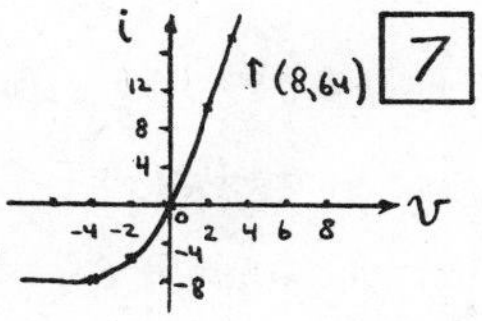

$$i_D = I_{DSS}\left(2\left(1 - \frac{v_{GS}}{V_P}\right)\left(\frac{v_{DS}}{+V_P}\right) - \left(\frac{v_{DS}}{V_P}\right)^2\right)$$

For $v = -4V$, Source and drain exchanged, operation in

   Pinchoff, $i_D = I_{DSS} = 8\,mA$

For $v = -2V$, source and drain exchanged, triode

   $i_D = 8\left(2(1)\frac{2}{4} - \left(\frac{2}{4}\right)^2\right) = 8\left(1 - \frac{1}{4}\right) = 6\,mA$

For $v = 0$, $i_D = 0$

For $v = 2$, $i_D = 8\left(2\left(1 - \frac{-2}{4}\right)\left(\frac{2}{4}\right) - \left(\frac{2}{4}\right)^2\right) = 8\left(\frac{3}{2} - \frac{1}{4}\right)$

         $= 12 - 2 = 10\,mA$

For $v = 4$, $i_D = 8\left(2\left(1 - \frac{-4}{4}\right)\left(\frac{4}{4}\right) - \left(\frac{4}{4}\right)^2\right) = 8(2(2)1 - 1) = 24\,mA$

For $v = 8$, $i_D = 8\left(2\left(1 - \frac{-8}{4}\right)\left(\frac{8}{4}\right) - \left(\frac{8}{4}\right)^2\right) = 8(2(3)2 - 4) = 64\,mA$

$\boxed{5}$ $i_D = K(v_{GS} - V_t)^2$; $K = 0.25\,mA/V^2$, $V_t = 2V$

     For $v_{GS} = 10V$, $i_D = 0.25(10-2)^2 = 16\,mA$

For $v_{GS} = 6V$, $i_D = 0.25(6-2)^2 = 4\,mA$

For $v_{GS} = 4V$, $i_D = 0.25(4-2)^2 = 1\,mA$

$\boxed{6}$ Triode operation: $i_D = K\left(2(v_{GS} - V_t)v_{DS} - v_{DS}^2\right)$

$\frac{1}{r_{DS}} = \frac{\partial i_D}{\partial v_{DS}} = K\left(2(v_{GS} - V_t) - 2v_{DS}\right) \rightarrow K(2(v_{GS} - V_t))$ for

small v_{DS}. Thus $r_{DS} \approx \frac{1}{2K(v_{GS} - V_t)}$

Now $K = \frac{1}{2}\mu_n C_{ox}\frac{W}{L} = \frac{10\mu A/V^2}{2}(10) = 50\mu A/V^2$

and $V_t = 1V$. Thus

for $v_{GS} = 2V$, $r_{DS} = \frac{1}{2(50)(2-1)} = 10k\Omega$

for $v_{GS} = 5V$, $r_{DS} = \frac{1}{2(50)(5-1)} = 2.5k\Omega$

$\boxed{7}$ $V_t = C + \gamma\sqrt{V_{SB}}$, and $1 = C + \gamma\sqrt{0} \rightarrow C = 1V$

Now for $V_{SB} = 0$ to 9 and $\gamma = 1$, V_t varies from

$1 + 1\sqrt{0} = \underline{\underline{1V}}$ to $1 + 1\sqrt{9} = \underline{\underline{4V}}$

$\boxed{8}$ $CV = I T \rightarrow V = \frac{10\times10^{-3}\times100\times10^{-9}}{10^{-12}} = \underline{1000V}$ $\boxed{7}$

$\underline{Breakdown}$ of the gate insulator is likely !

$\boxed{9}$ Pinchoff: $i_D = K(v_{GS} - V_t)^2$, $V_t = 1.5V$

   ie $5 = K(-3 - (-1.5))^2 = K(1.5)^2$

whence $K = \frac{5}{1.5^2} = 2.\dot{2}\,mA/V^2$

For $v_{SG} = 4.5V$, $i_D = \frac{5}{(1.5)^2}(4.5-1.5)^2 = \underline{20mA}$

Triode: $i_D = K\left(2(v_{GS} - V_t)v_{DS} - v_{DS}^2\right)$

For v_{DS} small, $i_D = K(2(v_{GS} - V_t)v_{DS})$

For $v_{SG} = 3V$, $i_D = 2.\dot{2}(2)(3-1.5)v_{SD} \rightarrow r_{SD} = \frac{v_{SD}}{i_D} = \frac{1}{4.4(1.5)} = \underline{150\Omega}$

For $v_{SG} = 4.5V$, $r_{SD} = \frac{1}{2.\dot{2}(2)(4.5-1.5)} = \underline{75\Omega}$

$\boxed{10}$ At $I_D \approx 4mA$, $r_o = \frac{8-4}{4.4-4} = \frac{4}{0.4} = \underline{10k}$

and $V_A \approx r_o I_D = 10^4 \times 4\times10^{-3} = \underline{40V}$

Note: $i_D = K(v_{GS} - V_t)^2\left(1 + \frac{v_{DS}}{V_A}\right) \rightarrow 4 = K(4-V_t)^2\left(1 + \frac{4}{V_A}\right)$

and $4.4 = K(4-V_t)^2\left(1 + \frac{8}{V_A}\right)$. Dividing $1.1 = \frac{1 + 8/V_A}{1 + 4/V_A}$

or $1.1 + 4.4/V_A = 1 + 8/V_A \rightarrow 0.1 = \frac{3.6}{V_A}$ or $V_A = 36V$

$\boxed{11}$ R_{G1} $+10$ R_D $10k$ $i_D = \frac{3V}{10k}$ and $i_D = K(v_{GS} - V_t)^2$ $\boxed{7}$

$5V$ $3V$ $= 0.3 = 5(5-3-V_t)^2 = 0.3\,mA$

R_{G2} R_S $10k$ ie $(2-V_t)^2 = 1 \rightarrow 2 - V_t = \pm 1$

or $V_t = \underline{1V}$, whence $i_D = \underline{0.3\,mA}$ and $v_D = 10 - 10k(0.3) = 7V$

and $v_{DS} = 7 - 3 = \underline{4V}$

Now for $K_2 = 10K_1 = 3mA/V^2$, $i_D = 3(v-1)^2$ and $\frac{5-v}{10k}$

Thus $5 - v = 30(v-1)^2 = 30v^2 - 60v + 30$

or $30v^2 - 59v + 25 = 0 \rightarrow v = \frac{59 \pm \sqrt{59^2 - 4(25)(30)}}{60}$

or $v = 1.35V$, whence $v_S = 5 - 1.35 = 3.65V$ and

$i_D = \underline{0.365\,mA}$, $v_D = 10 - 3.65 = 6.35V$

and $v_{DS} = 6.35 - 3.65 = \underline{2.7\,V}$

$\boxed{12}$ $i_D = K(v_{GS} - V_t)^2 = .050(v-2)^2$ and $i_D = \frac{5-v}{10k}$

Thus $5 - v = 0.5(v-2)^2$ or $10 - 2v = v^2 - 4v + 4$

$v^2 - 2v - 6 = 0 \rightarrow v = \frac{2 \pm \sqrt{4 - 4(-6)}}{2} = 3.65$

and $i_D = \frac{5-3.65}{10k} = \underline{135\mu A}$

Now if $K = 100\mu A/V^2 \rightarrow 5 - v = 1(v-2)^2$

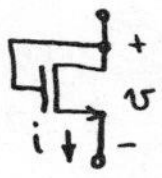

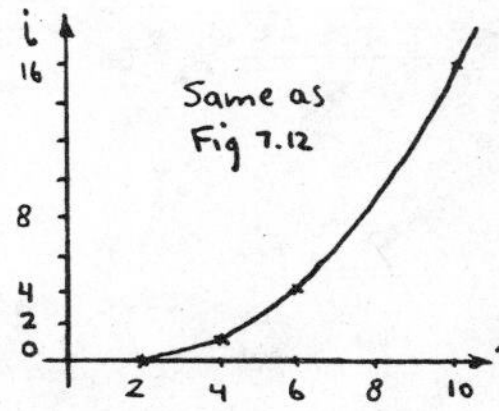

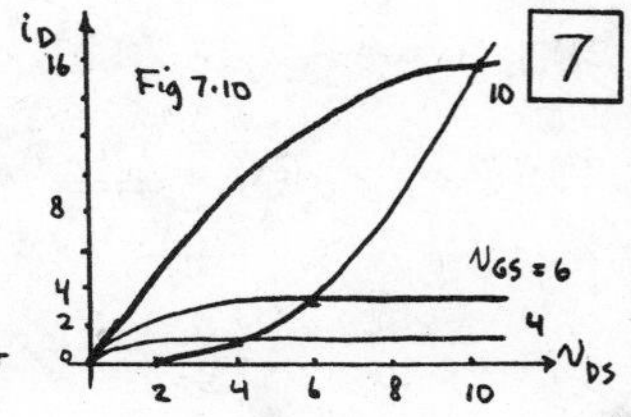

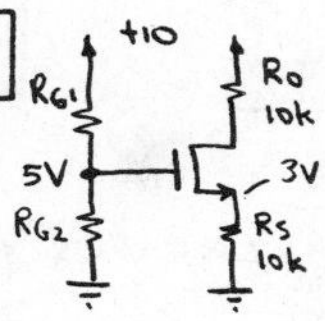

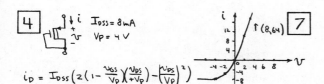

7

Thus $v^2 - 3v - 1 = 0 \rightarrow v = \frac{3 \pm \sqrt{9-(-4)}}{2} = 3.30$

and $i_D = \frac{5-v}{10k} = \underline{170\mu A}$

Now $\frac{\Delta i}{i}\% = \frac{170-135}{135} \times 100 = \underline{\underline{26\%}}$

for $\frac{\Delta K}{K}\% = \frac{100-50}{50} \times 100 = \underline{\underline{100\%}}$ } a 4 to 1 reduction!

13

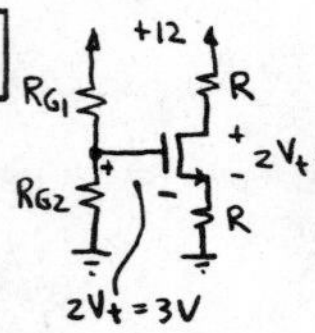

$V_t = 1.5V$, $K = 0.5\ mA/V^2$

$i = \frac{12-3}{2R} = \frac{4.5}{R}$ and $i = K(v_{GS} - V_t)^2$

$= 0.5(3-1.5)^2 = 1.125\ mA$

Now $R = 4.5/1.125 = 4k\Omega$, whence $v_G = 3 + 4k(1.125) = 7.5V$

For $R_{G2} = \underline{2.2M\Omega}$, $\frac{2.2}{R_t} \cdot 12 = 7.5 \rightarrow R_t = \frac{2.2}{7.5} \times 12 = 3.52M$

Thus $R_{G1} = 3.52 - 2.2 = \underline{\underline{1.32M\Omega}}$

ⓐ Now for $V_t = 3V$, $i_D = 0.5(v-3)^2$ and $i = \frac{7.5-v}{4} \rightarrow$

$7.5 - v = 2(v^2 - 6v + 9) = 2v^2 - 12v + 18 \rightarrow 2v^2 - 11v + 10.5 = 0$

or $4v^2 - 22v + 21 = 0$, whence $v = \frac{22 \pm \sqrt{22^2 - 4(4)(21)}}{8}$

or $v = 4.27V$, $i_D = \frac{7.5-4.27}{4} = \underline{\underline{0.807\ mA}}$

and $v_{DS} = 12 - 2(7.5 - 4.27) = \underline{\underline{5.54V}}$

ⓑ Now for $V_t = 1.5V$ but $K = 1mA/V$:

7

$i_D = 1(v-1.5)^2$ and $i_D = \frac{7.5-v}{4}$

or $7.5 - v = (2v-3)^2 = 4v^2 - 12v + 9$

Thus $4v^2 - 11v + 1.5 = 0 \rightarrow v = \frac{11 \pm \sqrt{11^2 - 4(4)(1.5)}}{8} = 2.61V$

for which $i_D = \frac{7.5-2.61}{4k} = \underline{1.22mA}$

and $v_{DS} = 12 - 2(7.5-2.61) = \underline{\underline{2.22V}}$

14

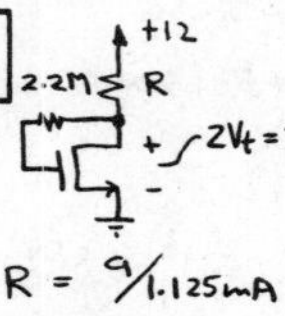

$K = 0.5mA/V^2$, $V_t = 1.5V$

$i = \frac{12-3}{R} = 9/R$ and $i = 0.5(3-1.5)^2 = 1.125$

$\therefore R = 9/1.125mA = \underline{\underline{8k\Omega}}$, $RG = \underline{\underline{2.2M}}$

ⓐ For $V_t = 3V$, $i_D = \frac{12-v}{8}$ and $i_D = 0.5(v-3)^2$, whence

$12 - v = 4(v^2 - 6v + 9) = 4v^2 - 24v + 36$

$4v^2 - 23v + 24 = 0 \rightarrow v = \frac{23 \pm \sqrt{23^2 - 4(4)(24)}}{8} = \underline{\underline{4.38V}}$

and $i_D = \frac{12-4.38}{8} = \underline{\underline{0.953\ mA}}$

ⓑ For $V_t = 1.5V$, but $K = 1mA/V^2$, $i_D = \frac{12-v}{8}$ and $1(v-1.5)^2 \rightarrow$

$12 - v = 8(v^2 - 3v + 2.25) = 8v^2 - 24v + 18$

$8v^2 - 23v + 6 = 0 \rightarrow v = \frac{23 \pm \sqrt{23^2 - 4(8)(6)}}{16} = \underline{\underline{2.58V}}$

and $i_D = \frac{12-2.58}{8} = \underline{\underline{1.18\ mA}}$

15 $C_{in\,equiv.} = 1 + 1(1-(-10)) = \underline{\underline{12pF}}$ **7**

16 $i_D = K(v_{GS} - V_t)^2 \rightarrow g_m = \frac{\partial i_D}{\partial v_{gs}} = 2K(v_{GS} - V_t)$

ⓐ $g_m = 2(0.05)(3-2) = \underline{\underline{0.1\ mA/V}}$

ⓑ $g_m = 2(0.5)(2.5-2) = \underline{\underline{0.5mA/V}}$

17 $i_D = K(v_{GS} - V_t)^2$ biassed at $V_{GS} = 4V$ and with

a signal $v_{gs} = v \sin \omega t$: $i_D = K(V_{GS} + v \sin \omega t - V_t)^2$

or $i_D = K(V_{GS} - V_t)^2 + 2K(V_{GS} - V_t) v \sin \omega t + K v^2 \sin^2 \omega t$

But $\sin^2 x = 1/2 - 1/2 \cos 2x$

$\therefore$ Fundamental component is $2K(V_{GS} - V_t)v$, $|V_t| = 2V$

Second harmonic comp. is $Kv^2/2$

1% distortion when $\frac{Kv^2}{2} = \frac{1}{100} \cdot 2K(V_{GS} - V_t)v$

or $v = \frac{4}{100}(4-2) = \underline{\underline{80mV}}$ peak

18 Gain $= -g_m R_L' = -1(10k \| 50k) = \underline{\underline{-8.33\ V/V}}$

$R_{in} = \frac{10M}{1 - \text{gain}} = \frac{10M}{1 + 8.33} = \underline{\underline{1.07M\Omega}}$

19 $K = \frac{1}{2} \mu_n C_{ox} \left(\frac{W}{L}\right) = \frac{20\mu A}{2}\left(\frac{100}{6}\right) = 167\mu A/V^2$ **7**

$i_D = K(v_{GS} - V_t)^2 \left(1 + \frac{v_{DS}}{V_A}\right)$,

Including the effects of r_o: $i_D = 100\mu A = 167(v_{GS} - 1.5)^2 \left(1 + \frac{5}{50}\right)$

or $v_{GS} = \sqrt{\frac{100}{167(1.1)}} + 1.5 = 0.738 + 1.5 = 2.24V$

and $g_m = 2K(v_{GS} - V_t)\left(1 + \frac{v_{DS}}{V_A}\right)$

or $g_m = 2(167)(1.1)(2.24 - 1.5) = 271\mu A/V^2$

and $g_{mb} = \chi g_m = 0.1(271) = 27.1\mu A/V$

and $1/r_o = \partial i_D / \partial v_{DS} = \frac{K}{V_A}(v_{GS} - V_t)^2 = \frac{167}{50}(2.24 - 1.5)^2 = 1.82\ \mu A/V$

whence $r_o = 549k\Omega$

Now excluding the effect of r_o on bias:

$v_{GS} = \sqrt{\frac{100}{167}} + 1.5 = 0.774 + 1.5 = 2.27V$

$g_m = \sqrt{2\mu_n C_{ox} \frac{W}{L} I_D} = \left(2 \times 20\left(\frac{100}{6}\right) 100\right)^{1/2} = 258\mu A/V$

(Note this is $271/\sqrt{1.1}$)

$g_{mb} = 0.1(258) = 25.8\mu A/V$

and $r_o = \frac{50}{100\mu A} = 500k\Omega$, lower by 10%

since bias point is higher!

20 $i_D = K(v_{GS} - V_t)^2$ 7

$$g_m = \frac{\partial i_D}{\partial v_{GS}}\bigg|_{\substack{i_D = I_D \\ v_{GS} = V_{GS}}} = 2K(V_{GS} - V_t) = \frac{2 I_D}{V_{GS} - V_t}$$

21

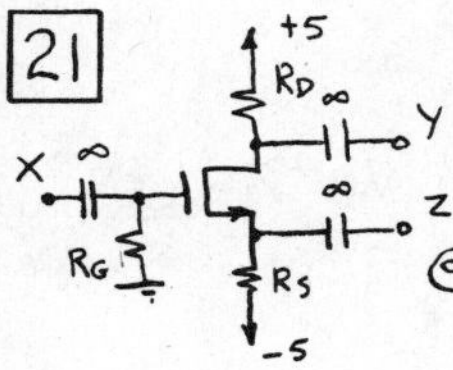

$V_t = 1V$, $K = 0.4\ mA/V^2$, $VA = 40V$

Select $R_G = \underline{10M\Omega}$

(a) Output ± 1V with RD as large as possible implies operation to the edge of pinchoff, ie $v_D = v_G - V_t$, for the highest possible v_G. For gain from X to Y ≥ 1, v_G goes at most to +1, allowing v_D to go as low as 0V, from its bias point, seen to be at +1V.

$i_D = K(v_{GS} - V_t)^2 \rightarrow 0.1 = 0.4(v-1)^2$

or $v^2 - 8v + 3 = 0 \rightarrow v = \frac{8 \pm \sqrt{64-48}}{8} = 1.5V$

$\therefore\ V_G = 0,\ V_S = -1.5,\ V_D = 1.0 \rightarrow R_S = \frac{5-1.5}{0.1} = \underline{35k\Omega}$

and $R_D = \frac{5-1}{0.1} = \underline{40k\Omega}$.

Note the current due to r_o, ie $\frac{1+1.5}{40}(0.1) \approx 6\mu A$ is small.

(b) $g_m = 2K(v_{GS} - V_t) = 2(0.4)(1.5-1) = \underline{0.4mA/V}$ 7

$r_o \approx V_A/I_D = \frac{40}{0.1} = \underline{400k\Omega}$

$r_s = 1/g_m = 1/0.4 = \underline{2.5k\Omega}$

(c) $\text{Gain}_{x-y} = -\frac{R_G}{R_G+R} \times g_m(r_o \| R_D \| R_L)$

$= -\frac{10}{10+1} \times 0.4(400\|40\|40)k = \underline{-6.92\ V/V}$

(d) $\text{Gain}_{x-z} = \frac{R_S}{R_S + 1/g_m} = \frac{35k}{35k+2.5k} = \underline{0.9\dot{3}\ V/V}$

$R_{out\,z} = 2.5k \| 35k = \underline{2.\dot{3}k\Omega}$

(e)

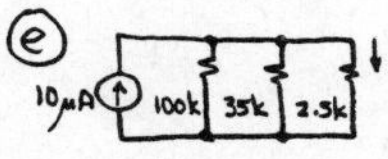

$i_s = 10\mu A \left(\frac{100k\|35k}{100k\|35k + 2.5k}\right) = 9.12\mu A$

$\therefore\ i_D = 9.12\mu A$

and $v_y = i_D R = 9.12\mu A \times 40k = \underline{0.365V}$

22

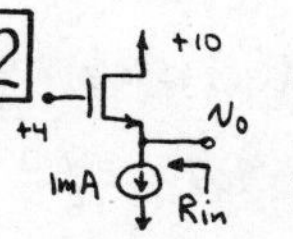

$V_t = 2V$, $K = 0.25\ mA/V^2$, $r_o = \infty$

$i_D = K(v_{GS} - V_t)^2 \rightarrow 1 = 0.25(v-2)^2$

$4 = v^2 - 4v + 4 \rightarrow v^2 - 4v = 0 \rightarrow v = \phi$ or $4V$

$\therefore\ V_o = V_G - V_{GS} = 4 - 4 = \underline{0V}$

and $g_m = 2K(v_{GS} - V_t) = 2(1/4)(4-2) = 1mA/V$

$R_{in} = 1/g_m \| \infty = \underline{1k\Omega}$

23

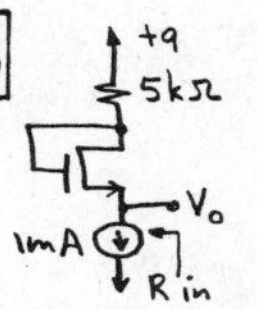

$V_t = 2V$, $K = 0.25mA/V^2$, (See **22**) 7

$i_D = 1mA$, $V_{GS} = 4V$, $V_D = 9 - 5(1) = 4V = V_G$

$V_o = V_S = V_G - V_{GS} = 4 - 4 = \underline{0V}$

$R_{in} = 1/g_m + 5k = 1k + 5k = \underline{6k\Omega}$

24

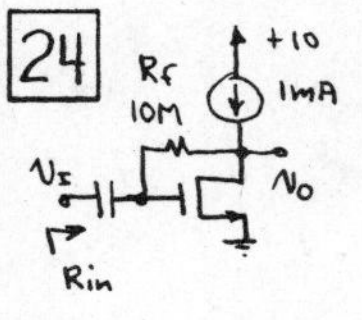

$V_t = 2V$, $K = 0.25mA/V^2$, $r_o = 100k\Omega$

$i_D = 1mA$, $v_{GS} = 4V$: Check $i_D = 0.25(4-2)^2$

$v_D = V_o = \underline{4V}$

$g_m = 2K(v_{GS} - V_t) = 2(0.25)(4-2) = 1mA/V$

$\text{Gain}\ v_o/v_I = -g_m(r_o \| R_F) = -1\times10^{-3}(10^5 \| 10^7) = \underline{-99}$

$R_{in} = \frac{10M\Omega}{1 - \text{gain}} = \frac{10^7}{1+99} = \underline{100k\Omega}$

25

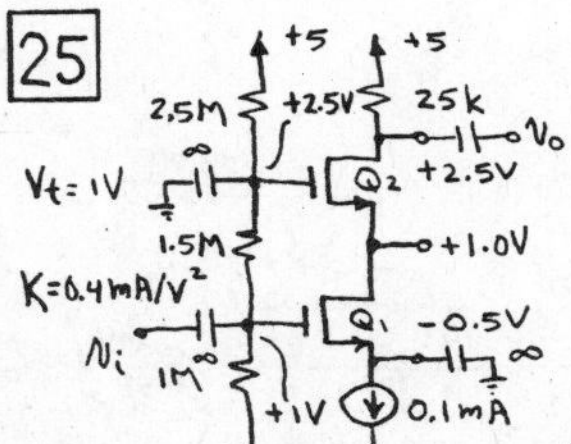

$0.1 = 0.4(V_{GS}-1)^2 \rightarrow V_{GS} = 1.5V$

See $V_{G1} = \underline{+1V}$, $V_{S1} = \underline{-0.5V}$

$V_{D1} = \underline{+1V}$, $V_{G2} = \underline{+2.5V}$

$V_{D2} = \underline{+2.5V}$

$g_m = 2K(V_{GS} - V_t) = 2 \times 0.4 \times 0.5 = \underline{0.4mA/V}$

Gains: $\frac{v_{o1}}{v_i} = -g_{m1}(1/g_{m2}) = \underline{-1\ V/V}$ 7

$\frac{v_o}{v_i} = \frac{v_{o2}}{v_i} = -g_{m1} R_D = -0.4(25k) = \underline{-10\ V/V}$

$R_{in} = 1M \| 1.5M = \frac{1 \times 1.5}{2.5} = \underline{0.6M\Omega}$

26 $K = 0.5mA/V^2$, $|V_t| = 1V$, $r_o = \infty$,

(a) Cut off: $i_D = \underline{0mA}$, $v_{SD} = \underline{10V}$

(b) zero-biassed depletion: $i_D = K(v_{GS} - V_t)^2 = 0.5(0-1)^2 = \underline{0.5mA}$

$v_D = 5k(0.5) = 2.5V$, $v_{SD} = 10 - 2.5 = \underline{7.5V}$

(c) $i_D = 0.5(v-1)^2$ and $i_D = \frac{10-v}{5} \rightarrow 10 - v = 2.5(v^2 - 2v + 1)$

$20 - 2v = 5v^2 - 10v + 5$

ie $5v^2 - 8v - 15 = 0 \rightarrow v = \frac{8 \pm \sqrt{64 - 5(4)(-15)}}{10} = 2.7V$

Thus $i_D = \frac{10-2.7}{5k} = \underline{1.46mA}$ and $v_{DS} = \underline{2.7V}$

(d) Ignore current in gate bias circuit

$v = v_{GS} = 1/2\, v_{DS}$: $i_D = 0.5(v-1)^2$ and $i_D = \frac{10-2v}{5}$

$\rightarrow 10 - 2v = 2.5v^2 - 5v + 2.5$ or $20 - 4v = 5v^2 - 10v + 5$

ie $5v^2 - 6v - 15 = 0 \rightarrow v = \frac{6 \pm \sqrt{36 - (4)(5)(-15)}}{10} = 2.43V$

Thus $v_{DS} = 2(2.43) = \underline{4.86V}$ and $i_D = \frac{10 - 4.86}{5} = \underline{1.03mA}$

7

(e) $i_D = 0.5(v-1)^2$ and $i_D = v/4 \rightarrow v = 2(v-1)^2$

or $v = 2v^2 - 4v + 2$

Thus $2v^2 - 5v + 2 = 0 \rightarrow v = \frac{5 \pm \sqrt{25-16}}{4} = 0.5V$

$\therefore i_D = \frac{0.5}{4} = \underline{\underline{0.125mA}}$, $v_D = 10 - 32(.125) = \underline{\underline{6V}}$

and $v_{DS} = 6 - 0.5 = 5.5V$

(f) $V_G = \frac{2}{2+8} \times 10 = 2V$

$\therefore i_D = 0.5(v_{GS}-1)^2 = 0.5(2-1)^2 = \underline{\underline{0.5mA}}$

$v_{DS} = 10 - 10(0.5) = \underline{\underline{5V}}$

(g) $V_G = 5V$, $i_D = 0.5(v-1)^2$ and $i_D = \frac{5-v}{6}$

from which $5 - v = 3(v-1)^2 = 3v^2 - 6v + 3$

or $3v^2 - 5v - 2 = 0 \rightarrow v = \frac{5 \pm \sqrt{25-4(-2)(3)}}{6} = 2V$

$\therefore i_D = \frac{5-2}{6} = \underline{\underline{0.5mA}}$ and $v_{DS} = 10 - 6(0.5) - 6(0.5) = \underline{\underline{4V}}$

(h) $V_G = \frac{1.5}{1.5+8.5} \times 10 = 1.5V$, $i = 0.5(v-1)^2$ and $\frac{1.5+v}{16}$

whence $1.5 + v = 8(v^2 - 2v + 1) = 8v^2 - 16v + 8$

or $8v^2 - 17v + 6.5 = 0 \rightarrow v = \frac{17 \pm \sqrt{17^2 - 4(6.5)(8)}}{16}$

or $v = \frac{17 \pm 9}{16} = 0.5$. Thus $v_S = 0.5 + 1.5 = 2.0V$,

$v_D = 10 - \frac{32}{16}(2.0) = 6.0$, $v_{DS} = 6 - 2 = \underline{\underline{4V}}$ and $i_D = \frac{2}{16} = \underline{\underline{0.125mA}}$

27 $K = 0.5\ mA/V^2$, $|V_t| = 1V$ 7

(a) $I_1 = 0.5(0-1)^2 = \underline{\underline{0.5mA}}$

(b) $I_D = 0.5mA = 0.5(v-1)^2 \rightarrow v^2 - 2v + 1 = 1 \rightarrow v = 2$

$\therefore V_2 = 10 - 2 = \underline{\underline{8V}}$

(c) Symmetry $\rightarrow V_3 = \underline{\underline{5V}}$

(d) Symmetry $\rightarrow V_5 = 10/3 = \underline{\underline{3.\dot{3}V}}$, $V_4 = 20/3 = \underline{\underline{6.\dot{6}V}}$

(e) Symmetry $\rightarrow V_6 = \underline{\underline{5V}}$

(f) $I_7 = 0.5(0-1)^2 = \underline{\underline{0.5mA}}$

(g) $V_G = 5V$, Symmetry $\rightarrow V_8 = \underline{\underline{5V}}$

(h) $i_{D_{top}} = 0.5(0-1)^2 = 0.5\ mA$.

Lower 2 transistors each conduct 0.25mA in triode mode

$i_D = K(2(v_{GS} - V_t)v_{DS} - v_{DS}^2) \rightarrow 0.25 = 0.5(2(0-(-1))v - v^2)$

or $1 = 2(2v - v^2) = 4v - 2v^2 \rightarrow 2v^2 - 4v + 1 = 0$

whence $v = \frac{4 \pm \sqrt{16 - 4(2)}}{4} = 0.293V$

$\therefore V_9 = \underline{\underline{0.293\ V}}$

28 7

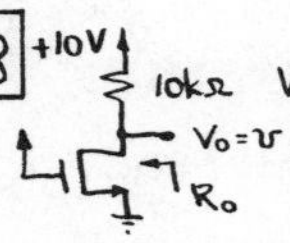

$10k\Omega$ $V_t = 1V$, triode operation:

$i_D = K(2(v_{GS} - V_T)v_{DS} - v_{DS}^2)$

(a) For $K = .05mA/V^2$: $i_D = .05(2(10-1)v - v^2)$ and $i_D = \frac{10-v}{10}$

whence $10 - v = 0.5(18v - v^2)$, $20 - 2v = 18v - v^2$

or $v^2 - 20v + 20 = 0 \rightarrow v = 20 \pm \sqrt{20^2 - 80} = 1.056\ V$

ie $V_o = \underline{1.056V}$

$(R_o)^{-1} = \frac{\partial i_D}{\partial v_{DS}} = K(2(v_{GS} - V_t) - 2v_{DS}) = .05(2(9) - 2(1.06)) = 0.794$

whence $R_o = \frac{1}{.794} = 1.26k\Omega$

and $R_{out} = 1.26k \| 10k = \underline{\underline{1.12k\Omega}}$

(b) For $K = 0.5mA/V^2$: $i_D = 0.5(18v - v^2)$ and $i_D = \frac{10-v}{10}$

whence $10 - v = 5(18v - v^2) = 90v - 5v^2$

or $5v^2 - 91v + 10 = 0 \rightarrow v = \frac{91 \pm \sqrt{91^2 - 4(5)(10)}}{10} = \underline{\underline{0.111V}} = V_o$

$1/R_o = 0.5(2(9) - 2(.111)) = 8.89$

$R_o = 1/8.89 = 0.112k$

$\therefore R_{out} = 0.112 \| 10 = \underline{\underline{0.111k\Omega}}$

(c) For $K = 5mA/V^2$: $i_D = 5(18v - v^2)$ and $i_D = \frac{10-v}{10}$

whence $10 - v = 50(18v - v^2) = 900v - 50v^2$

$50v^2 - 901v + 10 = 0 \rightarrow v = \frac{901 \pm \sqrt{901^2 - 4(10)(50)}}{100} = .011V$ 7

Thus $V_o = \underline{0.011V}$

$1/R_o = 5(2(9) - 2(.011)) = 89.9 \rightarrow R_o = .0111k$

$R_{out} \doteq \underline{\underline{.011k\Omega}}$

29

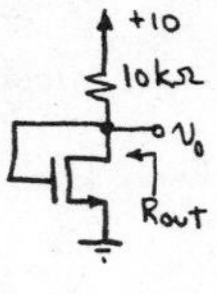

$V_t = 1V$, Pinchoff operation

$i_D = K(v_{GS} - V_t)^2$

$g_m = \frac{\partial i_D}{\partial v_{GS}} = 2K(v_{GS} - V_t)$

(a) $K = 0.05mA/V^2$: $i_D = 0.05(v-1)^2$ and $i_D = \frac{10-v}{10}$

whence $10 - v = 0.5(v^2 - 2v + 1)$, $20 - 2v = v^2 - 2v + 1$

or $v^2 - 19 = 0 \rightarrow v = \pm\sqrt{19} = \underline{4.36V} = V_o$

$g_m = 2(.05)(4.36-1) = .336\ mA/V \rightarrow 1/g_m = 2.98k$

$R_{out} = 1/g_m \| 10k = \underline{\underline{2.30k\Omega}}$

(b) $K = 0.5mA/V^2$: $i_D = 0.5(v-1)^2$ and $i_D = \frac{10-v}{10}$

whence $10 - v = 5(v^2 - 2v + 1) = 5v^2 - 10v + 5$

or $5v^2 - 9v - 5 = 0 \rightarrow v = \frac{9 \pm \sqrt{81 - 4(-5)(5)}}{10} = \underline{\underline{2.25}}V = V_o$

$g_m = 2(0.5)(2.25-1) = 1.25mA/V \rightarrow 1/g_m = 0.8K$, $R_{out} = 0.8k \| 10k = \underline{\underline{0.74k\Omega}}$

7

(c) $K = 5\ mA/V^2$: $i_D = 5(v-1)^2$ and $i_D = \frac{10-v}{10}$

whence $10 - v = 50(v^2 - 2v + 1) = 50v^2 - 100v + 50$

or $50v^2 - 99v + 40 = 0 \rightarrow v = \frac{99 \pm \sqrt{99^2 - 40(50)(4)}}{100} = 1.41\ V = V_o$

$g_m = 2(5)(1.41 - 1) = 4.1\ mA/V \rightarrow 1/g_m = 0.243\ k$

$R_{out} = 0.243k \| 10k = \underline{\underline{0.238\ k\Omega}}$

30

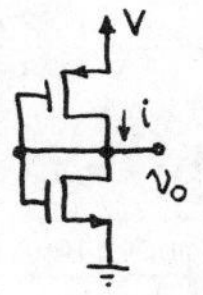

$|V_t| = 1V$, $K = .05\ mA/V^2$

v_o From symmetry $v_o = V/2$

$i = K(V/2 - V_t)^2$

For $V = 5V$, $V_o = \underline{\underline{2.5V}}$, $i = .05(2.5-1)^2 = \underline{\underline{.1125\ mA}}$

For $V = 10V$, $V_o = \underline{\underline{5.0V}}$, $i = .05(5-1)^2 = \underline{\underline{0.80\ mA}}$

For $V = 15V$, $V_o = \underline{\underline{7.5V}}$, $i = .05(7.5-1)^2 = \underline{\underline{2.11\ mA}}$

31

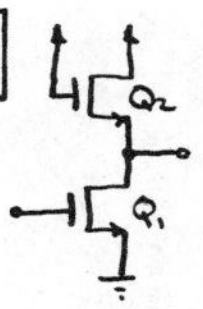

$A_v = -\sqrt{\frac{(W/L)_1}{(W/L)_2}} = -\sqrt{\frac{W_1/L_1}{W_1/10 / 10L_1}} =$

$= -\sqrt{10 \times 10} = \underline{\underline{-10\ V/V}}$

32 7

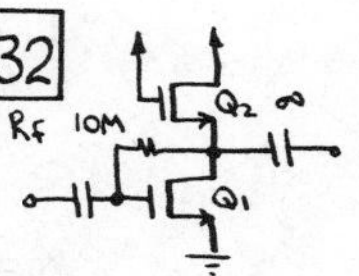

$V_A = 50$, $K_1 = 270\ \mu A/V^2$

$K_2 = 30\ \mu A/V^2$, $I_D = 2\ mA$

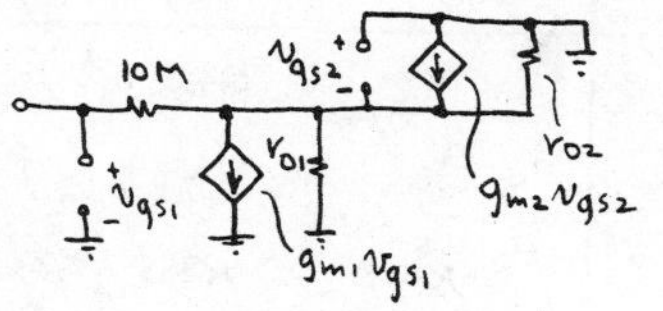

$g_m = 2K(v_{GS} - V_t) = 2K\sqrt{I_D/K}$, $r_o = \frac{V_A}{I_D}$

$\text{Gain} = -g_{m1}(1/g_{m2} \| r_{o1} \| r_{o2} \| R_f)$

$= -2K_1\sqrt{I_D/K_1}\left\{\frac{1}{2K_2}\sqrt{K_2/I_D} \| \frac{V_A}{I_D} \| \frac{V_A}{I_D} \| R_f\right\}$

$= -\underbrace{2(270)\sqrt{\frac{2000}{270}}}_{1.47\ mA/V}\left\{\frac{1}{\underbrace{2(30)\sqrt{\frac{2000}{30}}}_{1/0.49\ mA/V}} \| \frac{50}{2} \| \frac{50}{2} \| 10^4\right\}$

$= -1.47(2k \| 25k \| 25k \| 10^4 k) = -1.47(1.72k)$

$= \underline{\underline{-2.53\ V/V}}$

33 Symmetry: $V_2 = 12/3 = 4V$, $V_1 = 2(12/3) = 8V$

(a) $I = K(v_{GS} - V_t)^2 = 5(4-2)^2 = 5(4) = 20\ \mu A$

(b) $i_{D1} = 5(v_1 - 2)^2$ and $i_{D2} = 1(v_2 - 2)^2$ and $i_{D3} = 5(v_3 - 2)^2$

7

Now $i_{D1} = i_{D2} = i_{D3}$, $v_1 = v_3$ and $v_1 + v_2 + v_3 = 12$

$\therefore v_2 - 2 = \pm\sqrt{5}(v_1 - 2) = 2.24v_1 - 4.48 \rightarrow v_2 = 2.24v_1 - 2.48$

and $2v_1 + v_2 = 12 \rightarrow 2.24v_1 - 2.48 + 2v_1 = 12$

or $4.24v_1 = 14.48 \rightarrow v_1 = 3.415$, $v_2 = 12 - 2(3.415) = 5.17$

$\therefore V_2 = \underline{\underline{3.41\ V}}$, $V_1 = 3.415 + 5.17 = \underline{\underline{8.59V}}$

and $I = 5(3.415 - 2)^2 = \underline{\underline{10.01\ \mu A}}$

34 $I = I_{DSS2} = \underline{\underline{1\ mA}}$

$i_3 = K(v_{GS} - V_t)^2 = 0.5(v-2)^2 = 1 \rightarrow (v-2)^2 = 2$

$v - 2 = 1.414$, $v = 3.41$

$\therefore V_1 = 10 - 3.41 = \underline{\underline{6.59}}\ V$

$V_2 = -10 + 3.41 = \underline{\underline{-6.59}}\ V$

35 See Eq 7.66 : $\text{Gain} = -\frac{g_{m1}}{g_{m2}} \times \frac{1}{1+\chi}$

$\therefore \sqrt{\frac{(W/L)_1}{(W/L)_2}} = (1+\chi)\,\text{gain} = 1.2(10) = 12$

$\therefore (W/L)_2 = \frac{(W/L)_1}{144} = \frac{9}{144} = \underline{\underline{.0625}}$

36 7

$i_D = K(v_{GS} - V_t)^2$, $g_m = 2K(v_{GS} - V_t)$

or $g_m = 2K\sqrt{I_D/K}$

$A_v = \frac{-g_{m1}}{g_{mb2}} = -\frac{g_{m1}}{g_{m2}} \times \frac{1}{\chi} = \sqrt{K_1/K_2} \times \frac{1}{\chi}$

$= \sqrt{4} \times \frac{1}{0.2} = \underline{\underline{-10\ V/V}}$

37 $\text{Gain} = -g_{m1}/g_{m2} = -\sqrt{K_1/K_2}$

(a) $K_2 = K_1$: $V_o = V_{DD}/2 = \underline{\underline{2.5V}}$, $\text{Gain} = \underline{\underline{-1}}\ V/V$

(b) $K_2 = 0.1K_1$: gain $= -\sqrt{10} = \underline{\underline{-3.16}}\ V/V$

$i_D = K_1(v_1 - 2)^2$ and $i_D = K_2(v_2 - 2)^2$ and $v_1 + v_2 = 5$

$\therefore v_2 - 2 = \sqrt{K_1/K_2}(v_1 - 2) = 3.16(5 - v_2 - 2) = 9.49 - 3.16v_2$

$\therefore 4.16v_2 = 11.49 \rightarrow v_2 = 2.76\ V$

$V_o = 5 - 2.76 = \underline{\underline{2.24\ V}}$

(c) $K_2 = 0.01K_1$: gain $= -\sqrt{100} = \underline{\underline{-10}}\ V/V$

$v_2 - 2 = 10(v_1 - 2) = 10(5 - v_2 - 2) = 30 - 10v_2$

$11v_2 = 32 \rightarrow v_2 = 2.91$

$V_o = 5 - 2.91 = \underline{\underline{2.08}}\ V$

38 $|V_t| = 2V$ $\quad i_D = K(v_{GS}-V_t)^2$ or $K(2(v_{GS}-V_t)v_{DS}-v_{DS}^2)$ **7**

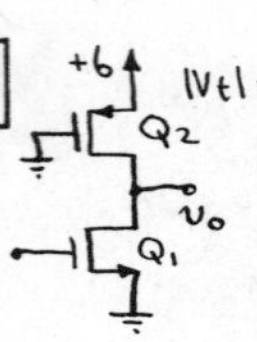

v_I \ v_O	ⓐ $K_1/K_2=1$	ⓑ $K_1/K_2=10$	ⓒ $K_1/K_2=100$
obvious → 0	6	6	6
3	5.87	4.45	0.83
6	3 (symmetry)	0.205	0.02

ⓐ $K_1 = K_2 = K$:

For $v_I = 3V$: $i_{D1} = K(3-2)^2 = K$, $i_{D2} = K(2(6-2)v - v^2)$

Thus $1 = 8v - v^2$ or $v^2 - 8v + 1 = 0 \rightarrow v = \frac{8 \pm \sqrt{64-4}}{2} = .127V$

$V_O = 6 - 0.127 = \underline{\underline{5.87}}\,V$

For $v_I = 6V$: Symmetrical drive : $V_O = \underline{\underline{3V}}$

ⓑ $K_1 = 10K_2 = 10K$:

For $v_I = 3V$: $i_{D1} = 10K(3-2)^2 = 10K$ and $i_{D2} = K(8v - v^2)$

or $10 = 8v - v^2$, $v^2 - 8v + 10 = 0 \rightarrow v = \frac{8 \pm \sqrt{64-40}}{2} = 1.55V$

$V_O = 6 - 1.55 = \underline{\underline{4.45}}\,V$

For $v_I = 6V$: Q_1 triode : $i_{D2} = K(6-2)^2 = 16K$

$i_{D1} = 10K(2(6-2)v - v^2) = 10K(8v - v^2)$

7

or $16 = 10(8v - v^2)$ or $10v^2 - 80v + 16 = 0$

whence $v = \frac{80 \pm \sqrt{80^2 - 640}}{20} = 0.205$

$V_O = \underline{\underline{0.205V}}$

ⓒ $K_1 = 100K_2 = 100K$:

For $v_I = 3V$: $i_{D2} = K(6-2)^2 = 16K$ and $i_{D1} = 100K(2(3-2)v - v^2)$

or $100v^2 - 200v + 16 = 0 \rightarrow v = \frac{200 \pm \sqrt{200^2 - 400(16)}}{200} = .083$

$V_O = \underline{\underline{0.083}}\,V$

For $v_I = 6V$: $i_{D2} = 16K$ and $i_{D1} = 100K(8v - v^2)$

whence $100v^2 - 800v + 16 = 0 \rightarrow v = \frac{800 \pm \sqrt{800^2 - 4(100)(16)}}{200} = .020V$

$V_O = \underline{\underline{0.02\,V}}$

39 ⓐ

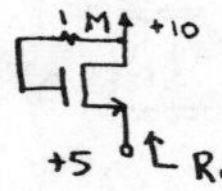

$V_t = 2V$, $K = .025\,mA/V^2$

$i_D = K(v_{GS} - V_t)^2$, $g_m = 2K(v_{GS} - V_t)$

$g_m = 2(.025)(5-2) = 0.15\,mA/V$

$R_{in} = 1/g_m = \underline{\underline{6.67\,k\Omega}}$

ⓑ

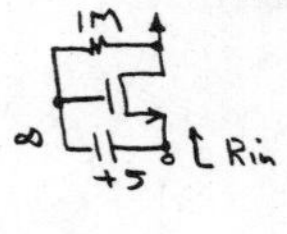

a) For $r_o = \infty$, $R_{in} = \underline{\underline{1M\Omega}}$

b) For $r_o = 1/3\,M$, $R_{in} = 1/3 \| 1 = \underline{\underline{1/4\,M\Omega}}$

ⓒ **7**

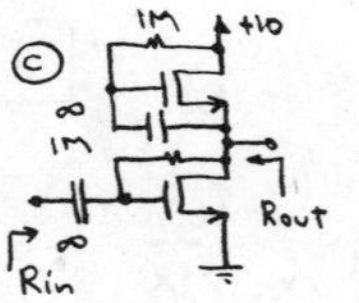

$g_m = 5\,mA/V$

$Gain = -g_m(1M \| 1M \| r_o \| r_o) = -\frac{g_m}{2}(1M \| r_o)$

$= -\frac{5}{2}\left(\frac{1M\,r_o}{1M + r_o}\right) = -25$ (as measured)

$\therefore 1000\,r_o = 10(r_o + 1000) \rightarrow r_o(990) = 10^4$, $r_o = \underline{\underline{10.1\,k\Omega}}$

$R_{out} = \frac{1M \| 10.1k}{2} = \underline{\underline{5.0\,k\Omega}}$

$R_{in} = \frac{1M}{1-(-25)} = \underline{\underline{38.5\,k\Omega}}$

40

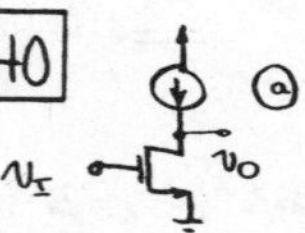

ⓐ See directly : $\frac{v_o}{v_I} = -g_m r_o$

ⓑ For cascade , see directly : Gain $= (g_{m1} r_{o1})(g_{m2} r_{o2})$

41 ⓐ See directly : $\left.\frac{i_o}{v_I}\right|_{v_O=0} = g_{m1}$

ⓑ

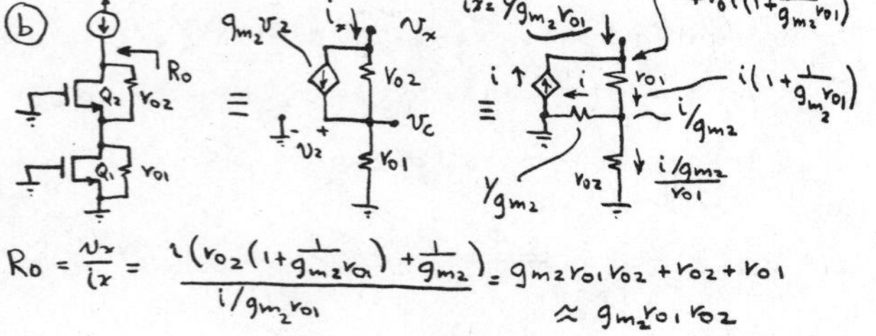

$R_O = \frac{v_x}{i_x} = \frac{i\left(r_{o2}\left(1 + \frac{1}{g_{m2} r_{o1}}\right) + \frac{1}{g_{m2}}\right)}{i/g_{m2} r_{o1}} = g_{m2} r_{o1} r_{o2} + r_{o2} + r_{o1}$

$\approx g_{m2} r_{o1} r_{o2}$

ⓒ **7**

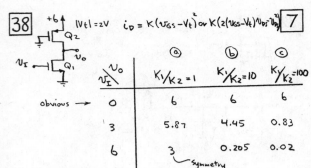

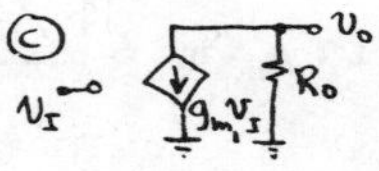

See $v_o/v_{I\,(oc)} = -g_{m1}(g_{m2} r_{o1} r_{o2})$

$= \underline{\underline{-(g_{m1} r_{o1})(g_{m2} r_{o2})}}$

as in P7.40 but with only 1 current source and 1 transistor type!

42 By symmetry $V_{GS2} = V_{GS1} = 8V/2 = 4V$

$i_{D1} = i_{D2} \doteq i_{D3} = K(v_{GS} - V_t)^2 = 5(4-2)^2 = 20\mu A$

$\therefore R = \frac{8-6}{20\mu A} = \frac{2}{20} \times 10^6 = \underline{\underline{100\,k\Omega}}$

43 $i_D = K(v_{GS} - V_t)^2$: $i = 0.05(v-2)^2$ and $i = \frac{12-v}{10k}$

Whence $12 - v = 0.5(v^2 - 4v + 4)$, $24 - 2v = v^2 - 4v + 4$

or $v^2 - 2v - 20 = 0 \rightarrow v = \frac{2 \pm \sqrt{4 + 4(20)}}{2} = 5.58$

$\therefore i = \frac{12 - 5.58}{10} = 0.642\,mA$, $V_o = 12 - 5(0.642) = \underline{\underline{8.79V}}$

44 $L_1 = L_2 = L_3$, $I_1 = 20\mu A$, $W_1 = 10\mu m$

$I_2 = 20\mu A \rightarrow W_2 = 10\mu m$

$I_3 = 100\mu A \rightarrow W_3 = 50\mu m$

45 Each of Q_1, Q_2, Q_2 share the supply **7**

equally with $V_{DS1} = V_{DS2} = V_{DS3} = \frac{15}{3} = 5$. Ignoring r_o,

$I_{D2} = I_{D4}$ since $V_{GS2} = V_{GS4}$, $\therefore I_{D5} = I_{D2}$

and $V_{G5} = V_{G2} = +10$. Thus $V_O = V_{S5} = V_{S2} = \underline{\underline{+5V}}$

46 See due device matching that $V_{SD3} = V_{SG3} =$

$V_{DS4} = V_{GS4} = V_{GS2} = V_{SG1} = V_{SD1} = V_{DS2} = 5V$

For $K = 25\mu A/V^2$, $V_t = 2$, $i_D = 25(5-2)^2 = 225\mu A$

$g_m = 2K(v_{GS} - V_t) = 2(25)(5-2) = 150\mu A/V$.

Currents from Q_1, Q_2 add in 100k with $\frac{v_o}{v_a} = -150\times10^{-6}\times10^5$

$= -15 = \frac{v_o}{v_b}$ also. Combining $v_o = -15(v_a + v_b)$

Thus $v_o = 5 - 15(10mV)(\sin\omega t + \sin \omega t + \phi)$

For $\phi = 0$, $v_o = 5 - .15\sin\omega t - .15\sin\omega t = 5 - 0.3\sin\omega t$

For $\phi = 90°$, $v_o = 5 - .15\sin\omega t - .15\sin(\omega t + 90°) = 5 - .212\sin(\omega t + 45°)$

For $\phi = 180°$, $v_o = 5 - .15\sin\omega t + .15\sin\omega t = 5 - 0$

ie $v_o = 0.3V, 0.212V, 0V$ for $\phi = 0, 90°, 180°$ respectively

47 **7**

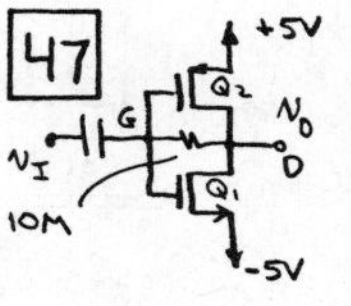

$K = 25\mu A/V^2$, $V_t = 2V$, $V = 0$

$i = 25(5-2)^2 = 225\mu A \rightarrow I_{D1} = I_{D2} = 225\mu A$

$g_m = 2(25)(5-2) = 0.15 mA/V$

For $r_o = \infty$, gain $= -2\times0.15\times10^{-3}(10^7) = \underline{\underline{-3000 V/V}}$

For $r_o = \frac{|V_A|}{I_D} = \frac{180}{225\times10^{-6}} = 0.8\times10^6\Omega$,

gain $= -2\times0.15\times10^{-3}(10^7 \| 0.8\times10^6 \| 0.8\times10^6)$

$= -.3\times10^{-3}(.385\times10^6) = \underline{\underline{-115.4 V/V}}$

and $R_{in} = \frac{R_f}{1-\text{gain}} = \frac{10^7}{116.4} = \underline{\underline{85.9 k\Omega}}$

For $1M\Omega$ source, nominal gain $= -\frac{10M}{1M} = -10$, but

actual $v_o/v_i = -\frac{85.9k}{1M + 85.9k}\times 115.4 = \underline{\underline{-9.13 V/V}}$

Alternatively, gain $v_o/v_i = \frac{-R_2/R_1}{1 + (1 + R_2/R_1)/A} = \frac{-10}{1 + 11/115.4} = -9.13 V/V$

Q_1 in pinchoff while while v_D remains 2 volts below v_G (as v_G goes negative). That is peak output for

$v_o - v_g = 2$ or $v_o - (-\frac{v_o}{115.4}) = 2 \rightarrow v_o = 1.98 V_{peak}$

ie Q_1, Q_2 in pinchoff for $v_o = \pm 1.98V$ peak or smaller

48 **7**

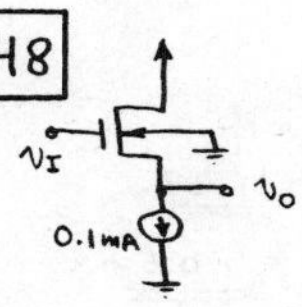

$I = 0.1mA$, $W = 100\mu m$, $L = 8\mu m$

$\mu_n C_{ox} = 100\mu A/V^2$, $V_t = 1V$, $V_A = 100V$

$\chi = 0.1$

$\therefore K = \frac{1}{2}\mu_n C_{ox} W/L = \frac{100}{2}\times\frac{100}{8} = \underline{\underline{625\mu A/V^2}}$

$r_o = \frac{V_A}{I_D} = \frac{100}{0.1mA} = \underline{1M\Omega}$

$g_m = 2K(v_{GS} - V_t) = 2K\sqrt{i_D/K} = 2\sqrt{K i_D} = 2\sqrt{625\times100}$

or $g_m = \underline{500\mu A/V} \rightarrow r_s = 1/g_m = 1/500 = \underline{2k\Omega}$, $r_{sB} = \frac{2k}{\chi} = \underline{20k\Omega}$

Gain $= +\frac{20k \| 1M}{2k + 20k\|1M} = \frac{19.6}{21.6} = \underline{0.907}$ (with no load)

$R_{out} = 2k \| 20k \| 1M = \underline{1.82k\Omega}$

Gain with $10k\Omega$ load is $\frac{10}{1.82 + 10}\times0.907 = \underline{\underline{0.767 V/V}}$

49

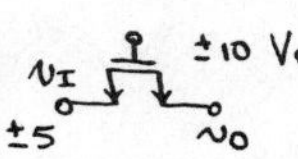

$K = 25\mu A/V^2$, $V_t = 2V$

Triode operation: $i_D = K(2(v_{GS} - V_t)v_{DS} - v_{DS}^2)$

Channel resistance $= \frac{v_{DS}}{i_D} = \frac{1}{2K(v_{GS} - V_t)}$

For $V_c = +10$ and $v_i = +5$, $r_{chan} = \frac{1}{2(25\times10^{-6})(10-5-2)} = \underline{\underline{6.\dot{6}k\Omega}}$

For $V_c = +10$ and $v_i = -5$, $r_{chan} = \frac{1}{2(25\times10^{-6})(10-(-5)-2)} = \underline{\underline{1.54k\Omega}}$

Loop Resist: $\frac{6.67}{R}\times100 = 1 \rightarrow R = 6.67\times100 = \underline{\underline{667k\Omega}}$

50 CMOS switch, $K = 25\mu A/V^2$, $V_t = 2V$, $V_c = \pm5V$ **7**

$v_i = \pm 5V$

At extremes of signal: $r_{chan} = \frac{1}{2(25\times10^{-6})(5-(-5)-2)} = \underline{\underline{2.5k\Omega}}$

for one device and open for the other.

At mid range, ie $v_i = 0$, there are 2 channels in parallel

with each $r_{chan} = \frac{1}{2(25\times10^{-6})(5-0-2)} = 6.67k\Omega$ and

an equivalent resistance of $6.\dot{6}\|6.\dot{6}$ or $\underline{\underline{3.\dot{3}k\Omega}}$

Thus the loop resistance for 1% switch loss must exceed

$100\times 3.\dot{3}k = \underline{\underline{333k\Omega}}$

51 For operation around 0 volts,

$r_{switch} = \frac{1}{2}\times\frac{1}{2(25\times10^{-6})(5-0-2)} = 3.\dot{3}k\Omega$

For $C = 1000pF$, cutoff frequency is $\frac{1}{2\pi RC}$

$= \frac{1}{2\pi\times3.\dot{3}\times10^3\times1000\times10^{-12}} = \underline{\underline{47.8 kHz}}$

1 $i_C = I_S e^{v_{BE}/V_T}$ **8**

whence $v_{BE} = V_T \ln i_C/I_S = 25 \ln \frac{10\times10^{-3}}{10^{-14}} = 690.8\text{ mV}$ or $\underline{\underline{0.691\text{ V}}}$

2 $i_C = 10\times10^{-14} e^{\frac{700}{25}} = 144.6$ or $\underline{\underline{145\text{ mA}}}$

3 $i_B = \frac{i_C}{\beta} = \frac{10}{100} = \underline{\underline{0.1\text{ mA}}}$

New $i_C = \beta(1\mu A) = 100(1\mu A) = 100\mu A = \underline{\underline{0.1\text{ mA}}}$

4 $\beta = \frac{i_C}{i_B} = \frac{10\times10^{-3}}{15\times10^{-6}} = \underline{\underline{667}}$

5 $I_E = I_B + I_C = 5 + .05 = \underline{\underline{5.05\text{ mA}}}$

$\beta = \frac{I_C}{I_B} = \frac{5\times10^{-3}}{50\times10^{-6}} = \underline{\underline{100}}$

$\alpha = \frac{I_C}{I_E} = \frac{5}{5.05} = \underline{\underline{0.990}}$

Verification: $\alpha = \frac{100}{101} = 0.990099$

$\beta = \frac{\alpha}{1-\alpha} = \frac{100/101}{1-100/101} = 100$ OK

and $\beta = \frac{.990099}{1-0.990099} = 100$ OK

But $\beta = \frac{0.990}{1-0.990} = \frac{0.99}{.01} = 99$!!

6 Leakage doubles for each 10°C rise: **8**

$\therefore$ 10 nA @ 25°C becomes $10\times10^{-9}\times2^{\frac{125-25}{10}} = 1024\times10^{-8}$

or $\underline{\underline{10.24\ \mu A}}$ at 125°.

7

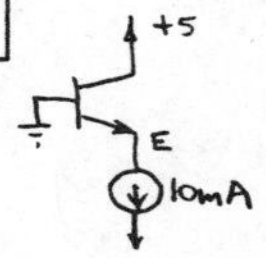

$\beta = 100$, $I_S = 10^{-14}$ A

$I_B = \frac{10}{\beta+1} = \frac{10}{101} = \underline{\underline{.099\text{ mA}}}$

$I_C = \frac{\beta}{\beta+1}\times10 = \underline{\underline{9.90\text{ mA}}}$

$v_{BE} = V_T \ln \frac{9.90\times10^{-3}}{10^{-14}} = \underline{\underline{0.6905\text{ V}}}$

$V_E = -0.691$ V

8

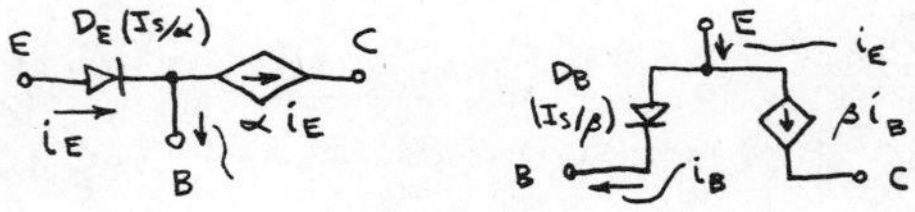

9

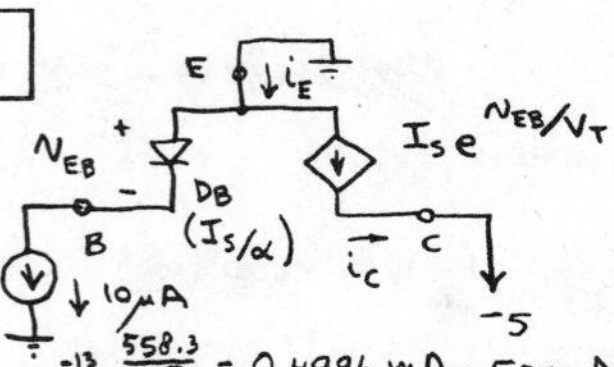

$I_S e^{v_{EB}/V_T}$

$I_S = 10^{-13}$ A, $\beta = 50$

$V_{EB} = V_T \ln \frac{10\times10^{-6}}{10^{-13}/50} = .5583\text{ V}$

$V_B = \underline{\underline{-0.5583\text{ V}}}$

$i_C = 10^{-13} e^{\frac{558.3}{25}} = 0.4996\text{ mA} = 500\mu A$. Directly: $i_C = \beta i_B = 50(10) = \underline{\underline{500\mu A}}$

10 $v_{BE} = 0.700 + V_T \ln \frac{10}{1} = 0.7576\text{ V} \approx 0.76\text{ V}$ **8**

$v_{BE} = 0.700 + V_T \ln \frac{10^{-3}}{1} = 0.5273\text{ V} \simeq 0.53\text{ V}$

11 $i_E = 5\text{ mA}$, $i_B = 1\text{ mA} \rightarrow i_C = 5 - 1 = 4\text{ mA}$

$\beta_R = \frac{i_C}{i_B} = \frac{4}{1} = \underline{\underline{4}}$; $\alpha_R = \frac{i_C}{i_E} = \frac{4}{5} = \underline{\underline{0.80}}$

12 $\beta = 100$, $|V_{BE}| = 0.7$

(a) $V_E = \underline{\underline{-0.700\text{ V}}}$; $I_E = \frac{10-0.7}{10k} = \underline{\underline{0.93\text{ mA}}}$

$I_B = \frac{I_E}{\beta+1} = \frac{0.93}{101} = \underline{\underline{9.2\mu A}}$;

$V_C = 10 - 10(0.930 - 0.0092) = \underline{\underline{0.792\text{ V}}}$

(b) $V_E = \underline{\underline{+0.700\text{ V}}}$; $I_E = \frac{10-0.7}{5k} = \underline{\underline{1.86\text{ mA}}}$

$I_C = \frac{\beta}{\beta+1} I_E = \frac{100}{101}(1.86) = \underline{\underline{1.842\text{ mA}}}$

$V_C = -15 + 5(1.842) = \underline{\underline{-5.79\text{ V}}}$

13 $\beta = \infty$, $|V_{BE}| = 0.7$

(a) $V_B = \underline{\underline{0.0\text{ V}}}$, $V_E = \underline{\underline{-0.7\text{ V}}}$

(b) $V_E = \underline{\underline{+0.7\text{ V}}}$, $V_C = -15 + 5\left(\frac{10-0.7}{5}\right) = \underline{\underline{-5.7\text{ V}}}$

14 **8**

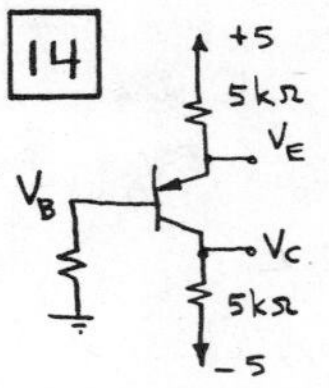

Measure $V_E = 1.0$ V

Conclude: $V_B = 1.0 - 0.7 = \underline{\underline{0.3\text{ V}}}$

$I_B = \frac{0.3}{20k} = \underline{\underline{0.015\text{ mA}}}$

$I_E = \frac{5-1}{5k} = \underline{\underline{0.80\text{ mA}}}$

$I_C = 0.80 - .015 = \underline{\underline{0.785\text{ mA}}}$

$V_C = -5 + 5(0.785) = \underline{\underline{-1.075\text{ V}}}$

$\beta = \frac{0.785}{0.015} = \underline{\underline{52.3}}$; $\alpha = \frac{0.785}{0.800} = \underline{\underline{0.98}}$

15

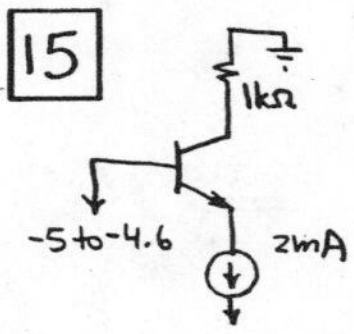

$\Delta V_B = +0.4$ V

$\Delta V_E = \underline{\underline{+0.4}}$ V

$\Delta V_C = \underline{\underline{0.0}}$ V

16 $i_C = I_S e^{v_{BE}/V_T}$

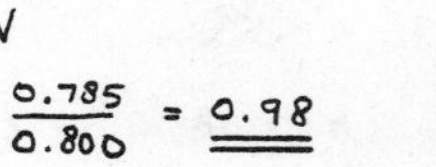

Use T.C of $-2.2\text{ mV/°C} \rightarrow \Delta T_s = \frac{715-685}{2.2} = \underline{\underline{13.6°C}}$ rise, eventually

In 1 minute, $\Delta T_1 = \frac{715-700}{2.2} = 6.82°C$ rise

$T = T_\infty + (T_0 - T_\infty)e^{-t/\tau}$: $\frac{6.8}{1} = \frac{13.6}{\tau} \rightarrow \tau = \frac{13.6}{6.8} = \underline{\underline{2\text{ minutes}}}$

25 $I_C = 1mA$, $I_B = 0.01mA \rightarrow \beta = \frac{1}{.01} = \underline{\underline{100}}$ **8**

$g_m = I_C/V_T = \frac{1}{25} = \underline{\underline{40mA/volt}}$, $r_\pi = \beta/g_m = \frac{100}{40\times10^{-3}} = \underline{\underline{2.5k\Omega}}$

26 $r_\pi = \frac{V_T}{I_B}$, $r_e = \frac{V_T}{I_E}$, $I_B = \frac{I_E}{\beta+1}$

whence $r_\pi = \frac{V_T}{I_E/(\beta+1)} = (\beta+1)\frac{V_T}{I_E} = (\beta+1)r_e$

27 (A) (a) Ground base → $R_{in} = r_e$ directly

(b)

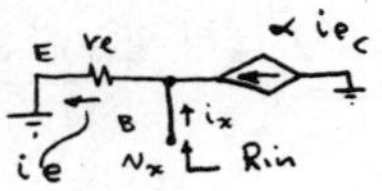

$i_e = v_x/r_e$, $i_x = i_e - \alpha i_e = (1-\alpha)i_e$

$R_{in} = \frac{v_x}{i_x} = \frac{v_x}{(1-\alpha)i_e} = \frac{v_x}{(1-\alpha)v_x/r_e} = \frac{r_e}{1-\alpha}$

But $\alpha = \frac{\beta}{\beta+1}$ and $\frac{1}{1-\alpha} = \frac{1}{1-\beta/_{\beta+1}} = \beta+1$

Thus $R_{in} = \frac{r_e}{1-\alpha} = r_e(\beta+1)$

(B)

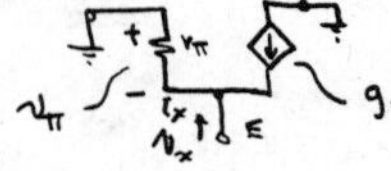

(a) Ground base → $v_\pi = -v_x$

$i_x = \frac{v_x}{r_\pi} + g_m v_x$

$R_{in} = \frac{v_x}{i_x} = \frac{v_x}{\frac{v_x}{r_\pi} + g_m v_x} = \frac{1}{1/r_\pi + g_m}$; But $r_\pi = \frac{\beta}{g_m}$

or $g_m = \beta/r_\pi \rightarrow R_{in} = \frac{r_\pi}{\beta+1} = r_e$

(b) Ground emitter → $R_{in} = r_\pi$ directly

28 $|gain| = g_m R_C = 40mA/V(10k\Omega) = \underline{\underline{400}}$ V/V **8**

Since $g_m = \frac{I_C}{V_T}$, reducing I_C by 2, lowers gain to $\underline{\underline{200}}$ V/V

29 For Fig 8.26 : $\beta = 50$, $V_{BE} = 0.7$

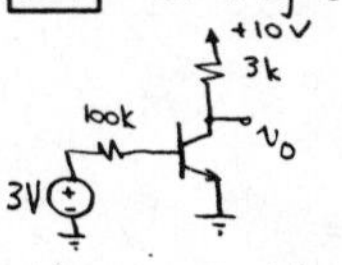

$I_B = \frac{3-0.7}{100k} = 23\mu A$

$I_C = 50(23\mu A) = 1.15mA$

$V_C = 10 - 3k(1.15) = 6.55V$; $g_m = \frac{I_C}{V_T} = \frac{1.15mA}{25mV} = 46mA/V$

$r_\pi = \frac{\beta}{g_m} = \frac{50}{46} = 1.09k$

Gain $= -\frac{1.09}{100+1.09}(46)3k = \underline{\underline{-1.5}}$ V/V

Useable Signals : Cuts off for input $= \frac{10-6.55}{1.5} = \underline{2.3V}$(neg)

Saturates for input $= \frac{6.55-0.7}{1.5} = \underline{3.9V}$(pos)

Thus the largest useable input is $\underline{\underline{2.3V}}$ peak (below 3.0V)

Saturation occurs at high β when $v_o \le 0.7$, for which

$I_C = \frac{10-0.7}{3k} = 3.1mA$ and $\beta \geq \frac{3.1}{23\times10^{-3}} = \underline{\underline{135}}$

30 **8**

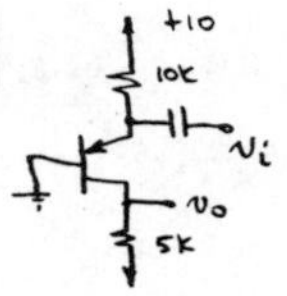

$I_E = \frac{10-0.7}{10k} = .93mA$

$r_e = \frac{V_T}{I_E} = \frac{25}{.93} = 26.9\Omega$

For $\beta = \infty$, $\alpha = 1$

For $\beta = 10$, $\alpha = \frac{10}{11} = 0.909$

Gain $= +\frac{\alpha R_L}{r_e} = \frac{1\times5}{26.9} = \underline{\underline{186}}$ V/V or $0.909(186) = \underline{\underline{169}}$ V/V

31

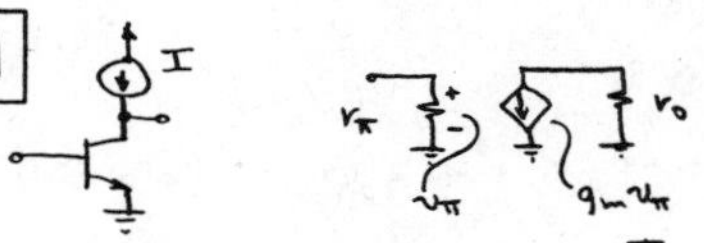

Gain $= -g_m r_o$ where $g_m = \frac{I_C}{V_T}$, $r_o = V_A/I_C$

∴ Gain $= -\frac{I_C}{V_T}\cdot\frac{V_A}{I_C} = \boxed{\frac{-V_A}{V_T}}$

Now for $V_A = 100V$, gain $= -\frac{100}{25mV} = \underline{\underline{-4000}}$

32

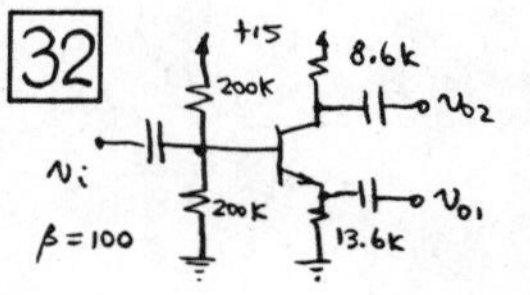

From Fig E 8.18 with resistors doubled

For high β, $V_B = 7.5V$, $V_E = 6.8V$

$I_E = \frac{6.8}{13.6} = 0.5mA$, $r_e = 50\Omega$

For no load, $\frac{v_{o1}}{v_i} = \frac{R_E}{r_e+R_E} = \frac{13.6}{.05+13.6} = \underline{\underline{.996}}$ V/V

$\frac{v_{o2}}{v_i} = \frac{-\alpha R_C}{r_e+R_E} = \frac{-.99(8.6)}{.05+13.6} = \underline{\underline{-.624}}$ V/V

For 10kΩ loads : $\frac{v_{o1}}{v_i} = \frac{13.6\|10k}{13.6\|10k+.05} = \underline{\underline{0.991}}$ V/V **8**

$\frac{v_{o2}}{v_i} = \frac{-0.99(8.6\|10k)}{8.6\|10k+.05} = \underline{\underline{-0.788}}$ V/V

33 Fig E8.19 :

$\frac{v_y}{v_i} = g_m R_L' = \frac{\alpha}{r_e}R_L' = \frac{1\cdot 8k\|8k}{25} = \underline{\underline{160}}$ V/V

$\frac{v_z}{v_i} = \frac{R_L}{r_e+R_L} = \frac{1k}{25+1k} = \underline{\underline{0.976}}$ V/V

34

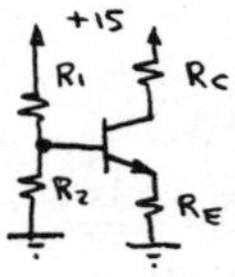

For $I_E = 10mA$ with $\beta = \infty$

and $I_{Bias} = I_E/10$, $V_{BB} = \frac{V_{CC}}{3} = 5V$

$R_2 = \frac{5}{1} = 5k\Omega$, $R_1 = 2R_2 = 10k\Omega$

$R_E = \frac{5-0.7}{10} = 430\Omega$, $R_C = R_E = 430\Omega$

Now for finite β, $I_E = \frac{V_{BB}-0.7}{R_{BB}/_{\beta+1} + R_E} = \frac{4.3}{3.3\bar{3}/(\beta+1)+0.43}$

For $\beta = 100$, $I_E = \frac{4.3}{3.33/101+.43} = \underline{\underline{9.3mA}}$

$I_C = 0.99(9.3) = 9.2mA$

$V_{CE} = 15 - 9.2(.43) - 9.3(.43) = \underline{\underline{7.05V}}$

For $\beta = 10$, $I_E = \frac{4.3}{3.33/11+.43} = \underline{5.87mA}$

$I_C = 5.34mA$, $V_{CE} = 15 - 5.34(.43) - 5.87(.43) = \underline{\underline{10.18V}}$

17 $I_C = 1mA @ V_{CE} = 1V$ and $I_C = 1.2mA @ V_{CE} = 11V$ **8**

$r_o = \frac{\Delta V}{\Delta I} = \frac{11-1}{1.2-1} = \underline{50 k\Omega}$

Also $r_o \approx \frac{V_A}{I} \rightarrow V_A = r_o I = 50k(1mA) = \underline{\underline{50V}}$

18 $|V_{BE}| = 0.7$, $\beta = 100$

(a) Assume active : $V_E = 2-0.7 = \underline{1.3V}$

$I_E = 1mA$; $I_C = \frac{1 \times 100}{101} = 0.99 mA$

$V_C = 6-3(0.99) = \underline{\underline{3.03V}} \rightarrow \therefore$ active

(b) Assume active ; $V_E = 1.0+0.7 = \underline{1.7V}$

$I_E = \frac{6-1.7}{10k} = 0.43 mA \approx I_C$

$V_C = 0+10(0.43) \gg V_B \rightarrow \therefore$ saturated

(c) Assume active ; $V_E = -5+0.7 = \underline{-4.3V}$

$I_E = \frac{9.5+4.3}{200k} = 0.4965 mA$

$I_C = I_E \frac{100}{101} = 0.492 mA$

$V_C = -50+.492(20k) = \underline{\underline{-40.2V}} \rightarrow \therefore$ active

(d) Assume active : $V_E = \underline{\underline{-20.7V}}, I_E = \frac{30-20.7}{5k} = 1.86 mA$

$V_C = -1.86\left(\frac{100}{101}\right)(2k) - 10 = \underline{\underline{-13.68V}} \rightarrow \therefore$ active

19 (a) $V_B = +2+0.7 = \underline{\underline{2.7V}}$; $I_B = \frac{12-2.7}{100k} = \underline{\underline{93\mu A}}$ **8**

Assume active :

For $\beta = 50$, $V_C = 12 - 1.5(50)\frac{93}{1000} = \underline{\underline{5.025V}} \rightarrow \therefore$ active

For $\beta = 100$, $V_C = 12 - 1.5(100)\frac{93}{1000} = \underline{neg} \rightarrow \therefore$ saturated

(b) $V_B = 10-0.7 = \underline{\underline{9.3V}}$; $I_B = \frac{9.3}{10^6} = \underline{\underline{9.3\mu A}}$

Assume active :

For $\beta = 50$, $V_C = 9.3(50)18k = \underline{\underline{8.37V}} \rightarrow \therefore$ active

For $\beta = 100$, $V_C = 9.3(100)18k \gg \underline{\underline{10V}} \rightarrow \therefore$ saturated

20 See Fig 8.20 $\rightarrow \beta = \infty$, $I_B = \underline{0}$, $V_{BB} = 5V$

$V_B = \underline{\underline{5V}}$, $V_E = \underline{\underline{4.3V}}$, $I_E = \frac{4.3V}{3k} = \underline{\underline{1.4\dot{3} mA}}$

$I_C = \left(\frac{\infty}{\infty+1}\right) I_E = \underline{\underline{1.4\dot{3} mA}}$, $V_C = 15-5(1.4\dot{3}) = \underline{\underline{7.83V}}$

21 $\beta = 50$, $V_{BE} = 0.7$; $V_{BB} = \frac{0.47}{1+0.47} \times 9 = 2.878V$

$R_{BB} = 470k \| 1M = 319.7k\Omega \rightarrow V_E = \frac{30k(51)}{30k(51)+319.7k} \times (2.878-0.7) = \underline{\underline{1.802V}}$

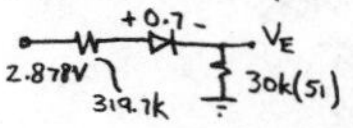

$V_B = 1.802+0.7 = \underline{\underline{2.50V}}$; $I_E = \frac{1.802}{30k} = \underline{\underline{0.060mA}}$

$I_C = \frac{50}{51}(.060) = \underline{\underline{.059mA}}$, $I_B = \frac{.060}{51} = \underline{\underline{1.18\mu A}}$, $V_C = 9-50(0.59) = \underline{\underline{6.06V}}$

22

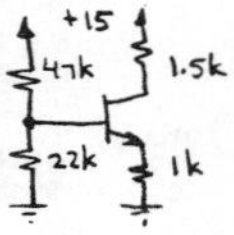

8

$\beta = 30$; $V_{BB} = \frac{22}{47+22} \times 15 = 4.78V$

$R_{BB} = 22 \| 47 = 15.0 k\Omega$

$V_E = \frac{31}{31+15}(4.78-0.7) = \underline{\underline{2.82V}}$

$V_B = 2.82+0.7 = \underline{\underline{3.52V}}$; $I_E = \frac{2.82}{1k} = \underline{\underline{2.82mA}}$

$I_C = \frac{30}{31}(2.82) = \underline{\underline{2.73 mA}}$, $V_C = 15-1.5(2.73) = \underline{\underline{10.9V}}$

$I_B = \frac{2.82}{31} = \underline{\underline{91\mu A}}$

23

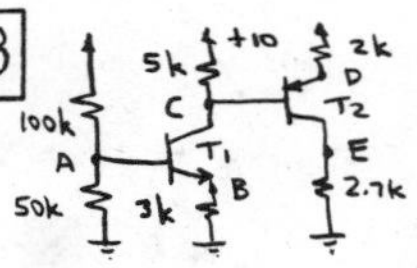

For $\beta = \infty$: $V_A = \underline{\underline{3.\dot{3}V}}$,

$V_B = 3.33-0.7 = \underline{\underline{2.63V}}$

$I_{E1} = \frac{2.63}{3} = \underline{\underline{0.877mA}}$

$V_C = 10-5(0.877) = \underline{\underline{5.62V}}$, $V_D = 5.62+0.7 = \underline{\underline{6.32V}}$

$I_{E2} = \frac{10-6.32}{2} = \underline{\underline{1.84mA}}$, $V_E = (1.84)(2.7) = \underline{\underline{4.97V}}$

For $\beta = 100$, $V_{AA} = 3.\dot{3}V$, $R_{AA} = 50k \| 100k = 33.\dot{3}k$

$V_B = \frac{101(3)}{101(3)+33.3}(3.\dot{3}-0.7) = \underline{\underline{2.37V}}$

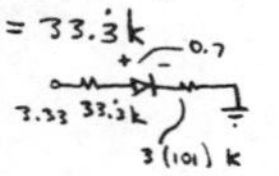

$V_A = 2.37+0.7 = \underline{\underline{3.07V}}$, $I_{E1} = \frac{2.37}{3k} = \underline{\underline{0.79mA}}$

$I_{C1} = \frac{100}{101}(0.79) = \underline{\underline{0.782mA}}$

$R_{C_{Eq}} = 5k \| 202k = 4.88k$, $V_{C_{Eq}} = 10 - \frac{5}{207}(0.7) = 9.98$

$V_C = 9.98 - 4.88(.782) = \underline{\underline{6.16V}}$, $V_D = 6.16+0.7 = \underline{\underline{6.86V}}$ **8**

$I_{E2} = \frac{10-6.86}{2} = \underline{\underline{1.57mA}}$, $I_{C2} = \frac{100}{101}(1.57) = \underline{\underline{1.55mA}}$

$V_E = 1.55(2.7) = \underline{\underline{4.20V}}$

24 For $v_{be} = \underline{10mV}$, $e^{v_{be}/V_T} = 1.49$ and $1 + \frac{v_{be}}{V_T} = 1.40$

Thus terms ignored $= 1.49 - 1.40 = \underline{\underline{.09}}$ or $\frac{.09}{.40} \times 100$ or

$\underline{\underline{22.5\%}}$ of $v_{be}/V_T = x$

For $e^x - (1+x) = 0.1x \rightarrow e^x - 1 = 1.1x$ or $x' = \frac{e^x - 1}{1.1}$

Try $x = 0.1 \rightarrow x' = .096$

$x = 0.2 \rightarrow x' = .2013$

$x = 0.19 \rightarrow x' = .1902$

$x = 0.189 \rightarrow x' = .1891$

ie $v_{be}/V_T = 0.189 \rightarrow v_{be} = 0.189(25) = \underline{\underline{4.7mV}}$ for $\underline{10\%}$

For $e^x - (1+x) = 0.01x \rightarrow e^x - 1 = 1.01x$ or $x' = \frac{e^x - 1}{1.01}$

Try $x = .01 \rightarrow x' = .00995$

$x = .02 \rightarrow x' = .0200$

ie $v_{be}/V_T = .020 \rightarrow v_{be} = .020(25) = \underline{\underline{0.5mV}}$ for $\underline{1\%}$

35 **8**

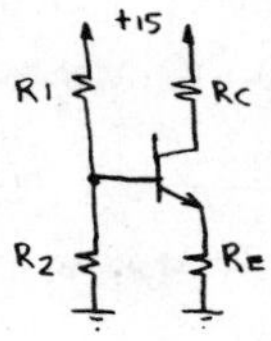

$R_2 = \frac{5V}{10mA} = 500$

$R_1 = 2R_2 = 1k\Omega$, $R_E = R_C = 430\Omega$

$R_{BB} = R_1 \| R_2 = 333\Omega$

$I_E = \frac{4.3}{.33\dot{3}/(\beta+1) + 0.43}$

For $\beta = 100$, $I_E = \frac{4.3}{.33\dot{3}/101 + .43} = \underline{\underline{9.92\ mA}}$

$I_C = 0.99(9.92) = 9.82\ mA$

$V_{CE} = 15 - .43(9.82) - .43(9.92) = \underline{\underline{6.51\ V}}$

For $\beta = 10$, $I_E = \frac{4.3}{.33\dot{3}/11 + .43} = \underline{9.35\ mA}$

$I_C = \frac{10}{11}(9.35) = 8.50\ mA$

$V_{CE} = 15 - .43(8.50) - .43(9.35) = \underline{\underline{7.32V}}$

36

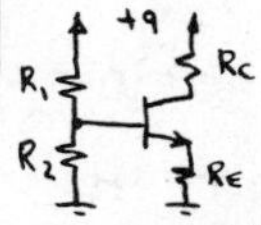

$V_{BB} = 3V$, $R_1 \| R_2 = R$

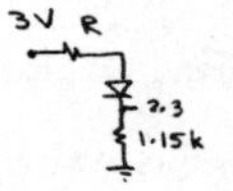

$R_E = \frac{3-0.7}{2\ mA} = 1.15k\Omega$

For β reducing from ∞ to 100, $\frac{1.15(101)}{1.15(101)+R} = 0.9(1)$

or $R = \frac{1.15(101)}{0.9} - 1.15(101) = 12.9k\Omega$

$\frac{R_1R_2}{R_1+R_2} = \frac{2R_2R_2}{3R_2} = \frac{2}{3}R_2 \rightarrow R_2 = 19.36K$ and $R_1 = 38.7k$. Use $\underline{\underline{R_2 = 18k}}$

and $R_1 = \underline{\underline{36k}}$, $R_E = \underline{\underline{1.2k}}$, $R_C = \frac{3}{2.3}(1.2) = 1.57k$ or $\underline{\underline{1.6k\Omega}}$

37 **8**

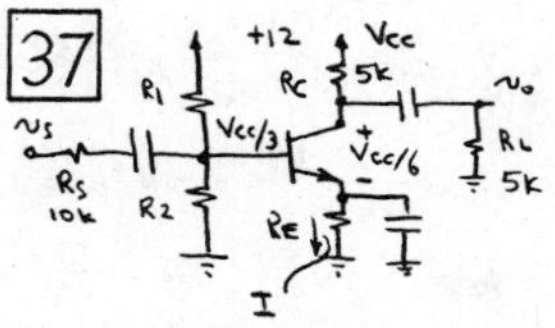

$R_L = 5k$, $R_C = R_L = \underline{\underline{5k}}$

$R_E = \frac{\frac{12}{3} - 0.7}{I} = 3.3/I$

$(R_E + 5)I = 12 - 12/6 = 10$

ie $\left(\frac{3.3}{I} + 5\right)I = 10 \rightarrow 3.3 + 5I = 10$, $I = \frac{10-3.3}{5} = \underline{\underline{1.34\ mA}}$

$R_E = \frac{3.3}{1.34} = \underline{\underline{2.46\ k\Omega}}$; $R_2 = 10R_E = \underline{\underline{24.6\ k\Omega}}$

$R_1 = 2(24.6) = \underline{\underline{49.2k\Omega}}$. Now for $\beta = 100$, $V_E = \frac{248.5}{248.5 + 16.4} \cdot 3.3$

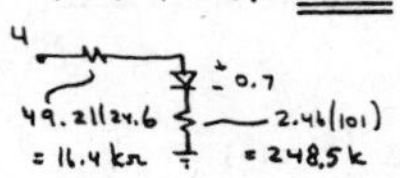

or $V_E = 3.096V \rightarrow I_E = \frac{3.096}{2.46} = \underline{1.26mA}$

for which $r_e = \frac{25}{1.26} = 19.8\Omega$

and $R_{in} = (\beta+1)r_e \| R_1 \| R_2 = (101(19.8)) \| 24.6 \| 49.2 = \underline{\underline{1.78k\Omega}}$

Gain direct $= -\frac{\alpha R_L'}{r_e} = -\frac{100}{101}\frac{(5/2\ k)}{19.8} = \underline{\underline{-125 V/V}}$, from base to load

Gain $\frac{v_o}{v_s} = -\frac{1.78}{10 + 1.78}(125) = \underline{\underline{-18.9 V/V}}$

38

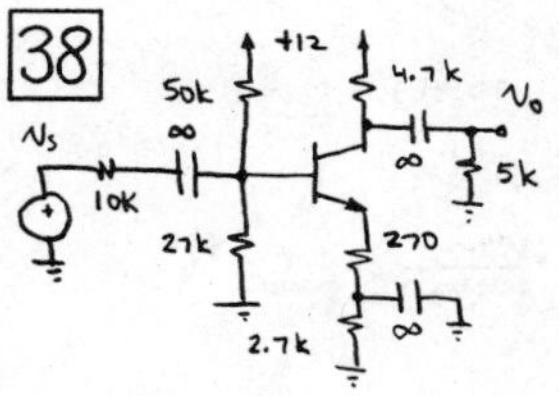

Bias for $\beta = \infty$

$V_B = V_{BB} = \frac{27}{50+27} \times 12 = 4.21V$

$V_E = 4.21 - 0.7 = 3.51V$

$I_E = \frac{3.51}{2.7 + .27} = 1.18mA$

$r_e = \frac{25}{1.18} = 21.2\Omega$

For $\beta = 150$, R_{in} at base $= (151(21.2)) \| 27k \| 50k = \underline{12.52k}$ **8**

Gain $\frac{v_o}{v_s} = \frac{12.52}{10 + 12.52} \times \frac{(4.7k\|5k)}{21.2 + 270}\frac{150}{151} = \underline{\underline{-4.59\ V/V}}$ (2.42)

For $v_{be} = 10mv$, $v_o = \frac{4.7k\|5k}{21.2}\frac{150}{151} \times 10mV = \underline{\underline{1.134V}}$

and $v_s = \frac{1.134}{4.59} = \underline{\underline{.247V}}$

39 For $R_1 = 5k$, $R_2 = 2.7k$, $R_{in_{base}} = 2.7k \| 5.0k \| 151(21.2)$

or $\underline{\underline{1.68k\Omega}}$. Thus gain becomes $-4.59 \times \frac{10 + 12.52}{12.52} \times \frac{1.68}{1.68+10}$

or $\underline{\underline{-1.19\ V/V}}$

40

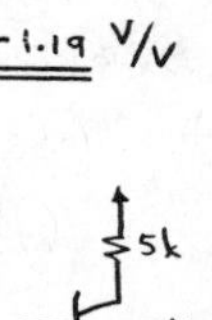

For $v_{be} = 10mV$, $v_o = 40 \times 10 \times 5 = \underline{\underline{2V}}$

With added 175Ω in emitter (whose $r_e = 25\Omega$)

$v_{b_{peak}} = \frac{10}{25} \times (175 + 25) = \underline{\underline{80\ mV}}$

Minimum collector-base bias voltage $= 2.00 + 0.08 = \underline{2.08V}$

For $i_E = 1mA$ and base to ground bias $= \frac{V_{CC}}{3}$, then

$V_{CC} = 5(1) + 2.08 + V_{CC}/3 \rightarrow 2/3\ V_{CC} = 7.08$

$\therefore V_{CC_{min}} = \frac{3(7.08)}{2} = \underline{\underline{10.62\ V}} \rightarrow$ Use 12V

41 **8**

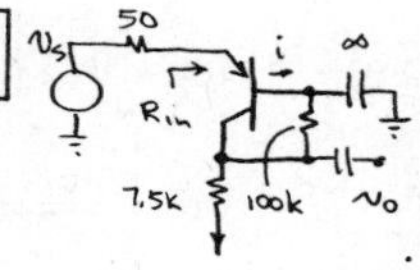

$\beta = 100$, $V_{EB} = 0.7$

$(.05)101i + 0.7 + i(100k) + 101i(7.5) = 5V$

ie $i = \frac{5 - 0.7}{5.05 + 100 + 757.5} = 4.99$ or $\underline{5\mu A}$

$i_C = 5\mu A(100) = \underline{\underline{0.5\ mA}}$, $r_e = \frac{25}{0.5} = 50\Omega$, $R_{in} = \underline{\underline{50\Omega}}$

$v_o/v_s = \frac{7.5k \| 100k}{50 + 50} = \underline{\underline{69.8\ V/V}}$

For v_{be} restricted to 10mV, max. input = 20mV and

max output $= 20(69.8) = 1.396V$

However $V_{BC} = 5\mu A(100k) = 0.5V$. Saturation limits the

input signal to $\frac{0.5}{69.8} = 7.2mV$. Thus the overall

limit, produced by the transistor leaving the

active region : $\hat{v}_s = \underline{\underline{7.2mV}}$

42

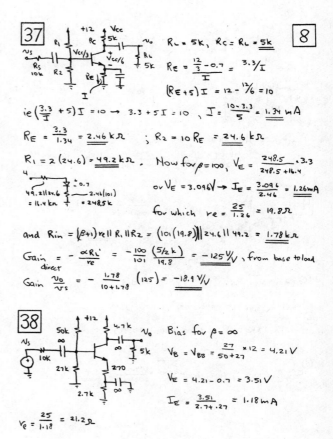

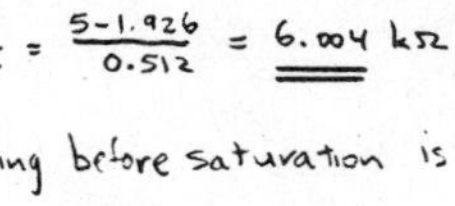

$\beta = 100$

For $i_C = 500\mu A$,

$i_{50} = 500 + 5 + \frac{700\ mV}{100\ k} = 512\mu A$

$V_A = 50(512) = -26mV$, $V_B = -726mV$, $V_C = -726 - 12\mu A(100k) = \underline{-1.926V}$

$R_C = \frac{5 - 1.926}{0.512} = \underline{\underline{6.004\ k\Omega}}$. Here the maximum collector

swing before saturation is $-1.926 + .726 = \underline{\underline{1.2V}} > 0.5V$ without R_B

43 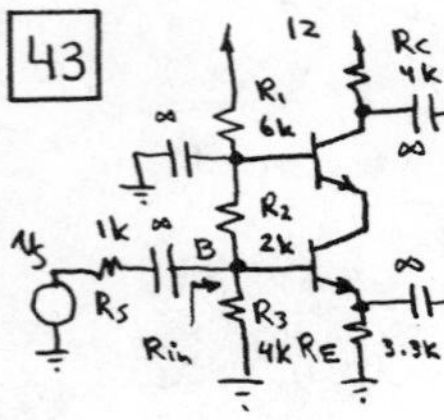

8

Approximate Analysis:

$V_B = \frac{4}{4+2+6} \times 12 = 4V$

$V_E = 3.3V$, $I_E = \frac{3.3}{3.3} = 1mA$

$r_e = 25\Omega$, $r_\pi = 101(25) = 2.525k$

$R_{in} = 2.525 \| 4k \| 2k = 0.872k$

$\text{Gain} = -\frac{4k\|4k}{25} \times \left(\frac{100}{101}\right)^2 \times \frac{.872}{1+.872} = -36.5 \text{ or } \underline{\underline{-37\ V/V}}$

45 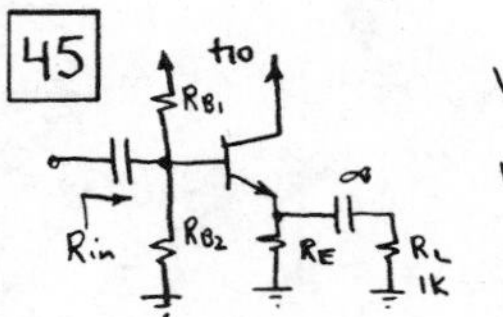

8

$V_{BB} = 5V$, β high , $V_E = 5-0.7 = 4.3$

$R_E = \frac{4.3V}{10mA} = \underline{\underline{430\Omega}}$

For 10% drop in I_E at $\beta = 100$,

4.3, R/2, 430(51)

$\frac{430(51)}{R/2 + 430(51)} \times 4.3 = 0.9(4.3) \rightarrow R = 4.87k$

Use $R_{B1} = R_{B2} = \underline{4.7k}$

$R_{in} = \left(101(430 \| 1k)\right) \| \frac{4.7k}{2} = 30.4k \| 2.35k = \underline{\underline{2.18\ k\Omega}}$

44 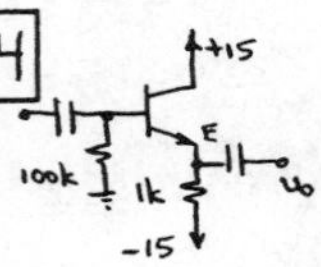

$V_E = -15 + \frac{101k}{100k + 101k}(15-0.7) = -7.81V$

(a) $I_E = \frac{15-7.81}{1k} = \underline{\underline{7.18mA}} \rightarrow r_e = \frac{25}{7.18} = 3.48\Omega$

(b) $R_{in} = 100k \| 101(1.003k) = \underline{\underline{50.3k}}$

$\text{Gain} = \frac{1000}{1000+3.5} = \underline{\underline{0.997\ V/V}}$ for no load

$R_{out} = 3.48 \| 1k = \underline{\underline{3.47\Omega}}$

(c) For $R_L = 1k$: $R_{in} = 100k \| 101(.5035k) = \underline{\underline{33.7k}}$

$\text{Gain} = 0.997 \times \frac{1k}{1k+3.5} = \underline{.994\ V/V}$

(d) For $R_S = 10k$, gain $= .994 \times \frac{33.7}{10+33.7} = \underline{\underline{0.767\ V/V}}$

46

$\beta = 100$, $I_E = 2.5mA$, $r_e = \frac{25mV}{2.5mA} = 10\Omega$

R_{out} (with $R_S = 10k\Omega$) $= 10 + \frac{10k}{101} = \underline{\underline{109\Omega}}$

No Load gain $= \underline{1.000\ V/V}$

Gain with $1k\Omega$ load $= \frac{1k}{0.109k + 1k} = \underline{\underline{0.902\ V/V}}$

For 1k load, the largest possible negative output swing is $-1k(2.5mA) = \underline{\underline{-2.5V}}$. Largest possible positive output is $3 + 0.2 - 0.7 = \underline{\underline{2.5\ V}}$. Thus the largest possible output signal is $\pm\ \underline{\underline{2.5V}}$

47 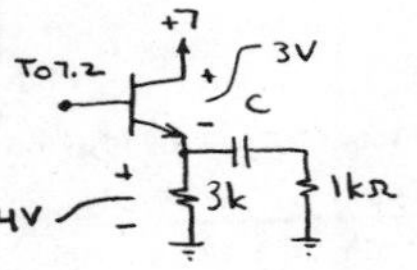

8

$v_{o-} = \frac{1}{3+1}(4V) = \underline{\underline{-1V}}$

$v_{o+} = 3 - 0.7 + .2 = \underline{\underline{+2.5V}}$

48 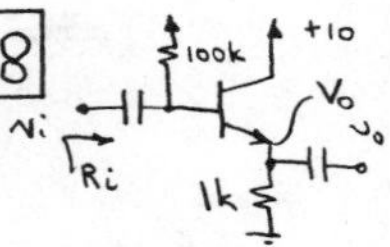

For $\beta = \infty$, $V_B = +10V$, $V_E = \underline{\underline{9.3V}} = V_o$

$I_E = \underline{\underline{9.3mA}}$, $r_e = 2.7\Omega$

$v_o/v_i = \frac{1k}{2.7 + 1k} = \underline{\underline{.997\ V/V}}$

$R_i = \underline{\underline{100k\Omega}}$

For $\beta = 100$, $V_E = \frac{101(1k)}{101(1k) + 100k} \times 9.3 = \underline{\underline{4.67V}} = V_o$

$I_E = \underline{\underline{4.67mA}}$, $r_e = \frac{25}{4.67} = 5.35\Omega$

$v_o/v_i = \frac{1k}{1k + 5.4} = \underline{\underline{0.995}}$

$R_i = 100k \| (101(1k + 5.4)) = \underline{\underline{50.4\ k\Omega}}$

49 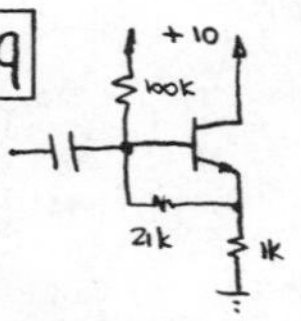

For $\beta = \infty$, $i_{21} = \frac{0.7}{21k} = 33.3\mu A$

$V_B = +10 - (100k(33.3\mu A)) = 6.67\ V$

$V_E = 6.67 - 0.7 = \underline{\underline{5.97V}}$

$I_E = \underline{\underline{5.97\ mA}}$, $r_e = 4.2\Omega$, $v_o/v_i = \underline{\underline{.9958\ V/V}}$

8

$R_i = 100k \| \frac{21k}{1 - .9958} = 100k \| 5M \simeq \underline{\underline{98k\Omega}}$

For $\beta = 100$: $V_E = \frac{101(1)}{100 + (101)1} \times (6.67 - 0.7) = \underline{\underline{3.0\ V}} = V_o$

$I_E = \underline{3mA}$, $r_e = \frac{25}{3} = 8.3\Omega$

$v_o/v_i = \frac{1k}{1k + 8.3} = \underline{\underline{.9918\ V/V}}$

$R_i = 100k \| \frac{21}{1 - .9918} \| (101(1.0083)) = 100k \| 2.6M \| 102k \simeq \underline{\underline{50k}}$

50 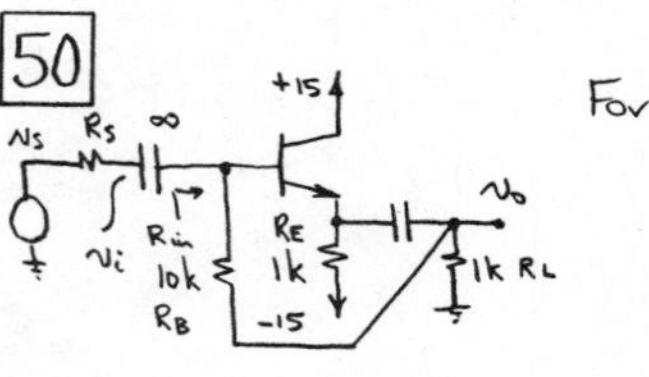

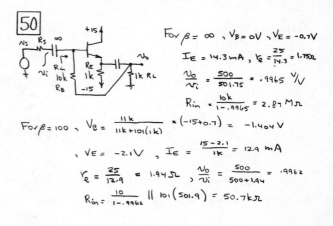

For $\beta = \infty$, $V_B = 0V$, $V_E = -0.7V$

$I_E = 14.3mA$, $r_e = \frac{25}{14.3} = 1.75\Omega$

$\frac{v_o}{v_i} = \frac{500}{501.75} = .9965\ V/V$

$R_{in} = \frac{10k}{1 - .9965} = 2.87M\Omega$

For $\beta = 100$, $V_B = \frac{11k}{11k + 101(1k)} \times (-15 + 0.7) = -1.404V$

, $V_E = -2.1V$, $I_E = \frac{15 - 2.1}{1k} = 12.9\ mA$

$r_e = \frac{25}{12.9} = 1.94\Omega$, $\frac{v_o}{v_i} = \frac{500}{500 + 1.94} = .9962$

$R_{in} = \frac{10}{1 - .9962} \| 101(501.9) = 50.7k\Omega$

(next)

8

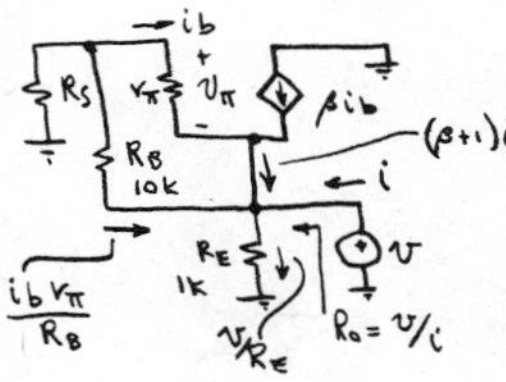

$$i = \frac{v}{R_e} - (\beta+1)i_b - i_b\frac{r_\pi}{R_B}$$

See $v = -\left(R_S\left(i_b + \frac{i_b r_\pi}{R_B}\right) + i_b r_\pi\right)$

whence $i_b = \dfrac{-v}{R_S + r_\pi\left(1+\frac{R_S}{R_B}\right)}$

Thus $i/v = 1/R_o = \dfrac{1}{R_E} + \dfrac{\left(\beta+1+\frac{r_\pi}{R_B}\right)}{R_S + r_\pi\left(1+\frac{R_S}{R_B}\right)}$

ie $\boxed{1/R_o = \dfrac{1}{R_e} + \dfrac{\beta+1}{R_S + r_\pi\left(1+\frac{R_S}{R_B}\right)} + \dfrac{1}{R_S + R_B\left(1+\frac{R_S}{r_\pi}\right)}}$

Now when $R_S = 0$: $1/R_o = \dfrac{1}{R_E} + \dfrac{\beta+1}{r_\pi} + \dfrac{1}{R_B}$

ie $R_o = R_E \parallel r_e \parallel R_B \approx r_e = 1.9\,\Omega$

Now when $R_S = 100k$, $R_B = 10k$ and (for convenience) $\beta = 99$, $r_e = 2$, $r_\pi = 200$

$$R_o(k\Omega) = 1 \parallel \left(\frac{100}{100} + \frac{0.2}{100}\left(1+\frac{100}{10}\right)\right) \parallel \left(100 + 10\left(1+\frac{100}{.2}\right)\right)$$

$$= 1 \parallel 1.022 \parallel 5110 \approx \underline{0.505\,k\Omega}$$

51

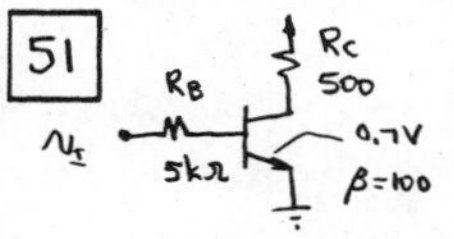

For $V_{CB} = 0$, $I_C = \dfrac{5-0.7}{500} = \dfrac{4.3}{500} = 8.6\,mA$

$I_B = \dfrac{8.6}{100} = \underline{86\,\mu A}$

Thus $V_I = 700\,mV + 86\times10^{-6}\times 5k = \underline{1.13\,V}$

$r_e = \dfrac{V_T}{I_E} = \dfrac{\alpha V_T}{I_C} = \dfrac{100}{101}\,\dfrac{25}{8.6} = 2.88\,\Omega$, $r_\pi = 101(2.88) = 290.7\,\Omega$

Gain $= \dfrac{v_o}{v_i} = -\dfrac{\beta R_L'}{R_B'} = \dfrac{-100\,(0.5)}{5 + .291} = -9.45 \approx \underline{-9.5\,V/V}$

52 8

(a)

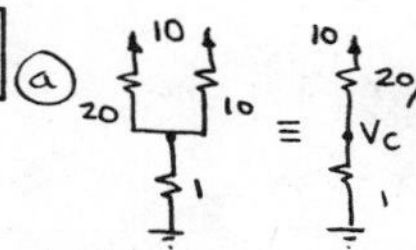

$V_C = \dfrac{1}{1+\frac{20}{3}} \times 10 = \dfrac{20}{23} = 1.3\,V$

$I_C = \dfrac{10-1.3}{10k} = .87\,mA$

$I_B = \dfrac{10-1.3}{20k} = .435\,mA$, $\beta_{forced} = \dfrac{0.87}{0.435} = 2$

(b)

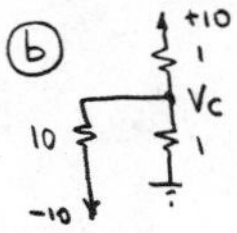

$10 - V_C = V_C + \dfrac{V_C + 10}{10} \rightarrow V_C = \dfrac{9}{2.1} = 4.29\,V$

$I_C = 4.29\,mA$, $I_B = \dfrac{4.29+10}{10} = 1.429\,mA$

$\beta_{forced} = \dfrac{4.29}{1.429} = 3$

(c)

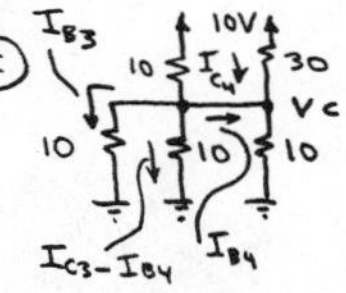

$V_C = \dfrac{10/3}{\frac{10}{3} + \frac{30}{4}} \times 10 = 3.08\,V$

$I_{C4} = \dfrac{10-3.08}{30k} = .23\,mA$

$I_{B4} = \dfrac{3.1}{10k} - .23 = .08\,mA$; Thus $\beta_{forced\,4} = \dfrac{0.23}{0.08} = 2.9$

$I_{C3} - I_{B4} = 0.31 \rightarrow I_{C3} = 0.31 + .08 = 0.39\,mA$

$I_{B3} = 0.31\,mA$. Thus $\beta_{forced\,3} = \dfrac{0.39}{0.31} = 1.26$

53

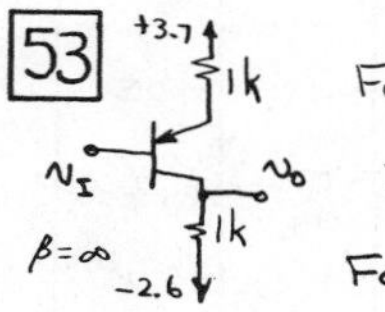

For $V_i = +2V$, $V_E = 2.7V$, $I_E = \dfrac{3.7-2.7}{1k} = 1\,mA$

$I_C = 1\,mA$, $V_C = -2.6 + 1(1) = -1.6$

For $V_i = 0V$, $V_E = 0.7$, $I_E = \dfrac{3.7-0.7}{1k} = 3\,mA$

Assume active, ie $I_C = 3mA$, $V_C = -2.6 + 1(3) = +0.4$, ie just at sat.

8

For $V_i = -2V$, transistor saturated:

$V_E = -2 + 0.7 = -1.3V$, $V_C = -1.3 - 0.3 = -1.6V$

Check: $V_i = +1V$:

$I_E = \dfrac{3.7-1.7}{1} = 2\,mA$

$V_C = -2.6 + 1(2) = -0.6$

For $V_i = -1V$:

$V_E = -0.3$, $V_C = -0.6V$

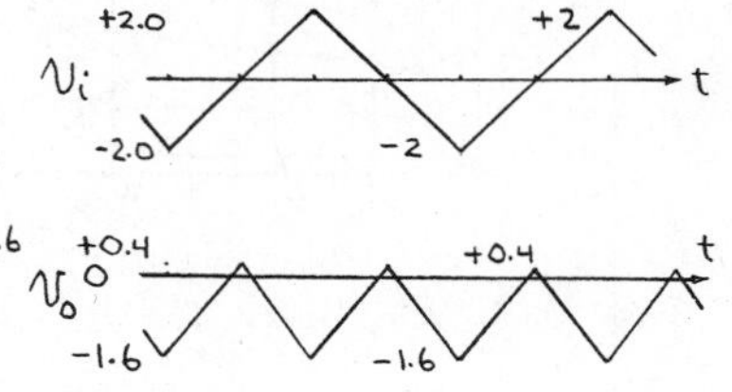

54 $\beta = \infty$, $|V_{BE}| = 0.7V$, $|V_{CE\,sat}| = 0.3V$

For $V_A = 0$, see the circuit is balanced with respect to the supplies and $V_C = -V_D = 0.7V$ and $V_E = 0$

For $V_A = v$, a small positive voltage, $V_B = v$ (as $\beta = \infty$)

Thus $V_C = 0.7 + v$ and $V_D = -0.7 + v$ and the current through the upper transistor (T_1) is reduced by $\dfrac{v}{10k}$ while that through the lower (T_2) increases by $\dfrac{v}{10k}$. Thus the net current in the output $10k\Omega$ is $\dfrac{2v}{10k}$ directed inward and $V_E = -10k\left(\dfrac{2v}{10k}\right) = -2v$.

Thus for inputs around zero, the gain is -2 until T_1 or T_2 saturate. 8

For T_1 saturated with $V_E = v$

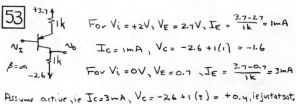

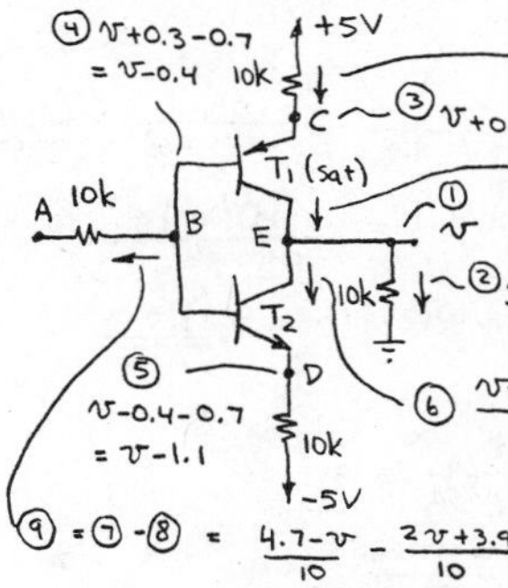

(1) v

(2) $\dfrac{v}{10}$

(3) $v + 0.3$

(4) $v + 0.3 - 0.7 = v - 0.4$

(5) $v - 0.4 - 0.7 = v - 1.1$

(6) $\dfrac{v - 1.1 - (-5)}{10} = \dfrac{3.9 + v}{10}$

(7) $\dfrac{5 - (v + 0.3)}{10} = \dfrac{4.7 - v}{10}$

(8) $\dfrac{v}{10} + \dfrac{3.9 + v}{10} = \dfrac{2v + 3.9}{10}$

(9) = (7) − (8) = $\dfrac{4.7 - v}{10} - \dfrac{2v + 3.9}{10} = \dfrac{0.8 - 3v}{10}$

(10) $V_A = v - 0.4 - \left(\dfrac{0.8 - 3v}{10}\right)10 = 4v - 1.2$

ie $V_A = 4V_E - 1.2$ or $\boxed{V_E = \dfrac{V_A + 1.2}{4}}$ implying again $\dfrac{dV_E}{dV_A} = 1/4$

Edge of saturation of T_1 occurs when the input current is 0, ie $\dfrac{0.8-3v}{10} = 0$ or $V_E = v = \dfrac{0.8}{3} = 0.267V$

at which point, $V_A = V_B = v - 0.4 = .267 - 0.4 = -0.133V$

Check: $V_E = \dfrac{-.133 + 1.2}{4} = 0.267\,V$ as expected

Now as the input is lowered from $-0.133V$,

the output falls, reaching 0V when

$V_E = 0 = \frac{V_A + 1.2}{4} \rightarrow V_A = -1.2V$

For T_2 saturated by positive inputs, from the symmetry of the situation:

$V_E = \frac{V_A - 1.2}{4}$, the slope of the transfer characteristic (gain) = 1/4 and $V_E = 0$ when $V_A = +1.2$ V

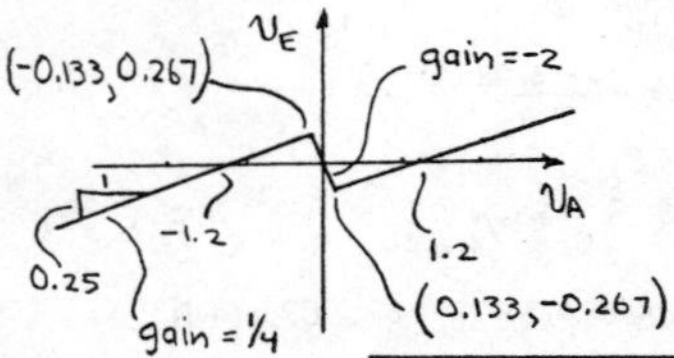

Voltage at	A	B	C	D	E
	0	0	0.7	-0.7	0
	1	+.35	+1.05	-.35	-.05
	2	+.60	+1.3	-0.1	+.20
	-4	-1.1	-0.4	-1.8	-0.70
	-5	-1.35	-0.65	-2.05	-0.95

55

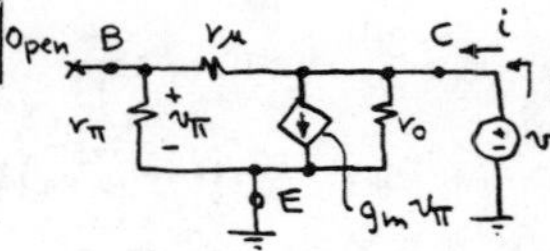

$v_\pi = \frac{r_\pi}{r_\mu + r_\pi} \times v$, $i = \frac{v}{r_o} + g_m v_\pi + \frac{v}{r_\mu + r_\pi}$

$\therefore 1/R_o = i/v = \left\{ 1/r_o + \frac{g_m r_\pi}{r_\mu + r_\pi} + \frac{1}{r_\mu + r_\pi} \right\}$

$= 1/r_o + \frac{1}{\frac{r_\mu}{g_m r_\pi} + \frac{1}{g_m}} + \frac{1}{r_\mu + r_\pi}$

$\therefore \boxed{R_o} = r_o \| \frac{r_\mu}{\beta} \| r_\mu \approx \boxed{r_o \| r_\mu/\beta}$

56

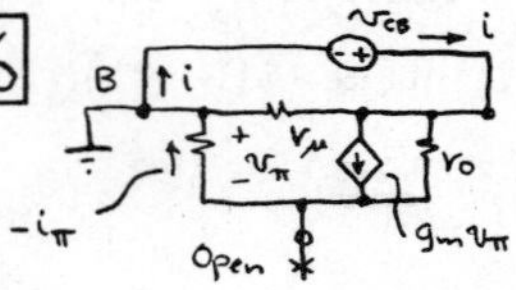

See $i = \frac{v_{CB}}{r_\mu} - i_\pi$

But $-i_\pi = g_m v_\pi + \frac{v_{CB} - (-v_\pi)}{r_o}$

or $-i_\pi = g_m i_\pi r_\pi + \frac{v_{CB}}{r_o} + \frac{i_\pi r_\pi}{r_o}$

or $-i_\pi \left(1 + g_m r_\pi + \frac{r_\pi}{r_o}\right) = \frac{v_{CB}}{r_o}$

or $-i_\pi = \frac{v_{CB}}{r_o(1 + g_m r_\pi + r_\pi/r_o)}$

$\therefore 1/R_o = \frac{i}{v_{CB}} = \frac{\frac{v_{CB}}{r_\mu} - i_\pi}{v_{CB}} = \frac{1}{r_\mu} + \frac{1}{r_o(1 + \beta + r_\pi/r_o)}$

Thus $R_o \approx r_\mu \| (\beta + 1) r_o$

(next)

Now for $r_\mu = 10 \beta r_o$

$I_E = 10$ mA, $V_{CB} = 1$ V, $I_C = 9.900$ mA

$I_E = 10$ mA, $V_{CB} = 11$ V, $I_C = 9.908$ mA

See $\beta = \frac{I_C}{I_B} = \frac{I_C}{I_E - I_C} = \frac{9.900}{10 - 9.900} = \underline{\underline{99}}$

$R_o = r_\mu \| (\beta+1) r_o = \frac{11 - 1}{9.908 - 9.900} = \frac{10}{.008 \times 10^{-3}} = \underline{\underline{1.25 M\Omega}}$

ie $1.25 \times 10^6 = (10(99) r_o) \| (100 r_o) = \frac{10(99)(100) r_o^2}{1090 r_o} = 90.8 r_o$

whence $r_o = \underline{\underline{13.8k}}$, $r_\mu = 10(99)13.8k = \underline{\underline{13.7 M\Omega}}$

57

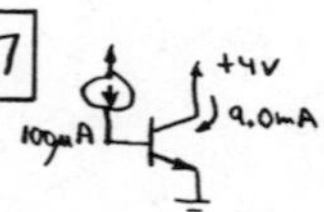

$\beta_{dc} = \frac{9000}{100} = \underline{\underline{90}}$

$\beta_{ac} = \frac{(10-9) \times 10^3}{10} = \underline{\underline{100}}$

58

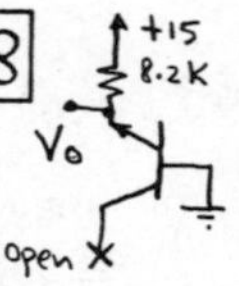

$V_o = 6.8$ V, ie BV_{EBO} with breakdown current = $\frac{15 - 6.8}{8.2K} = 1.0$ mA

59

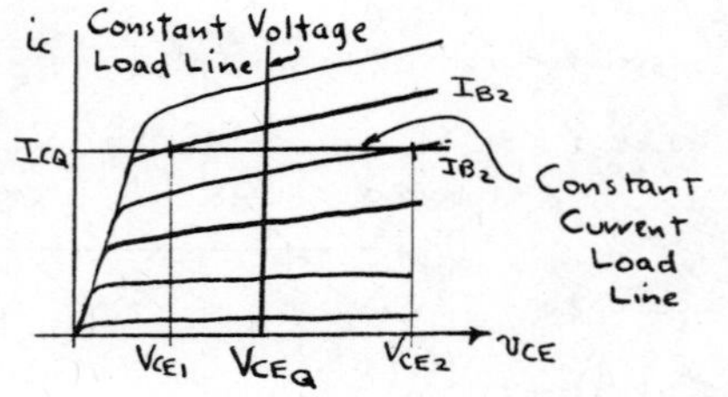

See $V_{CE_2} - V_{CE_1}$ large for $I_{B2} - I_{E1}$ small for current load

60

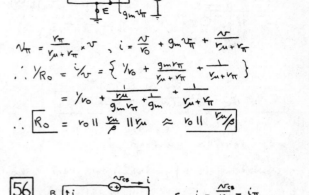

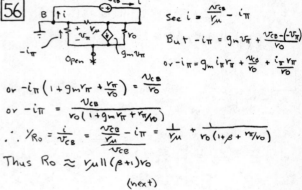

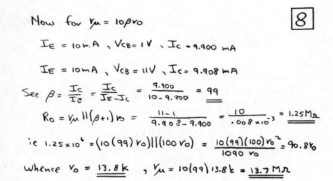

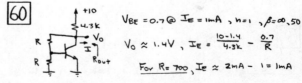

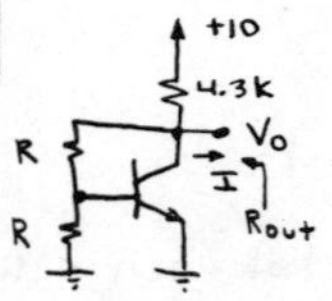

$V_{BE} = 0.7$ @ $I_E = 1$mA, $n = 1$, $\beta = \infty, 50$

$V_o \approx 1.4V$, $I_E = \frac{10 - 1.4}{4.3k} - \frac{0.7}{R}$

For R = 700, $I_E \approx 2mA - 1 = 1mA$

and $V_{BE} = 0.7$, $V_o = \underline{\underline{1.40V}}$. Here $r_e = 25\Omega$

For R = 7k, $I_E = 2mA - 0.1mA = 1.9mA$, $V_{BE} = 700 + V_T \ln \frac{1.9}{1}$

or 716 mV, for which $V_o \approx 2 V_{BE} = \underline{1.432V}$. Here $r_e = 13.16\Omega$

@ For Rout, apply a test voltage v and measure i →

$i = \frac{v}{4.3k} + \frac{v}{2R} + v \times \frac{R \| r_\pi}{R + R \| r_\pi} \times \frac{\alpha}{r_e}$

Thus Ro consists of a parallel combination of 4.3k, 2R and $\frac{R + R \| r_\pi}{R \| r_\pi} \times \frac{r_e}{\alpha}$

8

The latter term $\frac{R + R\|r_\pi}{R\|r_\pi} \cdot \frac{r_e}{\alpha} = \left(\frac{R}{\frac{r_\pi \times R}{r_\pi + R}} + 1\right)\frac{r_e}{\alpha}$

$= \left(\frac{R}{r_\pi} + 2\right)\frac{r_e}{\alpha}$

Now for $\beta = \infty$, $R = 700$, $R_o = 4.3k \| 1.4k \| 2(25) = \underline{\underline{47.7\,\Omega}}$

$R = 7k$, $R_o = 4.3k \| 1.4k \| 2(13.2) = \underline{\underline{26.1\,\Omega}}$

for $\beta = 50$, $R = 700$, $R_o = 4.3k \| 1.4k \| \left(\frac{700}{51(25)} + 2\right)(25) =$

$= \underbrace{4.3k \| 1.4k}_{1.06k} \| \underbrace{2.55(25)}_{63.8} = \underline{\underline{60.2\,\Omega}}$

$R = 7k$, $R_o = 1.06k \| \left(\frac{7000}{51(13.2)} + 2\right)13.2 =$

$= 1.06k \| (12.4)(13.2) = \underline{\underline{142\,\Omega}}$

For V_o: For 7k, $V_o = .716 + 7\left(\frac{0.716}{7} + \frac{1.9}{51}\right) = \underline{\underline{1.69\text{ V}}}$ } no load

(I=0) For 0.7k, $V_o = .700 + 0.7\left(\frac{0.7}{0.7} + \frac{1}{51}\right) = \underline{\underline{1.414\text{ V}}}$

(b) For $R = 7k$, $\beta = 50$, $I = 1\text{mA}$ → $I_E = 1.9 - 1 = 0.9\text{mA}$

$V_{BE} = 700 + V_T \ln \frac{0.9}{1} = 639\text{ mV}$, $r_e = \frac{25}{0.9} = 28\,\Omega$

Now $V_o = .639 + 7\left(\frac{.639}{7} + \frac{0.9}{51}\right) = 1.401\text{V}$

Thus as I varies from 0 to 1mA, V_o falls from

$\underline{\underline{1.69\text{V}}}$ to $\underline{\underline{1.40\text{V}}}$

(a) V_o for $\beta = \infty$ and $I = 0$ } For $R = 700$, $V_o = 2(0.70) = \underline{\underline{1.40\text{V}}}$

$R = 7k$, $V_o = 2(0.716) = \underline{\underline{1.43\text{V}}}$

9

1 $v_{O1} = v_{O2} = 5 - 1.25k(0.98)\frac{0.8\text{mA}}{2} = \underline{\underline{4.51\text{V}}}$

2 Q_1 is on. $v_{C1} = 5 - 1.25k(0.98)(0.8\text{ mA}) = \underline{\underline{4.02\text{V}}}$

$v_{C2} = \underline{\underline{5\text{V}}}$

3 $v_I = -0.7$, $v_E = 0.0\text{V}$, $v_{C2} = \underline{-5\text{V}}$

$v_{C1} = -5 + \frac{5}{1k} \times 1k = 0$ → ∴ saturated and

$v_{C1} = -0.7 + (0.7 - 0.3) = \underline{\underline{-0.3\text{V}}}$

4 $i_{E1} = 0.90\,I$, $i_{E2} = 0.10\,I \rightarrow i_{C1} = 9 i_{C2}$

But $i_C = I_S e^{v_{BE}/nV_T}$ or $v_{BE} = V_T \ln i_C/I_S$, $n = 1$

$\therefore v_{BE1} - v_{BE2} = V_T(\ln i_{C1} - \ln I_S - (\ln i_{C2} - \ln I_S))$

$= V_T(\ln i_{C1} - \ln i_{C2}) = V_T \ln \frac{i_{C1}}{i_{C2}} = V_T \ln 9$

$= \underline{\underline{54.9\text{ mV}}}$

5 $\frac{i_{E1}}{I} = \frac{1}{1 + e^{\Delta V/V_T}}$, $\Delta V = v_{B1} - v_{B2}$ **9**

ΔV mV	i_{E1}/I	Normalized Differences
0	0.500	
		$\frac{0.5 - 0.45}{5\text{ mV}} = 10.0$
5	0.450	
		9.8
10	0.401	
		9.4
15	0.354	
		8.8
20	0.310	
		7.9
30	0.231	
		6.3
40	0.168	
		4.9
50	0.119	

6 $e^{v_d/2V_T} = 1 + \frac{v_d}{2V_T} + \frac{1}{2!}\left(\frac{v_d}{2V_T}\right)^2 + \cdots$

(1st dropped)/(last included) $= \frac{\frac{1}{2!}\left(\frac{v_d}{2V_T}\right)^2}{v_d/2V_T} = \frac{1}{2!}\cdot\frac{v_d}{2V_T}$

i.e. $\boxed{\text{ratio} = \frac{v_d}{4V_T}}$

For $v_d = 2V_T$, ratio $= \frac{2V_T}{4V_T} = \underline{\underline{1/2}}$

For $v_d = V_T$, ratio $= \underline{\underline{1/4}}$

For ratio = 0.1, $\frac{v_d}{4V_T} = 0.1 \rightarrow v_d = 0.4V_T = 0.4(25) = \underline{\underline{10\text{mV}}}$

7 $I_{E1} = I_{E2} = 2\text{mA} \rightarrow r_{e1} = r_{e2} = \frac{25}{2} = 12.5\,\Omega$ **9**

$\therefore v_o = \frac{100\text{mV}}{2(12.5) + 2(100)} \times \alpha(2k) = \underline{\underline{0.8\dot{8}\text{ V}}}$

8 $v_o/v_i = \frac{2(10k)}{1/g_m + 1/g_m} = \frac{10k}{1/10} = \underline{\underline{100\text{ V/V}}}$

9 $r_e = 25\,\Omega$, gain $= \frac{100}{101} \times \frac{2k}{150 + 2(25)} = \underline{\underline{9.9\text{ V/V}}}$

$R_{in} = (\beta+1)(200) = 101(200) = \underline{\underline{20.2\text{ k}\Omega}}$

10 $R_{in} = 10\text{k}\Omega$, Gain (dido) = 100

$10k = (\beta+1)\,2r_e \rightarrow (\beta+1) r_e = 5$

$100 = \frac{5k}{r_e} \times \frac{\beta}{\beta+1} = \frac{5\beta}{5} \rightarrow \underline{\underline{\beta = 100}}$

$r_e = \frac{5}{101} = 49.5\,\Omega$, $I/2 = \frac{25}{49.5} = .505\text{mA}$

$I = 1.01\text{ mA} \approx \underline{1\text{mA}}$

11 $\beta = 100$, $r_e = \frac{25}{5} = 5\,\Omega$

$R_{in} = 101(2(5) + 2(10)) = \underline{\underline{3030\,\Omega}}$

Gain $= \frac{100}{101} \cdot \frac{1k}{30} = \underline{\underline{33.0}}$

12 $r_e = \frac{25}{.25} = 100\Omega$ **9**

Differential Out: $G_D = \frac{10k}{100} = 100$, $G_{cm} = 0$] CMRR $= \underline{\underline{\infty}}$

Single-Ended Out: $G_D = \frac{100}{2} = 50$, $G_{cm} = \frac{10k}{4M} = .0025$] CMRR $= \frac{50}{.0025} = \underline{\underline{20{,}000}}$

13 $\frac{10k}{2R} = 10^{-40/20} \rightarrow R = \frac{10k}{2\times10^{-2}} = 5\times10^{5} = \underline{\underline{500k}}$

(or) $10k/2R = .01 \rightarrow R = \frac{10}{0.02}k = 500k$

14 $A_{cm_{do}} = \frac{R_C}{2R}\times\frac{\Delta R_C}{R_C}$, $A_{cm_{seo}} = \frac{R_C}{2R}$

$\therefore \frac{\Delta R_C}{R_C} = 10^{\frac{(-80+40)}{20}} = \frac{1}{100} \rightarrow \underline{\underline{1\%}}$ mismatch

ie $\frac{R_{C1}}{R_{C2}} = \frac{R_C+\Delta R_C}{R_C} = 1 + \frac{\Delta R_C}{R_C} = 1.01$

15 Currents split 2/3 in the larger and 1/3 in the other.

$v_{o1} = \frac{2}{3}\times\frac{v_{cm}}{R}\times R_C = \frac{20k}{3M}\times v_{cm}$

$v_{o2} = \frac{1}{3}\times\frac{v_{cm}\times R_C}{R} = \frac{10k}{3M}\times v_{cm}$

$\frac{v_{o1}-v_{o2}}{v_{cm}} = \frac{20k-10k}{3M} = \frac{10^4}{3\times10^6} = 3.\dot{3}\times10^{-3}$

ie common mode gain $= \underline{\underline{3.\dot{3}\times10^{-3}}} \equiv 20\log_{10}3.\dot{3}\times10^{-3} = \underline{\underline{-49.5\,dB}}$

16 $\beta = 200$, $V_A = 100V$, $r_\mu = 10\beta r_o$ **9**

$I_C = 50\mu A$, $r_o = \frac{V_A}{I_C} = \frac{100}{50\times10^{-6}} = 2M\Omega$, $r_\mu = 10(200)(2) = 4G\Omega$

$R_{cm} = r_\mu/2 \,\|\, \left((\beta+1)\left(\frac{r_o}{2}\|R\right)\right) = \frac{4\times10^9}{2}\,\|\left(201\left(\frac{2\times10^6}{2}\|4\times10^6\right)\right)$

$= 2000M \,\|\, 160.8M = \underline{\underline{149\,M\Omega}}$

Note R_C was ignored as small with respect to r_o, r_μ

$R_{dm} = (\beta+1)(2r_e) = 201(2)\left(\frac{25}{0.1/2}\right) = \underline{\underline{201\,k\Omega}}$

17

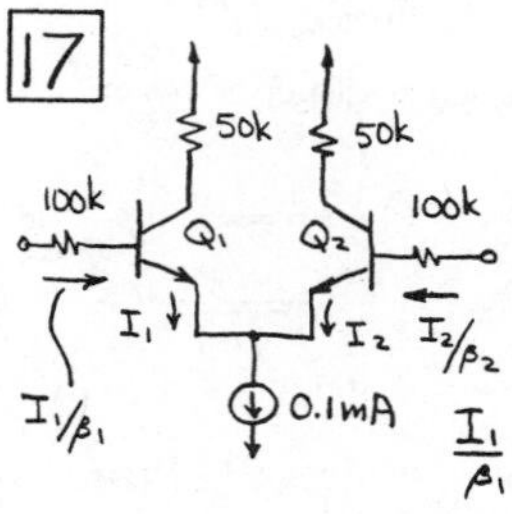

Let $\beta_1 = 200 + 10\%\times200 = 220$

$\beta_2 = 200 - 10\%\times200 = 180$

DC bias $I_1 = 0.05 + \Delta I$

$I_2 = 0.05 - \Delta I$

$\frac{I_1}{\beta_1}\times100 + V_{BE1} = \frac{I_2}{\beta_2}\times100 + V_{BE2}$

$V_{BE1} - V_{BE2} = \frac{I_2\times100}{180} - \frac{I_1\times100}{220}$

ie $V_T\ln I_1/I_S - V_T\ln I_2/I_S = I_2/1.8 - I_1/2.2$

or $V_T\ln I_1/I_2 = I_2/1.8 - I_1/2.2$

or $V_T\ln\frac{0.05+\Delta I}{0.05-\Delta I} = \frac{0.05-\Delta I}{1.8} - \frac{0.05+\Delta I}{2.2}$

(next)

Now $V_T\ln\frac{1+\Delta I/.05}{1-\Delta I/.05} = 0.05\left(\frac{1}{1.8}-\frac{1}{2.2}\right) - \Delta I\left(\frac{1}{1.8}+\frac{1}{2.2}\right)$ **9**

Approximate: $\ln\frac{1+x}{1-x} \simeq \ln(1+2x) \approx 2x$

Thus $V_T\times\frac{2\Delta I}{0.05} = 0.05\left(\frac{1}{1.8}-\frac{1}{2.2}\right) - \Delta I\left(\frac{1}{1.8}+\frac{1}{2.2}\right)$

Whence $\Delta I = .0025\ mA$

Thus $I_1 = .0525\ mA$, $I_2 = .0475\ mA$

For common-mode gain:

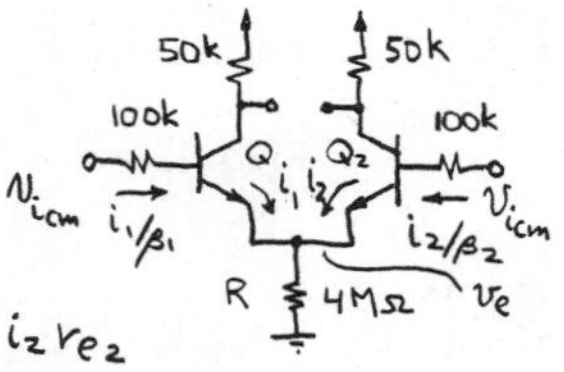

$r_{e1} = \frac{25}{.0525} = 476\Omega$

$r_{e2} = \frac{25}{.0475} = 526\Omega$

$i_1/\beta_1\times100 + i_1 r_{e1} = i_2/\beta_2\times100 + i_2 r_{e2}$

ie. $i_1/i_2 = \frac{100/180 + 0.526}{100/220 + 0.476} = 1.16$

But $(i_1+i_2) = v_e/R \rightarrow v_e = 2.16\,i_2 R$

Now $v_{icm} = i_2/\beta_2\times100 + i_2 r_{e2} + v_e$

or $v_{icm} = \frac{i_2}{1.8} + i_2(0.526) + 2.16\,i_2\times4000$

or $i_2 = v_{icm}/\left(1/1.8 + 0.526 + 2.16(4000)\right) \approx \frac{v_{icm}}{2.16\times4000}$

and $i_1 = 1.16\,i_2 = \frac{1.16\,v_{icm}}{2.16\times4000}$

Now $v_o = (i_1-i_2)R_C = 0.16\,i_2 R_C = \frac{0.16\,v_{icm}\times50}{2.16\times4000}$

Thus $A_{cm} = \frac{v_o}{v_{icm}} = \frac{0.16\times50}{2.16\times4000} = \underline{\underline{9.3\times10^{-4}\,V/V}} \equiv -60.6\,dB$

18

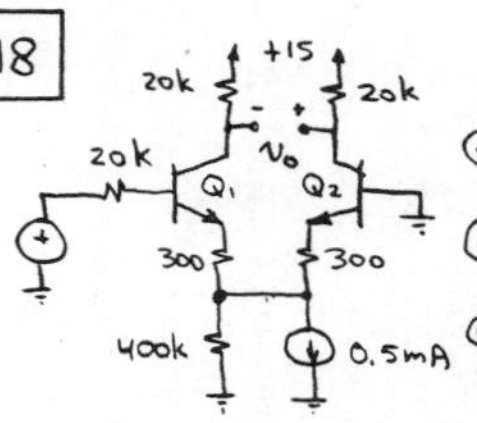

$\beta = 100$, $r_e = \frac{25}{0.25} = 100\Omega$ **9**

ⓐ $R_{id} = (\beta+1)(2(100+300)) = \underline{\underline{80.8\,k\Omega}}$

ⓑ $Gain_d = \frac{100}{101}\times\frac{20k}{800}\times\frac{80.8}{20+80.8}\times2 = \underline{\underline{39.6\,V/V}}$

ⓒ $Gain_{cm} = \frac{20k}{2(400k)}\times2\left(\frac{1}{100}\right) = \underline{\underline{5\times10^{-4}\,V/V}}$

ⓓ CMRR $= 20\log_{10}\frac{39.6}{5\times10^{-4}} = \underline{\underline{98\,dB}}$

ⓔ $R_{icm} = \frac{r_\mu}{2}\,\|\left(\left(R\,\|\,\frac{r_o}{2}\right)(\beta+1)\right)$

where $r_o = \frac{V_A}{I_C} = \frac{100}{.25} = 400k$, $r_\mu = 10\beta r_o = 10(10^2)(4\times10^5) = 4\times10^8\Omega$

Whence $R_{icm} = 200M\,\|\left((400k\,\|\,200k)\right)101 = 13.5M\,\|\,200M = \underline{\underline{12.6\,M\Omega}}$

19 $I_{S2} = 2I_{S1} \rightarrow i_{c1} \doteq I/3$, $i_{c2} \doteq 2I/3$

$V_{o1} = \frac{R_C I}{3}$, $V_{o2} = \frac{2R_C I}{3} \rightarrow$ Output offset $= V_{o2} - V_{o1} = \frac{R_C I}{3}$

Small signal analysis: $r_{e1} = \frac{V_T}{I/3}$, $r_{e2} = \frac{V_T}{2I/3}$

To rebalance making $i_{c1} = i_{c2}$, need $\Delta i_c = (2/3 - 1/2)I = I/6$

Required input, $\Delta v_d = I/6\,(r_{e1}+r_{e2}) = I/6\,(V_T)\left(\frac{1}{I/3}+\frac{1}{2I/3}\right)$

or $\Delta v_d = \frac{V_T}{6}(3 + 3/2) = 3/4\,V_T = \underline{\underline{0.75V_T}}$

Large signal analysis: $i_1 = I_S e^{V_1/V_T} = I/2$; $i_2 = 2I_S e^{V_2/V_T} = I/2$

$\therefore e^{\frac{V_1-V_2}{V_T}} = 2 \rightarrow \Delta V = V_1 - V_2 = V_T\ln 2 = \underline{\underline{0.693\,V_T}}$

9

Bias/offset Currents : $I = 0.1\,mA$, $\beta_1 = \beta_2 = 100$

Bias current $= \left(\frac{0.1}{3} + \frac{2(0.1)}{3}\right)/101 = \underline{1\mu A}$

Offset current $= \left(\frac{2}{3} - \frac{1}{3}\right)\frac{0.1}{101} = \underline{\frac{1}{3}\mu A}$

20 $V_{BB} = \frac{R_2}{R_1+R_2} \times V_{CC}$

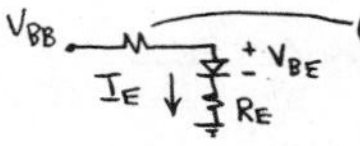

$$I_E = \frac{V_{BB} - V_{BE}}{\frac{R_1 \| R_2}{\beta+1} + R_E}, \quad I_O = \alpha I_E = \alpha \times \frac{\frac{R_2}{R_1+R_2} \times V_{CC} - V_{BE}}{\frac{1}{\beta+1}\frac{R_1 R_2}{R_1+R_2} + R_E}$$

21

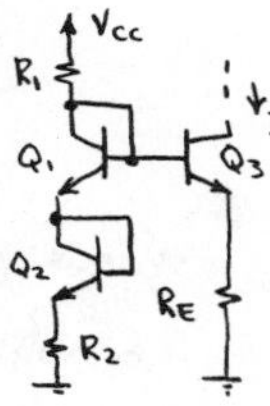

$\beta \gg 1$: V_{BE} are all the same if

$$\frac{V_{CC} - 2V_{BE}}{R_1 + R_2} = I_O R_E$$

If V_{BE} all same :

$$V_{CC} = I_O R_E + V_{BE} + R_1\left(\frac{I_O R_E - V_{BE}}{R_2}\right)$$

or $V_{CC} R_2 = I_O R_E R_2 + V_{BE} R_2 + R_1 I_O R_E - R_1 V_{BE}$

$$\text{or } I_O = \frac{V_{CC} R_2 - V_{BE} R_2 + V_{BE} R_1}{R_E R_2 + R_E R_1} = \frac{V_{CC}\frac{R_2}{R_1+R_2} + V_{BE}\frac{(R_1 - R_2)}{R_1+R_2}}{R_E}$$

See independant of V_{BE} if $R_1 = R_2$

for which $I_O = \frac{V_{CC}/2}{R_E}$

Actually $\frac{I_O}{\alpha} = \frac{V_{CC}}{2R_E} \rightarrow I_O = \frac{\alpha V_{CC}}{2R_E}$

9

For 15V, $\alpha = 1$, $V_{BE} = 0.7$, $I_O = 1mA$

$$R_1 = R_2 = R_E\left(1 - \frac{2(0.7)}{15}\right)$$

$$R_E = \frac{V_{CC}}{2 I_O} = \frac{15}{2(1)} = 7.5k\Omega$$

$$R_1 = R_2 = 7.5\left(1 - \frac{1.4}{15}\right) = \underline{6.8k\Omega}$$

Lowest useable output voltage $= \frac{15}{2} + 0.3 = \underline{7.8V}$

22

$$\frac{I}{(\beta+1) I} \times 100 = \frac{100}{101} = \underline{0.99\,\%}$$

23

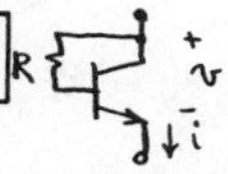

$$r = v/i = r_e + \frac{R}{\beta+1}$$

24

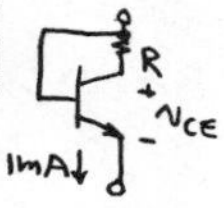

$$v_{CE} = v_{BE} - R i_C$$

$$V_{CE} + v_{ce} = V_{BE} + v_{be} - R I_C - r i_c$$

$v_{ce} = v_{be} - R i_c = r_e i_e - R i_c = 0$ when $\underline{R = r_e/\alpha} = 1/g_m$

$R = \underline{25\Omega}$ at 1mA

25 $R = \frac{5 - 0.7}{1mA} = 4.3k\Omega$,

$v_C \le 0.3$ is likely OK. $v_C \le 0$ is assured.

26 **9**

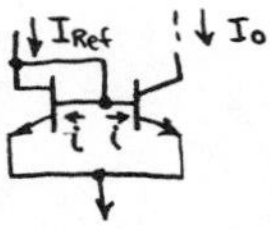

$$I_O = \beta i, \quad I_{Ref} = \beta i + 2i$$

$$I_O/I_{Ref} = \frac{\beta}{\beta+2} = \frac{1}{1 + 2/\beta}$$

$I_O/I_{Ref} \geq 90\,\%$ for $1 = (1 + 2/\beta)0.9$ or $1 - .9 = \frac{1.8}{\beta}$

or $\beta = \frac{1.8}{.1} = \underline{18}$

$I_O/I_{Ref} \geq 99\,\%$ for $1 = (1 + 2/\beta)(0.99)$ or $1 - .99 = \frac{1.98}{\beta}$

or $\beta = \frac{1.98}{.01} = \underline{198}$

27

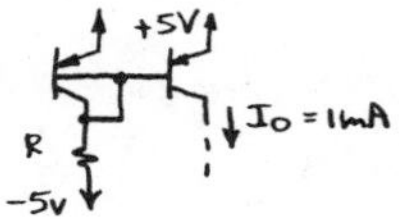

$$R = \frac{5 - (-5) - 0.7}{1mA} = \underline{9.3\,k\Omega}$$

$$r_o = \frac{V_A}{I_C} = \frac{100}{1mA} = 100k\Omega$$

$\therefore$ at $+4.3V$, $I_O = 1mA$

and at $-5.0V$, $I_O = 1mA + \frac{5+4.3}{100k} = 1.093\,mA$

$\therefore$ Change in output current is $\underline{0.093}$ mA over $+4.3/-5$

28 $\beta = 100$, $r_o = \frac{100}{1mA} = 100k\Omega$, $R_{o_{wilson}} = \beta r_o/2$

I_O ranges from 1mA @ +3.6V to $1 + \frac{3.6+5}{100(100k/2)}$

or 1.0017 mA @ −5V for a change of $\underline{1.7\mu A}$ or

only $\frac{1.7}{1000} \times 100 = \underline{1.7\,\%}$. Note $R = \frac{5-(-5)-2(0.7)}{1mA} = \underline{8.6k\Omega}$

29 **9**

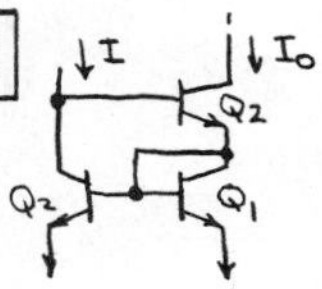

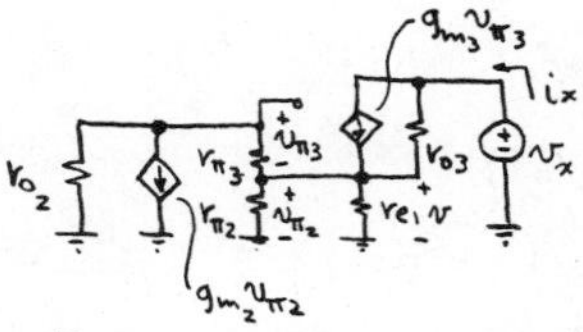

Ignore r_{o2} as $\gg r_{\pi 3}$. T_1, T_2, T_3 operate at essentially same I.

and their corresponding parameters are equal (β, g_m, r_π)

$$\text{See } i_x = \frac{v}{r_{e_1}} + \frac{v}{r_{\pi_2}} + g_{m2} v = v\left(\frac{1}{r_e} + \frac{1}{r_\pi} + g_m\right)$$

$$= v\left(\frac{1}{r_e} + \frac{1}{(\beta+1) r_e} + \frac{\beta}{\beta+1}\cdot\frac{1}{r_e}\right) = v\left(\frac{\beta+1+1+\beta}{(\beta+1) r_e}\right) = \frac{2v}{r_e}$$

$$\text{Also } i_x = \frac{v_x - v}{r_{o_3}} - g_{m_2} v\, r_{\pi_3} g_{m_3} = \frac{v_x - v}{r_o} - g_m^2 r_\pi v$$

$$\therefore v_x = r_o \frac{2v}{r_e} + v + g_m^2 r_\pi r_o v = v\left(1 + \frac{2 r_o}{r_e} + g_m^2 r_\pi r_o\right)$$

$$\text{Thus } R_o = \frac{v_x}{i_x} = \frac{v\,(1 + 2r_o/r_e + g_m^2 r_\pi r_o)}{2v/r_e}$$

$$= \left(r_e + 2r_o + \frac{r_e \beta}{(\beta+1)} \times \frac{1}{r_e} \times \frac{\beta}{\beta+1} \times \frac{1}{r_e} \times (\beta+1) r_e \times r_o\right)/2$$

$$= r_e/2 + r_o + \frac{\beta \alpha r_o}{2} \approx \boxed{\frac{\beta r_o}{2}} \text{ as stated}$$

30

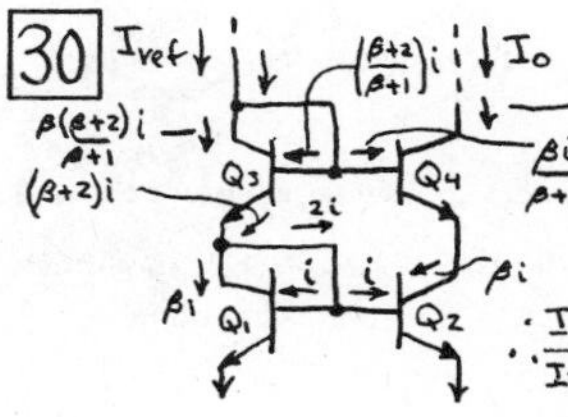

$$\text{See } I_{ref} = \left(\frac{\beta(\beta+2)}{\beta+1} + \frac{\beta+2}{\beta+1} + \frac{\beta}{\beta+1}\right) i$$

$$= \frac{\beta^2 + 2\beta + \beta + 2 + \beta}{\beta+1} \times i$$

$$= \frac{\beta^2 + 4\beta + 2}{\beta+1} \times i$$

$$\therefore \frac{I_O}{I_{ref}} = \frac{\frac{\beta^2}{\beta+1}}{\frac{\beta^2 + 4\beta + 2}{\beta+1}} = \frac{1}{1 + \frac{4}{\beta} + \frac{2}{\beta^2}}$$

9

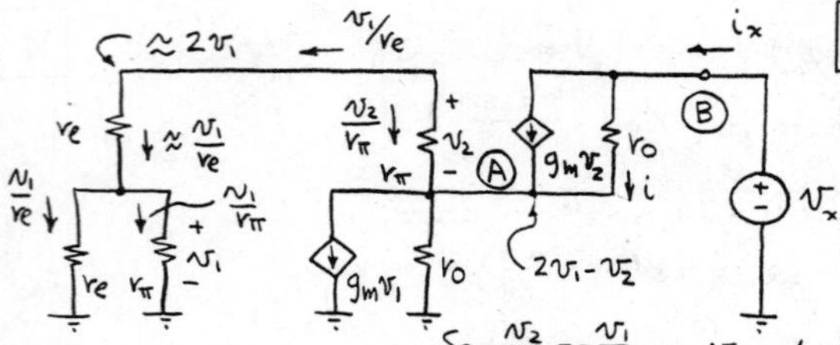

See $\frac{v_2}{r_\pi} = -\frac{v_1}{r_e} \rightarrow v_2 = -(\beta+1)v_1$ - ①

Node Eq. at Ⓐ: $g_m v_1 + \frac{2v_1 - v_2}{r_o} = \frac{v_2}{r_\pi} + g_m v_2 + i$

Thus $i = g_m v_1 + \frac{2v_1}{r_o} - \frac{v_2}{r_o} - \frac{v_2}{r_\pi} - g_m v_2$

With ① $\rightarrow i = v_1\left[g_m + 2/r_o + (\beta+1)/r_o + (\beta+1)/r_\pi + g_m(\beta+1)\right]$ - ②

At output: $v_x = i r_o + 2v_1 - v_2 = i r_o + 2v_1 + (\beta+1)v_1$ {with ①}

With ② and $g_m = (\beta+1)/r_\pi$

$v_x = v_1\left[g_m r_o + 2 + \beta + 1 + g_m r_o + g_m r_o(\beta+1) + 2 + \beta + 1\right]$

or $v_x = v_1\left[2\beta + 6 + g_m r_o(\beta+3)\right]$

or $v_x = v_1(\beta+3)(2 + g_m r_o) \approx v_1 \beta g_m r_o$ -- - ③

Now $i_x = i + g_m v_2 = v_1\left(g_m + \frac{2}{r_o} + \frac{\beta+1}{r_o} + \frac{\beta+1}{r_\pi} + g_m(\beta+1) - g_m(\beta+1)\right)$

ie $i_x = v_1\left(g_m + \frac{2}{r_o} + \frac{\beta+1}{r_o} + \frac{\beta+1}{r_\pi}\right) = v_1\left(2g_m + \frac{\beta+3}{r_o}\right) \approx 2g_m v_1$ - ④

From ③, ④, $R_{out} = v_x/i_x = \frac{v_1 \beta g_m r_o}{2 g_m v_1} = \frac{\beta r_o}{2}$

31

9

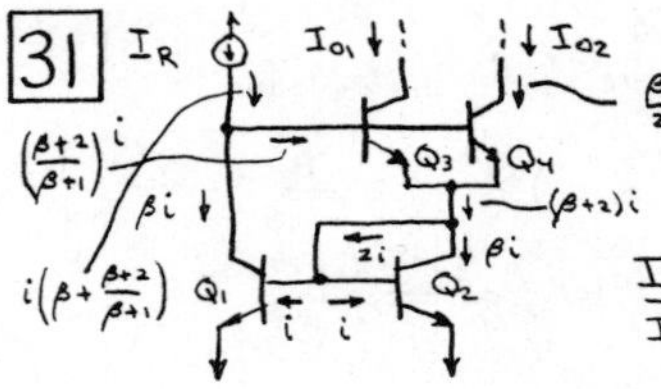

$\frac{I_{O2}}{I_R} = \frac{\beta/2\left(\frac{\beta+2}{\beta+1}\right)i}{\left(\frac{\beta+2}{\beta+1} + \beta\right)i}$

$\frac{I_{O1}}{I_R} = \frac{I_{O2}}{I_R} = \frac{1}{2} \times \frac{\beta^2 + 2\beta}{\beta^2 + 2\beta + 2} = \frac{1}{2} \times \frac{1}{1 + \frac{2}{\beta^2 + 2\beta}}$

32

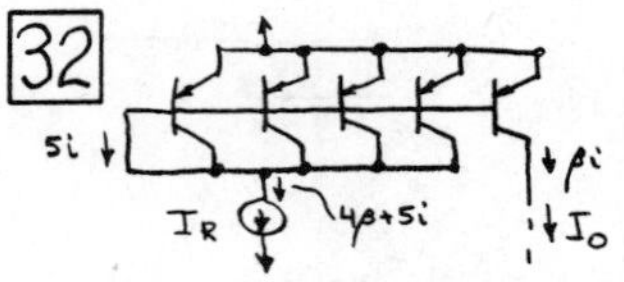

$\frac{I_O}{I_R} = \frac{\beta i}{(4\beta+5)i} = \frac{1}{4}\,\frac{1}{1 + \frac{5}{4\beta}}$

33

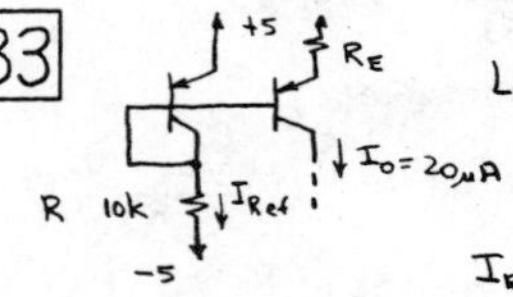

Largest R is 10k – use for R

Ignore β, $V_{EB} = 0.7$ @ 1mA

$I_{Ref} = \frac{(5 - 0.7 - (-5))}{10k} \doteq 0.93mA$

$i_C = I_S e^{V_{EB}/V_T} \rightarrow V_{EB1} - V_{EB2} = V_T \ln \frac{i_{C1}}{i_{C2}} = 25 \ln \frac{930}{20} = 95.99mV$

$\therefore R_E = \frac{95.99}{20\mu A} = 4.8k\Omega$. Highest output is 5-0.7 = 4.3V where $I_O = 20\mu A$.

Now from Eq 9.78, $R_o = (1 + g_m(R_E \| r_\pi))r_o$

9

Since β is high, $R_o = (1 + g_m R_E)r_o$ where

$\frac{1}{g_m} \approx \frac{25mV}{20\mu A} = 1250\Omega$ and $r_o = \frac{100V}{20\times10^{-6}} = 5M\Omega$

or $R_o = \left(1 + \frac{4800}{1250}\right)5\times10^6 = 24.2M\Omega$

Thus for Vo at -5, increase in Io is $\frac{5+4.3}{24.2M} = 0.384\mu A$,

For Vo ranging from -5 to +4.3, Io ranges from 20.4 to 20.0μA

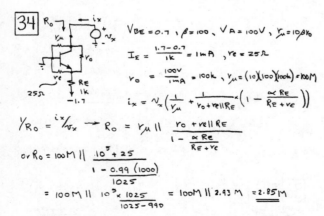

34

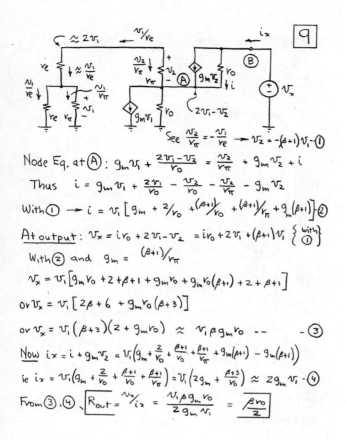

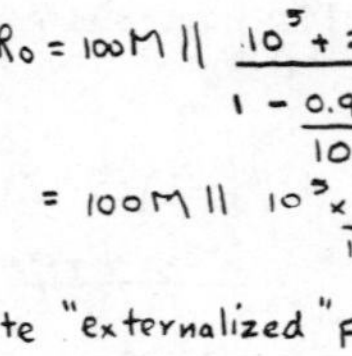

$V_{BE} = 0.7$, $\beta = 100$, $V_A = 100V$, $r_\mu = 10\beta r_o$

$I_E = \frac{1.7 - 0.7}{1k} = 1mA$, $r_e = 25\Omega$

$r_o = \frac{100V}{1mA} = 100k$, $r_\mu = (10)(100)(100k) = 100M$

$i_x = v_x\left(\frac{1}{r_\mu} + \frac{1}{r_o + r_e \| R_E}\times\left(1 - \frac{\alpha R_E}{R_E + r_e}\right)\right)$

$1/R_o = i_x/v_x \rightarrow R_o = r_\mu \| \frac{r_o + r_e \| R_E}{1 - \frac{\alpha R_E}{R_E + r_e}}$

or $R_o = 100M \| \frac{10^5 + 25}{1 - \frac{0.99(1000)}{1025}}$

$= 100M \| 10^5 \times \frac{1025}{1025 - 990} = 100M \| 2.93M = 2.85M$

Note "externalized" parameters used above as an alternative to complete modelling. Only the α generator is implicit

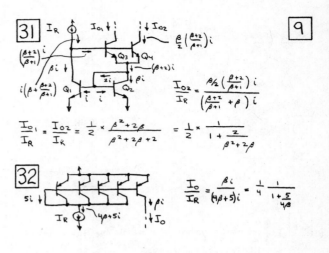

35 Assume $|V_{BE}| = 0.7$, $\beta = \infty$

9

See $V_{C1} = 10 - 0.7 = 9.3V$, $V_{C2} = -10 + 0.7 = 9.3 = V_{B2,7,8,9}$

$I_{R1} = \frac{9.3 - (-9.3)}{10k} = 1.86mA$, $I_{C7} = I_{C8} = 1.86mA$

$I_{R4} = 2(1.86) = 3.72mA$, $V_{C7} = 0 - 1(3.72) = -3.72V$

$I_{C9} = I_{C10} = I_{C11} = 1.86mA$, $V_{B10,11} = V_{C9,10} = 4.3V$

$I_{R5} = 1.86mA$, $V_{C11} = 1.86V$, $V_{B1,3,4} = 9.3V$

$I_{C1} = I_{C3} = I_{C4} = I_{R1} = 1.86mA$, $V_{C3} = 2(1.86) = 3.72V$

$I_{C6} = I_{C5} = I_{C4} = 1.86mA$, $V_{C5} = V_{B5,6} = 0.7V$

$V_{C6} = 5 - 1(1.86) = 3.14V$

36

$I_O/I_{Ref} = \frac{5i\beta}{\beta i + 6i} = 5 \times \frac{1}{1 + \frac{6}{\beta}}$

37 Need $V_{C1} = V_{C2} = +12$, $V_{C5} = 13$, for which $V_{E7} = 13.7$

$R_{C1} = R_{C2} = \frac{15-12}{0.25} = 12k\Omega$, $R_{C5} = \frac{15-13}{1} = 2k\Omega$, $R_{E7} = \frac{15-13.7}{1} = 1.3k$

Common mode range extends from +12 to -14.3+0.7 = -13.6V

38 $\beta = \infty$, $|V_{BE}| = 0.7V$ **9**

R_Ω	I mA	V_1	V_2	V_3	V_4	V_5
10k	2	−0.7	5	0.7	−0.7	−5.7
100k	0.2	−0.7	5	0.7	−0.7	−5.7

39 For $v > 0$, $i = \frac{v}{R}$ for $v_{C2} \le v$ {or $v + 0.4$ or so}

For a tap on R, the output voltage range is extended: eg. for a tap at 0.1R, to $v_2 \le 10v$

40

(a)

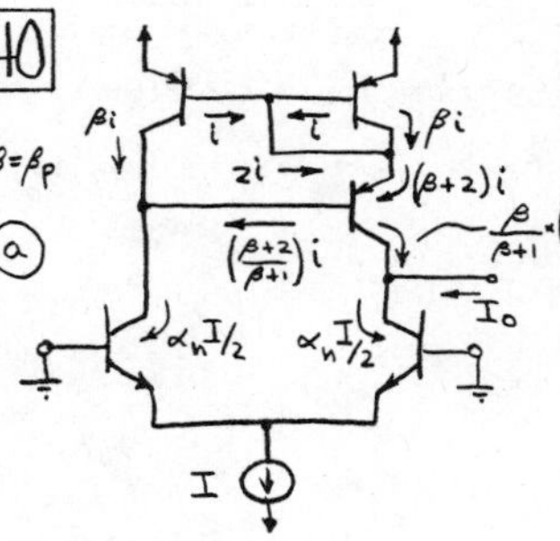

For balance at the left

$$\alpha_n I/2 = i\left(\beta + \frac{\beta+2}{\beta+1}\right)$$

$$= i\,\frac{(\beta^2+2\beta+2)}{\beta+1}$$

ie. $i = \alpha_n I/2 \times \frac{\beta}{\beta^2+2\beta+2}$

(next)

At output: $I_o = \alpha_n I/2 - \frac{\beta}{\beta+1}(\beta+2)\alpha_n I/2\left(\frac{\beta}{\beta^2+2\beta+2}\right)$ **9**

ie. $I_o = \alpha_n I/2 \left\{\frac{\beta^2+2\beta+2-\beta^2-2\beta}{\beta^2+2\beta+2}\right\}$

$$= \alpha_n I/2\ \frac{2}{\beta^2+2\beta+2} = \frac{\alpha_n I}{\beta^2+2\beta+2}$$

or $I_o \approx \frac{\alpha_n I}{\beta_p^2}$

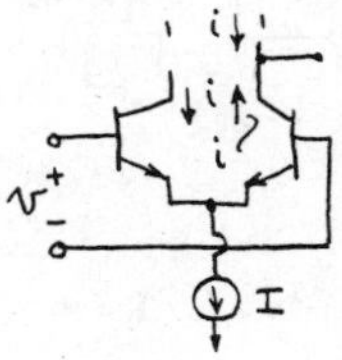

(b) To reduce $I_o \approx I/\beta_p^2$ to zero, apply an input voltage v as shown and adjust its value so $2i = I/\beta_p^2$

But $i = \frac{v}{2r_e} = \frac{v}{2V_T/(I/2)}$

whence $I/\beta_p^2 = \frac{2v}{2V_T} \times I/2$ or $v = \frac{2V_T}{\beta_p^2}$

Thus $V_{off} = 2V_T/\beta_p^2$

(c) For $\beta_p = 25$

$$V_{off} = \frac{2(25)}{25^2} = 0.08\,mV$$

41 **9**

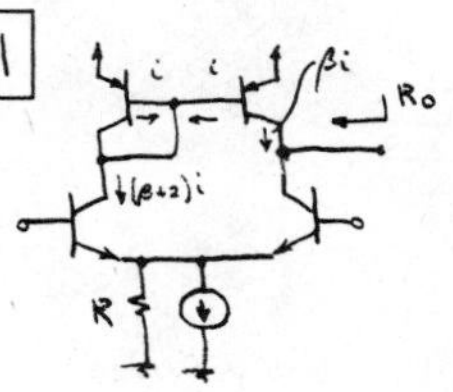

$$\frac{v_{ocm}}{v_{icm}} = \left(\frac{R_o}{2R} - \frac{\beta}{\beta+2} \times \frac{R_o}{2R}\right)$$

$$= \frac{R_o}{2R}\left(\frac{2}{\beta+2}\right)$$

$$\frac{v_{od}}{v_{id}} = \frac{R_o}{2r_e} \cdot \frac{\beta}{\beta+2} + \frac{R_o}{2r_e}$$

$$= \frac{R_o}{2r_e}\left(\frac{2\beta+2}{\beta+2}\right)$$

$$CMRR = \frac{\frac{R_o}{2r_e}\left(\frac{2\beta+2}{\beta+2}\right)}{\frac{R_o}{2R}\left(2/\beta+2\right)} = \frac{g_m}{\alpha_n} R \times (\beta_p + 1) \approx g_m R \beta_p$$

42 Output resistance of the modified circuit is $r_o \| \frac{\beta r_o}{2} = \frac{r_o\,\beta r_o/2}{r_o + \beta r_o/2} = \frac{\beta}{\beta+2} \times r_o$, or about 2x normal

Open circuit gain is $\frac{v_o}{v_i} = \frac{\beta}{\beta+2} r_o \left(\frac{\alpha}{2r_e} + \frac{\alpha}{2r_e}\right)$

or $\frac{\beta_p}{\beta_p+2} \times g_{m_n} r_o$, assuming $r_{o_n} = r_{o_p} = r_o$!

43 $I_{DSS} = 2mA$, $|V_p| = 2V$, $I = 0.5mA$

For all of 0.5mA in one device, $i_D = I_{DSS}\left(1 - \frac{v_{GS}}{V_P}\right)^2$

or $0.5 = 2\left(1 - \frac{v}{2}\right)^2 \rightarrow v = 1$ volt, ie $v_{GS_1} = 1V$. To cutoff the other $v_{GS2} = -2V$. Required $v_d = 2 - 1 = 1V$

44 $I_{DSS} = 2mA$, $|V_P| = 2V$, $I = 2mA$, $R_o = 100k$ **9**

$$g_m = \frac{2I_{DSS}}{V_P}\sqrt{\frac{I_D}{I_{DSS}}} = \frac{2(2)}{2}\sqrt{\frac{1}{2}} = 1.414\,mA/V$$

$$G_{d_{do}} = g_m R_L = 1.414(10k) = 14.14\,V/V$$

$$G_{cm_{do}} = \frac{1.01(10^4)}{200k} - \frac{0.99(10^4)}{200k} = \frac{2}{100} \times \frac{10^4}{2 \times 10^5} = 10^{-3}$$

$$CMRR = \frac{14.1}{10^{-3}} = 14 \times 10^{-3} = -37.1\,dB$$

Output offset $= 10k(1mA)\frac{2}{100} = 0.2$ Volts, but gain is 14.1 → input offset $= \frac{200\,mV}{14.14} = 14.1\,mV$

45

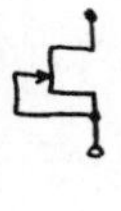

$I_{DSS} = 2mA$, $|V_P| = 2V$, $V_A = 100V$

$$r_o = \frac{V_A}{I_D} = \frac{100}{2 \times 10^{-3}} = 50\,k\Omega$$

46

$I_{DSS} = 8mA$, $V_P = -2$, $V_A = 100$, $I_D = 2mA$

$r_o = \frac{V_A}{I_D} = \frac{100}{2} = 50k\Omega$, $i_D = I_{DSS}\left(1 - \frac{v_{GS}}{V_P}\right)^2$

or $2 = 8\left(1 - \frac{v_{GS}}{2}\right)^2 \rightarrow v_{GS} = 1V$. Thus $R = \frac{1V}{2mA} = 500\Omega$

$$g_m = \frac{2I_{DSS}}{V_P}\sqrt{\frac{I_D}{I_{DSS}}} = \frac{2(8)}{2}\sqrt{\frac{2}{8}} = 4\,mA/V$$

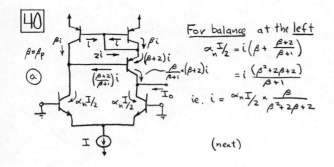

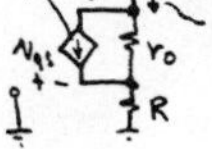

i_x $\frac{1}{R_o} = \frac{i_x}{v_x} = \frac{1}{r_o + R\|r_s}\left(1 - \frac{R}{r_s+R}\right) = \frac{r_s}{r_s+R} \times \frac{1}{r_o + \frac{Rr_s}{r_s+R}}$

$$= \frac{r_s}{r_o(r_s+R) + Rr_s} = \frac{1}{R + r_o(1 + R/r_s)} \rightarrow R_o = R + r_o(1 + g_m R)$$

Here $R_o = R + r_o(1 + g_m R) = 0.5 + 50(1 + 4 \times 0.5)$

$= \underline{150.5\,k\Omega}$

47

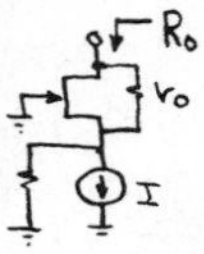

$I_{DSS} = 8mA,\ V_P = -2V,\ V_A = 100V$

$I = 2mA,\ r_o = \frac{100}{2} = 50k,\ g_m = 4mA/V$

From [46] $R_o = R + r_o(1 + g_m R)$

Now for $R = \infty$, $R_o = \infty + \cdots = \infty$

for $R = \frac{100}{I} = 50k$, $R_o = 50 + 50(1 + 4 \times 50) = 202(50k)$

or 10.1M

48 $W/L = 20$, $\mu C_{ox} = 20\mu A/V^2$, $K = \frac{1}{2}\mu C_{ox}\frac{W}{L} = \frac{1}{2}(20)(20)$

ⓐ or $K = \underline{200\mu A/V^2}$. Operation at $(V_{SS} - V_T) = 0.2$ for

$i_D = K(V_{GS} - V_T)^2 = 200(0.2)^2 = 8\mu A \rightarrow \therefore\ I = \underline{16\mu A}$

ⓑ $g_m = 2K(V_{GS} - V_T) = 2(200)(0.2) = \underline{80\mu A/V}$

ⓒ For full switching, $16\mu A = 200(v_{GS1} - V_T)^2$

and $0 = 200(v_{GS2} - V_T)^2 \rightarrow v_{GS2} = V_T$

$\therefore\ v_{GS1} - v_{GS2} = \sqrt{\frac{16}{200}} = \frac{4}{10} \cdot \frac{1}{\sqrt{2}} = \underline{.2828\,V} = v_{D\,full switch}$

ⓓ $r_o = \frac{V_A}{I_D} = \frac{24V}{8\mu A} = \underline{3M\Omega}$

ⓔ $K_1 = 1.04 K_2 = 200\mu A/V^2$, $i_D = K(v_{GS} - V_T)^2$

$\therefore\ v_{GS1} - V_T = \sqrt{\frac{8}{K_1}}$, $v_{GS2} - V_T = \sqrt{\frac{8}{K_2}}$ $\Big\}$ $v_{GS1} - v_{GS2} = \frac{\sqrt{8}}{\sqrt{K_1}}(1 - \sqrt{1.04})$

$= \sqrt{\frac{8}{200}}(.0198) = \underline{3.96mV}$

ⓕ For mirror load, $R_L = r_o/2$

$\text{Gain} = \frac{g_m R_L + g_m R_L}{2} = 80 \times 10^{-6} \times \frac{3 \times 10^6}{2} = \underline{120\ V/V}$

49 Cascode mirror (Fig 9.31b, 9.32b)

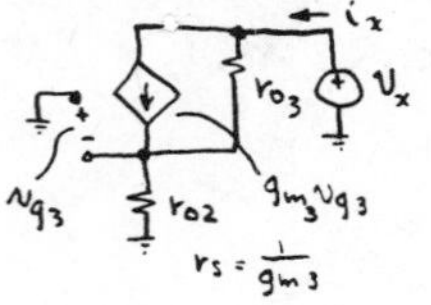

$\frac{1}{R_o} = \frac{i_x}{v_x} = \frac{1}{r_{o3} + r_s \| r_{o2}} \times \left(1 - \frac{r_{o2}}{r_s + r_{o2}}\right)$

$= \frac{r_s}{r_s + r_{o2}} \times \frac{1}{r_{o3} + \frac{r_s r_{o2}}{r_s + r_{o2}}}$

$= \frac{r_s}{r_s r_{o3} + r_{o2} r_{o3} + r_s r_{o2}}$

Thus $R_o = r_{o3} + \frac{r_{o2} r_{o3}}{r_s} + r_{o2} = r_{o2} + r_{o2} r_{o3} g_{m3} + r_{o3}$

as required. Note also $R_o = r_{o2} + r_{o3}(1 + g_{m3} r_{o2})$, a Miller formulation.

50 As suggested, assume all gates are grounded: Use result in [49]

$R_{o1} = r_{o1}$

$R_{o2} = R_{o1} + r_{o2} + g_{m2} R_{o1} r_{o2} = r_{o1} + r_{o2} + g_{m2} r_{o1} r_{o2}$

$R_{o3} = R_{o2} + r_{o3}(1 + g_{m3} R_{o2})$

$= r_{o1} + r_{o2}(1 + g_{m2} r_{o1}) + r_{o3}(1 + g_{m3}(r_{o1} + r_{o2}(1 + g_{m2} r_{o1})))$

$\approx g_m^2 r_o^3$ for all devices the same.

51 $i_D = K(v_{GS} - V_T)^2$

$\frac{\partial i_D}{\partial K}\Big|_{V_T\ const.} = (v_{GS} - V_T)^2 \rightarrow \Delta i_{D_K} = \Delta K (v_{GS} - V_T)^2$

$\frac{\partial i_D}{\partial V_T}\Big|_{K\ const.} = -2K(v_{GS} - V_T) \rightarrow \Delta i_{D_V} = -2K(v_{GS} - V_T)\Delta V_T$

Now $\Delta I_D = \Delta i_{D_K} + \Delta i_{D_V}$

and $\frac{\Delta I_D}{I_D} = \frac{\Delta i_{D_K} + \Delta i_{D_V}}{I_D} = \frac{\Delta K}{K} - \frac{2\Delta V_T}{(v_{GS} - V_T)}$ as req'd.

52 Assume the circuit "turns on" and I flows

$I_{D1} = K_1(v_{GS} - V_T)^2 = K_1(IR - V_T)^2 = I$ due to T_3 and T_4. Thus

$IR - V_T = \sqrt{I/K_1}$, or $IR = V_T + \sqrt{\frac{2I}{\mu_n C_{ox}(W/L)_1}}$ as req'd.

For $\mu C_{ox} = 20\mu A/V^2$ and $(W/L)_1 = 25$, $V_T = 1V$,

$I = 10\mu A$ when $10R = 1 + \sqrt{\frac{2 \times 10}{20 \times 25}} = 1 + 1/5$

or $R = \frac{1.2}{10} = \underline{.12\,M\Omega}$

Note that while positive feedback is provided by the loop Q_3, Q_2, Q_4, the gain is limited, and negative feedback is provided by Q_1 through Q_2, in increasing amounts as I↑

53 Assume I flows establishing operation of a positive feedback loop whose gain is controlled by Q_6 whose resistance lowers as I↑.

See $\boxed{IR = V_T \ln I/I_S}$ with $700 = V_T \ln \frac{1mA}{I_S}$

Thus for $I = 10\mu A \rightarrow R = \frac{1}{10 \times 10^{-6}}\left(700 + 25 \ln \frac{10 \times 10^{-6}}{1 \times 10^{-3}}\right) \times 10^{-3}$

or $R = \underline{58.4\,k\Omega}$

54 Gain of 1st stage $= \frac{(5k + 5k) \| (101)(2+2)}{2(10 + 40)} \cdot \frac{100}{101}$

$= \frac{10k \| 404}{100} \cdot \frac{100}{101} = \underline{3.84}$

55 $I_{E1} = I_{E2} = 0.25\,mA \rightarrow r_{e1} = r_{e2} = 100\Omega$

$I_{E3} = I_{E4} = 1mA \rightarrow r_{e3} = r_{e4} = 25\Omega$

When $R_{E3} = R_{E4} = 25\Omega$ introduced, R_{in} of 2nd stage doubles to $101(2(25+25)) = 10100\Omega$:

Gain of 1st stage $= \frac{(20k+20k)\|(10.1k)}{2(100+100)} = \underline{20.16}$ V/V (was 22.4)

R_{in} of 1st stage $= 101(2(100+100)) = \underline{40.4k}$ (doubled)

Overall gain $= \frac{8513}{22.4}(20.16)\times \frac{1}{2} = \underline{\underline{3831}}$ V/V ($\approx \frac{1}{2}$)
↑ due R_{E3}, R_{E4}

56 R_5 replaced by a 1mA source

A_3 changes from -6.42 V/V to $-\frac{303.5}{2.325} = \underline{\underline{130.5}}$ V/V
see P 537

Overall gain changes from 8521 to

$\frac{8513}{6.42}\times 130.5 = \underline{\underline{1.73\times 10^5}}$

57 Gain now depends more strongly on load, that is its output resistance has risen

Eg. $r_{i4} = (\beta+1)(r_{e8} + R_6 \| R_L)$, which for 100Ω load becomes $101(5 + 3k\|100) = \underline{\underline{10.3k}}$, (not 303k)

New gain $= \frac{173\times 10^3}{303.5}\times 10.3 = \underline{\underline{5871}}$ V/V

The gain of the original amplifier loaded by 100Ω is $8513 \times \frac{100}{100+152} = \underline{\underline{3381}}$ V/V, ie not as good!

58

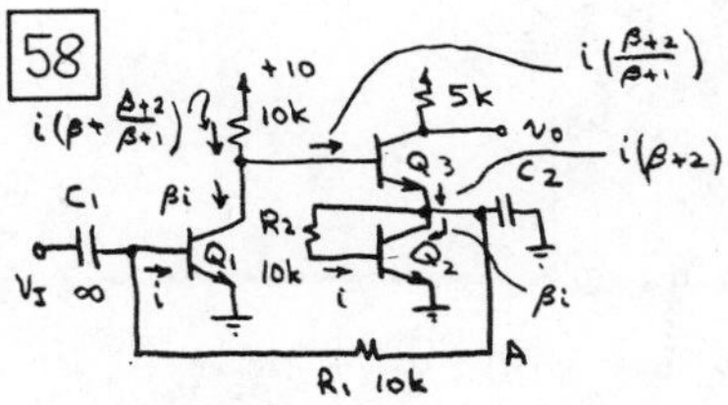

$\beta = 100$, $V_{BE} = 0.7$

$10 - 10k\left(\beta + \frac{\beta+2}{\beta+1}\right)i - 0.7 - 10k(i) - 0.7 = 0$

$10 - 10\left(100 + \frac{102}{101}\right)i - 1.4 - 10i = 0$

$8.6 - 1010i - 10i = 0 \rightarrow i = \frac{8.6}{1020} = 8.43\,\mu A$

$I_{E1} = 101(8.43) = .852\,mA$, $I_{E_3} = \frac{102}{101}(8.43) = .85\,mA$

$V_o = -\frac{100}{101}(.85)\times 5k + 10 = \underline{\underline{5.74V}}$

For $C_2 = \infty$: $r_{in3} = 101\,\frac{25}{.85} = 2970\Omega$, $r_{e3} = 29.4$, $r_{e1} = 29.3$

gain $= \frac{100}{101}\left(\frac{10k\|2.97k}{29.3}\right)\cdot\frac{5k}{29.4}\times\frac{100}{101} = 13\times 10^3$ V/V

For $C_2 = 0$: $R_{E3} = R_1 \| \frac{R_2 + r_{\pi 2}}{\beta+1} = 10k\|\left(\frac{10k}{101} + 29.4\right) = 128\Omega$

$R_{in3} = 101(29.4 + 128) = 15.9k$

Gain $\frac{v_o}{v_I} = \frac{100}{101}\frac{(10k\|15.9)}{29.3}\times\frac{100}{101}\frac{5k}{128+29.1} = 6.54\times 10^3$

R_{in} for $C_2 = \infty$, $R_{in} = 101(29.3)\|10k = \underline{2.28k\Omega}$

for $C_2 = 0$, Gain to node A is $-\frac{6.54\times 10^3\times 0.128k\times 101}{5k \qquad 100}$

or -169

Thus $R_{in} = 101(29.3)\|\frac{10k}{(1-(-169))} = \underline{\underline{57.7\Omega}}$

This is an interesting feedback topology as we shall see in Chapter 12

1

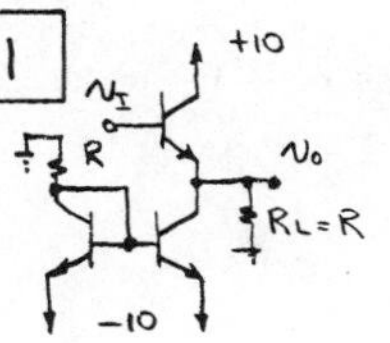

$v_o = R_L i_Q = R\left(\frac{0-10+0.7}{R}\right) = \underline{\underline{-9.3V}}$

2

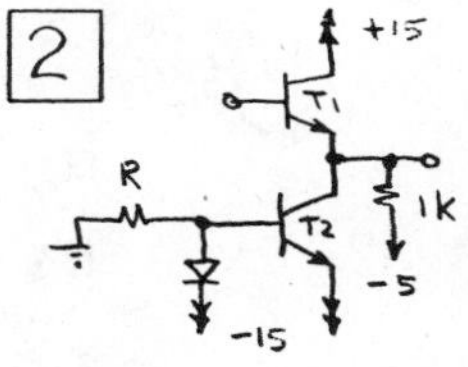

For $v_o = -10V$

$i_{c_2} = \frac{-5-(-10)}{1k} = \underline{\underline{5mA}}$

$R = \frac{15-0.7}{5mA} = \underline{2.86\,k\Omega}$

For follower gain of 0.98,

$\frac{1k}{r_e + 1k} = 0.98 \rightarrow r_e = \frac{1}{.98} - 1 = 20\Omega$

for which $I_{E1} = \frac{25mV}{20\Omega} = \underline{\underline{1.25}}\,mA$ as a minimum.

The required $R = \frac{15-0.7}{5+1.25} = \underline{\underline{2.29\,k\Omega}}$

For $\bar{v}_o = +10$, $I_{E1} = \frac{10+5}{1k} + 5 + 1.25 = \underline{\underline{21.25\,mA}}$

3

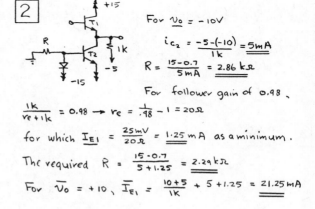

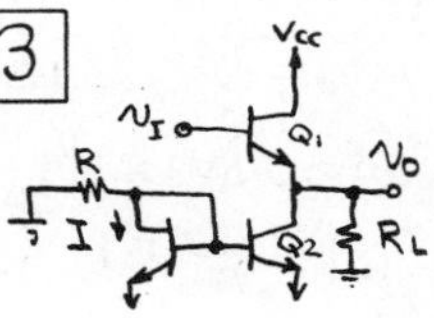

$R_L = \frac{V_{cc}}{I}$

10

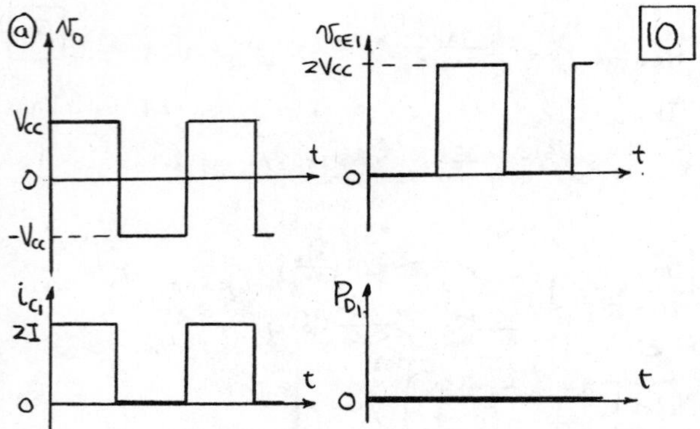

Av. pwr. dissipation in Q_1: For sq. wave is 0

For sine wave is $\frac{1}{2} V_{cc} I$

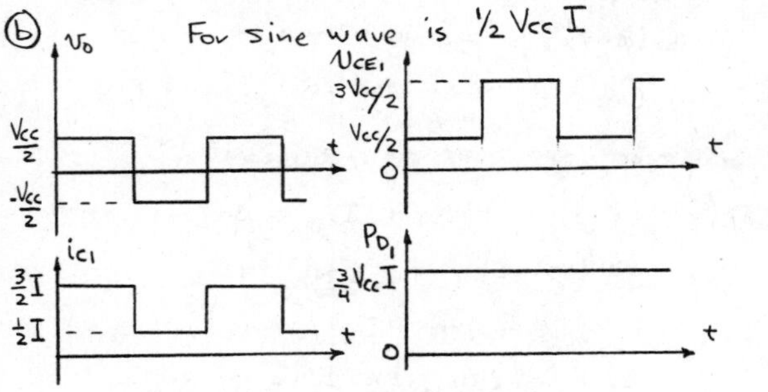

Av. pwr. dissipation in Q_1: $\overline{P_{D1}} = \frac{3}{4} V_{cc} I$, for sq. wave and $\frac{7}{8} V_{cc} I$ for corresponding sine wave.

4 ⓐ **10**

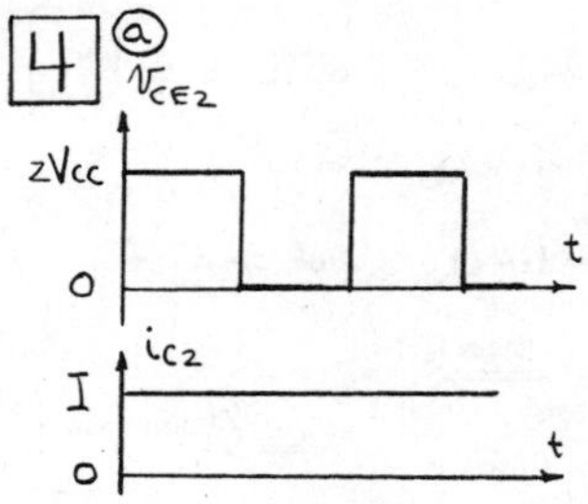

For v_o with p-p value of $2V_{cc}$, average power dissipation in Q_2 is $\left(\frac{2V_{cc}+0}{2}\right)I = V_{cc}I$

Since I is constant, $\overline{P_{D2}}$ depends only on the average of the waveform, indep. of its shape and magnitude.

ⓑ

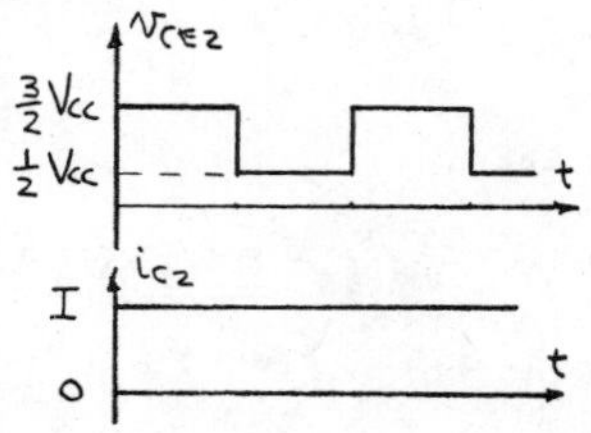

Thus $\overline{P_{D2}}$ is $V_{cc}I$, the same for all cases.

5 **10**

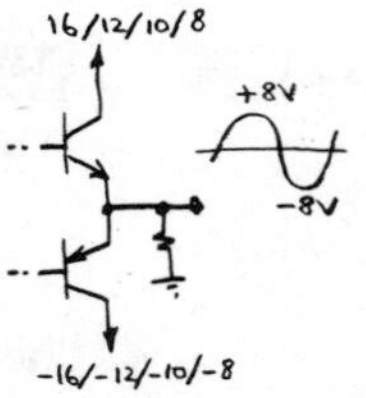

Power delivered to the load: $\left(\frac{8}{\sqrt{2}}\right)^2 / 100 = 0.32\,W$

Average power from the supply:

Negative : 100 mA (V_{cc})
Positive : 100 mA (V_{cc})
} Total 200 V_{cc}

For ±16 V : $P_s = 200(16) = 3.2\,W$, Effic. $= \frac{.32}{3.2} \times 100 = 10\%$

±12 V :	2.4 W	13.3%
±10 V :	2.0 W	16 %
±8 V :	1.6 W	20%

6

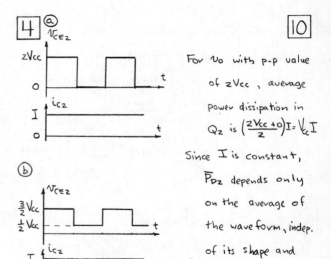

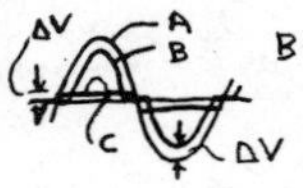

B = A − C

$v_o = (V + \Delta V)\sin\omega t - \frac{4\Delta V}{\pi}\left(\sin\omega t + \frac{1}{3}\sin 3\omega t + \frac{1}{5}\sin 5\omega t + \cdots\right)$

RMS values: For a square wave of peak ΔV: $1.00\Delta V$

For its fundamental: $\frac{4\Delta V}{\pi}\frac{1}{\sqrt{2}} = 0.90\Delta V$

For its harmonics: $\Delta V\sqrt{1-0.9^2} = 0.436\Delta V$

For composite, fundamental is $(V + \Delta V - 1.27\Delta V)\sin\omega t = (V - 0.27\Delta V)\sin\omega t$ whose rms is $\left(\frac{V - 0.27\Delta V}{\sqrt{2}}\right)$

10

and harmonics have an rms of $0.436\Delta V$

$\therefore THD = \frac{0.436\,\Delta V\sqrt{2}}{V - 0.27\Delta V} \times 100 = \boxed{\frac{61.6\Delta V}{V - 0.27\Delta V}}$

Now for ΔV = 0.5V :

For V = 1 volt, $THD = \frac{61.6(0.5)}{1 - 0.27(0.5)} = \underline{\underline{35.6\%}}$

For V = 10V, $THD = \frac{61.6(0.5)}{10 - 0.27(0.5)} = \underline{\underline{3.12\%}}$

7 ⓐ

$P_{out} = \frac{(\hat{V}_o/\sqrt{2})^2}{R_L} = \frac{(5/\sqrt{2})^2}{10} = \underline{\underline{1.25\,W}}$

$P_{S+} = P_{S-} = \frac{1}{\pi}\frac{\hat{V}_o}{R_L}V_{cc} = \frac{1}{\pi} \times \frac{5}{10} \times 5$

$P_S = \frac{2}{\pi} \times \frac{5^2}{10} = \underline{\underline{1.59\,W}}$

Power loss in each transistor $= \frac{1.59 - 1.25}{2} = \underline{\underline{0.17\,W}}$

$\eta = \frac{\pi}{4}\frac{\hat{V}_o}{V_{cc}} = \frac{\pi}{4}\frac{5}{5} = \underline{\underline{78.6\%}}$ (Check: $\eta = \frac{1.25}{1.59} = .786$)

ⓑ $P_{out} = \frac{(1/\sqrt{2})^2}{10} = \underline{\underline{.05\,W}}$

$P_S = \frac{2}{\pi} \times \frac{1}{10} \times 5 = \underline{\underline{0.318\,W}}$

$P_L/\text{trans} = \frac{0.318 - .05}{2} = \underline{\underline{0.134\,W}}$

$\eta = \frac{\pi}{4}\frac{1}{5} = \underline{\underline{15.7\%}}$

8 For square wave output: **10**

$P_{out} = \frac{V_o^2}{R_L}$, $P_S = 2\left(\frac{1}{2} \times \frac{V_o}{R_L} \times V_{cc}\right) = \frac{V_o V_{cc}}{R_L}$

$\eta = \frac{V_o^2/R_L}{V_o V_{cc}/R_L} = V_o/V_{cc}$

For $V_o = 5V$: $P_{out} = \frac{5^2}{10} = \underline{\underline{2.5W}}$, $P_S = \frac{5 \times 5}{10} = \underline{\underline{2.5W}}$

$\eta = \underline{\underline{100\ \%}}$

For $V_o = 1V$: $P_{out} = \frac{1^2}{10} = \underline{\underline{0.1W}}$, $P_S = \frac{1 \times 5}{10} = \underline{\underline{0.5W}}$

$\eta = \frac{0.1}{0.5} \times 100 = \underline{\underline{20\ \%}}$

9 $P_{D_{max\ each}} = \frac{V_{cc}^2}{\pi^2 R_L} = \frac{(23(1.1)(1.1))^2}{\pi^2\, 8(0.90)} = 10.9W$

(versus 6.7W normally)

10

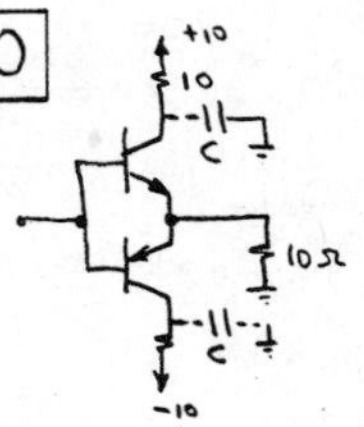

No Capacitor : Peak output $= \frac{\pm 10}{2} = \underline{\underline{\pm 5V}}$

With Large Capacitor :

Peak output voltage $= V_p$

Peak output current $= V_p/10$

Av output current $= \frac{1}{2} V_p/10$; Av drop in 10Ω in supply $= V_p/2$

Max peak output $V_p \rightarrow V_p/2 + V_p = 10 \rightarrow V_p = \underline{\underline{6.67\ V}}$

10

For a small capacitor, Vout reduces

For $V_{out} = 0.9 V_p = 0.9(6.67) = 6.0V$

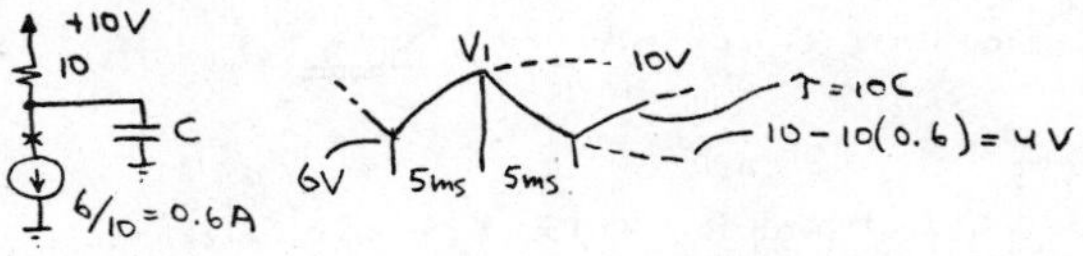

See from symmetry $\frac{V_1 - 6}{10 - 6} = \frac{6 - V_1}{4 - V_1} \rightarrow 10 - 6 = V_1 - 4$

or $V_1 = 10 - 6 + 4 = 8V$. Now $(10-6)e^{-\frac{5}{\tau}} = 2$

or $2 = e^{5/\tau} \rightarrow 5/\tau = \ln 2 \rightarrow \tau = 5/\ln 2 = 7.21\ ms$

$C = \frac{7.21 \times 10^{-3}}{10} = \underline{\underline{721\,\mu F}}$

11

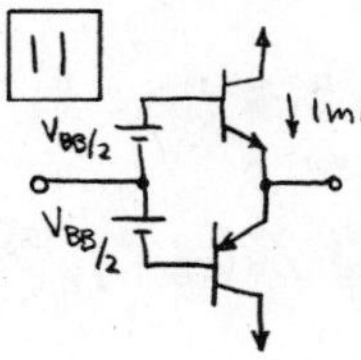

(a) For $|V_{BE}| = 0.7$ @ 1mA

$V_{BB} = \underline{1.4V}$

(b) For $|V_{BE}| = 0.7V$ @ 10mA

$V_{BB} = \frac{2}{1000}(700 + V_T \ln 1/10)$

$= \underline{\underline{1.285V}}$

(c) For $I_S = 10^{-14}A$, $V_{BB} = 2\left(\frac{25}{1000}\right) \ln \frac{10^{-3}}{10^{-14}} = \underline{\underline{1.266V}}$

12 Use data from p564 : $V_{BB} = 1.186$ for $I_Q = 2mA$ **10**

With 10 ohm load use data for 100Ω at 10× the output to provide $i_L, i_N, i_P, V_{BEn}, V_{EBp}, R_{out}$

$v_I = v_O + \frac{V_{BEp} - V_{BEn}}{2}$, v_O/v_I is calculated directly

$v_O/v_i = \frac{10}{R_{out} + 10}$

v_O	i_L (mA)	i_N	i_P	V_{BEn}	V_{EBp}	v_I	v_O/v_I	R_{out} (Ω)	v_O/v_i
0	0	2	2	.593	.593	0	1	6.25	.615
+.1	10	10.4	0.4	.634	.552	0.141	.71	2.32	.81
−.1	−10	0.4	10.4	.552	.634	−.141	.71	2.32	.81
+1	100	100.04	.04	.691	.495	1.098	.91	0.25	.976
−1	−100	.04	100.04	.495	.691	−1.098	.91	0.25	.976

13 $V_{BB} = 1.4 \rightarrow \frac{V_{BB}}{2} = 0.7 \rightarrow I_Q = \underline{\underline{1mA}}$

$i_L = \frac{1V}{100\Omega} = 10mA$, $i_P = i_N + i_L$, $i_N = i_P - i_L$

$i_N i_P = I_Q^2 \rightarrow i_P^2 - i_L i_P - I_Q^2 = 0$

$i_P = \frac{i_L \pm \sqrt{i_L^2 + 4I_Q^2}}{2} = \frac{10 + \sqrt{10^2 + 4(1^2)}}{2} = \underline{\underline{10.099\ mA}}$

$i_N = \frac{1}{10.099} = \underline{\underline{.099\ mA}}$

10

$v_{BE_N} = 700 - 25\ln\frac{.099}{1} = 642mV$

$v_{EBP} = 700 - 25\ln\frac{10.099}{1} = 758mV$

$v_{in} = \frac{-758 + 642}{2000} - 1 = -1.058V$

Thus for an output step of −1V requires an input step of −1.058V.

Largest positive step $= 10 - 6 = \underline{\underline{4V}}$

Largest negative step $= 6 - 0 = \underline{\underline{6V}}$

14

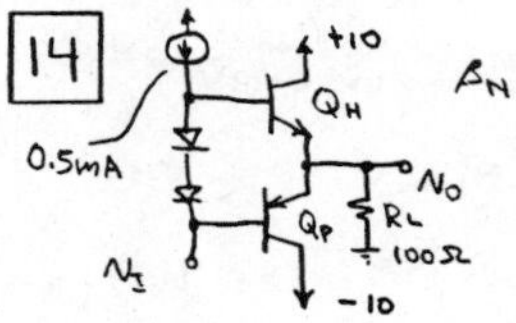

$\beta_N = 50$: Junctions are the same

$I_Q = \underline{0.5mA}$. Output swings to $\underline{\underline{-10V}}$ and up to

$0.5(51)100 = \underline{\underline{2.55V}}$. For +10V out, $I_{bias} = \frac{10}{100(51)} = \underline{\underline{1.96mA}}$

15 $I_Q = 2(1) = \underline{\underline{2mA}}$, $i = I_S e^{v/V_T}$

At 25°C, $\frac{2}{1000} = I_S e^{700/25} \rightarrow I_S = \frac{2}{1000} e^{-700/25}$

At 125°C, $I = I_S (1.14)^{100} e^{700/\left(25\frac{(273+125)}{273+25}\right)}$

$= \frac{2}{1000} e^{-700/25} e^{700/33.9} (1.14)^{100} = \underline{\underline{863\ mA}}$

Quiescent Power in each output transistor:

at 25°C = 2mA × 20V = $\underline{\underline{40 mW}}$

at 125°C = 86.3mA × 20 = $\underline{\underline{1.73 W}}$

16 Repeat problem 10.15 but with half coupling and using −2mV/°C rise for V_j

At 25°C

For diode: $10^{-3} = I_s e^{700/25} \rightarrow I_s = 10^{-3} e^{-700/25}$

For transistor: $I = 2 I_s e^{700/25} = 2 \times 10^{-3} e^{-700/25} e^{700/25} = 2mA$

At 125°C for transistor junction, diode is at $25 + \frac{100}{2} = 75°C$ and diode voltage reduces to $700 - 2\left(\frac{125-25}{2}\right) = 600 mV$

For transistor: $I = 2(10^{-3}) e^{-700/25} \times e^{600/25\left(\frac{273+125}{273+25}\right)} \times (1.14)^{100}$

or $I = \underline{\underline{43.1 mA}}$

17 $|V_{t_{1,2,3,4}}| = 1V$, $K_{3,4} = 1mA/V^2$, $K_{1,2} = n\,mA/V^2$

(a) I_{bias} keeps diode string operating at $2v_{GS}$ and $v_{GS1} + v_{GS2} = 2v_{GS}$. Since $K_{1,2} = nK_{3,4}$, $\underline{\underline{I_Q = nI_{bias}}}$

(b) $g_{m1} = g_{m2} = g_m$

Small signal gain $= \frac{1k}{1k + 1/g_m \| 1/g_m} = 0.99$

$\therefore 1/g_m = 2\left(\frac{1k}{0.99} - 1k\right) = 20.2\Omega$, or $g_m = \underline{\underline{49.5 mA/V}}$

$i_D = k(v_{GS} - V_t)^2 \rightarrow g_m = 2k(v_{GS} - V_t) = 2k\sqrt{i_D/k}$

For diodes $0.1 = 1(v_{GS} - 1)^2 \rightarrow v_{GS} = \sqrt{0.1} + 1 = 1.316V$

$\therefore g_m = 2nk(v_{GS} - V_t)$ or $49.5 = 2n(1)(.316)$

or $n = \frac{49.5}{2(.316)} = \underline{\underline{78.3}}$ and $I_Q = \underline{\underline{7.83 mA}}$

18 $v_O = 5$, $I_L = \frac{5}{100} = 50mA$, $\beta_{min} = \frac{50}{1} = \underline{\underline{50}}$

That $v_I = -0.7$ for $v_O = 0$ implies $\underline{0.7V}$ junctions

For $\beta = 55$, $i_{BN} = \frac{50}{55} = .909 mA$ and $I_D = 1 - .909 = .0909$

and $v_D = 700 + 25 \ln \frac{.0909}{1.00 - 5/55} = \underline{\underline{.642V}}$

Also $i_N^2 - i_L i_N - I_Q^2 = 0 \rightarrow i^2 - 50i - 5^2 = 0$

or $i = \frac{50 \pm \sqrt{50^2 + 4(25)}}{2} = \underline{\underline{50.49 mA}} = i_N$

$\therefore i_P = 50.49 - 50 = .49 mA$

$V_{EBP} = 700 + 25 \ln \frac{0.49}{5.0} = .642$

$\therefore v_I = 5.0 - .642 = 4.36V$

But the $i_N i_P$ approach assumes constant V_{BE}, which is not the case here! Alternatively, Assume Q_P off and Q_N on:

For $\beta = 55$: $I_{EN} = 50$, $V_{BEN} = 700 + 25 \ln \frac{50}{5} = 0.76V$

and $I_{B_N} = \frac{50}{55+1} = 0.9 mA$. Thus diode current is ≈ 0.1mA for which $V_D = 700 - 60$ or $0.64V$

$\therefore v_I = 5 + 0.76 - 2 \times 0.64 = 4.48V$

and $V_{EBP} = 5 - 4.48 = 0.52V$ for which $I_{EP} \approx 4\mu A$, negligible as assumed.

For $\beta = 100$ $V_{BEN} = 0.76$, $I_{BN} \approx 0.5$, $I_D \approx 0.5mA$

$V_D = 0.68$, $V_I = 5 + 0.76 - 2 \times 0.68 = 4.4V$

and $V_{EBP} \approx 0.6V$ for which $I_{EP} \approx 90\mu A$, still small (wrt 50mA)

19

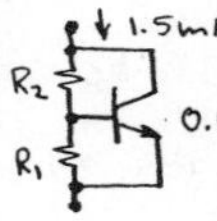

$R_1 = R_2 = 1.2k\Omega$

For $\beta = \infty$, $I_{R_1} = I_{R_2} = \frac{0.6}{1.2k} = 0.5mA$

and $I_C = 1mA$, and $V_{CE} = 2(0.6) = \underline{\underline{1.2V}}$

Assuming V_{BE} fixed

For $\beta = 100$, $1.5 = 0.5 + (\beta+1) i_b \rightarrow i_b = \frac{1}{\beta+1} = 9.9\mu A$

and $V_{CE} = 0.6 + 1.2(.5 + .0099) = \underline{1.212V}$

For $\beta = 10$, $1.5 = 0.5 + 11 i_b \rightarrow i_b = \frac{1}{11} = .0909 mA$

and $V_{CE} = 0.6 + 1.2(0.5 + .091) = \underline{1.31 V}$

20 $T_J = 50 + 3°C/W(30W) = \underline{140°C}$

$V_{BE_{140}} = 800 - 2.0(140 - 25) = \underline{\underline{570 mV}}$

21 $T_{A_{max}} = 175 - 13(10) = 45°$ ambient

22 T_J max was 150°C; now 200°C. Assume Θ_{JA} same

(a) At 62.5°C/W, extra power rating is $\frac{50}{62.5} = 0.8W$

ie it is now 2.8W

(b) Now at 50°C ambient, $P_{Dmax} = \frac{200-50}{62.5} = 2.4\,W$ 10

(c) $T_{JA\,1W} = 25 + 62.5 = 87.5$ as before

23 For $T_j = 100°C$

(a) $\theta_{JA} = 62.5°C/W$ as before

(b) P_{Do} at 25°C ambient is $(100-25)/62.5 = \underline{\underline{1.2W}}$

(c) P_{Dmax} at 50°C ambient is $(100-50)/62.5 = \underline{\underline{0.8W}}$

(d) Operation at 25°C and 1W is OK

24 $T_J = 25 + 100(1.6) = 185°C$

25 $\theta_{JC} = \frac{180-50}{50} = \underline{2.6°C/W}$

At 30W : $T_C = 180 - 2.6(30) = 102°C$

$T_S = 102 - 30(0.6) = \underline{\underline{84°C}}$

$\theta_{SA} = \frac{84-39}{30} = \underline{\underline{1.5°C/W}}$ or $1/\theta_{SA} = \frac{1}{1.5} = .6\dot{6}\ W/°C$

For Heat Sink : Conductance $= \frac{1}{4.5}\ W/°C/cm = .2\dot{2}\ W/°C/cm$

$\therefore$ need $\frac{.6\dot{6}}{.2\dot{2}} = \underline{\underline{3\,cm}}$ of sink !

26 Double sink size : $\theta_{SA} = \frac{1.5}{2}°C/W$ 10

$\therefore T_j = 50\left(\frac{1.5}{2} + 0.4 + 1.4\right) + 25 = \underline{152.5°C}$

New power level $= \frac{200-25}{\frac{1.5}{2}+0.4+1.4} = \underline{\underline{68.6\,W}}$

Additional power $= 68.6 - 50 = \underline{\underline{18.6\,W}}$

27 Fig 10.24 : $\beta = 200$

For $v_i = 0$, base currents cancel → $\underline{\underline{I_{in} = 0}}$ for

$R_L = \infty$ or 100Ω

For $v_i = \pm 10$: $v_i = +10V$, $R_L = \infty$

$i_{c1} = 0.88$, $i_{b1} = \frac{0.88}{200} = 4.4\mu A$
$i_{c2} = 4.87$, $i_{b2} = \frac{4.87}{200} = 24.4\mu A$
} $i_{in} = \underline{\underline{20\mu A}}$ directed in.

$v_i = +10$, $R_L = 100$

$i_{c1} = 0.38$, $i_{b1} = 1.9\mu A$
$i_{c2} = 4.87$, $i_{b2} = 24.4\mu A$
} $i_{in} = \underline{\underline{22.5\mu A}}$ directed in

$v_i = -10$, $R_L = \infty$ → $i_{in} = \underline{\underline{20\mu A \text{ outward}}}$

$v_i = -10$, $R_L = 100$ → $i_{in} = \underline{\underline{22.5\mu A \text{ outward}}}$

28 Fig 10.24, R_1, R_2 replaced by 2.87mA sources 10

v_I	R_L	i_{c1}	i_{c2}	i_{c3}	i_{c4}	v_o
0	∞	2.87	2.87	2.87	2.87	0
0	100	2.87	2.87	2.87	2.87	0
+10	∞	2.87	2.87	2.87	2.87	+10
+10	100	2.37	2.87	100	.082	9.91
−10	∞	2.87	2.87	2.87	2.87	−10
−10	100	2.87	2.37	.082	100	−9.91

See detail below:

For $v_I = +10V$, $v_O \approx 10V$, $I_L \approx \frac{10}{100} = 100mA$

$i_N^2 - i_L i_N - I_Q^2 = 0$, $i^2 - 100i - 2.87^2 = 0$

$i = \frac{+100 \pm \sqrt{100^2 + 4(2.87)^2}}{2} = 100.082$

ie $i_{c3} = 100.082$, $i_{c4} = .082$, $i_{b3} = \frac{100}{200} = .5\,mA$

$i_{c1} = 2.87 - 0.5 = 2.37$, $i_{c2} = 2.87$

$v_O = v_I + v_{BE1} - v_{BE3}$

$v_{BE1} = V_T \ln \frac{2.37\times10^{-3}}{3.3\times10^{-14}} = .625$
$v_{BE2} = V_T \ln \frac{100\times10^{-3}}{3.3\times10^{-14}} = .718$
} $v_O = 10.0 + .625 - .718 = 9.91\,V$

29 10

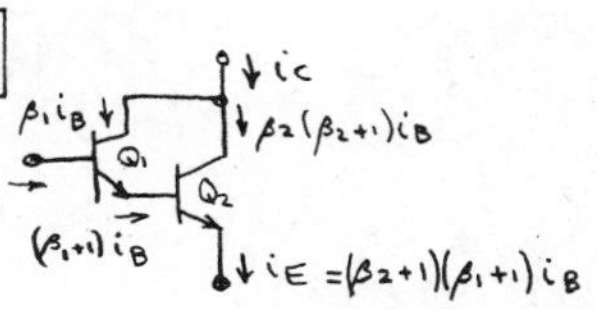

$i_C = i_B[\beta_1 + \beta_2(\beta_1+1)]$
$i_E = i_B(\beta_1+1)(\beta_2+1)$
} $\boxed{\beta = \beta_1\beta_2 + \beta_1 + \beta_2}$

$v_{BE} = v_{BE2} + v_{BE1} = V_T \ln \frac{\alpha_2 i_E}{I_{S2}} + V_T \ln \frac{\alpha_1 i_E/(\beta_2+1)}{I_{S1}}$

or $v_{BE} = V_T \ln \frac{\alpha_1\alpha_2 i_E^2}{(\beta_2+1)I_{S1}I_{S2}}$

or $\boxed{v_{BE} = V_T \ln \frac{\beta_1\beta_2\ i_C}{(\beta_1+1)(\beta_2+1)^2 I_{S1}I_{S2}}}$

At $I_E = 10mA$

$V_{BE} = \frac{25\times10^{-3}\ln(100)(100)(10^{-2})^2}{(101)(101)^2(3.3\times10^{-14})(3.3\times10^{-15})} = \underline{\underline{1.264V}}$

$\beta = 100^2 + 100 + 100 = \underline{\underline{10200}}$

$I_B = \frac{10}{10200} \approx \frac{10}{(101)^2} = \underline{\underline{.98\mu A}}$

$I_C = 10 - .00098 = \underline{\underline{9.99902\,mA}}$

30 **10**

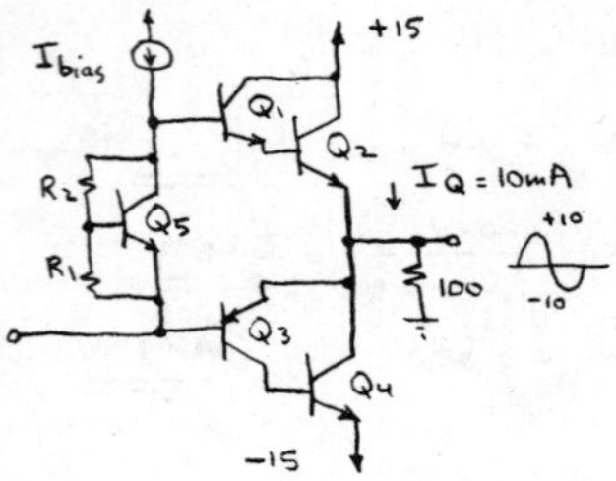

Q	I_S	β
2, 4	10^{-13}	50
1, 5	10^{-14}	100
3	10^{-14}	50

$I_L = \frac{10}{100} = 100mA$, $I_{B1} = \frac{100}{50(100)} = 20\mu A$, $I_{bias} = 2(20) = 40\mu A$

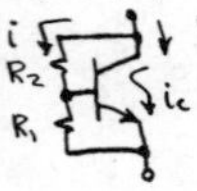

$\frac{40-i}{20-i} = \frac{5}{1} \rightarrow 40 - i = 100 - 5i$
$4i = 60$, $i = 15\mu A$

No Load $I_{B1} = 0$, $I_{bias} = 40\mu A$, $i = 15\mu A$,

$i_{C5} = 25\mu A$, $v_{BE5} = V_T \ln \frac{25\times10^{-6}}{10^{-14}} = 541\ mV$

$R_1 = \frac{541\times10^{-3}}{15\times10^{-6}} = \underline{\underline{36k}}$, $I_{R2} = \frac{541\times10^{-3}}{36k} + \frac{25}{100} = 15.28\mu A$

$\underline{I_Q = 10mA}$: $I_{E2} = 10\ mA \longrightarrow v_{BE2} = V_T \ln \frac{10(\frac{50}{51})\times10^{-3}}{10^{-13}} = 633mV$

$I_{E1} = \frac{10}{50} = 0.2mA \rightarrow v_{BE1} = V_T \ln \frac{0.2\times10^{-3}(100/101)}{10^{-14}} = 593mV$

$I_{E4} = 10mA \rightarrow v_{BE4} = v_{BE2} = 633mV$

$I_{C3} = 0.2mA \rightarrow v_{BE3} = V_T \ln \frac{0.2\times10^{-3}}{10^{-14}} = 593mV$

$V_{B1-3} = 633 + 593 + 593 = 1.819V$, $V_{R2} = 1.819 - .541 = 1.278V$

$R_2 = \frac{1.278\ V}{15.28\mu A} = \underline{\underline{83.6k}}$

Input Voltage for $v_O = 0$ is $0 - V_{BE3} = \underline{\underline{-0.593V}}$

10

For $\underline{v_O = -10V}$, $i_L = 100mA$

$i^2 - i_L i - I_Q = 0$, $i^2 - 100i - 10^2 = 0$

$i = \frac{+100 \pm \sqrt{100^2 + 400}}{2} = 101\ mA$

ie $i_{E4} = 101mA$, $i_{B4} = \frac{101}{51} = 1.98mA$

$v_{BE3} = V_T \ln \frac{1.98\times10^{-3}}{10^{-14}} = 650mV$.

Thus for $v_O = -10V$, $v_I = -10 - 0.65 = \underline{\underline{-10.65V}}$

$\underline{\text{For } v_O = +10V}$, $i_L = 100mA$

$i_{E2} = 101mA$, $i_{E1} = \frac{101}{51} = 1.98mA$, $i_{B1} = \frac{1.98}{101} = 19.6\mu A$

$v_{BE2} = V_T \ln \frac{101\frac{50}{51}\times10^{-3}}{10^{-13}} = 691$, $v_{BE1} = V_T \ln \frac{1.98\times10^{-3}}{10^{-14}} \times \frac{100}{101} = 535mV$

$I_{bias} = 40$, $i_{B1} = 19.6\mu A$, $i_{R2} = 15\mu A$

$\therefore i_{C5} \simeq 40 - 19.6 - 15 = 5.4\mu A$, $v_{BE5} = V_T \ln \frac{5.4\times10^{-6}}{10^{-14}} = 503mV$

$\therefore v_I = 10 + 0.691 + .535 - .503\left(\frac{84+36}{36}\right) = \underline{\underline{9.55\ V}}$

31

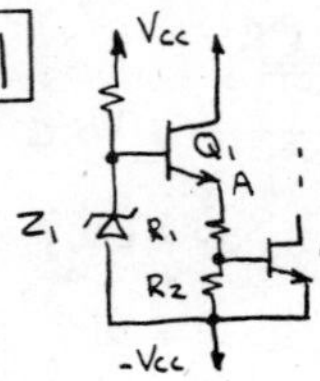

$V_{Z1} = 6.8V$, $+400\ ppm/°C$

$I_S = 10^{-15}A$, $\beta = 100$

$I_{C1} = 100\mu A$ @ 25°C, $I_{C2} = 1mA$ @ 150°C

Temp Coeff – V_{BE}: $-2m/°C$, I_S: $+14\%/°C$

10

$v_{BE1} = V_T \ln \frac{100\times10^{-6}}{10^{-15}} = 633\ mV$, $R_1 + R_2 = \frac{6.800 - .633}{100\mu A} = 61.7k$

$i_C = I_S e^{v_{BE}/V_T}$

$\underline{\text{At } 150°C}$ $I_S = 10^{-15}(1.14)^{15-25} = 1.297\times10^{-8}$

$V_T = \frac{25(273+150)}{273+25} = 35.5$

$\therefore v_{BE2} = 35.5 \ln \frac{1\times10^{-3}}{1.297\times10^{-8}} = 400\ mV$

$V_A = 6.8(1.0004)^{150-25} - .633 + 2(150-25) = 6.77\ V$

$\therefore \frac{R_2}{R_1+R_2}(6.77) = .400 \rightarrow R_2 = 61.7k\left(\frac{.400}{6.77}\right) = \underline{\underline{3.64\ k}}$

$R_1 = 61.7 - 3.64 = \underline{\underline{58\ k}}$

$\underline{\text{At } 25°C}$ $V_{B2} = \frac{3.64}{58 + 3.64} \times (6.8 - .63) = .364\ V$

$i_{C2} = 10^{-15} e^{\frac{364}{25}} = \underline{\underline{2.1\ nA}}$

An iterative process indicates $i_{C2} = 100\mu A$ at about 129 °C for this design.

32 $V_{BE} = 0.7$, $\beta_{npn} = 100$, $\beta_{pnp} = 20$. Label Q_3 emitter as A, and the centre of R_1 as B. See $V_A \approx 1.4V$, $I_{R1} = \frac{20 - 0.7 - 1.4}{50k} = .358mA$

$I_{B3} = I_{E4} = \frac{.358}{20} = 17.9\mu A$, $I_{E1} = I_{B2} = \frac{17.9}{20} = .895\mu A$, $V_{B1} = V_{B2} = 150k(.895) = .134V$

$I_{B6} = I_{B5} = \frac{20}{21} \times \frac{358}{100} = 341\mu A$, $V_O = V_B = \frac{20 - 0.7 + .134 + 2(0.7)}{2} = \underline{\underline{10.42V}}$

33 Find transconductance from bases of Q_1, Q_2 to output at collectors Q_4, Q_6 of Fig 10.30 **10**

From **32**, $r_{e3} = r_{e4} = \frac{25mV}{.358mA} = 69.8\Omega$

$r_{e1} = r_{e2} = \frac{25mV}{17.9\mu A} = 1396 \equiv \frac{1396}{21} = 66.5$ in emitter of Q_3, Q_4

$r_{e5} = r_{e6} = \frac{25}{.341} = 73.3\Omega$

$g_m = \frac{1}{2(69.8) + 2(66.5) + 1k \| (25k + 25k)} \times 2 = 1.596mA/V$

$r_d = (150k + 150k) \| (21)(21)\left(\frac{2}{g_m}\right) = 194k\Omega$

34 $I_{C3} = I_{C4} = 0.9(10) = 9mA$, $V_{BE3} = V_T \ln \frac{9\times10^{-3}}{10^{-13}} = 631\ mV$

$I_{C1} = I_{C2} = 0.1(10) - \frac{9}{100} = 0.91mA$, $V_{BE1} = V_T \ln \frac{.91\times10^{-3}}{10^{-14}} = 631\ mV$

Thus $R_5 = R_6 = \frac{631 - 631}{9\times10^{-3}} = 0$

Now $R_1 = R_2 = \frac{15 - 0.63}{1mA} = \underline{14.37k}$ (use 15 kΩ)

$I_L = 100\mu A$ – (ignore I_{B3}), $I_{C5} = 50mA$

$I_{B5} = \frac{50}{21} = 2.38mA$, $I_{E3} = 50mA$, $I_{C3} = \frac{100}{101}(50) = 49.5mA$

$I_{R3} = 49.5 - 2.38 = 47.12\ mA$, $V_{BE5} = V_T \ln \frac{50\times10^{-3}}{10^{-12}} = 616mV$

$\therefore R_3 = \frac{616\times10^{-3}}{47.12\times10^{-3}} = \underline{\underline{13.07\Omega}} = R_4$ – (use 13 Ω)

35 | **10**

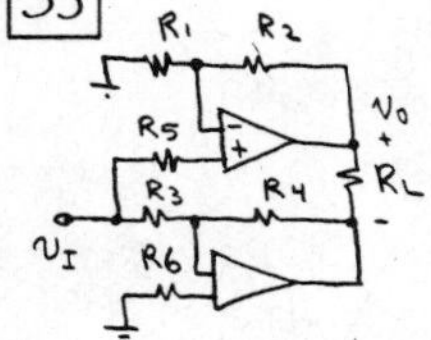

$R_2 = R_4 = \underline{\underline{100\,k}}$

Required gain $\frac{v_O}{v_I} = 10 \rightarrow$ Half gain $= 5$

$5 = \frac{R_2}{R_1} + 1 \rightarrow R_1 = \frac{R_2}{4} = 25\,k\Omega$

$R_3 = \frac{100}{5} = \underline{20\,k\Omega}$

$R_5 = \frac{100}{4+1} = \underline{\underline{20\,k\Omega}}$, $R_6 = \frac{100}{5+1} = \underline{\underline{16.\dot{6}\,k\Omega}}$

36

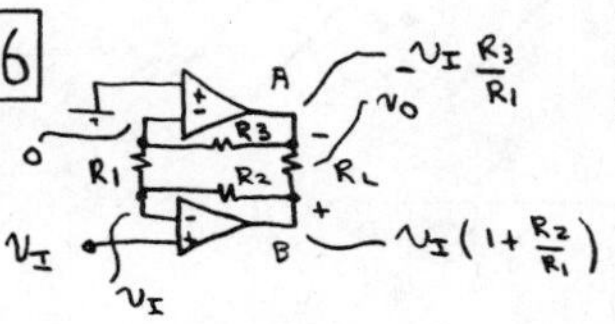

$\boxed{\text{Gain} = \frac{v_O}{v_I} = \left(1 + \frac{R_2}{R_1} + \frac{R_3}{R_1}\right)}$

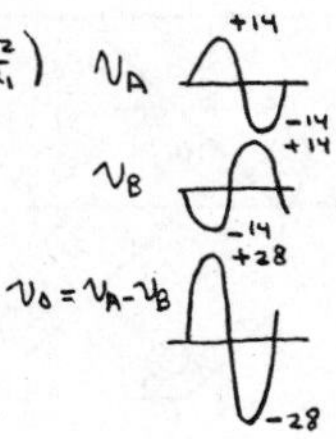

Peak to peak of largest sine wave is $\underline{\underline{56\,V}}$

$\text{Gain} = 20 = \left(1 + \frac{R_2}{R_1}\right) + \frac{R_3}{R_1}$

$= 10 + 10$

$\rightarrow R_3 = 10 R_1 = \underline{\underline{100k}}$

$R_2 = (10-9) R_1 = \underline{\underline{90k}}$

37 | **10**

$i_{D1} = \frac{1}{2} C_{ox} W U_{sat} (v_{GS} - V_t)$

$i_{D2} = \frac{1}{2} \mu_n C_{ox} (W/L)(v_{GS} - V_t)^2$

At $v_{GS} - V_t = 4$, $L = 2\mu m = 2 \times 10^{-4}$ cm

and $U_{sat} = 5 \times 10^6$ cm/sec

For $i_{D1} = i_{D2}$ $\mu_n = \frac{L}{(v_{GS} - V_t)} U_{sat} = \frac{2 \times 10^{-4}}{4} \times 5 \times 10^6 = 250\,cm^2/Vs$

38

For velocity saturation, $i_D = \frac{1}{2} C_{ox} W U_{sat} (v_{GS} - V_t)$

$g_m = \frac{\partial i_D}{\partial v_{GS}} = \frac{1}{2} C_{ox} W U_{sat}$, a constant indep. of v_{GS}

For square law, $i_D = \frac{1}{2} \mu_n C_{ox} \left(\frac{W}{L}\right)(v_{GS} - V_t)^2$

$g_m = \frac{\partial i_D}{\partial v_{GS}} = \mu_n C_{ox} \left(\frac{W}{L}\right)(v_{GS} - V_t)$

$\therefore g_{m_{VS}} = \frac{1}{2} \frac{L \cdot U_{sat}}{V_{GS} - V_t} \times g_{m_{SL}}$

39 | **10**

$V_t = 2V$ with $TC = -3\,mV/°C$

$K = 100\,mA/V^2$; $|V_{BE}| = 0.7$ with $TC = -2\,mV/°C$, $\beta = \infty$

$i_D = K(v_{GS} - V_t)^2$ or $10 = 100(v-2)^2 \rightarrow v = 2.316\,V$

$R = \frac{(2.316) \times 2}{10\,mA} = \underline{463\,\Omega}$

Voltage across $Q_5 + Q_6 = 2(2.316 + 1.4) = 7.432\,V$

$R_2 = R_4 = \frac{0.7V}{50\mu A} = \underline{\underline{14k}}$

$2V_{GS}$ changes by $2(-3)$ or $-6\,mV/°C$

To compensate, need $R_3 = 2R_4$ with V_{BE6} thermally coupled to Q_5, Q_6 and $TC = -2\,mV/°C$

$R_3 = 2(14k) = \underline{\underline{28\,k\Omega}}$, $V_{CE6} = 3(0.7) = 2.1$

$V_{CE5} = 7.432 - 2.1 = 5.33$,

$\therefore R_1 = \frac{5.33 - 0.7}{0.7} \cdot R_2 = \underline{\underline{92.6\,k}}$

$R_G = 100\,\Omega$ or so

1 | **11**

(a) $\frac{v_o}{v_i} = \frac{R_1}{R_1 + R_2 \| 1/Cs} = \frac{R_1}{R_1 + \frac{R_2}{Cs(R_2 + 1/Cs)}}$

or $\frac{v_o}{v_i} = \frac{R_1(1 + R_2 Cs)}{R_1 R_2 Cs + R_1 + R_2}$

or $\frac{v_o}{v_i} = \frac{s + \frac{1}{R_2 C}}{s + \frac{1}{(R_1 \| R_2) C}}$ or directly $\frac{\frac{1}{R_2} + sC}{\frac{1}{R_1} + \frac{1}{R_2} + sC}$

(b) $\frac{v_o}{v_i} = \frac{R_1 + sL}{R_1 + R_2 + sL} = \frac{s + \frac{1}{L/R_1}}{s + \frac{1}{L(R_1 + R_2)}}$

2

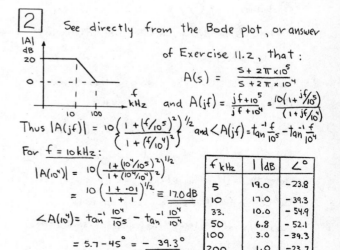

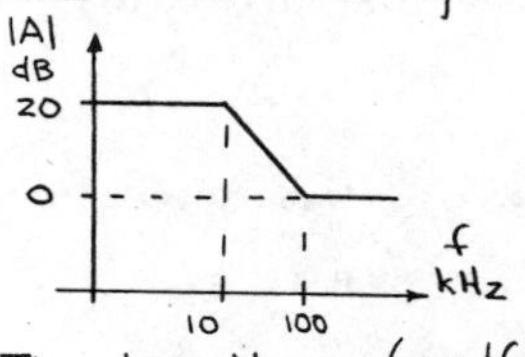

See directly from the Bode plot, or answer of Exercise 11.2, that:

$A(s) = \frac{s + 2\pi \times 10^5}{s + 2\pi \times 10^4}$

and $A(jf) = \frac{jf + 10^5}{jf + 10^4} = \frac{10(1 + jf/10^5)}{(1 + jf/10^4)}$

Thus $|A(jf)| = 10 \left\{ \frac{1 + (f/10^5)^2}{1 + (f/10^4)^2} \right\}^{1/2}$ and $\angle A(jf) = \tan^{-1} \frac{f}{10^5} - \tan^{-1} \frac{f}{10^4}$

For $\underline{f = 10\,kHz}$:

$|A(10^4)| = 10 \left(\frac{1 + (10^4/10^5)^2}{1 + (10^4/10^4)^2} \right)^{1/2}$

$= 10 \left(\frac{1 + .01}{1 + 1} \right)^{1/2} \equiv \underline{\underline{17.0\,dB}}$

$\angle A(10^4) = \tan^{-1} \frac{10^4}{10^5} - \tan^{-1} \frac{10^4}{10^4}$

$= 5.7 - 45° = \underline{\underline{-39.3°}}$

f kHz	| |dB	∠°
5	19.0	−23.8
10	17.0	−39.3
33.	10.0	−54.9
50	6.8	−52.1
100	3.0	−39.3
200	1.0	−23.7

3 **11**

$$T(s) = \frac{10s}{(1+s/10)(1+\frac{s}{1000})}$$

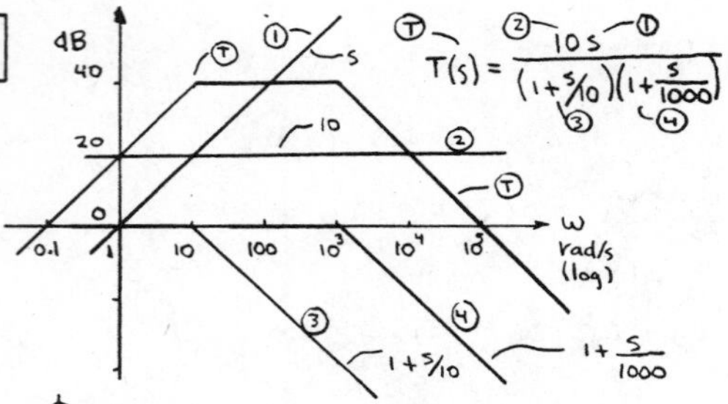

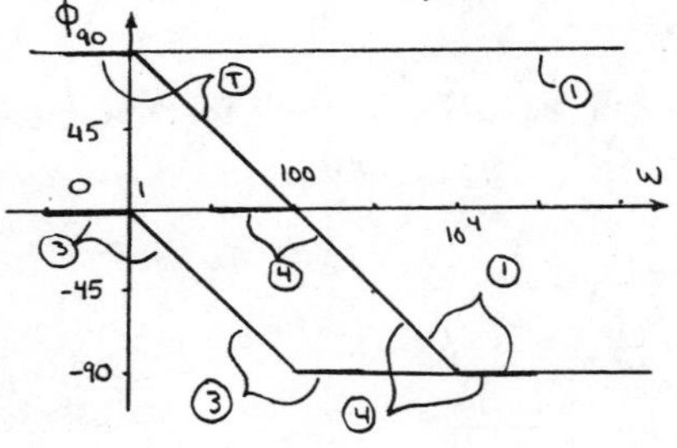

ω	|G| dB	∠φ°
1	20	84
10	37	45
100	40	0
1000	37	-45
10^4	20	-84
10^5	0	-90

4 See explanation following: **11**

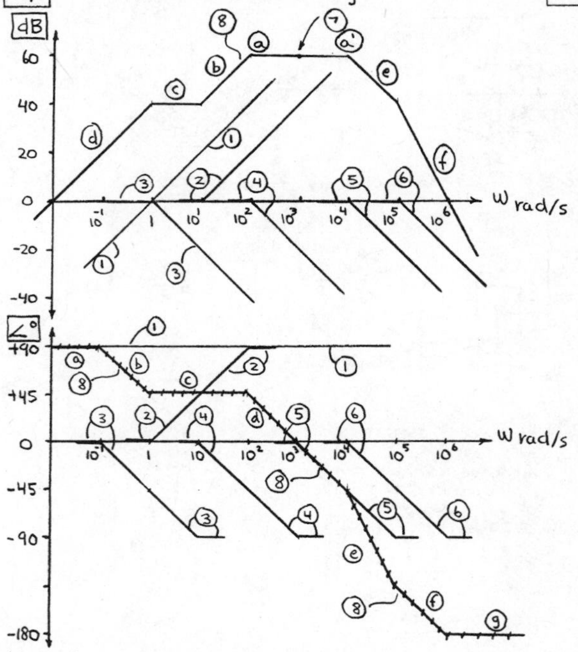

Key: ① Zero at 0 rad/s, ② zero at 10, ③ pole at 1 rad/s

④ pole at 10^2, ⑤ pole at 10^4, ⑥ pole at 10^5 rad/s

⑦ gain of 10^3 at 10^3 rad/s, ⑧ Overall Response

11

For the magnitude plot: The characteristics of each pole and zero are plotted with respect to the 0 dB axis (see keyed items ① thru ⑥). The zeros at 0 and 10 rad/s compensate the poles at 1 and 100 rad/s allowing a flat midband response to begin at 10^2 rad/s. The gain of 10^3 at 10^3 rad/s establishes point ⑦, from which the overall response ⑧ is drawn in the order ⓐ thru ⓓ and ⓐ', ⓔ, ⓕ

For the phase plot: The corresponding phases of the zeros and poles are first plotted as deviations from 0° (see keyed items ① thru ⑥). The net angle is found by summation as ⑧. Note the interesting effects of placement of the critical frequencies: The zero at 10 between poles at 1 and 100 leads to a region of small (zero) phase change. The rapid variation of phase (at 90°/decade) above 10^4 rad/s is due to the proximity (a factor of 10) of the upper 2 poles.

11

5 One could follow the approach used in **4** or:

For magnitude: Note at 10^5 rad/s that the response is locally flat since there is only a single pole and a single zero at lower frequencies. Thus construct the plot in the sequence shown, ⓐ through ⓘ

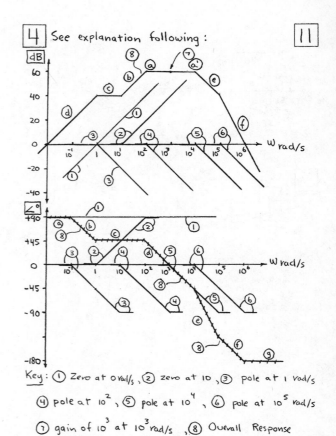

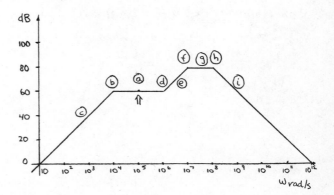

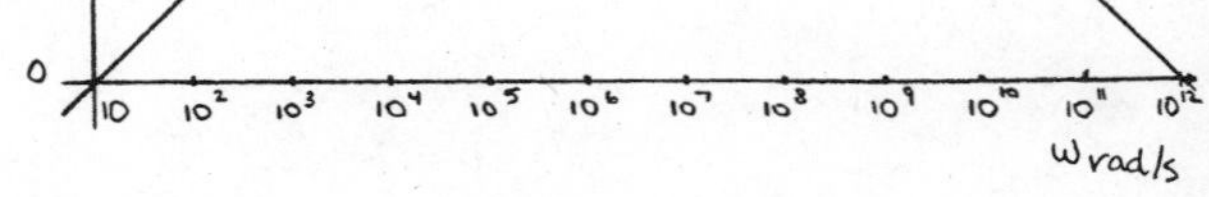

11

For phase: Sketch the basic zero and pole components, then add:

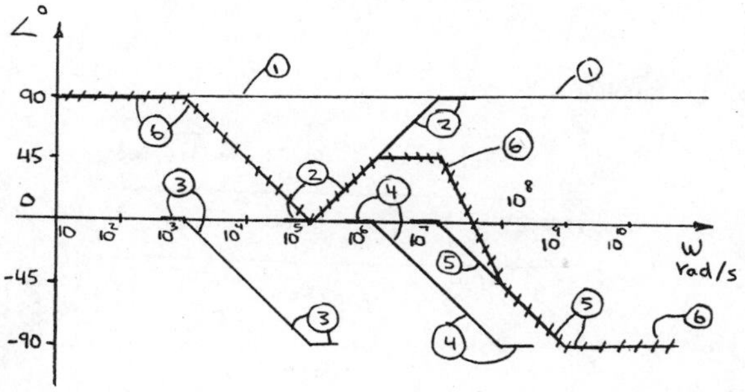

① Zero at 0, ② zero at 10^6, ③ pole at 10^4

④ pole at 10^7, ⑤ pole at 10^8, ⑥ overall

See peak gain occurs midway between 10^7 and 10^8, say at 33×10^6 rad/s with gain of 80 dB (ie 10^4 V/V) and phase of about 0°

6

11

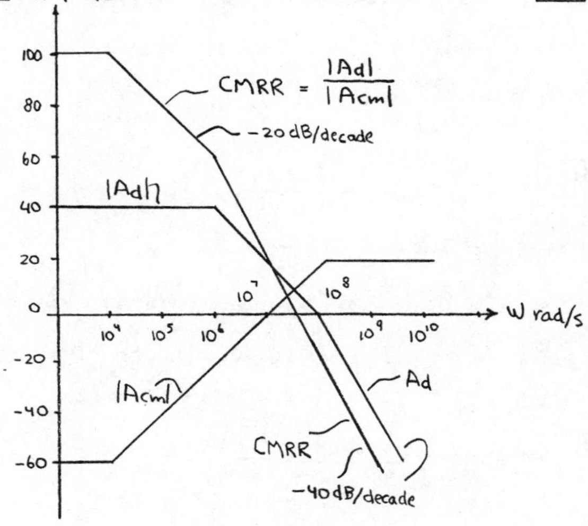

See CMRR at 10^7 rad/s is +20 dB

7 $\tan^{-1} \omega/a = 1^\circ$ for $\omega/a = \tan 1^\circ = \underline{.0175}$ 11

or at $\omega = 0.0175$ of a, the corner frequency

8

$$| \, | = \frac{1}{\left(1+\frac{\omega^2}{\omega_o^2}\right)^{n/2}} \quad , \quad \phi = -n \tan^{-1}\left(\frac{\omega}{\omega_o}\right)$$

(a) The magnitude is low by 3dB at ω_H where $\frac{1}{\left(1+\left(\frac{\omega_H}{\omega_o}\right)^2\right)^{n/2}} = \frac{1}{\sqrt{2}}$, or $1+\left|\frac{\omega_H}{\omega_o}\right|^2 = 2^{1/n}$, or

for $\omega_H/\omega_o = \sqrt{2^{1/n}-1}$

(b) The phase shift is 45° at ω_ϕ where $-n \tan^{-1}\left(\frac{\omega_\phi}{\omega_o}\right) = -45^\circ$ or $\omega_\phi/\omega_o = \tan \frac{45^\circ}{n}$

n	ω_H/ω_o	ω_ϕ/ω_o
1	1	1
2	0.642	0.414
3	0.509	0.268
4	0.434	0.199

9 $$T(s) = -\frac{K(1+s/1)(1+s/10)}{(1+s/5)(1+s/100)}$$ 11

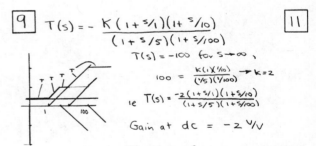

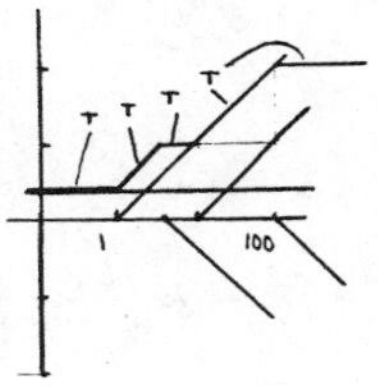

$T(s) = -100$ for $s \to \infty$,

$100 = \frac{K(1)(1/10)}{(1/5)(1/100)} \to K = 2$

ie $T(s) = \frac{-2(1+s/1)(1+s/10)}{(1+s/5)(1+s/100)}$

Gain at dc $= -2$ V/V

The 3dB frequency occurs at ω where $\frac{(1+\omega^2)(1+(\omega/10)^2)}{(1+(\omega/5)^2)(1+(\omega/100)^2)} = 1/2$ whence $\omega_L = 98.5$ r/s

More easily using Eq 11.18 : $\omega = \omega_L \approx \sqrt{\omega_{p1}^2 + \omega_{p2}^2 - 2\omega_{z1}^2 - 2\omega_{z2}^2}$

or $\omega_L = \sqrt{25 + 10^4 - 2 - 200} = 99.1$ rad/s

10 $$T(s) = -k \frac{(1+s/1)(1+s/10)}{(1+s/10)(1+s/100)} = -k \frac{(1+s/1)}{(1+s/100)}$$

Gain as $s \to \infty$ $T(\infty) = -\frac{k(1)}{1/100} = -100 \to k = 1$

$\therefore T(s) = -\frac{(1+s/1)}{(1+s/100)}$

Gain at dc = 1 ; pole at 100 rad/s dominant

Low 3dB frequency $\omega_L = 100$ rad/s

11 $T_L(s) = \dfrac{K s^2(1+s/10)}{(1+s/100)(1+s/50)(1+s/5)}$ **11**

$\omega_L \approx (100^2 + 50^2 + 5^2 - 2(10^2))^{1/2} = (10{,}000 + 2500 + 25 - 200)^{1/2}$

or $\omega_L \approx 111$ rad/sec

12 $F_H(s) = \dfrac{K(1+s/10^6)}{(1+s/10^5)(1+s/10^7)}$, $F_H(0) = K = -100$

$\therefore F_H(s) = \dfrac{-100(1+s/10^6)}{(1+s/10^5)(1+s/10^7)}$

$\underline{\omega_H}$: ⓐ By dominant pole approx: $\omega_H = 10^5$ rad/s

ⓑ By sum of squares approx: $\omega_H = 1/\left(\left(\frac{1}{10^5}\right)^2 + \left(\frac{1}{10^7}\right)^2 - 2\left(\frac{1}{10^6}\right)^2\right)^{1/2}$

or $\omega_H = \dfrac{10^5}{(1 + 10^{-4} - .02)^{1/2}} = 1.01 \times 10^5$ rad/sec

ⓒ Exactly: $\dfrac{1 + \omega^2/10^{12}}{(1+\omega^2/10^{10})(1+\omega^2/10^{14})} = 1/2$

or $2 + 2\omega^2/10^{12} = 1 + \omega^4/10^{24} + \omega^2(1/10^{10} + 1/10^{14})$ → Let $\omega^2/10^{10} = x$

$\therefore 1 + .02x = x^2/10^4 + x^2 + x^2/10^4 \rightarrow x^2 \times 10^{-4} + x(.9801) - 1 = 0$

Whence $x \approx \frac{1}{0.98} \doteq 1.02 = \omega^2/10^{10} \rightarrow \omega = 1.01 \times 10^5$ r/s $= \omega_H$

For zero lowered to 10^5 rad/s, $T_L' = \dfrac{-100}{(1+s/10^7)}$

for which $\omega_H = 10^7$ rad/s, a great improvement!

13 **11**

ⓐ

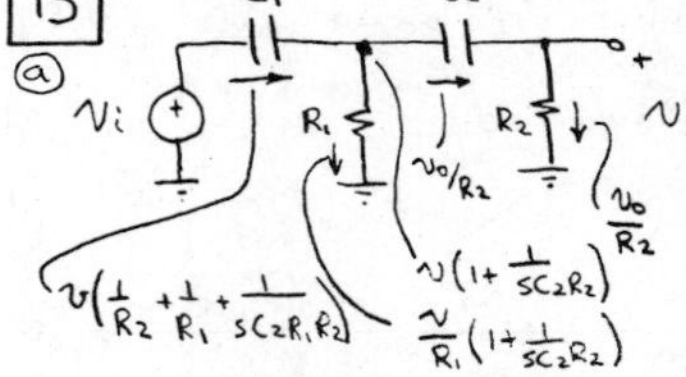

$v_i = v_o\left[\left(1 + \frac{1}{sC_2R_2}\right) + \frac{1}{sC_1R_2} + \frac{1}{sC_1R_1} + \frac{1}{s^2C_1C_2R_1R_2}\right]$

ie $\dfrac{v_o}{v_i} = \dfrac{1}{\frac{1}{s^2C_1C_2R_1R_2} + \frac{1}{sC_2R_2} + \frac{1}{sC_1R_1} + \frac{1}{sC_1R_2} + 1}$

$= \dfrac{s^2}{s^2 + s\left(\frac{1}{C_1R_1} + \frac{1}{C_1R_2} + \frac{1}{C_2R_2}\right) + \frac{1}{C_1C_2R_1R_2}}$ } as required

ⓑ Poles:

i) $C_1 = C_2 = 1\mu F$, $R_1 = R_2 = 10k\Omega$

$s^2 + s\left(\frac{1}{10} + \frac{1}{10} + \frac{1}{10}\right) + \frac{1}{100} \rightarrow s^2 + s(0.3) + 0.01 = 0$

ie poles at $s = -0.038$, $s = -0.261$ or $\underline{\underline{38.2}}$, $\underline{\underline{261}}$ rad/s

ii) $C_1 = 10C_2 = 1\mu F$, $R_2 = 10R_1 = 100k\Omega$

$s^2 + s\left(\frac{1}{10} + \frac{1}{10} + \frac{1}{100}\right) + \frac{1}{100} \rightarrow s^2 + s(.21) + .01 = 0$

with poles at $\underline{\underline{73}}$ rad/s and $\underline{\underline{137}}$ rad/s

iii) $C_2 = 10C_1 = 1\mu F$, $R_1 = 10R_2 = 10k\Omega$

$s^2 + s\left(\frac{1}{10} + \frac{1}{10} + 1\right) + \frac{1}{100} \rightarrow s^2 + s(1.2) + .01 = 0$

with poles at $\underline{\underline{8.4}}$ rad/s and $\underline{\underline{1192}}$ rad/s

ⓒ For $T(s) = \dfrac{s^2}{s^2 + as + b}$ **11**

Exact $\omega_L = \omega_L = \left(\dfrac{(a^2 - b) + \sqrt{(a^2-b)^2 - 4b^2}}{2}\right)^{1/2}$

i) $a = 0.3$, $b = 0.01 \rightarrow \omega_L = 285$ rad/s

ii) $a = 0.21$, $b = 0.01 \rightarrow \omega_L = 192$ rad/s

iii) $a = 1.2$, $b = 0.01 \rightarrow \omega_L = 1196$ rad/s

ⓓ By dominant pole approx:

i) 261 rad/s ii) 137 rad/s iii) 1192 rad/s

ⓔ By sum of squares approx:

i) 264 rad/s ii) 155 rad/s iii) 1192 rad/s

ⓕ By short-circuit time constants:

$\omega_L = \dfrac{1}{C_2R_2} + \dfrac{1}{C_1(R_1 \| R_2)}$

i) 300 rad/s ii) 210 rad/s iii) 1200 rad/s

14 $R_{eq} = R_{G1} \| R_{G2} = 2.2 \| 10M = 1.803M$

$R_{C1} = 100k + 1.803M = 1.903M$

$C_{C1} = \dfrac{1}{2\pi \times 100 \times 1.90 \times 10^6} = \underline{\underline{836pF}}$

Use $\underline{\underline{1000pF}} \rightarrow f = \dfrac{1}{2\pi(1.9 \times 10^6)10^{-9}} = \underline{\underline{83.6Hz}}$

15 **11**

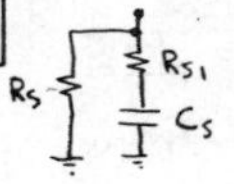

$Z_S = \dfrac{R_S(R_{S1} + \frac{1}{C_Ss})}{R_S + R_{S1} + \frac{1}{C_Ss}}$

Z_S becomes infinite when $R_S + R_{S1} + \frac{1}{C_Ss} = 0$ at $s = \dfrac{-1}{(R_S + R_{S1})C_S}$. Thus by introducing R_{S1}, the zero is lowered, from $\frac{-1}{R_SC_S}$ to $\frac{1}{(R_S + R_{S1})C_S}$. At the same time the pole lowers as well, from $\dfrac{1}{C_S(R_S \| 1/g_m)}$ to $\dfrac{1}{C_S(R_{S1} + R_S \| 1/g_m)}$

16 $C_{C2} = \dfrac{1}{2\pi \times 100\,(10^4 + 10^4 \| 10^5)} = \underline{\underline{.0834\mu F}}$: $\underline{\underline{\text{Use } 0.1\mu F}}$

17

$I_{DSS} = 1mA$, $V_P = -2V$

$i_D = I_{DSS}\left(1 - \frac{v_{GS}}{V_P}\right)^2 = 1\left(1 - \frac{1}{2}\right)^2 = 1/4$ mA

$g_m = \dfrac{2I_{DSS}}{-V_P}\left(1 - \frac{v_{GS}}{V_P}\right) = \frac{2(1)}{2}\left(1 - \frac{1}{2}\right) = 0.5$ mA/V

$r_s = 1/g_m = 2k\Omega$

Gain at high frequencies $= -\dfrac{10}{2 + 1.1} = -3.22 \equiv \underline{\underline{10.2dB}}$

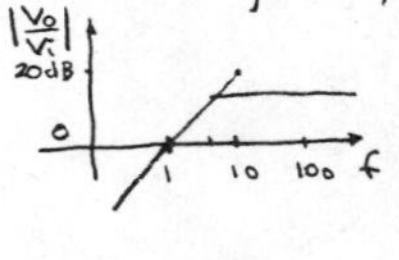

$f = \dfrac{1}{2\pi(10^{-5})(2 + 1.1)\times 10^3} = \underline{\underline{5.13 Hz}}$

Generally $\dfrac{V_o}{V_i}(s) = \dfrac{-R_o}{R_s + 1/g_m + \frac{1}{sC_s}}$

18 | 11

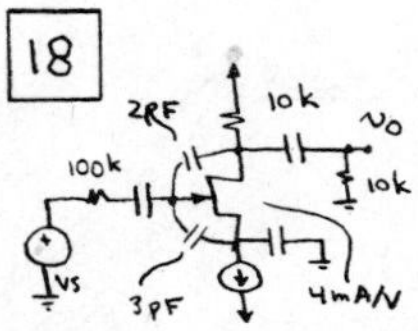

Basic gain $= -g_m(R_D \| R_L)$

$= -4\times10^{-3}(10k \| 10k) = -20$

$v_o/v_s = -20\left(\frac{1}{1+0.1}\right) = -18.2$

$R_T = 1M \| 100k = 90.9k$, $C_T = 3 + 2(1+20) = 45\,pF$

Dominant cutoff, $f_{p1} = \frac{1}{2\pi \times 90.9\times10^3 \times 45\times10^{-12}} = 38.9\,kHz$

$f_{p2} \approx \frac{g_m}{2\pi C_{gs}} = \frac{4\times10^{-3}}{2\pi \times 3\times10^{-12}} = 212\,MHz$

$f_Z = \frac{g_m}{2\pi C_{gd}} = \frac{4\times10^{-3}}{2\pi\times2\times10^{-12}} = 318\,MHz$

Exact solution from Eq. 11.51 gives $f_{p1} = 38.9\,kHz$ and

$f_{p2} = 239\,MHz$

19 | 11

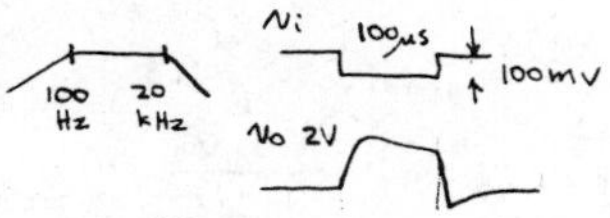

$t_r = t_f = \frac{.35}{f_H} = \frac{.35}{20\times10^3} = 17.5\,\mu s$

$Sag = \frac{T}{\tau}\times100$ and $\tau = \frac{1}{2\pi f} \rightarrow Sag = 2\pi f T \times 100$

$= 2\pi(100)100\times10^{-6}\times100 = 6.3\%$

20

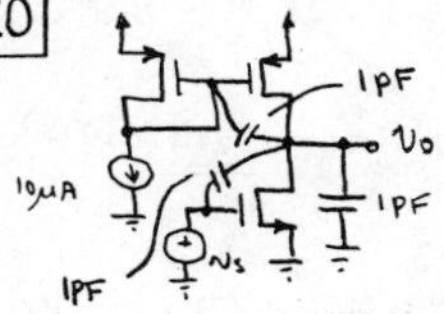

$k = \frac{1}{2}\mu_n C_{ox} W/L = \frac{20}{2}(64) = 640\,\mu A/V^2$

$i_D = k(v_{GS} - V_t)^2$

$g_m = 2k\sqrt{i_D/k} = 2(640)\sqrt{\frac{10}{640}}$

$= 160\,\mu A/V$

$r_o = \frac{V_A}{I_D} = \frac{50}{10\times10^{-6}} = 5\,M\Omega$

$Gain = -g_m(r_{o1} \| r_{o2}) = -160\times10^{-6}\times\frac{5}{2}\times10^6 = -400$

Output pole $= f_p = \frac{1}{2\pi R_T C_T} = \frac{1}{2\pi(5/2\times10^{-6})(1+1+1)\times10^{-12}} = 21.2\,kHz$

Output zero $= f_Z = \frac{g_m}{2\pi C_{gd}} = \frac{160\times10^{-6}}{2\pi\times1\times10^{-12}} = 25.5\,MHz$

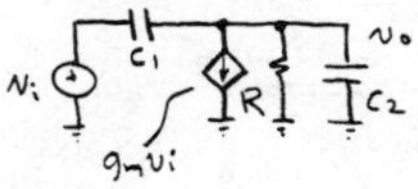

$sC_2 v_o + v_o/R + g_m v_i = sC_1(v_i - v_o)$

$\frac{v_o}{v_i} = \frac{-(g_m - sC_1)}{s(C_1+C_2) + 1/R}$

with right-half plane zero at $\omega_Z = g_m/C_1$ and pole $\omega_p = \frac{1}{R(C_1+C_2)}$

21 | 11

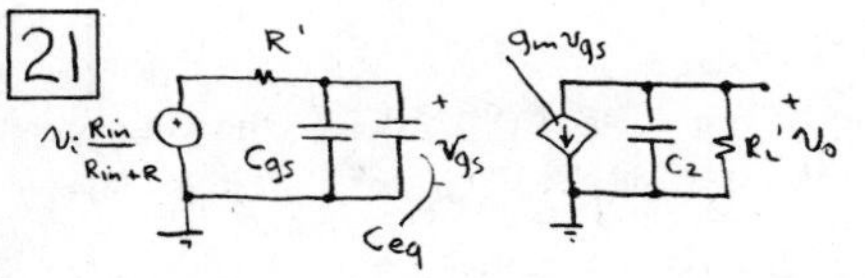

$\omega_{p1} = \frac{1}{\left(C_{gs} + C_{gd}(1+g_m R_L') + C_{gd}(R_L'/R')\right)R'}$

whence $C_{eq} = C_{gd}\left[(1+g_m R_L') + R_L'/R'\right]$

$\omega_{p2} = \frac{C_{gs} + C_{gd}(1 + g_m R_L' + R_L'/R')}{C_{gs}C_{gd}R_L'}$

whence $C_2 = \frac{C_{gd}}{1 + \frac{C_{gd}}{C_{gs}}(1 + g_m R_L' + R_L'/R')}$

Now $C_{gd} = C_{gs} = 1\,pF$, $g_m = 4\,mA/V$, $R' = 80.8k$, $R_L' = 3.\dot{3}k$

$\therefore C_{eq} = 1(1 + 4(3.33) + 3.\dot{3}/80.8) = 14.4\,pF$

$C_2 = 1/(1 + 1/1(1 + 4(3.33) + 3.\dot{3}/80.8))$

$= 1/(1 + 14.4) = .065\,pF$

For which $f_{p1} = \frac{1}{2\pi\times80.8\times10^3\times(1+14.4)\times10^{-12}} = 127.9\,kHz$

$f_{p2} = \frac{1}{2\pi(3.3\times10^3)\times.065\times10^{-12}} = 734.6\,MHz$

as expected

22 | 11

$I_E = 10\,mA \rightarrow r_e = \frac{V_T}{I_E} = \frac{25\times10^{-3}}{10\times10^{-3}} = 2.5\Omega$

$i_c = \frac{120\times10^{-3}}{10.0} = 1.2\,mA$, $i_b = \frac{13.9-3.9}{1k} = 10\,\mu A$

$h_{fe} = \frac{1.2\times10^{-3}}{10\times10^{-6}} = 120$, $r_\pi = (h_{fe}+1)r_e = 121(2.5) = 302.5$

$(r_\pi + r_x) = \frac{3.9-0.6}{10} = 330\Omega$, $r_x = 330 - 302.5 = 27.5\Omega$

$g_m = \frac{120}{121}\times\frac{1}{2.5} = 397\,mA/V$

Note that if I_C were known to be 10mA (as measured using the 100Ω collector resistor),

$g_m = 400\,mA/V$, $r_\pi = \frac{h_{fe}}{g_m} = \frac{120}{400\,mA/V} = 300\Omega$

$r_x = 330 - 300 = 30\Omega$

23

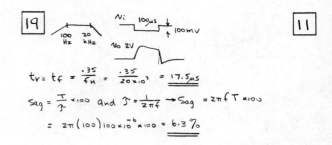

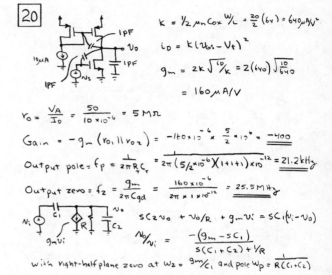

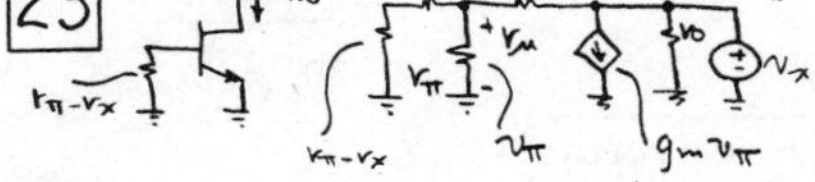

$i_x = v_x\left(\frac{1}{r_o} + \frac{1}{r_\mu + r_\pi/2} + g_m\frac{1}{r_\mu + r_\pi/2}\cdot r_\pi/2\right)$

$1/R_o = \frac{i_x}{v_x}\left(1/r_o + \frac{1}{r_\mu} + \frac{1}{r_\mu(2/\beta)}\right)$

$r_\mu >> r_\pi/2$, $g_m r_\pi = \beta$

$\therefore R_o = r_o \| r_\mu \| \frac{2r_\mu}{\beta}$

24 | 11

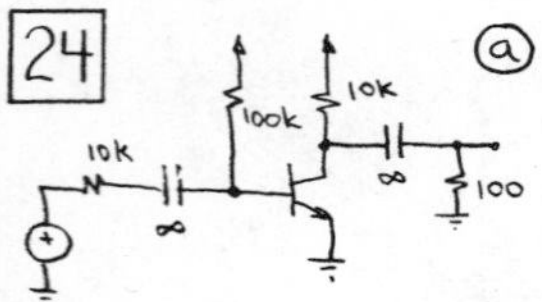

ⓐ Approximately:

$$h_{ie} = \frac{5\,mV}{(15-5)\,mV} = \underline{\underline{5\,k\Omega}}$$

$$h_{fe} = \frac{20/100}{(15-5)/10k} = \underline{\underline{200}}$$

Better: Base current $= \frac{(15-5)10^{-3}}{10\times10^3} - \frac{5\times10^{-3}}{100\times10^3} = (1-.05) = .95\,\mu A$

Collector current $= \frac{20\,mV}{100} + \frac{20\,mV}{10^4} = 202\,\mu A$

$$\therefore h_{fe} = \frac{202}{0.95} = \underline{\underline{212.6}}$$

$$h_{ie} = \frac{5\,mV}{.95\,\mu A} = \underline{\underline{5.26\,k\Omega}}$$

ⓑ For $r_x = 50\,\Omega$, $r_\pi = 5260 - 50 = \underline{\underline{5210}}\,\Omega$

$$r_e = \frac{5210}{212.6+1} = \underline{\underline{24.39\,\Omega}}$$

$$g_m = \frac{\alpha}{r_e} = \frac{\beta}{\beta+1}\times\frac{1}{r_e} = \frac{212.6}{213.6}\times\frac{1}{24.39} = \underline{\underline{40.81\,mA/V}}$$

$$I_E = \frac{25}{24.39} = \underline{\underline{1.025\,mA}}$$

ⓒ $h_{re} = \frac{1\,mV}{5\,V} = 0.2\times10^{-3} = \underline{\underline{2\times10^{-4}}}$

Use low a frequency to avoid the effect of C_μ shunting r_μ

ⓓ $h_{re} = \frac{r_\pi}{r_\pi + r_\mu} = \frac{5210}{r_\mu + 5210} = 2\times10^{-4} \rightarrow r_\mu = \underline{\underline{26\,M\Omega}}$

$$f = \frac{1}{2\pi RC} = \frac{1}{2\pi\times26\times10^6\times1\times10^{-12}} = \underline{\underline{6.12\,kHz}}$$

ⓔ $h_{oe} = \frac{i_c}{v_c} = \left(\frac{8\times10^{-3}}{100}\right)\frac{213}{214} = \underline{\underline{15.9\,\mu A/V}}$

$$r_o = \left(h_{oe} - \frac{h_{fe}}{r_\mu}\right)^{-1} = \left(15.9\times10^{-6} - \frac{213}{26\times10^6}\right)^{-1} = \underline{\underline{129.5\,k\Omega}}$$

25 $g_m = \frac{2\,mA}{25\,mV} = \underline{\underline{80\,mA/V}}$, $\beta = \underline{\underline{100}}$ | 11

$$r_e = \frac{\beta}{\beta+1}\times\frac{1}{g_m} = \frac{100}{101}\cdot\frac{1}{80} = \underline{\underline{12.38\,\Omega}}$$

$$r_\pi = (\beta+1)r_e = 101(12.38) = \underline{\underline{1250\,\Omega}}$$

$$r_x = h_{ie} - r_\pi = 1350 - 1250 = \underline{\underline{100\,\Omega}}$$

$$r_\mu = \frac{r_\pi}{h_{re}} = \frac{1250}{5\times10^{-5}} = \underline{\underline{25\,M\Omega}}$$

$$r_o = \left(h_{oe} - \frac{h_{fe}}{r_\mu}\right)^{-1} = \left(2.4\times10^{-5} - \frac{100}{25\times10^6}\right)^{-1} = \underline{\underline{50\,k\Omega}}$$

$$V_A = 50\times10^3\times2\times10^{-3} = \underline{\underline{100\,V}}$$

26 $g_m = \frac{1}{25} = 40\,mA/V$,

$$\omega_T = \beta_o\omega_\beta = \frac{g_m}{C_\pi + C_\mu} = \frac{40\times10^{-3}}{(1+10)\times10^{-12}} = 3.64\,Grad/s$$

$$\omega_\beta = \frac{3.64}{150} = 24.2\,Mrad/s$$

27 $C_d = C_\pi - C_j = 10 - 2 = 8\,pF$ @ 1mA

At 0.1mA, $C_d = \frac{0.1}{1}\times 8\,pF = 0.8\,pF$

$$\omega_{T_{0.1}} = \frac{g_m}{C_\pi + C_\mu} = \frac{4\times10^{-3}}{(0.8+2+1)\times10^{-12}} = 1.05\,Grad/s$$

$$\omega_{T_1} = \frac{g_m}{C_\pi + C_\mu} = \frac{40\times10^{-3}}{(10+1)\times10^{-12}} = 3.64\,Grad/s$$

28 $g_m = \frac{0.2\,mA}{25\,mV} = 8\,mA/V$ | 11

$$f_T = \frac{g_m}{2\pi(C_\pi + C_\mu)} \rightarrow C_\pi + C_\mu = \frac{g_m}{2\pi f_T} = \frac{8\times10^{-3}}{2\pi(3\times10^9)}$$

or $C_\pi + C_\mu = 424\,pF \rightarrow C_\pi = .424 - 0.1 = \underline{\underline{.324\,pF}}$

29 $G.B = f_T(1) = 10^9\,Hz = \beta f$

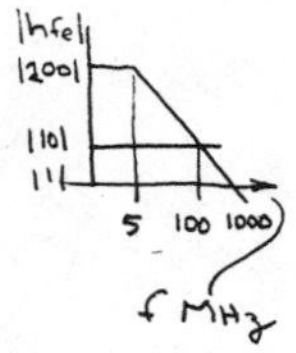

$h_{fe} = 10$ at $\frac{10^9}{10} = 10^8\,Hz = 100\,MHz$

$$f_\beta = \frac{f_T}{\beta_o} = \frac{10^9}{200} = 5\times10^6 = 5\,MHz$$

$$\omega_\beta = 2\pi f_\beta = 31.4\,Mrad/sec$$

30

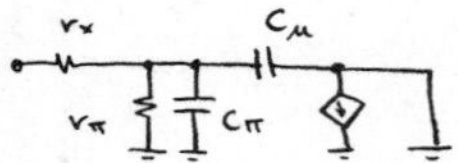

$$\omega_\beta = \frac{1}{r_\pi(C_\pi + C_\mu)}$$

$$Z_{in}(s) = r_x + r_\pi \| \frac{1}{(C_\pi + C_\mu)s} = r_x + \frac{r_\pi/(C_\pi+C_\mu)s}{r_\pi + \frac{1}{(C_\pi+C_\mu)s}}$$

$$= r_x + \frac{r_\pi}{1 + r_\pi(C_\pi + C_\mu)s}$$

$$= r_x + r_\pi\frac{(1 - j(C_\pi + C_\mu)r_\pi\omega)}{1 + r_\pi^2(C_\pi + C_\mu)^2\omega^2} = r_x + \frac{r_\pi(1 - j\frac{\omega}{\omega_\beta})}{1 + (\omega/\omega_\beta)^2}$$

Real part $Z(s) = r_x + r_\pi/(1 + (\omega/\omega_\beta)^2) \leq 1.1\,r_x$

for $r_\pi/(1 + (\omega/\omega_\beta)^2) \leq 0.1 r_x \leq r_\pi/100$, at frequencies where $1 + (\omega/\omega_\beta)^2 \geq 100$ or $\underline{\underline{\omega \geq 10\,\omega_\beta}}$

31 | 11

	I_E mA	r_e Ω	g_m mA/V	r_π kΩ	β_o	f_T MHz	C_μ pF	C_π pF	f_β MHz
ⓐ	1	25	39.6	2.525	100	400	2	13.8	4
ⓑ	1	25	39.7	3.133	124.3	497	2	10.7	4
ⓒ	1	25	39.6	2.525	100	400	2	13.8	4
ⓓ	10	2.5	396	.252	100	400	2	155.6	4
ⓔ	0.1	250	3.96	25.25	100	100	2	4.3	4
ⓕ	1	25	36.4	.275	10	400	2	12.5	40
ⓖ	1.38	18.1	50.3	.199	10	800	1	9	80

$r_e = V_T/I_E$, $g_m = \frac{\alpha}{r_e}$, $r_\pi = (\beta+1)r_e$, $f_T = \frac{1}{2\pi}\frac{g_m}{C_\pi + C_\mu}$, $f_\beta = \frac{f_T}{\beta_o}$

ⓐ $r_e = \frac{25}{1} = 25$, $f_\beta = \frac{400}{100} = 4$, $g_m = \frac{100}{101}\frac{1}{25} = 39.6\,mA/V$

$$C_\pi = \frac{g_m}{2\pi(f_T)} - C_\mu = \frac{39.6\times10^{-3}}{2\pi(400\times10^6)} - 2\times10^{-12} = 13.8\,pF$$

ⓑ $f_\beta = \frac{1}{2\pi(C_\pi + C_\mu)r_\pi} \rightarrow r_\pi = \frac{1}{2\pi f_\beta(C_\pi + C_\mu)} = \frac{1}{2\pi\times4\times10^6(12.7\times10^{-12})} = 3.13k$

$\beta = \frac{3133}{25} - 1 = 124.3$, $g_m = \frac{124.3}{125.3}\times\frac{1}{25} = 39.7$, $f_T = 4(124.3) = 497$

ⓒ $C_\mu = \frac{1}{f_\beta(2\pi r_\pi)} - C_\pi = 15.76 - 13.8 = 2\,pF$, $\beta = \frac{400}{4} = 100$, $r_e = \frac{2525}{101}$

ⓓ $C_\pi = \frac{\alpha/r_e}{2\pi f_T} - C_\mu = \frac{396}{2\pi(400)} - 2 = 157.6 - 2 = 155.6$, ⓖ $\beta = \frac{800}{80} = 10$

ⓔ $C_\pi = \frac{.396}{2\pi(100\times10^6)} - 2 = 4.3\,pF$, ⓕ $C_\pi = \frac{36.4}{2\pi(400)} - 2 = 12.5$ ⓖ $g_m = 2\pi f_T(C_\pi + C_\mu)$

32 (a) 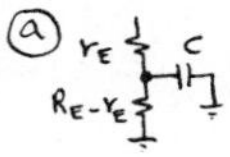 or (b) 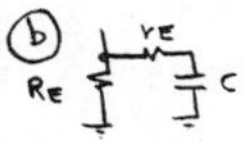

11

(a) $R_E' = (R_E - r_E) \parallel \left(\frac{r_\pi + r_x + R_B \parallel R_S}{(\beta+1)} + r_E\right)$

$W_Z = \frac{1}{C_E(R_E - r_E)}$

(b) $R_E' = r_E + R_E \parallel \left(\frac{r_\pi + r_x + R_B \parallel R_S}{\beta+1}\right)$

$W_Z = \frac{1}{C_E(R_E + r_E)}$

W_Z is the value of s for which $Z_E = \infty$ or $1/Z_E = 0$

$1/Z_E = \left(\frac{1}{R_E} + \frac{1}{r_E + 1/sC_E}\right)$ or $-R_E = \frac{1}{sC_E} + r_E$ or $s = -\frac{1}{C_E(r_E + R_E)}$

33 Bias: $\beta = \infty$, $I_{C3} = I_{C2} = I_{C1} = \frac{11.4 - 1.4}{10k} = 1mA$

$V_O = 11.4 - 5(1) = 6.4V$, $r_{e1,2,3} = 25\Omega$

$\underline{C=0}$: Gain $= \frac{-\alpha R_L}{r_e + r_e \parallel r_\pi} = -\frac{R_L}{2r_e} = -100$

$R_{in} = \frac{v_i}{i_i} = \frac{v_i}{i_{b1} + i_{c3} + i_{10k}}$ for which $i_{b1} = 0$

since $\beta = \infty$, $i_{c3} = \frac{v_i}{2r_e}$ through mirror and $i_{10k} = \frac{v_i}{10k}$

$\therefore R_i = \frac{1}{1/2r_e + 1/10k} = 50\Omega \parallel 10k \simeq 49.8\,\Omega$

$\underline{C=\infty}$: Gain $= \frac{-R_L}{r_e} = -200$

$R_{in} = 10k$ (since no feedback)

$\underline{C \text{ finite}}$: $\frac{v_o}{v_i} = \frac{-R_L}{r_e + r_e \parallel \frac{1}{Cs}} = \frac{-R_L}{r_e + \frac{r_e}{1 + r_e Cs}}$

11

or $\frac{v_o}{v_i} = -\frac{R_L(1 + r_e Cs)}{r_e\,(2 + r_e Cs)} = -\frac{R_L}{2r_e}\left(\frac{1 + r_e Cs}{1 + \frac{r_e}{2}Cs}\right)$

For $C = 1\mu F$, $W_Z = \frac{1}{25 \times 10^{-6}} = 40$ krad/s, $W_P = 80$ krad/s

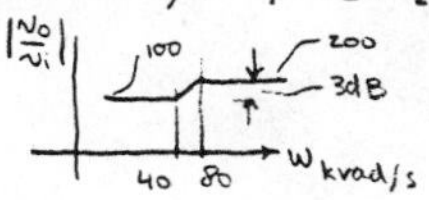

34 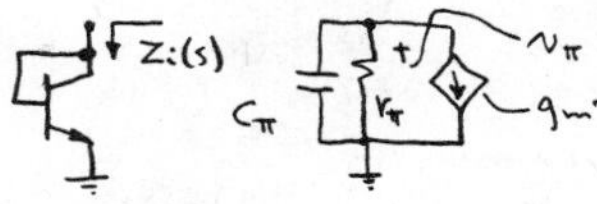

$Z_i = r_e \parallel \frac{1}{C_\pi s}$

$Z_i = \frac{r_e / C_\pi s}{r_e + 1/C_\pi s} = \frac{r_e}{1 + r_e C_\pi s}$

$\tan^{-1} Z_i(s) = 45°$ at $\omega = \frac{1}{r_e C_\pi}$ or $f = \frac{1}{2\pi r_e C_\pi}$

ie at $f \approx \frac{f_T}{\alpha}$ for $C_\mu \ll C_\pi$

or $f \simeq \frac{400\,MHz}{100/101} = \underline{\underline{404\,MHz}}$ or higher for larger C_μ

35 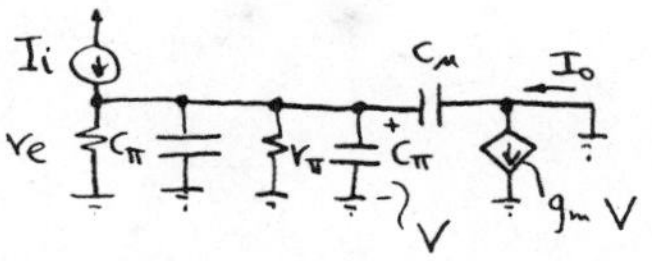

$I_I = 1mA$, $r_e = 25$

$f_T = 400\,MHz$

$C_\mu = 2pF$, $\beta_0 = 100$

$C_\pi = \frac{g_m}{2\pi f_T} - C_\mu = \frac{100/101}{25 \times 2\pi \times 400 \times 10^6} - 2pF = 13.8\,pF$

$V = \frac{I_i}{1/r_{e1} + 1/r_{\pi 2} + s(C_{\pi 1} + C_{\pi 2} + C_{\mu 2})}$,

11

$I_o = (g_{m2} - sC_{\mu 2})V$

$\therefore \frac{I_o}{I_i} = \frac{g_m - sC_\mu}{1/r_e + 1/r_\pi + s(2C_\pi + C_\mu)}$

See $W_Z = g_m / C_\mu = \frac{1}{r_e C_\mu}$

$w_p = \frac{1}{(2C_\pi + C_\mu)(r_e \parallel r_\pi)} = \frac{1}{r_e(2C_\pi + C_\mu)}$ } for large β

$f_Z = \frac{1}{2\pi \times 25 \times 2 \times 10^{-12}} = 3.18\,GHz$

$f_P = \frac{1}{2\pi \times 25\,(2(13.8) + 2) \times 10^{-12}} = 215\,MHz$

36 Assume one capacitor is shorted while the other is calculated: $R_{C1} = 10k + 10k \parallel (100 + 1k) = 10.99k$

$R_{CE} = 1k \parallel \frac{1}{101}\times(1k + 100 + 10k \parallel 10k) = 57\Omega$

For equal contribution to cut off: $10.99 C_{C1} = 57 C_E$

or $\frac{C_E}{C_{C1}} = \frac{10990}{57} = \underline{\underline{193}}$

37 $10mA \to r_e = 2.5\Omega$; $f_T = 100MHz \to C_\pi = \frac{1}{2\pi \times 2.5 \times 10^8} - 5$

or $C_\pi = 637 - 5 = 632$ pF. Input pole: $f_{P1} = \frac{1}{2\pi(2.5 \parallel 200 \parallel 50)(632 \times 10^{-12})}$

or $f_{P1} = \underline{\underline{107\,MHz}}$. Output pole: $f_{P2} = \frac{1}{2\pi(5 \times 10^{-12})(500 \parallel 500)} = \underline{\underline{127\,MHz}}$

38 $V_{E1} = 3V$, $V_{C1} = V_{E2} = 4.5V$, $V_{C2} = 6V$

11

$I_{E1} = I_{E2} = 0.1mA \to R_E = \frac{3}{0.1} = \underline{\underline{30k\Omega}} = R_C$

$I_{BN} = 10\mu A \to R_3 = \frac{3.7}{10\mu A} = \underline{\underline{370k}}$, $R_2 = \frac{4.5 - 3}{10\mu A} = \underline{\underline{150k\Omega}}$

$R_1 = \frac{9 - (4.5 + 0.7)}{10\mu A} = \underline{\underline{380\,k\Omega}}$, $r_{e1} = r_{e2} = 250\Omega$

i) Input Resistance:

(a) For $\beta = \infty \to R_2 \parallel R_3 = 150k \parallel 370k = \underline{\underline{107k\Omega}}$

(b) For $\beta = 100 \to 107k \parallel 101(250) = \underline{\underline{20.4\,k\Omega}}$

ii) Gain: $\beta = \infty$

(c) For no load $\to$ gain $= -\frac{\alpha^2 R_L}{r_e} = \frac{-30k}{250} = \underline{\underline{-120}}$

(d) For 10k load $\to$ gain $= -\frac{30k \parallel 10k}{250} = -120 \times \frac{10}{10 + 30} = \underline{\underline{-30}}$

iii) $C_\pi = \frac{g_m}{2\pi f_T} - C_\mu = \frac{50/51}{2\pi(250)(100 \times 10^6)} - 1 = 6.37 - 1 = 5.37\,pF$

(e) Gain $= -\frac{107 \parallel 51(250)}{107 \parallel 51(250) + 10k} \times \left(\frac{50}{51}\right)^2 \times \frac{30k \parallel 10k}{250} = \underline{\underline{-15.36\,V/V}}$

(f) $f_{P1} = \frac{1}{2\pi((51 \times 250) \parallel 10) \times 10^3\,(5.37 + 1(1+1)) \times 10^{-12}} = \underline{\underline{3.86\,MHz}}$

$f_{P2} = \frac{1}{2\pi(250)(5.37 + 1) \times 10^{-12}} = \underline{\underline{100\,MHz}}$

$f_{P3} = \frac{1}{2\pi(30/4) \times 10^3 \times 1 \times 10^{-12}} = \underline{\underline{21.2\,MHz}}$

(g) $f_H = \left(\frac{1}{3.86^2} + \frac{1}{100^2} + \frac{1}{21.2^2}\right)^{-1/2} = \underline{\underline{3.80\,MHz}}$

39 $r_e = 25\,\Omega$, $\beta = 100$, $C_\pi = 5\,pF$, $C_\mu = 1\,pF$ **11**

$$f_{P_{RC}} = \frac{1}{2\pi (5k) 1\times 10^{-12}} = \underline{\underline{31.8\,MHz}}$$

$$f_{P_{12}} = \frac{1}{2\pi (25)(5+1)10^{-12}} = \underline{\underline{106\,MHz}}$$

For input pole $r_\pi = 101(25) = 2525\,\Omega$

For $R_S = 1k$, $R_T = 2.525 \| 1k = .716\,k$

$$f_1 = \frac{1}{2\pi (716)(5 + 1(1+1))\times 10^{-12}} = 31.75\,MHz$$

For $R_S = 10k$, $R_T = 2.525 \| 10k = 2.016\,k$

$$f_{1_{10}} = \frac{1}{2\pi(2016)(7)\times 10^{-12}} = \underline{11.28\,MHz}$$

Upper cutoff

(a) $R_S = 1k$: $f_{H_1} = \left(\left(\frac{1}{31.8}\right)^2 + \left(\frac{1}{31.75}\right)^2\right)^{-1/2} = \underline{\underline{22.5\,MHz}}$

(b) $R_S = 10k$: $f_{H_{10}} = \left(\left(\frac{1}{31.8}\right)^2 + \left(\frac{1}{11.28}\right)^2\right)^{-1/2} = \underline{\underline{10.6\,MHz}}$

f_{H_1} reduces to 21.9 MHz if f_{P12} included

f_{H10} is unaffected

40 (a) $\underline{\underline{V_A = 0.7}}$, $I_{bias} = \frac{0.7}{6.8k} = .103 \simeq 0.1\,mA$ **11**

$V_{B2} = 1.4$, $V_C = 0.7/6.8\,(6.8 + 6.8 + 33) = 4.8V \simeq \underline{\underline{5V}}$

$I_{4.5} = \frac{10 - 4.8}{4.5} = 1.083\,mA$, $V_B = \underline{\underline{0.7V}}$

$I_C \simeq 1\,mA$, $r_{e1} = r_{e2} = 25\,\Omega$

(b) $$\frac{v_o}{v_I} = -\frac{\frac{6.8}{2}k \| (101)25}{1k + \frac{6.8}{2}k \| (101)25} \times \frac{4.5k \| 5k \| 33k}{25} \cdot \left(\frac{100}{101}\right)^2 = \underline{\underline{-51.4}}$$

(c) For C_{C1}, $R_T = 1 + 2.525 \| 6.8/2 = 1.449\,k$

$$f_{P1} = \frac{1}{2\pi (1)\times 10^{-6} (1.449\times 10^3)} = 110\,Hz$$

For C_{C2}, $R_T = 5K + 4.5k \| 33k = 8.96k$

$$f_{P2} = \frac{1}{2\pi (0.1)\times 10^{-6} (8.96\times 10^3)} = 177.6$$

$f_L \simeq 178 + 110 = 288\,Hz$

or $f_L' = (178^2 + 110^2)^{1/2} = \underline{\underline{209\,Hz}}$

41 **11**

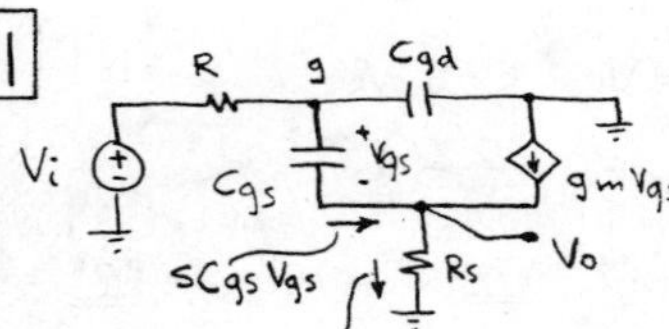

$V_o = (g_m + sC_{gs})V_{gs}R_s$

$$\frac{V_o}{sC_{gs}V_{gs}} = R_s + \frac{g_m R_s}{sC_{gs}}$$

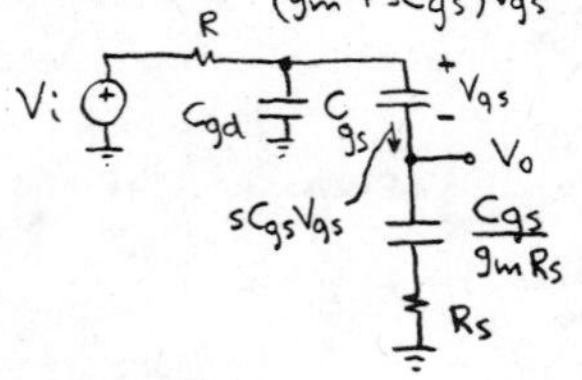

$V_o = 0$ at $R_s + \frac{1}{s_z \frac{C_{gs}}{g_m R_s}} = 0$

whence $s_z = -\frac{g_m}{C_{gs}}$

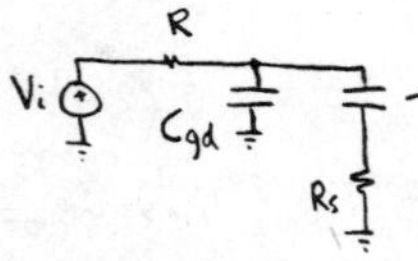

$$\sim C_{gs}\left(\frac{1 \times \frac{1}{g_m R_s}}{1 + \frac{1}{g_m R_s}}\right) = C_{gs}\frac{1}{1 + g_m R_s}$$

Using open-circuit time constant technique:

$\tau_1 = C_{gd} R$, $\tau_2 = (R + R_S)\frac{C_{gs}}{1 + g_m R_s}$ with correspondingly

a pole at $\frac{1}{2\pi \times 10^{-12} \times 10^5} = 1.59\,MHz$ (dominant),

a pole at $\frac{1}{2\pi \times (100+10)\times 10^{+3} \times \frac{2\times 10^{-12}}{1 + 20}} = 15.2\,MHz$

and a zero at $\frac{-1}{2\pi \times 2\times 10^{-12} \times \frac{1}{2\times 10^{-3}}} = 159\,MHz$

Midband gain is $A_m = \frac{R_s}{R_s + 1/g_m} = \frac{10k}{10k + 500} = 0.952$

42 **11**

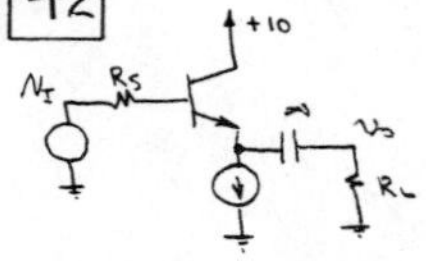

$R_S = 1K, 10k, 100k$; $R_L = 1k$; $r_e = 12.5$

$\beta_o = 100$, $f_T = 400\,MHz$, $C_\mu = 2pF$

$$C_\pi = \frac{\beta/\beta+1}{2\pi r_e f_T} - C_\mu = \frac{\frac{100}{101}}{2\pi(12.5)400\times 10^6} - 2$$

$= 31.5 - 2 = 29.5\,pF$

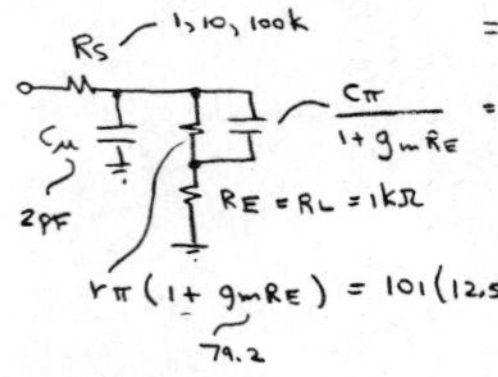

$$\frac{C_\pi}{1 + g_m R_E} = \frac{29.5}{1 + \frac{100}{101}\times\frac{1}{12.5}\times 1000} = 0.368\,pF$$

$r_\pi(1 + g_m R_E) = 101(12.5)(80.2) = 101K$ (79.2)

Method of Open Circuit Time Constants:

$R_S = 1k$ $\tau_1 = (1k \| 102k)(2) = .2nsec$; $\tau_2 = (101k \| 2k)(.368) = .72nsec$ } $2.72 \rightarrow f_H = \frac{1}{2\pi(2.72)} = \underline{\underline{58.5\,MHz}}$

$R_S = 10k$ $\tau_1 = (10k \| 102k)(2) = 18nsec$; $\tau_2 = (101k \| 11k)(.368) = 3.65nsec$ } $21.65 \rightarrow f_H = \frac{1}{2\pi(21.65)} = \underline{\underline{7.35\,MHz}}$

$R_S = 100k$ $\tau_1 = (100k \| 102k)(2) = 100nsec$; $\tau_2 = (101k \| 101k)(.368) = 18.6nsec$ } $118.6 \rightarrow f_H = \frac{1}{2\pi(118.6)} = \underline{\underline{1.34\,MHz}}$

With dominant poles for $R_S = 1, 10, 100\,k$ of

$\underline{\underline{79.6}}, \underline{\underline{8.84}}, \underline{\underline{1.59}}$ MHz respectively and a zero at $\frac{-1}{2\pi C_\pi/g_m}$

or 430 MHz

43 (a) DC bias: (note Q_1, Q_2 labelling) **11**

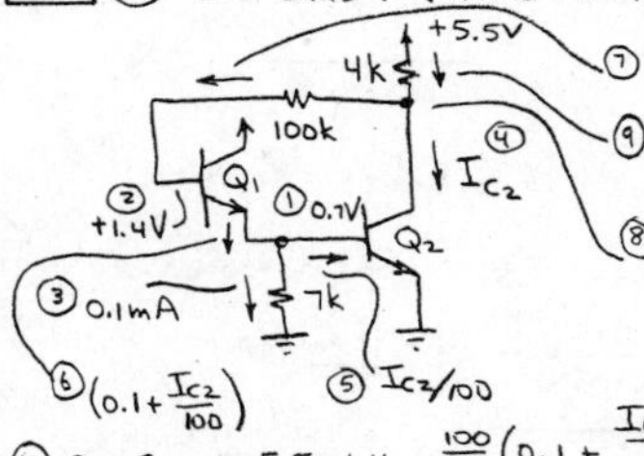

⑦ $(0.1 + \frac{I_{C2}}{100})/101$

⑨ $\dfrac{5.5 - 1.4 - \frac{100}{101}(0.1 + \frac{I_{C2}}{100})}{4}$

⑧ $1.4 + \frac{100}{101}(0.1 + \frac{I_{C2}}{100})$

⑩ At C_2: $\dfrac{5.5 - 1.4 - \frac{100}{101}(0.1 + \frac{I_{C2}}{100})}{4} = \dfrac{0.1 + \frac{I_{C2}}{100}}{101} + I_{C2}$

or $\dfrac{5.5-1.4}{4} - \dfrac{100 \times 0.1}{4 \times 101} - \dfrac{0.1}{101} = I_{C2}\left[1 + \dfrac{1}{100 \times 101} + \dfrac{100}{100 \times 101 \times 4}\right]$

whence $I_{C2} \simeq \underline{1 mA}$, $V_{C2} = 1.5(1) V$

$I_{E1} = 0.1 + \dfrac{I_{C2}}{100} = 0.1 + 0.01 = 0.11 mA$

$I_{C1} = \alpha I_{E1} = 0.99 \times 0.11 \simeq \underline{0.11 mA}$

(b)

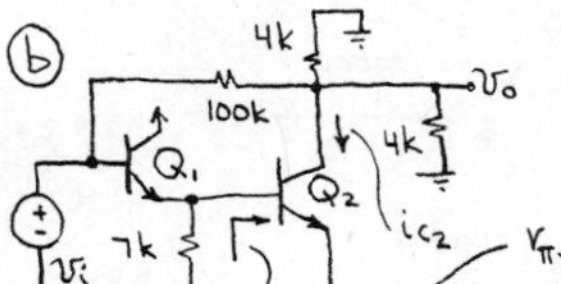

$r_{e1} \simeq \dfrac{25}{0.11} = 227\Omega$

$r_{e2} \simeq \dfrac{25}{1} = 25\Omega$

$r_{\pi 2} = (\beta+1) r_{e2} \doteq 101 \times 25 = 2.525 k\Omega$

$\dfrac{v_{e1}}{v_i} = \dfrac{7 \| 2.525}{7 \| 2.525 + 0.227} = 0.89 V/V$

$i_{c2} = g_{m2} v_{b2} = g_{m2} v_{e1} = g_{m2} \times 0.89 v_i = 40 \times 0.89 v_i$

Node equation at C_2: $i_{c2} + \dfrac{v_o}{4} + \dfrac{v_o}{4} + \dfrac{v_o - v_i}{100} = 0$

ie. $40 \times 0.89 v_i + v_o(1/4 + 1/4 + 1/100) - 0.01 v_i = 0$

whence $v_o/v_i = \dfrac{-(40 \times 0.89 - 0.01)}{1/4 + 1/4 + 1/100} = \underline{\underline{-69.8 V/V}}$ **11**

For R_{in}:

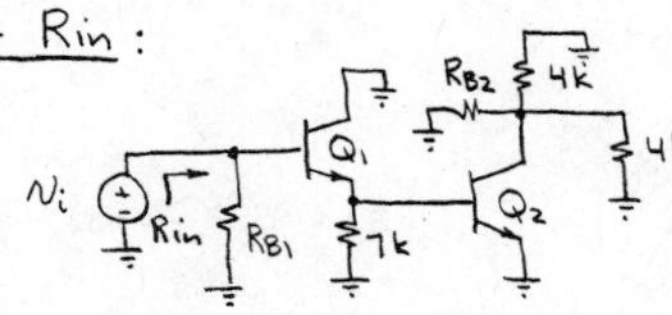

See:

$v_i/R_{B1} = \dfrac{v_i - v_o}{R_B} = \dfrac{v_i + 69.8 v_i}{R_B} \rightarrow R_{B1} = \dfrac{R_B}{70.8} = \dfrac{100}{70.8} = \underline{\underline{1.4 k\Omega}}$

$v_o/R_{B2} = \dfrac{v_o - v_i}{R_B} = \dfrac{v_o - (-v_o/69.8)}{R_B} \rightarrow R_{B2} \simeq R_B = \underline{\underline{100 k\Omega}}$

Now $R_{in} = R_{B1} \| \{(\beta+1)[r_{e1} + 7 \| 2.525]\}$

$= 1.4 \| 101(227 + 7 \| 2.525) \simeq \underline{1.4 k\Omega}$

For R_{out}:

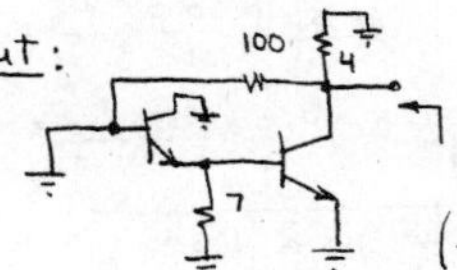

$R_{out} = 4 \| 100 = \underline{3.85 k\Omega}$

(for low impedance input shown)

For overall gain: $v_o/v_s = \dfrac{v_{b1}}{v_s} \times \dfrac{v_o}{v_{b1}} = \dfrac{R_{in}}{R_s + R_{in}} \times (-69.8)$

ie $v_o/v_s = -\dfrac{1.4}{4 + 1.4} \times 69.8 = \underline{\underline{-10.1 V/V}}$

(c) For input low-frequency pole at f_{PL1}

$f_{PL1} = \dfrac{1}{2\pi C_{C1}(R_s + R_{in})} = \dfrac{1}{2\pi \times 10^{-6} \times (4 + 1.4) \times 10^3}$

$= \dfrac{1000}{2\pi \times 5.4} = \underline{\underline{29.5 Hz}}$

For output low-frequency pole at f_{PL2} **11**

$f_{PL2} = \dfrac{1}{2\pi C_{C2}(R_L + R_{out})} = \dfrac{1}{2\pi \times 10^{-6} \times (4 + 3.85) \times 10^3} = \underline{\underline{20.3 Hz}}$

Note that R_{out} is properly one for which calculation includes the effect of R_s. It is somewhat smaller than the value use here and f_{PL2} is higher than 20Hz

Using Eq (11.18), $f_L \simeq \sqrt{f_{PL1}^2 + f_{PL2}^2} = \sqrt{29.5^2 + 20.3^2} = \underline{\underline{35.8 Hz}}$

(d) For the upper cutoff f_H

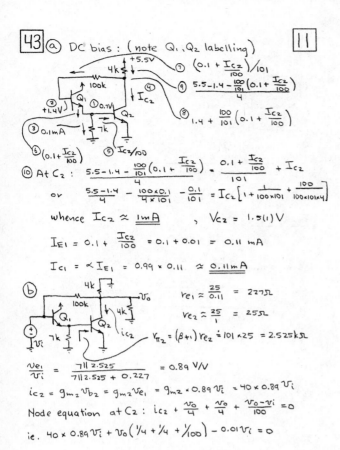

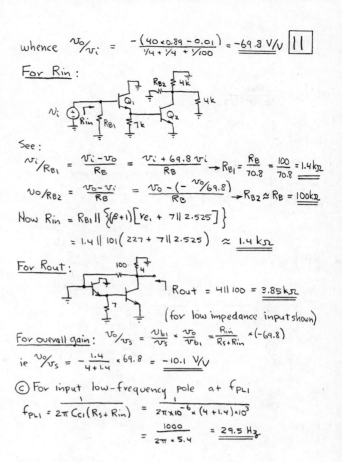

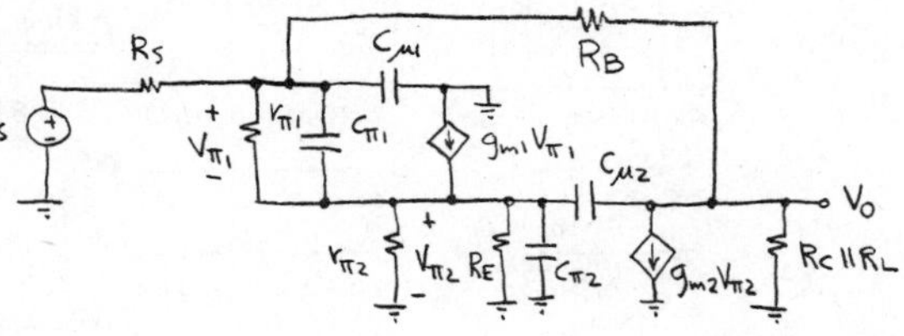

$\omega_{T2} = g_{m2}/(C_{\pi 2} + C_{\mu 2})$, whence

$C_{\pi 2} + C_{\mu 2} = 40 \times 10^{-3}/(2\pi \times 400 \times 10^6) = 15.9 pF$

$C_{\mu 2} = 2pF \rightarrow C_{\pi 2} = 13.9 pF$

$C_{d2} = 13.9 - C_{je} = 12.9 pF$, $C_{d1} = 12.9 \times \dfrac{0.11}{1} = 1.4 pF$

$C_{\pi 1} = 1.4 + 1 = 2.4 pF$, $C_{\mu 1} = 2pF$

To simplify matters, replace R_B by R_{B1} and R_{B2} and follow the method of Example 11.9 (See Fig 11.32 and page 649) **11**

Here $R_{\mu 1} = R_s \| R_{in} = 4 \| 1.4 \simeq 1 k\Omega$

$R_{\pi 1} = r_{\pi 1} \| \dfrac{(R_s \| R_{B1}) + (R_E \| r_{\pi 2})}{1 + g_{m1}(R_E \| r_{\pi 2})}$

$= 23 \| \dfrac{(4 \| 1.4) + (7 \| 2.525)}{1 + 40 \times 0.11 \times (7 \| 2.525)} = 307\Omega$

$C_T = C_{\pi 2} + C_{\mu 2}(1 + g_{m2}(R_L \| R_C \| R_{out}))$

$= 13.9 + 2(1 + 40(4 \| 4 \| 100)) = 94.3 pF$

$R_T = (R_E \| r_{\pi 2}) \| ((r_{\pi 1} + (R_s \| R_{B1}))/(\beta+1))$

$= 7 \| 2.525 \| \left(\dfrac{23 + (4 \| 1.4)}{101}\right) = 211\Omega$

Thus $\tau = C_{\mu 1} R_{\mu 1} + C_{\pi 1} R_{\pi 1} + C_T R_T + C_{\mu 2}(R_L \| R_C \| R_{out})$

$= 2 \times 1 + 2.4 \times 0.307 + 94.3 \times 0.211$

$+ 2(4 \| 4 \| 100)$

$= 24.6 ns$

$\therefore f_H = \dfrac{1}{2\pi\tau} = \dfrac{1}{2\pi \times 24.6 \times 10^{-9}} = \underline{\underline{6.5 MHz}}$

44 $r_e = \frac{25}{5} = 5\,\Omega$, $\beta = 50$, $r_\pi = 255\,\Omega$ **11**

$f_T = 1\,GHz$, $C_\mu = 1\,pF$

$C_\pi = \frac{50/51}{2\pi(10^9)(5)} - 1 = 31.2 - 1 = 30.2\,pF$

Basic gain, base — collector $= -\frac{50}{51} \times \frac{5000}{5} = -980$

appropriate for symetric excitation

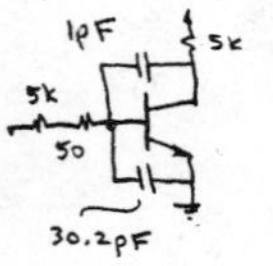

$f_H = \frac{1}{2\pi(30.2 + 1(1+980))((5k+50)\|255)} = 648\,kHz$

Overall gain $= -(980) \times \frac{255}{5050 + 255} = -47.1\,V/V$

45 $r_E = 100$ added: basic gain $= \frac{-50}{51} \times \frac{5000}{105} = -46.7$

$r_{in} = 51(105) = 5355$. Overall gain $= -46.7 \times \frac{5355}{5050+5355} = -24.0$

$f_H \simeq \frac{1}{2\pi((30.2(1 - \frac{100}{100+5}) + 1(1+46.7))(5050\|5355)} = 1.25\,MHz$

GB product $= 1.25 \times 24 = 30\,MHz$ } Same

GB product of original $= .647 \times 47.1 = 30.5\,MHz$ }

46 **11**

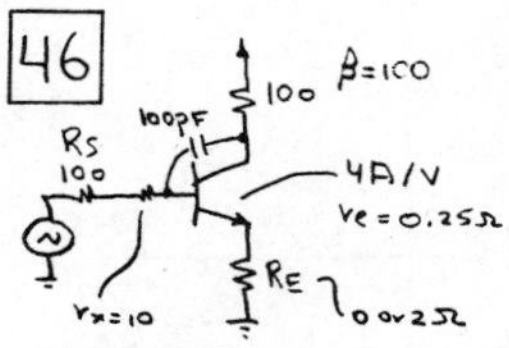

$f_T = 100\,MHz$, $C_\mu = 100\,pF$

$C_\pi = \frac{1}{2\pi(.25)100\times10^6} - 100 = 6266\,pF$

$r_\pi = 101(.25) = 25.25\,\Omega$

For $R_E = 0$: Basic gain $= -\frac{100}{101} \times \frac{100}{.25} = -396$

Overall gain $= -396 \times \frac{25.25}{10 + 100 + 25.25} = -73.9\,V/V$

$f_H = \frac{1}{2\pi(110\|25.25)(6266 + 100(1+396))} = 169\,kHz$

$GBP = (73.9)(.169) = 12.49\,MHz$

For $R_E = 2\,\Omega$

$r_{in} = 101(.25 + 2) = 227\,\Omega$

Basic gain $= -\frac{100}{101} \times \frac{100}{2.25} = -44.0$

Overall gain $= -44\left(\frac{277.3}{110 + 277.3}\right) = -31.5\,V/V$

$f_H = \frac{1}{2\pi(110\|227)(6266(1 - \frac{2}{2+.25}) + 100(1+44))} = 413\,kHz$

$GBP = (31.5 \times .413) = 13.01\,MHz$

47 **11**

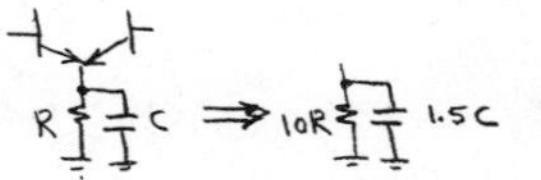

See at very low freq.
CMRR ↑ by 20 dB

but at frequencies above $\omega = 1/RC$, CMRR ↓

$20 \log 1.5 = 3.5\,dB$

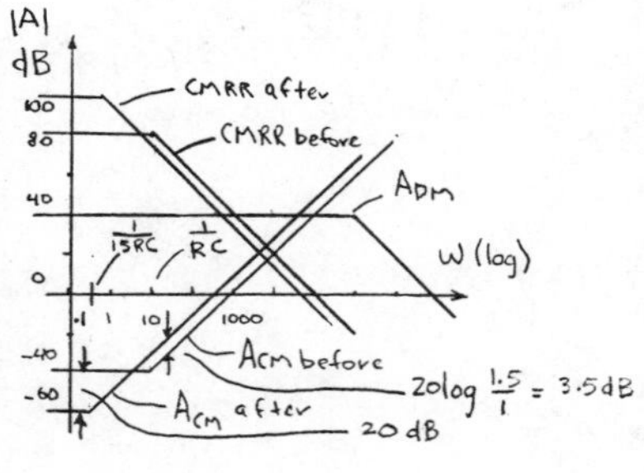

48

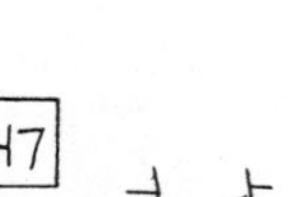

$r_e = 250\,\Omega$, $\beta = 50$, $r_\pi = 12.75k$, $r_{in} = 2(12.75)k$

gain $= \frac{50}{51} \times \frac{10^4}{2(250)} \times \frac{2(12.75)}{10 + 2(12.75)} = 14.08\,V/V$

$C_\pi = \frac{50/51}{2\pi \times 10^9 \times 250} - 0.5 = 0.624 - 0.5 = .124\,pF$

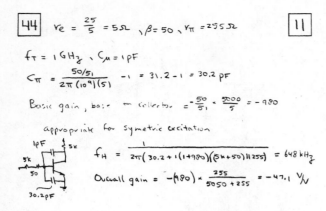

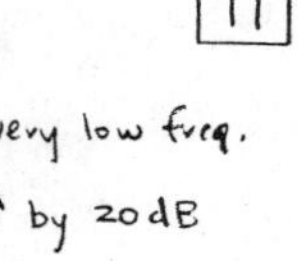

Input pole: $\frac{1}{2\pi(10k\|25.5k)(.5 + \frac{.124}{2})\times10^{-12}} = 39.4\,MHz$

Output pole: $\frac{1}{2\pi(10k)(0.5)\times10^{-12}} = 31.8\,MHz \rightarrow f_H = \left(\frac{1}{39.4^2} + \frac{1}{31.8^2}\right)^{-1/2} = 24.7\,MHz$

49 **11**

ⓐ $g_m = 20\,mA/V$, $r_e = 50\,\Omega$, $r_\pi \simeq 5\,k\Omega$

$C_\pi + C_\mu = \frac{20 \times 10^{-3}}{2\pi \times 400 \times 10^6} = 8\,pF$; $C_\mu = 2\,pF \rightarrow C_\pi = 6\,pF$

$A_M = \frac{R_{in}}{R_{in} + R_s} \times -g_m R_C = \frac{5}{10+5} \times (-20) \times 10 = -66.7\,V/V$

$f_H = \frac{1}{2\pi(R_s\|r_\pi)(C_\pi + C_\mu(1 + g_m R_C))} = \frac{1}{2\pi(10\|5)\times10^3(6 + 2(1+200))\times10^{-12}}$

$= 117\,kHz$

ⓑ $g_m = 20\,mA/V$, $r_e = 50\,\Omega$, $r_\pi \simeq 5\,k\Omega$

$C_\pi = 6\,pF$, $C_\mu = 2\,pF$

$A_M = \frac{R_{in}}{R_{in} + R_s} \times -g_m R_C = \frac{5}{10+5} \times (-20) \times 10 = -66.7\,V/V$

Now $f_1 = \frac{1}{2\pi R_s'(C_{\pi 1} + 2C_{\mu 1})} = \frac{1}{2\pi(10\|5)\times10^3 \times 10 \times 10^{-12}} = 4.8\,MHz$

$f_2 = \frac{1}{2\pi C_{\pi 2} r_{e2}} = \frac{1}{2\pi \times 6 \times 10^{-12} \times 50} = 530\,MHz$

$f_3 = \frac{1}{2\pi C_{\mu 2} R_L'} = \frac{1}{2\pi \times 2 \times 10^{-12} \times 10 \times 10^3} = 8.0\,MHz$

For f_H, neglect f_2 and use f_1, f_3 as follows:

$2 = (1 + (f_H/f_1)^2)(1 + (f_H/f_2)^2) \rightarrow f_H = 3.8\,MHz$

ⓒ Small-signal parameters are as in ⓐ, ⓑ

$A_M = \frac{R_{in}}{R_{in} + R_s} \times \frac{\alpha R_C}{2 r_e} = \frac{2(5)}{2(5) + 10} \times \frac{10}{0.1} = 50\,V/V$

At input: $f_{P1} = \frac{1}{2\pi(R_s\|(2r_\pi))(C_\pi/2 + C_{\mu 1})} = \frac{1}{2\pi \times 5 \times 10^3 \times (3/2 + 2)\times10^{-12}}$

$= 6.4\,MHz$

11

At output : $f_{P2} = \frac{1}{2\pi \times 10\times10^{3} \times 2\times10^{-12}} = 8$ MHz

Now from $2 = (1 + f_H^2/6.4^2)(1 + f_H^2/8^2)$

$f_H = 4.6$ MHz

(d) Small-signal parameters are as in (a) above

$R_{in} = (\beta_1+1)(r_{e1} + (\beta_2+1)r_{e2}) \approx 100(5.05) = 505$ kΩ

$A_M = \frac{R_{in}}{R_{in}+R_s} \times \frac{r_{\pi2}}{r_{\pi2}+r_{e1}} \times (-g_{m2}R_C) = \frac{505}{515}\times\frac{5}{5.05}(-20\times10) = -194$ V/V

For f_H, following Example 11.9 :

$R_s' = R_s = 10$kΩ , $C_T = C_{\pi2} + C_{\mu2}(1 + g_{m2}R_L')$

ie $C_T = 6 + 2(1 + 20\times10) = 408$pF , $R_{\mu1} = R_s \| R_{in} = 10\|505 = 9.8$k

$R_{\pi1} = r_{\pi1} \| \left(\frac{R_s' + R_{E1}'}{1 + g_m R_E'}\right) = 5 \| \frac{10+5}{1+20(5)} = 144$Ω

$R_T = R_{E1} \| \left(\frac{r_{\pi1} + R_s'}{\beta_1 + 1}\right) = 5 \| \frac{5+10}{101} = 144$Ω

$R_{\mu2} = R_L = 10$kΩ

Thus $\tau = C_{\mu1}R_{\mu1} + C_{\pi1}R_{\pi1} + C_T R_T + C_{\mu2}R_{\mu2}$

$= 2(9.8) + 6(0.144) + 408(0.144) + 2(10) = 99.2$ ns

whence $f_H = \frac{1}{2\pi\tau} = \frac{1}{2\pi(99.2\times10^{-12})} = 1.6$MHz

(next)

11

(e) The circuit is a (folded) cascode whose small-signal parameters are as in (a):

Here $R_{in} = r_{\pi1} = 5$kΩ

$A_M = -\frac{R_{in}}{R_{in}+R_s} \times g_{m1} \times \alpha_2 \times R_C = \frac{-5}{10+5}\times 20\times10 = -66.7$ V/V

For f_H :

$f_1 = \frac{1}{2\pi R_s'(C_{\pi1} + 2C_{\mu1})} = \frac{1}{2\pi(10\|5)\times10^{3}\times10\times10^{-12}} = 4.8$MHz

$f_2 = \frac{1}{2\pi C_{\pi2} r_{e2}} = \frac{1}{2\pi(6\times10^{-12})\times50} = 530$MHz

$f_3 = \frac{1}{2\pi C_{\mu2} R_L'} = \frac{1}{2\pi(2\times10^{-12})\times10\times10^{3}} = 8$ MHz

The results are the same as in (b) (as should be expected) and f_H = 3.8 MHz

(f) From an ac point of view, this circuit is the same as (c) above.

Thus A_M = 50 V/V and f_H = 4.6 MHz

12

1 $A_f = \frac{A}{1+A\beta} \rightarrow A = A_f + A\beta A_f \rightarrow A = \frac{A_f}{1-A_f\beta}$

For $\beta = .0100$, $A_f = 99$ if $A = \frac{99}{1-99(.01)} = 9900$

, $A_f = 99.9$ if $A = \frac{99.9}{1-99.9(.01)} = 99{,}900$

2

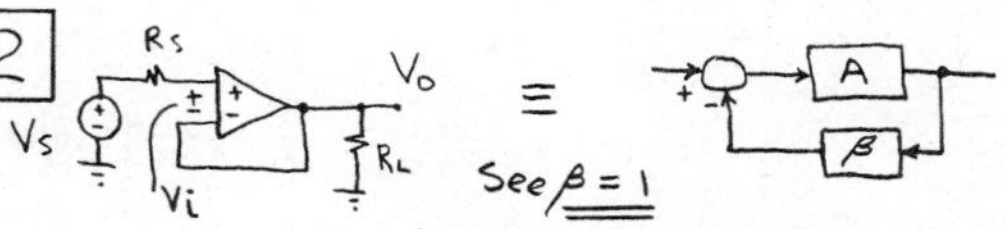

See $\beta = 1$

For $A = 10$, $A_f = \frac{A}{1+\beta A} = \frac{10}{1+10(1)} = 0.909$ V/V

Amount of feedback $= 1 + A\beta = 1 + 10(1) = 11 \equiv 20\log_{10}(11) = 20.83$dB

For $V_s = 1$ V, $V_o = 0.909$V , $V_i = (1 - 0.909) = 0.091$ V

See $\frac{\partial A_f}{\partial A} = \frac{1}{1+A\beta} + \frac{A(-1)}{(1+A\beta)^2}\times\beta = \frac{1+A\beta-A\beta}{(1+A\beta)^2} = \frac{1}{(1+A\beta)^2}$

$\therefore \frac{\partial A_f}{A_f} = \frac{1}{(1+A\beta)^2}\times\frac{(1+A\beta)}{A}\times\partial A = \frac{1}{(1+A\beta)}\frac{\partial A}{A}$

Thus if A reduces by 10%, A_f reduces by $\frac{10}{1+A\beta}$

or $\frac{10}{1+10(1)} = 0.909$%

3 For $\beta = 1$, $A = 1 \rightarrow A_f = \frac{A}{1+A\beta} = \frac{100}{1+100(1)} = 0.990$ V/V

Amt. of feedback $= 1 + A\beta = 1 + 100 = 101 \equiv 20\log_{10}(101) = 40.09$dB

For $V_s = 1$V, $V_o = 0.990099$V, $V_i = (1 - 0.990099) = 0.009901\text{V} \approx 0.01$V

12

$\frac{\partial A_f}{A_f} = \frac{1}{1+A\beta}\times\frac{\partial A}{A}$.

For 10% reduction in A, a reduction of $\frac{10\%}{1+A\beta} = \frac{10}{101}$ or 0.099% in A_f

4

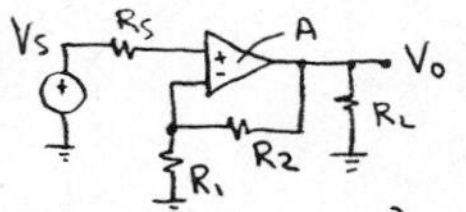

(a) $\beta = \frac{R_1}{R_1 + R_2}$

(b) For $A = 10^3$ and $A_f = 100$,

$A_f = \frac{A}{1+\beta A} \rightarrow 100 = \frac{10^3}{1+10^3\beta}$. Thus $\beta = \frac{10^3/100 - 1}{10^3} = \frac{10-1}{10^3} = 9\times10^{-3}$

Thus $R_1/(R_1+R_2) = 9\times10^{-3} \rightarrow R_1(1 - 9\times10^{-3}) = R_2(9\times10^{-3})$

and $R_2/R_1 = \frac{1-9\times10^{-3}}{9\times10^{-3}} = \frac{1}{9\times10^{-3}} - 1 = 111.1$

Amount of feedback $= 1 + A\beta = 1 + 10^3(9\times10^{-3}) = 10 \rightarrow 20$dB

For $V_s = 0.1$V, $V_o = 0.1(100) = 10$V

, $V_i = \frac{10}{1000} = 0.01$V

, $V_f = 10(9\times10^{-3}) = 9\times10^{-2} = 0.09$V

Check: 0.1 = 0.09 + 0.01 ✓

$\frac{\partial A_f}{A_f} = \frac{\partial A/A}{1+A\beta} = \frac{\partial A/A}{A/A_f}$

Thus if A↓ by 20%, then A_f↓ by $\frac{20}{10^3/10^2} = 2$%

5 Gain Desensitivity factor $= (1+A\beta) = \frac{A}{A_f} = \frac{10^4}{10^3} = 10$ **12**

ie $\frac{\partial A_f}{A_f} = \frac{1}{1+A\beta} \cdot \frac{\partial A}{A}$

Approximately: As $A \downarrow 10\%$, $A_f \downarrow \frac{10}{10} = 1\% \rightarrow A_f = 990$

As $A \downarrow 50\%$, $A_f \downarrow \frac{50}{10} = 5\% \rightarrow A_f = 950$

Exactly: $A_f = \frac{A}{1+\beta A} \rightarrow 1+\beta A = \frac{A}{A_f} = \frac{10^4}{10^3} = 10$

$\beta = \frac{10-1}{A} = 9 \times 10^{-4}$

Now if $A \rightarrow 9000$, $A_f = \frac{9000}{1+(9/10^4) \times 9000} = \frac{9000}{9.1} = 989$

, a drop of $\frac{1000-989}{1000} = 1.1\%$

Now if $A \rightarrow 5000$, $A_f = \frac{5000}{1+(9/10^4) \times 9000} = \frac{5000}{9.1} = 909.1$

, a drop of $\frac{1000-909.1}{1000} = 9.1\%$

6 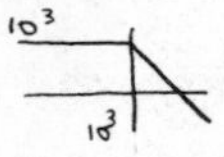

$f_{H_f} = (1+A_m\beta) f_H$, $A_m = 10^3$, $f_H = 10^3$

For $\beta = 0.1$, $f_{H_f} = (1+10^3 \times 0.1)(10^3) = \underline{\underline{101\,kHz}}$

7 $A_m = 10^3$, $f_L = 10^3\,Hz$, $A_f = 10$

$(1+A\beta) = \frac{A}{A_f} = \frac{10^3}{10} = 100$

Now $f_{L_f} = f_L/(1+A\beta) = \frac{10^3}{10} = \underline{\underline{10\,Hz}}$

8 $A = \frac{A_m}{(1+s/\omega_H)(1+s/100\omega_H)}$ **12**

$1/A = \frac{1}{A_m}(1+s/\omega_H)(1+s/100\omega_H)$

$A_f = \frac{A}{1+\beta A} = \frac{1}{1/A + \beta} = \frac{1}{\frac{1}{A_m}(1+s/\omega_H)(1+s/100\omega_H) + \beta}$

$= \frac{A_m}{1+A_m\beta + \frac{s}{\omega_H}(1.01) + \frac{s^2}{10^2\omega_H^2}}$

$= \frac{A}{1+A_m\beta} \times \frac{1}{1 + \frac{1.01s}{\omega_H(1+A_m\beta)} + \frac{s^2}{10^2\omega_H^2(1+A_m\beta)}}$

$= \frac{1000}{11} \times \frac{1}{1 + \frac{1.01}{11\omega_H}s + \frac{s^2}{1100\omega_H^2}}$

or $1 + \frac{1.01}{11}x + \frac{x^2}{1100} = 0 \rightarrow x^2 + 101x + 1100 = 0$

$\rightarrow x = -14.42, -88.6$

$\therefore$ poles are at $\underline{\underline{12.42\,\omega_H}}$ and $\underline{\underline{88.6\,\omega_H}}$

and gain is $\underline{\underline{90.9}}$ V/V

9 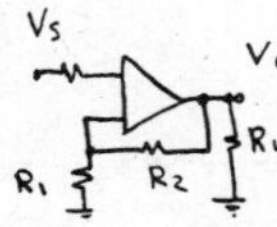

$A = 10^5$, $f_p = 10\,Hz$, $R_1 = 1k$, $R_2 = 9k$

$\beta = \frac{R_1}{R_1+R_2} = \underline{\underline{10^{-1}}}$,

$(1+A\beta) = 1 + 10^5 \times 10^{-1} = 10^4 + 1$

$\therefore$ 3dB cutoff at $10(10^4) = \underline{\underline{10^5\,Hz}}$

Low frequency gain $A_f = \frac{A}{1+\beta A} = \frac{10^5}{1+10^4} = \underline{\underline{9.999}}$ V/V

10 $A = 10^3$, $f_p = 10^3$, $\beta = 0.1$ **12**

$(1+A\beta) = 1 + 10^3 \times 10^{-1} = 101$

$f_{3dB} = 10^3(101) = \underline{\underline{1.01 \times 10^5\,Hz}}$

Low frequency gain $= \frac{A}{1+\beta A} = \frac{10^3}{1+10^3 \times 10^{-1}} = \frac{10^3}{101} = \underline{\underline{9.90\,V/V}}$

11 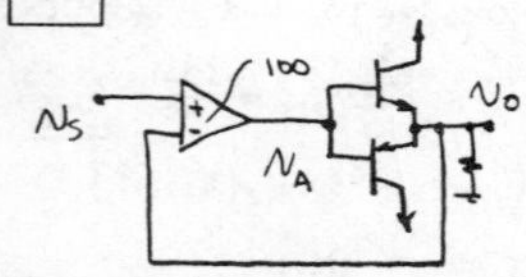

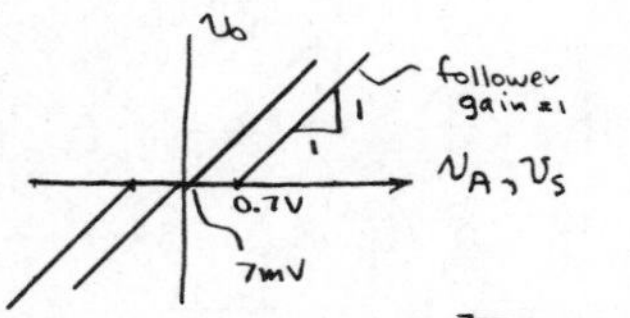

Dead band is reduced by the amplifier gain to $\pm \frac{700}{100} = \underline{\underline{\pm 7mV}}$

Outside the band $A_f = \frac{A}{1+\beta A} = \frac{100 \times 1}{1+1(100 \times 1)} = \frac{100}{101} = \underline{\underline{0.990\,V/V}}$

12 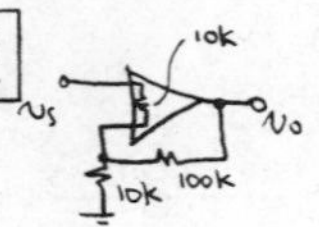

See Fig 12.12 with $R_s = 0$, $r_o = \infty$

$R_{icm} = \infty$, $R_{id} = 10k$, gain $= \mu$

$A = \frac{R_{id}}{R_{id} + (R_1 \| R_2)} \times \mu = \frac{10}{10+9.09}\mu = 0.524\mu$

Here $\beta = \frac{10}{100+10} = \frac{1}{11} = .0909$, $A_f = 10$, $A = \frac{A_f}{1-\beta A_f} = \frac{10}{1-1/11 \times 10} = \underline{\underline{110}}$

$R_i = 10 + 10 \| 100 = 19.09\,k\Omega$, $R_{if} = (1+A\beta)R_i = (1+\frac{110}{11})19.09$

or $R_{if} = 11(19.09) = \underline{\underline{210\,k\Omega}}$

12

Alternatively using Millers Theorem (for which the gain element is assumed to have zero output resistance). To ensure conditions apply:

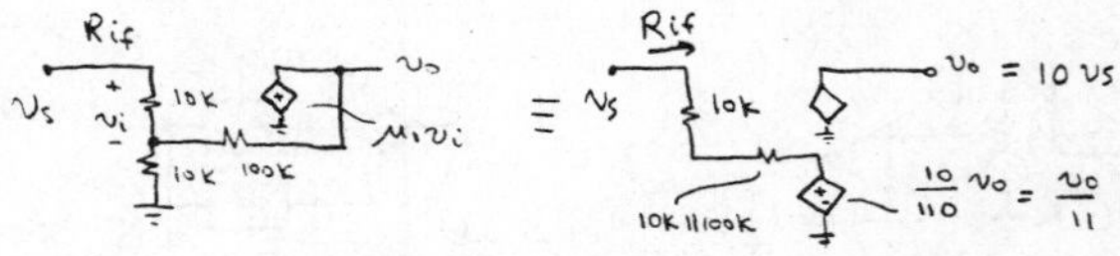

From Miller $R_{if} = \frac{R_i}{1 - \text{gain}} = \frac{10k + 10k \| 100k}{1 - 10(\frac{1}{11})} = \frac{19.09k}{1/11}$

$= 11(19.09) = 210\,k\Omega$

13 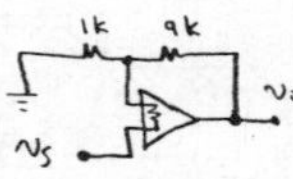

Series-Shunt Feedback,

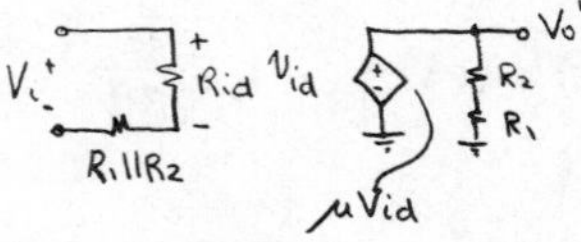

$A = \frac{R_{id}}{R_{id} + (R_1 \| R_2)} \times \mu$

$= \frac{10}{10 + 9 \| 1}\mu = 0.917\mu$

$R_i = R_{id} + R_1 \| R_2 = 10.9\,k$; $\beta = 0.1$

$Z_{if} = 10.9 \times 10^3 (1 + 0.917 \times 0.1 \mu)$

$= 10.9\,k + \frac{10.9 \times 10^3 \times 0.917 \times 0.1 \times 10^4}{1 + s/(2\pi \times 100)} = 10.9k + \frac{10^7}{1 + \frac{s}{2\pi \times 100}}$

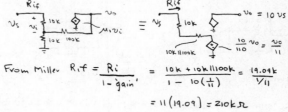

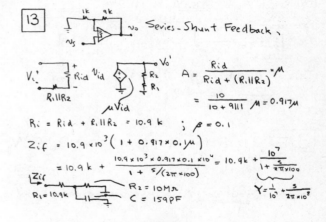

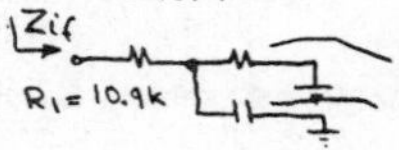

$R_2 = 10\,M\Omega$
$C = 159\,pF$

$Y = \frac{1}{10^7} + \frac{s}{2\pi \times 10^9}$

14 $\quad A=100$, $R_0=1000$ $\quad$ Shunt Sampling : $R_{of} = \dfrac{R_0}{1+A\beta}$ $\boxed{12}$

$1+A\beta = \dfrac{R_0}{R_{of}} = \dfrac{1000}{100} = 10$

$A_f = \dfrac{A}{1+\beta A} = \dfrac{100}{10} = \underline{\underline{10 \, ^V/_V}}$

For unity gain application , $\beta=1$

and $R_{of} = \dfrac{R_0}{1+(100)1} = \dfrac{1000}{101} = \underline{\underline{9.90 \, \Omega}}$

15 $\quad A=10^4$, $f_c=100Hz$ $\qquad A(s) = \dfrac{10^4}{1+\frac{s}{2\pi 100}}$

$1000 \qquad \beta=0.1$

$Z_{of} = \dfrac{R_{of}}{1+A\beta} = \dfrac{10^3}{1+\frac{(10^4)10^{-1}}{1+\frac{s}{2\pi100}}} = \dfrac{1}{Y_{of}}$

$\therefore \; Y_{of} = \dfrac{1}{10^3} + \dfrac{1}{1+\frac{s}{2\pi\times10^2}}$

ie $R_1 = 1000\,\Omega$

$R_2 = 1\,\Omega$, $L = \dfrac{1}{2\pi\times10^2} = 1.59\,mH$

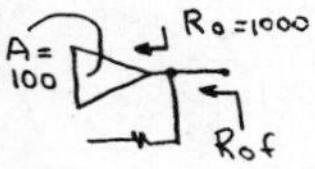

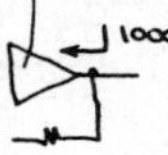

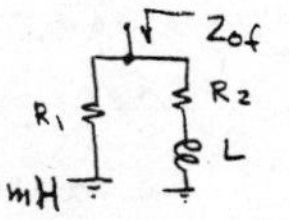

16 $\quad \beta=100$

$20k \quad +10.7$

R_s $\quad Q_1 \; Q_2 \qquad Q_3$

$N_s \quad 10k \qquad 9k \qquad R_{of} \quad 2k$

$1mA \qquad R_1 \qquad 5mA$

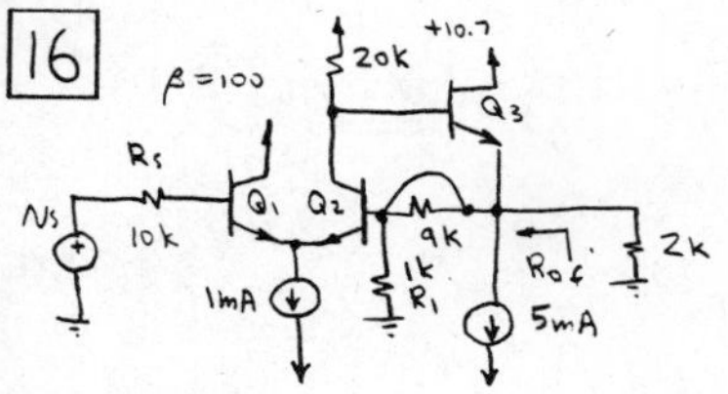

$r_{e_1}=r_{e_2} = 50\,\Omega$

$r_{e_3} = 5\,\Omega$

$r_{\pi_1} = 5050\,\Omega$

A Circuit:

$20k$

R_s

$N_s \quad 10k \qquad N_0$

$1k \; 2k$

$R_i = 0$

$A = \dfrac{5050(2)}{10100+10,000} = \dfrac{100}{101} \times \dfrac{20k||(101)(2k||1k)}{2(50)} = \underline{76.7} \, ^V/_V$

$\beta = \underline{1} \, ^V/_V$

$A_f = \dfrac{A}{1+A\beta} = \dfrac{76.7}{1+1(76.7)} = \underline{.987} \, ^V/_V$

$R_0 = \left(5+\frac{20k}{101}\right)||2k||1k = 155.6\,\Omega$

$R_{of} = \dfrac{R_0}{1+A\beta} = \dfrac{155.6}{1+76.7} = 2.00\,\Omega = R_{of}'||R_L$

$\rightarrow R_{of}' = \dfrac{R_{of}R_L}{R_L-R_{of}} = \dfrac{2(2k)}{2k-2} = \underline{2.002\,\Omega}$

$R_i = 10k+2(5.05)+0 = 20.1\,k\Omega$

$R_{if} = R_i(1+A\beta) = 20.1(77.7) = 1.56\,M\Omega$

$R_{if}' = R_{if}-R_s = \underline{1.55\,M\Omega}$

17

$10k \quad 20k$

R_2

$9k \quad R_1 \; 1k \qquad 2k$

$1\mu F$

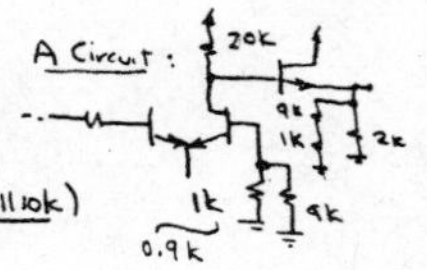

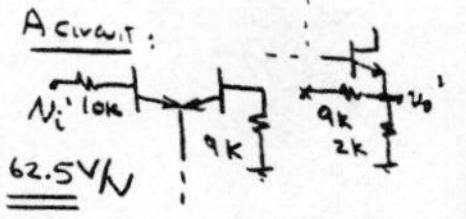

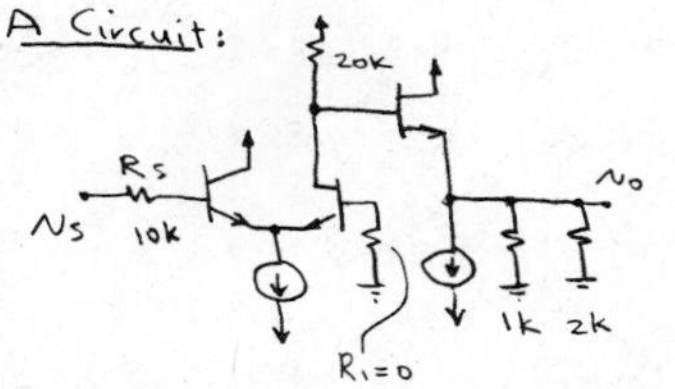

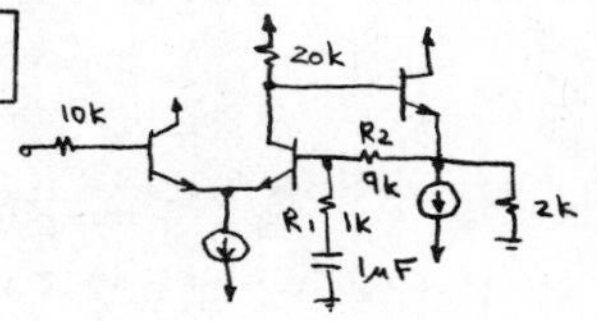

At high Frequencies , R_1 is in effect grounded and result is same

---

in Exercise 12.5 , ie $A=85.7\,V/V$, $\beta=0.1\,V/V$, $A_f=8.96\,V/V$ $\boxed{12}$

$R_{if} = 191\,k$, $R_{of}' = 19.1\,\Omega$:

Check solution (with Values as in $\boxed{16}$)

$A = \dfrac{10.1}{10.1+10+0.9} \times \dfrac{100}{101} \times \left(\dfrac{20k||101(5+2k||10k)}{2(50)}\right)$

$\times \dfrac{2k||10k}{(2k||10k)+5} \approx \underline{85.1}\,V/V$

$\beta = \dfrac{1}{1+9} = \dfrac{1}{10} = .01\,V/V$; $1+A\beta = 1+85.1(0.1) = 9.51$

$A_f = \dfrac{A}{1+A\beta} = \dfrac{85.1}{9.51} = \underline{8.95\,V/V}$

$R_0 = \left(5+\frac{20k}{101}\right)||2k||10k = 181\,\Omega \rightarrow R_{of} = \dfrac{181}{9.51} = \underline{19.0}$

$R_{of}' = \dfrac{19.0(2k)}{2k-19.0} = \underline{19.2\,\Omega}$

$R_i = 10k+10.1k+0.9k = 21k \rightarrow R_{if} = 21k(9.51) = 200k$

$R_{if}' = 200k-10k = \underline{190k}$

At low frequencies : C is open

$N_i:10k \qquad 9k \qquad 9k \; 2k$

$A = \dfrac{10.1}{10.1+10+0.9} \times \dfrac{100}{101} \times \dfrac{20k||101(2k+5)}{2(50)} \times \dfrac{2k}{2k+5} \approx \underline{62.5\,V/V}$

$\beta = \underline{1}\,V/V$; $1+A\beta = 1+62.5 = 63.5$; $A_f = \dfrac{62.5}{63.5} = \underline{0.984\,V/V}$

$R_0 = 2k||\left(\frac{20k}{101}+5\right) = 184\,\Omega \rightarrow R_{of} = \dfrac{184}{63.5} = 2.90 \rightarrow R_{of}' = \underline{2.91\,\Omega}$

$R_i = 10k+10.1k+9k = 29.1k \rightarrow R_{if} = 29.1(63.5) = \underline{1.85\,M\Omega}$

$R_{if}' = 1.85M-10k = \underline{1.84\,M\Omega}$

For frequencies from low to high , the gain $\boxed{12}$

rises from $.984\,V/V$ to $8.95\,V/V$:

$R_1 \quad R_2$
$1k \quad 9k$
$1\mu F$

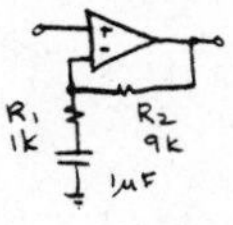

For an ideal op amp , gain $= \left(1+\frac{Z_2}{Z_1}\right) = \dfrac{Z_1+Z_2}{Z_1}$

which is zero where $Z_1+Z_2 = 0$

ie $R_1 + \frac{1}{s_z C} + R_2 = 0$ or $s_z = -\dfrac{1}{C(R_1+R_2)}$

for which $W_z = \dfrac{1}{1\times10^{-6}\times10^4} = \dfrac{100}{1} = \underline{100}\,rad/s$

Whence $W_p = \dfrac{8.95}{1}\times100 = \underline{895\,rad/s}$

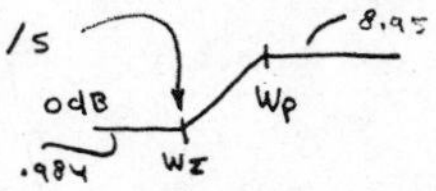

$0dB \qquad 8.95$
$.984 \quad W_z$

18

$100\,mA/V \quad 10k$

$1\,V/mA$

$R_{of} = R_0(1+A\beta) = 10k(1+100mA/V \times 1V/mA)$

$= 10k(101) = \underline{1.01\,M\Omega}$

19

[circuit diagrams]

A circuit $\qquad \beta circuit$

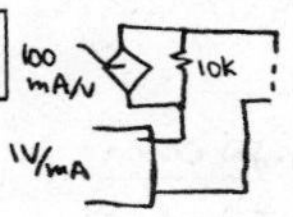

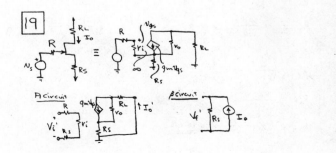

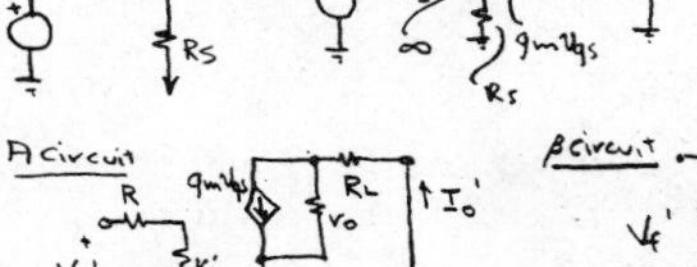

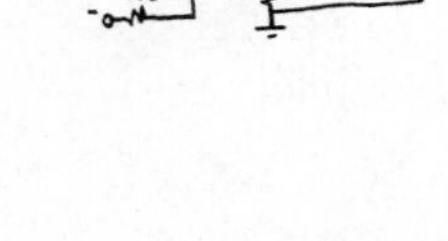

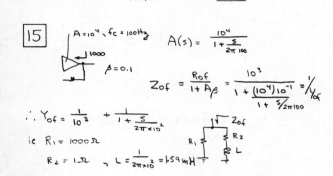

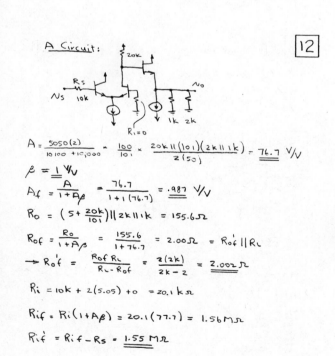

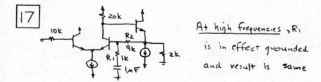

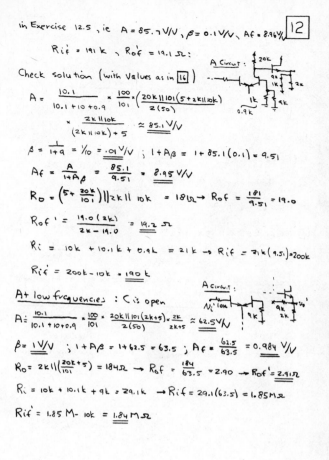

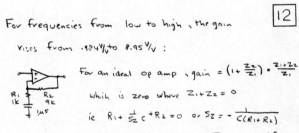

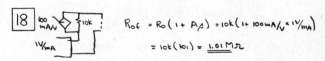

12

(a) $A = \frac{I_o'}{V_i'} = g_m \frac{r_o}{R_L + R_s + r_o}$

$\beta = \frac{V_f'}{I_o'} = R_s$

$A_f = \frac{A}{1+\beta A} = \frac{g_m \frac{r_o}{R_L+R_s+r_o}}{1 + R_s\, g_m \frac{r_o}{R_L+R_s+r_o}} = \frac{g_m r_o}{R_L + R_s + r_o + R_s g_m r_o}$

$R_o = R_L + R_s + r_o$

$R_{of} = (R_L + R_s + r_o)\left(1 + \frac{R_s g_m r_o}{R_L+R_s+r_o}\right) = R_L + R_s + r_o + R_s g_m r_o$

$R_{of}' = R_{of} - R_L = r_o(1 + g_m R_s) + R_s$

$R_i = \infty$, $R_{if} = \infty$

(b) From BJT example (Eq 12.27) : use r_{oo} for r_π

$R_{of}' = R_s + r_o + \frac{g_m r_{oo} R_E}{r_{oo} + R + R_s}\, r_o = R_s + r_o + \frac{g_m R_E}{1 + \frac{R+R_s}{r_{oo}}} \times r_o$

and as $r_{oo} \to \infty$, $R_{of}' = R_s + r_o + g_m R_E r_o = R_s + r_o(1 + g_m R_E)$

For gain : $A_f = \frac{g_m r_{oo}}{R_s(1 + g_m r_{oo}) + r_{oo} + R} = \frac{g_m}{R_s(1/r_{oo} + g_m) + 1 + \frac{R}{r_{oo}}}$

$= \frac{g_m}{g_m R_s + 1} = \frac{1}{1/g_m + R_s}$, the value obtained above when $r_o \to \infty$ as it was approximated when Eq 12.22 obtained from Eq 12.20

20 **12**

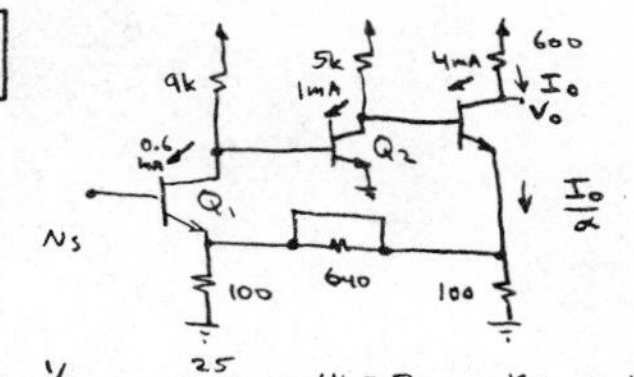

$\beta = 100$, $r_o = \infty$

β Circuit

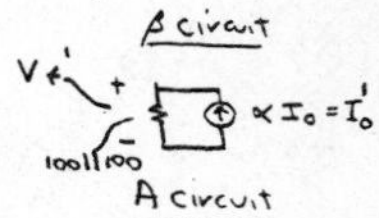

$r_{e1} \approx 1/g_{m1} = \frac{25}{0.6} = 41.7\,\Omega$, $r_{\pi 1} = 4170$

$1/g_{m2} = \frac{25}{1} = 25$, $r_{\pi 2} = 2500$

$1/g_{m3} = \frac{25}{4} = 6.25$, $r_{\pi 3} = 625$

A Circuit

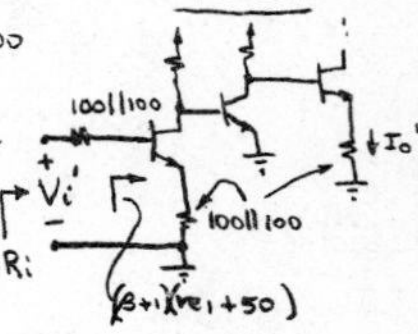

$A = \frac{I_o'}{V} = \frac{100}{101} \times \frac{9k \| 2.5k}{41.7 + 50} \times \frac{5k \| 101(50 + 6.25)}{25} \times \frac{100}{101} \times \frac{1}{6.25+50} \approx \underline{\underline{40 A/V}}$

$\beta = \frac{V_f'}{I_o'} = \underline{\underline{50 V/A}} \to A\beta = 40 A/V \times 50 V/A = \underline{\underline{2000}}$

$A_f = \frac{A}{1+A\beta} \approx \frac{40 A/V}{2000} = \underline{\underline{20 mA/V}}$

$V_o/V_s = -20 \times \frac{100}{101} \times 0.6 \approx \underline{\underline{-12 V/V}}$

$R_i = 50 + 101(41.7 + 50) = 9.26\,k\Omega$

$R_{if} = 9.26(1 + A\beta) = 9.26(2000) = \underline{\underline{18.5 M\Omega}}$

21 **12**

See Ex 12.6 : $A = 20.8$ A/V, $\beta = 12\,\Omega$,

$A_f = 83$ mA/V. Thus $(1 + A\beta) = \frac{A}{A_f} = \frac{20.8}{83 \times 10^{-3}} = 250.6$

or $(1 + A\beta) = 1 + 20.8(12) = 250.6$

$f_H = 1 MHz \to f_{Hf} \approx 250 MHz$!

It is likely that secondary poles would affect this result in practice.

22

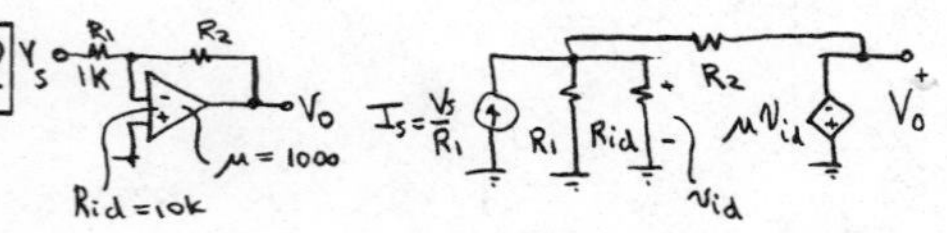

$A_f = \frac{V_o}{I_s} = \frac{V_o}{V_s} \times R_1 = 10 \times 1 = 10\,k\Omega$

(pb) A Circuit

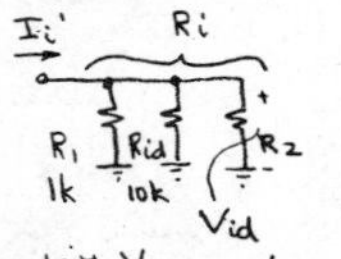

$R_i = 1 \| 10 \| R_2$

$A = \frac{V_o}{I_i'} = \frac{-\mu V_{id}}{V_{id}/R_i} = -\mu R_i$

$\beta = -1/R_2$

$A_f = \frac{A}{1+A\beta} = \frac{-\mu R_i}{1 + \mu R_i/R_2} = -10\,k\Omega$

$R_{if} = \frac{R_i}{1 + \frac{\mu R_i}{R_2}} = \frac{-A_f}{\mu} = \frac{10k}{1000} = 10\,\Omega$

$R_{if}' = (1/10 - \frac{1}{1000})^{-1} = \underline{\underline{10.1\,\Omega}}$

23 **12**

(a) shunt - series : $R_i \downarrow$, $R_o \uparrow$

(b) series - series : $R_i \uparrow$, $R_o \uparrow$

(c) shunt - shunt : $R_i \downarrow$, $R_o \downarrow$

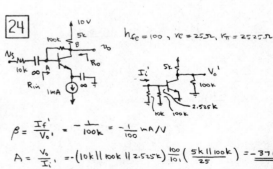

24

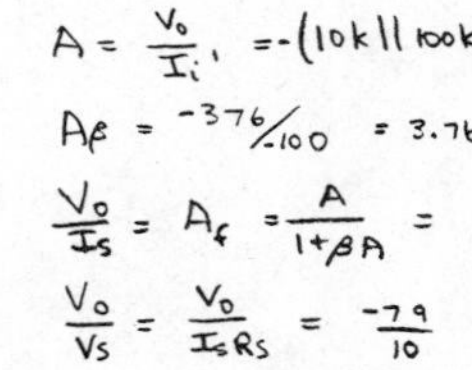

$h_{fe} = 100$, $r_e = 25\,\Omega$, $r_\pi = 2525\,\Omega$

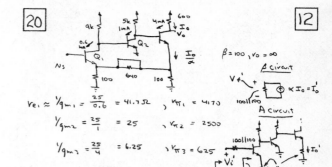

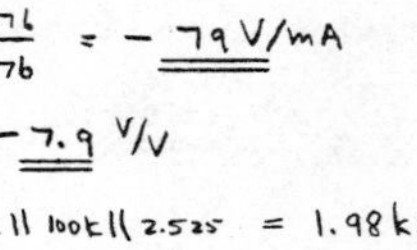

$\beta = \frac{I_f'}{V_o'} = -\frac{1}{100k} = -\frac{1}{100}$ mA/V

$A = \frac{V_o}{I_i'} = -(10k \| 100k \| 2.525k)\frac{100}{101}\left(\frac{5k \| 100k}{25}\right) = \underline{\underline{-376}}\ k\Omega$

$A\beta = -376/-100 = 3.76 \to 1 + A\beta = 4.76$

$\frac{V_o}{I_s} = A_f = \frac{A}{1+\beta A} = \frac{-376}{4.76} = \underline{\underline{-79 V/mA}}$

$\frac{V_o}{V_s} = \frac{V_o}{I_s R_s} = \frac{-79}{10} = \underline{\underline{-7.9}}$ V/V

$R_i = R_s \| R_f \| r_\pi = 10k \| 100k \| 2.525 = 1.98\,k\Omega$

$R_{if} = \frac{R_i}{1 + A\beta} = \frac{1.98k}{4.76} = 415\,\Omega$

$1/R_{if}' = 1/R_{if} - 1/R_s = \frac{1}{.419} - \frac{1}{10} = 2.39 \to R_{if}' = \underline{\underline{433\,\Omega}} = R_{in}$

$R_o = R_C \| R_f = 5k \| 100k = 4.76k \to R_{of} = \frac{4.76}{4.73} = \underline{\underline{1.006\,k\Omega}} \approx 1\,k\Omega$

12

Directly Gain A-B $= \frac{-100}{101}\left(\frac{5k \| 100k}{25}\right) = -188.6$

$R_{in} = \frac{100k}{1+188.6} \| (101)(25) = 527 \| 2525 = \underline{\underline{436\,\Omega}}$

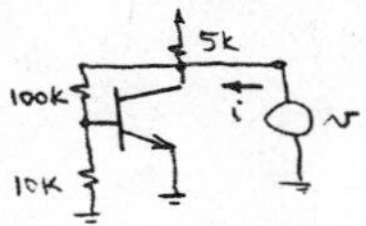

For R_o: Apply a test voltage v

$$i = v\left(\frac{1}{5k} + \frac{1}{102k}\left(1 + \frac{10}{10+2.525} \times 100\right)\right)$$

(h_{fe})

$= .992\,v$

$R_o = \frac{v}{i} = \frac{1}{.992} = \underline{\underline{1008\ k\Omega}}$

Gain $v_o/v_s = \frac{-.436}{10+.436}(188.6) = \underline{\underline{-7.88\ V/V}}$

25

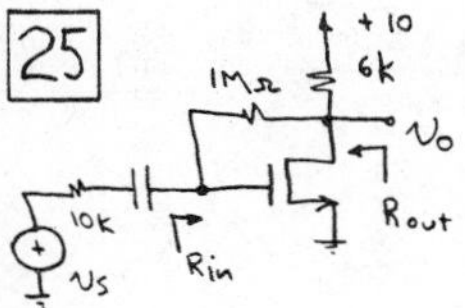

$i_D = k(v_{GS} - V_T)^2$

$i = 0.25(v-2)^2 = \frac{10-v}{6}$

$3(v-2)^2 = 20 - 2v$

or $3v^2 - 12v + 12 = 20 - 2v \rightarrow 3v^2 - 10v - 8 = 0$

Thus $= \frac{+10 \pm \sqrt{10^2 + 12(8)}}{2(3)} = 4 \rightarrow i = 0.25(4-2)^2 = \underline{\underline{1mA}}$

and $v_o = 10 - 6(1) = \underline{\underline{4V}} \rightarrow g_m = 2k(v_{GS} - V_T) = 2(.25)(4-2) = 1mA/V$

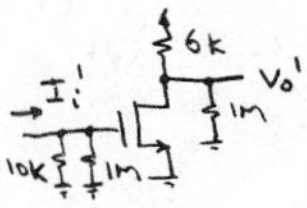

$\beta = \frac{I_f'}{V_o'} = -\frac{1}{1M\Omega} = -10^{-3}\ mA/V$

$A = \frac{V_o'}{I_i'} = -(10k \| 1M)(1 \times 10^{-3})(6k \| 1M) = -59.05k$

$A\beta = (-10^{-3}\ mA/V)(-59.05\ k\Omega) = 59.05 \times 10^{-3}$

12

$\frac{V_o}{I_s} = A_f = \frac{A}{1+\beta A} = -\frac{59.05k}{1 + 59.05 \times 10^{-3}} = -55.76k$

$\frac{V_o}{V_s} = \frac{V_o}{I_s R_s} = \frac{-55.76k}{10k} = \underline{\underline{-5.58\ V/V}}$

$R_i = R_s \| R_f = 10k \| 1M = 9.9k \rightarrow R_{if} = \frac{R_i}{1+\beta A} = \frac{9.9k}{1.059} = 9.35k$

$R_{if}' = \frac{1}{1/R_{if} - 1/R_s} = \frac{1}{1/9.35k - 1/10k} = \underline{\underline{143.8\ k\Omega}} = R_{in}$

$R_o = R_o \| R_f = 6k \| 1M \approx 6k \rightarrow R_{of} = \frac{R_o}{1.059} = \underline{\underline{5.67k}} = R_{out}$

Direct Analysis: Gain (gate to drain) $= -1mA/V \times 6k = -6\,V/V$

$R_{in} = \frac{1M}{1+6} = \underline{\underline{142.9\,k}}$

For Rout, drive the output with with v_x and find i_x

$i_x = v_x\left(\frac{1}{6} + \frac{1}{1000} + \frac{10}{10+1000} \times 1mA/V\right) = v_x(0.1776)$

$\therefore R_{out} = \frac{v_x}{i_x} = \frac{1}{.1776} = \underline{\underline{5.63k}}$

$\frac{V_o}{V_s} = -\frac{142.9}{10+142.9} \times 6 = \underline{\underline{-5.61\ V/V}}$

26 **12**

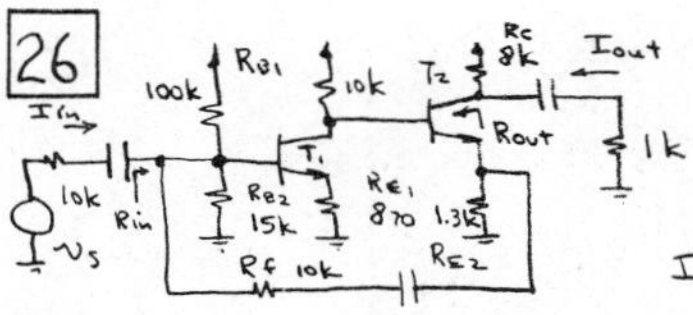

$\beta = 100$

From Ex 12.4:

$I_{E1} = I_{E2} = 1mA$, $r_{e1} = r_{e2} = 25\Omega$

For A: $V_{\pi 1} = I_i'\left[R_s \| (R_{E2} + R_F) \| R_B \| ((\beta+1)(r_{e1} + R_{E1}))\right] \times \left(\frac{r_{e1}}{r_{e1} + R_{E1}}\right)$

ie $V_{\pi 1} = K I_i' \rightarrow$ In 12.4, $K_o = (10k \| 11.3k \| 13.0k \| (101)(25)) \times 1 = 1.316$

Here, $K_n = (10k \| 11.3k \| 13.0k \| (101)(25+870)) \times \frac{25}{25+870} = .1011$

All of the other components of A remain the same.

Thus $A = \frac{I_o'}{I_i'} = A(\text{from Ex 12.4}) \times \frac{K_n}{K_o} = -434.6 \times \frac{.1011}{1.316} = -33.39$

$\beta = \frac{I_o'}{I_f'} = -\frac{1.3}{1.3+10} = -.115$

$1 + A\beta = 1 + (-33.39)(-.115) = 4.84$

$A_f = \frac{I_o}{I_s} = \frac{A}{1+A\beta} = \frac{-33.9}{4.84} = -6.90$

Now $\frac{I_{out}}{I_{in}} \approx \frac{I_{out}}{I_s} = \frac{R_{C2}}{R_L + R_{C2}} \times \frac{I_o}{I_s} = \frac{8}{1+8} \times (-6.90) = \underline{\underline{-6.13\ A/A}}$

$R_i = R_s \| (R_{E2} + R_F) \| R_B \| (\beta+1)(r_{e1} + R_{E1}) = 10k \| 11.3k \| 13.0k \| 90.4 = 3.62k$

$R_{if} = \frac{R_i}{1+A\beta} = \frac{3.62}{4.84} = 748\,\Omega \rightarrow R_{in} = \frac{1}{1/R_{if} - 1/R_s} = \frac{1}{1/.748 - 1/10} = \underline{\underline{808\,\Omega}}$

$R_o = 1.08\ M\Omega$ (From Ex 12.4)

$R_{of} = 1.08(4.84) = 5.23M$ and $R_{out} = 5.23M - (R_L \| R_C) = \underline{\underline{5.23M}}$

27 See Example 12.4 and **26** **12**

For A: $f_L = 1kHz = \frac{1}{2\pi C\left(R_{E1} \| r_{e1} + \frac{(R_B \| (R_F + R_{E2}) \| R_s)}{\beta+1}\right)}$

Whence $C = \frac{1}{2\pi(10^3) \times 870 \| (25 + \frac{3.77k}{101})} = \underline{\underline{2.74\,\mu F}}$

For Feedback, $f_{Lf} = \frac{1kHz}{1+A\beta} = \frac{1kHz}{51} = \underline{\underline{19.6\ Hz}}$

where $(1+A\beta)$ is the value at midband, with E_1 grounded, found in Ex 12.4

28 For opamp, $\mu = 10^4$ and $f_T = 10^6\,Hz \rightarrow f_H = \frac{10^6}{10^4} = 100Hz$

A Circuit:

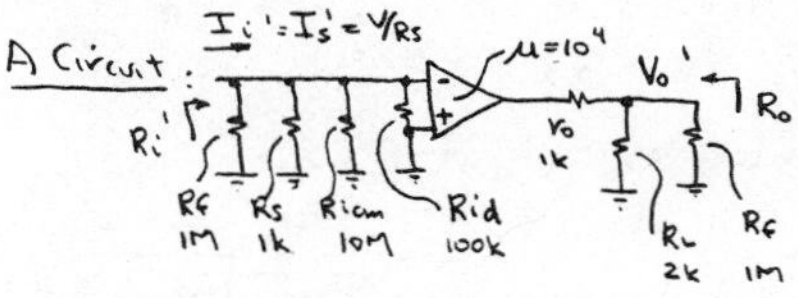

$\beta = \frac{I_f'}{V_o'} = \frac{-1}{R_f} = -10^{-6}$

$A = \frac{V_o'}{I_i'} = -(R_f \| R_s \| R_{icm} \| R_{id})(10^4)\left(\frac{R_L \| R_f}{R_L \| R_f + r_o}\right)$

$= \frac{-1}{10^{-3}(10^{-3} + 1 + 10^{-4} + 10^{-2})}(10^4)\left(\frac{2k \| 1M}{2k \| 1M + 1k}\right) = \frac{10^3}{1.011} \times 10^4 \times (.666)$

$= -6.587M$

$A_f = \frac{A}{1+\beta A} = \frac{-6.587 \times 10^6}{1 + 6.587 \times 10^6 \times 10^{-6}} = -0.868 \times 10^6 = \frac{V_o}{I_s} = \frac{V_o R_s}{V_s}$

$\frac{V_o}{V_s} = \frac{A_f}{R_s} = -\frac{0.868 \times 10^6}{10^3} = \underline{\underline{-868\ V/V}}$

$R_i = 1M \| 1k \| 10M \| 100k = 1.011k \rightarrow R_{if} = \frac{1.011}{7.587} = \underline{\underline{0.133k}}$

$R_{in} = \frac{1}{\frac{1}{.133} - \frac{1}{1}} = \underline{\underline{154\Omega}}$

$R_o = 1k \| 2k \| 1M = 667\Omega \rightarrow R_{of} = \frac{667}{7.587} = 87.9\Omega$

$R_{out} = \frac{1}{1/R_{of} - 1/R_L} = \frac{1}{1/.0879 - 1/2} = \underline{\underline{91.8\Omega}}$

$f_H = \frac{10^6}{10^4} = 100\,Hz \rightarrow \omega_H = 2\pi(100) = 628$ rad/s

$\mu(s) = \frac{\mu_m}{1+\frac{s}{628}} = \frac{10^4}{1+s/628} \rightarrow A(s) = \frac{6.587\times10^6}{1+s/628}$

$1+\beta A(s) = 1 + \frac{6.587\times10^6}{1+s/628}\cdot10^{-6} = 1+\frac{6.59}{1+s/628}$

$Z_{if} = \frac{1.0111}{1+\frac{6.59}{1+s/628}} \rightarrow 1/Z_{if} = \frac{1}{1.0111} + \frac{1}{.152+s(2.42\times10^{-3})}$

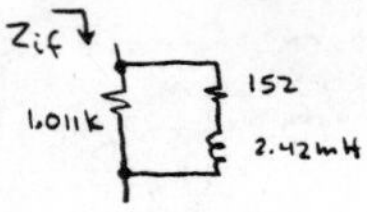

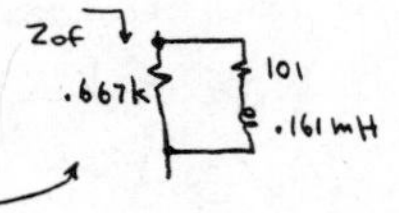

$Z_{of} = \frac{0.667}{1+\frac{6.59}{1+s/628}} \rightarrow 1/Z_{of} = \frac{1}{.667} + \frac{1}{.101+.000161s}$

29

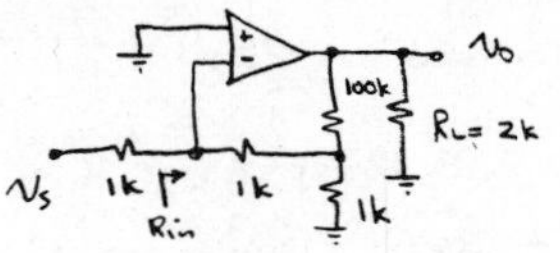

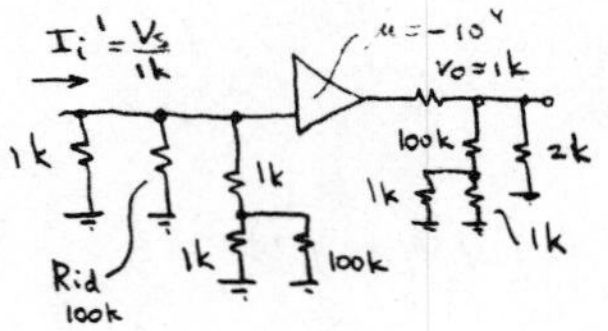

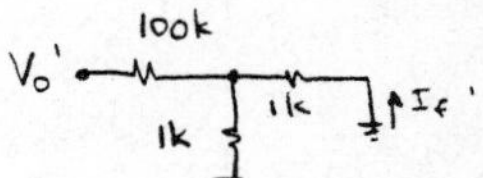

$\beta = \frac{I_f'}{V_o'} \rightarrow I_f' = -\frac{1}{2}\,\frac{V_o'}{100k+0.5k}$

$\beta = \underline{\underline{-4.975\times10^{-6}}}$ A/V

$A = \frac{V_o'}{I_i'} = \frac{(1k\|100k\|1.99k)\times10^4}{.661k}\times\frac{2k\|100.5k}{2k\|100.5k+1k} = \underline{\underline{-4.38\times10^6}}$

$1+A\beta = 1+(-4.975)(-4.38\times10^6) = 22.79$

$A_f = \frac{A}{1+A\beta} = \frac{-4.38\times10^6}{22.79} = -192k = V_o/I_s$

$\frac{V_o}{V_s} = \frac{V_o}{R_s I_s} = \frac{A_f}{R_s} = \underline{\underline{-192\,V/V}}$

$R_i = 1k\|100k\|1.99k = .661k$, $R_{if} = \frac{.661}{22.79} = 29\Omega$

$R_{in} = \frac{1}{\frac{1}{.029}-1/1} = \underline{\underline{29.7\Omega}}$

$R_o = 1k\|2k\|65k = 0.662k$, $R_{of} = \frac{.662}{22.79} = 29\Omega$

$R_{out} = \frac{1}{\frac{1}{.029}-\frac{1}{2}} = \underline{\underline{29.4\Omega}}$

30

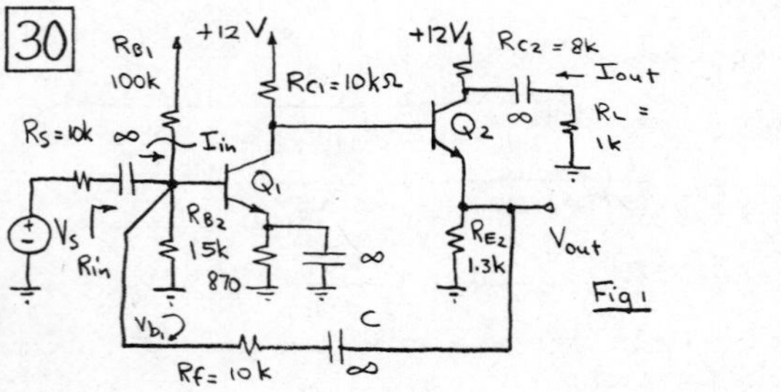

Fig 1

The dc conditions are the same as in Example (12.4):

$I_{C1} = 1mA$, $I_{C2} = 1mA$, $r_{e1} = r_{e2} = 25\Omega$, $g_{m1} = g_{m2} = 40mA/V$

$r_{o1} = r_{o2} = 100k\Omega$, $r_{\pi1} = r_{\pi2} = 2.5k\Omega$

The feedback is of the shunt-shunt type:

The A circuit is:

$R_i = R_S\|R_f\|R_{B1}\|R_{B2}\|r_{\pi1}$

$= 10\|10\|100\|15\|2.5 = 1.48k\Omega$

$A = \frac{V_{out}'}{I_i'} = R_i(-g_m)\{R_{C1}\|r_{o1}\|((\beta_o+1)(r_{e2}+R_{E2}\|R_f))\}\times\frac{R_{E2}\|R_f}{R_{E2}\|R_f+r_{e2}}$

$= -1.48\times40\{10\|100\|(101(.025+1.3\|10))\}\times\frac{1.3\|10}{1.3\|10+.025}$

$= -489.3\,k\Omega$

$\beta = \frac{I_f'}{V_{out}'} = -\frac{1}{R_f} = -0.1\,mA/V$

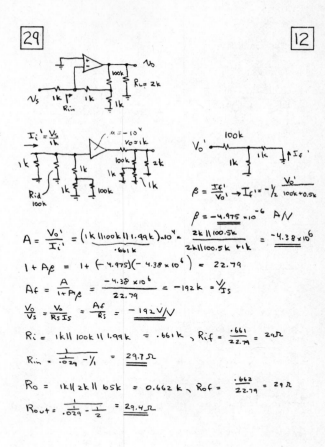

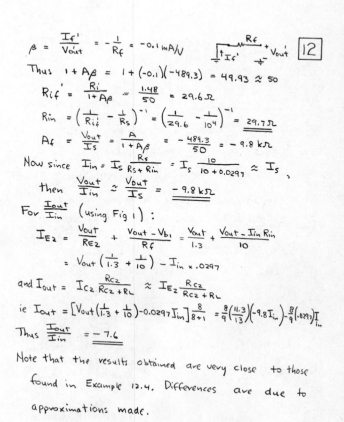

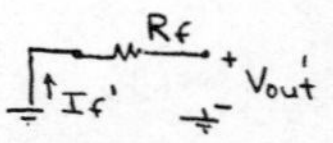

Thus $1+A\beta = 1+(-0.1)(-489.3) = 49.93 \approx 50$

$R_{if}' = \frac{R_i}{1+A\beta} = \frac{1.48}{50} = 29.6\Omega$

$R_{in} = \left(\frac{1}{R_{if}'}-\frac{1}{R_s}\right)^{-1} = \left(\frac{1}{29.6}-\frac{1}{10^4}\right)^{-1} = \underline{29.7\Omega}$

$A_f = \frac{V_{out}}{I_s} = \frac{A}{1+A\beta} = -\frac{489.3}{50} = -9.8\,k\Omega$

Now since $I_{in} = I_s\frac{R_s}{R_s+R_{in}} = I_s\frac{10}{10+0.0297} \approx I_s$,

then $\frac{V_{out}}{I_{in}} \approx \frac{V_{out}}{I_s} = \underline{\underline{-9.8\,k\Omega}}$

For $\frac{I_{out}}{I_{in}}$ (using Fig 1):

$I_{E2} = \frac{V_{out}}{R_{E2}} + \frac{V_{out}-V_{b1}}{R_f} = \frac{V_{out}}{1.3} + \frac{V_{out}-I_{in}R_{in}}{10}$

$= V_{out}\left(\frac{1}{1.3}+\frac{1}{10}\right) - I_{in}\times.0297$

and $I_{out} = I_{C2}\frac{R_{C2}}{R_{C2}+R_L} \approx I_{E2}\frac{R_{C2}}{R_{C2}+R_L}$

ie $I_{out} = \left[V_{out}\left(\frac{1}{1.3}+\frac{1}{10}\right)-0.0297I_{in}\right]\frac{8}{8+1} = \frac{8}{9}\left(\frac{11.3}{13}\right)(-9.8I_{in})-\frac{8}{9}(.0297)I_{in}$

Thus $\frac{I_{out}}{I_{in}} = \underline{\underline{-7.6}}$

Note that the results obtained are very close to those found in Example 12.4. Differences are due to approximations made.

31 **12**

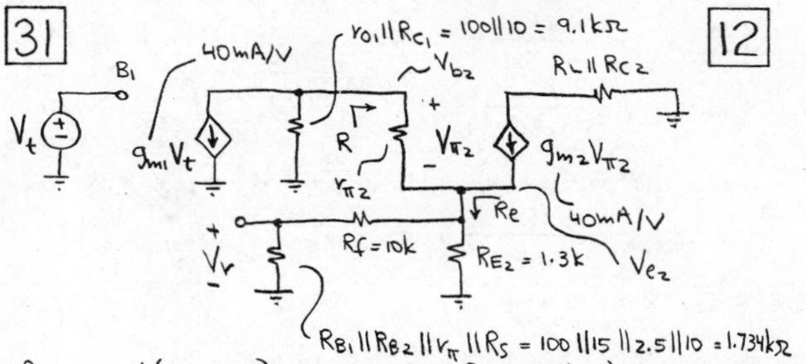

$Re = 1.3 \| (10 + 1.73) = 1.17\,k\Omega$, $R = r_{\pi 2} + (\beta+1)Re = 2.5 + 101(1.17) = 104.7\,k\Omega$

$$V_{b2} = -g_{m1} V_t (r_{o1} \| R_{C1} \| R)$$
$$= -40\, V_t (100 \| 10 \| 104.7) = -334.9\, V_t$$
$$V_{e2} = V_{b2} \times \frac{Re}{Re + r_{e2}} = -334.9\, V_t \times \frac{1.17}{1.17 + 0.025} = -327.9\, V_t$$
$$V_r = V_{e2} \times \frac{1.734}{1.734 + 10} = -48.4\, V_t$$

Thus $A\beta = -\frac{V_r}{V_t} = \underline{\underline{48.4}}\ V/V$

(compared to 50 found in Example 12.4)

32 **12**

(a)

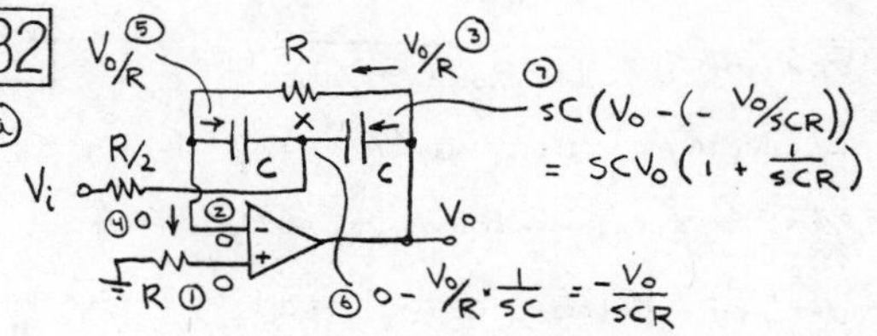

Node equation at X: $\frac{V_i - (-V_o/sCR)}{R/2} + \frac{V_o}{R} + sCV_o\left(1 + \frac{1}{sCR}\right) = 0$

$$\frac{2}{R} V_i + \frac{V_o}{R}\left(\frac{2}{sCR} + 1 + sCR + 1\right) = 0$$

whence $V_o/V_i = \frac{-2}{sCR + 2 + 2/sCR} = \frac{-2\frac{s}{CR}}{s^2 + 2\frac{s}{CR} + \frac{2}{(CR)^2}}$

Thus the poles of the circuit are the roots of the polynomial $\left[s^2 + s\frac{2}{CR} + \frac{2}{(CR)^2}\right]$

(b)

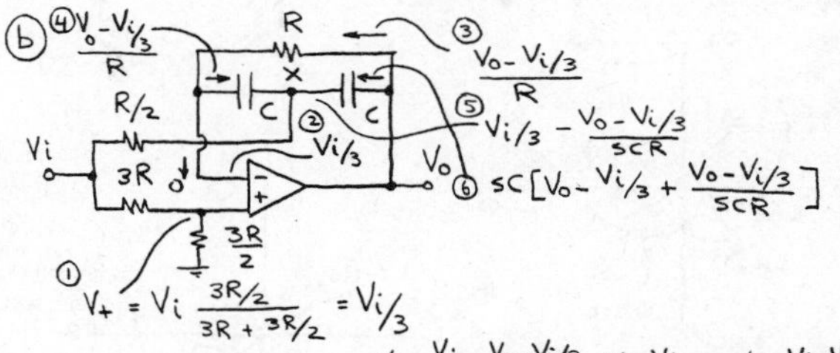

① $V_+ = V_i \frac{3R/2}{3R + 3R/2} = V_i/3$

Node equation at X: $\frac{V_i - \frac{V_i}{3} + \frac{V_o - V_i/3}{sCR}}{R/2} + \frac{V_o - \frac{V_i}{3}}{R} + sC\left(V_o - \frac{V_i}{3} + \frac{V_o - \frac{V_i}{3}}{sCR}\right) = 0$

$$V_i\left(\frac{4}{3} - \frac{2}{3sCR} - \frac{1}{3} - \frac{sCR}{3} - \frac{1}{3}\right) = V_o\left(\frac{2}{sCR} + 1 + sCR + 1\right)$$

whence $V_o/V_i = \frac{-\left(\frac{sCR}{3} - \frac{2}{3} + \frac{2}{3sCR}\right)}{sCR + 2 + 2/sCR}$

12

ie $V_o/V_i = -\frac{1}{3} \times \frac{s^2 - s\frac{2}{CR} + \frac{2}{(CR)^2}}{s^2 + s\frac{2}{CR} + \frac{2}{(CR)^2}}$

Thus the poles of this circuit are the roots of the polynomial $\left[s^2 + s\frac{2}{CR} + \frac{2}{(CR)^2}\right]$

Thus we conclude that both circuits have the same poles (or natural modes). This is easily verified by grounding the input voltage in each circuit. The result for both is the feedback loop:

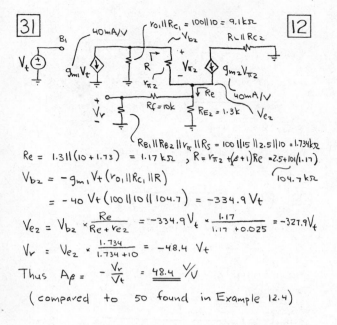

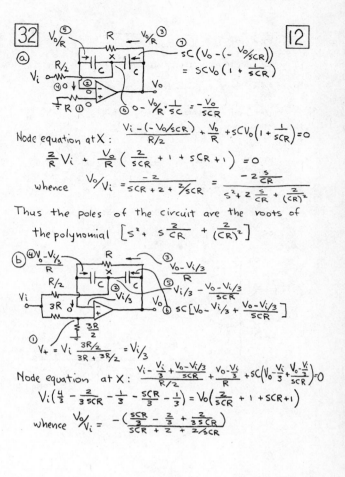

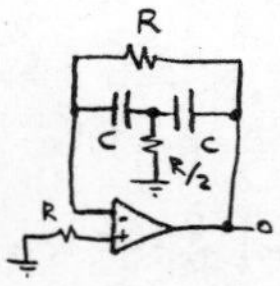

Two circuits with the same feedback loop, have identical poles.

33 **12**

$$A(s) = \frac{10^5}{(1 + s/100)(1 + s/10^4)(1 + s/10^4)}$$

$\angle A(\omega) = -\tan^{-1}\frac{\omega}{100} - 2\tan^{-1}\frac{\omega}{10^4}$. The total phase shift is 180° at ω_c where $\tan^{-1}\frac{\omega_c}{100} + \tan^{-1}\frac{\omega_c}{10^4} = 180$. Solve by trial and success: a) at $\omega_c = 10^4$, $\tan^{-1}100 + 2\tan^{-1}1 = 89.4 + 2(45)$ or 179.4°; b) at $\omega_c = 1.01 \times 10^4$, $\angle = \tan^{-1}101 + 2\tan^{-1}1.01$ or 179.99°.

Conclude that the phase angle is 180° at about $\underline{\underline{10^4\ rad/s}}$ where $|A(10^4)| = \frac{10^5}{(1+(10^2)^2)^{\frac{1}{2}}(1+1^2)^{\frac{1}{2}}(1+1^2)^{\frac{1}{2}}} = \underline{\underline{500}}\ V/V$

Critical $\beta = \beta_{max} = \frac{1}{500} = \underline{\underline{.002}}$, for which corresponding closed loop gain is $A_f = \frac{10^5}{1 + 10^5(\frac{1}{500})} = 497.5$ or $\underline{\underline{500}}$. For a gain margin of 20 dB, $\beta = \frac{.002}{10} = .0002$ and $A_f = \frac{10^5}{1 + 10^5(1/5000)} = 4762$

34 For $A(s) = \frac{10^5}{(1+s/100)(1+s/10^4)^2}$ **12**

plot $A\beta$, $|A\beta|$ radially vs. $\angle A\beta = \phi$, for $\beta = 1, 10^{-3}$

Since β is frequency independant, $\angle A\beta = \angle A$.

W (rad/sec)	$\lvert A\rvert \times 10^{-5}$	$\angle A$	$\lvert A\rvert$	$\lvert A/1000\rvert$
0	1	0°	10^5	100
100	.707	45°	70.7×10^3	70.7
10^3	≈.01	95.7°	9.85×10^3	9.85
10^4	1/200	180°	500	0.5
∞	1	0	10^5	100
			↑ $\beta=1$	↑ $\beta=10^{-3}$

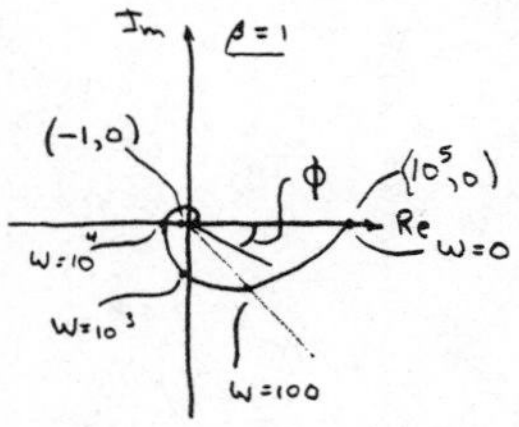

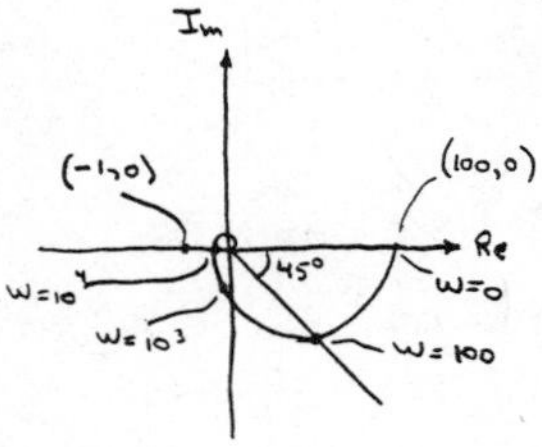

35 $A = \frac{+10^3}{1+s/10^4}$, $\beta = \frac{k}{(1+s/10^4)^2}$ $\Big\}$ $A\beta = \frac{10^3 k}{(1+s/10^4)^3}$ **12**

Potentially unstable where $\tan^{-1}\frac{w}{10^4} = 60° \rightarrow w = 10^4(1.732)$

and $\frac{10^3 k}{(1+(1.732)^2)^{3/2}} \geq 1$

or for $k \geq 8\times10^{-3}$

That is stable for $k \leq \underline{\underline{8\times10^{-3}}}$ and $A\beta < 8$

36 $A(s) = \frac{1000}{(1+s/10^4)(1+s/10^5)^2}$

Critical frequency $w \rightarrow \tan^{-1}\frac{w}{10^4} + 2\tan^{-1}\frac{w}{10^5} = 180$

Try $w = 10^5 \rightarrow \tan^{-1}10 + 2\tan^{-1}1 = 84.2 + 90 = 174.2$

$w = 1.1\times10^5 \rightarrow 84.8 + 2(47.7) = 180.25$

$\therefore w_C = \underline{\underline{1.1\times10^5}}$ rad/s

at which $|A| = \frac{1000}{\left(\left(1+\left(\frac{1.1\times10^5}{10^4}\right)^2\right)\left(1+\left(\frac{1.1\times10^5}{10^5}\right)^2\right)^2\right)^{1/2}} = 40.97$

For stability $\beta < \frac{1}{40.97} = \underline{\underline{.0244}}$

37 $A(s) = \frac{10^5}{\left(1+\frac{s}{2\pi(10)}\right)\left(1+\frac{s}{2\pi(10^4)}\right)}$ **12**

$\beta = \frac{R_1}{R_1+R_2} \rightarrow$ nominal gain $= 1/\beta = \frac{R_1+R_2}{R_1} = 100$

Thus $\beta = \frac{1}{100}$

$|A\beta| = 1$ when $\frac{10^5\times10^{-2}}{\left(1+\left(\frac{f}{10}\right)^2\right)^{1/2}\left(1+\left(\frac{f}{10^4}\right)^2\right)^{1/2}} = 1$

or $\left(1+\left(\frac{f}{10}\right)^2\right)\left(1+\left(\frac{f}{10^4}\right)^2\right) = 10^6$

or $1 + \frac{f^2}{10^8} + \frac{f^2}{10^2} + \frac{f^4}{10^{10}} = 10^6$

or $10^{10} + f^2(10^8) + f^4 = 10^{16}$

or $f^4 + 10^8 f^2 - 10^{16} = 0 \rightarrow f^2 = \frac{-10^8 \pm \sqrt{10^{16}+4(10)^{16}}}{2}$

or $f^2 = .618\times10^8 \rightarrow f = \underline{.786\times10^4}$ Hz

Now at 7.86 kHz, $\angle A\beta = \tan^{-1}(786) + \tan^{-1}(.786) = 128.1°$

and Phase Margin $= 180 - 128.1 = \underline{51.9°}$

38 $A(s) = \frac{10^4}{\left(1+\frac{s}{2\pi10^3}\right)\left(1+\frac{s}{2\pi\times10^6}\right)\left(1+\frac{s}{4\pi\times10^6}\right)}$

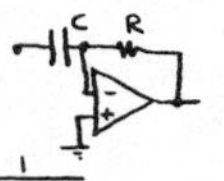

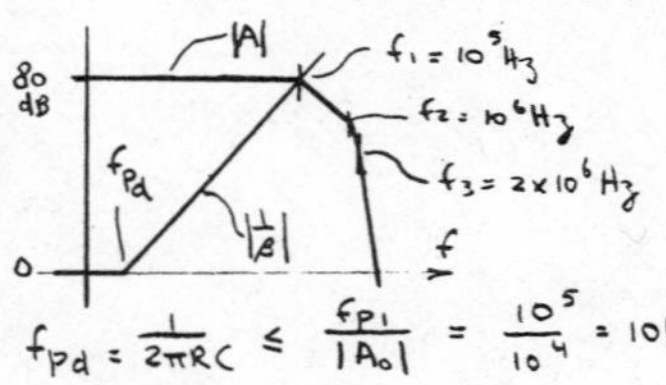

$\beta = \frac{\frac{1}{Cs}}{\frac{1}{Cs}+R} = \frac{1}{1+RCs}$

For 20 dB rate of closure, operation as shown:

$f_{Pd} = \frac{1}{2\pi RC} \leq \frac{f_{P1}}{|A_0|} = \frac{10^3}{10^4} = 10\text{Hz} \rightarrow RC \leq \frac{1}{2\pi\times10} = \underline{\underline{15.9\text{ msec}}}$

39 $(R_1+R_2)/R_2 = 100 = 1/\beta$ **12**

$A(s) = \frac{10^5}{1+s/\omega_H} \rightarrow A_f = \frac{A}{1+\beta A} = \frac{10^5/1+\frac{s}{\omega_H}}{1+\frac{10^3}{1+s/\omega_H}}$

or $A_f(s) = \frac{10^5}{10^3+1+s/\omega_H} \approx \frac{100}{1+s/(10^3\omega_H)}$

and $A_f(f) = \frac{100}{1+jf/10^3 f_H}$. Gain is 1 and $\phi = -90°$

at $f = 10^4$ Hz $\rightarrow \frac{100}{10^4/10^3 f_H} = 1$ or $\frac{10^5}{10^4} f_H = 1$

or $\underline{\underline{f_H = 0.1\text{ Hz}}}$

40 Normalize by substituting p for $\frac{s}{2\pi\times10^6}$

$\therefore$ response in Fig 12.37 becomes

$A(p) = \frac{10^5}{(1+p/0.1)(1+p/1)(1+p/10)}$

Phase margin is 90° when $\tan^{-1}\frac{f}{0.1} + \tan^{-1}f + \tan^{-1}\frac{f}{10} = 90°$

or (from the figure) where $f = 0.3$. As a check, note that

$\tan^{-1}\frac{0.3}{0.1} + \tan^{-1}0.3 + \tan^{-1}\frac{0.3}{10} = 89.98°$. The

Corresponding actual frequency is $0.3\times10^6 = \underline{\underline{300\text{kHz}}}$,

at which $|A| = \frac{10^5}{((1+3^2)(1+.3^2)(1+.03^2))^{1/2}} = 0.303\times10^5$

and for which $|A\beta| = 1$ when $\beta = \frac{1}{.303\times10^5} = 3.3\times10^{-5}$

and the Corresponding $A_f = \frac{10^5}{1+3.3} = \underline{\underline{23.2\times10^3}}$ V/V

12

For Φ margin of 45°: $\tan^{-1}\frac{f}{0.1} + \tan^{-1} f + \tan^{-1}\frac{f}{10} = 135°$

From graph frequency $\approx 10^6$ Hz, for which $f = 1$. Check:

$\tan^{-1} 10 + \tan^{-1} 1 + \tan^{-1} 0.1 = 84.29 + 45 + 5.7 = 135°$ as req'd.

At 1 MHz, $|A| = \dfrac{10^5}{\left((1+10^2)(1+1^2)(1+0.1)^2\right)^{1/2}} = \underline{\underline{7000}}$

For $|A\beta| = 1$, $\beta = 1/7000$ and at low frequencies

$$A_f = \frac{10^5}{1 + 10^5/7000} = \underline{\underline{6542}}$$

41

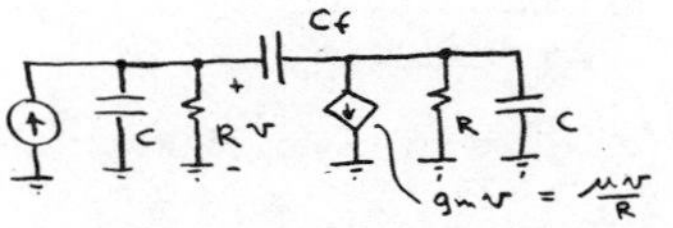

$g_m = \mu/R$

$$\omega_{p1}' = \left(CR + CR + C_f\left((\mu/R)RR + R + R\right)\right)^{-1}$$
$$= \left(2CR + C_f R(\mu+2)\right)^{-1}$$

For $C_f = 0$, $\omega_{p1} = \dfrac{1}{2CR}$

With C_f, $\omega_{p1}' = \dfrac{1}{2CR} \cdot \dfrac{1}{\ell}$

$\therefore 2\ell CR = 2CR + C_f R(\mu+2) \rightarrow C_f = \dfrac{2\ell CR - 2CR}{(\mu+2)R} = \underline{\underline{C \cdot \dfrac{2(\ell-1)}{\mu+2}}}$

or $C_f = \underline{\underline{\dfrac{C(\ell-1)}{1+\mu/2}}}$

42 (a) 12

$f_{P1} = 0.1$ MHz, $f_{P2} = f_{P3} = 1$ MHz

$C_1 = 100$ pF, $C_2 = 5$ pF, $g_m = 40$ mA/V

$0.1 \times 10^6 = 1/(2\pi \times 100 \times 10^{-12} \times R_1) \rightarrow R_1 = \dfrac{1}{2\pi \cdot 10^{-5}} = \dfrac{100}{2\pi}$ kΩ

$10^6 = 1/(2\pi \times 5 \times 10^{-12} \times R_2) \rightarrow R_2 = \dfrac{1}{10^{-5}\pi} = \dfrac{100}{\pi}$ kΩ

Connecting C_f across the output of the input stage the first pole is moved to f_D':

$f_D' = 1/(2\pi(C_f + C_1)R_1) \rightarrow \dfrac{10^6}{10^5} = 1/\left(2\pi(C_f + C_1) \times \frac{100}{2\pi} \times 10^3\right)$

whence $C_f + C_1 = \dfrac{1}{10^6} = 1\,\mu$F and $\underline{\underline{C_f \approx 1\,\mu F}}$

Connecting C_f in the feedback path (ie using Miller comp.) will move the second pole much higher and the first pole is moved to f_{P1}':

$f_{P1}' \approx 1/(2\pi g_m R_2 C_f R_1)$, or

$\dfrac{10^6}{10^5} = 1/\left(2\pi \times 40 \times 10^{-3} \times \frac{100}{\pi} \times 10^3 \times C_f \times \frac{100}{2\pi} \times 10^3\right)$

whence $C_f = \dfrac{\pi}{4 \times 10^9} = \underline{\underline{785.4 \text{ pF}}}$

Now, the second pole is at

$f_{P2}' = g_m C_f / \left(2\pi(C_1 C_2 + C_f(C_1 + C_2))\right)$

$= \dfrac{40 \times 10^{-3} \times 785.4 \times 10^{-12}}{2\pi(100 \times 5 + 785.4 \times 105) \times 10^{-24}} = \underline{\underline{60.3 \text{ MHz}}}$

(b) 12

$f_{P1} = f_{P2} = f_{P3} = 10^6$

$C_1 = 100$ pF, $C_2 = 5$ pF, $g_m = 40$ mA/V

$10^6 = 1/2\pi C_1 R_1 = \dfrac{1}{2\pi \times 100 \times 10^{-12} \times R_1} \rightarrow R_1 = \dfrac{10}{2\pi}$ kΩ

$10^6 = 1/2\pi C_2 R_2 = \dfrac{1}{2\pi \times 5 \times 10^{-12} \times R_2} \rightarrow R_2 = \dfrac{100}{\pi}$ kΩ

Connecting C_f across the output of the first stage moves the first pole to f_D'

$f_D' = 1/(2\pi(C_1 + C_f)R_1) \rightarrow \dfrac{10^6}{10^5} = \dfrac{1}{2\pi(C_1 + C_f) \times 10^4/2\pi}$

whence $C_1 + C_f = 10^{-5}$ F and $\underline{\underline{C_1 \approx 10\,\mu F}}$

Connecting C_f in the feedback path (using Miller comp.) moves the second pole much higher with the first pole at f_{P1}'

$f_{P1}' = 1/(2\pi g_m R_2 C_f R_1)$, or

$\dfrac{10^6}{10^5} = 1/\left(2\pi \times 40 \times 10^{-3} \times 10^5/\pi \times C_f \times 10^4/\pi\right)$

whence $C_f = \dfrac{\pi}{4 \times 10^8} = \underline{\underline{7.85 \text{ nF}}}$

Now, the second pole is at

$f_{P2}' \approx g_m / (2\pi(C_1 + C_2))$

$= \dfrac{40 \times 10^{-3}}{2\pi(105 \times 10^{-12})} = \underline{\underline{60.6 \text{ MHz}}}$

(c) 12

$f_{P1} = 0.1$ MHz, $f_{P2} = 1$ MHz, $f_{P3} = 10$ MHz

$C_1 = 50$ pF, $C_2 = 5$ pF

$10^5 = \dfrac{1}{2\pi \times 50 \times 10^{-12} \times R_1} \rightarrow R_1 = \dfrac{100}{\pi}$ kΩ

$10^6 = \dfrac{1}{2\pi \times 5 \times 10^{-12} \times R_2} \rightarrow R_2 = \dfrac{100}{\pi}$ kΩ

Connecting C_f across the output of the first stage moves the first pole f_{P1} to f_D'

$f_D' = 1/(2\pi(C_f + C_1)R_1) \rightarrow \dfrac{10^6}{10^5} = \dfrac{1}{2\pi(C_f + C_1) \cdot 10^5/\pi}$

whence $C_1 + C_f = \dfrac{1}{2 \times 10^6} = 0.5\,\mu$F and $\underline{\underline{C_f \approx 0.5\,\mu F}}$

Connecting C_f in the feedback path (using Miller Comp) moves the second pole to a much higher frequency and moves the first pole to f_{P1}'

$f_{P1}' \approx 1/(2\pi g_m R_2 C_f R_1)$, or

$\dfrac{10^7}{10^5} = 1/\left(2\pi \times 40 \times 10^{-3} \times 10^5/\pi \times C_f \times 10^5/\pi\right)$

whence $C_f = \underline{\underline{39.3 \text{ pF}}}$

Now, the second pole is at

$f_{P2}' = g_m C_f / \left(2\pi(C_1 C_2 + C_f(C_1 + C_2))\right)$

$= \dfrac{40 \times 10^{-3} \times 39.3 \times 10^{-12}}{2\pi[50 \times 10^{-12} \times 5 \times 10^{-12} + 39.3 \times 10^{-12} \times 55 \times 10^{-12}]} = \underline{\underline{104 \text{ MHz}}}$

43 Eq. 12.64, 65 **12**

$\omega_{p1}' = \frac{1}{g_m R_2 C_f R_1}$ for $\omega_{p1} = \frac{1}{C_1 R_1}$

$\omega_{p2}' = \frac{g_m C_f}{C_1 C_2 + C_f(C_1 + C_2)}$ for $\omega_{p2} = \frac{1}{C_2 R_2}$

With $R_1 = R_2 = C$, $C_2 = C_1/10 = C$, $C_f >> C$, $g_m = \frac{100}{R}$

$\omega_{p1} = \frac{1}{10RC} \rightarrow \omega_{p1}' = \frac{1}{\frac{100}{R} \times R \times C_f \times R} = \frac{1}{100 C_f R}$,

a reduction by more than a factor of 10

$\omega_{p2} = \frac{1}{RC} \rightarrow \omega_{p2}' = \frac{\frac{100}{R} C_f}{(10C)C + C_f(10C + C)}$ which for $C_f >> C$

becomes $\omega_{p2}' = \frac{100 C_f}{R C_f (11C)} = \frac{9.1}{RC}$, an increase by nearly a factor of 10.

44

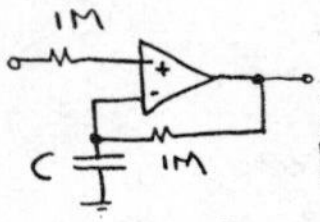

$A(\frac{s}{2\pi}) = A(p) = \frac{10^4}{(1 + p/10^5)(1 + p/10^6)(1 + p/10^7)}$

For $\beta = 1$:

Dominant pole 10^4 below lowest (at 10^5),

at $f_p = 10\ Hz$. $f_p = \frac{1}{2\pi RC} \rightarrow C = \frac{1}{2\pi \times 10 \times 10^6} = .0159\ \mu F$

45 **12**

$f_{p1} = 10^5 = \frac{1}{2\pi C_1 R_1} = \frac{1}{2\pi \times 150 \times 10^{-12} \times R_1}$

whence $R_1 = 10.61\ k\Omega$

$f_{p2} = 10^6 = \frac{1}{2\pi C_2 R_2} = \frac{1}{2\pi \times 5 \times 10^{-12} \times R_2}$

whence $R_2 = 31.83\ k\Omega$

Assume that pole splitting moves the pole at f_{p2} to a much higher frequency. This permits us to place the new dominant pole at $\frac{f_{p3}}{10^4}$

Thus $\frac{2 \times 10^6}{10^4} = \frac{1}{2\pi g_m R_2 C_f R_1}$

and $C_f = 10^4/(2 \times 10^6 \times 2\pi \times 40 \times 10^{-3} \times 31.83 \times 10^3 \times 10.61 \times 10^3)$

or $C_f = 58.9\ pF$, for which (from Eq 12.65)

$f_{p2}' = \frac{g_m C_f}{2\pi(C_1 C_2 + C_f(C_1 + C_2))}$

$= \frac{40 \times 10^{-3} \times 58.9 \times 10^{-12}}{2\pi(150 \times 5 + 58.9 \times 155) \times 10^{-24}} = \frac{40 \times 58.9 \times 10^9}{2\pi(750 + 58.9 \times 155)}$

$= 38\ MHz$

46 **12**

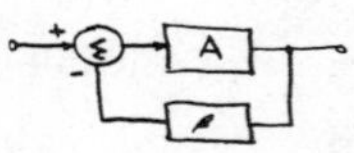

A neg, β pos → Positive Feedback

A neg, β neg → Negative Feedback

A pos, β neg → Positive Feedback

$A_f = \frac{A}{1 + \beta A}$ A pos, β pos → Negative Feedback

- For $A\beta$ negative and $|A\beta| << 1$, $|A_f| > |A|$
- For $A\beta = -0.9$, $A_f = \frac{A}{1 - 0.9} = 10A$
- For $A\beta = -1.0$, $A_f = \infty$, ie output with no input!

47

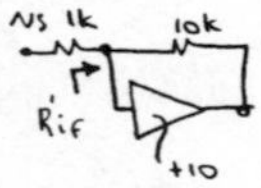

Break the loop

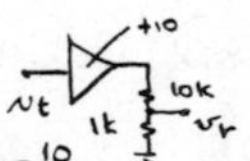

Loop Gain $= A\beta = -\frac{v_r}{v_t} = -\frac{10}{11}$

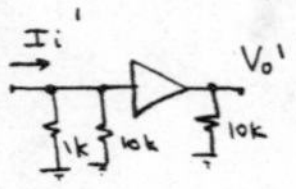

$A = \frac{V_o'}{I_i'} = (1k \| 10k)10 = \frac{100}{11}\ k\Omega$

$\beta = \frac{V_o'}{I_f'} = -\frac{1}{10\ k\Omega}$

$1 + A\beta = 1 - \frac{10}{11} = 1/11 \rightarrow A_f = \frac{V_o}{I_s} = \frac{A}{1 + A\beta} = \frac{100/11}{1/11} = 100\ k\Omega$

$R_i = 1k \| 10k = \frac{10}{11} k\Omega \rightarrow R_{if} = \frac{10/11}{1/11} = 10\ k\Omega$

$R_{if}' = \frac{1}{1/10 - 1/1} = \frac{1}{-9/10} = -\frac{10}{9} = -1.11\ k\Omega$

$V_o/V_s = \frac{V_o}{I_s R_s} = \frac{100\ k\Omega}{1\ k\Omega} = 100$

48 **12**

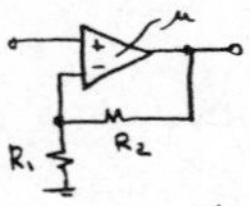

Series-Shunt Feedback

$A = +\mu$, $\beta = \frac{R_1}{R_1 + R_2}$

$A_f = \frac{\mu}{1 + \mu \times \frac{R_1}{R_1 + R_2}}$

For $\mu = 1$: a) $R_1 = R_2 = R \rightarrow A_f = \frac{1}{1 + 1(1/2)} = 2/3 = 0.667\ V/V$

b) $R_2 = 0 \rightarrow A_f = \frac{1}{1 + 1 \times 1} = 1/2 = 0.5\ V/V$

c) $R_1 = \infty \rightarrow A_f = \frac{1}{1 + \frac{\infty}{\infty}} = 1/2 = 0.5\ V/V$

49

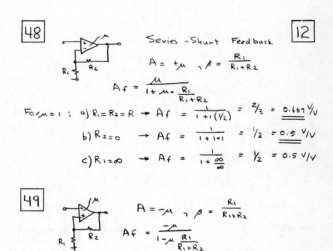

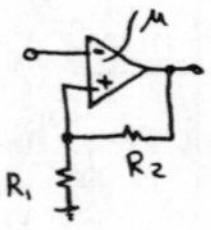

$A = -\mu$, $\beta = \frac{R_1}{R_1 + R_2}$

$A_f = \frac{-\mu}{1 - \mu \frac{R_1}{R_1 + R_2}}$

For $\mu = 1$: a) $R_1 = R_2 = R \rightarrow A_f = \frac{-1}{1 - 1(1/2)} = -2$

b) $R_2 = 0 \rightarrow A_f = \frac{-1}{1 - 1(1)} = -\infty$

c) $R_1 = \infty \rightarrow A_f = \frac{-1}{1 - 1\frac{\infty}{\infty}} = -\infty$

For $\mu = 0.99$: a) $R_1 = R_2 = R \rightarrow A_f = \frac{-0.99}{1 - 0.99(1/2)} = -1.96$

b) $R_2 = 0 \rightarrow A_f = \frac{-0.99}{1 - 0.99} = -99$

c) $R_1 = \infty \rightarrow A_f = \frac{-0.99}{1 - 0.99(\frac{\infty}{\infty})} = -99$

1 **13**

(a) For $\pm 15V$, $I_5 = \frac{V_{CC}+V_{EE}-0.7-0.7}{39k} = \frac{28.6}{39k} = \underline{\underline{0.733\ mA}}$

(b) For $\pm 5V$, $I_5 = \frac{5+5-0.7-0.7}{39k} = \underline{\underline{0.2205\ mA}}$

2 Using data from table 13.1 :

From V_{CC}, Current is $I_+ = I_{12}+I_{13A}+I_{13B}+I_9+I_8+I_{14}$

or $730+180+550+19+19+154 = \underline{\underline{1652\ \mu A}}$

To V_{EE}, excluding the overload currents, I_{22}, I_{24},

$I_- = I_{11}+I_{10}+I_5+I_6+I_7+I_{16}+I_{17}+I_{23}+I_{20}$

or $730+19+9.5+9.5+10.5+16.2+550+180+154$

or $\underline{\underline{1678.7\ \mu A}}$

Obviously the supply currents should be the same. The difference is due, for example to using I_{16} and not I_{R9}, part of which is included in I_{17}

Quiescent Power $= 1.6(8)mA(15V+15V) = \underline{\underline{50.4\ mW}}$

4 **13**

Differential input for breakdown is $7+7+0.7+0.7 = \underline{\underline{15.4\ V}}$

5 For pnp: $I_S = 10^{-14}A$, $\beta = 50$, $V_A = 50V$, $I_C = 1mA$

$\therefore V_{EB} = V_T \ln I_C/I_S = V_T \ln \frac{1\times10^{-3}}{10^{-14}} = \underline{\underline{633\ mV}}$

$g_m = I_C/V_T = 1/25 = \underline{\underline{40\ mA/V}}$

$r_e = \alpha/g_m = \frac{50}{51}\times\frac{1}{40} = 24.5\Omega \approx \underline{\underline{25\Omega}}$

$r_\pi = (\beta+1)r_e = 51(24.5) = 1.2495k \approx \underline{\underline{1.25k\Omega}}$

$r_o = V_A/I_C = 50/1 = \underline{\underline{50k\Omega}}$

$r_\mu = 10\beta r_o = 10(50)(50k) = \underline{\underline{25\ M\Omega}}$

6 For npn: $I_S = 10^{-14}A$, $\beta = 200$, $V_A = 125V$, $I_C = 0.1mA$

$\therefore V_{BE} = V_T \ln \frac{10^{-4}}{10^{-14}} = \underline{\underline{576\ mV}}$

$g_m = I_C/V_T = 0.1/25 = \underline{\underline{4\ mA/V}}$

$r_e = \alpha/g_m = \frac{200}{201}\times\frac{1}{4} \approx \underline{\underline{250\Omega}} \rightarrow r_\pi = 201(r_e) = \underline{\underline{50k\Omega}}$

$r_o = 125/0.1 = \underline{\underline{1.25\ M\Omega}}$

$r_\mu = 10\beta r_o = 10(200)(1.25\times10^6) = 2.5\times10^9 = \underline{\underline{2.5\ G\Omega}}$

3 **13**

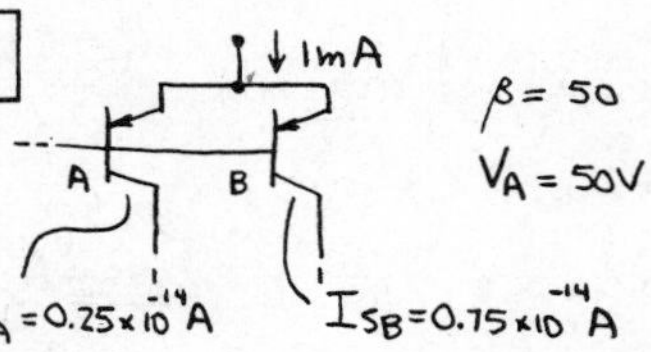

$\beta = 50$

$V_A = 50V$

The emitter current will split by junction size, 3x more going to T_B than to T_A.

Thus $I_{EA} = \underline{\underline{0.25mA}}$, $I_{EB} = \underline{\underline{0.75mA}}$

Now $i_C = I_S e^{V_{EB}/V_T} = i_E/\alpha$ and $r_e = \frac{V_T}{I_E}$

$\therefore V_{EB} = V_T \ln \frac{I_E}{\alpha I_S} = V_T \ln \frac{0.25\times10^{-3}}{50/51 \times 0.25\times10^{-14}} = \underline{\underline{634mV}}$

and $r_{eA} = \frac{25mV}{0.25mA} = \underline{\underline{100\Omega}}$; $r_{eB} = \frac{25mV}{0.75mA} = \underline{\underline{33.\dot{3}\Omega}}$

and $r_{e\,Total} = r_{eA} \| r_{eB} = \frac{25mV}{1mA} = \underline{\underline{25\Omega}}$

Also $r_{\pi\,Total} = (\beta+1)r_{e\,Total} = 51(25) = \underline{\underline{1.275\ k\Omega}}$

Now $r_o = \frac{V_A}{I_C} = \frac{V_A}{\alpha I_E}$ and $r_\mu \simeq 10\beta r_o$

Thus $r_{oA} = \frac{50}{0.25\times10^{-3}(50/51)} = 204k\Omega \approx \underline{\underline{200k\Omega}}$

and $r_{oB} = 204/3 = \underline{\underline{68\ k\Omega}}$

Thus $r_{\mu A} = 10(50)(204k) = 102\ M\Omega \approx \underline{\underline{100\ M\Omega}}$

and $r_{\mu B} = 102/3 = \underline{\underline{34\ M\Omega}}$

7 **13**

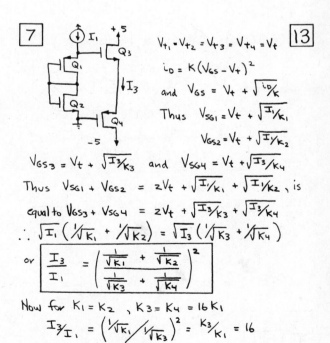

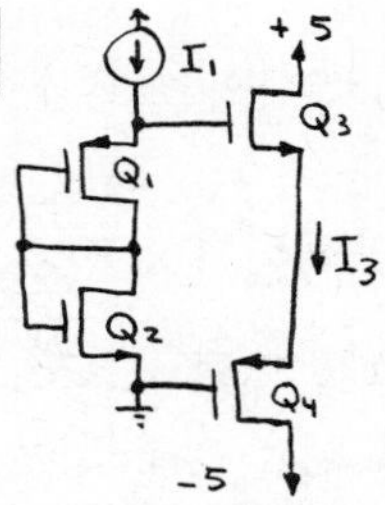

$V_{t1} = V_{t2} = V_{t3} = V_{t4} = V_t$

$i_D = K(V_{GS}-V_t)^2$

and $V_{GS} = V_t + \sqrt{i_D/K}$

Thus $V_{SG1} = V_t + \sqrt{I_1/K_1}$

$V_{GS2} = V_t + \sqrt{I_1/K_2}$

$V_{GS3} = V_t + \sqrt{I_3/K_3}$ and $V_{SG4} = V_t + \sqrt{I_3/K_4}$

Thus $V_{SG1} + V_{GS2} = 2V_t + \sqrt{I_1/K_1} + \sqrt{I_1/K_2}$, is equal to $V_{GS3} + V_{SG4} = 2V_t + \sqrt{I_3/K_3} + \sqrt{I_3/K_4}$

$\therefore \sqrt{I_1}\left(1/\sqrt{K_1} + 1/\sqrt{K_2}\right) = \sqrt{I_3}\left(1/\sqrt{K_3} + 1/\sqrt{K_4}\right)$

or
$$\boxed{\frac{I_3}{I_1} = \left(\frac{\frac{1}{\sqrt{K_1}} + \frac{1}{\sqrt{K_2}}}{\frac{1}{\sqrt{K_3}} + \frac{1}{\sqrt{K_4}}}\right)^2}$$

Now for $K_1 = K_2$, $K_3 = K_4 = 16K_1$

$I_3/I_1 = \left(\frac{1/\sqrt{K_1}}{1/\sqrt{K_3}}\right)^2 = K_3/K_1 = 16$

Thus for $I_1 = 0.1\ mA$, $I_3 = \underline{\underline{1.6\ mA}}$

8 **13**

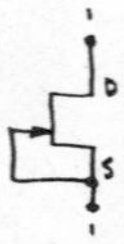

(a) $I_{DSS} = I_{REF} = \underline{0.73\,mA}$

(b) $I_D = I_{DSS}\left(1 + \frac{V_{DS}}{V_A}\right)$

For ±5V, $I_D = 0.5\left(1 + \frac{10-1.4}{50}\right) = \underline{0.59\,mA}$

For ±15V, $I_D = 0.5\left(1 + \frac{30-1.4}{50}\right) = \underline{0.79\,mA}$

(c) Minimum supply $\pm V_m$, such that

$2V_m - 1.4 = V_p = 2 \rightarrow 2V_m = 3.4V$ or $V_m = 1.7V$

∴ use $\underline{\pm 1.7V}$ supplies at least

9

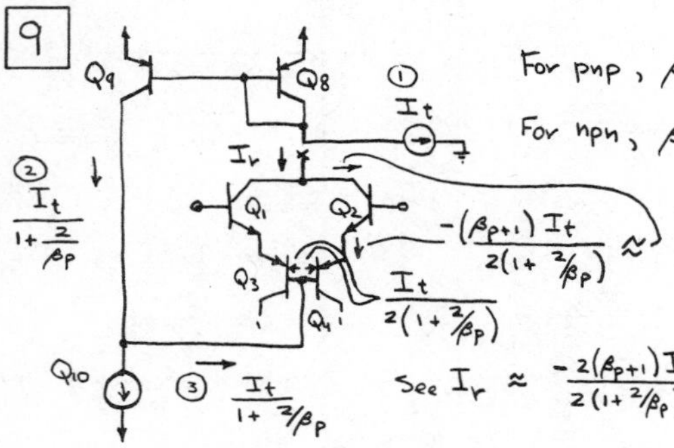

For pnp, β_p

For npn, $\beta_n >> 1$

See $I_r \approx \frac{-2(\beta_p+1)I_t}{2(1+2/\beta_p)} \approx -\beta_p I_t$

Thus $(A\beta)_{cm} = -\frac{I_r}{I_t} = \beta_p = 50$

Amount of feedback $= (1+A\beta) = 51$ or $20\log 51 = \underline{34\,dB}$

10 **13**

Assume $I_{C1} \approx I_{C2} = 9.5\,\mu A$

$I_{B1} = \frac{9.5}{175} = .05429\,\mu A$

$I_{B2} = \frac{9.5}{225} = .04222\,\mu A$

$I_B = \frac{I_{B1}+I_{B2}}{2} = \underline{48.25\,nA}$

and $I_{offset} = I_{B1} - I_{B2} = .01207\,\mu A = \underline{12.1\,nA}$

11

For $|V_{BE}| = 0.6$, $|V_{CE}| = 0.6 - 0.2 = 0.4$ near saturation

Thus, negative limit is $-15 + 0.6 + 0.6 + 0.4 + 0.6 = \underline{-12.8V}$

and, positive limit is $+15 - 0.6 + 0.2 = \underline{+14.6V}$

12

From table 13.1: $I_{C17} = 550\,\mu A$, $I_{C16} = 16.2\,\mu A$ } $I_S = 10^{-14}A$

∴ $V_{BE17} = V_T \ln \frac{550\times10^{-6}}{10^{-14}} = 618.3\,mV$

and $V_{BE16} = V_T \ln \frac{16.2\times10^{-6}}{10^{-14}} = 530.1\,mV$

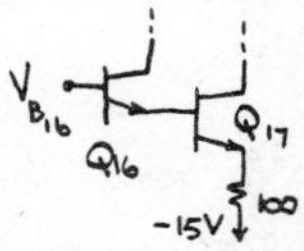

Thus $V_{B16} = -15 + 100(550\times10^{-6}) + .618 + .530 = \underline{-13.8\,V}$

13 **13**

(a) If both I_S double, I_Q doubles

(b) If one doubles: Let $I_{Q\,original} = I_O$, $I_{Q\,new} = I_N$

Thus $2V_T \ln I_O/I_S = V_T(\ln I_N/I_S + \ln I_N/2I_S)$

ie $\ln(I_O/I_S)^2 = \ln(I_N^2/2I_S^2) \rightarrow \frac{I_N}{\sqrt{2}I_S} = \frac{I_O}{I_S}$

or $I_N = \sqrt{2}\,I_O$. See I_Q increases to $1.414\,I_Q$,

that is increases by $\underline{41.4\%}$

(c) If one halved, one doubles:

See $2V_T \ln I_O/I_S = V_T\left(\ln \frac{I_N}{2I_S} + \ln \frac{2I_N}{I_S}\right)$

$= 2V_T \ln I_N/I_S + V_T(\ln 2 - \ln 2)$

$= 2V_T \ln I_N/I_S$

See I_Q stays the same

14

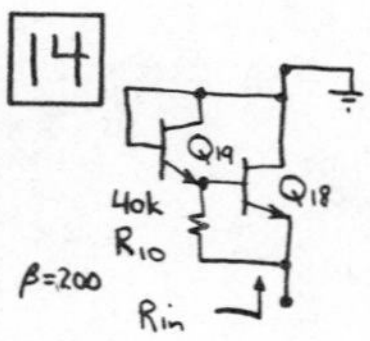

$I_{E18} = 165\,\mu A \rightarrow r_{e18} = 151.5\Omega$

and $r_{\pi 18} = 201(151.5) = 30.45\,k\Omega$

$I_{E19} = 15.8\,\mu A \rightarrow r_{e19} = 1582\,\Omega$

(next)

13

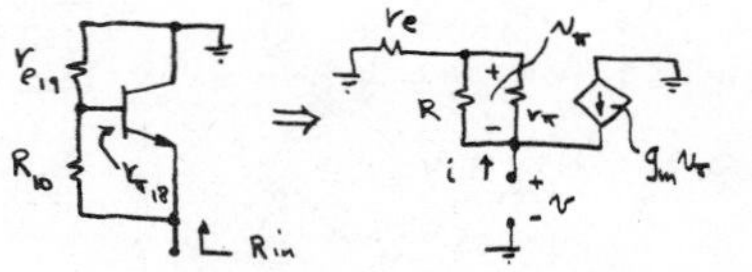

$R||r_\pi = 40k||30.45k = 17.3k\Omega$

See $1/R_{in} = i/v = \frac{1}{r_e + R||r_\pi} + \frac{g_m(R||r_\pi)}{r_e + R||r_\pi}$

or $1/R_{in} = \frac{1}{(17.3+1.6)k} + \frac{\frac{1}{151.5}\times\frac{200}{201}(17.3k)}{(17.3+1.6)k} = \frac{1}{18.9} + \frac{1}{18.9/113.6}$

Thus $R_{in} = \frac{18.9}{114.6} = \underline{165\,\Omega}$

Check: $R_{in} \approx 151.5 + \frac{1582}{201} = 159\Omega$ ✓

15

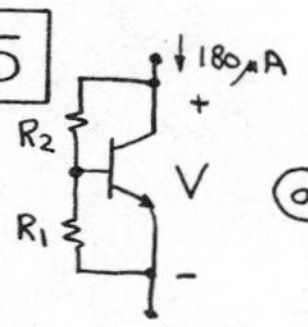

$\beta = 200$, $I_S = 10^{-14}$, $V = 1.118V$

(a) $I_E = 180/2 = 90\,\mu A \rightarrow r_e = \frac{25}{90} = 278\Omega$

$r_\pi = 201(278) = 55.9\,k\Omega$

$V_{BE} = V_T \ln \frac{90\times10^{-6}\times 200/201}{10^{-14}} = \underline{573\,mV}$

$R_1 = \frac{573\times10^{-3}}{90\times10^{-6}} = \underline{6.37\,k\Omega}$

$I_{R2} = 90 + \frac{90}{201} = 90.45\,mA \rightarrow R_2 = \frac{1.118 - .573}{90.45} = \underline{6.025\,k\Omega}$

See [14]: $\frac{1}{R_{in}} = \frac{1}{6.025 + 6.37||55.9}\left(1 + 200\left(\frac{6.37}{6.37+55.9}\right)\right)$

or $R_{in} = \frac{11.74}{1+20.46} = \underline{547\Omega}$

Now for $\beta = 100$, assuming the current split is about

13

the same: $I_E = 90\mu A \rightarrow I_B = \frac{90}{101} = 0.89\mu A$

$V = 573 + (90 + 0.89)(6.025) = \underline{\underline{1.121 V}}$ (vs 1.118), a rise of 3 mV. Now $\frac{1}{R_{in}} = \frac{1}{6.025 + 6.37 \| 55.9/2}\left(1 + \frac{100 \times 6.37}{6.37 + 55.9/2}\right)$

or $R_{in} = \frac{11.21}{1 + 18.56} = \underline{\underline{572\Omega}}$

(b) $I_E = 180 \times 0.9 = 162\mu A \rightarrow r_e = 154.3\Omega$, $r_\pi = (201) r_e = 31k\Omega$

$V_{BE} = V_T \ln \frac{162\left(\frac{200}{201}\right) \times 10^{-6}}{10^{-14}} = \underline{\underline{588 mV}}$

$R_1 = \frac{588}{180 - 162} = 32.6 k\Omega$

$I_{R2} = 18 + \frac{162}{201} = 18.81\mu A \rightarrow R_2 = \frac{1.118 - .588}{18.81} = \underline{28.2k}$

$\frac{1}{R_{in}} = \frac{1}{28.2 + 32.6 \| 31.0}\left(1 + \frac{200(32.6)}{31 + 32.6}\right) = \frac{103}{44.1}$

$R_{in} = \frac{44.1}{103} = \underline{\underline{428\Omega}}$

Now for $\beta = 100$, say $I_E = 162 \rightarrow I_B = \frac{162}{101} = 1.60\mu A$

and $V = 588 + (18 + 1.6)(28.2) = \underline{\underline{1.141 V}}$, a rise of 23 mV

$\frac{1}{R_{in}} = \frac{1}{28.2 + 32.6 \| 31/2}\left(1 + \frac{100(32.6)}{31/2 + 32.6}\right) = 68.8/38.7$

$R_{in} = \frac{38.7}{68.8} = \underline{\underline{563\Omega}}$

16 $V = V_{BE18} + V_{BE19} = V_T\left(\ln i/I_S + \ln \frac{(180 - i)}{I_S}\right)$ 13

for $i = I_{E18}$. Thus $V = V_T \ln\left(\frac{i(180 - i)}{I_S^2}\right)$ is a maximum when $i(180 - i)$ is maximum, where $\frac{\partial}{\partial i}(180i - i^2) = 0$ or $180 - 2i = 0$ or $i = 180/2$ or where the current splits equally, for which

$V_{BE} = V_T \ln \frac{90 \times 10^{-6}}{10^{-14}} = 573 mV$, $V = 2(573) = \underline{\underline{1.146 V}}$

and $R_{10} = \frac{573 \times 10^{-3}}{90 \times 10^{-6}} = \underline{\underline{6.36 k\Omega}}$

17

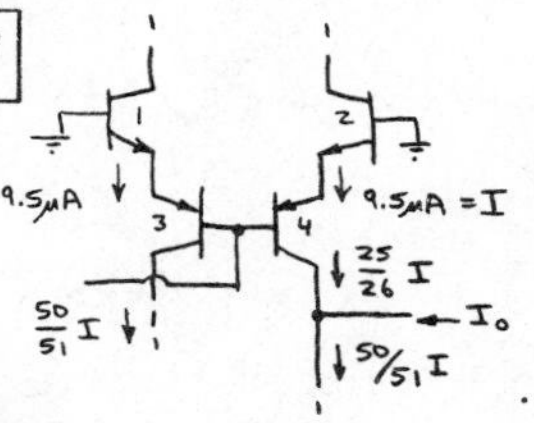

$I_o = \left(\frac{50}{51} - \frac{25}{26}\right) \times 9.5\mu A = .179\mu A$

$V_{off} = I_o / G_{m1}$, where

$1/G_{m1} = 5.26 k\Omega$

$\therefore V_{off} = 0.179 \times 5.26 \times 10^{-3} = \underline{\underline{0.94 mV}}$

18 Eq. 13.10: $\frac{\Delta I}{I} = \frac{\Delta R}{R + \Delta R + r_e}$ where $R = 1k\Omega$, $r_e = 2.63k\Omega$

$I = 9.5\mu A$ and $\Delta I = \left(\frac{50}{51} - \frac{25}{26}\right) 9.5\mu A = .0189(9.5\mu A)$

$\therefore \frac{\Delta R}{R} = 0.0189\left(1 + \frac{\Delta R}{R} + 2.63\right) \rightarrow \frac{\Delta R}{R} = .068$ or $\approx \underline{\underline{7\%}}$

19 Eq 13.10: $\frac{\Delta I}{I} = \frac{\Delta R}{R + \Delta R + r_e}$ 13

For R_1 or R_2 shorted, $\frac{\Delta I}{I} = \frac{R}{R + R + r_e} = \frac{1}{2 + 2.63} = \frac{1}{4.63}$

$\therefore \Delta I = \frac{9.5 \times 10^{-6}}{4.63} = G_{m1} V_{off}$

$\therefore V_{off} = \frac{9.5 \times 10^{-6}}{4.63} \times 5.26 \times 10^{3} = \underline{\underline{10.8 mV}}$

20 Reducing $\frac{\Delta R}{R}$ by factor of 10 reduces common mode gain by 10 → CMRR increases by 10 or $\underline{20dB}$

21 $i_6 = i_3 = \frac{v_{icm}}{2r_e + \frac{2R_o}{\beta_3 + 1}} \times \frac{\beta_3}{\beta_3 + 1} = \frac{v_{icm}\,\beta_3}{2R_o + 2(\beta_3 + 1) r_e}$

Corresp: $i_4 = \frac{v_{icm}\,\beta_4}{2R_o + 2(\beta_4 + 1) r_e}$

$i_o = v_{icm}\left(\frac{\beta_3}{2R_o + 2(\beta_3 + 1) r_e} - \frac{\beta_4}{2R_o + 2(\beta_4 + 1) r_e}\right)$

ie $G_{mcm} = i_o / v_{icm} = \frac{55}{2(R_o + 56 r_e)} - \frac{50}{2(R_o + 51 r_e)}$

But $R_o = 2.43 M\Omega$ and $r_e = \frac{1}{2(0.19)} = 2.63 k\Omega$

$\therefore G_{mcm} = \frac{55}{2(2.43 + 56 \times .0026)} - \frac{50}{2(2.43 + 51 \times .0026)} = 0.92\mu A/V$

$CMRR = \frac{.19 \times 10^{-3}}{.92 \times 10^{-6}} = 207 \equiv \underline{\underline{46.3 dB}}$

22 Assuming potential offsets are cancelled by feedback and that $i_{C5} = i_{C6} = 9.5\mu A$, 13

$r_e \simeq \frac{25 \times 10^{-3}}{9.5 \times 10^{-6}} = 2.63 k\Omega$. Note that for differential input, gain is due to sum of 2 (equal) parts $= \frac{G}{2} + \frac{G}{2}$

(a) R_1 shorted: gain becomes $\frac{G}{2} \times \frac{2.63}{1 + 2.63} + \frac{G}{2} = 0.86\,G$

(b) R_2 shorted: gain becomes $\frac{G}{2} \times \frac{3.63}{2.63} + \frac{G}{2} = 1.19\,G$

(c) Both shorted: gain is the same, ie G

23 $\beta_n = 200$, $\beta_p = 50$, $V_{An} = 125V$, $V_{Ap} = 50V$, $r_\mu = 10\beta r_o$

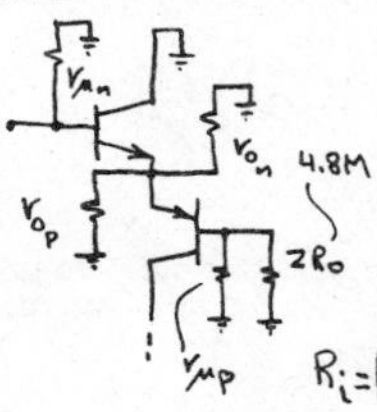

$r_e = \frac{25 \times 10^{-3}}{9.5 \times 10^{-6}} = 2.63 k\Omega$

$r_{on} = \frac{125}{9.5 \times 10^{-6}} = 13.2M$, $r_{\mu n} = 10(200)(13.2) = 26 G\Omega$

$r_{op} = \frac{50}{9.5 \times 10^{-6}} = 5.3M$, $r_{\mu p} = 10(50)(5.3) = 2.6 G\Omega$

$R_i = \left(\left(\left(\frac{4.8M \| 2.6G}{51} + 2(2.6k)\right) \| (13.2M \| 5.3M)\right)(201)\right) \| 26G$

or $R_i = ((99.4k \| 3.8M)\, 201) \| 26G = 19.5 M\Omega$

And $R_{if} \simeq R_i(A\beta + 1) \approx 19.5M \times 51 = \underline{\underline{995 M\Omega}}$

But as feedback directly affects only $2R_o \| r_{op} = 4.8M$, likely

$R_{if} \simeq \left(\left(\left(\frac{4.8M \times 51}{51}\right) \| 13.2 \| 5.3\right) 201\right) \| 26G = \underline{424 M\Omega}$, ie $R_{icm} \gtrsim 400M$

24 **13**

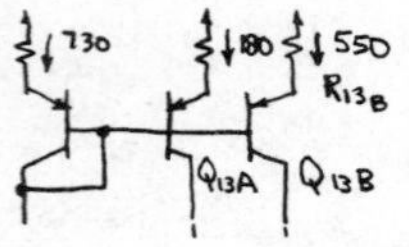

$R_{13B} = R$

$R_{13A} = \frac{550}{180} R = 3.06R$

$R_{12} = \frac{550}{730} R = .753R$

Assume that the common base line has low impedance:

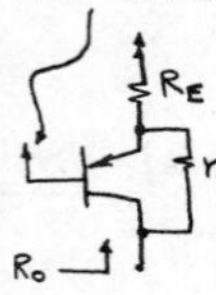

$\frac{1}{R_o} = \frac{1}{r_o}\left(1 - \frac{\alpha R_E}{R_E + r_e}\right)$ and for $\beta >> 1$

$R_o \simeq r_o\left(1 + \frac{R_E}{r_e}\right)$

Now for Q_{13B}, $r_e = \frac{25}{550} = 45.5\Omega$,

$r_o = V_A/I = \frac{50}{550\mu A} = 90.9k\Omega$, $r_\mu = 10\beta r_o = 10(50)(90.9) = 45.5M\Omega$

For Q_{17}, $\beta_n = 200$, $V_{An} = 125V$, $r_{o17} = \frac{125}{550\mu A} = 227\,k\Omega$

$r_{e17} = \frac{25}{550\mu A} = 45.5\,\Omega$, $R_{E17} = 100$

$\therefore R_{o17} = 227k\left(1 + \frac{100}{45.5}\right) = 227(3.2) = 726\,k\Omega$

and $R_{o13B} = 90.9\left(1 + \frac{R}{45.5}\right)$ is required to be 726k

Thus $1 + \frac{R}{45.5} = 7.99 \rightarrow R = R_{13B} = 45.5(6.99) = \underline{318\Omega}$

and $R_{13A} = 3.06(318) = \underline{973\Omega}$, $R_{12} = 0.753(318) = \underline{239\Omega}$

when $R_{o13B} = R_{o17}$

25 **13**

$f_P = f_T/A_o = \frac{5\times10^6}{10^6} = 5\,Hz$

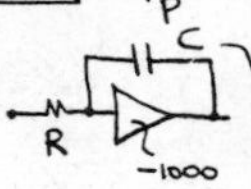

$C = 50pF \rightarrow f_P = \frac{1}{2\pi RC(1-\text{gain})}$

$\therefore R \geq \frac{1}{2\pi\times5(50\times10^{-12})(1001)} = \underline{637\,k\Omega}$

26

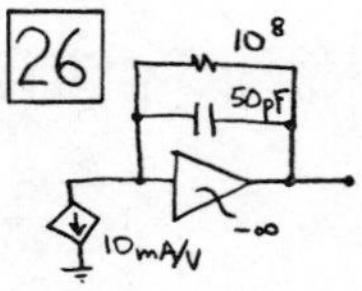

DC gain $= 10\times10^{-3}\times10^8 = \underline{10^6\,V/V}$

$RC = 10^8\times50\times10^{-12} = 50\times10^{-4}$

$f_c = \frac{1}{2\pi\times50\times10^{-4}} = \underline{31.8\,Hz}$

$f_T = 31.8\,Hz\times10^6 = \underline{31.8\,MHz}$

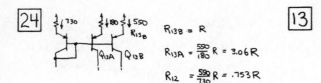

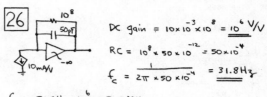

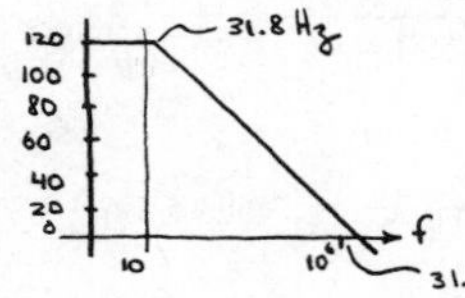

$G_m = 10mA/V = \frac{I}{2V_T} \rightarrow$

$I = 2(25\times10^{-3})(10\times10^{-3}) = \underline{50\mu A}$

$CV = IT \rightarrow$

$V/T = I/C = \frac{50\times10^{-6}}{50\times10^{-12}} = \underline{1V/\mu sec}$

27

Eq 3.27: $f_M = \frac{SR}{2\pi V_{o\,max}} = \frac{10\times10^6\,V/s}{2\pi(10V)} = \underline{159\,kHz}$

For 741 topology:

Eq 13.42: $f_t = \frac{SR}{2\pi(4V_T)} = \frac{10\times10^6}{2\pi(4)(25\times10^{-3})} = \underline{15.9\,MHz}$

and $\omega_t = \underline{100\times10^6\ \text{rad/s}}$

28 **13**

(a) $I_{E1} = I_{E2} = 50\mu A \simeq I_{E3} = I_{E4}$

$I_{E7} \approx 1mA \rightarrow I_{B7} = 10\mu A$

$I_{C5} = 0.99\,mA$, $I_{E5} = \frac{0.99}{\alpha} = 1mA = I_{E6} = I_{E7}$

$\therefore r_{e1} = \frac{25\times10^{-3}}{50\times10^{-6}} = 500\Omega$, $r_{e5} = 25\Omega$

(b) Gain for $1k\Omega$ load $= A_v$

$$A_v = \left(\frac{2\left(\frac{100}{101}\right)\times\frac{101\times25}{2}}{500+500}\right)\times\left\{\frac{100}{101}\times\frac{(1k+25)101}{25}\times\frac{1k}{1k+25} + \frac{1k}{25}\right\}$$

mirror; via Q_5, Q_6; via Q_6

$= 2.5(4000+40) = \underline{10.1\times10^3\ V/V}$

(c) For $1k\Omega$ load, gain of $Q_5 = -\frac{100}{101}\frac{(101)(1k+25)}{25} = -4100$

$f_P = \frac{1}{2\pi R_{eq}C_{eq}}$, $R_{eq} = \frac{101(25)}{2} = \frac{2525}{2}\Omega$

$C_{eq} = C(1-(-4100)) = 4101$

$\therefore C = \frac{1}{2\pi\left(\frac{2525}{2}\right)(10^3)(4101)} = 3.07\times10^{-2}\mu F \approx \underline{.003\mu F}$

29 **13**

$V_t = 1V$, $\mu_n C_{ox} = 20\mu A/V^2$, $\mu_p C_{ox} = 10\mu A/V^2$

$V_A = 25V$. Now from results of 13.23, v_{GS6} was 1.5V

and $(W/L)_6$ was $\frac{100}{10}$ for which $i_{D6} = \frac{1}{2}(20)\left(\frac{100}{10}\right)(1.5-1)^2 = 25\mu A$

Now for v_{GS6} the same and $(W/L) \rightarrow \frac{120}{10}$

i_{D6} becomes $\frac{1}{2}(20)\left(\frac{120}{10}\right)(1.5-1)^2 = \underline{30\mu A}$

Thus the additional output current is $30-25 = 5\mu A$.

The output resistance is $r_{o6} \| r_{o7} = \frac{1}{2}\,\frac{25V}{25\mu A} = 500k\Omega$

Thus output offset resulting is $-5\times10^{-6}\times0.5\times10^6 = \underline{-2.5V}$

Since the open loop gain is 3125 V/V, the compensating input offset is $\frac{2.5}{3125} = \underline{0.8\,mV}$

30

For the two sides: $I = K(V_{GS}-V_t)^2$ for Q_3

and $I + \Delta I = K(V_{GS}-V_t-\Delta V_t)^2 = I\left(1 - \frac{\Delta V_t}{V_{GS}-V_t}\right)^2$ for Q_4

or $I + \Delta I \simeq I\left(1 - \frac{2\Delta V_t}{V_{GS}-V_t}\right) \rightarrow \Delta I = -I\times\frac{2\Delta V_t}{V_{GS}-V_t}$

ie $\Delta I = -\frac{2I}{V_{GS}-V_t}\times\Delta V_t = -g_{m3}\Delta V_t$

Corresponding input offset $= \frac{\Delta I}{g_{m1}} = \frac{g_{m3}}{g_{m1}}\times\Delta V_t = \frac{50}{625}\times2mV$

or $\underline{1.6\,mV}$

31

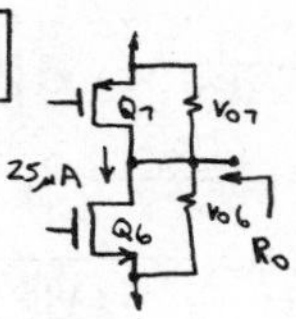

$V_A = 25V$

$r_o = \frac{25V}{25\mu A} = 1M\Omega$

$R_o = 1M \| 1M = \underline{\underline{0.5M\Omega}}$

32

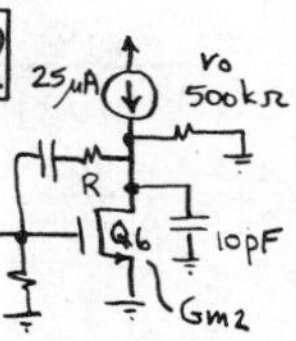

$R_1 = \frac{1}{2}\frac{V_A}{I_D} = \frac{25}{2(12.5)\times10^{-6}} = 1M\Omega$

$G_{m1} = 62.5\mu A/V$, $G_{m2} = 100\mu A/V$

$\omega_z = \frac{-1}{C_c(1/G_{m2} - R)}$ at ∞, if

$R = 1/G_{m2} = \frac{1}{100\times10^{-6}} = \underline{10k\Omega}$

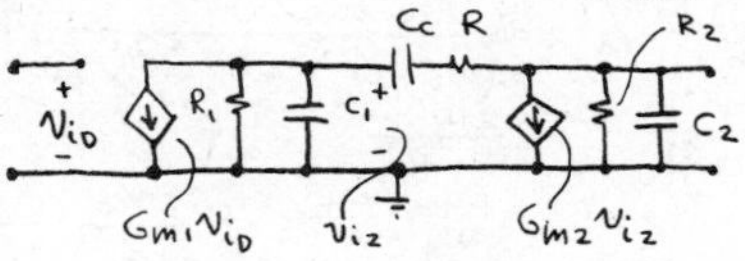

$\omega_{p1} = \frac{1}{G_{m2}R_2C_cR_1}$, $\omega_{p2} = \frac{G_{m2}C_c}{C_1C_2 + C_c(C_1+C_2)} \approx \frac{G_{m2}}{C_2}$

$A_o = G_{m1}R_1G_{m2}R_2$, $\omega_t = A_o\omega_{p1} = G_{m1}/C_c$

At ω_t, ω_{p2} introduces an excess 10° shift → $\omega_{p2} = \frac{100\times10^{-6}}{10\times10^{-12}} = 10^7/s$

$\tan^{-1}\frac{\omega_t}{10^7} = 10° \rightarrow \omega_t = .176\times10^7 = \underline{1.76\times10^6}$ rad/s

$\therefore C_c = \frac{G_{m1}}{\omega_t} = \frac{62.5\times10^{-6}}{.176\times10^7} = \underline{\underline{35.5pF}}$, $f_t = \frac{1}{2\pi}\times1.76\times10^6 = \underline{\underline{280kHz}}$

Slew Rate $V/T = I/C = \frac{2(12.5\times10^{-6})}{35.5\times10^{-12}} = \underline{\underline{0.70\ V/\mu s}}$

33 $\omega_z = \frac{-1}{C_c(1/G_{m2} - R)}$, $G_{m2} = 100\mu A/V$, $G_{m1} = 62.5\mu A/V$

$\omega_t = 2\pi\times1\times10^6 = 6.28\times10^6$ rad/s

$C_c = \frac{G_{m1}}{\omega_t} = \frac{62.5\times10^{-6}}{6.28\times10^6} = \underline{10pF}$

$\omega_{p2} \approx \frac{G_{m2}}{C_2} = \frac{100\times10^{-6}}{10\times10^{-12}} = 10^7$ rad/s

$\omega_{p1} = \frac{\omega_t}{A_o} = \frac{6.28\times10^6}{3125} = 2.01$ krad/s

For 80° margin: $\tan^{-1}\frac{6.28\times10^6}{2.01\times10^3} + \tan^{-1}\frac{6.28\times10^6}{10^7} - \tan^{-1}\frac{6.28\times10^6}{\omega_z} = 180 - 80 = 100$

ie $90 + 32.1 + \tan^{-1}\frac{6.28\times10^6}{\omega_z} = 100$

or $\omega_z = +\frac{6.28\times10^6}{\tan(100-90-32.1)} = -15.46\times10^6$ rad/s

and $\left(\frac{1}{G_{m2}} - R\right) = -\frac{1}{10\times10^{-12}\times15.5\times10^6} = -6466\ \Omega$

whence $R = \frac{1}{100\times10^{-6}} + 6466 = \underline{16.47}k\Omega$

and $SR = \frac{2(12.5\times10^{-6})}{10\times10^{-12}} = \underline{\underline{2.5V/\mu sec}}$

34 $W/L = 120/8$, $|V_t| = 1V$, $V_A = 25V$, $\mu_nC_{ox} = 20\mu A/V^2$, $\mu_pC_{ox} = 10\mu A/V^2$

Bias, ignoring r_o : All devices conduct $\underline{12.5\mu A}$

$K_n = \frac{1}{2}\mu_nC_{ox}W/L = \frac{1}{2}\times20\times\frac{120}{8} = 150\mu A/V^2$, $K_p = 75\mu A/V^2$

$v_{GSn} - V_t = \sqrt{\frac{12.5}{150}} = 0.289 \rightarrow v_{GSn} = \underline{\underline{1.289}}\ V$

$v_{GSp} - V_t = \sqrt{\frac{12.5}{75}} = 0.408 \rightarrow v_{GSp} = \underline{\underline{1.408}}\ V$

$g_{mn} = 2K(v_{GS} - V_t) = 2(150)(.289) = \underline{86.7\mu A/V}$, $g_{mp} = \underline{61.2\mu A/V}$

$r_o = \frac{V_A}{I_D} = \frac{25}{12.5\times10^{-6}} = \underline{2M\Omega}$ for each

For cascodes assume Eq 9.133 applies and that lower sources are cascodes with large R_o:

$\therefore$ At output $R_o = \left(r_o(2 + g_{mp}r_o)\right) \| \left(r_o(2 + g_{mn}r_o)\right)$

$= \left(2\times10^6(2 + 61.2\times10^{-6}\times2\times10^6)\right) \| \left(2\times10^6(2 + 86.7\times10^{-6}\times2\times10^6)\right)$

$= 249 \| 351 = \underline{146}\ M\Omega$

Gain $= 2\times\frac{146\times10^6}{2(1/61.2\times10^{-6})} = \underline{\underline{8935}}\ V/V$

Compensation: $\omega_p = \frac{1}{C_L\times146\times10^6} = \frac{\omega_t}{8935} = \frac{2\pi\times10^6}{8935} = 703/s$

$\therefore C_L = \frac{1}{703\times146\times10^6} = \underline{\underline{9.74\ pF}}$

Slew Rate: $SR = V/T = I/C = \frac{25\times10^{-6}}{9.74\times10^{-12}} = \underline{\underline{2.57}}\ V/\mu s$

Output Range: Neg: $-2.2 - 1 = \underline{\underline{-3.2V}}$

Pos: $+5 - 2(1.408) + 1 = \underline{\underline{3.2V}}$

1 Want $\omega_{3dB} = 10^4$ rad/s, $R_S, R_T = 10k\Omega$ } $L' = \frac{L}{10^4}\times10^4 = L$

$C' = \frac{C}{10^4}\times\frac{1}{10^4} = C\times10^{-8}$

Thus

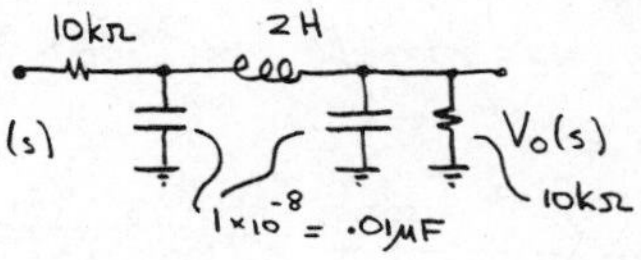

2 Butterworth Nth order : $|T(j\omega)| = \frac{1}{\sqrt{1+\omega^{2N}}}$

5th order → $|T(j\omega)| = \frac{1}{\sqrt{1+\omega^{10}}}$

ω	0.5	0.7	0.8	0.9	1.0	2.0	3.0
| |	.9995	.986	.95	.86	.707	.031	.004
dB	−.004	−.12	−.44	−1.3	−3.0	−30.3	−47.7

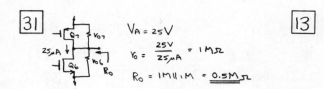

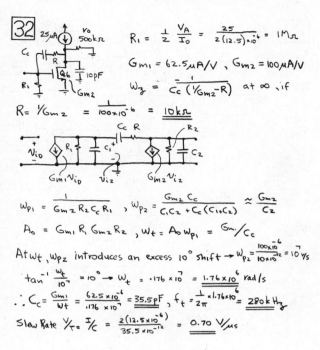

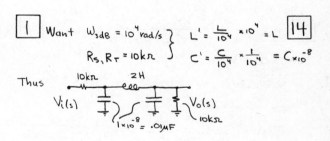

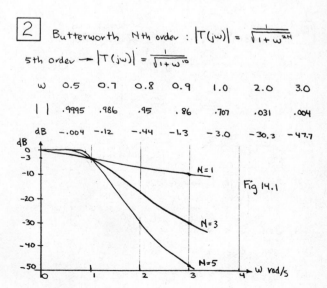

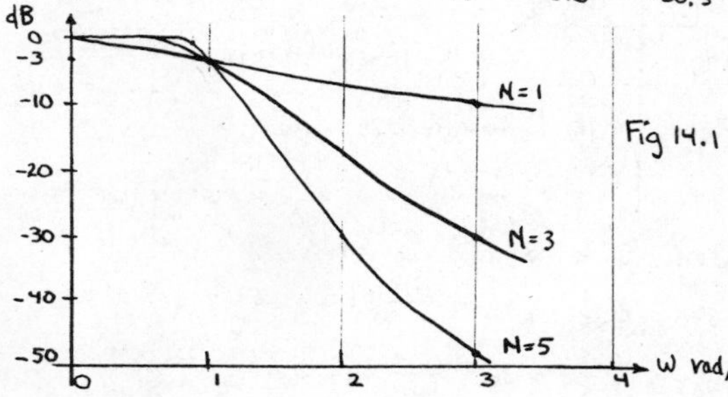

Fig 14.1

3 Characteristic equation: $s^2 + s(\omega_o/Q) + \omega_o^2 = 0$ **14**

with roots $P_1, P_2 = -\frac{\omega_o}{2Q} \pm j\omega_o\sqrt{1 - 1/4Q^2}$

(a) $\omega_o = 100$ rad/s, $Q = \infty$ →

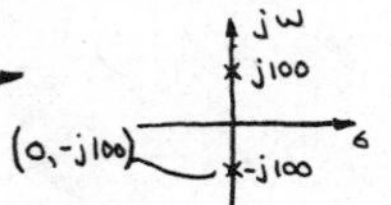

$s = 0 \pm j100$

(b) $\omega_o = 50$ rad/s, $Q = 1$

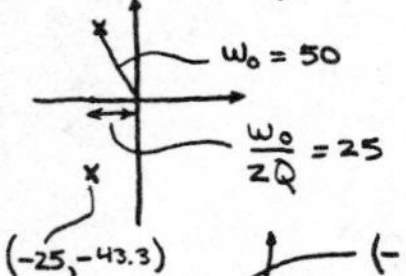

$s = -25 \pm j43.3$

(c) $\omega_o = 10$ rad/s, $Q = 0.5$

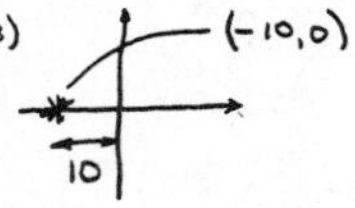

$s = -10$ and -10

, a double pole

(d) $\omega_o = 100$, $Q = 0.1$

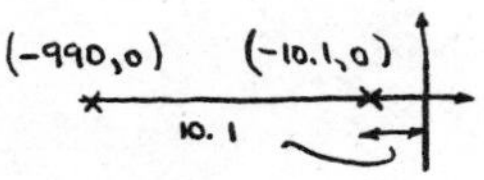

$s^2 + s(1000) + 10^4 = 0$

$\rightarrow s = \frac{-1000 \pm \sqrt{10^6 - 4\times10^4}}{2} = -990$ or -10.1

4 Low pass: $T(s) = \frac{n_o}{s^2 + s\,\omega_o/Q + \omega_o^2}$, $\omega_o = 10$ rad/s

Unity gain at dc → $s = 0$, $T(s) = \frac{n_o}{\omega_o^2} = 1 \rightarrow n_o = \omega_o^2 = 100$

Maximally flat:

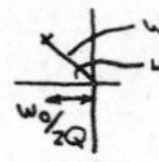

$2\left(\frac{\omega_o}{2Q}\right)^2 = \omega_o^2 \rightarrow \frac{2}{4Q^2} = 1, Q = \frac{1}{\sqrt{2}}$

$\therefore$ $T(s) = \frac{100}{s^2 + 1.414s + 100}$

5 High Pass: $T(s) = \frac{n_2 s^2}{s^2 + s(\omega_o/Q) + \omega_o^2}$, $\omega_o = 10$ **14**

Unity gain at ∞ → $s = \infty$, $T(s) = \frac{n_2 s^2}{s^2} \rightarrow n_2 = 1$

Maximally flat: $Q = 0.707 \rightarrow T(s) = \frac{s^2}{s^2 + 14.14s + 100}$

6 $T(s) = \frac{n_1 s}{s^2 + s\,\omega_o/Q + \omega_o^2} \rightarrow T(j\omega) = \frac{n_1 j\omega}{(\omega_o^2 - \omega^2) + j\frac{\omega\omega_o}{Q}}$

$|T(j\omega)|^2 = \frac{n_1^2\omega^2}{(\omega_o^2-\omega^2)^2 + \frac{\omega^2\omega_o^2}{Q^2}}$ and $|T(j\omega_o)|^2 = \frac{n_1\omega_o^2}{\omega_o^4/Q^2} = \frac{n_1^2 Q^2}{\omega_o^2}$

Thus $\left|\frac{T(j\omega)}{T(j\omega_o)}\right|^2 = \frac{\omega^2\omega_o^2/Q^2}{(\omega_o^2-\omega^2)^2 + \frac{\omega^2\omega_o^2}{Q^2}}$

For 3dB frequencies $\frac{1}{2} = \frac{\omega^2\omega_o^2/Q^2}{(\omega_o^2-\omega^2)^2 + \omega^2\omega_o^2/Q^2}$

or $(\omega_o^2-\omega^2)^2 + \frac{\omega^2\omega_o^2}{Q^2} = \frac{2\omega^2\omega_o^2}{Q^2}$

$(\omega_o^2-\omega^2)^2 = \frac{\omega^2\omega_o^2}{Q^2} \rightarrow \omega_o^2 - \omega^2 = \pm\frac{\omega\omega_o}{Q}$

ie $\omega^2 \pm \frac{\omega\omega_o}{Q} - \omega_o^2 = 0$

Whence $\omega = \left(\mp \omega_o/Q \pm \sqrt{\omega^2\omega_o^2/Q^2 + 4\omega_o^2}\right)/2$

or $\omega = \mp\frac{\omega_o}{2Q} \pm \sqrt{\omega_o^2 + (\omega_o/2Q)^2}$

Positive roots are $\omega_{1,2} = \sqrt{\omega_o^2 + \left(\frac{\omega_o}{2Q}\right)^2} \pm \frac{\omega_o}{2Q}$

Thus $\omega_1 - \omega_2 = \omega_o/Q$

$\omega_1\omega_2 = \left(\omega_o^2 + \left(\frac{\omega_o}{2Q}\right)^2\right) - \left(\frac{\omega_o}{2Q}\right)^2 = \omega_o^2$

7 $T(s) = n_2\left(\frac{s^2 + \omega_n^2}{s^2 + s(\omega_o/Q) + \omega_o^2}\right)$ – notch **14**

For $s = 0$, $T(0) = n_2\omega_n^2/\omega_o^2 = 1$

For $\omega_n = 100$ rad/s, $\omega_o = 10$ rad/s, $n_2 = \frac{10^2}{100^2} = 1/100$

$\omega_o/Q = 10/0.5 = 20$

$\therefore T(s) = \frac{(s/10)^2 + 100}{s^2 + 20s + 100} = \frac{1}{100} \times \frac{s^2 + 10^4}{s^2 + 20s + 100}$

8 All-pass: $T(s) = \frac{s^2 - s(\omega_o/Q) + \omega_o^2}{s^2 + s(\omega_o/Q) + \omega_o^2}$

$T(\omega) = \frac{-j\omega\omega_o/Q + \omega_o^2 - \omega^2}{+j\omega\omega_o/Q + \omega_o^2 - \omega^2}$; $\phi = -2\tan^{-1}\frac{\omega\omega_o}{Q(\omega_o^2 - \omega^2)}$

For $\omega_o = 1$, $Q = 1$

$\phi = -2\tan^{-1}\frac{\omega}{1-\omega^2} \rightarrow \frac{\omega}{1-\omega^2} = \tan(-\phi/2)$

ϕ	$\tan\frac{-\phi}{2}$	
-90	1	$\rightarrow \omega = 1-\omega^2, \omega^2+\omega-1=0, \omega = \frac{-1\pm\sqrt{1+4}}{2} = -1.615, \underline{0.615}$
-180	0	$\rightarrow \omega = 0, \pm1 \rightarrow \omega = 1$
-270	-1	$\rightarrow \omega^2 - 1 = \omega, \omega^2-\omega-1=0, \omega = \underline{+1.615}, -0.615$

At $\omega = 0$, $\phi = -2\tan^{-1} 0 = 0$

$\omega = 0.1$, $\phi = -2\tan^{-1}\frac{0.1}{1-.01} = -11.5°$

$\omega = 0.3$, $\phi = -2\tan^{-1}\frac{0.3}{1-.09} = -36.5°$

14

$\omega = 3$, $\phi = -2\tan^{-1}\frac{3}{1-9} = +41.1°$, $318.9°$

$\omega = 10$, $\phi = -2\tan^{-1}\frac{10}{1-100} = +11.5°$, $348.5°$

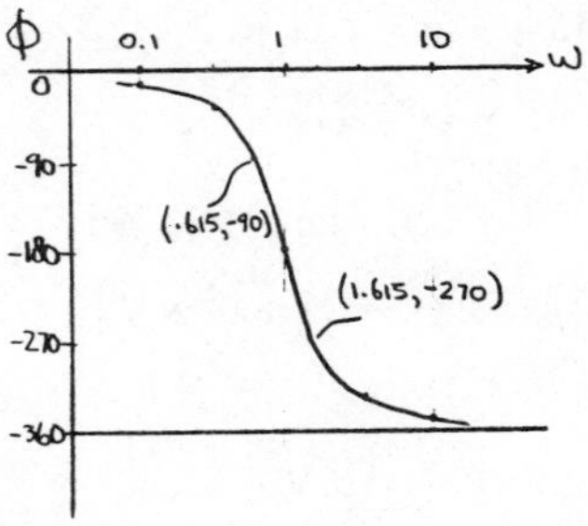

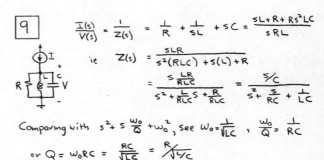

9 $\frac{I(s)}{V(s)} = \frac{1}{Z(s)} = \frac{1}{R} + \frac{1}{sL} + sC = \frac{sL + R + Rs^2LC}{sRL}$

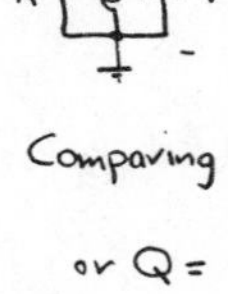

ie $Z(s) = \frac{sLR}{s^2(RLC) + s(L) + R}$

$= \frac{s\frac{LR}{RLC}}{s^2 + \frac{L}{RLC}s + \frac{R}{RLC}} = \frac{s/C}{s^2 + \frac{s}{RC} + \frac{1}{LC}}$

Comparing with $s^2 + s\frac{\omega_o}{Q} + \omega_o^2$, see $\omega_o = \frac{1}{\sqrt{LC}}$, $\frac{\omega_o}{Q} = \frac{1}{RC}$

or $Q = \omega_o RC = \frac{RC}{\sqrt{LC}} = R/\sqrt{L/C}$

10 **14**

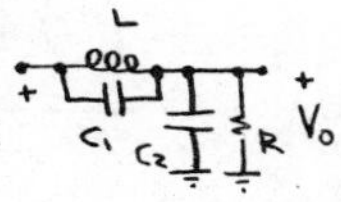

$w_o = \frac{1}{\sqrt{LC}}$, $C = C_1 + C_2$

$w_n = \frac{1}{\sqrt{LC_1}}$

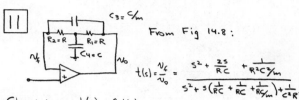

For $w_n = 1.1\, w_o$, $\frac{1}{\sqrt{LC_1}} = \frac{1.1}{\sqrt{LC}} \rightarrow C_1 = \frac{C}{1.21} = \frac{C_1 + C_2}{1.21}$

ie $1.21 C_1 = C_1 + C_2$, $0.21 C_1 = C_2$, $\underline{\underline{C_1 = 4.76 C_2}}$

For $w \ll w_o$, $|T| = \underline{1}$

For $w \gg w_o$, $T = \frac{\frac{1}{wC_2}}{\frac{1}{wC_1} + \frac{1}{wC_2}} = \frac{C_1}{C_1 + C_2} = \frac{C_1}{1.21 C_1} = \underline{\underline{0.826}}$

Note also $(w_o/w_n)^2 = 1/(1.1)^2 = .826$ ✓

11

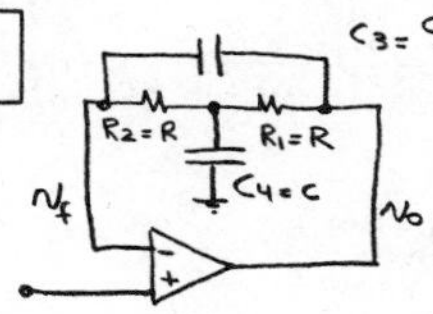

From Fig 14.8:

$$t(s) = \frac{v_t}{v_o} = \frac{s^2 + \frac{2s}{RC} + \frac{1}{R^2C^2/m}}{s^2 + s\left(\frac{1}{RC} + \frac{1}{RC} + \frac{1}{RC/m}\right) + \frac{1}{C^2R^2}}$$

Closed Loop: $L(s) = A\,t(s)$

Poles are solution of $1 + L(s) = 0$ or $L(s) = -1$

or $t(s) = -1/A \rightarrow 0$ for large A.

Now for $t(s) = \frac{N(s)}{D(s)}$, poles are solutions of $N(s) = 0$

or $s^2 + \frac{2}{RC}s + \frac{1}{R^2C^2/m} = 0$, whence $w_o = \frac{\sqrt{m}}{RC}$, $\frac{w_o}{Q} = \frac{2}{RC}$

or $Q = \frac{w_o RC}{2} = \frac{\sqrt{m}}{2}$. Thus $\boxed{m = 4Q^2}$ and $\boxed{RC = \frac{2Q}{w_o}}$

12 **14**

Closed loop poles of Fig 14.9, are, from Fig 14.8a, solutions of $s^2 + s\left(\frac{1}{C_1} + \frac{1}{C_2}\right)\frac{1}{R_3} + \frac{1}{C_1C_2R_3R_4} = 0$

With $C_1 = C_2 = C \rightarrow s^2 + \frac{2s}{R_3C} + \frac{1}{C^2R_3R_4} = 0$, $C = 1nF$

Now $\frac{1}{(C^2R_3R_4)^{1/2}} = w_o = 10^4 \rightarrow R_3R_4 = \left(\frac{1}{10^4 \times 10^{-9}}\right)^2 = 10^{10}$

and $\frac{w_o}{Q} = \frac{2}{R_3C} \rightarrow R_3 = \frac{2Q}{w_oC} = \frac{2/\sqrt{2}}{10^4 \times 10^{-9}} = \underline{\underline{141.4\,k\Omega}}$

and $R_4 = \frac{10^{10}}{\sqrt{2} \times 10^5} = \frac{10^5}{\sqrt{2}} = \underline{\underline{70.7\,k\Omega}}$

13

From Fig 14.8a $t(s) = \frac{s^2 + \frac{2}{RC} + \left(\frac{1}{RC}\right)^2}{s^2 + s\left(\frac{3}{RC}\right) + \left(\frac{1}{RC}\right)^2}$

or $t(s) = \frac{s^2 + \frac{2s}{\tau} + \frac{1}{\tau^2}}{s^2 + \frac{3}{\tau}s + \frac{1}{\tau^2}}$

Poles at $s = -\left(3/\tau \pm \sqrt{\left(\frac{3}{\tau}\right)^2 - \frac{4}{\tau^2}}\right) \times \frac{1}{2} = \frac{1}{\tau}\left(\frac{-3 \pm \sqrt{5}}{2}\right)$

or $s = \underline{\underline{-2.62/\tau}}$ and $\underline{\underline{\frac{-0.38}{\tau}}}$

Zeros at $s = -\left(2/\tau \pm \sqrt{\left(\frac{2}{\tau}\right)^2 - \frac{4}{\tau^2}}\right) \times \frac{1}{2} = \underline{\underline{-\frac{1}{\tau}}}$ {ie 2 coincident zeroes}

For closed loop operation, poles are zeros of $t(s)$ and are coincident at $\underline{\underline{-\frac{1}{\tau}}}$

14 **14**

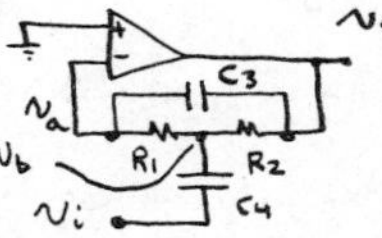

$R_1 = R_2 = R$, $C_4 = C$, $C_3 = C/16$

Currents at (a) sum to zero

ie $\frac{v_o}{1/C_3s} = -\frac{v_b}{R}$

At (b) $\frac{v_b}{R} + \frac{v_b - v_o}{R} + \frac{v_b - v_i}{1/Cs} = 0$

or $v_b\left(\frac{2}{R} + Cs\right) = v_iCs + v_o/R$

$v_b = \frac{v_iCs + v_o/R}{2/R + Cs} \rightarrow -Rv_oC_3s = \frac{v_iCs + v_o/R}{2/R + Cs}$

Thus $v_i = \frac{v_o}{Cs}\left(-RC_3s(2/R + Cs) - 1/R\right)$

or $\frac{v_o}{v_i} = \frac{-1}{R\,C_3/C\,(2/R + Cs) + 1/RCs} = \frac{-RCs}{2RC_3s + RRCC_3s^2 + 1}$

ie $\boxed{\frac{v_o}{v_i}(s) = \frac{-s/RC_3}{s^2 + \frac{2}{RC}s + \frac{1}{R^2CC_3}}}$, that is $\underline{\underline{\text{bandpass}}}$

with $w_o = \frac{1}{R\sqrt{CC_3}} = \frac{4}{RC}$

Now $\frac{w_o}{Q} = \frac{2}{RC} \rightarrow Q = \frac{w_oRC}{2} = \frac{\frac{4}{RC} \times RC}{2} = \underline{\underline{2}}$

Gain at $w_o \rightarrow \frac{v_o}{v_i}(jw_o) = \frac{-jw_o/RC_3}{-w_o^2 + jw_o \times \frac{2}{RC} + w_o^2}$

$= \frac{-C}{2C_3} = \frac{-C}{2(C/16)} = \underline{\underline{-8\ V/V}}$

15 **14**

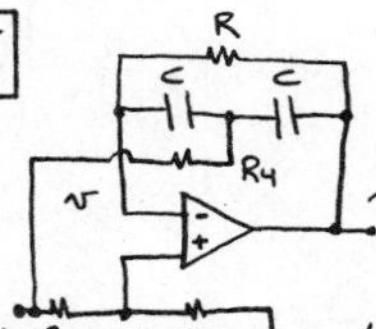

$R_4 = R/4Q^2$, $CR = \frac{2Q}{w_o}$, $\alpha = 1$

$v = \frac{R_2}{R_1 + R_2}v_i \rightarrow v_i = \left(1 + \frac{R_1}{R_2}\right)v = kv$

$\rightarrow (v_o - v_t)Cs + (v - v_t)Cs = \frac{v_t - kv}{R_4}$

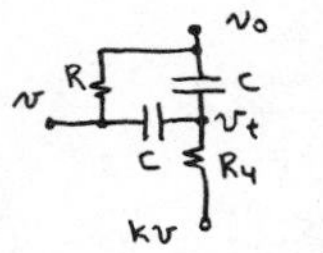

$v_o + v - 2v_t = \frac{v_t}{R_4Cs} - \frac{kv}{R_4Cs}$

$v_o + v\left(1 + \frac{k}{R_4Cs}\right) = v_t\left(2 + \frac{1}{R_4Cs}\right)$ ①

and $(v - v_t)Cs = \frac{v_o - v}{R}$

$v - v_t = \frac{v_o}{RCs} - \frac{v}{RCs} \rightarrow v_t = v\left(1 + \frac{1}{RCs}\right) - \frac{v_o}{RCs}$ ②

②→① , $v_o + v\left(1 + \frac{k}{R_4Cs}\right) = \left(v\left(1 + \frac{1}{RCs}\right) - \frac{v_o}{RCs}\right)\left(2 + \frac{1}{R_4Cs}\right)$

$\therefore v_o + v + \frac{kv}{R_4Cs} = 2v + \frac{2v}{RCs} + \frac{v}{R_4Cs} + \frac{v}{RR_4C^2s^2} - \frac{2v_o}{RCs} - \frac{v_o}{RR_4C^2s^2}$

$v_o\left(1 + \frac{2}{RCs} + \frac{1}{RR_4C^2s^2}\right) = v\left(1 - \frac{k}{R_4Cs} + \frac{2}{RCs} + \frac{1}{R_4Cs} + \frac{1}{RR_4C^2s^2}\right)$

$$\therefore \boxed{\frac{v_o}{v} = \frac{v_o}{v_i/k} = \frac{\frac{1}{RR_4C^2s^2} + \frac{1}{s}\left(\frac{2}{RC} + \frac{1-k}{R_4C}\right) + 1}{\frac{1}{RR_4C^2s^2} + \frac{1}{s}\left(\frac{2}{RC}\right) + 1}}$$

ⓐ For $\underline{\text{All-pass}}$: $-\frac{2}{RC} = \frac{2}{RC} + \frac{1-k}{R_4C} \rightarrow 1 - k = -\frac{4}{RC}(R_4C)$

or $k = \frac{4R_4}{R} + 1 = 1 + \frac{4(R/4Q^2)}{R} = 1 + \frac{1}{Q^2}$

Thus $\boxed{\frac{R_2}{R_1 + R_2} = 1/k = \frac{1}{1 + 1/Q^2} = \frac{Q^2}{Q^2 + 1}}$

ⓑ For $\underline{\text{Notch}}$: $\frac{2}{RC} + \frac{1-k}{R_4C} = 0 \rightarrow k = 1 + \frac{2R_4}{R} = 1 + \frac{1}{2Q^2}$; $\boxed{\frac{R_2}{R_1 + R_2} = \frac{1}{k} = \frac{Q^2}{Q^2 + 0.5}}$

16 **14**

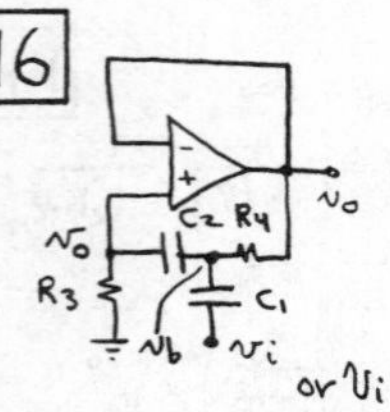

$$v_b = \frac{v_o}{R_3}\times\frac{1}{C_2 s} + v_o = v_o\left(1+\frac{1}{R_3C_2s}\right)$$

$$\text{Current in } C_1 = \frac{v_o}{R_3} + \frac{v_b - v_o}{R_4}$$

$$\therefore\ v_i = \frac{1}{C_1 s}\left(\frac{v_o}{R_3} + \frac{v_b - v_o}{R_4}\right) + v_b$$

$$\text{or } V_i = v_o\left(\frac{1}{R_3C_1s} + \frac{1}{R_3R_4C_1C_2s^2} + 1 + \frac{1}{R_3C_2s}\right)$$

Thus $$v_o/v_i = \frac{s^2}{s^2 + s\left(\frac{1}{R_3C_1} + \frac{1}{R_3C_2}\right) + \frac{1}{R_3R_4C_1C_2}}$$, a <u>high-pass function</u> with high frequency <u>gain of 1</u> and 2 zeros at dc. Comparing denom. with $s^2 + \frac{s\omega_o}{Q} + \omega_o^2$,

see $\omega_o^2 = \frac{1}{R_3R_4C_1C_2}$ and $\omega_o/Q = \left(\frac{1}{R_3C_1} + \frac{1}{R_3C_2}\right)$

For $C_1 = C_2 = 10\,nF$, $Q = 1/\sqrt{2}$, $\omega_o = 10^3$ rad/s

See $R_3 = \frac{1/\sqrt{2}}{10^3}\left(\frac{1}{10^{-8}} + \frac{1}{10^{-8}}\right) = \underline{\underline{141.4\,k\Omega}}$

and $R_4 = \frac{1}{\omega_o^2 R_3C_1C_2} = \frac{1}{(10^3)^2(141.4\times10^3)(10^{-8})^2} = \underline{\underline{70.7\,k\Omega}}$

17

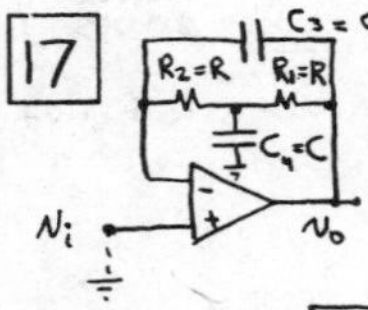

$\omega_o = \frac{\sqrt{m}}{RC}$

$Q = \frac{\sqrt{m}}{2}$

Comp. ⇒ Trans.

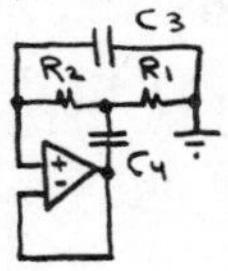

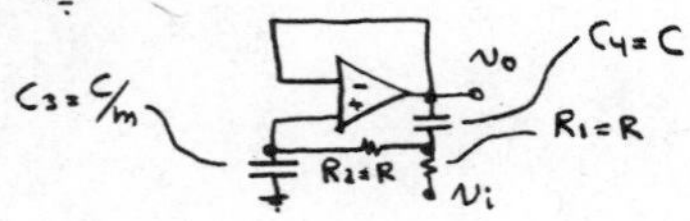

Choose Input for Lowpass function via R_1

14

See directly that circuit has a dc gain of unity and a transfer function $\frac{v_o}{v_i}(s) = \frac{1}{s^2 + \frac{s\omega_o}{Q} + \omega_o^2}$

with $\omega_o = \frac{\sqrt{m}}{RC}$, $Q = \frac{\sqrt{m}}{2}$

For maximally flat, $Q = \frac{1}{\sqrt{2}} = \frac{\sqrt{m}}{2} \rightarrow m = 2$. For 10 kHz and $R = 10^4$

$\omega_o = \frac{\sqrt{m}}{RC} \rightarrow C = \frac{\sqrt{m}}{\omega_o R} = \frac{\sqrt{2}}{2\pi\times10^4\times10^4} = 2251\,pF$

$\therefore\ C_4 = \underline{\underline{2251\,pF}}$, $C_3 = \underline{\underline{1125\,pF}}$, $R_1 = R_2 = \underline{\underline{10\,k\Omega}}$

18 Bandpass: $t(s) = \frac{n_1 s}{s^2 + s\left(\frac{\omega_o}{Q}\right) + \omega_o^2}$

For gain of 1 at $\omega_o \rightarrow 1 = \frac{n_1 j\omega_o}{-\omega_o^2 + j\omega_o^2/Q + \omega_o^2}$

whence $n_1 = \omega_o/Q$

$$\therefore\ 1 - t(s) = \frac{s^2 + s(\omega_o/Q) + \omega_o^2 - \omega_o/Q\, s}{s^2 + s(\omega_o/Q) + \omega_o^2}$$

$$= \frac{s^2 + \omega_o^2}{s^2 + s(\omega_o/Q) + \omega_o^2}\text{, a notch at } \omega_o$$

Verification:

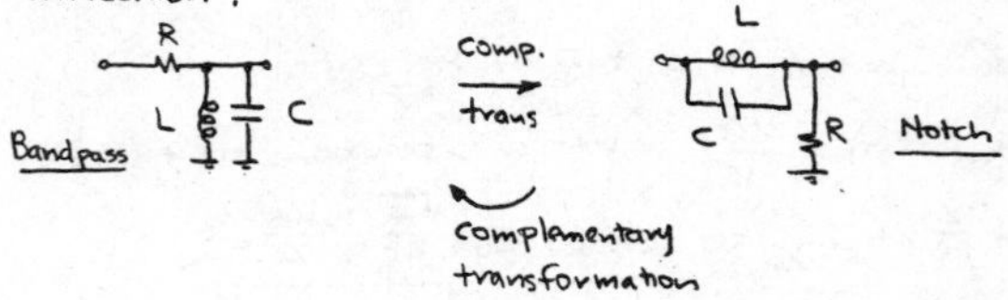

19 **14**

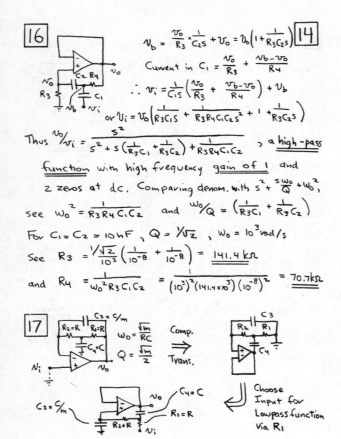

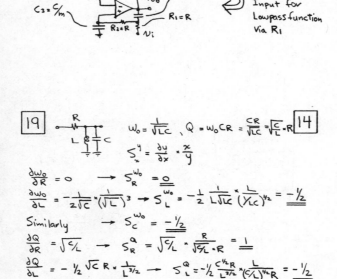

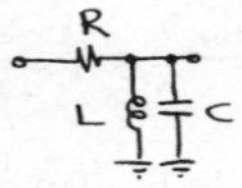

$\omega_o = \frac{1}{\sqrt{LC}}$, $Q = \omega_o CR = \frac{CR}{\sqrt{LC}} = \sqrt{\frac{C}{L}}\times R$

$S_x^y = \frac{\partial y}{\partial x}\times\frac{x}{y}$

$\frac{\partial\omega_o}{\partial R} = 0 \longrightarrow S_R^{\omega_o} = \underline{\underline{0}}$

$\frac{\partial\omega_o}{\partial L} = -\frac{1}{2\sqrt{C}}\times\left(\frac{1}{\sqrt{L}}\right)^3 \rightarrow S_L^{\omega_o} = -\frac{1}{2}\frac{1}{L\sqrt{LC}}\times\frac{L}{(1/LC)^{1/2}} = \underline{\underline{-1/2}}$

Similarly $\longrightarrow S_C^{\omega_o} = \underline{\underline{-1/2}}$

$\frac{\partial Q}{\partial R} = \sqrt{C/L} \longrightarrow S_R^Q = \sqrt{C/L}\times\frac{R}{\sqrt{C/L}\cdot R} = \underline{\underline{1}}$

$\frac{\partial Q}{\partial L} = -\frac{1}{2}\sqrt{C}R\times\frac{1}{L^{3/2}} \longrightarrow S_L^Q = -\frac{1}{2}\frac{C^{1/2}R}{L^{3/2}}\times\frac{L}{(C/L)^{1/2}R} = \underline{\underline{-1/2}}$

$\frac{\partial Q}{\partial C} = \frac{1}{2}\frac{R}{\sqrt{L}}\times C^{-1/2} \longrightarrow S_C^Q = \frac{1}{2}\times\frac{R}{\sqrt{LC}}\times\frac{C}{(\sqrt{C/L})R} = \underline{\underline{1/2}}$

20

(a) $y = uv \rightarrow S_x^y = \frac{dy}{dx}\cdot\frac{x}{y} = \frac{x}{uv}\left(u\frac{\partial v}{\partial x} + v\frac{\partial u}{\partial x}\right) = S_x^v + S_x^u$

(b) $y = u/v \rightarrow S_x^y = \frac{dy}{dx}\cdot\frac{x}{y} = \frac{x}{u/v}\left(\frac{-u}{v^2}\frac{\partial v}{\partial x} + \frac{1}{v}\frac{\partial u}{\partial x}\right) = S_x^u - S_x^v$

(c) $y = ku \rightarrow S_x^y = \frac{\partial y}{\partial x}\cdot\frac{x}{y} = k\frac{\partial u}{\partial x}\cdot\frac{x}{ku} = S_x^u$

(d) $y = u^n \rightarrow S_x^y = \frac{\partial y}{\partial x}\cdot\frac{x}{y} = nu^{n-1}\frac{\partial u}{\partial x}\cdot\frac{x}{u^n} = n\frac{x}{u}\cdot\frac{\partial u}{\partial x} = nS_x^u$

(e) $y = f_1(u),\ u = f_2(x) \rightarrow S_x^y = \frac{\partial y}{\partial x}\cdot\frac{x}{y} = \frac{\partial f_1}{\partial u}\times\frac{\partial u}{\partial x}\times\frac{x}{f_1}$

$= \frac{\partial f_1}{\partial u}\times\frac{\partial f_2}{\partial x}\times\frac{x}{f_1} = \frac{\partial f_1}{\partial u}\times\frac{u}{f_1}\times\frac{\partial f_2}{\partial x}\times\frac{x}{f_2}$, since $u = f_2$

$= S_u^y\times S_x^u$

21 **14**

The circuit of Fig 14.13b is obtained from that in Fig 14.9 via the complementary transformation. Thus both have the same characteristic equation and hence the same pole sensitivities. Therefore we can use the results of example 14.1: from which

$S_A^{\omega_o} = 0$

$S_A^Q \approx \frac{2Q^2}{A}$

22 **14**

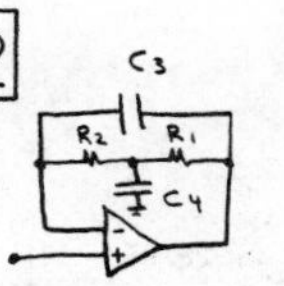

From Fig 14.8 poles are roots of $s^2 + s\left(\frac{1}{R_1}+\frac{1}{R_2}\right)\frac{1}{C_4} + \frac{1}{R_1R_2C_3C_4} = 0$

See $w_o = \frac{1}{\sqrt{R_1R_2C_3C_4}}$, $\frac{w_o}{Q} = \frac{1}{C_4}\left(\frac{1}{R_1}+\frac{1}{R_2}\right)$

Thus $Q = \dfrac{\frac{1}{\sqrt{R_1R_2C_3C_4}}}{\frac{1}{C_4}\left(\frac{1}{R_1}+\frac{1}{R_2}\right)} = \sqrt{C_4/C_3} \times \frac{R_1R_2}{R_1+R_2} \times \frac{1}{\sqrt{R_1R_2}}$

or $Q = \sqrt{C_4/C_3} \times \frac{\sqrt{R_1R_2}}{R_1+R_2}$

$\frac{\partial w_o}{\partial C_4} = -\frac{1}{2}\frac{1}{\sqrt{R_1R_2C_3C_4} \times C_4} \rightarrow S_{C_4}^{w_o} = -\frac{1}{2}\frac{w_o}{C_4} \times \frac{C_4}{w_o} = -\frac{1}{2}$

Likewise $S_{C_3}^{w_o} = S_{R_1}^{w_o} = S_{R_2}^{w_o} = -\frac{1}{2}$

Now for $R_1 = R_2$, $Q = \frac{1}{2}\sqrt{C_4/C_3}$, and

$\frac{\partial Q}{\partial C_4} = \frac{1}{2} \times \frac{1}{2} \times \frac{1}{\sqrt{C_3C_4}} \rightarrow S_{C_4}^{Q} = \frac{1}{4} \times \frac{1}{\sqrt{C_3C_4}} \times \frac{C_4}{\frac{1}{2}\sqrt{C_4/C_3}} = \frac{1}{2}$

$\frac{\partial Q}{\partial C_3} = \frac{-1}{2} \times \frac{1}{2}\frac{\sqrt{C_4}}{C_3^{3/2}} \rightarrow S_{C_3}^{Q} = -\frac{1}{4}\sqrt{\frac{C_4}{C_3}} \times \frac{1}{C_3} \times \frac{C_3}{\frac{1}{2}\sqrt{C_4/C_3}} = -\frac{1}{2}$

$\frac{\partial Q}{\partial R_1} = \sqrt{\frac{C_4}{C_3}}\left\{\frac{\sqrt{R_2}}{R_1+R_2} \times \frac{1/2}{\sqrt{R_1}} + \frac{\sqrt{R_1R_2}}{(R_1+R_2)^2}\right\}$

$\rightarrow S_{R_1}^{Q} = \sqrt{\frac{C_4}{C_3}}\left(\frac{1}{2} \times \sqrt{\frac{R_2}{R_1}} \times \frac{1}{R_1+R_2} + \frac{\sqrt{R_1R_2}}{(R_1+R_2)^2}\right)\dfrac{R_1}{\sqrt{\frac{C_4}{C_3}}\frac{\sqrt{R_1R_2}}{R_1+R_2}}$

which for $R_1 = R_2 \rightarrow S_{R_1}^{Q} = \frac{1}{2} + \frac{R_1}{R_1+R_2} = 1$

Similarly $S_{R_2}^{Q} = 1$

23 **14**

$w_o = \frac{1}{\sqrt{C_2C_6R_1R_3R_5/R_4}}$

$Q = R_7\sqrt{\frac{C_6R_4}{C_2R_1R_3R_5}}$

For w_o:

$\frac{\partial w_o}{\partial C_2} = -\frac{1}{2}\frac{1}{\sqrt{C_6R_1R_3R_5/R_4}} \times \frac{1}{(C_2)^{3/2}} \rightarrow S_{C_2}^{w_o} = \left(\frac{\partial w_o}{\partial C_2}\right) \times \frac{C_2}{w_o} = -\frac{1}{2}$

$\therefore S_{C_2}^{w_o} = S_{C_6}^{w_o} = S_{R_1}^{w_o} = S_{R_3}^{w_o} = S_{R_5}^{w_o} = -\frac{1}{2}$

and $S_{R_4}^{w_o} = +\frac{1}{2}$

For Q:

Similarly $S_{C_2}^{Q} = S_{R_1}^{Q} = S_{R_3}^{Q} = S_{R_5}^{Q} = -\frac{1}{2}$

$S_{C_6}^{Q} = S_{R_4}^{Q} = +\frac{1}{2}$

$S_{R_7}^{Q} = +1$

24

For $t(s) = \frac{n_1 s}{s^2 + s(w_o/Q) + w_o^2}$, $t(jw_o) = \frac{n_1 jw_o}{-w_o^2 + jw_o(w_o/Q) + w_o^2}$

$|t(jw)| = 2$ for $n_1\frac{Q}{w_o} = 2 \rightarrow n_1 = \frac{2w_o}{Q}$

For complementary Xform: $1 - t = \dfrac{s^2 + s(w_o/Q) + w_o^2 - \frac{2w_os}{Q}}{s^2 + s(w_o/Q) + w_o^2}$

$= \dfrac{s^2 - s(w_o/Q) + w_o^2}{s^2 + s(w_o/Q) + w_o^2}$

—an all-pass function

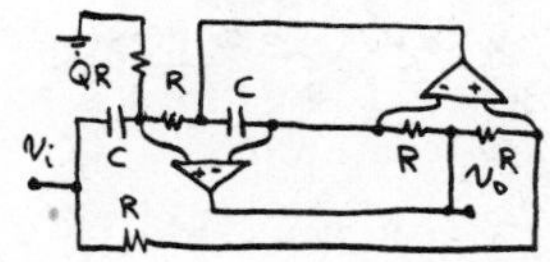

25 **14**

$\frac{V_{hp}}{V_i} = \frac{n_2 s^2}{s^2 + s(w_o/Q) + w_o^2}$, $V_{bp} = \frac{-w_o}{s}V_{hp}$, $V_{lp} = \frac{w_o^2}{s^2}V_{hp}$

$CR = 1/w_o$, $R_3/R_2 = 2Q - 1$ and $n_2 = 2 - 1/Q$

For $f_o = 10kHz$, $Q = 50$, $R = 10k\Omega$

$C = \frac{1}{2\pi \times 10^4 \times 10^4} = 1591pF$

$R_3/R_2 = 2(50) - 1 = 49$, $n_2 = 2 - 1/50 = 1.98$

$R_1 = \underline{10k\Omega}$, $R_2 = \underline{10k\Omega}$, $R_3 = \underline{490k\Omega}$, $C = \underline{1591pF}$

$V_{bp} = \frac{-n_2w_os}{s^2 + s(w_o/Q) + w_o^2} \times V_i$

At w_o, $|\ | = \frac{n_2w_o}{w_o/Q} = n_2Q = Q(2 - 1/Q) = 2Q - 1 = 99$

$\therefore$ Centre frequency gain is $\underline{-99}$

26

From Eq 14.28 and Fig 14.17a

$V_{lp} = -\frac{w_o}{s} \times -\frac{w_o}{s} \times V_{hp} = \dfrac{\frac{w_o^2}{s^2}n_2s^2}{s^2 + s(\frac{w_o}{Q}) + w_o^2} = \dfrac{n_2w_o^2}{s^2 + s(\frac{w_o}{Q}) + w_o^2}$

$CR = 1/w_o$, $R = 10k\Omega$, $f_o = 10kHz$, $Q = 1/\sqrt{2}$

$C = \frac{1}{2\pi 10^4 \times 10^4} = 1591pF$

$R_d = QR = \frac{1}{\sqrt{2}} \times 10^4 = 7.07k\Omega$

See low frequency gain $= n_2 = 1 \rightarrow R_g = R/n_2 = 10k\Omega$

27 **14**

$V_o = R_7\left(\frac{V_{lp}}{R_4} + \frac{V_{bp}}{R_5} + \frac{V_{hp}}{R_6}\right)$

$\frac{V_o}{V_i} = R_7\left(\frac{w_o^2}{R_4s^2} - \frac{w_o}{R_5s} + \frac{1}{R_6}\right) \times \frac{n_2's^2}{s^2 + s(w_o/Q) + w_o^2}$

$= n_2'\frac{R_7}{R_6} \times \dfrac{\left(s^2 - \frac{w_os}{R_5/R_6} + \frac{w_o^2}{R_4/R_6}\right)}{\left(s^2 + sw_o/Q + w_o^2\right)}$ impliments

a notch, ie $\frac{V_o}{V_i} = \dfrac{n_2(s^2 + w_n^2)}{s^2 + \frac{sw_o}{Q} + w_o^2}$

if $\underline{R_5 = \infty}$, $\frac{w_o^2}{R_4/R_6} = w_n^2$ or $\underline{R_4 = R_6\left(\frac{w_o}{w_n}\right)^2}$

where $\underline{R_6 \text{ is arbitrary}}$, and $n_2 = n_2'\frac{R_7}{R_6}$

or $R_7 = R_6[n_2/n_2']$. Now n_2' is the gain at high frequencies of the high-pass function, ie $n_2' = 2 - 1/Q$. Thus $\underline{R_7 = R_6\left[\frac{n_2}{2 - 1/Q}\right]}$

28

$R_{eq} = \frac{T_c}{C_1} = \frac{1/(100 \times 10^3)}{C_1}$

For 1pF $\rightarrow R_{eq} = \frac{10^{-5}}{10^{-12}} = 10^7 = \underline{10M\Omega}$

For 10pF $\rightarrow R_{eq} = \frac{10^{-5}}{10 \times 10^{-12}} = 10^6 = \underline{1M\Omega}$

29 $CV = IT \rightarrow Q = CV = 1\times10^{-12}\times1 = \underline{1pC}$ **14**

For 1pC/cycle at 100kHz, $I = \frac{Q}{T} = \frac{10^{-12}}{10^{-5}} = 10^{-7} = \underline{0.1\mu A}$

$Q = CV \rightarrow \Delta V = \frac{Q}{C_f} = \frac{10^{-12}}{10\times10^{-12}} = \underline{0.1V}$

clock cycles for saturation $= \frac{10V}{0.1V} = \underline{100}$

Slope of output: 10V in $100\times10\mu s$ or 1V in $100\mu s$

, ie $\underline{10^4 V/s}$

30 Ex 14.15 with clock frequency doubled (to 400kHz)

Clock period reduces by 2. Resistors reduce by a factor of 2 for the same integrating capacitors (ie C_1, C_2). Compensate by halving all other caps:

$\therefore$ New C_3, C_4, C_5, C_6 are $\underline{3.14}, \underline{3.14}, \underline{0.157}, \underline{0.157}$ pF

(or) Directly: $f_0 = 10kHz, Q = 20, A_{f_0} = 1, C_1 = C_2 = 20pF = C$

$C_3 = C_4 = W_0 T_c C = 2\pi\times10^4 \times \frac{1}{400\times10^3}\times20\times10^{-12} = \underline{3.14\,pF}$

$C_5 = C_4/Q = \frac{3.14}{20} = \underline{0.157\,pF}$, $C_6 = C_5 \times A_{f_0} = \underline{0.157pF}$

31 Ex 14.15 for $Q = 40$, $C_1 = C_2 = 20pF = C$ **14**

$f_0 = 10kHz$, unity centre gain, $f_c = 200kHz$

$C_3 = C_4 = W_0 T_c C = 2\pi\times10^4\times\frac{1}{200\times10^3}\times20\times10^{-12} = \underline{6.28pF}$

$C_5 = W_0 T_c C/Q = \frac{6.28\,pF}{40} = \underline{1.57pF}$

$C_6 = C_5 A_{f_0} = C_5\times1 = \underline{1.57pF}$

32 Low frequency gain of LP is $\frac{R_4}{R_6} \rightarrow \frac{C_6}{C_4} = 1$

$W_{3dB} = W_0 = \frac{1}{T_c}\sqrt{\frac{C_3C_4}{C_2C_1}}$

Use $C_1 = C_2 = C = \underline{10pF}$

$\therefore C_3 = C_4 = KC = W_0 T_c C = 10^4 \times \frac{1}{10^5}\times C = C/10 = \underline{1pF}$

Now $C_6 = C_4 = \underline{1pF}$

and $C_5 = C_4/Q = \frac{1pF}{1/\sqrt{2}} = \underline{1.414\,pF}$

33

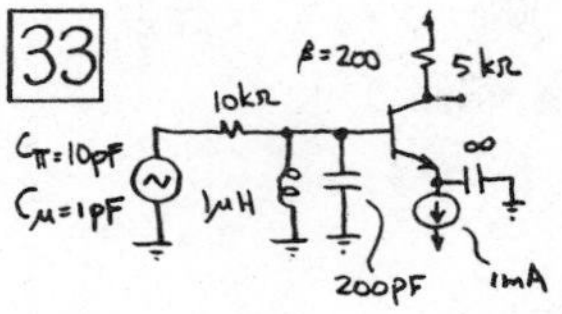

$r_e = 25\Omega$, $r_\pi = 201(25) = 5.025k\Omega$

gain $= -\frac{200}{201}\times\frac{5k}{25} = -199 \approx -200 V/V$

$C_T = 10 + 1(199+1) = 210\,pF$

(next)

$W_0 = \frac{1}{\sqrt{LC}} = (1\times10^{-6}\times(200+210)\times10^{-12})^{-1/2} = \underline{49.4\times10^6/s}$ **14**

Centre frequency gain $= -\frac{200}{201}\times\frac{5k}{25}\times\frac{5.025}{10+5.025} = \underline{-66.6 V/V}$

Bandwidth, $B = \frac{1}{CR} = \frac{1}{410\times10^{-12}\times(5.025\|10)\times10^3} = \underline{729.4\ krad/s}$

$Q = \frac{W_0}{B} = \frac{49.4\times10^6}{729.4\times10^3} = \underline{67.7}$

34 $Q = \frac{WL}{r_s} = \frac{R_p}{WL}$

Thus $R_p = QWL = 200\times2\pi\times10^6\times10\times10^{-6} = \underline{12.57k\Omega}$

$W_0 = 2\pi f_0 = \frac{1}{\sqrt{LC}} \rightarrow LC = \frac{1}{(2\pi f_0)^2}$

Thus $C = \frac{1}{L(2\pi f_0)^2} = \frac{1}{10\times10^{-6}(2\pi\times10^6)^2} = \underline{2533}\,pF$

$B = 1/CR \rightarrow R = \frac{1}{CB} = \frac{1}{2533\times10^{-12}\times10\times10^3\times2\pi} = 6283\,\Omega$

Now $R_{par} \| R_p = R$

$R_{par} = \frac{RR_p}{R_p - R} = \frac{6.28\times12.6}{12.6-6.28} = \underline{12.56\,k\Omega}$

35

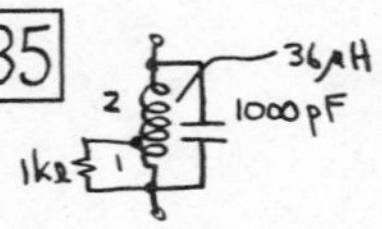

$f_0 = \frac{1}{2\pi\sqrt{LC}} = \frac{1}{2\pi(36\times10^{-6}\times1000\times10^{-12})^{1/2}} = \underline{838.8\ kHz}$

$R_{p\,equiv.} = n^2 R_L = 3^2\times1k = \underline{9k\Omega}$

Bandwidth, $B_f = \frac{1}{2\pi CR} = (2\pi\times1000\times10^{-12}\times9\times10^3)^{-1} = \underline{17.7kHz}$

$Q = f_0/B_f = 838.8/17.7 = \underline{47.4}$

36

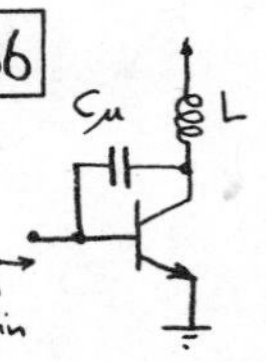

14

$WC_\mu \ll \frac{1}{WL} \rightarrow W^2 < \frac{1}{LC_\mu}$

ie operation is well below resonance

gain $= -g_m jWL$

$Y_{in} = \frac{1}{r_\pi} + jC_\pi W + jWC_\mu(1 - (-jWL)g_m)$

$= \frac{1}{r_\pi} + jW(C_\pi + C_\mu) - W^2 LC_\mu g_m$

or $Y_{in} = \left(\frac{1}{r_\pi} - W^2 C_\mu L g_m\right) + jW(C_\pi + C_\mu)$ as required

or $Y_{in} = \frac{1 - \beta W^2 C_\mu L}{r_\pi} + jW(C_\pi + C_\mu)$

37 $W = W_0(1 + \delta W/W_0)$ with $\frac{\delta W}{W_0} \ll 1$ so $W^2 = W_0^2(1 + \frac{2\delta W}{W_0})$

(a) Eq 14.4: $T(jW) = \frac{n_1 jW}{-W^2 + jW\frac{W_0}{Q} + W_0^2}$, a bandpass fun.

and $T(jW_0) = \frac{n_1 jW_0}{jW_0^2/Q} = \frac{n_1 Q}{W_0}$

$\therefore |T(jW)| = n_1 W\left((WW_0/Q)^2 + (W_0^2 - W^2)^2\right)^{-1/2}$

$= \frac{\frac{n_1 W}{WW_0}\cdot Q}{\sqrt{1 + Q^2\left(\frac{W_0^2 - W^2}{W_0 W}\right)^2}}$, but $W_0^2 - W^2 = -2W_0\delta W$

$\therefore |T(jW)| = \frac{n_1 Q/W_0}{\sqrt{1 + Q^2\left(\frac{2\delta W}{W}\right)^2}} = \frac{|T(jW_0)|}{\sqrt{1 + 4Q^2\left(\frac{\delta W}{W_0}\right)^2}}$

since $W \approx W_0$ as $\frac{\delta W}{W_0} \ll 1$

14

(b) For N bandpass sections, synchronously tuned in cascade, half power level occurs where $\left(\frac{1}{1+4Q^2\left(\frac{\delta\omega}{\omega_o}\right)^2}\right)^N = 1/2$, or $\left(1+4Q^2\left(\frac{\delta\omega}{\omega_o}\right)^2\right)^N = 2$

$\rightarrow 1+4Q^2\left(\frac{\delta\omega}{\omega_o}\right)^2 = 2^{1/N}$ or $\delta\omega = \frac{\omega_o}{2Q}\sqrt{2^{1/N}-1}$

$\therefore$ Bandwidth, $B = 2\delta\omega = \frac{\omega_o}{Q}\sqrt{2^{1/N}-1}$

38 (a)

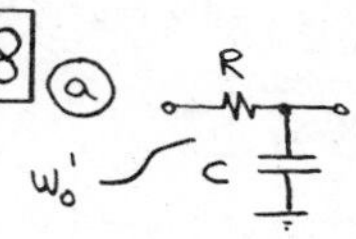

For the low-pass prototype: $T'(s) = \frac{\omega_o'}{s+\omega_o'}$

and $|T'(j\omega)| = \frac{\omega_o'}{(+\omega^2+\omega_o'^2)^{1/2}}$ with $|T'(0)| = 1$

Now the 2nd-order bandpass response around ω_o, with $\omega_o' \leftarrow \frac{\omega_o}{2Q}$, is $|T(j\omega)| = \frac{\frac{\omega_o}{2Q}}{\left((\delta\omega)^2+\left(\frac{\omega_o}{2Q}\right)^2\right)^{1/2}}$

or $|T(j\omega)| = \frac{\frac{\omega_o}{2Q}}{\frac{\omega_o}{2Q}\left(1+4Q^2\left(\frac{\delta\omega}{\omega_o}\right)^2\right)^{1/2}} = \frac{1}{\left(1+4Q^2\left(\frac{\delta\omega}{\omega_o}\right)^2\right)^{1/2}}$

having unity magnitude at $\omega = \omega_o$, ie $\delta\omega = 0$

or $|T(j\omega)| = \frac{|T(j\omega_o)|}{(1+4Q^2(\delta\omega/\omega_o)^2)^{1/2}}$ otherwise.

177A ←

14

(b) For N synchronously-tuned sections in cascade; response is down 3 dB when $\left(|T|/|T_o|\right)^N = 1/\sqrt{2}$

ie $\left(|T|/|T_o|\right)^2 = \frac{1}{2^{1/N}}$ or $1+4Q^2\left(\frac{\delta\omega'}{\omega_o}\right)^2 = 2^{1/N}$

or $\left(\frac{\delta\omega'}{\omega_o}\right)^2 = \frac{1}{4Q^2}\left(2^{1/N}-1\right) \rightarrow \frac{\delta\omega'}{\omega_o} = \frac{1}{2Q}\sqrt{2^{1/N}-1}$

Now for bandpass section, $B = 2\delta\omega' = \frac{\omega_o}{Q}\sqrt{2^{1/N}-1}$,

from which, for the basic section, $Q = \frac{\omega_o}{B}\sqrt{2^{1/N}-1}$

Thus $|T(j\omega)|_{overall} = |T(j\omega)|^N = \frac{|T(j\omega_o)|_{overall}}{\left(1+4Q^2\left(\frac{\delta\omega}{\omega_o}\right)^2\right)^{N/2}}$

$= \frac{|T(j\omega_o)|_{overall}}{\left(1+4\frac{\omega_o^2}{B^2}\left(2^{1/N}-1\right)\left(\frac{\delta\omega}{\omega_o}\right)^2\right)^{N/2}}$

$= \frac{|T(j\omega_o)|_{overall}}{\left(1+4\left(2^{1/N}-1\right)\left(\frac{\delta\omega}{B}\right)^2\right)^{N/2}}$

(c) i) For bandwidth 2B, $\delta\omega = \pm B$

Atten. $= 20\log_{10}\left(1+4\left(2^{1/N}-1\right)1\right)^{-N/2} = -10N\log_{10}\left(2^{2+1/N}-3\right)$

→ N:	1	2	3	4	5
Atten.(dB)	−6.70	−8.49	−9.28	−9.79	−10.13

(next)

14

ii) 3dB bandwidth is $\delta\omega = \pm B/2$

For 30dB bandwidth, $\frac{\delta\omega}{B} = x$

Thus $-30 = -20\frac{N}{2}\log\left(1+4\left(2^{1/N}-1\right)x^2\right)$

or $3 = N\log\left(1+4\left(2^{1/N}-1\right)x^2\right)$

or $x = \left(\frac{10^{3/N}-1}{4\left(2^{1/N}-1\right)}\right)^{1/2}$

Ratio of 30dB to 3dB bandwidth $= \frac{2Bx}{B} = 2x$

→ N	1	2	3	4	5
Ratio (2x)	31.6	8.6	5.7	5.0	4.5

39 See Fig. 14.31 and Eq. 14.55 and 14.56

(a) For the narrowband approximation, variation of Ω around 0 is equivalent to $\delta\omega$ around ω_o. Thus a low-pass maximally flat filter of bandwidth (B/2) and order N for which $|T| = \left(1+\left(\Omega/(B/2)\right)^{2N}\right)^{-1/2}$ is transformed to a bandpass maximally flat filter of bandwidth (B/2), order N and center frequency ω_o for which

$|T| = \left(1+\left(\frac{\delta\omega}{B/2}\right)^{2N}\right)^{-1/2}$

14

(b) For bandwidth 2B, $\delta\omega = B$

and $|T| = \left(1+\left(\frac{B}{B/2}\right)^{2N}\right)^{-1/2} = \left(1+2^{2N}\right)^{-1/2}$, thus

N	1	2	3	4	5
|T|	0.447	0.242	0.124	0.062	0.031
|T| dB	−6.99	−12.3	−18.1	−24.1	−30.1

For 30-dB bandwidth, $-30\text{ dB} = 20\log x \rightarrow x = 10^{-\frac{30}{20}}$

or $x = 0.0316 = 1/31.6$

$\therefore 1+\left(\frac{\delta\omega'}{B/2}\right)^{2N} = (31.6)^2 = 999 \rightarrow \left(\frac{\delta\omega'}{B/2}\right)^{2N} = 998$

Thus ratio of the 30-dB bandwidth ($2\delta\omega'$) to the 3-dB bandwidth (B) is $\frac{2\delta\omega'}{B} = \frac{\delta\omega'}{B/2} = 998^{\frac{1}{2N}}$

N	1	2	3	4	5
ratio	31.6	5.62	3.16	2.37	1.99

40 See Fig. 14.3 and Fig 14.31

Low Pass prototype has poles $-1, -0.5 \pm j\sqrt{3}/2$ and unity bandwidth. For bandwidth $B/2$, poles should be at $-B/2$ and $\frac{B}{2}\left(-\frac{1}{2} \pm j\frac{\sqrt{3}}{2}\right)$

Band Pass: transformed filter has poles (approx.) at $-B/2 \pm j\omega_o$, $-B/4 \pm j(\omega_o + \sqrt{3}B/4)$ and $-B/4 \pm j(\omega_o - \sqrt{3}B/4)$

Note the ideal j axis coordinate should be $\sqrt{\omega_o^2 - \left|\frac{B}{2}\right|^2} \approx \omega_o$

For the 3 circuits:

① $\omega_{o1} = \omega_o$, $B_1 = B$, $Q_1 = \omega_o/B$

② $\omega_{o2} = \omega_o + \frac{\sqrt{3}B}{4}$, $B_2 = B/2$, $Q_2 \approx 2\omega_o/B$

③ $\omega_{o3} = \omega_o - \frac{\sqrt{3}B}{4}$, $B_3 = B/2$, $Q_3 \approx 2\omega_o/B$

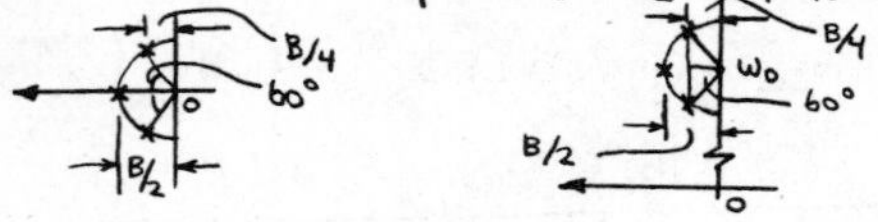

41 From Fig. 14.32, amplifier must have 180° shift and a gain of at least 20 dB at ω_o.

42

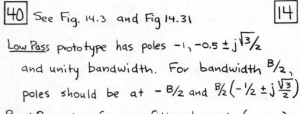

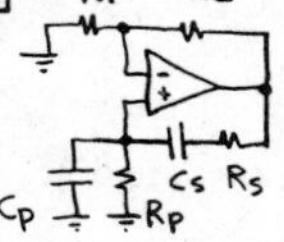

$$\beta = \frac{Z_P}{Z_P + Z_S} = \frac{1}{1 + Z_S Y_P}$$

$$= \frac{1}{1 + (R_S + \frac{1}{sC_S})(sC_P + \frac{1}{R_P})}$$

$$= \frac{1}{1 + \frac{R_S}{R_P} + \frac{C_P}{C_S} + sC_P R_S + \frac{1}{sC_S R_P}}$$

$$\text{or } \beta = \frac{\frac{s}{R_S C_P}}{s^2 + s\left(\frac{1}{R_S C_P} + \frac{1}{R_S C_S} + \frac{1}{R_P C_P}\right) + \frac{1}{R_S C_S R_P C_P}}$$

$A\beta = \left(1 + \frac{R_2}{R_1}\right)\beta$ and oscillation if $|A\beta| \geq 1$ at $\angle A\beta = 0°$

See $\angle A\beta = 0$ at $\omega = \boxed{\omega_o = \frac{1}{\sqrt{R_S C_S R_P C_P}}}$ at which

$$A\beta = (1 + R_2/R_1)\frac{(1/R_S C_P)}{1/R_S C_P + 1/R_S C_S + 1/R_P C_P}$$

$A\beta = 1$ when $1 + R_2/R_1 = 1 + C_P/C_S + R_S/R_P$

or $\boxed{R_2/R_1 = C_P/C_S + R_S/R_P}$

ⓐ For $C_S = C$, $R_S = R$, $C_P = C/10$, $R_P = 10R$

$$\omega_o = \left(CR\frac{C}{10} \cdot 10R\right)^{-1/2} = \frac{1}{RC}$$

$$R_2/R_1 = \frac{C/10}{C} + \frac{R}{10R} = 1/5 \rightarrow R_1 = 5R_2$$

ⓑ For $C_S = C/2$, $R_S = R$, $C_P = 2C$, $R_P = R$

$$\omega_o = ((C/2)R(2C)R)^{-1/2} = \frac{1}{RC}$$

$$R_2/R_1 = \frac{C}{C} + \frac{2R}{R/2} = 5 \rightarrow R_2 = 5R_1$$

(next)

ⓓ For $C_S = C$, $R_S = 10R$, $C_P = C$, $R_P = R/10$

$$\omega_o = \left(C(10R)C(R/10)\right)^{-1/2} = \frac{1}{RC}$$

$$R_2/R_1 = \frac{C}{C} + \frac{10R}{R/10} = 101 \rightarrow R_2 = 101R_1$$

ⓔ For $C_S = C$, $R_S = R/10$, $C_P = C$, $R_P = 10R$

$$\omega_o = (C(R/10)C(10R))^{-1/2} = \frac{1}{RC}$$

$$R_2/R_1 = \frac{C}{C} + \frac{R/10}{10R} = 1.01 \rightarrow R_2 = 1.01R_1$$

43 See Fig 14.35:

Let $R_5 + R_6 = x$ kΩ. Now for $R_5 = 1$ kΩ, $R_6 = (x-1)$ kΩ

Now $v_b = v_o - (v_o + 15)\frac{1}{x} = v_o(1 - 1/x) - \frac{15}{x}$

Through the bridge, at ω_o, $v_1 = v_o/3$

Thus $v_b = 0.7 + v_1 = 0.7 + v_o/3 = v_o(1 - 1/x) - \frac{15}{x}$

Now for a 10 V p-p output, $v_o = 5$ V

and $0.7 + 5/3 = 5(1 - 1/x) - 15/x = 5 - \frac{20}{x} = 2.3\dot{6}$

whence $\frac{20}{x} = 2.6\dot{3}$ and $x = \frac{20}{2.6\dot{3}} = 7.595$

Thus $R_6 = 7.595 - 1 = \underline{\underline{6.60\text{ k}\Omega}}$.

∴ Likewise $R_3 = 6.60$ kΩ

For R_3, R_6 open, $x = \infty$

$\therefore 0.7 + v_o/3 = v_o(1) - 0 \rightarrow \frac{2}{3}v_o = 0.7$

$\therefore v_o = \frac{3(0.7)}{2} = 1.05$ V

Thus output is $\underline{\underline{2.1\text{ V}}}$ p-p for $R_3 = R_6 = \infty$

44 The circuit in Fig 14.36 oscillates at (about) 1 kHz (See Exercise 14.23). To raise the frequency of oscillation to 10 kHz while using the same resistance values we must reduce the capacitors by a factor of 10. Thus each capacitor becomes $\underline{1.6\text{ nF}}$.

At f = 10 kHz, the op amp provides an excess phase of 5.7° (which we will assume to be a phase lag which, furthermore, is constant around 10 kHz). Thus the circuit will oscillate at the frequency for which the phase shift of the Wien bridge is +5.7° (thus resulting in 0 phase around the loop). From Eq(14.62) the phase shift of the Wien bridge can be seen as $\phi = -\tan^{-1}\frac{1}{3}\left(\omega CR - \frac{1}{\omega CR}\right)$. **14**

where $C = 1.6\,nF$, $R = 10\,k\Omega$. Thus $\tan 5.7° = \frac{\frac{1}{\omega CR} - \omega CR}{3}$

For $\omega = \omega_o - \Delta\omega$ with $\omega_o = 1/CR$

$$3\tan^{-1} 5.7° = \frac{1}{(\omega_o - \Delta\omega)/\omega_o} - \frac{(\omega_o - \Delta\omega)}{\omega_o}$$

ie $0.3 = \left(\omega_o^2 - \omega_o^2 + 2\Delta\omega\,\omega_o - \Delta\omega^2\right)/\omega_o(\omega_o - \Delta\omega)$

or $0.3 = \frac{(2\omega_o - \Delta\omega)\Delta\omega}{(\omega_o - \Delta\omega)\,\omega_o} \approx \frac{2\omega_o \cdot \Delta\omega}{\omega_o \times \omega_o} = \frac{2\Delta\omega}{\omega_o}$

$\therefore\ \Delta\omega = 0.15\,\omega_o$ or $\Delta f = 0.15 \times 10^4 = 1500\,Hz$

Thus the new frequency of oscillation is <u>8.5 kHz</u>

<u>To restore operation</u> to 10kHz we must arrange that at 10kHz, the Wien bridge provides a phase angle of 5.7°. For the bridge,

$$t(s) = \frac{Z_p}{Z_p + Z_s} = \frac{1}{1 + Y_p Z_s} = \frac{1}{1 + (1/R_p + sC)(R + 1/sC)}$$

$$= 1/(1 + R/R_p + 1 + sCR + 1/sCR_p)$$

or $t(j\omega) = 1/((2 + R/R_p) + j(\omega CR - 1/\omega CR_p))$

for which $\phi = -\tan^{-1}\left((\omega CR - 1/\omega CR_p)/(2 + R/R_p)\right)$

Thus $\tan^{-1} 5.7° = \left(\frac{1}{2 + R/R_p}\right) \times \left(\frac{1}{\omega CR_p} - \omega CR\right)$ **14**

where $\omega = 2\pi \times 10^4$, $C = 1.6 \times 10^{-9}\,F$, $R = 10^4\,\Omega$

ie $0.1 = \frac{1}{2 + 10^4/R_p}\left(\frac{1}{2\pi \times 10^4 \times 1.6 \times 10^{-9} R_p} - 2\pi \times 10^4 \times 1.6 \times 10^{-9} \times 10^4\right)$

or $0.1 = \frac{1}{2 + 10^4/R_p}\left(\frac{1}{10^{-4} R_p} - 1\right)$

ie $0.2 + 10^3/R_p = 10^4/R_p - 1 \rightarrow 1.2 = \frac{10^4 - 10^3}{R_p}$

Thus $R_p = \frac{10^4 - 10^3}{1.2} = \underline{\underline{7.5\,k\Omega}}$

<u>Note</u> that we must also make

$$1 + R_2/R_1 = 2 + 10^4/R_p = 2 + \frac{10}{7.5}$$

ie $R_2/R_1 = 1 + 10/7.5 = \underline{\underline{2.33}}$ (rather than 2 as before)

45 **14**

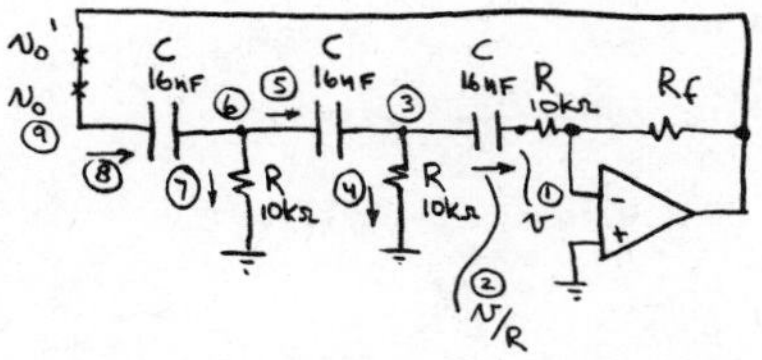

③ $v + \frac{1}{Cs} \times \frac{v}{R} = v + \frac{v}{sCR}$, ④ $\frac{v + \frac{v}{sCR}}{R} = \frac{v}{R} + \frac{v}{sCR^2}$,

⑤ $\frac{2v}{R} + \frac{v}{sCR^2}$, ⑥ $v + \frac{v}{sCR} + \frac{1}{sC}\left(\frac{2v}{R} + \frac{v}{sCR^2}\right) = v + \frac{3v}{sCR} + \frac{v}{s^2C^2R^2}$

⑦ $\frac{v}{R} + \frac{3v}{sCR^2} + \frac{v}{s^2C^2R^3}$ ⑧ $=$ ⑦ $+$ ⑤ $= \frac{3v}{R} + \frac{4v}{sCR^2} + \frac{v}{s^2C^2R^3}$

⑨ $v + \frac{3v}{sCR} + \frac{v}{s^2C^2R^2} + \frac{3v}{sCR} + \frac{4v}{s^2C^2R^2} + \frac{v}{s^3C^3R^3} = v_o$

See $v_o = v + \frac{6v}{sCR} + \frac{5v}{s^2C^2R^2} + \frac{v}{s^3C^3R^3}$

Loop gain $= L(s) = \frac{-v_o'}{v_o} = \frac{R_f/R\ v}{v\left(1 + \frac{6}{sCR} + \frac{5}{s^2C^2R^2} + \frac{1}{s^3C^3R^3}\right)}$

or $L(s) = \frac{s^3 R_f/R}{s^3 + \frac{6s^2}{RC} + \frac{5s}{R^2C^2} + \frac{1}{R^3C^3}}$

Now $L(j\omega) = \frac{R_f/R\,(-j\omega^3)}{-j\omega^3 + j\frac{5\omega}{R^2C^2} - \frac{6\omega^2}{RC} + \frac{1}{C^3R^3}}$ is real ($\phi = 0$)

when $\frac{6\omega^2}{RC} = \frac{1}{R^3C^3}$ or $\omega_o = \frac{1}{\sqrt{6}} \times \frac{1}{RC} = \frac{0.408}{RC}$

at which $|L(j\omega_o)| = \frac{R_f/R\,(-j\omega_o^3)}{+j\left(-\omega_o^3 + \frac{5\omega_o}{R^2C^2}\right)} = \frac{R_f/R\ \omega_o^2}{-\omega_o^2 + \frac{5}{R^2C^2}}$

ie $|L(j\omega_o)| = \frac{\frac{R_f}{R}\left(\frac{1}{6}\right)\frac{1}{R^2C^2}}{-\left(\frac{1}{6}\right)\frac{1}{R^2C^2} + \frac{5}{R^2C^2}} = \frac{R_f}{29R}$ **14**

Now loop gain $|L| = 1$ when $\underline{R_f = 29R}$

For $C = 16\,nF$, $R = 10\,k\Omega$, $R_f = \underline{290\,k\Omega}$ and

$$f_o = \frac{1}{2\pi\sqrt{6} \times 10^4 \times 16 \times 10^{-9}} = \underline{\underline{406\,Hz}}$$

46 In Fig. 14.39, break the loop at x.

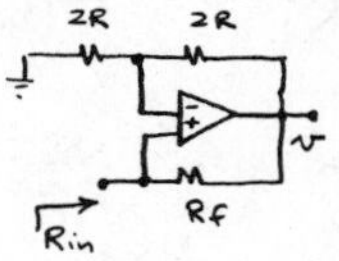

From Ex 3.5, $R_{in} = -R_f\frac{2R}{2R} = -R_f$

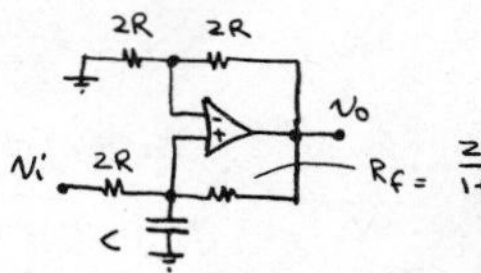

$R_f = \frac{2R}{1+\Delta}$ $\Rightarrow$

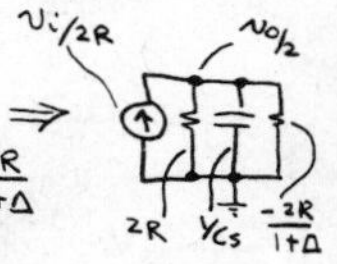

Now $2R \parallel \frac{-2R}{1+\Delta} = \frac{-2R \times \frac{2R}{1+\Delta}}{2R - \frac{2R}{1+\Delta}} = \frac{-(2R)^2}{-2R + 2R + 2R\Delta} = -\frac{2R}{\Delta}$

$\therefore\ v_o/2 = \frac{v_i}{2R}\left(\frac{-2R}{\Delta} \parallel \frac{1}{Cs}\right) = \frac{v_i}{2R}\left(\frac{-2R/\Delta \times 1/Cs}{1/Cs - 2R/\Delta}\right) =$

or $v_o = \frac{2v_i}{2R} \times \frac{-2R}{\Delta - 2RCs} = \frac{v_i}{RCs - \Delta/2}$, an ideal integrator for $\Delta = 0$

Now, overall, $L(s) = -\frac{1/Cs}{R} \times \frac{1}{RCs - \Delta/2} = \frac{-1}{s^2R^2C^2 - sRC\Delta/2}$

Now $L(s) = 1$ when $s^2R^2C^2 - sRC\Delta/2 + 1 = 0$, the char. eq.

with poles $s = \frac{\frac{RC\Delta}{2} \pm \sqrt{R^2C^2(\frac{\Delta}{2})^2 - 4R^2C^2}}{2R^2C^2} = \frac{\Delta/2 \pm 2j(1 - (\Delta/4)^2)^{1/2}}{2RC}$

Now for $\Delta \ll 1$, $(1-(\frac{\Delta}{4})^2)^{1/2} \approx (1 - \frac{1}{2}(\frac{\Delta}{4})^2)$

$\therefore\ s = \frac{\Delta/2 \pm j(2-(\frac{\Delta}{4})^2)}{2RC}$

or $s \approx \frac{1}{RC}(\Delta/4 \pm j)$, in the right half plane!

47 The transmission of the filter normalized with respect to the transmission at the center frequency is $|T(\omega)| = \frac{\omega\omega_0/Q}{\sqrt{(\omega_0^2-\omega^2)^2 + \frac{\omega^2\omega_0^2}{Q^2}}} = \frac{\frac{1}{Q}(\frac{\omega_0}{\omega})}{\sqrt{((\frac{\omega_0}{\omega})^2-1)^2 + (\frac{1}{Q}\frac{\omega_0}{\omega})^2}}$.

Now Q = 20:

Relative to the amplitude of the fundamental:

(a) the second harmonic = 0

(b) 3rd harmonic $= \frac{1}{3} \times \frac{\frac{1}{20}\times\frac{1}{3}}{((1/9-1)^2+(1/20 \times 1/3)^2)^{1/2}} = 6.25\times10^{-3}$

(c) 5th harmonic $= \frac{1}{5}\times\frac{\frac{1}{20}\times 1/5}{((1/25-1)^2+(1/20\times1/5)^2)^{1/2}} = 2.08\times10^{-3}$

(d) 4th harmonic = 0 = 6th harmonic = 8th = 10th

7th harmonic $= \frac{1}{7}\times\frac{\frac{1}{20}\times 1/7}{((1/49-1)^2+(1/20\times1/7)^2)^{1/2}} = 1.04\times10^{-3}$

9th harmonic $= \frac{1}{9} \times \frac{\frac{1}{20}\times 1/9}{((1/81-1)^2+(1/20\times1/9)^2)^{1/2}} = 0.62\times10^{-3}$

Thus $\frac{\text{RMS value of 2nd to 10th harmonic}}{\text{RMS of fundamental}}$ is

$(6.25^2+2.08^2+1.04^2+0.62^2)^{1/2}\times10^{-3} = 6.7\times10^{-3}$ or 0.7%

48 (a) $\omega_0 = \frac{1}{\sqrt{LC}}$

Gain $= \frac{\alpha R_C}{2r_e}$ → $R_C = 2r_e$ for gain of 1

$r_e = \frac{V_T}{I/2} = \frac{2V_T}{I}$ and $R_C = \frac{4V_T}{I} = (\frac{100\text{ mV}}{I\text{ mA}})\Omega = 0.1/I$ kΩ

(b) For $R_C = 1/I$ (kΩ, note)

Gain $= \frac{1/I}{2(\frac{2V_T}{I})} = \frac{1}{4\times25\times10^{-3}} = 10$

For BJT's turning on and off, output goes from V_{CC} to $V_{CC} - R_C I$ or $V_{CC}-1$, ie output is a square wave of amplitude 1 V_{pp}, whose fundamental component has a pp amplitude of $4/\pi = 1.27$ V

180 B C

1

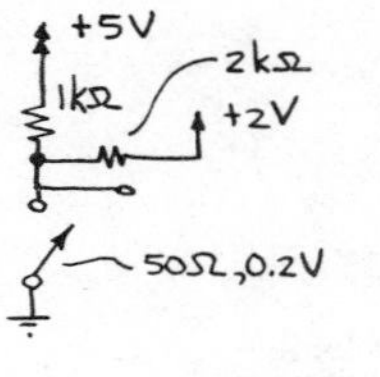

$V_{OH} = 2 + \frac{2}{2+1}(5-2) = 4V$

$V_{OL} = 0.2 + \frac{50}{50+1000\|2000}\times(4-0.2)$

$= 0.465V$

2

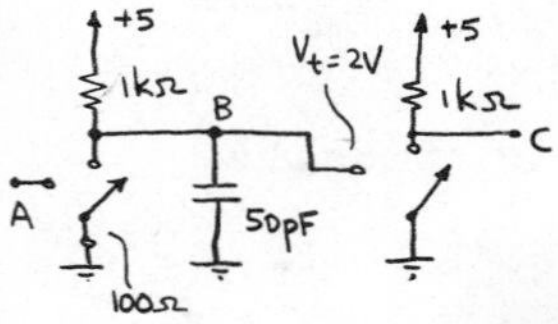

To close:

$t_{cl} = (10 + t_r + 10)$ ns

$v_B = (5 - \frac{0.1}{1+0.1}\times5)(1-e^{-t/\tau_1}) + \frac{0.1}{1+0.1}\times5$

$= 5-(5-0.454)e^{-t/\tau_1}$

where $\tau_1 = 1k\Omega\times50pF = 50ns$

Now $v_B = 5-4.545e^{-t_r/50} = 2.0$

Whence $e^{-t_r/50} = \frac{3}{4.545} = 0.66$

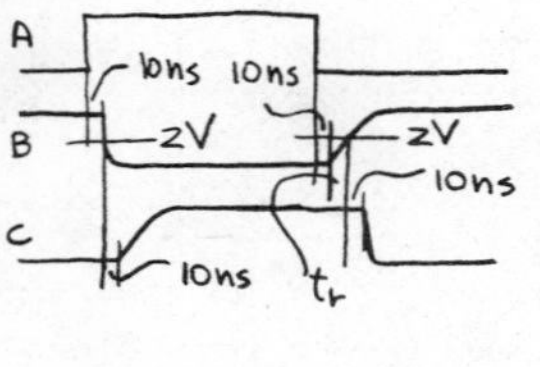

Thus $t_r = 0.4154(50) = 20.8$ ns

and $t_{close} = 10 + 10 + 20.8 = 40.8$ ns

To open: $v_B = (5-\frac{0.1}{1+0.1}\times5)e^{-t/\tau_2} + \frac{0.1}{1+0.1}(5)$

$= 4.545e^{-t/\tau_2} + 0.454$

where $\tau_2 = (100\|1000)50pF = 4.545$ nsec

Now $2.0 = 4.545e^{-t_f/4.545} + 0.454$

and $e^{t_f/4.545} = \frac{2-.454}{4.545} = 0.340$

Thus $t_f = 1.08\times4.545 = 4.9$ nsec

and $t_{open} = 10+10+4.9 = 24.9$ ns

3

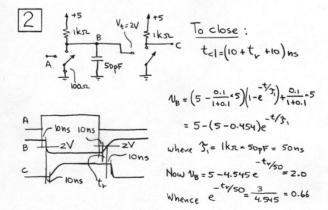

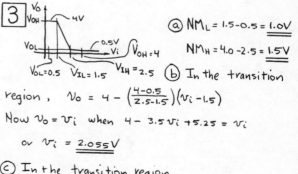

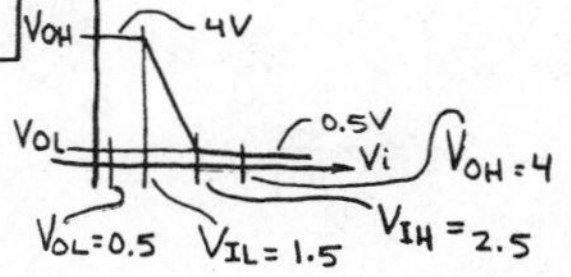

(a) $NM_L = 1.5-0.5 = 1.0V$

$NM_H = 4.0-2.5 = 1.5V$

(b) In the transition region, $v_O = 4 - (\frac{4-0.5}{2.5-1.5})(v_I - 1.5)$

Now $v_O = v_I$ when $4 - 3.5v_I + 5.25 = v_I$

or $v_I = 2.055$ V

(c) In the transition region,

gain $= -\frac{4-0.5}{2.5-1.5} = -3.5$ V/V

4 **15**

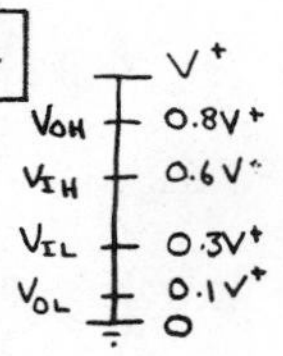

$NM_L = 0.3 - 0.1 = \underline{0.2\,V^+}$

$NM_H = 0.8 - 0.6 = \underline{0.2\,V^+}$

$V_{trans} = 0.6 - 0.3 = \underline{0.3\,V^+}$

For $NM = 1.0V$, $0.2V^+ = 1V$

whence $V^+ = 1/0.2 = \underline{5V}$

5

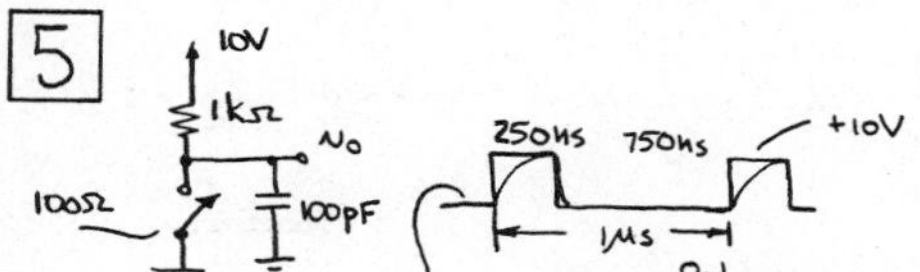

$v_{OL} = 10 \times \frac{0.1}{0.1+1} = 0.909V$

For switch closed, $v_{OL} = 0.909\,V$ and a current of 9.09 mA flows from the supply, both for 3/4 cycle.

As well, current is required for capacitor charging:

Capacitor charge change $= C\Delta V = 100\times10^{-12}\times(10 - 0.909) = Q$

or 909.1 pcoulombs. This charge is supplied by the 10V source every cycle. Energy from supply/cycle $= \int_{cycle} iv\,dt = 10\int_{cycle} i\,dt = 10Q/\text{cycle}$

or 9091 pJ/cycle.

15

Thus average power from supply for cap. charging $= 9091\times10^{-12}\times10^{6}\,Hz = 9.091\,mW$

Now total supply current $= \frac{9.091}{10} + \frac{3}{4}(9.09) = \underline{7.73mA}$

and total supply power $= 7.73\times10 = \underline{77.3\,mW}$

For the loss in switch:

Dc component: 9.09 mA in 100Ω for 3/4 of a cycle:

Energy/cycle $= (9.09\times10^{-3})^2\times100\times0.75\times10^{-6}$

Power $= 9.09^2\times10^{-6}\times75\times10^{-6}\times10^{6} = 6.2\,mW$

Capacitor component:

Energy lost/cycle $= \frac{1}{2}C\times10^2 - \frac{1}{2}C(0.909)^2$

$= \frac{1}{2}(100\times10^{-12})(100 - .826) = 4959\,pJ$

Power loss $= 4958\times10^{-12}\times10^{6} = 4.96\,mW$

Thus total power dissipation in the switch $= 6.2 + 5.0 = \underline{11.2\,mW}$

6 For rising input: $t = \frac{t_r}{2} + t_{PHL} + \frac{t_{THL}}{2} = \frac{20}{2} + 20 + \frac{30}{2} = \underline{45\,ns}$

For falling input: $t = \frac{t_f}{2} + t_{PLH} + \frac{t_{TLH}}{2} = \frac{20}{2} + 30 + \frac{40}{2} = \underline{60\,ns}$

For 4 gates: $t_P = 2t_{PLH} + 2t_{PHL} = 2(20+30) = \underline{100\,ns}$

7 **15**

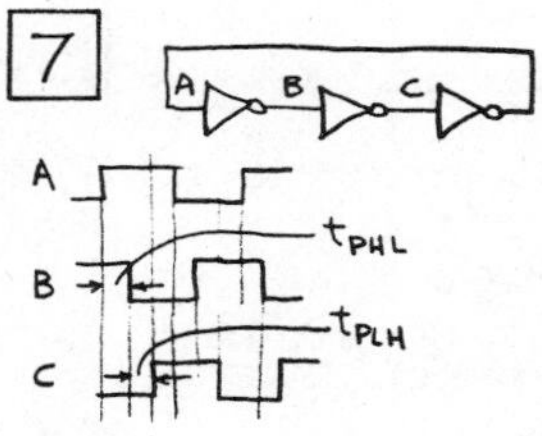

1 cycle incorporates $2(3) = 6$ transitions

For $t_p = 50nsec$,

$f_{osc} = \frac{1}{2\times3\times50\times10^{-9}} = \frac{10^9}{3(100)} = 3.\dot{3}\,\underline{MHz}$

For $t_{PLH} = 60\,ns$, $t_{PHL} = 40\,ns$, period $T = 3(t_{PLH} + t_{PHL})$

or $T = 3(40 + 60) = 300ns$ and $f_{osc} = \frac{1}{300\times10^{-9}} = \underline{3.\dot{3}\,MHz}$

8

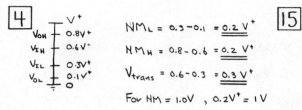

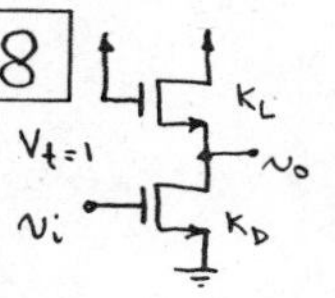

$K_R = \frac{K_D}{K_L} = 9$, $i_D = k(v_{GS} - V_t)^2$

(a) For $V_O = V_{DD} - 2V_t$:

$i_{DL} = K_L(2V_t - V_t)^2 = K_L V_t^2$

and $i_{DD} = K_D(v_i - V_t)^2 = i_{DL}$

$\therefore\ v_i - 1 = \left(\frac{K_L}{K_D}\right)^{1/2}(1)^2 = \frac{1}{3} \rightarrow v_i = \underline{1.3\dot{3}\,V}$

(b) For $v_O = v_i$:

Generally $(v_i - 1) = \frac{1}{\sqrt{K_R}}(V_{DD} - v_O - 1) \rightarrow v_i = 1 + \frac{1}{3}(4 - v_O)$

Now for $v_O = v_i \rightarrow v_i = 1 + \frac{4 - v_i}{3} \rightarrow 3v_i = 7 - v_i$

or $v_i = 7/4 = \underline{1.75V}$

(c) For $v_O = V_t = 1$, $v_i = 1 + 1/3(4 - 1) = \underline{2V}$

15

(d) For $\frac{dv_O}{dv_i} = -1$

Note first that in the region where both devices are pinched of, and $v_i = 7/3 - v_O/3$, $\frac{\partial v_i}{\partial v_O} = -1/3$ or $\frac{\partial v_O}{\partial v_i} = -3$, that is for v_i somewhat above 1V, the slope is -3.

Thus $\frac{\partial v_O}{\partial v_i} = -1$ occurs with the driver in the triode region for which $i_D = K(2(v_{GS} - V_t)v_{DS} - v_{DS}^2)$

or $i_{D_D} = K_D(2(v_i - 1)v_O - v_O^2) = i_{DL} = K_L(4 - v_O)^2$

or $16 - 8v_O + v_O^2 = 9(2v_i v_O - 2v_O - v_O^2)$

ie $16 - 8v_O + v_O^2 = 18v_i v_O - 18v_O - 9v_O^2$

or $10v_O^2 + 10v_O + 16 = 18v_O v_i$ -- (1)

Now $\frac{\partial (1)}{\partial v_O} \rightarrow 20v_O + 10 = 18v_i + 18v_O\frac{\partial v_i}{\partial v_O} = 18v_i - 18v_O$

since $\frac{\partial v_O}{\partial v_i} = 1$. Thus $18v_i = 38v_O + 10$.

Substituting in (1), $10v_O^2 + 10v_O + 16 = 38v_O^2 + 10v_O$

or $28v_O^2 = 16 \rightarrow v_O = \frac{4}{\sqrt{28}} = 0.756$, for which v_i

is $v_i = \frac{38(0.756) + 10}{18} = \underline{2.15V}$

9 Using detail of **8** for $K_R = 36$

For both Q_D, Q_L in pinchoff: $(v_i - V_t) = \frac{1}{\sqrt{K_R}}(V_{DD} - v_O - V_t)$

or $v_i = 1 + \frac{1}{6}(4 - v_O) = \frac{10 - v_O}{6}$

(a) For $v_O = V_{DD} - 2V_T = 5 - 2 = 3$, $v_i = \frac{10-3}{6} = \underline{\underline{1.17V}}$

(b) For $v_O = v_i$, $v_i = \frac{10 - v_i}{6} \rightarrow 6v_i = 10 - v_i$ or $v_i = \frac{10}{7} = \underline{\underline{1.43V}}$

(c) For $v_O = V_t = 1$, $v_i = \frac{10-1}{6} = \frac{9}{6} = \underline{\underline{1.5V}}$

(d) For $\frac{\partial v_O}{\partial v_i} = -1$, from **8**,

$$16 - 8v_O + v_O^2 = 36(2(v_i - 1)v_O - v_O^2) = 72 v_i v_O - 72 v_O - 36 v_O^2$$

or $37 v_O^2 + 64 v_O + 16 = 72 v_O v_i$ --- (1)

$\frac{\partial}{\partial v_O} \rightarrow 74 v_O + 64 = 72 v_i + 72 v_O \frac{\partial v_i}{\partial v_O} = 72 v_i - 72 v_O$

since $\frac{\partial v_O}{\partial v_i} = -1$, Thus $72 v_i = 146 v_O + 64$

Now from (1), $37 v_O^2 + 64 v_O + 16 = 146 v_O^2 + 64 v_O$

ie $109 v_O^2 = 16$ or $v_O = \left(\frac{16}{109}\right)^{1/2} = 0.383$

and $v_i = \frac{146(0.383) + 64}{72} = \underline{\underline{1.67V}}$

(e)xtra!: Note maximum "gain" $\frac{\partial v_O}{\partial v_i} = -6$

10 For each case $V_{OH} = 5 - 1 = 4V$, $v_i = V_{OH}$

(a) At $v_O = 4V$, $i_{D2} = 0$; all of i_{D1} is available to cap.

For $K_R = 9$, $i_D = 9 \times \mu A/V^2(4-1)^2 = \underline{\underline{81\mu A}} = i_{cap}$

For $K_R = 36$, $i_{D1} = 36 \times 1\mu A/V^2(4-1)^2 = \underline{\underline{324\mu A}} = i_{cap}$

(b) At $v_O = 3V$, both devices in pinchoff.

As load, $i_{D2} = 1\mu A/V^2(5-3-1)^2 = 1\mu A$

For $K_R = 9$, capacitor current $= 81 - 1 = \underline{\underline{80\mu A}} = i_{cap}$

For $K_R = 36$ $\quad 324 - 1 = \underline{\underline{323\mu A}} = i_{cap}$

(c) At $v_O = 1V$, Q_1 in triode operation, Q_2 in pinchoff.

As load, $i_{D2} = 1\mu A/V^2(5-1-1)^2 = 9\mu A$

For driver, $i_{D1} = K_R(2(4-1)1 - 1^2) = 5K_R$

For $K_R = 9$, $i_{D1} = 5(9) = 45\mu A$; $i_{cap} = 45 - 9 = \underline{\underline{36\mu A}}$

For $K_R = 36$, $i_{D1} = 5(36) = 180\mu A$; $i_{cap} = 180 - 9 = \underline{\underline{171\mu A}}$

11 $V_t = V_{t0} + \gamma(\sqrt{V_{SB} + 2\phi_F} - \sqrt{2\phi_F})$. For load V_{OH} lowest for V_t largest, ie when $V_{t0} = 1.5V$ and $\gamma = 1V^{1/2}$.

Lowest $V_{OH} = v = 5 - (1.5 + 1(\sqrt{v + 0.6} - \sqrt{0.6}))$

or $v = 3.5 - \sqrt{v + 0.6} + \sqrt{0.6}$

or $v + 0.6 = (3.5 + .775 - v)^2 = v^2 - 8.54v + 18.3$

ie $v^2 - 9.54v + 17.7 = 0 \rightarrow v = \frac{9.54 \pm \sqrt{9.54^2 - 4(17.7)}}{2}$

or $v = \underline{\underline{2.52V}}$, ½ of the supply!

12 From Ex 15.1: $K_1(2(v_i - V_{t1})v_O - v_O^2) = K_2(V_{DD} - v_O - V_{t2})^2$ (1)

$K_1 = 9K_2$, $v_i = V_{OH} = 3.4V$, $v_O = V_{OL} = v$?

$V_{t2} = V_{to2} + \gamma(\sqrt{V_{OL} + 2\phi_F} - \sqrt{2\phi_F})$ and initially $V_{OL} \approx 0.3$

$\rightarrow V_{t2} = 1 + 0.5(\sqrt{0.3 + 0.6} - \sqrt{0.6}) = 1 + 0.5(.18) = 1.09 \approx \underline{\underline{1.1V}}$

Now for $V_{t2} = 1.1V$, $9(2(3.4 - 1)v - v^2) = (5 - v - 1.1)^2$

or $43.2v - 9v^2 = (3.9 - v)^2 = 15.2 - 7.8v + v^2$

Thus $10v^2 - 51v + 15.2 = 0 \rightarrow v^2 - 5.1v + 1.52 = 0$

whence $v = \frac{-5.1 \pm \sqrt{5.1^2 - 4(15.2)}}{2} = \underline{\underline{0.318V}} = V_{OL}$

Now for $V_{IH} = 2.2$ where (with no body effect) $\frac{\partial v_O}{\partial v_i} = -1$

and $v_O = 0.8V$, $V_{t2} = 1 + 0.5(\sqrt{0.8 + 0.6} - \sqrt{0.6}) = \underline{1.20V}$

For revised V_{IH}, $K_1(2(v_i - V_{t1})v_O - v_O^2) = K_2(V_{DD} - v_O - V_{t2})^2$

$\frac{\partial}{\partial v_i} \rightarrow K_1(2(v_i - V_{t1})\frac{\partial v_O}{\partial v_i} + 2v_O - 2v_O\frac{\partial v_O}{\partial v_i}) = K_2(-2)(V_{DD} - v_O - V_{t2})\frac{\partial v_O}{\partial v_i}$

Now $v_i = V_{IH} = v$ where $\frac{\partial v_O}{\partial v_i} = -1$ and $K_1 = 9K_2$

ie $9(2(v - 1)(-1) + 2v_O - 2v_O(-1)) = -2(5 - v_O - 1.2)(-1)$

or $-18v + 18 + 36v_O = 7.6 - 2v_O$

or $38v_O = 18v - 10.4 \rightarrow v = \frac{38v_O + 10.4}{18}$

Now from (1) $9(2(v - 1)v_O - v_O^2) = (5 - v_O - 1.2)^2$

or $18vv_O - 18v_O - 9v_O^2 = v_O^2 - 7.6v_O + 14.44$

or $10v_O^2 + 10.4v_O + 14.44 = 18vv_O = 38v_O^2 + 10.4v_O$

Thus $28v_O^2 = 14.44 \rightarrow v_O = 0.718$

and $v = \frac{38(0.718) + 10.4}{18} = \underline{\underline{2.09V}} = V_{IH}$

Now $V_{IL} = \underline{\underline{1.0}}$, $V_{IH} = \underline{\underline{2.09}}$, $V_{OH} = \underline{\underline{3.40}}$, $V_{OL} = \underline{\underline{0.32}}$

Thus $NML = 1.0 - .32 = \underline{\underline{0.68}}$, $NM_H = 3.40 - 2.09 = \underline{\underline{1.31V}}$

13 $V_t = V_{t0} + \gamma(\sqrt{V_{SB} + 2\phi_F} - \sqrt{2\phi_F})$

or $2 = 1 + \gamma(\sqrt{3 + 0.6} - \sqrt{0.6})$

whence $\gamma = \frac{2 - 1}{1.897 - .775} = \underline{\underline{0.89}}$

14

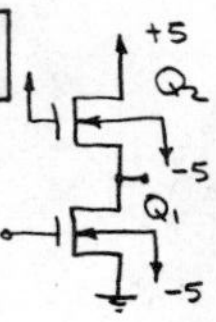

15

$V_t = V_{to} + \gamma\left(\sqrt{V_{SB}+2\phi_F} - \sqrt{2\phi_F}\right)$

For Q_1: $V_t = 0 + 0.5\left(\sqrt{5+0.6} + \sqrt{0.6}\right) = 0.80$

For Q_2:

For V_{OH}, assume $V_{OH} \approx +3.5$

$\therefore V_t = 0 + 0.5\left(\sqrt{5+3.5+0.6} - \sqrt{0.6}\right) = 1.13V$

$\therefore V_{OH} = 5 - 1.13 = 3.87$

for which $V_t = 0 + 0.5\left(\sqrt{5+3.87+0.6} - \sqrt{0.6}\right) = 1.15V$

$\therefore V_{OH} = 5 - 1.15 = 3.85\,V$

For V_{OL}, assume $V_{OL} \approx 0.5$

$V_t = 0 + 0.5\left(\sqrt{5+0.5+0.6} - \sqrt{0.6}\right) = 0.85V$

Now $i_{D2} = K_2(V_{DD} - v_O - V_{t2})^2 = K_2(5 - 0.85 - v_O)^2$

$= K_2(4.15 - v_O)^2 = i_{D1}$

and $i_{D1} = K_1\left(2(V_{OH} - V_{t_1})v_O - v_O^2\right)$

$= 9K_2\left(2(3.85 - 0.80)v_O - v_O^2\right)$

$\therefore (4.15 - v_O)^2 = 9(6.1v_O - v_O^2)$

or $17.22 - 8.30v_O + v_O^2 = 54.9v_O - 9v_O^2$

ie $10v_O^2 - 63.2v_O + 17.22 = 0$

whence $v_O = \dfrac{+63.2 \pm \sqrt{63.2^2 - 4(10)(17.22)}}{2(10)} = 0.29V$

15

$\therefore V_{OL} \approx \underline{\underline{0.30V}}$ and $V_{OH} = \underline{\underline{3.85V}}$

15 For Fig 15.11d, consider t_{PLH}

Q_2 in pinchoff: $i_D = K(v_{GS} - V_t)^2 = K(V_{DD} - v_O - V_t)^2$

$K = \frac{1}{2}\mu_n C_{ox}\frac{W}{L} = \frac{1}{2} \times 20 \times \frac{1}{3} = 3.3\dot{3}\mu A/V^2,\ V_t = 1V$

Now let $i_D = i$, $v_O = v$

$\therefore i = 3.3\dot{3}(5 - 1 - v)^2 = 3.\dot{3}(4 - v)^2$

$v = \frac{1}{C}\int i\,dt = \frac{0.3\dot{3} \times 10^{-6}}{0.1 \times 10^{-12}}\int (4 - v)^2 dt$

$\therefore \frac{dv}{dt} = (4 - v)^2\frac{K}{C}$. Output ranges from 0.3 to 4

$\therefore \int_{0.3}^{\frac{4+0.3}{2}} \frac{dv}{(4-v)^2} = \frac{K}{C}\int_0^{t_P} dt \rightarrow \frac{K}{C}t_p = \frac{1}{4-v}\Big]_{0.3}^{2.15}$

or $t_p = \frac{C}{K}\left(\frac{1}{4-2.15} - \frac{1}{4-0.3}\right) = \frac{C}{K}(0.270)$

or $t_p = \frac{0.1 \times 10^{-12}}{3.3 \times 10^{-6}} \times 0.27 = \underline{\underline{8.1\,nsec}}$

Compare this with estimate of 6.4 nsec which was low since average current in Eq 15.15 overestimates the actual value (, the characteristic being concave)

16 Eq 15.11: $K_1(2(v_i - V_{t_1})v_O - v_O^2) = K_2(V_{DD} - v_O - V_{t_2})^2$

15

Assume $V_{t_1} = V_{t_2} = 1V$, $v_i = V_{OH} = 5 - 1 = 4V$ and $v_O = V_{OL} = 1V$

For $K_1 = K_R K_2$: $K_R(2(4-1)1 - 1^2) = (5 - 1 - 1)^2$

Thus $K_R = \frac{3^2}{5} = \underline{1.8}$, that is the driver is only 1.8 times as wide as the load for V_O

Since $\left(\frac{W}{L}\right)_1 = 3$, $\left(\frac{W}{L}\right)_2 = \frac{3}{1.8} = \frac{5}{3} = 1.\dot{6} \rightarrow K_2 = \frac{1}{2} \times 20 \times 1.\dot{6} = \underline{\underline{16.\dot{6}}}$

Now $t_{PLH} = \dfrac{C\left(\frac{1}{2}(V_{OH} + V_{OL}) - V_{OL}\right)}{I_{LH}}$

where $I_{LH} = (i_{D2}(A) + i_{D2}(M))/2$, $i_D = K_2(V_{DD} - v_O - V_t)^2$

Here $i_{D_2}(A) = 16.\dot{6}(5 - 1 - 1)^2 = 150\mu A$

$i_{D2}(M) = 16.\dot{6}\left(5 - \frac{4+1}{2} - 1\right)^2 = 16.\dot{6}(1.5)^2 = 37.5\mu A$

$I_{LH} = \frac{150 + 37.5}{2} = 93.7\mu A$

$\therefore t_{PLH} = 0.1 \times 10^{-12}\left(\frac{1}{2}(4+1) - 1\right)/93.7 \times 10^{-6} = \underline{\underline{1.6\,ns}}$

17 Eq 15.15: $I_{LH} = \frac{1}{2}(i_D(A) + i_D(M))$. For $V_{OL} \approx 0$, $V_{OH} \approx V_{DD}$

$i_D(A) \approx K(V_{DD} - V_t)^2 = K(V_{DD}^2 - 2V_t V_{DD} + V_t^2)$ and

$i_D(M) \approx K(V_{DD}/2 - V_t)^2 = K\left(\frac{V_{DD}^2}{4} - V_t V_{DD} + V_t^2\right)$, whence

$I_{LH} = \frac{1}{2}K\left(V_{DD}^2 \times \frac{5}{4} - 3V_t V_{DD} + 2V_t^2\right)$

Now $I_{LH} = \frac{5}{8}K\left(V_{DD}^2 - \frac{12}{5}V_t V_{DD} + \frac{8}{5}V_t^2\right)$

15

$= \frac{5}{8}K\left(V_{DD}^2 - \frac{10}{5}V_t V_{DD} + \frac{5}{5}V_t^2\right)$

$+ \frac{5}{8}K\left(-\frac{2}{5}V_t V_{DD} + \frac{3}{5}V_t^2\right)$

ie $I_{LH} = \frac{5K}{8}(V_{DD} - V_t)^2 + KV_t\left(\frac{3}{8}V_t - \frac{1}{4}V_{DD}\right) \approx \frac{5K}{8}(V_{DD} - V_t)^2$

Check: For $V_{DD} = 5$, $V_t = 1$,

$\frac{5K}{8}(5-1)^2 = 10K$ while $K\left(3/8 - \frac{5}{4}\right) = -\frac{7}{8}K$ is smaller

Conclude $I_{LH} \approx \frac{5}{8}K(V_{DD} - V_t)^2$

18 Eq 15.19: $t_P = \frac{1}{2}t_{PLH} = \dfrac{0.4C}{K_2(V_{DD} - V_t)}$

Eq 15.20: $P_D = \frac{1}{2}K_2(V_{DD} - V_t)^2 V_{DD}$

Eq 15.21: $DP = 0.2C\,V_{DD}(V_{DD} - V_t)$

For $K_2 = 5\mu A/V^2$, $V_t = 1V$, $V_{DD} = 5V$, $C = 0.1\,pF$

$t_P = \frac{0.4(0.1)}{5(5-1)} = 2ns$

$P_D = \frac{5}{2}(5-1)^2 5 = 200\mu W$

$DP = 0.2(0.1)10^{-12}(5)(5-1) = 0.4 \times 10^{-12} = 0.4\,pJ$

(next)

15

K_2 $\mu A/V^2$	V_t V	V_{DD} V	C pF	t_p ns	P_D μW	DP pJ
5	1	5	0.1	2	200	0.4
1	1	5	0.1	10	40	0.4
5	0.5	5	0.1	1.78	253	0.45
5	1	10	0.1	.89	1012	0.90
5	1	5	1.0	20	200	4.0
1	0.5	5	0.1	8.9	50.6	0.45

19 $V_t = V_{to} + \gamma\left(\sqrt{V_{SB}+2\phi_F} - \sqrt{2\phi_F}\right)$

$i_D = K(v_{GS}-V_t)^2$ or $K\left(2(v_{GS}-V_t)v_{DS} - v_{DS}^2\right)$

(a) $V_{t_o} = -2V$, $K = 2.5\mu A/V^2$

$v_O = 0$, $i_D = 2.5(0+2)^2 = \underline{10\mu A}$

$v_O = 2.5V$, $V_t = -2 + 0.5(\sqrt{2.5+0.6} - \underbrace{\sqrt{0.6}}_{0.77}) = -2+0.5 = -1.5$

Pinchoff: $i_D = 2.5(0-(-1.5))^2 = \underline{5.63\mu A}$

$v_O = 4V$, $V_t = -2 + 0.5(\sqrt{4+0.6} - \sqrt{0.6}) = -2+.69 = -1.31$

Triode: $i_D = 2.5(2(0+1.31)1 - 1^2) = \underline{4.05\mu A}$

15

(b) $V_{t_o} = -3$, $K = 1.11\mu A/V^2$

$v_O = 0$, $V_t = -3$, $i_D = 1.11(0+3)^2 = \underline{10\mu A}$

$v_O = 2.5$, $V_t = -3 + 0.5 = -2.5V$

Pinchoff (barely): $i_D = 1.11(0+2.5)^2 = \underline{6.94\mu A}$

$v_O = 4V$, $V_t = -3 + 0.69 = -2.31V$

Triode: $i_D = 1.11(2(0+2.31)1 - 1^2) = \underline{4.02\mu A}$

(c) $V_{t_o} = -4$, $K = 0.625\mu A/V^2$

$v_O = 0$, $V_t = -4$, $i_D = 0.625(0+4)^2 = \underline{10\mu A}$

$v_O = 2.5V$, $V_t = -4 + 0.5 = -3.5V$

Triode: $i_D = 1.11(2(0+3.5)2.5 - 2.5^2) = \underline{7.03\mu A}$

$v_O = 4V$, $V_t = -4 + 0.69 = -3.31V$

Triode: $i_D = 1.11(2(0+3.31)1 - 1^2) = \underline{3.51\mu A}$

20 $i_D = K\left(2(v_{GS}-V_t)v_{DS} - v_{DS}^2\right)$, $1/r_o = \frac{\partial i_D}{\partial v_{DS}}$

At $v_O = V_{OH} = 5V$, $V_{tD} = -2.2V$, $K = 5.1\mu A/V^2$

Thus $1/r_o = K(2(0+2.2)) = 5.1\times10^{-6}(4.4) = 22.4\times10^{-6}$

whence $r_o = \underline{44.5\,K\Omega}$

21 Verify that $DP = \frac{1}{8\alpha}CV_{DD}^2$ where α depends on body effect: 15

For $V_{OL} = 0$, $i_{Do} = K_2(0-V_{to})^2 = K_2V_{to}^2$

For $V_{OL} = V_{DD}/2$, $V_t = V_{to} + \gamma(\sqrt{V_{DD}/2+0.6} - \sqrt{0.6})$

or $V_t = V_{to}(1+\Delta)$

whence, $i_{Dm} = K_2(0 - V_{to}(1+\Delta))^2 \approx K_2V_{to}^2(1+2\Delta)$

$\therefore$ average charging current $I_{LH} = K_2V_{to}^2\frac{(1+1+2\Delta)}{2}$

$= K_2V_{to}^2(1+\Delta)$

$\therefore t_{PLH} = \frac{C\left(\frac{V_{OH}+V_{OL}}{2} - V_{OL}\right)}{I_{LH}} = \frac{C\left(\frac{V_{DD}-V_{OL}}{2}\right)}{I_{LH}}$

For $V_{OL} \approx 0$, $t_{PLH} = \frac{CV_{DD}/2}{K_2V_{to}^2(1+\Delta)}$

Now $t_p \approx \frac{t_{PLH}+0}{2} = \frac{CV_{DD}/4}{K_2V_{to}^2(1+\Delta)}$

Assuming gate ½ on, ½ off $\rightarrow P_D = ½(K_2V_{to}^2)V_{DD}$

$\therefore \boxed{DP} = ½(K_2V_{to})V_{DD} \times \frac{CV_{DD}/4}{K_2V_{to}^2(1+\Delta)} = \boxed{\frac{1}{8}\frac{V_{DD}^2C}{\alpha}}$

where $\alpha = 1+\Delta = 1 + \frac{\gamma}{V_{to}}\left(\sqrt{V_{DD}/2+0.6} - \sqrt{0.6}\right)$

22 15

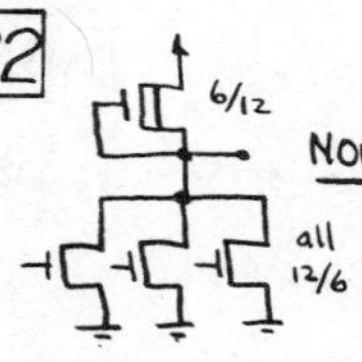

Area $= 6\times12 + 3(12\times6)$

$= 4(72) = \underline{288\mu m^2}$

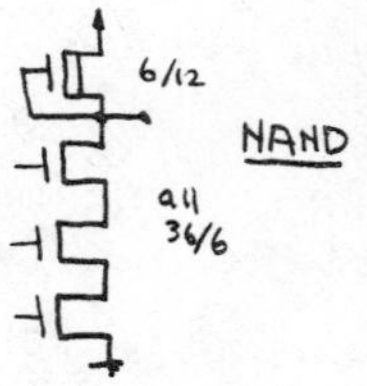

Area $= 6\times12 + 3(36\times6)$

$= 10(72) = \underline{720\mu m^2}$

23

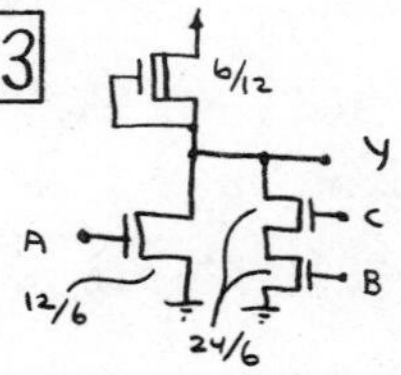

$\bar{Y} = A \vee (B.C)$

24

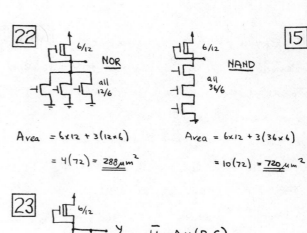

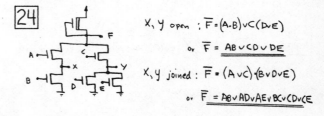

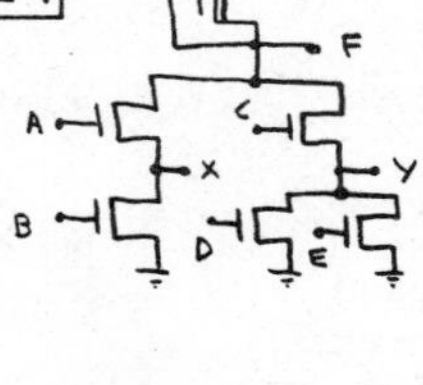

X, Y open: $\bar{F} = (A.B) \vee C(D \vee E)$

or $\bar{F} = \underline{AB \vee CD \vee DE}$

X, Y joined: $\bar{F} = (A \vee C)\cdot(B \vee D \vee E)$

or $\bar{F} = \underline{AB \vee AD \vee AE \vee BC \vee CD \vee CE}$

25 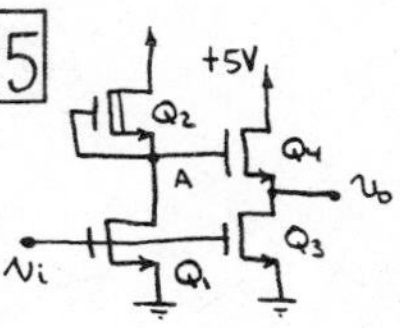

15

$W_1 = W_2 = 12$, $W_3 = 120$, $W_4 = 240$

$L_1 = L_2 = L_3 = L_4 = 6$, $V_{DD} = 5V$

$\mu C_{ox} = 20$, $V_{tE} = 1V$, $V_{tD} = -3V$

(a) $V_{AH} = \underline{+5V}$, $V_{OH} = 5 - 1 = \underline{4V}$

$\underline{V_{AL}}$: $I_{D2} = K_2(0 - V_t)^2 = \frac{1}{2}(20)(\frac{12}{6})(3^2) = 180\mu A$

For $V_{AL} = v$, $180 = K_1(2(5-1)v - v^2) = \frac{1}{2}(20)\frac{12}{6}(8v - v^2)$

or $180 = 20(8v - v^2) \rightarrow v^2 - 8v + 9 = 0$

whence $v = \frac{+8 \pm \sqrt{8^2 - 4(9}}{2} = \underline{1.35V} = V_{AL}$

$\underline{V_{OL}}$: For $V_{OL} \approx 0$, $i_{D4} = \frac{1}{2}(20)\frac{240}{6}(1.35-1)^2 = 49\mu A$

also $49 = i_{D3} = \frac{1}{2}(20)\frac{120}{6}(2(5-1)V_{OL} - V_{OL}^2) \approx 1600 V_{OL}$

whence $V_{OL} \approx \underline{0.03V}$

(b) Output low: Total supply current $= 180 + 49 = \underline{229\mu A}$

Output high: Total supply current $= \underline{0\mu A}$

(c) Peak Current (negative) with Q_4 cut off $= I_p$

$I_p = K_3(v_{GS} - V_t)^2 = \frac{1}{2}(20)(\frac{120}{6})(5-1)^2 = 3200\mu A = \underline{3.2mA}$

At $v_O = 4/2 = 2V$, $I_m = 200(2(5-1)2 - 2^2) = \underline{2.4mA}$

Av discharge current (to half V_{OH}) is $\frac{3.2 + 2.4}{2} = \underline{2.8mA}$

15

$\therefore t_{PHL} = \frac{CV}{I} = \frac{10 \times 10^{-12} \times 2}{2.8 \times 10^{-3}} = \underline{7.14 ns}$

(d) Going high: max current $I_p = K_4(v_{GS} - V_t)^2$

or $I_p = \frac{1}{2}(20)(\frac{240}{6})(5-1)^2 = \underline{6.4mA}$

Current at $v_O = 2$, $I_m = 400(5-2-1)^2 = \underline{1.6mA}$

Average charging current $= \frac{6.4 + 1.6}{2} = \underline{4.0mA}$

$\therefore t_{PLH} = \frac{10 \times 10^{-12} \times 2}{4 \times 10^{-3}} = \underline{5 nsec}$

26 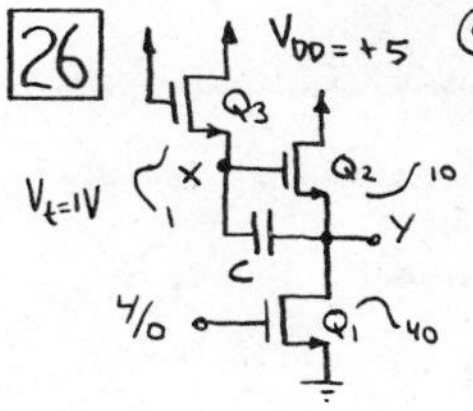

(a)

For $v_i = 4V$, $v_x = 5 - 1 = \underline{4V}$

$v_y = v \approx 0$, $i_{D1} = i_{D2}$

ie $40(2(4-1)v - v^2) = 10(4 - v - 1)^2$

or $24v - 4v^2 = 9 - 6v + v^2$

or $5v^2 - 30v + 9 = 0 \rightarrow v = \frac{+30 \pm \sqrt{30^2 - 4(5)9}}{10} = .32V$

ie $v_y = \underline{0.32V}$

(b) Q_1 cuts off, Q_2 forces Y to rise, Q_3 cuts off and X rises above 5V. v_y goes to 5V and v_x goes to $(5-1) + (5 - .32) = \underline{8.7V}$

(next)

15

(c) As Q_1 turns off, current available to drive the load is $i_{D2} = 10(4 - 0.32 - 1)^2 = \underline{72\mu A}$

(d) For v_y initially at +5V, and v_x at 8.7V, $i_{D2} = 0$ since $v_{DS} = 0$, and $i_{D1} = 40(4-1)^2 = \underline{360\mu A}$, all to load

(e)xtra: For v_y at 2V, $v_x = 8.7 - (5-2) = 5.7V$ and $i_{D2} \approx 10(5.7 - 2.0 - 1)^2 = 73\mu A$ and current available to drive output capacitance is $360 - 73 = 287\mu A$

27 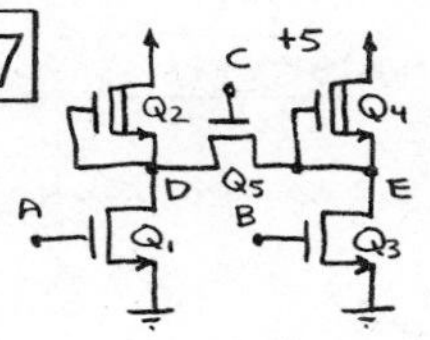

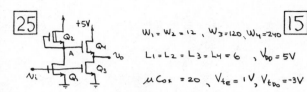

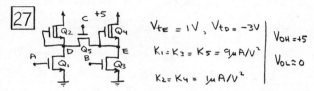

$V_{tE} = 1V$, $V_{tD} = -3V$

$K_1 = K_3 = K_5 = 9\mu A/V^2$

$K_2 = K_4 = 1\mu A/V^2$

$V_{OH} = +5$

$V_{OL} \approx 0$

Provided Q_1, Q_3 can either overpower Q_2 and Q_4

$\underline{\overline{E} = B \vee A.C}$, $\underline{\overline{D} = A \vee B.C}$

A, B both low, $V_D = V_E = \underline{+5V}$

A high, B low, C low $\rightarrow V_D = v$, $V_E = 5V$

See $i_2 = 1(0 - -3)^2 = 9\mu A = i_1 = 9(2(5-1)v - v^2)$

ie $9 = 9(8v - v^2)$ or $v^2 - 8v + 1 = 0 \rightarrow V_D = v = \frac{8 \pm \sqrt{8^2 - 4(1)(1)}}{2} = \underline{0.127V}$

15

Also A high, B high, C high or low, $V_D = V_E = 0.127V$

Now for A high, B low, C high, $V_D = v$

where $i_1 = 9(\ v - v^2) = 2(9)$ {from Q_2 and Q_4}

ie $v^2 - 8v \ \ 2 = 0 \rightarrow v = \frac{8 \pm \sqrt{8^2 - 4(2)(1)}}{2} = 0.258V$

ie $V_D = \underline{0.258}$

Also for V_E $V_D = v$

$i_5 = 9(2(5 - 0.258 - 1)(v) - v^2) = 9\mu A$

$v^2 - .48v + 1 = 0 \rightarrow v = \frac{+7.48 \pm \sqrt{7.48^2 - 4}}{2} = 0.136V$

$\therefore V_E = .258 + 0.136 = \underline{0.394}$

Thus levels at D, E are 0.127, 0.258, 0.394V {logic 0}

and 5.00V {logic 1}

28 See potentially, for Q_1, Q_3 large enough,

y is low if Q_1 and Q_5 conduct or Q_6 and Q_3 conduct

ie $\bar{y} = A.\bar{B} \vee B.\bar{A} \rightarrow y = \overline{A\bar{B} \vee \bar{A}B} = \bar{A}\bar{B} \vee AB$

licating a high output if both inputs are the

ame as each other — An Equivalence or $\overline{\text{EX-OR}}$

15

For a basic inverter $(W/L)_{load} = 6/12$ and $(W/L)_{driver} = 12/6$. Here for the EX-OR, use $(W/L)_2 = (W/L)_4 = (W/L)_7 = 6/12$. Now to lower Y via Q_1, Q_1 drives 2 loads while Q_5 (in series) drives 1 load. Now $(W/L)_1 = (W/L)_3 = (W/L)_5 = (W/L)_6$. Assume $v_{DS1,3} \approx 0$ so that Q_1, Q_3, Q_5, Q_6 operate in essentially the same (triode) mode with $r_{DS} = r$:

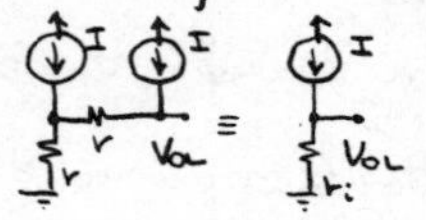

where I is the standard load and r_i is the triode resistance of the basic inverter. Now, see $V_{OL} = r(2I) + r(I) = r_i(I) \rightarrow r = \frac{r_i}{3}$

Thus $Q_{1,2,5,7}$ should be 3x wider than Q_{DI}

ie $(W/L)_1 = (W/L)_3 = (W/L)_5 = (W/L)_6 = \frac{3(12)}{6} = 36/6$

29 15

$K_n = 1/2\,(20)\,\frac{12}{6} = 5\mu A/V^2$

$K_p = 1/2\,(\frac{20}{2})\,\frac{24}{6} = 5\mu A/V^2$

In segment BC, $i_D = k(v_{GS} - V_t)^2$

where $v_{GS} = V_{DD}/2 = 2.5 \rightarrow i_D = 5(2.5-1)^2 = 11.25\mu A$

$r_o = \frac{V_A}{i_D} = \frac{100}{11.25\times10^{-6}} = 8.89\,M\Omega$

Slope of BC is gain:

$g_m = \frac{\partial i}{\partial v_{gs}} = 2k(v_{GS} - V_t) = 2(5)(2.5-1) = 15\mu A/V$

Gain $= -(g_m r_o/2 + g_m r_o/2) = -g_m r_o = -15\times10^{-6} \times 8.9\times10^{6} = -133\,V/V$

That is slope of BC segment is -133 V/V

For 10M feedback connection, $V_i = V_o = 2.5V$

Voltage gain $= -2g_m(\frac{r_o}{2} \| 10M) = -2(15)(\frac{8.9}{2} \| 10)$

$= -92.4$ V/V

$R_{in} = \frac{10M}{1 + 92.4} = 107\,k\Omega$

30 15

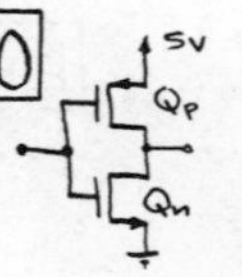

$K_n = 2K_p$, $|V_t| = 1V$

$V_{th} = v$ where

$i = k_n(v-1)^2 = k_p(5-v-1)^2$

or $2(v^2 - 2v + 1) = 16 - 8v + v^2 \rightarrow 2v^2 - 4v + 2 = v^2 - 8v + 16$

or $v^2 + 4v - 14 = 0$, whence $V_{th} = v = \frac{-4 \pm \sqrt{4^2 + 4(14)}}{2} = 2.24V$

For V_{IH}, Q_n in triode region: (Using Eq. 15.34)

$$2(2(v_i - V_t)v_o - v_o^2) = (V_{DD} - v_i - V_t)^2 \quad \text{--- ①}$$

$$\frac{\partial}{\partial v_i} \rightarrow 2\left(2(v_i - V_t)\frac{\partial v_o}{\partial v_i} + 2v_o - 2v_o\frac{\partial v_o}{\partial v_i}\right) = 2(V_{DD} - V_t - v_i)(-1)$$

Now for $V_{DD} = +5$, $V_t = 1$, $v_i = V_{IH}$, $\frac{\partial v_o}{\partial v_i} = -1$

$$2(2(V_{IH} - 1)(-1) + 2v_o + 2v_o) = -2(5 - 1 - V_{IH})$$

or $-2V_{IH} + 2 + 4v_o = -4 + V_{IH} \rightarrow 3V_{IH} = 6 + 4v_o$

or $V_{IH} = 2 + \frac{4}{3}v_o$ which with ① and substitutions above

$\rightarrow 2(2(V_{IH} - 1)v_o - v_o^2) = (4 - V_{IH})^2$

or $2(2(1 + \frac{4}{3}v_o)(v_o) - v_o^2) = (2 - \frac{4}{3}v_o)^2$

ie $4v_o + \frac{16}{3}v_o^2 - 2v_o^2 = 4 - \frac{16}{3}v_o + \frac{16}{9}v_o^2$

$18v_o + 24v_o^2 - 9v_o^2 = 18 - 24v_o + 8v_o^2$

or $7v_o^2 + 42v_o - 18 = 0 \rightarrow v_o = \frac{-42 \pm \sqrt{42^2 + 4(7)18}}{2(7)} = 0.402V$

15

whence $V_{IH} = 2 + \frac{4}{3}(.402) = 2.54$, for which $v_o = .402$

For V_{IL}, Q_p in triode region; $v_i = v\,(= V_{IH})$

$$\therefore 2(v-1)^2 = 1(2(5 - v - 1)(5 - v_o) - (5 - v_o)^2 \quad \text{--- ②}$$

$$\frac{d}{dv} \rightarrow 2(2)(v-1) = -2(4-v)\frac{\partial v_o}{\partial v} + 2(4)(-1)(5 - v_o) + 2(5 - v_o)\frac{\partial v_o}{\partial v}$$

Now for $\frac{\partial v_o}{\partial v} = -1 \rightarrow 4v - 4 = +8 - 2v - 40 + 8v_o - 10 + 2v_o$

whence $10v_o = 6v + 38 \rightarrow v_o = 0.6v + 3.8$

Substituting in ②: $2(v-1)^2 = 2(4-v)(1.2 - 0.6v) - (1.2 - 0.6v)^2$

or $2v^2 - 4v + 1 = 9.6 - 4.8v - 2.4v + 1.2v^2 - 1.44 + 1.44v - .36v^2$

or $1.16v^2 + 1.76v - 7.16 = 0 \rightarrow v = \frac{-1.76 \pm \sqrt{1.76^2 + 4(1.16)(7.16)}}{2.32} = 1.84V$

whence $v = 1.84V = V_{IL}$, for which $v_o = 0.6(1.84) + 3.8 = 4.90V$

Noise Margins $NM_H = 5 - 2.54 = 2.46V$

$NM_L = 1.84 - 0 = 1.84V$

31 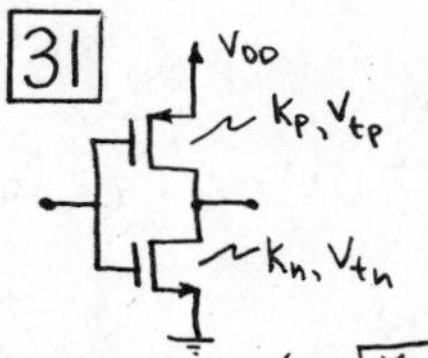

15

At V_{th}, both in pinchoff

ie $i_D = K_p(V_{DD}-V_{th}-|V_{tp}|)^2 = K_n(V_{th}-V_{tn})^2$

or $V_{DD}-V_{th}-|V_{tp}| = \sqrt{K_n/K_p}\,(V_{th}-V_{tn})$

Thus $V_{th}(1+\sqrt{K_n/K_p}) = V_{DD}-|V_{tp}| + \sqrt{K_n/K_p}\,V_{tn}$

or $$\boxed{V_{th} = \frac{V_{DD}-|V_{tp}|+\sqrt{K_n/K_p}\,V_{tn}}{1+\sqrt{K_n/K_p}}}$$

Now for $K_n = 2K_p$, $V_{tp} = -1$, $V_{DD} = 5$, $V_{th} = 5/2$

then $5/2 = \dfrac{5-1+\sqrt{2}\times V_{tn}}{1+\sqrt{2}}$

$\therefore V_{tn} = \dfrac{5/2\,(1.414+1)-4}{1.414} = \underline{\underline{1.44V}}$

32 For V_{IH}: n in triode, p in pinchoff;

$K_n = K_p = K$; let $V_{IH} = v$ at v_O; $V_{tn} = |V_{tp}| = 1$

$\therefore i_D = K(V_{DD}-v-1)^2 = K(2(v-1)v_O - v_O^2)$ --- (1)

or $(V_{DD}-1-v)^2 = 2(v-1)v_O - v_O^2$

$\frac{\partial}{\partial v} \rightarrow 2(V_{DD}-1-v)(-1) = 2v_O + 2(v-1)\frac{\partial v_O}{\partial v} - 2v_O\frac{\partial v_O}{\partial v}$

At $\frac{\partial v_O}{\partial v} = -1$, $-2V_{DD}+2+2v = 2v_O - 2v + 2 + 2v_O$

or $4v = 4v_O + 2V_{DD} \rightarrow v = v_O + V_{DD}/2$ --- (2)

Now (2) → (1), $(V_{DD}-1-v_O-\frac{V_{DD}}{2})^2 = 2(v_O - 1 + \frac{V_{DD}}{2})v_O - v_O^2$ **15**

For $V_{DD} = +10V$: $(10-1-v_O-5)^2 = 2(v_O-1+5)v_O - v_O^2$

ie $(4-v_O)^2 = 2(v_O+4)v_O - v_O^2$

or $16 - 8v_O + v_O^2 = 2v_O^2 + 8v_O - v_O^2$, whence $v_O = 1$

Thus $v = V_{IH} = 1 + 10/2 = \underline{\underline{6V}}$

Likewise $V_{IL} = 10-6 = \underline{\underline{4V}}$ | $NM_L = NM_H = \underline{4V}$

For $V_{DD} = +15V$: $(15-1-v_O-7.5)^2 = 2(v_O-1+7.5)v_O - v_O^2$

ie $(6.5-v_O)^2 = 2(v_O+6.5)v_O - v_O^2$

or $42.25 - 13v_O + v_O^2 = 2v_O^2 + 13v_O - v_O^2$

whence $26v_O = 42.25$, or $v_O = \frac{42.25}{26} = 1.625V$

Thus $v = V_{IH} = 1.625 + \frac{15}{2} = 9.125V$ | $NM_L = NM_H = \underline{5.875V}$

Likewise $V_{IL} = 15 - 9.125 = 5.875V$

33 For $V_t = 0.5, 1.5, 2.0$; $V_{DD} = 5V$; $K_n = K_p$

From **32** $V_{IH} = v_O + V_{DD}/2$

where $(V_{DD}/2 - V_t - v_O)^2 = 2(v_O - V_t + \frac{V_{DD}}{2})v_O - v_O^2$

For $V_{DD} = 5$: $V_{IH} = v_O + 2.5$ and $(5 - V_t - v_O)^2 = 2(v_O - V_t + 2.5)v_O - v_O^2$

For $V_t = 0.5$: $(2.5-0.5-v_O)^2 = 2(v_O-0.5+2.5)v_O - v_O^2$ **15**

ie $(2-v_O)^2 = 2(v_O+2)v_O - v_O^2$

or $4 - 4v_O + v_O^2 = 2v_O^2 + 4v_O - v_O^2 \rightarrow 8v_O = 4$

Thus $v_O = 0.5$, $V_{IH} = 0.5 + 2.5 = 3.0V$ | $NM_L = NM_H = 2V$

and from symmetry $V_{IL} = 5-3 = 2.0V$

For $V_t = 1.5$: $(2.5-1.5-v_O)^2 = 2(v_O-1.5+2.5)v_O - v_O^2$

ie $(1-v_O)^2 = 2(v_O+1)v_O - v_O^2$

or $1 - 2v_O + v_O^2 = 2v_O^2 + 2v_O - v_O^2 \rightarrow 4v_O = 1$

Thus $v_O = 0.25$, $V_{IH} = 0.25 + 2.5 = 2.75V$ | $NM = 2.25V$

$V_{IL} = 5 - 2.75 = 2.25V$

For $V_t = 2.0V$: $(2.5-2-v_O)^2 = 2(v_O-2+2.5)v_O - v_O^2$

ie $(0.5-v_O)^2 = 2(v_O+0.5)v_O - v_O^2$

or $0.25 - v_O + v_O^2 = 2v_O^2 + v_O - v_O^2 \rightarrow 2v_O = 0.25$

Thus $v_O = 0.125$, $V_{IH} = 0.125 + 2.5 = 2.625V$ | $NM = 2.375V$

$V_{IL} = 5 - 2.625 = 2.375V$

34 For the p device $K_p = \frac{1}{2}\times 10 \times 40 = 200\,\mu A/V^2$ } $= K$ **15**

and for the n device $K_n = \frac{1}{2}\times 20\times 20 = 200\,\mu A/V^2$

Now $i_D = K(2(v_{GS}-V_t)v_O - v_O^2)$ with $v_{GS} = V_{DD}$,

$v_O = 0.1V_{DD}$, $V_t = 1V$, for loads of either polarity.

For $V_{DD} = 5V$: $i_D = 200(2(5-1)(0.1\times5) - (0.1\times5)^2)$

$= 200(3 - 0.25) = \underline{0.55mA}$

To raise this to 1.55 mA, width of the devices must be increased by a factor of $\frac{1.55}{0.55} = \underline{2.82}$. For enlarged device:

At $V_{DD} = 10V$, $i_D = 2.82\times200\,(2(10-1)(0.1\times10) - 1^2) = \underline{\underline{4.51\,mA}}$

At $V_{DD} = 15V$, $i_D = 2.82\times200\,(2(15-1)1.5 - 1.5^2) = \underline{\underline{22.4\,mA}}$

35 For both devices: $K = \frac{1}{2}(20)(20) = 200\,\mu A/V^2$, $V_t = 2V$

Peak current during switching occurs at $v_I = V_{DD}/2$

and is $i_D = K(v_{GS} - V_t)^2 = 200(V_{DD}/2 - 2)^2$

For 5V: $i = 200(5/2 - 2)^2 = \underline{\underline{50\,\mu A}}$

For 10V: $i = 200(10/2 - 2)^2 = \underline{\underline{1.8\,mA}}$

For 15V: $i = 200(15/2 - 2)^2 = \underline{\underline{6.05\,\mu A}}$

36

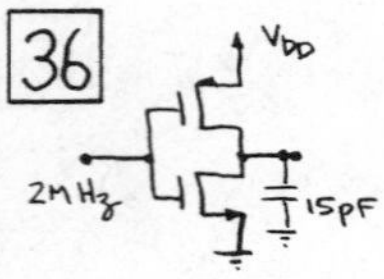

$Q = CV = IT$

For capacitor, average current from the supply, $I = \frac{CV_{DD}}{1/f}$. Power loss in the gate, $P = IV_{DD}$

For $V_{DD} = 5$, $I = \frac{15\times10^{-12}\times5}{1/2\times10^{6}} = \underline{\underline{0.15\,mA}}$

$P = 0.15(5) = \underline{\underline{0.75\,mW}}$

For $V_{DD} = 10$, $I = 15\times10^{-12}\times10\times2\times10^{6} = 0.30\,mA$ | Ex 15.17

$P = 0.30(10) = 3.0\,mW$

For $V_{DD} = 15$, $I = 15\times10^{-12}\times15\times2\times10^{6} = \underline{\underline{0.45\,mA}}$

$P = 0.45(15) = \underline{\underline{6.75\,mW}}$

37

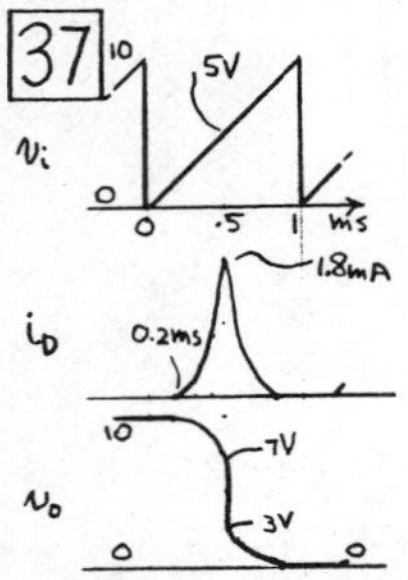

Gate is symmetric: $K = \frac{1}{2}(20)20 = 200\,\mu A/V^2$

i_D is 0 until $v_i = V_t = 2V$ at 0.2ms

At $v_i = 5$, $i_D = 200(5-2)^2 = 1.8\,mA$, the peak

$v_i = 4$, $i_D = 200(4-2)^2 = 0.8\,mA$

$v_i = 3$, $i_D = 200(3-2)^2 = 0.2\,mA$

Edge of pinchoff for $v_i = 5V$ is $5 \pm 2V$

During switching, charge transferred is

$$Q = 2\int_{0.2\times10^{-3}}^{0.5\times10^{-3}} i\,dt \quad \text{where } i = 200\times10^{-6}(v-2)^2 \text{ and } v = 0 + \frac{10t}{T} = 10^4 t$$

$$Q = 400\times10^{-6}\int_{0.2\times10^{-3}}^{0.5\times10^{-3}} (10^4 t - 2)^2\,dt$$

$$= 4\times10^{-4}\int_{2\times10^{-4}}^{5\times10^{-4}} (10^8 t^2 - 4\times10^4 t + 4)\,dt$$

$$= 4\times10^{-4}\left[\frac{10^8}{3}t^3 - 2\times10^4 t^2 + 4t\right]_{2\times10^{-4}}^{5\times10^{-4}}$$

$$= 4\times10^{-4}\left(\frac{10^8}{3}(10^{-9})(0.5^3-0.2^3) - 2(10^4)(10^{-6})(0.5^2-0.2^2) + 4(10^{-3})(0.5-0.2)\right)$$

$$= 4\times10^{-4}(10^{-3})(3.9 - 4.2 + 1.2) = 0.36\times10^{-6}\,C$$

Now average current $= \frac{0.36\times10^{-6}}{10^{-3}} = \underline{\underline{0.36\,mA}}$

Average power $= 10(0.36) = \underline{3.6\,mW}$ (from supply)

Peak current $= 200\times10^{-6}(10/2 - 2)^2 = \underline{1.8\,mA}$

Peak power for each device $= 1.8\,mA(5V) = \underline{\underline{9.0\,mW}}$

38 Eq 15.44

$$t_{PHL} = \frac{C}{K_n(V_{DD}-V_t)}\left[\frac{V_t}{V_{DD}-V_t} + \frac{1}{2}\ln\left(\frac{3V_{DD}-4V_t}{V_{DD}}\right)\right]$$

For $V_t = 0.1V_{DD}$

$$t_{PHL} = \frac{C}{K_n(0.9V_{DD})}\left(\frac{0.1}{0.9} + \frac{1}{2}\ln\left(\frac{3-0.4}{1}\right)\right) = \frac{0.654\,C}{K_n V_{DD}}$$

For $V_t = 0.2V_{DD}$, $t_{PHL} = \frac{C}{K_n V_{DD}}\times\frac{1}{0.8}\left(\frac{0.2}{0.8} + \frac{\ln 2.2}{2}\right) = \frac{0.805C}{K_n V_{DD}}$

For $V_t = 0.3V_{DD}$, $t_{PHL} = \frac{C}{K_n V_{DD}}\times\frac{1}{0.7}\left(\frac{0.3}{0.7} + \frac{\ln 1.8}{2}\right) = \frac{1.03C}{K_n V_{DD}}$

39 Refer to Fig 15.20. Let t_{THL1} denote the time for the output voltage to decrease from $0.9V_{DD}$ to $V_{DD} - V_t$. During t_{THL1}, the current in Q_H is constant at $K_n(V_{DD}-V_t)^2$, thus

$$t_{THL1} = \frac{C[0.9V_{DD} - (V_{DD}-V_t)]}{K_n(V_{DD}-V_t)^2} = \frac{C[V_t - 0.1V_{DD}]}{K_n(V_{DD}-V_t)^2} \quad \text{--- (1)}$$

For v_o below $(V_{DD}-V_t)$, Q_H operates in the triode region. The capacitor discharge is described by Eq (15.41):

$$\frac{K_n}{C}dt = \frac{1}{2(V_{DD}-V_t)}\times\frac{dv_o}{\frac{1}{2(V_{DD}-V_t)}v_o^2 - v_o}$$

To find t_{THL2}, the component of t_{THL} during which v_o decreases from $(V_{DD}-V_t)$ to $0.1V_{DD}$:

$$\frac{K_n}{C}t_{THL2} = \frac{1}{2(V_{DD}-V_t)}\int_{v_o=V_{DD}-V_t}^{v_o=0.1V_{DD}} \frac{dv_o}{\frac{1}{2(V_{DD}-V_t)}v_o^2 - v_o}$$

Now using $\int\frac{dx}{ax^2-x} = \ln(1 - 1/ax)$

$$\frac{K_n}{C}t_{THL2} = \frac{1}{2(V_{DD}-V_t)}\ln\left(1 - (2(V_{DD}-V_t))\frac{1}{v_o}\right)\Bigg]_{v_o=V_{DD}-V_t}^{v_o=0.1V_{DD}}$$

$$= \frac{1}{2(V_{DD}-V_t)}\left[\ln\left(1 - \frac{2(V_{DD}-V_t)}{0.1V_{DD}}\right) - \ln\left(1 - \frac{2(V_{DD}-V_t)}{V_{DD}-V_t}\right)\right]$$

$$= \frac{1}{2(V_{DD}-V_t)}\ln\left(\left(1 - \frac{2(V_{DD}-V_t)}{0.1V_{DD}}\right)\Big/(1-2)\right)$$

$$= \frac{1}{2(V_{DD}-V_t)}\ln\left(\frac{2(V_{DD}-V_t)}{0.1V_{DD}} - 1\right)$$

Thus $t_{THL2} = \frac{C}{2K_n(V_{DD}-V_t)}\ln\left[\frac{20(V_{DD}-V_t)}{V_{DD}} - 1\right]$ --- (2)

Now $t_{THL} = t_{THL1} + t_{THL2}$

ie $t_{THL} = \frac{C(V_t - 0.1V_{DD})}{K_n(V_{DD}-V_t)^2} + \frac{C}{2K_n(V_{DD}-V_t)}\ln\left(\frac{20(V_{DD}-V_t)}{V_{DD}} - 1\right)$

For the inverter in Exercise 15.18: $C = 0.1\,pF$

$K_n = \frac{1}{2}\times20\times10^{-6}\times\frac{10}{5} = 20\times10^{-6}\,A/V^2$, $V_{DD} = 5V$, $V_t = 1V$

$$\text{Thus } t_{THL} = \frac{0.1\times10^{-12}(1-0.5)}{20\times10^{-6}\times16} + \frac{0.1\times10^{-12}}{2\times20\times10^{-6}\times4}\ln\left(\frac{20\times4}{5} - 1\right)$$

$$= \left(\frac{50}{20\times16} + \frac{100}{8\times20}\ln 15\right)ns$$

$$= \left(0.16 + \frac{1}{1.6}\ln 15\right)ns = 0.16 + 1.69 = \underline{\underline{1.85\,ns}}$$

40 | 15

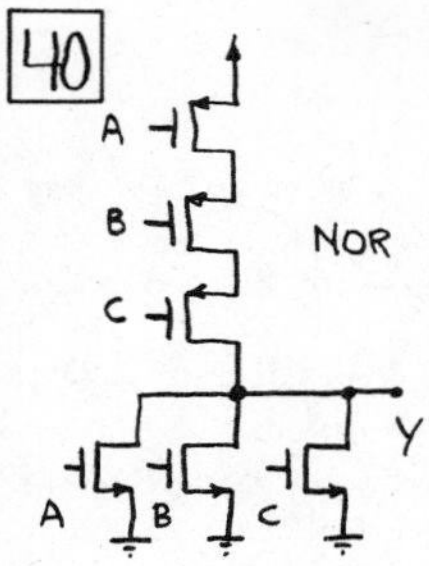

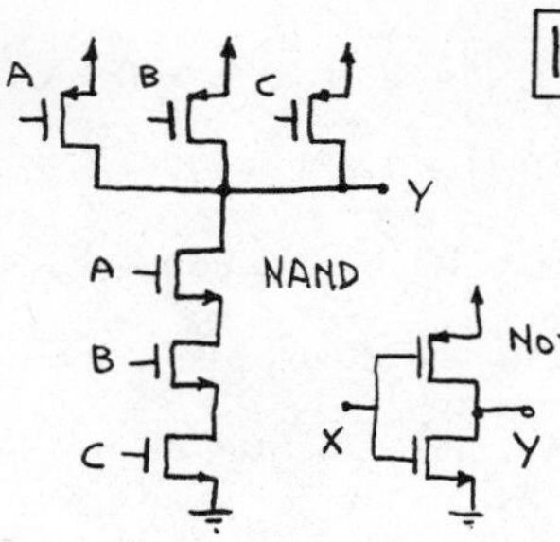

Basic device: $(W/L)_n = 2$, $L = 5\mu m \rightarrow W_n = 10\mu m$, $W_p = 20$

NOT: $W_n = 10\mu m$, $W_p = 20\mu m$, area $= 5(10+20) = 150\mu m^2$

NOR: $W_n = \underline{10\mu m}$, $W_p = \underline{60\mu m}$, area $= 3(5(10+60)) = \underline{1050\mu m^2}$

NAND: $W_n = \underline{30\mu m}$, $W_p = \underline{20\mu m}$, area $= 3(5(20+30)) = \underline{750\mu m^2}$

41

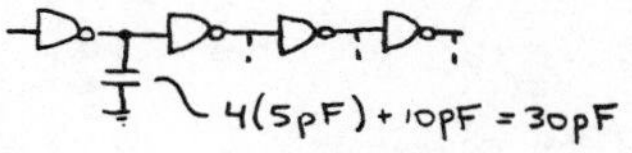

For each $t_P = (0.66\,ns/pF)C_L + 22\,ns$

Total Delay $= 4((0.66(30)) + 22) = \underline{167.2\,ns}$

42 $CV = IT$ | 15

Capacitor component current $I = \frac{50\times10^{-12} \times 10V}{10^{-3}s} = \underline{0.5\mu A/kHz}$

For $C_L = 0$, $I \simeq 0.6 - 0.5 = 0.1\mu A/kHz$

Now for 10V, 10^7 Hz, 100 pF

Current $= 10^4(0.1 + 2(0.5))10^{-6} = \underline{11\,mA}$

Power dissipation $= 10V(11mA) = \underline{110\,mA}$

43

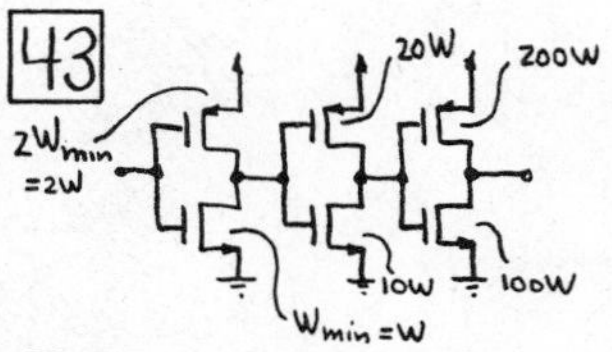

All devices have same length, L

For the simple inverter:

area $= LW(1+2)100 = 300LW$

For the buffered inverter, area $= LW(1+2+10+20+100+200)$

or 333 LW. Area ratio $= \frac{\text{Buffered}}{\text{Unbuffered}} = \frac{333}{300} = \underline{1.11}$

ie area increase (for devices alone) is $\underline{11\%}$

44 Unbuffered gate: $C_{in} = 5pF$, wiring $= 1pF$

Feedback Cap $= \frac{5-1}{50} = 0.08pF$. For Buffered gate:

$C_{in} = 1 + \frac{50(.08)}{10^2} = \underline{1.04pF}$, or less since input wiring smaller!

45 $K_n = \frac{1}{2}(20)\frac{12}{6} = 20\mu A/V^2$, $K_p = \frac{1}{2}(10)\frac{24}{6} = 20\mu A/V^2$ | 15

$|V_t| = 1V$, $V_{DD} = 5V$. Situation is symmetrical ($K_n = K_p = K$)

For $v_i = 2.5V$, for both devices in pinchoff, v_O ranges from $2.5 - 1 = 1.5V$ to $2.5 + 1 = 3.5V$.

(a)

For $v_i \geq 2.5V$, n channel device is in triode mode: $i = K(5 - v_i - 1)^2 = K(2(v_i - 1)v_O - v_O^2)$

or for $v_O = v$: $v^2 - 2v(v_i - 1) + (4 - v_i)^2 = 0$ --- (1)

For $v_i = 2.5V$: $v^2 - 3v + 2.25 = 0$

and $v = \frac{+3 \pm \sqrt{3^2 - 4(2.25)}}{2} = \underline{1.5V}$ {the edge of Pinchoff}

For $v_i = 2.75V$: $v^2 - 3.5v + 1.5625 = 0$

and $v = \frac{+3.5 \pm \sqrt{3.5^2 - 4(1.5625)}}{2} = \underline{0.525V}$

For $v_i = 3.0V$: $v^2 - 4v + 1 = 0$

and $v = \frac{4 \pm \sqrt{16 - 4(1)}}{2} = \underline{0.268V}$

For $v_i = 3.5V$: $v^2 - 5v + .25 = 0$

and $v = \frac{5 \pm \sqrt{25 - 1}}{2} = \underline{0.051V}$

For $v_i = 4.0V$: $v^2 - 6v + 0 = 0$

and $v = \underline{0V}$

From symmetry: for $v_i = 2.0$, 1.5, 1 | 15

$v_O = 5 - .268 = \underline{4.73}$, $5 - .051 = \underline{4.95}$, $5 - 0 = \underline{5}$ respectively

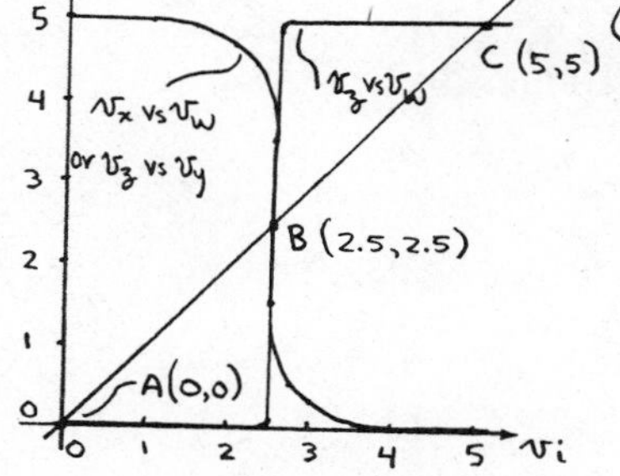

(b)

For v_Z vs v_W:

- when $v_W = 2.5$, v_X varies 1.5 to 3.5
- when v_Y is 1.5 or 3.5, v_Z is 4.95 or 0.05

(c) At B: $i_D = K(v_S - V_t)^2 = 20(2.5-1)^2 = 45\mu A$

$g_m = 20(2)(2.5-1) = 60\mu A/V$

$r_O = \frac{100V}{45\mu A} = \underline{2.22M\Omega}$

Gain per stage $= -(g_m \frac{r_O}{2} + g_m \frac{r_O}{2}) = -g_m r_O = -60 \times 2.\dot{2} = -133.\dot{3}$

Slope of the loop transfer characteristic is $(-133.\dot{3})^2 = \underline{17.8\times10^3\,V/V}$

Transition region width is $\frac{5-0}{133.3^2} = \underline{0.28mV}$

46 15

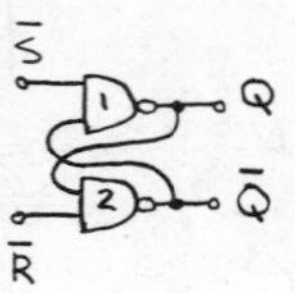

S	R	$\bar{S}$	$\bar{R}$	Q	$\bar{Q}$	Q_{n+1}
0	0	1	1	0/1	1/0	Q_n
0	1	1	0	0	1	0
1	0	0	1	1	0	1
1	1	0	0	0	0	?

47

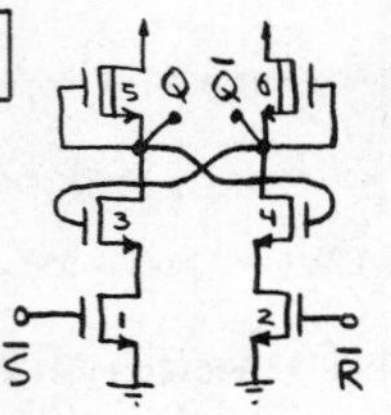

Rest state of $\bar{S}$, $\bar{R}$ is <u>high</u>

48

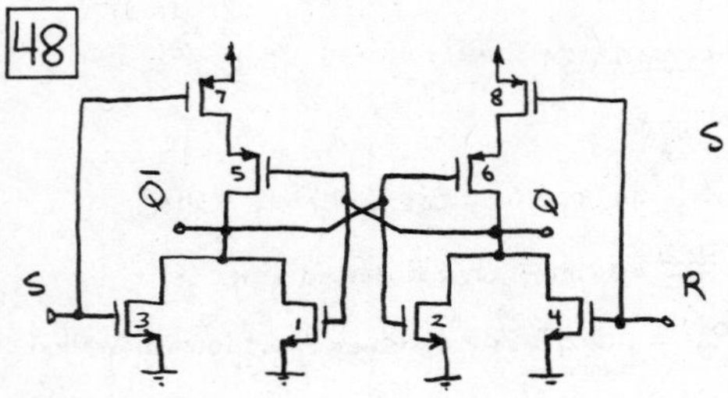

S, R rest <u>low</u>

49 15

Since $K_1 = K_2 = K_3 = K_4 = K$, bistable will regenerate into the reversed state when the common drain connection reaches $V_{critical}$ impelled by input current (say from Q5) while Q3 conducts, with its gate held at 0 momentarily by capacitance. Q5 operates in pinchoff while Q3 remains in triode op.

For triggering at $v_i = V_{DD}/2$ for $V_{critical} = V_{DD}/2$,

$$K5(2.5-1)^2 = K3[2(5-1)\times 2.5 - 2.5^2]$$

whence $\frac{K5}{K3} = \frac{20-6.25}{1.5^2} = 6.1$

<u>But</u> triggering requirement is actually somewhat less, since all that is required is that the drain of Q3 fall to $(V_{DD} - V_t - \epsilon)$ where Q4 begins to conduct enough to cause the loop gain to reach unity, while the gate of Q3 is still at ≈0V

For $\epsilon = 0$, $K5(2.5-1)^2 = K3[2[5-1]\times 1 - 1^2]$

whence $\frac{K5}{K3} = \frac{8-1}{1.5^2} = 3.1$. For $\epsilon > 0$ only a slightly larger ratio would be needed

50 15

CMOS

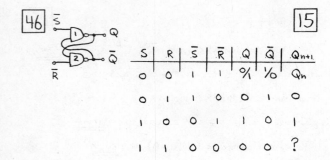

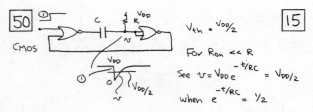

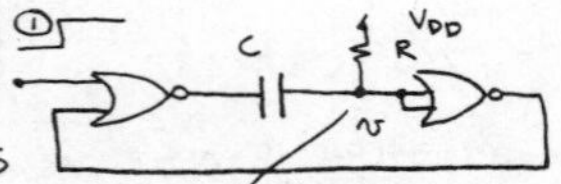

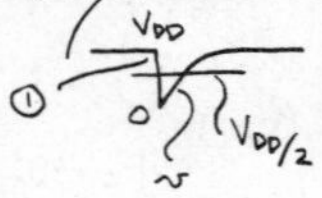

$V_{th} = V_{DD}/2$

For $R_{on} << R$

See $v = V_{DD} e^{-t/RC} = V_{DD}/2$

when $e^{-t/RC} = 1/2$

or $t = RC \ln 2$. Thus pulse interval $T = RC \ln 2 = \underline{0.693RC}$

(or) from Ex 15.24: $T = C(R+R_{on}) \ln\left(\frac{R}{R+R_{on}} \times \frac{V_{DD}}{V_{DD}-V_{th}}\right)$

See for $R_{on} << R$, $V_{th} = V_{DD}/2$, $T = C(R+0)\ln\left(\frac{R}{R+0} \times \frac{V_{DD}}{V_{DD}-V_{DD}/2}\right)$

or $T = RC \ln 2$ as found directly

51 $V_{DD} = 10$, $V_{th} = 5$, $R = 10k\Omega$, $R_{on} = 200\Omega$, $C = .001\mu F$

$T = C(R+R_{on}) \ln\left(\frac{R}{R+R_{on}} \times \frac{V_{DD}}{V_{DD}-V_{th}}\right)$

$= .001 \times 10^{-6}(10^4 + 200) \ln\left(\frac{10^4}{10^4+200} \times \frac{10}{10-5}\right) = \underline{\underline{6.86\mu s}}$

$\Delta V_1 = V_{DD} \frac{R}{R+R_{on}} = 10 \frac{10^4}{10^4+200} = \underline{9.8\ V}$

$\Delta V_2 = V_{DD} + V_{D1} - V_{th} = 10 + 0.7 - 5 = \underline{5.7\ V}$

Change in v_{O1} during T due to current in 200 Ω which changes from $\frac{10}{10k+200} = 0.98$ to $\frac{10-5}{10k} = 0.5$ mA. Change in v_{O1} is $200(0.98-0.50) = \underline{\underline{.096V}}$.

15

Peak current in G_1, as sink $= \frac{10}{10k+200} = \underline{\underline{0.98mA}}$

, as source $= \frac{10-0.5(200)-5-0.7}{200} = 21mA$

52 $T = C(R+R_{on}) \ln\left(\frac{R}{R+R_{on}} \times \frac{V_{DD}}{V_{DD}-V_{th}}\right)$

$R_{on} = 100\Omega$, $V_{DD} = 5V$, $V_{th} = 0.4(5) = 2V$, $C = 1\mu F$,

$T = 1s$, $R = ?$

Thus $1 = 10^{-6}(R+100) \ln\left(\frac{R}{R+100} \times \frac{5}{5-2}\right)$

See that R is large ≈ 1Meg, and $R_{on} <<< R$

$\therefore\ 1 = 10^{-6}(R) \ln\left(\frac{5}{3}\right)$

or $R = \frac{1 \times 10^6}{\ln 5/3} = \underline{\underline{1.96M\Omega}}$

53 Ex 15.25: $T = CR \ln\left(\frac{V_{DD}}{V_{DD}-V_{th}} + \frac{V_{DD}}{V_{th}}\right)$

$= .001 \times 10^{-6} \times 10^4 \ln\left(\frac{10}{10-10/2} + \frac{10}{10/2}\right)$

$= 13.86\mu sec$

$\therefore f = 1/T = \underline{\underline{72.1\ kHz}}$

1 $\alpha_F = 1.0$, $\alpha_R = 0.5$, $I_{SE} = 10^{-14}$ A **16**

$I_{SC} = \frac{\alpha_F I_{SE}}{\alpha_R} \simeq 2 I_{SE} = \underline{\underline{2\times10^{-14}\text{ A}}}$

Thus the collector junction is <u>twice as large</u> as EJ

See $\beta_R = \frac{\alpha_R}{1-\alpha_R} = \frac{0.5}{1-0.5} = \underline{\underline{1.0}}$

2

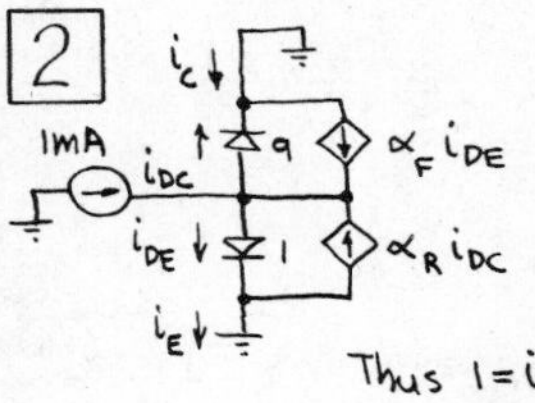

$\alpha_F \simeq 1.0$, $\alpha_R = \frac{\alpha_F I_{SE}}{I_{SC}} = 1\left(\frac{1}{9}\right) = .11$

Now at the base node, $\Sigma I = 0$

Thus $1 = i_{DC}(1-\alpha_R) + i_{DE}(\underbrace{1-\alpha_F}_{0}) = i_{DC}(1-\alpha_R)$

ie $i_{DC} = \frac{1}{1-\alpha_R} = \frac{1}{1-1/9} = \frac{9}{8} = 1.125$ mA.

The using the area ratio $i_{DE} = \frac{1}{9}(1.125)$ mA $= 0.125$ mA

Now $\alpha_F i_{DE} = 1 \times 0.125 = 0.125$ mA

$\alpha_R i_{DC} = 1/9\,(9/8) = 1/8 = 0.125$ mA

Check: $9/8 + 1/8 - 1/8 - 1/8 = 1$ as provided ✓

3 Eq. 16.15 → $i_B = \frac{I_S}{\beta_F} e^{v_{BE}/V_T} - \underbrace{I_S\left(\frac{1}{\beta_F} + \frac{1}{\beta_R}\right)}_{\text{small}}$ **16**

ie $i_B \approx \frac{I_S}{\beta_F} e^{v_{BE}/V_T}$

Now $\beta_F = \frac{\alpha_F}{1-\alpha_F} = \frac{0.99}{1-0.99} = 99$; $I_S = 10^{-15}$ A

$\therefore\ 10\times10^{-6} = \frac{10^{-15}}{99} e^{v_{BE}/V_T} \rightarrow v_{BE} = 25 \ln \frac{990\times10^{-6}}{10^{-15}} = \underline{\underline{690.5\text{ mV}}}$

For $\alpha = 0.98$, $\beta_F = \frac{0.98}{1-0.98} = 49$

and $v_{BE} = 25 \ln 490\times10^{9} = \underline{\underline{672.9\text{ mV}}}$

4 $i_E = 1$ mA ; Eq. 15.6 → $i_E \approx I_S/\alpha_F\, e^{v_{BE}/V_T}$

For $\alpha = 0.99$, $v_{BE} = 25 \ln \frac{(0.99)10^{-3}}{10^{-15}} = \underline{690.5\text{ mV}}$

For $\alpha = 0.98$, $v_{BE} = 25 \ln (0.98)10^{12} = \underline{690.3\text{ mV}}$

5

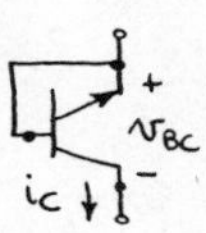

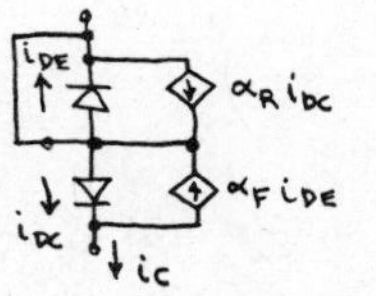

$i_C = i_{DC} - \alpha_F i_{DE}$

ie $i_C = I_{SC}(e^{v_{BC}/V_T} - 1) - \alpha_F I_{SE}(e^{v_{BE}/V_T} - 1)$, but $v_{BE} = 0$

$\therefore\ i_C = I_{SC}(e^{v_{BC}/V_T} - 1) - \alpha_F I_{SE}(1-1) = I_{SC}(e^{v_{BC}/V_T} - 1)$

or $\boxed{i_C = \frac{I_S}{\alpha}(e^{v_{BC}/V_T} - 1)}$

6 **16**

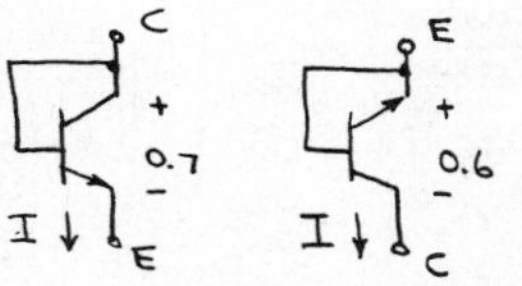

$i_E = I_{SE}(e^{v_{BE}/V_T} - 1) = I = i_C = I_{SC}(e^{v_{BC}/V_T} - 1)$

For forward conduction: $I_{SC} = I_{SE}\, e^{\frac{v_{BE}-v_{BC}}{V_T}}$

or $I_{SC} = I_{SE}\, e^{\frac{0.7-0.6}{V_T}} = I_{SE}\, e^{\frac{100}{25}} = 54.6\, I_{SC}$

Thus the collector junction is <u>54.6</u> times size of emitter

7 Eq. 16.16 : $V_{CEsat} = V_T \ln \frac{1 + (\beta_{forced}+1)/\beta_R}{1 - \beta_{forced}/\beta_F}$

Now $\beta_{forced} \approx 0$:

For Q_1: $\beta_F = 100$, $\beta_R = 1$

$V_{CEsat} = 25 \ln \frac{1+1/1}{1-0/100} = 25 \ln \frac{2}{1} = \underline{\underline{17.3\text{ mV}}}$

For Q_2: $\beta_F = \beta_R = 20$

$V_{CEsat} = 25 \ln \frac{1+1/20}{1-0} = 25 \ln 1.05 = \underline{\underline{1.22\text{ mV}}}$

For Q_3: $\beta_F = 1$, $\beta_R = 100$

$V_{CEsat} = 25 \ln \frac{1+1/100}{1} = 25 \ln 1.01 = \underline{\underline{0.25\text{ mV}}}$

8 $r_{CEsat} = \frac{(150-100)\text{mV}}{(20-2)\text{mA}} = \underline{2.78\ \Omega}$ **16**

$V_{CEsat} = V_T \ln \frac{1 + (\beta_{forced}+1)/\beta_R}{1 - \beta_{forced}/\beta_F}$

For $\beta_{forced} = \frac{2}{1} = 2 \rightarrow 100 = 25 \ln \frac{1 + 3/\beta_R}{1 - 2/\beta_F}$

For $\beta_{forced} = \frac{20}{1} = 20 \rightarrow 150 = 25 \ln \frac{1 + 21/\beta_R}{1 - 20/\beta_F}$

Thus $1 + 3/\beta_R = (1 - 2/\beta_F)e^4 = 54.6(1 - 2/\beta_F)$

$1 + 21/\beta_R = (1 - 20/\beta_F)e^6 = 403.4(1 - 20/\beta_F)$

Whence $3/\beta_R = 53.6 - 109.2/\beta_F$

and $1 + 21/\beta_R = 1 + 7(53.6 - 109.2/\beta_F) = 403.4 - 8068/\beta_F$

or $7304/\beta_F = 403.4 - 1 - 375.2 = 27.2 \rightarrow \beta_F = \frac{7304}{27.2} = \underline{\underline{268.5}}$

and $3/\beta_R = 53.6 - \frac{109.2}{268.5} \rightarrow \beta_R = \underline{\underline{0.056}}$

Check: $V_{CEsat} = 25 \ln\left(\frac{1 + (2+1)/0.056}{1 - 2/268.5}\right) = 100$ mV ✓

Thus Offset Voltage $= 100\text{ mV} - 2\text{mA}(2.78\Omega) = \underline{\underline{94.4\text{ mV}}}$

9 | 16

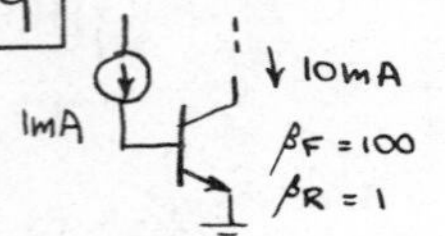

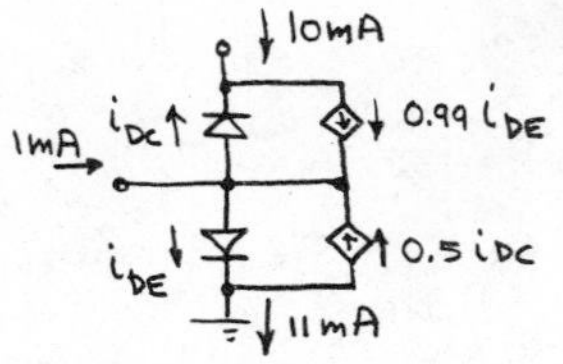

$\alpha = \frac{\beta}{\beta+1}$:

$\alpha_F = \frac{100}{101} = 0.99$, $\alpha_R = \frac{1}{1+1} = 0.5$

See $i_{DE} = 11 + 0.5\,i_{DC}$

and $i_{DC} + 10 = 0.99\,i_{DE} = 0.99\,(11 + 0.5\,i_{DC})$

$= 10.89 + 0.495\,i_{DC}$

Thus $0.505\,i_{DC} = 0.89 \rightarrow i_{DC} = \underline{\underline{1.76\text{ mA}}}$, $i_{DE} = \underline{\underline{11.88\text{ mA}}}$

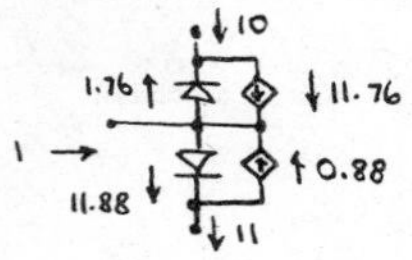

10

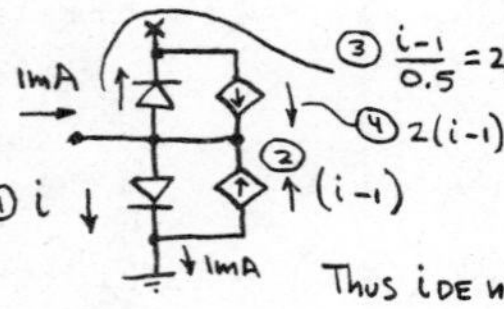

③ $\frac{i-1}{0.5} = 2(i-1)$ Now $0.99\,i = 2(i-1) = 2i-2$

Thus $1.01\,i = 2 \rightarrow i = 1.98\text{ mA}$

Thus i_{DE} now 1.98 mA

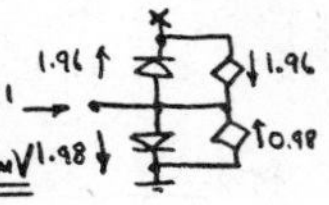

But i_{DE} was 11.88 mA $\rightarrow V_{BE}$ drops by $V_T \ln \frac{1.98}{11.88} = \underline{\underline{44.8\text{ mV}}}$

11 | 16

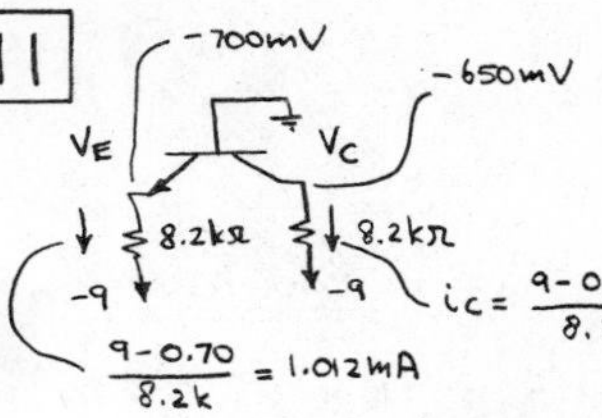

Assume β_F large

ie $\alpha_F = 1$

$i_C = \frac{9-0.65}{8.2k} = 1.018\text{ mA}$

$\frac{9-0.70}{8.2k} = 1.012\text{ mA}$

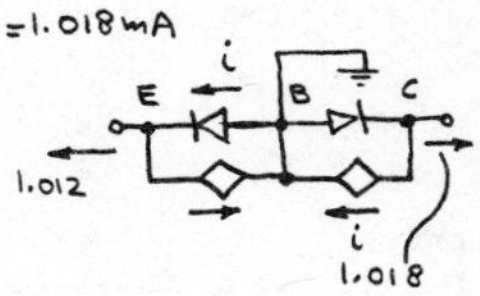

See $1.012 = i_{DE} - \alpha_R i_{DC}$ -- ①

$1.018 = i_{DC} - i_{DE}$ -- ②

Add: $i_B = 2.03 = (1-\alpha_R)\,i_{DC}$ -- ③

Now $\alpha_R I_{SC} = \alpha_F I_{SE} \approx I_{SE}$

and $i_{DE} = I_{SE}\,e^{700/V_T} = I_{SE}\,(1.446 \times 10^{12})$

$i_{DC} = I_{SC}\,e^{650/V_T} = \frac{I_{SE}}{\alpha_R}\,(1.957 \times 10^{11})$

Thus $i_{DE} = i_{DC}\,(\alpha_R)\,7.39$

From ② : $1.018 = i_{DC} - i_{DC}(\alpha_R)7.39 \rightarrow i_{DC} = \frac{1.018}{1-7.39\alpha_R}$

with ③ : $2.03 = \frac{(1-\alpha_R)\,1.018}{1-7.39\alpha_R}$

whence $2.03 - 2.03(7.39\alpha_R) = 1.018 - 1.018\alpha_R \rightarrow \alpha_R = 0.072$

and $\beta_R = \frac{\alpha_R}{1-\alpha_R} = \underline{\underline{0.078}}$

Alternatively: $\beta_{forced} = \frac{-1.018}{1.012+1.018} = -0.5$; $V_{CEsat} = V_T \ln \frac{1+(\beta_f+1)/\beta_R}{1-\beta_f/\beta_F}$

ie $100-650 \approx 25 \ln\left(1 + \frac{1-0.5}{\beta_R}\right) \rightarrow \beta_R = \frac{0.5}{e^2-1} = \underline{\underline{0.078}}$

12 | 16

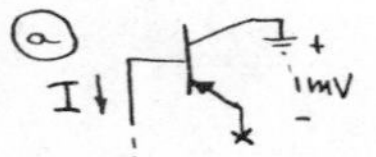

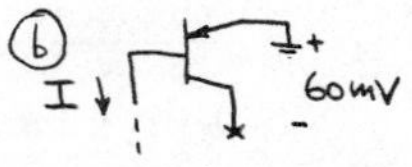

Eq. 16.16 : $V_{CEsat} = V_T \ln \frac{1 + (\beta_{forced}+1)/\beta_R}{1 - \beta_{forced}/\beta_F}$ -- ①

(a) Two approaches are possible :

i) Use ① with β_F and β_R reversed , with $\beta_{forced} = 0$

ie. $1 = 25 \ln\left(\frac{1 + (0+1)/\beta_F}{1-0}\right)$

or $1 + 1/\beta_F = e^{1/25} = 1.0408 \rightarrow \beta_F = \frac{1}{.0408} = \underline{\underline{24.5}}$

ii) Use ① directly with $\beta_{forced} = -1$ and $V_{CEsat} = -1\text{mV}$

ie. $-1 = 25 \ln\left(\frac{1 + (1-1)/\beta_R}{1-(-1)/\beta_F}\right) = 25 \ln(1 + 1/\beta_F)$

$\therefore \ln(1 + 1/\beta_F) = \frac{1}{25}$ or $\beta_F = \underline{\underline{24.5}}$ (as before)

(b) Directly: $60 = 25 \ln(1 + 1/\beta_R)$

or $1 + 1/\beta_R = e^{60/25} = 11.02 \rightarrow 1/\beta_R = 10.02$, $\beta_R = \underline{\underline{0.10}}$

13 $t_s = \tau_s \frac{I_{B2} - I_{CS}/\beta}{I_{B1} + I_{CS}/\beta}$

(a) For $I_B = 1\text{mA}$, excess base charge $= 20 \times 10^{-9}\left(1 - \frac{10}{100}\right) \times 10^{-3} = \underline{\underline{18\text{ pC}}}$

(b) For $I_B = 0.11\text{mA}$, excess base charge $= 20 \times 10^{-9}\left(0.11 - \frac{10}{100}\right) \times 10^{-3} = \underline{\underline{0.2\text{ pC}}}$

For (a) , $t_s = \frac{20(1-0.1)}{0.1+0.1} = \underline{\underline{90\text{ ns}}}$; For (b) , $t_s = \frac{20(.11-0.1)}{0.1+0.1} = \underline{\underline{1\text{ ns}}}$

14 | 16

$t_s = \tau_s \frac{I_{B2} - I_{CS}/\beta}{I_{B1} + I_{CS}/\beta}$

Now for $I_{B2} \gg I_{CS}/\beta$ and $I_{B1} = I_{B2}$, $t_s = 10\text{ns}$

Thus $\tau_s = \frac{t_s\,(I_{B1} + I_{CS}/\beta)}{(I_{B2} - I_{CS}/\beta)} = \frac{10\,(I_{B1}+0)}{(I_{B1}-0)} = \underline{\underline{10\text{ns}}}$

Now for a forward base current of 1mA and high β

with a reverse current of 0.25 mA, $t = \frac{10 \cdot 1}{0.25} = \underline{\underline{40\text{ns}}}$

15

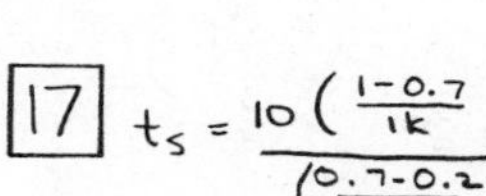

$t_s = 10\text{ns}\left(\frac{\frac{1-0.7}{1k} - 0}{\frac{0.7-0.2}{1k} + 0}\right)$

$= 10\,(0.3/0.5) = \underline{\underline{6\text{ ns}}}$

16 $t_s = \frac{10\left(\frac{10-0.7}{1k} - 0\right)}{\left(\frac{0.7-0}{1k} + 0\right)} = \frac{10(9.3)}{0.7} = \underline{\underline{133\text{ ns}}}$

17 $t_s = \frac{10\left(\frac{1-0.7}{1k} - \frac{20}{100}\right)}{\left(\frac{0.7-0.2}{1k} + \frac{20}{100}\right)} = \frac{10(0.3-0.2)}{(0.5+0.2)} = \underline{\underline{1.43\text{ns}}}$

18 **16**

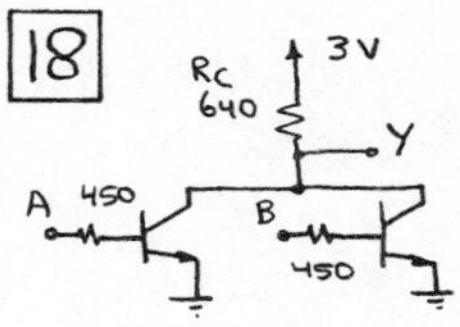

$v_B = 0,\ \beta_R = 0.1,\ \beta_F = 50$

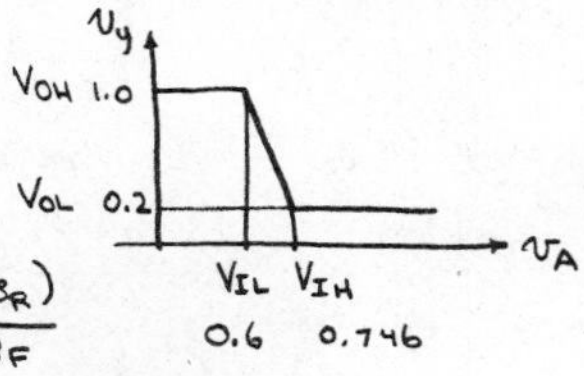

For V_{IH}:

$$V_{CEsat} = V_T \ln \frac{(1+(\beta_{forced}+1)/\beta_R)}{1-\beta_{forced}/\beta_F}$$

Thus $\dfrac{1+(\beta_f+1)/0.1}{1-\beta_f/50} = e^{\frac{200}{25}} = 2981$

ie $1 + 10\beta_f + 10 = 2981 - 59.6\beta_f \rightarrow \beta_f = \dfrac{2970}{69.6} = \underline{42.7}$

Now $V_{IH} = 0.7 + 0.45\left(\dfrac{3-0.2}{0.64}\right)/42.7 = \underline{0.746\,V}$

For NM: See $NM_H = 1.0 - 0.746 = \underline{0.254}$ V

$NM_L = 0.6 - 0.2 = \underline{0.40}$ V

19 (a) $I_{RC} = \dfrac{3-0.2}{0.640} = \underline{4.375\ mA}$

P_D in the low output state $= 3(4.375) = \underline{13.125 mW}$

(b) For $V_{OH} = 1V$, $I_{RC} = \dfrac{3-1}{0.640} = \underline{3.125 mA}$

$P_D = 3(3.125) = \underline{9.375\ mW}$

(c) Av power $= P_{AV} = (13.125 + 9.375)/2 = \underline{11.25}$ mW

(d) For $t_p = 10ns$, $DP = 10 \times 11.25 = \underline{112.5\ pJ}$

20 For Fig. 16.10, Assume $v_i = 0/4$, $v_o = 4/0$ **16**

v_i high: For +4V, $i_{R1} = \dfrac{4-3(0.7)}{2k} = 0.95 mA$

$i_{RC} = \dfrac{4-0}{4k} = 1.00 mA$ } $\underline{1.95 mA}$ total

For −2V, $i_{R2} = \dfrac{2+0.7}{5k} = \underline{0.54 mA}$

$P_D = 1.95(4) + 0.54(2) = \underline{8.88\ mW}$

v_i low: For +4V, $i_{R1} = \dfrac{4-0.7}{2k} = \underline{1.65 mA}$

For −2V, $i_{R2} = \dfrac{2-0.7}{5k} = \underline{0.26 mA}$

$P_D = 1.65(4) + 0.26(2) = \underline{7.12\ mW}$

Average power $= P_{AV} = (8.88 + 7.12)/2 = \underline{7.5 mW}$

21

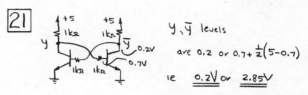

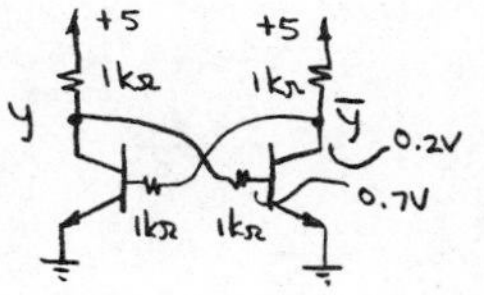

$Y, \bar{Y}$ levels are 0.2 or $0.7 + \frac{1}{2}(5-0.7)$

ie $\underline{0.2V}$ or $\underline{2.85V}$

22

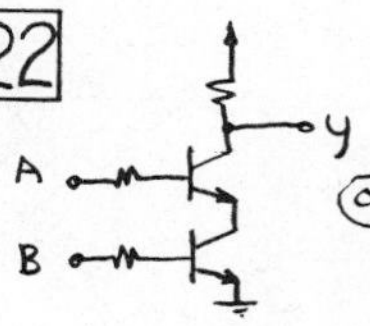

$Y = \bar{A} \vee \bar{B} = \overline{A \cdot B}$, ie NAND

(or) $\bar{Y} = A \cdot B \rightarrow Y = \overline{A \cdot B}$, ie NAND

23 **16**

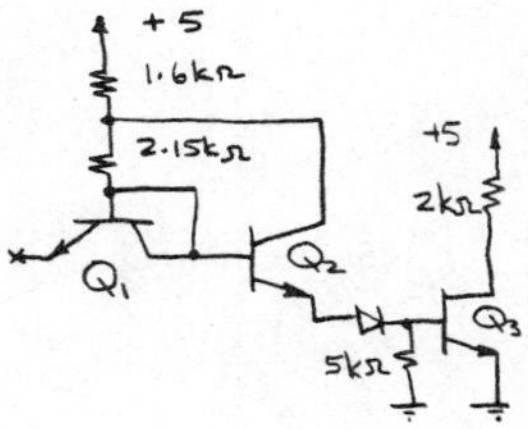

$\beta = 100$, $V_{BE} = 0.7V$

$i_{B3} = \dfrac{5-3(0.7)}{1.6 + \frac{2.15}{101}} - \dfrac{0.7}{5}$

$= 1.789 - 0.14 = \underline{1.65 mA}$

For Q_3, turnoff current $= \dfrac{0.7}{5k} = \underline{0.14 mA}$

Thus for turnoff, $t = 10 \times \dfrac{1.65 - \frac{5}{2k} \times \frac{1}{100}}{0.14 + \frac{5}{2k} \times \frac{1}{100}} = \dfrac{10(16.25)}{0.14 + .025} = \underline{98.5}$ ns

24 $\beta = \infty$, $V_{CEsat} = 0.2V$, $v_i = 0.2V$ or $5V$

$v_i = 5V$: $I_S = \dfrac{5-3(0.7)}{1.6k} + \dfrac{5-0.2}{2k} = \underline{4.21\ mA}$

(since the current in 2.15kΩ is zero)

$v_i = 0.2V$: $I_S = \dfrac{5-0.2-0.7}{1.6k+2.15k} = \underline{1.09 mA}$

Overall: $I_{Sav} = (4.21 + 1.09)/2 = \underline{2.65 mA}$

$P_{Dav} = 5(2.65) = \underline{13.3\ mW}$

25 **16**

$I_{Csat} = \dfrac{5-0.2}{2k} = 2.4 mA$, $I_{Bsat} = \dfrac{2.4}{\beta}$

Required base current $I_B = 4 I_{Bsat} = 9.6/\beta$

Current from $Q_2 = I_{E2} = 9.6/\beta + \dfrac{0.7}{5k} = \dfrac{9.6}{\beta} + 0.14$

But $I_{E2} = \dfrac{5-3(0.7)}{1.6 + 2.15/(\beta+1)}$

Thus $\dfrac{2.9}{1.6 + 2.15/(\beta+1)} = \dfrac{9.6}{\beta} + 0.14$

or $\dfrac{9.6 + .14\beta}{\beta} = \dfrac{2.9(\beta+1)}{1.6(\beta+1) + 2.15}$

or $9.6(1.6)(\beta+1) + 9.6 \times 2.15 + .14\beta(1.6)(\beta+1) + .14\beta(2.15) = 2.9\beta(\beta+1)$

or $15.36\beta + 15.36 + 20.64 + .224\beta^2 + .224\beta + .301\beta - 2.9\beta^2 - 2.9\beta = 0$

ie $\beta^2(2.676) - \beta(12.985) - 36 = 0$

whence $\beta = \dfrac{12.985 \pm \sqrt{12.985^2 + 4(36)(2.676)}}{2(2.676)} = 6.82$

ie minimum $\underline{\beta = 6.82}$

26

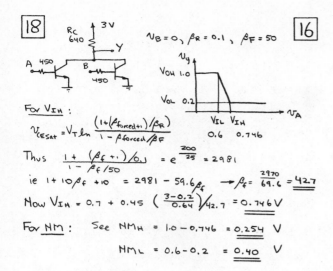

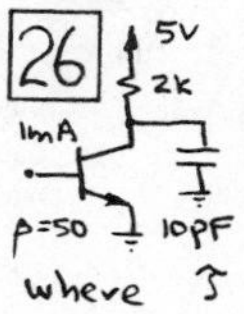

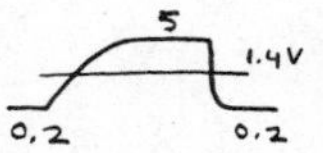

Rising Edge $v = 5 - 4.8e^{-t/\tau}$

(or) $v = 0.2 + (5-0.2)(1 - e^{-t/\tau})$

where $\tau = 2 \times 10^{3} \times 10 \times 10^{-12} = 20ns \rightarrow v = 5 - 4.8e^{-t_1/20} = 1.4$

whence $t_1 = -20 \ln \dfrac{3.6}{4.8} = 20(.288) = \underline{5.75 ns}$

(next)

16

Falling Edge : Output heads for 5 − 2k(1×50) or −95V, that is $v = 5 - (100)(1 - e^{-t/\tau})$

or $v = -95 + 100 e^{-t/\tau} = 1.4V$, whence

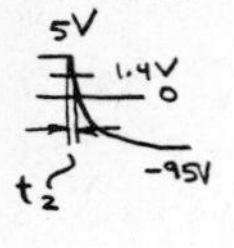

$t_2 = 20 \ln \frac{100}{96.4} = \underline{\underline{0.73\ ns}}$

27

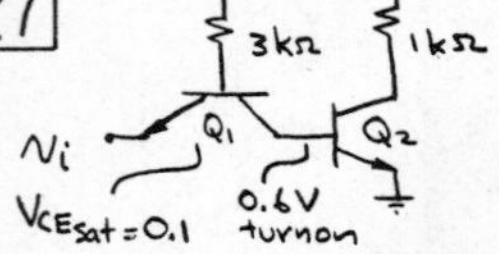

$V_{IL} = 0.6 - 0.1 = \underline{0.5V}$

28

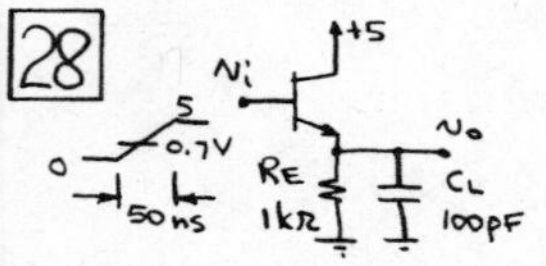

$\text{Delay} = \frac{0.7V}{5V} \times 50ns = \underline{7ns}$

$V_{o\,max} = 5 - 0.7 = \underline{\underline{4.3V}}$

$i_E = \frac{v_o}{R_E} + C\frac{dv_o}{dt}$

I_{Epeak} occurs just at ramp top $= \frac{4.3}{1k} + 100\times10^{-12} \times \frac{5V}{50\times10^{-9}}$

ie $I_{Ep} = \underline{\underline{14.3 mA}}$

29 16

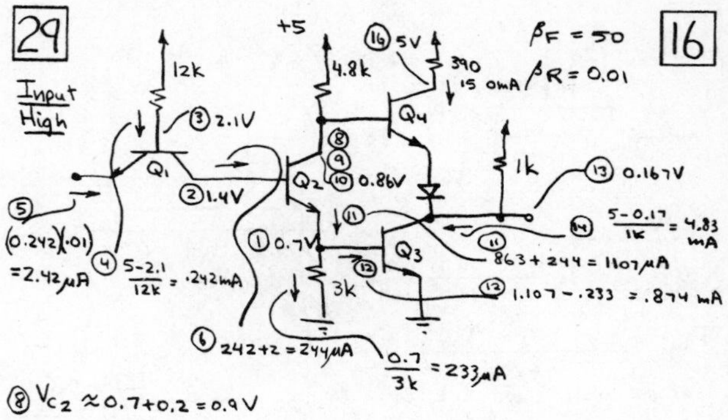

⑧ $V_{C2} \approx 0.7 + 0.2 = 0.9V$

⑨ $I_{C2} = \frac{5-0.9}{4.8k} = 0.854\,mA \rightarrow \beta_{forced\,2} = \frac{854}{244} = 3.5 = \beta f$

$V_{CEsat_2} = V_T \ln \frac{(1 + (\beta_f + 1)/\beta_R)}{(1 - \beta f/\beta_F)} = V_T \ln \frac{1 + 4.5/.01}{1 - 3.5/30} = 156mV$

⑩ $I_{C2} = \frac{5 - 0.7 - 0.16}{4.8k} = 0.863\,mA$

⑫ $V_{CE3} \approx 0.2$, $I_{C3} = \frac{5 - 0.2}{1k} = 4.8\,mA$

$\beta_{forced\,3} = \frac{4.8}{.874} = 5.49$, $V_{CEsat_3} = V_T \ln \frac{1 + 6.49/.01}{1 - 5.49/30} = 167mV$

30 16

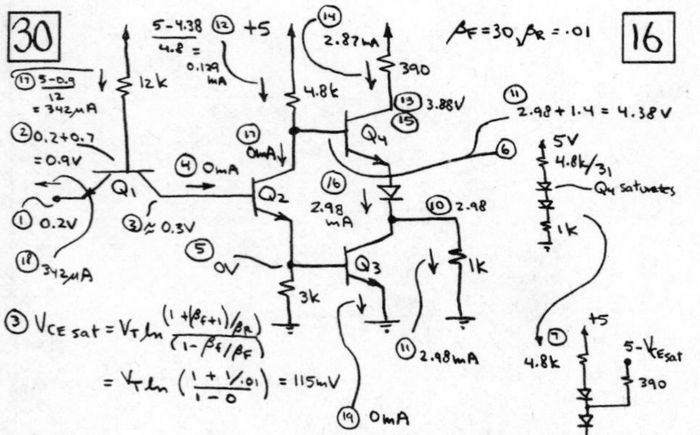

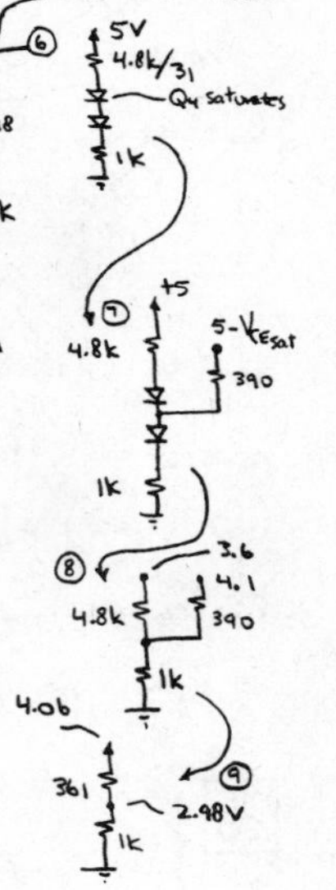

③ $V_{CE\,sat} = V_T \ln \frac{(1 + (\beta_f + 1)/\beta_R)}{(1 - \beta_f/\beta_F)}$

$= V_T \ln\left(\frac{1 + 1/.01}{1 - 0}\right) = 115mV$

⑬ $V_{C4} \approx 2.98 + 0.7 + 0.2 = 3.88V$

⑭ $(5 - 3.88)/390 = 2.87\,mA$

⑮ $\beta_{f_4} = \frac{2.87}{.129} = 22.25$

$V_{CEsat4} = V_T \ln \frac{(1 + (23.25)/.01)}{(1 - 22.25/30)} = .228V$ ≈ OK

31 16

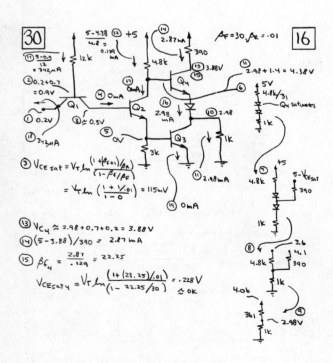

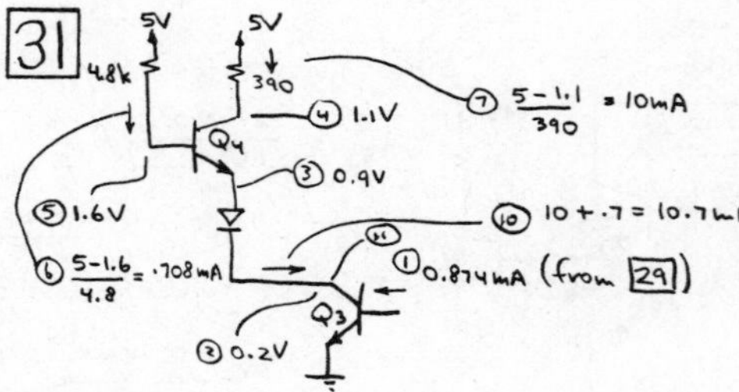

⑦ $\frac{5 - 1.1}{390} = 10mA$

⑩ $10 + .7 = 10.7mA$

① 0.874mA (from 29)

⑧ $\beta_{f_4} = \frac{10}{.708} = 14.1$

⑨ $V_{CEsat4} = V_T \ln\left(\frac{1 + (14.1+1)/.01}{1 - 14.1/30}\right) = 199\,mV$ ✓

⑪ $\beta_{f_3} = \frac{10.7}{.874} = 12.25 \rightarrow V_{CEsat3} = V_T \ln\left(\frac{1 + 13.25/.01}{1 - 12.25/30}\right) = .193V$ ✓

∴ <u>10.7 mA</u> flows in short circuit

32 For $i_L = 0, 1, 10, 100$ mA and $i_B = 2.5$ mA,

$\beta_{forced} = \beta_f = 0, 0.4, 4, 40$

Now $V_{CE\,sat} = V_T \ln\left(\frac{1 + (\beta_f + 1)/\beta_R}{1 - \beta_f/\beta_F}\right)$ for $\beta_F = 50$, $\beta_R = 5$

For $i_L = 0mA$, $\frac{1 + 1/5}{1} = 1.2 \rightarrow \underline{4.56\,mV}$

1, $\frac{1 + 1.4/5}{1 - 0.4/50} = \frac{1.28}{.992} = 1.29 \rightarrow \underline{6.37\,mV}$

10, $\frac{1 + 5/5}{1 - 4/50} = \frac{2}{.92} = 2.17 \rightarrow \underline{19.4\,mV}$

100, $\frac{1 + 41/5}{1 - 40/50} = \frac{9.2}{0.2} = 46 \rightarrow \underline{\underline{95.7\,mV}}$

16

Now at 0.5 mA, $R_{CEsat} = \frac{6.37 - 4.56}{1} = \underline{\underline{1.81\Omega}}$

5 mA, $R_{CEsat} = \frac{19.4 - 6.4}{9} = \underline{\underline{1.44\Omega}}$

50 mA, $R_{CEsat} = \frac{95.7 - 19.4}{90} = \underline{\underline{0.85\Omega}}$

33

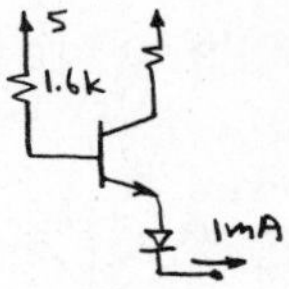

$v_o = 5 - 0.7 - 0.7 - \frac{1mA}{51}(1.6k) = \underline{\underline{3.57V}}$

$r_o = 25 + 25 + \frac{1.6k}{51} = \underline{\underline{81.4\Omega}}$

34 (a) For $\beta = \infty$, $V_{CEsat} = 0.2$, Q_4 saturates

at $\frac{0.7 - 0.2}{130} = \underline{\underline{3.85 mA}}$

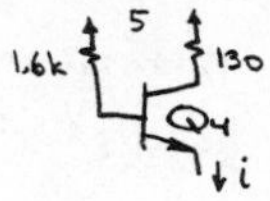

(b) For $\beta = 20$, Saturation for

$1.6k \frac{i}{21} - 0.13 i \frac{20}{21} = 0.7 - 0.2 \rightarrow 1.6i - 2.6i = 10.5$

or $i = \underline{\underline{10.5 mA}}$

35 For shorted output: $i_S = \frac{5 - 0.2 - 0.7}{130} = \underline{\underline{31.5 mA}}$

$i_B = \frac{5 - 1.4}{1.6k} = 2.25 mA$

$\beta_{min} = \frac{31.5}{2.25} = \underline{\underline{14}}$

36

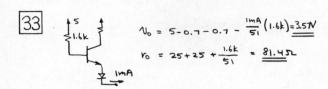

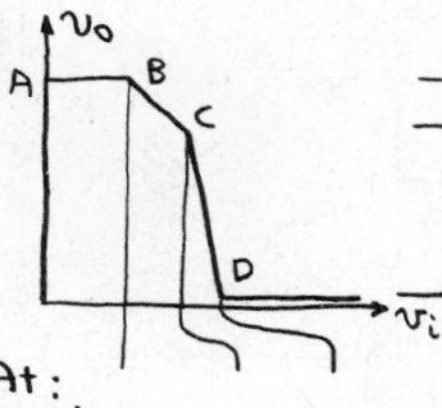

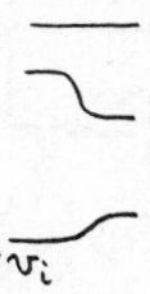

At:	25°C	−55°C	125°C
	3.70	3.38	4.10
	2.70	2.16	3.46
	0.10	0.10	0.10

16

At:

25°C	0.50	1.20	1.40
−55°C	0.66	1.52	1.72
125°C	0.30	0.80	1.00

25°C: $NM_L = 0.5 - 0.1 = 0.4V$

$NM_H = 3.7 - 1.4 = 2.3V$

−55°C: $NM_L = 0.66 - 0.10 = \underline{\underline{0.56V}}$

$NM_H = 3.38 - 1.72 = \underline{\underline{1.66V}}$

125°C $NM_L = 0.30 - 0.10 = \underline{\underline{0.20V}}$

$NM_H = 4.10 - 1.00 = \underline{\underline{3.10V}}$

37 For the supply: $I_{AV} = \frac{5+3}{2} = 4mA$, $P_{AV} = 5 \times 4 = 20mW$

Delay $T_{PAV} = \frac{18+12}{2} = 15ns$; $DP = 20 \times 10^{-3} \times 15 \times 10^{-9} = \underline{\underline{300pJ}}$

38 For inputs high, $I_{B1} = \frac{5 - 3(0.7)}{4k} = 0.725 mA$

Additional current per input $= 0.725 \times \beta_R = 0.725 \times 0.04 = \underline{\underline{29\mu A}}$

For 8 inputs extra current to base of Q_2 is $8(29) = \underline{\underline{232\mu A}}$

39 Any input high lowers output X. **16**

ie $\overline{X} = A \vee B \vee C \rightarrow X = \overline{A \vee B \vee C}$, a NOR Function

Alternatively: All inputs must be low to raise the output: ie $X = \bar{A}.\bar{B}.\bar{C} = \overline{A \vee B \vee C}$ by De Morgans Law

40 Q_7 turns off when Q_6 conducts $\frac{5-1.4}{4k} = \underline{\underline{0.9mA}}$

for which $V_{B6} = 1.4V$ and $v_{in} = \underline{\underline{1.4V}}$

41 (a) See Y is low if A is high or B and C are both high, ie $\overline{Y} = A \vee B.C \rightarrow \underline{\underline{Y = \overline{A \vee B.C}}}$

(or) Y is high if A is low and one or both of B or C is low, ie $Y = \bar{A}.(\bar{B} \vee \bar{C})$. These are equivalent by De Morgan's Law, ie $\overline{A \vee B.C} = \bar{A}.(\overline{B.C})$

$= \bar{A}.(\bar{B} \vee \bar{C})$

(b) V_{OL} produced when schottky diode in Q_1 conducts

ie $V_{OL} = 0.8 - 0.5 = \underline{\underline{0.3V}}$

V_{OH} produced by D_6, D_7 conducting, ie $V_{OH} = 0.5 + 0.8 = \underline{\underline{1.3V}}$

(c) **16**

For V_{IL}, Q_1 is at edge of conduction and D_1, D_4 (say) are conducting, ie $V_{IL} = 0.7 + 0.5 - 0.5 = \underline{\underline{0.7V}}$

For V_{IH}, Q_1 and D_4 are conducting heavily and D_1 begins to conduct, ie $V_{IH} = 0.8 + 0.5 - 0.5 = 0.8V$

(d) $NM_H = 1.3 - 0.8 = 0.5V$

$NM_L = 0.7 - 0.3 = 0.4V$

(e) For inputs low, $I_{supply} = \frac{2(2.5 - 0.5 - 0.3)}{4k} + \frac{2.5 - 1.3}{6k}$

ie $I_S = 0.85 + 0.20 = 1.05 mA$

For one input low, one high,

$I_S = \frac{1(2.5 - 0.5 - 0.3)}{4k} + \frac{1(2.5 - 0.8 - 0.5)}{4k} + \frac{2.5 - 0.3}{4k}$

$= 0.425 + 0.30 + 0.367 = 1.092 mA$

For inputs high, $I_S = 0.367 + 2(0.30) = 0.967 mA$

For which the smallest is 0.967 mA

the largest is 1.092 mA

the average is 1.03 mA

the variability is ±.06 mA

the result is 1.03 mA ± 5.7%

43 — 16

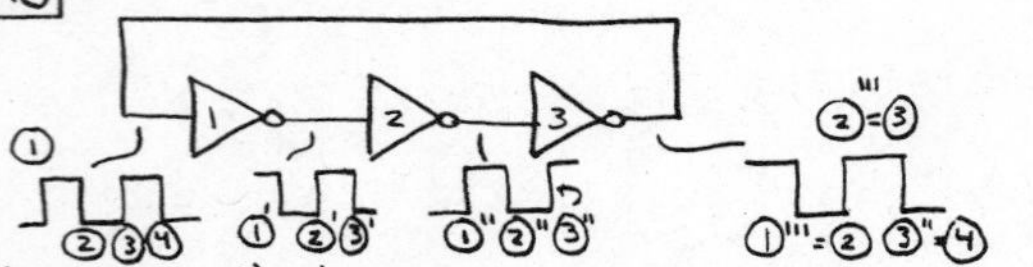

Notation: i) circled numbers indicate relative time, ① preceeding ②, etc

ii) prime notation indicates passage, thru a single stage of logic, of a generating event. For example ①' is induced by ① and follows it by one logic gate delay, while ①'' succeeds ①' correspondingly

iii) numbers may be in direct sequence, or with gaps intervening. Gaps are typically used to indicated independence or (at least) an unknown or uncertain relationship. Gaps allow for the retrospective insertion of new events.

iv) equivalence notation may be used to simplify notation, while emphasizing relationship and order. Thus ①''' = ② indicates a notable event, called ② which is initiated by ① and follows it by 3 logic delays.

Here, an initial rising transient at ①, propagates to create ②, 3 delay units later, then ③, 3 delay units later still, but of the same polarity as the event ①. Thus one cycle is of 6 delays duration. If, as in this case delay depends on the direction of change of signal level, then there are 3 of one and 3 of the other in a single cycle.

ie $f_{osc} = \dfrac{1}{3(3ns)+3(7ns)} = \dfrac{1}{30ns} = \underline{\underline{33.3\,MHz}}$

(or), following the signal transitions,

$f_{osc} = \dfrac{1}{3+7+3+7+3+7}$, with the same result.

44 — 16

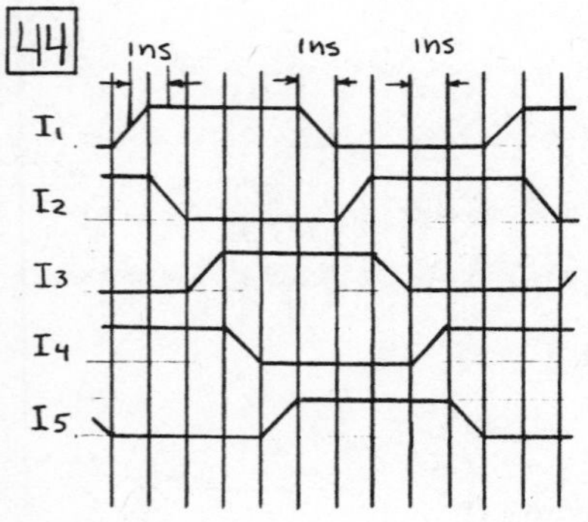

For:

rise time 1ns

fall time 1ns

prop. delay 1ns

See:

period = 2(5)1 = 10ns

$f_{osc} = \dfrac{1}{T} = 100\,MHz$

That is $Freq = f_{osc} = \dfrac{1}{2 \times 5 \times t_p} = \underline{\underline{100\,MHz}}$

45

$Y = \bar{A}B \vee A\bar{B} = \overline{A \vee \bar{B}} \vee \overline{\bar{A} \vee B}$

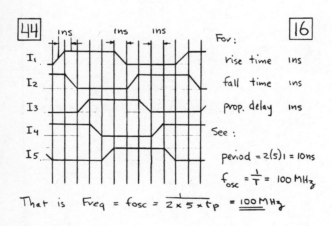

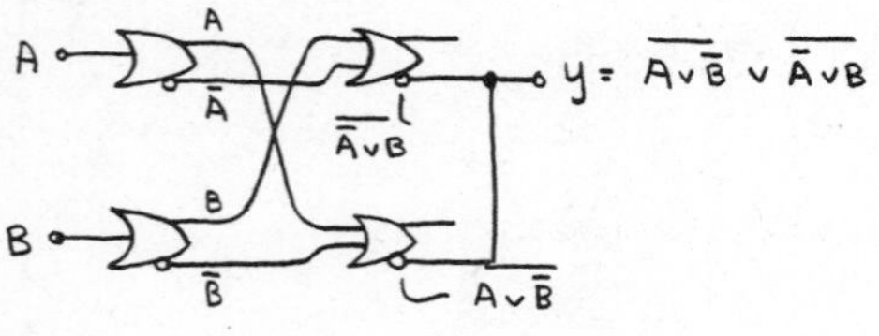

46 — 16

$\beta = 100$

At m: $I = \dfrac{-1.32 - 0.75 + 5.2}{779} = 4.02mA$, $r_{e_R} = \dfrac{V_T}{4.02/2} = 12.44\Omega$

$V_{O_m} \approx -1.32V \rightarrow I_{E2} = \dfrac{+2-1.32}{50} = 13.6mA$, $r_{e_2} = \dfrac{25}{13.6} = 1.84\Omega$

$Gain_m = \dfrac{100}{101}\,\dfrac{(245 \,\|\, 101(1.8+50))}{2(12.44)} \times \dfrac{50}{50+1.84}$

$= \dfrac{0.99(234)}{24.88} \times \dfrac{50}{51.8} = \underline{\underline{8.99}}\ V/V$

At x: $I_R = 0.99\,I$, $I_A = 0.01\,I$

$\therefore r_{e_R} = \dfrac{25}{4.02} = 6.28\Omega$, $r_{e_A} = 622\Omega$

$V_{O_L} \approx -1.77V \rightarrow I_{E2} = \dfrac{2-1.77}{50} = 4.6mA$, $r_{e_2} = 5.43\Omega$

$Gain_x = 0.99\left(\dfrac{245 \,\|\, 101(55.4)}{622+6.3}\right) \times \dfrac{50}{55.4} = \underline{\underline{0.34}}\ V/V$

At y: $I_R = 0.01\,I$, $I_A = 0.99\,I$

$r_{e_R} = 622\Omega$, $r_{e_A} = 6.28\Omega$

$V_{OH} \approx -0.88V \rightarrow I_{E2} = \dfrac{2-0.88}{50} = 22.4mA$, $r_{e2} = \dfrac{25}{22.4} = 1.12\Omega$

$Gain_y = 0.99\left(\dfrac{245 \,\|\, 101(51.1)}{622+6.3}\right) \times \dfrac{50}{51.1}$

$= 0.99\dfrac{(234)}{628.3} \times \dfrac{50}{51.1} = \underline{\underline{0.36}}\ V/V$

47 (a) 90% switching: **16**

$V_T \ln \frac{0.9}{1} = 2.63$, $V_T \ln \frac{0.1}{1} = 57.56$ } difference $= 54.9$ mV

$\therefore V_{IH} = .0549 - 1.32 = \underline{\underline{-1.265V}}$

$V_{IL} = -.0549 - 1.32 = \underline{\underline{-1.375V}}$

(b) 99.9% switching:

$V_T \ln 0.999 = .025$, $V_T \ln .001 = 172.7$ } difference $= 173$ mV

$\therefore V_{IH} = -1.32 + .173 = \underline{\underline{-1.147V}}$

$V_{IL} = -1.32 - .173 = \underline{\underline{-1.493V}}$

48 $V_{OH} = -0.88V$, $I_L = \frac{2-0.88}{50} = 22.4$ mA

$V_{OL} = -1.77V$, $I_L = \frac{2-1.77}{50} = 4.6$ mA

Power Lost: Resistors: $22.4(1.12) + 4.6(.23) = 26.16$ mW

Transistors: $22.4(0.88) + 4.6(1.77) = 27.8$ mW

50k: $2\frac{(5.2-1.32)^2}{50k} = 0.6$ mW

-5.2V supply: $\frac{-1.32-0.75+5.2}{779} \times 5.2 = 20.9$ mW

Total Power Loss $= 26.2 + 27.8 + 0.6 + 20.9 = \underline{\underline{75.5\text{ mW}}}$

49 $NM_H = 0.325$ **16**

For $\beta = 100$ ⟶

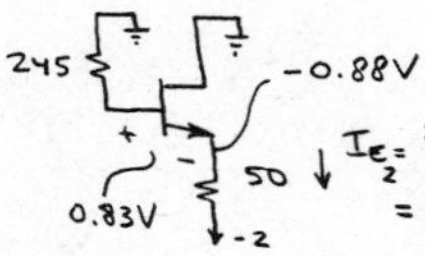

$I_{E_2} = \frac{2-0.88}{50} = 22.4$ mA

Now as β lowers and V_{E2} drops by $\frac{.325}{2} = 0.162V$, I_{E2} lowers by $\frac{.162}{50} = 3.2$ mA

and V_{BE} changes from 0.83 by $25 \ln \frac{22.4-3.2}{22.4} = -4$ mV to .826 V: Thus $\frac{245}{245+50(\beta+1)} \times (2-.826) = .88 - .826 + .162$

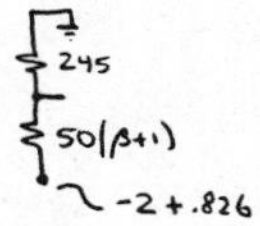

or $52.9 + 10.8(\beta+1) = 288$

$(\beta+1) = 21.7 \rightarrow \beta = 20.7$

50

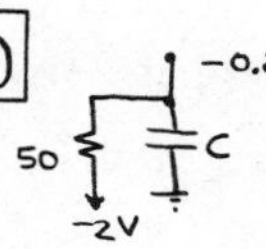

$V_o = -0.88 - (2.0 - 0.88)(1 - e^{-t/\tau}) = -1.77$

Now in 1ns, $-e^{-1/\tau} = \frac{-1.77+0.88}{-2.00+0.88} - 1 = -.205$

ie $e^{-1/\tau} = .205 \rightarrow -1/\tau = -1.585$

$\tau = \frac{1}{1.585} = .631$ ns

Thus $C = \frac{0.631}{50} = \underline{\underline{12.6\text{ pF}}}$

51 Propagation at $2/3(30) = 20$ cm/ns **16**

For 3.5 ns, line length $= \frac{3.5}{2(5)} = 0.35$ ns

equivalent to $20(0.35) = \underline{\underline{7\text{cm}}}$ long

52 E is low if (A and B) or (C and D) are low

ie $\bar{E} = \bar{A}.\bar{B} \vee \bar{C}.\bar{D} \rightarrow E = \overline{\bar{A}\bar{B} \vee \bar{C}\bar{D}}$

(or) E is high if (A or B) and (C or D) are high

ie $E = (A \vee B).(C \vee D)$

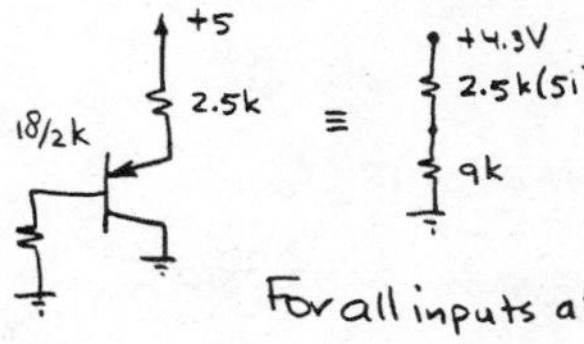

$\frac{9k}{2.5k(51)+9k} \times 4.3V = 0.284V$

For all inputs at 0V, $V_E = 0.7 + 0.284 = \underline{\underline{0.984V}}$

For A, C at +5V, $V_E = \underline{\underline{+5V}}$

EXTRA EXAM AND DESIGN PROBLEMS

EXAM AND DESIGN PROBLEMS

PREAMBLE

The Exam and Design questions which follow are inevitably of somewhat variable length and complexity.

Generally speaking, it is possible to remove parts and/or provide intermediate results, to reduce the length of an Exam question, or to add a constraint (as revealed in the long answer) to limit the scope of a Design.

(next)

If the answer to a part of an exam question seems unduly complex, yet the part is too interesting/important/exciting/peculiar/perverse to eliminate, the judious addition of the word approximate(ly) or its ilk, will allow the student more latitude in estimating a result. Note in general that answers provided are often more complex than maybe expected from a usual student, in order that a basis for evaluating the more thoughtful student be available.

Finally, note that design answers (A) are also inevitably less than complete!

1 Exam **1**

An AM broadcast station operates at a center (carrier) frequency of 1010kHz within an assigned band whose total width is 10kHz. What are the upper and lower frequency limits of this station's transmissions? What is the highest frequency square wave for which the first four non-zero harmonic components are transmitted? At what two broadcast-band frequencies does energy from the third harmonic of a 1kHz square wave appear? For a signal consisting of a single sine wave at 1kHz, and a modulation index, m, of 0.5, what fraction of the total energy transmitted lies in the sidebands?

(A) For AM transmission of a sine-wave signal at ω_s: $v_{AM}(t) = \hat{V}_c \cos \omega_c t + \frac{1}{2} m \hat{V}_c \left[\cos(\omega_c + \omega_s)t + \cos(\omega_c - \omega_s)t\right]$ **1**

Upper sideband edge $= 1010 + 10/2 = \underline{\underline{1015}}$ kHz

Lower sideband edge $= 1010 - 10/2 = \underline{\underline{1005}}$ kHz

Specified square wave of frequency f has frequency components at f, 3f, 5f, 7f

To (barely) accomodate 7f, 7f = 5000Hz, the square-wave fundamental can be no higher than $f = \frac{5000}{7} = \underline{\underline{714}}$ Hz. Perhaps to account for attenation at the band edge, one could consider a limitation of square-wave fundamental to 700 Hz for which the 7th harmonic (ie the 4th non-zero harmonic component) is 4.9kHz

The 3rd harmonic of 1kHz is at 3kHz, for which the corresponding band freq. are $\underline{\underline{1013}}$ and $\underline{\underline{1007}}$ kHz

For m=0.5, $\frac{\text{sideband energy}}{\text{total energy}} = \frac{(m/2)^2 + (m/2)^2}{1 + (m/2)^2 + (m/2)^2} = \frac{2(1/4)^2}{1 + 2(1/4)^2} = \underline{\underline{1/9}}$

1 **Design** 1

Design a Time-Division Multiplexing (TDM) System having 16 channels, each capable of faithfully reproducing at least 4 of the non-zero components of a 1kHz square wave. What is the required sampling rate and maximum sampling interval?

(A) For a 1kHz square wave, components exist at 1, 3, 5, 7 kHz. Thus a channel must be at least 7kHz wide. Input data must be sampled at 14 kHz or more. For 16 channels, the total sampling rate must be 14×16 = 224kHz and the sampling interval must be $\frac{1}{224\times10^3}$ = 4.5 μs or less.

1 **Exam** 2

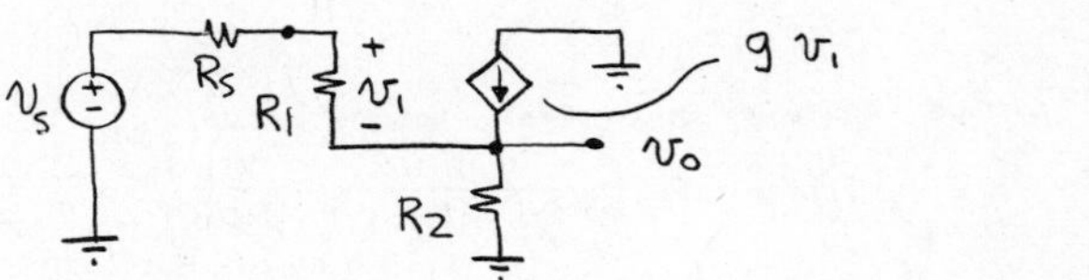

For the amplifier whose equivalent circuit is shown, find a Thevenin equivalent characterization in terms of v_s, R_s, R_1, R_2 and g. Use this with $R_s = R_1 = R_2 = 9/g = 10k\Omega$, to find v_o/v_s for an external load of 10kΩ.

(A) At the output node, $\frac{v_o}{R_2} = g v_1 + \frac{v_1}{R_1} = v_1\left(g + \frac{1}{R_1}\right)$

Thus $v_1 = \frac{v_o}{R_2 g + R_2/R_1}$

and $v_s = v_1 + v_o + \frac{v_1}{R_1}\times R_s = v_o + v_1(1 + R_s/R_1)$

$\therefore\ v_s = v_o\left(1 + \frac{1 + R_s/R_1}{R_2 g + R_2/R_1}\right) = v_o\left(1 + \frac{R_1 + R_s}{R_2(1+gR_1)}\right)$

Thus the Thevenin source voltage, $V_T = v_o$,

is $\boxed{V_T = \frac{R_2(1+gR_1)}{R_1 + R_s + R_2(1+gR_1)} \times v_s}$ 2

Now, short the output:

See $i_{os} = \frac{v_s}{R_s + R_1} + g v_1 = v_s\left(\frac{1}{R_s+R_1} + \frac{gR_1}{R_s+R_1}\right)$

or $i_{os} = \frac{1+gR_1}{R_s+R_1} \times v_s$

Thus the Thevenin source resistance, $R_T = \frac{V_T}{i_{os}}$,

is $R_T = \frac{R_2(R_s+R_1)}{R_1 + R_s + R_2(1+gR_1)} = \frac{R_2 \times \frac{R_s+R_1}{1+gR_1}}{R_2 + \frac{R_s+R_1}{1+gR_1}}$

or $\boxed{R_T = R_2 \| \left(\frac{R_s+R_1}{1+R_1 g}\right)}$

For $R_s = R_1 = R_2 = 9/g = 10k\Omega$ → $g = 9\times10^{-4}$

$V_T = \frac{10^4(1 + 9\times10^{-4}\times10^4)}{10^4 + 10^4 + 10^4(1+9\times10^{-4}\times10^4)} v_s = 0.8\dot{3}\, v_s$

$R_T = 10^4 \| \frac{10^4+10^4}{1+10^4\times9\times10^{-4}} = 10^4\|(0.2\times10^4) = 0.1\dot{6}\, k\Omega$

Thus $\left.\frac{v_o}{v_s}\right|_{\substack{10k\Omega \\ load}} = \frac{10^4}{10^4(1+0.1\dot{6})} \times 0.8\dot{3}\, v_s = \underline{\underline{0.714\ V/V}}$

2 **Exam** 2

Characterize the following circuit as a single time constant (STC) network using Miller's Theorem. For a positive pulse input of 5μs duration and 10mV peak, rising from 0V, sketch and label the output, providing values of rise and fall times, sag, overshoot and peak values where appropriate. What is the upper 3dB frequency of the v_o/v_s transfer characteristic.

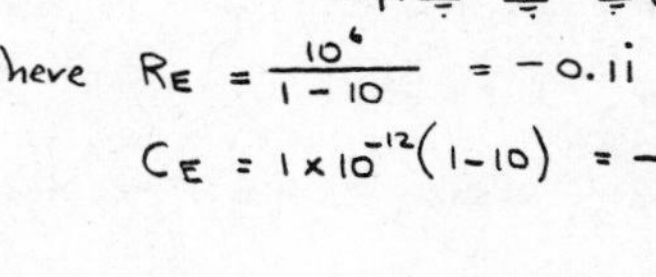

(A) ⇒

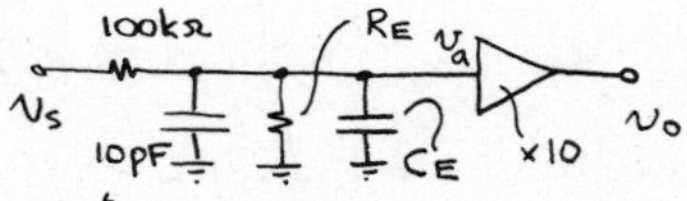

where $R_E = \frac{10^6}{1-10} = -0.1\dot{1}\ M\Omega$

$C_E = 1\times10^{-12}(1-10) = -9pF$

2

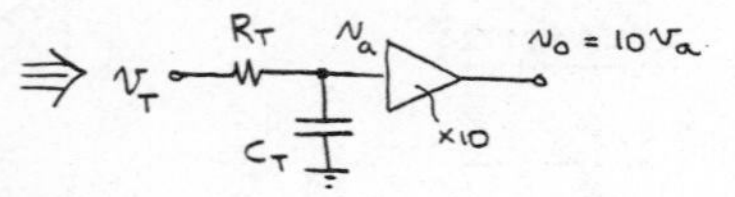

For the Thevenin equivalent input network:

$$v_T = \frac{R_E}{100k + R_E} \times v_s = \frac{-0.11\, v_s}{0.1 + (-0.11)} = \frac{0.11}{0.011} v_s = \underline{\underline{10 v_s}}$$

$$R_T = 100k \| R_E = 0.1M \| (-0.11M) = \frac{0.1(-0.11)}{0.1 - 0.11} = \frac{-.011M}{-.011} = \underline{\underline{1M}}$$

$$C_T = 10pF + C_E = 10 + (-9) = \underline{\underline{1pF}}$$

See an STC circuit with overall low-frequency gain of 100 V/V and $\tau = R_T C_T = 10^6 \times 1 \times 10^{-12} = 10^{-6} s = \underline{\underline{1 \mu s}}$

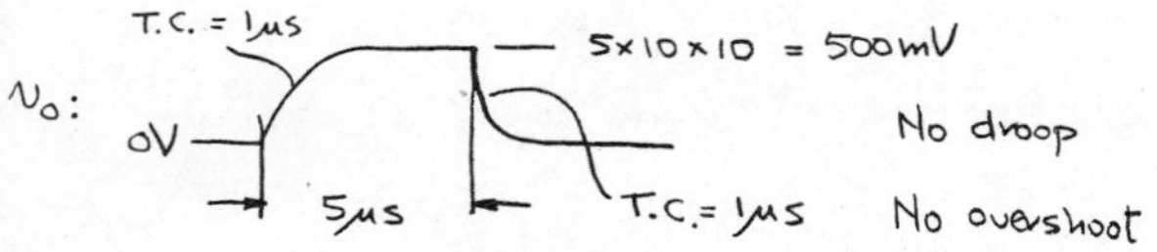

$$f_{3dB} = \frac{1}{2\pi \times 10^{-6}} = \underline{\underline{159 kHz}}$$

1 **Design** 2

Design a 3-stage amplifier to provide maximum voltage gain from a source whose output resistance is 1MΩ to a load of 10Ω. The available amplifier components are as follows:

Type	Gain (V/V)	Rin (Ω)	Rout (Ω)
ⓐ	10	1M	10
ⓑ	10	100k	1
ⓒ	100	100k	1k
ⓓ	1	10M	100
ⓔ	1000	100	100

- (Optionally, allow more than one amplifier of one type in a single design)
- What gain v_o/v_s does your design provide?

Ⓐ 2

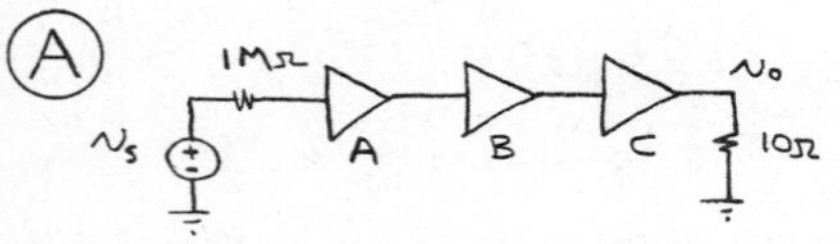

Several different design strategies are possible: The first uses a set of local optimizations; the second is somewhat more global; the third assumes that multiple units of one type are available. Finally .... !

For convenience amplifiers are named by a 3-tuple $x_A x_B x_C$ where each x is one of ⓐ through ⓔ.

Strategy 1:

① For the input stage, A, use the highest available input resistance. Thus choose ⓓ

② For the output stage, C, use the lowest available output resistance. Thus choose ⓑ

③ For the intermediate stage, B, use the stage which combines high Rin, low Rout and high gain. Thus consider ⓒ. This choice is generally less obvious than the others!

2

Thus consider the amplifier dcb, for which

$$v_o/v_s = 1 \times 100 \times 10 \times \frac{10^7}{10^7 + 10^6} \times \frac{10^5}{10^5 + 10^2} \times \frac{10^5}{10^5 + 10^5} \times \frac{10}{10+1} = \underline{\underline{413 V/V}}$$

Note generally that the process is iterative, and that in particular available intermediate stages, B, might motivate a second choice for A or C.

Thus consider the amplifier dca, for which

$$v_o/v_s = 1 \times 100 \times 10 \times \frac{10^7}{10^7 + 10^6} \times \frac{10^5}{10^5 + 10^2} \times \frac{10^6}{10^6 + 10^3} \times \frac{10}{10+10} = \underline{\underline{454}}$$

Clearly dca is superior to dcb although this was not particularly obvious.

Strategy 2: Look for the highest available gain (ie ⓔ) and place it in the most appropriate position. Since it has a very low input resistance, it should not be chosen for A. Since its output resistance is high (100 Ω) it is not ideal for C. 2

Thus consider amplifier deb:

$$v_o/v_s = 1\times 1000\times 10\times\frac{10^7}{10^7+10^6}\times\frac{100}{100+100}\times\frac{10^5}{10^5+10^2}\times\frac{10}{10+1} = 4132\ \text{V/V}$$

Strategy 3: Considering that multiple units of a single amplifier type are available, and even desirable if quantity pricing is considered, select the one with the highest gain.

Thus consider amplifier eee

$$v_o/v_s = 10^3\times 10^3\times 10^3\times\frac{10^2}{10^2+10^6}\times\frac{10^2}{10^2+10^2}\times\frac{10^2}{10^2+10^2}\times\frac{10}{10+100} = 2273\ \text{V/V}$$

Alternatively (using the next highest gain) consider ccc

$$v_o/v_s = 10^2\times 10^2\times 10^2\times\frac{10^5}{10^5+10^6}\times\frac{10^5}{10^5+10^3}\times\frac{10^5}{10^5+10^3}\times\frac{10}{10+10^3} = 9706\ \text{V/V}$$

See that the gain is higher since the input and output resistances are more appropriate!

Strategy 4: Consider writing a program to tabulate all possible combinations of stages. How many are there? What is the largest available gain?

1 Exam 3

For the circuit shown, using an op amp whose characteristics are ideal, unless otherwise specified:

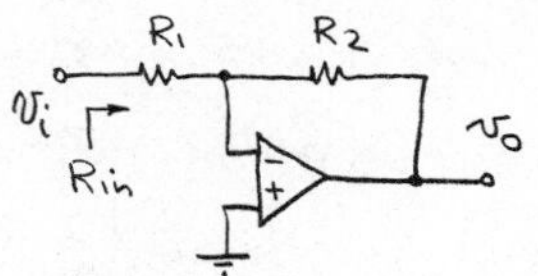

(a) What is the nominal gain v_o/v_i for $R_1 = 10\,k\Omega$, $R_2 = 100\,k\Omega$?

(b) What is the input resistance R_{in} for $R_1 = 1\,k\Omega$, $R_2 = 100\,k\Omega$?

(c) Choose R_1 and R_2 for a gain of -10 V/V and an input resistance of $100\,k\Omega$.

(d) For output saturation levels of ± 12 V, $R_1 = 10\,k\Omega$, $R_2 = 100\,k\Omega$ and $v_i = +2$ V, what is the current drawn from the input?

(e) If the ratio R_2/R_1 is chosen for a nominal gain of -10 V/V using an ideal amplifier, what is the actual gain of the overall circuit if an amplifier having a gain of 100 is used? 3

(f) For $R_2 = 1\,M\Omega$ and $R_1 = 10\,k\Omega$ and an amplifier whose input offset voltage is 1mV and bias current is 1μA, what total output offset voltage can result?

(g) For the situation described in (f), what bias-current compensation resistor is needed?

(h) With compensation as in (g) and offset current of 0.1μA, what total output offset can result (including the effect of input voltage offset)

A (a) $\frac{v_o}{v_i} = -\frac{R_2}{R_1} = -\frac{100k}{10k} = -10\ \text{V/V}$

(b) The negative terminal is virtual ground, thus $R_{in} = R_1 = 1\,k\Omega$

(c) $R_2/R_1 = 10$ and $R_1 = 100k \rightarrow R_2 = 10(100k) = 1M\Omega$

3

(d)

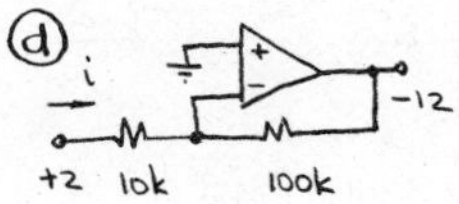

$$i = \frac{2-(-12)}{10k+100k} = 0.127\ \text{mA}$$

(e) $$\frac{v_o}{v_i} = \frac{-R_2/R_1}{1+(1+R_2/R_1)/A}$$

For a nominal gain of -10, $R_2/R_1 = 10$

and $$\frac{v_o}{v_i} = \frac{-10}{1+(1+10)/100} = \frac{-10}{1+11/100} = -9.009\ \text{V/V}$$

(f)

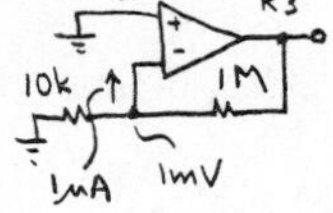

$$\text{Output offset} = 1mV\left(1+\frac{1M}{10k}\right)+1\mu A(1M) = 10^{-3}(101)+1 = 1.101\ \text{V}$$

(g) To compensate, $R_3 = R_1 \| R_2 = 10k \| 1M = 9.9\,k\Omega$ or $R_3 \simeq 10\,k\Omega$

(h) Compensated output offset
$$= (V_{io}+I_{io}R_3)\left(1+\frac{R_2}{R_1}\right) = \left(10^{-3}+10^{-7}(10^4)\right)\left(1+\frac{10^6}{10^4}\right) = 2\times 10^{-3}(101) = 0.202\ \text{V}$$

1 | Design/Exam | 3

The design is required of an amplifier having a gain of $-1000\ V/V$, an input resistance of $1\,M\Omega$ or more, the greatest possible bandwidth and a reasonable output offset. A quad op-amp is available for which each of the 4 op-amps have $A = 10^5$ and $f_t = 1\,MHz$. Bias current is $1\,nA$ or less and offset current $1/10$ as large. Input offset voltage is to be ignored (It can be assumed to be compensated by some unspecified means). The largest available precision resistor is $1\,M\Omega$. Consider designs with 1, 2, 3 op amps. In the case of multiple op amps, be careful to calculate the actual 3dB frequency. (Specify one of the topologies identified next for Exam use.)

Ⓐ Some possible topologies can be identified by considering the specifications in the following order: i) sign of gain, ii) input resistance, iii) gain magnitude (approximately), iv) bandwidth as implicit in the topology ($f_{3dB}\uparrow$ as closed-loop gain $\downarrow$), and v) offset as correctable. 3

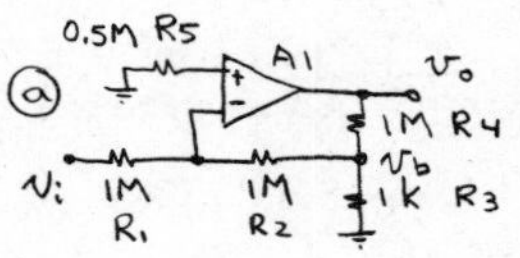

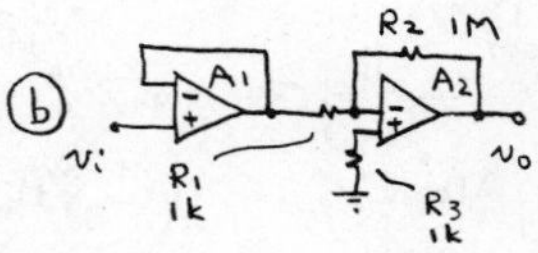

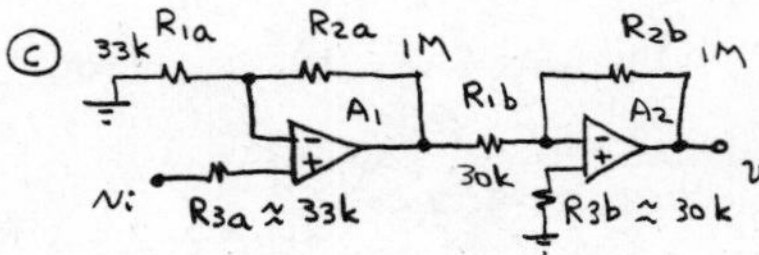

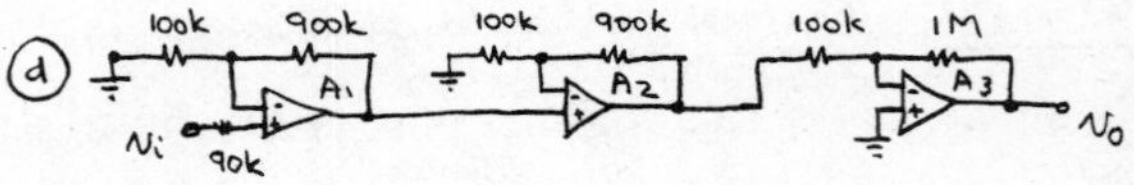

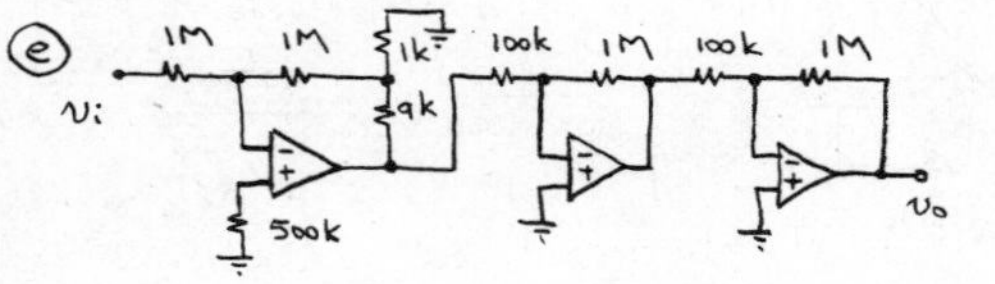

3

Analysis:

ⓐ Gain: Nominally $v_b/v_i = -1$

but $v_b = \frac{1k\|1M}{1k\|1M + 1M} \times v_o = .000998\,v_o$

$\therefore \frac{v_o}{v_i} = \frac{v_o}{v_b} \times \frac{v_b}{v_i} = 1/.000998 = -1002$

Thus for gain of exactly -1000, use $R_3 = 1002\,\Omega$

Finite gain: The gain of the (attenuated) amplifier, for which R_2 and R_1 close the loop, is A' where

$A' \simeq A \times \frac{R_3}{R_3 + R_4} = 10^5 \frac{10^3}{10^3 + 10^6} \simeq 100$

for which $v_b/v_i = \frac{-R_2/R_1}{1 + (1 + R_2/R_1)/A'} = \frac{-1}{1 + (1+1)/100} \simeq -0.98$

Thus the overall gain becomes $-980\ V/V$

This can be compensated by raising R_3, so

$\frac{R_3\|1M}{R_3\|1M + 1M} = \frac{0.98}{1000} \rightarrow 1 + \frac{1}{R_3\|1M} = \frac{1000}{.98} = 1020$

ie $\frac{R_3 + 1}{R_3} = 1019 = 1 + \frac{1}{R_3} \rightarrow R_3 = \frac{1}{1018} = 982\,\Omega$

Input Resistance: $R_{in} = R_1 = 1\,M\Omega$

Offset: Note that while bias current flowing in R_2 produces a voltage at v_b of only $10^6 \times 10^{-9} = 1\,mV$, V_o is 1000 times greater, or $1\,V$ 3

Thus $R_5 = R_1 \| R_2 = 0.5M$ is used to compensate.

For offset current $1/10$ as large, $v_{o_{off}}$ is reduced to $(1/10 \times 10^{-9} \times 0.5 \times 10^{-6})(1 + 1/1)\left(\frac{1}{1/1000}\right) = \underline{0.1V}$

Bandwidth: $f_{3dB} = \frac{f_t}{1 + R_2/R_1}$ for a simple circuit (Eq 3.12)

$\simeq \frac{f_t}{|\text{closed-loop gain}|}$ in general.

Here $f_{3dB} \simeq \frac{10^6}{1000} = \underline{1kHz}$

ⓑ Gain: Nominally $v_o/v_i = -\frac{10^6}{10^3} = -1000$

Finite gain: For $A = 10^5 \rightarrow \frac{v_o}{v_i} = \frac{-R_2/R_1}{1 + (1 + R_2/R_1)/A}$

or $v_o/v_i = -\frac{1000}{1 + 1001/10^5} = -990.1\ V/V$

For gain of -1000, lower R_1 to $990\,\Omega$

Input Resistance: $R_{in} \simeq \infty$ for follower input.

Offset: With $R_3 = R_1 \| R_2 \simeq 1k\Omega$

$v_{o_{off}} = \frac{1}{10} \times 10^{-9} \times 10^3 \times (1 + 1000) = \underline{0.1mV}$

Bandwidth For A_2, $f_{3dB} = \frac{f_t}{1 + R_2/R_1} = \frac{10^6}{1 + 10^6/10^3} \simeq 10^3\,Hz$

For A_1, $f_{3dB} = \frac{10^6}{1+0} = 10^6$ Hz **3**

Overall, f_{3dB} = 1 kHz

(c) Gain : Nominally, $v_o/v_i = \left(1+\frac{R_{2a}}{R_{1a}}\right)\left(-\frac{R_{2b}}{R_{1b}}\right)$

or $v_o/v_i = \left(1+\frac{10^6}{33\times10^3}\right)\left(-\frac{10^6}{30\times10^3}\right) = 31.3(33.3) = -1043\ V/V$

For $A = 10^5$, gain is $\frac{+31.3}{1+(1+30.3)/10^5} \times \frac{-33.3}{1+(1+33.3)/10^5}$

or $\approx \frac{1043}{(1.00035)^2} = 1042\ V/V$

For gain of −1000, $\frac{31.3\times10^6}{R_{1b}} = 1000$

or $R_{1b} = \frac{31.3\times10^6}{1000} = 31.3\ k\Omega$

Input Resistance : $R_{in} \approx \infty$

Offset : The offset of the first stage is multiplied by the gain of the second.

With $R_{3a} = 33k \| 1M \approx 33k$,

$V_{o\,off} = 33\times31\times\frac{1}{10}\times10^{-9}\times33\times10^3 = 3.3\ mV$

Bandwidth:

For A_1, $f_{3dB} = \frac{f_t}{1+R_2/R_1} = \frac{10^6}{1+10^3/33} = 31.9\ kHz$

For A_2, $f_{3dB} = \frac{10^6}{1+10^3/31.3} = 30.4\ kHz$

Overall $f_{3dB} \approx \frac{1}{\sqrt{(1/31.9)^2+(1/30.4)^2}} = 22\ kHz$

(d) Gain: Nominally, $\frac{v_o}{v_i} = \left(1+\frac{9}{1}\right)\left(1+\frac{9}{1}\right)(-10) = -10^3$ **3**

For $A = 10^5$, gain is essentially the same

Input Resistance : $R_{in} \approx \infty$

Offset : Comes essentially from first stage.

With compensation, $R_{3a} = 100k \| 900k = 90\ k\Omega$

$V_{o\,off} = 10\times10\times10\times\frac{1}{10}\times10^{-9}\times90\times10^3 = 9\ mV$

Bandwidth : For the inverter $f_{3dB} = \frac{10^6}{1+10^6/10^5} = 91\ kHz$

and 100 kHz for other 2 stages

Overall $f_{3dB} = 1/(10^2+10^2+11^2)^{1/2} = 55.8\ kHz$

(e) Very much like (d) except :

$V_{o\,off} = 10\times10\times20\times\frac{1}{10}\times10^{-9}\times0.5\times10^6 = 100\ mV$

Overall $f_{3dB} = 1/(11^2+11^2+11^2)^{1/2}\ MHz = 52.4\ kHz$

Conclude : (d) is best for 3 amplifiers

(c) is best for 2 amplifiers

(a) is all there is for 1 amp ?

1 Exam **4**

For 1mA diodes for which $n=2$, find an expression for v_o/v_s in terms of I. What is v_o/v_s for $I = 10\mu A$? 10 mA?

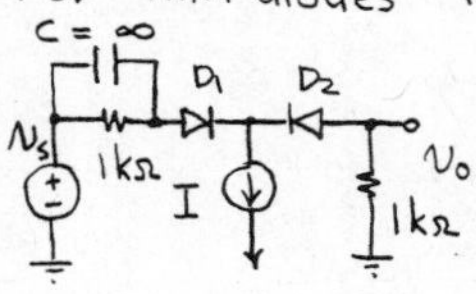

(A) DC calculation :

Through symmetry, $I_{D1} = I_{D2} = I/2$ mA

AC calculation :

Incremental resistance of each diode,

$r = \frac{nV_T}{I_D} = \frac{2\times25}{I/2} = \frac{100}{I}\ \Omega$

Since $C = \infty$, v_s appears at the anode of D_1

and $v_o/v_s = \frac{1000}{1000+100/I} = \frac{10I}{10I+1} = \frac{I}{I+0.1}$

ie $v_o/v_s = I/(I+0.1)$, I in mA

For $I = 10\mu A = 10^{-2}$ mA, $v_o/v_s = \frac{10^{-2}}{10^{-2}+10^{-1}} = \frac{1}{11} = 0.091\ V/V$

For $I = 10$ mA, $v_o/v_s = \frac{10}{10+0.1} = 0.99\ V/V$

2 Exam **4**

For a diode which conducts 100 mA at 0.8V and for which $n = 1.5$, find the current at 0.7V. For this diode, what is I_S? What is its incremental resistance at 100 mA and at 0.7V? For 2 such diodes in parallel supplied by 100 mA in total, what is the incremental resistance found?

(A) $I = I_S e^{v/nV_T}$

At 0.8V, $100 = I_S e^{\frac{800}{1.5(25)}} \rightarrow I_S = 100 e^{-\frac{800}{1.5(25)}}\ mA = 5.43\times10^{-11} A$

At 0.7V, $I = I_S e^{\frac{700}{1.5(25)}} = 100 e^{\frac{-800+700}{1.5(25)}} = 100 e^{\frac{-4}{1.5}} = 6.95\ mA$

for which $r = \frac{nV_T}{I} = \frac{1.5(25)}{6.95} = 5.4\ \Omega$

At 100 mA, $r = \frac{nV_T}{I} = \frac{1.5(25)}{100} = 0.375\ \Omega$

For 2 diodes in $\|$, $I = \frac{100}{2} = 50$ mA, for which $r = \frac{1.5(25)}{50} = 0.75\ \Omega$ for each or $\frac{0.75}{2} = 0.375\ \Omega$ for the pair (as seen directly)

1 **Design** 4

Design a shunt regulator using a string of junction diodes to provide a nominal output voltage of 5 volts from a (10 ± 2)V supply. Only 1mA diodes are available for which the 0.1 volt/decade of current change characteristic applies. The load current is nominally 1mA but it can vary from 0 to 2mA. The goal of your design is to reduce both the output voltage variation and power supply current. Consider in detail 2 designs which meet the nominal requirements, one which is intended simply to minimize the total supply current while the other uses a higher supply current to reduce the effect of load variation. For both designs, evaluate the highest and lowest output voltages produced. Select an adequate design.

4

(A)

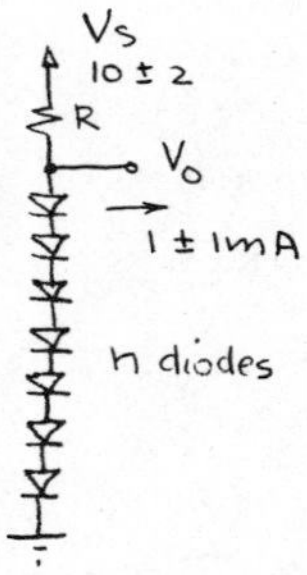

For diodes with 0.7V drop, the nominal requirement is for $\frac{5}{0.7} = 7+$ diodes

Thus one could use 7 diodes operating at slightly more than 1mA, or 6 diodes operating at somewhat more than 10mA.

Nominal Designs:

"1mA": $V_S = 10V$, $V_O = 5V$, $I_L = 1mA$, 7 diodes

Drop/diode $= \frac{5}{7} = 0.7143V = 0.70 + 0.1 \log \frac{I_D}{1}$

Nominal diode current, $I_D = 10^{\frac{0.7143 - 0.7000}{0.1}} = 1.39mA$

Current in R, $I_R = 1.39 + 1.00 = 2.39mA$

$R = \frac{10-5}{2.39} = 2.092\ k\Omega$

4

Use $R = 2.0k\Omega$ for which $I_R = \frac{10-5}{2} = 2.5mA$

"10mA": 6 diodes → drop/diode $= \frac{5}{6} = 0.8\dot{3}V$

$0.83\dot{3} = 0.700 + 0.1 \log_{10} I_D/1$

$\therefore I_D = 10^{\frac{0.8\dot{3} - 0.7}{0.1}} = 21.53mA$

and $I_R = 21.53 + 1 = 22.53mA$

$\therefore R = \frac{10-5}{22.53} = 0.222k\Omega$

Use $R = 220\Omega$ for which $I_R = \frac{10-5}{.22} = 22.7mA$

Extremes Analysis: $V_S = 8V$ to $12V$, $I_L = 0$ to $2mA$.

The highest output, V_{OH}, occurs at +12V and 0mA

The lowest output, V_{OL}, occurs at +8V and 2mA

For "1mA" design

V_{OH}: $I_{DH} = \frac{12 - V_{OH}}{2}$, $V_{OH} = 7(0.7 + 0.1 \log I_{DH})$

Iterate: $I_{DH} = 4mA$, $V_{OH} = 7(0.7 + 0.1 \log 4) = 5.32V$

$I_{DH} = \frac{12 - 5.32}{2} = 3.34\ mA$, $V_{OH} = 5.27V$

$I_{DH} = \frac{12 - 5.37}{2} = 3.36mA$, $V_{OH} = 5.27V$

$\therefore V_{OH} = 5.27V$

V_{OL}: $I_{DL} = \frac{8 - V_{OL}}{2} - 2$, $V_{OL} = 7(0.70 + 0.1 \log I_{DL})$

4

Iterate: $I_{DL} = 1mA$, $V_{OL} = 7(0.7 + 0.1 \log 1) = 4.9V$

$I_{DL} = \frac{8 - 4.9}{2} - 2 = -.45$, ie diodes cut off.

and $V_{OL} = 8 - 2k(2mA) = 4V$

$\therefore \Delta V = V_{OH} - V_{OL} = 5.27 - 4 = 1.27V$

Regulation $= \frac{1.27}{5} \times 100 = 25.4\%$

Not good!

For "10 mA" design:

V_{OH}: $I_{DH} = \frac{12 - V_{OH}}{0.22} - 0$, $V_{OH} = 6(0.7 + 0.1 \log I_{DH})$

Iterate: $I_{DH} = 24mA$, $V_{OH} = 6(0.7 + 0.1 \log 24) = 5.028$

$I_{DH} = \frac{12 - 5.028}{0.22} = 31.7\ mA$, $V_{OH} = 5.10V$

$I_{DH} = \frac{12 - 5.10}{0.22} = 31.4mA$, $V_{OH} = 5.10V$

$\therefore V_{OH} = 5.10V$

V_{OL}: $I_{DL} = \frac{8 - V_{OL}}{0.22} - 2$, $V_{OL} = 6(0.7 + 0.1 \log I_{DL})$

Iterate: $I_{DL} = 24mA$, $V_{OL} = 6(0.7 + 0.1 \log 24) = 5.028V$

$I_{DL} = \frac{8 - 5.028}{0.22} - 2 = 13.5mA$, $V_{OL} = 4.878V$

$I_{DL} = \frac{8 - 4.878}{0.22} - 2 = 12.19mA$, $V_{OL} = 4.852V$

$\therefore V_{OL} = 4.85V$, $\Delta V = V_{OH} - V_{OL} = 5.27 - 4.85 = 0.42$, $Reg = \frac{0.42}{5} \times 100 = 8.4\%$

OK - Use 6 diodes, $R = 220\Omega$

1 | Exam | 5

A full-wave rectifier bridge utilizing 4 1mA diodes has applied to it a 60Hz sine wave of 20V peak to peak amplitude. Assuming the diodes are characterized by a 0.1V/decade characteristic, sketch and label the output waveform assuming the load to be (a) a resistor in which the peak current flow is 0.1mA, (b) a 200μF capacitor (and no resistor), (c) a 200μF capacitor shunted by a 1kΩ resistor. In the latter case, make the assumption of small ripple and estimate the peak diode current.

(A) | 5

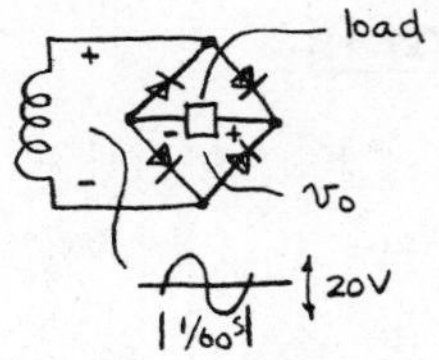

(a) v_o

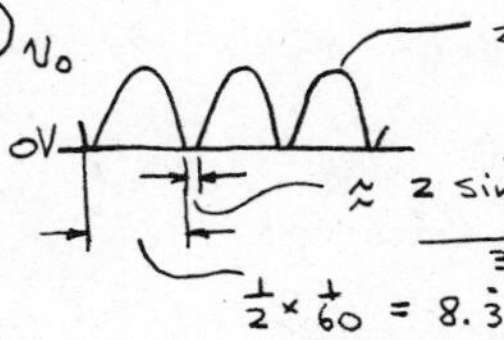

$20/2 - 2(0.7-0.1) = 10-1.2 = \underline{\underline{8.8V}}$

$\approx \dfrac{2\sin^{-1}\frac{0.5}{10}}{360} \times \dfrac{1}{60} = 0.26\,ms$

$\frac{1}{2} \times \frac{1}{60} = 8.\dot{3}\,ms$

(b)

10V (eventually for zero load)

(c)

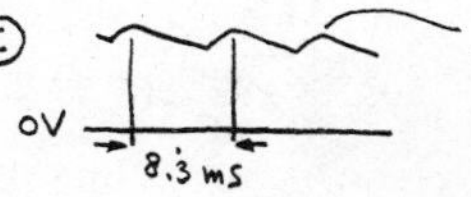

The diode current at the peak is due essentially to the resistor load of about $\frac{10V}{1k} \approx 10mA$ for which the diode drop is $0.7+0.1=0.8V$

$\therefore V_{peak} \approx 10 - 2(0.8) = \underline{\underline{8.4V}}$

Ripple: $V_{r_{pp}} = \dfrac{IT}{C} = \dfrac{8.4/1k \times 8.\dot{3}\times10^{-3}}{200\times10^{-6}} = \underline{\underline{0.35V}}$ | 5

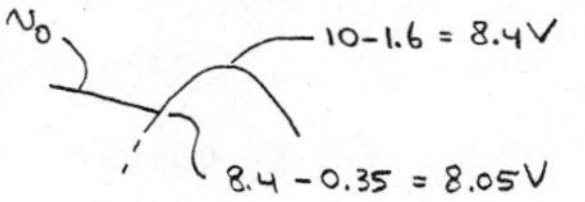

Peak Diode Current: Approach #1: Assume for $v_o = 8.05V$, that the diode drops are each 0.9V (corresponding to a diode current of 100 mA or so)

$\therefore$ diodes conduct when input rises to about $8.05 + 2(0.9) = 9.85V$. This will occur at an angle of $\sin^{-1}\frac{9.85}{10} = 80°$ at which the slope is $2\pi(60)\times 10\cos 80° = 655\,V/s$ and for which the peak diode current required to charge C would be $I = C\frac{V}{T} = 200\times10^{-6}\times 655 = 131mA$

Including the load the maximum diode current would be about $131 + 8.4 = \underline{\underline{139\,mA}}$.

Approach #2: Accept that conduction is for 10°, ie $\frac{1}{18}$ of a half cycle. Assume that the

5

diode current is essentially triangular and of peak value I_p, replacing the charge lost during most of the half cycle. Now average current $\approx 8.4mA$ in the 1k load

$\therefore \frac{1}{2} I_p \times \frac{10}{180} = 8.4 \times \frac{180}{360} \rightarrow I_p = \underline{\underline{151\,mA}}$

Approach #3: Ignore the variability of diode drop with current, and proceed otherwise as in approach #1. This is essentially the approach leading to Eq 5.10 (modified for full-wave operation). That is

$$i_{D_{max}} = \frac{I_L}{2}\left(1 + 2\pi\sqrt{2V_p/V_r}\right)$$

$$= \frac{8.4}{2}\left(1 + 2\pi\sqrt{\frac{2(8.4)}{0.35}}\right) = \underline{\underline{187mA}}$$

The actual current is somewhere between 139 and 187, and can be found more closely using approach #1 with additional care taken with diode drop and other calculations

2 **Exam** 5

Sketch the transfer characteristic of the following circuit under the conditions that the diodes are 0.1mA diodes with a 0.1V/decade characteristic. For what input and output voltages do the diodes conduct 0.1mA? and 0.01mA?

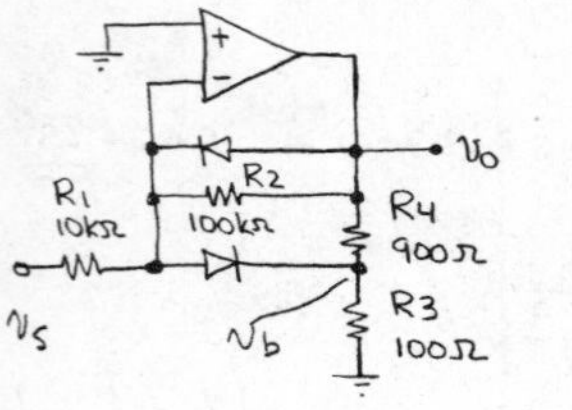

(A) For v_s around 0, $v_o = -10 v_s$, ie slope $= -10$ V/V

For v_s negative, D_2 conducts with v_o one diode drop positive

For v_s positive, D_1 conducts with v_o 10 diode drops negative, since the values of R_3, R_4 are low.

For v_s very positive, current in R_1 flowing in D_1 and R_4 lowers the gain toward

$$\frac{R_3 \| R_4}{R_1} \cdot \frac{1}{R_3/(R_1+R_4)} = R_4/R_1 \approx 0.1 \text{ V/V}$$

5

Ultimately for v_s very positive, v_o is 10 times a diode characteristic, ie shows 1 volt/decade of current change.

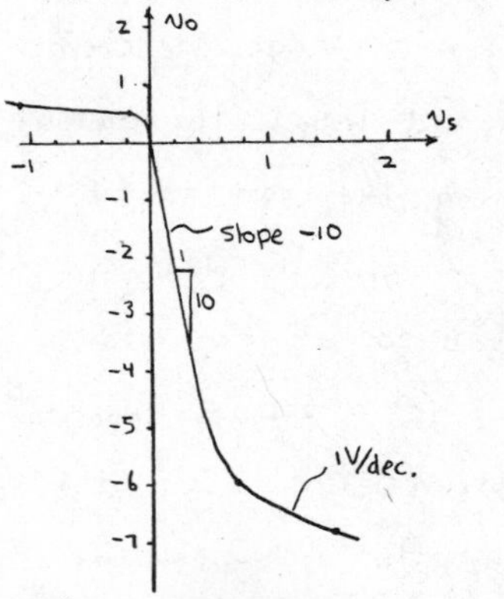

In the table below, (n) indicates calculation order and keys Detail below:

	D_2 conducts		D_1 Conducts	
I_D(mA)	0.1	.01	0.1	.01
v_b			(5) −0.7	(8) −0.6
v_o	(1) 0.7	(3) 0.6	(6) −7.09	(9) −6.009
v_s	(2) −1.07	(4) −0.16	(7) 1.709	(10) 0.701

Detail:

(2) $-10k\left(0.1 + \frac{0.7}{100k}\right) = -1.07\text{V}$; (4) $-10k\left(.01 + \frac{0.6}{100k}\right) = -0.16\text{V}$

(6) $-0.7 - \left(\frac{0.7}{0.1} + 0.1\right)0.9 = -7.09\text{V}$; (7) $10k\left(0.1 + \frac{7.09}{100k}\right) = 1.709\text{V}$

(9) $-0.6 - \left(\frac{0.6}{0.1} + .01\right)0.9 = -6.009\text{V}$; (10) $10k\left(.01 + \frac{6.01}{100k}\right) = 0.701\text{V}$

1 **Design** 5

The following circuit topology is being considered for use in a function generator, for the creation of square and triangular waveforms.

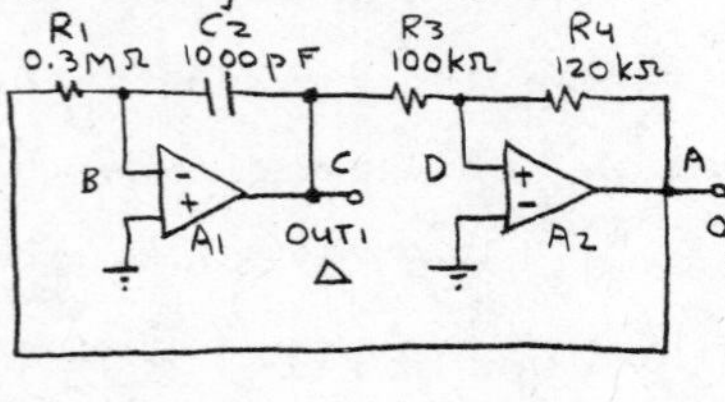

As shown, the oscillator, using op amps which limit at ±12V, has a nominal period of 1ms. In order to quantify the adequacy of the design as presented, evaluate the effect of various imperfections of individual components on performance parameters such as frequency, waveform amplitude, etc. Use a 1% variation of

5

such performance measures as a basis of comparison in an attempt to establish critical specifications such as bias current, offset current, offset voltage, gain, component tolerance, saturation limits etc.

Note the critical dependence of operation on amplifier limiting voltage. Assuming that such voltages are stable but variable upon manufacture from 12 to 14 volts, suggest a simple addition to compensate assuming that both saturation limits have the same magnitude. What must also be changed if the range of saturation limits extends to 10V? Augment your design with 2 diodes (and controls) to accomodate different values of $|L+|$ and $|L-|$ in the range 10V to 14V.

Suggest a way to incorporate switch-selection

5

of frequency down to 1 Hz and up to 100 kHz. If the square wave is to have rise/fall times of less than 10% of the period, what is the slew rate requirement on the amplifier.

Design a simple addition to allow the frequency in each range to be reduced continuously to 1/11 of the maximum. Note that this feature allows the ranges to overlap.

Suggest a simple means by which waveform symmetry can be adjusted to ensure that each half cycle has the same length. What are the secondary consequences of your choice?

5

(5) **Waveforms:**

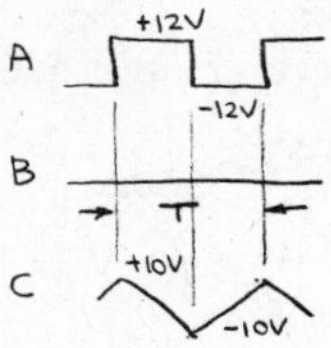

Half Period →

$$T/2 = \frac{1000\times10^{-12}\times 20}{12/0.3\times10^{6}}$$

$$= 500\times10^{-6}\,s$$

T = 1 ms

Performance: Legend – — indicates no effect

× indicates no problem for reasonable components

Performance Limitations Causing a 1% Change in a Performance Measure

Perform. Meas. / Circ. Parameter	Freq.	Half Period Symm.	□ Wave Amp.	□ Wave Offset	△ Wave Amp.	△ Wave Offset	△ Wave Linearity
R_1, C_2 %	1	—	—	—	—	—	—
R_3, R_4 %	1	—	—	—	1	—	—
$L_1\pm$	—	—	—	—	—	—	—
$L_2\pm$ % separately	1	1	1	2	1	2	—
$\lvert L_2\rvert\pm$ % together	—	—	0.5	—	0.5	—	—
A_{v1} V/V	×	×	×	×	×	×	7100

5

Par	Freq	Sym	□ Amp	□ Off.	△ Amp	△ Off.	△ Lin
A_{v2} V/V	7100	—	—	—	7100	—	—
I_{bias1} μA	—	0.5	—	—	—	—	—
I_{bias2} μA	—	1	—	—	1	1	—
$I_{offset1,2}$	×	×	×	×	×	×	×
$V_{offset1,2}$	—	×	×	×	—	×	—
Supply V	1	1	1	2	1	2	—

See from the table that the effect of passive components, L+, L– and power supply is quite direct, ie 1% change produces a 1% effect. For components this is OK since .1% or even 0.01% components are available at reasonable cost and/or can be trimmed to value (if stable). Likewise a well-regulated power supply is available at reasonable cost. But such is not the case for L+, L– of different manufacture. L+, L– are not well controlled!

5

Improvements

For |L+| = |L–| variable at manufacture from +12 to +14 V, add resistor R_5 to the output of A_2 as shown.

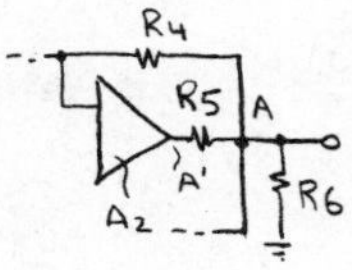

Adjust R_5 so the voltage at A is 12 V for V_C near one of its extreme values:

$$R_{5_{max}} \approx \frac{14V-12V}{\frac{12V}{120k}+\frac{12V}{300k}} = \frac{2}{0.14\,mA} = 14.2k \rightarrow \text{Use } 15\,k\Omega \text{ Var.}$$

Note that the current in R5 varies as V_C varies, causing V_A and I_{R_1} to vary and for the triangle at V_C to be nonlinear. This can be compensated (to the desired degree) by adding R6 from A to ground. For example chose $R_6 = 12\,k\Omega$ and $R_5 = 2\,k\Omega$ (Variable). Note that since the standardized value of $|V_A|$ is 12 V, that frequencies and amplitudes are as originally designed.

5

However if saturation limits (and or power supply variation) ranges down to 10V, a redesign for 10 V is necessary: Use $R_6 = 10k\Omega$, $R_5 = 4k\Omega$ (variable) (for ±14V max), $R_4 = 100k\Omega$, and $R_1 = 0.25M\Omega$. V_C as before is a ±10V triangle (just at the L± limits of A_1).

Now if $|L+|$ and $|L-|$ are not equal, replace R_5 by

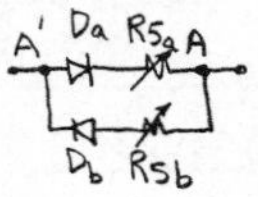

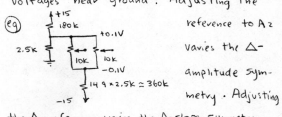

. This idea works (with R_4, R_1 changed and R_6 added) down to $|L+| \neq |L-|$ of 10.7V.

For switched frequency change from 1Hz to 100 kHz, us a 1-pole 5-position switch to change C_2 from $1\mu F$ to 10pF (or slightly less to compensate for wiring capacitance).

For operation at 100kHz, with 10μsec period, rise time $\leq \frac{1}{10}(10\mu s) = 1\mu s$.

∴ op amp slew rate $\geq 20 V/\mu s$ (ie quite high!)

5

To reduce the frequency continuously from 1x to 1/11 x nominal, connect the high voltage end of R_1 to the wiper of a $10k\Omega$ potentiometer used for R_6 whose lower lower end is connected to ground via $R_7 = 1k\Omega$. With R_6 adjusted low (for 1/11 frequency) offset voltage of A_1 can be 11x more serious.

A simple way to adjust waveforms for symmetry would be to connect the grounded inputs of A_1, A_2 to small variable voltages near ground: Adjusting the

(eg)

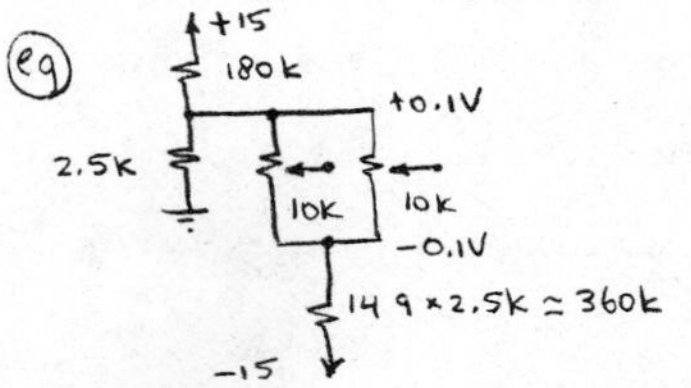

reference to A_2 varies the Δ-amplitude symmetry. Adjusting the A_1 reference varies the Δ-slope symmetry. Both control the □ wave duty-cycle symmetry.

6

ie $i_{D1} = 1mA$

(b) $V_A = -15 + 1 = -14V$

$V_B = 0V$

Since $i_{D2} = i_{D1}$ and both are in pinchoff, $v_{GS2} = v_{GS1}$

∴ $V_C = +1V$

$V_D = +1 - 1(0.1) = +0.9V$

$V_E = 15 - 10k(1mA) = +5V$

$V_F = 0V$

(c) $i_D = I_{DSS}\left(1 - \frac{v_{GS}}{V_P}\right)^2 \rightarrow g_m = \frac{\partial i_D}{\partial v_{GS}} = -2\frac{I_{DSS}}{V_P}\left(1 - \frac{v_{GS}}{V_P}\right)$

Here $g_{m2} = \frac{-2(4)}{(-2)}\left(1 - \frac{-1}{-2}\right) = 2mA/V$

(d) Resistance looking into gate is ∞

(e) $r_{s2} = 1/g_{m2} = \frac{1}{2 \times 10^{-3}} = 500\Omega$

∴ $v_o/v_s = \frac{\infty}{1M + \infty} \times \left(-\frac{10k \| 20k}{500 + 100}\right) = -11.1 V/V$

1 Exam 6

For the following JFET amplifier, $I_{DSS1} = I_{DSS2} = 4mA/V$ and $V_{P1} = V_{P2} = -2V$

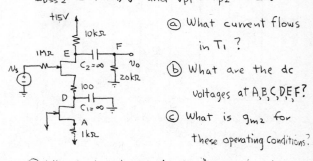

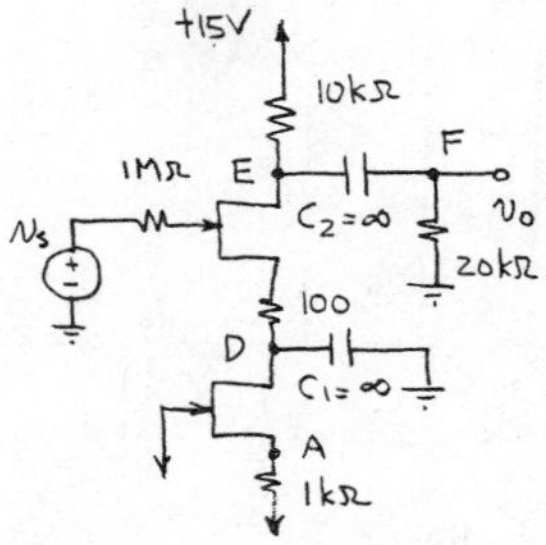

(a) What current flows in T_1?

(b) What are the dc voltages at A,B,C,D,E,F?

(c) What is g_{m2} for these operating conditions?

(d) What is the input resistance "looking into" the gate of T_2?

(e) What is the voltage gain v_o/v_s?

(A) (a) T_1 is self-biassed by resistor $R_S = 1k\Omega$.

$i_D = I_{DSS}\left(1 - \frac{v_{GS}}{V_P}\right)^2$ and $v_{GS} = -i_D R_S$

ie $i_D = 4\left(1 - \frac{-i_D(1)}{-2}\right)^2 = 4\left(1 - i_D + \frac{i_D^2}{4}\right) = 4 - 4i_D + i_D^2$

or $i_D^2 - 5i_D + 4 = 0 \rightarrow i_D = \frac{5 \pm \sqrt{25 - 4(4)}}{2} = 1$ or ~~4~~ mA

2 | Exam | 6

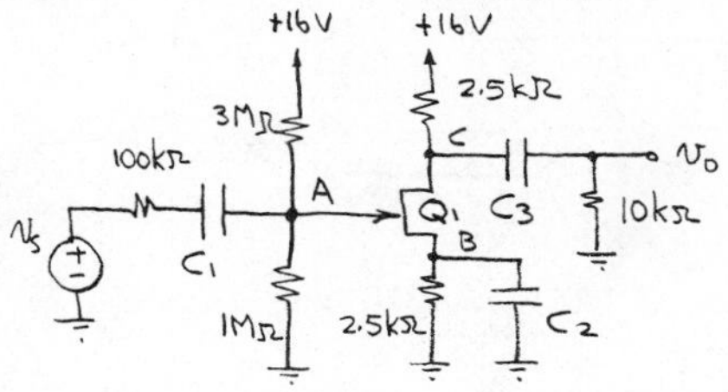

$I_{DSS} = 8\,mA$

$V_P = -2V$

C_1, C_2, C_3 are large

ⓐ What is the voltage at A, V_A ?

ⓑ What is the drain current, i_D ?

ⓒ What are the voltages at B, C, ie V_B, V_C ?

ⓓ What is g_m of the transistor ?

ⓔ What is the voltage gain, v_o/v_s ?

ⓕ For v_A having a sinewave component $\hat{V}\sin\omega t$, for what value of $\hat{V}$ is the harmonic distortion less than 1% ?
Use the fact that $\sin^2 x = \frac{1}{2}(1-\cos 2x)$

Ⓐ 6

ⓐ $V_A = \frac{1M}{1M+3M} \times 16V = \underline{4V}$

ⓑ $i_D = I_{DSS}\left(1-\frac{v_{GS}}{V_P}\right)^2$ and $i_D = \frac{V_A - v_{GS}}{R_S}$

Letting $v_{GS} = v \rightarrow \frac{4-v}{2.5} = 8\left(1-\frac{v}{-2}\right)^2$

or $4 - v = 20\left(1+v+\frac{v^2}{4}\right) = 20 + 20v + 5v^2$

ie $5v^2 + 21v + 16 = 0$

or $v = \frac{-21 \pm \sqrt{21^2 - 4(5)(16)}}{2(5)} = \frac{-21 \pm 11}{10} = -1V$

$\therefore V_B = 4-(-1) = 5V$

$i_D = \frac{5V}{2.5k} = \underline{\underline{2mA}}$

ⓒ $V_B = \underline{\underline{+5V}}$

$V_C = 16 - 2(2.5k) = \underline{\underline{11V}}$

ⓓ $g_m = \frac{\partial i_D}{\partial v_{GS}} = \frac{2I_{DSS}}{V_P}\left(1-\frac{v_{GS}}{V_P}\right) = \frac{2(8)}{2}\left(1-\frac{1}{2}\right) = \underline{\underline{4mA/V}}$

ⓔ Load on input source is $1M \| 3M = \frac{3M}{4} = 0.75M$

$\therefore \frac{v_o}{v_s} = -\frac{0.75}{0.1+0.75} \times 4 \times (2.5k \| 10k) = \underline{\underline{-7.06V/V}}$

ⓕ $i_D = 8\left(1-\frac{-1+\hat{V}\sin\omega t}{-2}\right)^2 = 2\left(2-1+\hat{V}\sin\omega t\right)^2$

$= 2(1 + 2\hat{V}\sin\omega t + \hat{V}^2\sin^2\omega t)$

$= 2\left(1 + 2\hat{V}\sin\omega t + \frac{\hat{V}^2}{2}(1-\cos 2\omega t)\right)$

Distortion $= \frac{\hat{V}^2/2}{2\hat{V}} = \frac{\hat{V}}{4} \le \frac{1}{100}$. Thus $\hat{V} \le \underline{\underline{40mV}}$ for 1% dist.

1 | Design | 6

Design a JFET amplifier, using one common-source and one common-drain stage, to couple a 1 megohm source to a 1 kilohm load. No direct current should flow in the load. Available n-channel JFETs have $I_{DSS} = 8mA$ and $V_T = -2V$. Power supplies of ± 10V are provided. An unlimited number of resistors of value up to 1MΩ are available. However capacitors are in limited supply and large ones are expensive. An ideal design would be one with a small number of relatively small capacitors. As well, it should maximize the available gain, while providing an output signal of at least ± 1 V. Use gain as a figure of merit.

Ⓐ Design 1: Conventional with 2 supplies 6

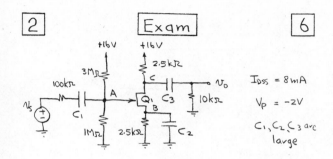

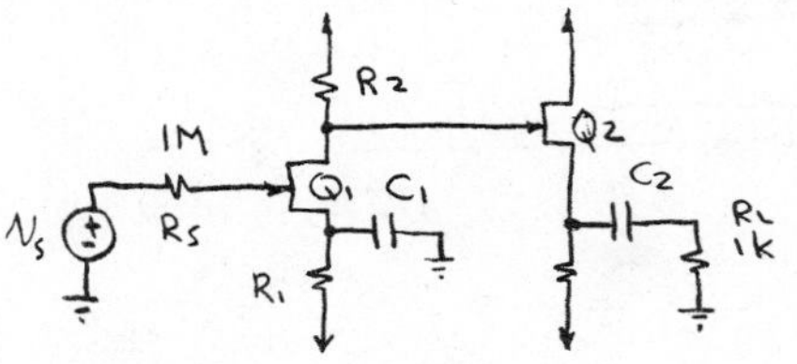

Generally, operate Q_1, Q_2 at relatively high currents for most gain. However, in view of JFET variability, compromise at $I_D = 2mA$ for which the stated FET requires $v_{GS} = -1V$, and provides $g_m = 4mA/V$. To allow for a −1V output signal and device variability, maintain $v_{DS} = 4V$ across the FET.

$\therefore R_1 = \frac{10+1}{2} = \underline{\underline{5.5k}}$, $R_2 = \frac{10-4-1}{2} = \underline{\underline{2.5k}}$

$R_3 = \frac{5+1+10}{2} = 8k$

Gain $= -4 \times 2.5 \times \frac{1 \| 8}{1/4 + 1 \| 8} = \underline{-7.8V/V}$

For a cutoff at f Hz, $C_1 = \frac{1}{2\pi f(1/g_{m1} \| R_1)}$, quite large

$C_2 = \frac{1}{2\pi f(1k + 1/g_{m2} \| R_3)} < C_1$

Design 2 : Eliminate C_1, the largest capacitor, by direct connection of source to ground : 6

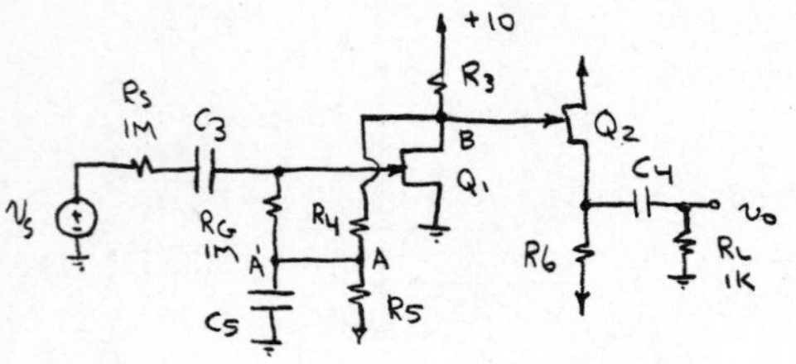

Use the same device currents and voltages as in D1:

$I_D = 2mA$, $V_A = -1V$, $V_B = 4V$,

Thus $R_3 = \frac{10-4}{2} = 3k$, $R_6 = \frac{4+1+10}{2} = 7.5k$

$R_G = 1M$ [10M would be better], $R_5 = 1M$ [likewise]

$R_4 = \frac{4+1}{\left(\frac{10-1}{1M}\right)} = \frac{5}{9} M = 0.5\dot{5} M \rightarrow$ use $560k\Omega$

Since R_G, R_5, R_4 are relatively low, need C_5 to eliminate Miller-effect reduction of R_{in}.

$$\text{Gain} = -\frac{1}{1+1} \times 4 \times 3 \times \frac{1117.5}{1/4 + 1117.5} = -4.67 \text{ V/V}$$

This is low due to $R_G = 1M$ (could put several $1M\Omega$ in series! wow!)

6

$$C_3 = \frac{1}{2\pi f(1M+1M)} \text{ is very small}$$

$$C_4 = \frac{1}{2\pi f(1K + 1/g_{m2} \| R_6)} \approx C_2$$

$$C_5 = \frac{1}{2\pi f\left(2M \| R_5 \| \frac{R_4}{1 + g_{m1} R_3 \| R_4}\right)} \approx 30 \times C_3 \text{ (middle size)}$$

C_5 can be reduced if higher-valued resistors were available and/or by introducing $R_F = 1M$ between nodes A and A'

Design 3 : Combines some of these features

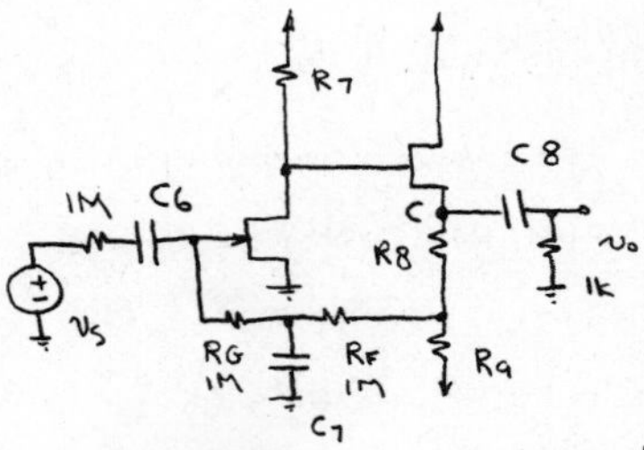

$V_A = -1V$, $V_B = +4V$, $V_C = +5$, $R_7 = \frac{10-4}{2} = 3k$

$R_9 = \frac{10-1}{2} = 4.5k$, $R_8 = \frac{5+1}{2} = 3k$

6

$$\text{Gain} = -\frac{1}{1+1} \times 4 \times 3 \times \frac{1117.5}{1/4 + 1117.5} = -4.67$$

$$C_6 = \frac{1}{2\pi f(1M+1M)} = C_3 \text{, is small}$$

$$C_7 = \frac{1}{2\pi f\left(2M \| \frac{1M}{1 + g_{m1} \frac{R_7 \times R_9}{1/g_{m2} + R_8 + R_9}}\right)} \approx C_5 \text{, is midde size}$$

$C_8 = C_4 = C_2$ is inevitable

C_7 can be reduced by resistor changes as stated. This is the best general-purpose topology for variable devices, since feedback compensates. In fact, as a result, a redesign is possible with less voltage across Q_1 and higher gain. The design is much improved if 10MΩ or 22MΩ resistors are used for R_G, R_F. The capacitor budget is lowest though/and spread among 3 units

1 **Exam** 7

For the amplifier shown, the enhancement MOS device has $K = 0.111 \text{ mA/V}^2$, $V_t = 2V$, and $|V_A| = 30V$. Find:

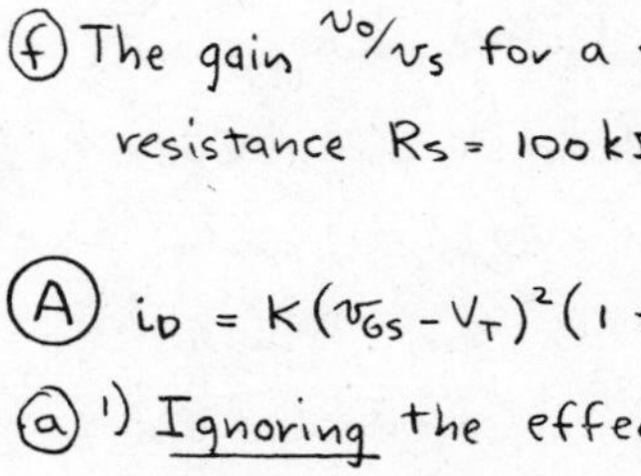

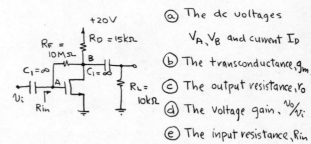

(a) The dc voltages V_A, V_B and current I_D

(b) The transconductance, g_m.

(c) The output resistance, r_o

(d) The voltage gain, v_o/v_i

(e) The input resistance, R_{in}

(f) The gain v_o/v_s for a source with source resistance $R_s = 100k\Omega$

(A) $i_D = K(v_{GS} - V_T)^2 \left(1 + \frac{v_{DS}}{V_A}\right)$ in general.

(a) 1) Ignoring the effect of V_A on biassing:

$v_{GS} = v_{DS} = v \rightarrow i_D = K(v - V_T)^2 = 0.11(v-2)^2$

But also $i_D = \frac{20 - v}{15} \rightarrow \frac{(v-2)^2}{9} = \frac{20-v}{15}$

ie $v^2-4v+4 = \frac{3}{5}(20-v) = 12-0.6v$ **7**

or $v^2-3.4v-8=0$

$$v = \frac{3.4 \pm \sqrt{3.4^2-4(-8)}}{2} = \frac{3.4 \pm 6.6}{2} = 5V$$

ie $V_A = \underline{+5V}$, $V_B = \underline{+5V}$, $i_D = \frac{20-5}{15} = \underline{1mA}$

2) Including $V_A = 30V$

$$i_D = \frac{1}{9}(v-2)^2\left(1+\frac{v}{30}\right) = \frac{20-v}{15}$$

or $(v-2)^2(30+v) = 18(20-v)$, a cubic

Iterate to a solution using $v = \sqrt{\frac{18(20-v)}{30+v}} + 2$

For $v = +5 \rightarrow v = \left(\frac{18(20-5)}{30+5}\right)^{1/2} + 2 = 4.78$

$v = 4.78 \rightarrow v = \left(\frac{18(20-4.78)}{(30+4.78)}\right)^{1/2} + 2 = 4.81$

$v = 4.81 \rightarrow v = \left(\frac{18(20-4.81)}{30+4.81}\right)^{1/2} + 2 = 4.80$

ie $V_A = \underline{4.8V}$; $V_B = \underline{4.8V}$, $i_D = \frac{20-4.8}{15} = 1.01mA \approx 1mA$

(b) Ignoring V_A, $g_m = \frac{\partial i_D}{\partial v_{GS}} = 2K(v_{GS}-V_T) = \frac{2}{9}(5-2) = \underline{0.6\dot{6}\ mA/V}$

(c) $1/r_o = \frac{\partial i_D}{\partial v_{DS}} = I_D/V_A \rightarrow r_o = \frac{30V}{1mA} = \underline{30k\Omega}$

(d) $\frac{v_o}{v_i} = -g_m(R_L \| R_D \| r_o) = -\frac{2}{3}(10k \| 15k \| 30k) = -\frac{2}{3}\left(\frac{30k}{3+2+1}\right) = \underline{-3.\dot{3}\ V/V}$

(e) Using Miller Effect: $R_{in} = \frac{10M}{1-(-3.\dot{3})} = \underline{2.31 M\Omega}$

(f) $\frac{v_o}{v_s} = -3.\dot{3}\left(\frac{2.31}{0.1+2.31}\right) = \underline{-3.19\ V/V}$

2 **Exam** **7**

For the amplifier shown, both devices are identical with $K = 0.\dot{1}\ mA/V^2$, $V_t = 2V$ and $|V_A| = 30$ V. For C_1, C_2, C_3 very large, find:

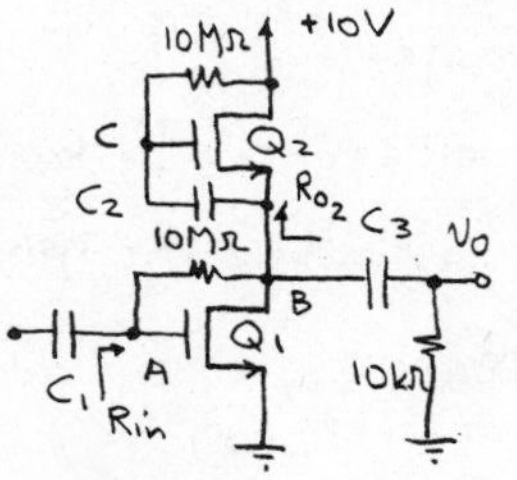

(a) The dc voltages, V_A, V_B, V_C and the operating drain current, I_D

(b) The transconductances, g_{m_1}, g_{m_2}, at the op. pt.

(c) The output resistances, r_{o1}, r_{o2}, at the op. pt.

(d) The load resistance presented by Q_2 (with C_2 connected as shown) to Q_1, ie R_{o2}

(e) The voltage gain, v_o/v_i

(f) The input resistance, R_{in}

(g) The gain, $\frac{v_o}{v_s}$, from a 100kΩ source.

(A) (a) Devices are identical and identically connected (for dc), thus they share the 10V supply equally **7**

$\therefore V_B = \underline{5V}$, $V_A = \underline{5V}$, $V_C = \underline{10V}$

Ignoring effect of r_o, ie for $V_A = \infty$

$I_D = K(v_{GS}-V_T)^2 = 0.\dot{1}(5-2)^2 = \underline{1mA}$

Note that for $V_A = 30$, an additional current $= 1\left(\frac{5}{30}\right)$ or 0.16 mA flows in Q_1, Q_2.

(b) $g_m = \frac{\partial i_D}{\partial v_{GS}} = 2K(v_{GS}-V_T) = 2(.\dot{1})(5-2) = 0.6\dot{6}\ mA/V$

ie $g_{m1} = g_{m2} = \underline{0.667}$ mA/V

(c) $r_{o1} = r_{o2} = V_A/I_D = 30/1 = \underline{30k\Omega}$

(d) With C_2 connected, v_{GS2} is held fixed, and $R_{o2} = 10M \| r_{o2} \approx \underline{30k\Omega}$

(e) Gain $v_o/v_i = -g_m(R_L \| r_{o1} \| R_{o2}) = -0.6\dot{6}(10k \| 30k \| 30k)$

$= -0.66\left(\frac{30k}{3+1+1}\right) = \underline{-4\ V/V}$

(f) Input Res., $R_{in} = \frac{10M}{1-(-4)} = \underline{2.0M\Omega}$

(g) Gain $v_o/v_s = -\frac{2}{0.1+2}(4) = \underline{-3.81\ V/V}$

1 **Design** **7**

Consider the design of an NMOS amplifier using two identical transistors for which $K = 62.5\ \mu A/V^2$ and $V_A = 30$ V and $V_t = 2V$. The amplifier is to consist of a common-source stage Q_1, directly coupled to a source follower stage Q_2, each biassed by a constant current of 1 mA. The input gate is to be directly coupled to the signal v_s for which $R_s = 1M\Omega$. The dc output voltage is to be 0V. The output is directly coupled to a grounded load of 10kΩ. A large capacitor C is available to bypass the common-source amplifier. A supply of +15V is provided.

(a) What is the required drain resistor, R_D?

(next)

7

(b) What is the overall gain, v_o/v_s?

(c) With nothing but a 3rd identical transistor, how can the gain be increased easily? By what factor?

(d) If a higher supply voltage can be found, what would you do to double the gain of the original design?

(A)

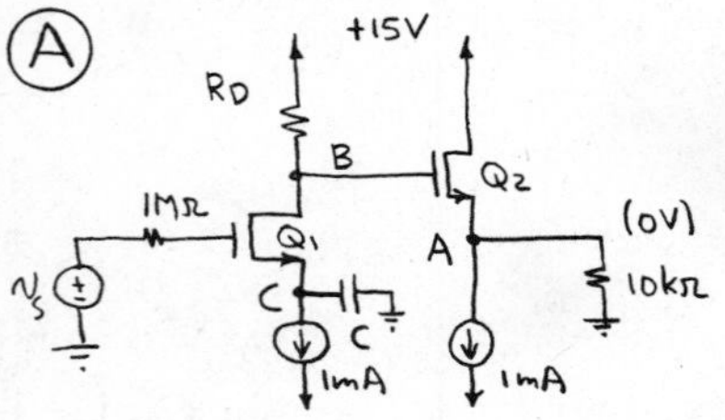

DC Calculations:

Ignoring V_A: $i_D = K(v_{GS}-V_T)^2$

For Q_2, $i_{D2} = 1\times10^{-3} = .0625\times10^{-3}(v_{GS}-2)^2$

Thus $v_{GS2} = \left(\frac{1}{.0625}\right)^{1/2} + 2 = 6V$

7

likewise $v_{GS1} = 6V$

Since $V_A = 0V$, $V_B = 6V$, $R_D = \frac{15-6}{1mA} = 9k\Omega$

Including V_A:

$i_D = K(v_{GS}-V_T)^2(1+\frac{v_{DS}}{V_A})$

For T_2: $v_{DS2} = 15V$

$\therefore (1+\frac{v_{DS}}{V_A}) = (1+\frac{15}{30}) = 1.5$.

Thus 1/3 of 1mA bias flows in r_{o2}

ie $1\times10^{-3} = 62.5\times10^{-6}(v_{GS}-2)^2(1.5)$

or $v_{GS2} = \left(\frac{1}{.0625\times1.5}\right)^{1/2} + 2 = 5.266V$

$\therefore$ for $v_o = 0 = V_A$, $V_B = +5.266V$

For T_1: total current remains 1mA flowing in $R_D \rightarrow R_D = \frac{15-5.266}{1mA} = 9.73k\Omega$

(b) For Q_1, Q_2, $I_D = 1mA$.

$g_m = 2K(v_{GS}-V_T) = 2\sqrt{K}\sqrt{I_D} = 2(62.5\times10^{-6}\times10^{-3})^{1/2} = 0.5$ mA/V

$r_o = V_A/I_D = 30/1mA = 30k\Omega$

Overall gain $= -0.5(9k\|30k)\frac{10k}{(\frac{1}{0.5})\|30k + 10k} = -2.91 V/V$

(c) With a third transistor, could

7

1) parallel Q_2, 2) parallel Q_1

For 2 devices in parallel, current reduces to $I_D/2$ in each, reducing g_m of each by $(\frac{1}{2})^{1/2}$ but increasing the g_m of the pair to $2(\frac{1}{2})^{1/2}$ or 1.414 of original, or to 0.707 mA/V.

Thus for Q_1 shunted, the overall gain increases to $1.414(-2.91)$ or -4.11 V/V, a factor of $\sqrt{2}$.

But for Q_2 shunted, the gain increases only to $-0.5(9k\|30k)\frac{10}{\frac{1}{.707}\|30+10} = -3.05 V/V$

Thus shunting Q_1 is best.

(d) To double the gain: 1) Raise V_{DD} and R_D

Ignoring r_o, use $R_D = 18k\Omega$ and $V_{DD} = 15+(18-9)1 = 24V$

Including r_o, find R_D so that $R_D\|30k = 2(9k\|30k)$

ie $\frac{1}{R_D}+\frac{1}{30} = \frac{1}{2}(\frac{1}{9}+\frac{1}{30}) \rightarrow R_D = \frac{1}{2(1/9-1/30)} = 25.7k\Omega$

and $V_{DD} = 15+(25.7-9)(1) = 31.7V$

2) Replace R_D by (1M, +12V, Q_3, C_2, R_o) . $R_o = 1M\|30k \simeq 30k$

Gain increases to $-0.5(30k\|30k)\times\frac{10}{0.5\|30+10} = -6.31 V/V$

1 Exam 8

For the amplifier shown, all capacitors are very large, and $|V_{EE}| = 0.7V$ independant of current level.

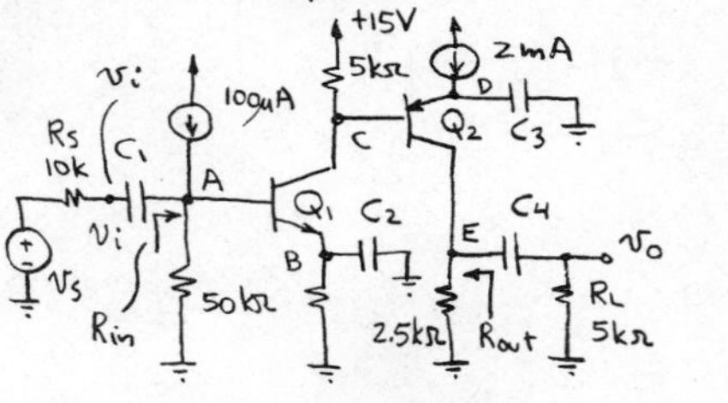

(a) For $\beta = \infty$, find dc voltages, V_A, V_B, V_C, V_D, V_E

(b) Find g_{m1}, g_{m2}

(c) Find the voltage gain from node A to node E, ie $\frac{v_e}{v_a}$, for $\beta = 50$ and $R_L = \infty$

(d) Find the input resistance, Rin

(e) Find the output resistance, Rout

(f) For a source v_s and source resistance of 10kΩ, and load of 5kΩ, find the gain v_o/v_s using the results in (c), (d), (e)

(g) For conditions as in (f) and linear operation

ensured by keeping $v_{be} \le 10\text{mV}$ peak, what is the largest v_o for which distortion is low?. What is the corresponding v_s? **8**

(A) For $\beta = \infty$, $V_A = 100 \times 10^{-6} \times 50 \times 10^{3} = \underline{5V}$

(a) $V_B = 5 - 0.7 = \underline{4.3V}$, $I_{C1} = \frac{4.3}{5k} = 0.86\text{mA}$

$V_C = 15 - 5(0.86) = \underline{9.7V}$,

$V_D = 9.7 + 0.7 = \underline{10.4V}$, $V_E = 2.5k(2\text{mA}) = \underline{+5V}$

(b) $r_{e1} = \frac{25\text{mV}}{0.86\text{mA}} = 29.1\Omega \rightarrow g_{m1} \approx \frac{1}{29.1} = \underline{34.4\text{mA/V}}$

$r_{e2} = \frac{25\text{mV}}{2\text{mA}} = 12.5\Omega \rightarrow g_{m2} \approx \frac{1}{12.5} = \underline{80}\ \text{mA/V}$

(c) $\frac{v_e}{v_a} = \left(-\frac{2.5k}{12.5} \times \frac{50}{51}\right)\left(-\frac{5k \| 51(12.5)}{29.1} \times \frac{50}{51}\right) = \underline{3735}\ \text{V/V}$

(d) $R_{in} = 50k \| (51(29.1)) = \underline{1.431\ k\Omega}$

(e) $R_{out} = 2.5\ k\Omega$

(f) $\frac{v_o}{v_s} = 3735 \times \frac{1.431}{1.431 + 10} \times \frac{5}{2.5 + 5} = 311.8 \simeq \underline{312}\ \text{V/V}$

(g) Critical level is reached in Q_2, such that

largest $v_o = 10\text{mV} \times \frac{2.5k \| 5k}{12.5} = \underline{1.3\dot{3}\ \text{V peak}}$

for which $v_s = \frac{1.3\dot{3}}{311.8} = \underline{4.28\ \text{mV}}$ peak

2 **Exam** **8**

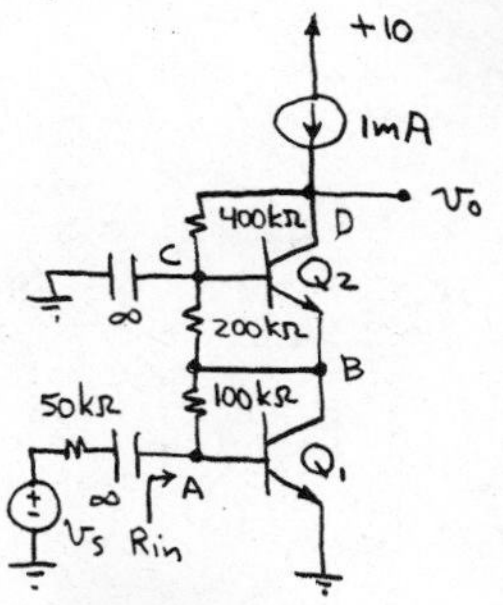

(a) For $V_{BE} = 0.7V$ and $\beta = \infty$, what are the voltages at nodes A, B, C, D?

(b) For $\beta = 100$, what does the voltage at D become?

(c) What is Rin corresponding?

(d) What is gain v_o/v_s corresponding?

(A) (a) For $\beta = \infty$, V_D rises until Q_2 and Q_1 conduct:

$V_A = \underline{0.7V}$, $I_{100k} = 0$; $V_B = \underline{0.7V}$, $V_C = \underline{1.4V}$

$I_{200k} = \frac{0.7}{200k} = 3.5\mu A$, $V_D = 1.4 + \frac{0.7}{200} \times 400 = \underline{2.8V}$

(b) Since the base resistors are large, assume $I_{C1} = I_{C2} = 1\text{mA}$

$\therefore I_{B1} = I_{B2} = \frac{1}{100} = 10\mu A$, $V_A = \underline{0.7V}$, $V_B = 0.7 + 0.1(10) = \underline{1.7V}$

$V_C = \underline{2.4V}$, and $V_D = 2.4 + 0.4M(10\mu A + 3.5\mu A) = \underline{7.8V}$

(c) $r_{e1} = r_{e2} = 25\Omega \rightarrow v_b/v_a \approx -1 \rightarrow R_{in} = \frac{100k}{1-(-1)} \| (101 \times 25) = \underline{2.40k\Omega}$

(d) $\frac{v_o}{v_s} \approx -\frac{400k}{25} \times \left(\frac{100}{101}\right)^2 \times \frac{2.4}{50 + 2.4} = \underline{-718.4}\ \text{V/V}$

1 **Design** **8**

Using npn transistors and current-sink biassing, design an amplifier, using one CE and 2CC stages and a ±15V supply, whose gain is negative and as large as possible, whose input and output are direct-coupled, whose input utilizes the signal source for biassing, whose input resistance exceeds 10kΩ, whose output voltage is approximately zero for an input of zero, whose output resistance is less than 100Ω, and whose output signal swing is at least ±2V with a 2kΩ load and transistors operating in a low-distortion mode, with less than ±10mV peak variation in v_{be}. Available transistors have $V_{BE} = 0.7V$ and nominal β of 200 with β varying from 100 to very large values. A single large capacitor is available for emitter bypassing. Three current sinks are available, whose values should be chosen to reduce the β-induced variability of device currents to ±10% or less. Two current sinks should have the same value, while the total supply current should be kept reasonably small. It is essential to reduce the number of resistors used. **8**

What gain does your design achieve between a 10kΩ source and 10kΩ load, for $\beta = \infty$?

(next)

(A) Consider:

8

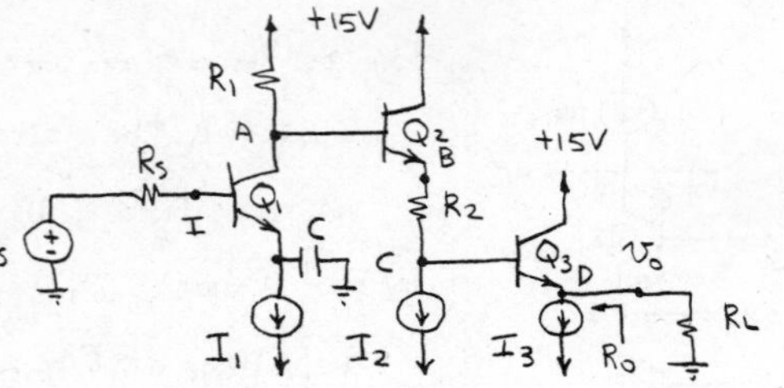

For small-signal operation : $\Delta v_{be} \le 10mV$.

Now $e^{10/25} = 1.49$. This implies that for linear operation, the collector current can vary from $2/3$ to 1.5 of nominal (ie increase by ½ or reduce by ⅓) during signal operation.

For I_3:

For $v_o = -2V$, the load requires $\frac{2V}{2k\Omega} = 1mA$, reducing the current in Q3 from nominal value I_3. For linear operation, $I_3/3 \ge 1mA$

or $I_3 \ge 3mA$

8

For $v_o = +2V$, the load requires 1mA, causing I_{C3} to increase from about 3mA to 4mA, an acceptable value < 1.5(3)

For I_2: $\beta = 200$ nominally, ranging from 100 to ∞

For $I_3 = 3mA$, $I_{B3} = \frac{3}{201 \text{ etc}} = 15\mu A \pm 15\mu A$

For a variation in I_{B3} of $\pm 15\mu A$ to represent less than $\pm 10\%$ variation in I_{E2},

$\frac{15\mu A}{I_2} \le 0.1$ or $I_2 \ge 150\mu A$

For I_1:

Input resistance $\ge 10k\Omega \rightarrow r_{e1} > \frac{10^4}{\beta_{min}+1} = \frac{10^4}{101} \simeq 100$

$\therefore I_1 \le \frac{25 \times 10^{-3}}{100} = 250\mu A$

ie $I_1 \le 250\mu A$

Consider a design where $I_3 = 3mA$, $I_1 = I_2 = 250\mu A$

For R_2: For $v_o = -2V$, Q_1 must stay away from saturation, say with $V_{CE} \ge 0$.

Now for β_1 very high, $v_I = 0V$ $\therefore v_A \ge 0$.

R_2 must be chosen to keep $v_A \ge 0$ while

$v_o \le 2V$. That is $R_2(I_2 + I_{B3}) = 0 - 0.7 - 0.7 - (-2)$ 8

or $R_2 = \frac{0.6}{0.25 + \frac{3.0}{201}} = \frac{0.6}{265\mu A} = 2.26 k\Omega$

Use $R_2 = 2.4 k\Omega$, a 5% standard value

For R_3: Consider nominal operation

With $V_o = 0V$, $V_A = 0 + 0.7 + 2.4k(0.265mA) + 0.7$

or $V_A = 2.04V$. Thus $R_3 = \frac{15 - 2.04}{\left(250 \times \frac{200}{201} + \frac{265}{201}\right) \times 10^{-6}} = 51.8k\Omega$

Use $R_3 = 51 k\Omega$, a 5% standard value.

For $v_o = +2V$, $i_L = \frac{2V}{2k} = 1mA$. Now for lowest β, (ie $\beta = 100$), $V_A = 2 + 0.7 + 2.4\left(0.25 + \frac{1}{101}\right) + 0.7 = 4.02V$

for which $I_{R1} = \frac{15 - 4.02}{51} = 0.215mA$.

Since this is > $2/3(250)$, Q_1 operates "linearly".

Output Resistance : $r_{e2} = \frac{25}{0.25} = 100\Omega$, $r_{e3} = \frac{25}{3} = 8.3\Omega$

Largest Ro occurs for $\beta = 100$ and is

$R_o = 8.3 + \frac{(2.4 + 0.1 + 51k/101)}{101} = 8.3 + 29.7 = 38\Omega < 100$ ✓

Overall : Total current = 3.0 + .25 + .25 = 3.5mA.

This could be reduced to 3.3mA, with the effect of raising the input resist.

8

above the spec. limit, but increasing the output variability as β changes.

Gain :

For $R_S = R_L = 10k\Omega$ and $\beta = \infty$

$r_{e1} = \frac{25}{.25} = 100 = r_{e2}$, $r_{e3} = \frac{25}{3} = 8.\dot{3}$, $r_{\pi 1} = r_{\pi 2} = r_{\pi 3} = \infty$

Gain $\frac{v_o}{v_s} = -1 \times \frac{51k}{100} \cdot \frac{1 \times 10k}{8.3 + 10k} = -510 V/V$

1 | **Exam** | 9

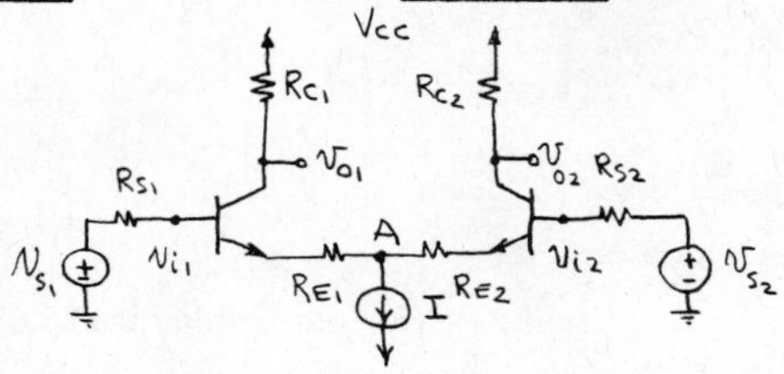

Unless otherwise specified, $I = 1mA$, $V_{CC} = +10V$, $V_{BE} = 0.7$, $\beta = 100$,

$R_{C1} = R_{C2} = 10k\Omega$, $R_{S1} = R_{S2} = 10k\Omega$, $R_{E1} = R_{E2} = 50\Omega$

Now, find:

(a) The dc output voltages, V_{o1}, V_{o2}, for $V_{s1} = V_{s2} = 0V$.

(b) The differential voltage gains $\frac{v_{o1}}{v_{id}} = \frac{v_{o1}}{v_{i1} - v_{i2}}$

and $\frac{v_{od}}{v_{id}} = \frac{v_{o1} - v_{o2}}{v_{i1} - v_{i2}}$

(c) The common-mode gains $\frac{v_{o1}}{v_{icm}}$

and $\frac{v_{od}}{v_{icm}} = \frac{v_{o1} - v_{o2}}{v_{icm}}$

if the source I has an output resistance, $R_o = 500k\Omega$

(d) The overall common-mode gain $\frac{v_{od}}{v_{scm}} = \frac{v_{o1} - v_{o2}}{(v_{s1} + v_{s2})/2}$

if $R_{s1} = 10k\Omega$, while $R_{s2} = 9k\Omega$ and $R_o = 500k\Omega$

(Note that this part is somewhat tricky)

(e) The correspond difference-mode gain 9

$$\frac{v_{od}}{v_{sd}} = \frac{v_{o1} - v_{o2}}{v_{s1} - v_{s2}}$$

(f) The corresponding CMRR in dB.

(A)

(a) For $V_{s1} = V_{s2} = 0$, and input circuits balanced

$$V_{o1} = 10 - 10k\left(\frac{100}{101}\right)\frac{1mA}{2} = \underline{5.05V} = V_{o2}$$

(b) For differential gains, use a DM half circuit with node A, a virtual ground.

$$r_{e1} = r_{e2} = \frac{25}{1/2} = 50\Omega$$

$$\therefore \text{ for one half circuit, } \frac{v_{o1}}{v_{d}/2} = \frac{v_{o1}}{v_{i1}} = \frac{-10k\left(\frac{100}{101}\right)}{50 + 50}$$

$$= -99.0\,V/V = 2\frac{v_{o1}}{v_d}$$

$$\text{Thus } \frac{v_{o1}}{v_{id}} = -\frac{99.0}{2} = -49.5\,V/V$$

$$\text{and } \frac{v_{od}}{v_{id}} = \frac{v_{o1} - v_{o2}}{v_{id}} = \frac{v_{o1}}{v_{id}} - \frac{v_{o2}}{v_{id}} = -49.5 - (-49.5) = \underline{\underline{-99.0\,V/V}}$$

(c) Using a CM half circuit,

$$\frac{v_{o1}}{v_{icm}} = \frac{-10k\left(\frac{100}{101}\right)}{50 + 50 + 2(500k)} = -.0099\,V/V = \frac{v_{o2}}{v_{icm}} \text{ as well}$$

$$\therefore \frac{v_{od}}{v_{icm}} = \frac{v_{o1} - v_{o2}}{v_{icm}} = -.0099 - (-.0099) = \underline{\underline{0\,V/V}}$$

(d) Equivalent input circuit is as follows: 9

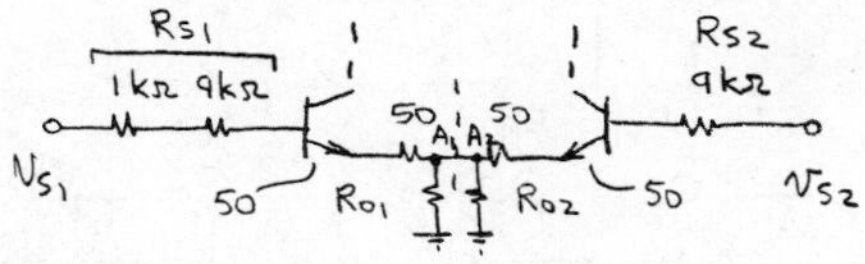

$R_{o1} \| R_{o2} = 500k$ where R_{o1}, R_{o2} chosen so $v_{A1} = v_{A2}$

and calculation can proceed with 2 "half" circ.

$$\text{See } \frac{v_{A1}}{v_{cm}} = \frac{R_{o1}}{50 + 50 + \frac{10k}{101}} = \frac{101 R_{o1}}{20.1k}$$

$$\frac{v_{A2}}{v_{cm}} = \frac{R_{o2}}{50 + 50 + \frac{9k}{101}} = \frac{101 R_{o2}}{19.1k}$$

$$v_{A1} = v_{A2} \text{ when } \frac{R_{o1}}{20.1} = \frac{R_{o2}}{19.2} \text{ or } \frac{R_{o1}}{R_{o2}} = \frac{20.1}{19.1} = 1.0523$$

$$\text{or } R_{o1} = 1.0523 R_{o2}$$

$$\text{But } R_{o1} \| R_{o2} = \frac{R_{o1} R_{o2}}{R_{o1} + R_{o2}} = 500k\Omega$$

$$\therefore \frac{1.052(R_{o2})(R_{o2})}{1.052 R_{o2} + R_{o2}} = 500k \rightarrow R_{o2} = \frac{500k\,(2.052)}{1.052} = 975.3k\Omega$$

$$\text{and } R_{o1} = 1.052 R_{o2} = 1026k\Omega$$

$$\therefore \frac{v_{od}}{v_{scm}} = \frac{v_{o1}}{v_{scm}} - \frac{v_{o2}}{v_{scm}} = \frac{10k \times 100/101}{50 + 50 + 1026k} - \frac{10k \times 100/101}{50 + 50 + 975.3k}$$

$$= 10k(100/101)\left(\frac{1}{1026.1k} - \frac{1}{975.4k}\right) = \underline{-.000501\,V/V}$$

More directly:

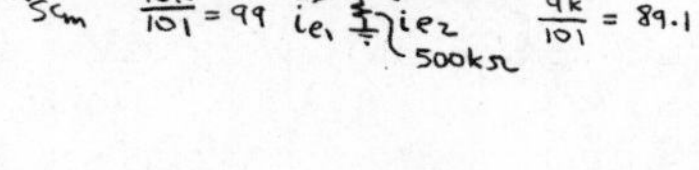

9

$$i_{e1} + i_{e2} \approx \frac{v_{scm}}{500k} = i_t$$

$$i_{e1} = \frac{50 + 50 + 89.1}{50 + 50 + 50 + 50 + 99 + 89.1} \times i_t = \frac{189.1}{388.1} i_t = 0.4872\,i_t$$

$$\frac{v_{od}}{v_{scm}} = -\frac{100}{101}\left(\frac{10k}{500k}\right)\left(.4872 - (1 - .4872)\right) = \underline{-.000505\,V/V}$$

(e) $$\frac{v_{od}}{v_{sd}} = -\frac{10k + 10k}{\frac{10k}{101} + 50 + 50 + 50 + 50 + \frac{9k}{101}} = \frac{-20k}{\frac{19k}{101} + 200} = \underline{\underline{-51.53}}$$

(f) $$\text{CMRR} = \frac{-51.53}{-5.05 \times 10^{-4}} = \underline{\underline{102\,854\,V/V}}$$

$$\text{or } 20\log_{10}(102.8 \times 10^3) = \underline{\underline{100.2\,dB}}$$

2 | Exam | 9

A CMOS amplifier utilizes an NMOS differential pair with a PMOS active load. The pair is biassed by a 20μA current sink. For all devices $K = 10\mu A/V^2$, $|V_t| = 1V$, and $|V_A| = 30V$. The input gates are biassed at 0V, and the positive supply is +10V.

(a) What is the voltage at the common source of the n-channel devices?

(b) What is the voltage at the common gate of the p-channel devices?

(c) What is the output voltage?

(d) What is the output resistance?

(e) What is the differential voltage gain?

(A) | 9

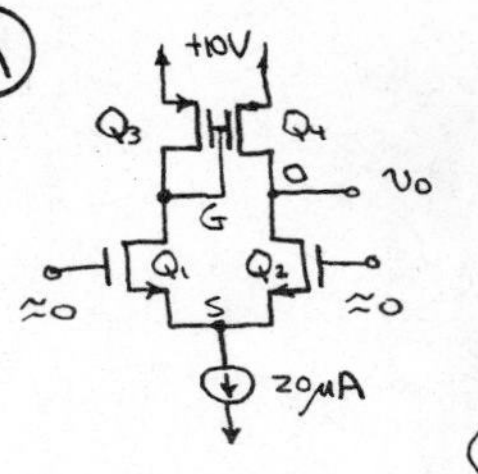

$K = 10\mu A/V^2$

$|V_t| = 1V$

$|V_A| = 30V$

(a) Ignoring V_A for bias calc.

$i_D = K(v_{GS} - V_t)^2 \rightarrow \frac{20}{2} = 10(v_{GS} - 1)^2$,

$v_{GS} - 1 = 1$, $v_{GS} = 2V \rightarrow V_S = \underline{\underline{-2V}}$

(b) Each p device conducts 10μA and $K = 10\mu A/V^2$, $|V_t| = 1V$. Thus $v_{GS} = 2V \rightarrow V_G = 10 - 2 = \underline{\underline{+8V}}$

(c) Symmetry (including r_o effects) imply that $V_o = V_G = \underline{\underline{+8V}}$

(d) For all devices, $r_o = \frac{V_A}{I_D} = \frac{30V}{10\mu A} = \underline{\underline{3 \times 10^6 \Omega}}$

∴ R_o of amplifier $= 3M \| 3M = \underline{\underline{1.5M\Omega}}$

(e) For Q_1, Q_2, $g_m = 2K(v_{GS} - V_t)$

ie $g_m = 2(10 \times 10^{-6})(2-1) = 20\mu A/V$

$\therefore \left|\frac{v_o}{v_d}\right| = 2\left(\frac{1.5 \times 10^6}{\frac{1}{20 \times 10^{-6}} + \frac{1}{20 \times 10^{-6}}}\right) = \frac{3}{2/20} = \underline{\underline{30 V/V}}$

1 | Design | 9

Design a direct-coupled BJT amplifier using an npn differential amplifier stage with active load, and an output follower incorporating an output resistor for level shifting. Employ current-mirror biassing using a single resistor, with the output stage operating at 10 times the current level of <u>each</u> input transistor. The output should be 0V for inputs of 0V, and capable of producing a peak output of ±1.5V when loaded by 10kΩ to ground. A supply of ±10V is available. For your design, specify all resistors used and relative device areas. What is the voltage gain with a 10kΩ load, and the differential input resistance, both for $\beta = 100$.

(A) Consider: | 9

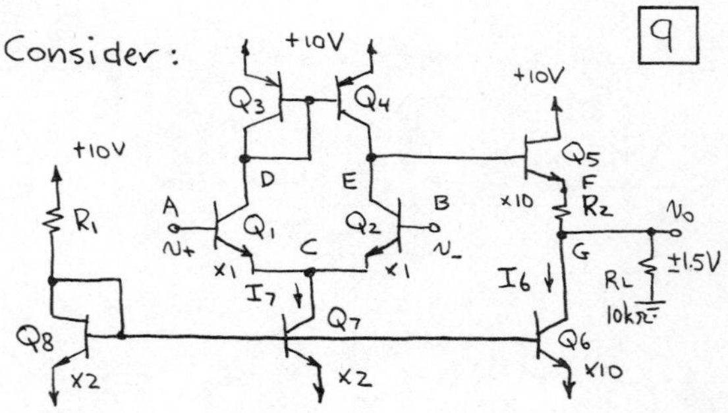

Topology is as shown. Assume $|V_{BE}| = 0.7V$

Transistors are area-scaled as shown (x1, x2 etc) for equal current densities.

For inputs near zero, ensure maximum output swing by arranging that V_E lies midway between saturation of Q_4 and Q_2. Using $V_{CB} = 0$ as the edge of saturation,

$V_E = \frac{10 - 0.7 - 0}{2} = 5.35V$

∴ $V_F = 5.35 - 0.7 = 4.65V$ and $I_6 R_2 = 4.65V$ — ①

For $v_o = -1.5V$, inputs near 0V, and Q_2 at

the edge of saturation, $V_E = 0V$, $V_F = -0.7V$ **9**

Thus the voltage across R_2 must be $-0.7-(-1.5) = 0.8V$. Thus $I_6 = \frac{0.8}{R_2} + \frac{1.5V}{10k}$ — ②

Now, from ①, $R_2 = \frac{4.65}{I_6}$

$\therefore I_6 = \frac{0.8}{4.65} I_6 + \frac{1.5}{10k} = 0.172 I_6 + 0.15 \text{ mA}$

$\therefore I_6 = \frac{0.15}{1-.172} = 0.181 \text{ mA}$

and $R_2 = \frac{4.65}{.181} = 25.7 k\Omega$

Use $R_2 = 27k\Omega$, for which $I_6 = \frac{4.65}{27k} = 172 \mu A$

For Q8 1/5 the size of Q6,

$R_1 = \frac{+10-(-10)-0.7}{172/5} = 0.561 \text{ M}$

Use $R_1 = 560 k\Omega$, $R_2 = 27k\Omega$, $I_6 = 172\mu A$, $I_7 = 34.4\mu A$

Differential input resistance $= 2(101 \times \frac{25\times10^{-3}}{34.4/2\times10^{-6}})$

or $202 \times 1.45k = 294 k\Omega$

Neglecting r_o, voltage gain, A_v, is

$$A_v = 2\left(\frac{100}{101}\right)\left(\frac{10k\times101}{1.45k+1.45k}\right)\left(\frac{10k}{10k+27k+\frac{25}{.172}}\right) = 185.6 \text{ V/V}$$

1 **Exam** **10**

Consider the Class AB output stage shown in which $|V_{BE}| = 0.7V$ at 100 mA for Q_N, Q_P and 1mA for Q_1. For all transistors, $n=1$, $\beta = 100$. $R_L = 10\Omega$

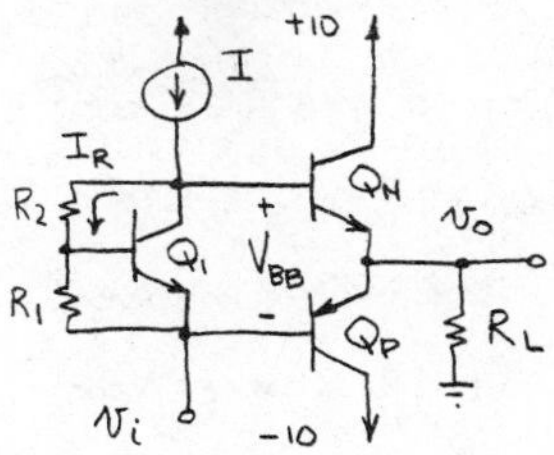

ⓐ For v_o of at least 5V positive, what is the smallest usable value of I?

ⓑ For v_o of 0V and a quiescent current of 10mA in Q_N, Q_P, what value of V_{EB} is required?

ⓒ For I = 10 mA and I_R = 1mA, what value of R_1 and R_2 are required to satisfy conditions ⓑ

ⓓ For the design in ⓒ with $V_o = 0V$ and $R_L = 10\Omega$

i) What value of v_i is needed?

ii) What small-signal gain, v_o/v_i, applies?

ⓔ For $v_o = +5V$, using an approximate analysis, estimate: **10**

i) the corresponding value of v_i

ii) the small-signal voltage gain.

Ⓐ ⓐ For $v_o = +5V$ and $\beta = 100$, $I_{BN} = \frac{5}{10} \times \frac{1}{101} = 4.95$ mA

Thus $I \gg$ 4.95 mA for $v_o \gg 5V$ across 10Ω

ⓑ For $I_{C_N} = 10$ mA, $V_{BE} = 700 + 25 \ln \frac{10}{100} = 642.4$ mV

Thus required $V_{BB} = 2(642.4)$ mV $= 1.285$ V

ⓒ For $\beta = 100$ and $I_{CN} = 10$mA, $I_{BN} = \frac{10}{100} = 0.1$mA

Now if $I_R = 1$mA and $I = 10$mA, $I_C = 10-1-0.1 = 8.9$ mA

$V_{BE} = 700 + \ln \frac{8.9}{1} = 754.7$ mV

For $I_R = 1$mA, $R_2 = \frac{1.285-0.755}{1mA} = 530\Omega$

and $R_1 = \frac{.755}{1-8.9/100} = 829\Omega$

ⓓ For $v_o = 0V$, $v_i = 0 - \frac{1.285}{2} = -0.645V$

There are two signal paths from v_i to v_o:

For Q_P, Q_N, $r_e = \frac{25mV}{10mA} = 2.5\Omega$

For Q_1, $r_e = \frac{25mV}{8.9mA} \times \frac{101}{100} = 2.84\Omega$ **10**

The equivalent resistance of the Q_1 circuit is $\approx \frac{1.285}{0.755} \times 2.84 = 4.8\Omega$

$\therefore$ output resistance of amplifier, R_o is

$R_o = 2.5 \| (2.5 + \frac{4.8}{101}) \approx 1.26\Omega$

$\therefore v_o/v_i = \frac{10}{1.26+10} = 0.888$ V/V

ⓔ For $v_o = +5V$, $i_L = \frac{5}{10} = 500$mA, $v_{BE_N} = 700 + 25\ln\frac{500}{100} = 740$ mV

and $i_{BN} = \frac{500}{101} = 4.95$ mA

$\therefore i_{C1} \approx 10-5-1 = 4$mA, $v_{BE_1} = 700 + 25 \ln \frac{4}{1} = 735$ mV

$\therefore V_{BB} = 735 + 530\left(\frac{735}{829} + \frac{4}{101}\right) = 1226$ mV

$\therefore v_i = +5 + 0.74 - 1.226 = 4.514V$

Thus $V_{BE_P} = 5.000 - 4.514 = .486V$

and $i_{EP} = 100mA\, e^{\frac{486-700}{25}} = 19.2\mu A$

$\therefore R_o$ is dominated by the Q_N path:

$R_o \approx \frac{25mV}{500mA} + \frac{25mV}{4mA} \times \frac{1226}{735} \times \frac{1}{101} = .05 + .103 = .153\Omega$

and $v_o/v_i = \frac{10}{10+0.153} = 0.985$ V/V

2 | Exam | 10

A power transistor is rated at $P_{Dmax} = 100W$ at a maximum junction temperature, T_{jmax}, of 200°C and case temperature, $T_C \le 25°C$. It is to be mounted on a heat sink of suitable size to allow it to operate with a dissipation of 50W at an ambient temperature of 40°C. If the connection to the heat sink involves a thermal resistance θ_{CS} of 0.5 °C/W, and the heat sink has a thermal conductance of 0.5W/°C per cm. of length, what length of heat sink is required? Assuming that an extremely large (infinite) heat sink is available, what is the largest thermal resistance that can be tolerated in connecting the transistor to it in this case?

(A) | 10

$\theta_{jc} = \frac{200-25}{100} = 1.75°C/W$

For a sink length l, $50\left(1.75+0.5+\frac{1}{0.5l}\right)+40 = 200$

ie $2.25 + \frac{1}{0.5l} = \frac{160}{50} = 3.2$

or $l = \frac{1}{0.5 \times 0.95} = 2.1\ cm$

For a very large sink, $50(1.75+\theta_{CS}) + 40 \le 200$

ie $\theta_{CS} \le \frac{200-40}{50} - 1.75 = 1.45°C/W$

1 | Design | 10

A design is required of the class AB output stage shown to meet the following constraints:

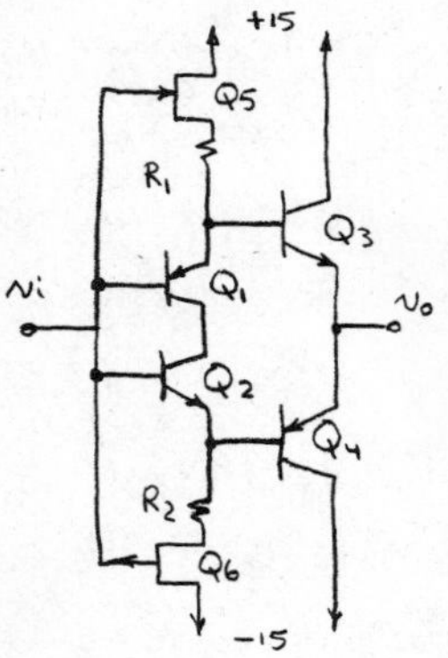

(1) Available FETs have $|V_P|$ in the range 2 to 4V and I_{DSS} in the range 6 to 12 mA, and are otherwise similar but not matched.

(2) Q3 and Q4 are 100 mA transistors, with β of 50 or more and $n = 1$.

(3) Q_1 and Q_2 have high β, but must be sized appropriately.

(4) The standing current in Q3 and Q4 must lie in the range 1 to 5mA, and at the high end.

(5) The peak current in Q3 or Q4 can be as high as 100 mA.

Your design should provide the relative junction sizes of Q_1 and Q_2 and values for resistors R_1 and R_2

10

(A) For the required peak current $|V_{BE}|_{1,2} = 0.7V$ and $I_{B_{1,2}} \le \frac{100}{50} = 2mA$

Consider the positive half circuit with $V_O = V_I$: R_1 must be chosen to provide 2mA plus the current in Q_1 for the least capable FET, namely one having low I_{DSS} and low V_P. For a minimal design let us assume that the current in Q_1 reduces to zero at peak.

$\therefore 2mA = 6mA\left(1 - \frac{v_{GS}}{-2}\right)^2$ and $v_{SG} = 2mA(R_1) + 0.7$

or $2 = 6\left(1 - \frac{2R_1 + 0.7}{2}\right)^2 = 6(0.65 - R_1)^2$

ie $0.65 - R_1 = \sqrt{1/3} = 0.577 \rightarrow R_1 = 0.65 - 0.577 = 0.73k$

To provide extra current (say for Q_1) use $R_1 = 68\,\Omega$ 10

But what is the maximum standing current in Q_1?

The standing current in Q_3 must range from 1 to 5 mA, and for Q_1 a factor k times Q_3 in size, the current in Q_1 can be as large as 5k mA. Thus for $\beta_3 = \infty$, $I_{DS_{max}} \times k < 5\text{mA}$

Now for $I_{C3} = 5\text{mA}$, $V_{BE3} = 700 + 25 \ln \frac{5}{100} = 0.625\text{V}$

I_{DS} is greatest for high I_{DSS} and high V_P

ie $I = 12\left(1 - \frac{v_{GS}}{-4}\right)^2$ and $v_{SG} = IR_1 + 0.625$

or $I = 12\left(1 - \frac{I(.068) + .625}{4}\right)^2$

$= 12(1 - .017I - .156)^2 = (2.92 - .0589I)^2$

$= 8.53 - 0.343I + .00347I^2$

and $.00347I^2 - 1.343I + 8.53 = 0$ where

ignoring I^2 term, $I \approx \frac{8.53}{1.343} = 6.4\text{mA}$

Thus $k = \frac{6.4}{5} = 1.28 \approx 1.3$

ie Q_1 should be 1.3 x the size of Q_3.

Now what is the minimum standing current in Q_3? It occurs with the least capable FET where $i_D = 6\left(1 - \frac{v_{GS}}{-2}\right)^2$ and $v_{SG} = i_D(.068) + V_{EB \text{ at } i_D}$. 10

Check for 1mA: $V_{EB} = 0.7 + .025 \ln \frac{1}{100(1.3)} = 0.578\text{V}$

$\therefore v_{SG} = 1(0.068) + 0.578 = 0.646\text{V}$

$i_D = 6\left(1 - \frac{0.646}{2}\right)^2 = 2.75\text{mA} > 1$, so OK

Thus Q_1 and Q_2 have an EB area 1.3 times that of Q_3 and Q_4 and $R_1 = R_2 = 68\,\Omega$

Note that a comment is due on the initial symmetry assumption (ie $V_O = V_I$): When Q_5 and Q_6 are opposite extremes, say Q_5 strongest, the extra current causes that in Q_1 to increase. Since the current in Q_2 is lower (fixed by Q_6), the excess flows in Q_4. Thus a small output offset exists corresponding to a few mA difference in a 100mA junction.

1 **Exam** 11

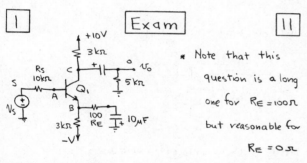

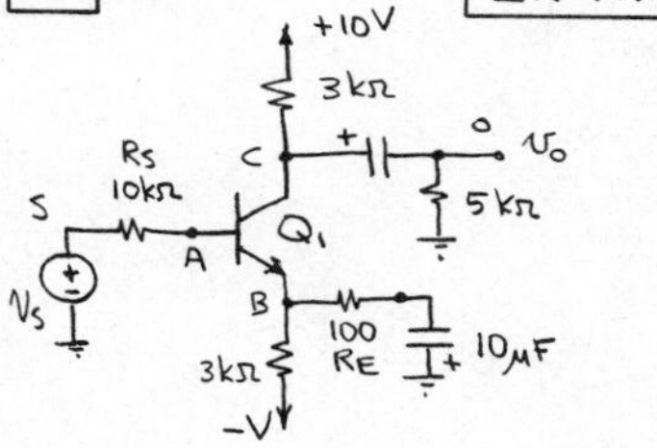

* Note that this question is a long one for $R_E = 100\,\Omega$ but reasonable for $R_E = 0\,\Omega$

In the circuit shown, Q_1 is biassed at $I_E = 2\text{mA}$, $h_{fe} = 150$, $f_T = 1\text{GHz}$, $C_\mu = 1\text{pF}$, $r_o = \infty$.

Find:

ⓐ The voltage gain, $A_m = v_o/v_s$.

ⓑ Two poles and a zero at low frequencies, that is f_1, f_2, f_3.

ⓒ An estimate of the lower 3dB frequency, f_L.

ⓓ The high-frequency input pole, f_3.

ⓔ An estimate of the upper 3dB frequency, f_H.

Ⓐ ⓐ $I_E = 2\text{mA} \rightarrow r_e = \frac{25}{2} = 12.5\,\Omega$ 11

Equivalent resistance in emitter $= 100 \| 3k = 96.8\,\Omega$

Gain $v_o/v_s = -\frac{3k\|5k}{12.5 + 96.8} \times \frac{150}{151} \times \frac{151(12.5 + 96.8)}{151(12.5 + 96.8) + 10k}$

$= -\frac{1.875k}{109.3} \times \frac{150}{151} \times \frac{16.5k}{26.5k} = -10.6\text{V/V}$

* For $R_E = 0$, $v_o/v_s = \frac{-3k\|5k}{12.5} \times \frac{150}{151} \times \frac{151(12.5)}{10k + 151(12.5)} = -23.7\text{V/V}$

ⓑ For output circuit, pole is

$f_2 = \frac{1}{2\pi \times 1 \times 10^{-6} \times (3k + 5k)} = 19.9\text{Hz}$

For emitter circuit, pole is

$f_1 = \frac{1}{2\pi \times 10 \times 10^{-6}\left(\left(\frac{10k}{151} + 12.5\right) \| (3k + 100)\right)} = 90.1\text{Hz}$

* For $R_E = 0$, $f_1 = \frac{1}{2\pi \times 10 \times 10^{-6}\left(12.5 + \frac{10k}{151}\right)} = 202\text{Hz}$

For the zero

* For $R_E = 0$, $f_Z = \frac{1}{2\pi \times 10 \times 10^{-6} \times 3k} = 5.3\text{Hz}$

For $R_E = 100\,\Omega$,

$Y_E(s) = \frac{1}{3k} + \frac{1}{0.1 + 1/Cs} = 1/3 + \frac{Cs}{1 + 0.1Cs}$

Now $Y_E(s)$ is zero when $\frac{Cs}{1 + 0.1Cs} = -1/3$

or $3Cs = -1 - 0.1Cs$, or $s = \frac{-1}{C(3.1)}$

Thus $f_Z = \frac{1}{2\pi \times 10 \times 10^{-6} \times 3.1k} = 5.13\text{Hz}$

11

(c) $f_1 = 90.1\ Hz$, $f_2 = 19.9\ Hz$

$\therefore f_L \simeq 90.1\ Hz$

$f_L \le 90.1 + 19.9 = 110 Hz$

$f_L \simeq (90.1^2 + 19.9^2)^{1/2} = \underline{92.3\ Hz}$

* For $R_E = 0$, $f_L \simeq \underline{202\ Hz}$

(d) For the input pole: (using a Miller interpretation of Eq 11.96)

$f_T = \frac{1}{2\pi} \times \frac{g_m}{C_\pi + C_\mu}$, $g_m = \frac{\alpha}{r_e} = \frac{150}{151} \times \frac{1}{12.5} = 79.5\ mA/V$

$C_\pi = \frac{g_m}{2\pi f_T} - C_\mu = \frac{79.5 \times 10^{-3}}{2\pi \times 10^9} - 1 \times 10^{-12} = 12.7 - 1 = 11.7 pF$

For C_T and R_T, use Miller's theorem twice, both for the base to collector circuit and for the base to emitter circuit:

For base to collector, gain is $\simeq \frac{-3k\|5k}{100 + 12.5} = -16.\dot{6}\ V/V$

For base to emitter, gain is $\simeq \frac{100}{100 + 12.5} = 0.8\dot{8}\ V/V$

$\therefore C_T = 1(1 - (-16.\dot{6})) + 11.7(1 - (+.8\dot{8})) = 17.\dot{6} + 1.30 = 19.0 pF$

$R_T = 10k \| \left(\frac{151(12.5)}{1 - (+.8\dot{8})}\right) = 6.29 k\Omega$

$\therefore f_3 = \frac{1}{2\pi \times 6.29 \times 10^3 \times 19 \times 10^{-12}} = \underline{1.33 MHz}$

* For $R_E = 0$, $C_T = 1(1 - (-\frac{3k\|5k}{12.5})) + 11.7 = 162.7\ pF$

11

$R_T = 10k \| (151 \times 12.5) = 1.59k$

$\therefore f_3 = \frac{1}{2\pi \times 162.7 \times 10^{-12} \times 1.59 \times 10^3} = \underline{0.615\ MHz}$

(e) The output pole, $f_4 = \frac{1}{2\pi \times 1pF \times (3k\|5k)} \simeq 85\ MHz$

$\therefore f_H = \underline{1.33\ MHz}$

* For $R_E = 0$, $f_H = \underline{0.615}\ MHz$

2 Exam 11

In the circuit shown, Q_1 is biassed for $g_{m_1} = 1mA/V$

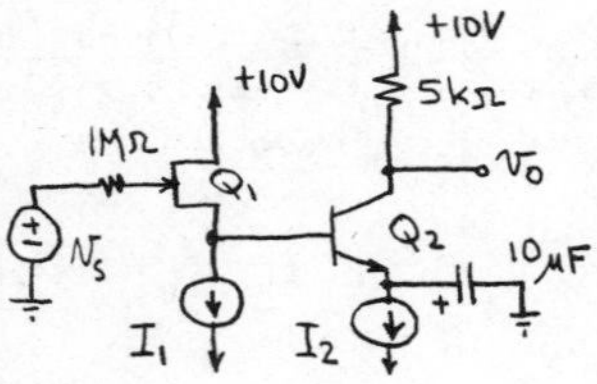

and Q_2 for $g_{m_2} = 40 mA/V$

$C_{gs_1} = C_{gd_1} = C_{ds_1} = 1pF$

$C_{\pi 2} = 10pF$, $C_{\mu 2} = 1pF$

$h_{fe_2} = 100$

Find:

(a) The voltage gain $A_m = v_o/v_s$

(b) The lower 3dB frequency, f_L

(c) The upper 3dB frequency, f_H

(A) (a) $r_{\pi 2} = \frac{\beta}{g_m} = \frac{100}{40 \times 10^{-3}} = 2.5k\Omega$, $r_s = \frac{1}{1mA/V} = 1k\Omega$

$\therefore v_o/v_s = -40 \times 5 \times \left(\frac{100}{101}\right) \times \frac{2.5}{2.5 + 1} = \underline{-141.4\ V/V}$

(b) Single pole due to $10\mu F$ at

$f_L = \frac{1}{2\pi \times 10 \times 10^{-6} \times \left(\frac{2.5k + 1k}{101}\right)} = \underline{459\ Hz}$

(next)

11

(c) For f_H:

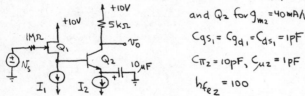

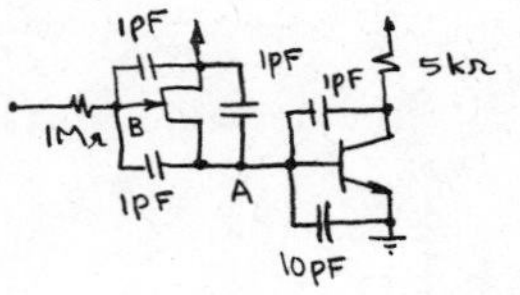

At A: $C_{T_A} = 1 + 10 + 1(1 + 40 \times 5) = 212\ pF$

$R_{T_A} = 2.5k \| 1k = 0.714 k\Omega$

At B: $C_{T_B} = 1 + 1(1 - \frac{2.5}{1 + 2.5}) = 1.29 pF$

$R_{T_B} = 1M\Omega$

$f_H \simeq \frac{1}{2\pi} \frac{1}{0.714 \times 10^3 \times 212 \times 10^{-12} + 10^6 \times 1.29 \times 10^{-12}}$

$\frac{1}{2\pi} \frac{1}{(0.151 + 1.29)\mu s} = \underline{110 kHz}$

Using 2 npn BJTs for which $h_{fe} = 100$, $f_T = 1\,GHz$, $C_\mu = 1\,pF$, $V_{BE} = 0.7V$, and a total bias current of 2 mA, design a broadband amplifier for use with a 10 kΩ source and a 10 kΩ load. Use constant current supplies for biassing wherever possible and direct-coupled load and source. A +15V voltage supply is available. The magnitude of the gain should be at least 100, with the largest possible bandwidth. Use as few capacitors as possible to establish a lower 3dB frequency at 100 Hz. Note that the source and load will accept reasonable dc bias currents.

Consider:

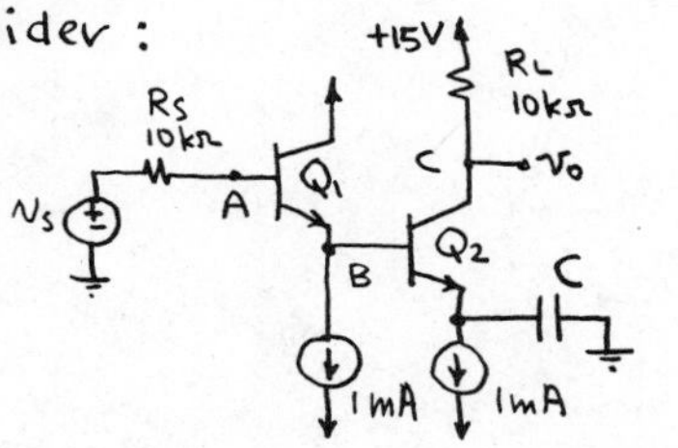

Overall:

For both Q_1, Q_2, $r_e = \frac{25}{1} = 25\Omega$, $r_\pi = 101(25) = 2.525k$

$$g_m = \frac{100}{101} \times \frac{1}{r_e} = 39.6\,mA/V$$

$$C_\pi = \frac{39.6 \times 10^{-3}}{2\pi \times 10^9} - 10^{-12} = 5.3pF$$

Gain: $$V_o/V_s = -\frac{100}{101} \times \frac{10k}{25} \times \frac{2.525}{2.525 + .025} \times \frac{10(2.525 + .025)}{10 + 101(2.525 + .025)} = -336.3\,V/V$$

Bandwidth:

At B, $C_T = 1pF\left(1 + \frac{10k}{25} \times \frac{100}{101}\right) + 5.3 = 397\,pF$

$$R_T = (101 \times 25) \| \left(25 + \frac{10k}{101}\right) = 118\Omega$$

$$f_B = \frac{1}{2\pi \times 397 \times 10^{-12} \times 118} = 3.40\,MHz$$

At C, $f_C = \frac{1}{2\pi \times 1 \times 10^{-12} \times 10^4} = 15.9\,MHz$

At A, $C_T = 1pF + 5.3pF\left(1 - \frac{2.525}{2.525 + .025}\right) \approx 1pF$

$$R_T = 10k \| (101(25 + 2.525k)) \approx 10k\Omega$$

$$f_A = \frac{1}{2\pi \times 10^4 \times 1 \times 10^{-12}} = 15.9\,MHz$$

For low cutoff at 100 Hz

$$C \simeq \frac{1}{2\pi \times 25 \times 100} = 63.6\,\mu F$$

Direction for redesign:

See have a surplus of gain with which to extend band width. See dominant pole is f_B, due mainly to Miller effect with C_μ. Consider:

(1) Shunting R_L by R_C to reduce the gain to -100. This reduces the gain across Q_2 to $\frac{100}{336} \times 400 = 119$ requiring that $R_L \| R_C = \frac{10k}{400} \times 119 = 2.975k = \frac{10k}{3.36}$ for which $R_C = \frac{10k}{3.36 - 1} = 4.24k$.

This change would raise f_C to $15.9 \times \frac{10}{2.975} = 53.4\,MHz$ and f_B to $\frac{1}{2\pi \times 118 \times (1(1 + 119) + 5.3) \times 10^{-12}} = 10.8\,MHz$ leaving f_A at 15.9 MHz

Overall $f_H \approx \left(\frac{1}{15.9^2} + \frac{1}{10.8^2} + \frac{1}{53.4^2}\right)^{-1/2} = 8.8\,MHz$

(2) Alternatively, including a resistor R_E in series with the emitter circuit of Q_2, to reduce the gain to 119.

Thus $\frac{100}{101} \times \frac{10k}{25 + R_E} = 119$

whence $R_E = 83.2 - 25 = 58.2\Omega$

in which case f_C stays at 15.9 MHz, but f_B rises: $R_{T_B} = (101(25 + 58.2)) \| \left(25 + \frac{10k}{101}\right) = 125\Omega$

$$C_{T_B} = 1\left(1 + \frac{10k}{25 + 58.2} \times \frac{100}{101}\right) + 5.3\left(1 - \frac{58.2}{25 + 58.2}\right)$$

$$= 120 + 1.59 = 122\,pF$$

$$\rightarrow f_B = \frac{1}{2\pi \times 122 \times 10^{-12} \times 125} = 10.4\,MHz$$

Overall f_H would not be as high as previous (8.8MHz).

But it can be raised to nearly 8.8MHz by bootstrapping $C_{\mu 1}$ as follows:

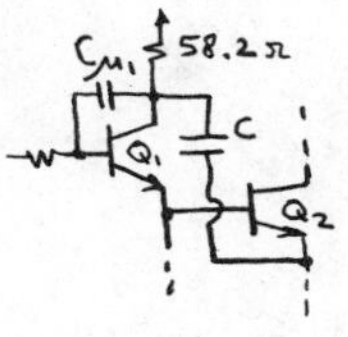

Here the upper end of $C_{\mu 1}$ moves about $\frac{58}{25 + 58} = 0.7$ times as much as its (input) lower end

$\therefore C_{T_A} = 1(1 - 0.7) = 0.3pF$

for which $f_A \approx 15.9 \times \frac{1}{0.3} = 53\,MHz$

For the latter cases (ie with $R_E = 58.2\Omega$), C can be reduced to $C = \frac{1}{2\pi \times 100 \times (58.2 + 25)} = 19.1\,\mu F$

11

Now, consider:

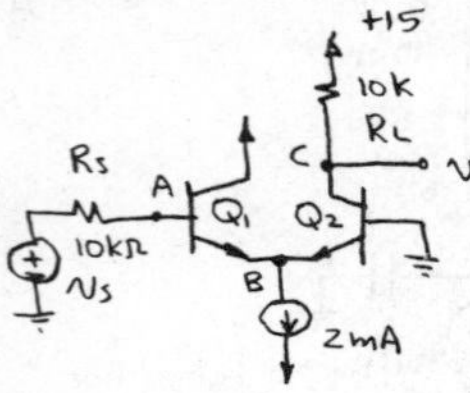

See $I_{E1} \simeq I_{E2}$, $r_{e1} = r_{e2} = 25\Omega$, $r_{\pi1} = r_{\pi2} \approx 2.5k$

$$\text{Gain} \approx \frac{2(2.5)}{2(2.5)+10} \times \frac{10k}{2(25)} = 66.\dot{6}$$

Thus the gain is a bit low. However there are no capacitors and the topology is simple. The gain could be raised by increasing the bias curren and/or hfe.

eg, $h_{fe} \approx \frac{10k}{25+25} = 200$ would suffice.

Bandwidth: $f_c = \frac{1}{2\pi \times 1 \times 10^{-12} \times 10k} = 15.9\text{ MHz}$

$R_{TA} = 10k \| (2.5k + 2.5k) = 3.3k$, $C_{TA} = \left(1 + \frac{5.3}{2}\right)\text{pF} = 3.65\text{ pF}$

$f_A = \frac{1}{2\pi \times 3.65 \times 10^{-12} \times 3.3 \times 10^3} = 13.2\text{ MHz}$

Thus $f_H = \left(\frac{1}{13.2^2} + \frac{1}{15.9^2}\right)^{-1/2} = \underline{\underline{10.2\text{ MHz}}}$

1 | Exam | 12

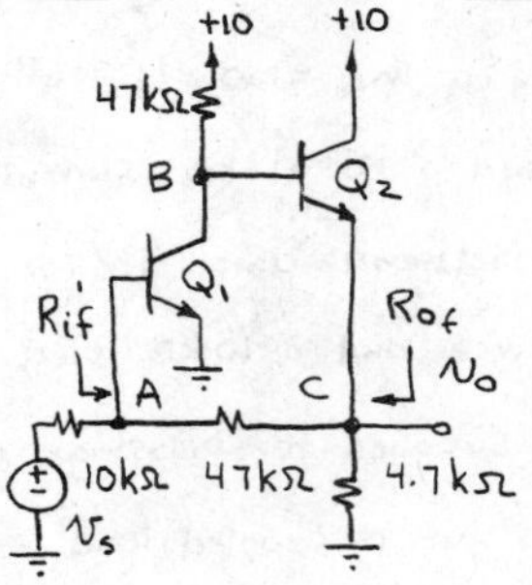

Analyse the circuit shown to find the loop gain $A\beta$, the small-signal voltage gain v_o/v_s, the input resistance R_{if}' (as shown) and the output resistance R_{of} (as shown). For Q_1, Q_2, $h_{fe} = 100$, $V_{BE} = 0.7V$.

(A) DC Bias: Use $\beta_{dc} = \infty$

$V_A = 0.7V$, $V_C = 0.7 + \frac{0.7}{10k} \times 47k = 3.99V$

$I_{E2} = \frac{3.99}{10k + 47k} + \frac{3.99}{4.7k} = 0.07 + 0.849 = \underline{\underline{0.919\text{ mA}}}$

$V_B = 3.99 + 0.7 = 4.69V$, $I_{C1} = \frac{10 - 4.69}{47k} = \underline{\underline{0.113\text{ mA}}}$

Gains: $r_{e1} = \frac{25}{0.113} = 221\Omega$, $r_{e2} = \frac{25}{0.919} = 27.2\Omega$

$r_{\pi1} = 101(221) = 22.3k\Omega$, $r_{\pi2} = 101(27.2) = 2.748\Omega$

12

Feedback analysis:

Convert to standard shunt-shunt form with $I_s = V_s / 10k\Omega$

A Circuit:

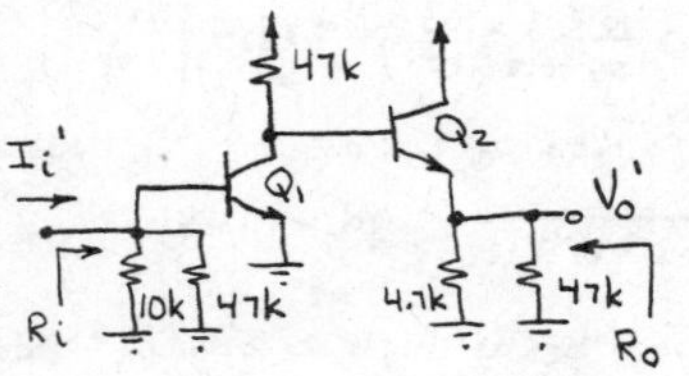

β Circuit:

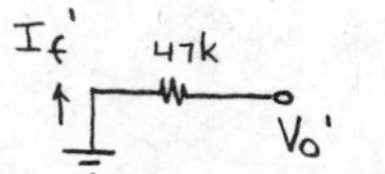

Load on emitter of $Q_2 = 4.7k \| 47k = 4.273k$

$R_o = 4.273k \| \left(27.2 + \frac{47k}{101}\right) = 442\Omega$

$R_i = 10k \| 47k \| 22.3k = 6.02k$

$$A = V_o'/I_i' = -6.02k \times \frac{100}{101} \times \frac{47k \| (101(27.2 + 4.273k))}{221} \times \frac{4.273k}{4.273k + 27.2} = \underline{\underline{-1137\text{ k}\Omega}}$$

$\beta = I_f'/V_o' = -\frac{1}{47k}$

Loop gain $A\beta = -1137k \times \frac{-1}{47k} = \underline{\underline{24.19}}\text{ V/V}$

$A_f = \frac{V_o}{I_s} = \frac{A}{1 + A\beta} = \frac{-1137k}{1 + 24.2} = -45.1\text{ k}\Omega$

12

Voltage gain $V_o/V_s = \frac{V_o}{10k\, I_s} = \frac{-45.1k}{10k} = \underline{\underline{-4.51\text{ V/V}}}$

Input Resistance with feedback $R_{if} = \frac{R_i}{1 + A\beta} = \frac{6.02k}{25.19} = 239\Omega$

Input Resistance excluding $R_s = R_{if}' = \left(\frac{1}{.239} - \frac{1}{10}\right)^{-1} = \underline{\underline{245\Omega}}$

Output Resistance with feedback $R_{of} = \frac{R_o}{1 + A_\beta} = \frac{442}{25.19} = \underline{\underline{17.5\Omega}}$

2 **Exam** 12

Consider an amplifier whose open-loop transfer function is characterized by 3 poles, at 10^5, 10^6 and 2×10^6 Hz, and for which the dc gain is 10^6. Following the rate-of-closure rule of thumb, what is the smallest closed-loop gain for which stability is assured with this amplifier? What gain and phase margins and approximate 3dB frequency correspond? If the dominant pole can be lowered, where must it be placed to allow a 20 dB reduction in closed-loop while maintaining similar margins

(A)

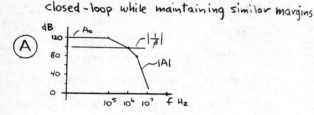

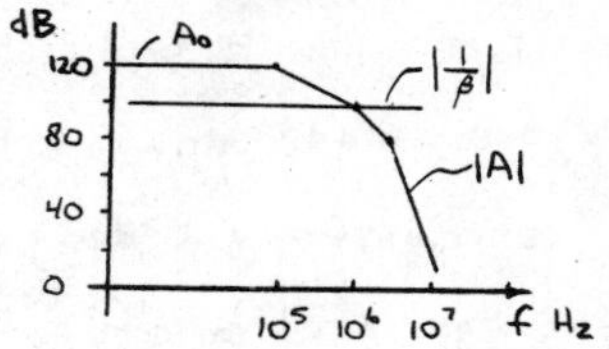

12

$$A(s) = \frac{10^6}{\left(1+\frac{s}{2\pi \times 10^5}\right)\left(1+\frac{s}{2\pi \times 10^6}\right)\left(1+\frac{s}{2\pi \times 2 \times 10^6}\right)}$$

The minimum value of $20\log_{10}(1/\beta)$ indicated by the 20 dB rate-of-closure rule is 100 dB

The corresponding closed-loop gain would be $\frac{10^6}{1+10^{-5} \times 10^6} = \underline{9.1 \times 10^5}$

At 10^6 Hz where $A\beta = 1$, the phase shift is

$$\theta = \tan^{-1}\frac{10^6}{10^5} + \tan^{-1}\frac{10^6}{10^6} + \tan^{-1}\frac{10^6}{2 \times 10^6}$$

$$= 84.3^\circ + 45^\circ + 26.6^\circ = 156^\circ$$

Thus the corresponding phase margin is $180 - 156 = \underline{\underline{24^\circ}}$

<u>For Gain margin</u>: Use a process of trial and success:

For $f = 1.3 \times 10^6$, $\theta = 85.6 + 52.4 + 33 = 171$

1.5×10^6, $\theta = 86.2 + 56.3 + 36.9 = 179.4$

$\therefore \theta = 180^\circ$ at $f \approx 1.5$ MHz

where $|A| = \frac{10^6}{((1+15^2)(1+1.5^2)(1+.75^2))^{1/2}} = 29.5 \times 10^3$

Now with $\beta = 10^{-5}$, $A\beta = 29.5 \times 10^3 \times 10^{-5} = 0.295 < 1$

Thus the gain margin is $20\log(.295) = \underline{\underline{-10.6 \text{ dB}}}$

12

The closed-loop 3dB frequency would be very slightly less than $\underline{\underline{1 \text{ MHz}}}$.

For a 20 dB reduction in closed-loop gain to be achieved by lowering the dominant pole, the pole must shift to $\frac{10^5}{10} = 10^4$ Hz. With this change, β can be raised to 10^{-4}, while maintaining the same margins, to produce a closed-loop gain of $\frac{10^6}{1+10^6 \times 10^{-4}} = \underline{9900}$

The 3dB frequency will be slightly closer to $\underline{\underline{1 \text{MHz}}}$ than previously.

1 **Design** 12

You are provided with 3 identical direct-coupled amplifiers, each having a nominal gain of 100, a pole at 10^5 Hz, differential inputs for which the differential input resistance is 10kΩ and the common-mode input resistance is 1MΩ, and an output resistance of 1000Ω. Your challenge is to create a direct-coupled composite amplifier having an overall stable gain of 100 using one or more feedback loops. The gain and phase margins should be reasonable, while the sensitivity of the overall gain to the gain of any individual amplifier, should be reduced. The overall input resistance Rin should be high while the output resistance Rout

12

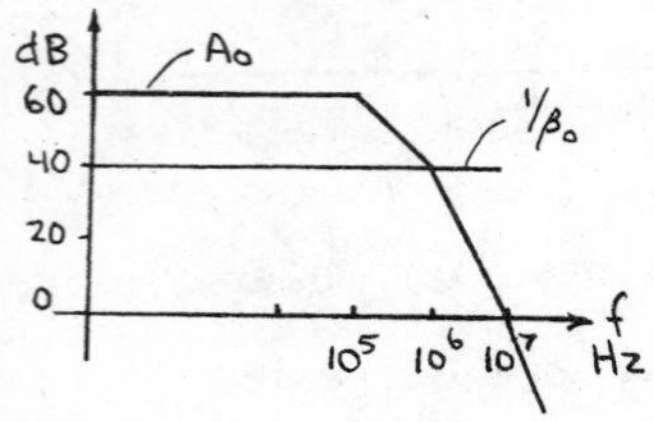

The Bode plot shows one possibility, that of a gain $A_o = 1000$ and poles at 10^5, 10^6, 10^7 Hz, enclosed in a loop for which $1/\beta_o \approx 100$.

The lowest pole is chosen to be that of the basic amplifier, for without capacitors there is no way to produce a lower frequency. The only way to shift poles upward is with feedback. The pole at 10^6 Hz is associated with a feedback loop for which the closed-loop gain is +10 (or −9) and that at 10^7 Hz with a loop for which the gain is +1.

Thus for a simple design, utilize one amplifier with no local feedback, one with gain of +1

12

should be low. Attempt to maximize the ratio (R_{in}/R_{out}). Assume availability of resistors up to and including 1MΩ, but no capacitors. Ignore amplifier bias and offset currents and offset voltages.

Ⓐ Alternatives:

① Consider the use of an overall feedback loop with greatest possible $A\beta$ in order to reduce Rout and raise Rin. But such a loop has 3 poles and must be stable for a closed-loop gain of 100 (40 dB). To allow this, the poles must be spread out, compensated or one made dominant. For a relatively straightforward design, consider the poles separated by a factor of 10:

12

for which $R_2/R_1 \approx 0$, and one with local feedback and a gain of +10. The local feedback stages with the greatest loop gain should be use either at the input or output to raise Rin or lower Rout of the basic stages before overall feedback is connected. As well it must be convenient to close the overall loop at the front end without reducing the input resistance. Thus try

ⓐ

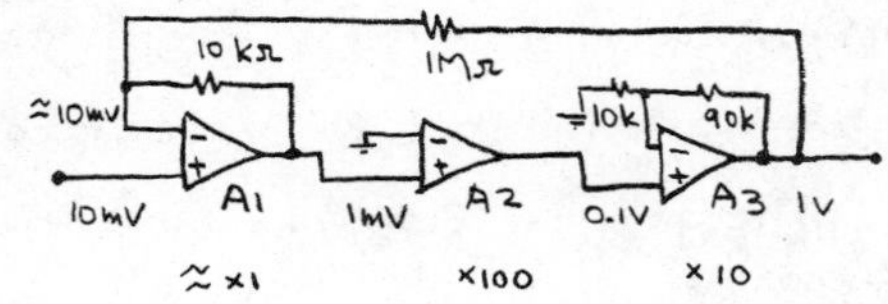

Here the voltage labels serve as a means for rapid analysis, starting with 1V at the output.

Now contrast this with other designs having less-global feedback:

12

ⓑ

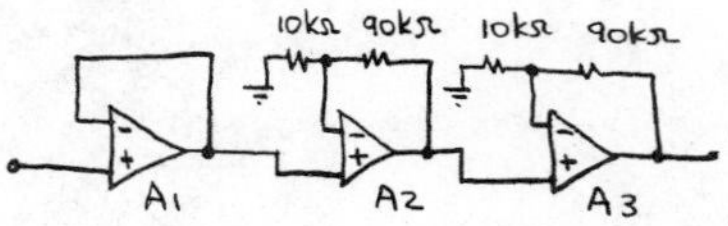

ⓒ

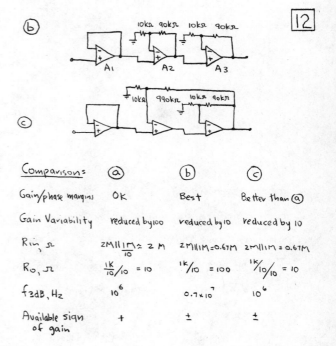

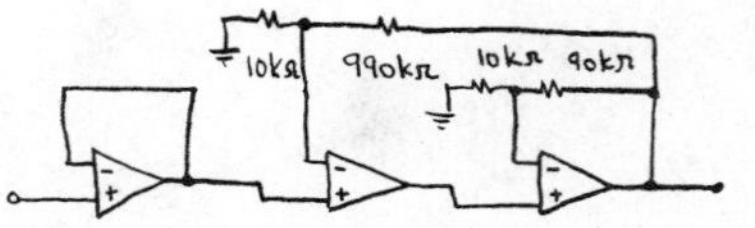

Comparisons	ⓐ	ⓑ	ⓒ
Gain/phase margins	OK	Best	Better than ⓐ
Gain Variability	reduced by 100	reduced by 10	reduced by 10
R_{in}, Ω	$2M \parallel \frac{1M}{10} \approx 2M$	$2M \parallel 1M = 0.67M$	$2M \parallel 1M = 0.67M$
R_o, Ω	$\frac{1K}{10}/10 = 10$	$1K/10 = 100$	$1K/10/10 = 10$
f_{3dB}, Hz	10^6	0.7×10^7	10^6
Available sign of gain	+	±	±

All comparitive calculations are quite approximate relying on the idea of multiplication by $A\beta$ or $1/A\beta$ where appropriate.

1 Exam 13

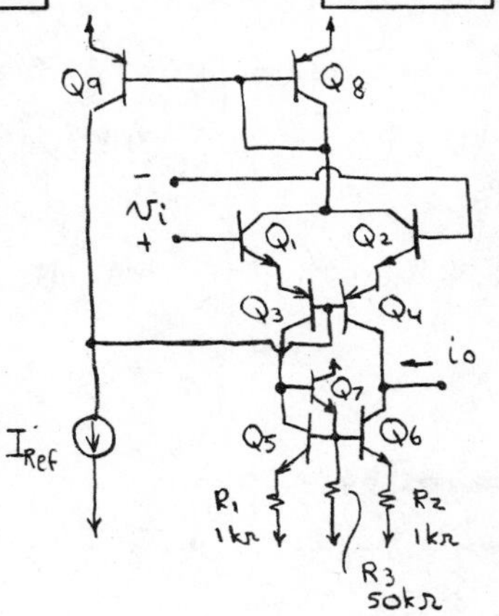

The circuit shown is the input stage of the 741 op amp.

(a) For $I_{Ref} = 20\mu A$, inputs joined at +3V, high β, and $|V_{BE}| = 0.7V$,

i) what are the currents in Q_3, Q_7?

ii) what are the voltages at the bases of Q_3 and Q_7?

13

(b) For $\beta_N = 250$ and $\beta_P = 50$

i) what is the differential input resistance, R_{id}?

ii) What is the transconductance $G_m = \frac{i_o}{v_i}$?

(c) If for each transistor, Including the I_{Ref} source, $V_A = 100V$,

i) What is the common-mode input resistance?

ii) What is the output resistance (shunting io), approximately?

(A)

(a) For high β, $I_R = 20\mu A \simeq I_{C9} = I_{C8} = 2I_{C1}$

$= 2I_{C2} = 2I_{C3} = 2I_{C4} = 2I_{C5} = 2I_{C6}$

i) $\therefore I_{C3} = \underline{10\mu A}$, $I_{C5} = 10\mu A$

$I_{C7} \simeq I_{R3} = \frac{0.7 + 10\mu A(1k)}{50k} = \underline{\underline{14.2\mu A}}$

13

ii) $V_{B3} = +3 - 0.7 - 0.7 = \underline{1.6V}$

$V_{B7} = -15 + 10\mu A(1k) + 0.7 + 0.7 = \underline{\underline{-13.59V}}$

(b) i) $r_{e1} = r_{e2} = r_{e3} = r_{e4} = \frac{25 \times 10^{-3}}{10 \times 10^{-6}} = 2500$

$\therefore R_{id} = 2(251(2.5) + 51(2.5)) = 2 \times 302 \times 2.5k = \underline{\underline{1.5M\Omega}}$

ii) For $v_i = v$, $i_o = \frac{v/2}{2.5+2.5} - \left(-\frac{v/2}{2.5+2.5}\right) = \frac{v}{5k}$

$\therefore G_m = i_o/v_i = \frac{v/5k}{v} = \frac{1}{5k} = \underline{200\mu A/V}$

(c) i) For CM input resistance, assume io flows in a low-resistance load. Thus for CM signals, the circuit reduces to that shown:

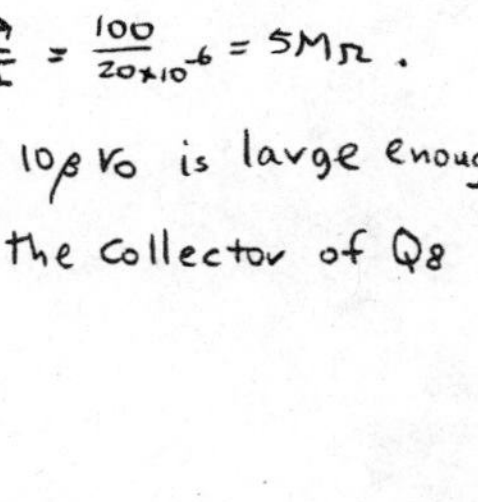

Here Rn is the resistor associated with Qn.

Since all transistors shown conduct the same current ($2\mu A$) all have the same $r_o = \frac{V_A}{I} = \frac{100}{20 \times 10^{-6}} = 5M\Omega$.

Assume that $r_{\mu n} \simeq 10\beta r_o$ is large enough to be ignored, and that the collector of Q8

13

$\therefore R_{icm}' \approx (\beta_{n+1})(R_1 \| R_3 \| (\frac{R_R \| R_9}{\beta_{p+1}}))$ --- (1)

But Q8 mirrors much of the base current of Q1, multiplied by (β_{n+1}), back to the base of Q3.

As well, a large part of the current ($\alpha_1 x$) in R_1 is returned to the collector of Q_1 where it essentially causes a cancellation of the R_1 part of the estimate in (1) above.

All the other resistors, namely R_3, R_R, R_9 are more simply connected as shunts in the loop through Q, Q8, Q9, Q3 whose loop gain (as seen directly in the current domain) is $(\beta_{p+1})(\alpha_n)\left(\frac{1}{1 + 2/\beta_n}\right) \approx \beta_P$

Thus R_{icm} (without R_1) is generally raised by β_P and becomes $(\beta_P)(\beta_{n+1})(R_3 \| \frac{R_9 \| R_R}{\beta_{p+1}})$

$\approx \beta_n \cdot \beta_P \left(R_3 \| \frac{R_R \| R_9}{\beta_P}\right)$

$= \beta_n \beta_P \left(\frac{\beta_P R_3 \| R_R \| R_9}{\beta_P}\right)$

$= \beta_n (R_R \| R_9) = \underline{\beta_n \frac{r_o}{2}}$

2 **Exam** 13

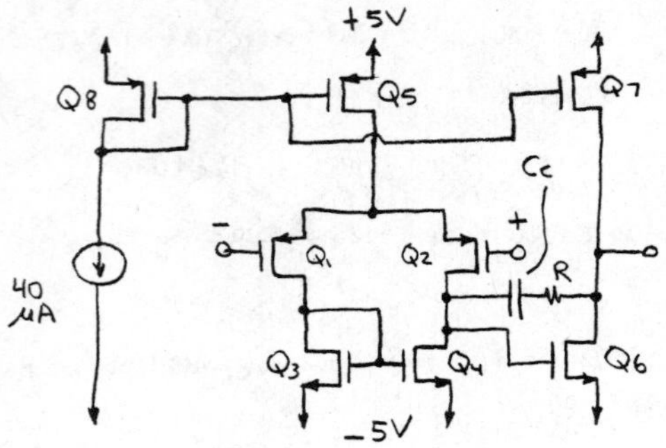

For the CMOS op amp shown, all transistors have $\frac{W}{L} = \frac{200}{8}$, except for Q3 and Q4 which have $\frac{W}{L} = \frac{100}{8}$. As well $\mu_n C_{ox} = 20\mu A/V^2$, $\mu_p C_{ox} = 10\mu A/V^2$, $|V_A| = 40V$ and $|V_t| = 1V$.

ⓐ Find the dc bias current in each device, and calculate the value of the dc open-loop gain.

ⓑ Find the value of R that will place the transmission zero at $s = \infty$ 13

ⓒ Find the value of C_c that will result in $f_t = 3MHz$.

ⓓ Calculate the value of the slew rate.

A

ⓐ $I_{D1} = I_{D2} = I_{D3} = I_{D4} = 20\mu A$

$I_{D8} = I_{D5} = I_{D7} = I_{D6} = 40\mu A$

ⓑ $g_{m1} = g_{m2} = \frac{2 I_{D1}}{V_{GS1} - V_t}$,

But $V_{GS1} - V_t = \sqrt{\frac{I_{D1}}{\frac{1}{2}\mu_p C_{ox}\left(\frac{W}{L}\right)_1}} = \sqrt{\frac{20}{\frac{1}{2} \times 10 \times \frac{200}{8}}} = 0.4V$

Thus $g_{m1} = g_{m2} = \frac{2 \times 20}{0.4} = 100\mu A/V$

$r_{o1} = r_{o2} = r_{o4} = \frac{V_A}{I_D} = \frac{40}{20} = 2M\Omega$

Gain of first stage $= g_{m1}(r_{o2} \| r_{o4})$

$= 100 \times (2 \| 2) = 100\ V/V$

$V_{GS6} - V_t = \sqrt{\frac{I_{D6}}{\frac{1}{2}\mu_n C_{ox}(W/L)_6}} = \sqrt{\frac{40}{\frac{1}{2} \times 20 \times 200/8}} = 1.4V$

$g_{m6} = \frac{2 I_{D6}}{V_{GS6} - V_t} = \frac{2 \times 40}{0.4} = 200\mu A/V$ 13

$r_{o6} = r_{o7} = \frac{V_A}{I_{D6}} = \frac{40}{40} = 1M\Omega$

Gain of second stage $= g_{m6}(r_{o6} \| r_{o7}) = 200(1 \| 1) = 100\ V/V$

Dc open-loop gain $= 100 \times 100 = \underline{10^4\ V/V}$

ⓑ The transmission zero is at

$s = \frac{1}{C_c\left(\frac{1}{G_{m2}} - R\right)}$ (see p 777)

where $G_{m2} = g_{m6} = 200\mu A/V$

For $s = \infty$, $R = \frac{1}{G_{m2}} = \frac{1}{200 \times 10^{-6}} = \underline{5k\Omega}$

ⓒ $\omega_t = \frac{G_{m1}}{C_c}$ where $G_{m1} = g_{m1} = g_{m2} = 100\mu A/V$

Thus $2\pi \times 3 \times 10^6 = 100 \times 10^{-6}/C_c$

or $C_c = \frac{100 \times 10^{-6}}{2\pi \times 3 \times 10^6} = \underline{5.3pF}$

ⓓ $SR = \frac{40\mu A}{C_c} = \frac{40 \times 10^{-6}}{5.3 \times 10^{-12}} = \underline{7.5 V/\mu s}$

1 **Exam** 14

ⓐ For the circuit shown, derive an expression for the transfer function $V_o(s)/V_i(s)$

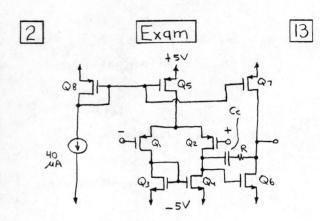

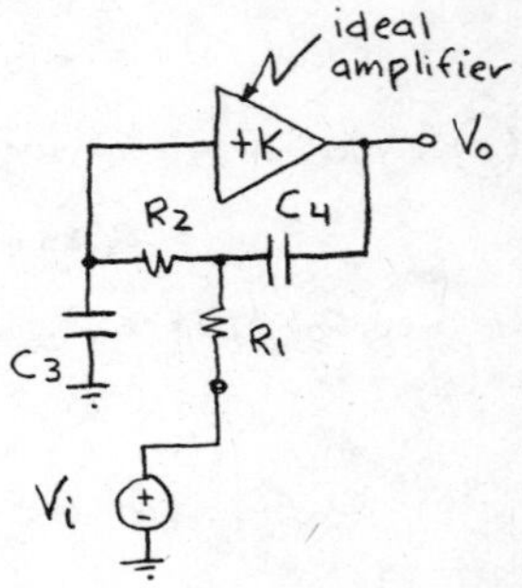

ⓑ What type of filtering function is realized by this circuit? Find ω_o, Q, and the dc gain

ⓒ For $R_1 = R_2 = 10k\Omega$ and $C_3 = 10nF$, find the values of C_4 and K to obtain $\omega_o = 10^4$ rad/s and $Q = 1/\sqrt{2}$.

ⓓ Calculate the sensitivity of ω_o relative to K and the sensitivity of Q relative to K.

ⓔ As K is varied, what is the locus

14

of the poles in the s plane?

(f) Find the value of K at which the circuit can sustain oscillations. At what frequency do these oscillations occur?

(A)

(a) $sC_3 \frac{V_o}{K}$

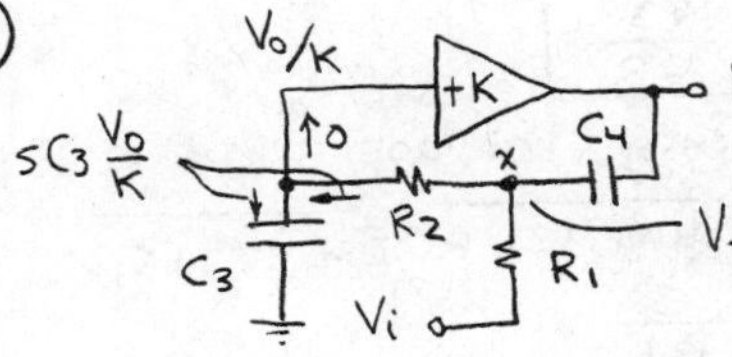

$V_x = \frac{V_o}{K} + sC_3 \frac{V_o}{K} R_2$

$= \frac{V_o}{K}(1 + sC_3R_2)$

Writing a node equation at x yields

$$sC_4(V_o - V_x) = sC_3\frac{V_o}{K} + \left(\frac{V_x - V_i}{R_1}\right)$$

Substituting for V_x, we obtain

$$sC_4V_o - sC_4\frac{V_o}{K}(1 + sC_3R_2)$$
$$= sC_3\frac{V_o}{K} + \frac{V_o}{KR_1}(1 + sC_3R_2) - \frac{V_i}{R_1}$$

Multiplying both sides by KR_1 and collecting terms gives

$$V_o[sC_3R_1 + 1 + sC_3R_2 + sC_4R_1(1 + sC_3R_2) - sKC_4R_1] = KV_i$$

14

Thus

$$\frac{V_o}{V_i} = \frac{K}{s^2C_3C_4R_1R_2 + s[C_4R_1(1-K) + C_3R_1 + C_3R_2] + 1}$$

$$= \frac{K/C_3C_4R_1R_2}{s^2 + s\left[\frac{1-K}{C_3R_2} + \frac{1}{C_4R_2} + \frac{1}{C_4R_1}\right] + \frac{1}{C_3C_4R_1R_2}}$$

(b) See a Low-Pass filter with

$$\omega_o = \frac{1}{\sqrt{C_3C_4R_1R_2}}$$

$$Q = \frac{1}{\sqrt{C_3C_4R_1R_2}} \Big/ \left[\frac{1-K}{C_3R_2} + \frac{1}{C_4R_2} + \frac{1}{C_4R_1}\right]$$

dc gain $= K$

(c) $10 \times 10^3 = 1/\sqrt{10 \times 10^{-9} \times C_4 \times 10^4 \times 10^4} \rightarrow C_4 = 10\text{nF}$

$\frac{1}{\sqrt{2}} = \frac{1}{1-K+1+1} = \frac{1}{3-K} \rightarrow K = 3 - \sqrt{2} = 1.586$

(d) Since ω_o is independant of K, $S_K^{\omega_o} = 0$

Since $Q = \frac{1}{3-K}$, $S_K^Q = \frac{\partial Q}{\partial K} \cdot \frac{K}{Q}$

or $S_K^Q = \frac{1}{(3-K)^2} \times \frac{K}{(1/3-K)} = \frac{K}{3-K}$

For $K = 1.586$, $S_K^Q = \frac{1.586}{3-1.586} = 1.12$

(e) Since ω_o remains constant as K varies, the root locus is a circle of radius equal to ω_o.

14

(f) For the circuit to sustain oscillations the poles must lie on the $j\omega$ axis, ie have $Q = \infty$:

ie $\infty = \frac{1}{3-K} \rightarrow K = 3$

Oscillation will have a frequency equal to ω_o, ie 10^4 rad/s

2 Exam 14

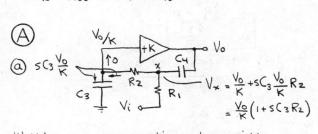

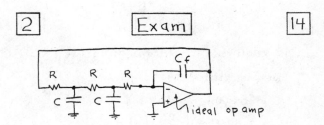

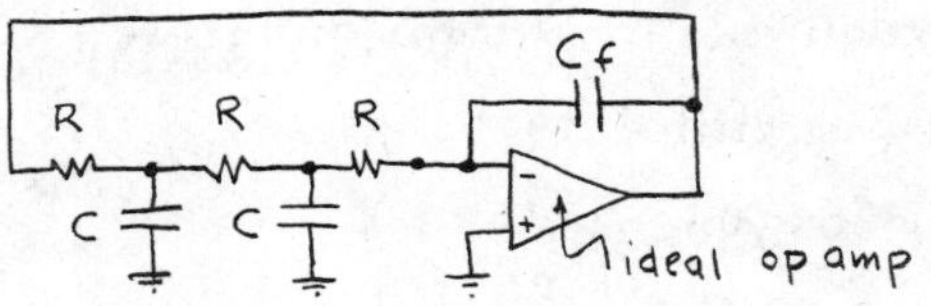

Show that the circuit shown can function as an oscillator. Find the frequency of oscillation ω_o as a function of the time constant CR. Also find the value of C_f required to sustain oscillations at ω_o. To ensure that oscillations start, should C_f be increased above or decreased below the value found?

(A) To show that the circuit can function as an oscillator, we find its loop gain and show that it can be made equal to unity. The loop gain is found by breaking the loop as shown: **14**

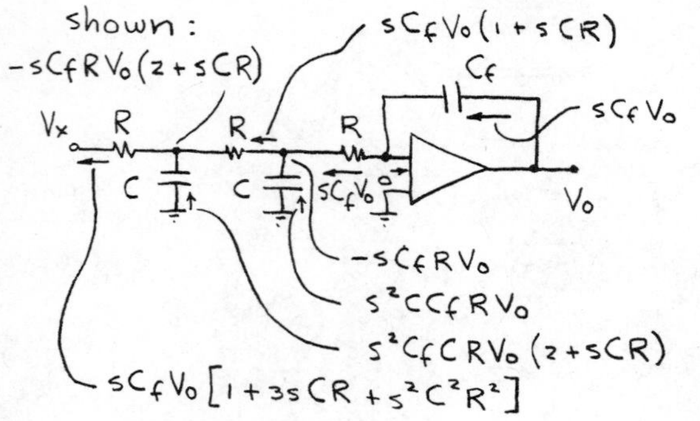

$$V_x = -sC_fRV_o(2+sCR) - sC_fRV_o(1+3sCR+s^2C^2R^2)$$
$$= -sC_fRV_o(3+4sCR+s^2C^2R^2)$$

Thus $L(s) = \dfrac{V_o(s)}{V_x(s)} = \dfrac{-1}{sC_fR(3+4sCR+s^2C^2R^2)}$

$$\therefore\ L(j\omega) = \frac{-1}{j\omega C_fR(3-\omega^2C^2R^2) - 4\omega^2CC_fR^2}$$ **14**

$L(j\omega)$ will become a real number at the frequency ω_0, where

$$3 - \omega_0^2C^2R^2 = 0$$

or $\boxed{\omega_0 = \dfrac{\sqrt{3}}{CR}}$

At this frequency, the loop gain is

$$L(j\omega_0) = \frac{1}{4\omega_0^2CC_fR^2} = \frac{1}{4\times\frac{3}{C^2R^2}CC_fR^2}$$
$$= \frac{C}{12C_f}$$

To obtain sustained oscillations, we select C_f to make $L(j\omega_0) = 1$, ie

$\boxed{C_f = \dfrac{C}{12}}$

To ensure that oscillations start, the loop gain is made slightly greater than 1. This is achieved by <u>decreasing</u> C_f

1 **Design** **14**

It is required to design an active-RC low-pass filter that has:

- dc gain = 1 (0 dB)
- 3-dB frequency = 1kHz
- transmission at f = 2kHz, at least 25dB below transmission at dc.

It has been decided to use a maximally-flat filter (known as a Butterworth filter). Such filters exhibit transmission functions of the type depicted in Fig 14.1. The transmission of a Butterworth filter of order N is given by $|T(j\omega)| = \dfrac{1}{\sqrt{1+\left(\frac{\omega}{\omega_{3dB}}\right)^{2N}}}$

Furthermore, it is known that an Nth order Butterworth filter has all its poles located on a circle in the s plane of radius ω_{3dB}, as shown in Fig. A. **14**

Provide a complete design for this filter.

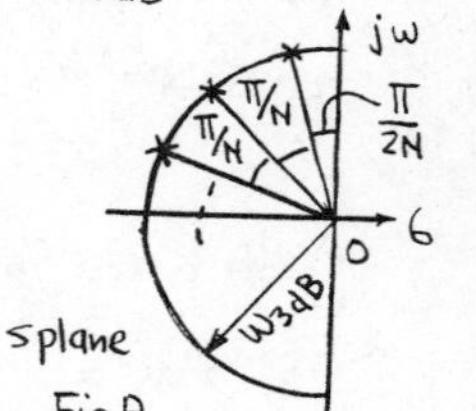

Fig A

(A)

First we must determine the required order (N) of the filter. The magnitude of transmission is given by

$$|T(j\omega)| = \frac{1}{\sqrt{1+\left(\frac{\omega}{\omega_{3dB}}\right)^{2N}}}$$

Thus the dc transmission is unity, and at $\omega = \omega_{3dB}$, $|T| = \frac{1}{\sqrt{2}}$ as should be the case. In our case $f_{3dB} = 1kHz$ and we require that at $f = 2kHz$ (ie $\frac{f}{f_{3dB}} = 2$),

14

$20\log|T|$ is a minimum of -25dB.

Thus $10\log(1+2^{2N}) \geq 25$ dB

or $1+2^{2N} \geq 10^{2.5}$

or $2^{2N} \geq 10^{2.5}-1$

$2N\log 2 \geq \log(10^{2.5}-1)$

or $N \geq \left(\frac{1}{2\log 2}\right)\log(10^{2.5}-1) = 4.15$

Since N must be an integer, we select

$N = \underline{5}$

Next we determine the poles of this filter using the graphical construction of Fig A, which in our case leads to that in Fig B:

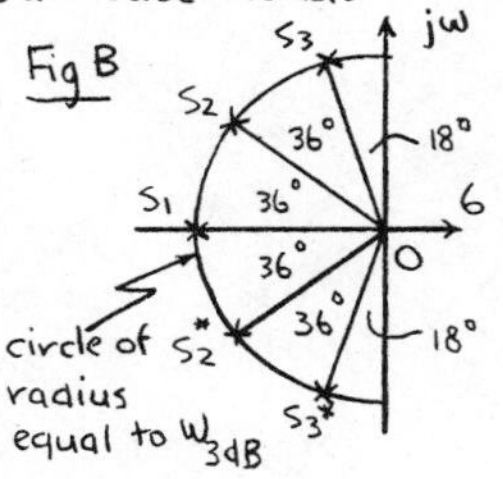

Thus we see that the filter has a real pole s_1,

$s_1 = -\omega_{3dB}$

and a pair of complex conjugate

14

poles, s_2, s_2^*, having

$\omega_{o2} = \omega_{3dB} = 2\pi\times 10^{+3}$ rad/s

$Q_2 = \frac{1}{2\cos 36^\circ} = 0.618$

and a pair of complex conjugate poles, s_3, s_3^* having $\omega_{o3} = \omega_{3dB} = 2\pi\times 10^3$ rad/s

$Q_3 = \frac{1}{2\cos 72^\circ} = 1.618$

The transfer function of the fifth-order filter is the product of the 3 low-pass transfer functions corresponding to s_1, (s_2 and s_2^*), (s_3 and s_3^*). If we arrange that each of the 3 functions has a unity dc gain, we obtain

$$T(s) = \frac{\omega_{3dB}}{s+\omega_{3dB}} \times \frac{\omega_{o2}^2}{s^2+s\left(\frac{\omega_{o2}}{Q_2}\right)+\omega_{o2}^2} \times \frac{\omega_{o3}^2}{s^2+s\left(\frac{\omega_{o3}}{Q_3}\right)+\omega_{o3}^2}$$

This function can be realized by cascading 3 active filters, each of which realizes one of the 3 functions in the product.

14

If each of the 3 sections has a low output resistance (obtained by taking the output at the output terminal of an op amp), then cascading will not change the individual transfer functions, and the overall transfer function realized will be the desired T(s)

The first section in the cascade is a first-order low-pass filter which can be realized using an RC circuit together with a buffering unity-gain amplifier, as shown in Fig C.

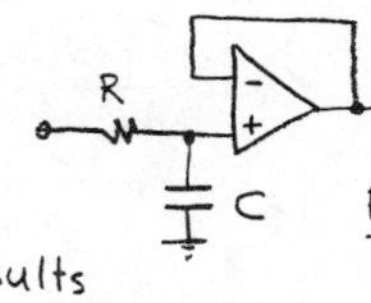

Fig C

For this circuit,

$CR = \frac{1}{\omega_{3dB}} = \frac{1}{2\pi\times 10^3}$

Selecting $C = \underline{10\text{nF}}$ results in $R = \underline{15.92}$ kΩ

Each of the second and third sections

14

realizes a second-order low-pass function with a low Q. Therefore we may use a single-op-amp realization such as that shown in Fig D:

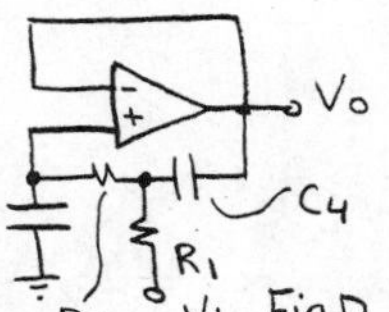

Fig D

Analysis shows that:

$$\frac{V_o}{V_i} = \frac{1/C_3C_4R_1R_2}{s^2+s\frac{1}{C_4}\left(\frac{1}{R_1}+\frac{1}{R_2}\right)+\frac{1}{C_3C_4R_1R_2}}$$

Thus $\omega_0 = \frac{1}{\sqrt{C_3C_4R_1R_2}}$

$$Q = \frac{1}{\sqrt{C_3C_4R_1R_2}} \Big/ \left[\frac{1}{C_4}\left(\frac{1}{R_1}+\frac{1}{R_2}\right)\right]$$

Selecting $R_1 = R_2 = R$, $C_4 = C$ and $C_3 = C/m$ gives the following design equations:

$CR = \frac{2Q}{\omega_0}$, $m = 4Q^2$

Thus for the second section in the cascade we obtain the following component values: $CR = \frac{2\times 0.618}{2\pi\times 10^3}$

$m = 4\times 0.618^2$.

For $C_4 = \underline{10\text{nF}}$, $C_3 = \underline{6.55}$ nF, $R_1 = R_2 = \underline{19.67\text{k}\Omega}$

For the third section in the cascade: 14

$$CR = \frac{2 \times 1.618}{2\pi \times 10^3} \quad , \quad m = 4 \times 1.618^2$$

For $C_4 = \underline{10\,nF}$, $C_3 = \underline{955\,pF}$, $R_1 = R_2 = \underline{51.50\,k\Omega}$

The complete filter is shown below:

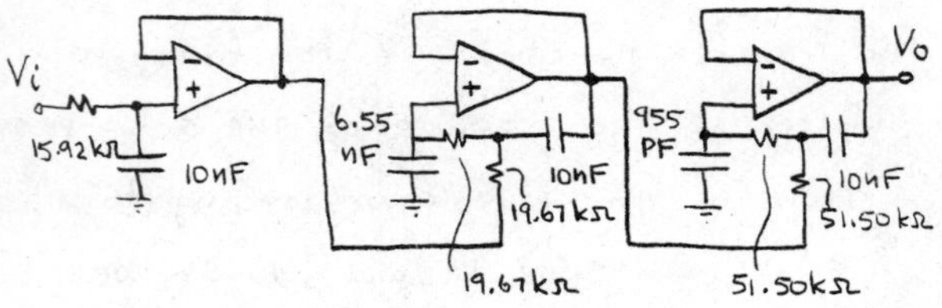

$\underline{Fig\ E}$

---

1 Exam 15

An NMOS Inverter with depletion load
has $V_{tE} = 1V$, $K_R = 4$, $V_{tDo} = -2V$, $\left(\frac{W}{L}\right)_E = 2$,
$\mu_n C_{ox} = 40\,\mu A/V^2$, $2\phi_F = 0.6V$, $\gamma = 0.5\,V^{1/2}$
and $V_{DD} = 5V$. Find:

(a) V_{OH}

(b) V_{tD} near $v_o = V_{OH}$

(c) V_{IL} (for $\frac{\partial v_o}{\partial v_I} = -1$)

(d) V_{OL}

(e) NM_L

(f) An estimate of t_{PHL} for a 0.5pF load.

(A)

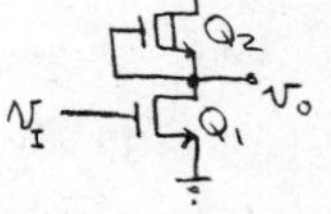

(a) $V_{OH} = V_{DD} = \underline{5V}$

(b) For v_o near $V_{OH} = 5V$

$$V_{tD} = V_{tDo} + \gamma\left(\sqrt{v_o + 2\phi_F} - \sqrt{2\phi_F}\right)$$
$$= -2 + 0.5\left(\sqrt{5 + 0.6} - \sqrt{0.6}\right) = \underline{1.20V}$$

(c) For V_{IL} : $v_{GS1} = v$, $\frac{K_1}{K_2} = K_R$, Q_1 is 15
in pinchoff while Q_2 in triode :

$$K_1(v - V_{tE})^2 = K_2\left(2|V_{tD}|(V_{DD} - v_o) - (V_{DD} - v_o)^2\right)$$
$$4(v-1)^2 = 2(1.2)(5 - v_o) - (5 - v_o)^2 \quad -- \textcircled{1}$$

Differentiate :

$$2 \times 4(v-1) = 2.4(-1)\frac{\partial v_o}{\partial v} - 2(5 - v_o)(-1)\frac{\partial v_o}{\partial v}$$

For $\frac{\partial v_o}{\partial v} = -1$: $8v - 8 = 2.4 - 10 + 2v_o$

$$v = (0.4 + 2v_o)/8 = 0.05 + 0.25v_o \quad -- \textcircled{2}$$

$\textcircled{2} \rightarrow \textcircled{1}$

$$4(.05 + .25v_o - 1)^2 = 2.4(5 - v_o) - (5 - v_o)^2$$

or $4(-.95 + .25v_o)^2 = 12 - 2.4v_o - 25 + 10v_o - v_o^2$

or $.25v_o^2 - 1.9v_o + 3.61 = 7.6v_o - v_o^2 - 13$

or $1.25v_o^2 - 9.5v_o + 16.61 = 0$

$$\rightarrow v_o = \frac{+9.5 \pm \sqrt{9.5^2 - 4(16.61)(1.25)}}{2(1.25)} = 4.87V$$

and $v = V_{IL} = \frac{0.4 + 2(4.87)}{8} = \underline{1.268V}$

(d) For V_{OL} : $v_I = V_{OH} = 5V$
Q_1 in triode and Q_2 in pinchoff with $V_{SB} \approx 0V$

$$K_1\left(2(V_{DD} - V_{tE})V_{OL} - V_{OL}^2\right) = K_2(0 - V_{tDo})^2 \quad \boxed{15}$$

ie $4(2(5-1)V_{OL} - V_{OL}^2) = 2^2$

$$V_{OL}^2 - 8V_{OL} + 1 = 0$$

$$V_{OL} = \frac{8 \pm \sqrt{8^2 - 4}}{2} = \underline{0.127V}$$

(e) $NM_L = V_{IL} - V_{OL} = 1.268 - .127 = \underline{1.14V}$

(f) For t_{PHL} : $K_1 = \frac{1}{2} \times 40 \times 2 = 40\,\mu A/V^2$, $K_2 = \frac{40}{4} = 10\,\mu A/V^2$

With V_o high , $i_{D1} = 40(5-1)^2 = 640\,\mu A$

V_o at 2.5V, $V_{tD} = -2 + 0.5\left(\sqrt{2.5 - 0.6} - \sqrt{0.6}\right)$
$$= 1.51V$$

$i_{D2} = 10(0 - 1.51)^2 = 23\,\mu A$

$i_{D1} = 40(2(5-1)2.5 - 2.5^2) = 550\,\mu A$

$\therefore$ Average discharge current $= \frac{640 + 550 - 23}{2} = 584\,\mu A$

$\therefore t_{PHL} = \frac{0.5 \times 10^{-12} \times 2.5}{584 \times 10^{-6}} = \underline{2.1\,nsec}$

2 | Exam | 15

A CMOS inverter utilizes devices for which $|V_{tn}| = |V_{tp}| = 1V$, $K_n = K_p = 10\mu A/V^2$ and a supply of +5V. Evaluate the critical inputs, V_{IH} (where $\frac{\partial v_O}{\partial v_I} = -1$) and the threshold V_{th} of the inverter for

i) no load

ii) with a load R = 50k connected to +5V.

(A)

For V_{th}

i) For no load, by virtue of symmetry, $V_{th} = \frac{5}{2} = 2.5V$

(ii) For 50k load, the threshold is raised to v

where $K_p(5-v-1)^2 + \frac{5-2.5}{R} = k_n(v-1)^2$

or $10\times10^{-6}(4-v)^2 + \frac{2.5}{50\times10^3} = 10\times10^{-6}(v-1)^2$

or $16 - 8v + v^2 + 5 = v^2 - 2v + 1$

15

or $6v = 20 \rightarrow v = \frac{20}{6} = 3.3\dot{3}V$

For V_{IH}:

i) For no load, $V_{IH} = v_i$, $v_O = v$

Q_n operates in triode, Q_p in pinchoff.

$\therefore K_p(5-v_i-1)^2 = k_n(2(v_i-1)v - v^2)$

$(4-v_i)^2 = 2(v_i-1)v - v^2$ --- (1)

Take $\frac{\partial}{\partial v_i}$

$2(4-v_i)(-1) = 2v + (v_i-1)\frac{\partial v}{\partial v_i} - 2v\frac{\partial v}{\partial v_i}$

Where $\frac{\partial v}{\partial v_i} = -1$, $-2(4-v_i) = 2v - (v_i-1) + 2v$

ie $-8 + 2v_i = 2v - v_i + 1 + 2v$

or $3v_i = 4v + 9 \rightarrow v_i = \frac{4}{3}v + 3$ --- (2)

(2)→(1), $(4 - \frac{4}{3}v - 3)^2 = 2(\frac{4}{3}v + 3 - 1)v - v^2$

$(1 - \frac{4}{3}v)^2 = \frac{8}{3}v^2 + 4v - v^2$

$1 - \frac{8}{3}v + \frac{16}{9}v^2 = \frac{4}{3}v^2 + 4v$

$\frac{4}{9}v^2 - \frac{20}{3}v + 1 = 0$

$4v^2 - 60v + 9 = 0$

$\therefore v = \frac{60 \pm \sqrt{60^2 - 4(4)(9)}}{2(4)} = 0.1515$

15

$\therefore V_{IH} = v_i = \frac{4}{3}(.1515) + 3 = 3.02V$

For $R = 50k\Omega$ load to 5V:

$10^{-5}(5-v)^2 + \frac{5-v}{50k} = 10^{-5}(2(v_i-1)v - v^2)$

$(4-v_i)^2 + 2(5-v) = 2(v_i-1)v - v^2$ - (3)

$\frac{\partial}{\partial v_i} \rightarrow 2(4-v_i)(-1) + 2(-\frac{\partial v}{\partial v_i}) = 2v + (v_i-1)\frac{\partial v}{\partial v_i} - 2v\frac{\partial v}{\partial v_i}$

$\frac{\partial v}{\partial v_i} = -1 \rightarrow -2(4-v_i) + 2 = 2v - (v_i-1) + 2v$

$-8 + 2v_i + 2 = 2v - v_i + 1 + 2v$

$3v_i = 4v + 7$

$v_i = \frac{4}{3}v + \frac{7}{3}$ --- (4)

(3)→(4), $(4 - \frac{4}{3}v - \frac{7}{3})^2 + 2(5-v) = 2(\frac{4}{3}v + \frac{7}{3} - 1)v - v^2$

$(\frac{5}{3} - \frac{4}{3}v)^2 + 10 - 2v = \frac{8}{3}v^2 + \frac{8}{3}v - v^2$

$25 - 40v + 16v^2 + 90 - 18v = 24v^2 + 24v - 9v^2$

$1v^2 - 82v + 115 = 0$

$v = \frac{82 \pm \sqrt{82^2 - 4(115)}}{2} = 1.43V$

$\therefore v_{IH} = v_i = \frac{4}{3}(1.43) + \frac{7}{3} = 4.24V$

1 | Design | 15

Design a CMOS astable multivibrator, using a CMOS IC consisting of 4 two-input NAND gates, a 5V supply and a small number of other components. There are several requirements, possibly in conflict.

(a) The circuit should operate only when the signal STOP is low, producing a square-wave output.

(b) The output waveform should be as close as possible to a "standard" digital signal, that is resembling the output of a gate driven by a "standard" digital signal.

(c) The output should go low when STOP goes low.

(d) The first and last cycles of the

15

oscillation should be as close as possible to all the rest

ⓔ Following the rise of STOP, the last cycle should complete as normally as possible.

ⓕ When STOP is high, the power dissipation should be low (but possibly not zero)

ⓖ It would be desirable to impliment $GO = \overline{STOP}$ and an output signal of high quality which is LOW when STOP is high.

15

Ⓐ Consider:

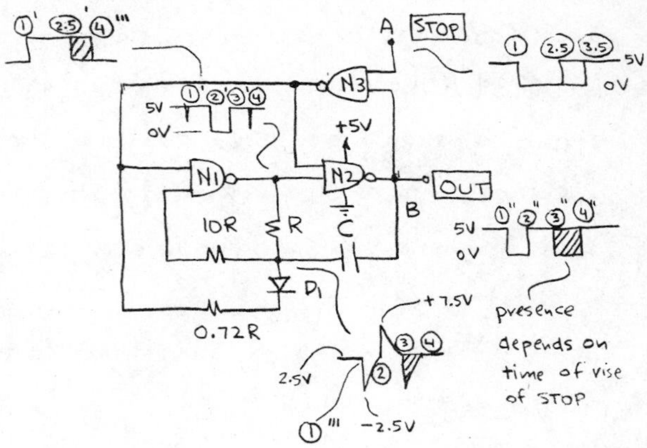

The notation ⓝ indicates relative timing with the event (n.5) occuring between ⓝ and (n+1). ⓝ' indicates an event which closely follows (and is driven by) ⓝ and produces ⓝ'' which preceeds (and causes) ⓝ''' etc.

The diode D_1 and extra resistor attempt to establish the startup voltage on the capacitor

15

near to the gate threshold in an attempt to ensure that the first cycle of operation is similar to the rest. A threshold of $V_{DD}/2$ is assumed.

The additional resistor is $R_x = \frac{5/2 - 0.7}{\frac{5/2}{R}} = .72R$

Gate N3 inhibits the action of STOP while OUT is low, ensuring that a cycle, on started, will be complete. N2 and N3 for a bistable.

The basic multivibrator (N_1, N_2) follows Fig 15.36 with 10R added to reduce the effect of the input protection diodes in N_1.

The additional gate can be used as an inverter to provide $\overline{OUT}$ or GO (but not both.

Note that the output of N1 is not a "standard" signal since the gain of N_1 is not large. As well it has "glitches" which are too small to set N_2N_3.

1

Exam

16

An npn BJT for which $n = 1$, $\beta_F = 200$ and $\beta_R = 0.2$, operates in the normal active mode at $i_E = 1mA$, with $V_{BE} = 700mV$. As well, when switching off from normal saturated mode with forward base current, reverse base current and saturated collector current all equal, a storage time of 10 nsec is measured:

ⓐ What value of I_s applies?

ⓑ If the device is operated in the active mode with the emitter and collector leads interchanged, and with 1mA flowing in the collector lead, what voltage must exist between base and collector leads?

ⓒ If the device is operated in the normal mode, but with the collector open circuited, what value of V_{CEsat} would be found? 16

ⓓ What is the storage time constant for this transistor?

ⓔ When operated at a forced β of 50, with a reverse base current 1/10 that of the forward drive, what storage time do you expect?

Ⓐ

ⓐ $i_E = \frac{I_S}{\alpha_F}\left(e^{v_{BE}/nV_T} - 1\right) - I_S\left(e^{v_{BC}/nV_T} - 1\right)$ -- ①

For normal active mode: $V_{BE} \gg V_T$, V_{BC} is 0 or -ve.

Thus $i_E = \frac{I_S}{\alpha_F} e^{v_{BE}/V_T}$ -- ②

ie $1 \times 10^{-3} = \frac{I_S}{200/201} e^{\frac{700}{25}}$

whence $I_S = 1 \times 10^{-3} \times \frac{200}{201} \times e^{\frac{-700}{25}} = 6.88 \times 10^{-16}$ A

ⓑ For this situation (from ②)

$i_C = \frac{I_S}{\alpha_R} e^{v_{BC}/V_T}$

or $v_{BC} = V_T \ln \frac{\alpha_R i_C}{I_S}$

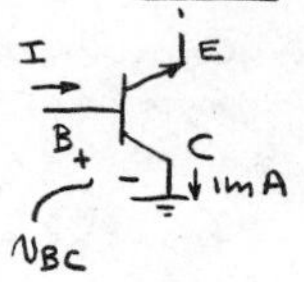

ie $v_{BC} = 25 \ln \frac{0.2}{1+0.2} \times \frac{1 \times 10^{-3}}{6.88 \times 10^{-16}} = 655$ mV 16

ⓒ If $i_E = 1$mA, $i_C = 0$, → $i_B = 1$mA

$\beta_F = 200$, $\beta_R = 0.2$, $\beta_{forced} = \beta_f = \frac{0}{1mA} = 0$

$V_{CEsat} = 25 \ln \frac{1 + (\beta_f + 1)/\beta_R}{1 - \beta_f/\beta_F}$

$= 25 \ln \frac{1 + (0+1)/0.2}{1 - 0/200}$

$= 25 \ln (1+5) = 44.8$ mV

ⓓ

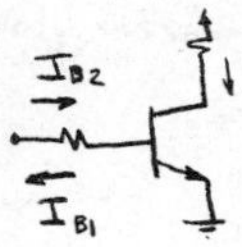

$t_s = \tau \frac{I_{B2} - \frac{I_{Csat}}{\beta_F}}{I_{B1} + \frac{I_{Csat}}{\beta_F}}$

ie $10ns = \tau \frac{1 - 1/200}{1 + 1/200}$

ie $\tau = 10ns \times \frac{1.005}{.995} = 10.1$ ns

ⓔ $t_s = 10.1 \frac{I/50 - I/200}{\frac{1}{10} \times I/50 + I/200} = 10.1\left(\frac{20-5}{20+5}\right) = 21.64$ ns

2 Exam 16

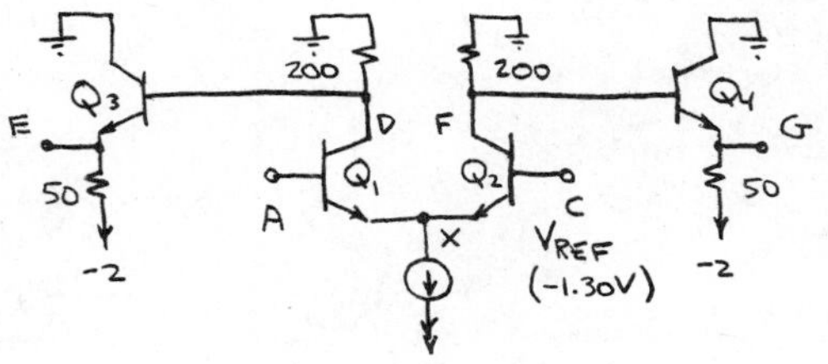

The particular circuit shown is being considered as a candidate for an ECL logic family: Transistors used exhibit $V_{BE} = 0.75$V at 1mA, n=1, and $\beta \geq 50$

ⓐ Using the node labels given, indicate the means by which a second input (B) can be added?

ⓑ At what output does the logic OR function (A+B) appear?

ⓒ What value of V_{OH} do you expect?

ⓓ What value of V_{OL} do you expect? (Use $\beta = \infty$ in your calculation for simplicity) 16

ⓔ What is the nominal switching threshold?

ⓕ For what values of input do the currents in Q1 and Q2 differ by a factor of 10?

Ⓐ ⓐ

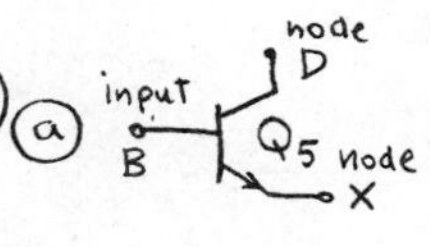

ⓑ Take the OR output from node G.

ⓒ For V_{OH}:

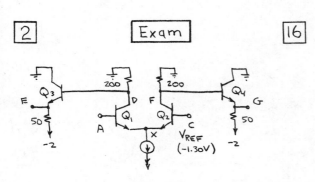

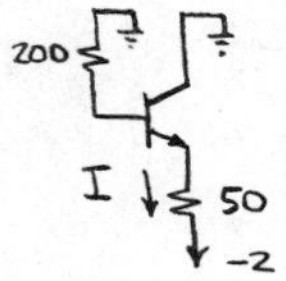

$V_{BE} = 0.75$ at 1mA, n=1, $\beta = 50$

∴ $50 I + \frac{I}{51} \times 200 + V_{BE} = 2000$ -- ①

$V_{BE} = (750 + 25 \ln I/1)$ mV -- ②

From ① $I = \frac{2000 - V_{BE}}{53.92}$ -- ③

Now iterate with ②, then ③

For I = 20 mA, $V_{BE} = 750 + 25 \ln 20 = 824.9$ mV

$I = \frac{2000 - 825}{53.9} = 21.8$, $V_{BE} = 750 + 25 \ln 21.8 = 827$ mV

$I = \frac{2000 - 827}{53.9} = 21.8$ mA, $V_{BE} = 827$ mV ✓

$\therefore V_{OH} = -2 + \frac{21.75(50)}{1000} = -0.9125V$ 16

(d) For V_{OL}: Say Q_2 conducting

$V_F = 0 - 0.2(5) = -1.0V$

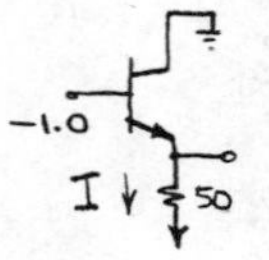

$-1 - V_{BE} - .05\,I = -2$

$I = \frac{1 - V_{BE}}{.05}$ and $V_{BE} = 0.75 + .025 \ln I$

Iterate: $I = 1$, $V_{BE} = 0.75V$

$I = \frac{1-0.75}{.05} = 5mA$, $V_{BE} = 0.75 + .025 \ln 5 = 0.790V$

$I = \frac{1-0.79}{.05} = 4.2mA$, $V_{BE} = 0.786$

$I = \frac{1-0.786}{.05} = 4.28mA$, $V_{BE} = 0.786$

$\therefore V_{OL} = -1 - 0.786 = -1.786V$

(e) The centre of the input switching range, $V_{th} = -1.30V$

(f) $I_1 = 10 I_2$ implies

$\Delta V_{BE} = 25 \ln 10 = 57.6mV$

Currents split 10 to 1 for inputs

of $-1.300 + 57.6 = -1.242V$

and $-1.300 - 57.6 = -1.358V$

1 Design 16

A design is required of an ECL-like circuit for which the input differential pair is supplied by a constant current. In order to save power, the desire is to reduce the −5.2V supply to −2.5V. Using a suitable current mirror and 2 resistors, suggest a means by which this is possible, while maintaining the usual ECL specifications: switched current of 4mA, threshold center of −1.3V a nominal collector swing of 1volt, and terminated output followers using 50Ω and −2V. Consider how temperature compensation of switching threshold center can be provided to account for the variation with temperature of

16

V_{OH} and V_{OL}. As well suggest how a −2V supply can be created simply from −2.5V in the context of this gate. Use $V_{BE} = 0.75V$ @ 1mA, $n = 1$, $\beta > 50$

(A)

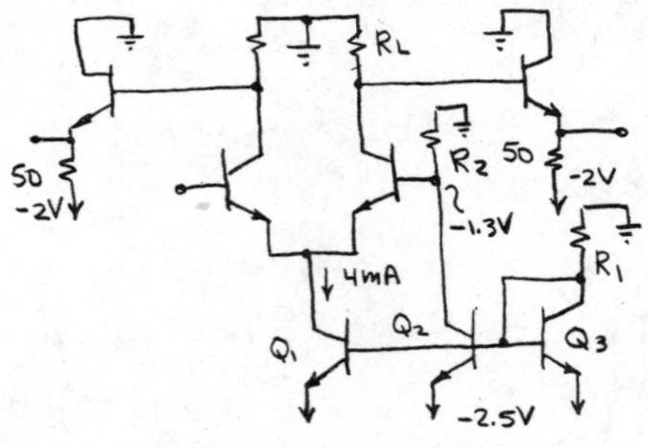

At 4mA, $V_{BE} = 0.75 + .025 \ln \frac{4}{1} = 0.7846V$

$R_1 = \frac{2.5 - 0.745}{4} = 429\Omega$

$R_2 = \frac{1.3V}{4mA} = 325\Omega$

$R_L = \frac{1.0V}{4mA} = 250\Omega$

(next)

16

For Temperature effects:

For each δ reduction in V_{BE},

I_{R_1} increases by $\frac{\delta}{429}$

V_{OL} rises by $(\delta - \frac{\delta}{429} \times 250) = 0.417\delta$

V_{OH} rises by δ directly.

$\therefore$ Center of output $V_{OA} = \frac{V_{OL}+V_{OH}}{2}$ rises by $\frac{\delta + .417\delta}{2} = .708\delta$

But threshold lowers by $325 \times \frac{\delta}{429} = 0.758\delta$

Compensate by adding a diode-connected transistor Q_4 at the ground end of R_2. The new value of R_2, $R_2' = \frac{1.30 - .785}{4} = 129\Omega$

Now the threshold centre rises by $\delta - \frac{129}{429}\delta = 0.708\delta$ compensating (perfectly!) the rise in output centering.

For −2V: Note that the loading on −2V for each balanced loaded gate is nearly constant. Consider joining the lower ends of 50Ω together to a diode to −2.5V. Select diode for 0.5V @ 25mA or so.

1.1 DATA CONVERTERS—AN INTRODUCTION

Digital Processing of Signals

Most physical signals, such as those obtained at transducer outputs, exist in analog form. Some of the processing required on these signals is most conveniently performed in an analog fashion. For instance, in instrumentation systems it is quite common to use a high-input-impedance high-gain high-CMRR differential amplifier right at the output of the transducer. This is usually followed by a filter whose object is to eliminate interference. However, further signal processing is usually required, which can range from simply obtaining a measurement of signal strength to performing some algebraic manipulations on this and related signals to obtain the value of a particular system parameter of interest, as is usually the case in systems intended to provide a complex control function. Another example of signal processing can be found in the common need for transmission of signals to a remote receiver.

All such forms of signal processing can be performed by analog means. In previous chapters we encountered circuits for implementing a number of such tasks. However, an attractive alternative exists: It is to convert, following some initial analog processing, the signal from analog to digital form and then use economical, accurate, and convenient digital ICs to perform *digital signal processing*. Such processing can in its simplest form provide us with a measure of the signal strength as an easy-to-read number (consider, for example, the digital voltmeter). In more involved cases the digital signal processor can perform a variety of arithmetic and logic operations that implement a *filtering algorithm*. The resulting *digital filter* does many of the same tasks that an analog filter performs—namely, eliminate interference and noise. Yet another example of digital signal processing is found in digital communications systems, where signals are transmitted as a sequence of binary pulses, with the obvious advantage that corruption of the amplitudes of these pulses by noise is, to a large extent, of no consequence.

Once digital signal processing has been performed, we might be content to display the result in digital form, such as a printed list of numbers. Alternatively, we might require an analog output. Such is the case in a telecommunications system, where the usual output may be speech. If an analog output is desired, then obviously we need to convert the digital signal back to an analog form.

It is not our purpose here to study the techniques of digital signal processing. Rather, we shall examine the interface circuits between the analog and digital domains. Specifically, we shall study the basic techniques and circuits employed to convert an analog signal to digital form (analog-to-digital or simply A/D conversion) and those used to convert a digital signal to analog form (digital-to-analog or simply D/A conversion). Digital circuits are studied in Chapters 15 and 16.

Sampling of Analog Signals

The principle underlying digital signal processing is that of *sampling* the analog signal. Figure 1.1 illustrates in a conceptual form the process of obtaining samples of an analog signal. The switch shown closes periodically under the control of a periodic pulse signal (clock). The closure time of the switch, τ, is relatively short, and the samples obtained are stored (held) on the capacitor. The circuit of Fig. 1.1 is known as a *sample-and-hold* (S/H) circuit. In Chapter 6 we presented a circuit implementation of the S/H building block.

Between the sampling intervals—that is, during the *hold* intervals—the voltage level on the capacitor represents the signal samples we are after. Each of these voltage levels is then fed to the input of an A/D converter, which provides an N-bit binary number proportional to the value of signal sample.

The fact that we can do our processing on a limited number of samples of an analog signal, while ignoring the analog-signal details between samples, is based on the sampling theorem [see Lathi (1965)].

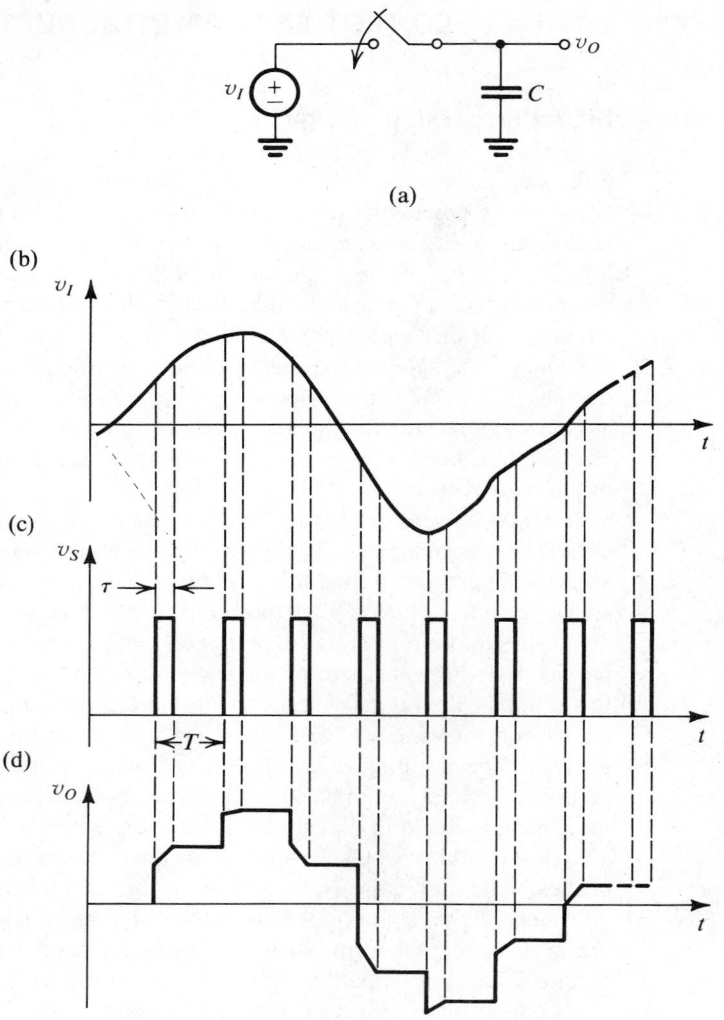

Fig. 1.1 Process of periodically sampling an analog signal. (a) Sample-and-hold (S/H) circuit. The switch closes τ second every period. (b) Input signal waveform. (c) Sampling signal (control signal for the switch). (d) Output signal (to be fed to A/D converter).

Signal Quantization

Consider an analog signal whose values range from 0 to + 10 V. Let us assume that we wish to convert this signal to digital form and that the required output is a 4-bit[1] signal. We know that a 4-bit binary number can represent 16 different values, 0 to 15; it follows that the *resolution* of our conversion will be 0 V/15 = $\frac{2}{3}$ V. Thus an analog signal of 0 V will be represented by 0000, $\frac{2}{3}$ V will be represented by 0001, 6 V will be represented by 1001, and 10 V will be represented by 1111.

All of the above sample numbers were multiples of the basic increment ($\frac{2}{3}$V). A question now arises regarding the conversion of numbers that fall between these successive incremental levels. For instance, consider the case of 6.2-V analog level. This falls between 18/3 and 20/3. However, since it is closer to 18/3 we treat it as if it were 6 V and *code* it as 1001. This process is called *quantization*. Obviously errors are inherent in this process; such errors are called quantization errors. Using more bits to represent (encode or code) an analog signal reduces quantization errors but requires more complex circuitry.

The A/D and D/A Converters as Functional Blocks

Figure 1.2 depicts the functional block representations of A/D and D/A converters. As indicated, the A/D converter accepts an analog sample v_A and produces an N-bit *digital word*. Conversely, the D/A converter accepts an n-bit digital word and produces an analog

[1]*Bit* stands for *b*inary dig*it*.

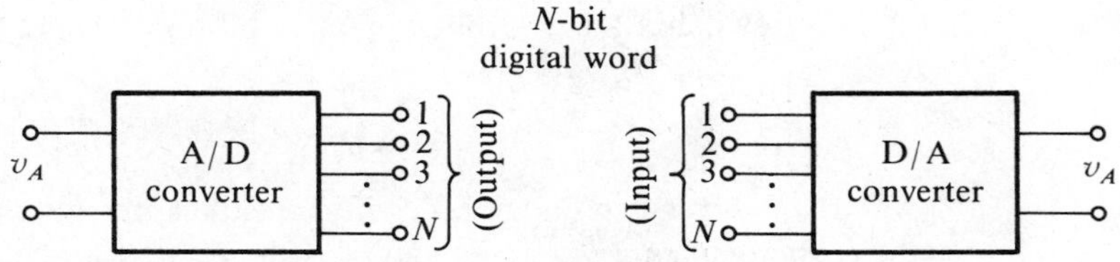

Fig. 1.2 The A/D and D/A converters as circuit blocks.

sample. The output samples of the D/A converter are often fed to a sample-and-hold circuit. At the output of the S/H circuit a staircase waveform, such as that in Fig. 1.3, is obtained. The staircase waveform can then be smoothed by a low-pass filter, giving rise to the smooth curve shown as a broken line in Fig. 1.3. In this way an analog output signal is reconstructed. Finally, note that the quantization error of an A/D converter is equivalent to $\pm\frac{1}{2}$ least significant bit (b_N).

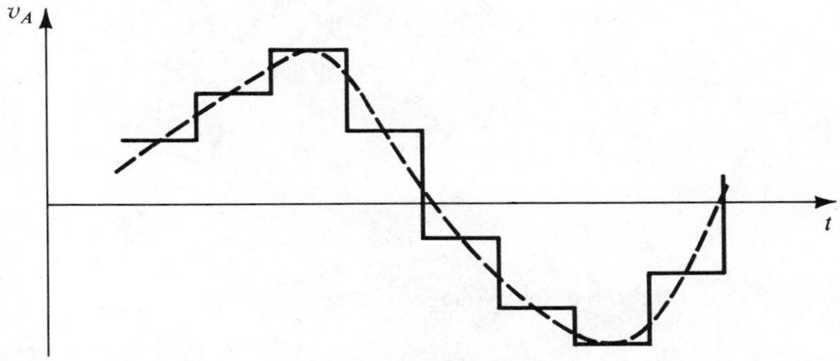

Fig. 1.3 The analog samples at the output of a D/A converter are usually fed to a sample-and-hold circuit to obtain the staircase waveform shown. This waveform can then be filtered to obtain the smooth waveform, shown as a broken line with filter delay removed.

Exercise

1.1 An analog signal in the range 0 to +10 V is to be converted to an 8-bit digital signal. What is the resolution of the conversion in volts? What is the digital representation of an input of 6 V? What is the representation of an input of 6.2 V? What is the error made in the quantization of 6.2 V in absolute terms and as a percent of the input? as a percent of full scale? What is the largest possible quantization error as a percent of full scale?

Ans. 0.0392 V; 10011001; 10011110; −0.0064 V; −0.1%; −0.064%; 0.196%

1.2 D/A CONVERTER CIRCUITS

Basic Circuit Using Binary-Weighted Resistors

Figure 1.4 shows a simple circuit for an N-bit D/A converter (or DAC, as it is sometimes called). The circuit consists of a reference voltage V_{ref}, N binary-weighted resistors R, $2R$, $4R$, $8R$, . . . , $2^{N-1}R$, N single-pole double-throw switches S_1, S_2, . . . , S_N, and an op amp together with its feedback resistance $R_f = R/2$.

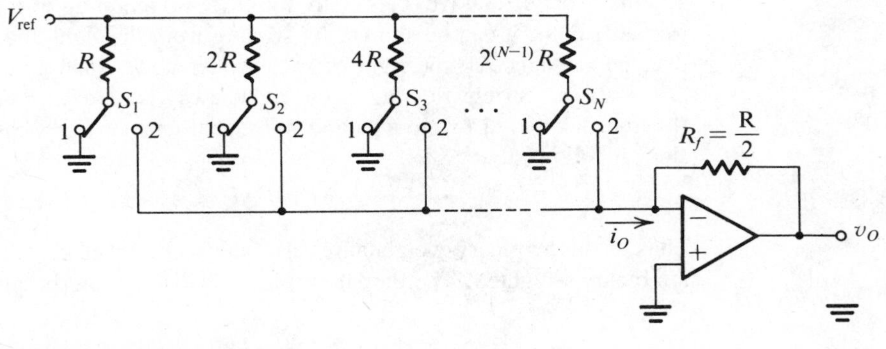

Fig. 1.4 An N-bit D/A converter.

The switches are controlled by an N-bit digital input word D,

$$D = \frac{b_1}{2^2} + \frac{b_2}{2^2} + \cdots + \frac{b_N}{2^N} \tag{1.1}$$

where b_1, b_2, and so on are bit coefficients that are either 1 or 0. Note that the bit b_N is the *least significant bit* (LSB) and b_1 is the *most significant bit* (MSB). In the circuit in Fig. 1.4, b_1 controls switch S_1, b_2 controls S_2, and so on. When b_i is 0 switch S_i is in position 1, and when b_i is 1 switch S_i is in position 2.

Since position 1 of all switches is ground and position 2 is virtual ground, the current through each resistor remains constant. Each switch simply controls where its corresponding current goes: to ground (when the corresponding bit is 0) or to virtual ground (when the corresponding bit is 1). The currents flowing into the virtual ground add up, and the sum flows through the feedback resistance R_f. The total current i_O is therefore given by

$$\begin{aligned} i_O &= \frac{V_{\text{ref}}}{R} b_1 + \frac{V_{\text{ref}}}{2R} b_2 + \cdots + \frac{V_{\text{ref}}}{2^{N-1}R} b_N \\ &= \frac{2V_{\text{ref}}}{R}\left(\frac{b_1}{2^1} + \frac{b_2}{2^2} + \cdots + \frac{b_N}{2^N}\right) \end{aligned}$$

Thus

$$i_O = \frac{2V_{\text{ref}}}{R} D \tag{1.2}$$

and the output voltage v_o is given by

$$v_o = -i_O R_f = -V_{\text{ref}} D \tag{1.3}$$

which is directly proportional to the digital word D, as desired.

It should be noted that the accuracy of the DAC depends critically on (1) the accuracy of V_{ref}, (2) the precision of the binary-weighted resistors, and (3) the perfection of the switches. Regarding the third point, we should emphasize that these switches handle analog signals; thus their perfection is of considerable interest. While the offset voltage and the finite on resistance are not of critical significance in a digital switch, these parameters are of immense importance in *analog switches*. The use of FETs to implement analog switches was discussed in Chapters 6 and 7. Also, we shall shortly see that in a practical circuit implementation of the DAC the binary-weighted currents are generated by current sources. In this case the analog switch can be realized using the differential-pair circuit, as will be shown.

A disadvantage of the binary-weighted resistor network is that for a large number of bits ($N > 4$) the spread between the smallest and largest resistances becomes quite large. This implies difficulties in maintaining accuracy in resistor values. A more convenient scheme exists utilizing a resistive network called the R-2R ladder.

R-2R Ladders

Figure 1.5 shows the basic arrangement of a DAC using an R-2R ladder. Because of the small spread in resistance values, this network is usually preferred to the binary-weighted scheme discussed above, especially for $N > 4$. Operation of the R-2R ladder is straightforward. First, it can be shown, by starting from the right and working toward the left, that the resistance to the right of each ladder node, such as that labeled X, is equal to $2R$. Thus the current flowing to the right, away from each node, is equal to the current flowing downward to ground, and twice that current flows into the node from the left side. It follows that

$$I_1 = 2I_2 = 4I_3 = \cdots = 2^{N-1}I_N$$

Thus, as in the binary-weighted resistive network, the currents controlled by the switches are binary weighted. The output current i_O will therefore be given by

$$i_O = \frac{V_{\text{ref}}}{R} D$$

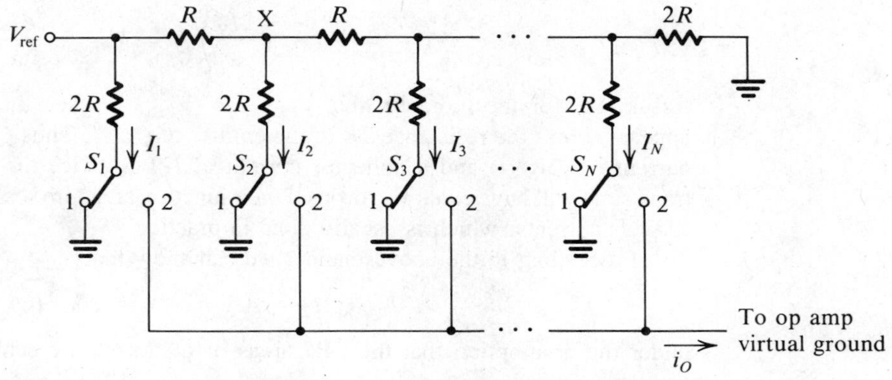

Fig. 1.5 Basic circuit configuration of a DAC utilizing an *R*-2*R* ladder network.

A Practical Circuit Implementation

A practical circuit implementation of the DAC utilizing an R-2R ladder is shown in Fig. 1.6. The circuit utilizes BJTs to generate binary-weighted constant currents $I_1, I_2, \ldots,$ I_N, which are switched between ground and virtual ground of an output summing op amp (not shown). We shall first show that the currents I_1 to I_N are indeed binary weighted, with I_1 corresponding to the MSB and I_N corresponding to the LSB of the DAC.

Starting at the two rightmost transistors, Q_N and Q_t, we see that if they are matched their emitter currents will be equal and are denoted (I_N/α). Transistor Q_t is included to provide proper termination of the R-2R network. The voltage between the base line of the BJTs and node N will be

$$V_N = V_{BE_N} + \left(\frac{I_N}{\alpha}\right)(2R)$$

where V_{BE_N} is the base-emitter voltage of Q_N. Since the current flowing through the resistor R connected to node N is $(2I_N/\alpha)$, the voltage between node B and node (N − 1) will be

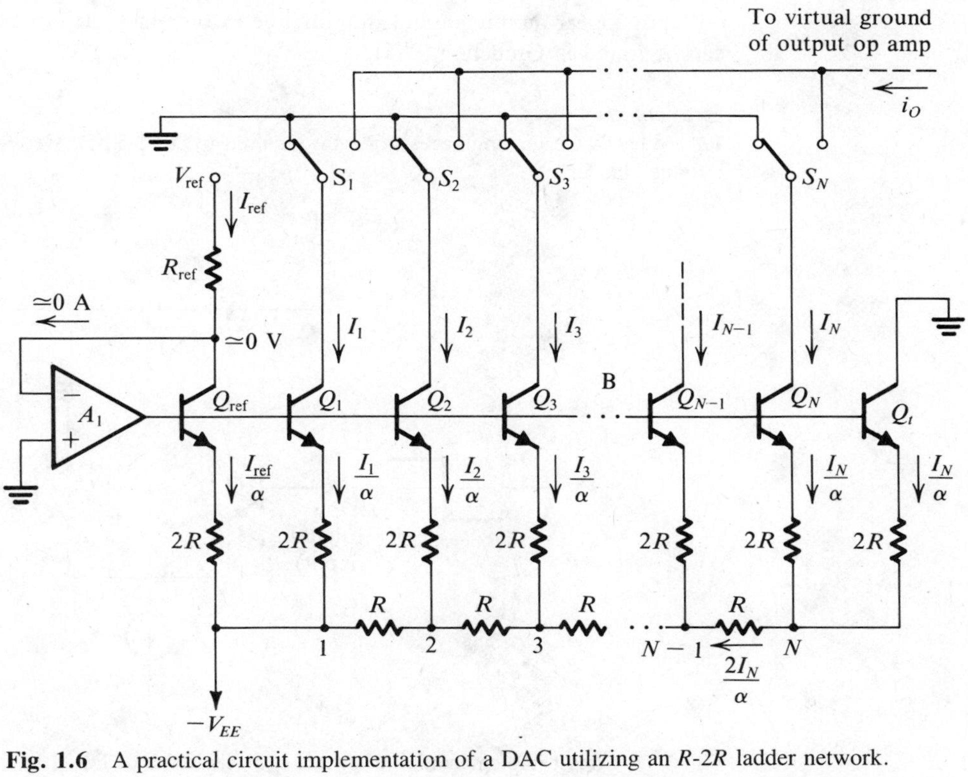

Fig. 1.6 A practical circuit implementation of a DAC utilizing an *R*-2*R* ladder network.

$$V_{N-1} = V_N + \left(\frac{2I_N}{\alpha}\right) R = V_{BE_N} + \frac{4I_N}{\alpha} R$$

Assuming, for the moment, that $V_{BE_{N-1}} = V_{BE_N}$, we see that a voltage of $(4I_N/\alpha)R$ appears across the resistance $2R$ in the emitter of Q_{N-1}. Thus Q_{N-1} will have an emitter current of $(2I_N/\alpha)$ and a collector current of $(2I_N)$, twice the current in Q_N. The two transistors will have equal V_{BE} drops if their junction areas are scaled in the same proportion as their currents, which is usually done in practice.

Proceeding in the above manner we can show that

$$I_1 = 2I_2 = 4I_3 = \cdots = 2^{N-1}I_N$$

under the assumption that the EBJ areas of Q_1 to Q_N are scaled in a binary-weighted fashion.

Next consider op amp A_1, which, together with the reference transistor Q_{ref}, forms a negative-feedback loop. A virtual ground appears at the collector of Q_{ref} forcing it to conduct a collector current $I_{\text{ref}} = V_{\text{ref}}/R_{\text{ref}}$ independent of whatever imperfections Q_{ref} might have. Now, if Q_{ref} and Q_1 are matched, their collector currents will be equal,

$$I_1 = I_{\text{ref}}$$

Thus, the binary-weighted currents are directly related to the reference current, independent of the exact values of V_{BE} and α. Also observe that op amp A_1 supplies the base currents of all the BJTs.

Current Switches

Each of the single-pole double-throw switches in the DAC circuit of Fig. 1.6 can be implemented by a circuit such as that shown in Fig. 1.7 for switch S_m. Here I_m denotes the current flowing in the collector of the mth bit transistor. The circuit is a differential pair with the base of the reference transistor Q_{mr} connected to a suitable dc voltage V_{bias}, and the digital signal representing the mth bit b_m applied to the base of the other transistor Q_{ms}. If the voltage representing b_m is higher than V_{bias} by a few hundred millivolts, Q_{ms} will turn on and Q_{mr} will turn off. The bit current I_m will flow through Q_{ms} and onto the output summing line. On the other hand, when b_m is low, Q_{ms} will be off and I_m flows through Q_{mr} to ground.

The current switch of Fig. 1.7 is simple and features high-speed operation. It suffers, however, from the fact that part of the current I_m flows through the base of Q_{ms} and thus does not appear on the output summing line. More elaborate circuits for current switches can be found in Grebene (1984).

Exercises

1.2 What is the maximum resistor ratio required by a 12-bit D/A converter utilizing a binary-weighted ladder?

Ans. 2048.

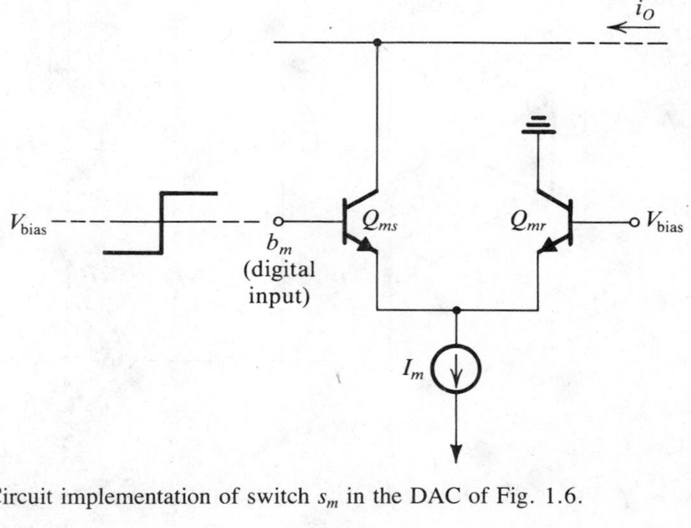

Fig. 1.7 Circuit implementation of switch s_m in the DAC of Fig. 1.6.

1.3 If the input bias current of an op amp, used as the output summer in a 10-bit DAC, is to be no more than that equivalent to $\frac{1}{4}$ LSB, what is the maximum current required to flow in R_f for an op amp whose bias current is as great as 0.5 μA?
Ans. 2.046 mA

1.3 A/D CONVERTER CIRCUITS

There exist a number of A/D conversion techniques varying in complexity and speed of conversion. In the following we shall discuss two simple but slow schemes, one complex (in terms of the amount of circuitry required) but extremely fast method, and finally a method particularly suited for MOS implementation.

The Feedback-Type Converter

Figure 1.8 shows a simple A/D converter that employs a comparator, an up-down counter, and a D/A converter. In Section 5.8 we discussed the comparator operator. An up-down counter is simply a counter that can count either up or down depending on the binary level applied at its up-down control terminal. Because the A/D converter of Fig. 1.8 employs a DAC in its feedback loop it is usually called a feedback-type A/D converter. It operates as follows: With a 0 count in the counter, the D/A converter output, v_O, will be zero and the output of the comparator will be high, instructing the counter to count the clock pulses in the up direction. As the count increases, the output of the DAC rises. The process continues until the DAC output reaches the value of the analog input signal, at which point the comparator switches and stops the counter. The counter output will then be the digital equivalent of the input analog voltage.

Operation of the converter of Fig. 1.8 is slow if it starts from zero. This converter however, tracks incremental changes in the input signal quite rapidly.

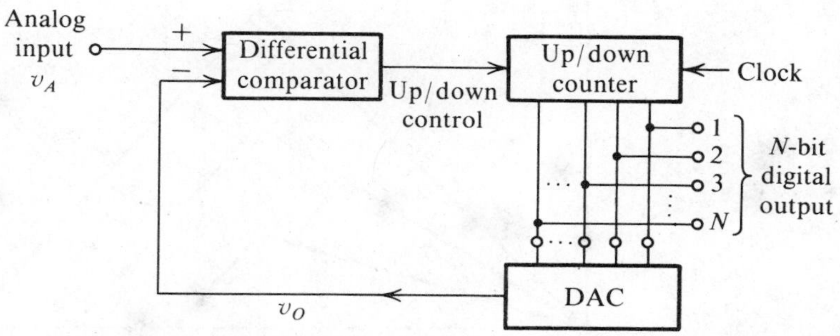

Fig. 1.8 A simple feedback-type A/D converter.

The Dual-Slope A/D Converter

A very popular high-resolution (12- to 14-bit) (but slow) A/D conversion scheme is illustrated in Fig. 1.9. To see how it operates, refer to Fig. 1.9 and assume that the analog input signal is negative. Prior to the start of the conversion cycle, switch S_2 is closed, thus discharging capacitor C and setting $v_1 = 0$. The conversion cycle begins with opening S_2 and connecting the integrator input through switch S_1 to the analog input signal. Since v_A is negative, a current $I = v_A/R$ will flow through R in the direction away from the integrator. Thus v_1 rises linearly with a slope of $I/C = v_A/RC$, as indicated in Fig. 1.9b. Simultaneously, the counter is enabled and it counts the pulses from a fixed-frequency clock. This phase of the conversion process continues for a fixed duration T_1. It ends when the counter accumulates a fixed count denoted n_{ref}. Usually, for N-bit converter, $n_{\text{ref}} = 2^N$. Denoting the peak voltage at the output of the integrator V_{peak}, we can write with reference to Fig. 1.9b

$$\frac{V_{\text{peak}}}{T_1} = \frac{v_A}{RC} \tag{1.4}$$

At the end of this phase, the counter is reset to zero.

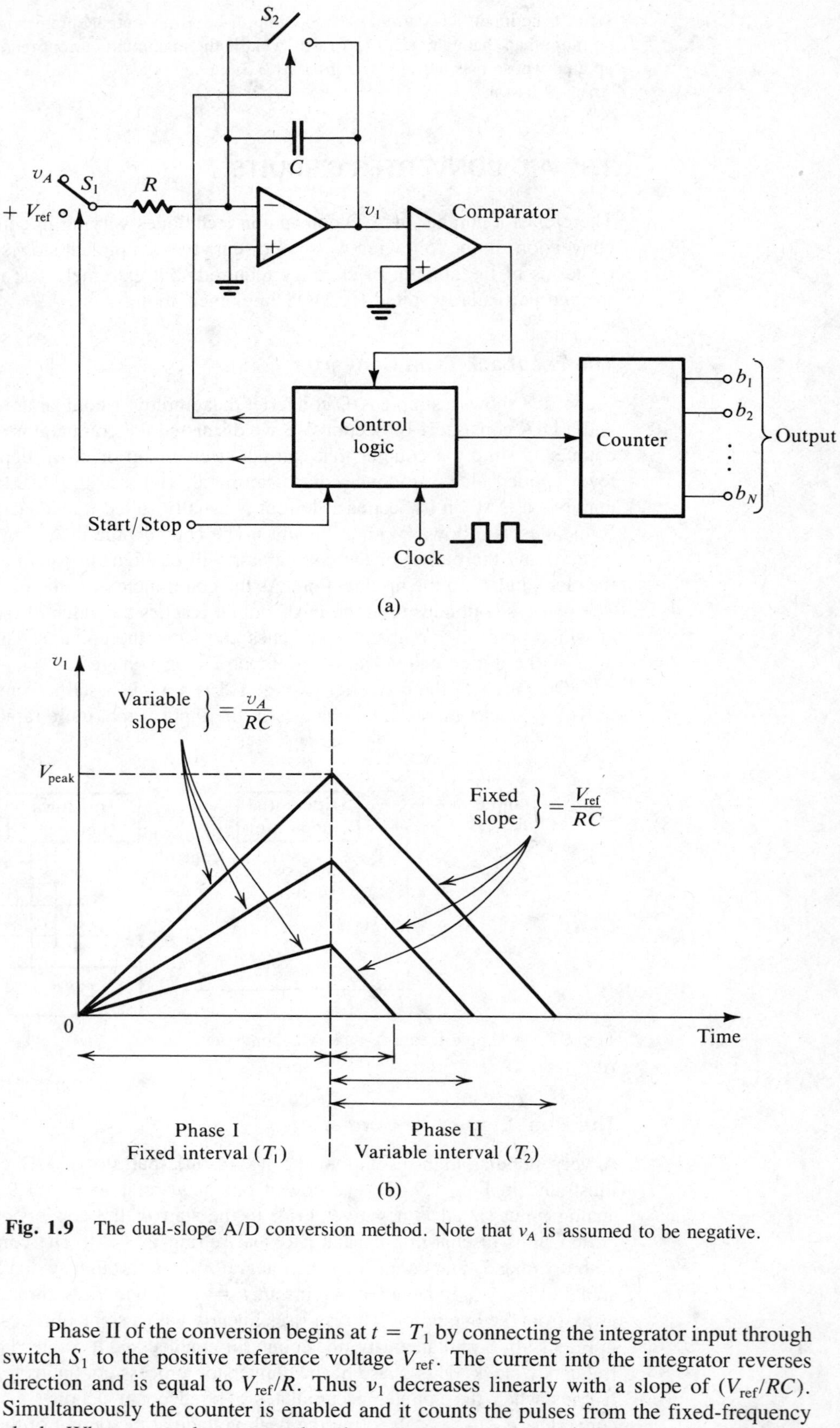

Fig. 1.9 The dual-slope A/D conversion method. Note that v_A is assumed to be negative.

Phase II of the conversion begins at $t = T_1$ by connecting the integrator input through switch S_1 to the positive reference voltage V_{ref}. The current into the integrator reverses direction and is equal to V_{ref}/R. Thus v_1 decreases linearly with a slope of (V_{ref}/RC). Simultaneously the counter is enabled and it counts the pulses from the fixed-frequency clock. When v_1 reaches zero volts, the comparator signals the control logic to stop the counter. Denoting the duration of phase II by T_2, we can write, by reference to Fig. 1.9b,

$$\frac{V_{peak}}{T_2} = \frac{V_{ref}}{RC} \tag{1.5}$$

Equations (1.4) and (1.5) can be combined to yield

$$T_2 = T_1 \left(\frac{v_A}{V_{\text{ref}}}\right) \tag{1.6}$$

Since the counter reading, n_{ref}, at the end of T_1, is proportional to T_1 and the reading, n, at the end of T_2, is proportional to T_2, we have

$$n = n_{\text{ref}} \left(\frac{v_A}{V_{\text{ref}}}\right) \tag{1.7}$$

Thus the content of the counter,[2] n, at the end of the conversion process is the digital equivalent of v_A.

The dual-slope converter features high accuracy, since its performance is independent of the exact values of R and C. There exist many commercial implementations of the dual-slope method, some of which utilize CMOS technology.

The Parallel or Flash Converter

The fastest A/D conversion scheme is the simultaneous, parallel, or flash conversion illustrated in Fig. 1.10. Conceptually, flash conversion is very simple. It utilizes $2^N - 1$ comparators to compare the input signal level with each of the $2^N - 1$ possible quantization levels. The outputs of the comparators are processed by an encoding-logic block to provide the N bits of the output digital word. Note that a complete conversion can be obtained within one clock cycle.

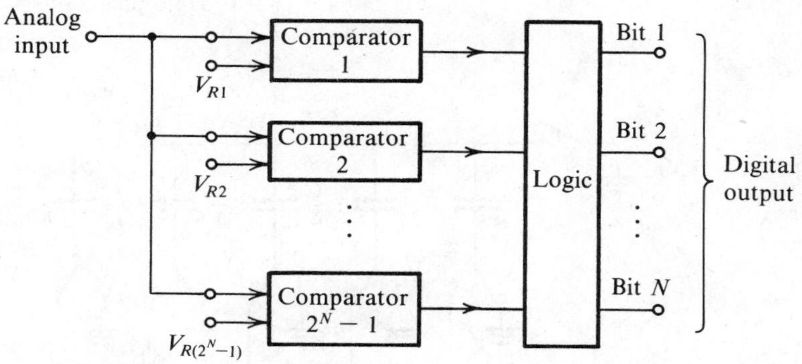

Fig. 1.10 Parallel, simultaneous, or flash A/D conversion.

Although flash conversion is very fast, the price paid is a rather complex circuit implementation. Variations on the basic technique have been successfully employed in the design of IC converters.

The Charge-Redistribution Converter

The last A/D conversion technique we shall discuss is particularly suited for CMOS implementation. As shown in Fig. 1.11, the circuit utilizes a binary-weighted capacitor array, a voltage comparator, analog switches, and control logic (not shown). The circuit shown is for a 5-bit converter; capacitor C_T serves the purpose of terminating the capacitor array, making the total capacitance equal to the desired value of $2C$.

Operation of the converter can be divided into three distinct phases, illustrated in Figs. 1.11a, b, and c. In the sample phase (Fig. 1.11a) switch S_B is closed, thus connecting the top plate of all capacitors to ground and setting v_O to zero. Meanwhile, switch S_A is connected to the analog input voltage v_A. Thus the voltage v_A appears across the total capacitance of $2C$, resulting in a stored charge of $2Cv_A$. Thus during this phase a sample of v_A is taken and a proportional amount of charge is stored on the capacitor array.

[2]Note that n is *not* a continuous function of v_A, as might be inferred from Eq. (1.7). Rather, n takes on discrete values corresponding to the quantized levels of v_A.

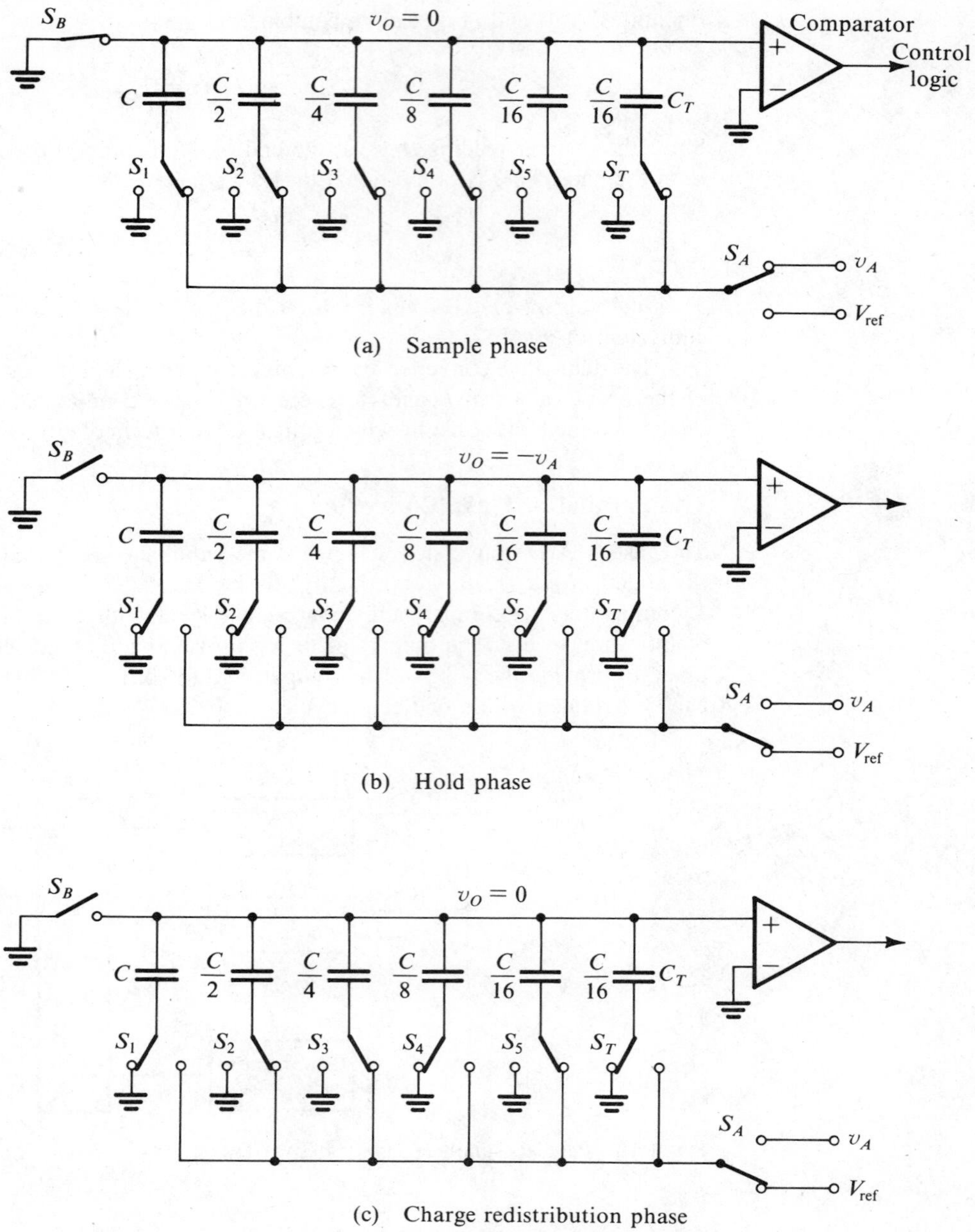

Fig. 1.11 Charge-redistribution A/D converter suitable for CMOS implementation.

During the hold phase (Fig. 1.11b), switch S_B is opened and switches S_1 to S_5, and S_T are thrown to the ground side. Thus the top plate of the capacitor array is open-circuited while their bottom plates are connected to ground. Since no discharge path has been provided, the capacitor charges must remain constant with the total equal to $2Cv_A$. It follows that the voltage at the top plate must become $-v_A$. Finally, note that during the hold phase S_A is connected to V_{ref} in preparation for the charge-redistribution phase.

Next we consider the operation during the charge-redistribution phase illustrated in Fig. 1.11c. First, switch S_1 is connected to V_{ref}. The circuit then consists of V_{ref}, a series capacitor C and a total capacitance to ground of value C. This capacitive divider causes a voltage increment of $V_{ref}/2$ to appear on the top plates. Now if v_A is greater than $V_{ref}/2$, the net voltage at the top plate will remain negative, which means that S_1 will be left in its new position as we move on to switch S_2. If, on the other hand, v_A was smaller than $V_{ref}/2$, then the net voltage at the top plate would become positive. The comparator will detect this situation and signal the control logic to return S_1 to its ground position and then to move on to S_2.

Next, switch S_2 is connected to V_{ref} which causes a voltage increment of $V_{ref}/4$ to appear on the top plate. If the resulting voltage is still negative, S_2 is left in its new position; otherwise, S_2 is returned to its ground position. We then move on to switch S_3, and so on until all the bit switches S_1 to S_5 have been tried.

It can be seen that during the charge-redistribution phase the voltage on the top plate will be reduced incrementally to zero. The connection of the bit switches at the conclusion of this phase gives the output digital word; a switch connected to ground indicates a 0 value for the corresponding bit, whereas connection to V_{ref} indicates a 1. The particular switch configuration depicted in Fig. 1.11c is for $D = 01101$. Observe that at the end of the conversion process, all the charge is stored in the capacitors corresponding to "1" bits; the capacitors of the "0" bits have been discharged

The accuracy of this A/D conversion method is independent of the value of stray capacitances from the bottom plate of the capacitors to ground. This is because the bottom plates are connected either to ground or to V_{ref}; thus the charge on the stray capacitances will not flow into the capacitor array. Also, because both the initial and the final voltages on the top plate are zero, the circuit is also insensitive to the stray capacitances between the top plates and ground.[3] The insensitivity to stray capacitances makes the charge-redistribution technique a reasonably accurate method capable of implementing A/D converters with as many as 10 bits.

Exercises

1.4 Consider the 5-bit charge-redistribution converter in Fig. 1.11 with $V_{ref} = 4$ V. What is the voltage increment appearing on the top plate when S_5 is switched? What is the full-scale voltage of this converter? If $v_A = 2.5$ V which switches will be connected to V_{ref} at the end of conversion?
Ans. $\frac{1}{8}$ V; $\frac{31}{8}$ V; S_1 and S_3

1.5 Express the maximum quantization error of an N-bit A/D converter in terms of its least significant bit (LSB) and in terms of its full-scale analog input V_{FS}.
Ans. $\pm\frac{1}{2}$ LSB; $V_{FS}/2(2^N - 1)$

PROBLEMS

1.1 An analog signal in the range 0 to +10 V is to be digitized with a quantization error of less than 1% of full scale. What is the number of bits required? What is the resolution of the conversion? If the range is to be extended to ±10 V with the same requirement, what is the number of bits required? For an extension to a 0 to + 15 V range, how many bits are required? What is the corresponding resolution and quantization error?

***1.2** Consider Fig. 1.3. On the staircase output of the S/H circuit sketch the output of a simple low-pass RC circuit with a time constant that is **(a)** one-third of the sampling interval **(b)** equal to the sampling interval.

***1.3** Consider the DAC circuit of Fig. 1.4 for the cases $N = 2$, 4, and 8. What is the tolerance, expressed as $\pm x\%$, to which the resistors should be selected so as to limit the resulting output error to the equivalent of $\pm\frac{1}{2}$ LSB?

1.4 The BJTs in the circuit of Fig. P1.4 have their base-emitter junction areas scaled in the ratios indicated. Find I_1 to I_4 in terms of I.

1.5 A problem encountered in the DAC circuit of Fig. 1.6 is the large spread in transistor EBJ areas required when N is large. As an alternative arrangement consider using the circuit in Fig. 1.6 for 4 bits only. Then, feed the current in the collector of the terminating transistor Q_t to the circuit of Problem 1.4, thus producing currents for 4 more bits. In this way an 8-bit DAC can be implemented with a maximum spread in areas of 8. What is the total area of emitters needed in terms of the smallest device? Contrast this with the usual 8-bit circuit? Give the complete circuit of the converter thus realized.

***1.6** The circuit in Fig. 1.4 can be used to multiply an analog signal by a digital one by feeding the analog signal to the V_{ref} terminal. In this case the D/A converter is called a *multiplying DAC* or MDAC. Given an input sine-wave signal of 0.1 sin ωt volts, use the circuit of Fig. 1.4 together with an additional op amp to obtain $v_O = 10D \sin \omega t$ where D is the digital word given by Eq.

[3]The final voltage can deviate from zero by as much as the analog equivalent of the LSB. Thus the insensitivity to top-plate capacitance is not complete.

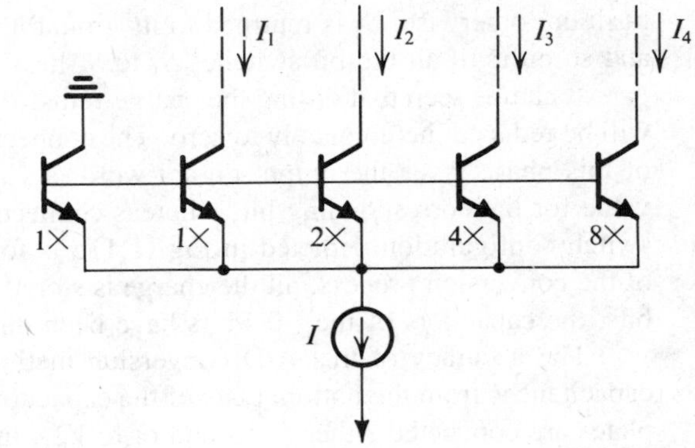

Fig. P1.4

(1.1) and $N = 4$. How many discrete sine-wave amplitudes are available at the output? What is the smallest? What is the largest? To what digital input does a 10-V peak-to-peak output correspond?

1.7 What is the input resistance seen by V_{ref} in the circuit of Fig. 1.5?

1.8 A 12-bit dual-slope ADC of the type illustrated in Fig. 1.9 utilizes a 1-MHz clock and has $V_{ref} = 10$ V. Its analog input voltage is in the range 0 to -10 V. The fixed interval T_1 is the time taken for the counter to accumulate a count of 2^N. What is the time required to convert an input voltage equal to the full-scale value? If the peak voltage reached at the output of the integrator is 10 V, what is the integrator time constant? If through aging R increases by 2% and C decreases by 1%, what does V_{peak} become? Does the conversion accuracy change?

1.9 The design of a 4-bit flash ADC as shown in Fig. 1.10 is being considered. How many comparators are required? For an input signal in the range of 0 to $+10$ V, what are the reference voltages needed? Show how they can be generated using a 10-V reference and several 1-k Ω resistors (how many?). If a comparison is possible in 50 ns and the associated logic requires 35 ns, what is the maximum possible conversion rate? Indicate the digital code you expect at the output of the comparators and at the output of the logic for an input of **(a)** 0 V, **(b)** $+5.1$ V, and **(c)** $+10$ V.

2.1 RANDOM-ACCESS MEMORY (RAM)

A computer system, whether a large machine or a microcomputer, requires memory for storing data and program instructions. Furthermore, within a given computer system there usually are various types of memory utilizing a variety of technologies and having different *access times*. Broadly speaking, computer memory can be divided into two types: *main memory* and *mass-storage* memory. The main memory is usually the most rapidly accessible memory and the one from which most, often all, instructions in programs are executed. The main memory is usually of the *random-access* type. A random-access memory (RAM) is one in which the time required for storing (writing) information and for retrieving (reading) information is independent of the physical location (within the memory) in which the information is stored.

Random-access memories should be contrasted with *serial* or *sequential* memories, such as disks and tapes, from which data are available only in the same sequence in which the data were originally stored. Thus, in a serial memory the time to access particular information depends on the memory location in which the required information is stored, and the average access time is longer than the access time of random-access memory. In a computer system, serial memory is used for mass storage. Items not frequently accessed, such as large parts of the computer operating system, are usually stored in a *moving-surface memory* such as magnetic disk or tape.

Another important classification of memory is whether it is a *read/write* or a *read-only* memory. Read/write (*R/W*) memory permits data to be stored and retrieved at comparable speeds. Computer systems require random access, read/write memory for data and program storage.

Read-only memories (ROM) permit reading at the same high speeds of R/W memories (or perhaps higher), but restrict the writing operation, ROMs can be used to store a microprocessor operating system program. They are also employed in operations that require table-lookup such as finding the values of mathematical functions. A popular application of ROMs is their use in video game cartridges. It should be noted that read-only memory is usually of the random-access type. Nevertheless, in the digital circuit jargon, the acronym RAM usually refers to read-write, random-access memory while ROM is used for read-only memory.

The regular structure of memory circuits has made them an ideal application for VLSI circuit design. Indeed, at any moment, memory chips represent the state of the art in packing density and hence integration level. At the present time chips containing 256K bits[1] are commercially available, while 1M-bit memory chips are being tested in research and development laboratories. In this section we shall study some of the basic circuits employed in VLSI RAM chips. Read-only memory circuits are studied in the next section.

Memory Chip Organization

The bits on a memory chip are either individually addressable, or addressable in groups of four or eight. As an example, a 64K-bit chip in which all bits are individually addressable is said to be organized as 64K words $\times$ 1 bit (or simply 64K $\times$ 1). Such a chip needs a 16-bit address ($2^{16} = 65{,}536 = 64K$). On the other hand, the 64K-bit chip can be organized as 16K words $\times$ 4 bits (16K $\times$ 4) in which case a 14-bit address is required. For simplicity we shall assume in our subsequent discussion that all the bits on a memory chip are individually addressable.

The bulk of a memory chip is the cells in which the bits are stored. Each memory cell is an electronic circuit capable of storing one bit. The storage cells on a chip are physically organized in a square matrix. As an example, Fig. 2.1 illustrates the organization of a 1K-bit chip. As indicated, the cell array has 32 rows and 32 columns. Each cell is connected to one of the 32 row lines, known rather loosely as *word lines*, and to one of the 32 column lines, known as *digit lines* or *bit lines*. A particular cell is selected by activating its word line and its digit line. This in turn is achieved by the row address decoder and the column address decoder. As indicated, five of the ten address bits form the *row address* and the other five address bits form the *column address*. The row address bits, labeled A_0 to A_4 are fed to the row address decoder, which selects one of the 32 word lines. Similarly, the column address bits, A_5 to A_9, are fed to the column address decoder, which selects one out of the 32 digit lines.

Address Buffers and Decoders

The address input terminals of a RAM chip are usually buffered using inverters. For instance, in an NMOS RAM the depletion-load circuits of Fig. 2.2 would be used. As indicated, the input buffers provide the true and the complement of the input address bits. Availability of the complements simplifies decoding. Each address decoder is usually a combinational circuit such as the NOR gate shown in Fig. 2.3. If, for instance, this NOR gate is used in the row address decoder, its output would be connected to one of the word lines and its inputs would be connected to the appropriate combination of address bits and their complements. This appropriate combination is selected so that the output of the NOR gate is high when we wish to select the particular word line to which it is connected.

Exercise

2.1 For the 1K-bit RAM shown in Fig. 2.1 find the address bits that are to be connected to the inputs of the NOR gate whose output is connected to row 18.
Ans. A_0, $\overline{A}_1$, A_2, A_3 and $\overline{A}_4$.

The complete NOR address decoder is usually connected in array form, as illustrated in Fig. 2.4.

[1]The capacity of a memory chip to hold binary information as binary digits (or bits) is measured in K-bit units, where 1K bit = 1,024 bits. Thus a 16K-bit chip contains 16,384 bits of memory, a 256K-bit chip contains 262,144 bits, and so on. Also, a 1M-bit chip contans 1,048,576 bits of memory.

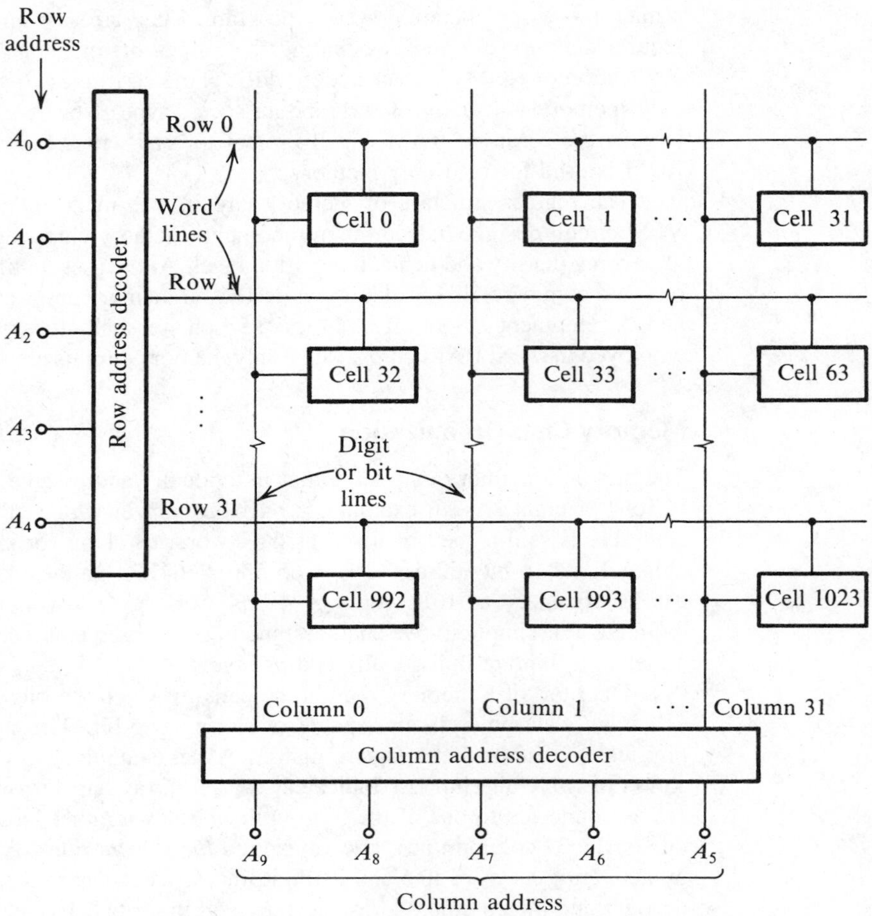

Fig. 2.1 Organization of a 1,024-bit chip. Note that from a system point of view this chip is organized as 1,024 words × 1 bit.

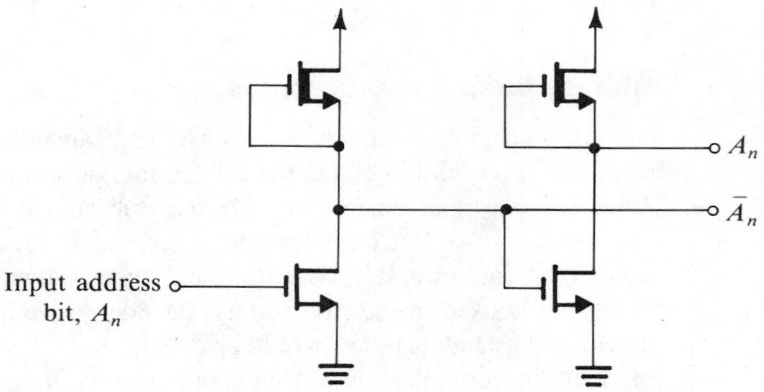

Fig. 2.2 A simple depletion-load address buffer.

Memory Chip Timing

The memory-access time is the time between the initiation of a read operation and the appearance of the output data. The memory-cycle time is the minimum time allowed between two consecutive memory operations. To be on the conservative side, a memory operation is usually taken to include both read and write (in the same location). MOS memories have access and cycle times in the range of 30 to 300 ns.

Static Memory Cell

There are basically two types of MOS RAMs: static and dynamic. Static RAMs utilize flip-flops as the storage cells. As will be seen shortly, these flip-flops have to be as simple as possible in order to minimize the silicon area per cell. This is very important since

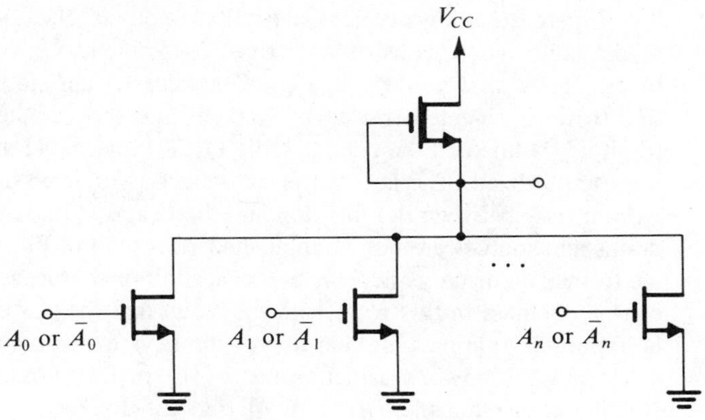

Fig. 2.3 A simple NOR decoder.

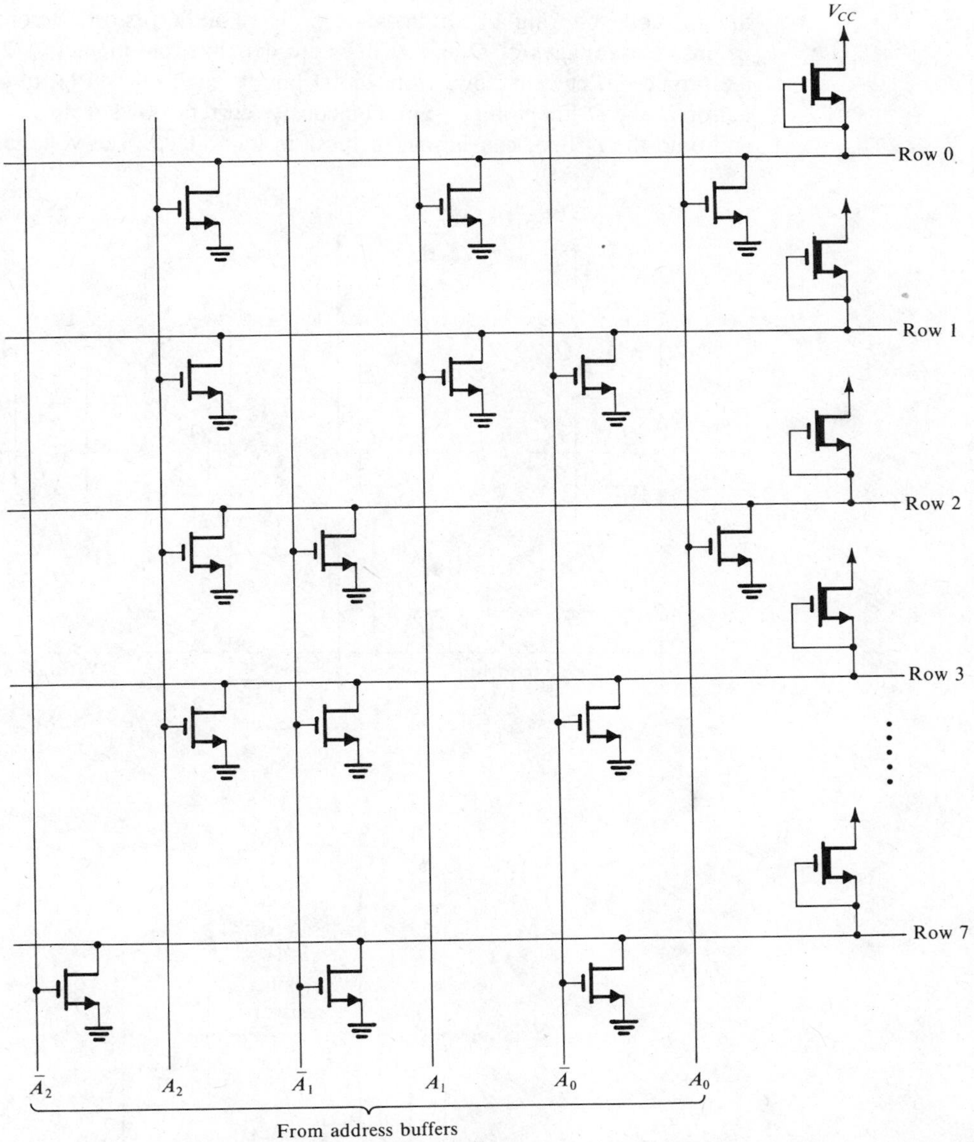

Fig. 2.4 A NOR address decoder in array form. One out of eight lines (row lines) is selected using a 3-bit address.

the cell array constitutes by far the largest part of the memory chip. Dynamic RAMs on the other hand store the binary data on capacitors, resulting in further reduction in cell area at the expense of more elaborate read and write circuitry. We shall discuss static RAMs first.

Figure 2.5 shows typical static RAM cells in NMOS and CMOS technology. Each of the cells shown consists of a flip-flop formed by cross-coupling two inverters, and two *access transistors,* Q_5 and Q_6. The access transistors are turned on when the word line (row) is selected (raised in voltage) and they connect the flip-flop to the column (digit or D) line and the $\overline{\text{column}}$, ($\overline{\text{digit}}$ or $\overline{D}$) line. Note that here both the digit and $\overline{\text{digit}}$ lines are utilized. The access transistors act as transmission gates allowing bidirectional current flow between the flip-flop and the D and $\overline{D}$ lines. (To emphasize this point, their drains and sources are not distinguished.) The cell of Fig. 2.5c utilizes load resistors that are formed in the polysilicon layer via an additional processing step. Large-valued resistors can be obtained in this way, with the result that the power dissipation per cell is low. It is important to appreciate that one of the keys to realizing large-capacity memory chips is keeping the power dissipation per bit as small as possible.

To access the memory cells of Fig. 2.5 for reading or writing, the voltage of the word line is raised, thus turning on the access transistors (Q_5 and Q_6). In this way, one side of the cell flip-flop is connected to the D line and the other side is connected to the $\overline{D}$ line. Consider as an example the read operation of the cell in Fig. 2.5a and assume that the cell is storing a 0. In this case Q_1 is on and Q_2 is off. Before the read operation begins, the voltages of D and $\overline{D}$ lines are equalized at about $V_{CC}/2$. When Q_5 and Q_6 are turned on, current flows from the D line through Q_5 and Q_1 to ground. This causes a drop in the D-line voltage. Simultaneously, current flows from V_{CC} through Q_4 and Q_6 and onto the $\overline{D}$ line, causing an increase in its voltage. The voltage signal that appears

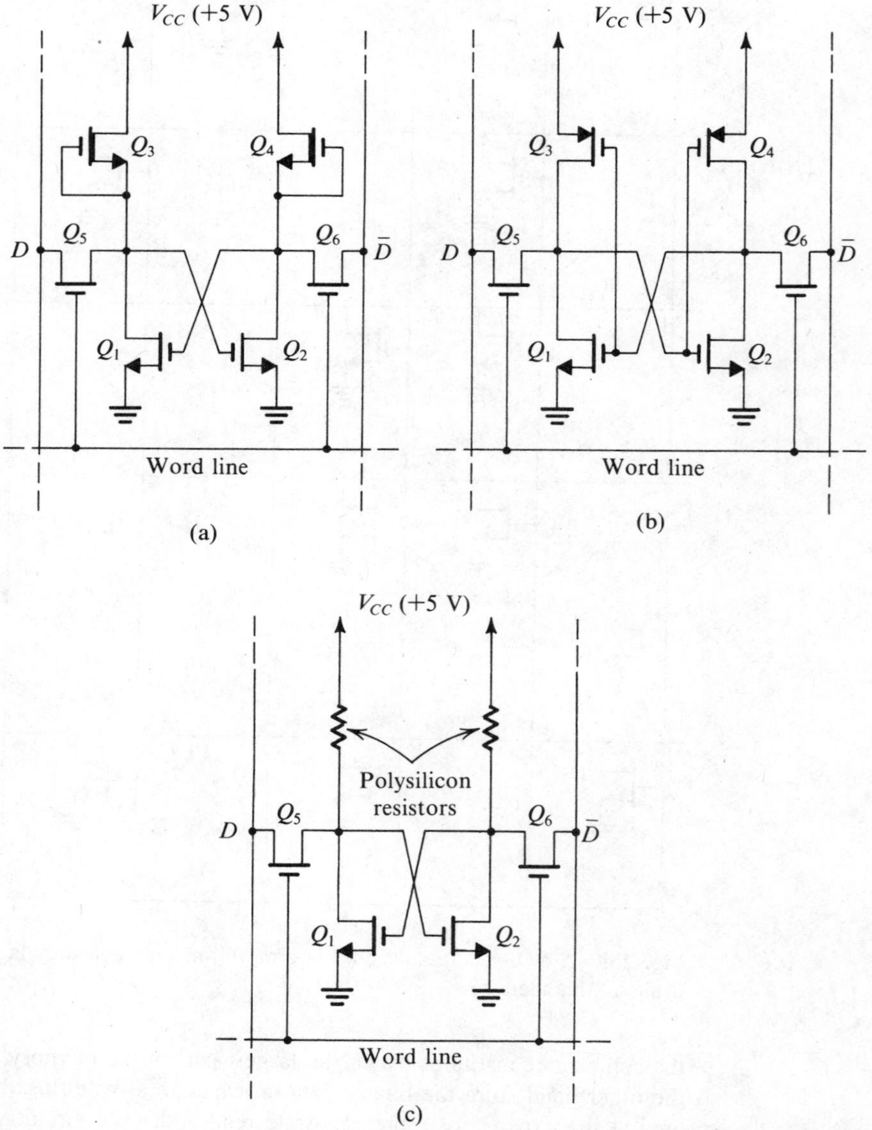

Fig. 2.5 Static RAM cells: (a) depletion load; (b) CMOS; and (c) polysilicon load.

between the D and $\overline{D}$ lines is then fed to the column *sense amplifier* (there is one sense amplifier per column). Only the sense amplifier in the selected column will be active, and its output is connected to the data output line of the chip.

From the above description we infer that the currents conducted by the flip-flop transistors, together with the capacitances of the D and $\overline{D}$ line (that is, between these lines and ground), determine the rise and fall times of the signals on the D and $\overline{D}$ lines. These times, in turn, contribute to the access time of the RAM. Another component of the access time is contributed by the nonzero rise time of the signal on the word line. This rise time is a result of the nonzero capacitance of the word line and the limited current-drive capability available from the output of the row decoder.

To speed up RAM operation, both components of time delay mentioned above have to be reduced. This is the reason the D and $\overline{D}$ lines are usually *precharged* to $V_{CC}/2$ before the read operation. In this way the signal swing on each of the two lines is reduced. This in turn reduces the time taken by the column sense amplifier to reliably detect the voltage difference between D and $\overline{D}$.

To complete our discussion of cell access, consider the write operation. The data bit to be written and its complement are transferred to the D and $\overline{D}$ lines, respectively. Thus, if a 1 is to be written, the D line is raised to V_{CC} and the $\overline{D}$ line is lowered to ground. The conducting transistors Q_5 and Q_6 then (see Fig. 2.5a) cause the high voltage to appear at the gate of Q_2 and the low voltage to appear at the gate of Q_1. The flip-flop is then forced into the state in which the drain of Q_1 is high and that of Q_2 is low. This state, which denotes a stored 1, will be maintained indefinitely unless changed by another write operation.

Exercises

2.2 A large static RAM (16K × 1) utilizing the cell shown in Fig. 2.5c requires 150 mW in standby (that is, when no reading or writing operations are carried out). If the standby current is nearly all required by the storage cells, what value (approximately) must the polysilicon resistors have if V_{CC} is + 5 V? If V_{CC} of the cell is reduced to +2 V during standby, what must the resistance be? In each case calculate the maximum current that can be drawn from the flip-flop at full voltage (5 V) without the loss of information that can occur if the drain of Q_1 or Q_2 is pulled below 1.5 V (V_t plus a safety margin). If the device K is designed to provide a low level ≤ 10 mV at the largest standing current and full voltage applied, what is the greatest current the flip-flop can sink while retaining an output ≤ 0.5 V (V_t less a safety margin). V_t = 1 V.
Ans. 2.73 MΩ; 1.09 MΩ; 1.28 μA and 3.2 μA; 0.21 mA

We next consider the circuits for sensing and data writing. Figure 2.6 shows the Mth column of a static RAM. When this column is selected, the gate of Q_9 goes high and Q_9 turns on—establishing a low voltage at the sources of Q_7, Q_8, Q_{10}, and Q_{11}. During a read operation the voltage signals appearing on the D and $\overline{D}$ lines are applied to the gates of Q_7 and Q_8, which operate as common source amplifiers, supplying amplified output signals at the chip Data out and $\overline{\text{Data out}}$ lines.

In a write operation, the input data bit and its complement are applied to the gates of transistors Q_{10} and Q_{11}, which operate as common-source amplifiers, supplying an amplified version of the input signal to D_M and $\overline{D}_M$. Finally, note that Q_{L1} and Q_{L2} act as load devices for the D and $\overline{D}$ lines.

Static RAMs can achieve very short access and cycle times. As an example, the Inmos IMS 1400, which is a 16K-bit static RAM fabricated in NMOS technology, has a 45-ns access time. The chip operates from a single 5-V supply and dissipates a maximum of 660 mW when operating. It has a "standby mode" in which it can hold its contents, but is not available for read or write operation. The power dissipation in the standby mode is reduced to 110 mW.

As a final note, we observe that static RAMs can keep their contents indefinitely, as long as the power supply is connected. Although a clock is used for gating and synchronization, it is not essential for memory chip operation. Dynamic RAMs, on the other hand, require a clock for their operation, as explained next.

Dynamic RAMs

In a dynamic MOS RAM, binary data are stored in the form of charge on the cell capacitor. A logic 0 is represented by no charge and hence a voltage close to zero; a logic 1 is represented by a capacitor voltage of value close to the power supply. Due to the various

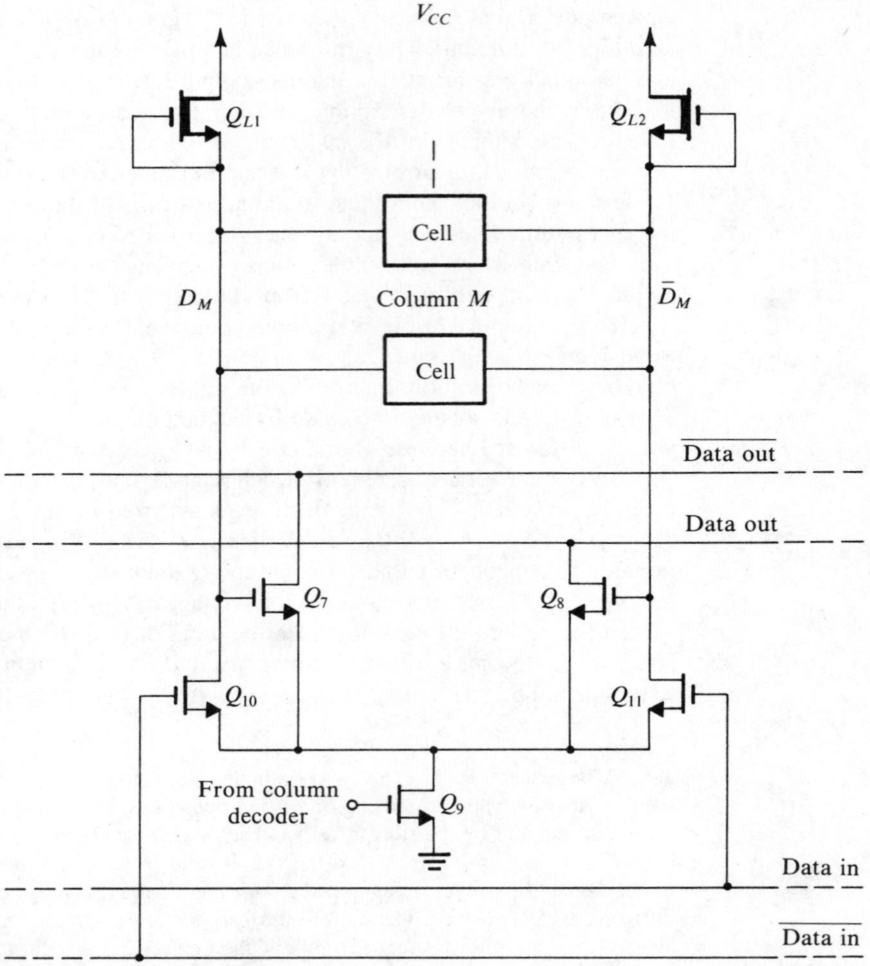

Fig. 2.6 Data-sensing and data-writing circuits for column M in a static RAM.

leakage effects that are inevitably present, the capacitor charge will leak off. Thus, essential to the proper operation of dynamic RAMs is the *refresh* operation. During refresh, the cell content is read and the data bit is rewritten, thus restoring the capacitor voltage to its proper value. The refresh operation must be performed every 2 to 4 ms. The need for periodically refreshing the dynamic memory chip implies the necessity of having a clock.

The periodic refresh operation necessary in a dynamic RAM requires additional circuitry. Nevertheless, because the memory cell is very simple, as we will see very shortly, dynamic RAMs achieve much greater packing density than is possible with their static counterparts. Roughly speaking, at any given time in the past few years the capacity of dynamic RAM chips has been about four times that of static RAMs.

The most common storage cell employed in dynamic RAMs is shown in Fig. 2.7. The cell consists of a single enhancement-mode *n*-channel MOSFET, known as the *access transistor*, and a storage capacitor C. The cell is appropriately known as the *one-transistor cell*.[2] The gate of the transistor is connected to the word (or row) line and its drain is connected to the digit (bit or column) line.

As in static RAMs, the row decoder selects a particular row by raising the voltage of its word line. This causes all the transistors in the selected row to become conductive, thereby connecting the storage capacitors of all the cells in the selected row to their respective digit lines. Thus the cell capacitor C is connected in parallel with the digit-line capacitance C_L as indicated in Fig. 2.8. Here it should be noted that typically C is about 0.05 pF and C_L is from 20 to 30 times larger. Now if the operation is a read and

[2]The name was originally used in order to distinguish this cell from earlier ones utilizing three transistors.

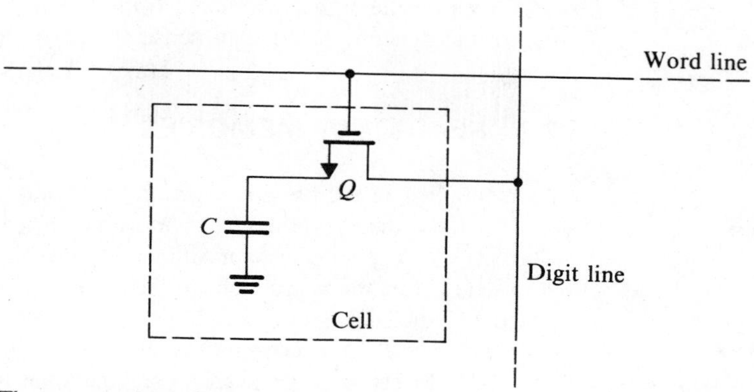

Fig. 2.7 The one-transistor dynamic RAM cell.

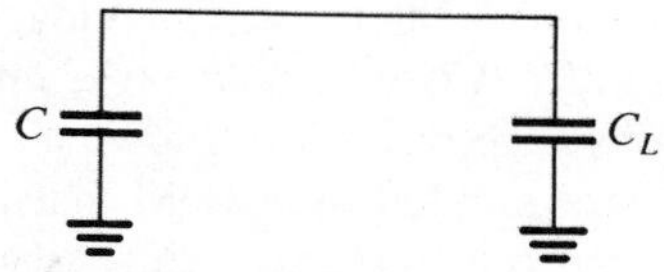

Fig. 2.8 When the voltage of the selected word line is raised, the transistor conducts, thus connecting the storage capacitor C to the digit-line capacitance C_L.

the cell is storing a logic 1, then the voltage on the cell capacitor C will cause a positive increment to appear across C_L. Since C_L is much greater than C, the voltage increment on C_L will be much smaller than the initial voltage on C. Obviously, if the cell is storing a logic 0, then no increment will appear on C_L.

The change of voltage on the digit line is detected and amplified by the column sense amplifier. The amplified signal is then impressed on the storage capacitor, thus restoring its signal to the proper level. In this way, all the cells in the selected row are refreshed. Simultaneously, the signal at the output of the sense amplifier of the selected column is fed to the data output line of the chip.

The write operation proceeds similarly to the read operation except that the data bit to be written, which is impressed on the data input line, is applied by the column decoder to the selected digit line. This data bit is thus stored on the capacitor of the selected cell. Simultaneously, all the other cells in the selected row are simply refreshed.

Although the read and write operations result in automatic refreshing of the selected row, provision must be made for the periodic refreshing of the entire memory every 2 to 4 ms, as specified for the particular chip. The refresh operation is carried out in a burst mode, one row at a time. During refresh, the chip will not be available for read or write operations. This, however, is not a serious matter since the interval required to refresh the entire chip is less than about 2% of the time between refresh cycles. In other words, the memory chip remains available for normal operation for more than 98% of the time.

Exercises

2.3 In a particular one-transistor-per-cell dynamic MOS memory utilizing a 64×64 array, the storage cell capacitance is 0.05pF, while the capacitance per cell on the digit line is 0.04 pF and the input capacitance of the sense amplifier and associated circuitry is 0.5 pF. If, after degeneration, the smallest signal allowed on the cell capacitance is 6 V, what is the corresponding signal available at the input of the sense amplifier when the access switch is closed?
Ans. 96.5 mV

2.4 A dynamic memory cell using a 0.05-pF capacitor and an MOS selection transistor employs 0- and 5-V levels for information storage. Sensing circuitry is adequate to permit the stored charge to decay to $1/e$ of its original value before refresh is required. The maximum allowed refresh interval for this design is 2 ms. What is the smallest equivalent resistance that can be allowed to shunt the storage capacitor? If the leakage phenomenon is best characterized as a current, what is the largest such current that can be tolerated?
Ans. 40×10^9 Ω; 79 pA

Because the signals available from dynamic RAM cells are very small, a critical part in the dynamic RAM is its sense amplifier (see Mostek, 1980).

2.2 READ-ONLY MEMORIES

As mentioned in the previous section, read-only memories (ROMs) are memories that contain fixed data patterns. They are used in a variety of digital system applications. Currently, a very popular application of ROMs is in microprocessor systems where they are used to store the instructions of the system operating program. ROMs are particularly suited for such an application because they are nonvolatile, that is, they retain their contents when the power supply is switched off.

A ROM can be viewed as a combinational logic circuit for which the input is the collection of address bits of the ROM and the output is the set of data bits retrieved from the addressed location. This viewpoint leads to the application of ROMs in code conversion—that is, in changing the code of the signal from one code (say, binary) to another. Code conversion is employed, for instance, in secure communication systems where the process is known as *scrambling*. It consists of feeding the code of the data to be transmitted to a ROM that provides corresponding bits in a supposedly secret code. The reverse process, which also uses a ROM, is applied at the receiving end.

In this section we will study various types of read-only memory. These include fixed ROM, which we refer to simply as ROM; programmable ROM (PROM); and erasable programmable ROM (EPROM).

A MOS ROM

Figure 2.9 shows a simplified 32-bit (or 8-word × 4-bit) MOS ROM. As indicated, the memory consists of an array of enhancement MOSFETs whose gates are connected to the word lines, whose sources are grounded, and whose drains are connected to the bit lines. Each bit line is connected to the power supply via a depletion-load device. A MOSFET exists in a particular cell if the cell is storing a 0; a cell storing a 1 has no MOSFET. This ROM can be thought of as 8 words of 4 bits each. The row decoder selects one of the 8 words by raising the voltage of the corresponding word line. The cell transistors connected to this word line will then conduct, thus pulling the voltage of the bit lines (to which transistors in the selected row are connected) down close to ground voltage (logic 0 level). The bit lines that are connected to cells (of the selected word) without transistors (that is, those cells that are storing 1s) will remain at the power-supply voltage (logic 1) because of the action of the pull-up depletion-load devices. In this way the bits of the addressed word can be read.

Mask Programmable ROMs

The data stored in the ROMs discussed above is determined at the time of fabrication, according to the user's specifications. However, in order to avoid having to custom design each ROM from scratch (which would be an extremely costly process), ROMs are manufactured using a process known as *mask programming*. As explained in Appendix A, integrated circuits are fabricated on a wafer of silicon using a sequence of processing steps that include photomasking, etching, and diffusion. In this way, a pattern of junctions and interconnections is created on the surface of the wafer. One of the final steps in the fabrication process consists of coating the surface of the wafer with a layer of aluminum and then selectively (using a mask) etching away portions of the aluminum, leaving aluminum only where interconnections are desired. This last step can be used to program (that is, store a desired pattern in) a ROM. For instance, if the ROM is made of enhancement MOS transistors as in Fig. 2.9, then MOSFETs are included at all bit locations, but only the gates of those transistors where 0s are to be stored are connected to the word lines; the gates of transistors where 1s are to be stored are not connected. This pattern is determined by the mask, which is produced according to the user's specifications.

The economic advantages of the mask programming process should be obvious: All ROMs are fabricated similarly; customization occurs only during one of the final steps in fabrication.

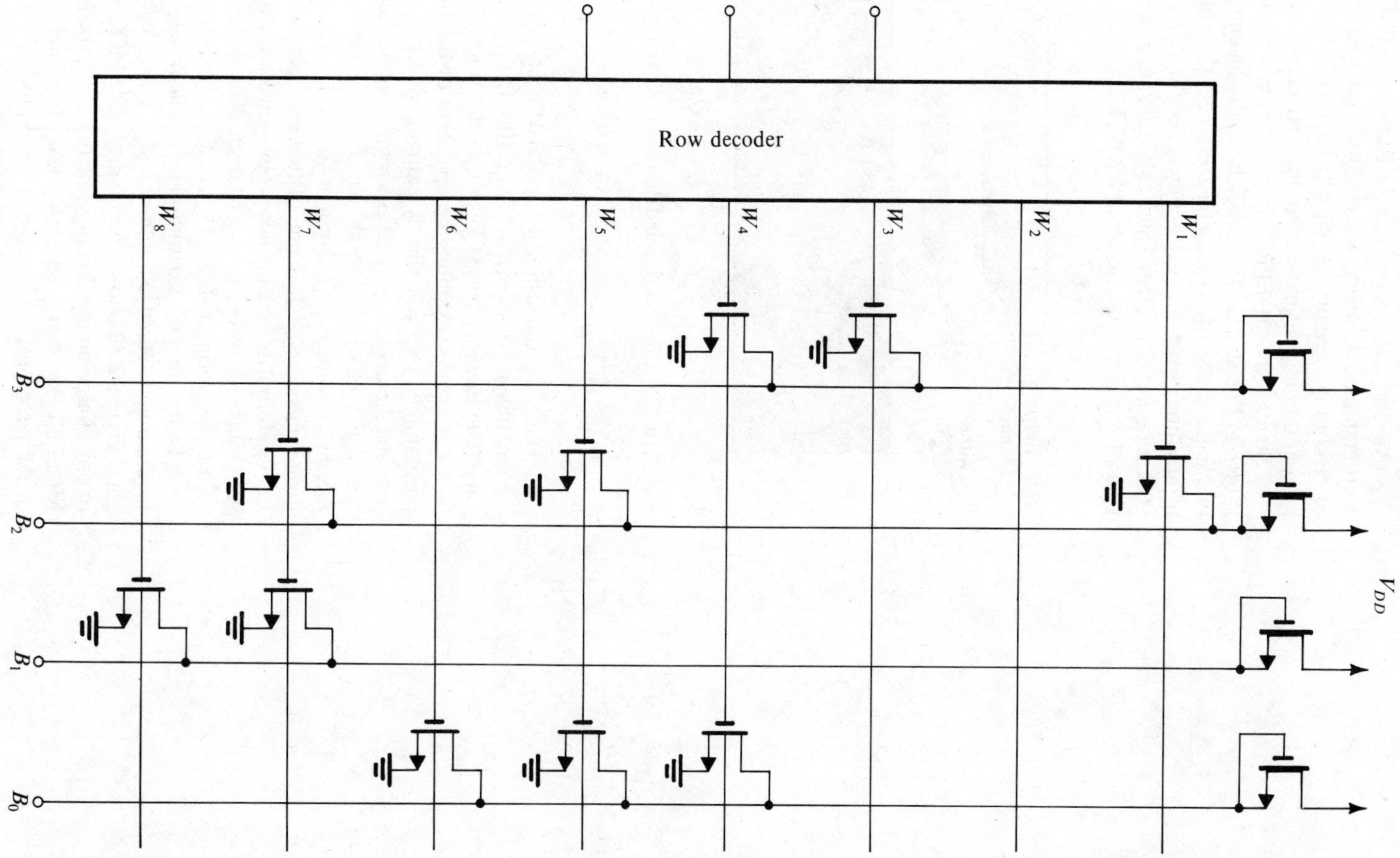

Fig. 2.9 A simple MOS ROM organized as 8 words × 4 bits.

Programmable ROMs (PROMs and EPROMs)

PROMs are ROMs that can be programmed by the user, but only once. A typical arrangement employed in BJT PROMs involves using polysilicon fuses to connect the emitter of each BJT to the corresponding digit line. Depending on the desired content of a ROM cell, the fuse can be either left intact or blown up using a large current. The programming process is obviously irreversible.

An erasable programmable ROM or EPROM is a ROM that can be erased and reprogrammed as many times as the user wishes. It is therefore the most versatile type of read-only memory. It should be noted, however, that the process of erasure and reprogramming is time-consuming and is intended to be performed only infrequently.

State-of-the-art EPROMs use variants of the memory cell whose cross section is shown in Fig. 2.10a. The cell is basically an enhancement-type n-channel MOSFET with two gates made of polysilicon material.[3] One of the gates is not electrically connected to any other part of the circuit; rather, it is left floating and is appropriately called a *floating gate*. The other gate, called a *select gate*, functions in the same manner as the gate of a regular enhancement MOSFET.

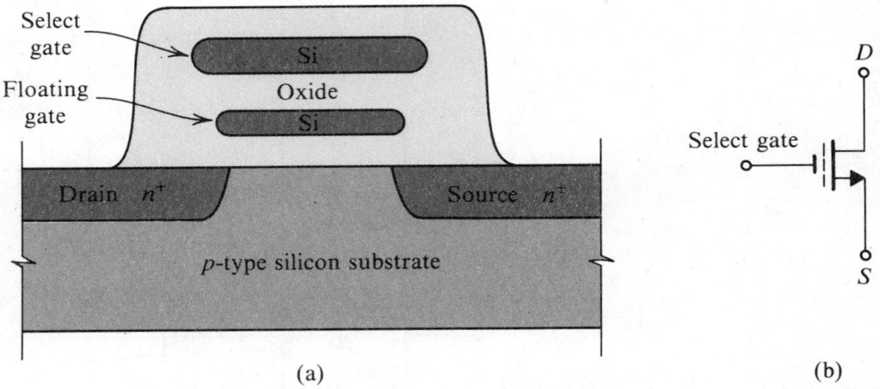

Fig. 2.10 (a) Cross section and (b) circuit symbol of the floating-gate transistor used as an EPROM cell.

The MOS transistor of Fig. 2.10a is known as a *floating-gate transistor* and is given the circuit symbol shown in Fig. 2.10b. In this symbol the broken line denotes the floating gate. The memory cell is known as the *stacked-gate cell*.

Let us now examine the operation of the floating-gate transistor. Before the cell is programmed (we will shortly explain what this means), no charge exists on the floating gate and the device operates as a regular n-channel enhancement MOSFET. It thus exhibits the i_D-v_{GS} characteristic shown as curve (a) in Fig. 2.11. Note that in this case the threshold voltage (V_t) is rather low. This state of the transistor is known as the *not-programmed state*. It is one of two states in which the floating-gate transistor can exist. Let us arbitrarily take the not-programmed state to represent a stored 1. That is, a floating-gate transistor whose i_D-v_{GS} characteristic is that shown as curve (a) in Fig. 2.11 will be said to be storing a 1.

To program the floating-gate transistor, a large voltage (16–20 V) is applied between its drain and source. Simultaneously, a large voltage (about 25 V) is applied to its select gate. Figure 2.12 shows the floating-gate MOSFET during programming. In the absence of any charge on the floating gate the device behaves as a regular n-channel enhancement MOSFET. An n-type inversion layer (channel) is created at the wafer surface as a result of the large positive voltage at the drain, the channel has a tapered shape.

The drain-to-source voltage accelerates electrons through the channel. As these electrons reach the drain end of the channel they acquire sufficiently large kinetic energy and are referred to as *hot electrons*. The large positive voltage on the select gate (greater than the drain voltage) establishes an electric field in the insulating oxide. This electric

[3]See Appendix A for a description of silicon-gate technology.

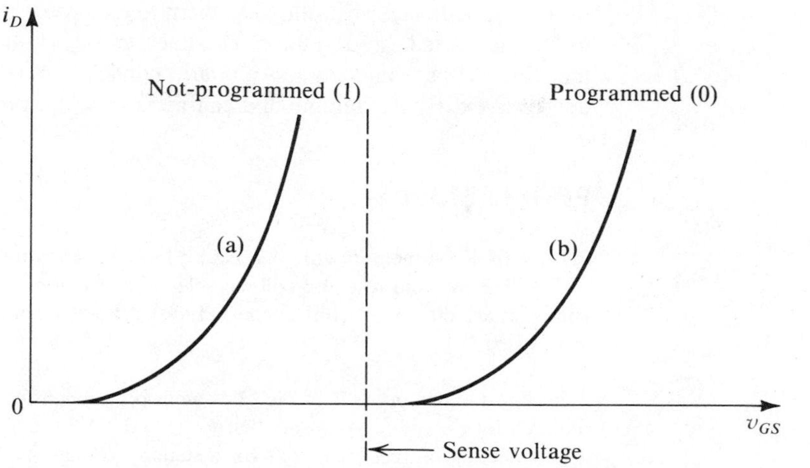

Fig. 2.11 Illustrating the shift in the i_D-v_{GS} characteristic of a floating-gate transistor as a result of programming.

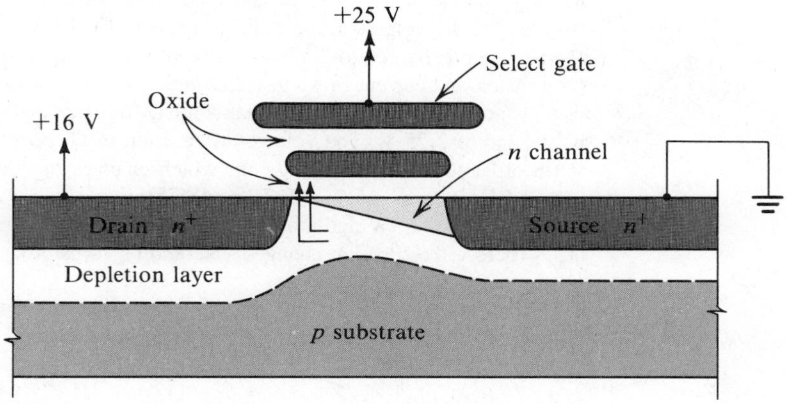

Fig. 2.12 The floating-gate transistor during programming.

field attracts the hot electrons and accelerates them toward the floating gate. In this way the floating gate is charged, and the charge that accumulates on it becomes trapped.

Fortunately, the process of charging the floating gate is self-limiting. The negative charge that accumulates on the floating gate reduces the strength of the electric field in the oxide to the point that it eventually becomes incapable of accelerating any more of the hot electrons.

Let us now inquire about the effect of the floating gate's negative charge on the operation of the transistor. The negative charge trapped on the floating gate will cause electrons to be repelled from the surface of the substrate. This implies that to form a channel, the positive voltage that has to be applied to the select gate will have to be greater than that required when the floating gate is not charged. In other words, the threshold voltage V_t of the programmed transistor will be higher than that of the not-programmed device. In fact, programming causes the i_D-v_{GS} characteristic to shift to that labeled (b) in Fig. 2.11. In this state, known as the *programmed state*, the cell is said to be storing a 0.

Once programmed, the floating-gate device retains its shifted i-v characteristic [curve (*b*)] even when the power supply is turned off. It fact, extrapolated experimental results indicate that the device can remain in the programmed state for as long as 100 years!

Reading the content of the stacked-gate cell is easy: A voltage V_{GS} somewhere between the low and high threshold values (see Fig. 2.11) is applied to the select gate. While a programmed device (one that is storing a 0) will not conduct, a not-programmed device (one that is storing a 1) will conduct heavily.

To return the floating-gate MOSFET to its not-programmed state, the charge stored on the floating gate has to be returned to the substrate. This *erasure* process can be accomplished by illuminating the cell with ultraviolet light of the correct wavelength (2,537 Å) for a specified duration. The ultraviolet light imparts sufficient photon energy to the trapped electrons, allowing them to overcome the inherent energy barrier and thus to be transported through the oxide, back to the substrate. To allow this erasure process, the EPROM package contains a quartz window. Finally, it should be mentioned that the device is extremely durable and can be erased and programmed many times.

PROBLEMS

2.1 A 64 K-bit memory chip is organized in a square array and utilizes the simple NOR decoder of Fig. 2.3 for both row and column selection. **(a)** How many inputs would each decoder need? **(b)** What are the address bits connected to the inputs of the NOR gate whose output is connected to row 251?

2.2 For the memory cell of Fig. 2.5c with polysilicon resistors of 1 MΩ, what is the W/L ratio required for Q_1 and Q_2 to ensure that $v_{DSon} \leq 0.1$ V? 0.2? What is the standby current and power in a collection of 16K such cells for a standby voltage of 2 V? Assume $V_t = 1$ V and $\mu_n C_{ox} = 20\ \mu A/V^2$.

****2.3** Consider the static RAM cell of Fig. 2.5a. Let $V_{CC} = +5$ V, $K_1 = K_2$, $K_3 = K_4$, $K_5 = K_6$, $V_{tE} = 1$ V, $V_{tD} = -3$ V and ignore the body effect. **(a)** With Q_5 and Q_6 off and the cell storing a 1, the voltage at the drain of Q_2 is to be 0.1 V. Find K_4 in terms of K_2. **(b)** The D and $\overline{D}$ lines are precharged to 3 V and the word line is raised to +5 V to read the stored 1. Transistor Q_5 turns on and current flows to the D line, raising its voltage by 0.25 V. The voltage at the drain of Q_1 is approximately 3.25 V. Meanwhile Q_6 turns on and current flows from the $\overline{D}$ line, lowering its voltage to 2.75 V. The voltage at the drain of Q_2 rises. We wish to limit this voltage to 0.75 V (in order to avoid turning Q_1 on, which changes the state of the flip-flop). Find the required value of K_6 in terms of K_2. **(c)** The cell is storing a 0 and we wish to write a 1 into it. The word line is raised to +5 V and the $\overline{D}$ line is lowered to 0 V. Find the voltage that appears at the drain of Q_2 (before the flip-flop changes state and Q_2 turns on).

2.4 For a dynamic RAM cell utilizing a capacitance of 0.01 pF, refresh is required within 2 ms. If a signal loss on the capacitor of 1 V can be tolerated, what is the largest acceptable leakage current present at the cell?

****2.5** Consider the one-transistor dynamic RAM cell in Fig. 2.7. For $V_{DD} = 5$ V, the digit-line voltages are either 0 or +5 V. To maximize the logic 1 level on C, arrangement is made to raise the word line from 0 to 7 V. $V_{tE} = 1$ V. For $C = 0.05$ pF, what value of K is required to ensure that C is charged to 4.5 V in 30 ns? [*Hint*: $\int dx/(ax^2 - x) = \ln(1 - 1/ax)$. You will also need the change of variables: $x = 5 - y$.]

TRANSPARENCY MASTERS

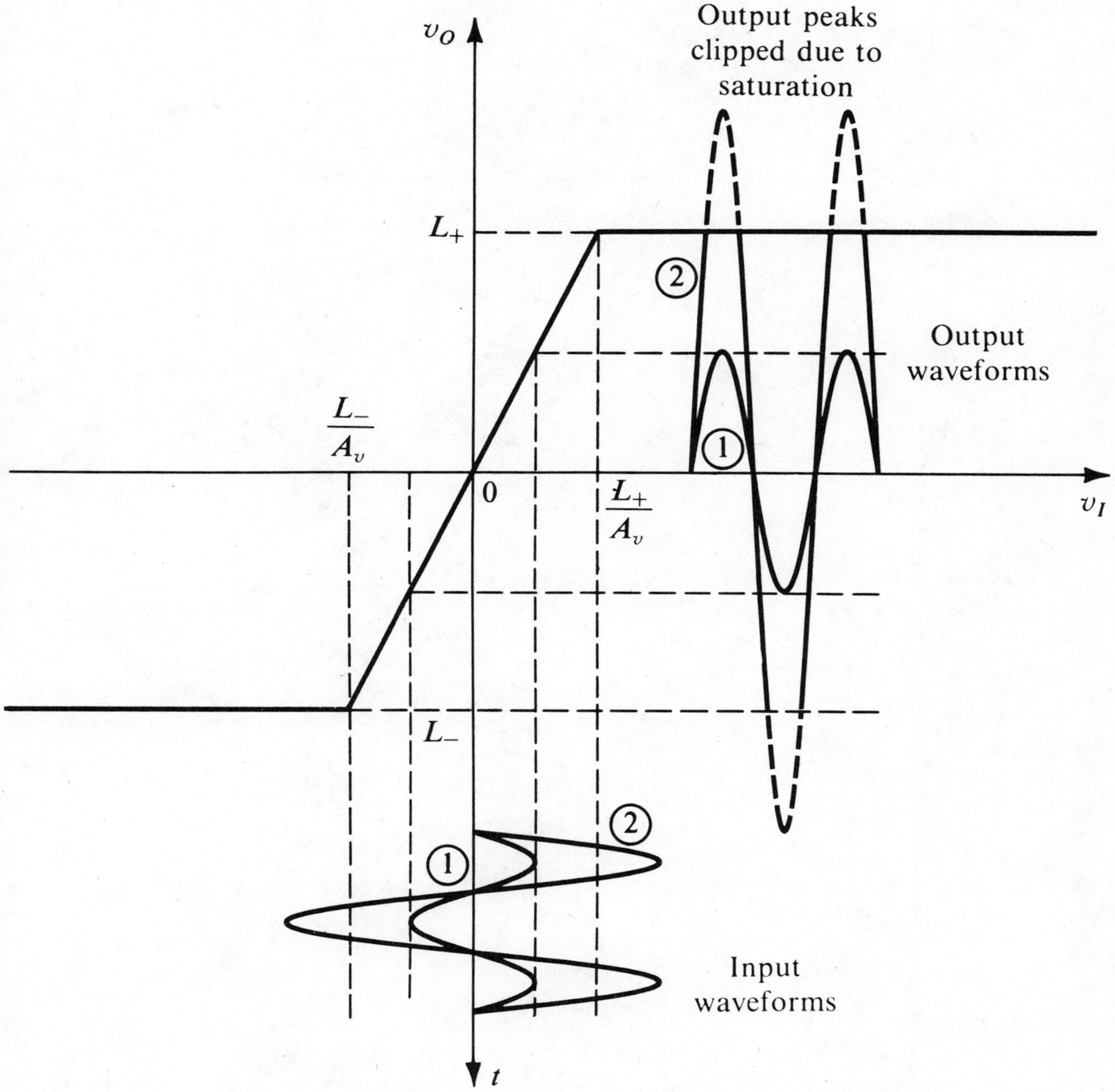

v_O
Output peaks clipped due to saturation
L_+
②
Output waveforms
$\frac{L_-}{A_v}$
①
0
$\frac{L_+}{A_v}$
v_I
L_-
②
①
Input waveforms
t

2.7

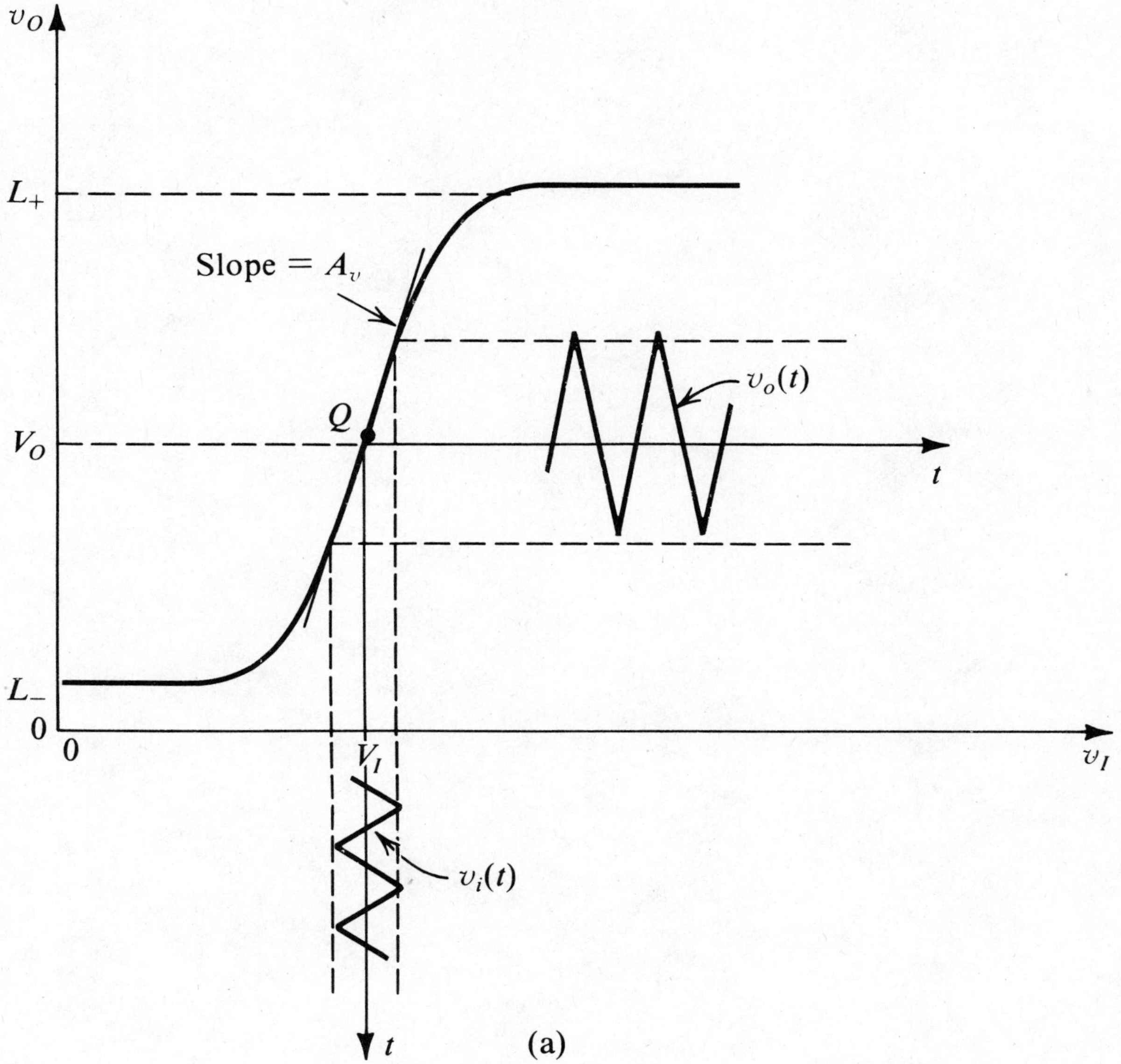

(a)

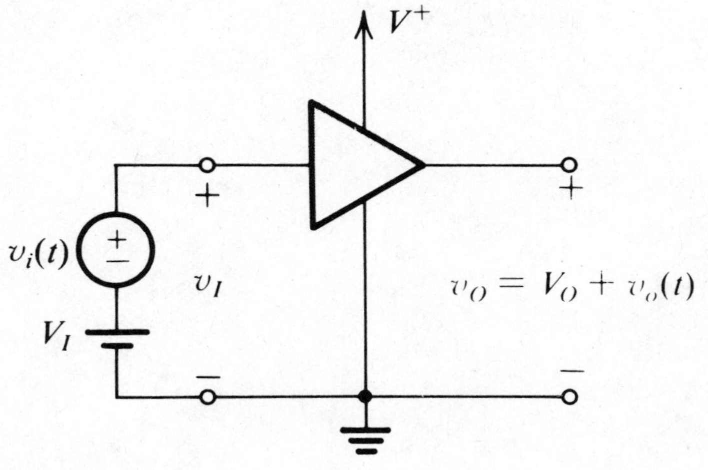

(b)

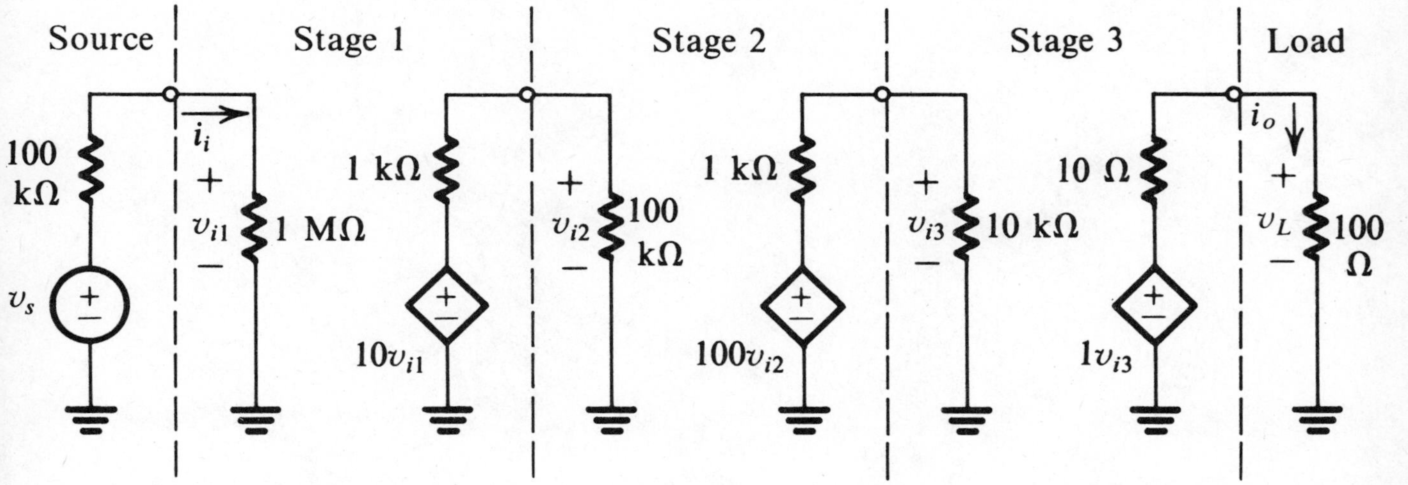

2.11

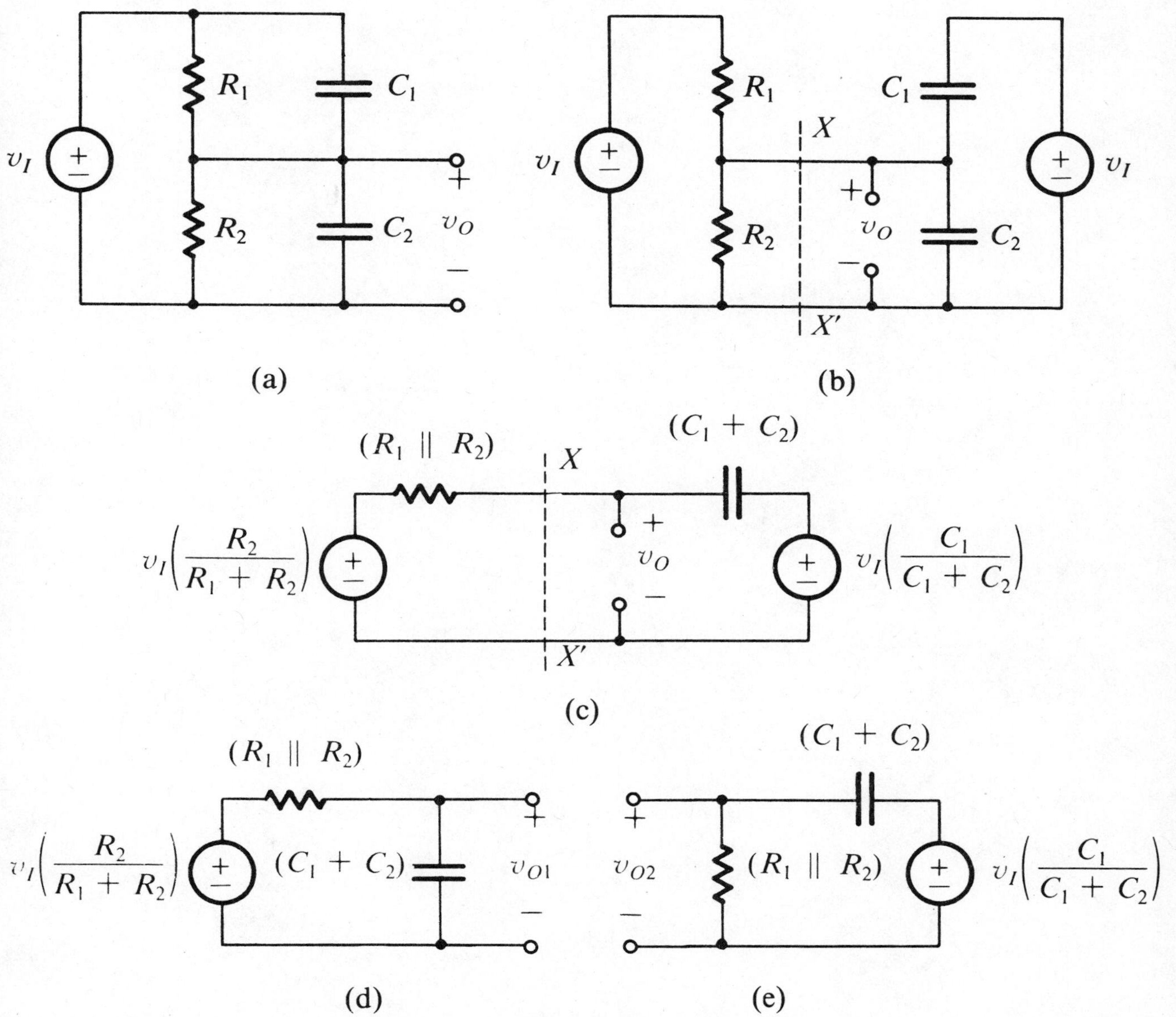

$$v_O = v_{O1} + v_{O2}$$

2.32

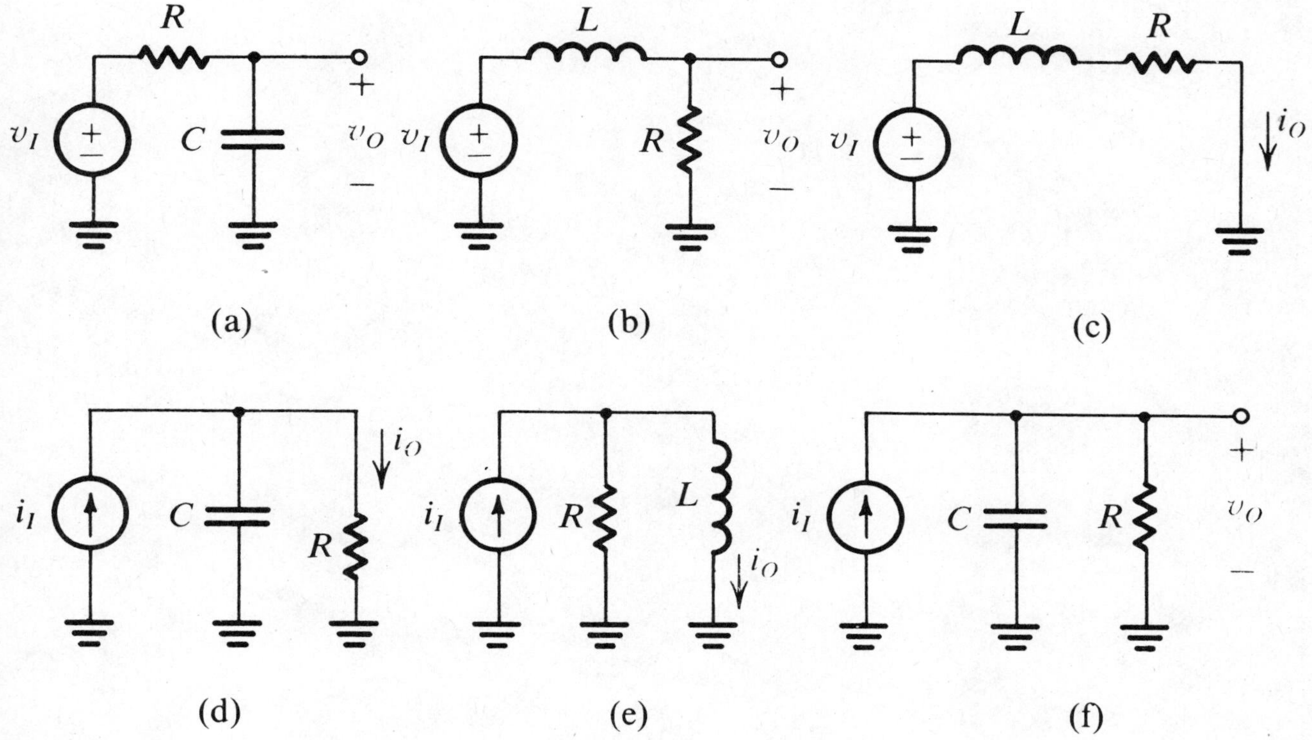

2.33

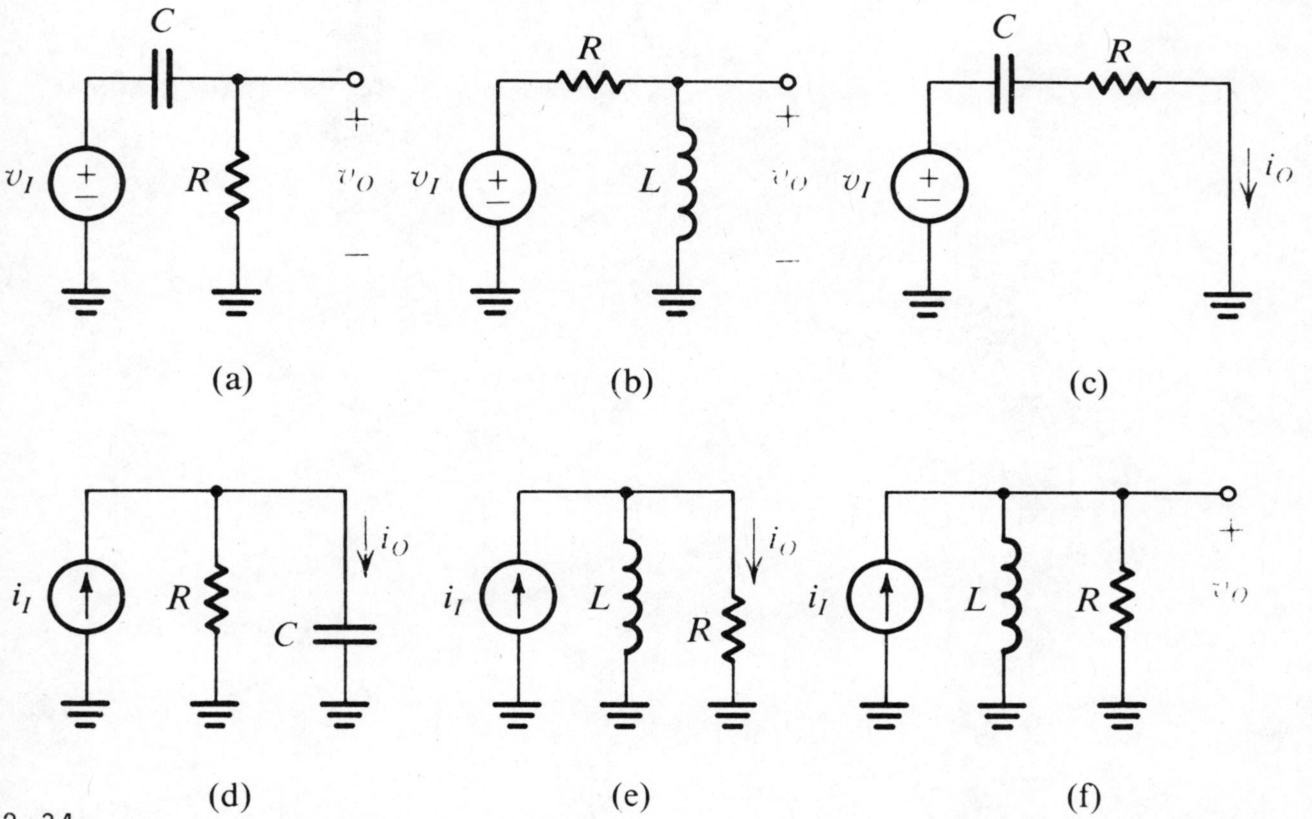

2.34

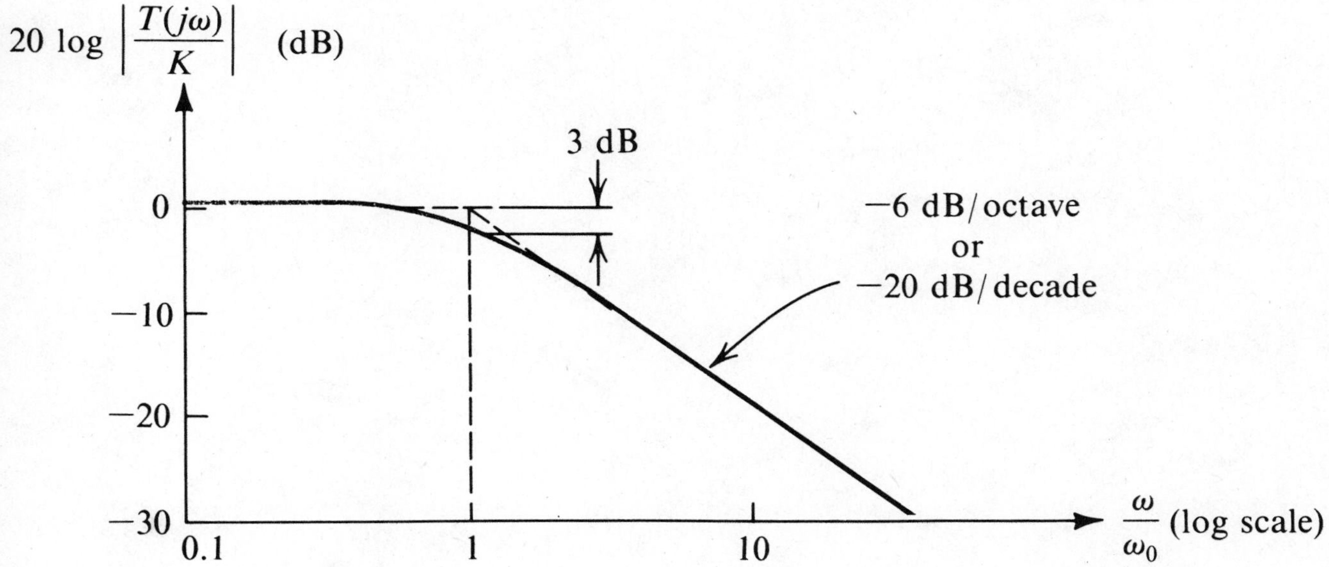

20 log |T(jω)/K| (dB)
3 dB
0
−6 dB/octave
or
−20 dB/decade
−10
−20
−30
0.1
1
10
ω/ω0 (log scale)

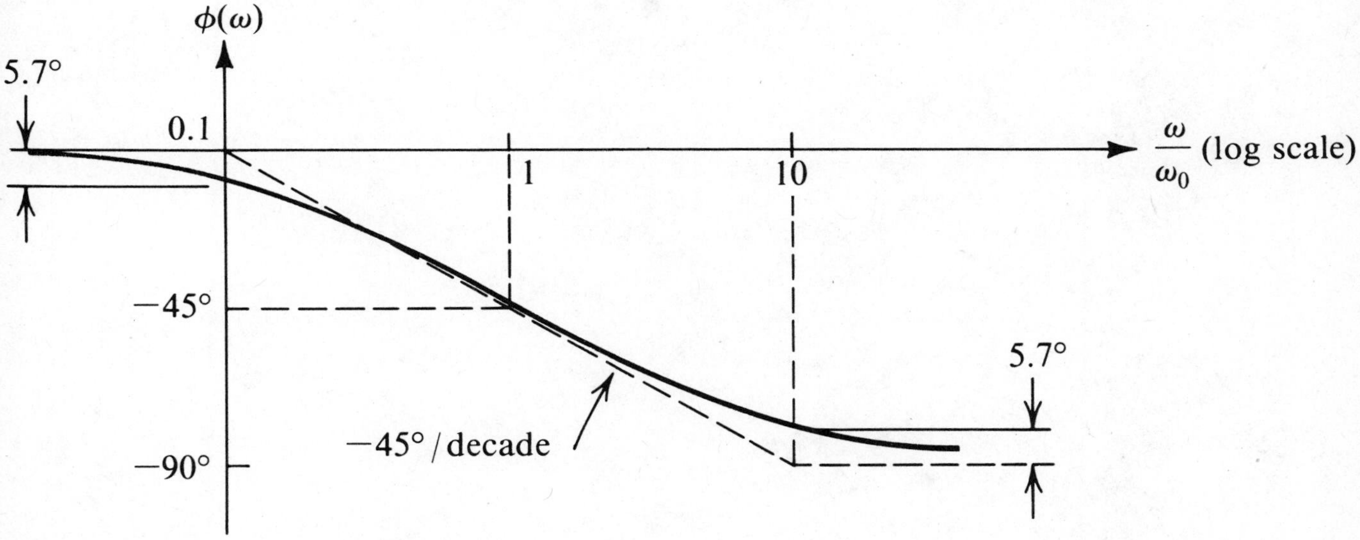

φ(ω)
5.7°
0.1
1
10
ω/ω0 (log scale)
−45°
5.7°
−45°/decade
−90°

2.35

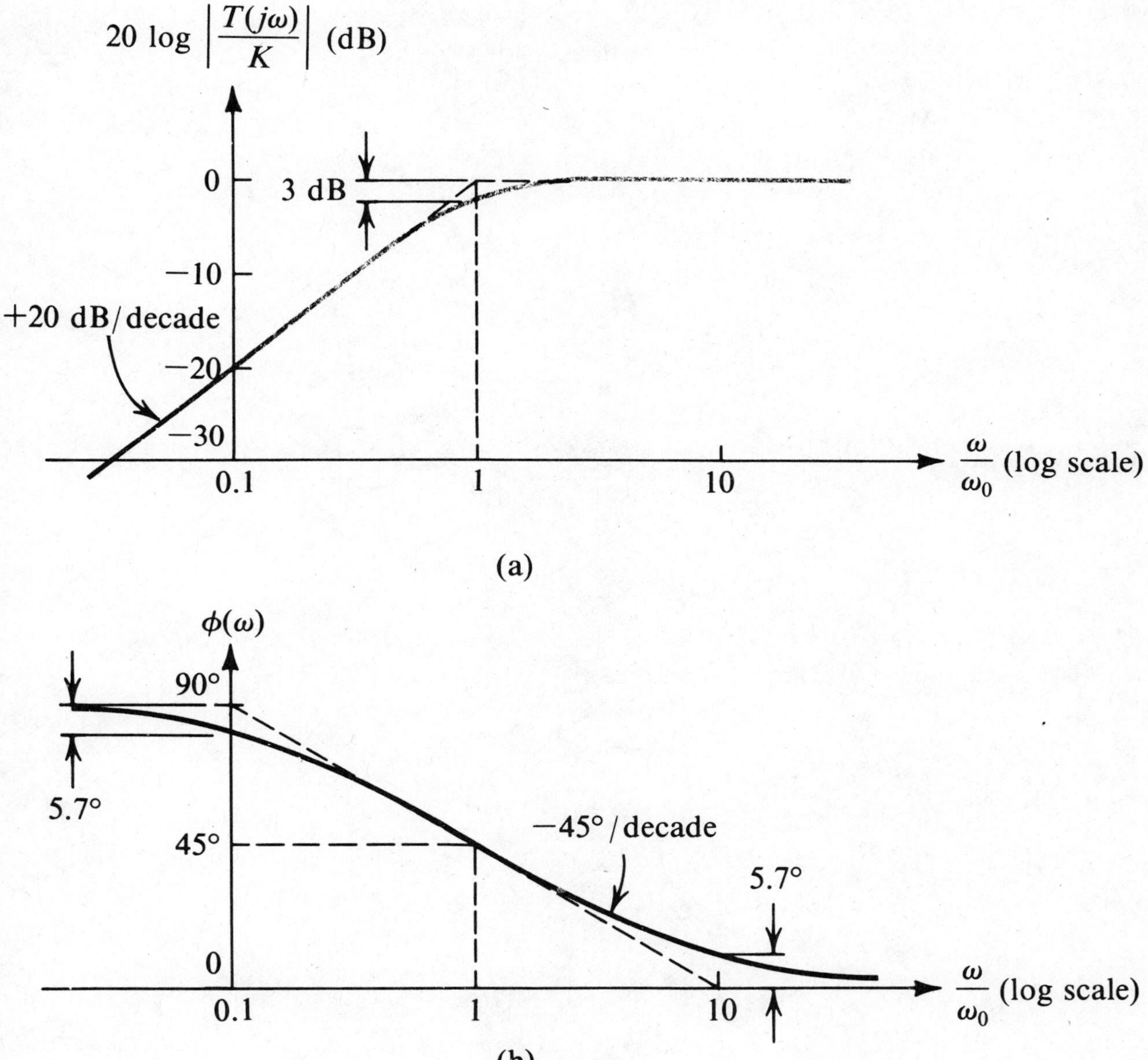
20 log |T(jω)/K| (dB)
0
3 dB
−10
+20 dB/decade
−20
−30
0.1
1
10
ω/ω0 (log scale)
(a)
φ(ω)
90°
5.7°
45°
−45°/decade
5.7°
0
0.1
1
10
ω/ω0 (log scale)
(b)

2.37

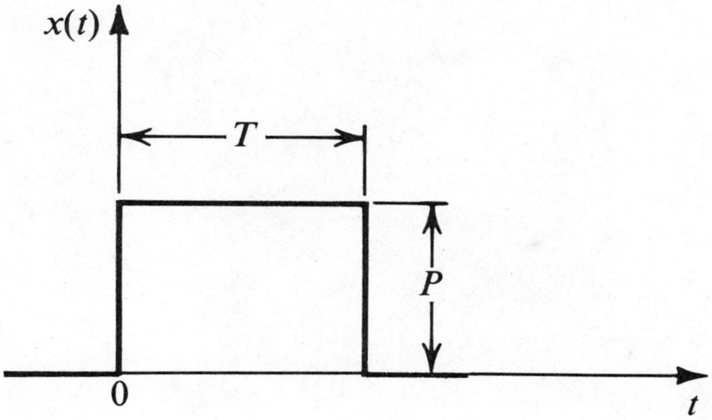

x(t)
T
P
0
t

2.41

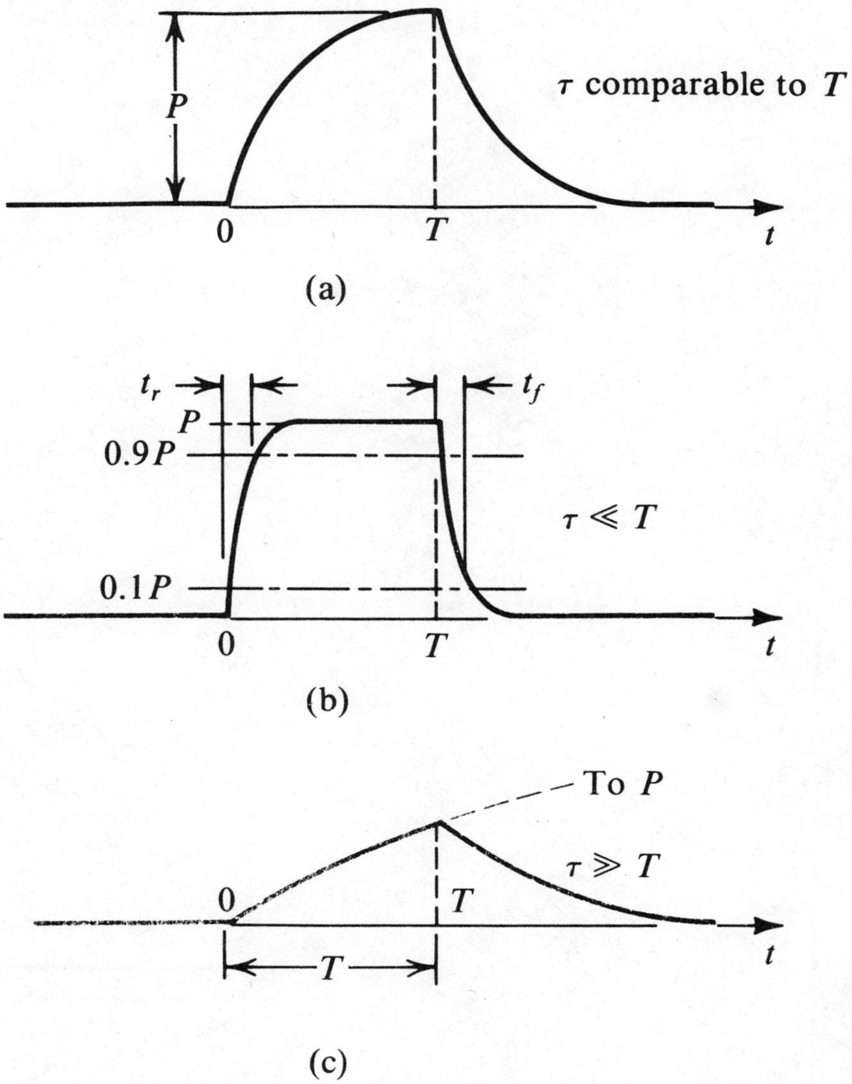

P
τ comparable to T
0
T
t
(a)
t_r
t_f
P
0.9P
0.1P
τ ≪ T
0
T
t
(b)
To P
τ ≫ T
0
T
t
T
(c)

2.42

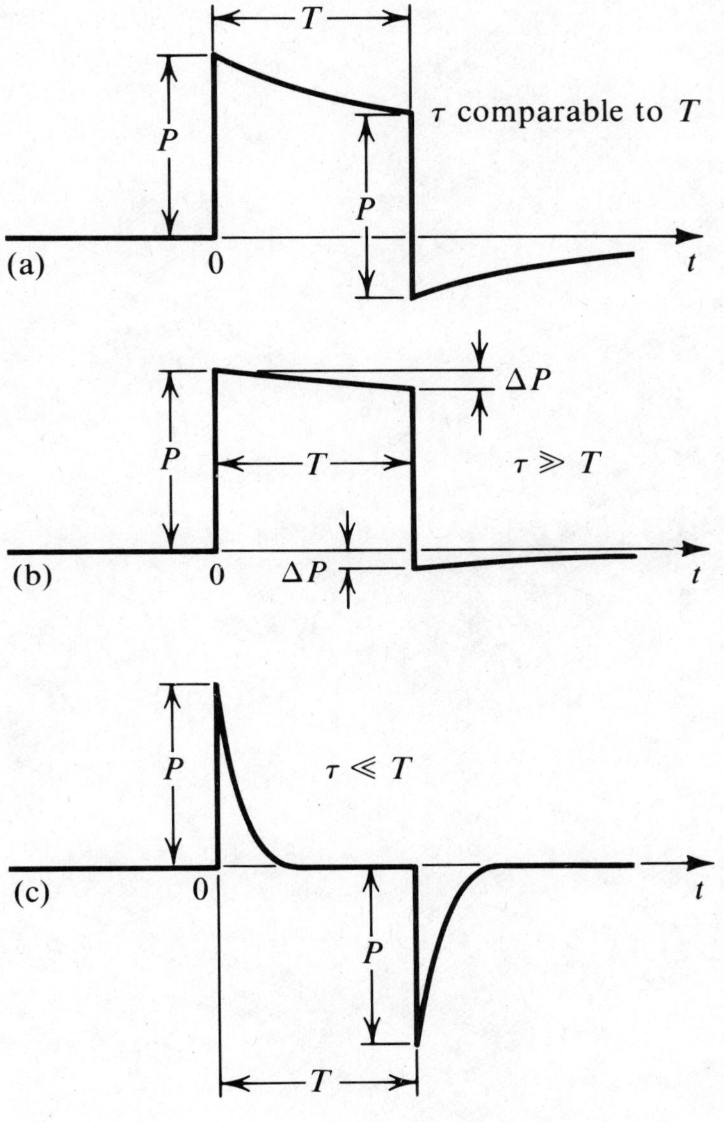

2.43

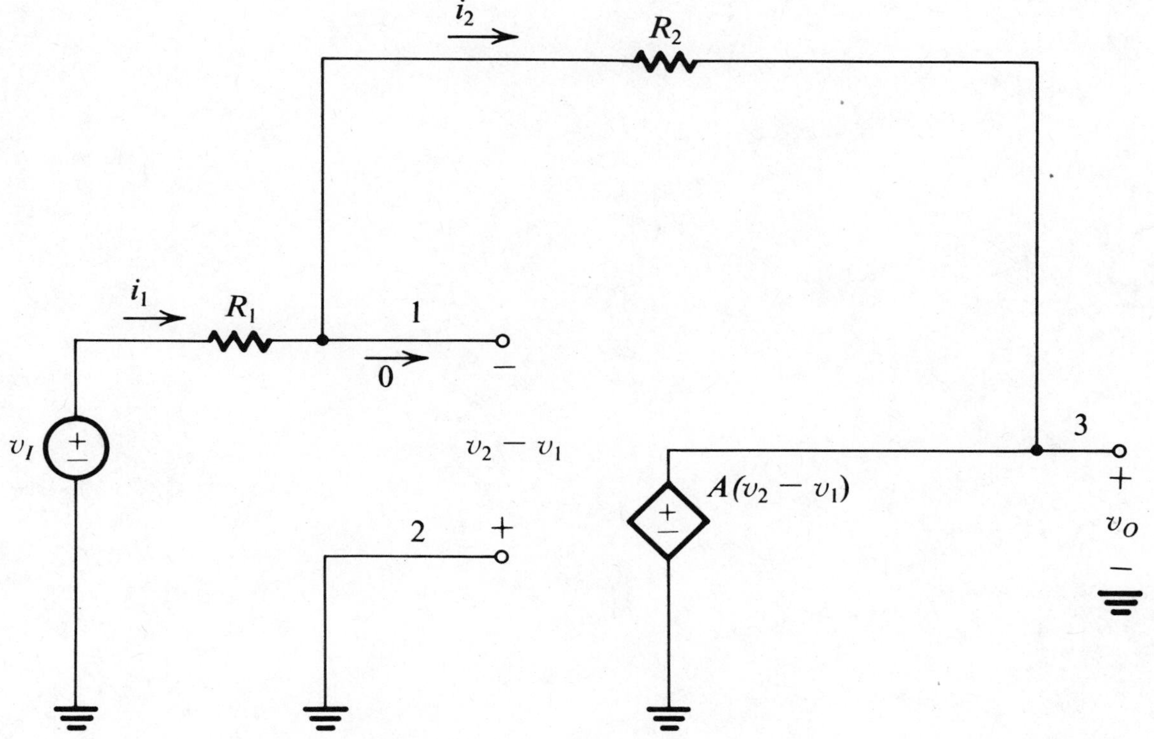

i_2
R_2
i_1
R_1
1
0
−
v_I
$v_2 - v_1$
3
$A(v_2 - v_1)$
+
v_O
−
2
+

(a)

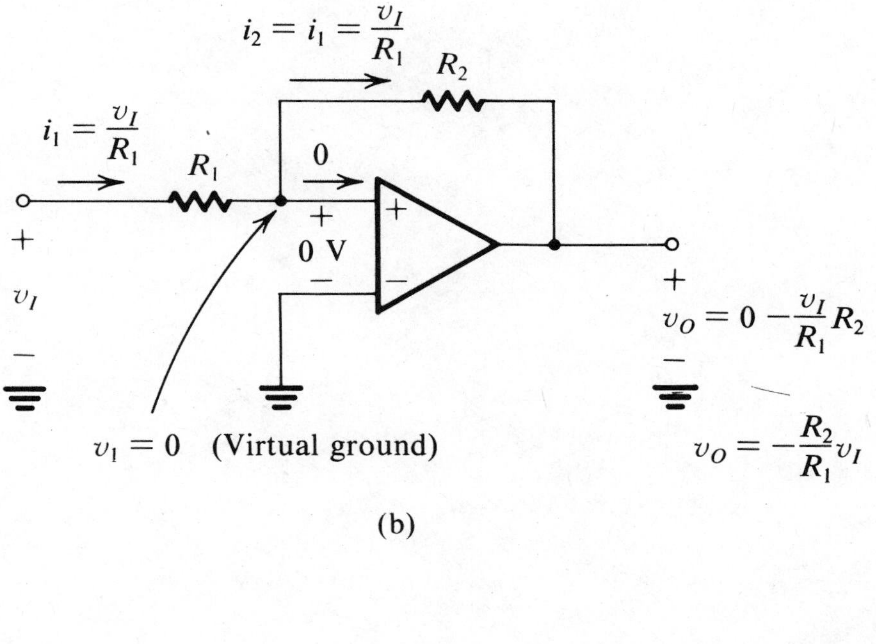

$i_2 = i_1 = \frac{v_I}{R_1}$
R_2
$i_1 = \frac{v_I}{R_1}$
R_1
0
+
0 V
−
+
−
+
v_I
−
+
$v_O = 0 - \frac{v_I}{R_1} R_2$
−
$v_O = -\frac{R_2}{R_1} v_I$
$v_1 = 0$ (Virtual ground)

(b)

3.5

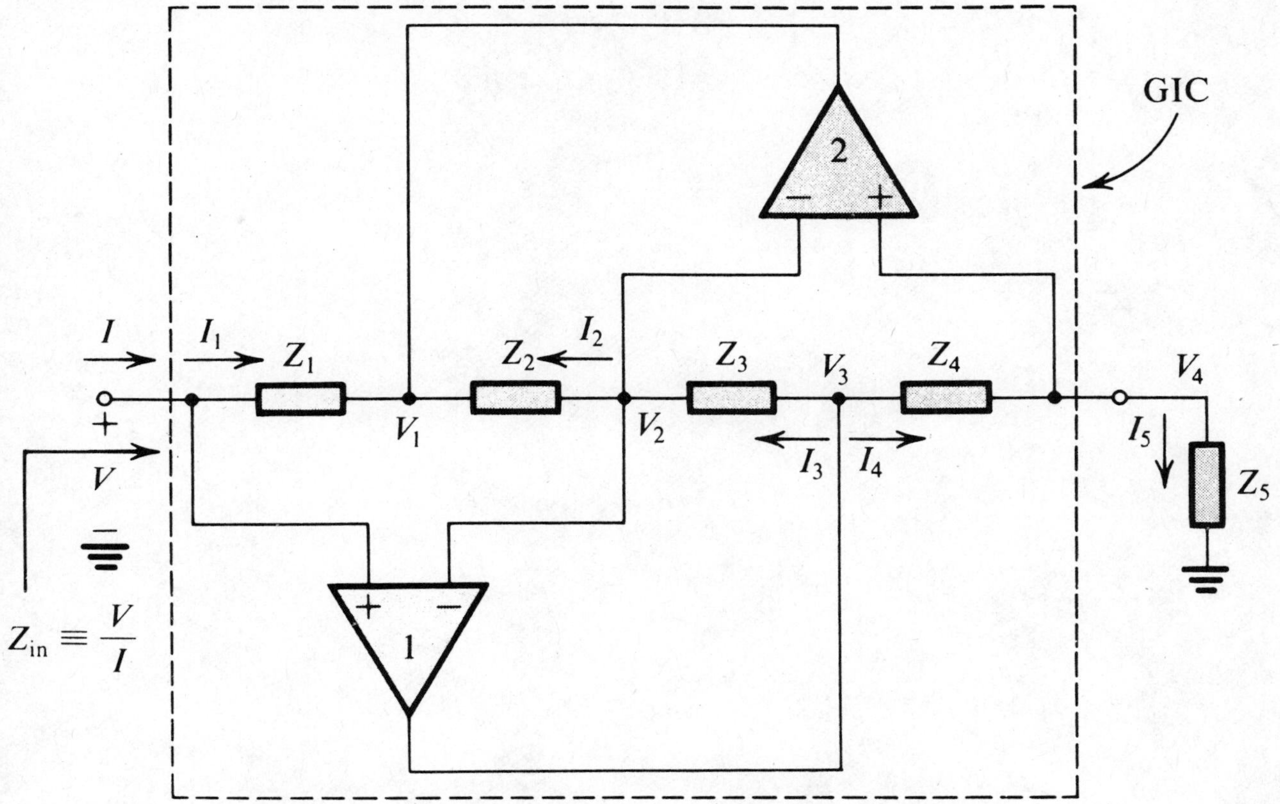

GIC
2
1
I
I_1
Z_1
Z_2
I_2
Z_3
V_3
Z_4
V_4
V_1
V_2
I_3
I_4
I_5
Z_5
V
$Z_{in} \equiv \frac{V}{I}$

3.24

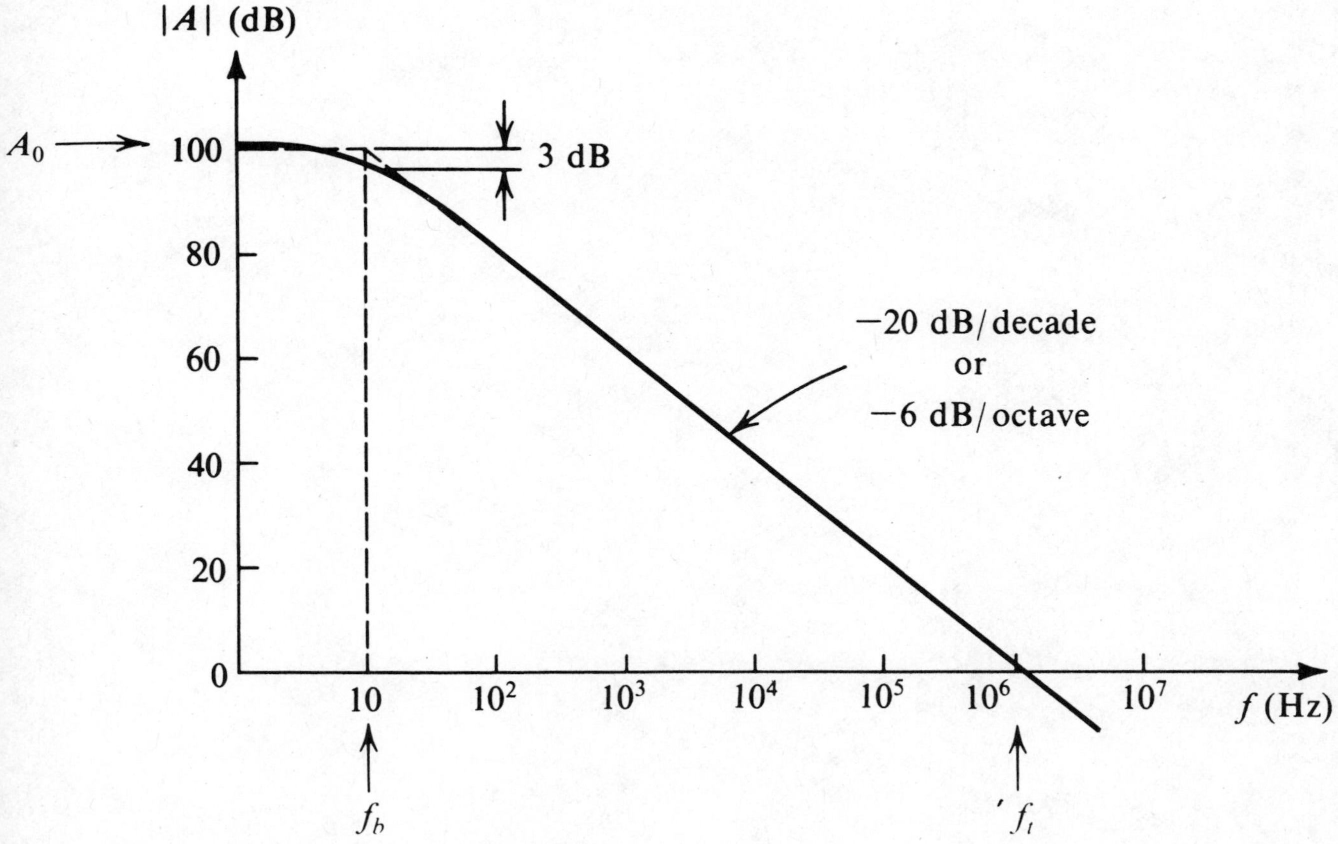

|A| (dB)
A_0
100
80
60
40
20
0
3 dB
−20 dB/decade
or
−6 dB/octave
10
10^2
10^3
10^4
10^5
10^6
10^7
f (Hz)
f_b
f_t

3.25

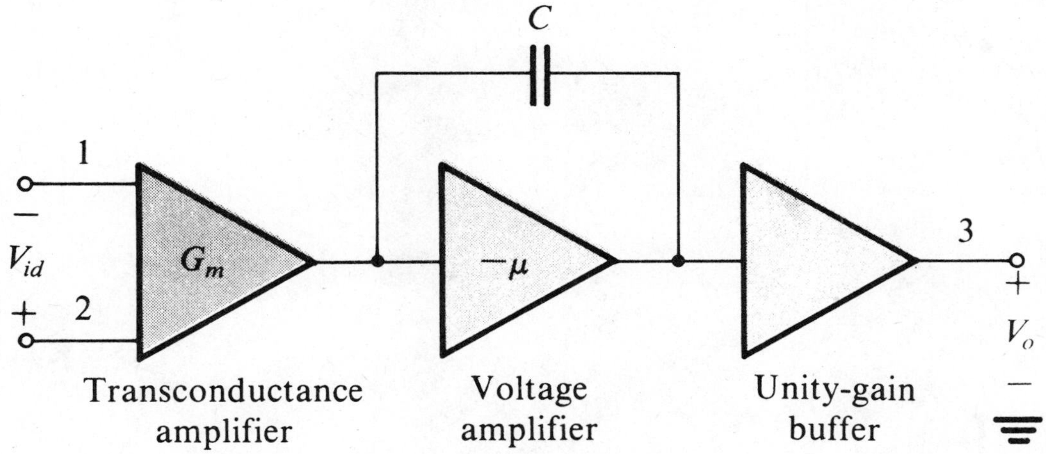
C
1
2
3
V_{id}
G_m
$-\mu$
+
−
V_o
Transconductance amplifier
Voltage amplifier
Unity-gain buffer

3.29

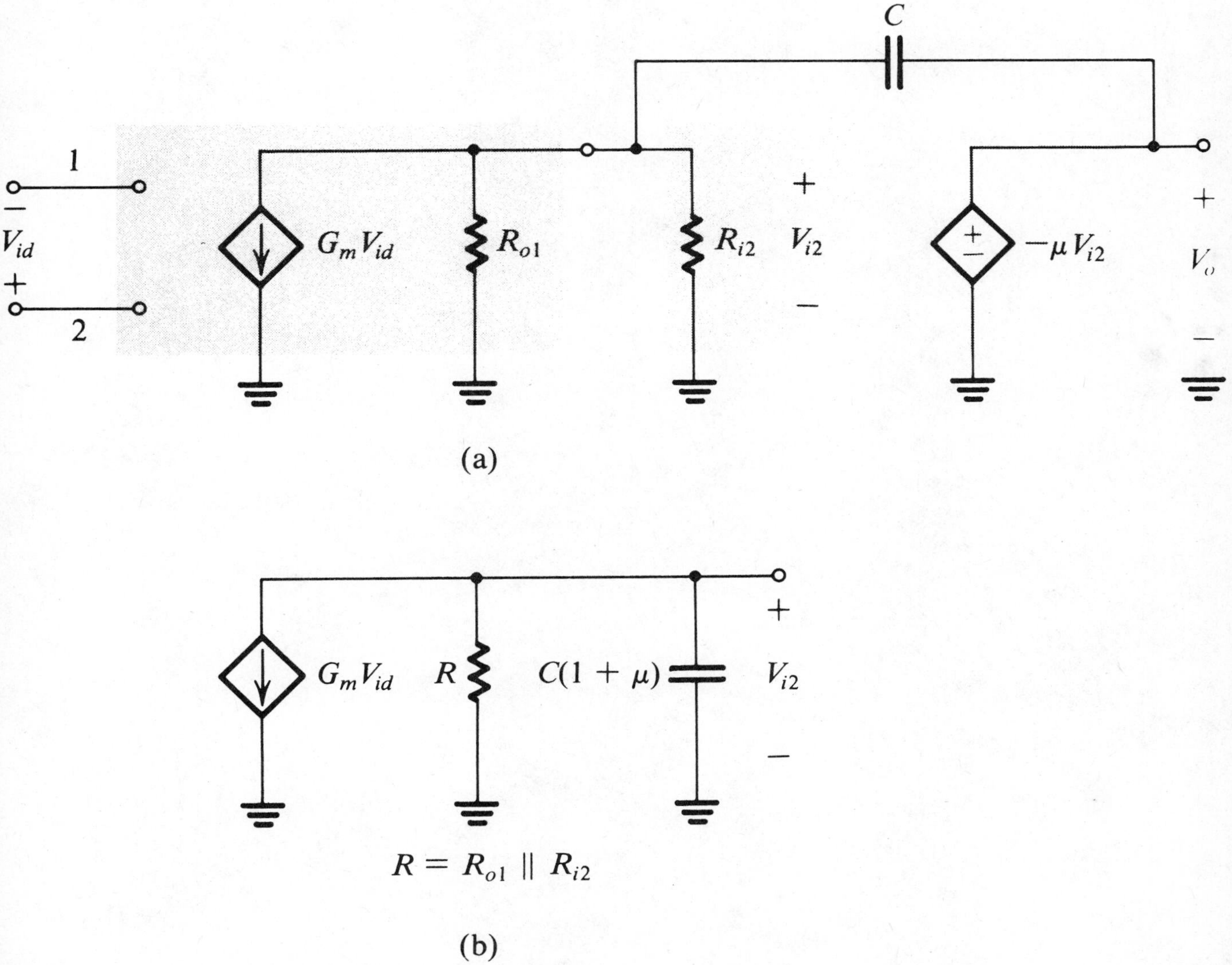
C
1
2
V_{id}
$G_m V_{id}$
R_{o1}
R_{i2}
V_{i2}
$-\mu V_{i2}$
V_o
(a)
$G_m V_{id}$
R
$C(1 + \mu)$
V_{i2}
$R = R_{o1} \parallel R_{i2}$
(b)

3.30

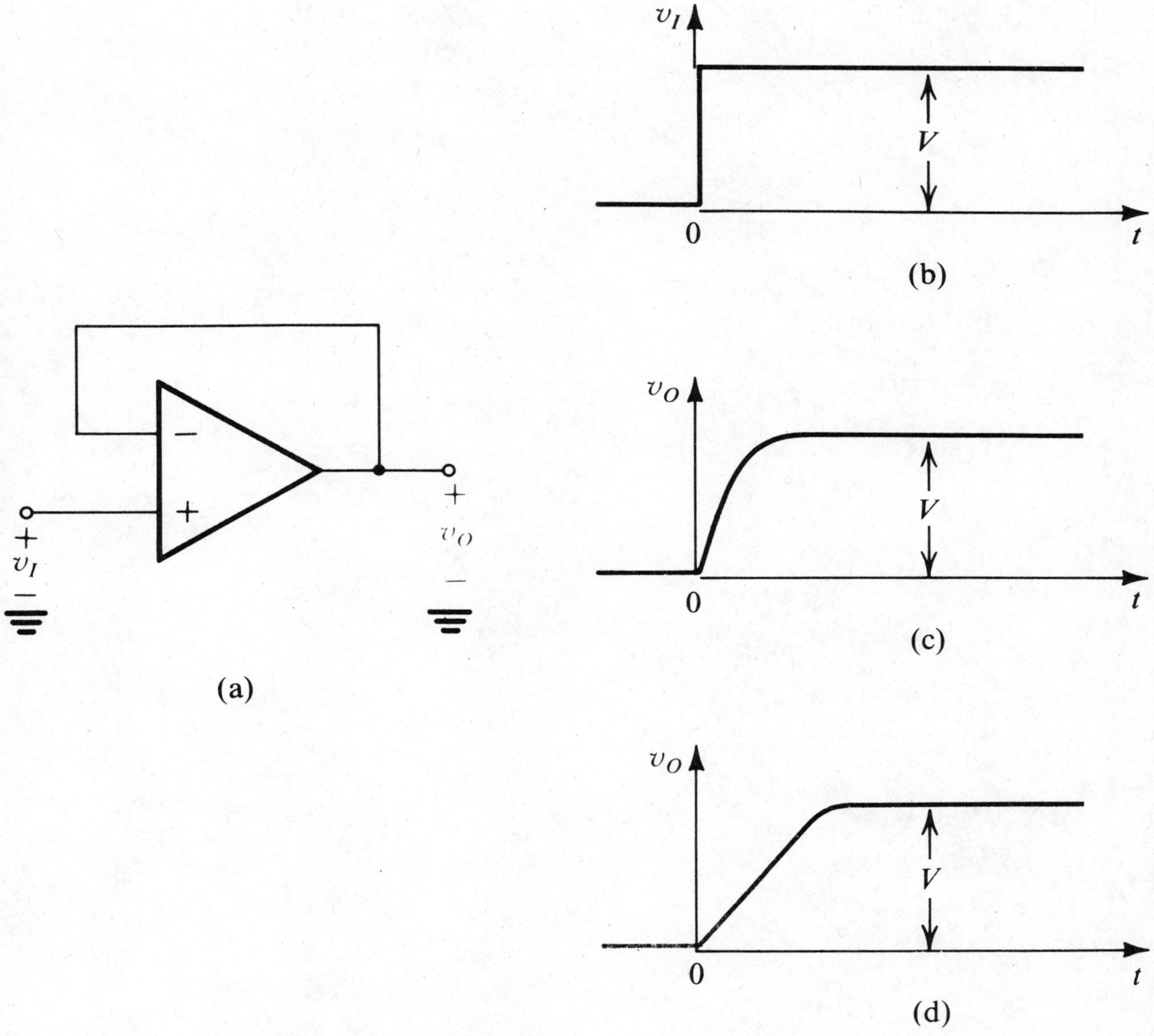

3.32

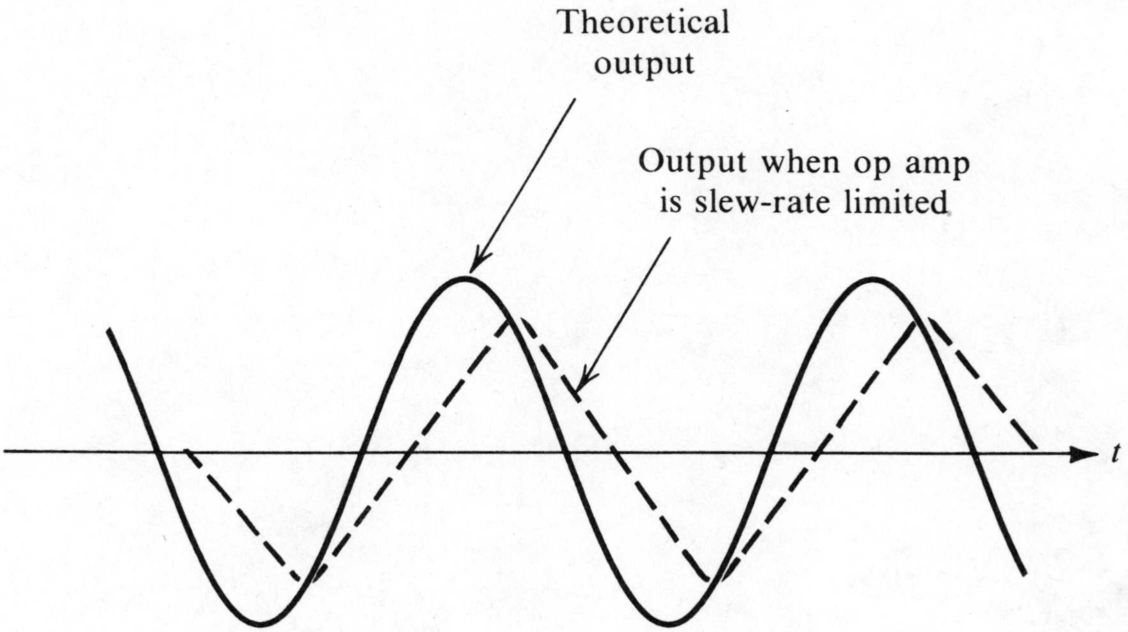
Theoretical
output
Output when op amp
is slew-rate limited
t

3.34

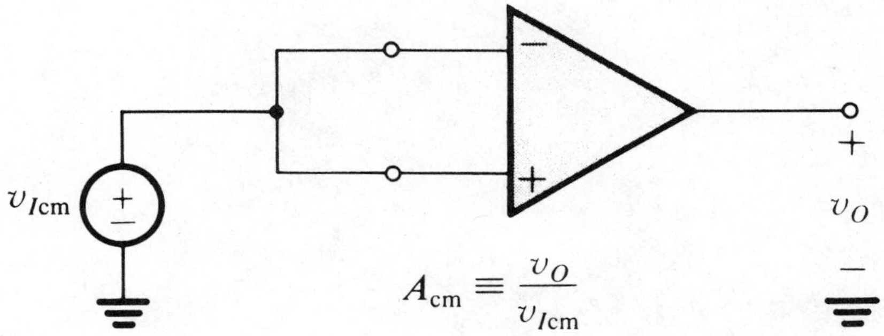
v_{Icm}
+
−
−
+
+
v_O
−
$A_{cm} \equiv \frac{v_O}{v_{Icm}}$

3.35

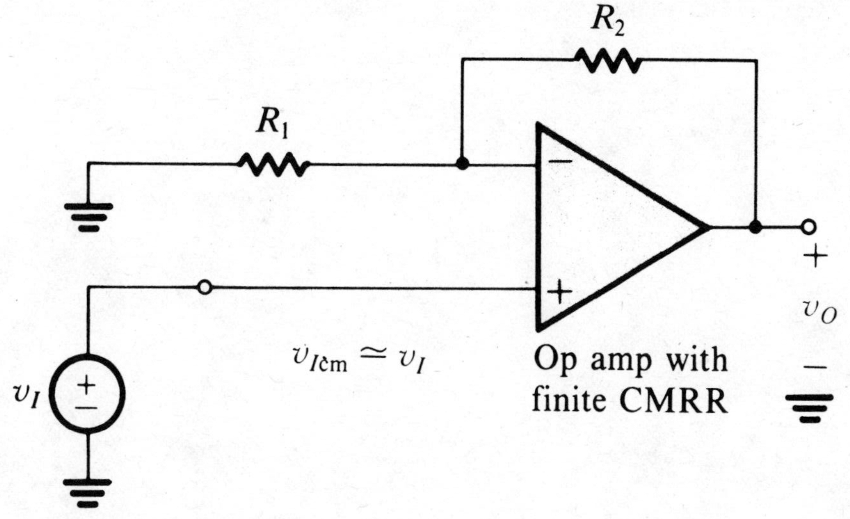

(a)

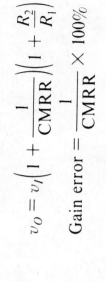

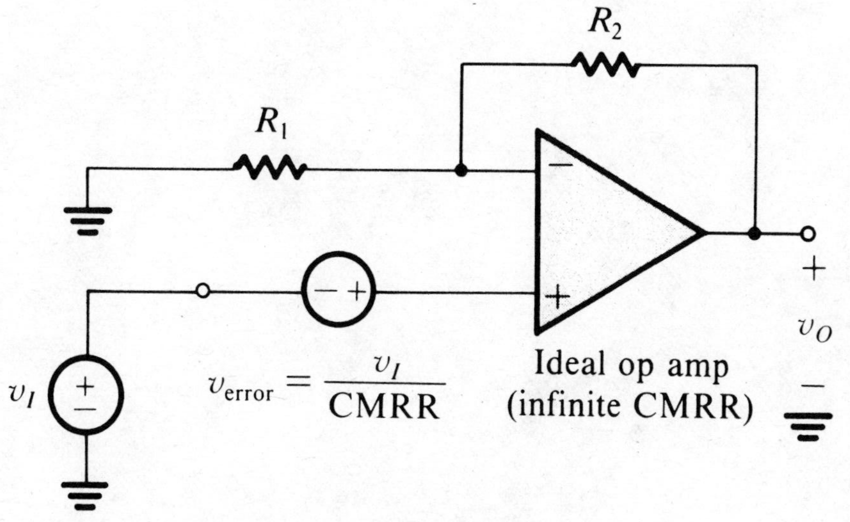

$$v_O = v_I\left(1 + \frac{1}{CMRR}\right)\left(1 + \frac{R_2}{R_1}\right)$$

$$\text{Gain error} = \frac{1}{CMRR} \times 100\%$$

(b)

3.36

3.37

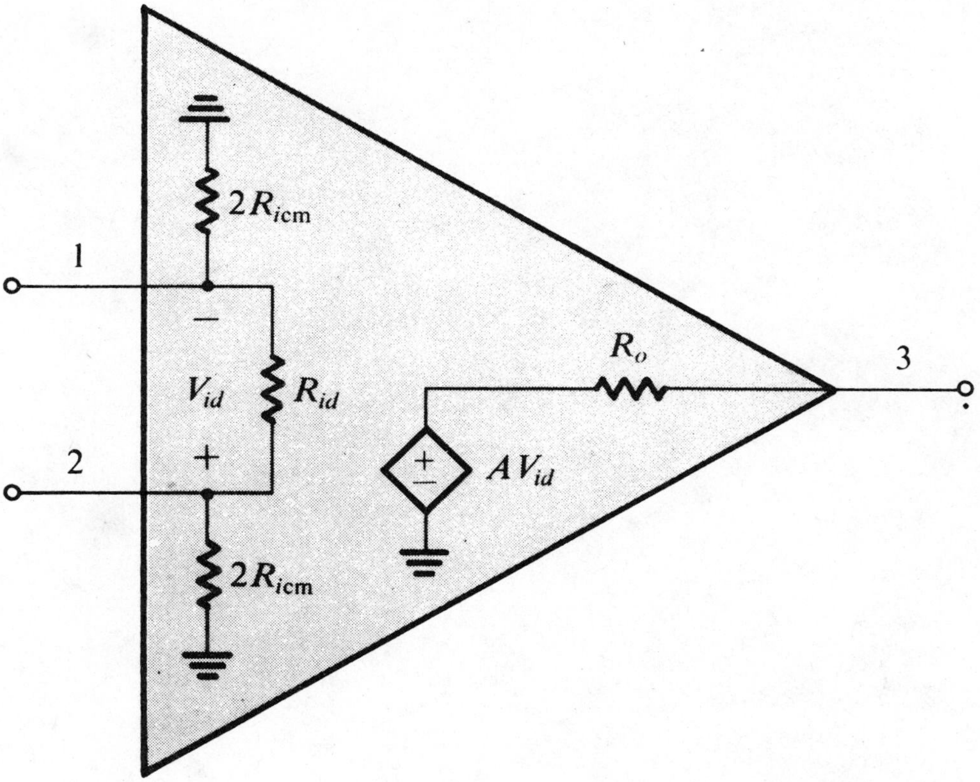

3.41

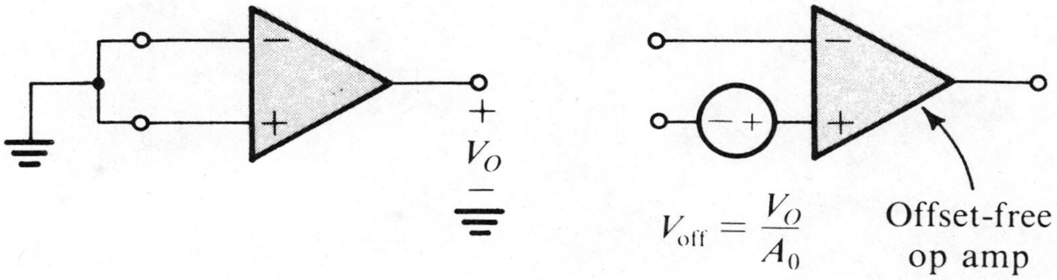

(a) (b)

3.42

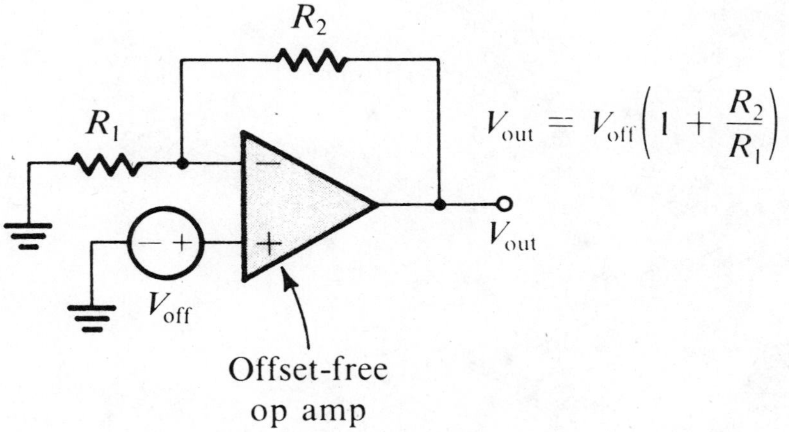

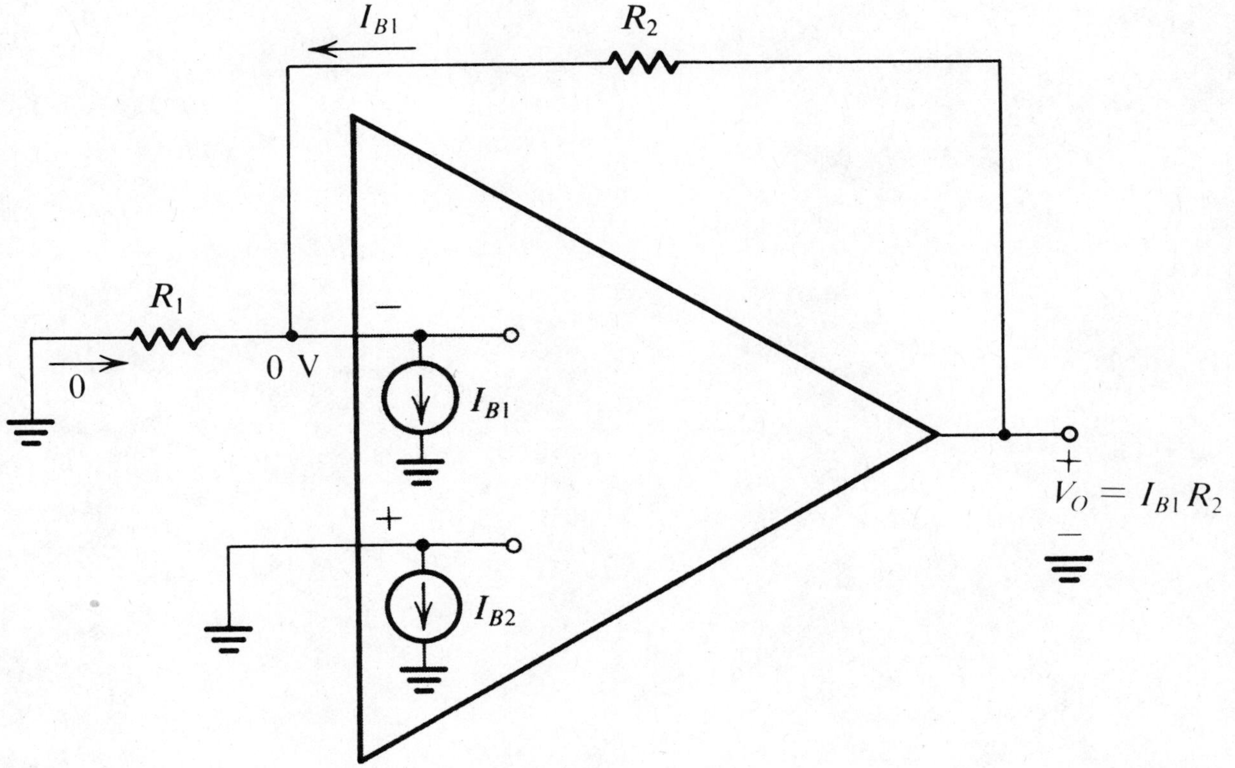
I_{B1}
R_2
R_1
−
0 V
0
I_{B1}
+
I_{B2}
+
$V_O = I_{B1} R_2$
−

3.45

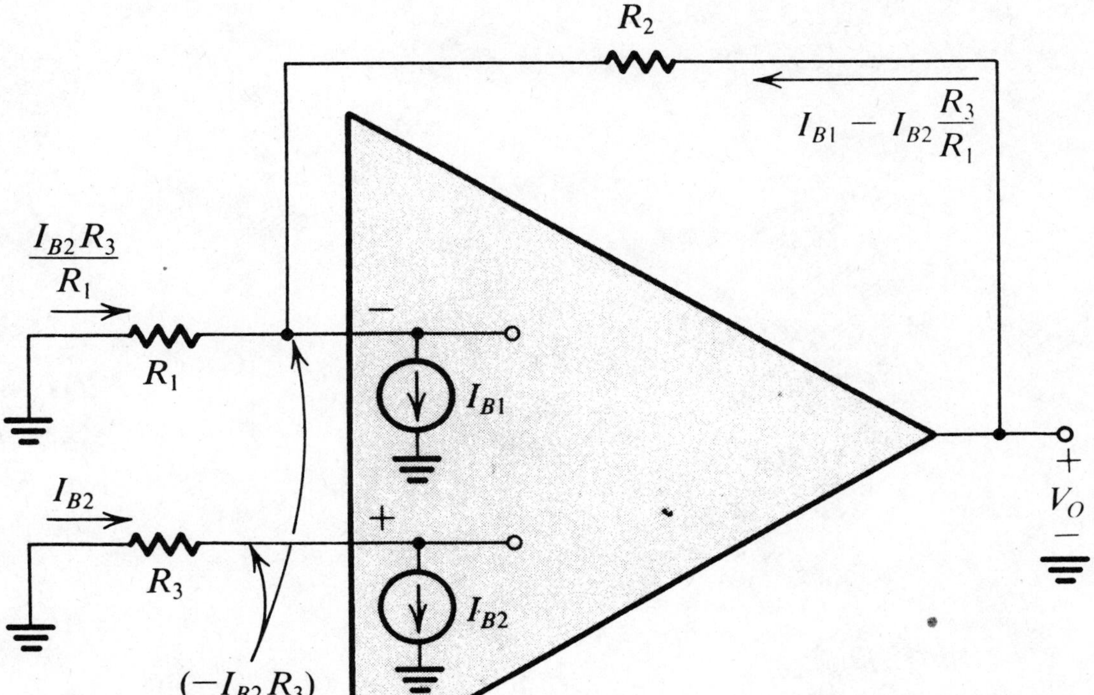
R_2
$I_{B1} - I_{B2}\frac{R_3}{R_1}$
$\frac{I_{B2} R_3}{R_1}$
−
R_1
I_{B1}
I_{B2}
+
R_3
I_{B2}
+
V_O
−
$(-I_{B2} R_3)$

3.46

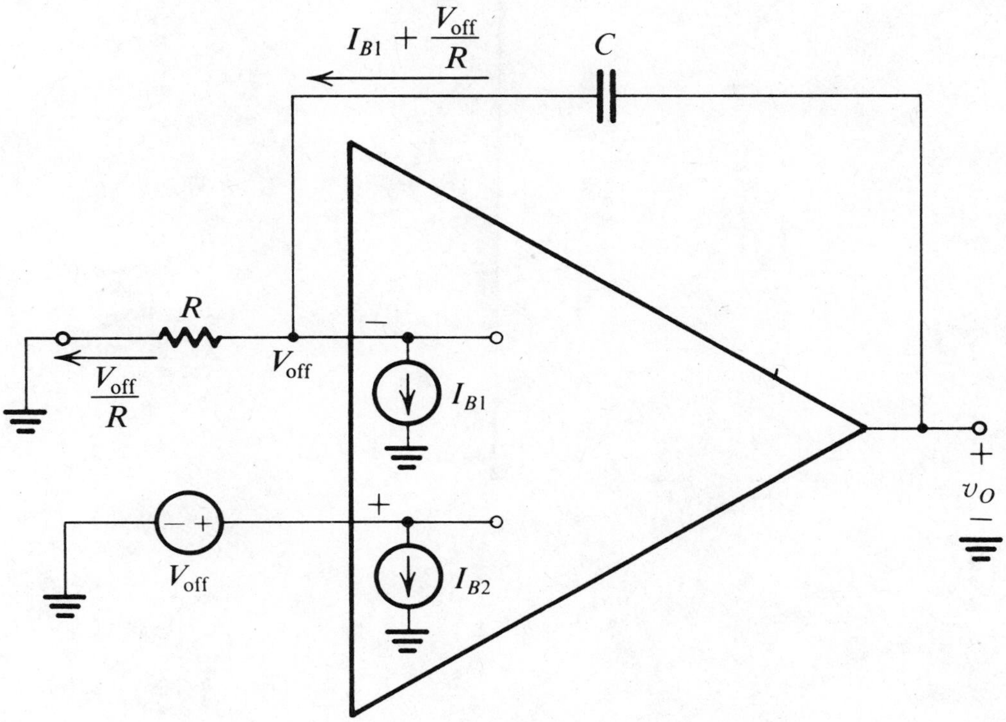

3.49

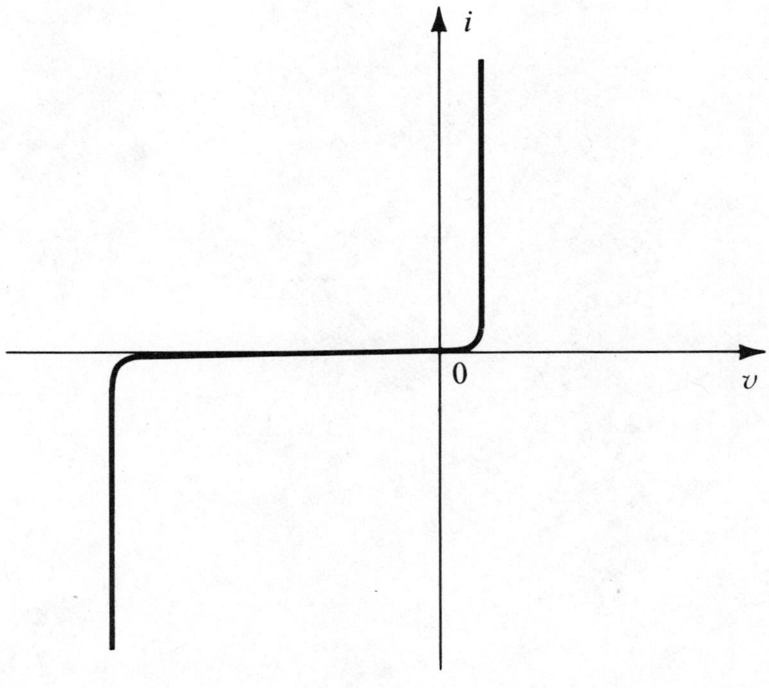

4.5

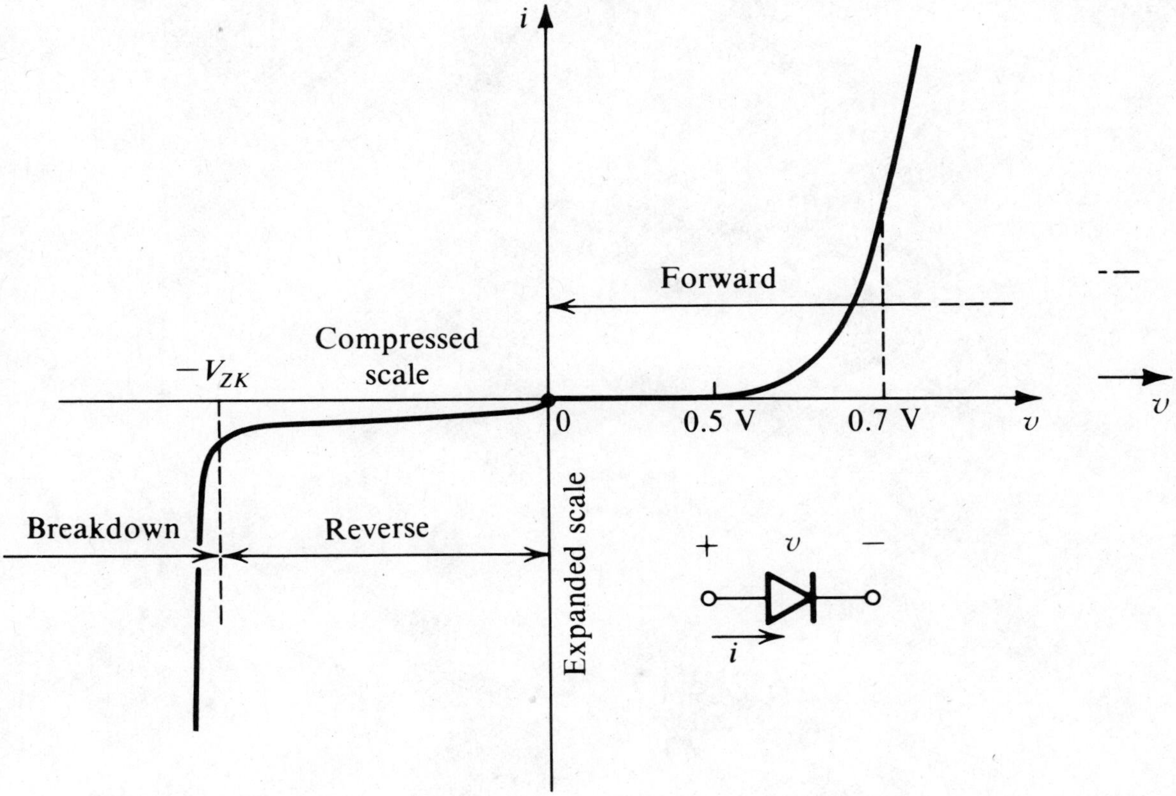

i
Forward
Compressed
scale
$-V_{ZK}$
0
0.5 V
0.7 V
v
v
Breakdown
Reverse
Expanded scale
+
v
−
i

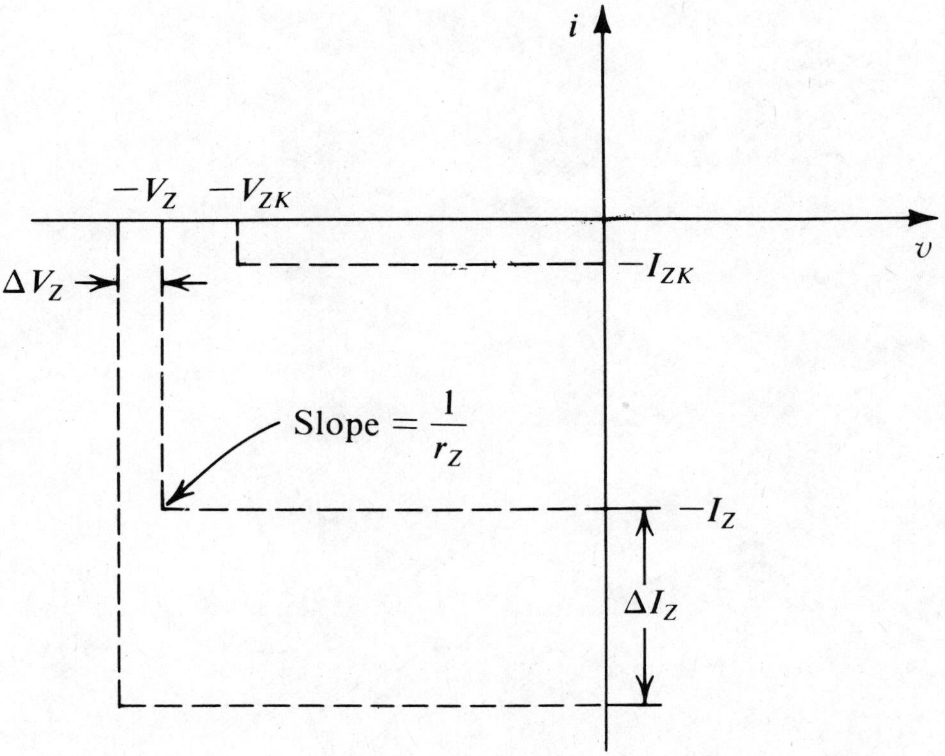

i
$-V_Z$
$-V_{ZK}$
v
$-I_{ZK}$
ΔV_Z
Slope = $\frac{1}{r_Z}$
$-I_Z$
ΔI_Z

4.6

4.8

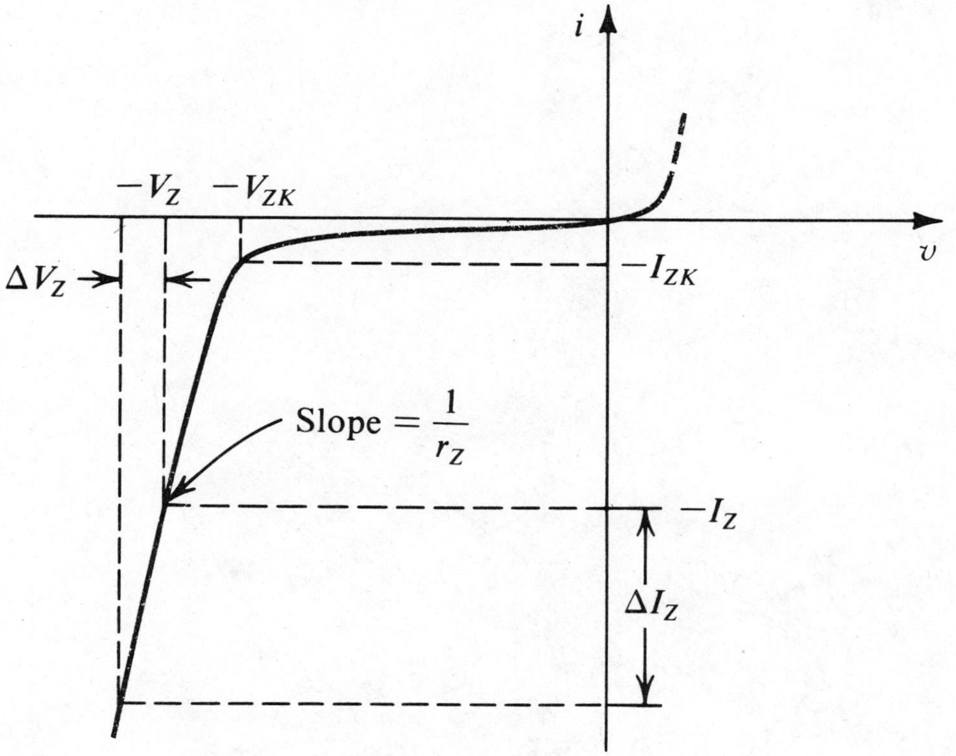

i
$-V_Z$
$-V_{ZK}$
v
ΔV_Z
$-I_{ZK}$
Slope = $\frac{1}{r_Z}$
$-I_Z$
ΔI_Z

4.13

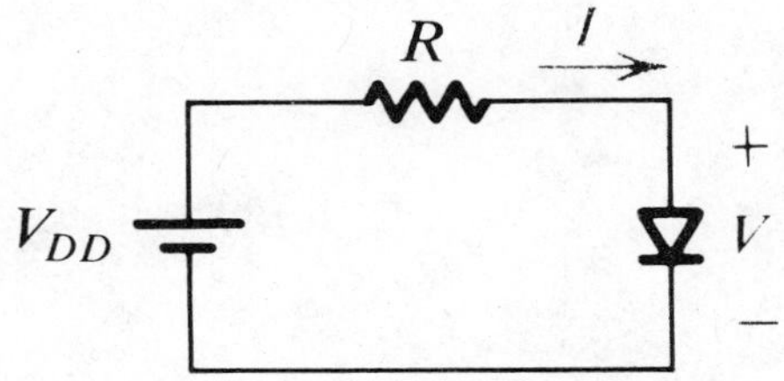

R
I
+
V_{DD}
V
−

4.14

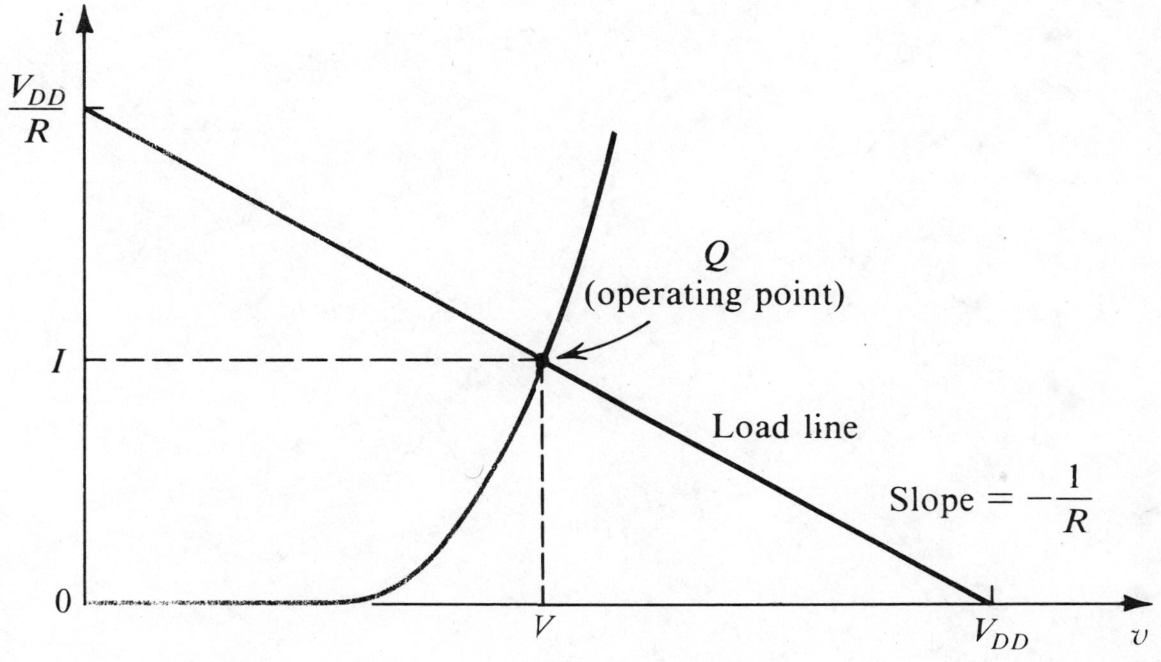

i
$\frac{V_{DD}}{R}$
Q
(operating point)
I
Load line
Slope = $-\frac{1}{R}$
0
V
V_{DD}
v

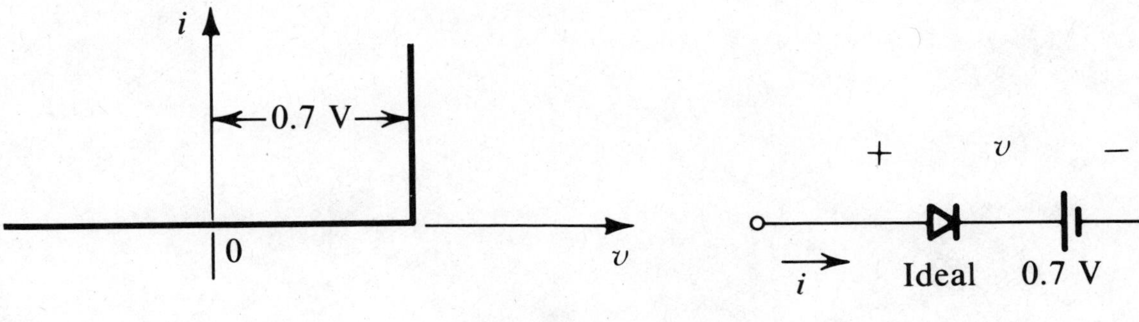

(a) (b)

4.16

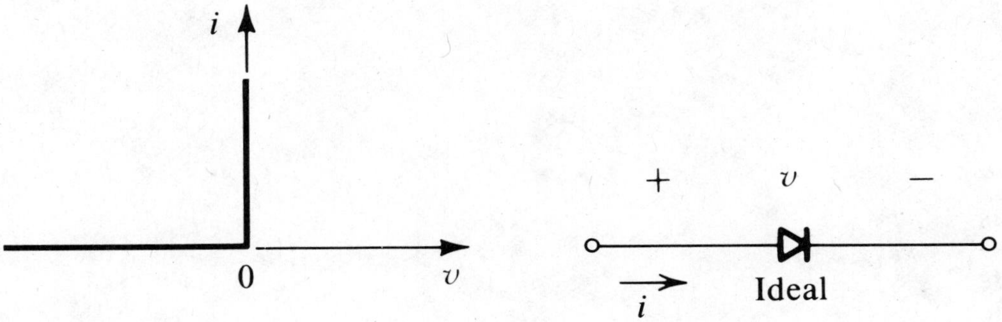

(a) (b)

4.17

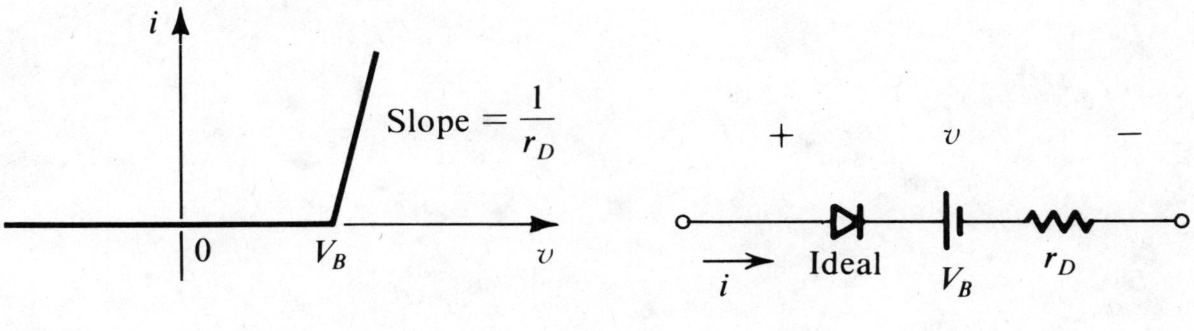

(a) (b)

4.18

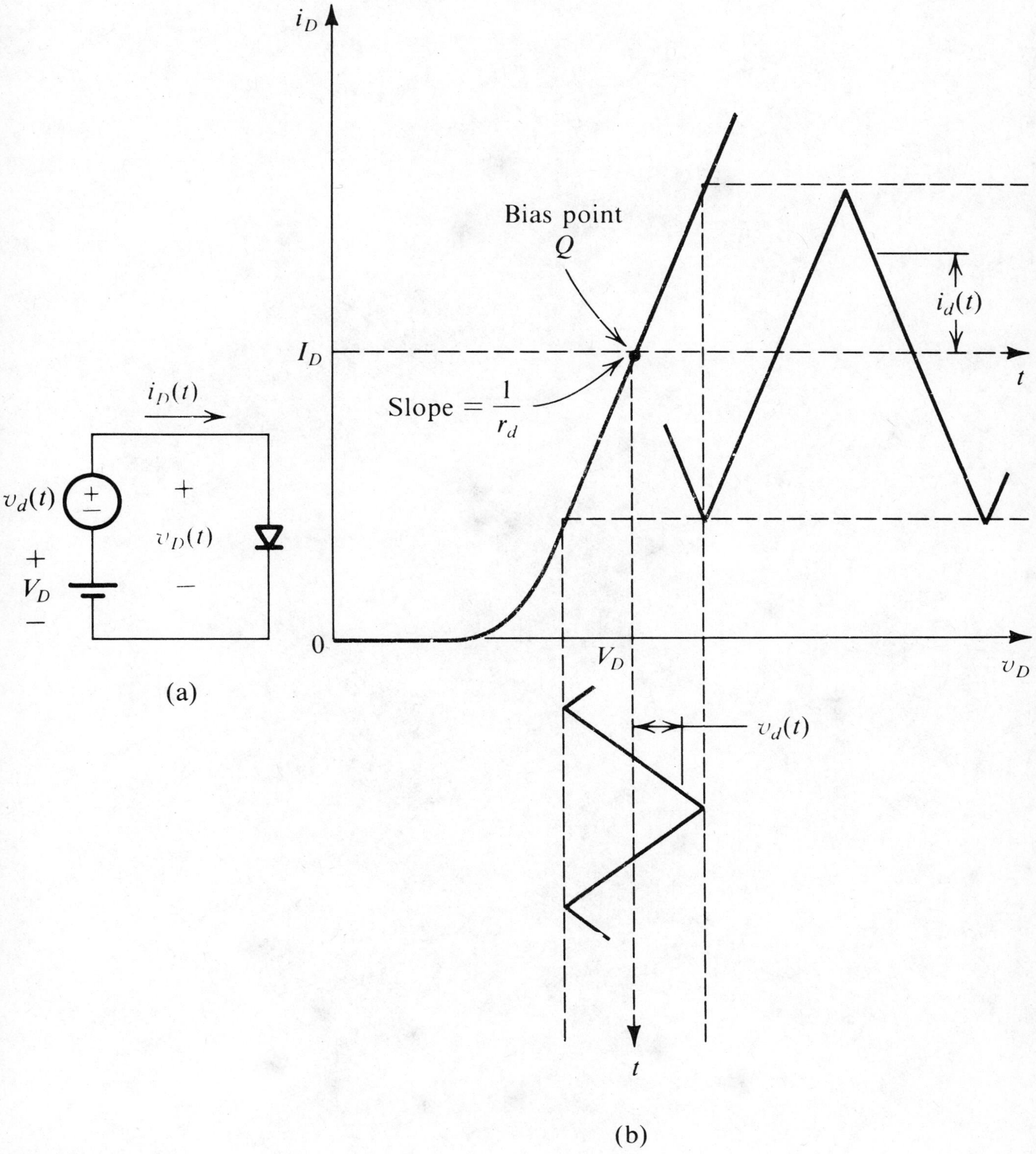

$i_D(t)$
$v_d(t)$
+
$v_D(t)$
−
+
V_D
−
(a)
i_D
Bias point
Q
I_D
Slope = $\frac{1}{r_d}$
$i_d(t)$
t
0
V_D
v_D
$v_d(t)$
t
(b)

4.20

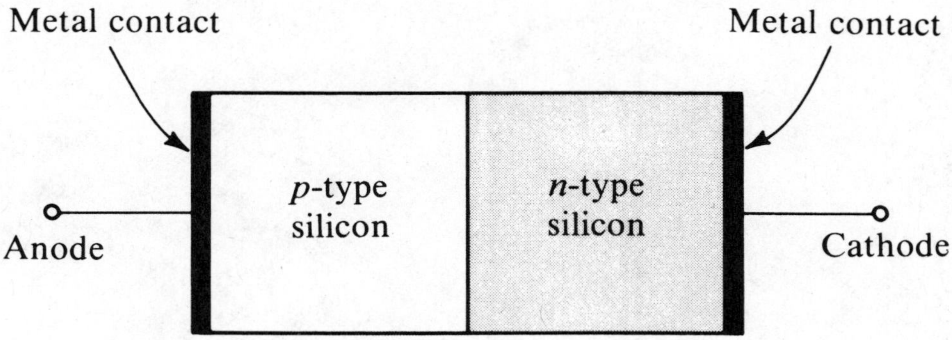

Metal contact
Metal contact
p-type
silicon
n-type
silicon
Anode
Cathode

4.23

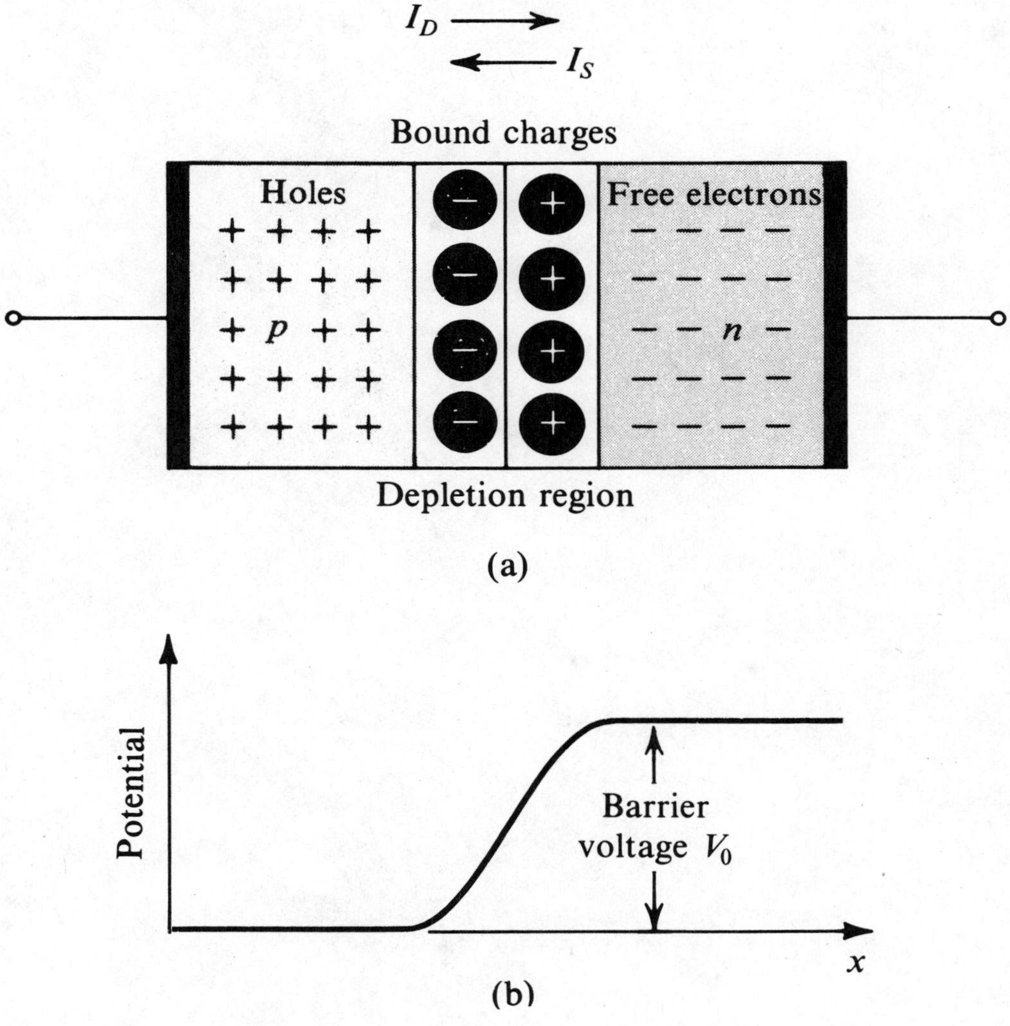

I_D
I_S
Bound charges
Holes
Free electrons
p
n
Depletion region
(a)
Potential
Barrier
voltage V_0
x
(b)

4.25

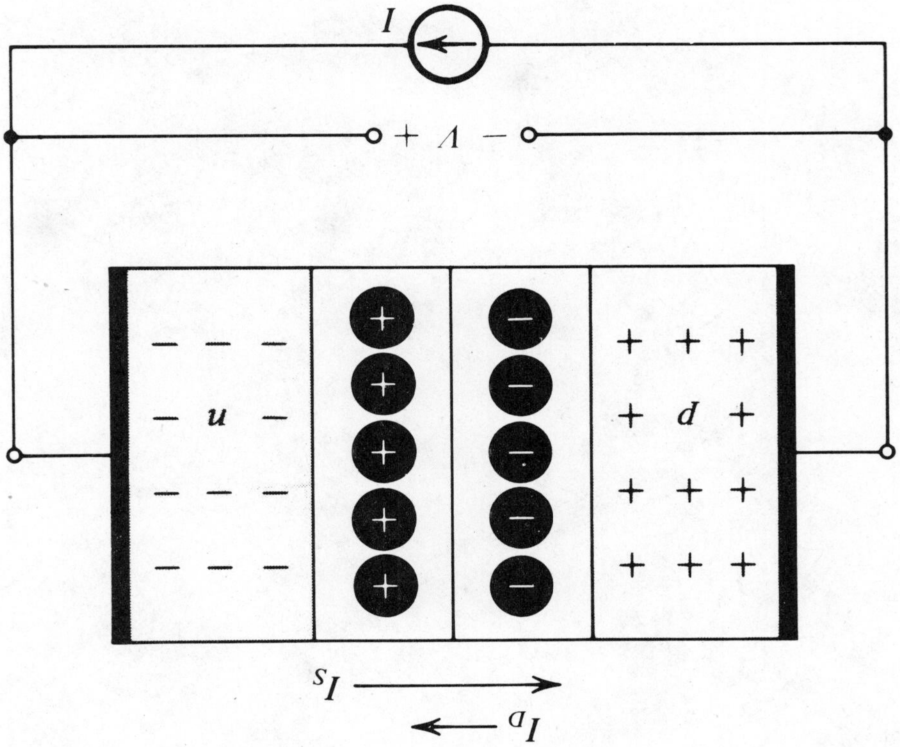

4.26

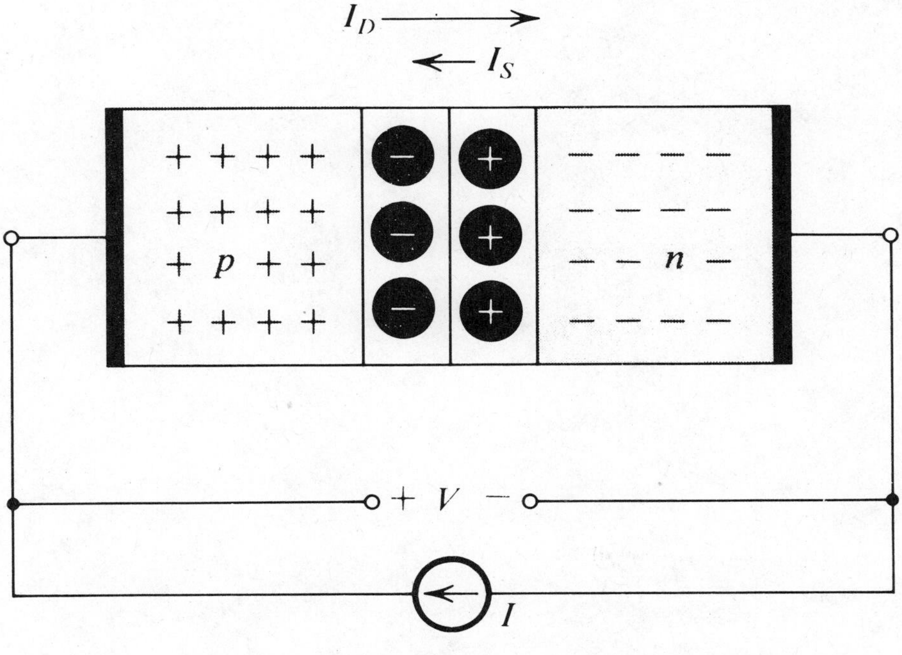

4.29

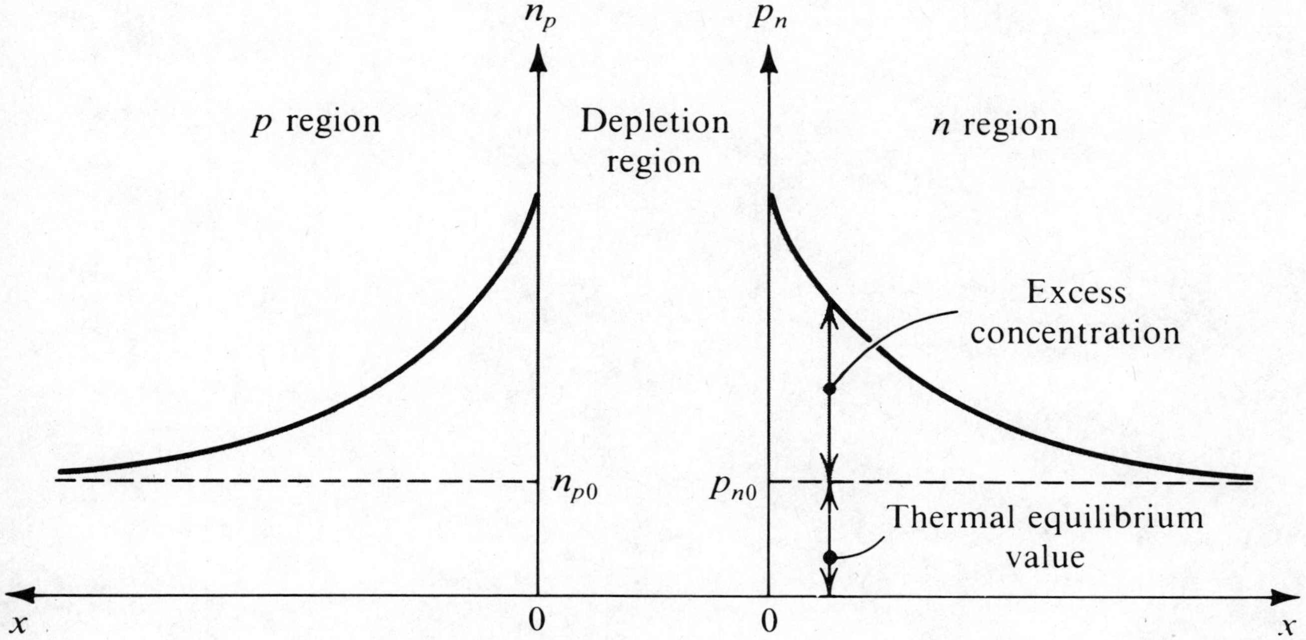
n_p
p_n
p region
Depletion region
n region
Excess concentration
n_{p0}
p_{n0}
Thermal equilibrium value
x
0
0
x

4.30

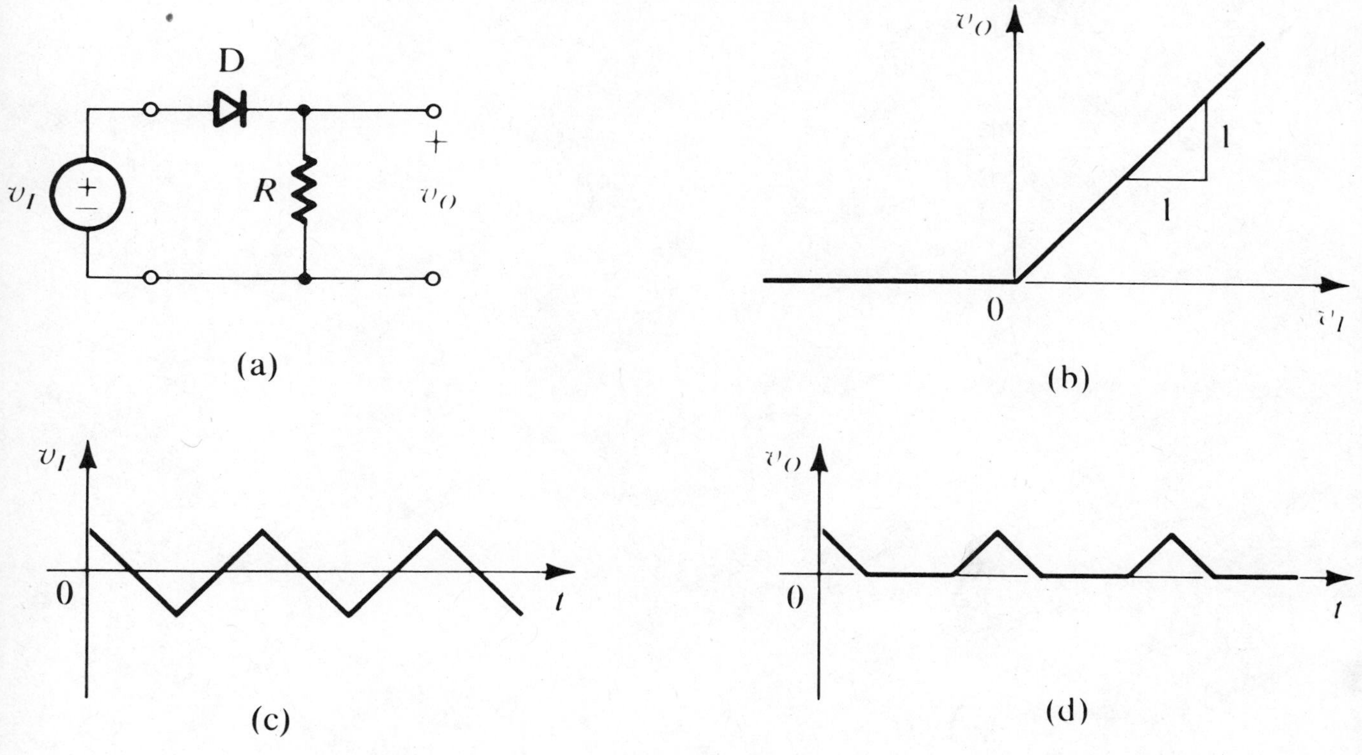

5.1

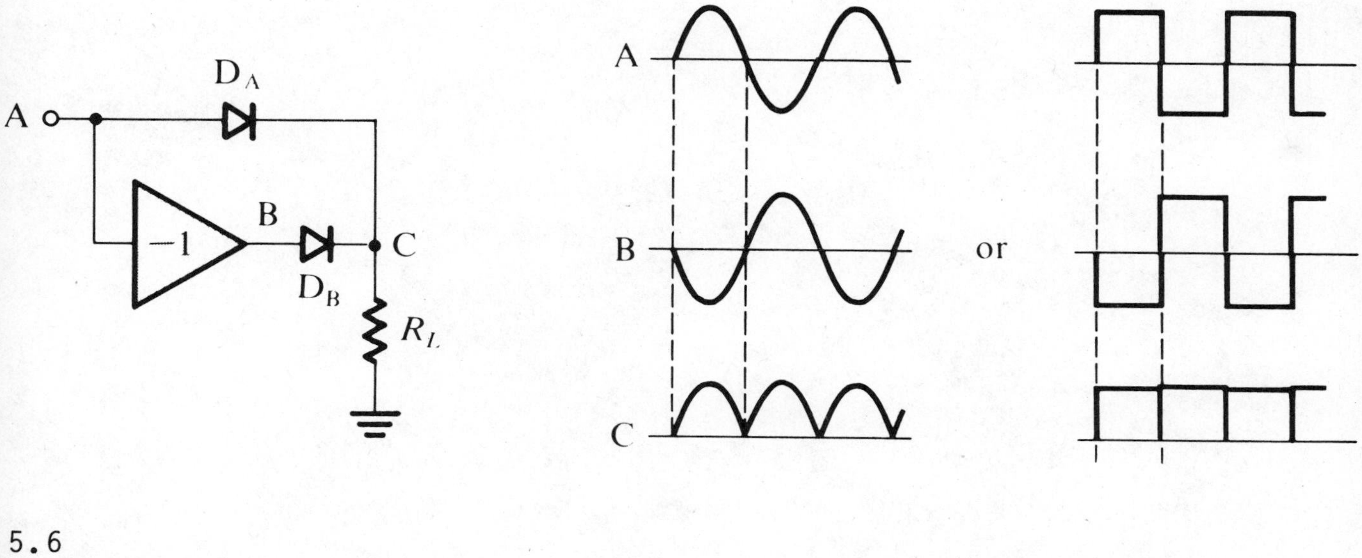

5.6

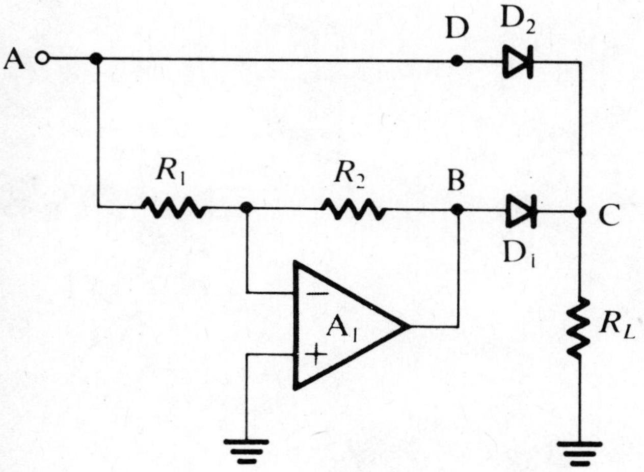
A
D
D2
R1
R2
B
C
D1
A1
RL

(a)

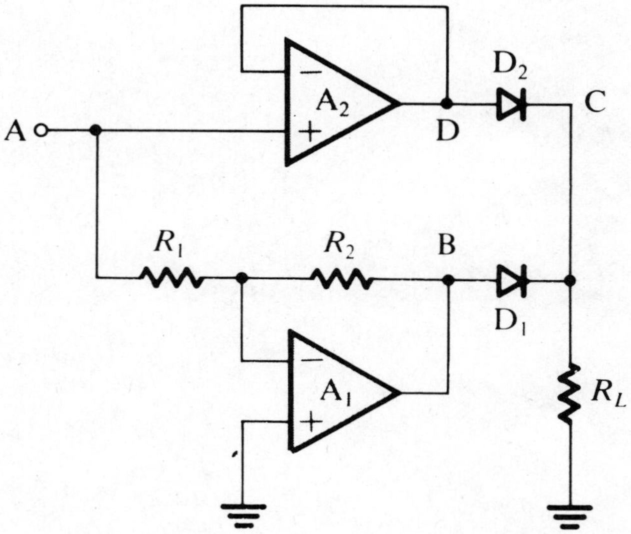
A2
D2
C
A
D
R1
R2
B
D1
A1
RL

(b)

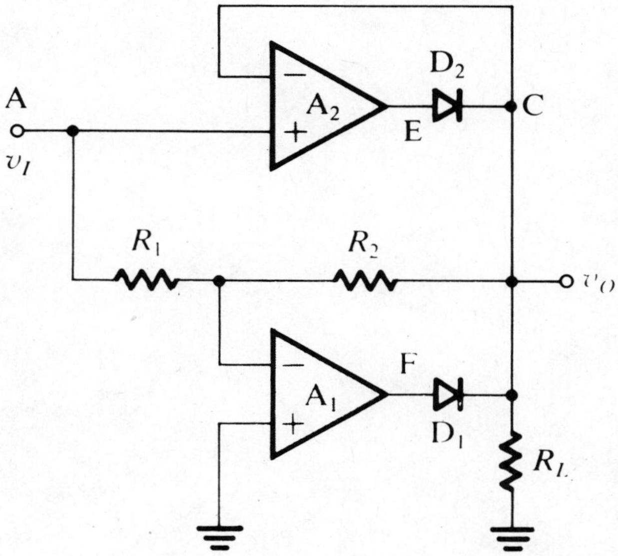
A
vI
A2
D2
C
E
R1
R2
vO
F
A1
D1
RL

(c)

5.7

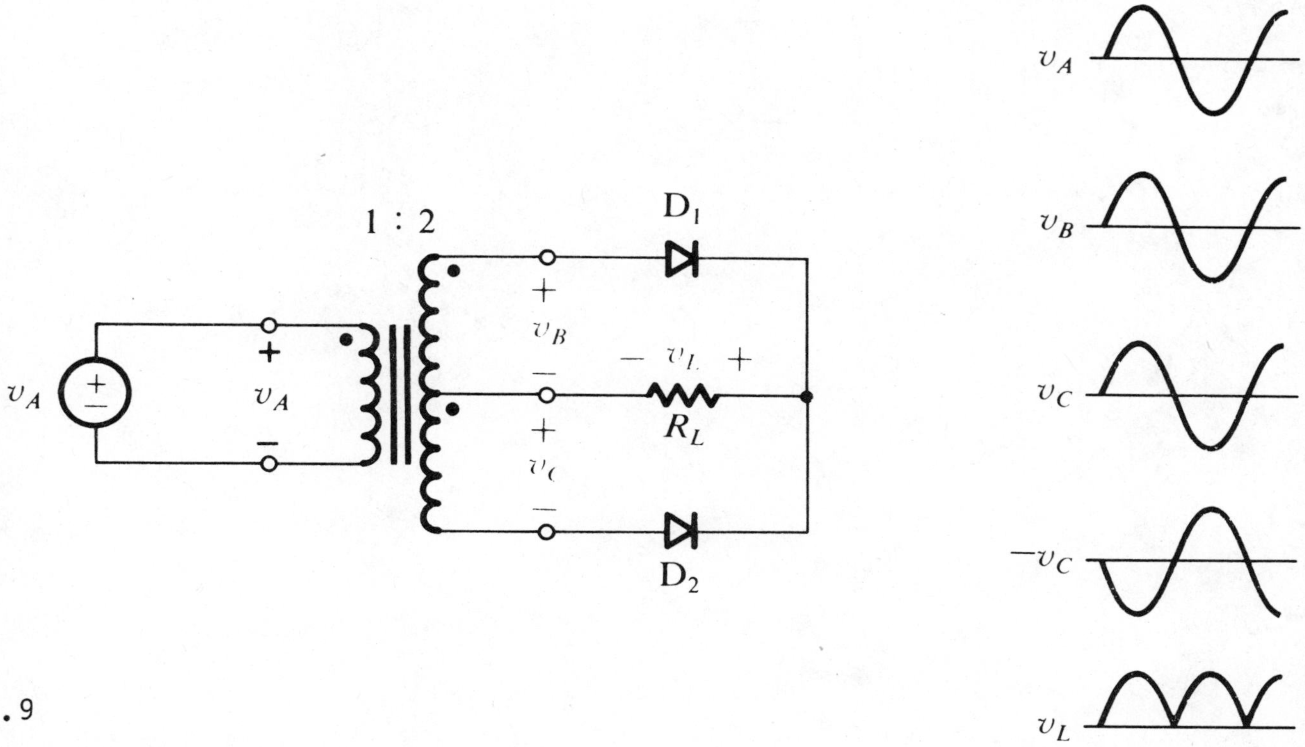
1 : 2
D1
D2
v_A
v_B
v_C
v_L
R_L
v_A
v_B
v_C
$-v_C$
v_L

5.9

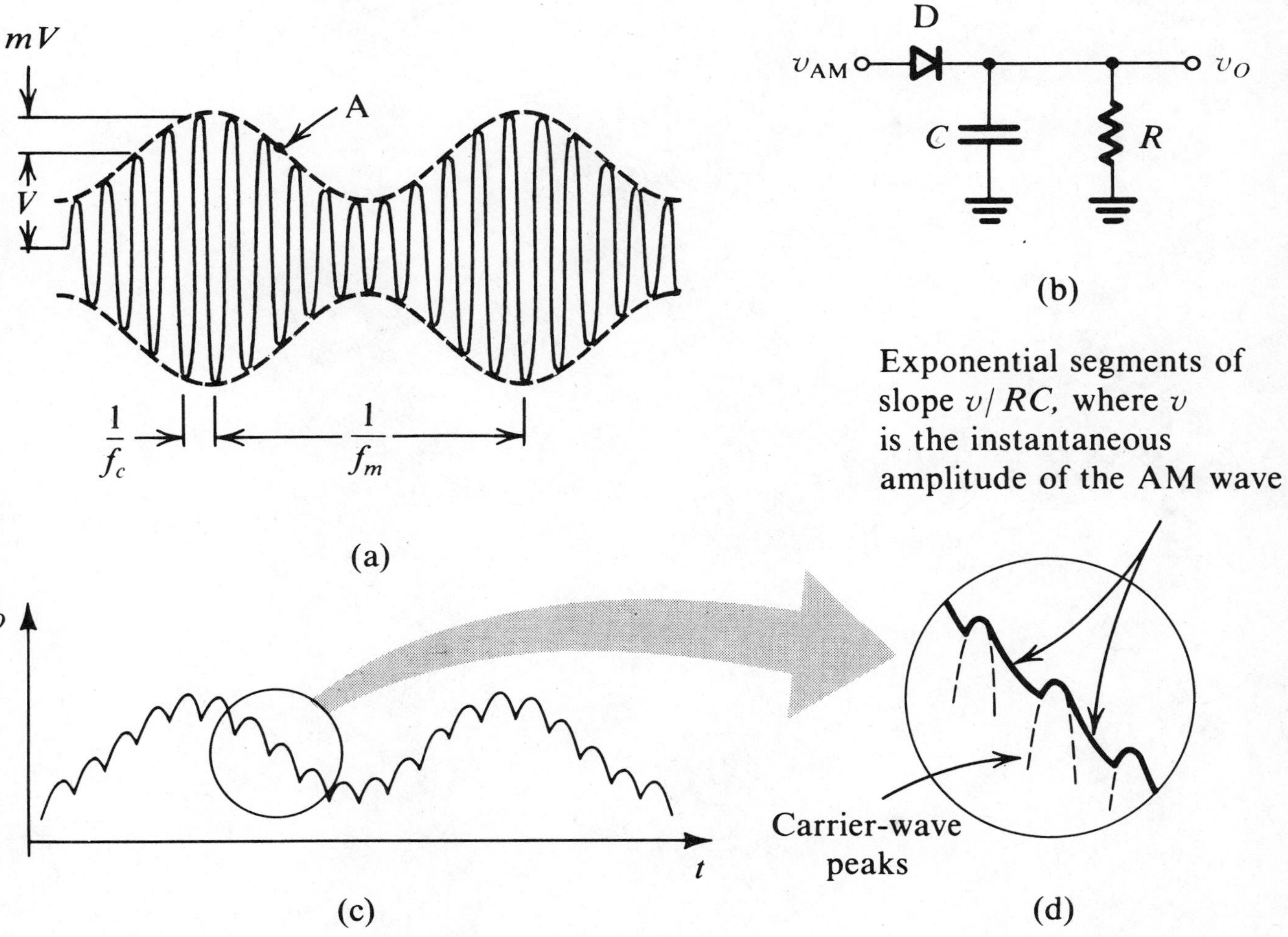
mV
A
V
1/f_c
1/f_m
(a)
D
v_AM
v_O
C
R
(b)
Exponential segments of slope v/RC, where v is the instantaneous amplitude of the AM wave
v_O
t
(c)
Carrier-wave peaks
(d)

5.21

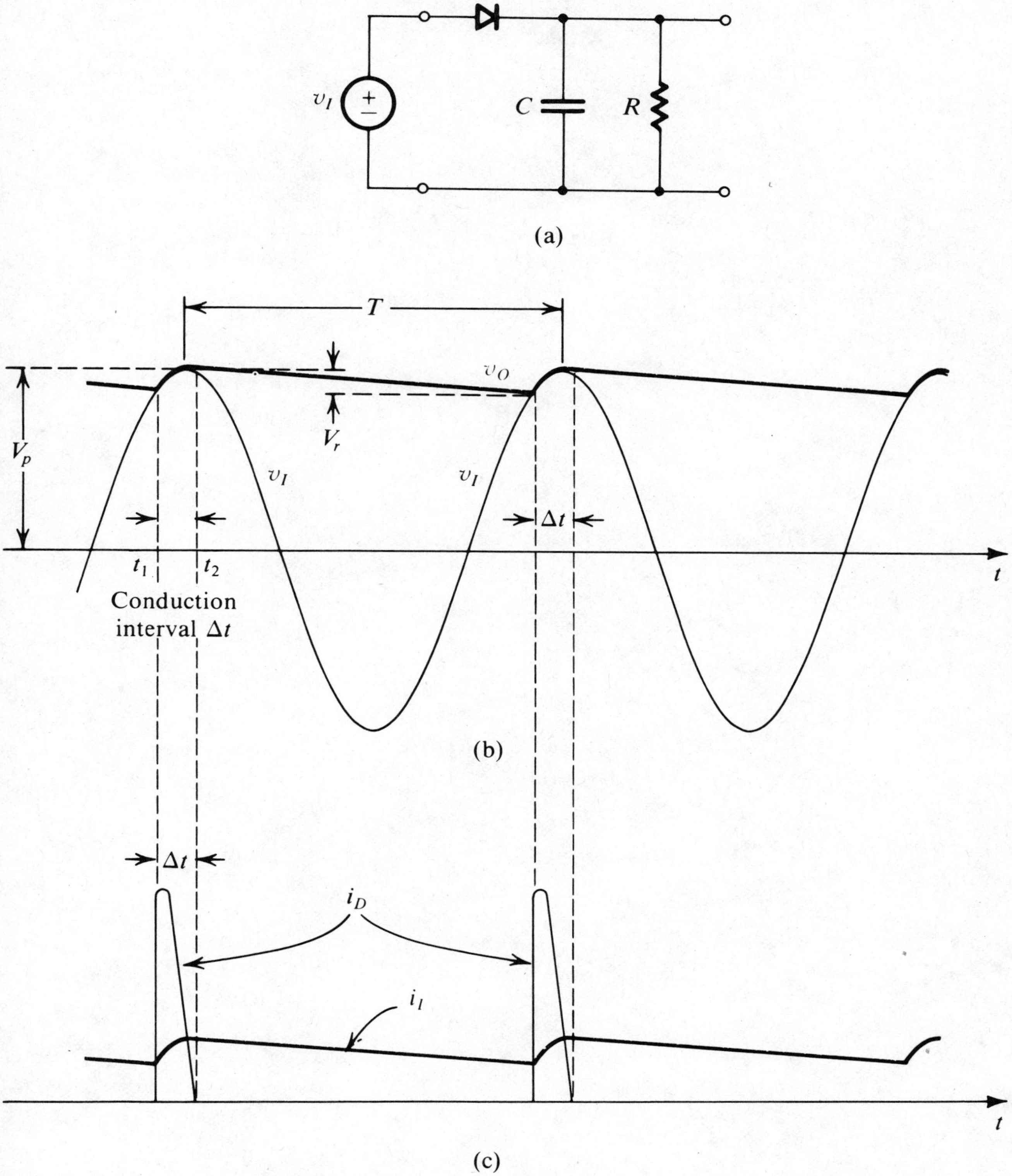

v_I
C
R
(a)
T
v_O
V_p
V_r
v_I
v_I
Δt
t_1
t_2
t
Conduction interval Δt
(b)
Δt
i_D
i_l
t
(c)

5.17

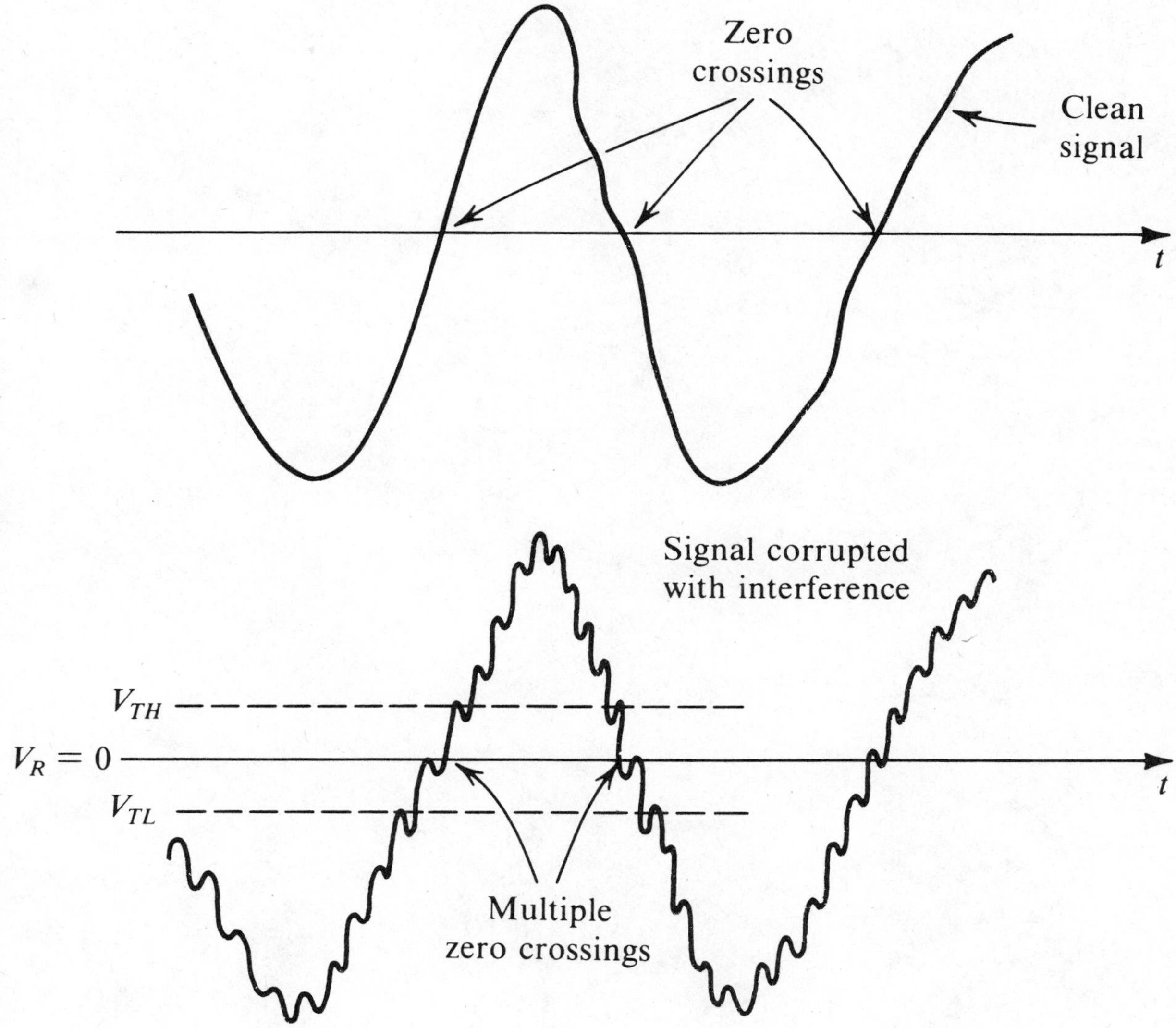
Zero
crossings
Clean
signal
t
Signal corrupted
with interference
V_{TH}
$V_R = 0$
V_{TL}
t
Multiple
zero crossings

5.30

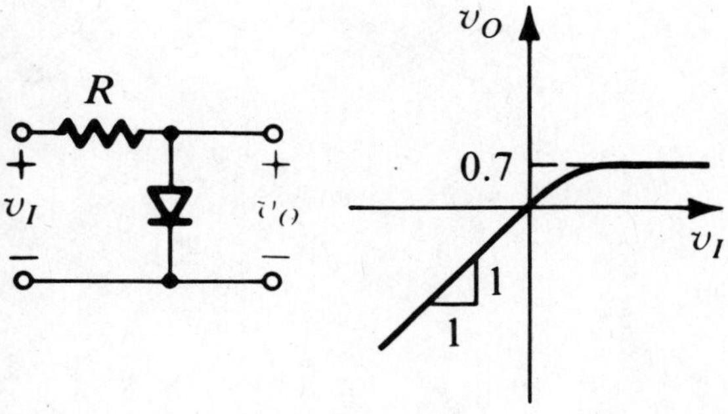
R
+
v_I
−
+
v_O
−
v_O
0.7
v_I
1
1

(a)

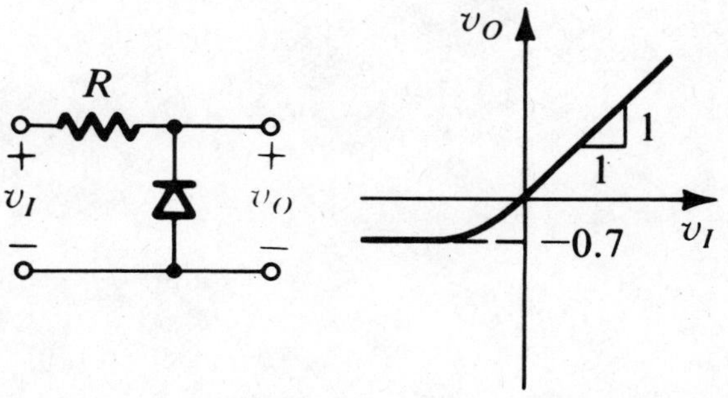
R
+
v_I
−
+
v_O
−
v_O
1
1
−0.7
v_I

(b)

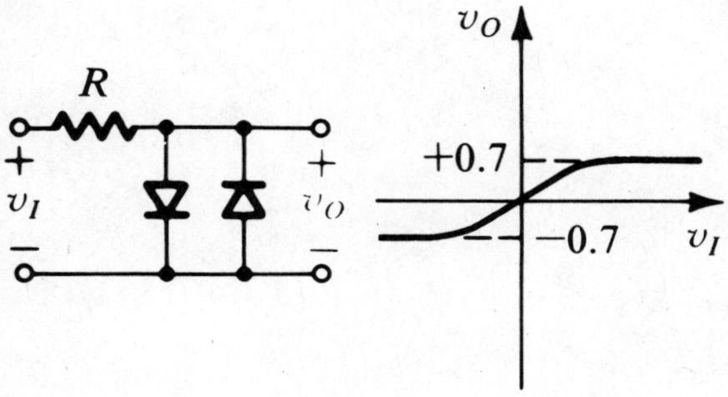
R
+
v_I
−
+
v_O
−
v_O
+0.7
−0.7
v_I

(c)

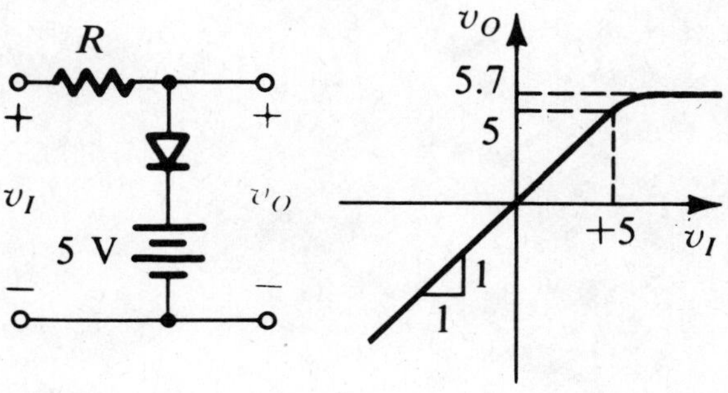
R
+
v_I
5 V
−
+
v_O
−
v_O
5.7
5
+5
v_I
1
1

(d)

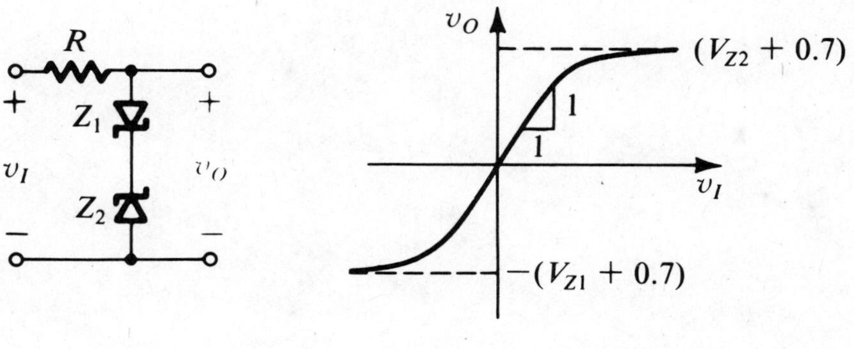
R
+
Z_1
v_I
Z_2
−
+
v_O
−
v_O
$(V_{Z2} + 0.7)$
1
1
v_I
$-(V_{Z1} + 0.7)$

(e)

5.32

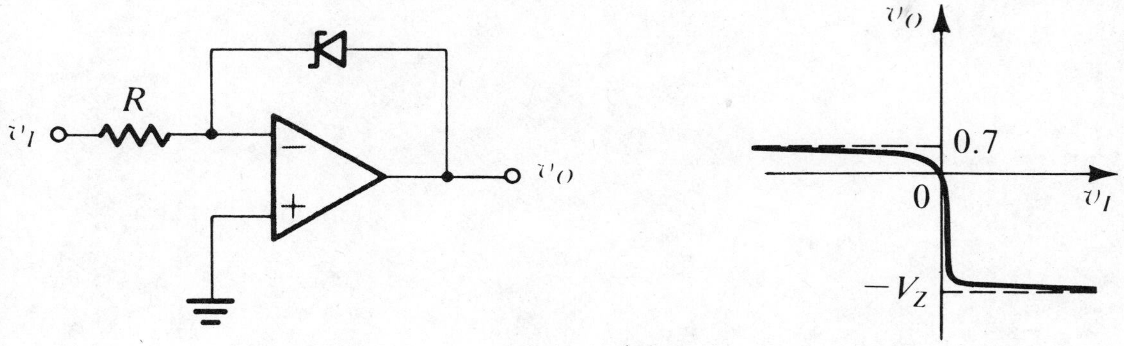

R
v_I
v_O
v_O
0.7
0
v_I
$-V_Z$

(a)

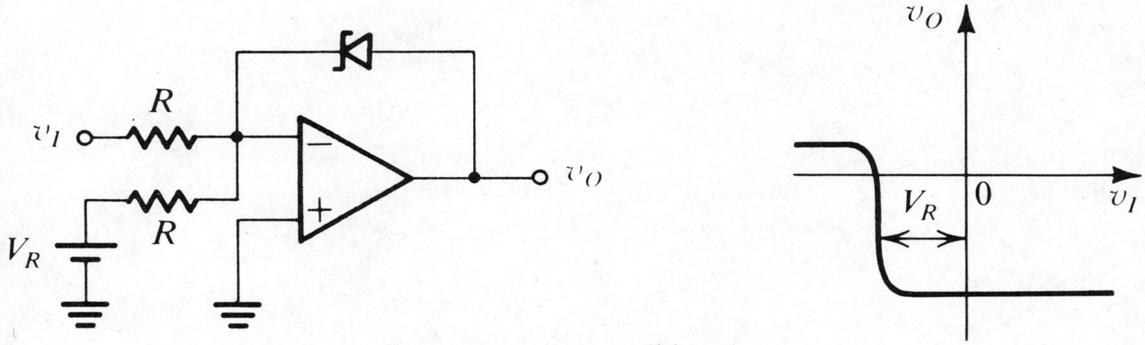

R
v_I
R
V_R
v_O
v_O
V_R
0
v_I

(b)

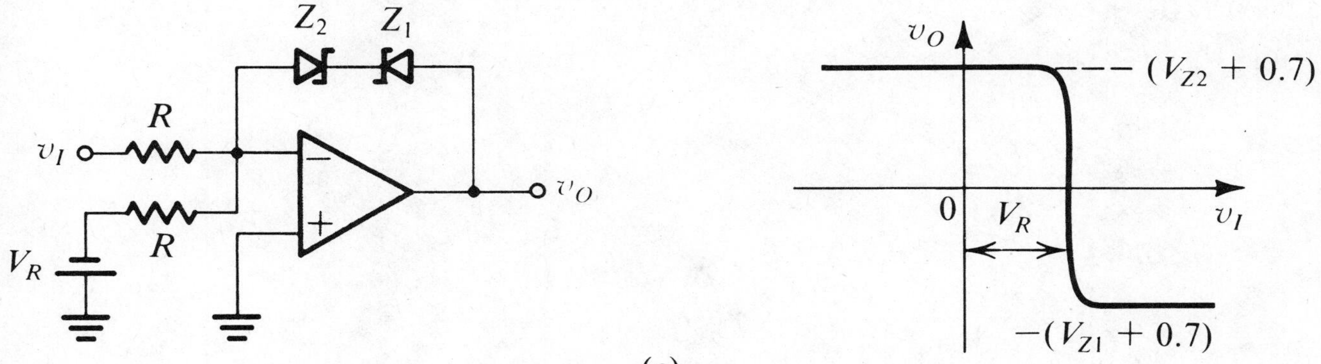

Z_2
Z_1
R
v_I
R
V_R
v_O
v_O
$(V_{Z2} + 0.7)$
0
V_R
v_I
$-(V_{Z1} + 0.7)$

(c)

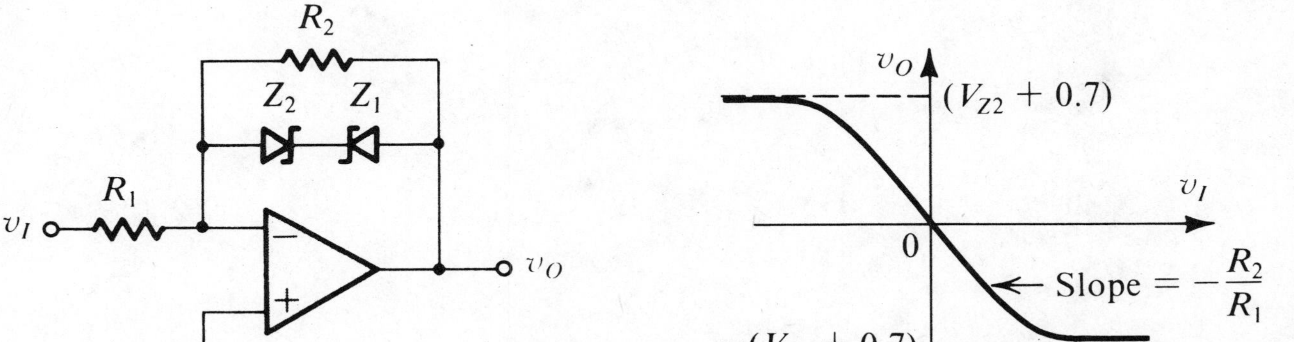

R_2
Z_2
Z_1
R_1
v_I
v_O
v_O
$(V_{Z2} + 0.7)$
v_I
0
Slope $= -\frac{R_2}{R_1}$
$-(V_{Z1} + 0.7)$

(d)

5.33

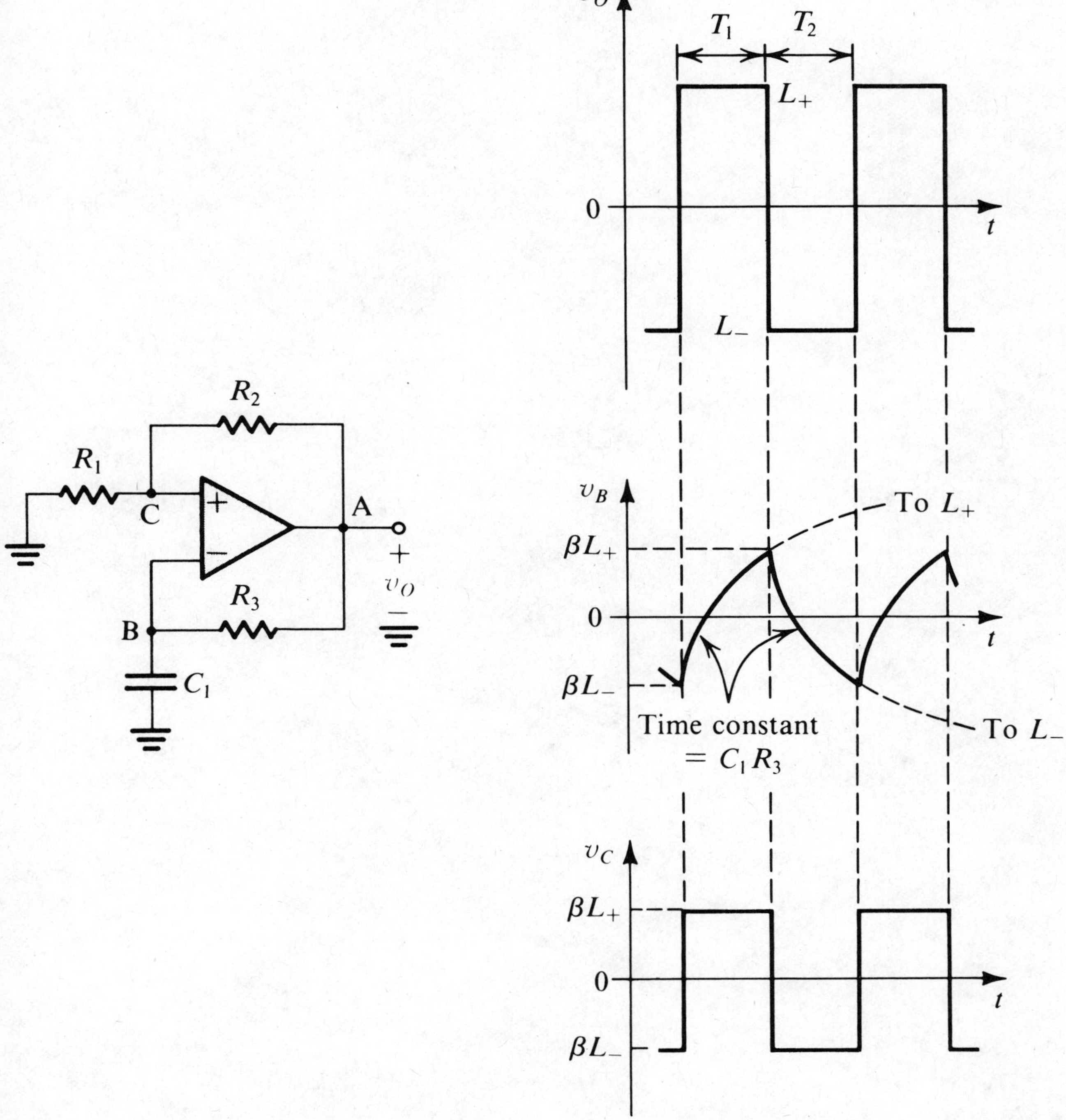

R2
R1
C
A
B
R3
C1
+
vO
−
vO
T1
T2
L+
0
t
L−
vB
To L+
βL+
0
t
βL−
Time constant
= C1R3
To L−
vC
βL+
0
t
βL−

5.36

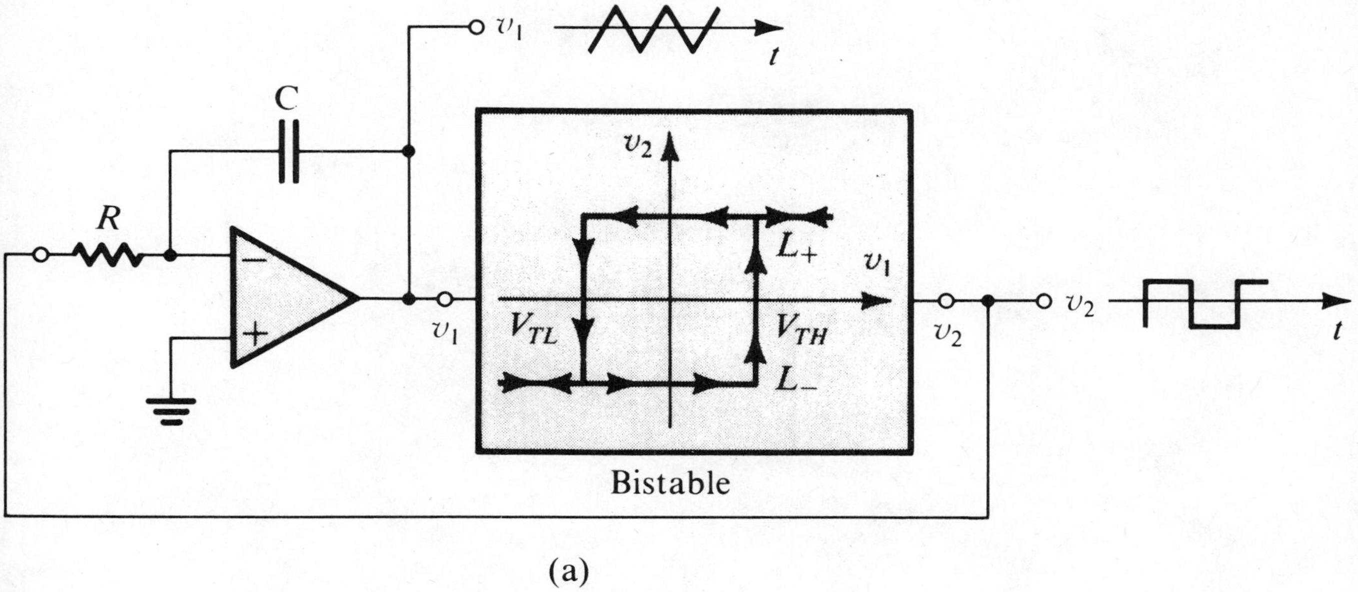

v_1
t
C
R
v_2
L_+
v_1
V_{TL}
V_{TH}
L_-
v_1
v_2
v_2
t
Bistable
(a)
v_2
T_1
T_2
L_+
0
t
L_-
T
(b)
v_1
Slope = $\frac{-L_+}{RC}$
T_1
T_2
V_{TH}
0
t
V_{TL}
Slope = $\frac{-L_-}{RC}$
(c)

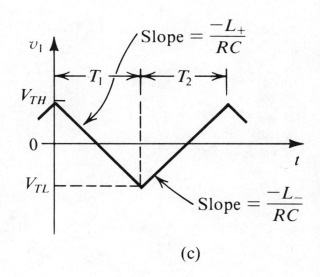

5.37

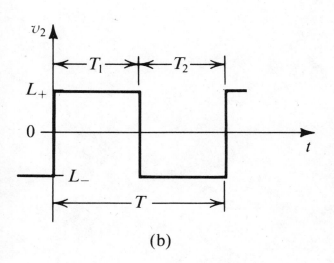

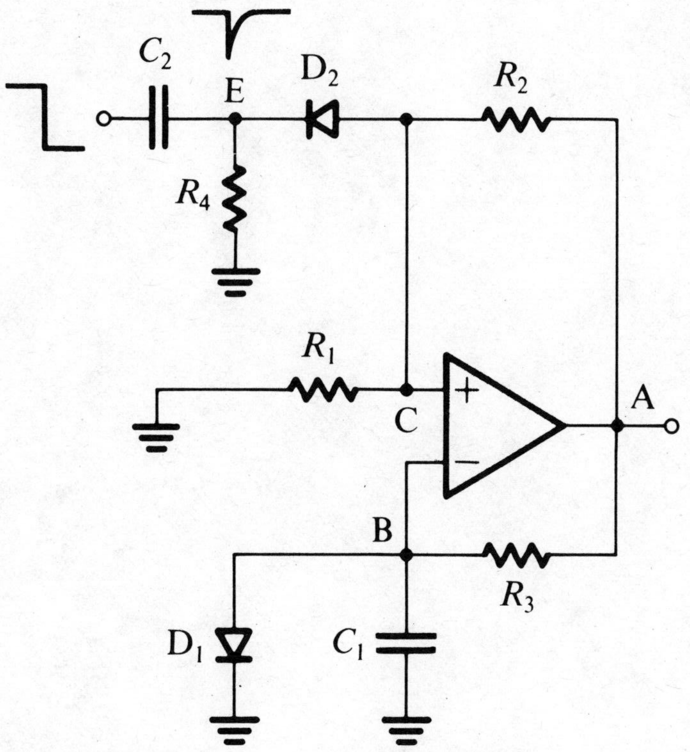

C2
E
D2
R2
R4
R1
C
A
B
R3
D1
C1

(a)

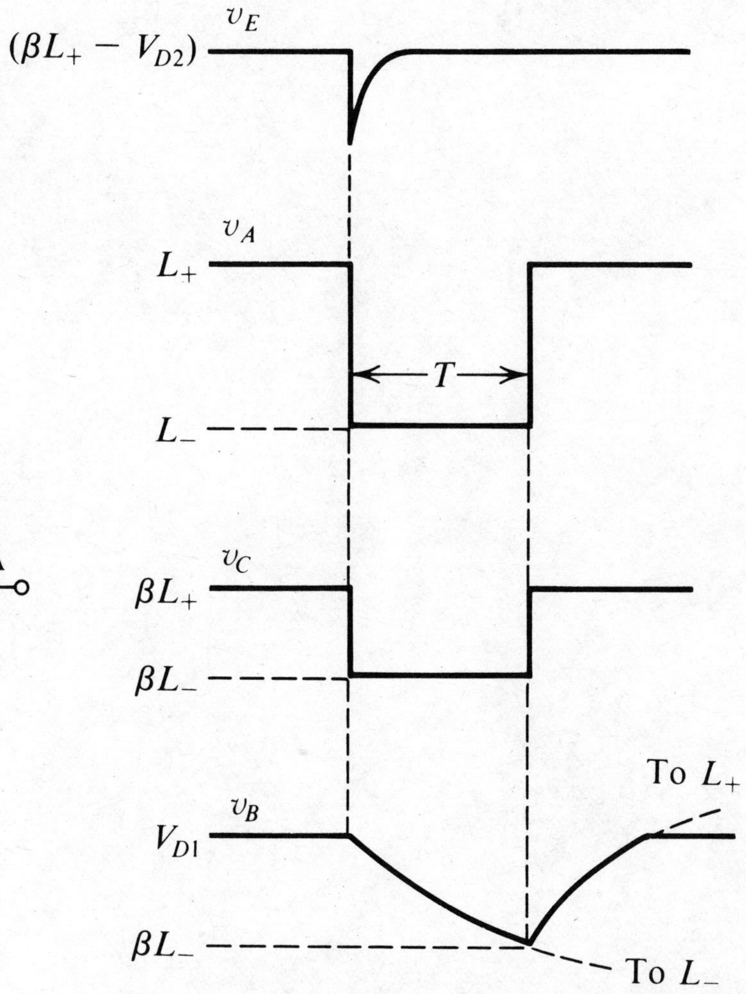

vE
(βL+ − VD2)
vA
L+
T
L−
vC
βL+
βL−
vB
VD1
βL−
To L+
To L−

(b)

5.38

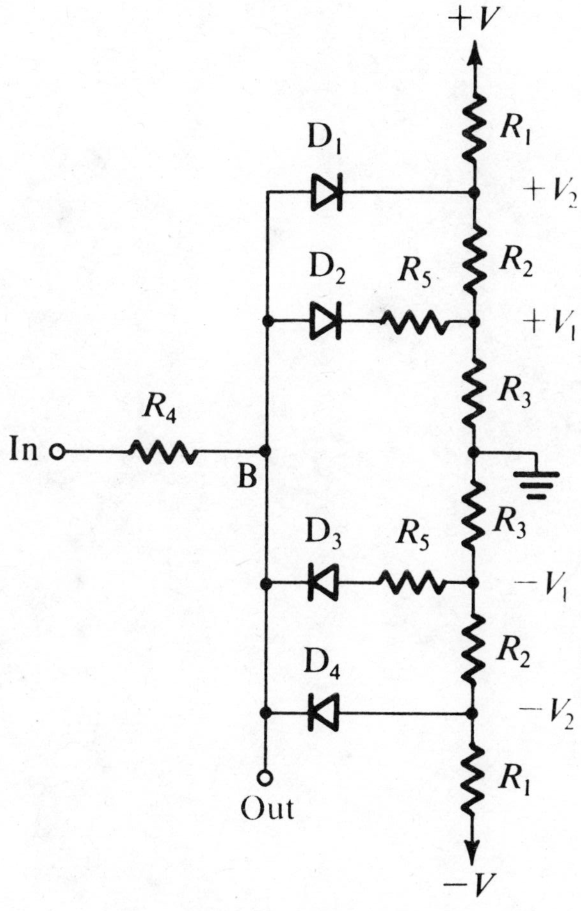
+V
D1
R1
+V2
D2
R5
R2
+V1
R3
R4
In
B
D3
R5
R3
−V1
D4
R2
−V2
R1
Out
−V

(a)

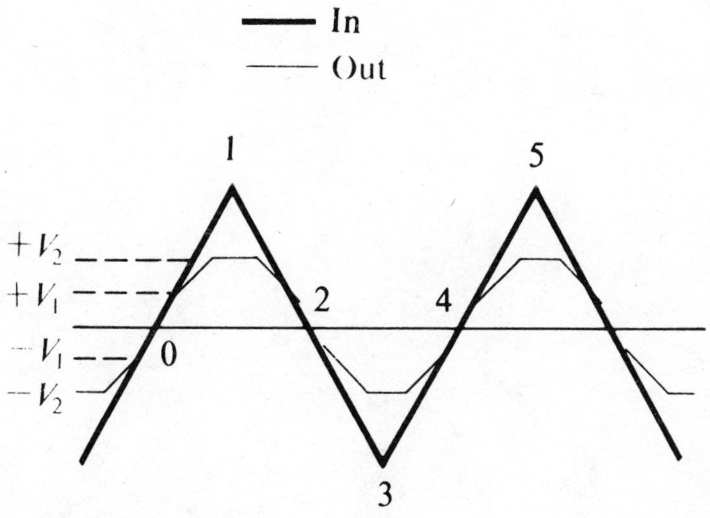
In
Out
1
5
+V2
+V1
2
4
−V1
0
−V2
3

(b)

5.39

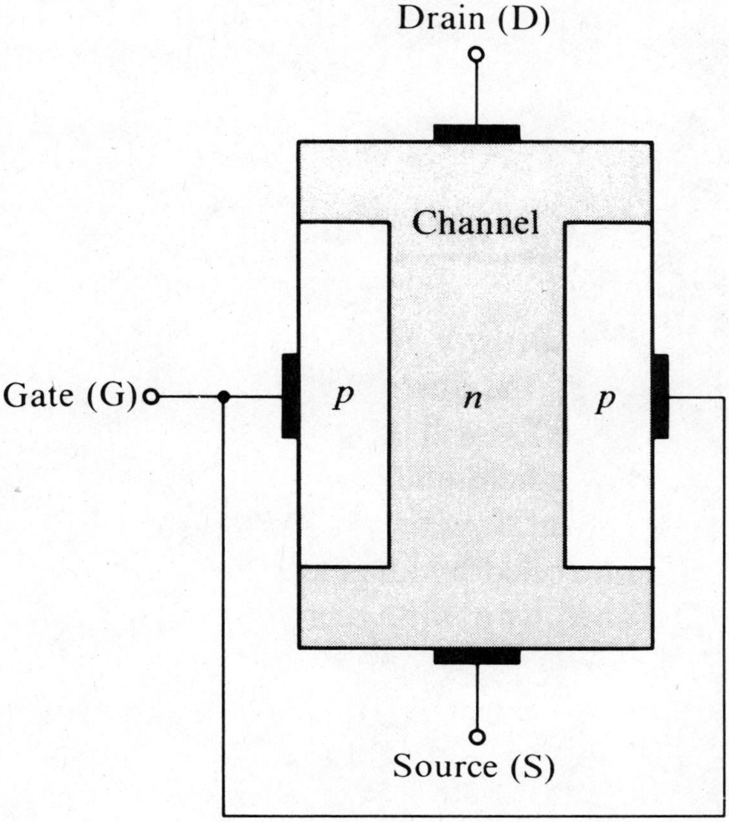

6.1

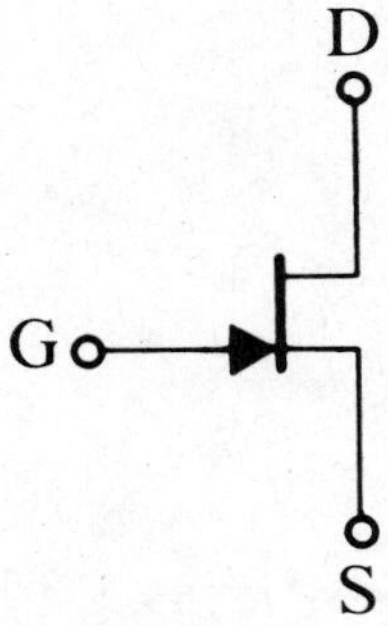

6.2

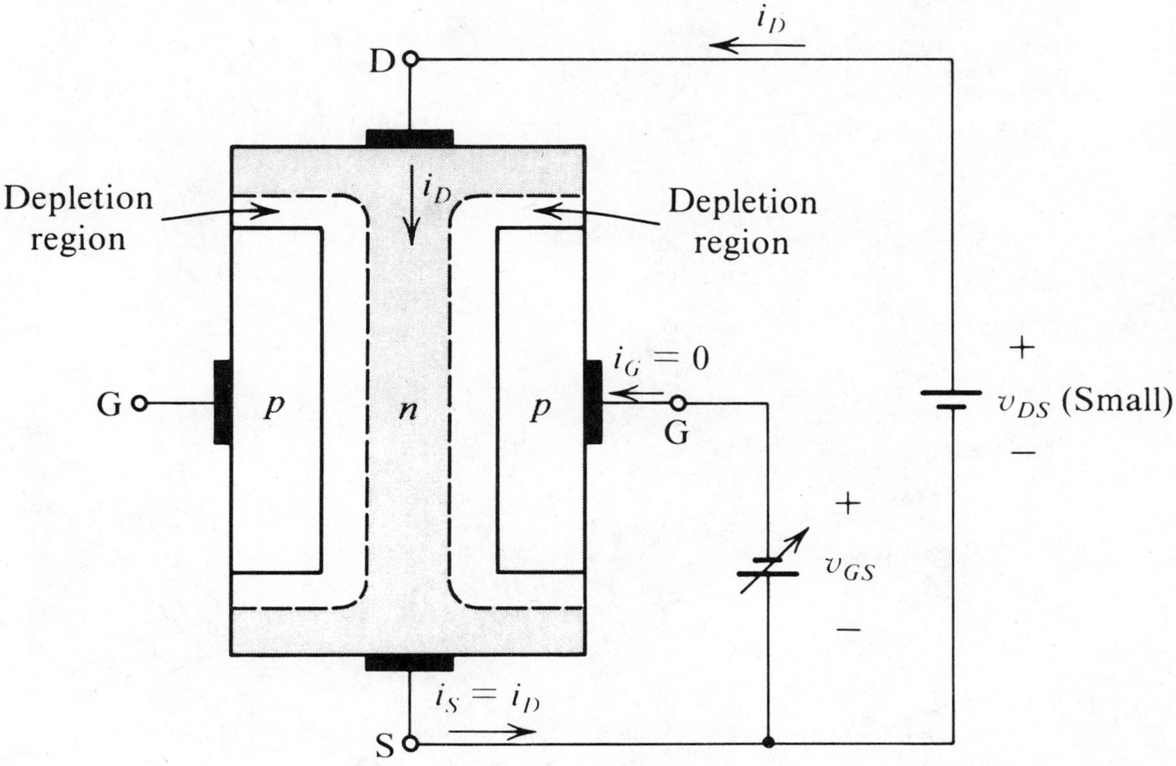
i_D
D
Depletion region
i_D
Depletion region
$i_G = 0$
G
p
n
p
G
+
v_{DS} (Small)
−
+
v_{GS}
−
$i_S = i_D$
S

6。3

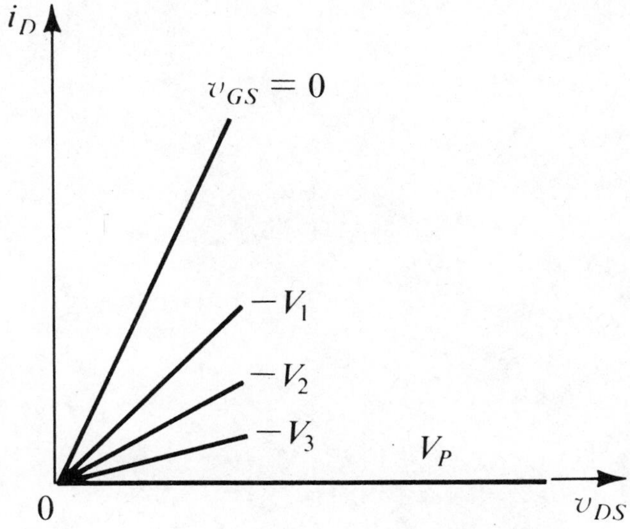
i_D
$v_{GS} = 0$
$-V_1$
$-V_2$
$-V_3$
V_P
0
v_{DS}

6。4

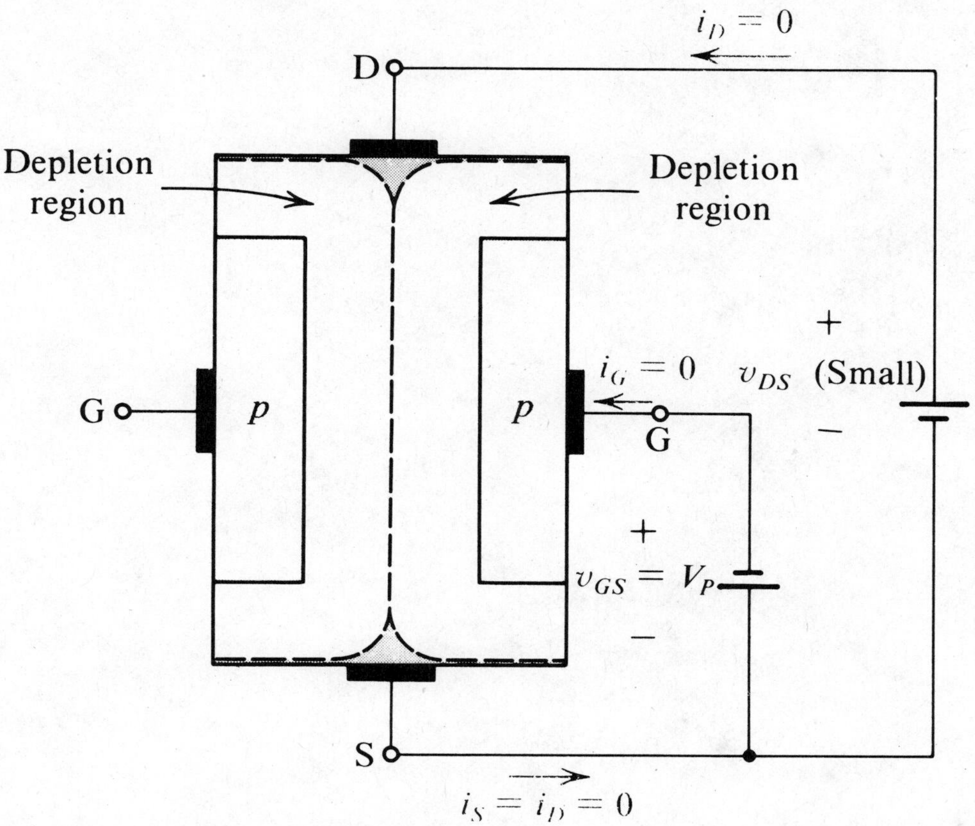

$i_D = 0$
D
Depletion region
Depletion region
p
p
G
$i_G = 0$
v_{DS} (Small)
G
$v_{GS} = V_P$
S
$i_S = i_D = 0$

6.5

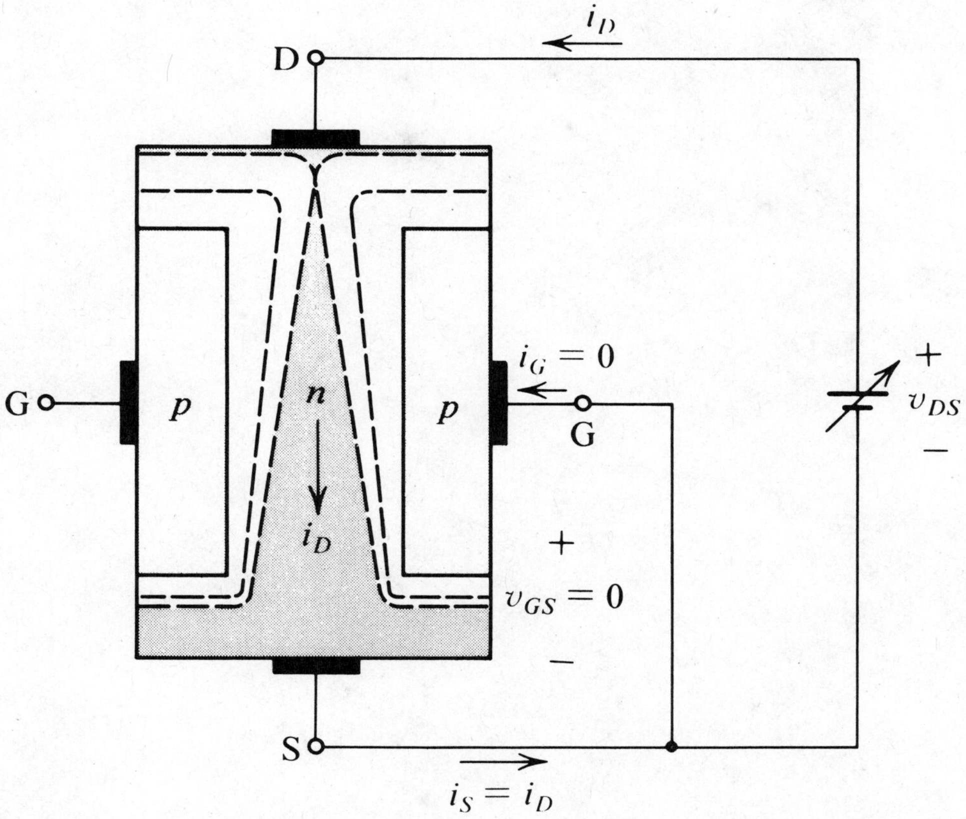

i_D
D
G
p
n
p
$i_G = 0$
G
v_{DS}
i_D
$v_{GS} = 0$
S
$i_S = i_D$

6.6

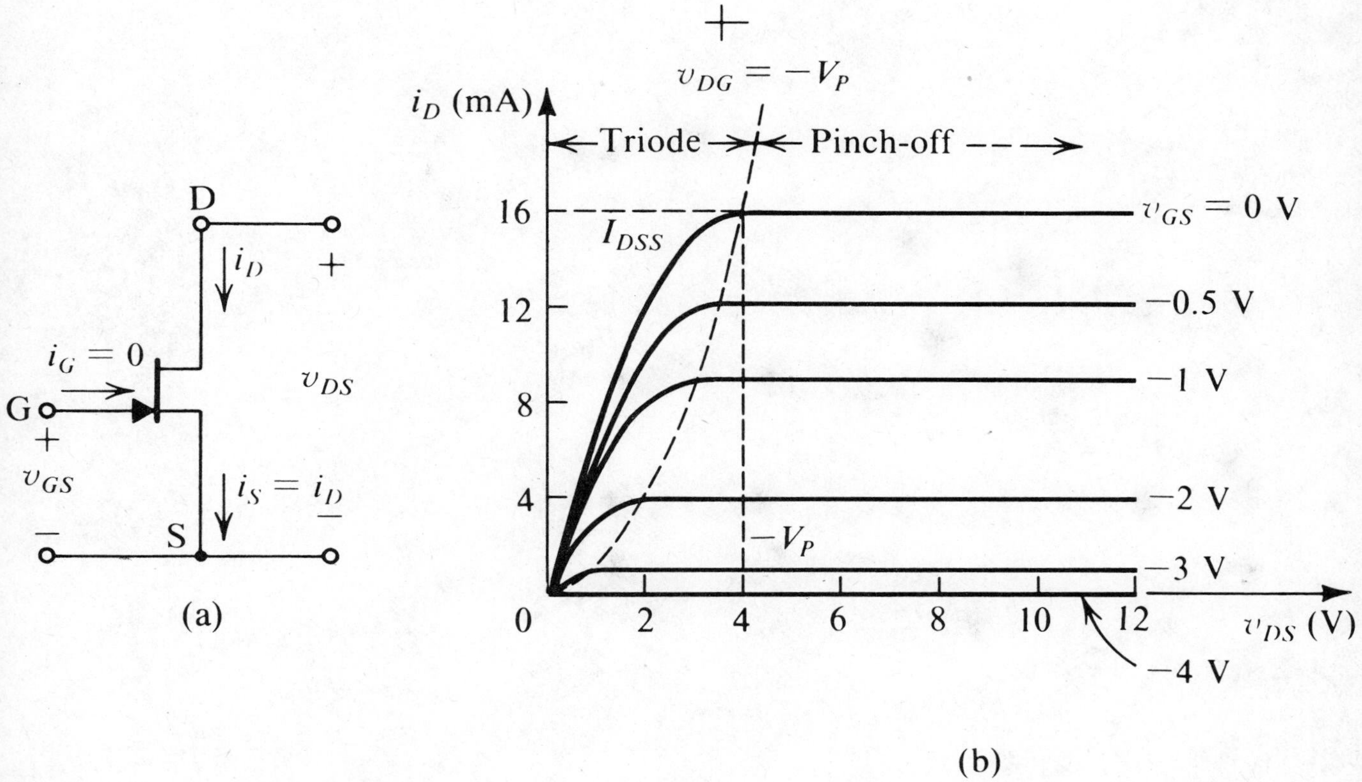
D
i_D
+
$i_G = 0$
v_{DS}
G
+
v_{GS}
$i_S = i_D$
−
S
−
(a)
+
$v_{DG} = -V_P$
i_D (mA)
Triode
Pinch-off
16
12
8
4
0
I_{DSS}
$v_{GS} = 0$ V
−0.5 V
−1 V
−2 V
−3 V
−4 V
$-V_P$
2
4
6
8
10
12
v_{DS} (V)
(b)

6.7

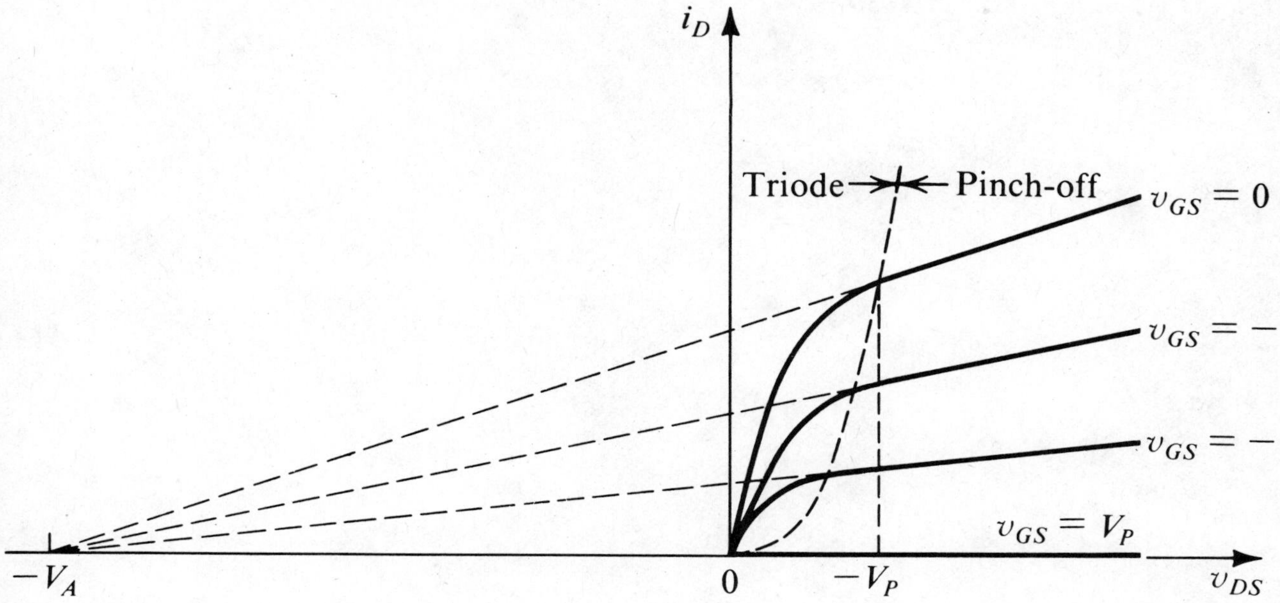

i_D
Triode
Pinch-off
$v_{GS} = 0$
$v_{GS} = -V_1$
$v_{GS} = -V_2$
$v_{GS} = V_P$
$-V_A$
0
$-V_P$
v_{DS}

6.10

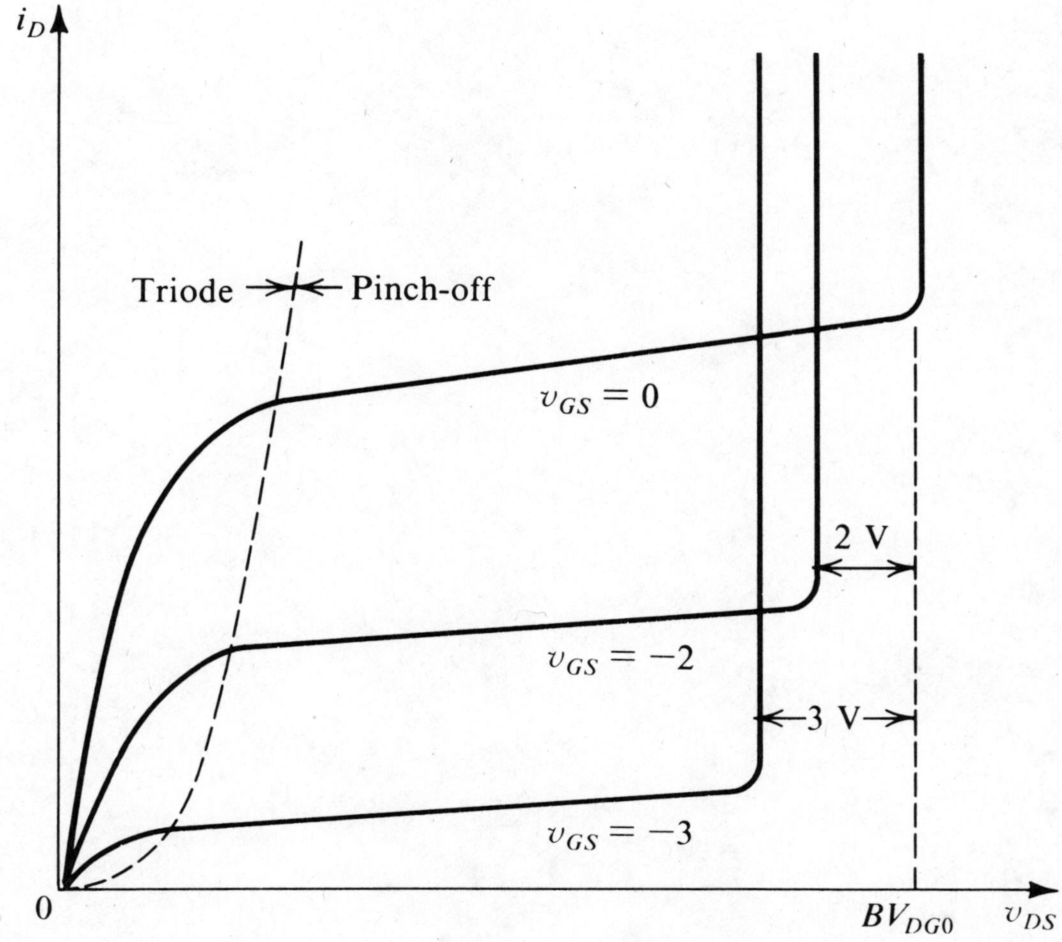

i_D
Triode
Pinch-off
$v_{GS} = 0$
2 V
$v_{GS} = -2$
3 V
$v_{GS} = -3$
0
BV_{DG0}
v_{DS}

6.11

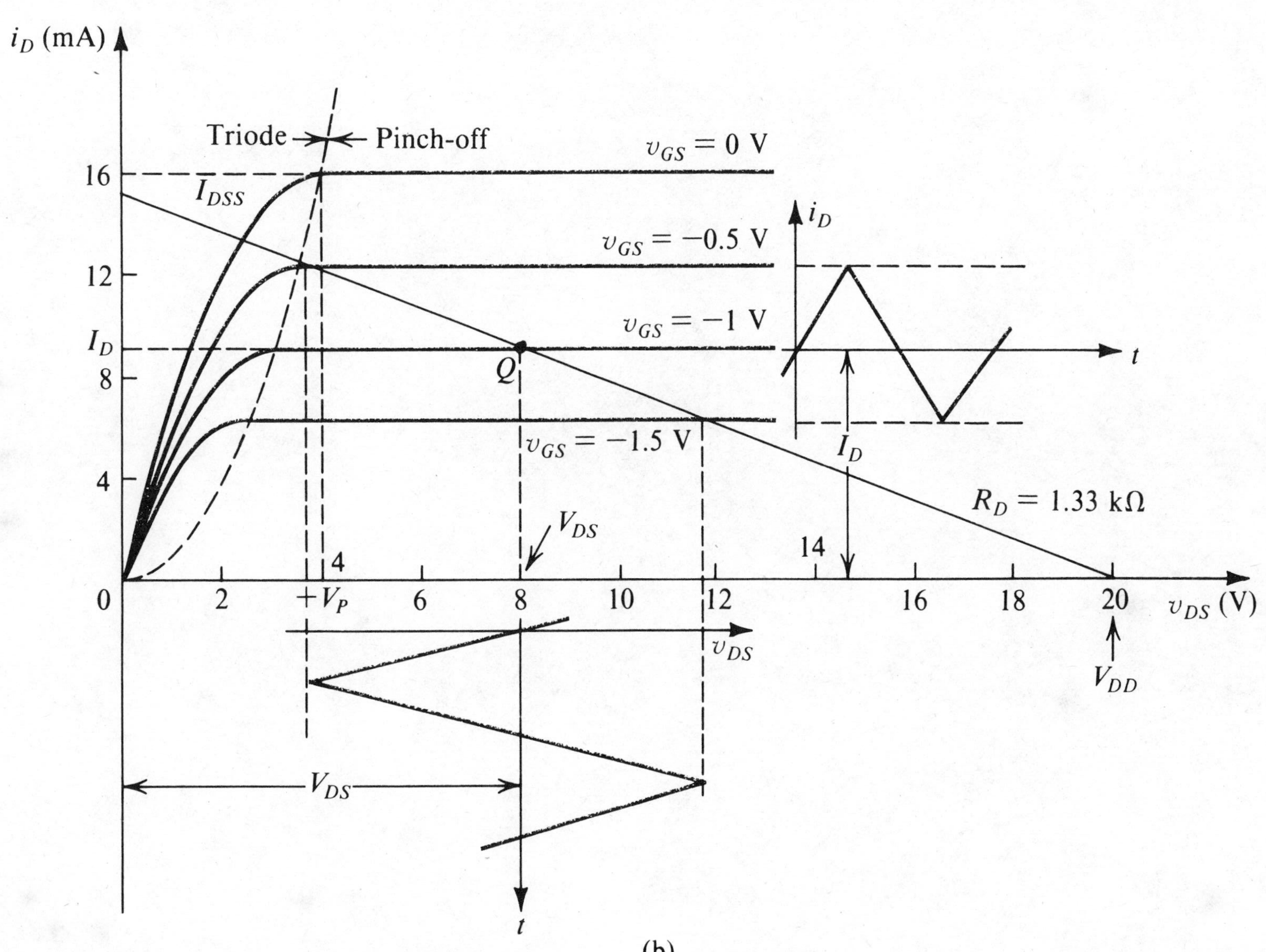

i_D (mA)
Triode
Pinch-off
$v_{GS} = 0$ V
I_{DSS}
$v_{GS} = -0.5$ V
$v_{GS} = -1$ V
$v_{GS} = -1.5$ V
i_D
t
I_D
Q
$R_D = 1.33$ kΩ
V_{DS}
16
12
8
4
0
2
4
$+V_P$
6
8
10
12
14
16
18
20
v_{DS} (V)
V_{DD}
v_{DS}
t

(b)

6.18

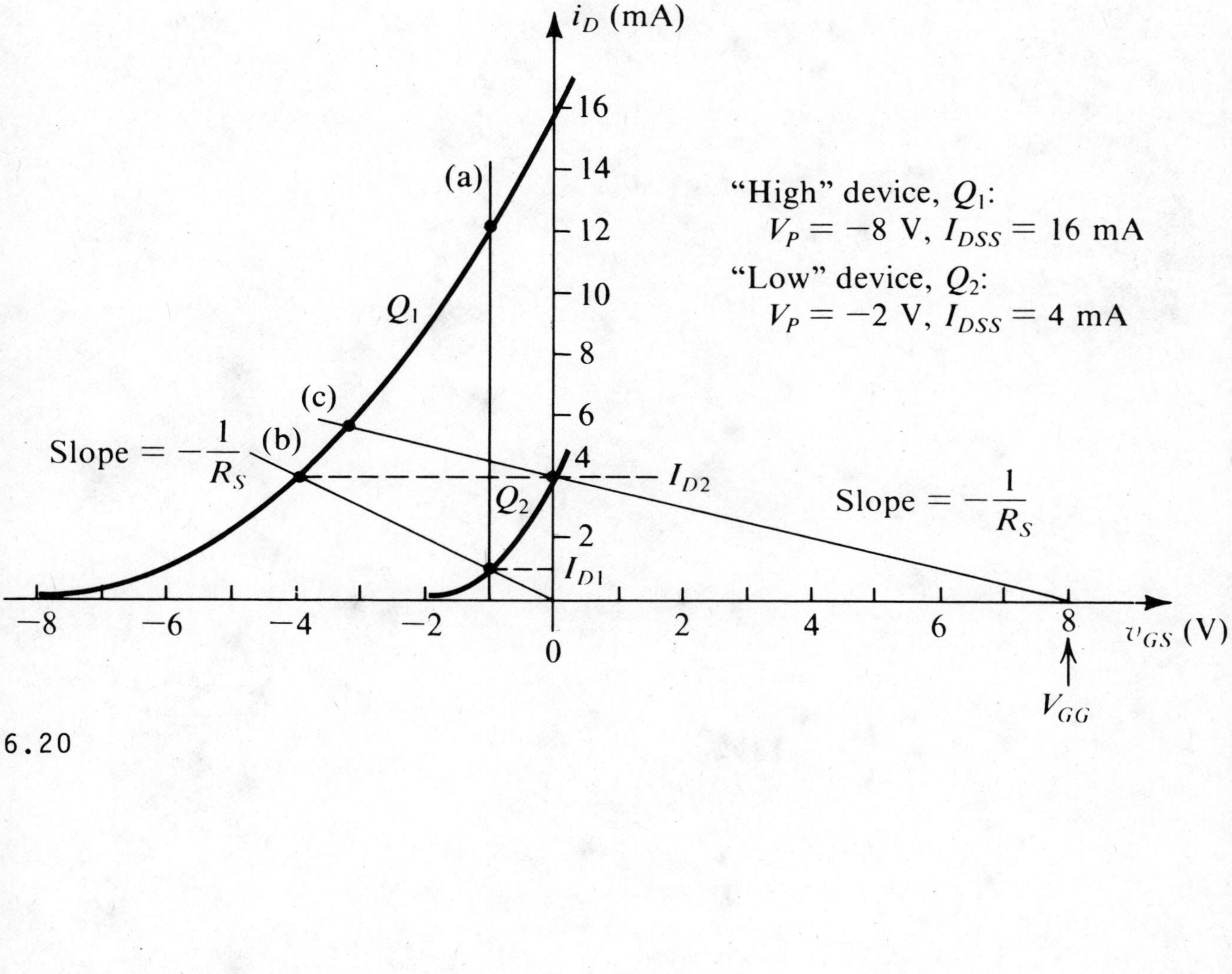

i_D (mA)
16
14
12
10
8
6
4
2
(a)
(b)
(c)
Q_1
Q_2
Slope $= -\frac{1}{R_S}$
I_{D2}
I_{D1}
"High" device, Q_1:
$V_P = -8$ V, $I_{DSS} = 16$ mA
"Low" device, Q_2:
$V_P = -2$ V, $I_{DSS} = 4$ mA
Slope $= -\frac{1}{R_S}$
−8
−6
−4
−2
0
2
4
6
8
v_{GS} (V)
V_{GG}

6.20

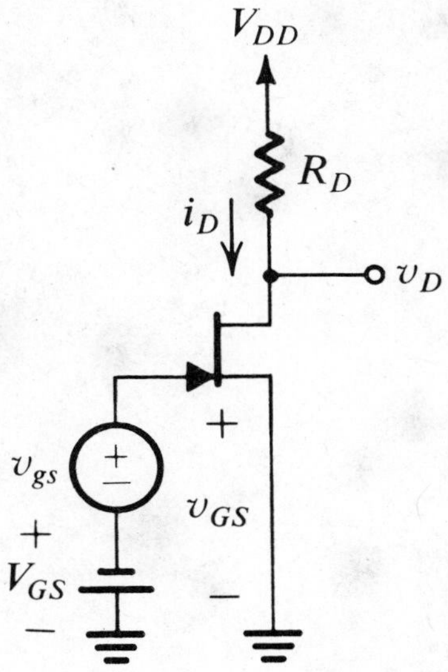

V_{DD}
R_D
i_D
v_D
v_{gs}
+
V_{GS}
−
+
v_{GS}
−

6.23

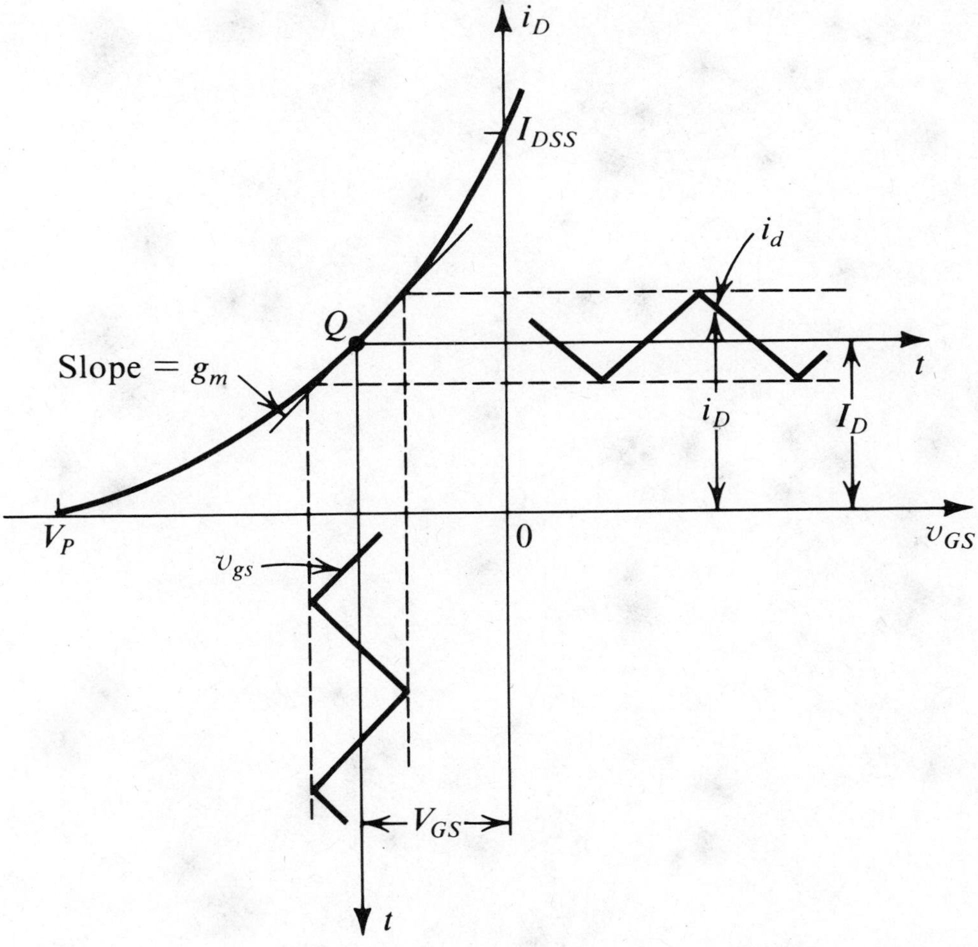

i_D
I_{DSS}
i_d
Q
Slope = g_m
t
i_D
I_D
V_P
0
v_{GS}
v_{gs}
V_{GS}
t

6.24

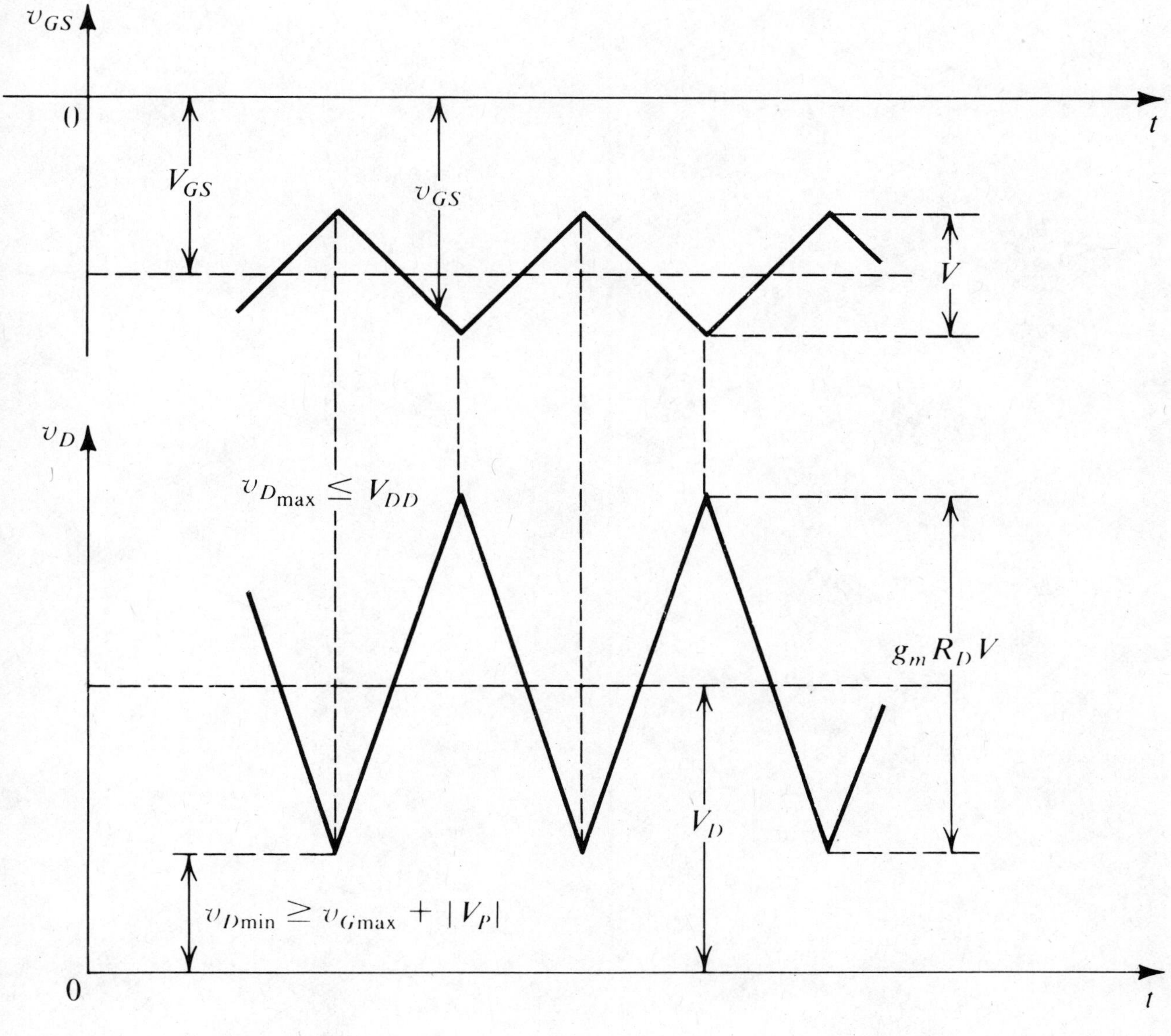

6.25

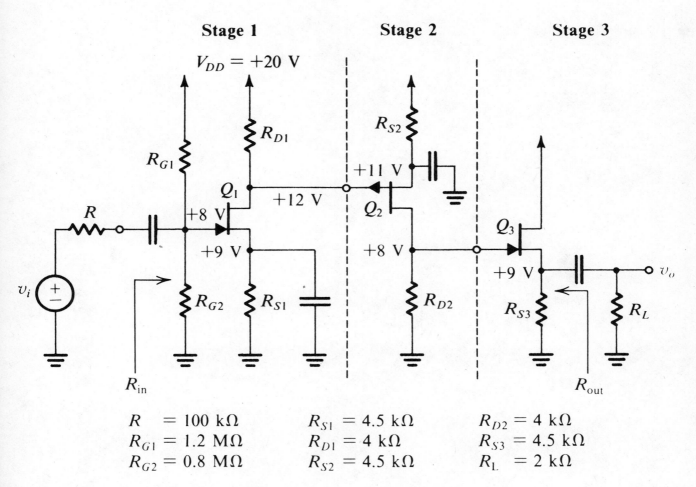

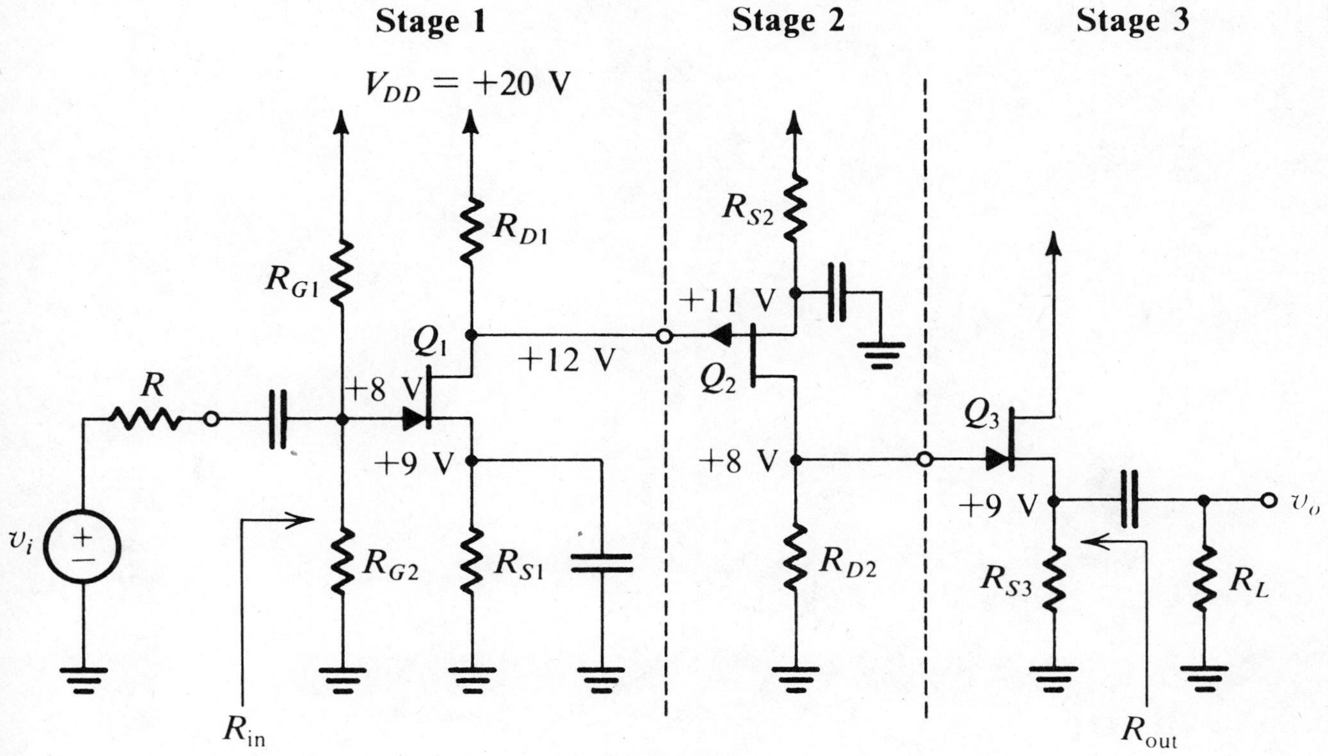

R = 100 kΩ
R_{G1} = 1.2 MΩ
R_{G2} = 0.8 MΩ

R_{S1} = 4.5 kΩ
R_{D1} = 4 kΩ
R_{S2} = 4.5 kΩ

R_{D2} = 4 kΩ
R_{S3} = 4.5 kΩ
R_L = 2 kΩ

All capacitances very large

6.34

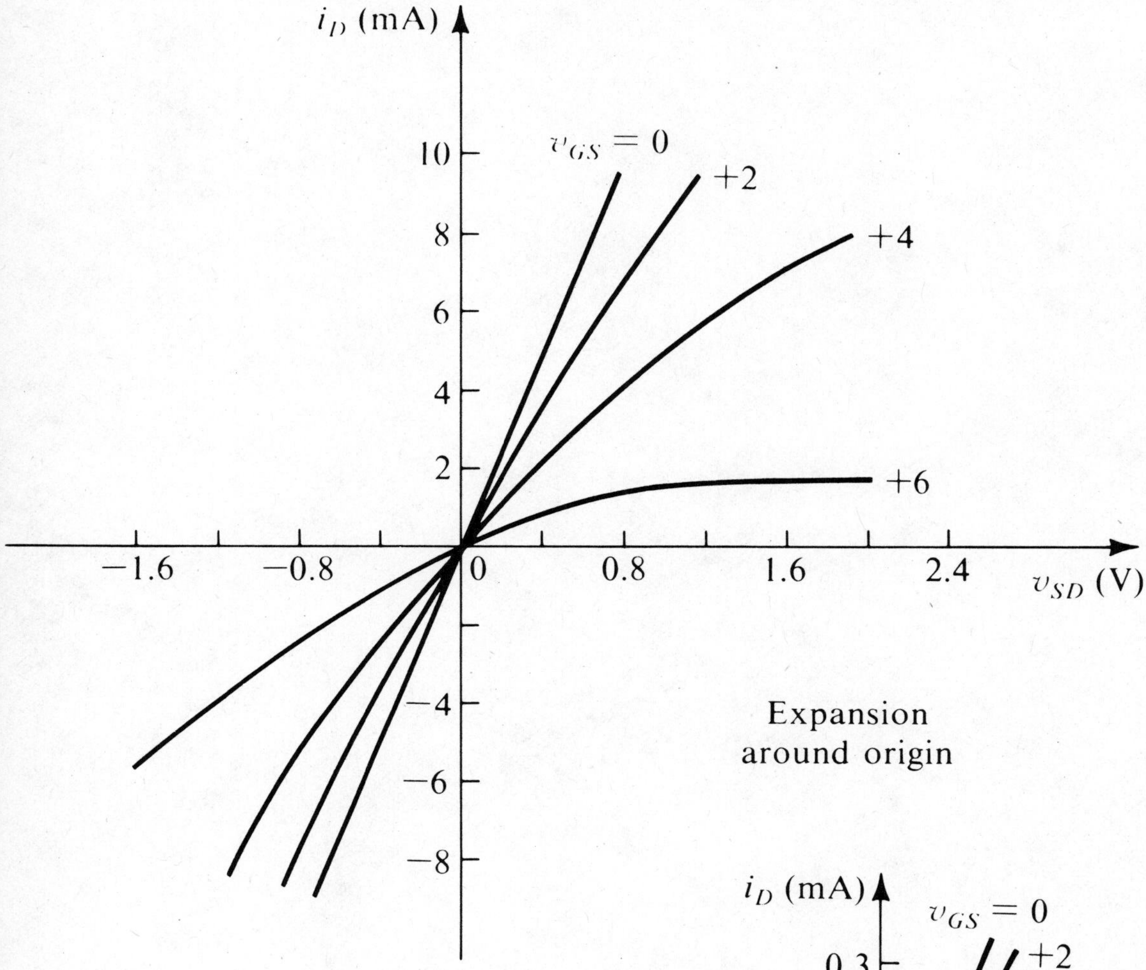

Expansion around origin

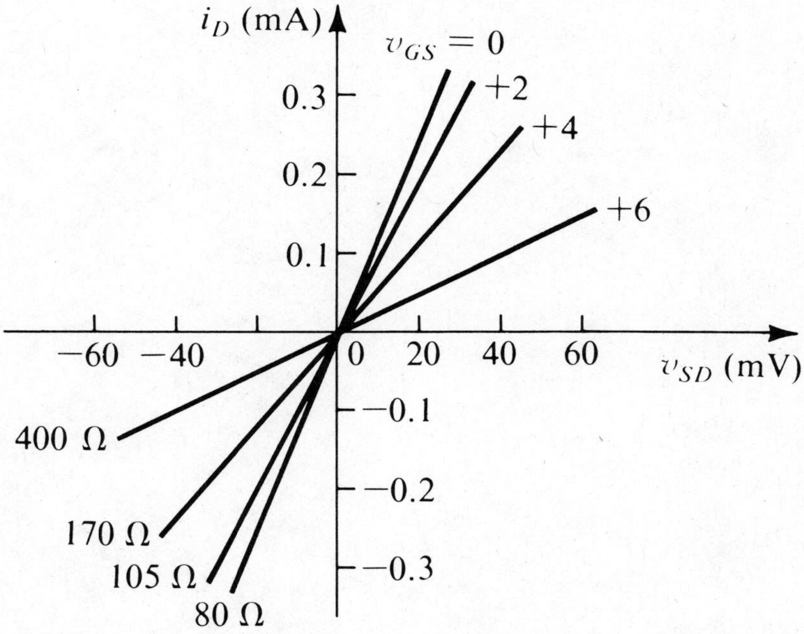

6.35

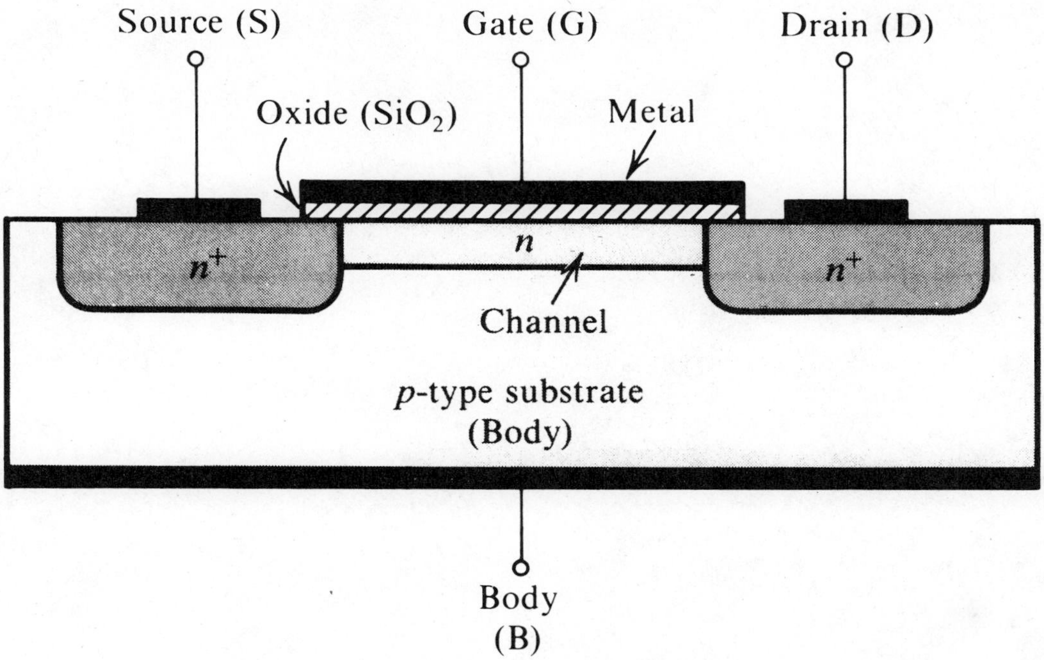
Source (S)
Gate (G)
Drain (D)
Oxide (SiO_2)
Metal
n^+
n
n^+
Channel
p-type substrate
(Body)
Body
(B)

7.1

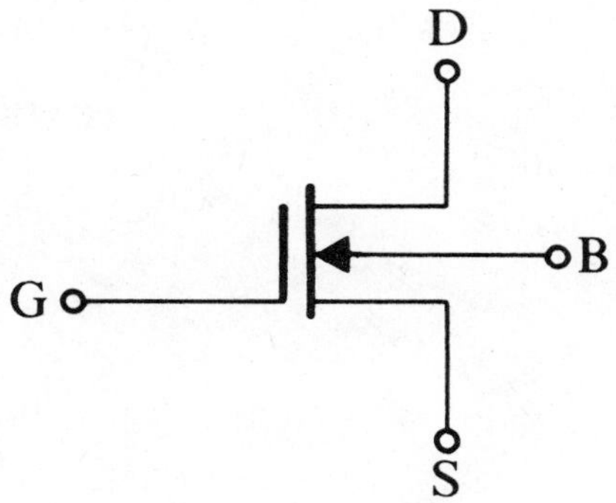
D
B
G
S

7.2

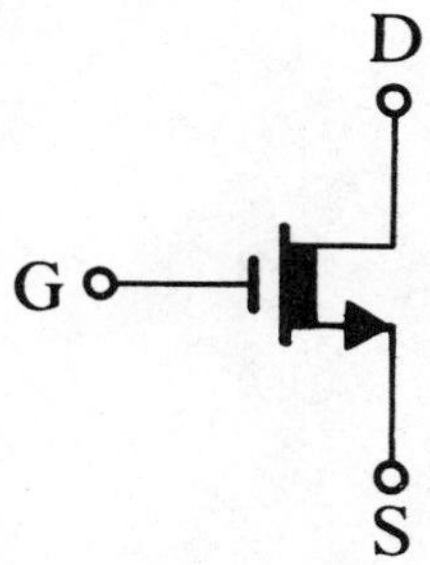
D
G
S

7.3

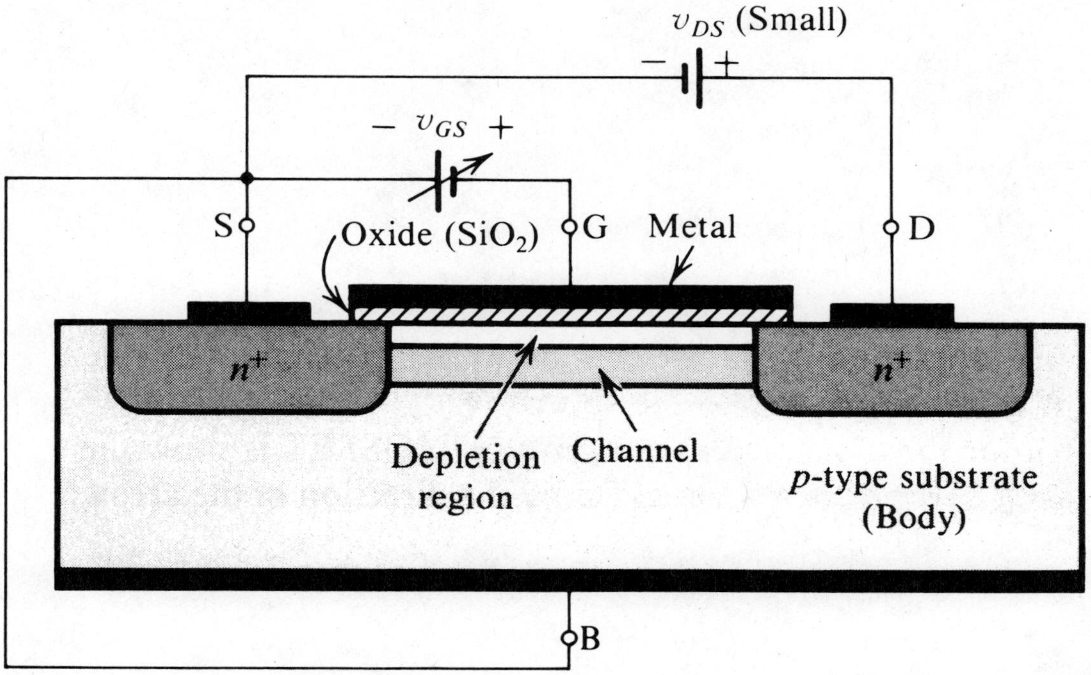

v_{DS} (Small)
− +
− v_{GS} +
S
G
D
Oxide (SiO_2)
Metal
n^+
n^+
Depletion region
Channel
p-type substrate (Body)
B

7.4

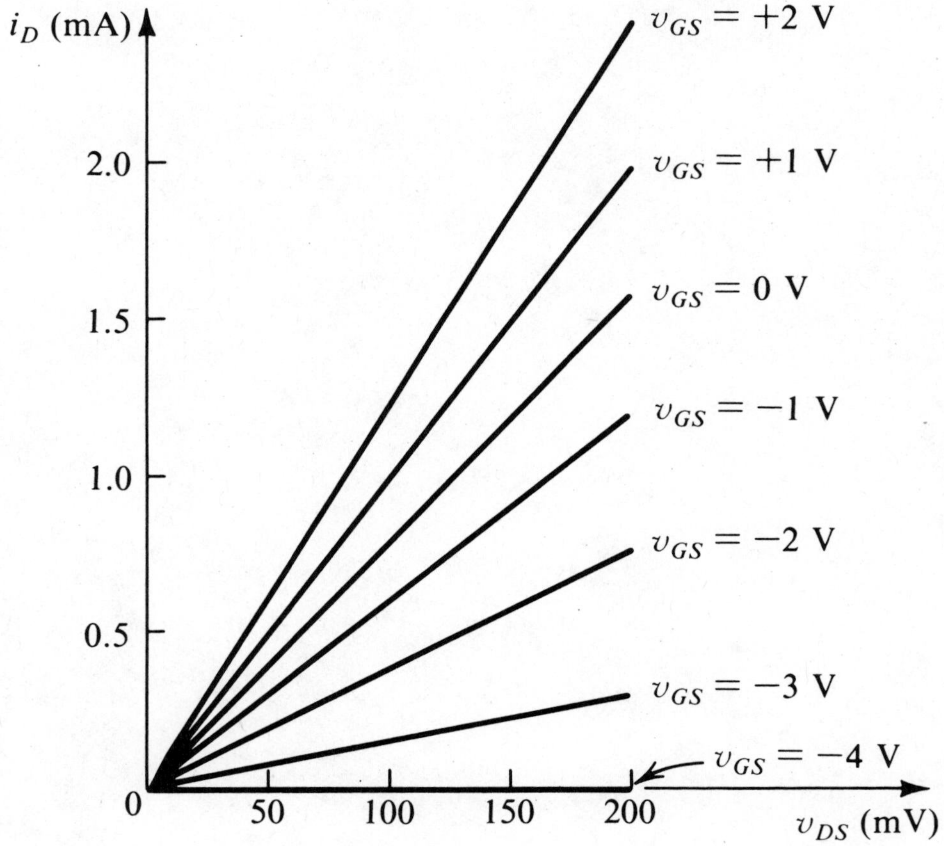

i_D (mA)
2.0
1.5
1.0
0.5
0
50
100
150
200
v_{DS} (mV)
$v_{GS} = +2$ V
$v_{GS} = +1$ V
$v_{GS} = 0$ V
$v_{GS} = -1$ V
$v_{GS} = -2$ V
$v_{GS} = -3$ V
$v_{GS} = -4$ V

7.5

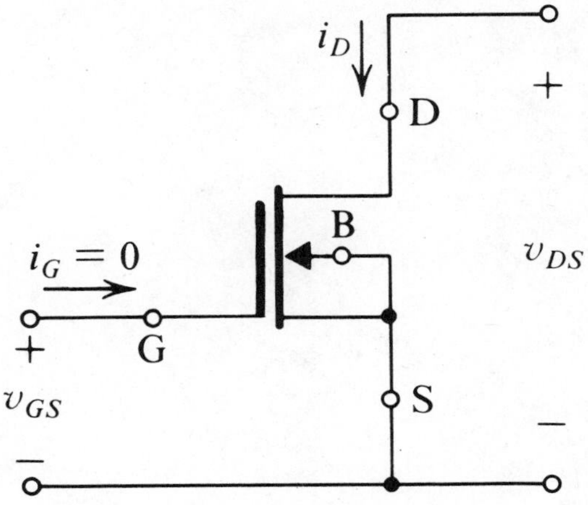

i_D
D
B
$i_G = 0$
v_{DS}
+
G
S
v_{GS}
−

(a)

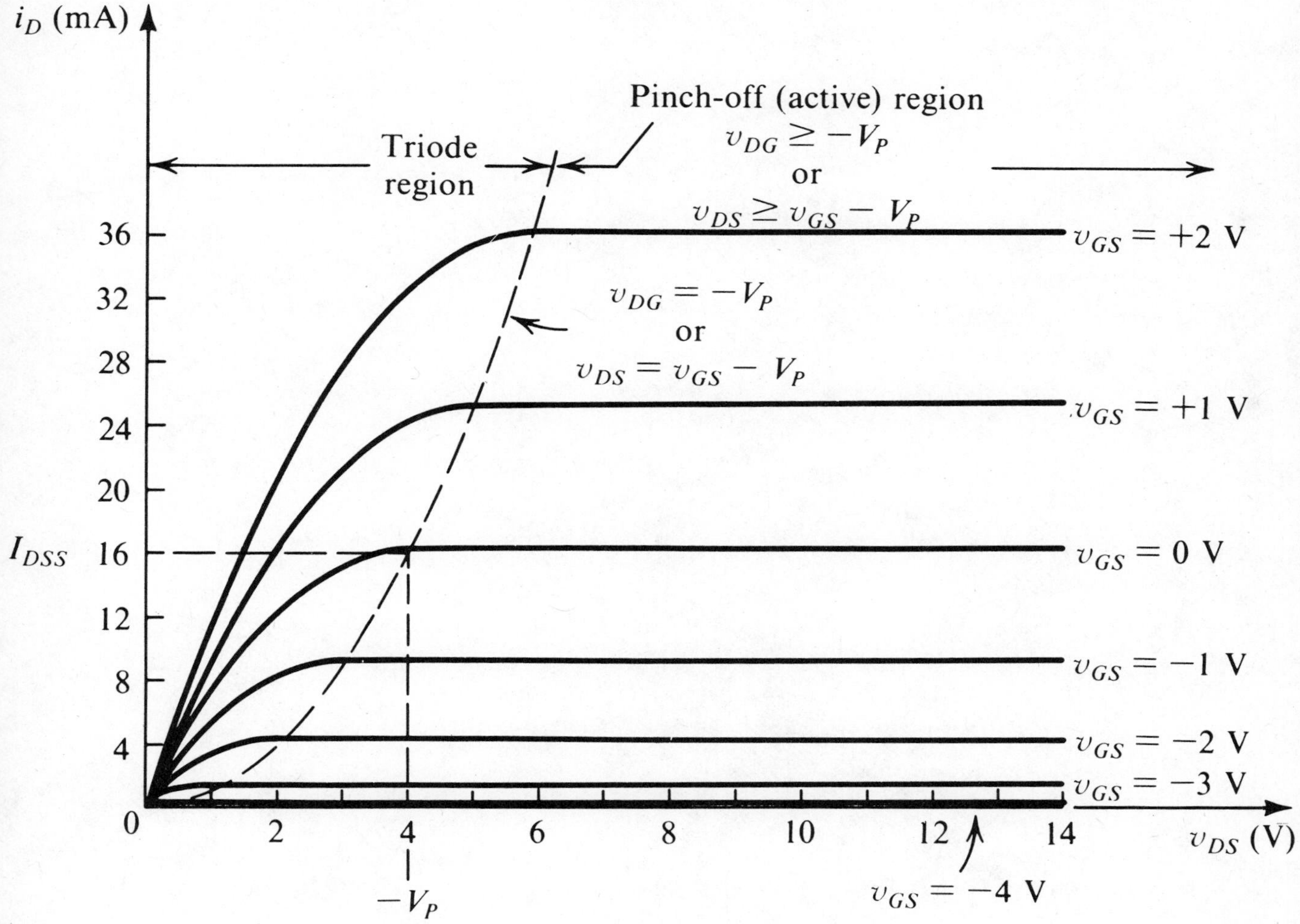

i_D (mA)
Pinch-off (active) region
$v_{DG} \geq -V_P$
or
$v_{DS} \geq v_{GS} - V_P$
Triode
region
36
32
28
24
20
I_{DSS} 16
12
8
4
0
2
4
6
8
10
12
14
v_{DS} (V)
$v_{DG} = -V_P$
or
$v_{DS} = v_{GS} - V_P$
$v_{GS} = +2$ V
$v_{GS} = +1$ V
$v_{GS} = 0$ V
$v_{GS} = -1$ V
$v_{GS} = -2$ V
$v_{GS} = -3$ V
$v_{GS} = -4$ V
$-V_P$

(b)

7.6

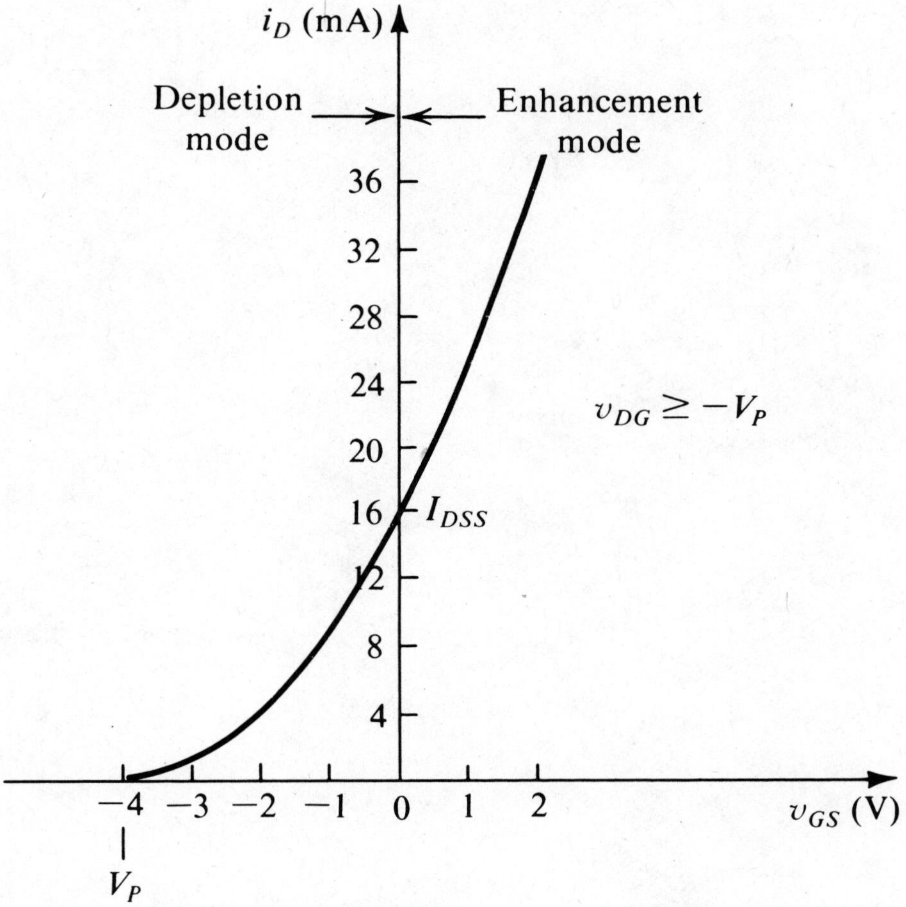
i_D (mA)
Depletion mode
Enhancement mode
36
32
28
24
20
16
12
8
4
I_{DSS}
$v_{DG} \geq -V_P$
−4
−3
−2
−1
0
1
2
v_{GS} (V)
V_P

7.7

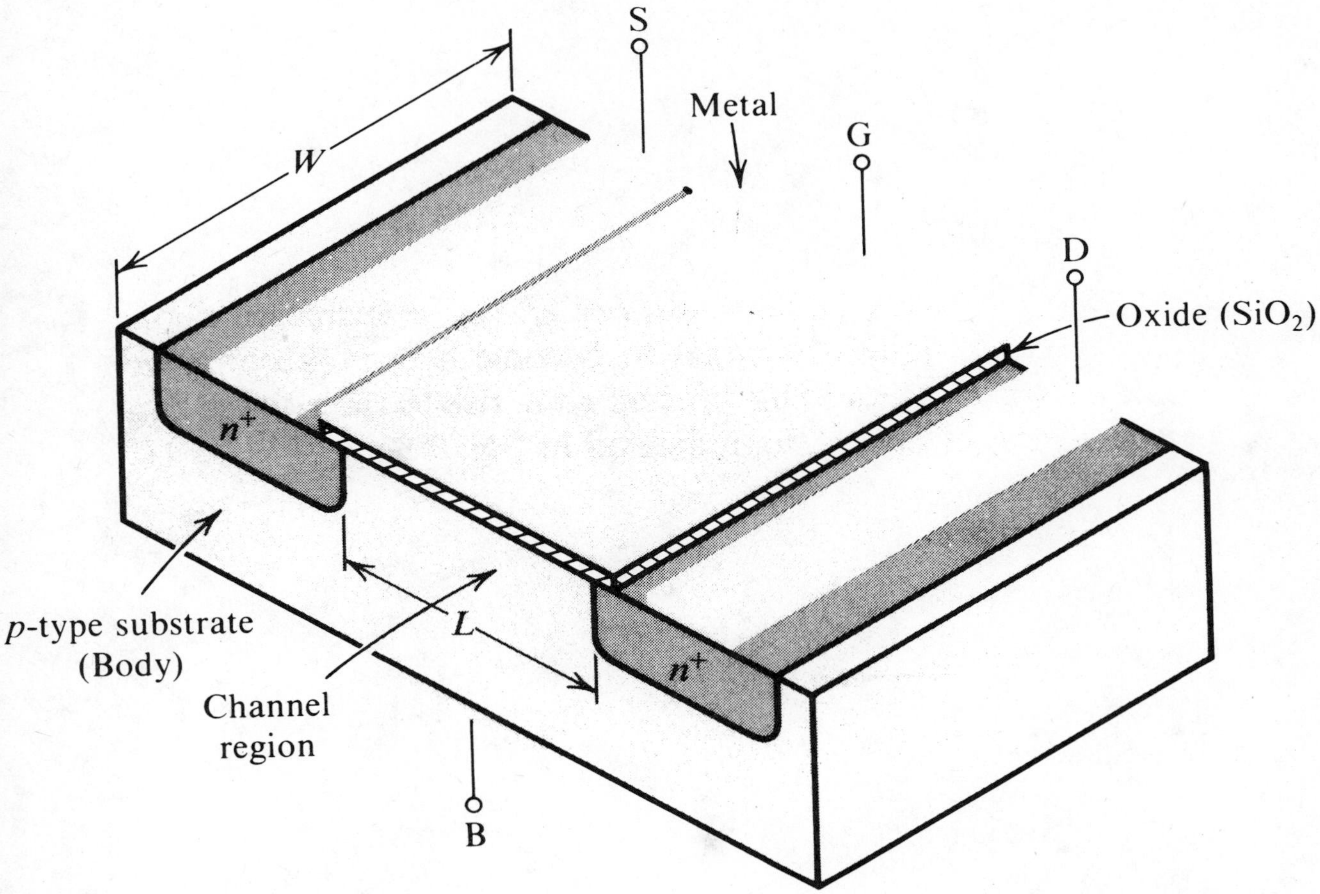
S
Metal
G
W
D
Oxide (SiO_2)
n^+
n^+
L
p-type substrate
(Body)
Channel
region
B

(a)

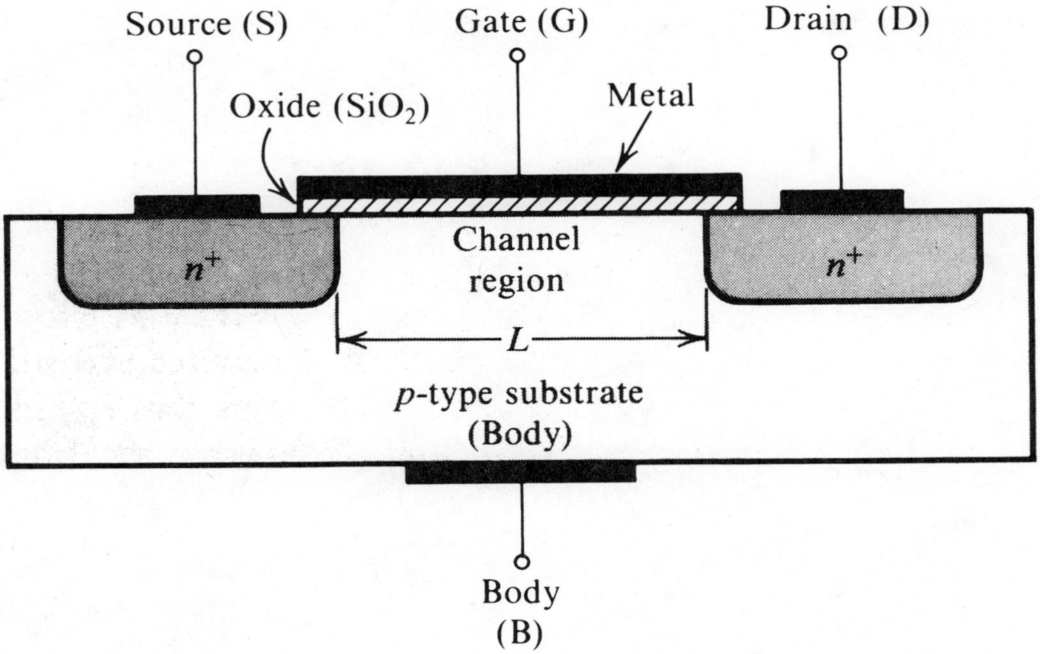
Source (S)
Gate (G)
Drain (D)
Oxide (SiO_2)
Metal
n^+
Channel
region
n^+
L
p-type substrate
(Body)
Body
(B)

(b)

7.9

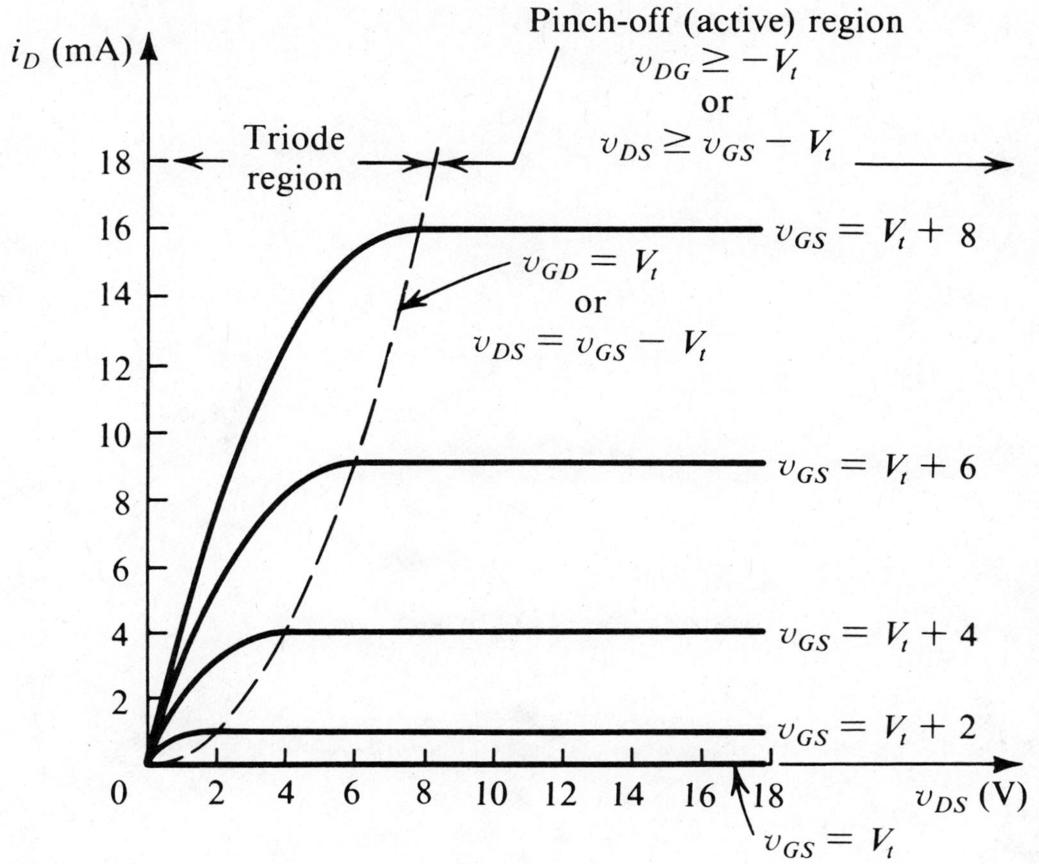
Pinch-off (active) region
$v_{DG} \geq -V_t$
or
$v_{DS} \geq v_{GS} - V_t$
i_D (mA)
Triode
region
$v_{GS} = V_t + 8$
$v_{GD} = V_t$
or
$v_{DS} = v_{GS} - V_t$
$v_{GS} = V_t + 6$
$v_{GS} = V_t + 4$
$v_{GS} = V_t + 2$
$v_{GS} = V_t$
v_{DS} (V)
0
2
4
6
8
10
12
14
16
18

7.10

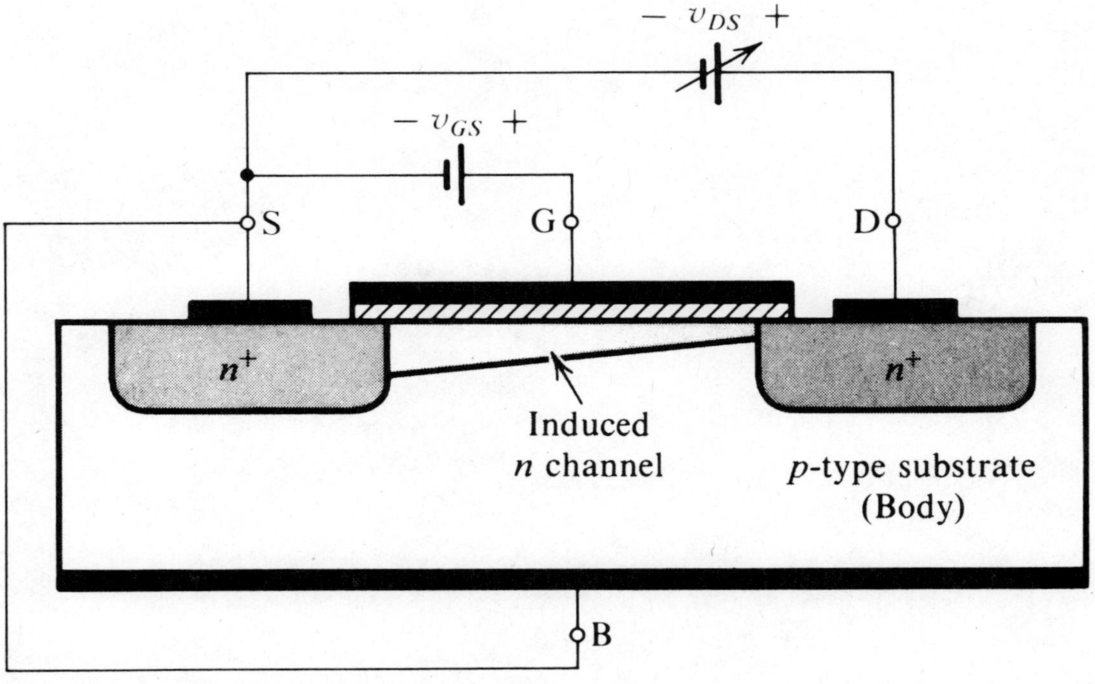
$- v_{DS} +$
$- v_{GS} +$
S
G
D
n^+
n^+
Induced
n channel
p-type substrate
(Body)
B

7.11

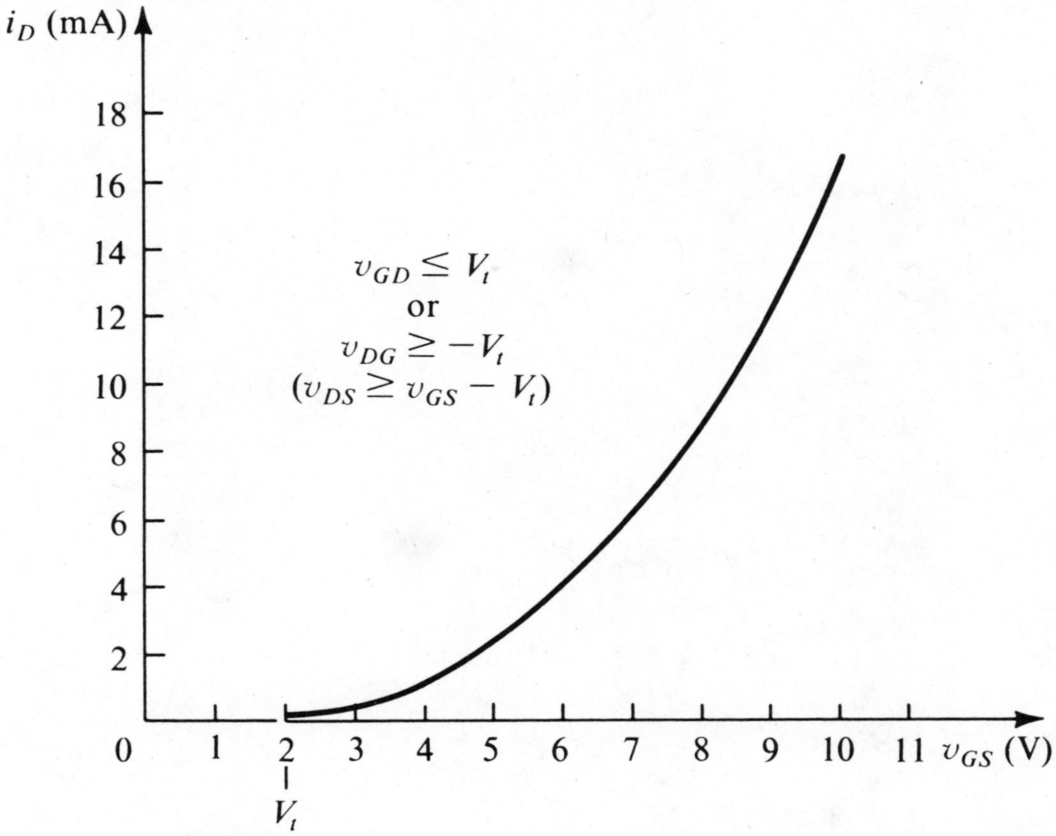

i_D (mA)
18
16
14
12
10
8
6
4
2
0
1
2
3
4
5
6
7
8
9
10
11
v_{GS} (V)
V_t
$v_{GD} \leq V_t$
or
$v_{DG} \geq -V_t$
$(v_{DS} \geq v_{GS} - V_t)$

7.12

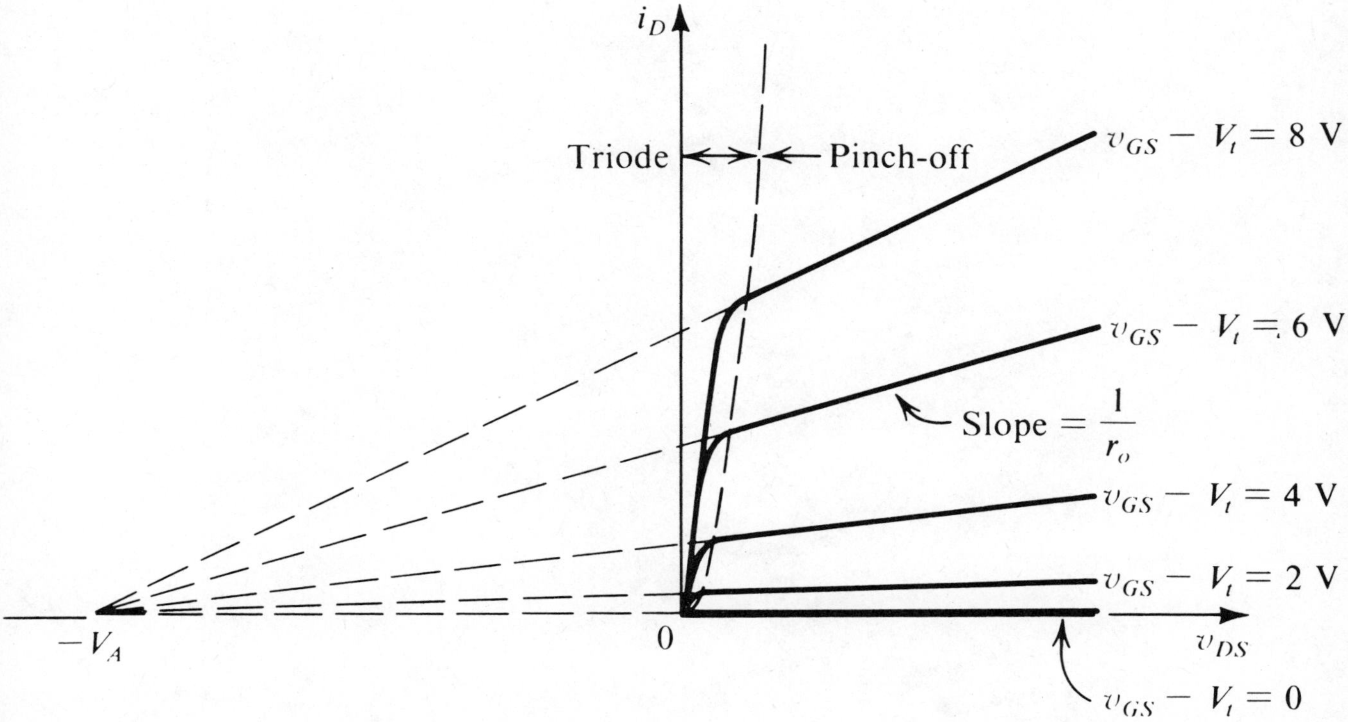

i_D
Triode
Pinch-off
$v_{GS} - V_t = 8$ V
$v_{GS} - V_t = 6$ V
Slope $= \frac{1}{r_o}$
$v_{GS} - V_t = 4$ V
$v_{GS} - V_t = 2$ V
$-V_A$
0
v_{DS}
$v_{GS} - V_t = 0$

7.13

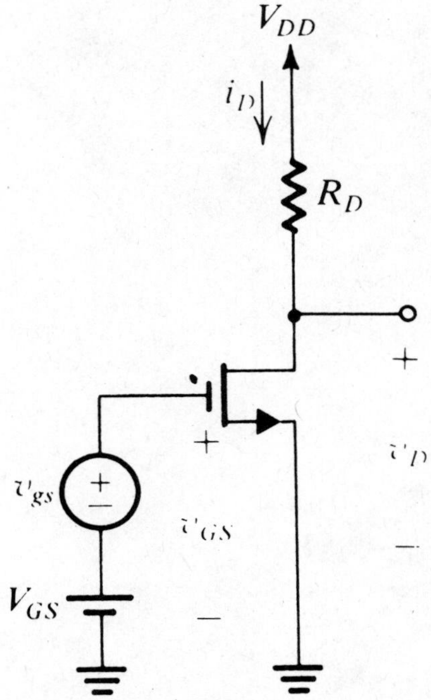

V_{DD}
i_D
R_D
+
v_D
−
+
v_{gs}
v_{GS}
V_{GS}
−

7.25

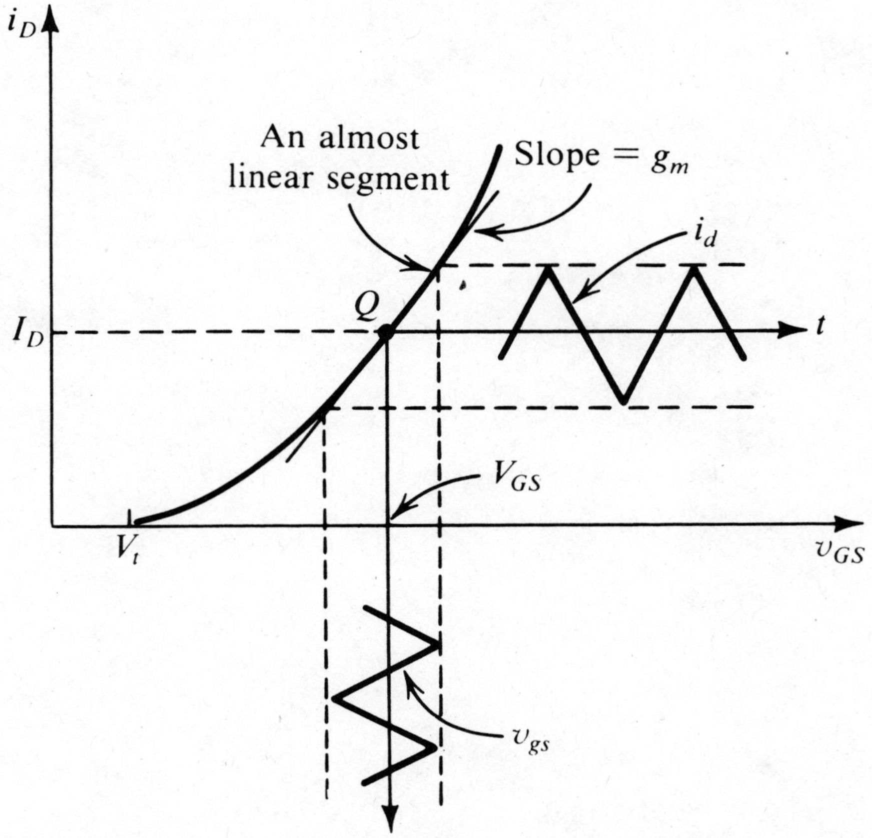

i_D
An almost
linear segment
Slope = g_m
i_d
Q
I_D
t
V_{GS}
V_t
v_{GS}
v_{gs}
t

7.26

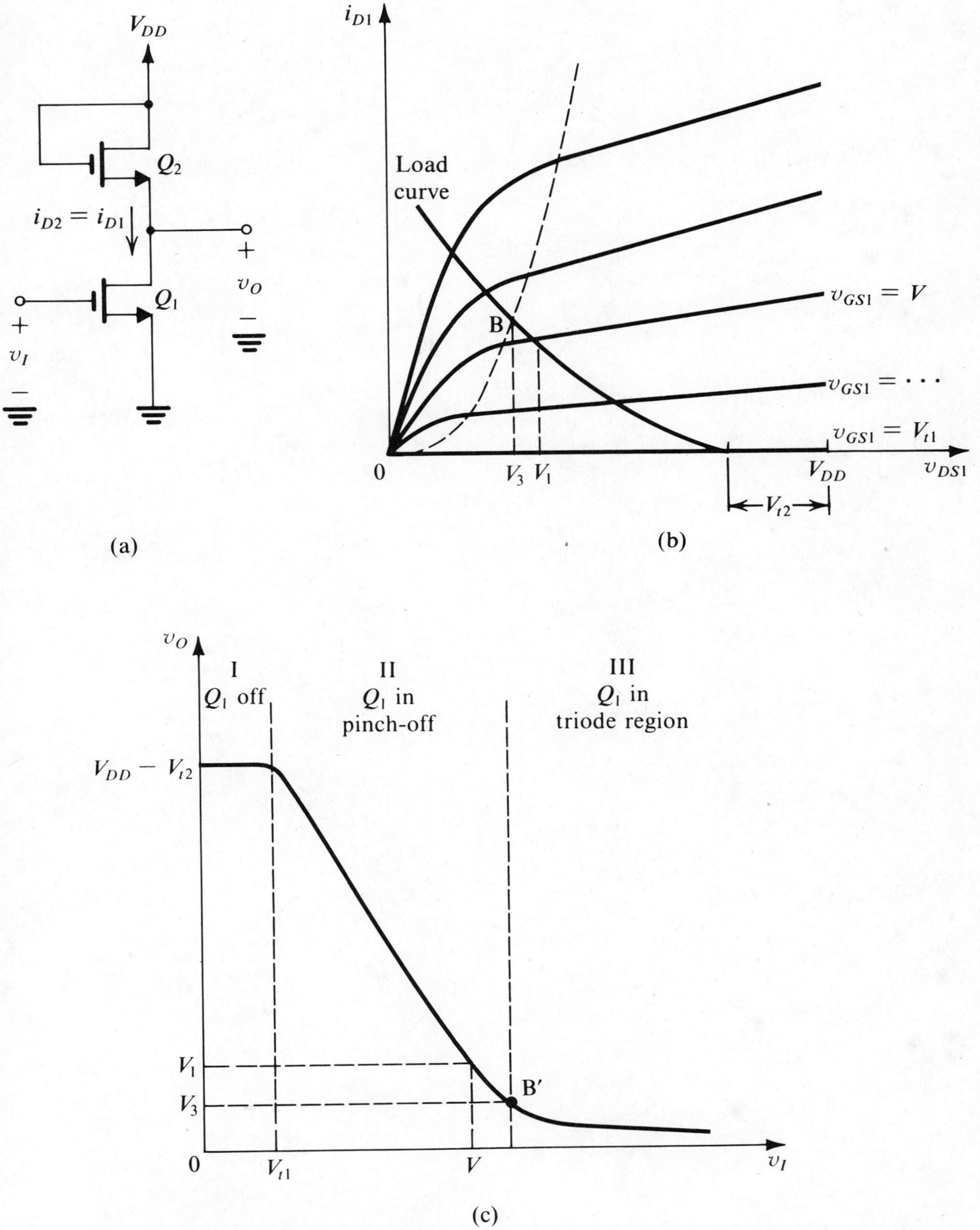

V_{DD}
Q_2
$i_{D2} = i_{D1}$
Q_1
+
v_O
−
+
v_I
−
(a)
i_{D1}
Load
curve
B
$v_{GS1} = V$
$v_{GS1} = \cdots$
$v_{GS1} = V_{t1}$
0
V_3 V_1
V_{DD}
v_{DS1}
V_{t2}
(b)
v_O
I
Q_1 off
II
Q_1 in
pinch-off
III
Q_1 in
triode region
$V_{DD} - V_{t2}$
V_1
V_3
B′
0
V_{t1}
V
v_I
(c)

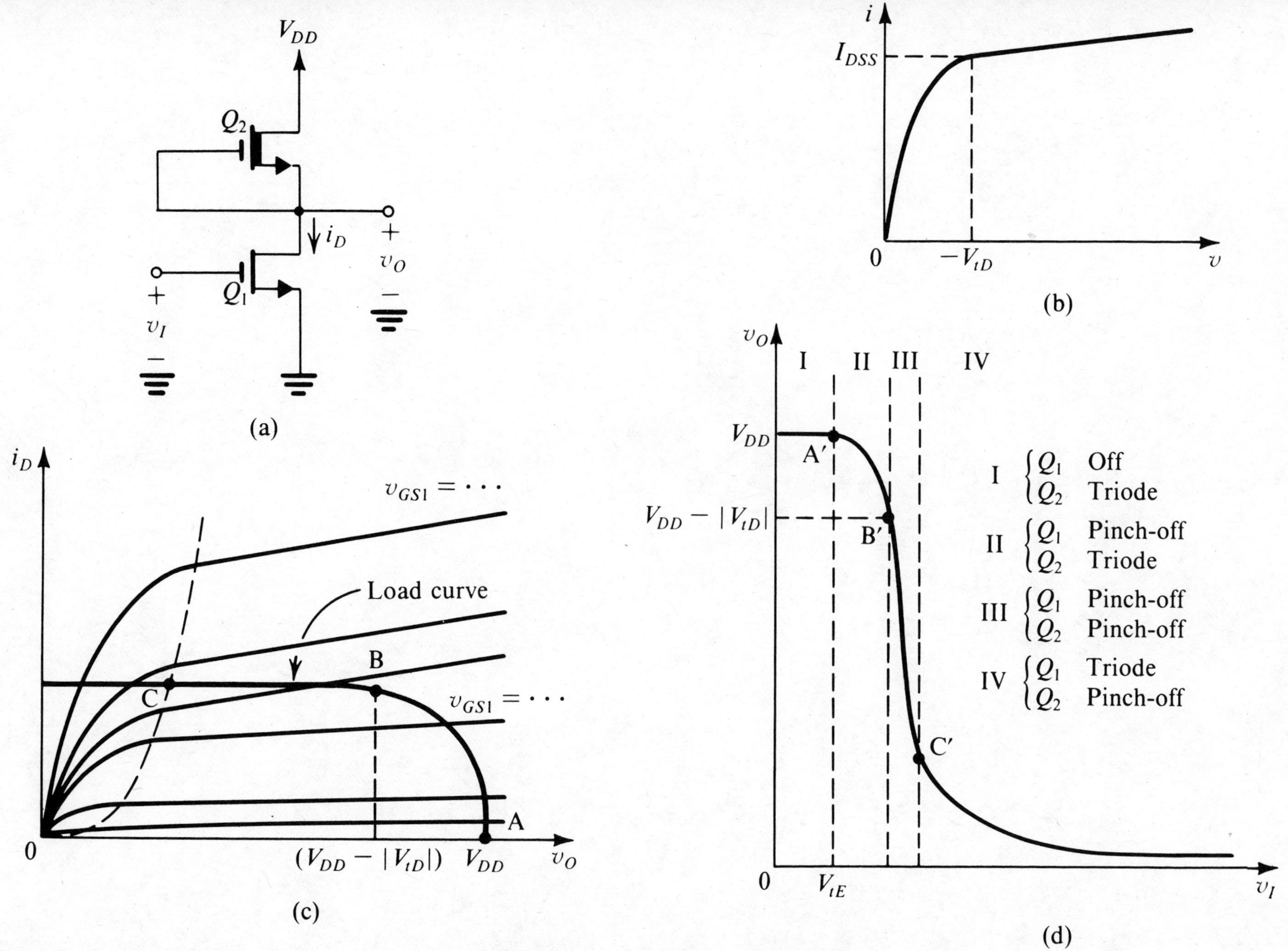

V_{DD}
Q_2
Q_1
i_D
v_I
v_O
(a)
i
I_{DSS}
0
$-V_{tD}$
v
(b)
i_D
$v_{GS1} = \cdots$
Load curve
B
C
$v_{GS1} = \cdots$
A
0
$(V_{DD} - |V_{tD}|)$
V_{DD}
v_O
(c)
v_O
I II III IV
V_{DD}
A′
$V_{DD} - |V_{tD}|$
B′
C′
0
V_{tE}
v_I
I Q_1 Off, Q_2 Triode
II Q_1 Pinch-off, Q_2 Triode
III Q_1 Pinch-off, Q_2 Pinch-off
IV Q_1 Triode, Q_2 Pinch-off
(d)

7.43

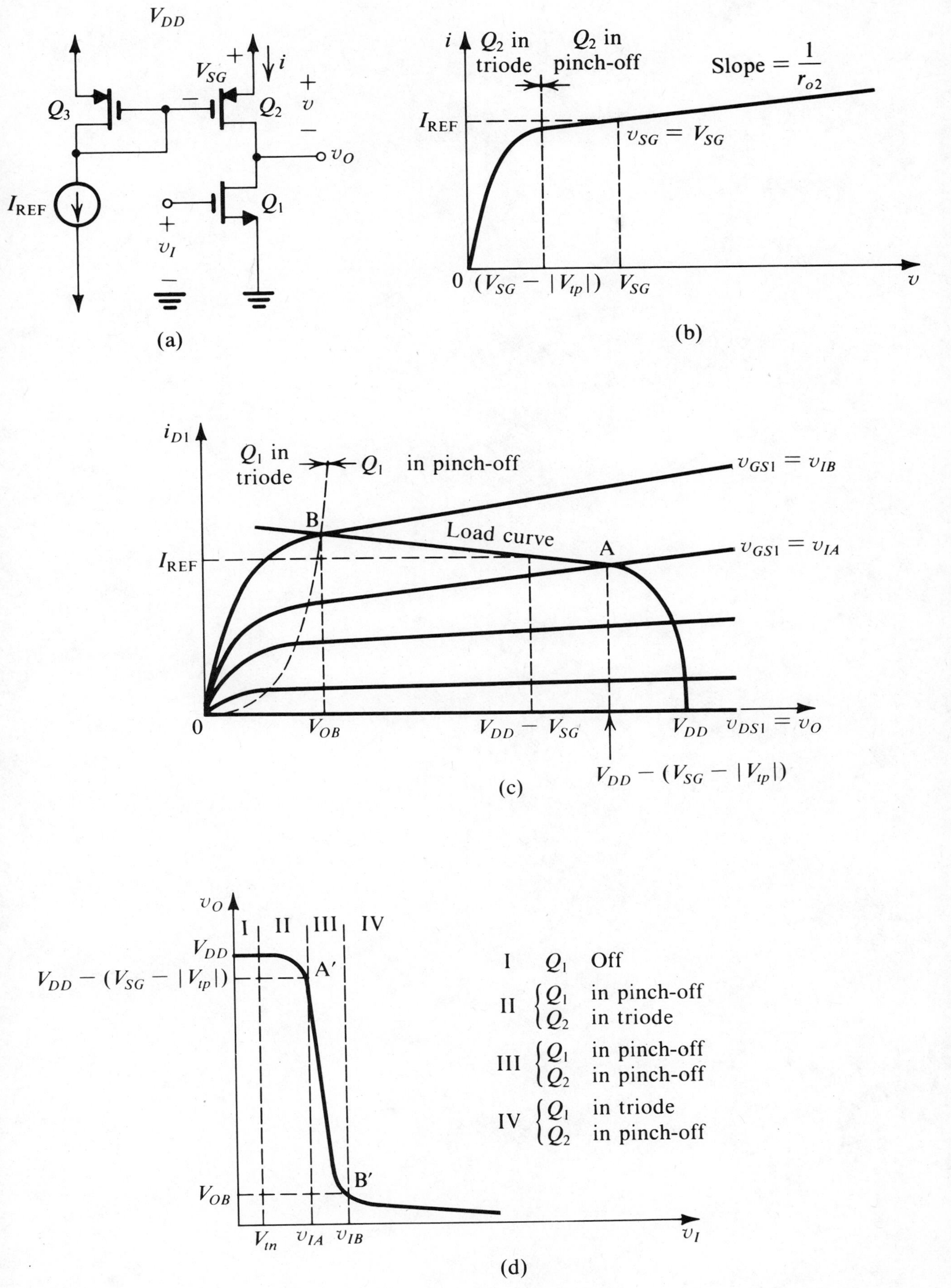
V_{DD}
Q_3
V_{SG}
i
Q_2
v
v_O
I_{REF}
Q_1
v_I
(a)
i
Q_2 in triode
Q_2 in pinch-off
Slope = $\frac{1}{r_{o2}}$
I_{REF}
$v_{SG} = V_{SG}$
0
$(V_{SG} - |V_{tp}|)$
V_{SG}
v
(b)
i_{D1}
Q_1 in triode
Q_1 in pinch-off
$v_{GS1} = v_{IB}$
B
Load curve
A
I_{REF}
$v_{GS1} = v_{IA}$
0
V_{OB}
$V_{DD} - V_{SG}$
V_{DD}
$v_{DS1} = v_O$
$V_{DD} - (V_{SG} - |V_{tp}|)$
(c)
v_O
I
II
III
IV
V_{DD}
$V_{DD} - (V_{SG} - |V_{tp}|)$
A′
B′
V_{OB}
V_{tn}
v_{IA}
v_{IB}
v_I
I Q_1 Off
II Q_1 in pinch-off, Q_2 in triode
III Q_1 in pinch-off, Q_2 in pinch-off
IV Q_1 in triode, Q_2 in pinch-off
(d)

7.46

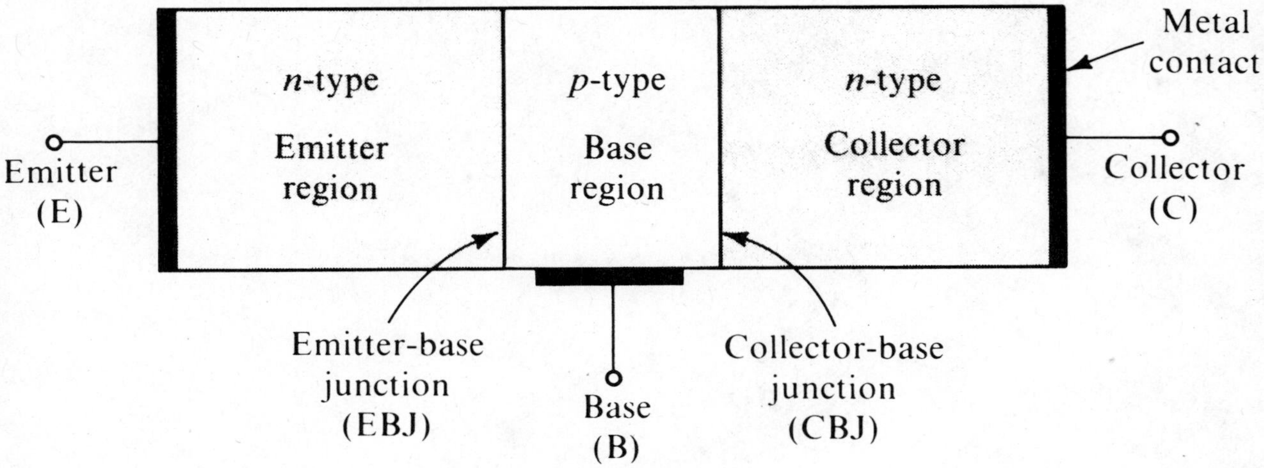
Metal contact
n-type
p-type
n-type
Emitter region
Base region
Collector region
Emitter (E)
Collector (C)
Emitter-base junction (EBJ)
Base (B)
Collector-base junction (CBJ)

8.1

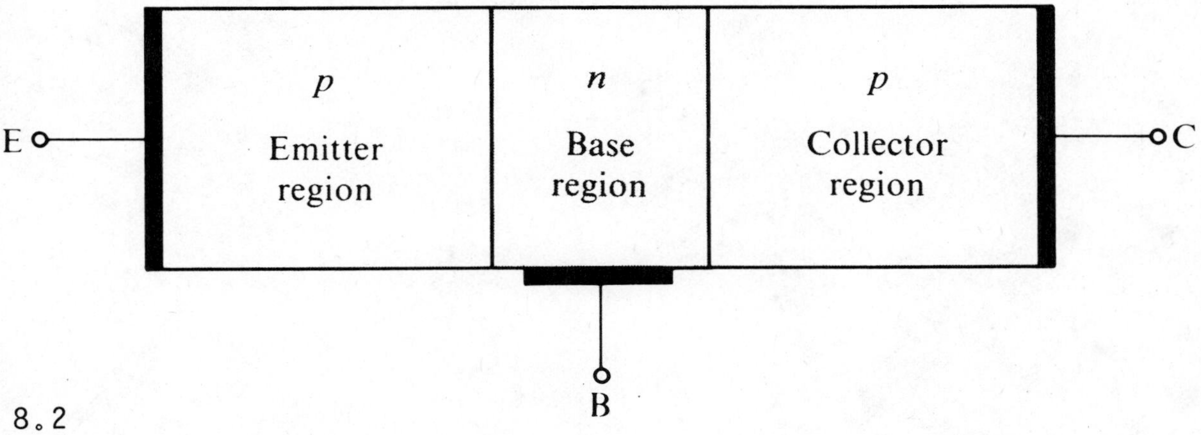
p
n
p
E
Emitter region
Base region
Collector region
C
B

8.2

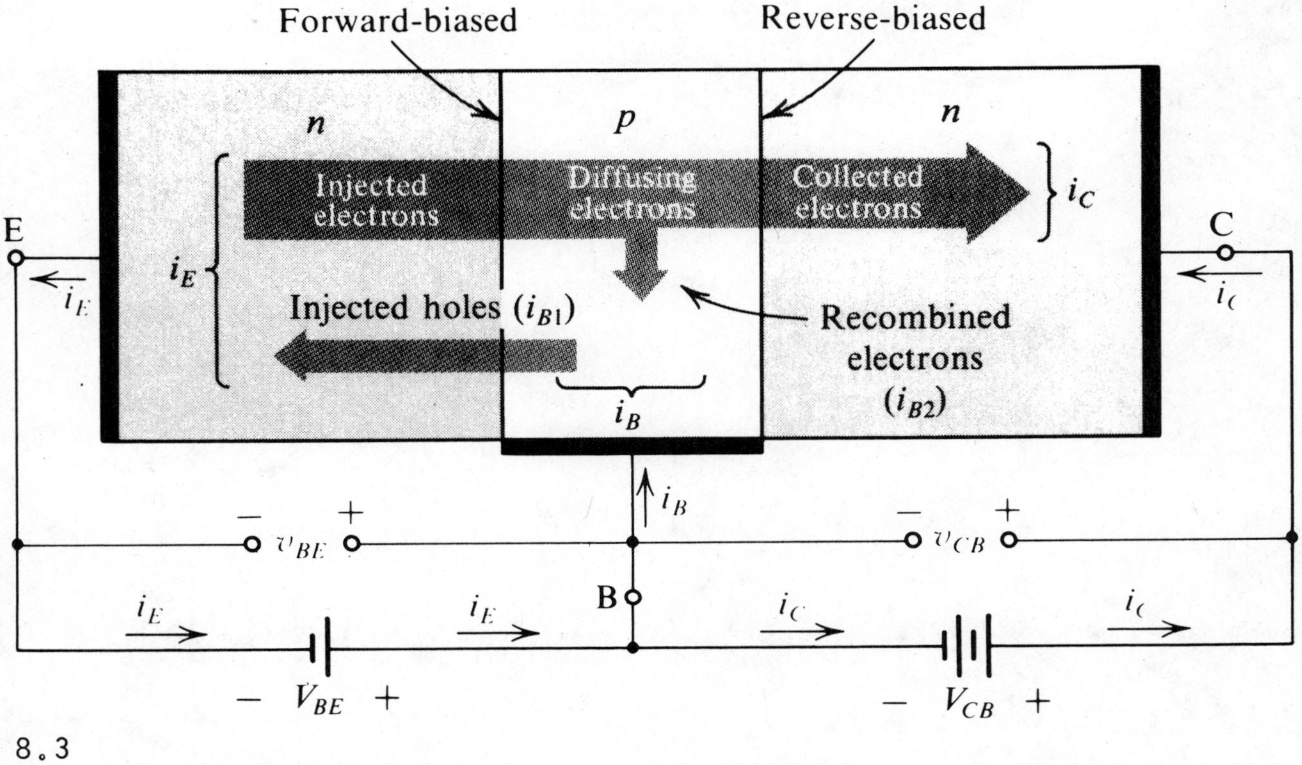
Forward-biased
Reverse-biased
n
p
n
Injected electrons
Diffusing electrons
Collected electrons
iC
E
C
iE
Injected holes (iB1)
Recombined electrons
(iB2)
iB
vBE
vCB
B
VBE
VCB

8.3

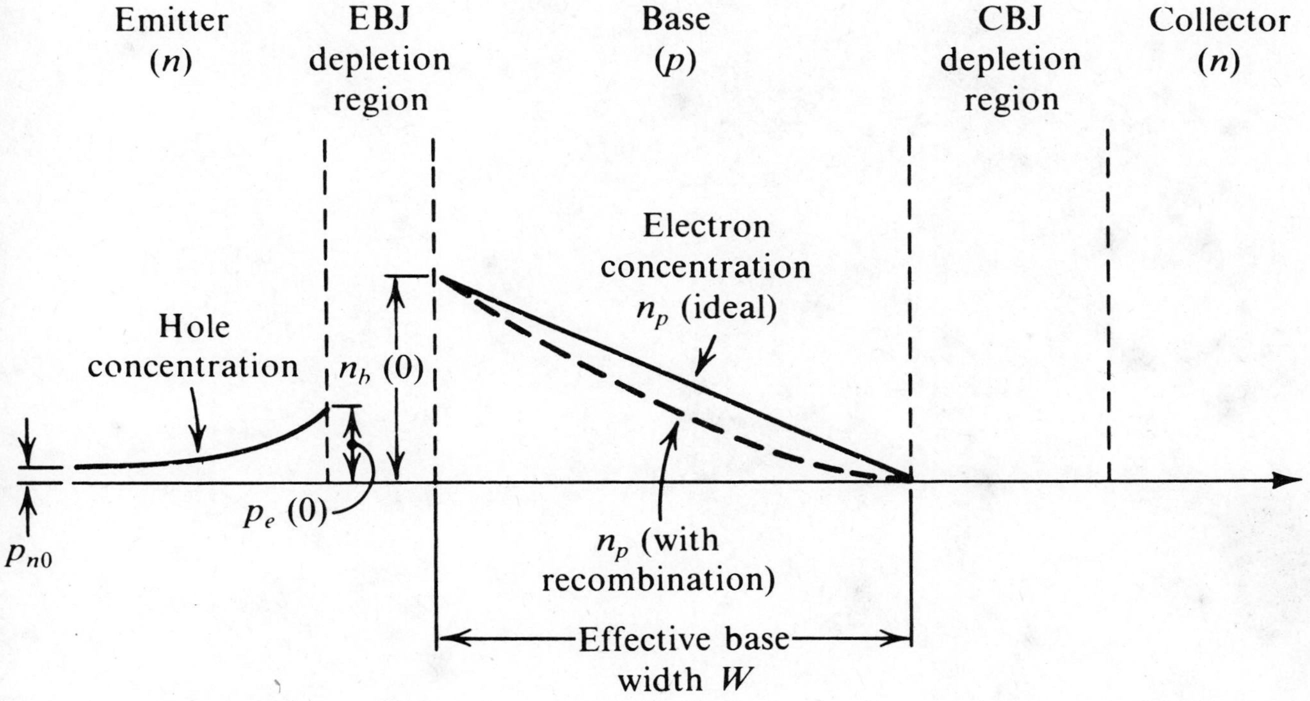
Emitter
(n)
EBJ
depletion
region
Base
(p)
CBJ
depletion
region
Collector
(n)
Electron
concentration
n_p (ideal)
Hole
concentration
n_b (0)
p_e (0)
p_n0
n_p (with
recombination)
Effective base
width W

8.4

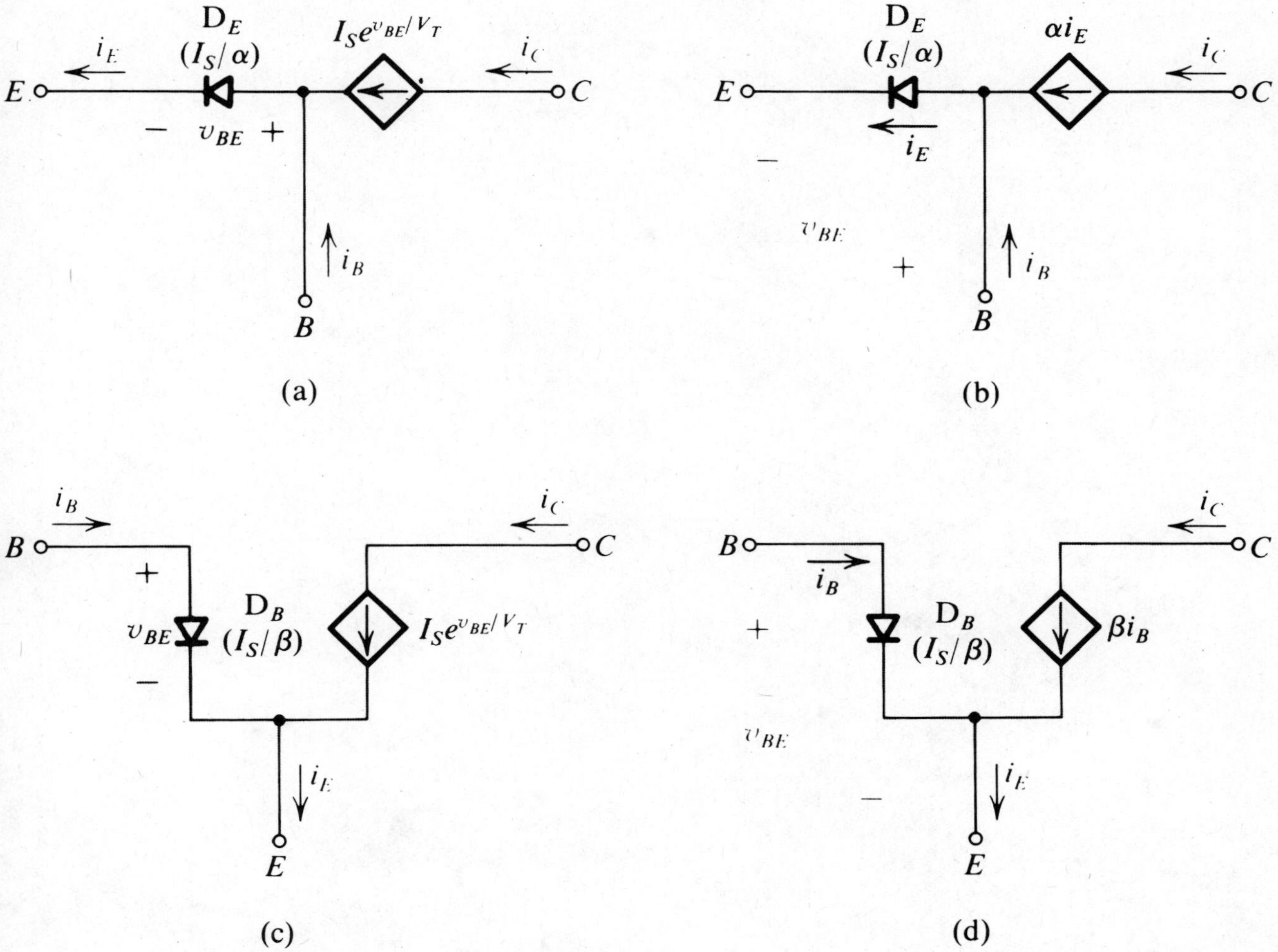
D_E
(I_S/α)
$I_S e^{v_{BE}/V_T}$
i_E
i_C
E
C
v_{BE}
i_B
B
(a)
D_E
(I_S/α)
αi_E
i_E
i_C
E
C
v_{BE}
i_B
B
(b)
i_B
i_C
B
C
v_{BE}
D_B
(I_S/β)
$I_S e^{v_{BE}/V_T}$
i_E
E
(c)
i_C
B
C
i_B
D_B
(I_S/β)
βi_B
v_{BE}
i_E
E
(d)

8.5

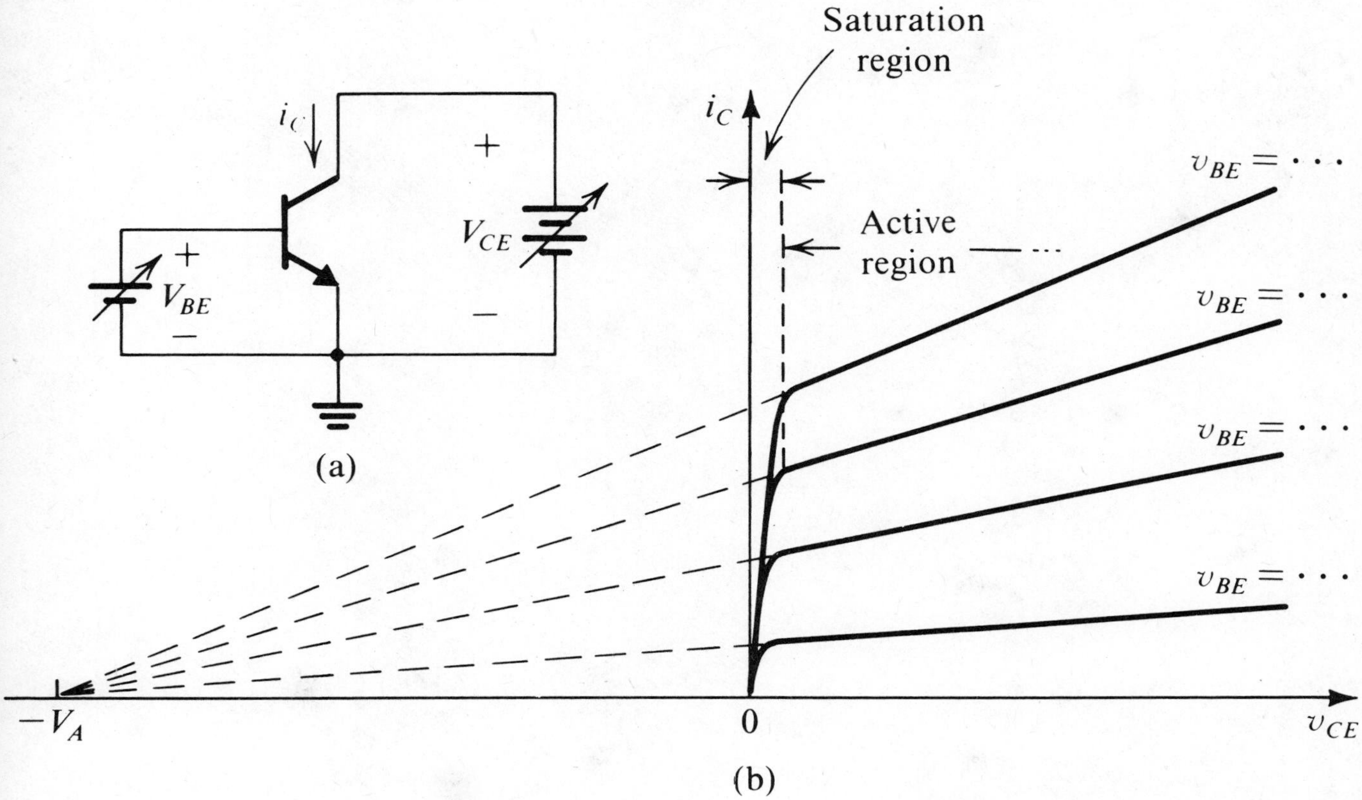
i_C
+
V_{CE}
−
+
V_{BE}
−
(a)
Saturation
region
i_C
Active
region
$v_{BE} = \cdots$
$v_{BE} = \cdots$
$v_{BE} = \cdots$
$v_{BE} = \cdots$
$-V_A$
0
v_{CE}
(b)

8.14

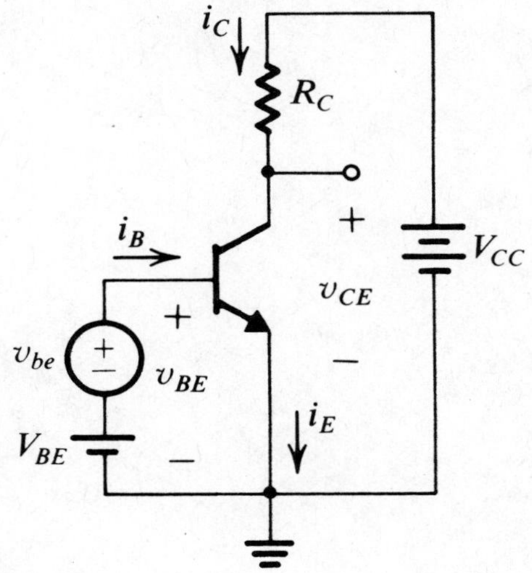

8.22

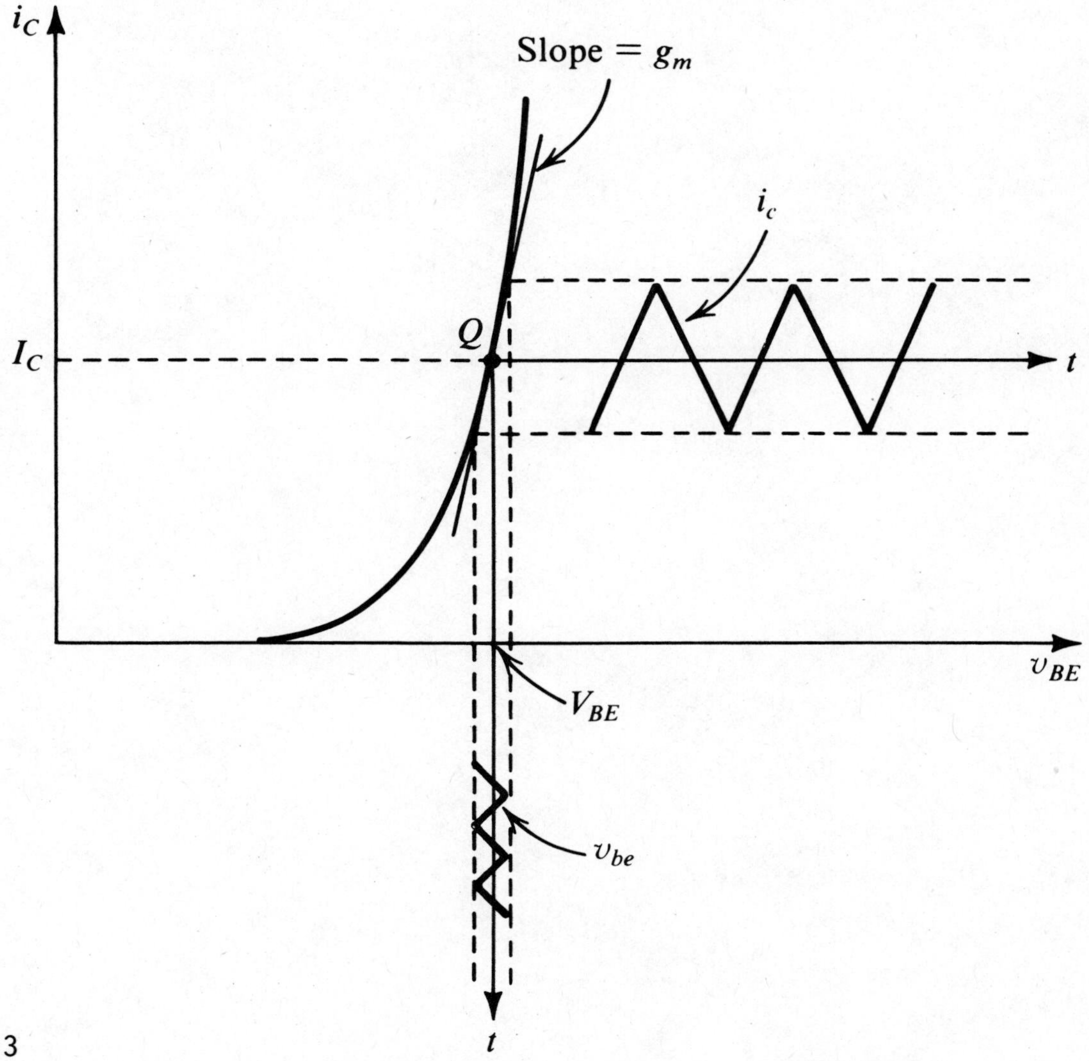

8.23

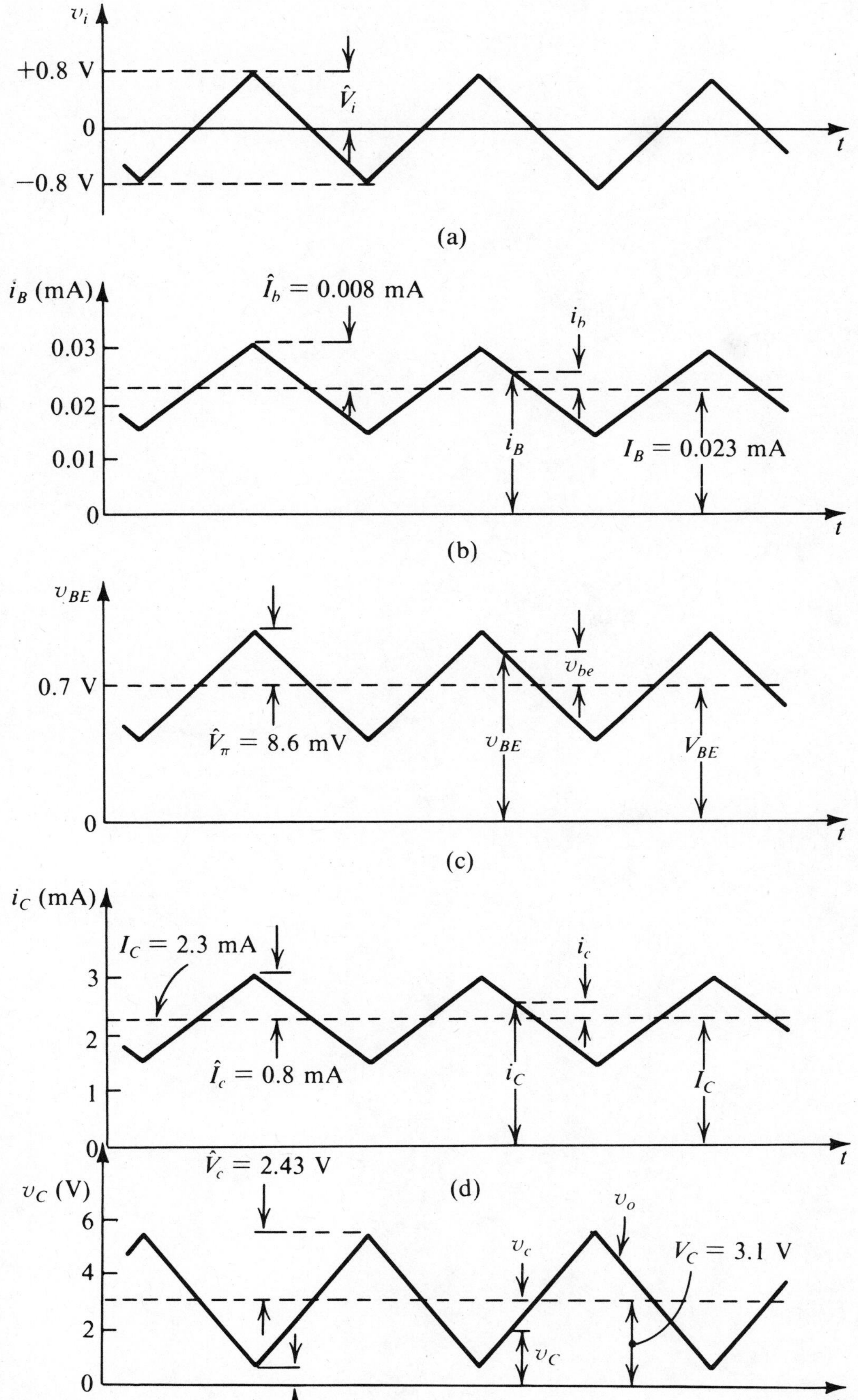

v_i
+0.8 V
$\hat{V}_i$
0
−0.8 V
t
(a)
i_B (mA)
$\hat{I}_b$ = 0.008 mA
0.03
0.02
0.01
0
i_b
i_B
I_B = 0.023 mA
t
(b)
v_{BE}
0.7 V
v_{be}
$\hat{V}_\pi$ = 8.6 mV
v_{BE}
V_{BE}
0
t
(c)
i_C (mA)
I_C = 2.3 mA
i_c
3
2
1
0
$\hat{I}_c$ = 0.8 mA
i_C
I_C
t
(d)
$\hat{V}_c$ = 2.43 V
v_C (V)
6
4
2
0
v_o
v_c
V_C = 3.1 V
v_C
0.67 V
t
(e)

8.37

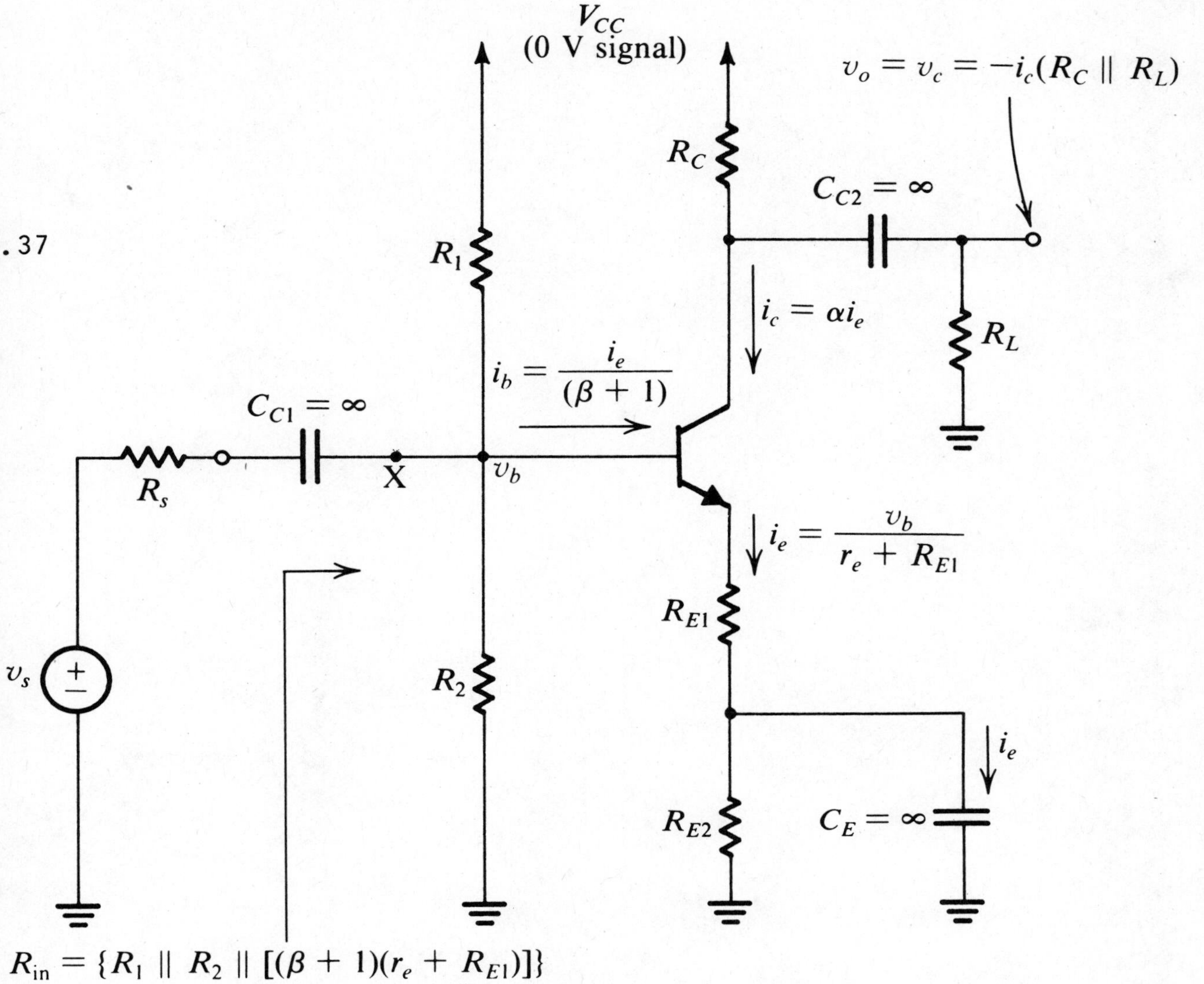

V_{CC}
(0 V signal)
$v_o = v_c = -i_c(R_C \parallel R_L)$
R_C
$C_{C2} = \infty$
R_1
$i_c = \alpha i_e$
R_L
$i_b = \frac{i_e}{(\beta + 1)}$
$C_{C1} = \infty$
R_s
X
v_b
$i_e = \frac{v_b}{r_e + R_{E1}}$
R_{E1}
v_s
R_2
i_e
R_{E2}
$C_E = \infty$
$R_{in} = \{R_1 \parallel R_2 \parallel [(\beta + 1)(r_e + R_{E1})]\}$

8.53

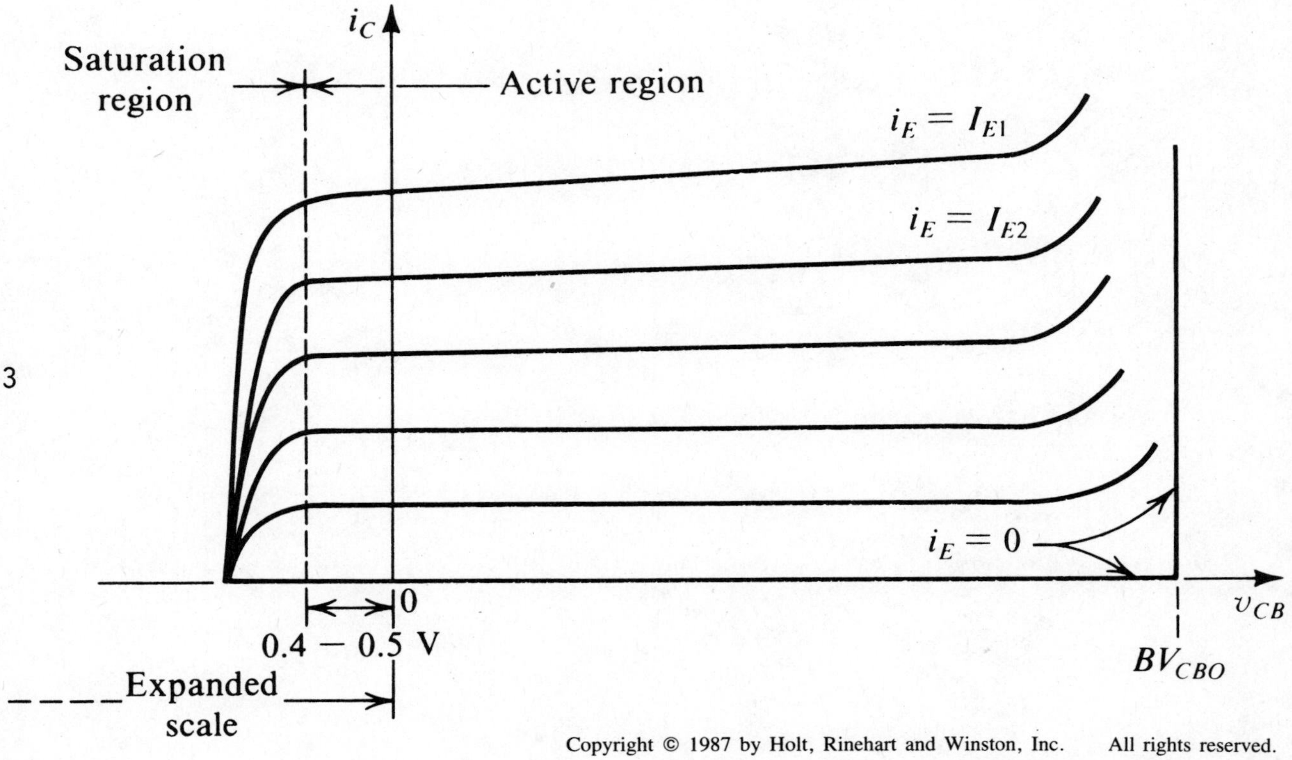

i_C
Saturation region
Active region
$i_E = I_{E1}$
$i_E = I_{E2}$
$i_E = 0$
0
v_{CB}
0.4 − 0.5 V
BV_{CBO}
Expanded scale

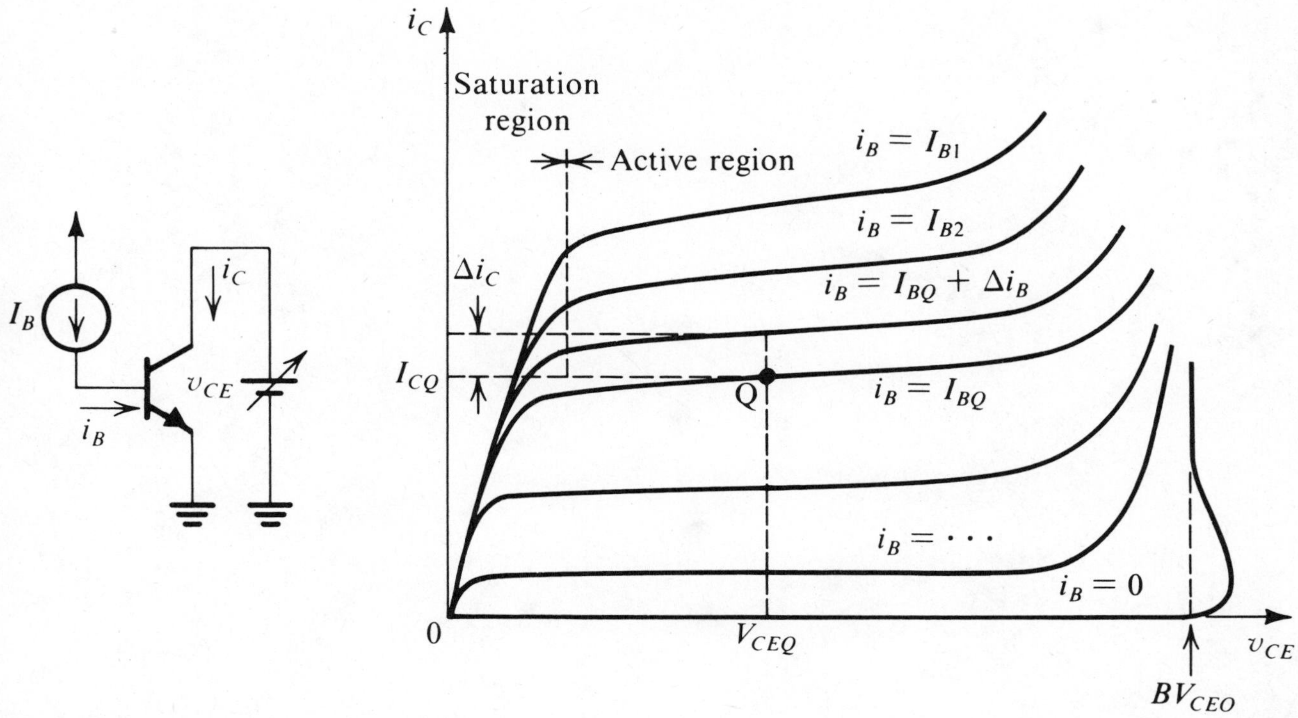
i_C
Saturation region
Active region
$i_B = I_{B1}$
$i_B = I_{B2}$
$i_B = I_{BQ} + \Delta i_B$
$i_B = I_{BQ}$
Δi_C
I_{CQ}
Q
$i_B = \cdots$
$i_B = 0$
0
V_{CEQ}
v_{CE}
BV_{CEO}
I_B
i_C
v_{CE}
i_B

8.55

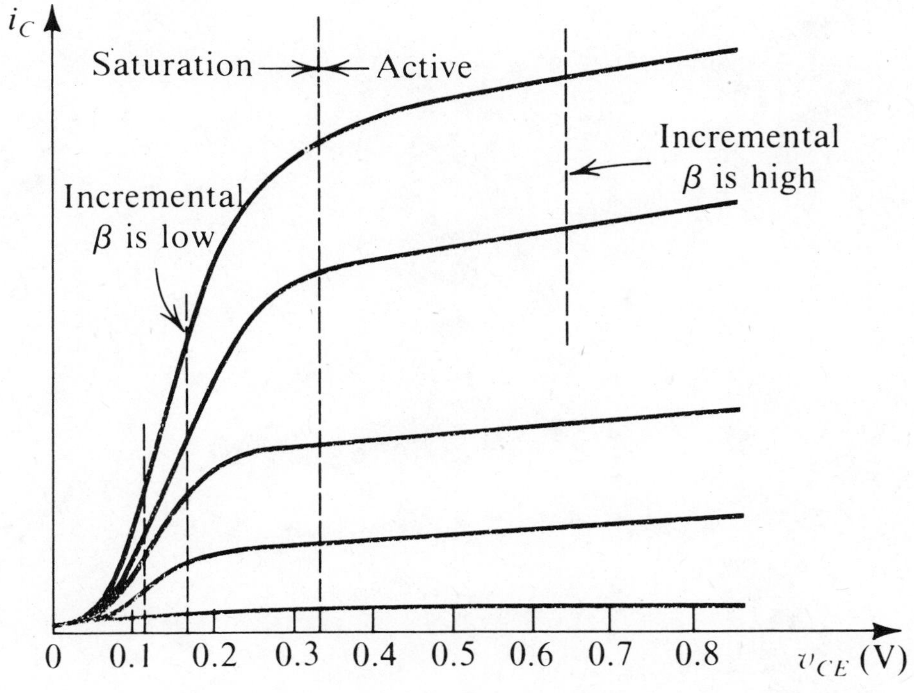
i_C
Saturation
Active
Incremental β is high
Incremental β is low
0
0.1
0.2
0.3
0.4
0.5
0.6
0.7
0.8
v_{CE} (V)

8.56

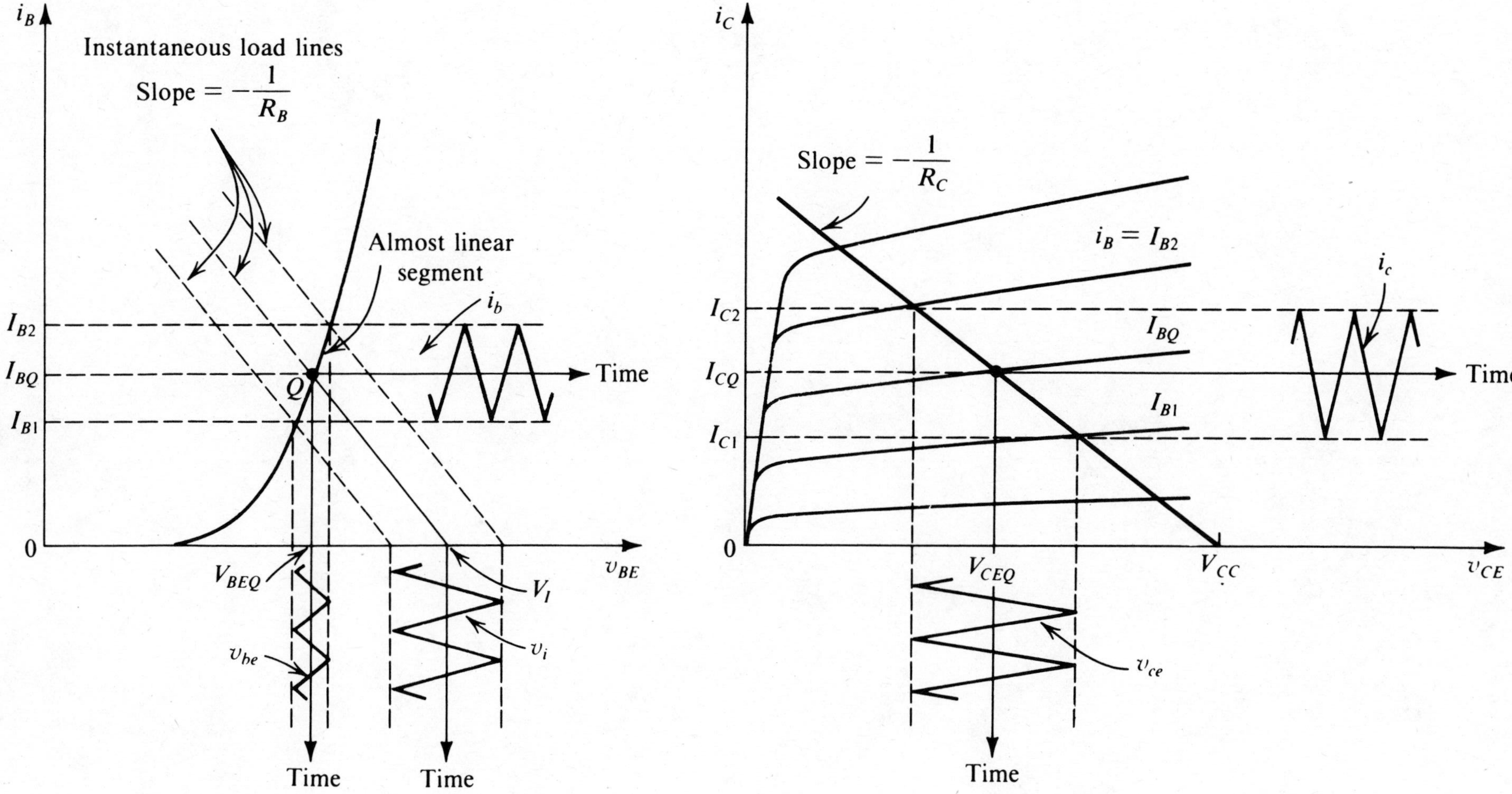

i_B
Instantaneous load lines
Slope $= -\frac{1}{R_B}$
Almost linear segment
i_b
I_{B2}
I_{BQ}
I_{B1}
Q
Time
0
V_{BEQ}
v_{BE}
V_I
v_i
v_{be}
Time
Time
i_C
Slope $= -\frac{1}{R_C}$
$i_B = I_{B2}$
i_c
I_{C2}
I_{BQ}
I_{CQ}
I_{B1}
I_{C1}
Time
0
V_{CEQ}
V_{CC}
v_{CE}
v_{ce}
Time

(a) (b)

8.62

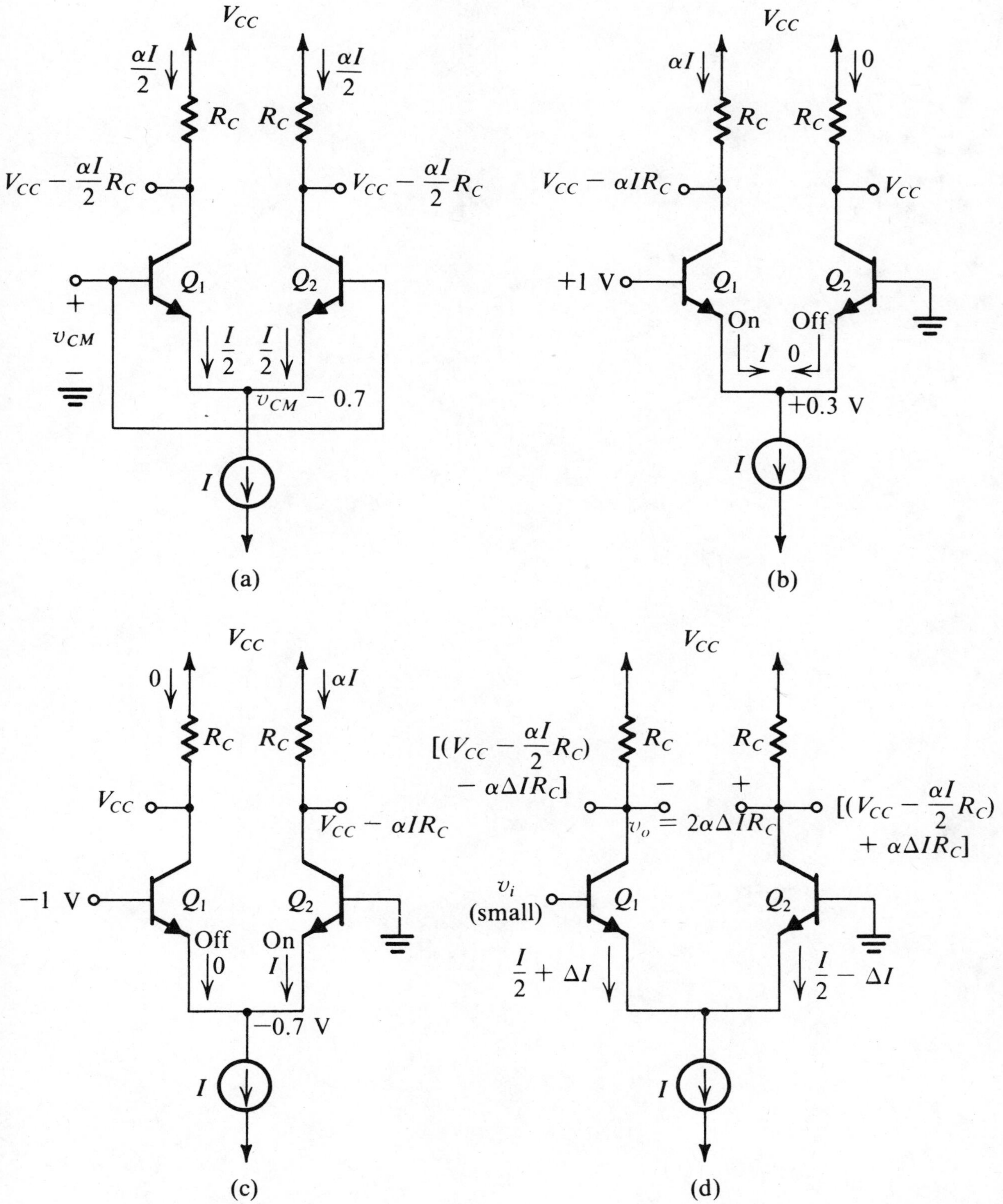

V_{CC}
$\frac{\alpha I}{2}$
R_C
$V_{CC} - \frac{\alpha I}{2} R_C$
Q_1
Q_2
+
v_{CM}
−
$\frac{I}{2}$
$v_{CM} - 0.7$
I
(a)
αI
0
$V_{CC} - \alpha I R_C$
V_{CC}
+1 V
On
Off
+0.3 V
(b)
−1 V
Off
On
−0.7 V
$V_{CC} - \alpha I R_C$
(c)
$[(V_{CC} - \frac{\alpha I}{2} R_C) - \alpha \Delta I R_C]$
$[(V_{CC} - \frac{\alpha I}{2} R_C) + \alpha \Delta I R_C]$
$v_o = 2\alpha \Delta I R_C$
v_i (small)
$\frac{I}{2} + \Delta I$
$\frac{I}{2} - \Delta I$
(d)

9.2

9.5

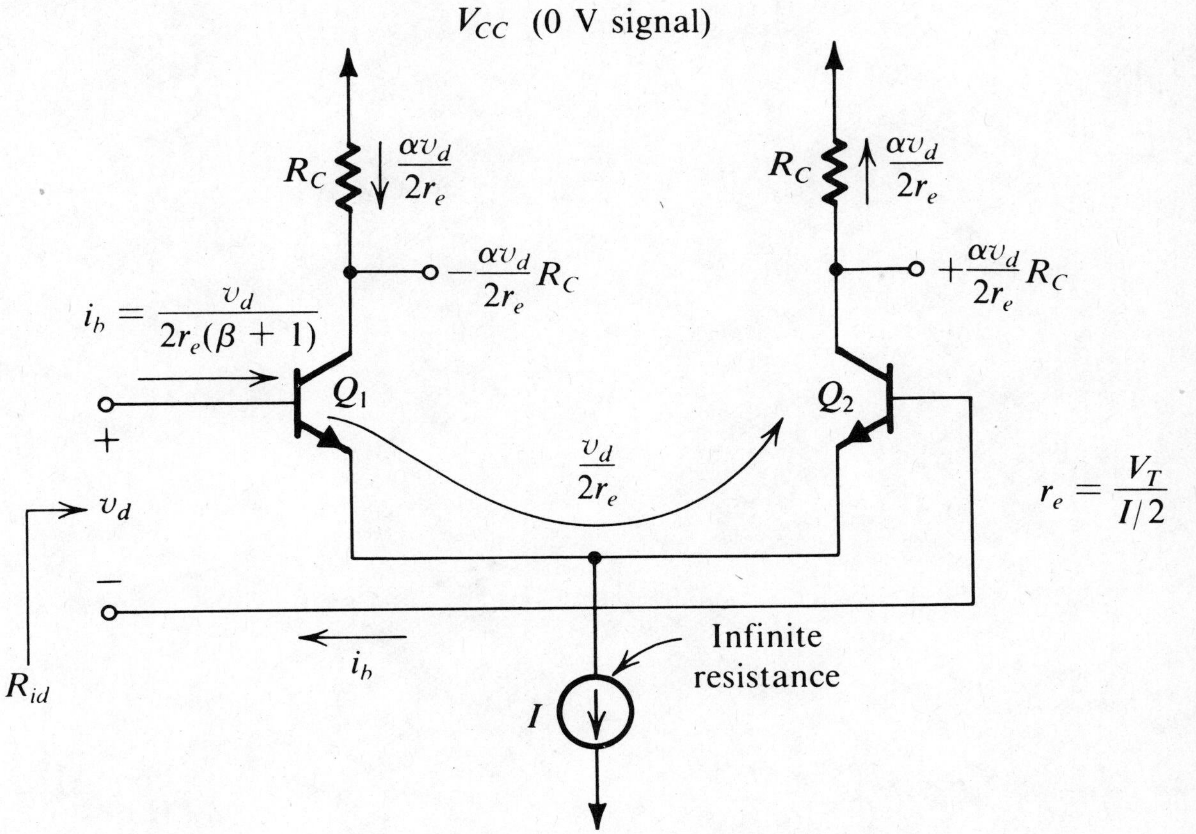
V_{CC} (0 V signal)
R_C
$\frac{\alpha v_d}{2r_e}$
R_C
$\frac{\alpha v_d}{2r_e}$
$-\frac{\alpha v_d}{2r_e}R_C$
$+\frac{\alpha v_d}{2r_e}R_C$
$i_b = \frac{v_d}{2r_e(\beta + 1)}$
Q_1
Q_2
+
v_d
−
$\frac{v_d}{2r_e}$
$r_e = \frac{V_T}{I/2}$
i_b
Infinite resistance
I
R_{id}

9.6

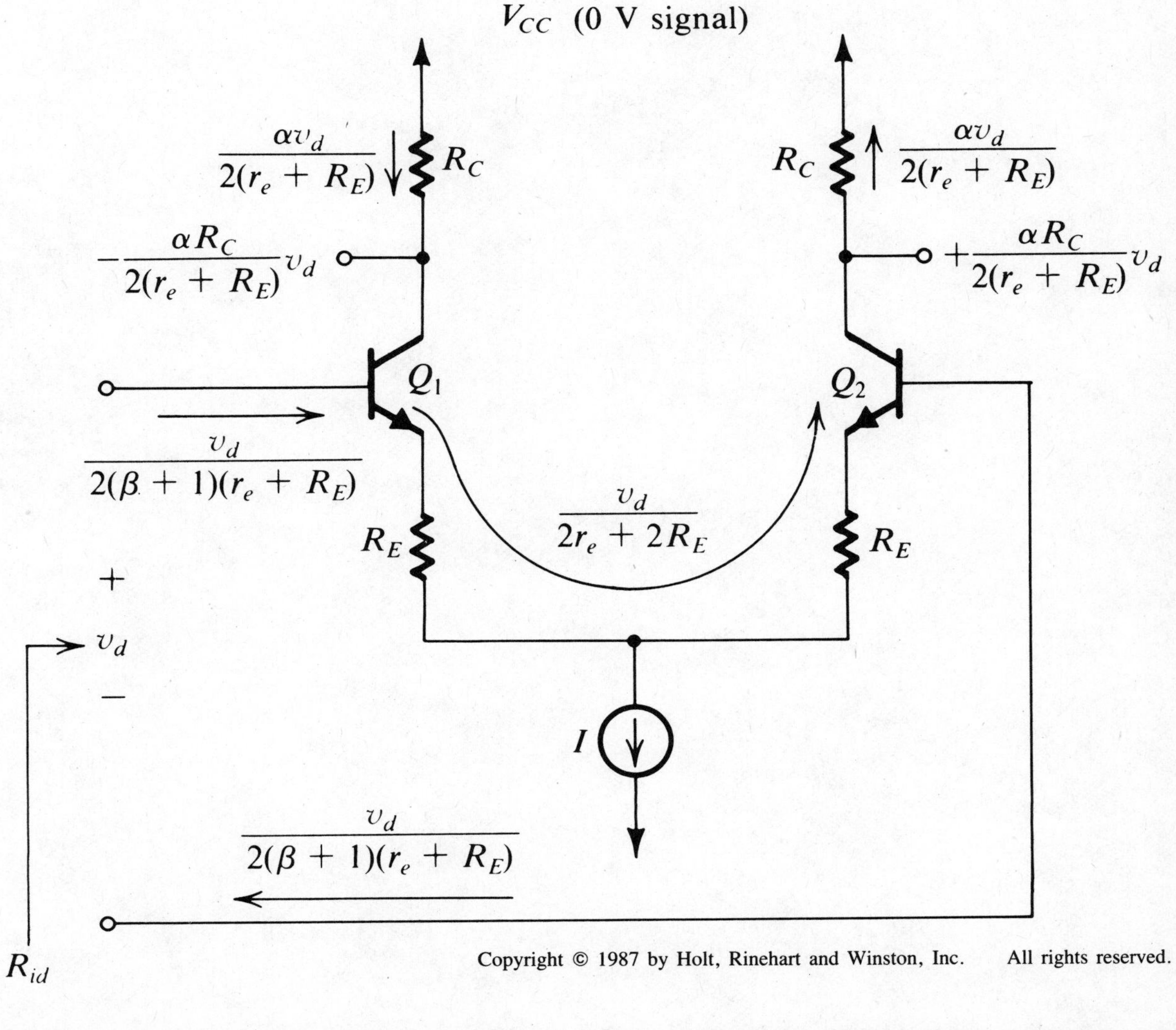
V_{CC} (0 V signal)
$\frac{\alpha v_d}{2(r_e + R_E)}$
R_C
R_C
$\frac{\alpha v_d}{2(r_e + R_E)}$
$-\frac{\alpha R_C}{2(r_e + R_E)}v_d$
$+\frac{\alpha R_C}{2(r_e + R_E)}v_d$
Q_1
Q_2
$\frac{v_d}{2(\beta + 1)(r_e + R_E)}$
R_E
$\frac{v_d}{2r_e + 2R_E}$
R_E
+
v_d
−
I
$\frac{v_d}{2(\beta + 1)(r_e + R_E)}$
R_{id}

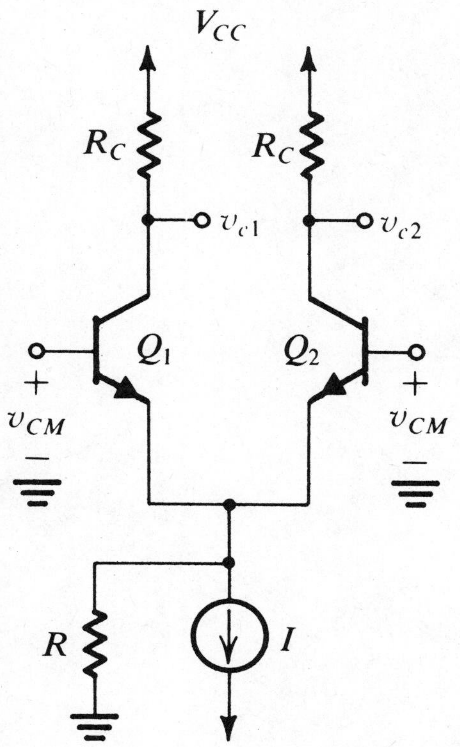

V_CC
R_C
R_C
v_c1
v_c2
Q_1
Q_2
+
v_CM
−
R
I

(a)

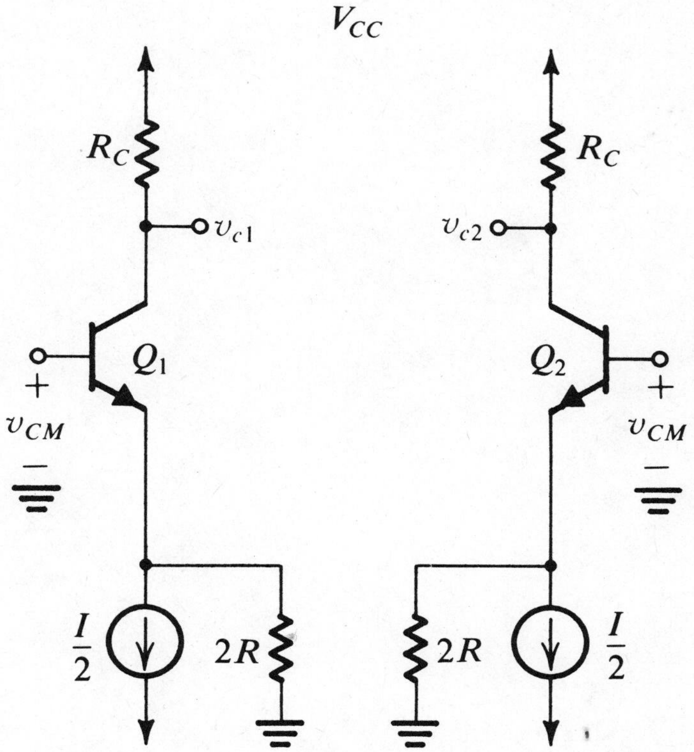

V_CC
R_C
R_C
v_c1
v_c2
Q_1
Q_2
+
v_CM
−
I/2
2R

(b)

9.10

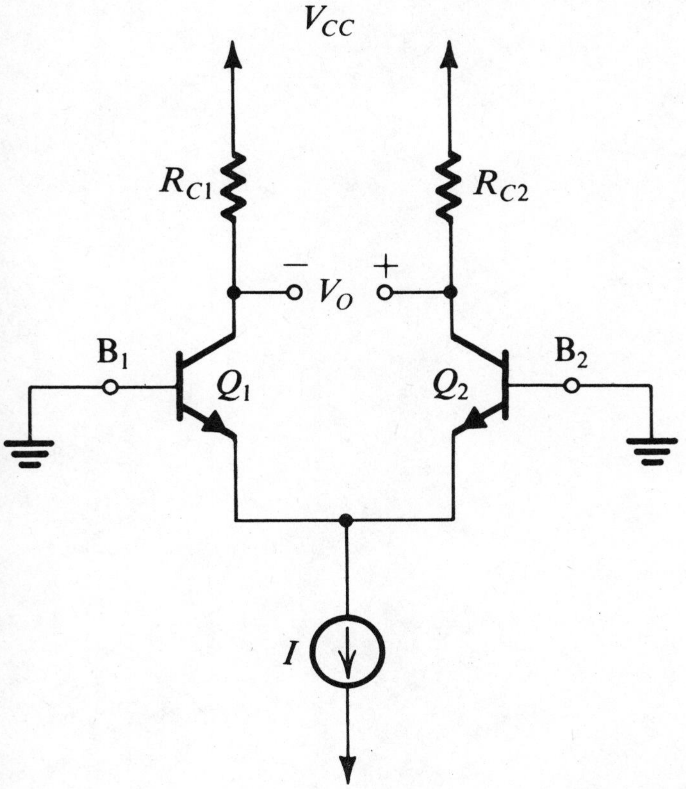

V_CC
R_C1
R_C2
− V_O +
B_1
B_2
Q_1
Q_2
I

(a)

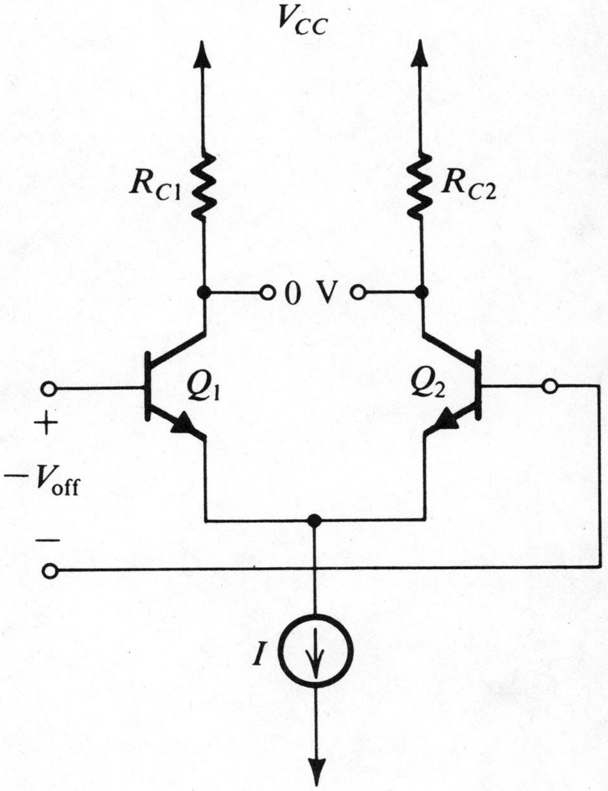

V_CC
R_C1
R_C2
0 V
Q_1
Q_2
+
−V_off
−
I

(b)

9.12

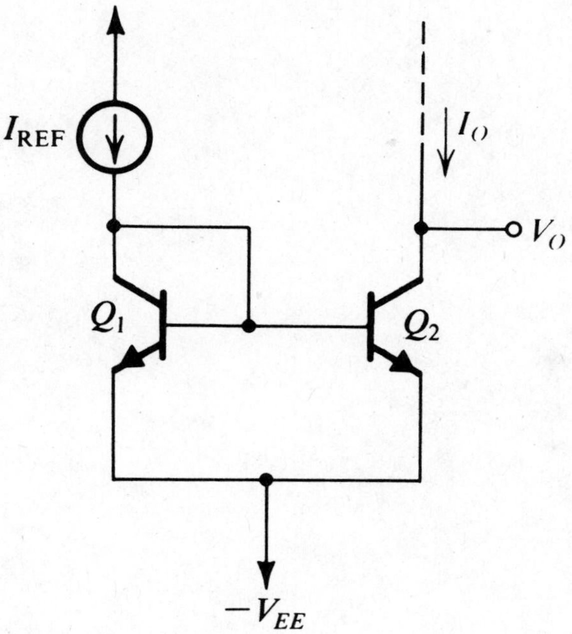

I_{REF}
I_O
V_O
Q_1
Q_2
$-V_{EE}$

9.14

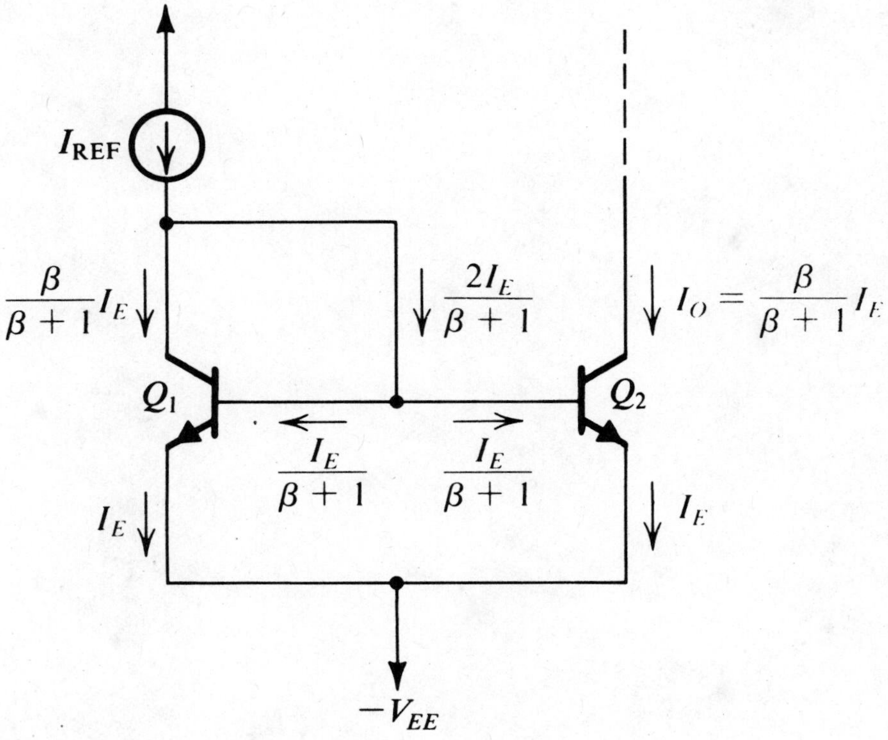

I_{REF}
$\frac{\beta}{\beta+1} I_E$
$\frac{2I_E}{\beta+1}$
$I_O = \frac{\beta}{\beta+1} I_E$
Q_1
Q_2
$\frac{I_E}{\beta+1}$
$\frac{I_E}{\beta+1}$
I_E
I_E
$-V_{EE}$

9.15

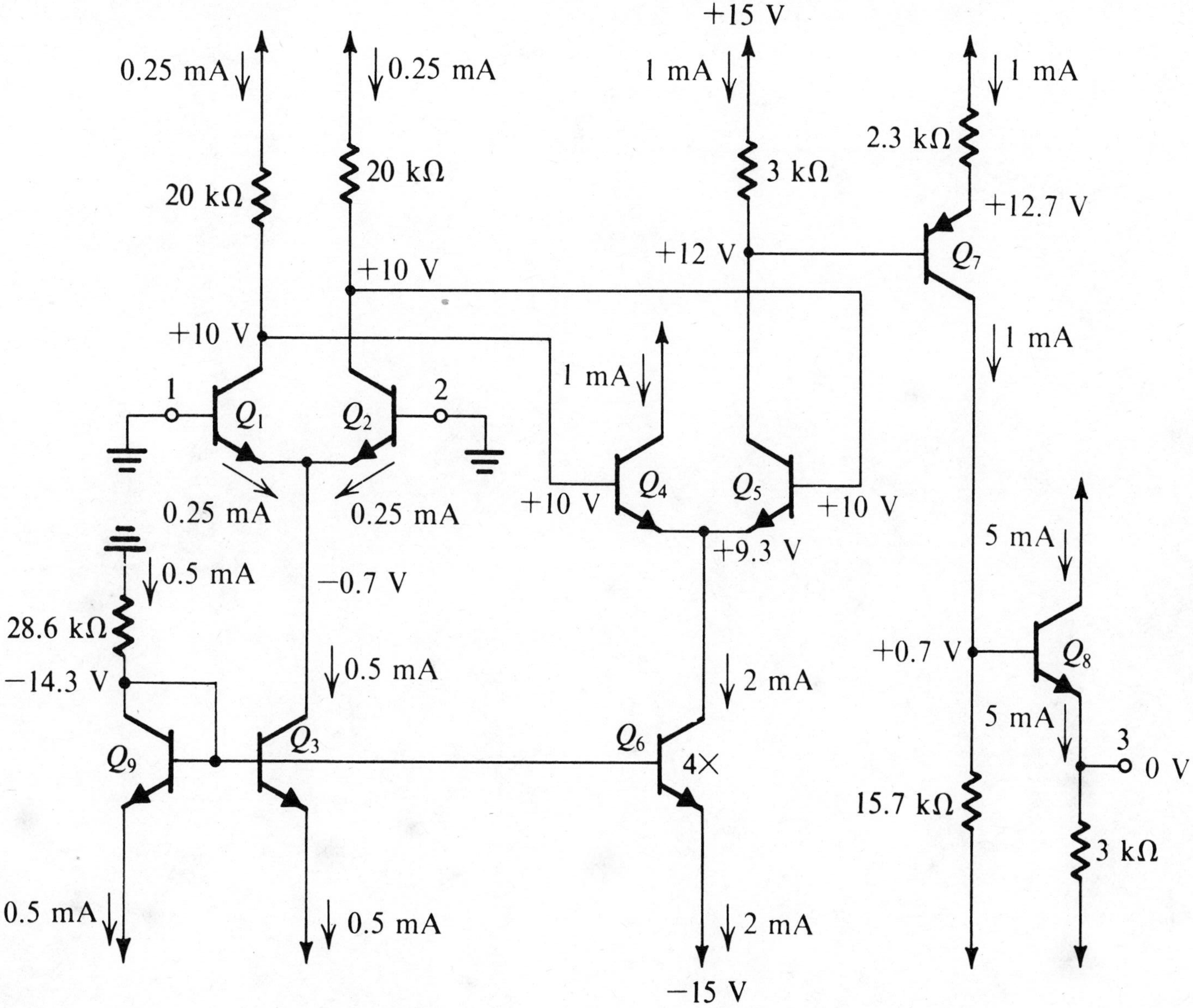
+15 V
0.25 mA
0.25 mA
1 mA
1 mA
20 kΩ
20 kΩ
3 kΩ
2.3 kΩ
+12.7 V
+12 V
+10 V
+10 V
Q1
Q2
Q7
1 mA
1
2
1 mA
Q4
Q5
+10 V
+10 V
0.25 mA
0.25 mA
+9.3 V
5 mA
0.5 mA
-0.7 V
28.6 kΩ
+0.7 V
Q8
-14.3 V
0.5 mA
2 mA
5 mA
Q9
Q3
Q6
4×
3
0 V
15.7 kΩ
3 kΩ
0.5 mA
0.5 mA
2 mA
-15 V

9.23

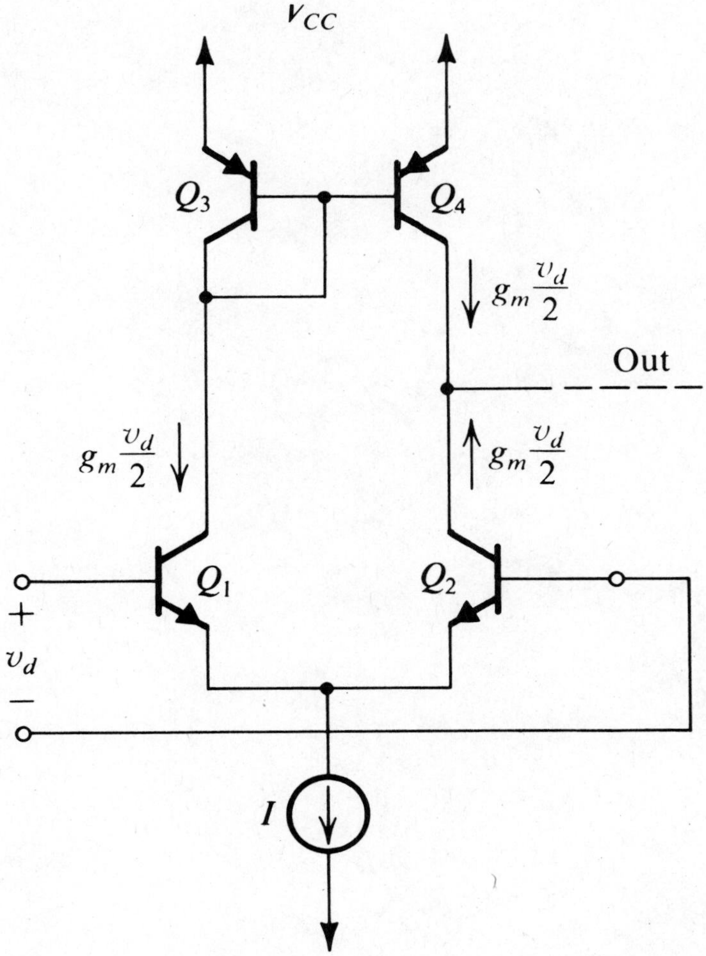
V_{CC}
Q_3
Q_4
$g_m \frac{v_d}{2}$
Out
$g_m \frac{v_d}{2}$
$g_m \frac{v_d}{2}$
Q_1
Q_2
+
v_d
−
I

9.24

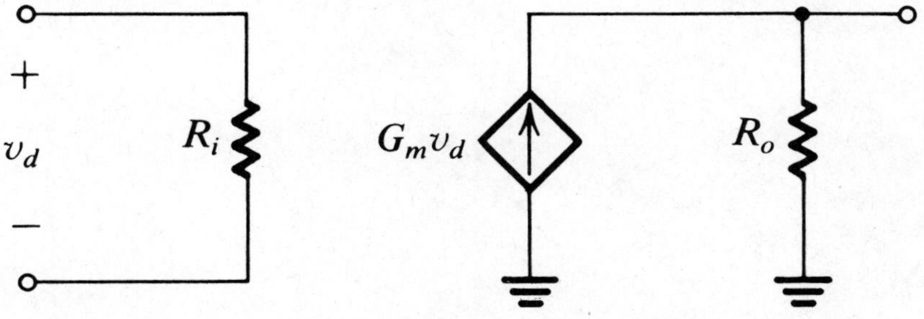
+
v_d
−
R_i
$G_m v_d$
R_o

9.25

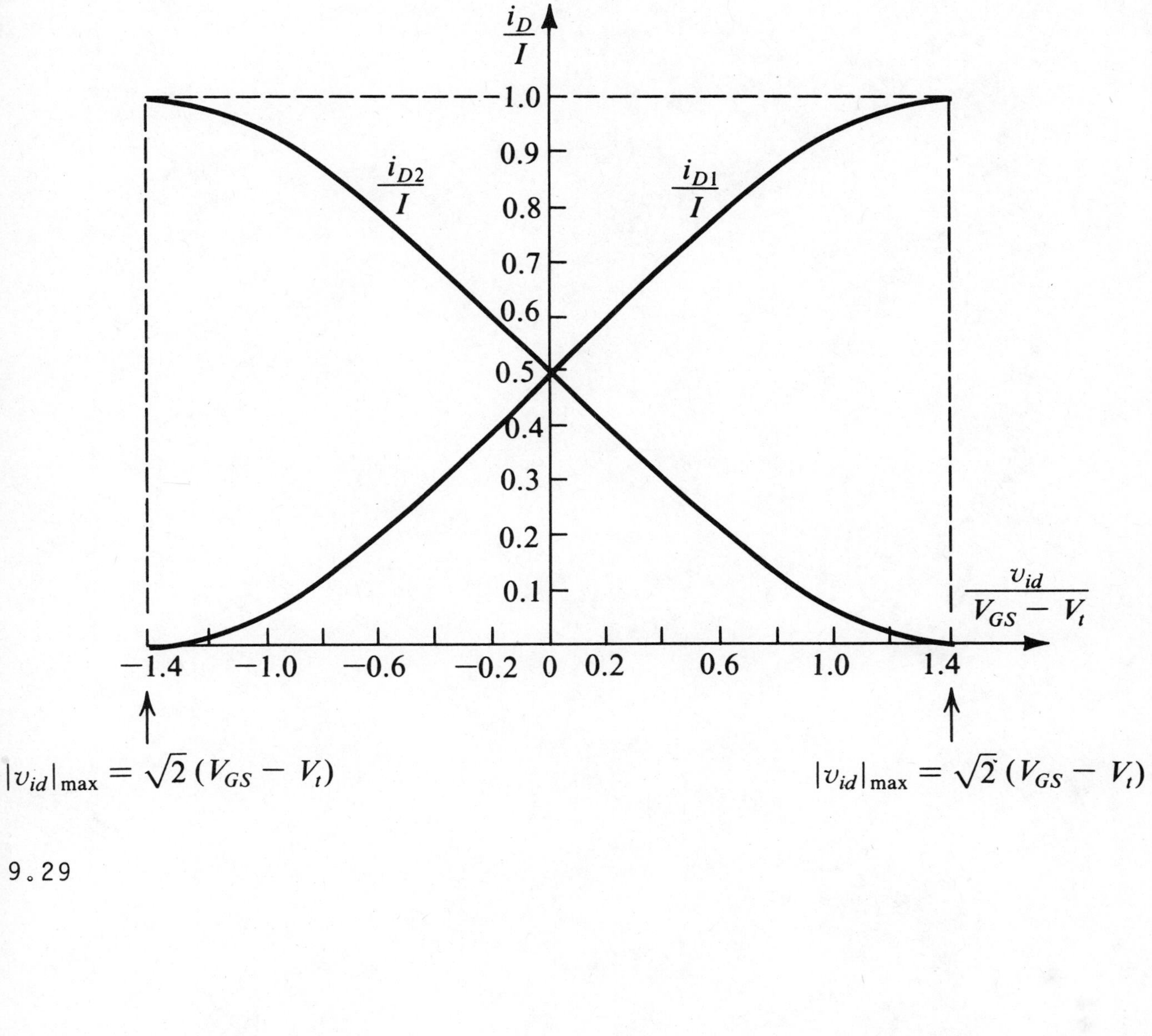

$\frac{i_D}{I}$
1.0
0.9
0.8
0.7
0.6
0.5
0.4
0.3
0.2
0.1
$\frac{i_{D2}}{I}$
$\frac{i_{D1}}{I}$
$\frac{v_{id}}{V_{GS} - V_t}$
−1.4
−1.0
−0.6
−0.2
0
0.2
0.6
1.0
1.4
$|v_{id}|_{max} = \sqrt{2}\,(V_{GS} - V_t)$
$|v_{id}|_{max} = \sqrt{2}\,(V_{GS} - V_t)$

9.29

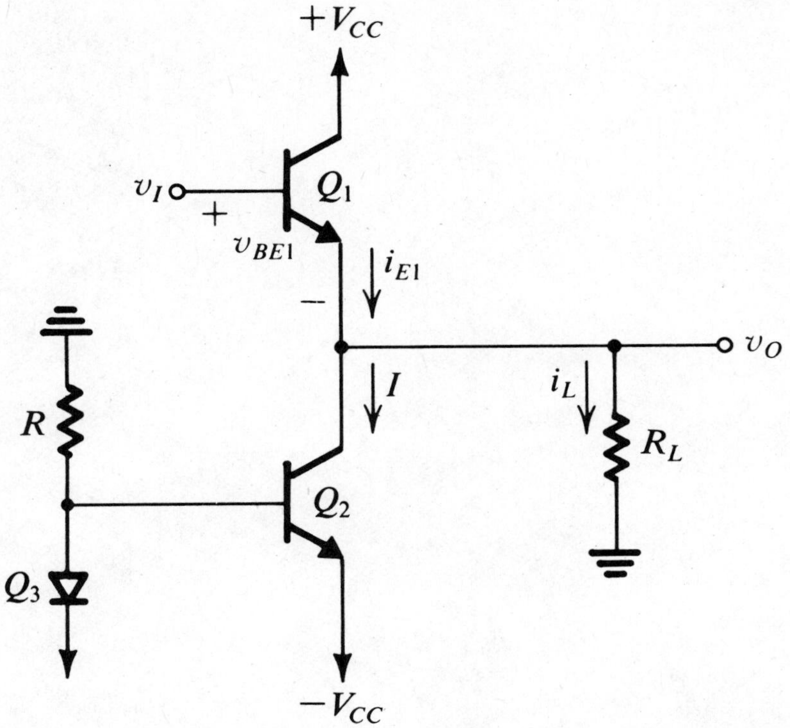

$+V_{CC}$
v_I
Q_1
+
v_{BE1}
i_{E1}
−
v_O
I
i_L
R
R_L
Q_2
Q_3
$-V_{CC}$

10.2

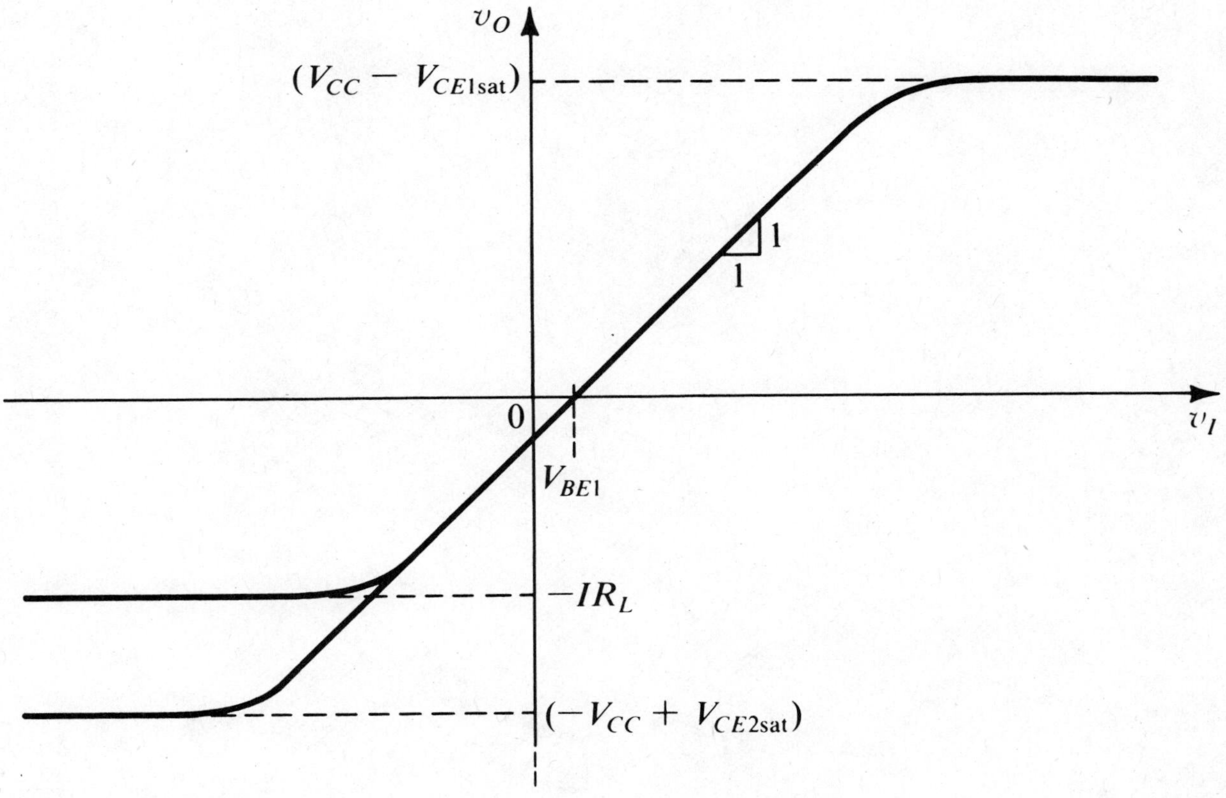

v_O
$(V_{CC} - V_{CE1\text{sat}})$
1
1
0
v_I
V_{BE1}
$-IR_L$
$(-V_{CC} + V_{CE2\text{sat}})$

10.3

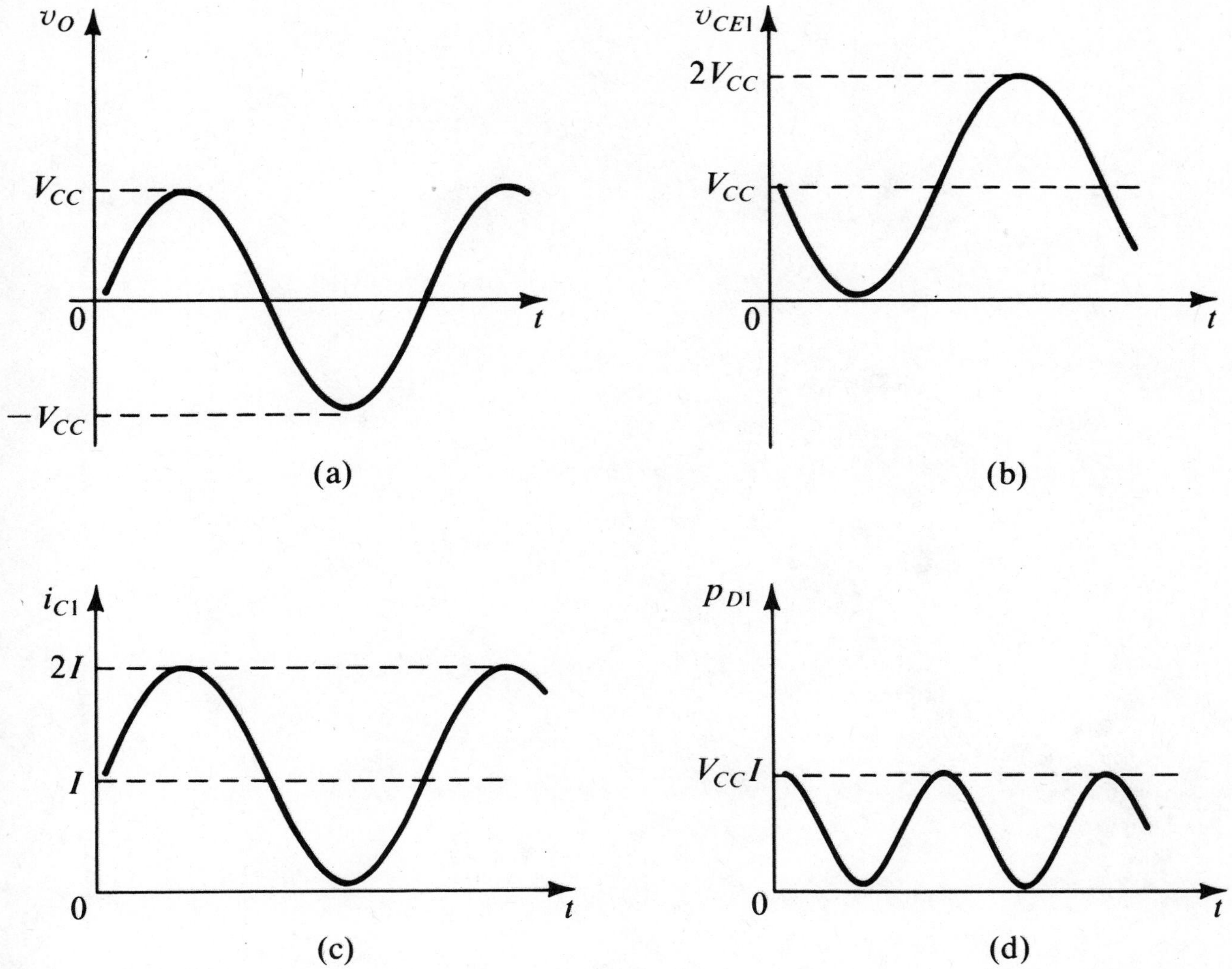
v_O
V_{CC}
0
$-V_{CC}$
t
(a)
v_{CE1}
$2V_{CC}$
V_{CC}
0
t
(b)
i_{C1}
$2I$
I
0
t
(c)
p_{D1}
$V_{CC}I$
0
t
(d)

10.4

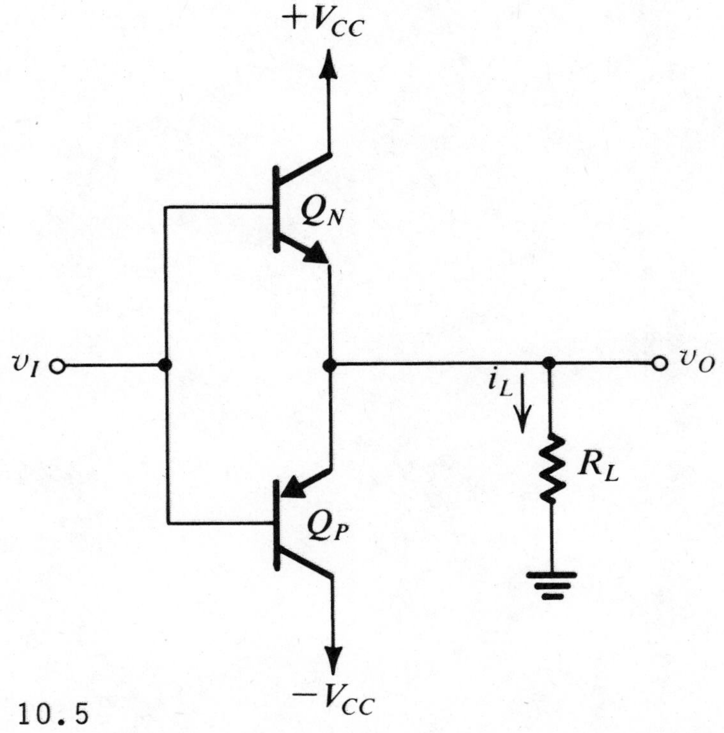
$+V_{CC}$
Q_N
v_I
v_O
i_L
R_L
Q_P
$-V_{CC}$

10.5

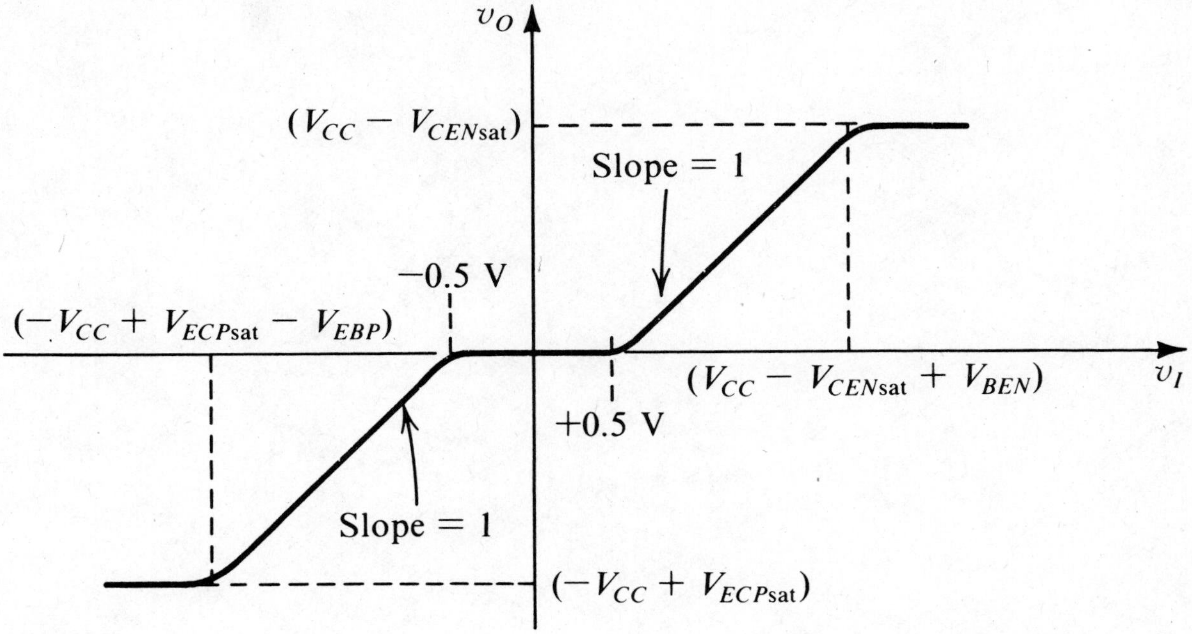
v_O
$(V_{CC} - V_{CEN\text{sat}})$
Slope = 1
−0.5 V
$(-V_{CC} + V_{ECP\text{sat}} - V_{EBP})$
$(V_{CC} - V_{CEN\text{sat}} + V_{BEN})$
v_I
+0.5 V
Slope = 1
$(-V_{CC} + V_{ECP\text{sat}})$

10.6

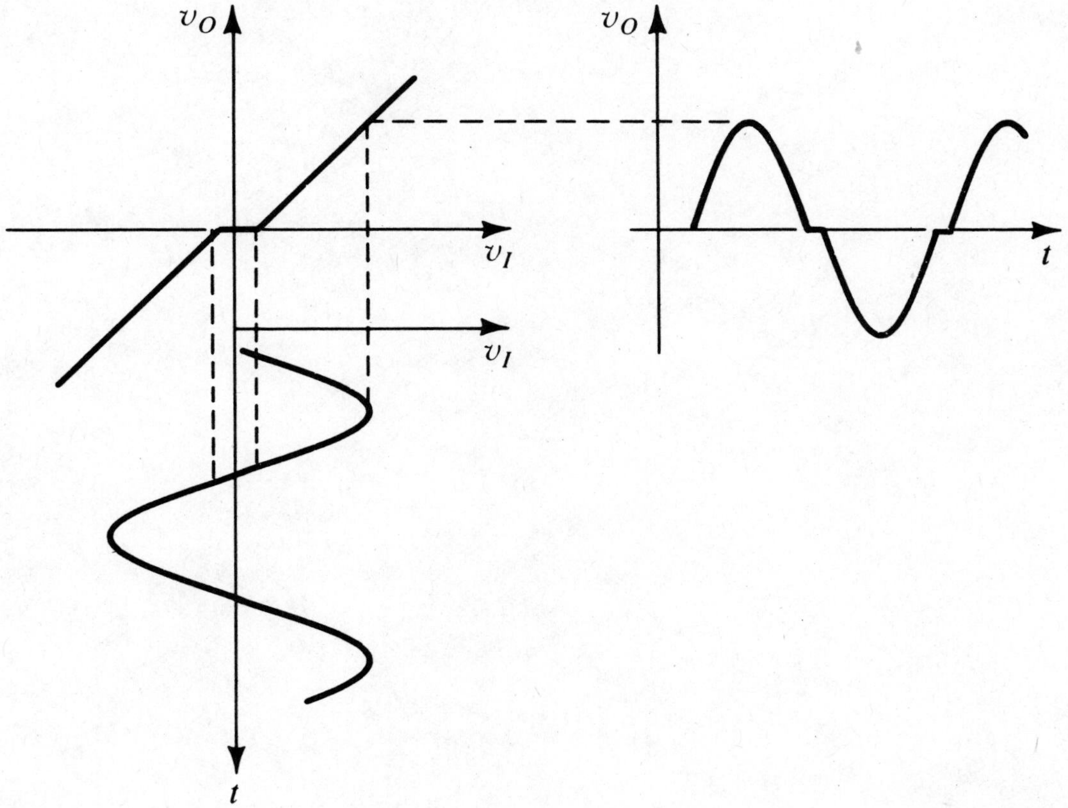
v_O
v_O
v_I
t
v_I
t

10.7

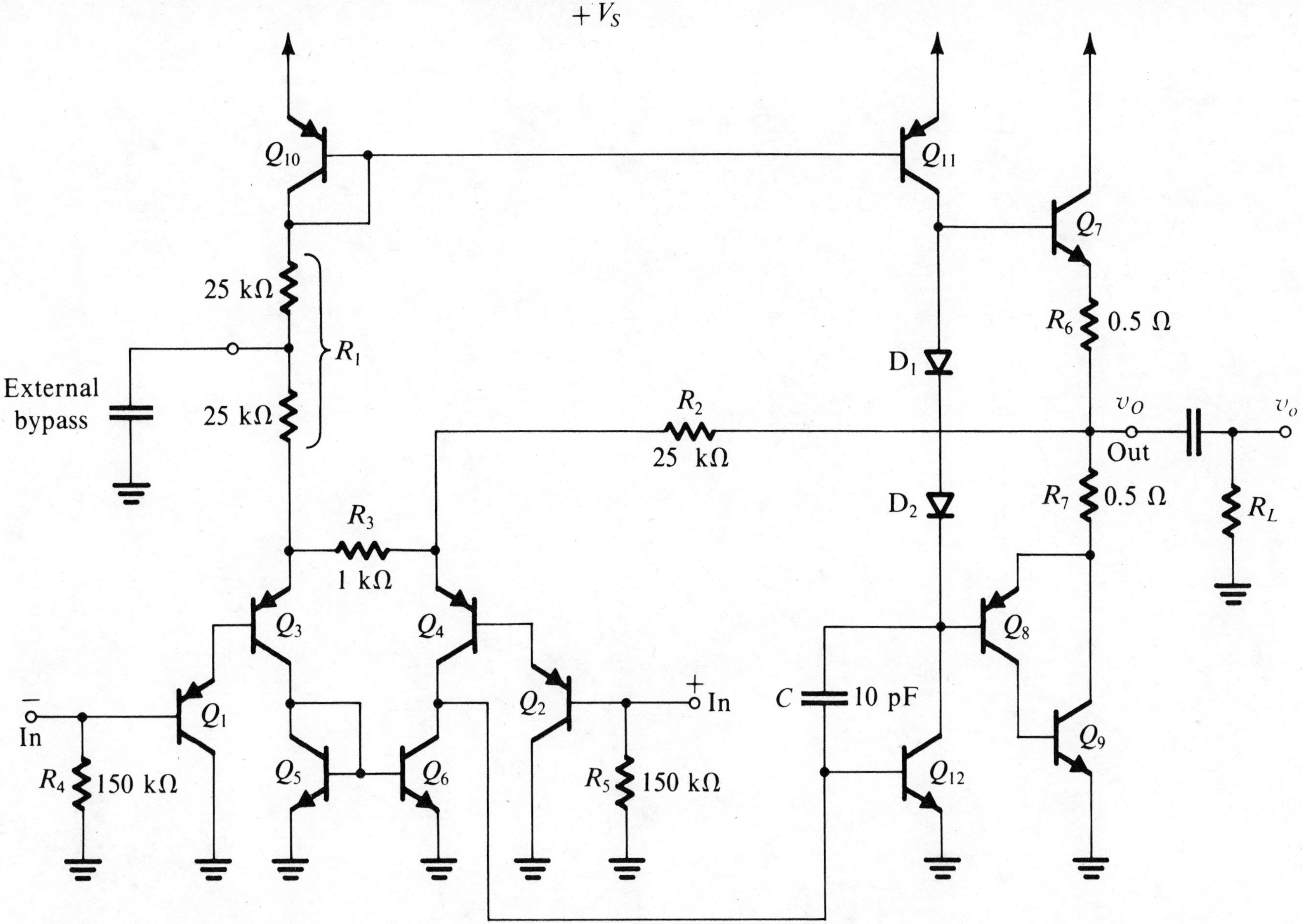
+ V_S
Q_{10}
Q_{11}
Q_7
25 kΩ
R_1
25 kΩ
External
bypass
R_6 0.5 Ω
D_1
R_2
25 kΩ
v_O
Out
v_o
D_2
R_7 0.5 Ω
R_L
R_3
1 kΩ
Q_3
Q_4
Q_8
Q_1
Q_2
− In
+ In
C 10 pF
Q_9
Q_5
Q_6
Q_{12}
R_4 150 kΩ
R_5 150 kΩ

10.30

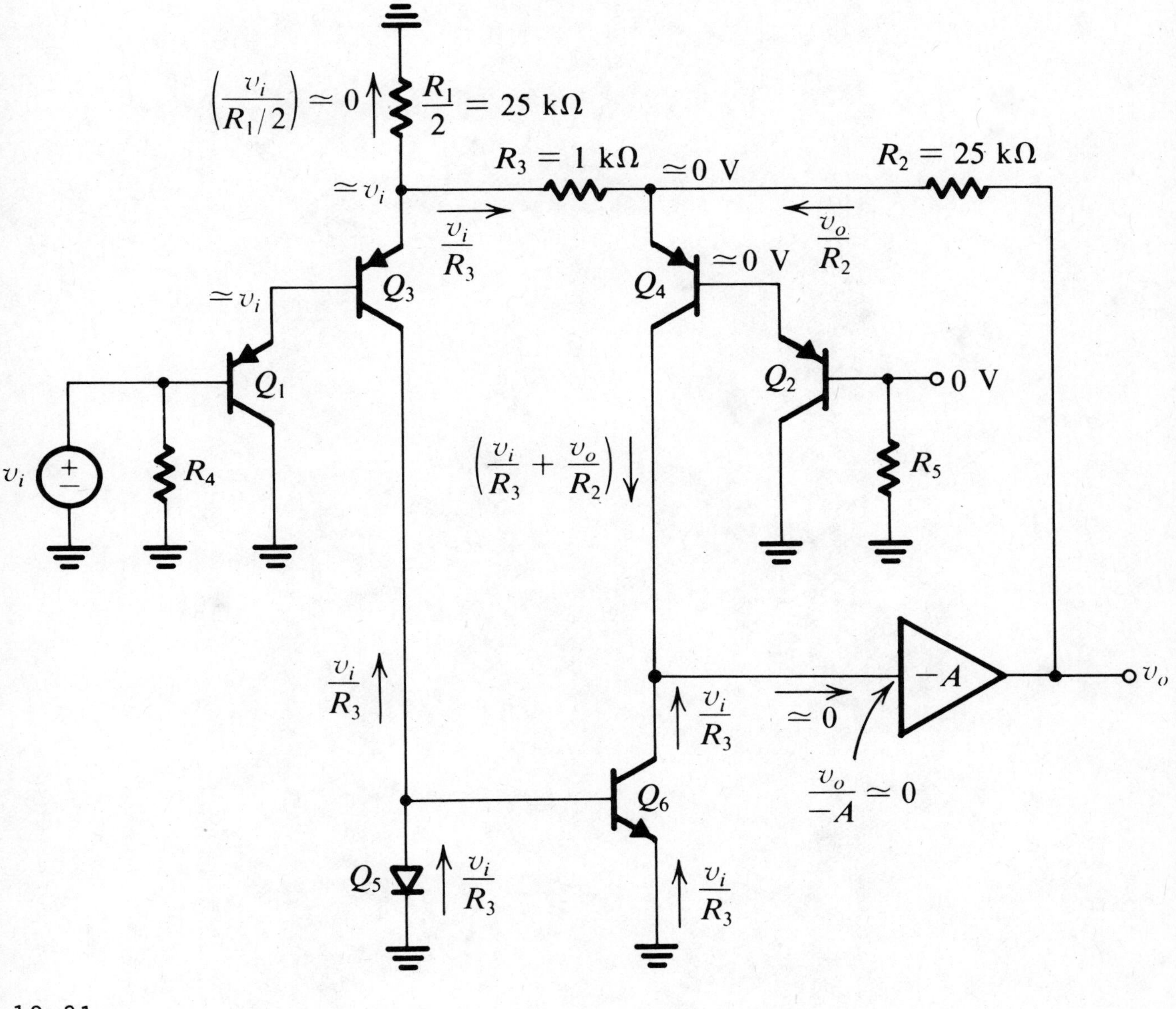

$\left(\frac{v_i}{R_1/2}\right) \simeq 0$
$\frac{R_1}{2} = 25\ \text{k}\Omega$
$R_3 = 1\ \text{k}\Omega$
$\simeq 0$ V
$R_2 = 25\ \text{k}\Omega$
$\simeq v_i$
$\frac{v_i}{R_3}$
$\frac{v_o}{R_2}$
$\simeq 0$ V
Q_3
Q_4
$\simeq v_i$
Q_1
Q_2
0 V
v_i
R_4
$\left(\frac{v_i}{R_3} + \frac{v_o}{R_2}\right)$
R_5
$\frac{v_i}{R_3}$
$-A$
v_o
$\frac{v_i}{R_3}$
$\simeq 0$
$\frac{v_o}{-A} \simeq 0$
Q_6
Q_5
$\frac{v_i}{R_3}$
$\frac{v_i}{R_3}$

10.31

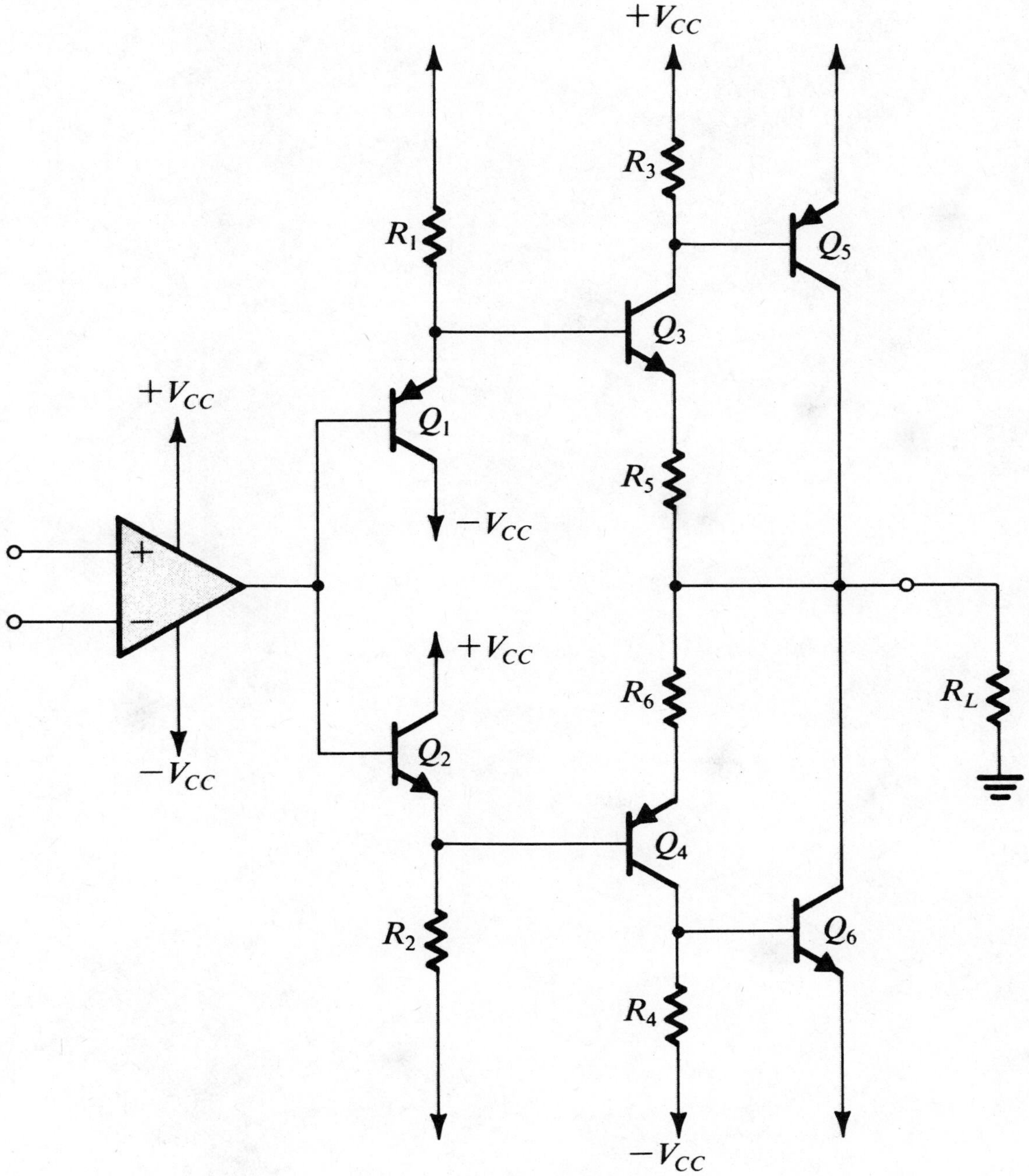

10.33

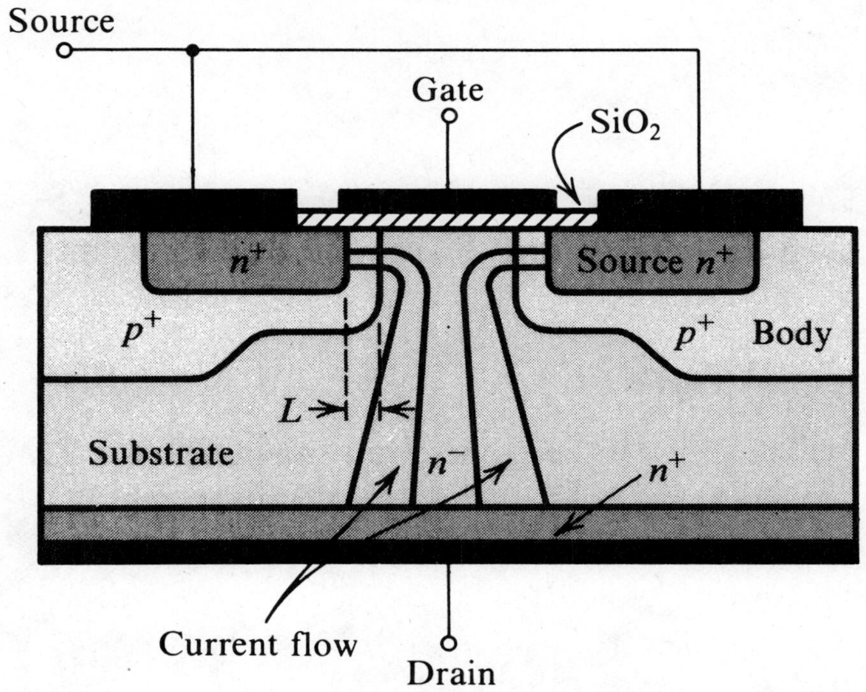

Source
Gate
SiO_2
n^+
Source n^+
p^+
p^+ Body
L
Substrate
n^-
n^+
Current flow
Drain

10.35

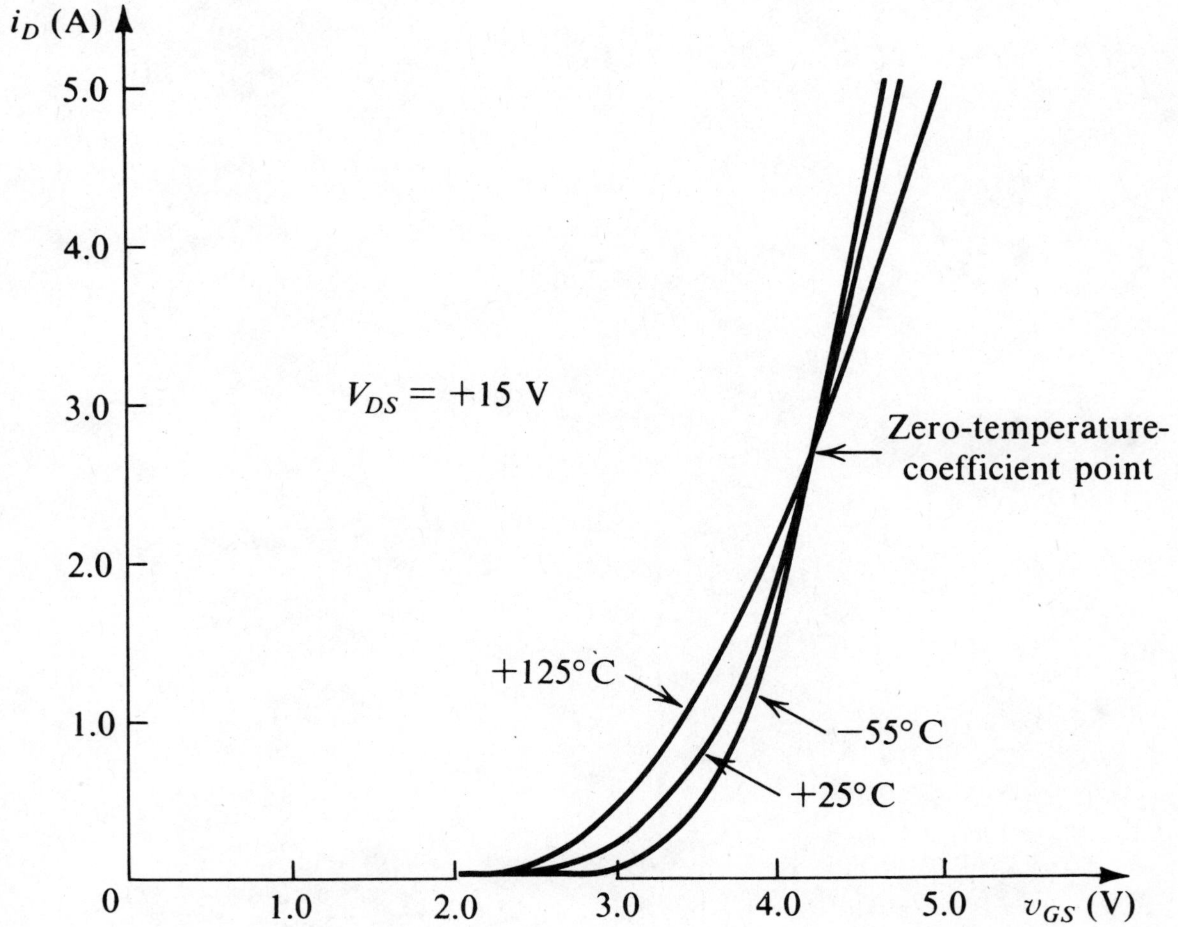

i_D (A)
5.0
4.0
3.0
2.0
1.0
0
1.0
2.0
3.0
4.0
5.0
v_{GS} (V)
$V_{DS} = +15$ V
Zero-temperature-coefficient point
+125°C
−55°C
+25°C

10.37

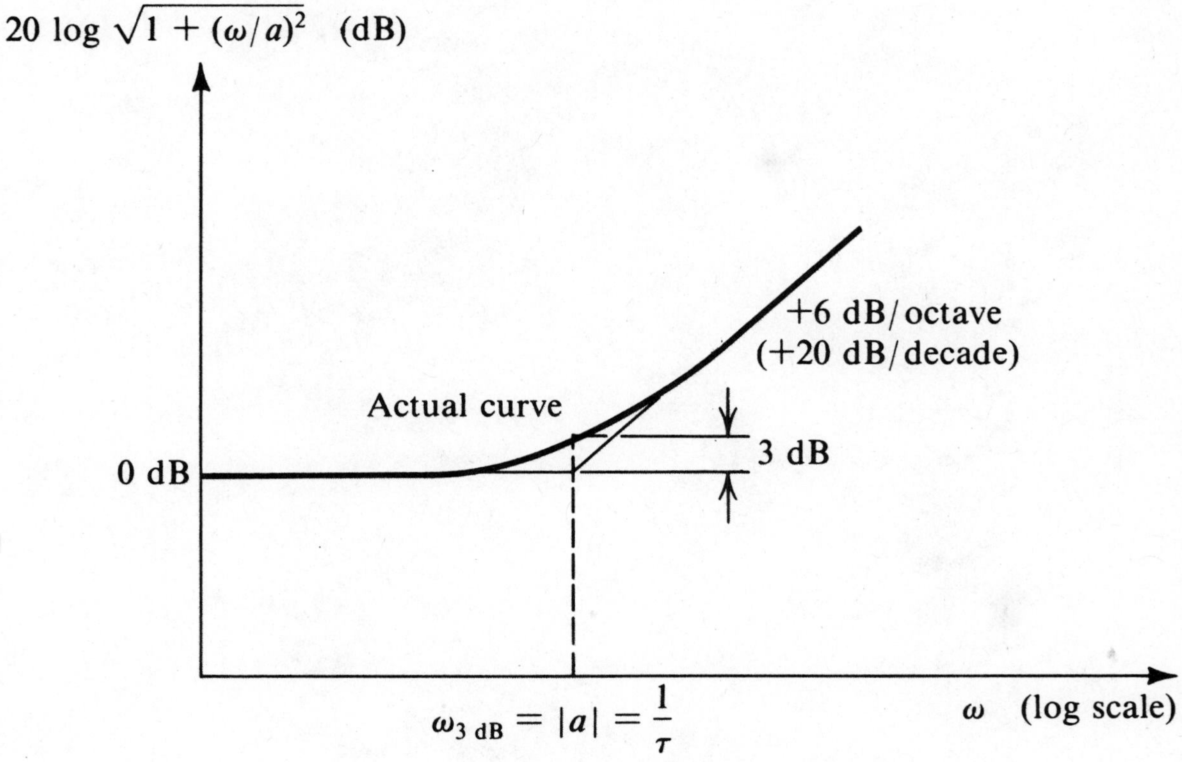

20 log $\sqrt{1 + (\omega/a)^2}$ (dB)
+6 dB/octave
(+20 dB/decade)
Actual curve
0 dB
3 dB
$\omega_{3\text{ dB}} = |a| = \frac{1}{\tau}$
ω (log scale)

11.1

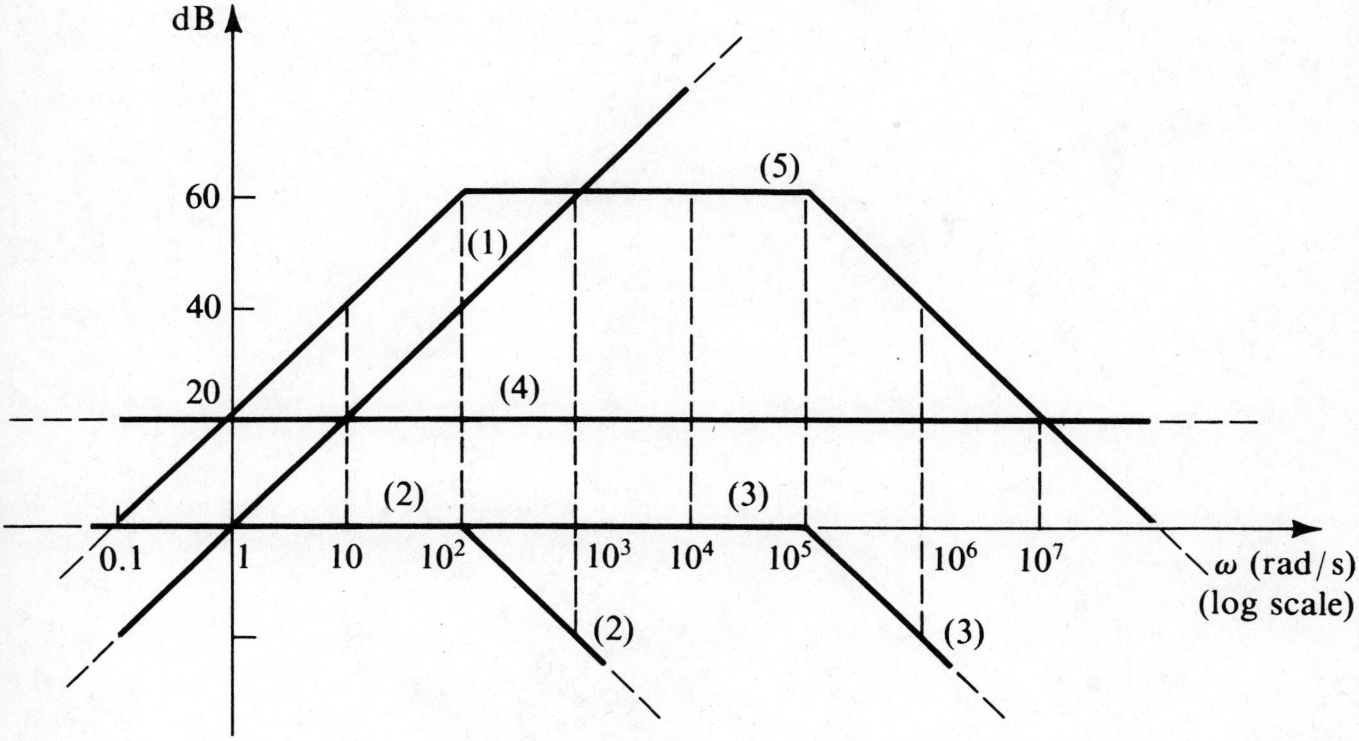
dB
60
40
20
(1)
(2)
(3)
(4)
(5)
(2)
(3)
0.1
1
10
10^2
10^3
10^4
10^5
10^6
10^7
ω (rad/s)
(log scale)

11.2

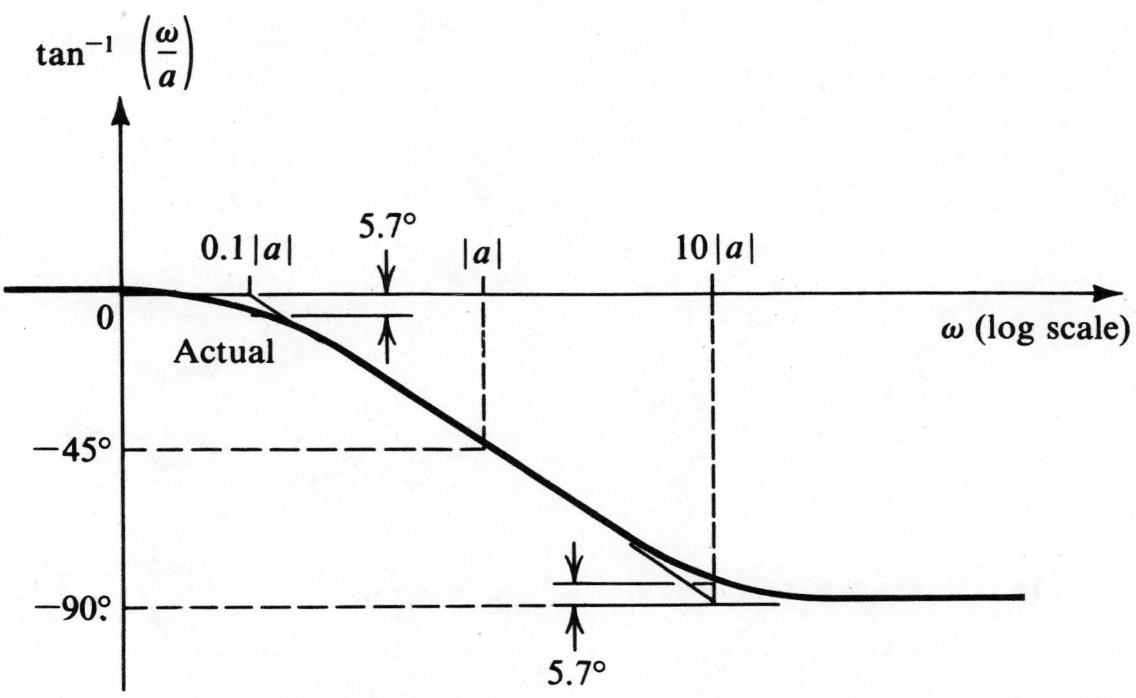

tan⁻¹ (ω/a)
0.1|a|
5.7°
|a|
10|a|
0
Actual
ω (log scale)
−45°
−90°
5.7°

11.3

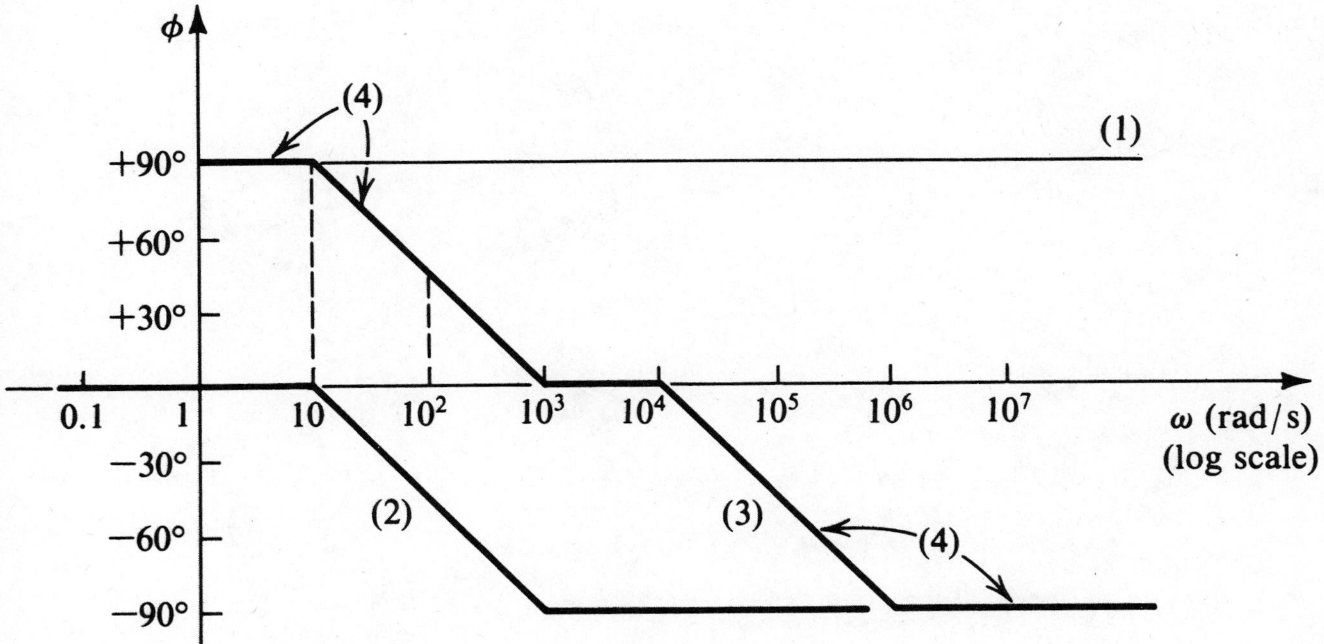

ϕ
(4)
(1)
+90°
+60°
+30°
0.1
1
10
10²
10³
10⁴
10⁵
10⁶
10⁷
ω (rad/s)
(log scale)
−30°
(2)
(3)
−60°
(4)
−90°

11.4

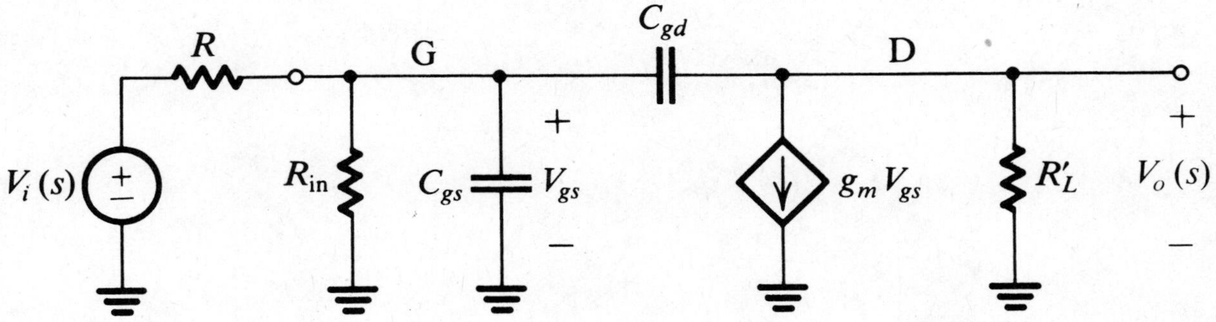

R
G
C_{gd}
D
$V_i(s)$
R_{in}
C_{gs}
+
V_{gs}
−
$g_m V_{gs}$
R'_L
+
$V_o(s)$
−

(a)

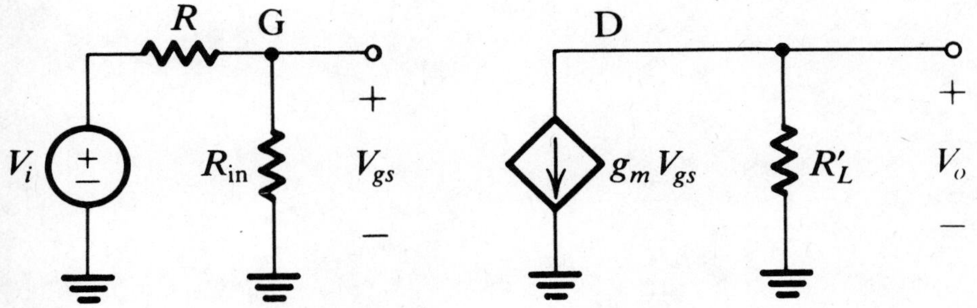

R
G
V_i
R_{in}
+
V_{gs}
−
D
$g_m V_{gs}$
R'_L
+
V_o
−

(b)

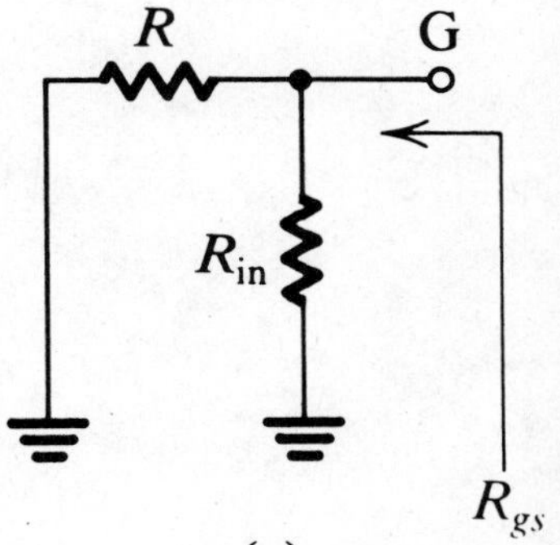

R
G
R_{in}
R_{gs}

(c)

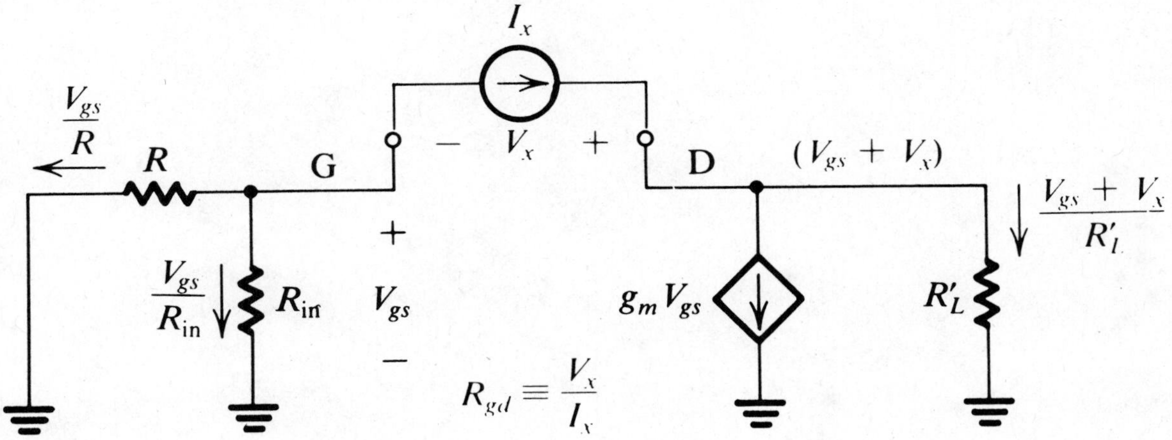

I_x
$\frac{V_{gs}}{R}$
R
G
−
V_x
+
D
$(V_{gs} + V_x)$
$\frac{V_{gs} + V_x}{R'_L}$
+
$\frac{V_{gs}}{R_{in}}$
R_{in}
V_{gs}
$g_m V_{gs}$
R'_L
−
$R_{gd} \equiv \frac{V_x}{I_x}$

(d)

11.8

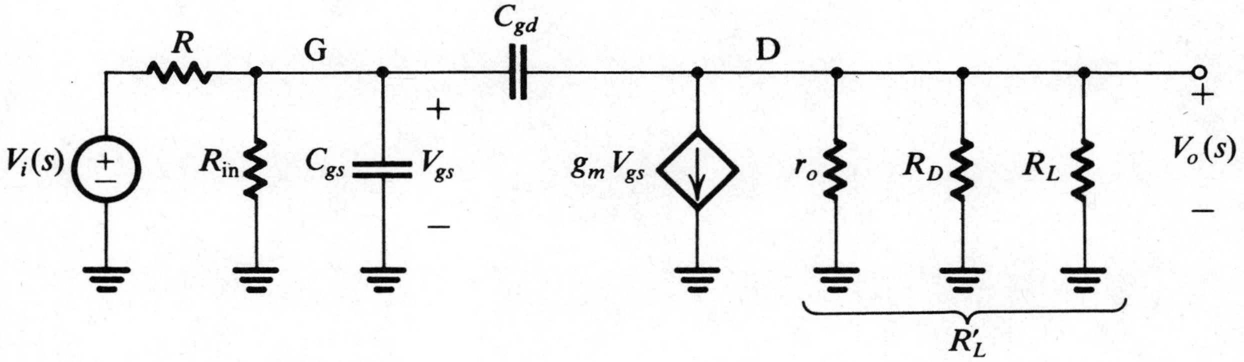
R
G
C_{gd}
D
$V_i(s)$
R_{in}
C_{gs}
V_{gs}
$g_m V_{gs}$
r_o
R_D
R_L
$V_o(s)$
R'_L

(a)

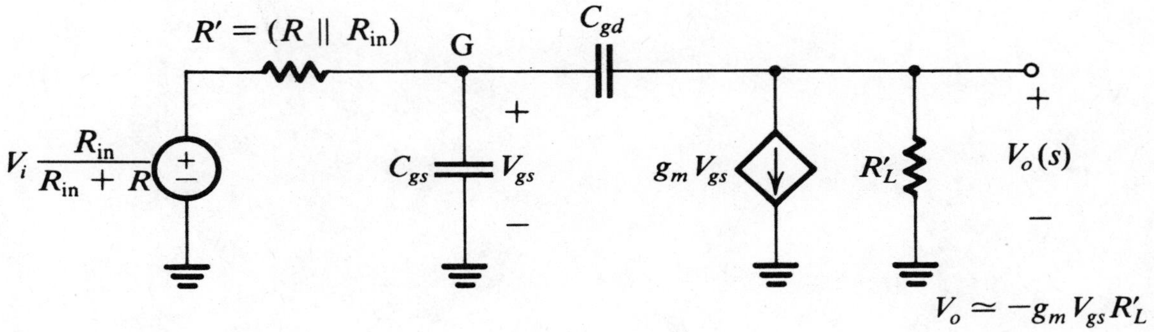
$R' = (R \parallel R_{in})$
G
C_{gd}
$V_i \dfrac{R_{in}}{R_{in} + R}$
C_{gs}
V_{gs}
$g_m V_{gs}$
R'_L
$V_o(s)$
$V_o \simeq -g_m V_{gs} R'_L$

(b)

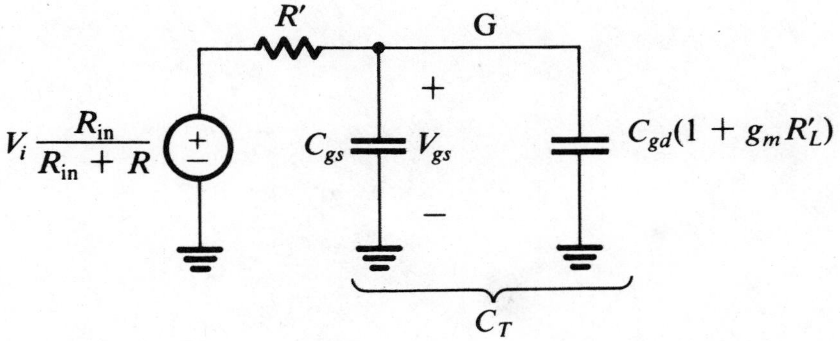
R'
G
$V_i \dfrac{R_{in}}{R_{in} + R}$
C_{gs}
V_{gs}
$C_{gd}(1 + g_m R'_L)$
C_T

(c)

11.12

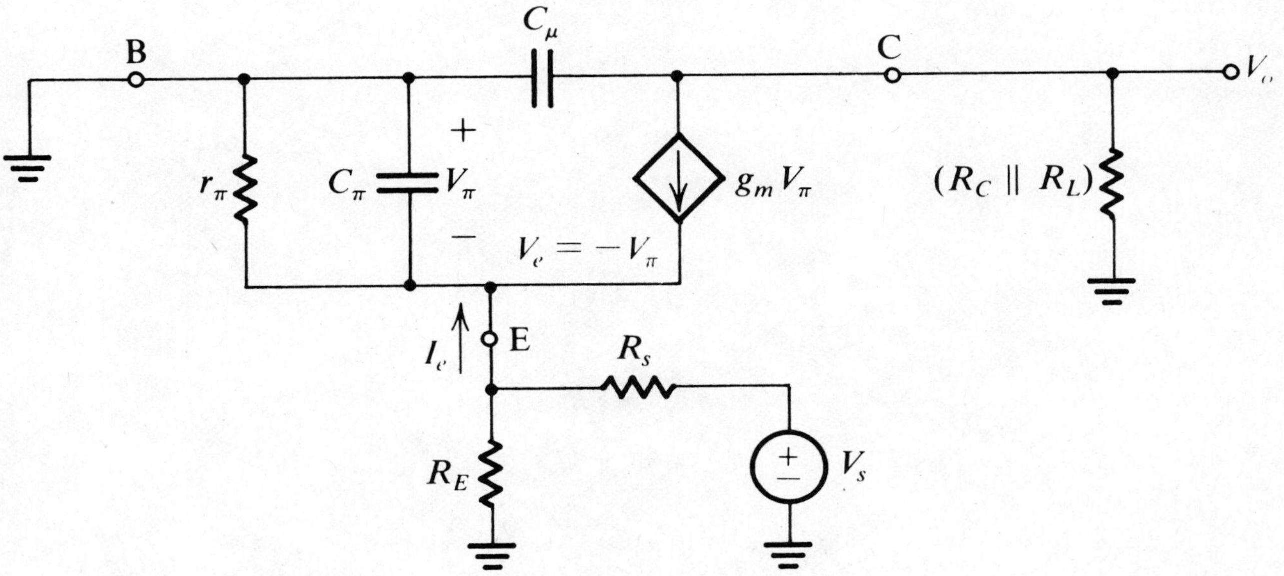

B
C_μ
C
V_o
+
r_π
C_π
V_π
$g_m V_\pi$
$(R_C \parallel R_L)$
−
$V_e = -V_\pi$
I_e
E
R_s
R_E
V_s

(a)

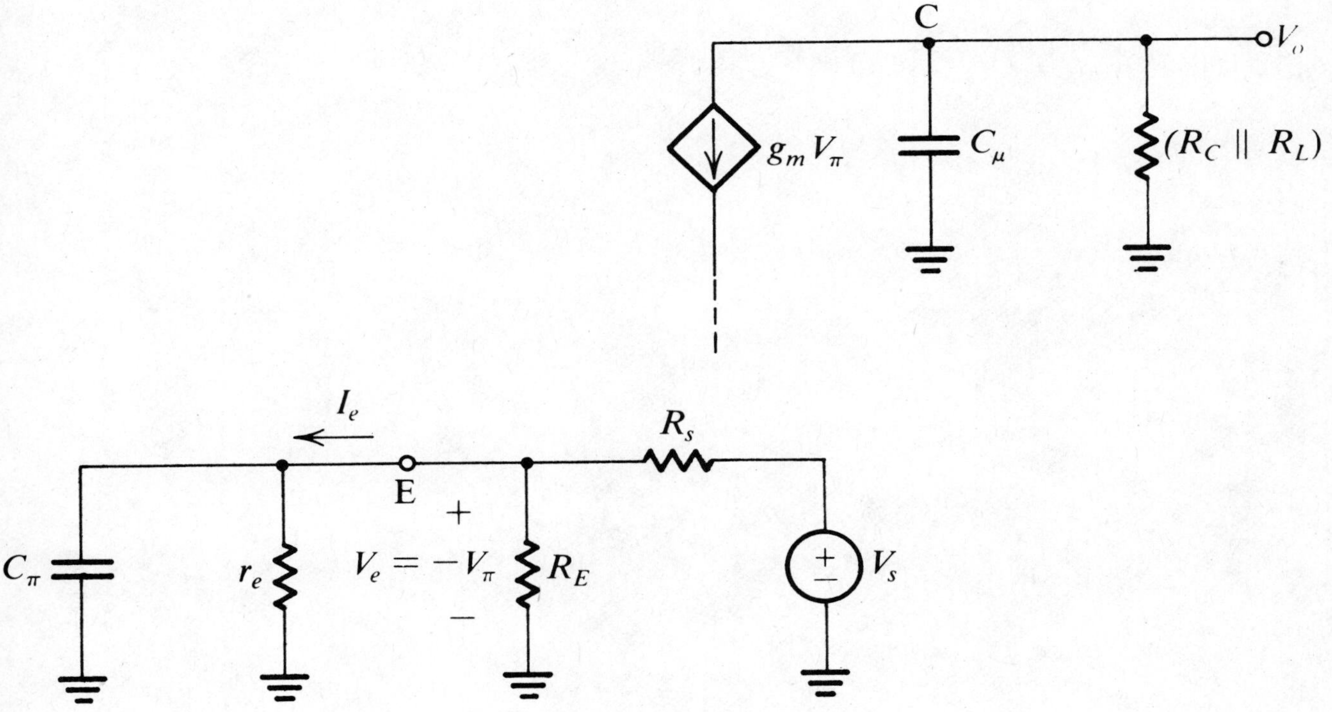

C
V_o
$g_m V_\pi$
C_μ
$(R_C \parallel R_L)$
I_e
R_s
E
+
C_π
r_e
$V_e = -V_\pi$
R_E
V_s
−

(b)

11.26

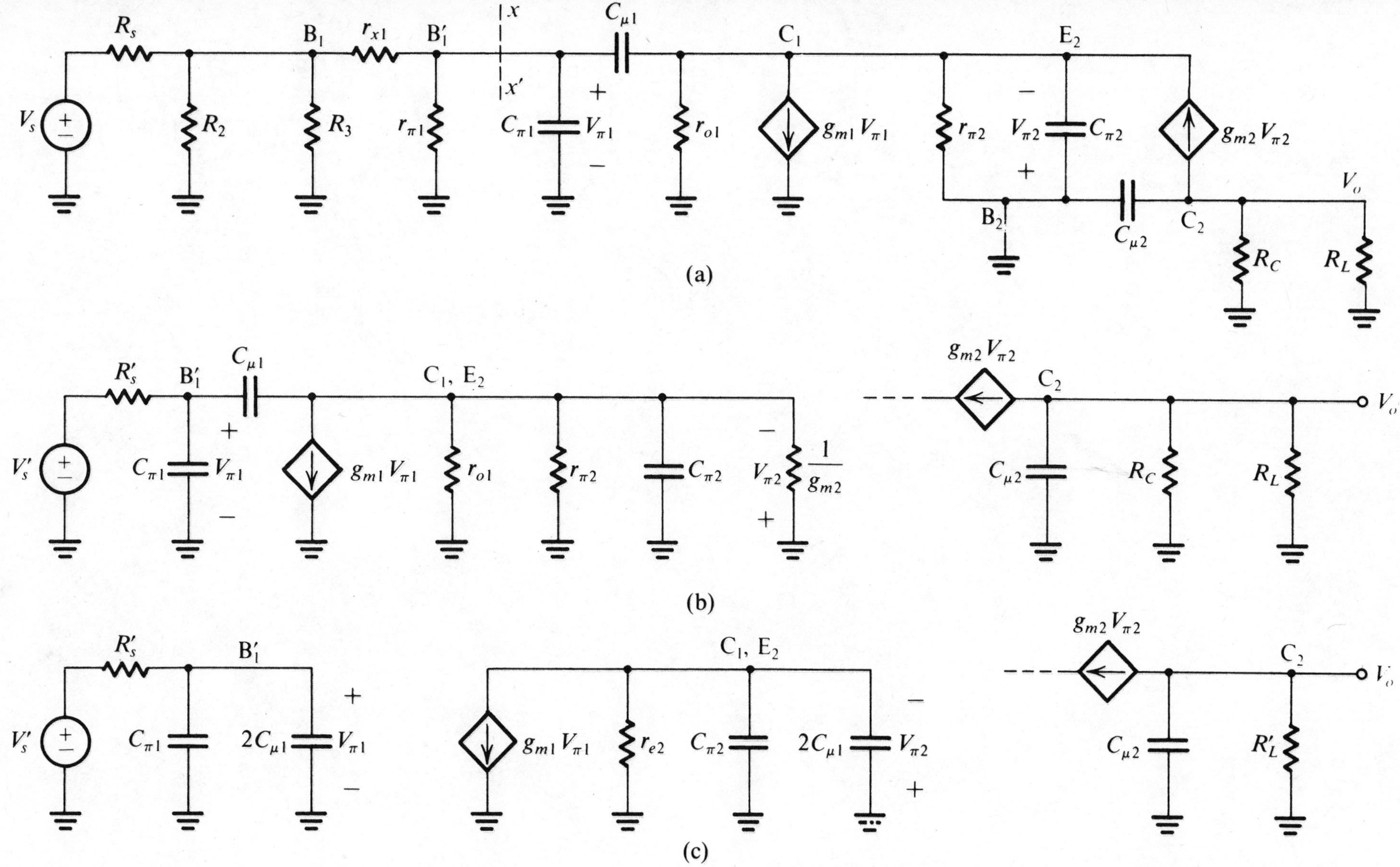

R_s
B_1
r_{x1}
B'_1
x
x'
$C_{\mu 1}$
C_1
E_2
V_s
R_2
R_3
$r_{\pi 1}$
$C_{\pi 1}$
$V_{\pi 1}$
r_{o1}
$g_{m1} V_{\pi 1}$
$r_{\pi 2}$
$V_{\pi 2}$
$C_{\pi 2}$
$g_{m2} V_{\pi 2}$
V_o
B_2
$C_{\mu 2}$
C_2
R_C
R_L
(a)
R'_s
B'_1
$C_{\mu 1}$
C_1, E_2
V'_s
$C_{\pi 1}$
$V_{\pi 1}$
$g_{m1} V_{\pi 1}$
r_{o1}
$r_{\pi 2}$
$C_{\pi 2}$
$V_{\pi 2}$
$\frac{1}{g_{m2}}$
$g_{m2} V_{\pi 2}$
C_2
V_o
$C_{\mu 2}$
R_C
R_L
(b)
R'_s
B'_1
C_1, E_2
V'_s
$C_{\pi 1}$
$2C_{\mu 1}$
$V_{\pi 1}$
$g_{m1} V_{\pi 1}$
r_{e2}
$C_{\pi 2}$
$2C_{\mu 1}$
$V_{\pi 2}$
$g_{m2} V_{\pi 2}$
C_2
V_o
$C_{\mu 2}$
R'_L
(c)

11.28

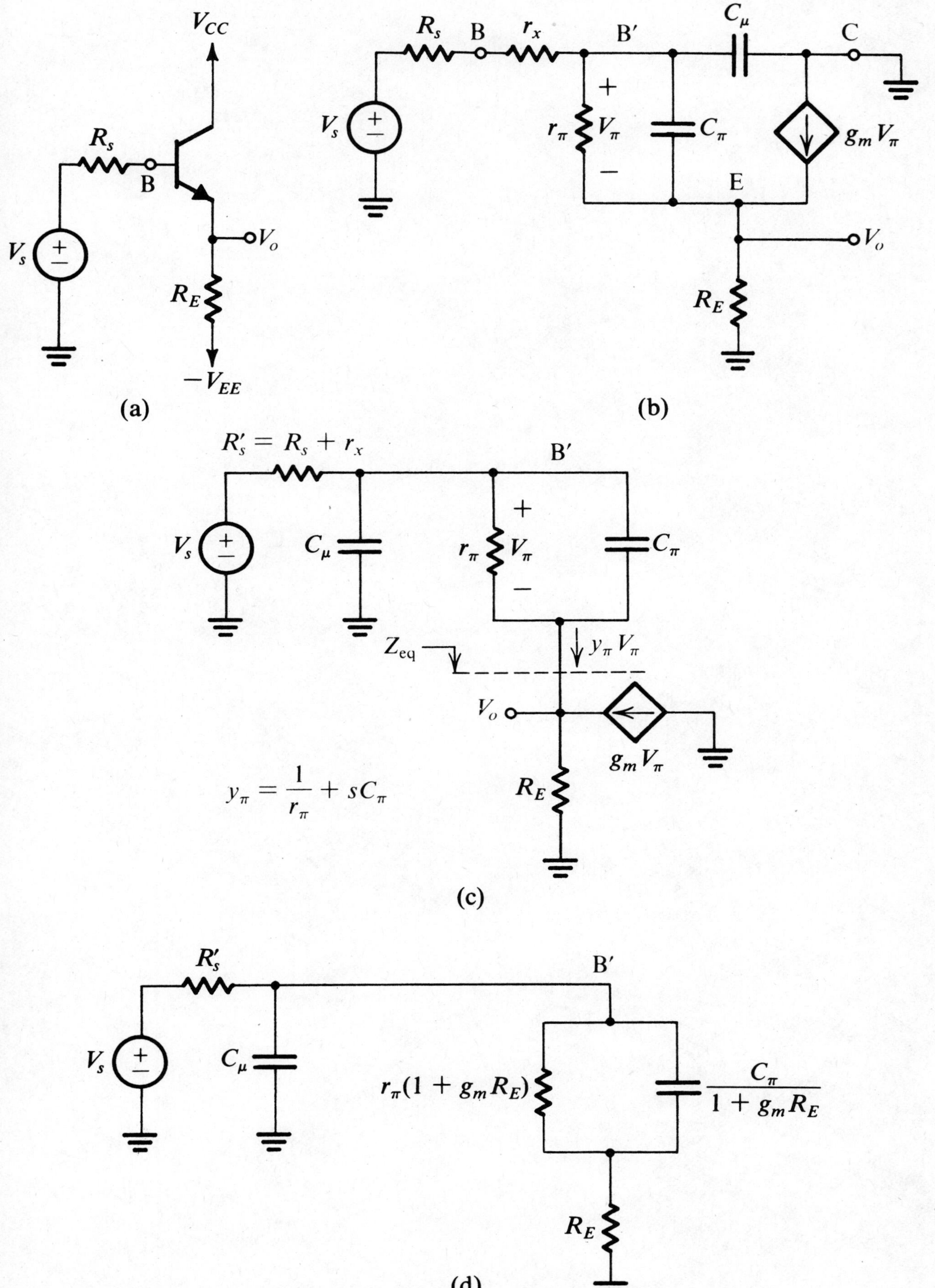

V_CC
R_s
B
V_s
V_o
R_E
−V_EE
(a)
R_s
B
r_x
B′
C_μ
C
V_s
r_π
V_π
C_π
g_m V_π
E
V_o
R_E
(b)
R′_s = R_s + r_x
B′
V_s
C_μ
r_π
V_π
C_π
Z_eq
y_π V_π
V_o
g_m V_π
R_E
y_π = 1/r_π + sC_π
(c)
R′_s
B′
V_s
C_μ
r_π(1 + g_m R_E)
C_π / (1 + g_m R_E)
R_E
(d)

11.29

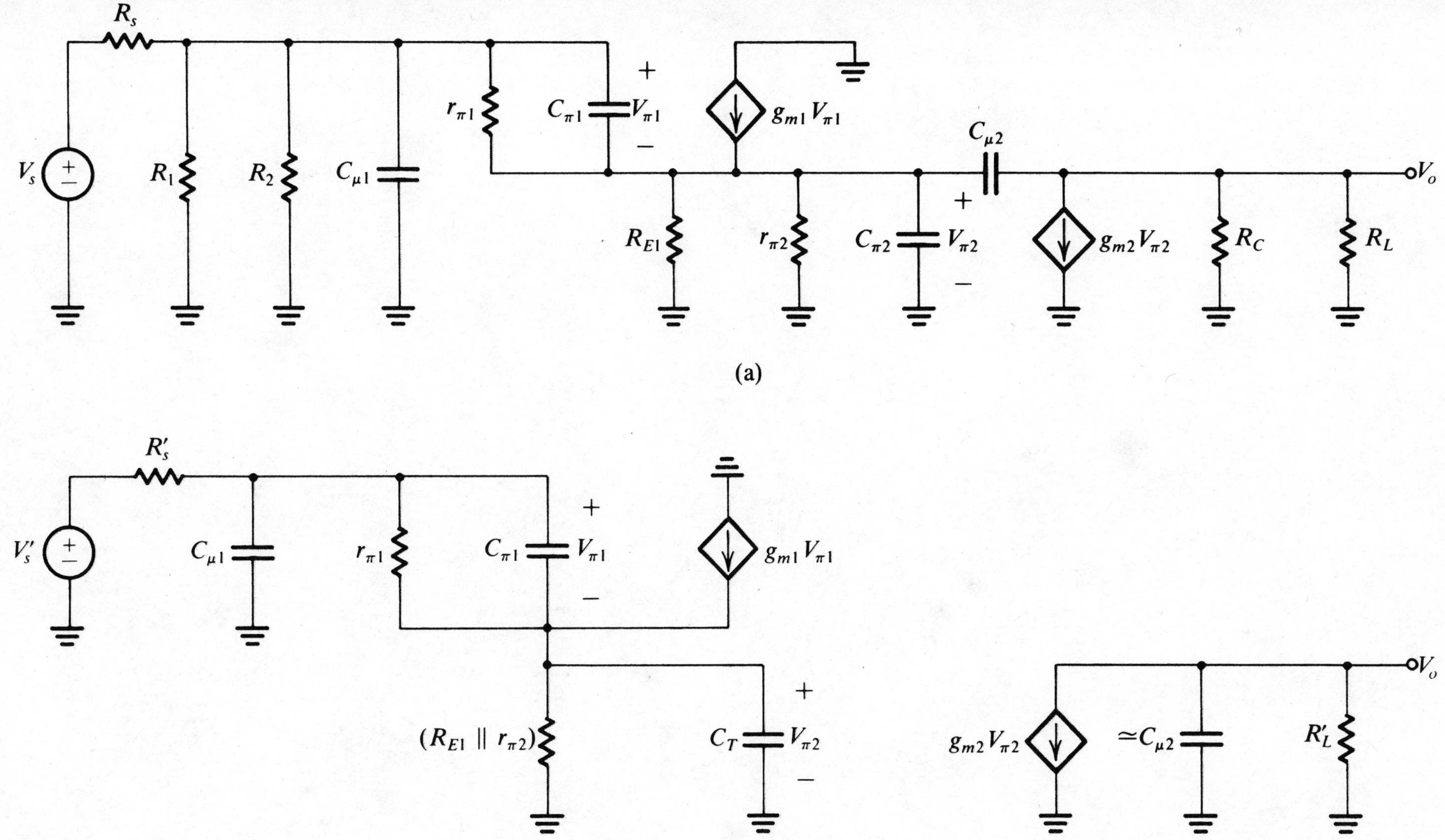
R_s
V_s
R_1
R_2
$C_{\mu 1}$
$r_{\pi 1}$
$C_{\pi 1}$
$V_{\pi 1}$
$g_{m1} V_{\pi 1}$
$C_{\mu 2}$
R_{E1}
$r_{\pi 2}$
$C_{\pi 2}$
$V_{\pi 2}$
$g_{m2} V_{\pi 2}$
R_C
R_L
V_o
R_s'
V_s'
$(R_{E1} \parallel r_{\pi 2})$
C_T
$\simeq C_{\mu 2}$
R_L'

(a)

(b)

11.32

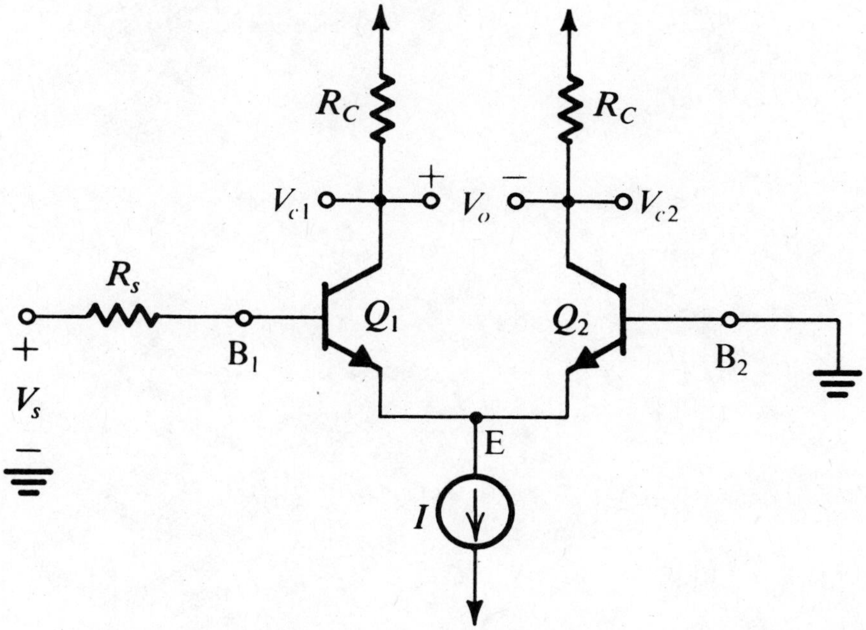
RC
RC
Vc1
+
Vo
−
Vc2
Rs
Q1
Q2
+
Vs
−
B1
B2
E
I

(a)

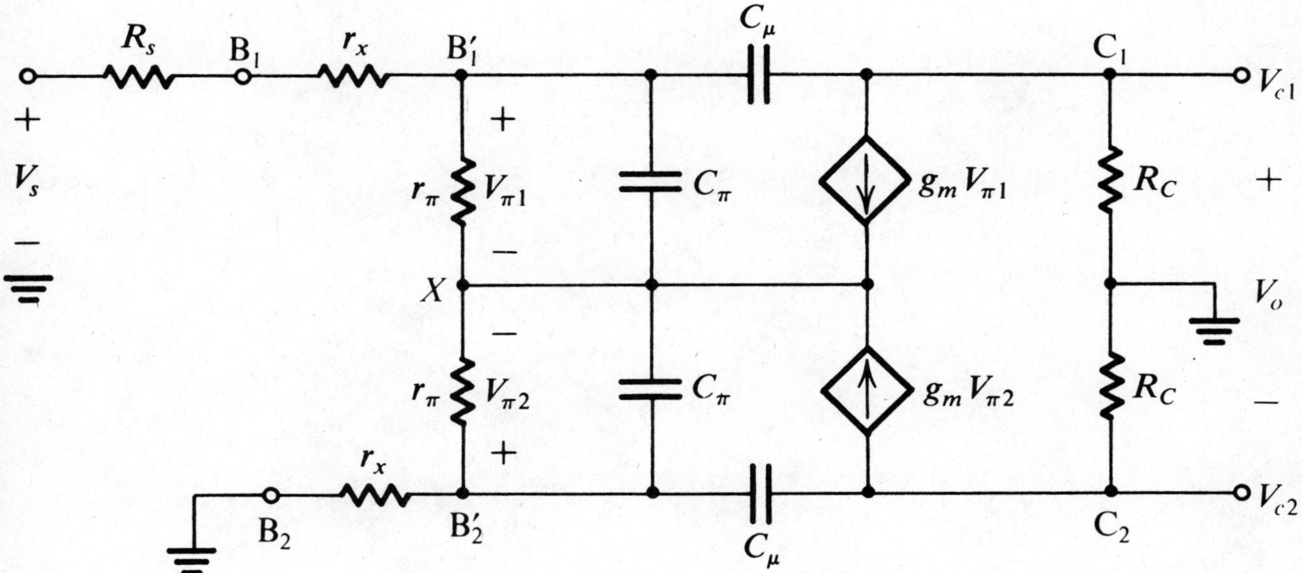
Rs
B1
rx
B′1
Cμ
C1
Vc1
+
Vs
−
+
rπ
Vπ1
−
Cπ
gm Vπ1
RC
+
X
Vo
−
rπ
Vπ2
+
Cπ
gm Vπ2
RC
−
rx
B2
B′2
Cμ
C2
Vc2

(b)

11.35 (a,b)

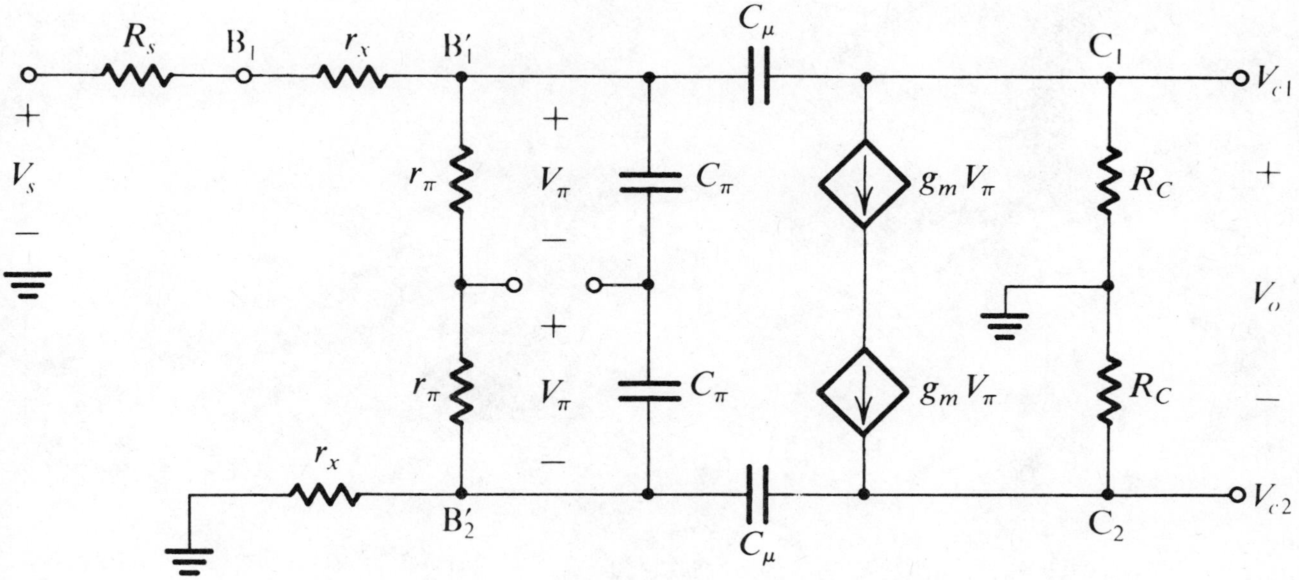

R_s
B_1
r_x
B_1'
C_μ
C_1
V_{c1}
+
V_s
—
r_π
+
V_π
—
C_π
$g_m V_\pi$
R_C
+
V_o
+
r_π
V_π
—
C_π
$g_m V_\pi$
R_C
—
r_x
B_2'
C_μ
C_2
V_{c2}

(c)

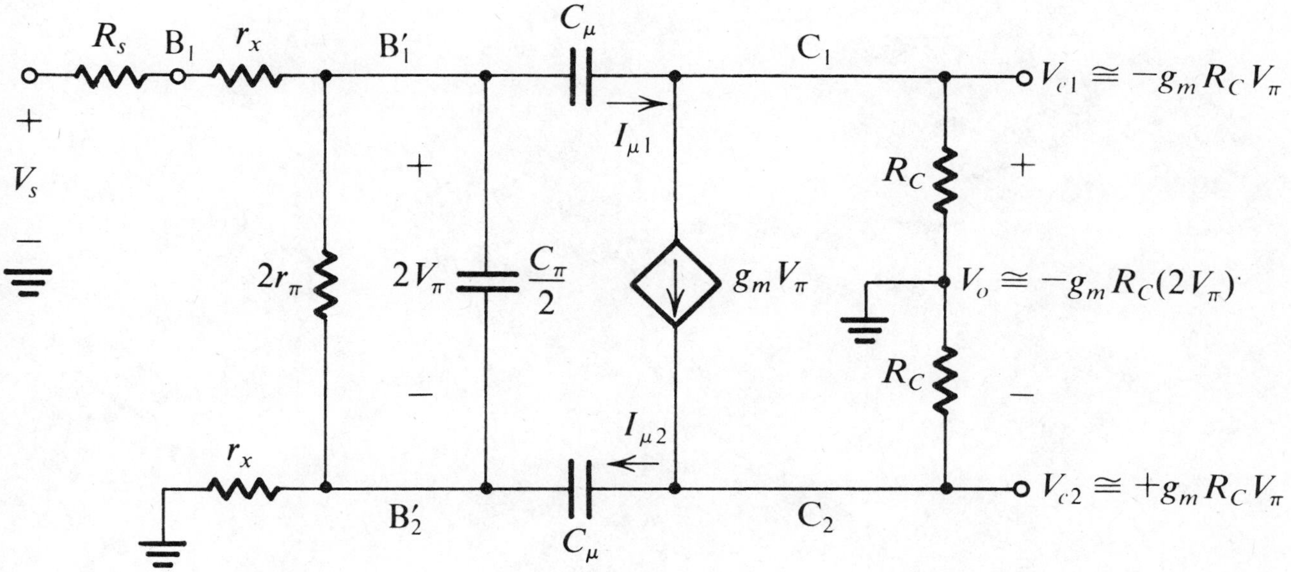

R_s
B_1
r_x
B_1'
C_μ
C_1
$V_{c1} \cong -g_m R_C V_\pi$
+
V_s
—
$I_{\mu 1}$
+
R_C
+
$2r_\pi$
$2V_\pi$
$\frac{C_\pi}{2}$
$g_m V_\pi$
$V_o \cong -g_m R_C (2V_\pi)$
—
R_C
—
$I_{\mu 2}$
r_x
B_2'
C_μ
C_2
$V_{c2} \cong +g_m R_C V_\pi$

(d)

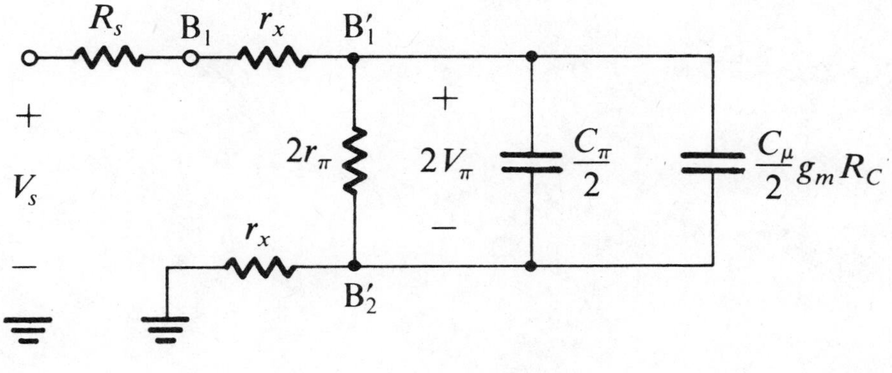

R_s
B_1
r_x
B_1'
+
+
V_s
—
$2r_\pi$
$2V_\pi$
$\frac{C_\pi}{2}$
$\frac{C_\mu}{2} g_m R_C$
—
r_x
B_2'

(e)

11.35 (c,d,e)

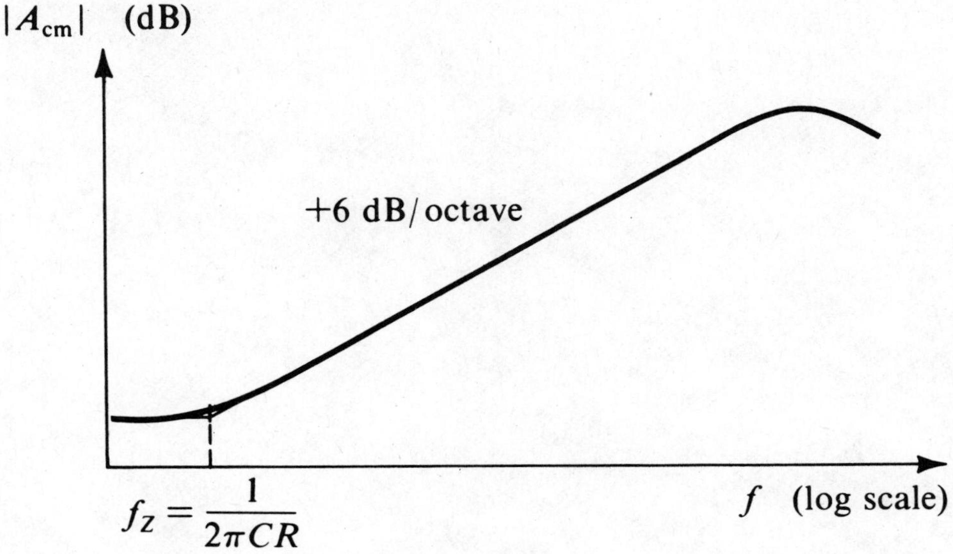
$|A_{cm}|$ (dB)
+6 dB/octave
$f_Z = \frac{1}{2\pi CR}$
f (log scale)

(a)

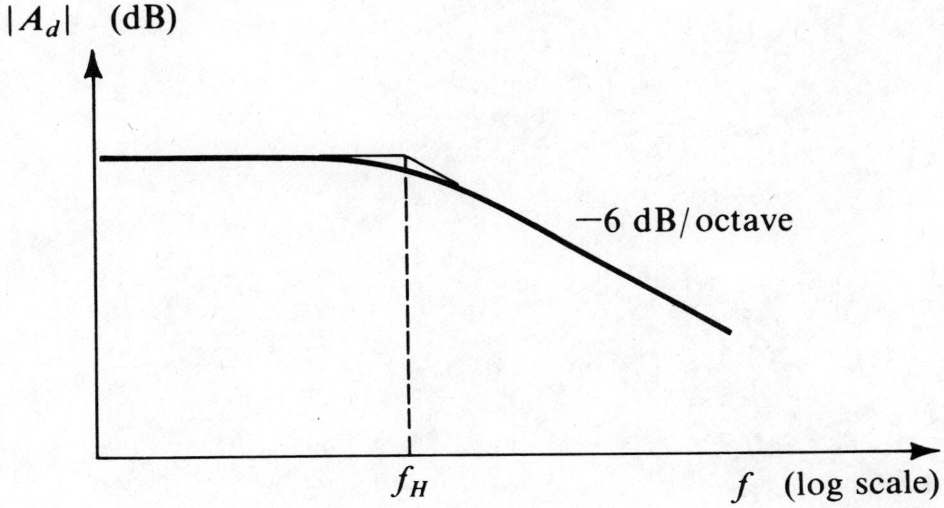
$|A_d|$ (dB)
−6 dB/octave
f_H
f (log scale)

(b)

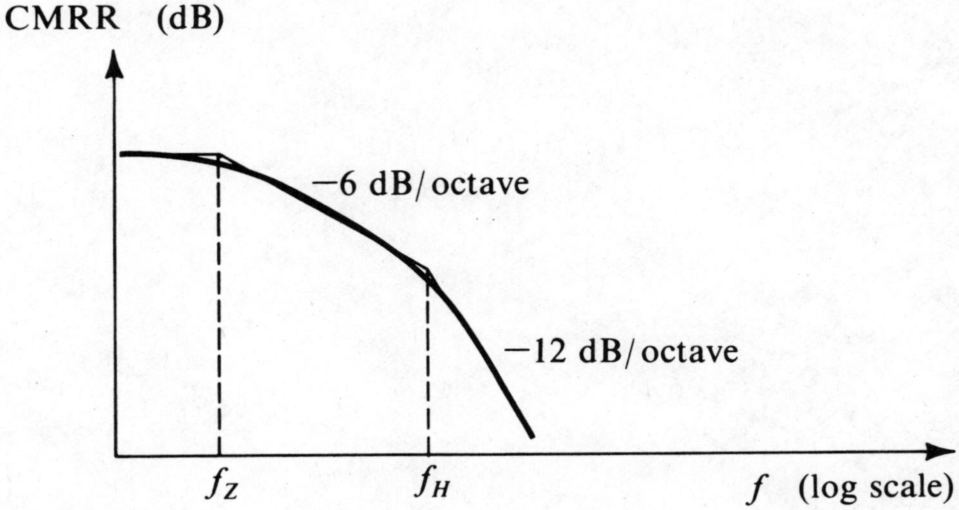
CMRR (dB)
−6 dB/octave
−12 dB/octave
f_Z
f_H
f (log scale)

(c)

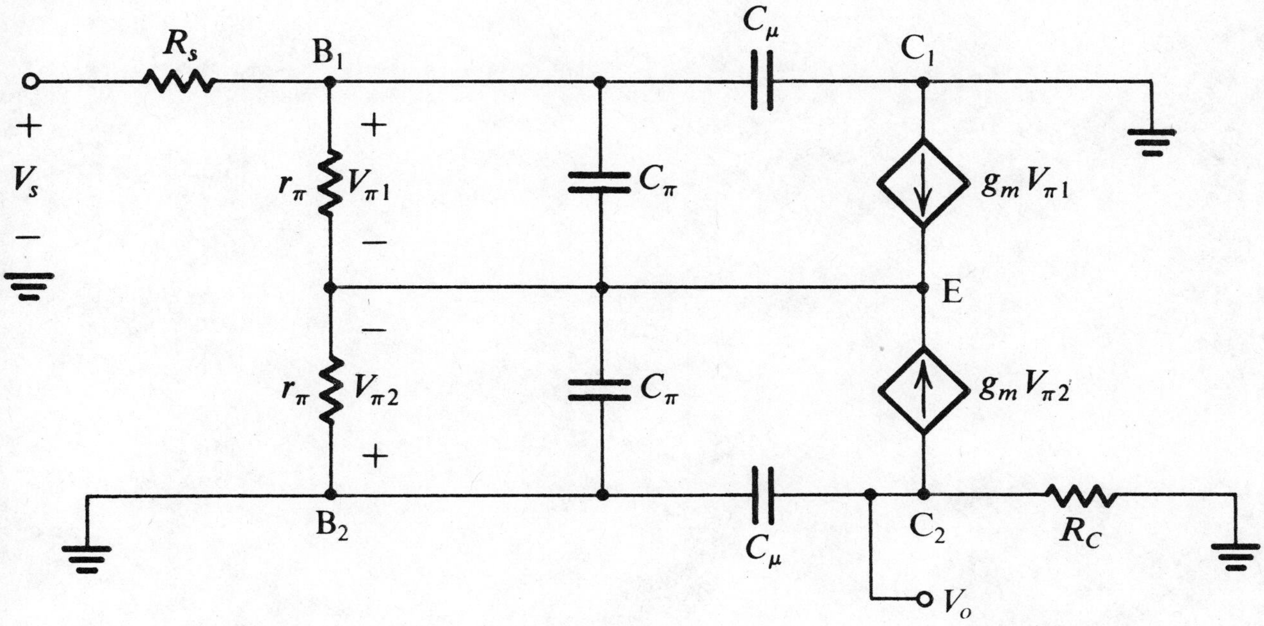

R_s
B$_1$
C_μ
C$_1$
+
V_s
−
+
r_π
$V_{\pi 1}$
−
C_π
$g_m V_{\pi 1}$
E
−
r_π
$V_{\pi 2}$
+
C_π
$g_m V_{\pi 2}$
B$_2$
C_μ
C$_2$
R_C
V_o

(a)

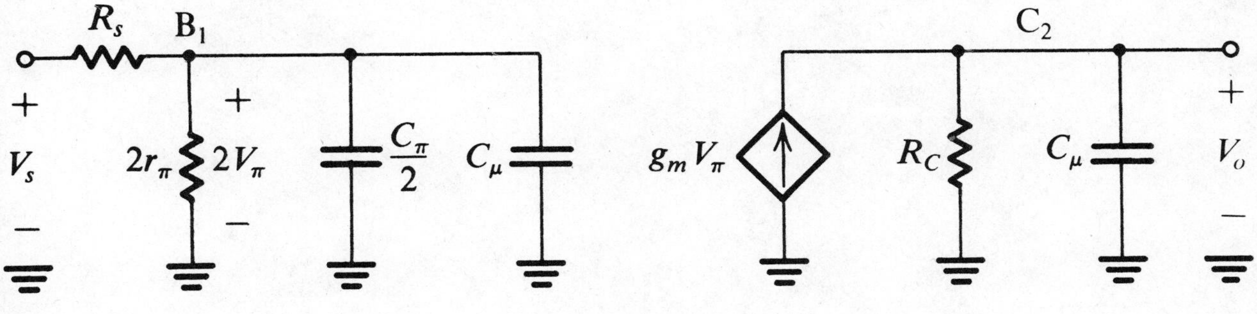

R_s
B$_1$
+
V_s
−
$2r_\pi$
$2V_\pi$
+
−
$\frac{C_\pi}{2}$
C_μ
C$_2$
$g_m V_\pi$
R_C
C_μ
+
V_o
−

(b)

11.40

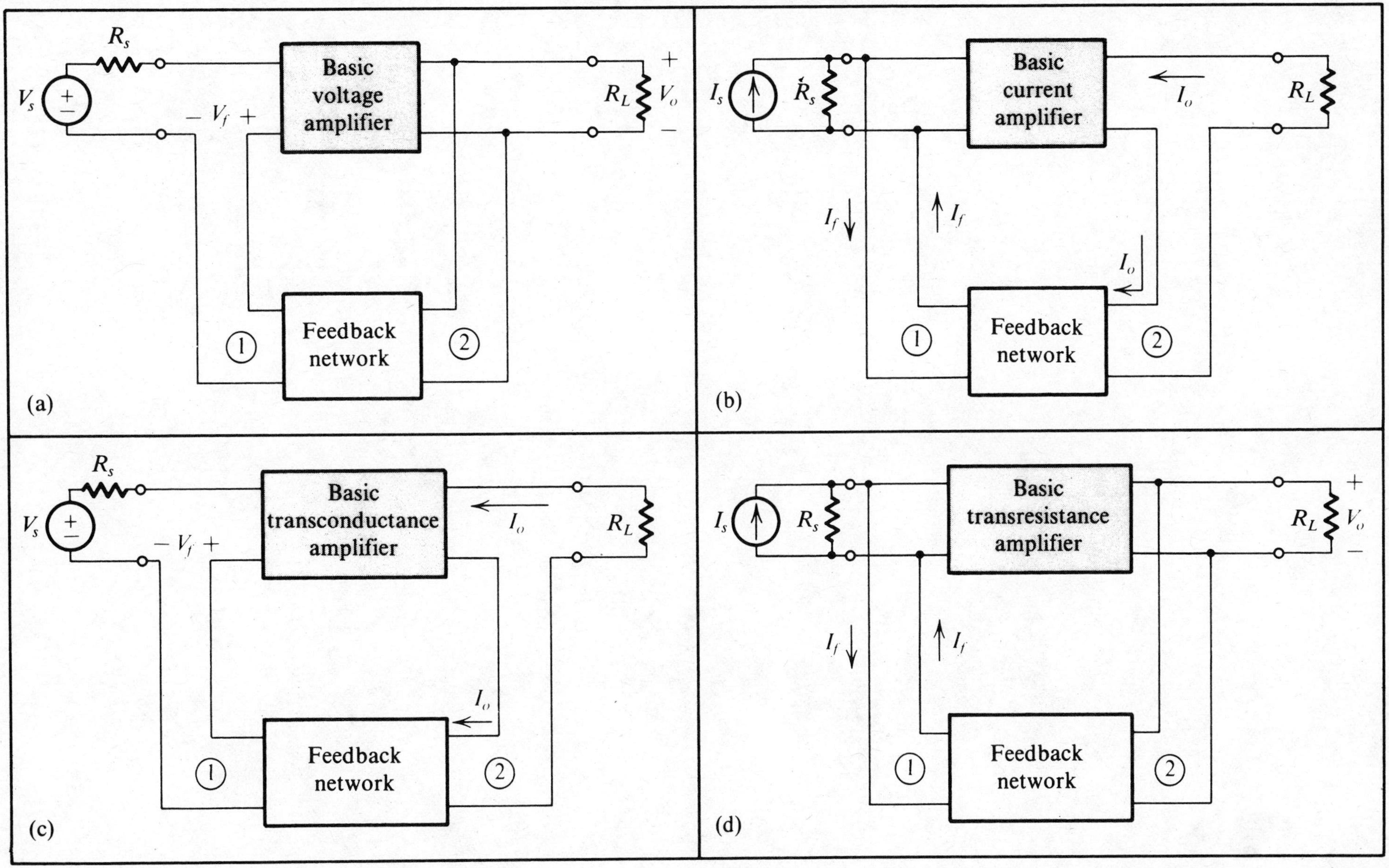

R_s
V_s
$-\ V_f\ +$
Basic voltage amplifier
R_L
V_o
Feedback network
1
2
(a)
I_s
R_s
Basic current amplifier
I_o
R_L
I_f
I_f
I_o
Feedback network
1
2
(b)
R_s
V_s
$-\ V_f\ +$
Basic transconductance amplifier
I_o
R_L
I_o
Feedback network
1
2
(c)
I_s
R_s
Basic transresistance amplifier
R_L
V_o
I_f
I_f
Feedback network
1
2
(d)

12.4

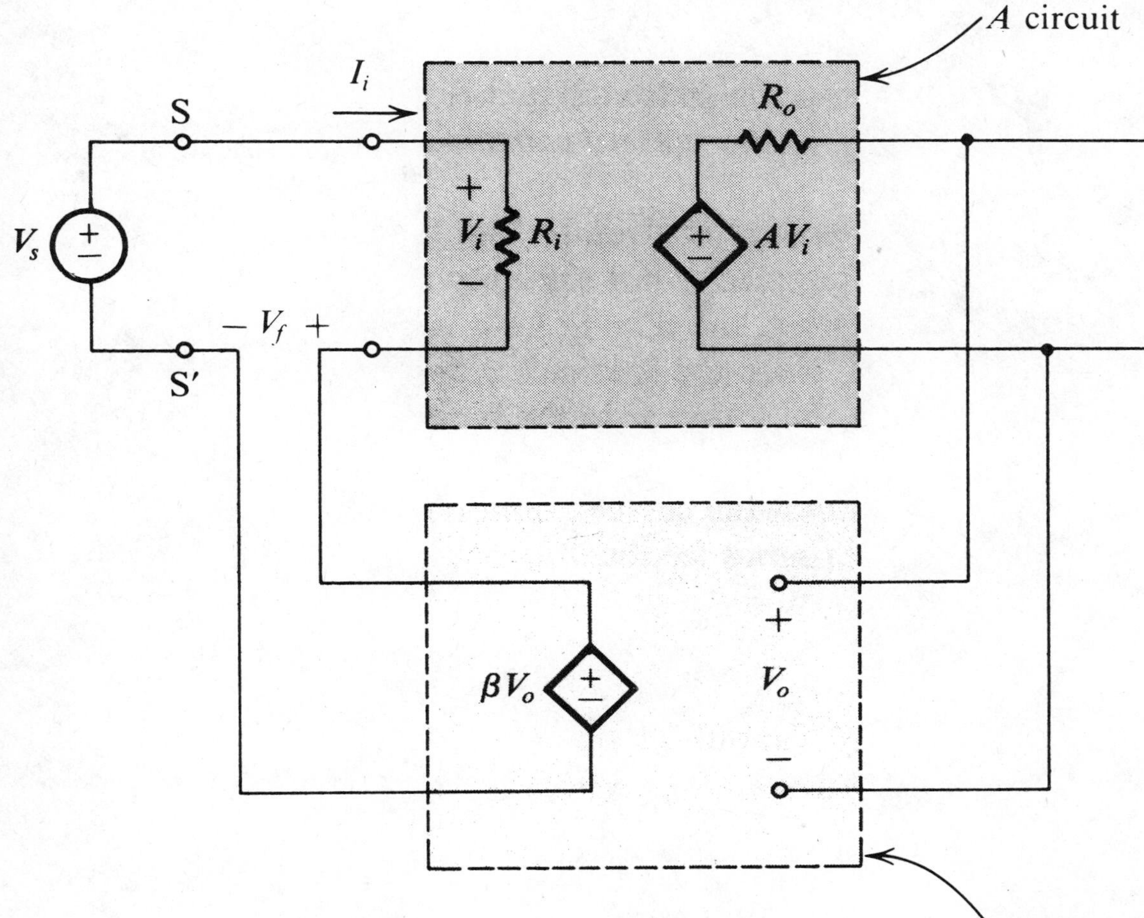
A circuit
I_i
S
R_o
O
+
V_i
R_i
AV_i
V_s
−
V_o
− V_f +
S′
O′
βV_o
+
V_o
−
β circuit
(a)

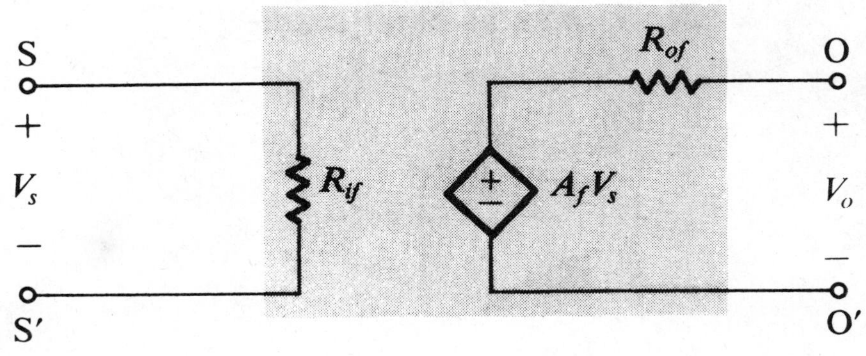
S
R_{of}
O
+
V_s
R_{if}
$A_f V_s$
V_o
−
S′
O′
(b)

12.8

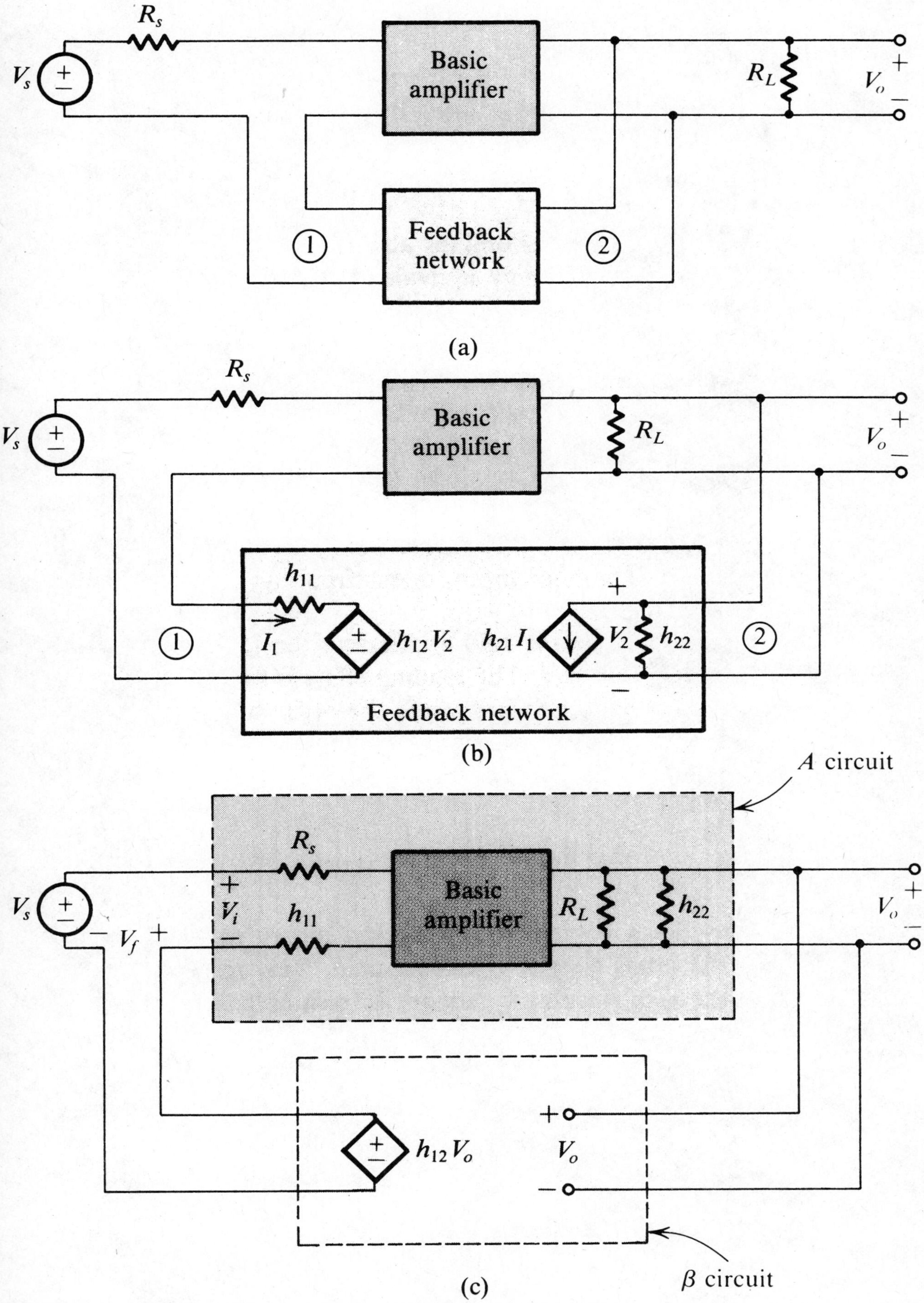
R_s
V_s
Basic amplifier
R_L
V_o
Feedback network
1
2
(a)
R_s
V_s
Basic amplifier
R_L
V_o
h_11
I_1
h_12 V_2
h_21 I_1
V_2
h_22
1
2
Feedback network
(b)
A circuit
R_s
V_s
V_i
h_11
Basic amplifier
R_L
h_22
V_o
V_f
h_12 V_o
V_o
β circuit
(c)

(a) The A circuit is

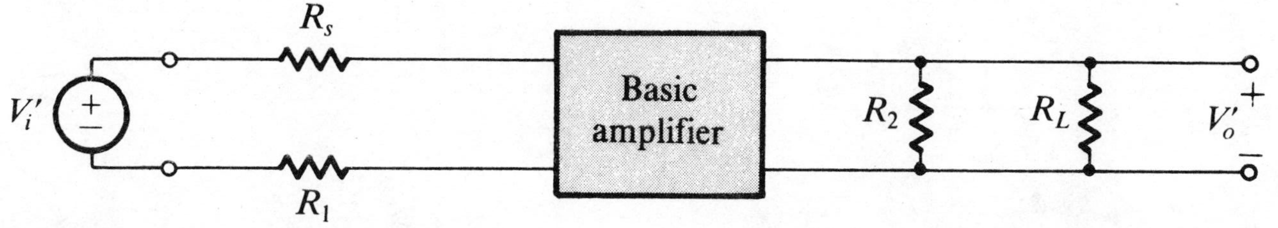

where R_1 is obtained from

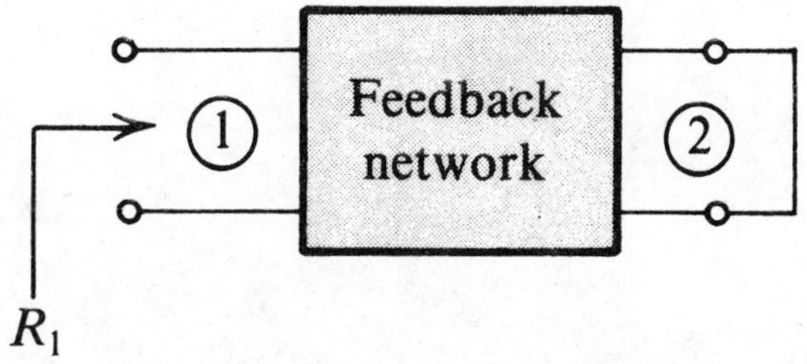

and R_2 is obtained from

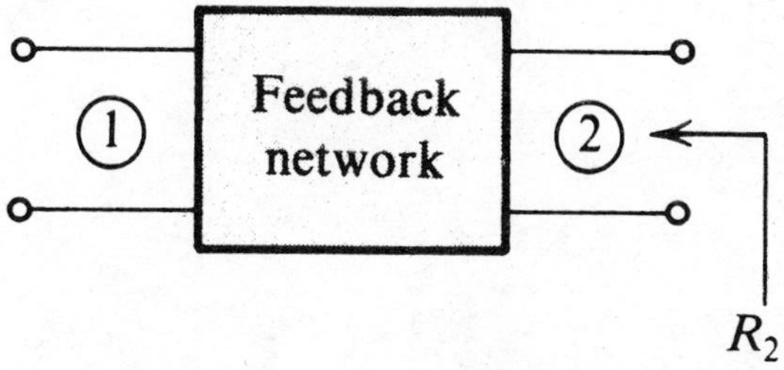

and the gain A is defined $A \equiv \frac{V_o'}{V_i'}$

(b) β is obtained from

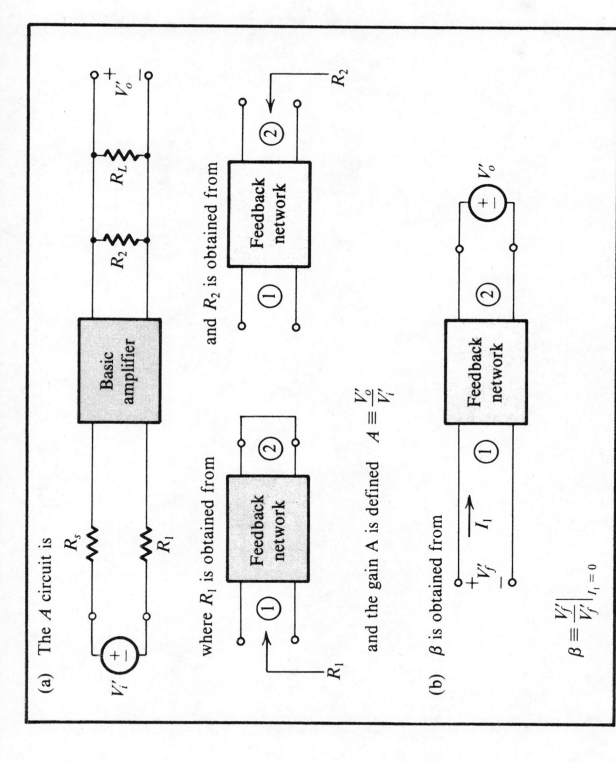

$$\beta \equiv \left. \frac{V_f'}{V_f'} \right|_{I_1 = 0}$$

12.11

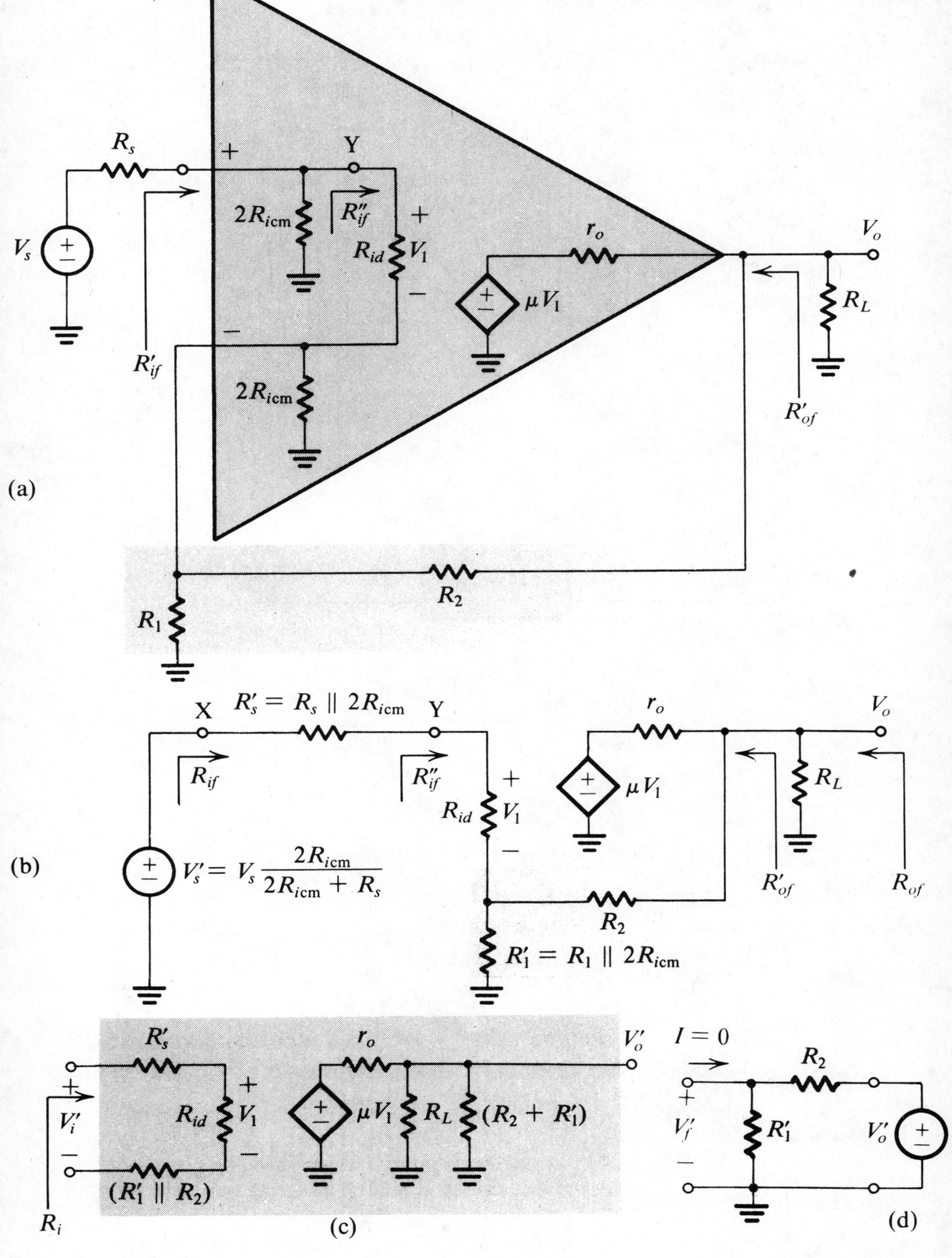

(a)
R_s
V_s
Y
$2R_{icm}$
R''_{if}
R_{id}
V_1
r_o
μV_1
V_o
R_L
R'_{if}
R'_{of}
R_2
R_1
(b)
X
$R'_s = R_s \parallel 2R_{icm}$
R_{if}
$V'_s = V_s \frac{2R_{icm}}{2R_{icm} + R_s}$
R'_{of}
R_{of}
$R'_1 = R_1 \parallel 2R_{icm}$
(c)
R'_s
V'_i
R_i
$(R'_1 \parallel R_2)$
V'_o
$(R_2 + R'_1)$
(d)
$I = 0$
V'_f
R'_1

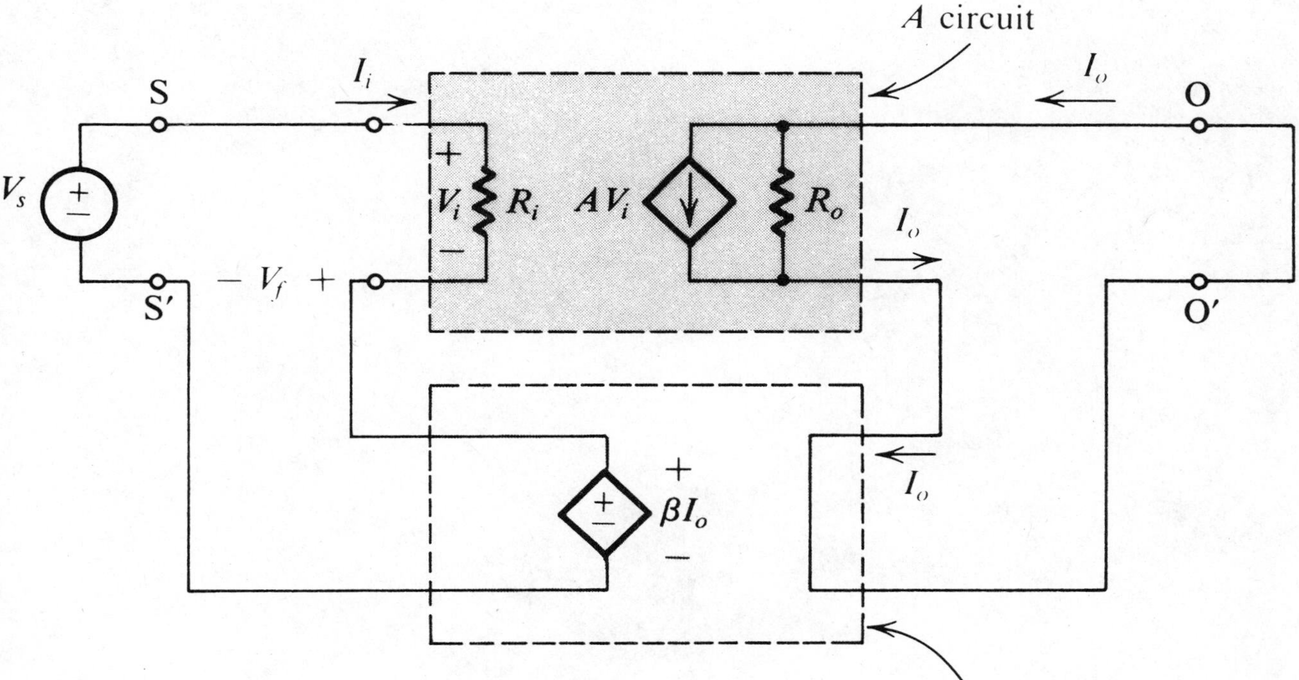
A circuit
S
I_i
I_o
O
V_s
+
V_i
R_i
AV_i
R_o
−
I_o
S′
$- V_f +$
O′
+
βI_o
−
I_o
β circuit

(a)

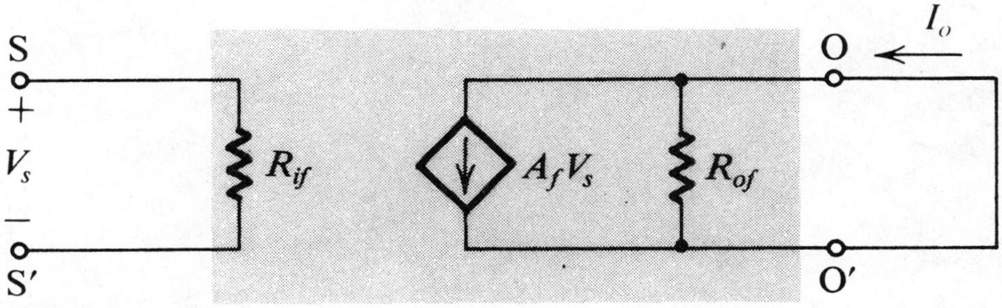
S
+
V_s
−
S′
R_{if}
$A_f V_s$
R_{of}
O
I_o
O′

(b)

12.13

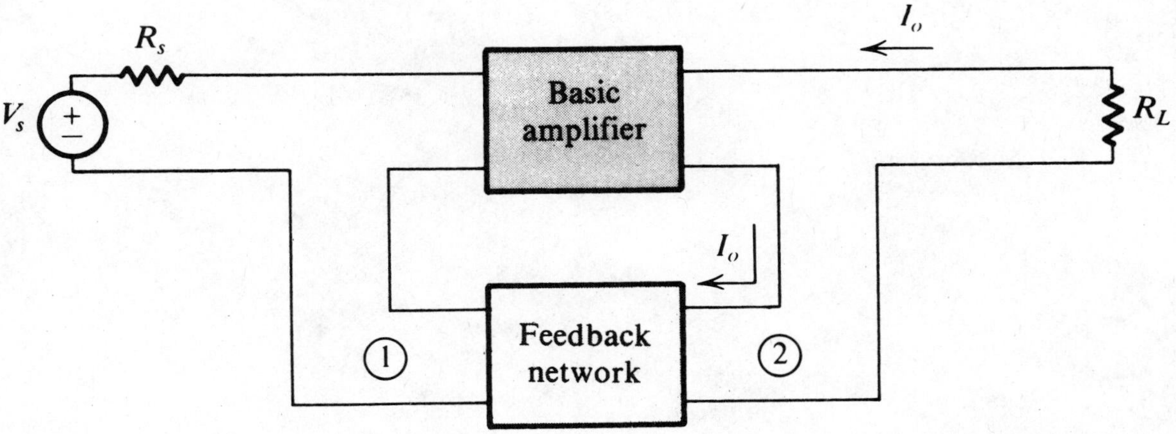

I_o
R_s
V_s
Basic amplifier
R_L
I_o
Feedback network
1
2

(a)

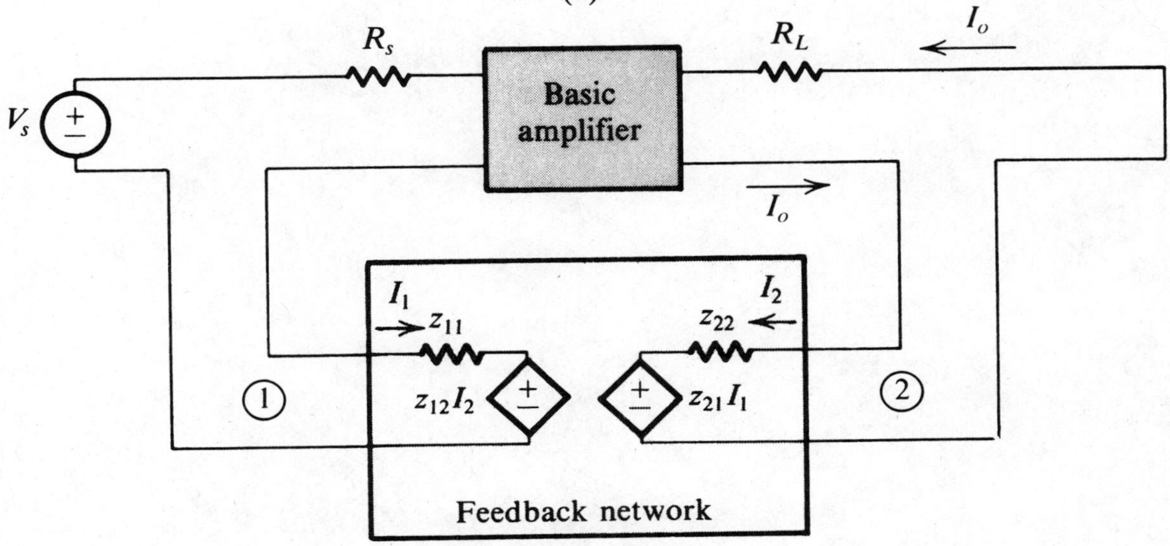

R_s
R_L
I_o
V_s
Basic amplifier
I_o
I_1
z_{11}
I_2
z_{22}
1
$z_{12}I_2$
$z_{21}I_1$
2
Feedback network

(b)

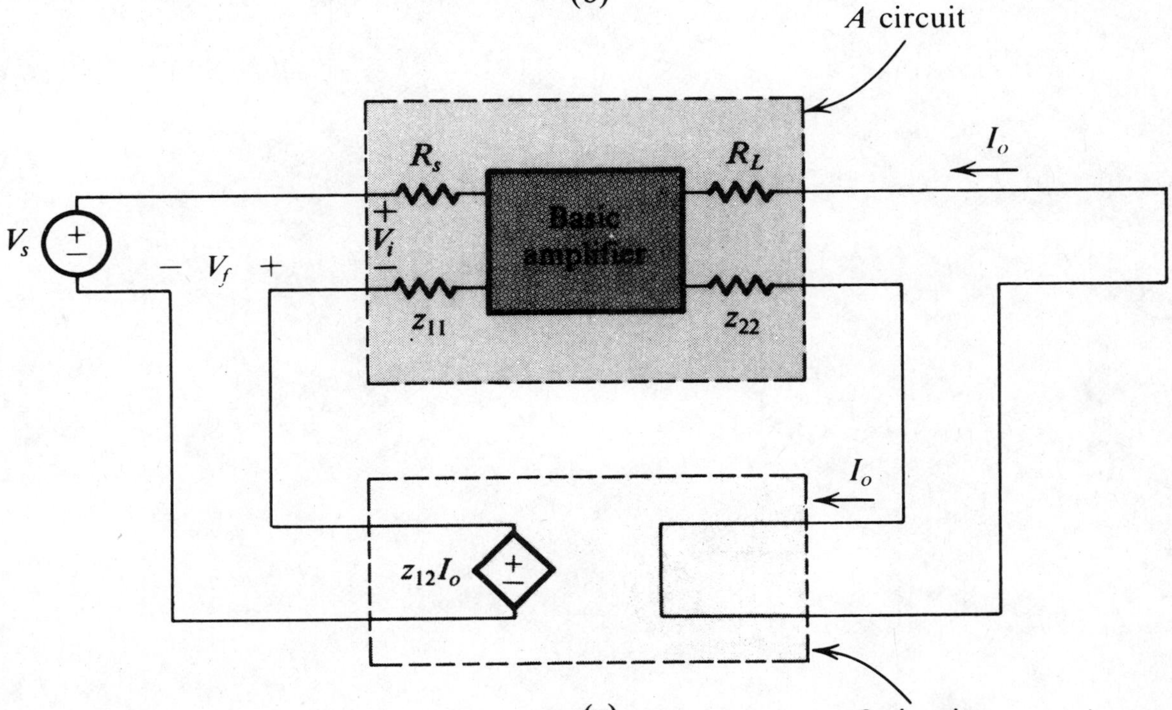

A circuit
I_o
R_s
R_L
V_s
Basic amplifier
$+$ V_i $-$
$-$ V_f $+$
z_{11}
z_{22}
I_o
$z_{12}I_o$
β circuit

(c)

(a) The A circuit is

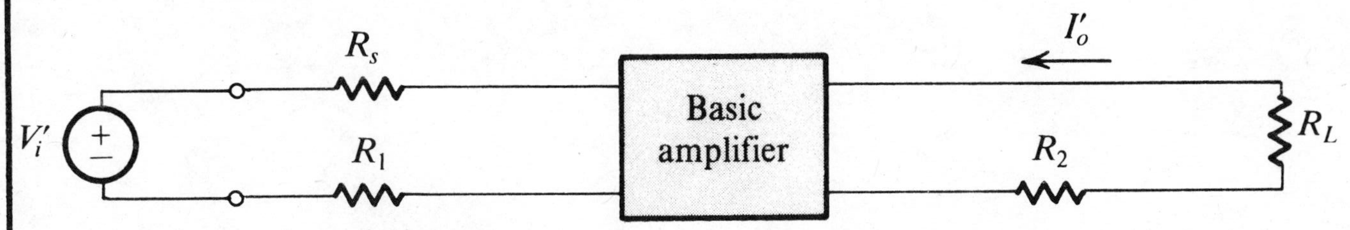

where R_1 is obtained from

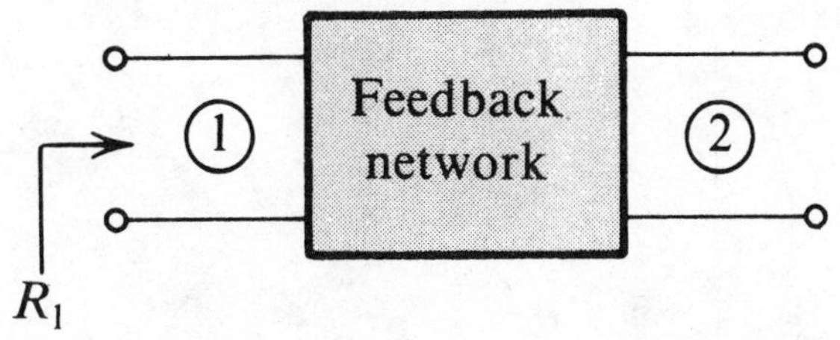

and R_2 is obtained from

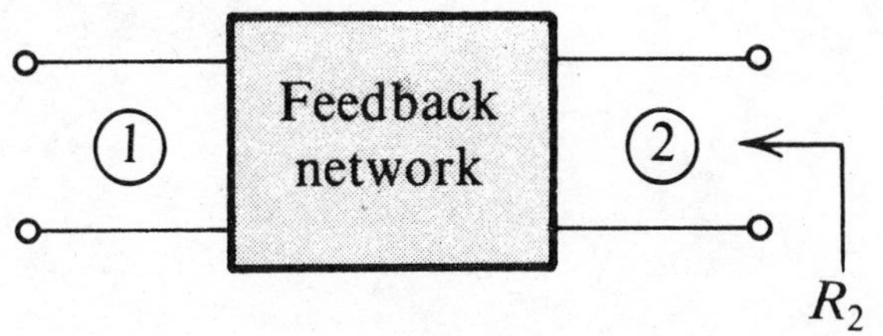

and the gain A is defined $A \equiv \frac{I_o'}{V_i'}$

(b) β is obtained from

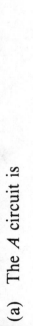

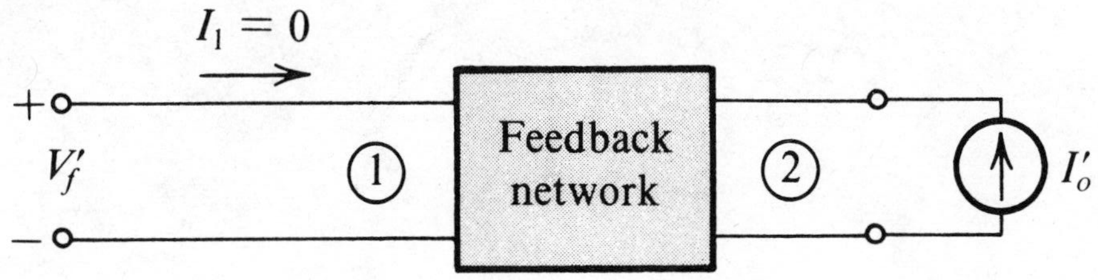

$$\beta \equiv \left.\frac{V_f'}{I_o'}\right|_{I_1 = 0}$$

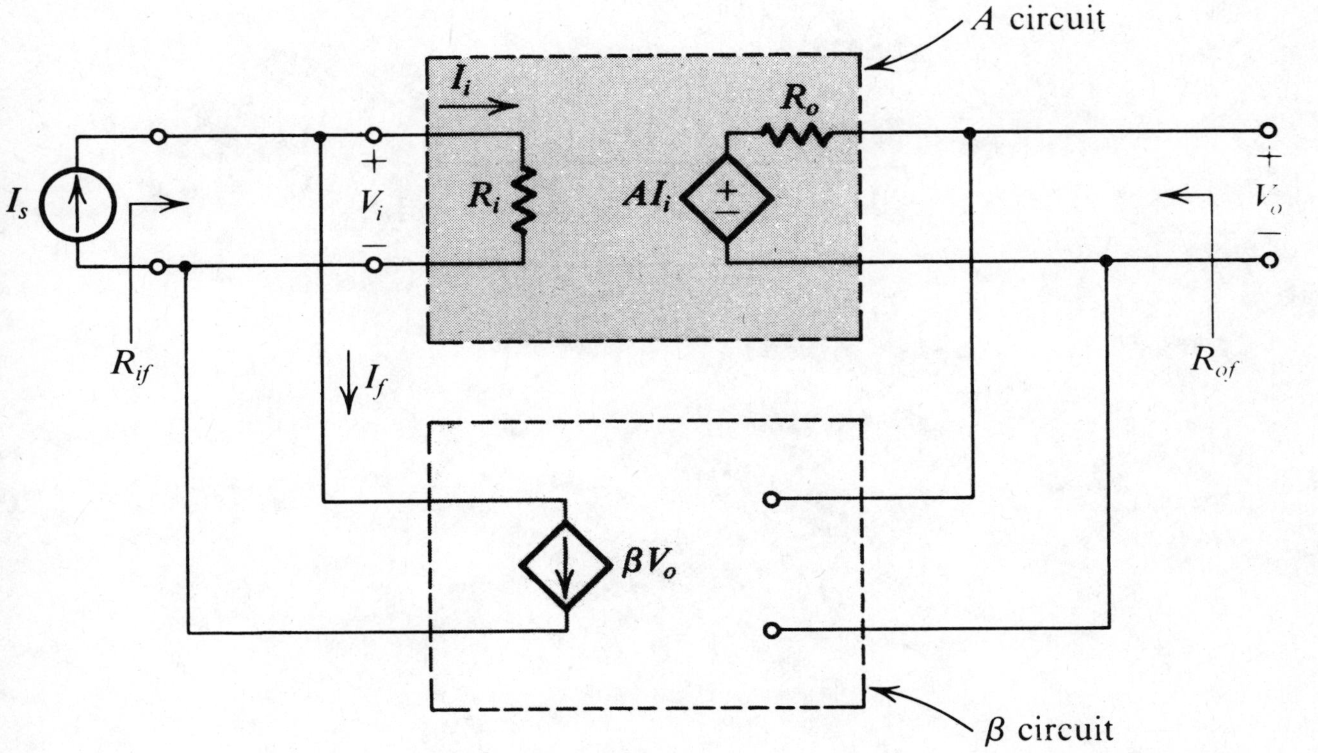
A circuit
I_i
R_o
I_s
V_i
R_i
AI_i
V_o
R_{if}
I_f
R_{of}
βV_o
β circuit

12.18

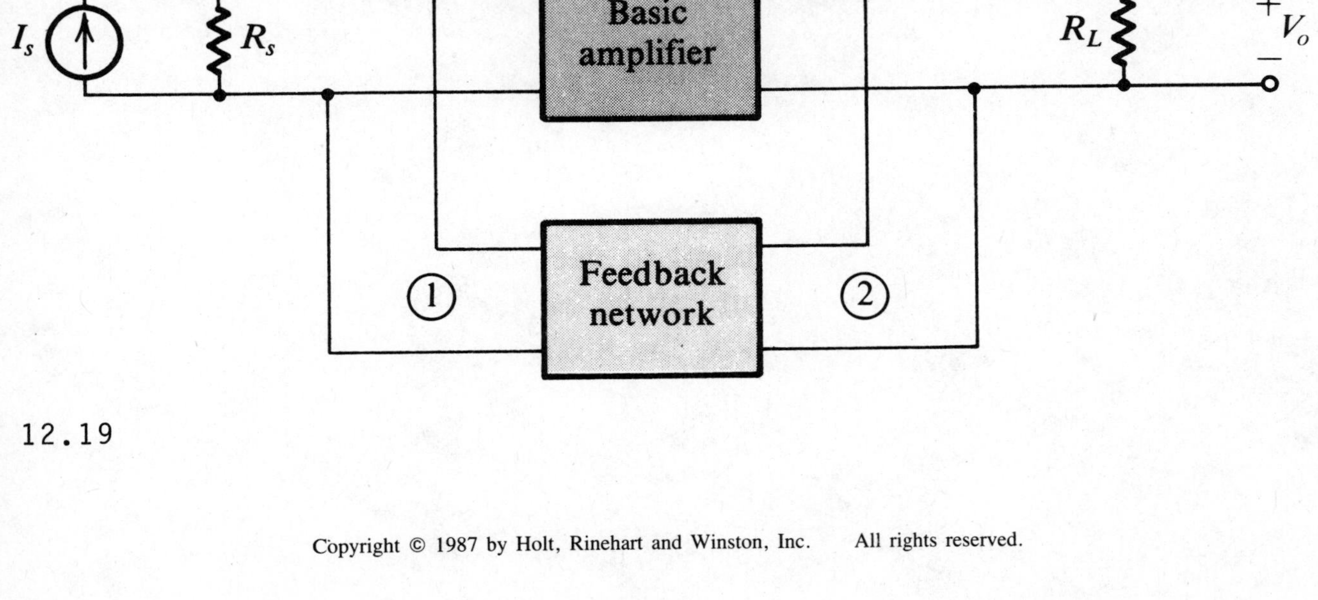
I_s
R_s
Basic amplifier
R_L
V_o
Feedback network
1
2

12.19

(a) The A circuit is

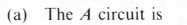

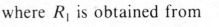

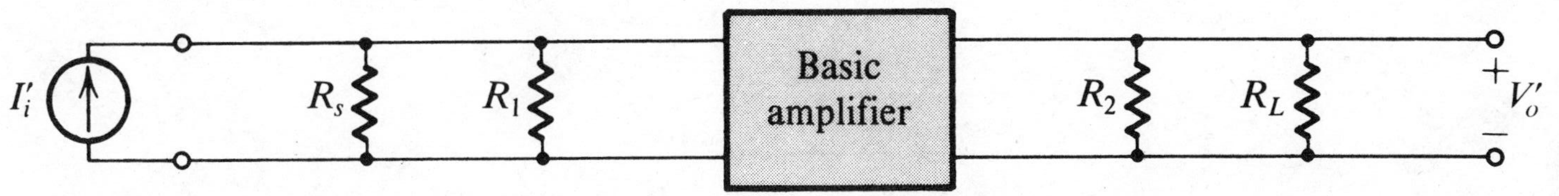

where R_1 is obtained from

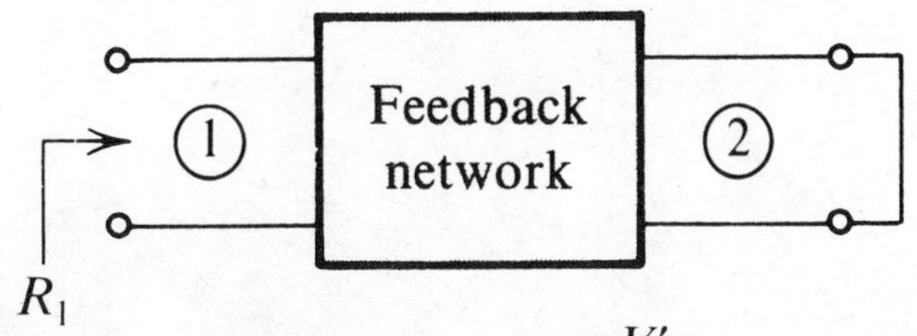

and R_2 is obtained from

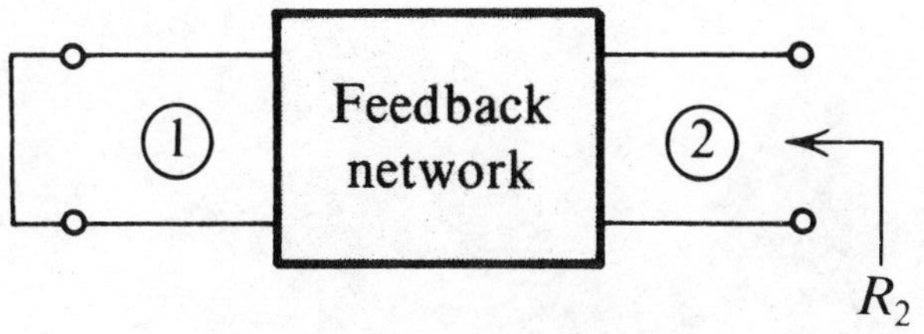

and the gain A is defined $A \equiv \frac{V_o'}{I_i'}$

(b) β is obtained from

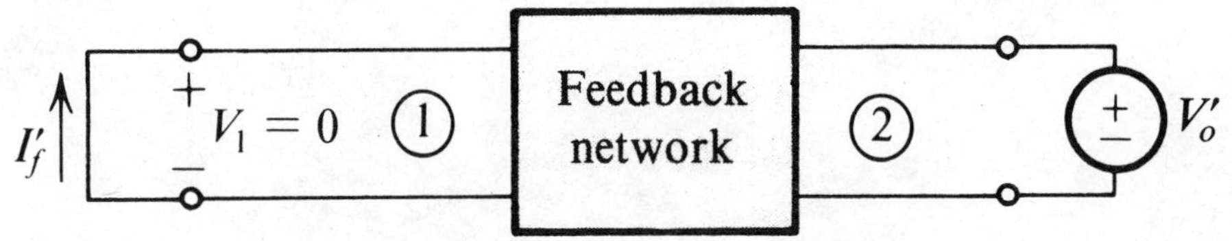

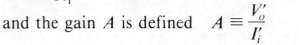

$$\beta \equiv \left. \frac{I_f'}{V_o'} \right|_{V_1 = 0}$$

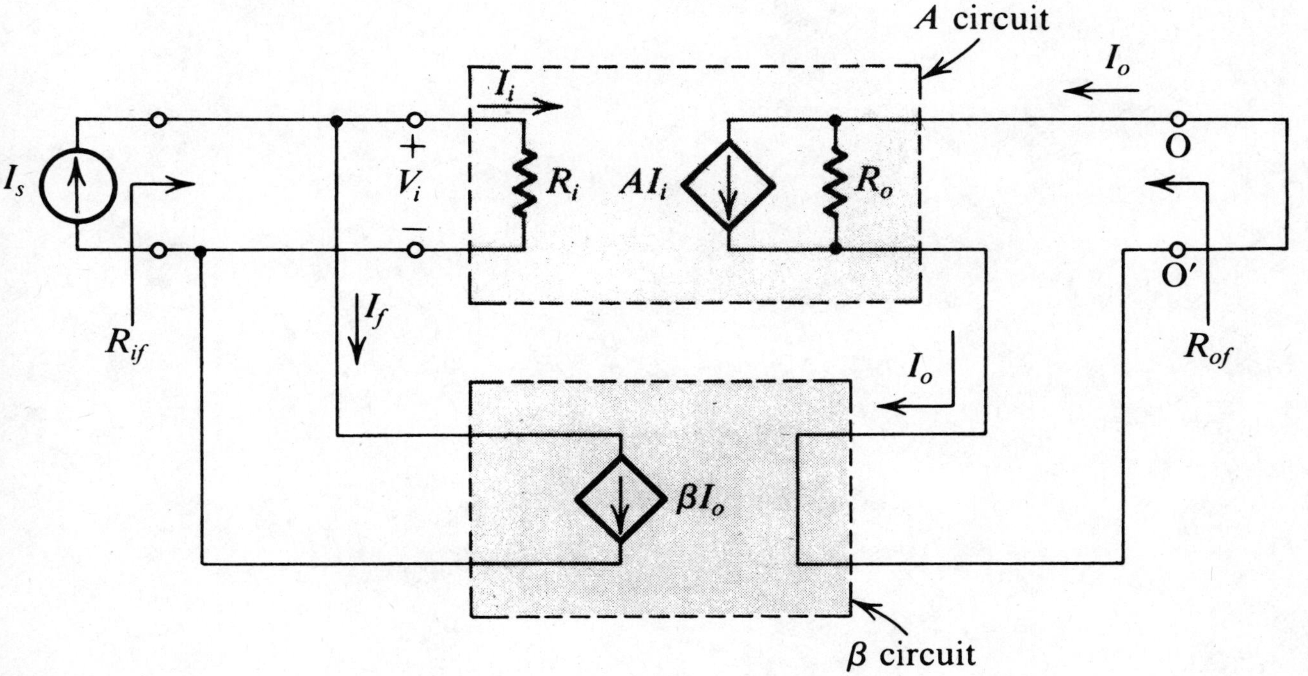
A circuit
I_o
I_i
I_s
+
V_i
−
R_i
AI_i
R_o
O
O′
I_f
R_{if}
I_o
R_{of}
βI_o
β circuit

12.22

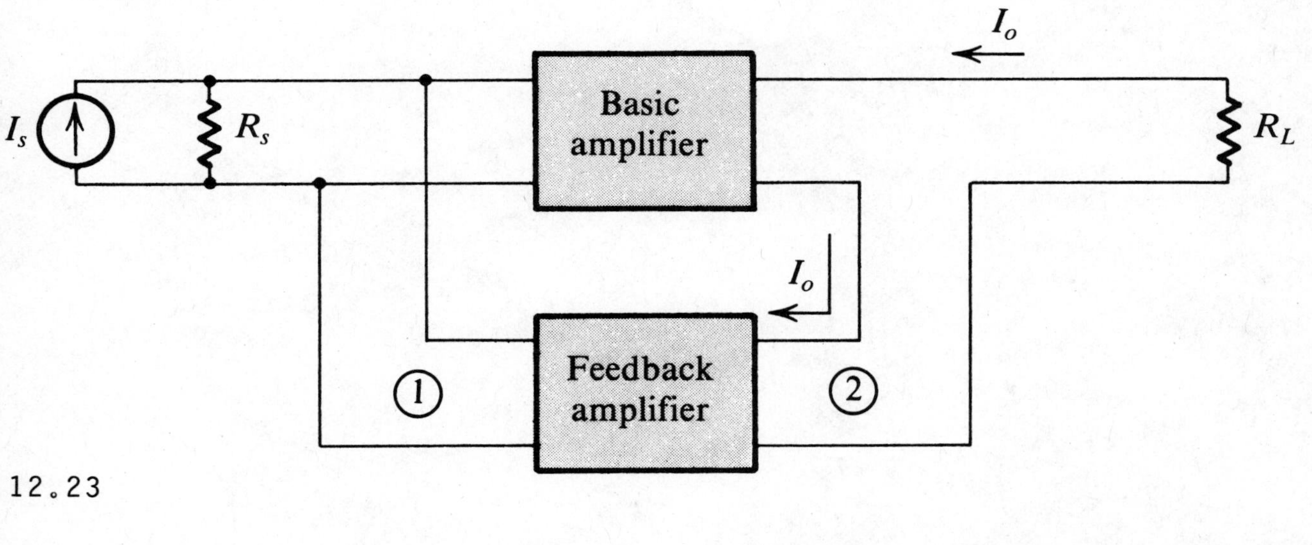
I_o
I_s
R_s
Basic amplifier
R_L
I_o
Feedback amplifier
1
2

12.23

(a) The A circuit is

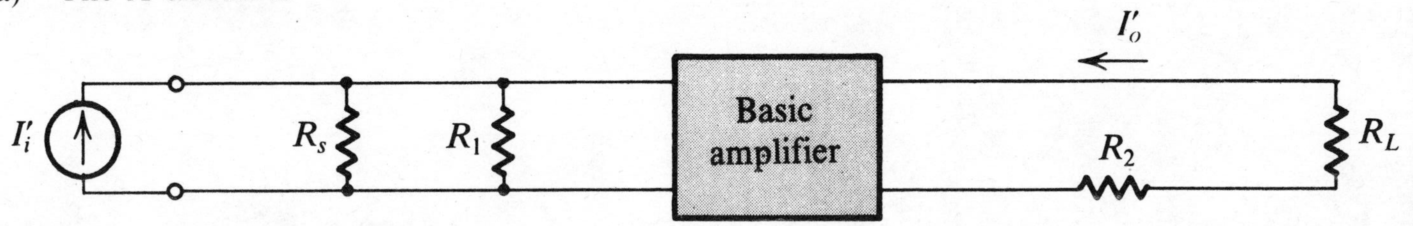

where R_1 is obtained from

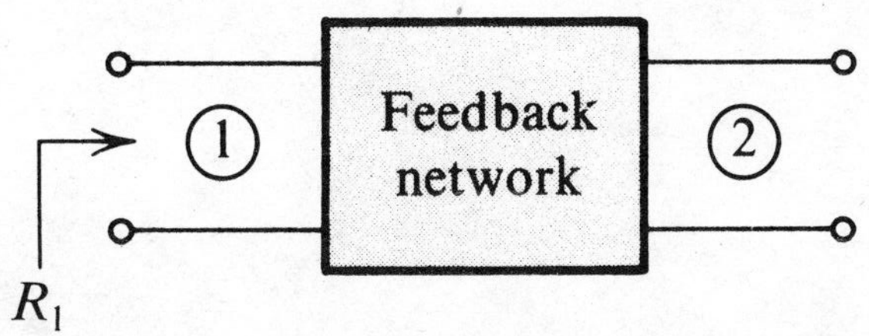

and R_2 is obtained from

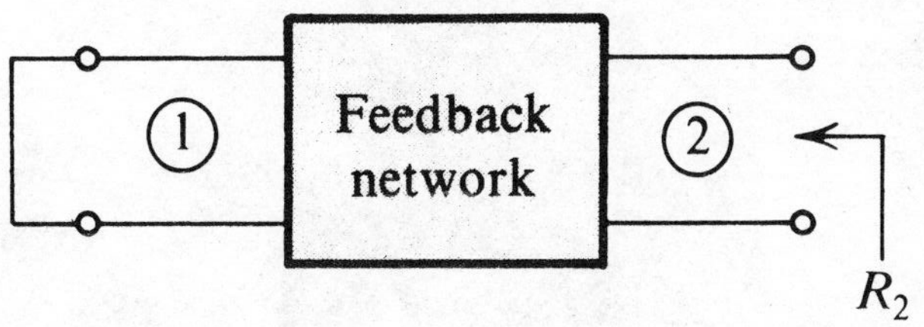

The gain A is defined as $A \equiv \frac{I'_o}{I'_i}$

(b) β is found from

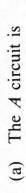

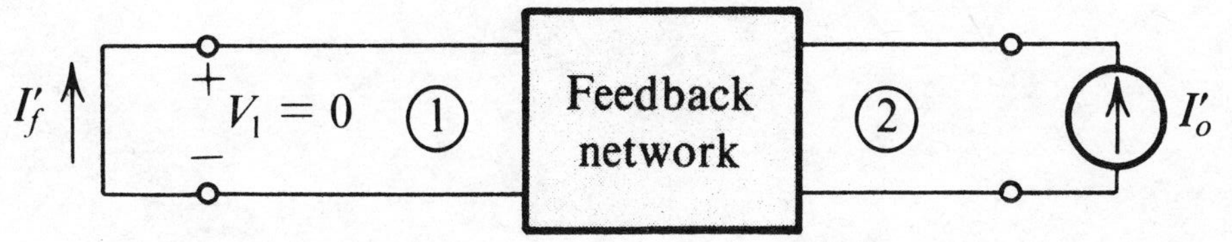

$$\beta \equiv \left.\frac{I'_f}{I'_o}\right|_{V_1 = 0}$$

12.24

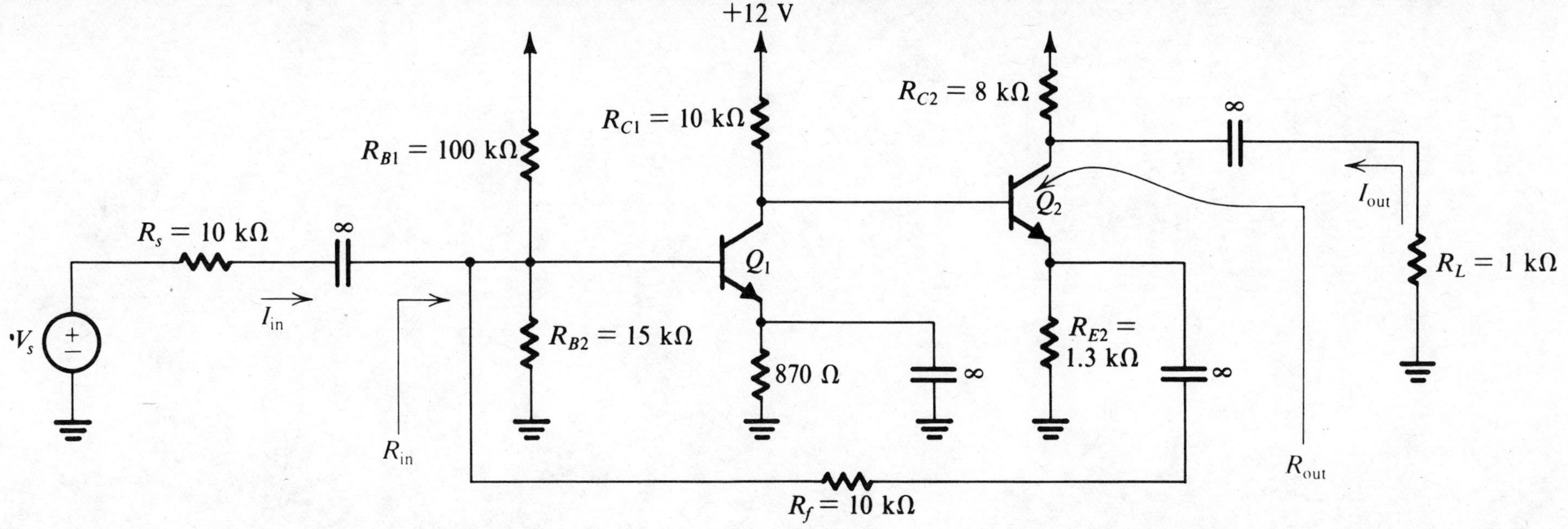
+12 V
$R_{C2} = 8\ k\Omega$
$R_{C1} = 10\ k\Omega$
$R_{B1} = 100\ k\Omega$
$R_s = 10\ k\Omega$
Q_1
Q_2
I_{out}
$R_L = 1\ k\Omega$
V_s
I_{in}
$R_{B2} = 15\ k\Omega$
870 Ω
$R_{E2} =$ 1.3 kΩ
R_{in}
R_{out}
$R_f = 10\ k\Omega$

(a)

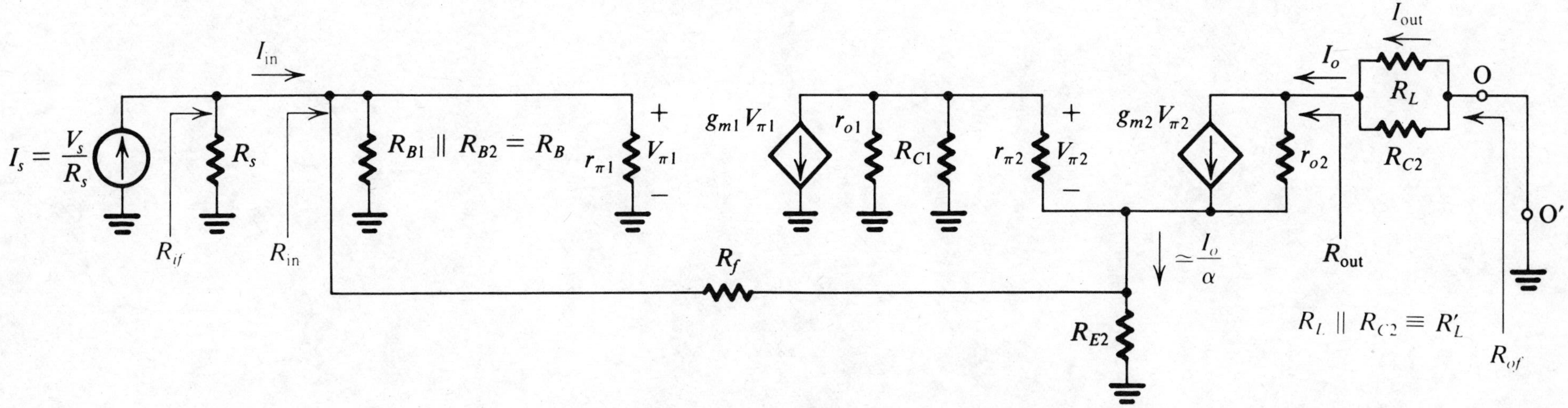
I_{in}
$I_s = \frac{V_s}{R_s}$
R_s
R_{if}
R_{in}
$R_{B1} \parallel R_{B2} = R_B$
$r_{\pi 1}$
$V_{\pi 1}$
$g_{m1} V_{\pi 1}$
r_{o1}
R_{C1}
$r_{\pi 2}$
$V_{\pi 2}$
$g_{m2} V_{\pi 2}$
r_{o2}
I_o
I_{out}
R_L
R_{C2}
O
O′
R_f
$\simeq \frac{I_o}{\alpha}$
R_{out}
R_{E2}
$R_L \parallel R_{C2} \equiv R'_L$
R_{of}

(b)

12.25

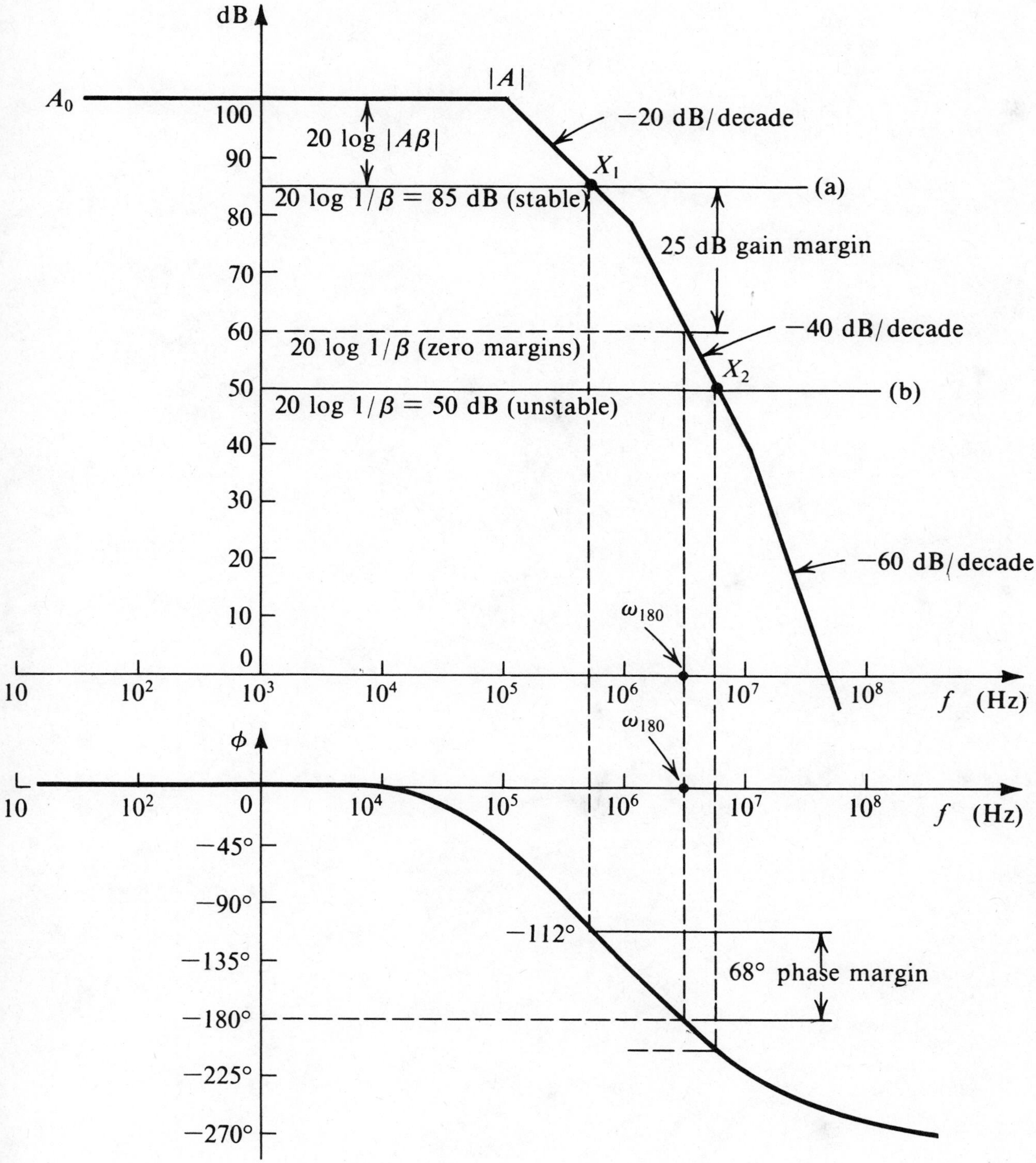
dB
|A|
A_0
100
90
80
70
60
50
40
30
20
10
0
20 log |Aβ|
−20 dB/decade
X_1
20 log 1/β = 85 dB (stable)
(a)
25 dB gain margin
20 log 1/β (zero margins)
−40 dB/decade
X_2
20 log 1/β = 50 dB (unstable)
(b)
−60 dB/decade
ω_{180}
10
10^2
10^3
10^4
10^5
10^6
10^7
10^8
f (Hz)
ω_{180}
ϕ
10
10^2
0
10^4
10^5
10^6
10^7
10^8
f (Hz)
−45°
−90°
−112°
−135°
68° phase margin
−180°
−225°
−270°

12.37

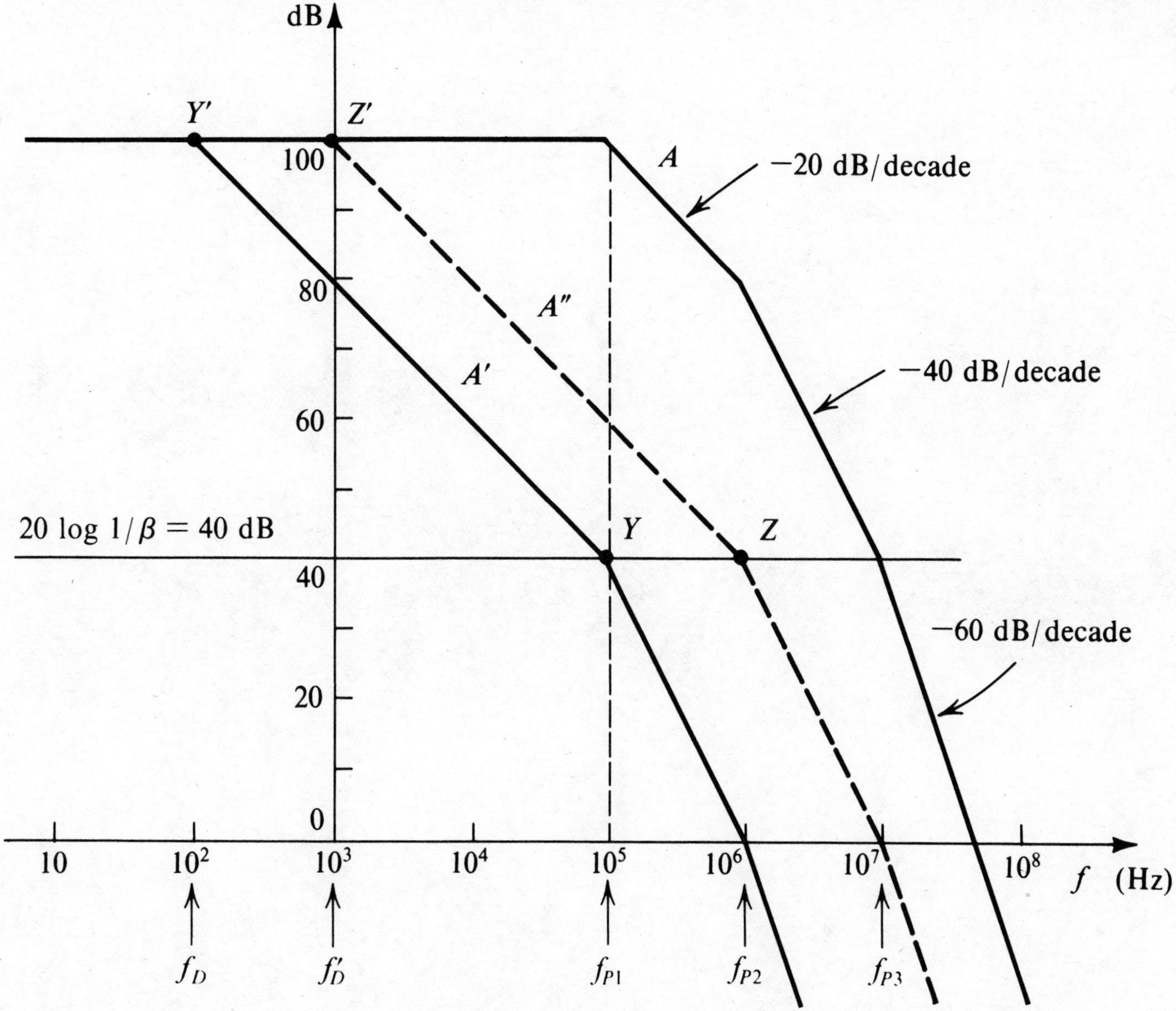
dB
Y′
Z′
100
80
60
40
20
0
A
A″
A′
Y
Z
−20 dB/decade
−40 dB/decade
−60 dB/decade
20 log 1/β = 40 dB
10
10²
10³
10⁴
10⁵
10⁶
10⁷
10⁸
f (Hz)
f_D
f′_D
f_P1
f_P2
f_P3

12.38

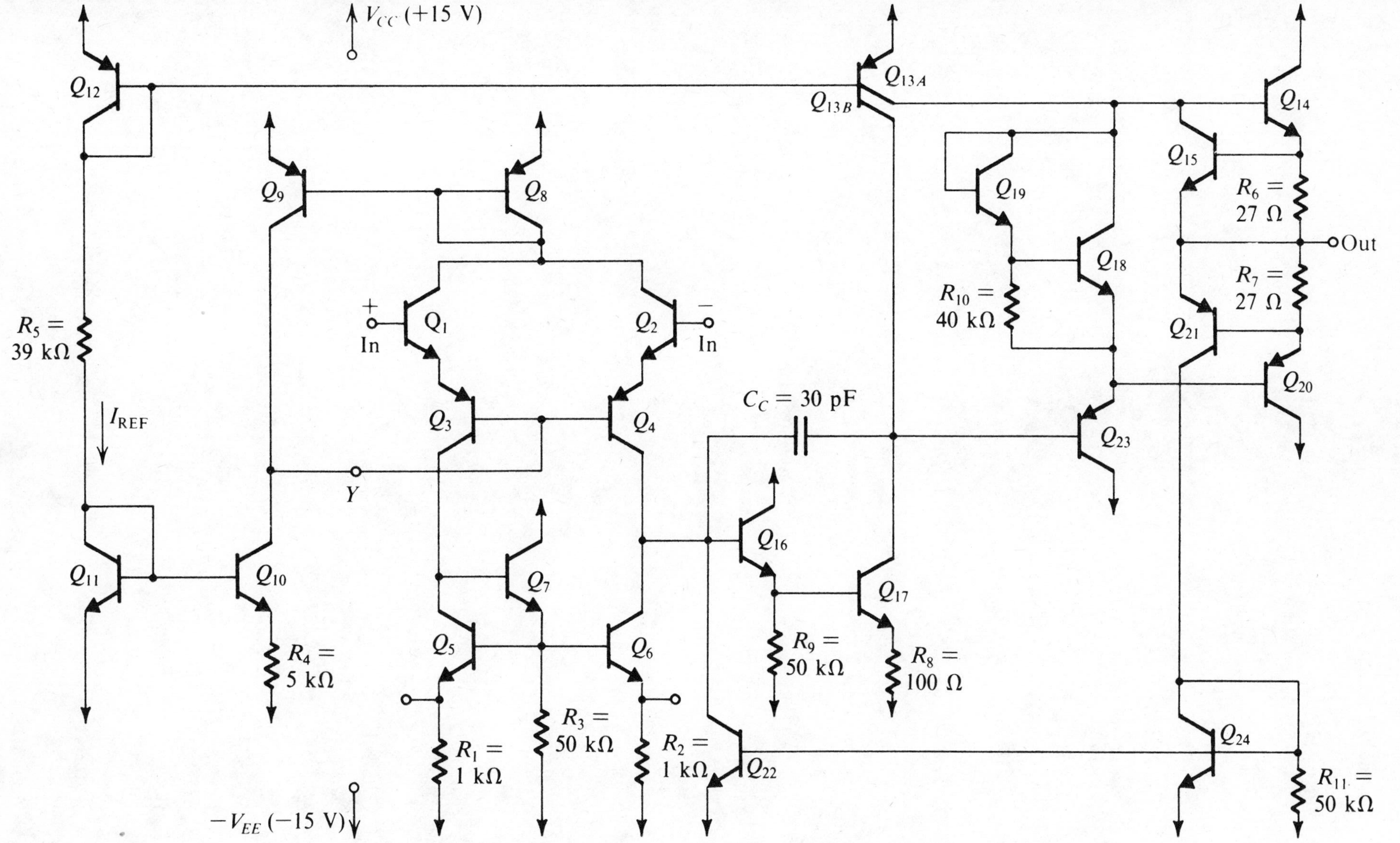

V_{CC} (+15 V)
Q_{12}
Q_{13A}
Q_{13B}
Q_{14}
Q_9
Q_8
Q_{19}
Q_{15}
$R_6 =$ 27 Ω
Out
Q_{18}
$R_{10} =$ 40 kΩ
$R_7 =$ 27 Ω
$R_5 =$ 39 kΩ
+
In
Q_1
Q_2
−
In
Q_{21}
Q_{20}
$C_C =$ 30 pF
I_{REF}
Q_3
Q_4
Q_{23}
Y
Q_{16}
Q_{11}
Q_{10}
Q_7
Q_{17}
Q_5
Q_6
$R_9 =$ 50 kΩ
$R_8 =$ 100 Ω
$R_4 =$ 5 kΩ
$R_3 =$ 50 kΩ
$R_1 =$ 1 kΩ
$R_2 =$ 1 kΩ
Q_{22}
Q_{24}
$R_{11} =$ 50 kΩ
$-V_{EE}$ (−15 V)

13.1

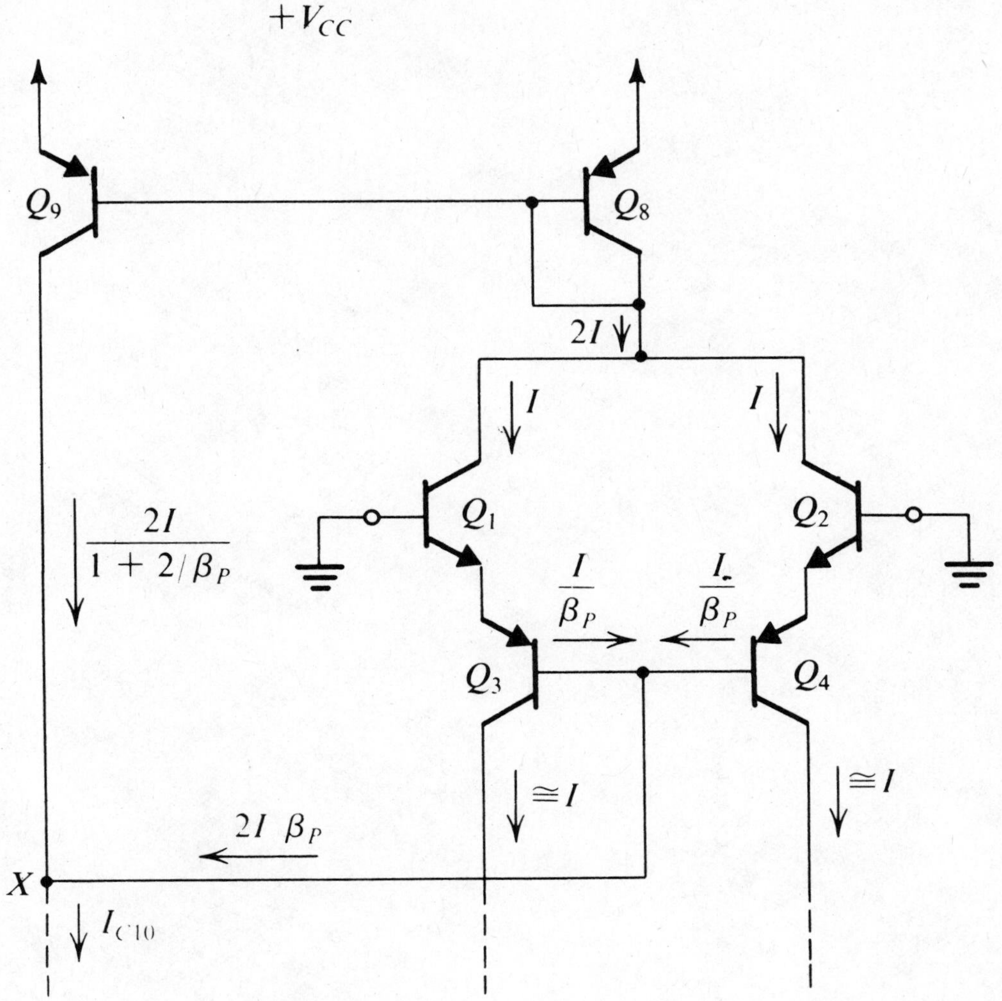

$+V_{CC}$
Q_9
Q_8
$2I$
I
I
Q_1
Q_2
$\frac{2I}{1 + 2/\beta_P}$
$\frac{I}{\beta_P}$
$\frac{I}{\beta_P}$
Q_3
Q_4
$\cong I$
$\cong I$
$2I\ \beta_P$
X
I_{C10}

13.3

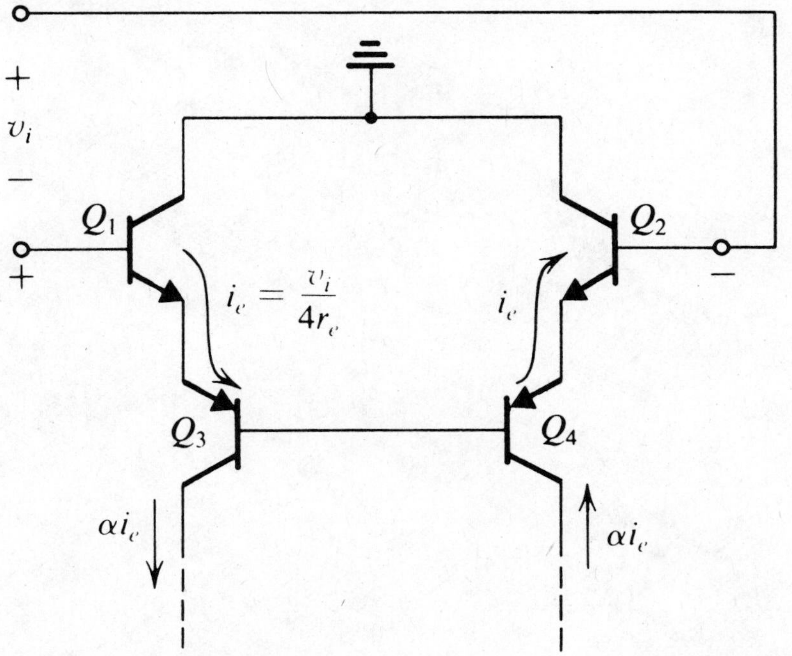

+
v_i
−
Q_1
+
Q_2
−
$i_e = \frac{v_i}{4r_e}$
i_e
Q_3
Q_4
αi_e
αi_e

13.6

13.7

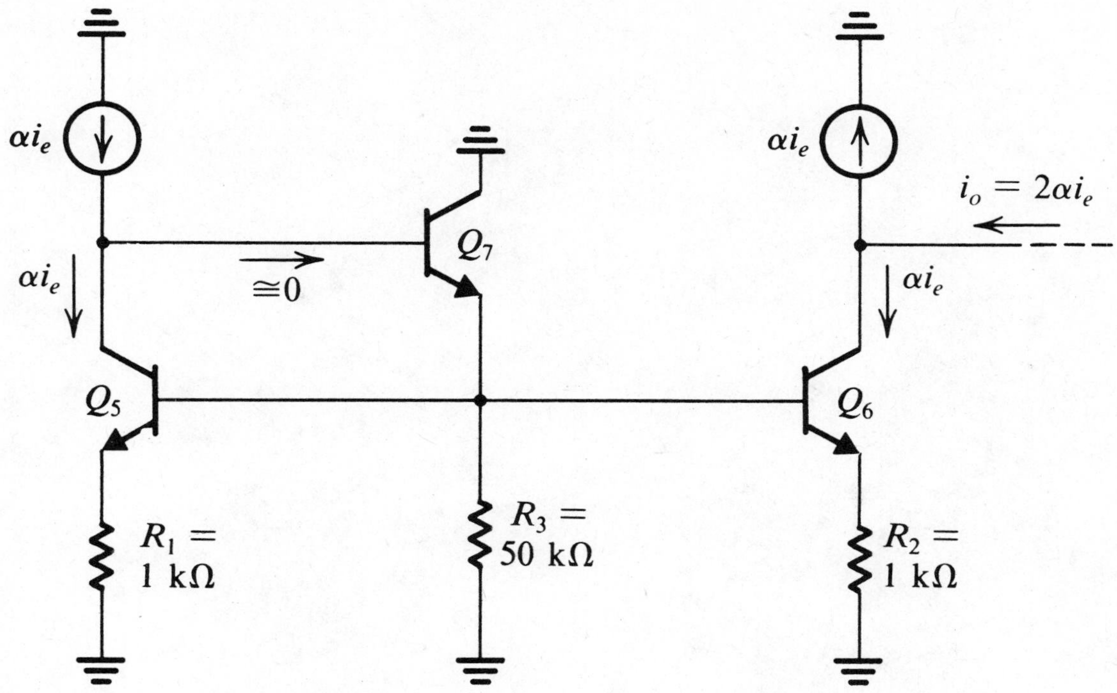

13.19

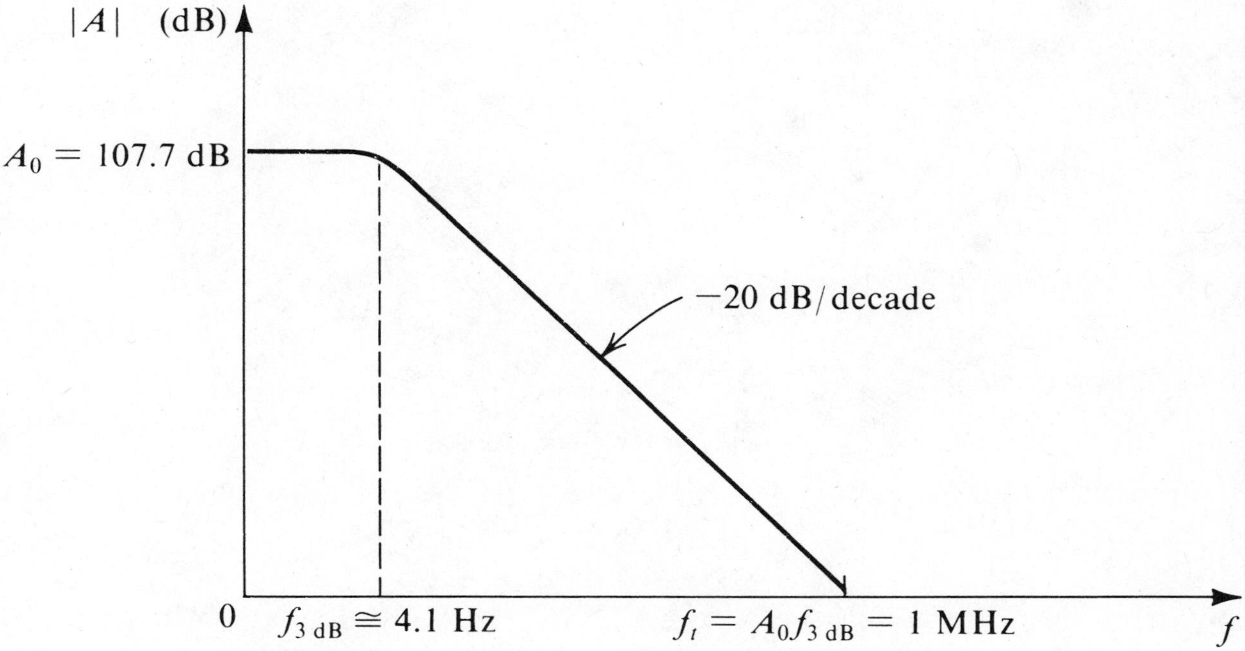

13.20

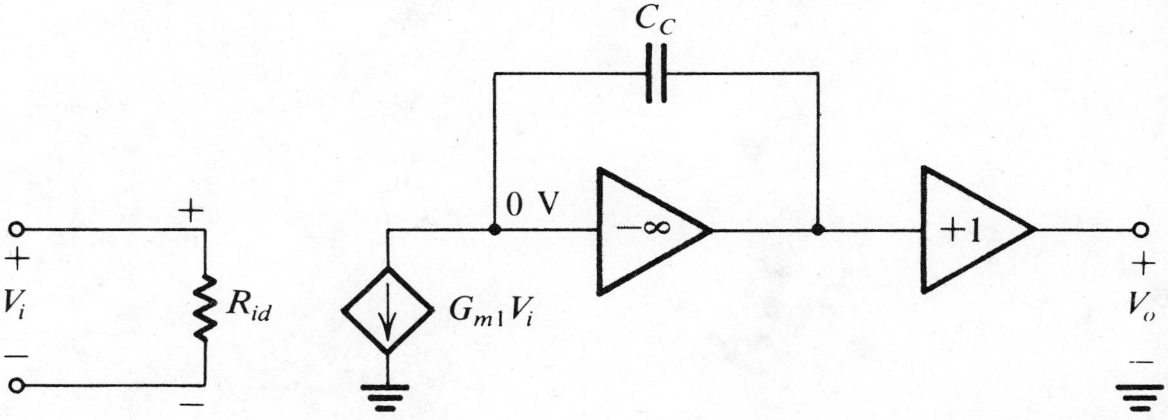

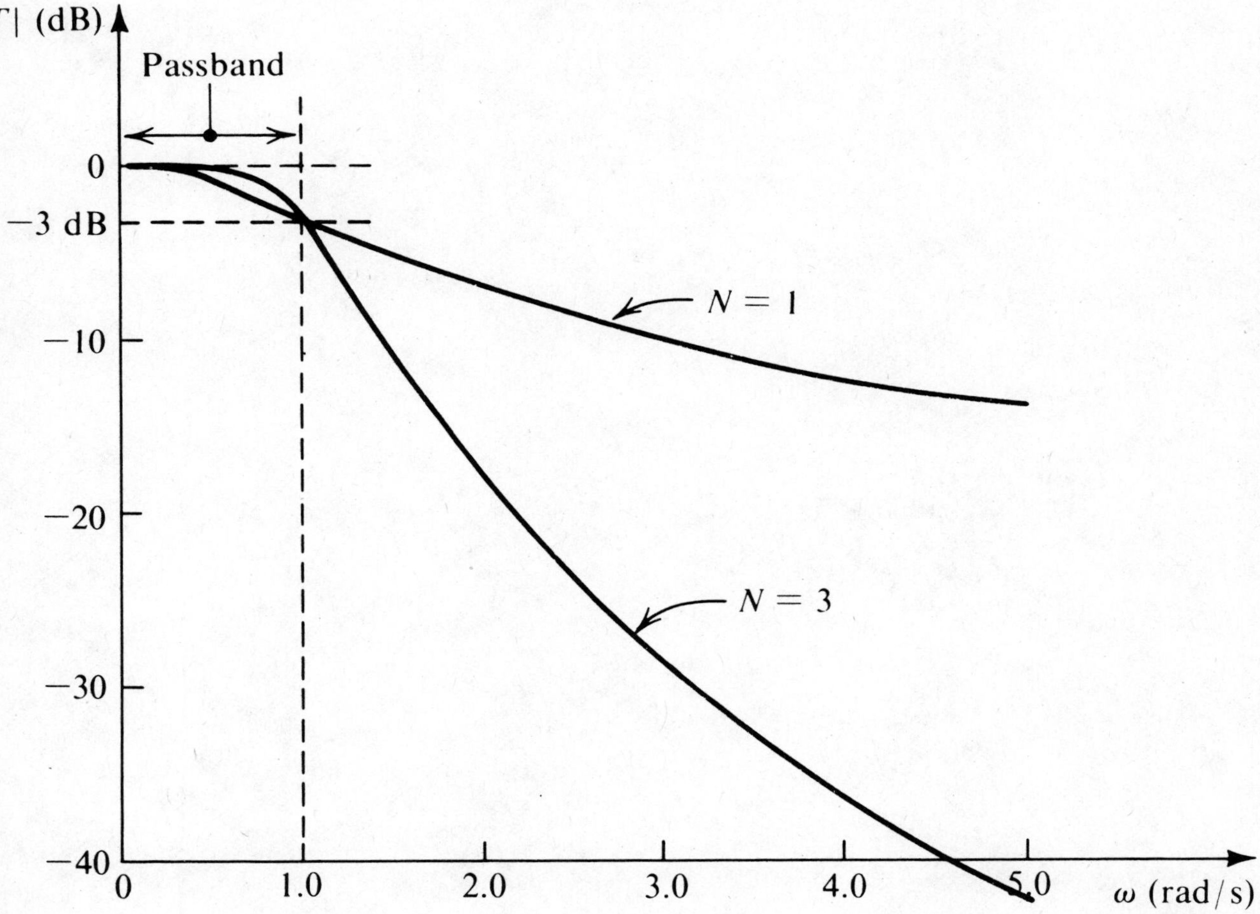

14.1

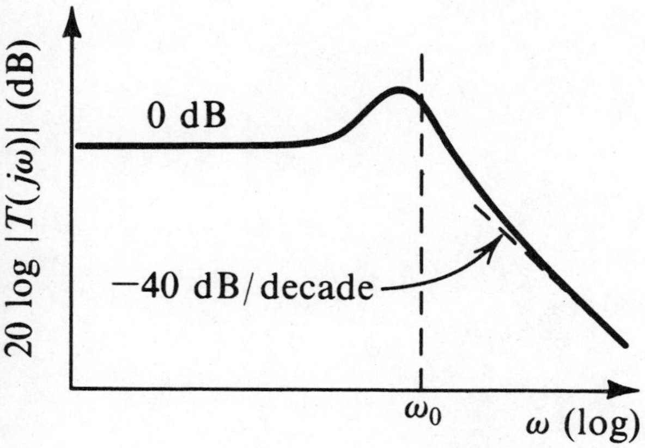

(a) Low pass (LP)

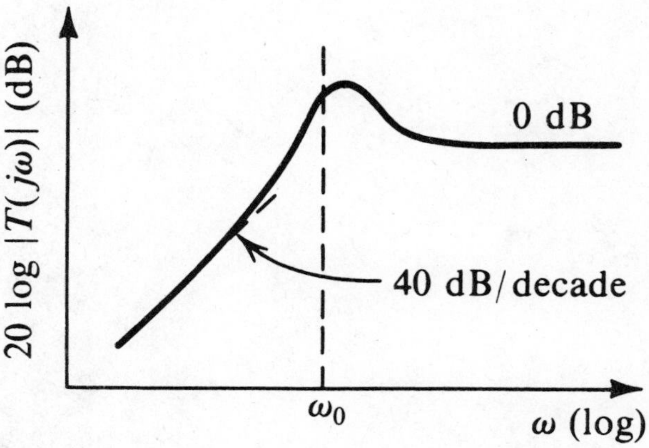

(b) High pass (HP)

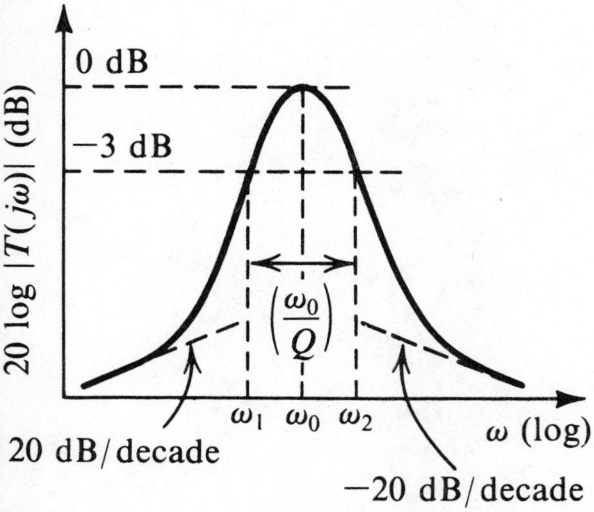

(c) Bandpass (BP)

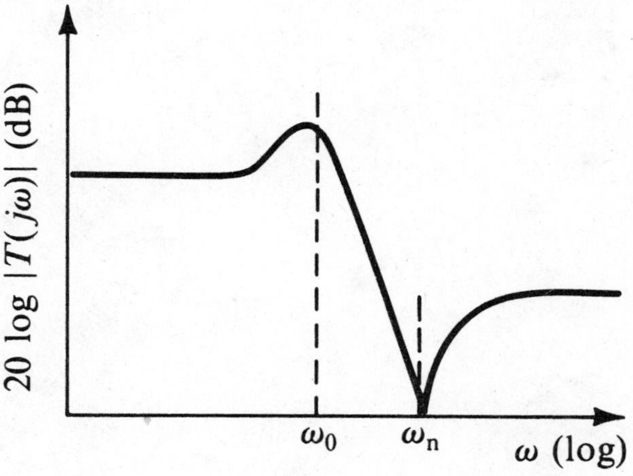

(d) Notch

14.5

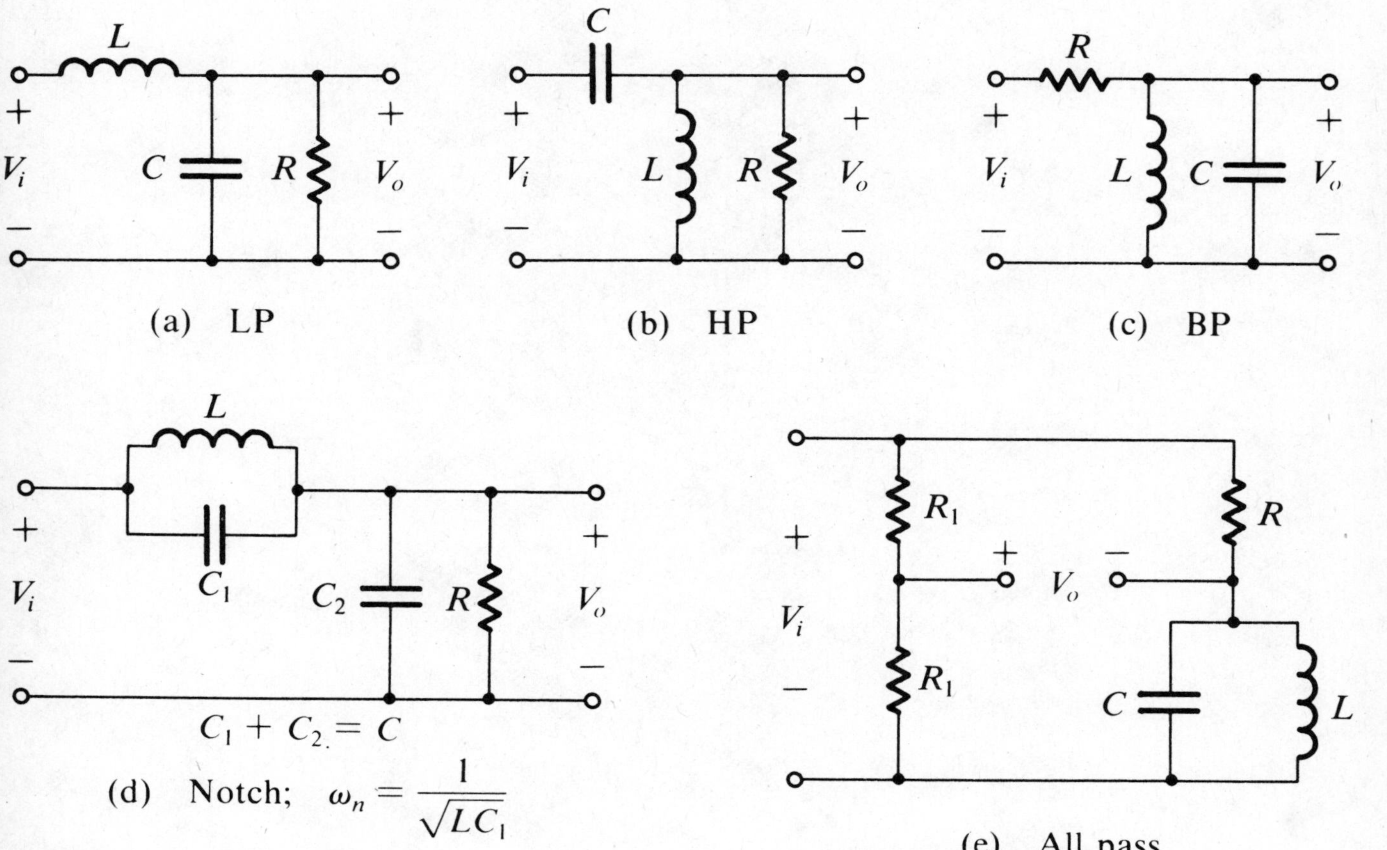
L
C
R
V_i
V_o
(a) LP
C
L
R
V_i
V_o
(b) HP
R
L
C
V_i
V_o
(c) BP
L
C_1
C_2
R
V_i
V_o
$C_1 + C_2 = C$
(d) Notch; $\omega_n = \frac{1}{\sqrt{LC_1}}$
R_1
R_1
R
V_i
V_o
C
L
(e) All pass

14.6

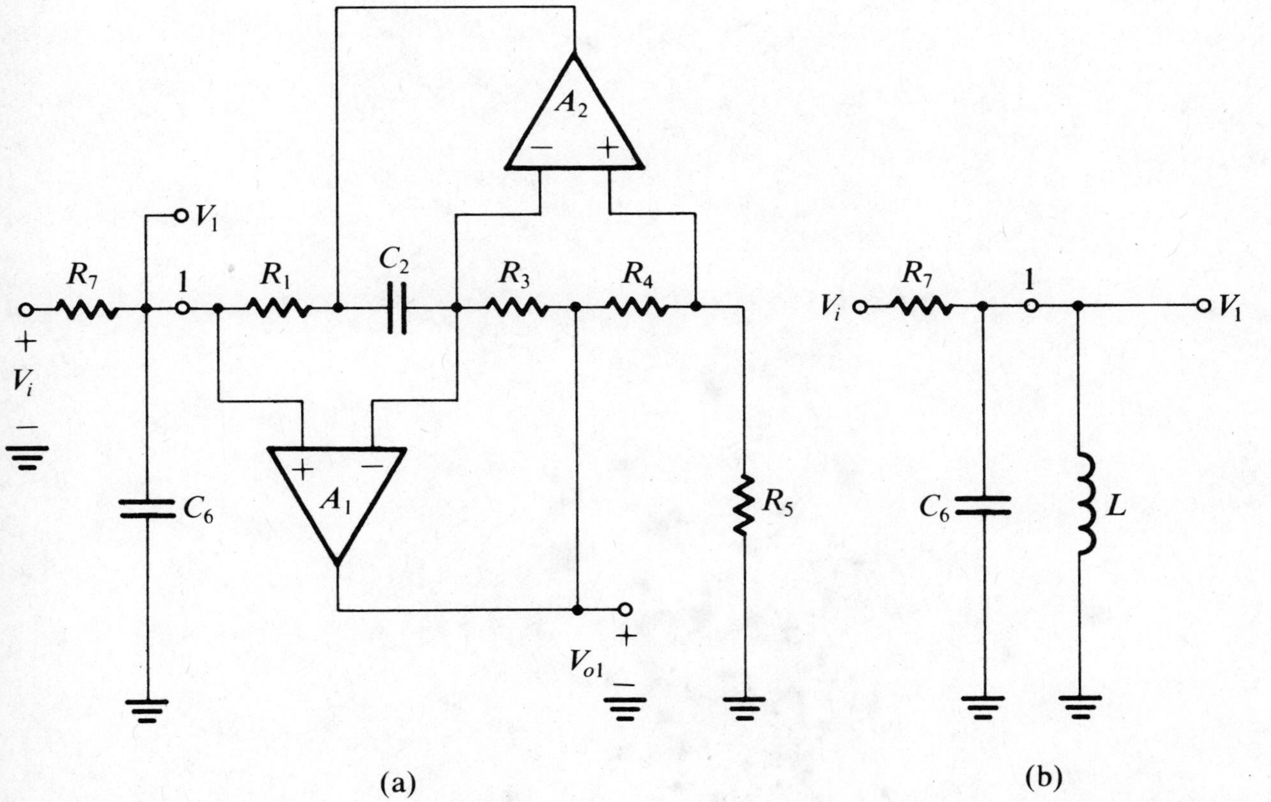
A_2
V_1
R_7
1
R_1
C_2
R_3
R_4
V_i
C_6
A_1
R_5
V_{o1}
(a)
R_7
1
V_i
V_1
C_6
L
(b)

14.15

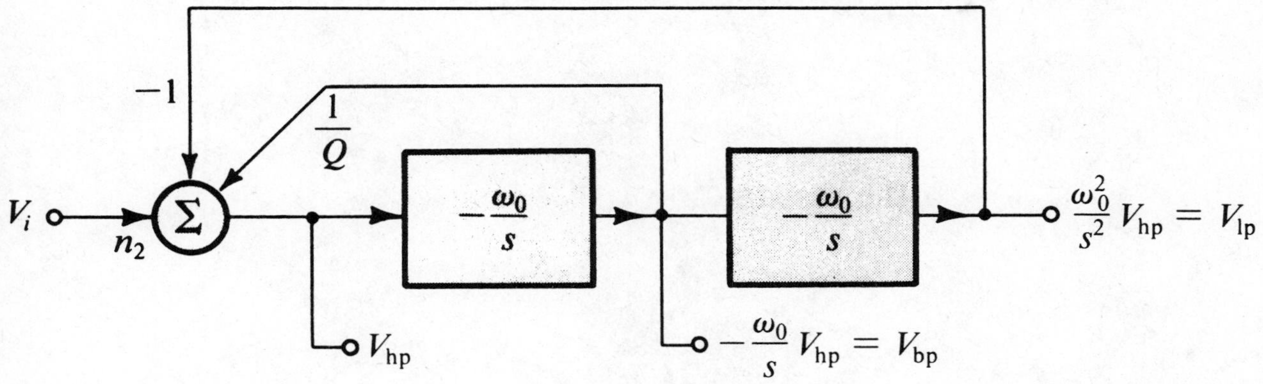

−1
$\frac{1}{Q}$
V_i
n_2
Σ
$-\frac{\omega_0}{s}$
$-\frac{\omega_0}{s}$
$\frac{\omega_0^2}{s^2} V_{hp} = V_{lp}$
V_{hp}
$-\frac{\omega_0}{s} V_{hp} = V_{bp}$

(a)

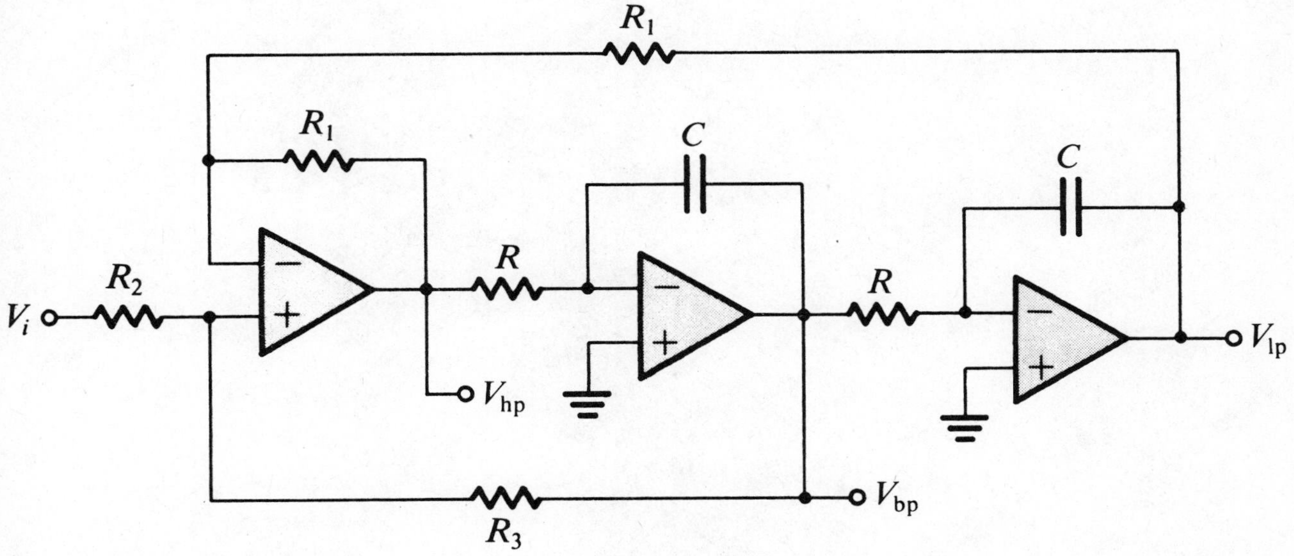

R_1
R_1
C
C
R_2
R
R
V_i
V_{hp}
V_{lp}
V_{bp}
R_3

(b)

14.16

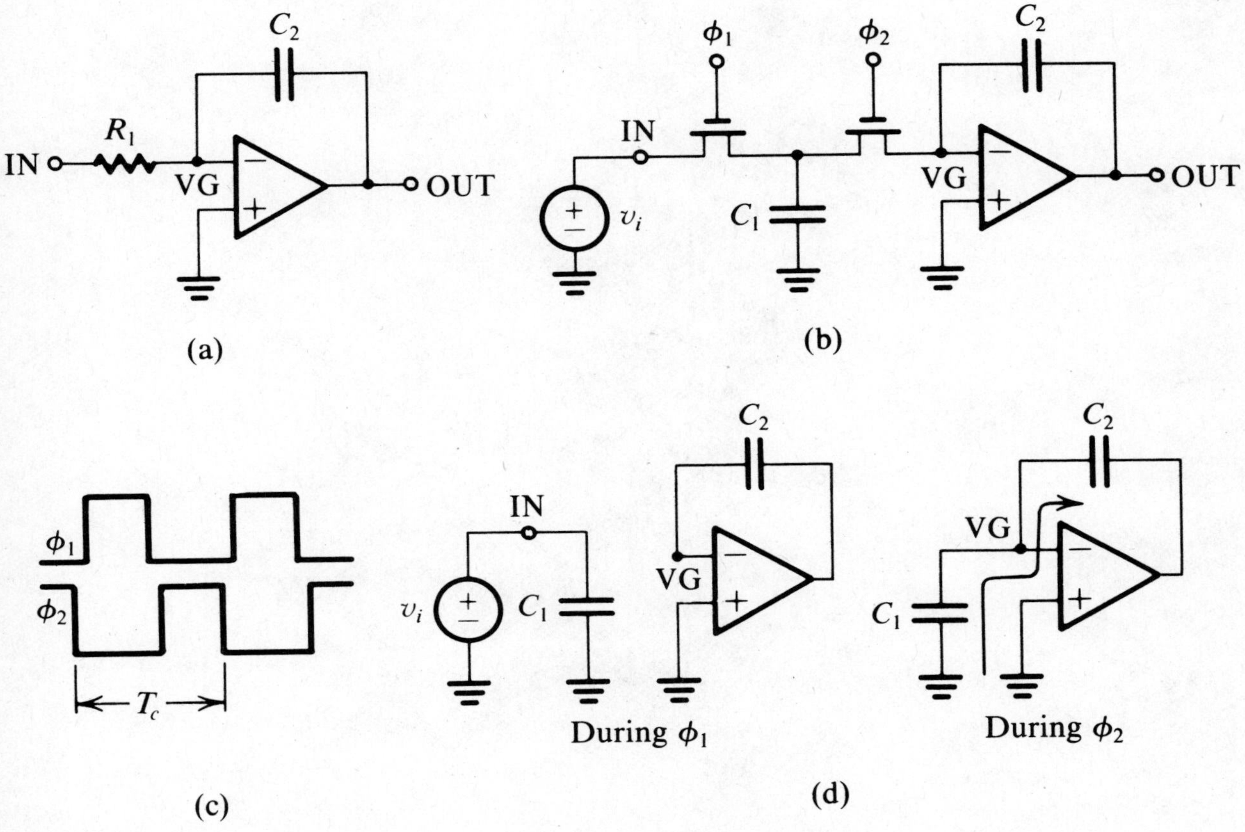
C2
R1
IN
VG
OUT
(a)
ϕ1
ϕ2
C2
IN
vi
C1
VG
OUT
(b)
ϕ1
ϕ2
Tc
(c)
C2
IN
vi
C1
VG
During ϕ1
C2
VG
C1
During ϕ2
(d)

14.18

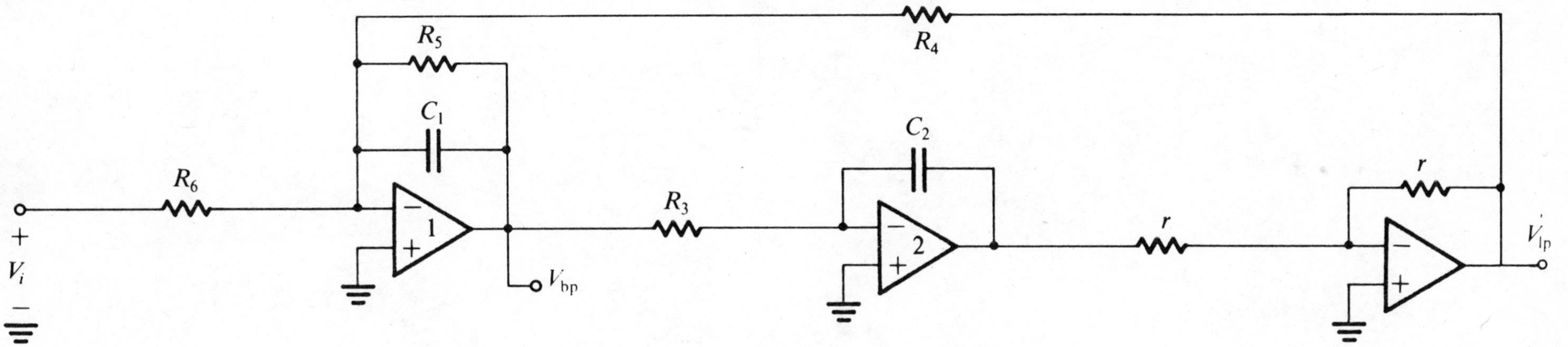

R_4
R_5
C_1
C_2
R_6
R_3
r
r
1
2
+
V_i
−
V_{bp}
V'_{lp}

(a)

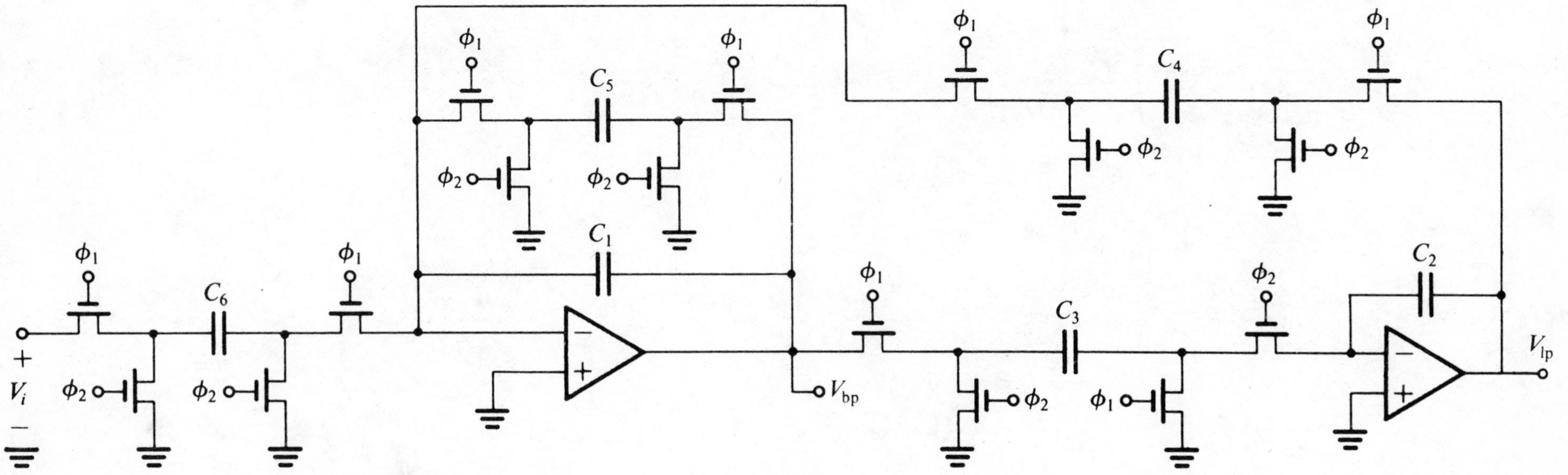

ϕ_1
ϕ_2
C_1
C_2
C_3
C_4
C_5
C_6
+
V_i
−
V_{bp}
V_{lp}

(b)

14.20

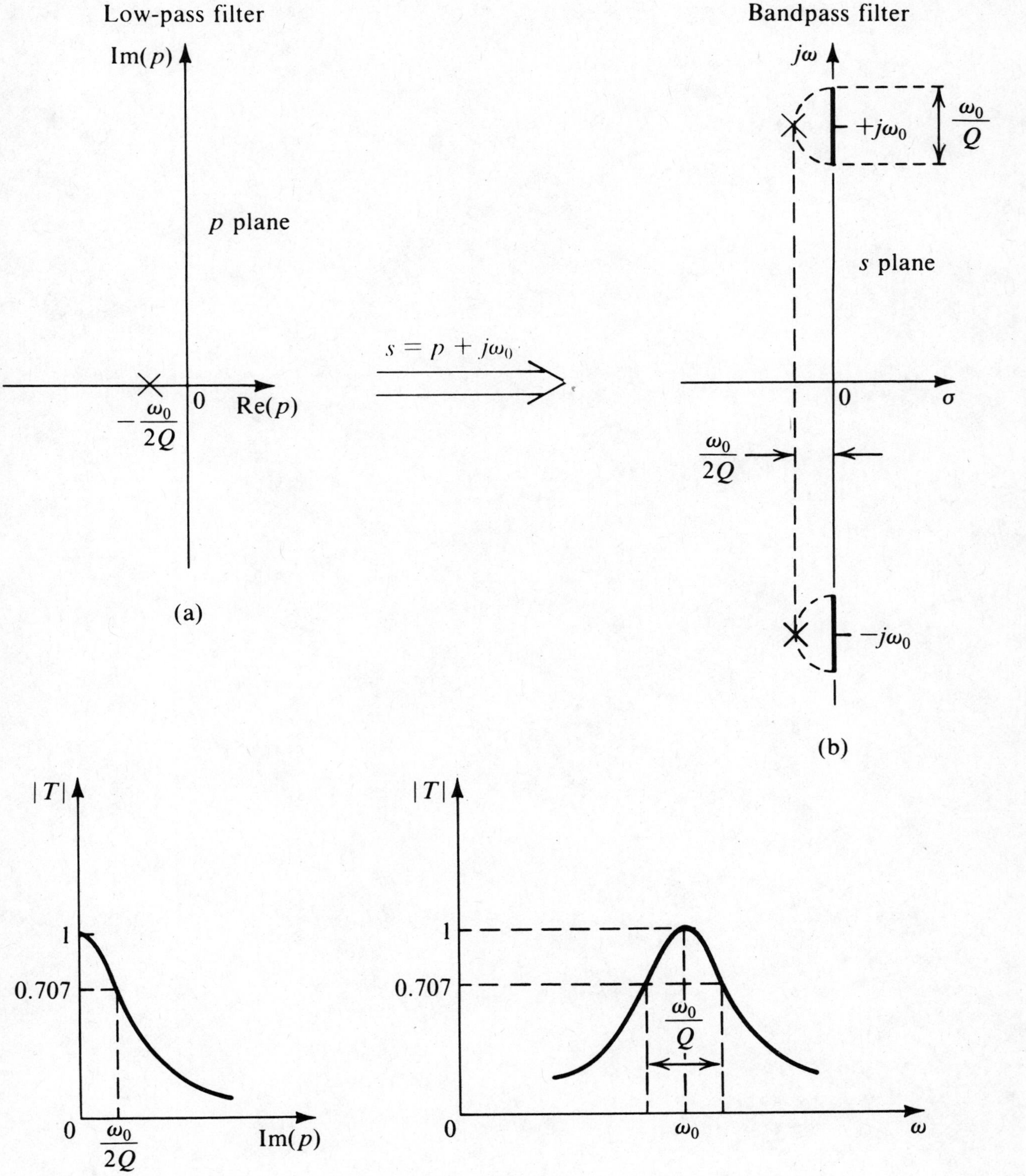

Low-pass filter
Bandpass filter
Im(p)
p plane
0
Re(p)
$-\frac{\omega_0}{2Q}$
$s = p + j\omega_0$
$j\omega$
$+j\omega_0$
$\frac{\omega_0}{Q}$
s plane
0
σ
$\frac{\omega_0}{2Q}$
$-j\omega_0$
(a)
(b)
$|T|$
1
0.707
0
$\frac{\omega_0}{2Q}$
Im(p)
(c)
$|T|$
1
0.707
$\frac{\omega_0}{Q}$
0
ω_0
ω
(d)

14.30

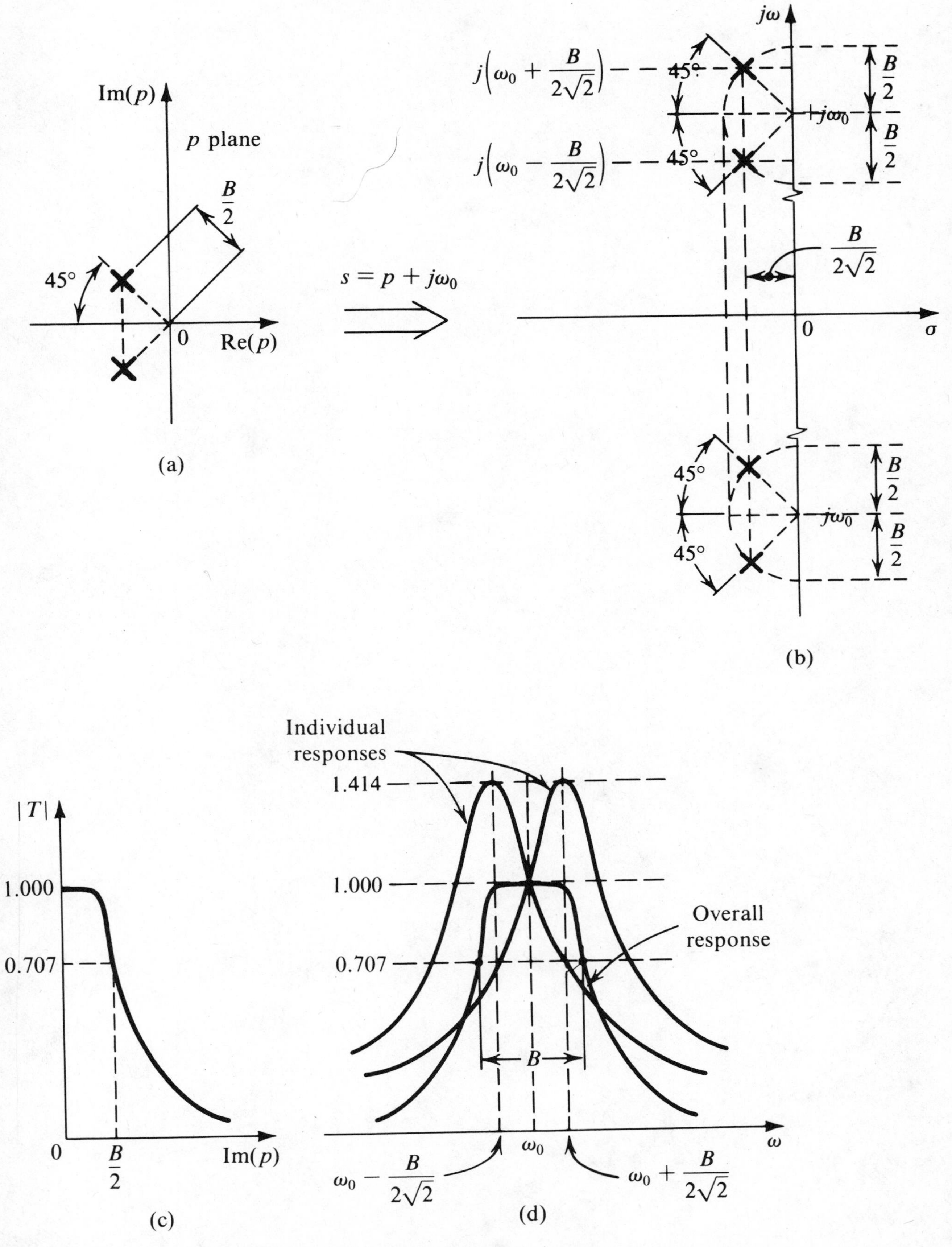
Im(p)
p plane
B/2
45°
0
Re(p)
(a)
s = p + jω0
jω
j(ω0 + B/(2√2))
j(ω0 − B/(2√2))
45°
jω0
B/2
B/(2√2)
0
σ
(b)
|T|
1.000
0.707
0
B/2
Im(p)
(c)
Individual responses
1.414
1.000
0.707
Overall response
B
ω0
ω
ω0 − B/(2√2)
ω0 + B/(2√2)
(d)

14.31

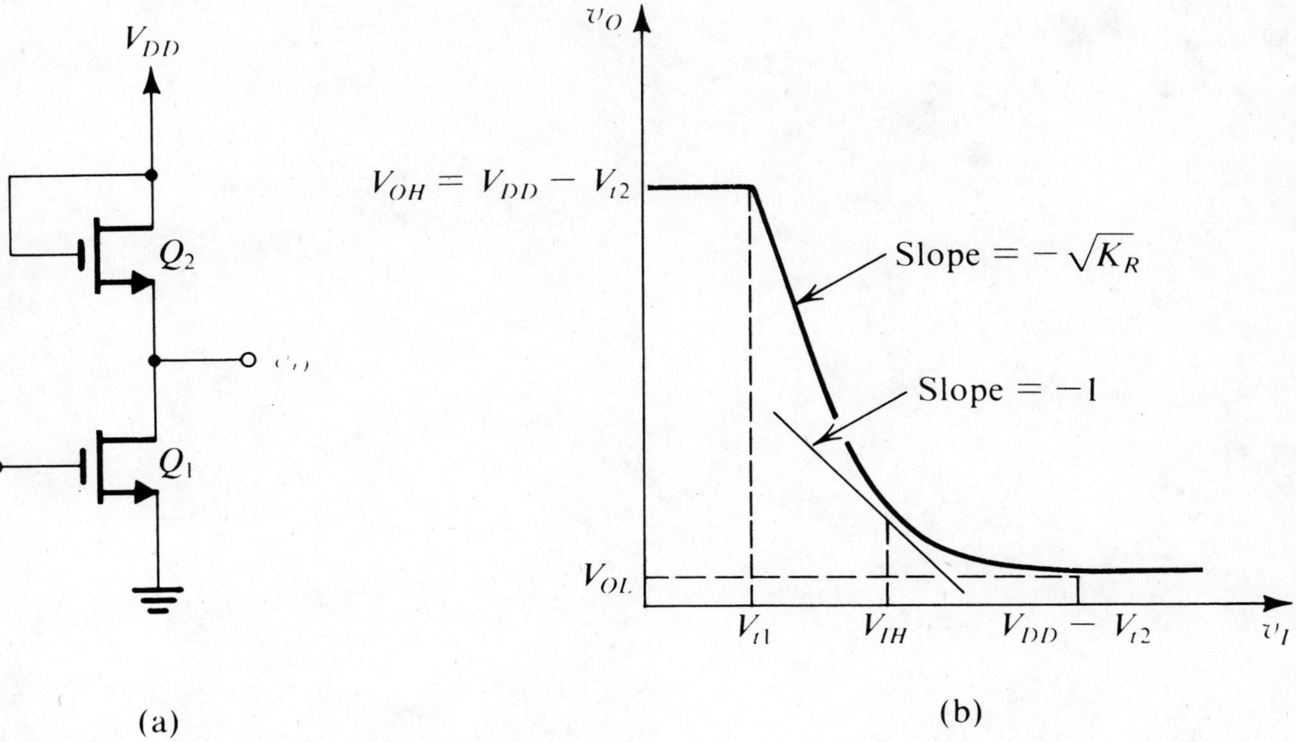

V_{DD}
Q_2
v_O
v_I
Q_1
(a)
v_O
$V_{OH} = V_{DD} - V_{t2}$
Slope $= -\sqrt{K_R}$
Slope $= -1$
V_{OL}
V_{t1}
V_{IH}
$V_{DD} - V_{t2}$
v_I
(b)

15.7

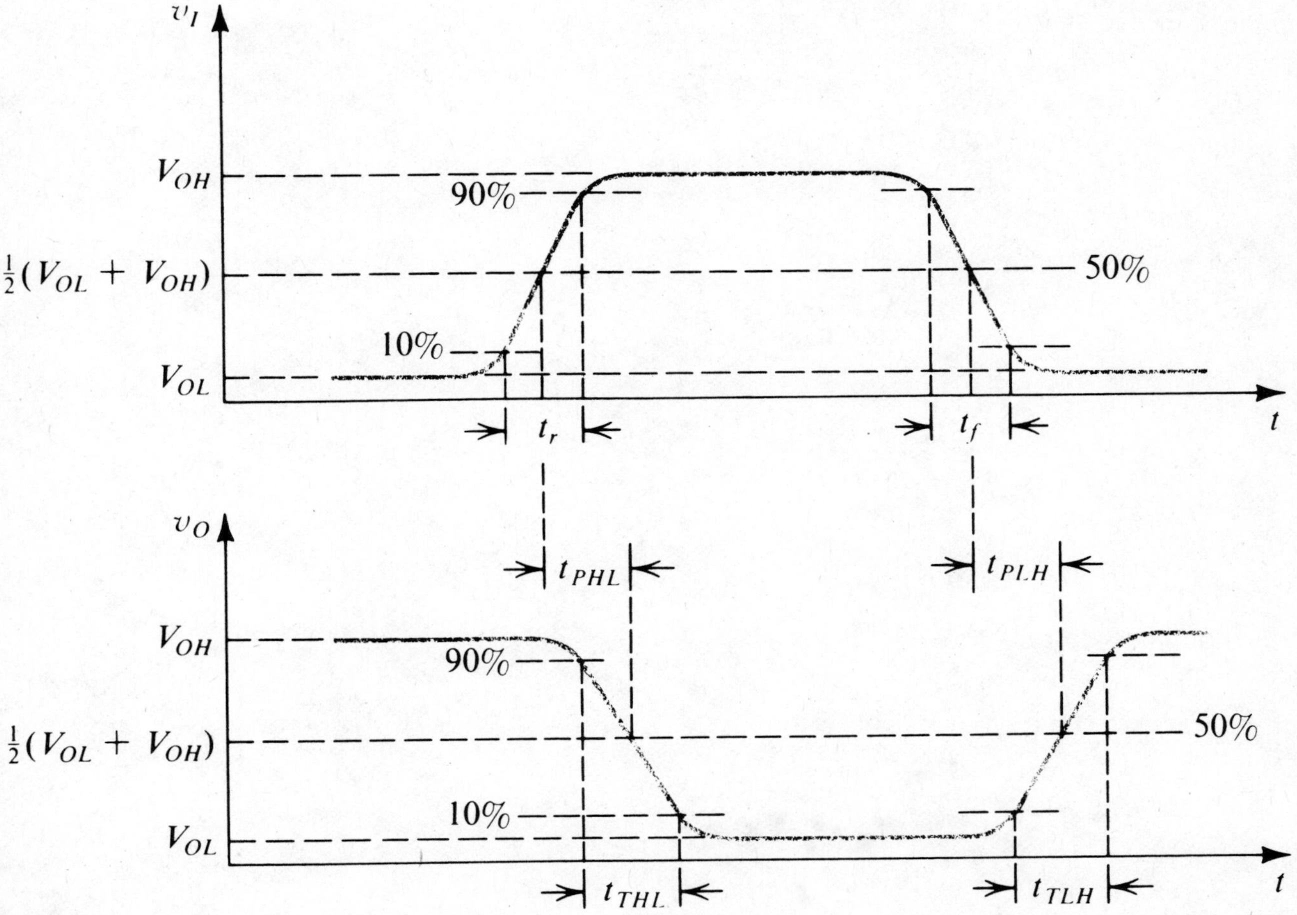

v_I
V_{OH}
90%
$\frac{1}{2}(V_{OL} + V_{OH})$
50%
10%
V_{OL}
t_r
t_f
t
v_O
t_{PHL}
t_{PLH}
V_{OH}
90%
$\frac{1}{2}(V_{OL} + V_{OH})$
50%
10%
V_{OL}
t_{THL}
t_{TLH}
t

15.9

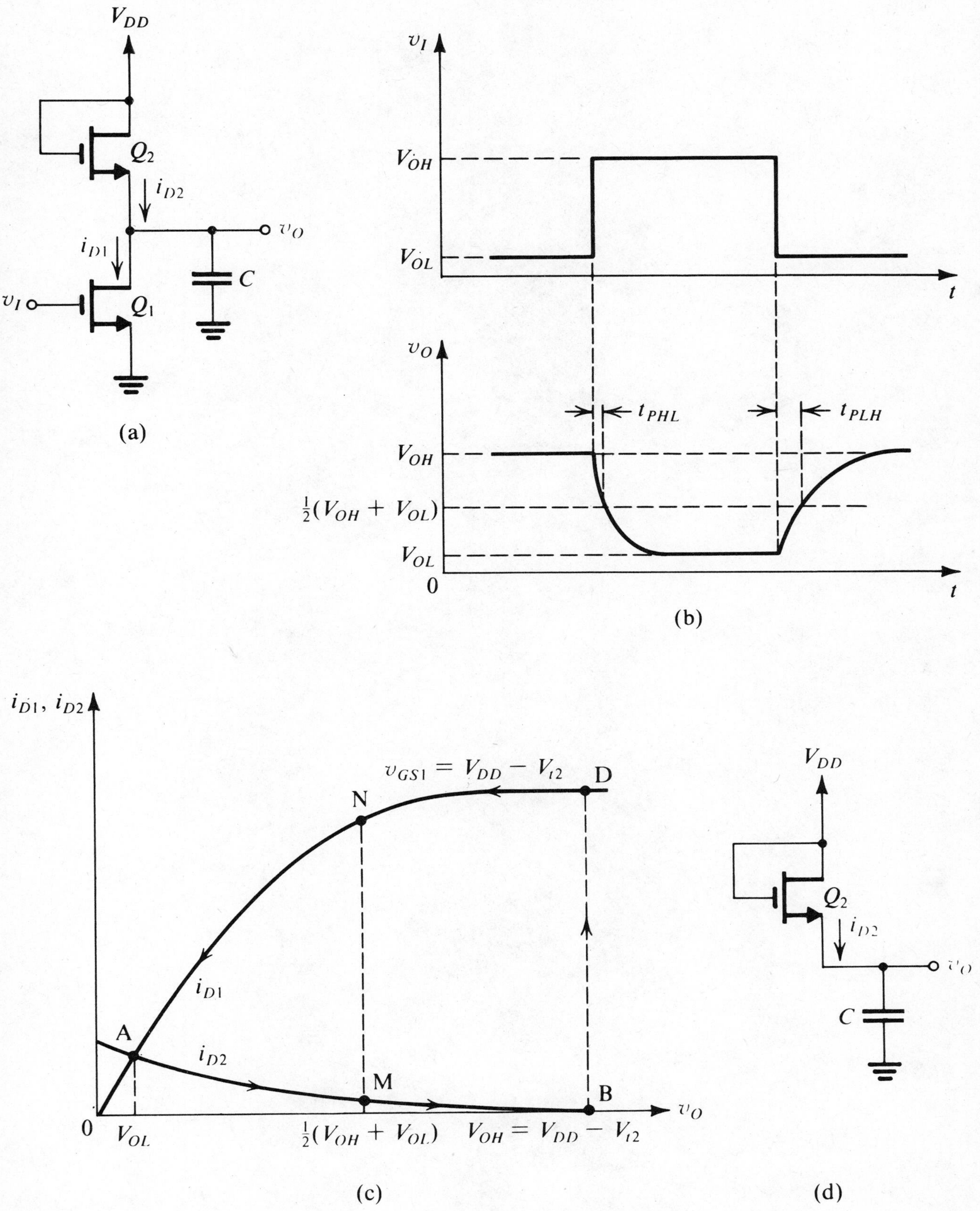

V_{DD}
Q_2
i_{D2}
i_{D1}
v_O
C
v_I
Q_1
(a)
v_I
V_{OH}
V_{OL}
t
v_O
t_{PHL}
t_{PLH}
V_{OH}
$\frac{1}{2}(V_{OH} + V_{OL})$
V_{OL}
0
t
(b)
i_{D1}, i_{D2}
$v_{GS1} = V_{DD} - V_{t2}$
D
N
i_{D1}
A
i_{D2}
M
B
v_O
0
V_{OL}
$\frac{1}{2}(V_{OH} + V_{OL})$
$V_{OH} = V_{DD} - V_{t2}$
(c)
V_{DD}
Q_2
i_{D2}
v_O
C
(d)

15.11

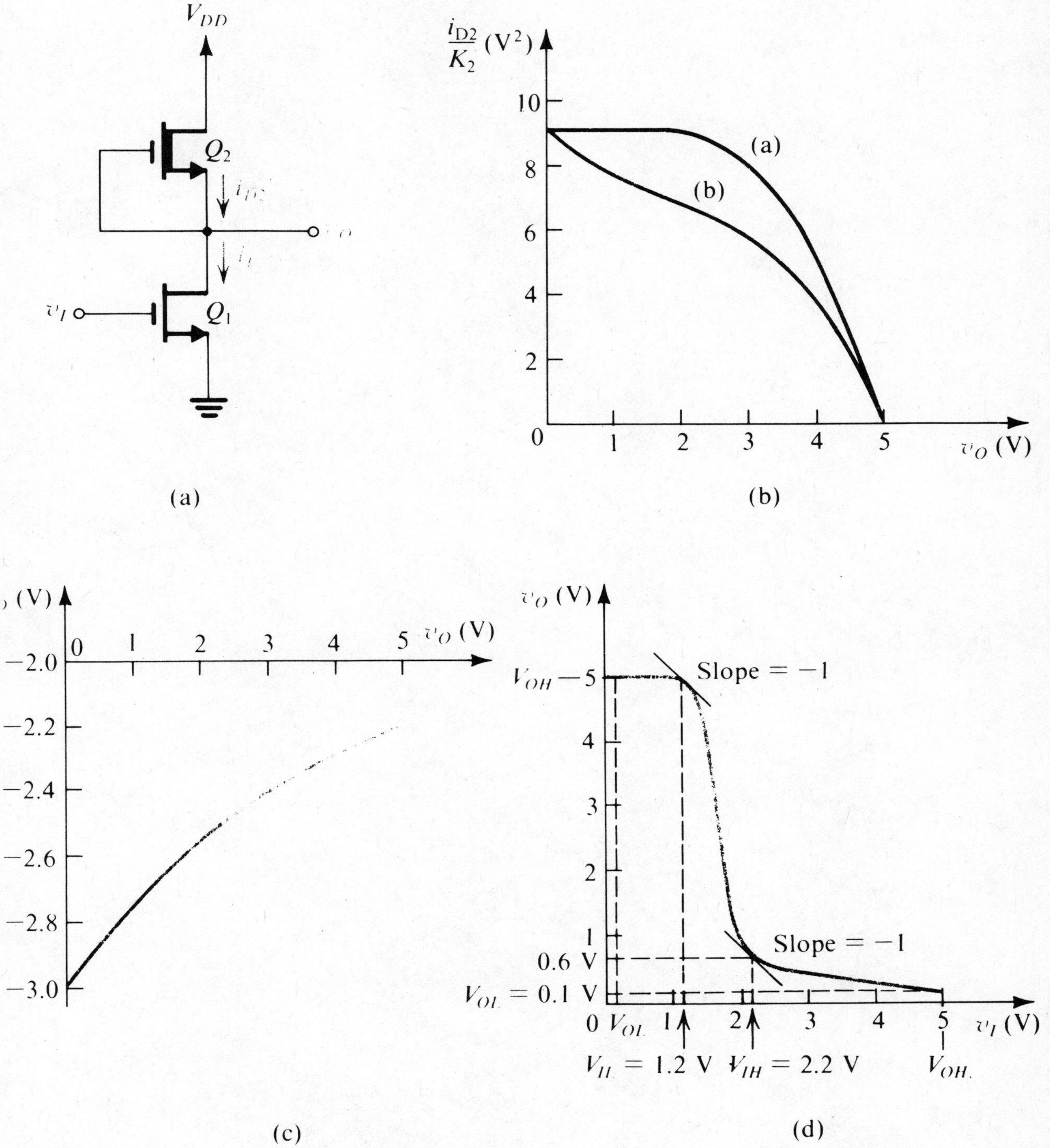
V_{DD}
Q_2
i_{D2}
v_O
i_1
v_I
Q_1
(a)
$\frac{i_{D2}}{K_2}$ (V^2)
10
8
6
4
2
0
1
2
3
4
5
v_O (V)
(a)
(b)
(b)
V_{tD} (V)
0
1
2
3
4
5
v_O (V)
−2.0
−2.2
−2.4
−2.6
−2.8
−3.0
(c)
v_O (V)
V_{OH} — 5
4
3
2
1
0.6 V
V_{OL} = 0.1 V
Slope = −1
Slope = −1
0 V_{OL}
1
2
3
4
5
v_I (V)
V_{IL} = 1.2 V
V_{IH} = 2.2 V
V_{OH}
(d)

15.12

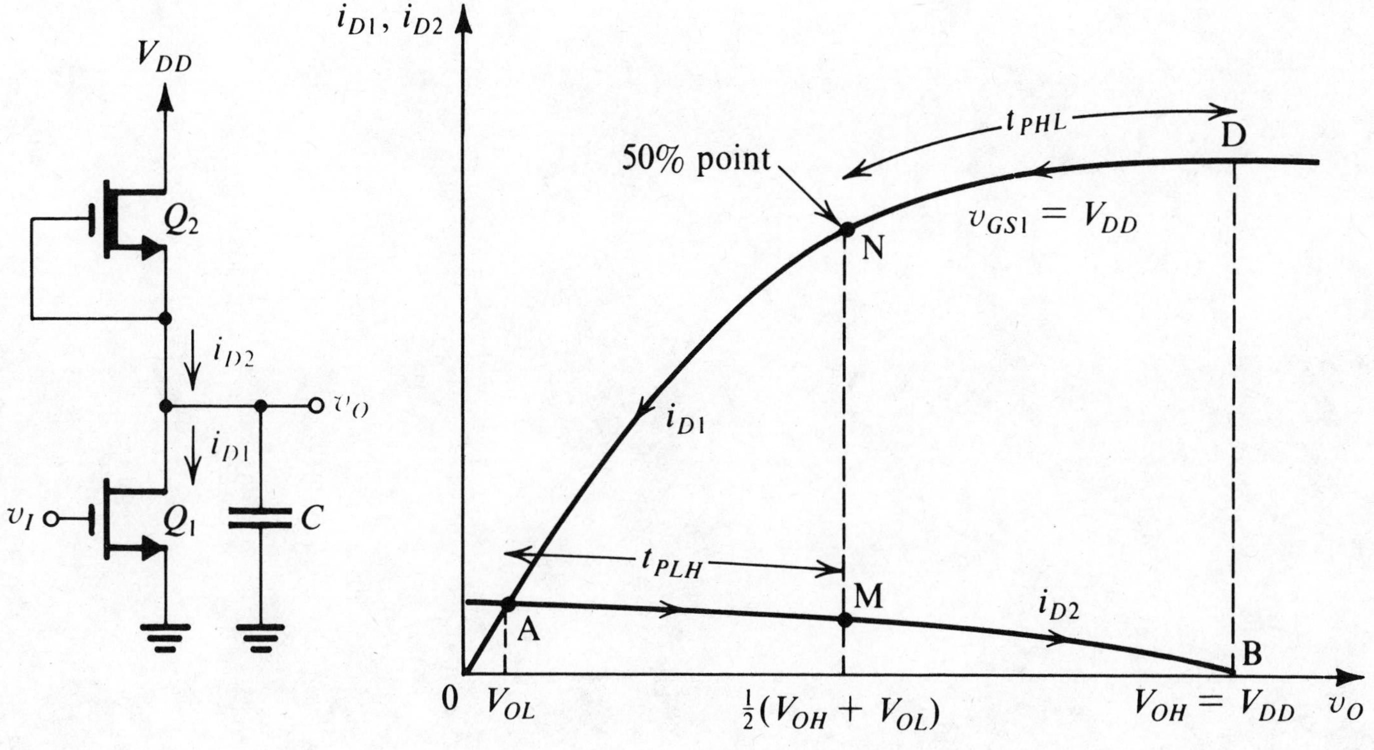

V_{DD}
Q_2
i_{D2}
v_O
i_{D1}
v_I
Q_1
C
i_{D1}, i_{D2}
t_{PHL}
D
50% point
N
$v_{GS1} = V_{DD}$
i_{D1}
t_{PLH}
M
i_{D2}
A
B
0
V_{OL}
$\frac{1}{2}(V_{OH} + V_{OL})$
$V_{OH} = V_{DD}$
v_O

(a)

(b)

15.13

15.16

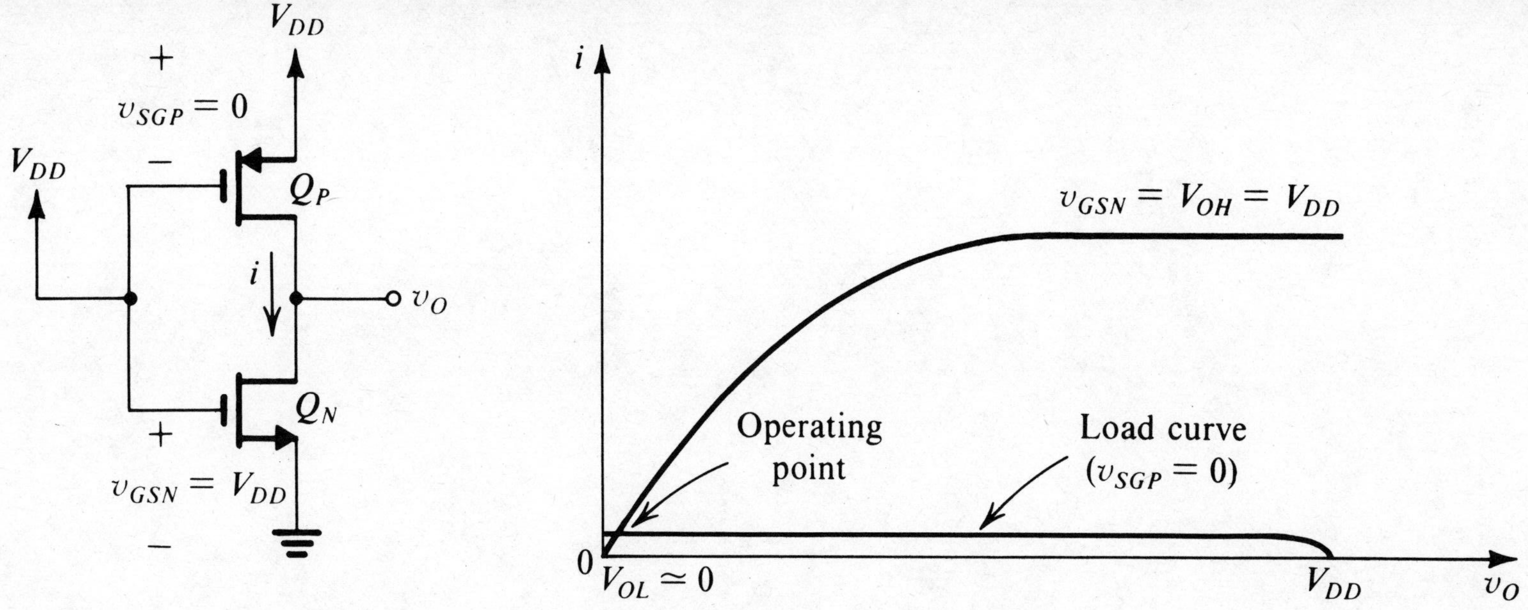
V_{DD}
+
$v_{SGP} = 0$
−
V_{DD}
Q_P
i
v_O
Q_N
+
$v_{GSN} = V_{DD}$
−
i
$v_{GSN} = V_{OH} = V_{DD}$
Operating point
Load curve ($v_{SGP} = 0$)
0
$V_{OL} \simeq 0$
V_{DD}
v_O

15.17

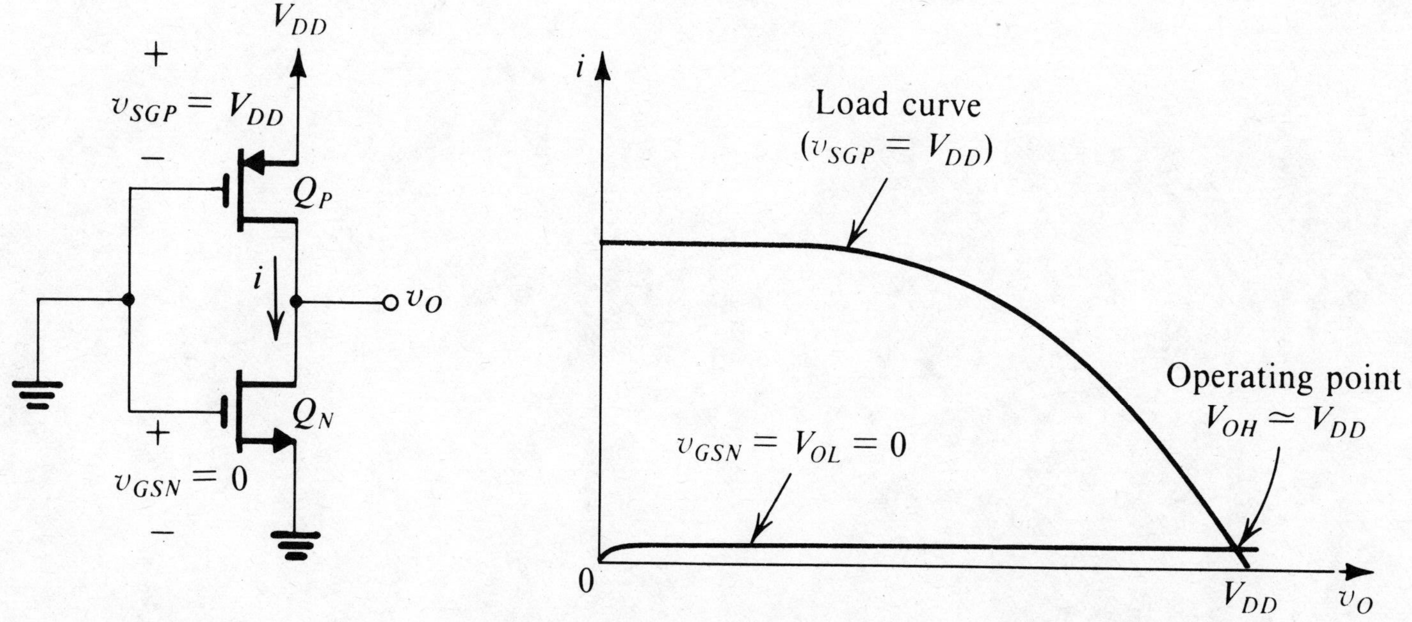
V_{DD}
+
$v_{SGP} = V_{DD}$
−
Q_P
i
v_O
Q_N
+
$v_{GSN} = 0$
−
i
Load curve ($v_{SGP} = V_{DD}$)
Operating point $V_{OH} \simeq V_{DD}$
$v_{GSN} = V_{OL} = 0$
0
V_{DD}
v_O

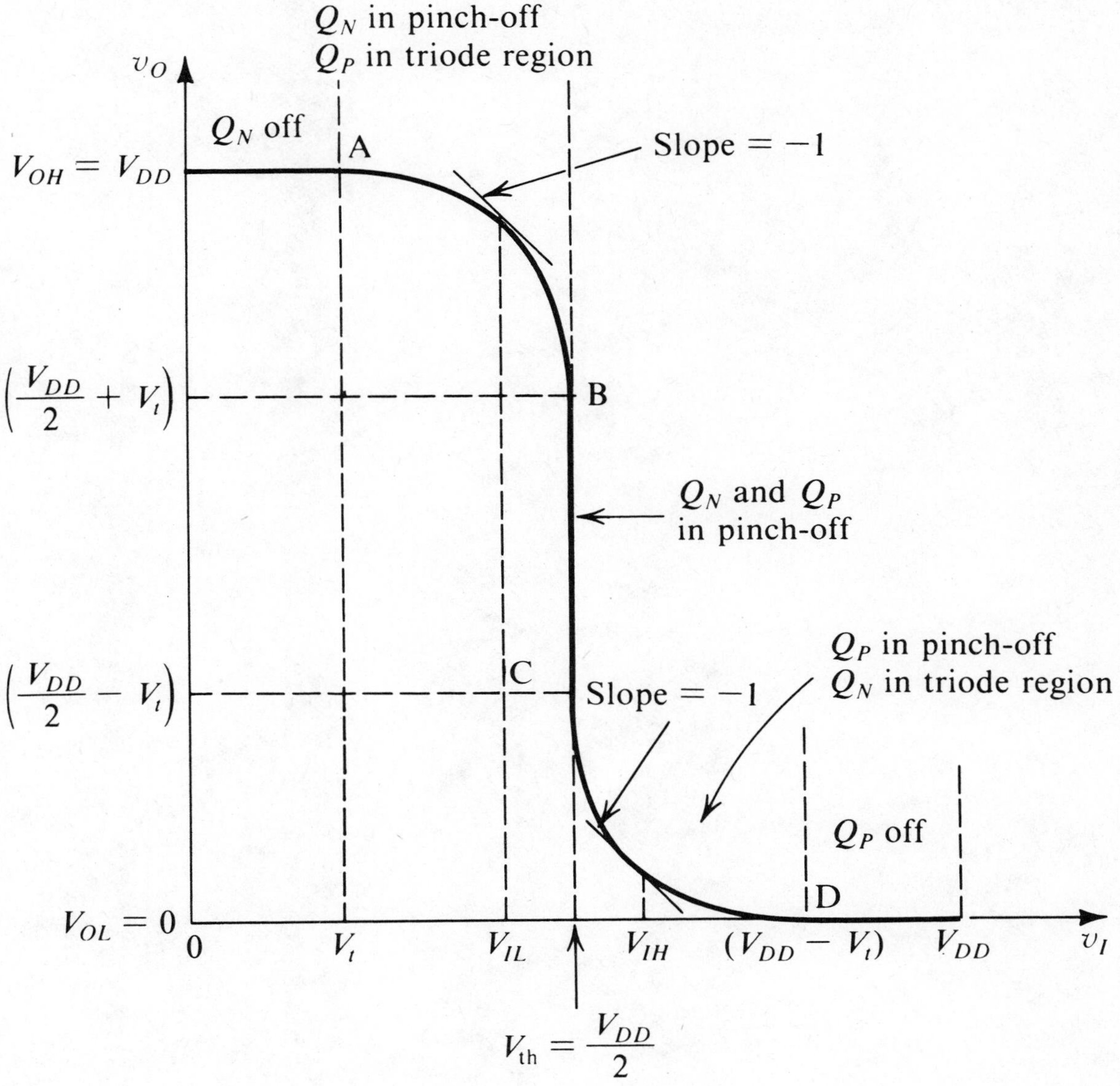

Q_N in pinch-off
Q_P in triode region
v_O
Q_N off
A
Slope = −1
$V_{OH} = V_{DD}$
$\left(\frac{V_{DD}}{2} + V_t\right)$
B
Q_N and Q_P in pinch-off
Q_P in pinch-off
Q_N in triode region
C
$\left(\frac{V_{DD}}{2} - V_t\right)$
Slope = −1
Q_P off
D
$V_{OL} = 0$
0
V_t
V_{IL}
V_{IH}
$(V_{DD} - V_t)$
V_{DD}
v_I
$V_{th} = \frac{V_{DD}}{2}$

15.18

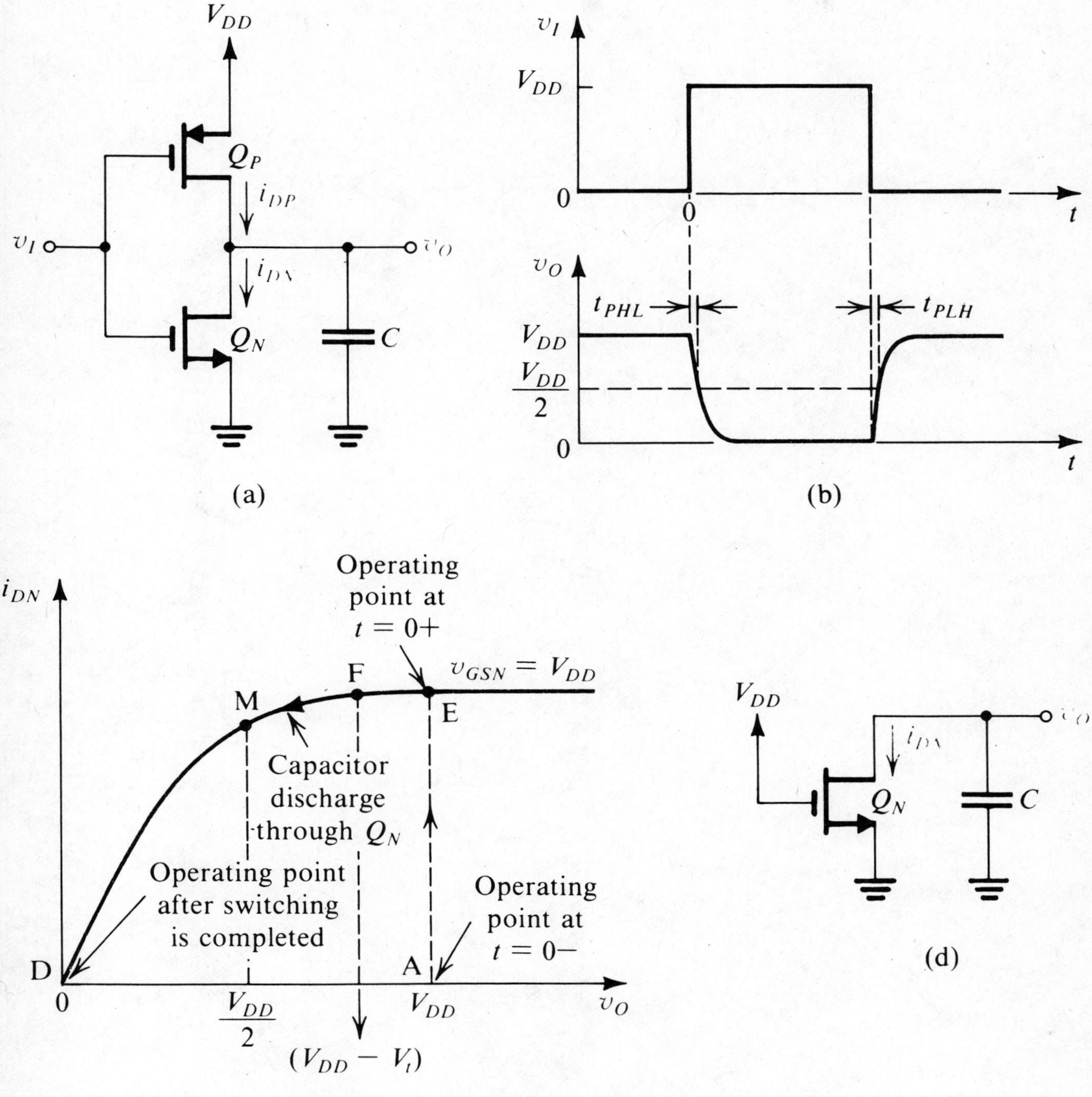
V_{DD}
Q_P
i_{DP}
v_I
v_O
i_{DN}
Q_N
C
(a)
v_I
V_{DD}
0
0
t
v_O
t_{PHL}
t_{PLH}
V_{DD}
$\frac{V_{DD}}{2}$
0
t
(b)
i_{DN}
Operating point at $t = 0+$
$v_{GSN} = V_{DD}$
F
M
E
Capacitor discharge through Q_N
Operating point after switching is completed
Operating point at $t = 0-$
D
A
0
$\frac{V_{DD}}{2}$
V_{DD}
v_O
$(V_{DD} - V_t)$
(c)
V_{DD}
v_O
i_{DN}
Q_N
C
(d)

15.20

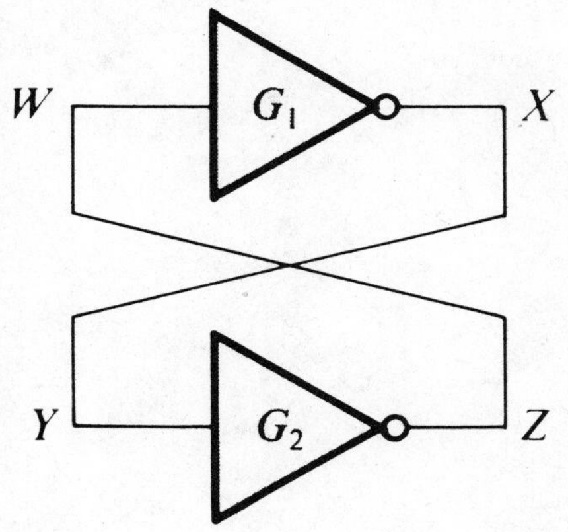
W
G1
X
Y
G2
Z

(a)

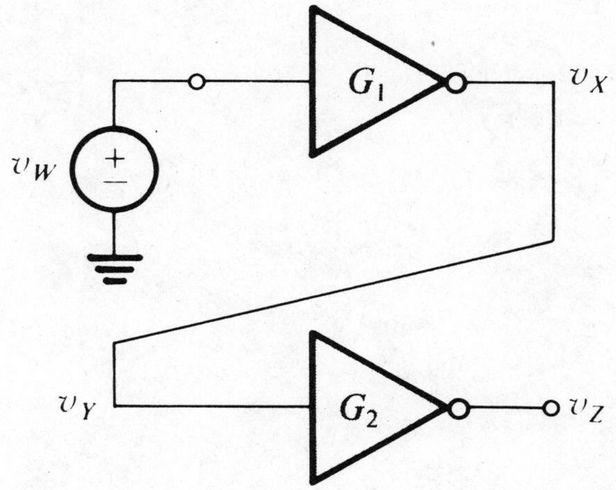
G1
vX
vW
+
−
vY
G2
vZ

(b)

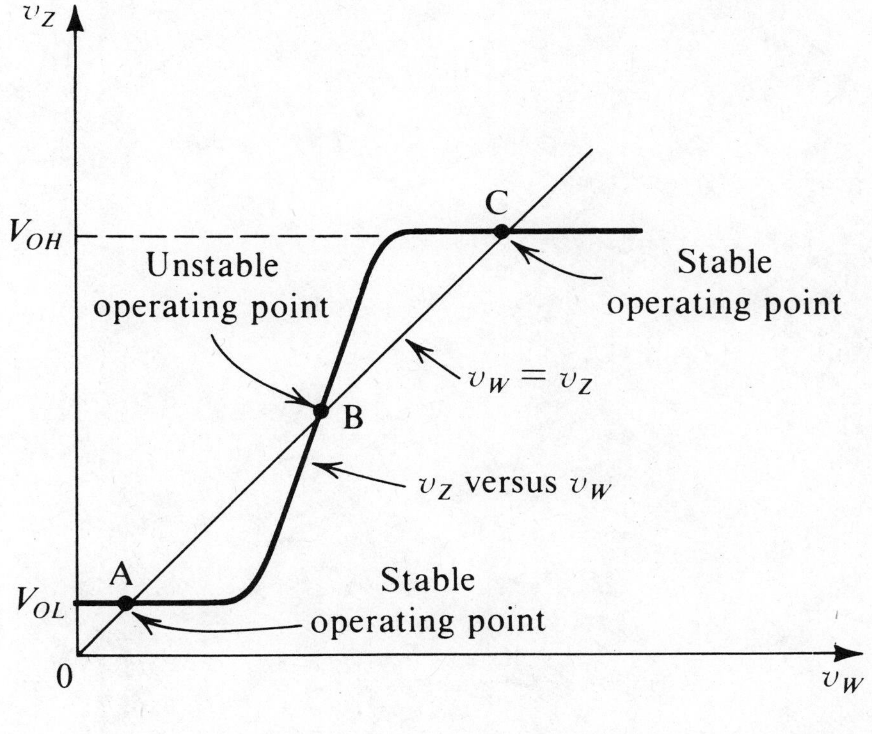
vZ
VOH
C
Unstable
operating point
Stable
operating point
vW = vZ
B
vZ versus vW
A
VOL
Stable
operating point
0
vW

(c)

15.25

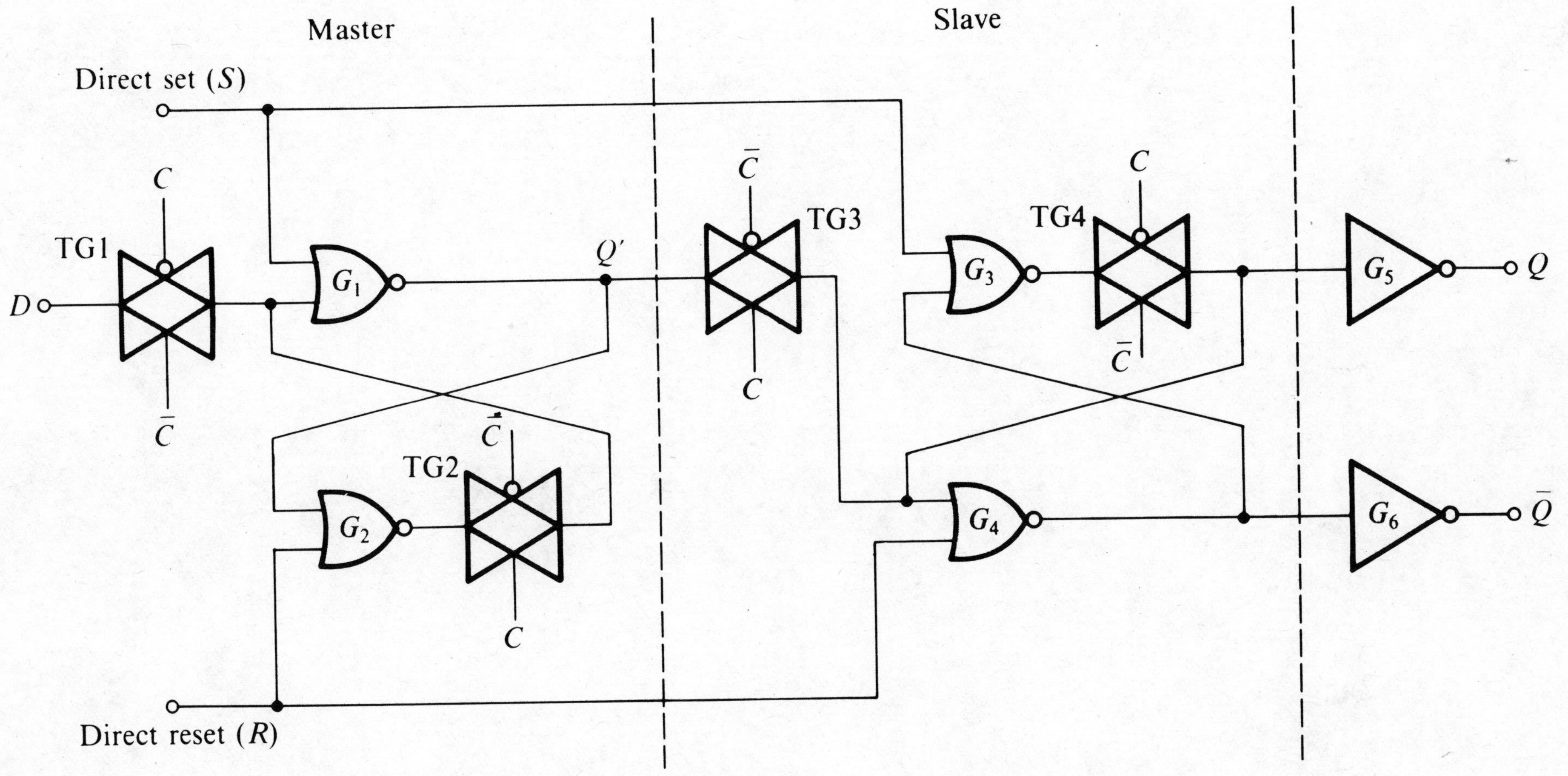
Master
Slave
Direct set (S)
Direct reset (R)
D
TG1
TG2
TG3
TG4
C
$\bar{C}$
G_1
G_2
G_3
G_4
G_5
G_6
Q′
Q
$\bar{Q}$

15.29

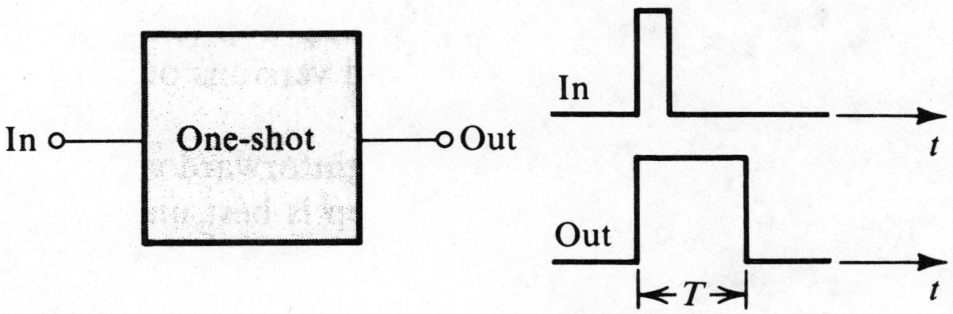

15.30

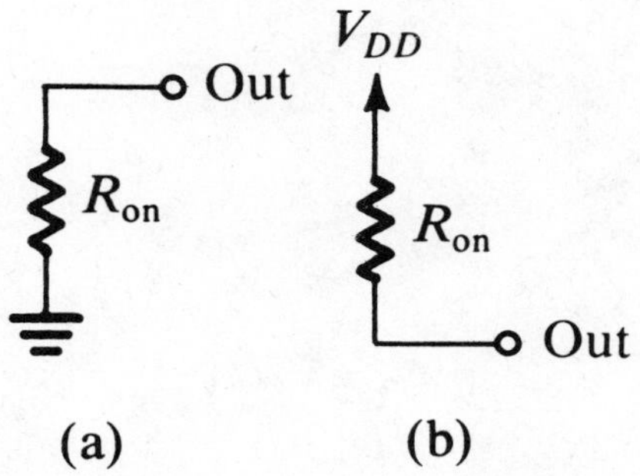

15.33

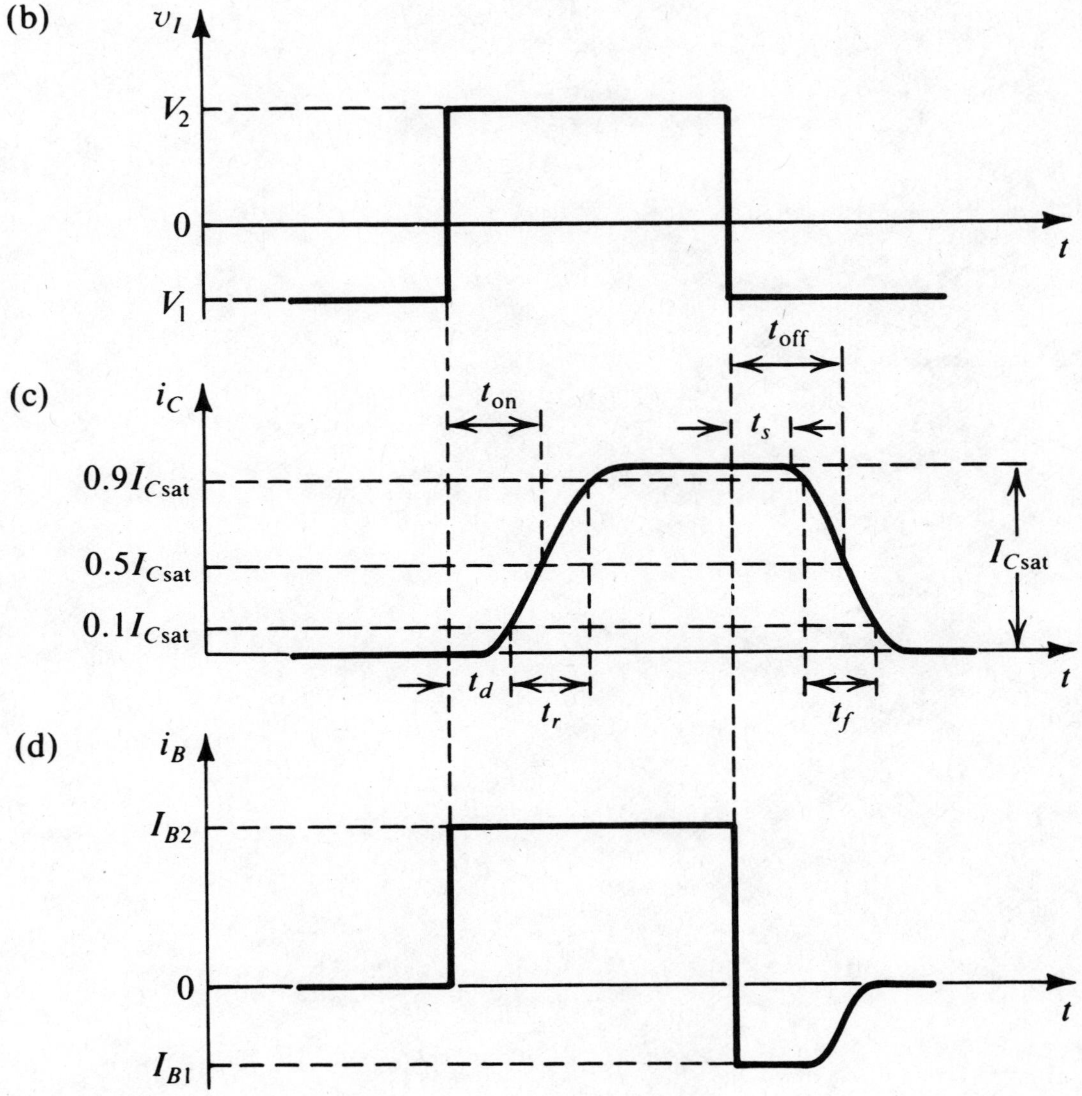
(b)
v_I
V_2
0
V_1
t
t_{off}
(c)
i_C
t_{on}
t_s
$0.9I_{Csat}$
$0.5I_{Csat}$
$0.1I_{Csat}$
I_{Csat}
t_d
t_r
t_f
t
(d)
i_B
I_{B2}
0
I_{B1}
t

16.5 (b,c,d)

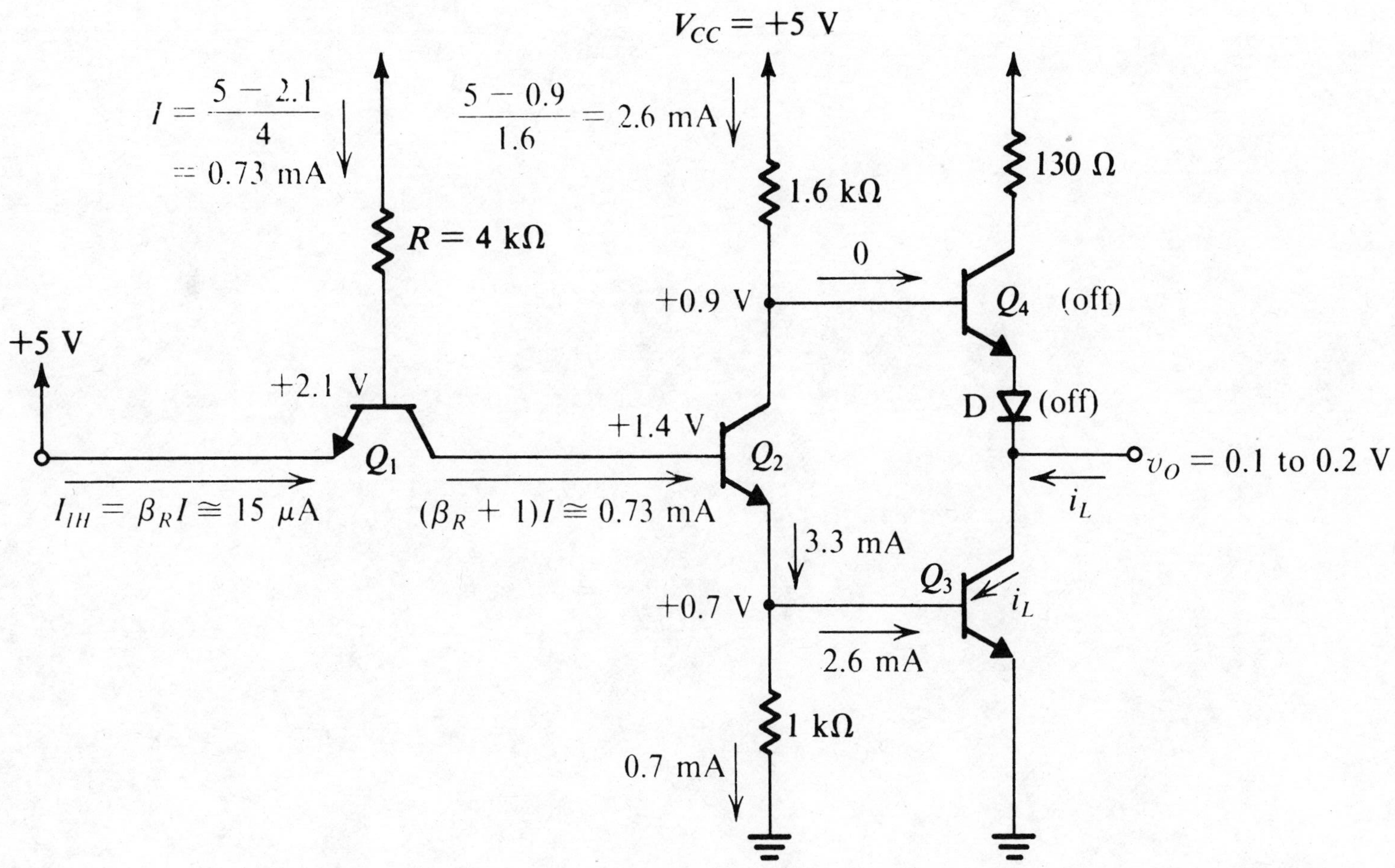
$V_{CC} = +5$ V
$I = \frac{5 - 2.1}{4}$
$= 0.73$ mA
$\frac{5 - 0.9}{1.6} = 2.6$ mA
130 Ω
1.6 kΩ
$R = 4$ kΩ
0
+0.9 V
Q_4 (off)
+5 V
+2.1 V
D (off)
+1.4 V
Q_1
Q_2
$v_O = 0.1$ to 0.2 V
i_L
$I_{IH} = \beta_R I \cong 15\ \mu$A
$(\beta_R + 1)I \cong 0.73$ mA
3.3 mA
Q_3
i_L
+0.7 V
2.6 mA
1 kΩ
0.7 mA

16.24

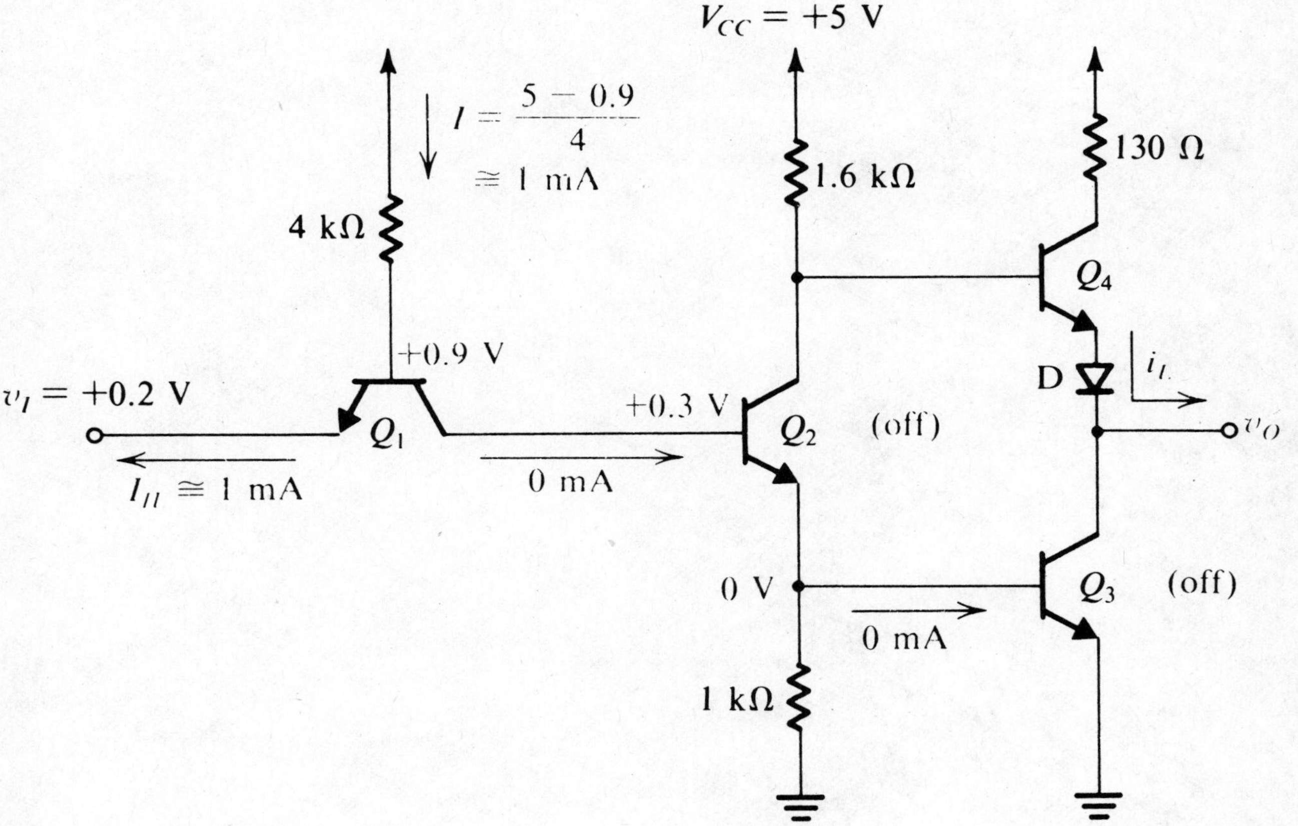

$V_{CC} = +5$ V
$I = \frac{5 - 0.9}{4}$
$\cong 1$ mA
4 kΩ
1.6 kΩ
130 Ω
Q_4
+0.9 V
D
i_L
$v_I = +0.2$ V
Q_1
+0.3 V
Q_2
(off)
v_O
$I_{IL} \cong 1$ mA
0 mA
0 V
Q_3
(off)
0 mA
1 kΩ

16.26

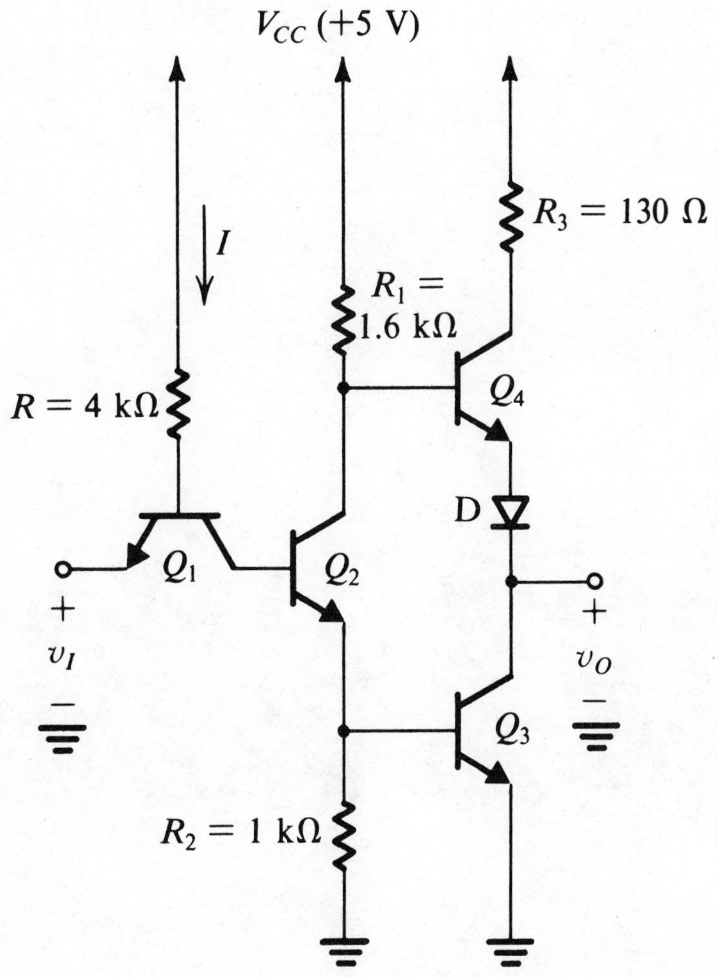
V_{CC} (+5 V)
I
$R = 4$ kΩ
$R_1 =$ 1.6 kΩ
$R_3 = 130$ Ω
Q_1
Q_2
Q_3
Q_4
D
$R_2 = 1$ kΩ
+
v_I
−
+
v_O
−

(a)

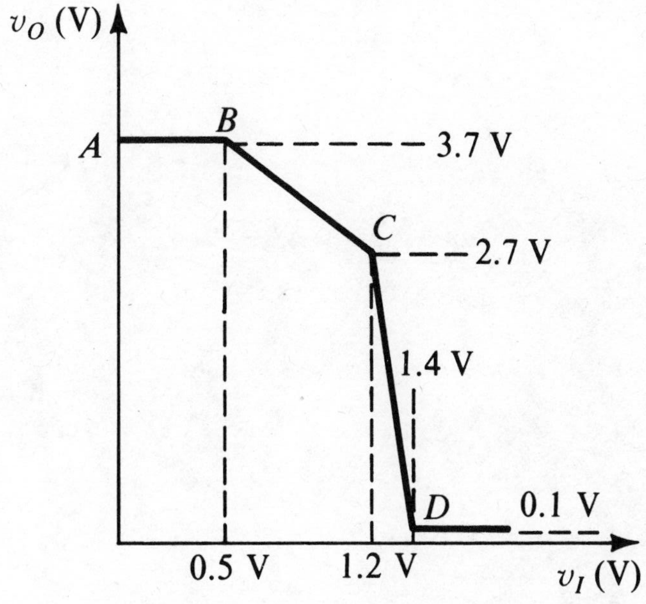
v_O (V)
A
B
C
D
3.7 V
2.7 V
1.4 V
0.1 V
0.5 V
1.2 V
v_I (V)

(b)

16.27

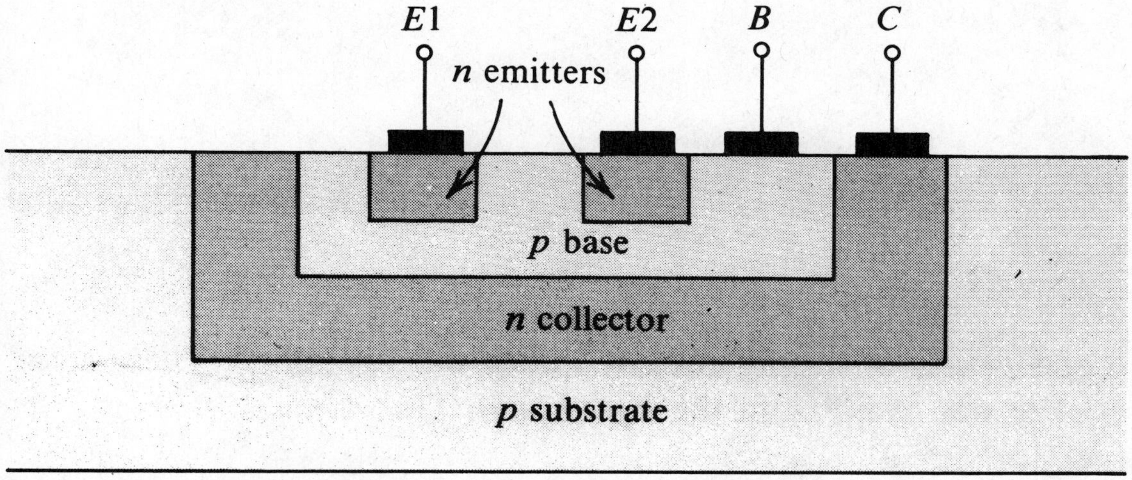
E1
E2
B
C
n emitters
p base
n collector
p substrate

16.29

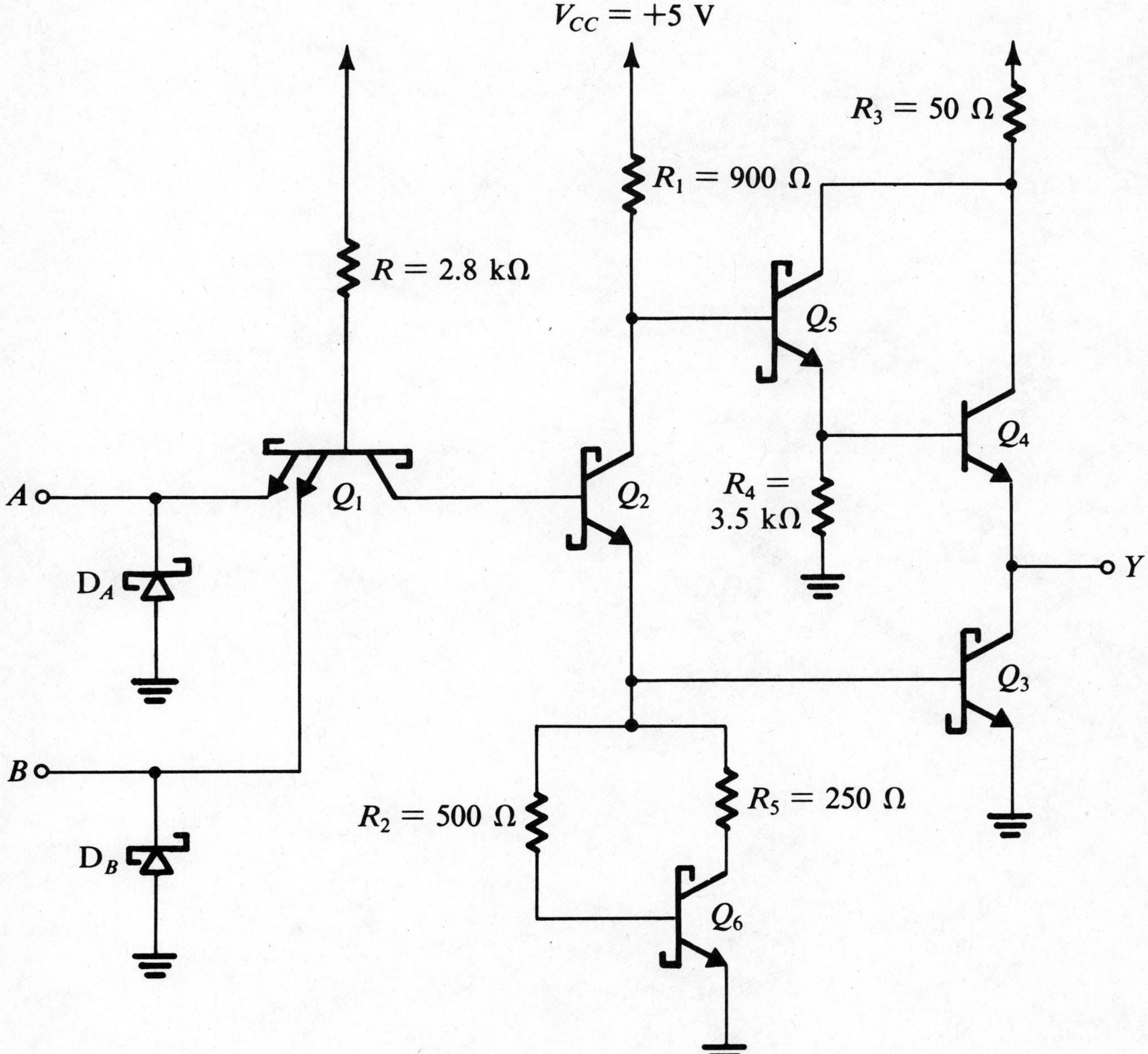
V_{CC} = +5 V
R_3 = 50 Ω
R_1 = 900 Ω
R = 2.8 kΩ
Q_5
Q_4
R_4 =
3.5 kΩ
A
Q_1
Q_2
D_A
Y
Q_3
B
R_5 = 250 Ω
R_2 = 500 Ω
D_B
Q_6

16.32

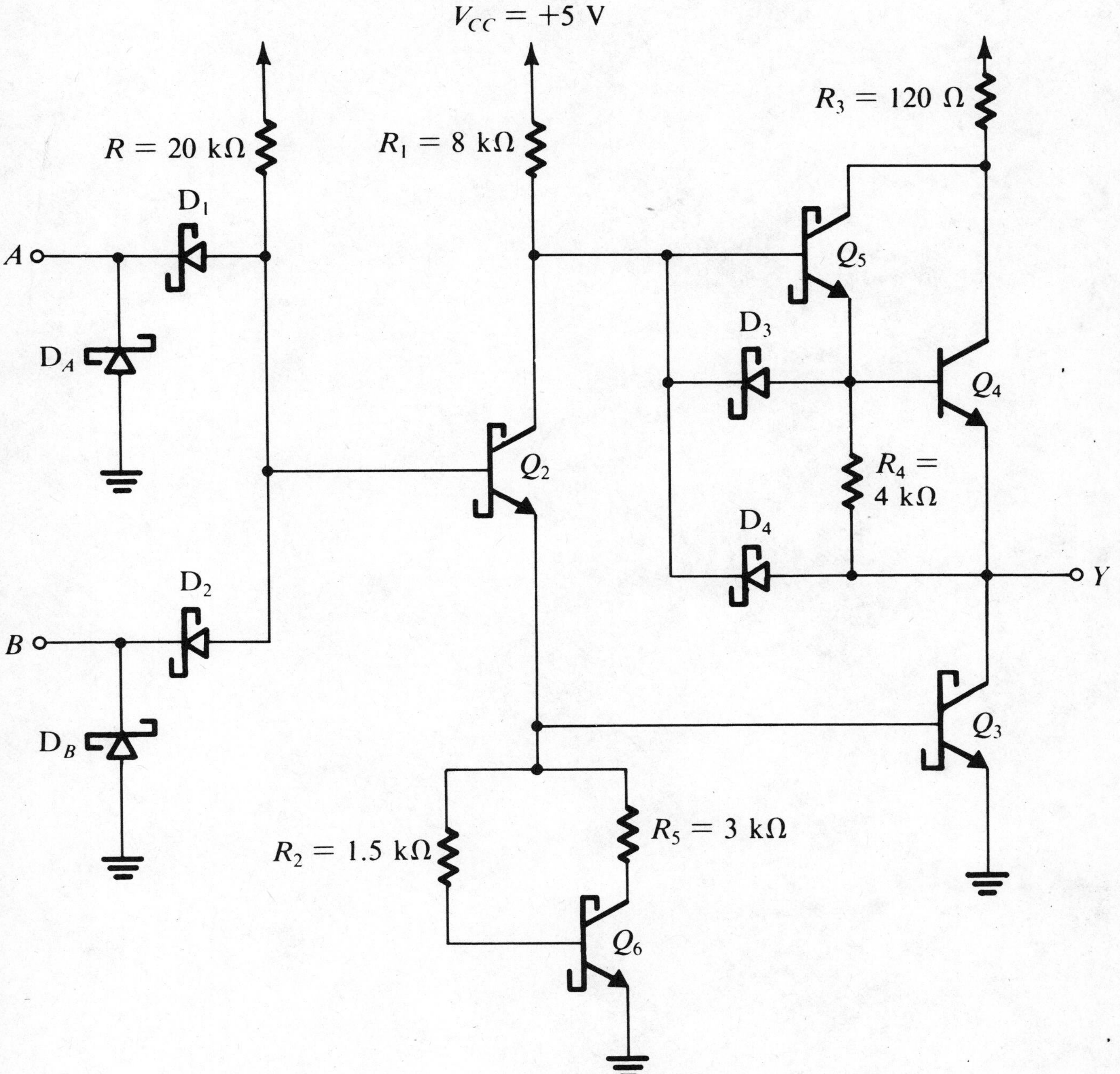

$V_{CC} = +5$ V
$R = 20$ kΩ
$R_1 = 8$ kΩ
$R_3 = 120$ Ω
D_1
A
D_A
Q_5
D_3
Q_4
Q_2
$R_4 =$
4 kΩ
D_4
D_2
Y
B
Q_3
D_B
$R_5 = 3$ kΩ
$R_2 = 1.5$ kΩ
Q_6

16.35

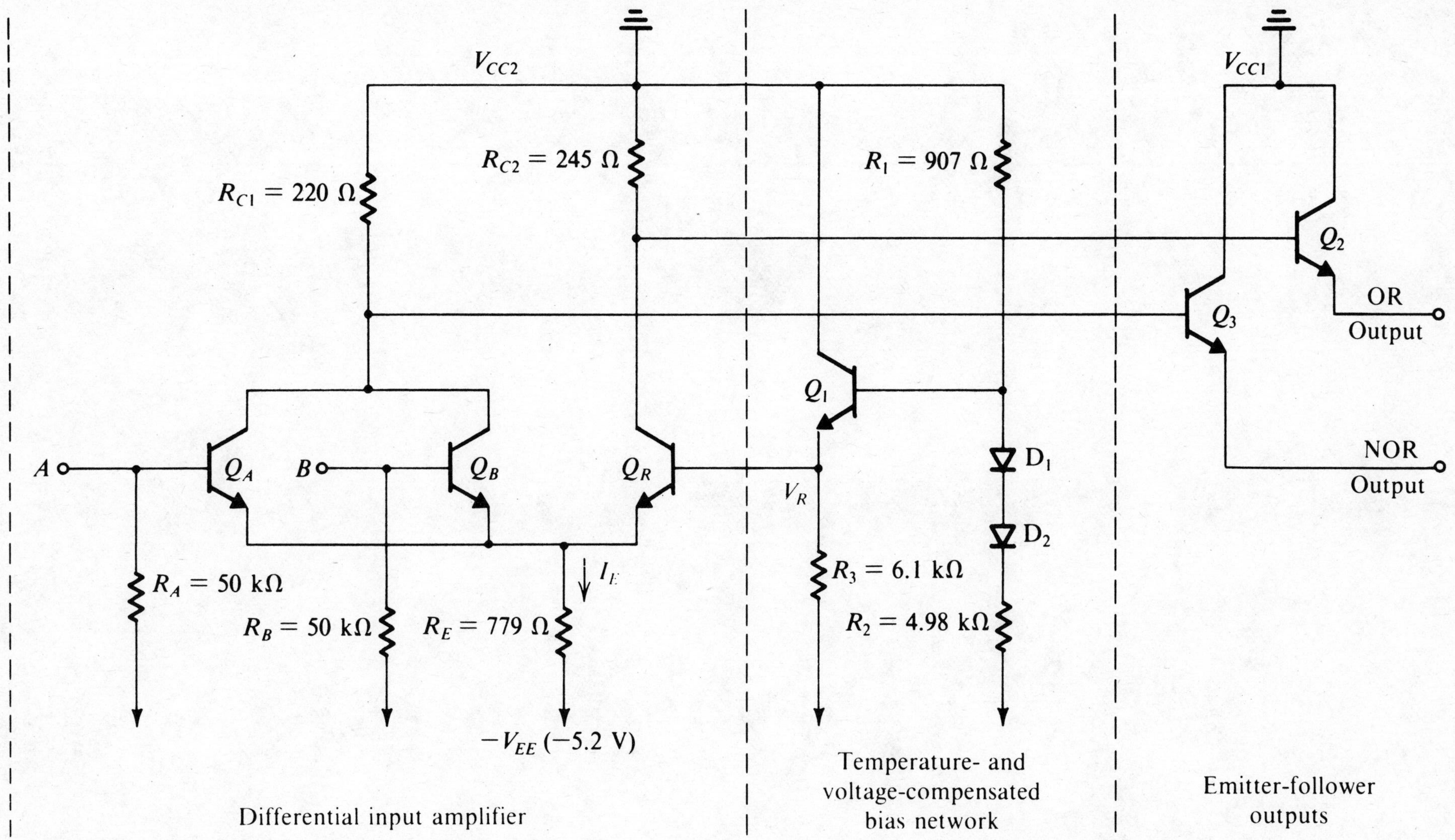

V_CC2
V_CC1
R_C1 = 220 Ω
R_C2 = 245 Ω
R_1 = 907 Ω
Q_2
OR
Output
Q_3
Q_1
A
Q_A
B
Q_B
Q_R
V_R
D_1
D_2
NOR
Output
I_E
R_A = 50 kΩ
R_B = 50 kΩ
R_E = 779 Ω
R_3 = 6.1 kΩ
R_2 = 4.98 kΩ
−V_EE (−5.2 V)
Temperature- and
voltage-compensated
bias network
Emitter-follower
outputs
Differential input amplifier

16.36

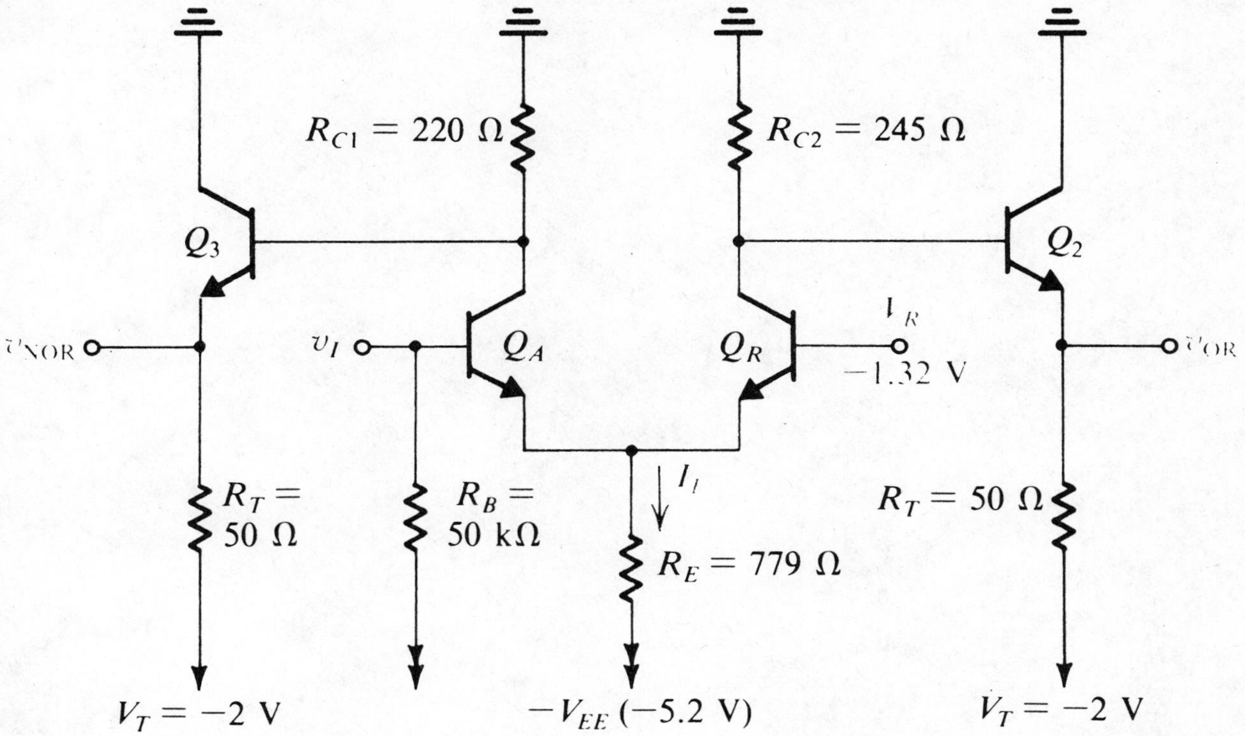
$R_{C1} = 220\ \Omega$
$R_{C2} = 245\ \Omega$
Q_3
Q_2
Q_A
Q_R
v_{NOR}
v_I
I_R
−1.32 V
v_{OR}
I_I
$R_T =$ 50 Ω
$R_B =$ 50 kΩ
$R_T = 50\ \Omega$
$R_E = 779\ \Omega$
$V_T = -2$ V
$-V_{EE}$ (−5.2 V)
$V_T = -2$ V

16.38

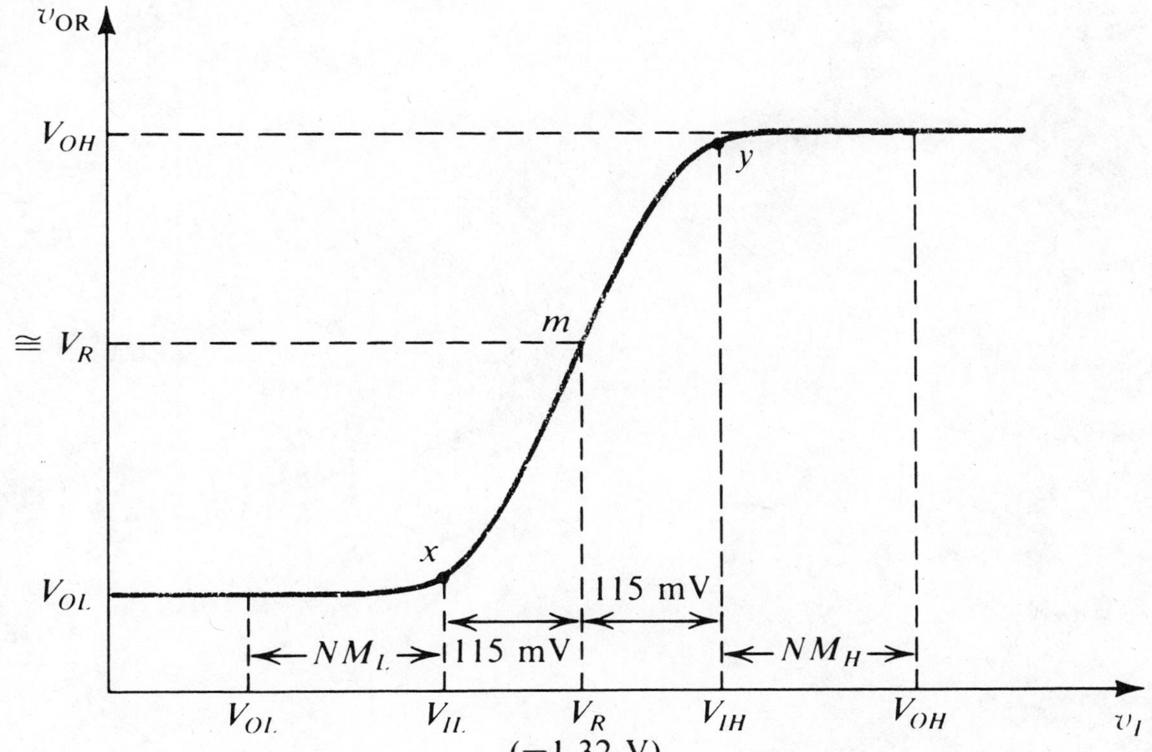
v_{OR}
V_{OH}
y
m
≅ V_R
x
V_{OL}
115 mV
NM_L
115 mV
NM_H
V_{OL}
V_{IL}
V_R
(−1.32 V)
V_{IH}
V_{OH}
v_I

16.39

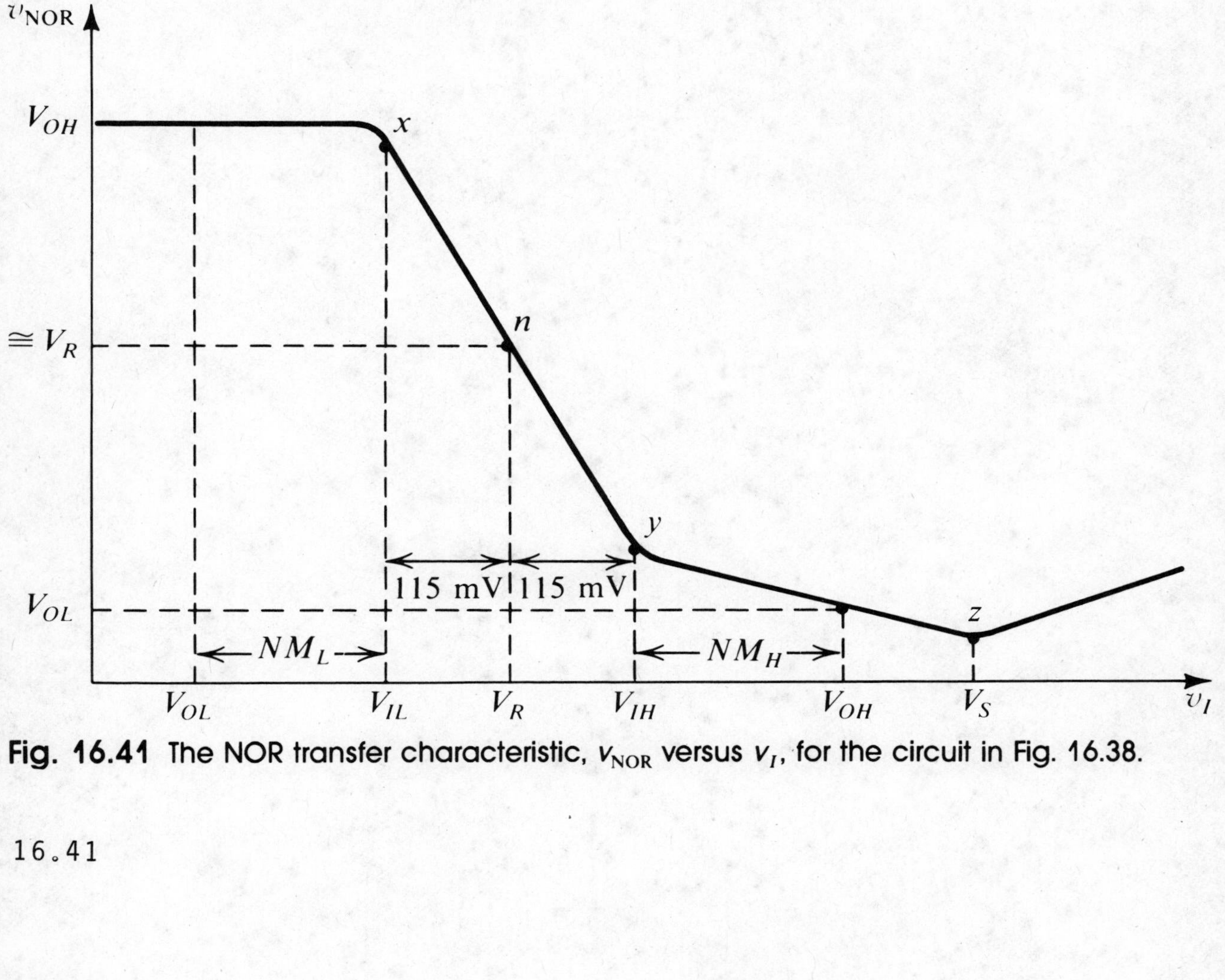

Fig. 16.41 The NOR transfer characteristic, v_{NOR} versus v_I, for the circuit in Fig. 16.38.

16.41